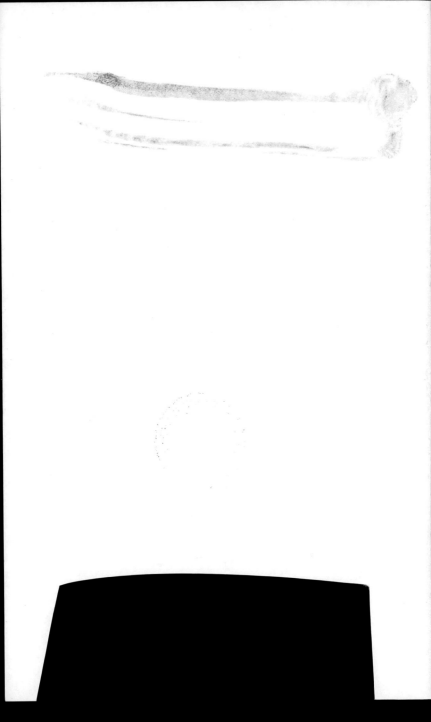

Cassell's

Concise
Latin-English
English-Latin
Dictionary

Compiled by

D. P. SIMPSON M.A.

Assistant Master and formerly Head of Classical Department at Eton College

CONTINUUM
London and New York

Published by Cassell Ltd, 1963
Reprinted 2000 by Continuum
Wellington House, 125 Strand,
London WC2R 0BB, England
370 Lexington Avenue, New York,
NY 10017-6550, USA

CASSELL'S NEW COMPACT LATIN-ENGLISH
ENGLISH-LATIN DICTIONARY
First edition 1963
Second edition 1965
Third edition 1966
Third edition, Fifth impression (title changed to
CASSELL'S CONCISE LATIN-ENGLISH
ENGLISH-LATIN DICTIONARY) 1977
Third edition, Tenth impression 1991
Reprinted 1992, 1994, 2000

ISBN 0 304 52263 5

Printed and bound in Great Britain
by The Bath Press, Bath

PREFACE

THE first Latin Dictionary published by Cassell appeared in 1854. It was the work of two Unitarian divines, J. R. Beard and his son Charles Beard, and consisted of two sections of equal length, Latin-English and English-Latin. The first of these sections was " revised, enlarged, and in part rewritten " for publication in 1886, by J. R. V. Marchant, who was for a short time a master at St. Paul's School, but later was called to the Bar, and became a County Court Judge. By 1892 the second section, English-Latin, had also been revised, and considerably shortened, by J. F. Charles, probably with help from Marchant. Charles had been a pupil, with Marchant, at the City of London School, and after graduating at London and Oxford he returned there as a master. The combined work of Marchant and Charles was reprinted at short intervals for the next sixty years. In 1927 a shortened version of it appeared, under the name of " Cassell's Compact Latin-English English-Latin Dictionary." This was prepared by Miss Millicent Thomas, M.A. (London), sometime Classics and Senior Mistress of Tottenham High School, and an assistant examiner in Classics for the University of London. She dispensed with most of the prolegomena printed by Marchant and Charles, and in her main text reduced both the length and the number of articles, leaving the rarer words out of account and removing the illustrative quotations from Latin authors. In her book, as in that of Marchant and Charles, the English-Latin section was little more than half as long as the Latin-English.

In 1959 Cassell published their " New Latin Dictionary." which was a complete revision by the present author of both sections of Marchant and Charles. The new "concise" dictionary follows as an abbreviation of this, the result of much the same process of selection and simplification as Miss Thomas applied to its predecessor.

This book resembles every other Latin dictionary so far produced by Cassell, in concerning itself with " classical " Latin, as used from about 200 B.C. to A.D. 100. It also conforms to the principle maintained since the time of Marchant and Charles, that the English-Latin section should be kept relatively short, in the hope that the user will refer from it to the Latin-English for fuller information. Both English and Latin words are treated in alphabetical order, except that adverbs appear under the adjectives from which they are derived, participles under verbs, and so on; certain synonyms, also, are grouped together within a single article. The spelling of Latin words is intended to correspond to what will be found in the more recent editions of Latin authors; I, i replaces J, j throughout, but V, v is retained. In the Latin-English section most vowels in Latin words are marked short (˘) or long (¯); in the English-Latin this has been done more sparingly, for the special purpose of distinguishing between words of similar form, or of indicating declension or conjugation.

D.P.S.

LIST OF SPECIAL TERMS

abbrev. abbreviated, abbreviation.
abl. ablative.
absol. absolute.
abstr. abstract.
acc. accusative.
act. active.
adj. adjective.
adv. adverb.
adversat. adversative.
architect. architectural.
c. common (both m. and f.).
class. classical.
coll. collective.
colloq. colloquial.
commerc. commercial.
compar. comparative.
concr. concrete.
conj. conjunction.
dat. dative.
dep. deponent.
dim. diminutive.
distrib. distributive.
e.g. exempli gratia (for example).
esp. especially.
etc. et cetera.
exclam. exclamatory.
f. feminine.
fig. figure, figurative.
foll. followed.
fut. future.
gen. general, generally.
genit. genitive.
gram., *grammat.* grammatical.
i.e. id est (that is).
imperf. imperfect.
impers. impersonal.
indecl. indeclinable.
indef. indefinite.
indic. indicative.
infin. infinitive.
interj. interjection.
interrog. interrogative.
intransit. intransitive.
logic. logical.
m. masculine.
medic. medical.
meton. by metonymy.
milit. military.
myth. mythological.
n. neuter.
naut. nautical.
neg. negative.
nom. nominative.
num. numeral.
obs. obsolete.
occ. occasionally.
opp. opposite (to).
partic. participle.
pass. passive.
perf. perfect.
pers. person.
personif. personified.
philosoph. philosophy, philosophical.
phr. phrase.
pl., *plur.* plural.
poet. poetical.
polit. political.
posit. positive.
prep. preposition.
pres. present.
pron. pronoun.
q.v. quod vide, quae vide (i.e. see article concerned).
reflex. reflexive.
relat. relative.
relig. religious.
rhet. rhetoric, rhetorical.
sc. scilicet (that is to say).
sing. singular.
subj. subjunctive.
subst. substantive.
superl. superlative.
t.t. technical term.
transf. transferred (i.e. used in altered sense).
transit. transitive.
voc. vocative.

CASSELL'S LATIN-ENGLISH DICTIONARY

A

A, a, the first letter of the Latin Alphabet.

a, ah, interj. *Ah!*

a, ab, abs, prep. with abl. (1) of motion or measurement in space, *from, away from.* (2) of time, *from, after.* (3) of separation, difference, change, *from*; so of position or number, *counting from*; and of the relation of part to whole, *out of, of.* (4) or origin and agency; especially with passive verbs, *by, at the hands of, because of.* (5) *viewed from, on the side of*: a tergo, *in the rear*; hence *in connexion with, as regards.*

ăbăcus -i, m. *a square board*; hence *sideboard, counting-board, gaming-board, ceiling panel.*

ăbălĭēnātĭo -ōnis, f. *transfer of property.*

ăbălĭēno -are, *to make alien, separate, estrange.*

ăbăvus -i, m. *great-great-grandfather.*

Abdēra -orum, n. pl., also -ae, f., *a town in Thrace, noted for the stupidity of its inhabitants.*

abdĭcātĭo -ōnis, f. *disowning, renunciation.*

[1]**abdĭco** -are, *to renounce, reject*; esp. of magistracies, *to abdicate*, often with reflex. and ablative of office.

[2]**abdīco** -dicĕre -dixi -dictum, in augury, *to disapprove of.*

abdo -dĕre -dĭdi -dĭtum, *to put away, withdraw, remove*; esp. *to secrete, hide.*

Hence partic. **abdĭtus** -a -um, *concealed, secret.* Adv. **abdĭtē.**

abdōmen -ĭnis, n. *belly*; hence *gluttony.*

abdūco -dūcĕre -duxi -ductum, *to lead* or *take away, detach, withdraw.*

ăbĕo -ire -ĭi -ĭtum, *to go away*; abi, *be off with you*; abi in malam rem, *go to the devil.* Transf., *to retire* from office; *to depart* from life, *die*; in discussion, *to digress*; in form, *to change*; of things, *to pass away, disappear, vanish; to pass over* from owner to owner.

ăbĕquĭto -are, *to ride off.*

ăberrātĭo ōnis, f. *escape, relief.*

ăberro -are, *to wander, deviate, escape.*

ăbhinc. (1) *hereafter.* (2) *ago*: abhinc annos tres, or annis tribus *three years ago.*

ăbhorreo -ēre, *to shrink back from*; hence *to be inconsistent with* or *opposed to*; a fide, *to be incredible.* Pres. part., as adj., *unseasonable, inappropriate.*

abicĭo -icĕre -iēci -iectum, *to throw down* or *away.* Transf., *to pronounce carelessly, break off abruptly; to get rid of, give up; to dash to the ground, weaken, dishearten.*

Hence partic. **abiectus** -a -um; of position, *low, common*; of character, *cowardly, mean;* of style, *without force, prosaic.* Adv. **abiectē,** *without spirit, meanly.*

abiectĭo -ōnis, f. *throwing away*; animi, *despondency, despair.*

ăbĭegnus -a -um, *of fir wood* or *deal.*

ăbĭēs ĕtis, f. *the silver fir*; meton., *anything made of deal*, such as *a ship* or *spear.*

ăbĭgo -ĕre -ēgi -actum, *to drive away*; of cattle, *to remove, steal.* Transf., *to banish, be rid of*: uxorem, *to divorce.*

ăbĭtĭo -ōnis, f. and **ăbĭtus** -ūs, m., *going away, departure; place of egress.*

abiūdĭco -are, *to take away by a judgment.*

abiungo -iungĕre -iunxi -iunctum, *to unharness*; hence *to estrange, detach.*

abiuro -are, *to abjure, deny on oath.*

ablātīvus -a -um, *ablative.*

ablēgātĭo -onis, f. *sending away, banishment.*

ablēgo -are, *to send away, remove to a distance.*

ablĭgūrĭo -ire, *to lick away*; hence *to squander.*

ablūdo -ĕre, *to be out of tune.*

ablŭo -lŭĕre -lŭi -lūtum. *to wash clean; to wash away.*

abnĕgo -are, *to deny, refuse.*

abnĕpōs -ōtis, m. *great-great-grandson.*

abneptis -is, f. *great-great-granddaughter.*

abnocto -are, *to stay out all night.*

abnormis -e, *irregular, unconventional.*

abnŭo -nŭĕre -nŭi, fut. partic. -nŭĭtūrus, *to refuse by a gesture, to deny.*

ăbŏleo -ēre -ēvi -itum, *to destroy, do away with.*

ăbŏlesco -ĕre -ēvi, *to perish.*

ăbŏlĭtĭo -ōnis, f. *removing, annulling, abolition.*

ăbolla -ae, f. *a cloak of thick woollen cloth.*

ăbōmĭno -are, and **ăbōmĭnor** -ari, dep. (1) *to deprecate*: quod abominor, *God forbid.* (2) *to hate, detest.*

ăbŏrĭor -ŏriri -ortus, dep.: of heavenly bodies, *to set*; poet., of the voice, *to fail.*

ăbŏriscor -i = aborior: q.v.

ăbortĭo -ōnis, f. *untimely birth, miscarriage.*

ăbortīvus -a -um, *prematurely born.*

ăbortus -ūs, m. *miscarriage.*

abrādo -radĕre -rāsi -rāsum, *to scrape off, shave.* Transf., *to squeeze out, to extort.*

abrĭpĭo -rĭpĕre -rĭpŭi -reptum *to, snatch away, drag off, remove, detach.*

abrōdo -rōdĕre -rōsi -rōsum, *to gnaw off*

abrŏgātĭo -ōnis, f. *annulling, repealing.*

abrŏgo -are. *to repeal, annul, remove, take away.*

abrŏtŏnum -i, n. and **abrŏtŏnus** -i, m. *southern-wood.*

abrumpo -rumpĕre -rūpi -ruptum, *to break off, sever; to remove, dissociate; to break off prematurely, destroy.*
Hence partic. **abruptus** -a -um, *steep, precipitous, abrupt, rough.* N. as subst., *a steep place.* Adv. **abruptē.**

abruptĭo -ōnis, f. *tearing away*; hence *divorce.*

abscēdo -cēdĕre -cessi -cessum, *to go away, depart, retire, desert.*

abscessĭo -ōnis, f. *going away, separation.*

abscessus -ūs, m. *going away, withdrawal.*

abscīdo -cīdĕre -cīdi -cīsum, *to cut off; to separate* or *take away.*
Hence partic. **abscīsus** -a -um, *precipitous, abrupt, short.*

abscindo -scindĕre -scĭdi -scissum, *to tear off, wrench away*; venas, *to cut open the veins*; poet., abscissa comas, *with her hair torn.* Transf., *to divide* or *separate.*

abscondo -condĕre -condi (-condĭdi) -condĭtum (-consum), *to conceal*; *to lose sight of*; pass., of stars, *to set.* Adv. from partic., **abscondĭtē,** *obscurely.*

absens -entis, *absent*; see also **absum.**

absentĭa -ae, f. *absence.*

absĭlĭo -ire, -ĭi or -ŭi, *to spring forth* or *away.*

absĭmĭlis -e, *unlike.*

absinthĭum -i, n. *wormwood.*

absisto -sistĕre -stĭti, *to go away* from a place or person; *to desist* from an action.

absŏlūtĭo -ōnis, f. (1) *acquittal.* (2) *perfection.*

absŏlūtōrĭus -a -um, *relating to acquittal.*

absolvo -solvĕre -solvi -sŏlūtum, *to loosen, to free*: of an accused person, *to acquit*; of a subject, *to dispose of, relate in full*; in gen. *to complete.*
Hence partic. **absŏlūtus** -a -um, *perfect, complete; unfettered, unconditional.* Adv. **absŏlūtē,** *perfectly, completely.*

absŏnus -a -um, *inharmonious, discordant, disagreeing.*

absorbĕo -ēre -ŭi, *to swallow, gulp down*; hence *to carry away, engross.*

absque, prep. with abl. *without.*

abstēmĭus -a -um, *temperate, abstemious.*

abstergĕo -tergēre -tersi -tersum, *to wipe off, clean away.*

absterrĕo -ēre, *to frighten away.*

abstĭnentĭa -ae, f. *self-denial, temperance*; sometimes *fasting.*

abstĭnĕo -tĭnēre -tĭnŭi -tentum: transit., *to hold back*; intransit., *to abstain.*
Hence present partic. **abstĭnens** -entis, *temperate.* Adv. **abstĭnenter.**

absto -are, *to stand aloof.*

abstrăho -trăhĕre -traxi, -tractum *to drag away*; hence *to remove, exclude, restrain.*

abstrūdo -trūdĕre -trūsi -trūsum, *to push away, hide.*
Hence partic. **abstrūsus** -a -um, *concealed, secret, abstruse*; of character, *reserved.*

absum, ăbesse, āfŭi. (1) *to be away, be absent* or *missing*; hence *to take no part* in a thing, *fail to help.* (2) *to be far away, be distant*; hence *to be far from* doing a thing, *to be free from* a fault.

absūmo -sūmĕre -sumpsi -sumptum, *to reduce, consume, waste, destroy.*

absurdus -a -um, *unmelodious, harsh.* Transf., *foolish, unreasonable, out of place*; of persons, *incapable.* Hence adv. **absurdē,** *harshly, discordantly; foolishly.*

ăbundantĭa -ae, f. *abundance, plenty; riches, wealth.*

ăbundē, *copiously, abundantly*; with est and genit., *there is plenty of* a thing.

ăbundo -are, *to overflow; to grow in abundance; to abound, be rich in,* esp. with abl.
Hence partic. **ăbundans** -antis, *overflowing; abundant, numerous; abounding in*; adv. **ăbundanter,** *abundantly, copiously.*

ăbusquĕ, prep. with abl., *from.*

ăbūsus -ūs, m. *using up, wasting.*

ăbūtor -ūti -ūsus, dep., with abl. (1) *to make full use of.* (2) *to abuse, waste*; esp. *to use a word wrongly.*

ac; see atque.

Ăcădēmĭa -ae, f., *the Academy,* a grove near Athens where Plato taught; meton., *the Academic school of philosophy.* Hence adj. **Ăcădēmĭcus** -a -um; n. pl. **Ăcădēmĭca,** *Cicero's treatise on the Academic philosophy.*

ăcălanthis and **ăcanthis** -ĭdis, f., *a small bird,* perhaps *siskin.*

ăcanthus -i, m. (1) *bear's foot, a plant.* (2) *a thorny evergreen tree.*

Ăcarnānĭa -ae, *Acarnania, a country in western Greece.*

Acca Lārentĭa, *a Roman goddess*; **Lārentālĭa** or **Accālĭa** -ĭum, n. pl. *her festival at Rome in December.*

accēdo -cēdĕre -cessi -cessum, *to approach, come near*; of persons, *to enter upon* a course; ad rem publicam, *to begin public life*; of things, *to be added*; huc accedit ut, *it is also true that, moreover.*

accĕlĕro -are: transit., *to quicken, accelerate*; intransit., *to hasten.*

accendo -cendĕre -cendi -censum, *to kindle, set alight, set on fire.* Transf., *to fire, inflame, excite.*

accensĕo -censēre -censum, *to reckon in addition.*
Hence partic. **accensus** -a -um, *reckoned with*; m. as subst., *an attendant*; in plural, **accensi,** *reserve troops, supernumeraries.*

acceptĭo -ōnis, f. *reception, acceptance.*

accepto -are, *to receive.*

acceptus -a -um, partic. from accipio; q.v.

accerso = arcesso; q.v.

accessĭo -ōnis, f. *a going* or *coming to; increase; a thing added, appendage.*
accessus -ūs, m. *approach, access; means of approach, entrance.*
[1]**accīdo** -cīdĕre -cīdi -cīsum, *to hew* or *hack at*; hence *to weaken, ruin.*
[2]**accĭdo** -cĭdĕre -cĭdi, *to fall down*; ad pedes, *to fall at a person's feet.* Transf., *to happen, fall out.*
accĭĕo -ēre, obs. form of accio; q.v.
accingo -cingĕre -cinxi -cinctum, *to gird on* a weapon; *to equip, arm* a person; with reflex., or in pass., *to arm oneself*, hence *to make oneself ready.*
accĭo -ire -īvi (-ĭi) -ītum, *to call, summon.*
accĭpĭo -cĭpĕre -cēpi -ceptum, *to take, receive, accept.* Esp. with the senses, *to hear, feel*, etc.; with the understanding, *to grasp, to learn*; also *to take, interpret* in a certain sense; of persons, *to receive hospitably*, or *to treat* in any particular manner; in business, acceptum referre, *to enter on the credit side* of an account book, hence *to consider oneself indebted to someone for a thing.*
Hence partic. **acceptus** -a -um, *welcome, pleasant, agreeable.*
accĭpĭter -tris, m. *a hawk.*
accītus -ūs, m. *a summons.*
Accĭus -a -um, *name of a Roman* gens; esp. of L. Accius, tragic poet (170-c. 85 B.C.).
acclāmātĭo -ōnis, f. *a loud cry.*
acclāmo -are, *to cry out* (in approval or otherwise); with acc. of person, *to name by acclamation.*
acclāro -are, *to make clear, reveal.*
acclīnis -e, *leaning towards, inclined to.*
acclīno -are, *to lean towards, incline to.*
acclīvis -e, *inclined upwards.*
acclīvĭtās -ātis, f. *upward slope.*
acclīvus -a -um, = acclivis; q.v.
accŏla -ae, m. or f. *neighbour*; as adj. *living near, neighbouring.*
accŏlo -cŏlĕre -cŏlŭi -cultum, *to live near.*
accommŏdātĭo -ōnis, f. (1) *proportion* or *adjusting.* (2) *courteousness, complaisance.*
accommŏdātus -a -um, partic. from accommodo; q.v.
accommŏdo -are, *to fit, put on* equipment, etc.; *to make suitable, adjust, adapt.*
Hence partic. **accommŏdātus** -a -um, *adapted, suitable*; adv. **accommŏdātē,** *agreeably.*
accommŏdus -a -um, *fit, adapted.*
accrēdo -crēdĕre -crēdĭdi -crēdĭtum, *to believe* (with dat.).
accresco -crescĕre -crēvi -crētum, *to grow, increase*; with dat., *to be joined to* a thing.
accŭbĭtĭo -ōnis, f. and **accŭbĭtus** -ūs, m. *the act of reclining at table.*
accŭbo -are, *to lie*, or *recline beside*, esp. at table; apud hominem, *to dine at a man's house.*
accumbo -cumbĕre -cŭbŭi -cŭbĭtum, *to lie down* or *recline*, esp. at table.
accŭmŭlātor -ōris, m. *one who heaps together.*
accŭmŭlo -are, *to heap up, accumulate*; *to heap* things *on* a person, *give in abundance; to ply, overwhelm* a person with things; *to increase.* Adv. from partic. **accŭmŭlātē,** *abundantly, copiously.*
accūrātĭo -ōnis, f. *accuracy, carefulness.*
accūro -are, *to take care of, prepare with care.*
Hence partic. **accūrātus** -a -um, *done with care, careful, exact, accurate.* Adv. **accūrātē.**
accurro -currere -curri (-cŭcurri) -cursum, *to run to*; of ideas, *to occur.*
accursus -ūs, m. *running, concourse.*
accūsābĭlis -e, *blameworthy.*
accūsātĭo -ōnis, f. *an accusation, indictment.*
accūsātor -ōris, m. *an accuser*; hence *an informer.*
accūsātōrĭus -a -um, *of* or *like an accuser*; adv. **accūsātōrĭē.**
accūsatrix -īcis, f. *a female accuser.*
accūso -are, *to accuse*; in gen., *to blame, find fault with.*
[1]**ăcer** -ĕris, n. *the maple tree* or *maple wood.*
[2]**ācer** -cris -cre, *sharp, cutting, keen.* Hence, to taste, *biting*; to touch, *sharp*; of sounds, *shrill*; of smells, *penetrating*; of sight, *keen*; of emotions, *painful*; of understanding or character, *quick, vigorous, energetic.* Adv. **ācrĭter,** *sharply, keenly.*
ăcerbĭtās -ātis, f. *bitterness, harshness, painfulness*; in plur., *calamities.*
ăcerbo -are, *to make bitter, to aggravate.*
ăcerbus -a -um, *bitter.* Hence, of sounds, *harsh*; of looks, *dark, gloomy*; of speech or writing, *bitter*; of events, etc., *painful, severe*; of persons, *morose*; from the notion of unripeness, *premature.* Adv. **ăcerbē,** *bitterly, harshly.*
ăcernus -a -um, *made of maple wood.*
ăcerra -ae, f. *a casket for incense.*
acervatim, *by accumulation*; dicere, *to sum up.*
ăcervo -are, *to heap up.*
ăcervus -i, m. *a heap, mass*; in logic, *argument by accumulation.*
ăcesco ăcescĕre ăcŭi, *to grow sour.*
ăcētum -i, n. *vinegar.*
Ăchāĭa or **Ăchāia** -ae, f., *the Greek country of Achaia, in the Peloponnese*, or in gen. *Greece*; after 146 B.C., *the Roman province of Achaea.* Hence adj. and subst. **Ăchaeus** and **Ăchīvus,** *Achaean, an Achaean* (or *Greek*).
Ăchātes -ae, m. *friend of Aeneas.*
Ăchĕron -ontis, m. (older form **Ăchĕruns** -untis) *mythol. river in the lower world; the lower world itself.*
Ăchillēs s, and **Ăchillēūs** -ei, m. *a Greek hero, son of Peleus and Thetis.* Adj. **Ăchillēus** -a -um.
Ăchīvus -a -um; see **Ăchaia.**
ăcĭdus -a -um, *sharp, sour.*

ăcĭēs -ei, f. *keenness, edge*; of the mind, *penetration, insight*; of the eye, *a piercing look* or *keen vision*; sometimes *the pupil of the eye*, or *the eye* itself. Milit., *battle-line*; hence *battle, battlefield*.

ăcīnăcēs -is, m. *a Persian sabre*.

ăcĭnus -i, m. and **ăcĭnum** -i, n. *a berry; the seed of a berry*.

ăcĭpenser -eris, also **ăcĭpensis** -is, m. *the sturgeon*.

āclys -ŷdis, f. *a small javelin*.

ăcŏnītum -i, n. *monk's hood, aconite*; in gen., *strong poison*.

acq- = adq-; q.v.

acrātŏphŏrum -i, n. *a vessel for unmixed wine*.

ācrēdŭla -ae, f. *a bird*, perhaps *thrush, owl*, or *nightingale*.

ācrĭcŭlus -a -um, *somewhat sharp in temper*.

ācrĭmōnĭa -ae, f. *sharpness, keenness*.

ācrĭtĕr, adv. from acer; q.v.

ācrŏāmă -ătis, n. *an entertainment*, esp. *musical; an entertainer*, i.e. *reader, actor*, or *singer*.

ācrŏāsis -is, f. *reading aloud, recitation*.

Ācrŏcĕraunĭa -orum, n. pl. *part of the Ceraunian mountains*; hence *any dangerous place*.

[1]acta -ae, f. *sea-shore, beach*; meton., *life at the seaside*.

[2]acta -orum, from partic. of ago; q.v.

Actaeon -ŏnis, m. *a hunter turned into a stag by Diana, and killed by his hounds*.

actĭo -ōnis, f. *action, doing*; gratiarum, *giving of thanks*. Esp. *the action of a magistrate, a proposal; in the theatre, a plot*; at law, *an action* or *the bringing of it* or *right to bring it*; also *a legal formula* or *speech on an indictment*.

actĭto -are, *to be busy, in law-court* or *theatre*.

Actĭum -i, n. *a promontory in Acarnania*, near which Augustus conquered Antony and Cleopatra (31 B.C.). Adj. **Actĭăcus** and **Actĭus** -a -um.

actor -ōris, m. (1) *a driver*. (2) *a doer*; esp. *a dramatic actor, player; a public speaker; the plaintiff in an action; a manager of property*.

actŭārĭŏlum -i, n. *a small skiff*.

actŭārĭus -a -um *swift*; actuaria (navis), *a fast-sailing vessel*.

actŭōsus -a -um, *active*; adv. **actŭōsē**.

actus -ūs, m. (1) *driving, movement*; esp. of cattle; hence *right of way for driving* cattle, etc. (2) *doing, action*, esp. on the stage; hence *the presentation of a piece on the stage*; also *a division of a piece, an act*.

actūtum, adv. *immediately, directly*.

ăcŭlĕātus -a -um, *provided with prickles* or *stings*; hence *pointed, stinging; hair-splitting, subtle*.

ăcŭlĕus -i, m. *sting, point*; fig., esp. in plur., *painful thoughts, cutting remarks*.

ăcūmen -ĭnis, n. *sharp point*; hence *the point* of remarks, etc.; *sharpness of intellect; cunning, trickery*.

ăcŭo -ŭĕre -ŭi -ūtum, *to sharpen, whet; to quicken, make expert; to inflame, encourage, incite*.

Hence partic. **ăcūtus** -a -um, *sharpened, pointed, acute*; to the hearing, *shrill*; to touch, *piercing*; of events, etc., *sharp, painful*; of minds, *sharp, keen, intelligent*; of orators, *effective*. Adv. **acūte,** *keenly, sharply*.

ăcus -ūs, f. *a needle, bodkin*; acu pingere, *to embroider*; acu rem tangere, *to hit the nail on the head*.

ăcūtŭlus -a -um *rather subtle*.

ăcūtus; see acuo.

ad, prep. with acc. (1) of motion, *towards, to* a person or place; ad Dianae (sc. aedem) *to Diana's temple*; ad me, *to my house*; often strengthened by usque. (2) of rest, *at* or *near*. (3) of time: either *to, until*, or *at, about*. (4) of other relations: *towards, for* a purpose; *concerning, bearing on; compared with, in addition to; in conformity with; approximating to, about; in consequence of* an event; *as far as, up to* a certain degree; ad summam, *on the whole*; ad verbum, *literally*.

ădactĭo -ōnis, f. *driving, compulsion*.

ădactus -ūs, m. *bringing to, application*.

ădaequē, *in like manner*.

ădaequo -are: transit., *to make equal*; hence *to compare*; intransit., *to match, come near to*.

ădămantēus -a -um, *hard as steel*.

ădămantĭnus -a -um, *made of steel*.

ădămas -antis, m. *the hardest steel, adamant*; poet., *anything firm, unyielding, durable*.

ădambŭlo -are, *to walk by* or *near*.

ădămo -are, *to fall in love with, find pleasure in*.

ădăpĕrĭo -ăpĕrire -ăpĕrui -ăpertum, *to open fully*.

ădauctus -ūs, m. *increase*.

ădaugĕo -ēre -auxi -auctum, *to increase, augment*.

ădaugesco, -ĕre, *to begin to increase*.

adbĭbo -bĭbĕre -bĭbi -bĭbĭtum, *to drink in*.

addenseo -ēre, and **addenso** -are, *to make thick* or *compact*.

addīco -dīcĕre -dixi -dictum, *to assent to*; in augury, *to promise well*; of a judge (especially the praetor), *to award*; of an auctioneer, *to knock down* a lot; of an owner, *to put up for sale*. Hence in gen., *to give up* or *over, doom, dedicate, surrender*; partic. **addictus,** *bound, pledged*.

addictĭo -ōnis, f. *a judge's award*.

addisco -discĕre -dĭdĭci, *to learn in addition*.

addĭtāmentum -i, n. *an addition*.

addo addĕre addĭdi addĭtum. (1) *to give, bring, place*; of feelings, *to inspire, cause*. (2) *to add, join*; esp. in speech or writing; adde, *or* adde huc, *or* eo, *add to this, take also into consideration*.

addŏcĕo -ēre, *to teach in addition*.

addŭbĭto -are, *to begin to doubt*.

addūco -dūcĕre -duxi -ductum. (1) *to bring* or *lead to* a person, place, or condition; of persons, *to bring to a certain state of mind, to influence, induce.* (2) *to draw to oneself, pull in*; hence *to contract*; partic. **adductus** -a -um, *contracted, taut*; of persons, *strict.* Compar. adv. **adductius.**

ădĕdo -esse -ēdi -ēsum, *to nibble, gnaw; to consume, waste away.*

ădemptĭo -ōnis, f. *taking away.*

ădĕō, adv., *to that point, so far*; often strengthened by usque; of space, *so far*; of time, *so long*; of degree, *so much, so, to such an extent*; sometimes, *even, what is more*; enclitically, with pron. or conjunction, *just.*

ădĕo -īre -ĭi -ĭtum, *to go* or *come to, approach, visit*; in ius, *to go to law*; of business, etc., *to undertake, undergo, incur*; adire hereditatem, *to enter on an inheritance.*

ădeps -ĭpis, c. *soft fat.*

ădeptĭo -ōnis, f. *attainment, obtaining.*

ădĕquĭto -are, *to ride to.*

ădesdum, or **ades dum,** *come hither.*

adfābĭlis -e, *easy to speak to, affable.*

adfābĭlĭtās -ātis, f. *affability.*

adfabrē, *in a workmanlike way.*

adfătim, *sufficiently, enough.*

adfātus -ūs, m. *address, speech.*

adfectātĭo -onis, f. *striving, eagerness.*

adfectātor -ōris, m. *a striver.*

adfectĭo -ōnis, f. *manner of being affected*; hence *relation* to a thing or person, or *change*, or *state, condition*; sometimes *favourable state of mind, good-will.*

adfecto -are, *to strive after, grasp at, aim at, aspire to*; polit. *to try to win over*; in literary style, *to affect*; partic. **adfectatus** -a -um, *studied.*

adfectus -ūs, m. *condition, disposition*; esp. of the mind, *a feeling*; often *friendly feeling, good-will.*

adfectus -a -um, partic. from adficio; q.v.

adfero adferre attŭli adlātum, *to carry to, bring to*; esp. of messages, and news; absol., *to bring news, report.* Transf., *to apply, bring to bear*; vim, *to offer violence; to cause, bring about; to bring forward* by way of excuse or reason; *to bring* by way of help, *contribute.*

adfĭcĭo -ficĕre -fēci -fectum, *to influence, work upon*; with adverbs, *to affect*; with abl. of nouns, *to treat with, present with*; nominem sepultura, *to bury*; poena, *to punish*, beneficio adfici, *to be benefited*; absol., of the body, *to affect adversely, weaken.*

Hence partic. **adfectus** -a -um, *affected, influenced*; with abl. *furnished with, treated with*; absol., of the body, *weakened, sick*; of undertakings, *worked upon*, and so *nearly finished.*

adfīgo -fīgĕre -fixi -fixum, *to fasten to, affix*; litteram ad caput, *to brand*; adfigi animis, *to be imprinted.*

adfingo -fingĕre -finxi -fictum, *to form* or *invent in addition.*

adfīnis -e *neighbouring*; hence *connected with, privy to*; also *related by marriage*; as subst., *a relative.*

adfīnĭtās -ātis, f., *relationship by marriage*; meton., *relations by marriage*; in gen., *union.*

adfirmatĭo -ōnis, f. *positive assertion.*

adfirmo -are *to strengthen; to support a statement, to prove; to assert as true.* Adv. from partic., **adfirmatē,** *positively.*

adflatus -ūs, m. *blowing* or *breathing on, breath*; maris, *sea breeze.* Transf. *inspiration.*

adflĕo -flēre -flēvi -flētum, *to weep at.*

adflictātĭo -ōnis, f. *pain, torture.*

adflicto -are, *to agitate, knock about harass, distress.*

adflictor -ōris, m., *a subverter.*

adflīgo -flīgĕre -flixi -flictum, *to dash, knock down, knock about; to weaken, discourage, injure*; causam susceptam, *to drop.*

Hence partic. **adflictus** -a -um, *damaged, shattered*; of spirits, *broken down, desponding*; of character, *vile, contemptible.*

adflo -are, *to blow on* or *breathe on.*

adflŭentĭa -ae, f. *overflow, abundance.*

adflŭo -flŭere -fluxi -fluxum. *to flow to, flow near*; of men, *to stream, to flock together.* Transf., *to flow freely, to be abundant*, with abl., *to abound in.*

Hence partic. **adflŭens** -entis, *rich, abounding.* Compar. adv. **adflŭentĭus.**

adfor -ari, dep. *to accost, address*; esp. *to say farewell* to the dead, and *to pray to* gods.

adfulgĕo -fulgēre -fulsi, *to shine, glitter; to shine upon, favour*, with dat.

adfundo -fundĕre -fūdi -fusum, *to pour upon*; colonia amne adfusa, *washed by a river*; adfundere se, or adfundi, *to prostrate oneself.* Transf., *to throw in, add.*

adgĕmo -ĕre, *to groan at*, with dat.

adgĕro -gĕrĕre -gessi -gestum, *to carry to, bring up.*

adgestus -ūs, m. *carrying to, accumulation.*

adglŏmĕro -are, *to wind on a ball*; hence *to add.*

adglūtĭno -are, *to glue to, fasten to.*

adgrăvesco -ĕre, *to grow worse* (of sickness).

adgrăvo -are, *to make heavier*; hence, *to make worse.*

adgrĕdĭor -grĕdi -gressus, dep. *to go to, approach*; with words, *to address*; of enemies, *to attack*; of business, etc., *to begin, undertake, attempt.*

adgrĕgo -are, *to add to the flock; so to attach, associate.*

adgressĭo -ōnis, f. *the introduction to a speech.*

ădhaerĕo -haerēre -haesi -haesum, *to hang to, stick to, adhere*; of places, *to border on, be near*; fig., *to depend on, cling to.*

adhaeresco -haerescĕre -haesi -haesum, *to hang on to, adhere.* Transf., *to*

cling to, hang on, attach oneself; in speaking, *to stick fast, stop.*
adhaesio -ōnis, f. and **adhaesus** -ūs, m. *adhering, clinging.*
ădhĭbĕo -ēre -ŭi -ĭtum, *to bring up to, apply, bring to bear*; of persons, *to invite, call in, employ* for a purpose; with adv., *to treat.*
ădhinnĭo -ire, *to neigh after, neigh at.*
ădhortātĭo -ōnis, f. *exhortation.*
ădhortātor -ōris, m. *one who exhorts.*
ădhortor -ari, dep. *to exhort, encourage* (esp. of soldiers).
ădhūc, of time, *hitherto, till now, till then; still, even now*; in gen., *besides, also*; with comparatives, *even, still.*
adiăcĕo -ēre, *to lie by the side of, be adjacent.* N. pl. of partic. as subst. **adiăcentĭa,** *the neighbourhood.*
adicĭo -icĕre -iēci -iectum, *to throw to*; hence *to cast, direct, apply*; also *to add*; at an auction, *to outbid.*
adiectĭo -ōnis, f. *addition, advance.*
adiectus -ūs, m. *addition.*
ădĭgo -ĭgĕre -ēgi -actum, *to drive, force, compel*; hominem ad iusiurandum, or iureiurando, *to put a man on his oath.*
ădĭmo -ĭmĕre -ēmi -emptum, *to take away.*

Hence partic. **ădemptus** -a -um, poet., *dead.*
ădĭpatus -a -um, *fatty, greasy*; n. pl. as subst., *pastry.* Transf., o style, *bombastic.*
ădĭpiscor -ĭpisci -eptus, dep. *to come up to, overtake*; hence *to obtain.* Perf. partic. adeptus, used passively, = *obtained.*
ădĭtĭo -ōnis, f. *approach.*
ădĭtus -ūs, m. *approach, access*; hence also *right* or *possibility of entrance*; homo rari aditus, *difficult of access*; concr., *an entrance to a place, approach.* Transf., *opportunity of obtaining.*
adiūdĭco -are, *to award as a judge, assign, grant.*
adiūmentum -i, n. *help, assistance.*
adiunctĭo -ōnis, f. *joining, addition, union*; rhet. *a limitation,* or *repetition.*
adiunctor -ōris, m., *one who joins.*
adiungo -iungĕre -iunxi -iunctum, *to join to, connect*; adiunctus fundus, *neighbouring*; of immaterial things, *to associate, impart*; of persons, *to attach,* esp. as partner, friend, etc.

Hence partic. **adiunctus** -a -um, *bound to, belonging to*; n. pl. as subst. *collateral circumstances.*
adiūro, -are, *to swear in addition*; *to swear to a thing, promise on oath.*
adiūto -are, *to be serviceable, help.*
adiūtor -ōris, m., *a helper, assistant, deputy.*
adiūtrix -īcis, f., of females and f. nouns, *an assistant, aid*; used of *reserve legions* under the empire.
adiŭvo -iŭvāre -iūvi -iūtum, *to help, assist, support.*
adlābor -lābi -lapsus, dep. *to glide to, flow to,* with dat or acc.
adlăbōro -are, *to labour at*; also *to add to by labour.*
adlacrĭmo -are, *to weep at.*
adlapsus -ūs, m., *a gliding approach.*
adlatro -are, *to bark at, rail at.*
adlaudābĭlis -e, *praiseworthy.*
adlecto -are, *to entice.*
adlēgātĭo -ōnis, f. *the sending of a person on a mission.*
adlēgo -are., *to send on private business, to commission*; adlegati, *deputies.* Transf., *to instigate, suborn*; *to adduce* or *allege in excuse.*
adlĕgo -lĕgĕre -lēgi -lectum, *to choose, elect.*
adlĕvāmentum -i, n., *a means of alleviation.*
adlĕvātĭo -ōnis, f., *a lifting up*; hence *alleviation.*
adlĕvo -are, *to lift up, erect*; hence *to lighten, alleviate*; pass., adlevari, *to be cheered.*
adlĭcĭo -lĭcĕre -lexi -lectum, *to allure, entice.*
adlīdo -līdĕre -līsi -līsum, *to strike against, dash against*; pass., adlidi, *to suffer damage.*
adlĭgo -are, *to tie to, bind to*; of wounds, *to bind up.* Transf., in gen., *to fetter, bind, confine*; esp. *to bind by friendship, obligations, promise,* etc.; pass., *to become an accomplice in, make oneself responsible for*; perf. partic. adligatus, *implicated, involved.*
adlĭno -lĭnĕre -lēvi -litum, *to smear on, bedaub.*
adlŏcūtĭo -ōnis, f. *an address*; esp. *a word of comfort.*
adlŏquĭum -i, n., *exhortation, encouragement, consolation.*
adlŏquor -lŏqui -lŏcūtus, dep. *to address*; esp. *to encourage, appeal to.*
adlūcĕo -lūcēre -luxi, *to shine at,* or *upon.*
adlūdo -lūdĕre -lūsi -lūsum, *to jest at, sport with*; of waves, *to play* or *dash upon.*
adlŭo -lŭĕre -lŭi, *to wash,* of the sea.
adlŭvĭēs -ēi, f., *a pool caused by flooding.*
adlŭvĭo -ōnis, f., *alluvial land.*
admātūro -are, *to hasten.*
admētĭor mētiri -mensus, dep. *to measure out to.*
Admētus -i, m. *husband of Alcestis.*
admĭnĭcŭlor -ari, dep. *to support, prop.*
admĭnĭcŭlum -i, n. *prop, support*; in gen., *aid, help.*
admĭnister -stri, m. *attendant, assistant.*
admĭnistra -ae, f. *a (female) helper.*
admĭnistrātĭo -ōnis, f. *the giving of help; direction, government.*
admĭnistrātor -ōris, m. *administrator, manager.*
admĭnistro -are. *to help, assist; to manage, direct, administer*: navem, *to steer.*
admīrābĭlis -e. *admirable; astonishing, strange.* Adv., **admīrābĭlĭter.**
admīrābĭlĭtās -ātis, f. *admirableness; admiration.*
admīrātĭo -ōnis, f. *admiration*; plur. *outbursts of admiration; wonder, astonishment.*

admīror -ari, dep. *to admire; to be astonished, to wonder.* Hence gerundive **admīrandus** -a -um, *admirable.*
admiscĕo -miscēre -miscŭi -mixtum (-mistum), *to mix with, to join*; admisceri novis sermonibus *to become familiar with.*
admissārĭus -i, m. *stallion.*
admissĭo -onis, f. *audience,* esp. with kings, etc.
admitto -mittĕre -mīsi -missum, *to send to, admit*; esp. of horses, *to let go, put to a gallop.* Transf., *to allow; to admit a crime to one's record,* so *to commit*; hence n. of partic. as subst. **admissum** -i, *a crime.*
admixtĭo -ōnis, f. *an admixture.*
admŏdĕrātē, *appropriately.*
admŏdum, *up to the measure, up to the mark*; hence, *completely.* With adjectives and other parts of speech, *wholly, quite*; puer admodum, *a mere boy*; with numbers, *just about*; in affirmative answers, *certainly.*
admŏnĕo -ēre -ŭi -ĭtum, *to admonish, remind,* of a fact or duty. N. of partic. as subst. **admŏnĭtum** -i, *an admonition.*
admŏnĭtĭo -ōnis, f. *a reminding*; esp. *a friendly admonition.*
admŏnĭtor -ōris, m. *one who reminds.*
admŏnĭtū, abl. sing. m., *by reminding, by warning.*
admordĕo -mordēre -morsum, *to bite at, gnaw*; fig. *to fleece.*
admōtĭo -ōnis, f. *moving to, application.*
admŏvĕo -mŏvēre -mōvi -mōtum, *to move to, bring up, apply*; manum operi, *to engage in a work*; manus nocentibus, *to lay hands on the guilty*; milit. *to bring up* war-machines or soldiers.
admūgĭo -ire, *to bellow after.*
admurmŭrātĭo -ōnis, f. *murmuring.*
admurmŭro -are, *to murmur at.*
adnăto -are, *to swim to or beside.*
adnecto -nectĕre -nexŭi -nexum, *to bind to, connect with.*
adnexus -ūs, m. *binding, connexion.*
adnītor -nīti -nīsus or -nixus, dep. *to press against, lean upon.* Transf., *to strive after.*
adno -are, *to swim to,* or *near,* or *beside.*
adnŏto -are, *to note, remark on.*
adnŭmĕro -are, *to count out, pay; to reckon in with,* with acc. and dat.
adnŭo -nŭĕre -nŭi -nūtum, *to nod to; to indicate by nodding; to nod assent to*; in gen., *to agree*; also *to agree to give* or *do* a thing.
[1]**ădŏlĕo** -ēre -ŭi, *to worship, offer sacrifice, burn a sacrifice; to sacrifice on* an altar; in gen., *to burn.*
[2]**ădŏlĕo** -ēre, *to smell.*
ădŏlescens = adulescens; q.v.
ădŏlesco -ŏlescĕre -ŏlēvi. (1) *to grow up, come to maturity.* (2) *to be heaped up,* or perhaps *to burn* (cf. adoleo).
Hence partic. **ădultus** -a -um, *grown up, adult, mature.*
Ădōnis -is or -ĭdis, *a beautiful young man, beloved of Venus.*
ădŏpĕrĭo -ŏpĕrire -ŏpĕrŭi -ŏpertum, *to cover* or *close.*
ădŏpīnor -ari, dep. *to guess.*
ădoptātĭo -ōnis, f. *adopting.*
ădoptĭo -ōnis, f. *the adoption of a child.*
ădoptīvus -a -um, *adopted, connected with adoption*; of plants, *grafted.*
ădopto -are, *to choose for oneself*; esp. *to adopt,* as child or grandchild; of plants, *to graft.*
ădŏr -oris, n. *a species of grain, spelt.*
ădōrātĭo -ōnis, f. *praying to, adoration.*
ădōrĕus -a -um, *of spelt*; f. as subst. *a reward for valour* (originally a gift of corn).
ădŏrĭor -ŏriri -ortus, dep. *to rise up at*; hence *to attack, set about, attempt, undertake.*
ădorno -are, *to prepare, furnish, provide*; *to adorn.*
ădōro -are, *to speak to*; esp. *to address* a deity, in worship or entreaty; sometimes *to ask* a deity for a thing.
adp-; see under app-.
adquīesco -quīescĕre -quīēvi quīētum, *to rest, repose, be undisturbed, find comfort.*
adquīro -quirĕre -quīsīvi -quīsītum, *to acquire, get,* esp. in addition to previous possessions.
adrādo -rādĕre -rāsi -rāsum, *to scrape, shave.*
adrectus -a -um, partic. from adrigo; q.v.
adrēpo -rēpĕre -repsi -reptum, *to creep up, glide gently to.*
Adrĭa = Hadria; q.v.
adrīdĕo -rīdēre -rīsi -rīsum, *to laugh to, to smile upon.* Transf., *to be favourable to; to please.*
adrĭgo rĭgĕre -rexi -rectum, *to erect, lift up*; hence *to excite, arouse.*
adrĭpĭo -rĭpĕre -rĭpŭi -reptum, *to seize, snatch, appropriate*; poet., terram velis, *to sail quickly to*; mentally, *to grasp, comprehend quickly*; legal, *to arrest, bring to court, accuse*; hence perhaps *to satirize.*
adrīsor -ōris, m. *a flatterer.*
adrōdo -rōdĕre -rōsi -rōsum, *to gnaw at.*
adrŏgans, partic. from adrogo; q.v.
adrŏgantia -ae, f. *assumption,* hence *pride, haughtiness.*
adrŏgo -are, polit., *to associate* in office; in gen., either *to take to oneself* (sibi), *to claim, assume,* or *to adjudge, grant to another* (dat.).
Hence partic. **adrŏgans** -antis, *assuming, arrogant, haughty*; adv. **adrŏganter.**
adsc-; see under asc-.
adsectātĭo -ōnis, f. *respectful attendance.*
adsectātor -ōris, m. *a companion, follower.*
adsector -ari, dep. *to follow, attend respectfully.*
adsĕcŭla (**adsecla**) -ae, m. *follower, servant, sycophant.*
adsensĭo -ōnis, *assent, agreement, applause*; philosoph. *belief in the reality of sensible appearances.*

adsensor -ōris, m. *one who assents* or *agrees.*

adsensus -ūs, m. *assent, agreement*; philosoph. *belief in the reality of sensible appearances*; poet., *echo.*

adsentātĭo -ōnis, f. *flattering assent* or *applause, flattery.*

adsentātĭuncŭla -ae, f. *trivial flattery.*

adsentātor -oris, m. *a flatterer.*

adsentātōrĭē, *flatteringly.*

adsentĭo -sentire -sensi -sensum, and **adsentĭor** -sentiri, -sensus, dep. *to assent to, agree with.*

adsentor -ari, dep. *to assent constantly*; hence *to flatter.*

adsĕquor -sĕqui -sĕcūtus, dep. *to follow after: to reach by following, to come up to, attain*; mentally, *to grasp.*

[1]**adsĕro** -sĕrĕre -sēvi -sĭtum, *to plant at* or *near.*

[2]**adsĕro** -sĕrĕre -sĕrŭi -sertum, *to lay hold* of a slave, and thereby either *claim him* or *declare him free*; in gen. *to set free, protect*, or *to claim.*

adsertor -ōris, m. *one who asserts the freedom* of another person *or claims him as his own.*

adservĭo -ire, *to assist, help.*

adservo -are, *to preserve, watch.*

adsessĭo -ōnis, f. *a sitting by the side of one* (to console).

adsessor -ōris, m. *one who sits by*, or *assists.*

adsĕvērātĭo -ōnis, f. *earnestness, vehemence*; esp. *vehement assertion, asseveration.*

adsĕvēro -are, *to be earnest*; esp. *to assert confidently* or *strongly*. Adv. from partic. **adsĕvēranter,** *earnestly.*

adsĭdĕo -sĭdēre -sēdi -sessum, *to sit near, sit beside*, esp. beside a person, *to give comfort, advice*, etc.; usually with dat. Hence, *to devote oneself to; to approximate to*; milit., *to besiege, blockade.*

adsīdo -sīdĕre -sēdi -sessum, *to sit down.*

adsĭdŭĭtās -atis, f. *continual presence, regular attention*. Hence *constancy; constant repetition*; epistularum, *regular correspondence.*

[1]**adsĭdŭus** -a -um, *continuously in one place*, or *one occupation*, in gen. *constant, persistent*. Adv. **adsĭdŭē** and **adsĭdŭō,** *continuously, without remission.*

[2]**adsĭdŭus** -i, m. *a taxpaying citizen.*

adsignātĭo -ōnis, f. *assignment, allotment.*

adsigno -are. (1) *to assign, allot*; hence *to impute, ascribe.* (2) *to seal*; hence to *impress upon.*

adsĭlĭo -sĭlire -sĭlŭi, *to leap to*, or *on.*

adsĭmĭlis -e, *like, similar.*

adsĭmŭlo -are, *to make like; to compare.*

Hence partic. **adsĭmŭlatus** -a -um, *similar, pretended, simulated.*

adsisto adsistĕre adstĭti or astĭti, *to place oneself at, to stand by*; at law, *to defend.*

adsŏlĕo -ēre, *to be accustomed*; ut adsolet, *as is usual.*

adsŏno -are, *to answer with a sound.*

adsp-; see under asp-.

adsterno -ĕre, *to strew* or *spread upon.*

adstĭpŭlātor -ōris, m. *a supporter.*

adstĭpŭlor -ari, dep. *to agree with.*

adsto -stare -stĭti, *to stand up, stand by* esp. *to stand by to help, to assist.*

adstrĕpo -ĕre, *to make a noise at*; esp. *to applaud.*

adstringo -stringĕre -strinxi -strictum, *to tighten, draw together, contract, make fast*; in writing or speech, *to compress*; of persons, *to bind, oblige*; with reflex., se adstringere, *to commit oneself to, become guilty of.*

Hence partic. **adstrictus** -a -um, *tight, compressed, drawn together; close-fisted, avaricious*; of oratory, *concise*; adv. **adstrictē.**

adstrŭo -strŭĕre -struxi -structum, *to build to* or *near*; hence *to add to.*

adstŭpĕo -ēre, *to be astonished at*, with dat.

adsuēfăcĭo -făcĕre -fēci -factum, *to accustom* a person *to* a thing.

adsuesco -suescĕre -suēvi -suētum: intransit., *to grow accustomed*: adsuevi, *I am accustomed*; transit., *to accustom*; poet., of things, *to make familiar.*

Hence partic. **adsuētus** -a -um, *customary, usual; accustomed to.*

adsuētūdo -ĭnis, f. *custom, use.*

adsuētus -a -um, partic. from adsuesco; q.v.

adsulto -are, *to leap violently upon; to attack, assault.*

adsultus -u, m. *leaping up, assault.*

adsum ădesse adfŭi, *to be present, to be at* or *near*; esp. *to be present and ready, to stand by*; hence, *to support, be favourable to*; sometimes *to be present for a special purpose*, esp. political or legal; of the mind, adesse animo *or* animis, *to attend*; of things, *to be near, at hand.*

adsūmo -sūmĕre -sumpsi -sumptum, *to take to oneself*, or *take in addition* a person or thing; hence *to claim, appropriate, call in*; in logic, *to state the minor premises of a syllogism.*

adsumptĭo -ōnis, f. *choice, adoption*; in logic, *the minor premise of a syllogism.*

adsumptīvus -a -um, *deriving its defence from an extraneous cause.*

adsŭo -ĕre, *to sew on.*

adsurgo -surgĕre -surrexi -surrectum, *to rise up, stand up*; with dat., *to rise in the presence of* a person, as a sign of respect: of feelings, *to rise, be aroused*; of style, *to become elevated*; of material things, *to rise up.*

adt-; see under att-.

ădūlātĭo -ōnis, f. *fawning, cringing, flattery.*

ădūlātor -ōris, m. flatterer.

ădŭlescens (**ădŏlescens**) -entis: as adj., *young, growing*; as subst., *a young man or young woman.*

ădŭlescentĭa -ae, f. *youth.*

ădŭlescentŭlus -i, m. *a young man.*

ădūlo -are, *to fawn* (*upon*).
ădūlor -ari, dep. *to fawn*; with acc. or dat., *to flatter, cringe before.*
ădulter -eri, m., **ădultĕra** -ae, f. *an adulterer, adulteress.*
ădulter -era -erum, adj. *adulterous.*
ădultĕrīnus -a -um, *adulterous; not genuine, forged.*
ădultĕrĭum -i, n. *adultery.*
ădultĕro -are, *to commit adultery, to defile.* Transf. *to falsify, defile, corrupt.*
ădultus -a -um, partic. from adolesco; q.v.
ădumbrātim, *in outline.*
ădumbrātĭo -ōnis, f. *a sketch.*
ădumbro -are, *to shade in, to sketch,* esp. in words. Partic. **ădumbrātus** -a -um, *sketched*; hence *imperfect, shadowy, unreal.*
ăduncĭtās -ātis, f. *a bending, curvature.*
ăduncus -a -um, *bent in, crooked.*
ădurgĕo -ēre, *to press against*; poet., *to pursue closely.*
ădūro -ūrĕre -ussi -ustum, *to set fire to, kindle, singe*; of frost or wind, *to nip.* Hence partic. **ădustus** -a -um, *burnt*: hominum color, *sunburnt.*
ădusquĕ: prep. with acc., *as far as*; adv. *thoroughly, entirely.*
advectĭcĭus -a -um, *brought from a distance, foreign.*
advecto -are, *to convey often.*
advectus -us, m. *conveying, carrying.*
advĕho -vĕhĕre -vexi -vectum, *to carry, bring, convey to* a place; pass., *to ride up, sail to,* etc.
advēlo -are, *to veil.*
advĕna -ae, c. *a stranger, foreigner.*
advĕnĭo -vĕnire -vēni -ventum, *to come to, arrive.* Transf., of time, *to come*; of events, *to happen, come near, break out*; of property, *to come to* an owner.
adventĭcĭus -a -um, *coming from without*; esp. *coming from abroad, foreign.*
advento -are, *to approach, come near.*
adventor -ōris, m. *a visitor, guest.*
adventus -ūs, m. *an arrival.*
adversārĭus -a -um. (1) *turned towards*; n. pl. as subst. *a day-book, journal, memorandum.* (2) *turned against, opposed, contrary*; as subst., m. and f. *an antagonist, rival*; n. pl., *the assertions of an opponent.*
adversor -ari, dep. *to oppose, resist.*
adversus -a -um, partic. from adverto; q.v.
adversus, adversum. Adv., *against, opposite*; adversum ire or venire, *go to meet.* Prep. with acc.: of place, *towards, opposite* ; of action, etc., *against, in answer to*; of behaviour, *towards*; of comparison, *compared with.*
adverto (**advorto**) -vertĕre -verti -versum, *to turn towards*; of the senses, etc. *to direct* towards an object; esp. of the mind, animum (or mentem) advertere, *to direct one's attention to, to perceive,* and of offences, *to punish*; of the object of attention, *to attract.* Hence partic. **adversus** -a -um, *turned towards, fronting, opposite*; solem adversum intueri, *to look straight at the sun*; adverso flumine, *against the stream*; venti adversi, *contrary winds*; hence, in gen., of persons and things, *opposed, unfavourable*; adversa valetudo, *ill health*; proelium, *unsuccessful*; n. as subst. *misfortune.*
advespĕrascit -avit, *evening approaches.*
advĭgĭlo -are, *to watch by, guard, be vigilant.*
advŏcātĭo -ōnis, f. *a calling to one's aid*; hence *legal assistance*; concr., *the bar.*
advŏco -are, *to summon, call*; esp. *to call to one's aid*: as legal t. t., *to call in as adviser, to consult an advocate.* M. of partic. as subst. **advŏcātus** -i, m. *one called in to help,* esp. in court as *witness* or *advocate.*
advŏlo -are, *to fly to*; hence *to hasten* or *rush to.*
advolvo -volvĕre -volvi -vŏlūtum, *to roll to*; of suppliants, advolvi, *or* se advolvere, *to throw oneself down* before a person.
advors- advort- = advers-, advert-; q.v.
ădўtum -i, n. *shrine*; poet., ex adyto cordis, *from the bottom of the heart.*
Aeăcus -i, m. *king of Aegina, grandfather of Achilles; after death a judge in the infernal regions.* Hence subst. **Aeăcĭdes** -ae, m. *a male descendant of Aeacus.*
aedēs (aedis) -is, f. *a building*; in sing., usually *a temple*; plur., *rooms,* or *a house*; of bees, *cells.*
aedĭcŭla -ae, f. *a small building,* esp. *a small temple* or *shrine*; in plur., *a little house.*
aedĭfĭcātĭo -ōnis. f.: abstr., *the act of building*; concr., *a building, structure.*
aedĭfĭcātor -ōris, m. *a builder, architect.*
aedĭfĭcĭum -i, n. *a building.*
aedĭfĭco -are, *to build, erect, establish; to create, frame.*
aedīlĭcĭus -a -um, *relating to the aediles*; m. as subst. *an ex-aedile.*
aedīlis -is, m. *an* aedile, *a public officer at Rome, in charge of streets, markets and public games.*
aedīlĭtās -ātis, f. *aedileship.*
aedĭtĭmus -i, and **aedĭtŭens** -entis, and **aedĭtŭus** -i, m. *keeper of a temple, sacristan.*
Aeēta and **Aeētēs** -ae, m., *king o Colchis, father of Medea.* Hence f. subst. **Aeētĭas** -ădis, and **Aeētīne** -es, = *Medea.*
Aegaeus -a -um, *Aegean*; n. as subst. **Aegaeum** -i, *the Aegean Sea.*
Aegātes -um, f. pl. *three islands off the west coast of Sicily.*
aeger -gra -grum, *sick, ill,* physically or mentally; aeger consilii, *infirm of purpose*; aegris oculis, *with envious eyes*; politically *unsound, mutinous.* M. as subst. *an invalid.* Adv. **aegrē** *with pain, regret* or *difficulty*; hence *hardly, scarcely* (cf. vix).

Aegeus -ĕi, m., *king of Athens, father of Theseus.*

Aegīna -ae, f. *an island near Athens.*

aegis -ĭdis, f. *an aegis,* or *shield,* esp. that of Jupiter or Minerva. Transf., *a protection, bulwark.*

Aegisthus -i, m. *murderer of Agamemnon, afterwards husband of Clytemnestra.*

aegrē, adv. from aeger; q.v.

aegreo -ēre, *to be sick.*

aegresco -ĕre, *to fall ill*; mentally, *to become troubled*; of bad things, *to become worse.*

aegrĭmōnĭa -ae, f., *grief, trouble of mind.*

aegrĭtūdo -ĭnis, f. *sickness,* esp. of the mind.

aegrōtātĭo -ōnis, f. *sickness,* of body or mind.

aegrōto -are *to be sick* or *ill,* in body or mind.

aegrōtus -a -um, *sick, ill,* in body or mind.

Aegyptus -i. (1) m., *a king of Egypt, brother of Danaus.* (2) f. *Egypt*; adj. **Aegyptĭus** and **Aegyptĭăcus** -a -um, *Egyptian.*

aelĭnos -i, m. *a dirge.*

Aemĭlĭus -a -um, *name of an old patrician family at Rome.* Hence adj. **Aemĭlĭanus** -a -um, *relating to the* gens Aemilia; *a surname of Scipio Africanus minor.*

Aemŏnia = Haemonia; q.v.

aemŭlātio -ōnis, f., *a striving after, emulation*; in bad sense, *jealousy, rivalry.*

aemŭlātor -ōris, m., *a rival, imitator.*

aemŭlor -ari, dep., *to rival, emulate*; with dat., *to envy.*

aemŭlus -a -um, *emulous, rivalling*; in bad sense, *jealous.* M. or f. as subst., *a rival,* esp. in love.

Aemus = Haemus; q.v.

Aenēās -ae, m., *son of Venus and Anchises, hero of Vergil's* Aeneid. Hence subst. **Aenĕădēs** -ae, m., *a male descendant of Aeneas*; **Aenēĭs** -ĭdos, f. *Vergil's Aeneid.*

ăēnĕus and **ăhēnĕus** -a -um, *made of copper* or *bronze; hard as bronze, brazen.*

aenigma -ătis, n., *a riddle, mystery.*

ăēnĭpēs -pĕdis, *brazen-footed.*

ăēnus (**ăhēnus**) -a -um, *made of copper* or *bronze*; poet., *hard as bronze.* N. as subst., *a brazen vessel.*

Aeŏles -um, m. *the Aeolians, Greeks living in Greece and Asia Minor.* Hence adj. **Aeŏlĭcus** and **Aeŏlĭus** -a -um, *Aeolic.*

Aeŏlĭa -ae, f. *north part of the coast of Asia Minor.*

Aeŏlus -i, m. *ruler of the Aeolian islands and of the winds.*

aequābĭlis -e, *like, similar, equal.* Transf., *equal to itself, uniform, consistent; fair, impartial.* Hence adv. **aequābĭlĭter,** *equably, uniformly, fairly.*

aequābĭlĭtās -ātis, f., *uniformity, equability*; hence *evenness* in style, *impartiality* in law.

aequaevus -a -um, *of equal age.*

aequālis -e, *even*; of places, *level.* Transf., *equal*; esp. of time, *of the same age, contemporary, coexistent.* M. or f. as subst., *a comrade, person of the same age.* Adv. **aequālĭtĕr,** *evenly, equally.*

aequālĭtās -ātis, f., *evenness*; of places, *smoothness.* Transf., *equality,* esp. *equality of age.*

aequănĭmĭtās -ātis, f. *impartiality.*

aequātĭo -ōnis, f. *making equal*; bonorum, *communism.*

Aequi -orum, m. *a people of central Italy.*

aequĭlībrĭtās -ātis, f. *equal distribution of natural forces.*

aequĭnoctĭālis -e, *equinoctial.*

aequĭnoctĭum -i, n., *the equinox.*

aequĭpăro (**aequĭpĕro**) -are, *to compare; to equal.*

aequĭtās -ātis, f., *uniformity, evenness.* Transf., *equanimity*; also *impartiality, fairness, justice.*

aequo -are. (1) *to make level* or *equal.* (2) *to compare.* (3) *to equal, come up to.*

aequor -ŏris, n., *a flat level surface*; esp. of a *plain,* or of *the sea*; rarely of *a river.*

aequŏrĕus -a -um, *belonging to the sea.*

aequus -a -um, adj. *equal.* (1) *equal in itself, even, level*; ex aequo loco loqui, *to speak in the senate*; milit., aequa frons, *a straight line.* (2) *equal to something else*: ex aequo, in aequo, *on even terms.* Transf., of places or times, *favourable, advantageous*; of battles, *even,* and so *indecisive*; of temper, *even, contented, easy*; aequo animo, *patiently, with resignation*; of behaviour, etc., *equal, impartial*; of persons, *fair*; aequum est, *it is just.* N. as subst. **aequum** -i, *level ground; fairness, equity.* Adv. **aequē,** *in like manner, equally; fairly, justly.*

āēr āĕris, m., *the lower air, the atmosphere.*

aerārĭus -a -um, *of* or *belonging to bronze* or *copper*; hence *belonging to* (*copper*) *money*; tribuni, *paymasters.* M. as subst. *a copper-smith*; in plur., aerarii, *the citizens of the lowest class in Rome.* N. as subst. *a treasury,* esp. *the public treasury at Rome.*

aerātus -a -um, *made of or fitted with copper* or *bronze*; hence *provided with money, rich.*

aerĕus -a -um, *made of* or *fitted with copper* or *bronze.*

aerĭfer -fĕra -fĕrum, *bearing brazen cymbals.*

aerĭpēs -pĕdis, *brazen-footed.*

āĕrĭus (**āĕrĕus**) -a -um, *belonging to the air, airy*; hence *high in the air, lofty.*

aerūgo -ĭnis, f., *the rust of copper, verdigris; rusty money.* Transf., *envy* or *avarice.*

aerumna -ae, f. *labour, toil, hardship.*

aerumnōsus -a -um, adj., *full of hardship.*

aes, aeris, n. *copper ore,* and *the alloy of copper, bronze.* Transf., *anything made of bronze; a vessel, statue,* *trumpet, kettle*; aera aere repulsa, *cymbals*; aes publicum, *public inscriptions.* Esp. *copper* or *bronze money*; aes grave, *the* as; aes signatum, *coined money*; also *money* generally, *pay*; aes alienum, *debt.*

Aeschÿlus -i, m. *an Athenian tragic poet.*

Aescŭlāpĭus -i, m. *the god of medicine.* Hence subst. **Aescŭlāpĭum** -i, n. *a temple of Aesculapius.*

aescŭlētum -i, n., *an oak forest.*

aescŭlĕus -a -um, *relating to the (winter) oak.*

aescŭlus -i, f. *the winter* or *Italian oak.*

Aesōn -ŏnis, m., *a Thessalian prince, father of Jason.* Hence subst. **Aesŏnĭdēs** -ae, m. *a male descendant of Aeson,* = *Jason*; adj. **Aesŏnĭus** -a -um.

Aesōpus -i, m. *a Greek fabulist of Phrygia.*

aestās -ātis, f. *summer*; hence *summer weather, summer heat.*

aestĭfer -fĕra -fĕrum, *heatbringing.*

aestĭmābĭlis -e, *valuable.*

aestĭmātĭo -ōnis, f. *an appraising in terms of money*; litis, *assessment of damages.* Transf., in gen., *valuation, worth, value.*

aestĭmātor -ōris, m. *one who estimates, an appraiser.*

aestĭmo (aestŭmo) -are, *to appraise, rate, estimate the value of*; litem, *to assess the damages in a law-suit*; in a wider sense, *to value* a thing or person; hence, in gen., *to judge.*

aestīvus -a -um, *relating to summer.* N. pl. as subst. **aestīva** -orum, *a summer camp*, and hence, *a campaign; summer pastures for cattle.*

aestŭārĭum -i, n., *low ground covered by the sea at high water; a firth, creek.*

aestŭo -are, *to be agitated* or *hot*; of liquids, *to boil, seethe*; fig., of emotional excitement, *to burn*; of perplexity, *to waver.*

aestŭōsus -a -um, *hot, agitated*; adv. **aestŭōsē.**

aestus -ūs, m., *agitation, heat*; of liquids, esp. of the sea, *seething, raging*; also of the sea's *tide*, and *spray*; fig., of persons, *dizziness*; also *emotional excitement, heat, fury,* and *perplexity, anxiety.*

aetās -ātis, f., *age*: of human life, either *a lifetime* or *a time of life, age*; id aetatis, *of that age*; bona (or iniens) aetas, flos aetatis, *youth*; aetas ingravescens, or provecta, *old age.* Meton., *the persons of a particular age*: aetas puerilis, *boys.* In gen., *time, age, a period of time, epoch.*

aetātŭla -ae, f., *youth.*

aeternĭtas -ātis, f., *eternity, immortality.*

aeterno -are, *to make eternal, immortalize.*

aeternus -a -um, *eternal, everlasting*: aeternum, or in aeternum, *for ever.*

aether -ĕris, acc. -ĕra, m., *the upper air*; poet., *heaven*, or *the upper world.*

aethĕrĭus -a -um, *of the air* or *upper air*; aqua, *rain*; poet., *heavenly,* or *belonging to the upper world.*

Aethĭŏpĭa -ae, f., *Ethiopia*; adj. **Aethĭŏpĭcus** -a -um. and **Aethĭops** -ŏpis, *Ethiopian, Negro.*

aethra -ae, f., *the upper air, clear sky.*

Aetna -ae and **Aetnē** -ēs, f. *Etna, a volcano in Sicily*; adj. **Aetnaeus** -a -um.

Aetōlĭa -ae, f., *Aetolia, a country in the west of Greece*; adj. **Aetōlus, Aetōlĭcus, Aetōlĭus** -a -um.

aevĭtās -ātis, f. = aetas; q.v.

aevum -in, n., also **aevus** -i, m., *eternity.* Transf., *time, lifetime,* or *time of life*; flos aevi, *youth*; in gen., *a period of time.*

Ăfĕr -fra -frum, adj. and subst., *African, from Africa*; esp. *from Carthage.* Hence subst. **Āfrĭca** -ae, f. *the continent of Africa*; esp. either *the country round Carthage* or *the Roman province of Africa.* Adj. **Āfrĭcānus** -a -um, *African, belonging to Africa*; esp. as a surname, conferred upon two of the Scipios. Also adj. **Āfrĭcus** -a -um; ventus Africus, *or simply* Africus, *the S.W. wind* (bringing rain and storms).

aff-; see under **adf-.**

Ăgămemnon -ŏnis, m. *leader of the Greek expedition to Troy.*

Ăgănippē -ēs, f. *a fountain in Boeotia, sacred to the Muses*; adj. **Ăgănippēus** -a -um, *sacred to the Muses.*

ăgāsō -ōnis, m. *a groom. lackey.*

ăgellus -i, m. *a little field.*

ăgēma -ătis, n. *a corps in the Macedonian army.*

Ăgēnor -ŏris, m. *father of Cadmus and Europa*; hence adj. **Ăgēnŏrĕus** -a -um, and subst. **Ăgēnŏrĭdēs** -ae, m. *a male descendant of Agenor.*

ăger, agri, m. *land, territory*; as cultivated, *a field; open country* (opp. towns); *land,* (opp. sea).

agg- (except agger and aggero); see **adg-.**

agger -ĕris, m. *heap, mound*; milit., *rampart*; poet., *any high place.*

aggĕro -are, *to form a mound, heap up, increase.*

ăgĭlis -e, *easily moved, light, nimble, active.*

ăgĭlĭtās -ātis, f. *quickness, agility.*

ăgĭtābĭlis -e, *easily moved, light.*

ăgĭtātĭo -ōnis, f., *movement, agitation, activity*; rerum magnarum, *management.*

ăgĭtātor -ōris, m. *driver*; esp. *charioteer.*

ăgĭto -are, *to put in motion, drive about* (cf. ago); of animals, *to drive* or *hunt*; of water, *to toss.* Transf. (1) *to vex, harry, trouble* persons, etc. (2) *to deal with, be engaged upon, argue, discuss, consider* a subject; *to maintain* a state of affairs; *to conduct* a business; *to keep* a holiday; *to spend* time; so, absol., *to live.*

Ăglăĭa -ae or **Ăglăĭē** -ēs, f. *one of the Graces.*

agmĕn -ĭnis, n. *a driving movement* or *a mass in (orderly)movement, a stream, band, train*; esp. milit., *an army on the march.*

agna -ae, f. *a ewe lamb.*

agnascor -nasci, -nātus, dep., of childdren, *to be born after their father's will.* M. of partic. as subst. **agnātus** -i, *a relation descended from a common ancestor in the male line; a child born into a family where a regular heir already exists.*

agnātĭo -ōnis, f. *relationship reckoned through males only.*

agnellus -i, m. *a little lamb.*

agnīnus -a -um, *of a lamb*; f. as subst., *lamb's flesh.*

agnĭtĭo -ōnis, f. *recognition*; in gen., *knowledge.*

agnōmen -ĭnis, n., *surname.*

agnosco -noscĕre -nōvi -nĭtum, *to know again, recognise; to know by inference* or *report, understand; to express knowledge, admit, acknowledge.*

agnus -i, m. *lamb.*

ăgo ăgĕre ēgi actum, *to set in motion, drive*; of animals, *to drive* or *hunt*; se agere, *to go*; animam, *to give up the ghost*; radices, *to strike root.* Transf., *to incite* to action; *to deal with, be engaged upon; to treat of* a subject; hoc agere, *to attend to the matter in hand*; pass., *to be concerned, be at stake*; actum est de, *it is settled about*, so *it is all over with*; bene agere cum homine, *to treat a person well*; grates, gratias, *to express thanks*; pacem, *to keep the peace*; of time, *to spend*; so absol., *to spend time, live*; on the stage, *to act, play*; primas partes, *to play the leading part*; legal and polit., *to take a matter up publicly*; agere (iure, or lege), *to go to law*; agere causam, *to plead a cause.* Pres. partic. **ăgens** -entis, as adj. *effective.*

ăgōn -ōnis, m. *a contest in the public games.*

ăgōnālĭa -ĭum and -orum, n. *a festival of Janus.*

agrārĭus -a -um, *relating to land*; m. pl. as subst., *the agrarian party*, aiming at a general distribution of public land.

agrestis -e, *belonging to the field* or *country; wild, rustic*; hence, *countrified, boorish, clownish.* M. as subst. **agrestis** -is, *a countryman.*

¹**agrĭcŏla** -ae, m. *farmer.*

²**Agrĭcŏla** -ae, m. Gnaeus Julius, *governor of Britain, and father-in-law of Tacitus.*

agricult-; see under cult-.

Agrĭgentum -i, n.; also **Acrăgās** -antis, m.; *a Doric town in S.W. Sicily.*

agrĭpĕta -ae, m. *a land-grabber, squatter.*

Agrippa -ae, m. *a Roman family name.*

Agrippīna -ae, f. *the name of several Roman women*, esp. *Nero's mother.* Hence **Colonia Agrippinensis** (now Cologne).

ah or **a**, *ah! oh!*

Ăhāla -ae, m., C. Servilius, *master of the horse under the dictator Cincinnatus*, 439 B.C.

ai, *ah!*, interjection of grief.

Āiax -ācis, m. *name of two Homeric heroes, sons of Telamon and of Oileus.*

āio, defective verb. *to say yes, to affirm, assert, state*; ain tu? *you don't say?* Hence pres. partic. **aiens** -entis, *affirmative.*

āla -ae, f. *a wing*; poet., of the *sails* or *oars* of a ship; of a man, *the armpit*; milit., *a wing, squadron.*

ălăbaster -stri, m., with pl. **ălăbastra**, *a perfume casket.*

ălăcer -cris -cre, and **ălacris** -e *quick, lively, animated.*

ălacrĭtās -ātis, f. *quickness, eagerness, animation.*

ălăpa -ae, f. *a box on the ear*, given by a master to his slave when freeing him.

ālārĭus -a -um, and **ālāris** -e, *belonging to the wings* of an army; m. pl. as subst., *allied troops.*

ālātus -a -um, *winged.*

ălauda -ae, f. *a lark*; also *the name of a legion formed by Caesar in Gaul*; in pl. **Ălaudae** -arum, *the soldiers of this legion.*

Alba -ae, *Alba Longa*, the oldest Latin town; hence adj. **Albānus** -a -um.

albātus -a -um, *clothed in white.*

albĕo -ēre, *to be white.*

albesco -ĕre, *to become white.*

albĭco -are, *to be white.*

albĭdus -a -um, *whitish.*

Albĭon -ōnis, f. *old name of Great Britain.*

Albis -is, m. *the Elbe.*

albŭlus -a -um, *whitish*; f. as subst. **Albŭla** -ae (sc. aqua), *old name of the Tiber.*

album -i; *see* albus.

albus -a -um, *white, dead white*; hence *pale* or *bright*; sometimes *making bright*; fig., *fortunate.* N. as subst. **album** -i, *white colour; a white writing-tablet, a list.*

Alcaeus -i, m. *a Greek lyric poet* (about 600 B.C.).

alcēdo -ĭnis and **alcȳŏn** -onis, f. *the kingfisher.* Hence n. pl. **alcēdōnĭa** -orum, *the kingfisher's time, quietness, calm.*

alces -is, f. *the elk.*

Alcestis -is, and **Alcestē** -ēs, f. *wife of Admetus, who saved her husband by dying for him.*

Alcēūs -ĕi and -ĕos, m. *grandfather of Hercules.* Hence subst. **Alcīdes** -ae, m. esp. of *Hercules.*

Alcĭbĭădēs -is, m. *an Athenian general, pupil of Socrates.*

Alcĭnŏus -i, m. *king of the Phaeacians, host of Odysseus.*

Alcmēna -ae, also **Alcmēnē** -ēs, f. *mother of Hercules.*

alcȳŏn = alcedo; q.v.

ālĕa -ae, f. *a game of dice, game of hazard*; hence *chance, risk, uncertainty.*

alĕātor -ōris, m. *dicer, gambler.*

ălĕātōrĭus -um, *of a gambler.*
ālec = allec; q.v.
ālĕs alĭtis, *winged*; hence *swift*; as subst., *a bird*, esp. *a large bird* or *bird of omen*; poet., *an omen, sign.*
ălesco -ĕre, *to grow up.*
Ălexander -dri, m. (1) = *Paris, son of Priam, king of Troy.* (2) *Alexander the Great* (356-323 B.C.), *king of Macedonia.* Hence **Alexandrīa** or **ēa** -ae, f. *a city founded by Alexander*, esp. *Alexandria in Egypt*; adj. **Ălexandrīnus** -a -um, *of Alexandria.*
alga -ae, f. *sea-weed.*
algĕo algēre alsi, *to be cold*; partic. **algens** -entis, *cold.*
algesco algescĕre alsi, *to catch cold.*
[1]**algĭdus** -a -um, *cold.*
[2]**Algĭdus** -i, m. *a mountain in Latium*; adj. **Algĭdus** -a -um, *of Algidus.*
algor -ōris, m. *cold.*
algus -ūs, = algor; q.v.
ălĭas, see under alius.
ălĭbī. (1) *elsewhere, at another place*; alibi . . . alibi, *here . . . there.* (2) *otherwise, in other respects.*
ălĭca -ae, f. *spelt*, or *a drink prepared from spelt.*
ălĭcŭbi, *anywhere, somewhere.*
ălĭcundĕ, *from anywhere, from somewhere.*
ălĭēnātĭo -ōnis, f. *a transference, alienation*; mentis, *aberration of mind.*
ălĭēnĭgĕna -ae, m. *strange, foreign*; as subst., *a foreigner.*
ălĭēnĭgĕnus -a -um, *of different elements, heterogeneous.*
ălĭēno -are, *to make something another's, let go, transfer; to estrange* one person from another; *to put* a thing *out of one's mind, forget*; with mentem, etc., *to cause a person to lose his reason*; pass., alienari, *to go out of one's mind.*
ălĭēnus -a -um, *belonging to another*; aes, *another's money*, and so *debt*; in gen., *strange, foreign, unrelated*; esp. of persons, *not at home, unfamiliar*, or *estranged, unfriendly*; of things, *unfavourable.* M. as subst., **alienus,** *a stranger*; n. as subst. **alienum,** *another person's property.*
ālĭger -gĕra -gĕrum, *winged.*
ălĭmentārĭus -a -um, *relating to food.*
ălĭmentum -i, n. (1) *food.* (2) *maintenance.*
ălĭmōnĭum -i, n. *nourishment.*
ălĭo; see under alius.
ălĭōquī and **ălĭōquīn.** (1) *otherwise, in other respects.* (2) *in general, in most respects.* (3) *else, in other conditions.*
ălĭorsum and **ălĭorsus.** (1) *in another direction, elsewhere.* (2) *in another manner.*
ālĭpēs -pĕdis, *having wings on the feet*; hence *swift*; m. pl. as subst., *horses.*
ălipta and **ăliptēs** -ae, m. *the anointer in the wrestling-school* or *the baths.*
aliqua, aliquamdiu, aliquammultus; see under aliquis.
ălĭquando, *at any time, once; sometimes, occasionally; at last.*
ălĭquantŭlus -a -um, *little, small*; n. as adv. *a little.*
ălĭquantus -a -um, *of some size, moderate.* N. as subst. **ălĭquantum** -i, *a good deal*; acc. aliquantum, and (with compar.) abl. aliquanto, *somewhat, considerably.*
ălĭquātĕnus, *to a certain degree.*
ălĭqui, aliquae, or aliqua, aliquod, adj. *some.*
ălĭquis aliquid, pron. *someone, something; anyone, anything.* N. aliquid often with partitive genit., *a certain amount or number of*; as adv., *in any respect.* Transf., *somebody* or *something great* or *significant.* Hence adv. **ălĭquō,** *some whither, in some direction*; adv. **ălĭquā,** *by some road, in some way*; adv. **ălĭquamdiu,** *for some time*; adj. **ălĭquammultus,** *considerable* in number or quantity.
ălĭquot, indecl., *some, several.*
ălĭquŏtiē(n)s, *several times.*
ălis, alid, old form of alius, aliud; q.v.
ălĭter; see under alius.
ālĭum or **allĭum** -i, *garlic.*
ălĭundĕ, *from some other direction*: alii aliunde, *from various directions.*
ălĭus -a -ud, adj. and pronoun, *another, other, different.* Distributively, *one, another*: alii . . . alii, *some . . . others*; alii alia censent, *some think one thing, some another.* In comparison, *other than*, followed by atque, quam, etc. Rarely, in plur., *all other, the rest*; in sing. = alter, *one of two.* Hence adv. **ălĭās.** (1) *at another time*; alius alias, *one person at one time, another at another.* (2) *otherwise.* Adv. **ălĭō,** *to another place*; alius alio *in various directions.* Transf., *to another person* or *object; for another end.* Adv. **ălĭtĕr.** (1) *otherwise, in another way*; alius aliter, *in different ways.* (2) *else, in other conditions.*
ălĭusmŏdi, *of another kind.*
all-, v. also under adl-.
allec or **ālec** -ēcis, n. *fish-pickle.*
Allecto or **Alecto,** *one of the three Furies.*
Allĭa (Alia) -ae, f. *river in Latium*; adj. **Allĭensis** -e.
Allobrox -ŏgis, and pl. **Allobrŏges** -um, m. *the Allobroges, a Gallic people.*
almus -a -um, *nourishing, kind.*
alnus -i, f. *the alder*; meton, *a ship of alderwood.*
ălo ălĕre ălŭi altum (or ălĭtum), *to nourish, support, rear, feed*; hence in gen., *to strengthen, increase, promote, advance.*

Hence partic. **altus** -a -um, *grown, great.* As seen from below, *high*, hence, of the voice, *shrill*; of character, dignity, rank, *lofty, noble.* As seen from above, *deep*; hence of quiet, *deep*; of thoughts, *secret, deep-seated*; of time, *reaching far back, ancient.* N. as subst. **altum** -i, either *height* or *depth*. Adv. **alte,** *highly* or *deeply*.

ălŏē -ēs, f., *the aloe; bitterness.*

Alpēs -ĭum, f. *the Alps*; adj. **Alpīnus** and **Alpĭcus** -a -um, *Alpine.*

Alphēus or **Alphēos** -i, m. *the chief river of the Peloponnese.*

alsĭus -a -um, *frosty, cold.*

altārĭa -ĭum, n. pl. *an erection upon an altar*; hence *high altars*, or *a high altar.*

alter -tĕra -tĕrum, *one of two, the one, the other*; as a numeral, *second*; unus et alter, *one or two*; in pl., of a *second set.* Hence of quality, *second, next best*; of similarity, *another, a second*; alter idem, *a second self*; of difference, *other, changed.*

altercātĭo -ōnis, f., *dispute, wrangling*; legal, *cross-examination.*

altercor -ari, dep. *to dispute, contend, quarrel*; legal, *to cross-examine, cross-question.*

alterno -are, *to do first one thing, then another*: transit, *to interchange*; intransit., *to alternate, waver.*

alternus -a -um, *one after the other, by turns, alternate, interchanging*; sermones, *dialogue*; of metre, *elegiac* (with hexameter and pentameter alternating).

altĕrŭter -utra -utrum, *one of two.*

altĭlis -e, *fattened, fed*; f. as subst. (sc. avis), *a fowl.*

altĭsŏnus -a -um, *sounding from on high; high-sounding, sublime.*

altĭtūdo -ĭnis, f. (1) *height*; hence *sublimity.* (2) *depth*; animi, *secrecy, reserve.*

altor -ōris, m, *nourisher, foster-father.*

altrix -īcis, f. *nurse, foster-mother.*

altus -a -um, **alte,** etc.; see under alo.

ălūcĭnor -ari, dep. *to wander in mind, dream, talk idly.*

ălumnus -a -um, adj. used as noun, *nursling, foster-child*; hence *pupil.*

ălūta -ae, f. *soft leather; a shoe, purse* or *patch.*

alvĕārĭum -i, n. *beehive.*

alvĕŏlus -i, m. *tray, trough, bucket; gaming-board.*

alvĕus -i, m. *a hollow, cavity, trough*; hence *boat*; also *the hold of a ship; bath-tub; bed of a stream; beehive; gaming-table.*

alvus -i, f. *belly, womb, stomach; hold of a ship, beehive.*

ămābĭlis -e, *amiable, lovely*; adv. **ămābĭlĭter.**

Ămalthēa -ae, f. either *a nymph, the nurse of Jupiter in Crete* or *the goat on the milk of which Jupiter was reared.*

āmandātĭo -ōnis, f. *a sending away.*

āmando -are, *to send away.*

ămans = partic. of amo; q.v.

āmănŭensis -is, m. *secretary, clerk.*

ămārăcĭnus -a -um, *made of marjoram*; n. as subst. *marjoram ointment.*

ămārăcus -i, c. and **ămārăcum** -i, n. *marjoram.*

ămărantus -i, m., *the amaranth.*

ămārĭtĭēs -ēi, f., *bitterness.*

ămārĭtūdo -ĭnis, f. *bitterness*; vocis, *harshness of voice.*

ămāror -ōris, m., *bitterness.*

ămārus -a -um, *bitter, pungent.* Hence, of things, *disagreeable, unpleasant*; of persons, *irritable*; of speech, *biting, acrimonious.* Adv. **ămārē,** *bitterly.*

ămātor -ōris, m. *a lover, friend, admirer*; esp. *the lover of a woman.*

ămātōrĭus -a -um, *loving, amorous*; n. as subst. *a love philtre.* Adv. **ămātōrĭē.**

ămātrix -īcis, f. *mistress, sweet-heart.*

Ămāzon -ŏnis, f.; gen. in plur. **Ămāzŏnes** -um, myth., *nation of female warriors.* Hence subst. **Ămāzŏnis** -ĭdis, f. = Amazon; adj. **Ămāzŏnĭcus, Ămāzŏnĭus** -a -um.

ambactus -i, m. *vassal.*

ambāges, abl. -e, f. (of sing. only abl. found) *a roundabout way, winding.* Hence, in speech, etc., either *circumlocution* or *obscurity, ambiguity.*

ambĕdo -esse -ēdi -ēsum, *to eat round, consume.*

ambĭgo -ĕre, *to go about* or *round.* Transf., (1) *to doubt, hesitate*; ambigitur, impers., *it is in doubt*; (2) *to dispute, contend.*

ambĭgŭĭtās -ātis, f. *ambiguity.*

ambĭgŭus -a -um, *moving from side to side, doubtful, uncertain, insecure, unreliable*; of speech, *ambiguous, obscure*; n. as subst. *uncertainty, doubt, ambiguity.* Adv. **ambĭgŭē,** *ambiguously, indecisively.*

ambĭo -īre -īvi -or -ĭi -ītum *to go round.* Hence (1) *to surround.* (2) *to go round* from person to person, *to approach, entreat, canvass* (for votes, help, etc.).

Ambĭŏrix -rīgis, m. *chief of the Eburones in Gallia Belgica.*

ambĭtĭo -ōnis, f. canvassing for office (in a lawful manner); in gen., *desire for office, popularity* or *fame.*

ambĭtĭōsus -a -um, *going round*; esp. *active in seeking office, popularity* or *fame; ambitious, ostentatious.* Adv. **āmbĭtĭōsē,** *ambitiously, ostentatiously.*

ambĭtus -ūs, m. *a going round, circuit, revolution.* Hence, of things, *border, edge* or *extent*; in speech, *circumlocution*; in relation to persons, *illegal canvassing for office, bribery, striving after popularity* or *effect.*

ambō -ae -ŏ, *both, two together.*

ambrŏsĭa -ae, f. *ambrosia, the food* or *unguent of the gods.*

ambrŏsĭus -a -um, *divine, immortal, ambrosial.*

ambūbāia -ae, f., *a Syrian flute-girl.*

ambŭlātĭo -ōnis, f. *a walk* or *place for walking.*

ambŭlātĭuncŭla -ae, f. *a little walk* or *place for walking, promenade.*

ambŭlo -are, *to walk, go for a walk, travel, march*: bene ambula, "*bon voyage*"; with acc., *to traverse.*

ambūro -ūrĕre -ussi -ustum, *to burn*

round, scorch; of cold, *to nip, numb*; in gen., *to injure.*

ămellus -i, m. *the purple Italian starwort.*

āmens -entis, *mad, insane, senseless.*

āmentĭa -ae, f. *madness, senselessness.*

āmento -are, *to furnish with a strap.*

āmentum -i, n. *a strap, thong.*

āmĕs -ĭtis, m. *a forked pole.*

ămĕthystĭnus -a -um, *amethyst-coloured*; n. pl. as subst., *dresses of amethyst colour.*

ămĕthystus -i, f. *an amethyst.*

amfractus = anfractus; q.v.

ămĭcĭo -ĭcīre -ĭcŭi or -ixi -ictum, *to clothe, wrap round, wrap up, cover, conceal.*

ămīcĭtĭa -ae, f. *friendship*; in plur., concrete, = *friends.*

ămīcĭtĭēs -ēi, f. = amicitia; q.v.

ămictus -ūs, m., *the putting on of a garment*, esp. *the toga.* Transf., *a garment, covering.*

ămīcŭla -ae, f. *a little mistress.*

ămĭcŭlum -i, n. *a mantle, cloak.*

ămīcŭlus -i, m. *a dear friend.*

ămīcus -a -um, *friendly, well-wishing, favourable.* M. as subst., **ămīcus** -i, *a friend*; in plur., *retinue*; f. as subst., **ămīca** -ae, *a friend* or *mistress.* Adv. **ămīcē** and **ămīcĭter,** *in a friendly manner.*

āmissĭo -ōnis, f. *loss.*

āmissus -ūs, m. = amissio; q.v.

ămĭta -ae, f. *a father's sister, aunt.*

āmitto -mittĕre -mīsi -missum, *to send away, let go, let slip*; hence, in gen., *to lose.*

Ammōn (Hammōn) (ōnis, m. *a Libyan deity,* worshipped at Rome under the name of Jupiter Ammon.

amnĭcŏla -ae, c. *dwelling by the riverside.*

amnĭcŭlus -i, m. *a little river.*

amnis -is, m. *a stream, river, torrent*; poet., *current, river water.*

ămo -are, *to love (passionately), be fond of;* amare se, *to be selfish* or *pleased with oneself*; amabo te, *or* amabo, *please, be so good*; with infin., *to like to* do a thing, also *to be wont, be accustomed.*

Hence partic. **ămans** -antis, *loving, fond*; as subst., *a lover.* Adv. **ămanter,** *lovingly.*

ămoenĭtās -ātis, f. *pleasantness,* esp. of places.

ămoenus -a -um, *pleasant, delightful,* esp. of places.

āmōlĭor -iri, dep. *to remove by an effort, set aside, get rid of*; amoliri se, *to take oneself off.*

ămōmum -i, n. *a shrub.*

ămor -ōris, m. *love, passion, fondness, desire*; meton., *an object of love, darling*; personified, *Love, Cupid.*

āmōtĭo -ōnis, f. *removal.*

āmŏvĕo -mŏvēre -mōvi -mōtum, *to move away,* withdraw; se amovere, *to depart*; in insulam, *to banish to an island*; of ideas or feelings, *to put aside.*

amphĭbŏlĭa -ae, f. *ambiguity, double meaning.*

Amphictyŏnes -aum, m. plur., *the Amphictyons, religious representatives of the Greek states.*

Amphīōn -ŏnis, m. *king of Thebes, husband of Niobe.*

amphĭthĕātrum -i, n. *amphitheatre.*

Amphitrītē -ēs, f. *wife of Neptune, goddess of the sea.*

amphŏra -ae, f. (1) *a two-handled jar.* (2) *a measure:* liquid, = about 7 gallons; of shipping, = about 1/40 of our ton.

amplector -plecti -plexus, dep., *to embrace, twine round, enclose, surround.* Transf., *to welcome, love, esteem*; in thought or speech, *to take in, consider, deal with; to include, comprise.*

amplexor -ari, dep. *to embrace; to welcome, love.*

amplexus -ūs, m. *encircling, embrace.*

amplĭfĭcātĭo -ōnis, f. *enlarging, heightening, amplification.*

amplĭfĭcātor -ōris, m. *one who enlarges.*

amplĭfĭco -are, *to enlarge, heighten, increase, magnify.*

amplĭo -are, *to enlarge, increase, magnify*; legal, *to adjourn a case.*

amplĭtūdo -ĭnis, f. *breadth, size; greatness, dignity, grandeur.*

amplus -a -um, *large, spacious, ample.* Transf., *great, important, honourable; eminent, distinguished*; amplissimi viri, *men of the highest position*; rhet., *grand, full.* Adv. **amplē** and **amplĭter** *fully, grandly.* Compar. adv. and n. subst., **amplĭus,** *more, further, besides*; with numerals, often = *more than.*

ampulla -ae, f. *flask, bottle.* Transf., *bombast.*

ampullor -ari, dep. *to speak bombastically.*

ampŭtātĭo -ōnis, f. *cutting off, pruning.*

ampŭto -are, *to cut off,* esp. of trees, *to lop, prune*; of limbs, *to amputate*; hence, in gen., *to remove, diminish*; amputata loqui, *to speak disconnectedly.*

Ămūlĭus -i, m. *king of Alba Longa, brother of Numitor.*

ămurca -ae, f. *oil-lees.*

ămygdălum -i, n., *almond.*

Ămyntas -ae, m., *name of several Macedonian kings.*

ămystis -ĭdis, f., *the emptying of a goblet at a draught.*

ăn, conj.: in direct questions, *or*; in indirect questions, *or whether.*

ănăbathrum -i, n. *a raised seat.*

ănădēma -ătis, n. *a head ornament, fillet.*

ănagnostēs -ae, m. *reader.*

ănălecta -ae, m. *a dining-room slave.*

ănălŏgĭa -ae, f. *proportion, comparison, analogy.*

ănăpaestus -a -um: pes, *a metrical foot, anapaest*; n. as subst. *a poem in anapaestic verse.*

ănăphŏra -ae, f. in rhetoric, *the repetition of a word at the beginning of several sentences.*

ănas ănătis, f. *duck.*
ănătĭcŭla -ae, f. *little duck.*
ănătŏcismus -i, m. *compound interest.*
Ănaxagoras -ae, m. *a Greek philosopher of the fifth century B.C.*
anceps -cĭpĭtis, *two-headed; hence with two peaks or edges.* Transf., *coming on* or *from both sides; of two natures; ambiguous, uncertain, undecided*; hence *dangerous*; n. as subst., *danger.*
Anchīsēs -ae, m. *father of Aeneas.* Hence subst. **Anchīsĭădēs** -ae m. *a male descendant of Anchises, Aeneas.*
ancīle -is, n., *a sacred shield, supposed to have fallen from heaven.*
ancilla -ae, f. *maid-servant, female slave.*
ancillāris -e *of a maid-servant.*
ancillor -ari, dep. *to serve* (*as a maid*).
ancillŭla -ae, f. a *little maid-servant.*
ancīsus -a -um, *cut round.*
Ancōn -onis, and **Ancōna** -ae, f. *a town on the Adriatic coast of Italy.*
ancŏra -ae, f. *an anchor*; ancoram tollere, *to weigh anchor.*
ancŏrāle -is, n. *a cable.*
ancŏrārĭus -a -um, *belonging to an anchor.*
Ancus (**Marcius**) -i, *fourth king of Rome.*
Ancȳra -ae, f. *capital of Galatia, in Asia Minor.*
andrŏgȳnus -i, m. or **andrŏgȳne** -es, f. *hermaphrodite.*
Andrŏmăchē -ēs and **-cha** -ae, f. *wife of Hector.*
Andrŏmĕdē -ēs, f. and **-da** -ae, f. *wife of Perseus.*
andrōn -ōnis, m., *corridor.*
Andrŏnīcus -i, m. L. Livius, *Roman dramatic and epic poet of the third century B.C.*
ānellus -i, m. *a little ring.*
ănēthum -i, n. *dill, anise.*
anfractus -ūs, m. *a turning, a bend*; solis, *revolution*; vallis, *winding.* Transf., *legal intricacies, circumlocution, digression.*
angellus -i, m. *a little corner.*
angĭportum -i, n. and **angĭportus** -ūs, m. *a narrow street.*
ango -ĕre, *to press tightly*; of the throat, *to strangle, throttle*; in gen., *to hurt, distress*; of the mind, *to torment, make anxious.*
angor -ōris, m. *compression of the throat, suffocation*; of the mind, *distress, anguish, trouble.*
anguĭcŏmus -a -um, *having snaky hair.*
anguĭfer -fĕra -fĕrum, *snake-bearing.*
anguĭgĕna -ae, m. *snake-born.*
anguilla -ae, f. *an eel.*
anguĭmănus -a -um, *snake-handed.*
anguĭnĕus -a -um, *of a snake, snaky.*
anguīnus -a -um, *snaky.*
anguĭpēs -pĕdis, *snake-footed.*
anguis -is, c. *a snake;* in astronomy, *the constellation Draco,* or *Hydra,* or *the Serpent.*
Anguĭtĕnens-entis, m., *the Snake-holder,* i.e. *the constellation Ophiuchus.*
angŭlātus -a -um, *angular, cornered.*
angŭlus -i, m. *a corner, angle*; esp. either *a quiet corner, retired spot,* or, fig., *an awkward corner, strait.*
angustĭae -arum, f. pl. *narrowness*; hence, of space, *a strait, narrow place*; spiritūs, *shortness of breath*; of time, *shortness*; of supplies, *shortness, poverty*; of circumstances, *difficulty, distress*; of disposition, *narrow-mindedness*; of reasoning, *subtlety.*
angustus -a -um, *narrow, confined*; habenae, *tightly-drawn reins*; spiritus angustior, *constricted breath*; of time, *short*; of supplies, *short, scarce*; of circumstances, *precarious, critical*; of mind or speech, *narrow, petty, limited*; of style, *brief, simple.* N. as subst. **angustum** -i, a narrow space. Adv. **angustē,** *narrowly, sparingly, in a narrow, confined manner*; of speech, *briefly.*
ănhēlĭtus -ūs, m. *puffing, panting.* Transf., in gen., *breath; exhalation, vapour.*
ănhēlo -are, *to puff, pant*; transit., *to pant out words*; also *to pant for a thing, desire eagerly.*
ănhēlus -a -um, *puffing, panting*; febris, *causing to pant.*
ănĭcŭla -ae, f. *a little old woman.*
ănīlis -e *belonging to* or *like an old woman.* Adv. **ănīlĭter.**
ănīlĭtās -ātis, f. *old age* (of women).
ănĭma -ae, f. *breath, wind, air.* Transf., *the breath of life, vital principle, soul*; animam edere, *to give up the ghost*; poet., *life-blood*; meton., *a living being*; sometimes = animus, *rational soul.*
ănĭmadversĭo -ōnis, f. *perception, observation, notice*; esp. *unfavourable notice; censure, blame, punishment.*
ănĭmadversor -ōris, m. *an observer.*
ănĭmadverto (**ănĭmadvorto**) -vertĕre -verti -versum *to turn or give the mind to.* Hence *to take notice of, attend to; to perceive, observe.* Esp. *to take notice of* a fault, *blame, censure, punish.*
ănĭmăl -ālis, n. *a living being, animal.*
ănĭmālis -e. (1) *consisting of air, airy.* (2) *living.*
ănĭmans -antis, *living*; as subst., *a living being, animal.*
ănĭmātĭo -ōnis, f. *animating*; hence, *a living being.*
ănĭmo -are. (1) (anima), *to animate, give life to.* (2) (animus), *to endow with a particular disposition.*

Hence partic. **animatus** -a -um. (1) *having life, alive.* (2) *having a disposition, inclined, disposed*; esp. *having courage, spirited.*
ănĭmōsus -a -um. (1) (anima), *full of breath, airy.* (2) (animus), *full of spirit* or *courage.* Adv. **ănĭmōsē,** *courageously.*
ănĭmŭla -ae, f. *a little soul, little life.*
ănĭmus -i, m. *the spiritual or rational principle of life in man.* More specifically: (1) *the seat of feeling, the heart*; animi causa, *for pleasure*; loc. (or genit.) animi, *at heart.* (2)

character, disposition; as a trait of character (esp. in plur.) *courage, spirit, vivacity*; also *pride, arrogance.* (3) *the seat of the will, intention:* habeo in animo, *I am resolved.* (4) *the seat of thought, intellect, mind, memory, consciousness.*

Ănĭo -ēnis, and poet. **Ănĭēnus** -i, m. *the Anio, a tributary of the Tiber.*

Anna -ae, f., *sister of Dido*; Anna Perenna, *an Italian goddess.*

annālis -e *lasting a year*, or *relating to a year.* M. as subst., usually plur. **annālēs** -ĭum, *yearly records, annals.*

anniversārĭus -a -um, *recurring every year.*

annōna -ae, f. *yearly produce, crop,* esp. of grain; *the price of provisions* (esp. corn), *the cost of living.*

annōsus -a -um, *full of years, long-lived.*

annōtĭnus -a -um, *a year old, belonging to last year.*

annus -i, m. *a circuit of the sun, year*; exeunte anno, *at the end of the year*; annos LXX natus, *seventy years old*; habere annos viginti, *to be twenty*; esp. *year of office*, or *of eligibility for office*; poet., *time of year, season.*

annŭus -a -um, *lasting for a year; returning every year, annual.* N. plur. as subst. *a salary, pension.*

anquīro -quīrĕre -quisivi -quīsītum, *to seek carefully, inquire after, investigate;* legal, *to set an inquiry on foot.*

ansa -ae, f. *a handle;* hence, *occasion, opportunity.*

ansātus -a -um, *with a handle*; homo, *a man with arms akimbo.*

anser -ĕris, m. *goose.*

Antaeus -i, m. *a giant killed by Hercules.*

ante. Adv., *before*, of place or time. Prep., *before*, of place or time; ante urbem conditam, *before the founding of the city*; of preference, *sooner than, above.*

antĕā, *before, formerly.*

antĕambŭlo -ōnis, m. *a footman to clear the way ahead.*

antĕcăpio -căpĕre -cēpi -ceptum, *to seize beforehand*; hence *to anticipate, not to wait for*; philosoph., antecepta informatio, *an innate idea.*

antĕcēdo -cēdĕre -cessi -cessum, *to go before, precede,* in space or time; *to excel* (with dat. or acc.).

Hence partic. **antĕcēdens** -entis, *preceding, antecedent.*

antĕcello -ĕre, *to be outstanding, excel* (with dat. or acc.).

antĕcessĭo -ōnis, f. *a preceding* or *going before*; philosoph., *the antecedent cause.*

antĕcursor -ōris, m. *a forerunner*; in pl., *pioneers.*

anteĕo -ire -ii *to go before*, in space or time; hence *to excel* (with dat. or acc.).

antĕfĕro -ferre -tŭli -lātum, *to carry before.* Transf., *to prefer*; *to anticipate, consider before.*

antĕfixus -a -um, *astened in front*; n. as subst. *ornaments fixed on roofs.*

antĕgrĕdĭor -grĕdi -gressus, dep. *to go before*; philosoph., of antecedent causes.

antehăbĕo -ēre, *to prefer.*

antĕhāc, *before this time, formerly.*

antĕlūcānus -a -um, *happening before daybreak.*

antĕmĕrīdĭānus -a -um, *before noon.*

antemitto -mittĕre -mīsi -missum, *to send before.*

antemna or **antenna** -ae, f. *a sail-yard.*

anteoccŭpātĭo -ōnis, f. *an exception.*

antĕpēs -pĕdis, m. *the forefoot.*

antĕpīlāni -orum, m. *front line soldiers* (i.e. *the* hastati *and* principes).

antĕpōno -pōnĕre -pŏsŭi -pŏsĭtum. *to place before, to prefer.*

antĕquam, conjunction, *before.*

antēs -ium, m. pl. *rows or ranks.*

antesignanus -i, m. usually plur., *soldiers chosen for a place in front of the standards*; hence, sing., *a leader.*

antesto (antisto) -stare -stĕti, *to stand before; to excel, surpass.*

antestor -ari, dep. legal, *to call as a witness.*

antĕvĕnĭo -vĕnire -vēni -ventum. *to come before, get the start of.* Transf., *to anticipate, prevent; to excel.*

antĕverto (-vorto) -vertĕre -verti -versum, *to come or go before, precede.* Transf., *to anticipate, prevent; to prefer.*

antĭcĭpātĭo -ōnis, f. *a preconception, innate idea.*

antĭcĭpo -are *to receive before, anticipate*; viam, *to travel over before.*

antīcus -a -um, *forward, in front.*

antidea, antideo, antidhac; see antea, anteeo, antehac, of which they are old forms.

Antĭgŏnē -ēs, f. and **Antĭgŏna** -ae, f. *daughter of Oedipus, put to death for burying her brother.*

Antĭgŏnus -i, m., *name of several of the successors of Alexander the Great.*

Antĭŏchīa or **Antĭŏchēa** -ae, f. *Antioch, name of several Asiatic towns.*

Antĭpăter -tri, m. *name of several kings of Macedonia.*

antīquārĭus -a -um *belonging to antiquity*; m. or f. as subst. *an antiquary.*

antīquitās -ātis, f. *antiquity, ancient times; the history of ancient times*; in plur., *the ancients.*

antīquĭtus v. antiquus.

antīquo -are, *to leave in its former state*; legem, *to reject a bill.*

antīquus -a -um, *coming before; previous, earlier*; absol., *old, ancient, primitive.* In compar. and superl., *preferred, more important.* M. pl. as subst. **antīqui** -orum, *the people of old time,* esp. *ancient authors.* Hence adv. **antīquē,** *in the ancient manner*; also **antīquĭtus,** *from of old* or *long ago.*

antistĕs -stĭtis, c. *a presiding priest* or *priestess.*

antistĭta -ae, f., *a presiding priestess.*

antisto, v. antesto.

antĭthĕton -i, n. *antithesis, opposition.*

Antĭum -i, n. *an old town of Latium on the sea-coast.*
antlĭa -ae, f., *a pump.*
Antōnīnus -i, m. *name of several Roman emperors.*
Antōnĭus -a -um, *the name of a Roman* gens.
antrum -i, n. *a cave, hollow.*
Ănūbis -bis or -bĭdis, m. *an Egyptian god.*
ānŭlārĭus -a -um, *of a ring*: m. as subst. *a ring-maker.*
ānŭlus -i, m. *a ring*; anulus equestris, *the badge of knighthood at Rome.*
[1]**ānus** -i, m. *the fundament.*
[2]**ănus** -ūs, f. *an old woman*; also used like adj., *old.*
anxĭĕtās -ātis, f., *anxiety, grief, anguish.*
anxĭfer -fĕra -fĕrum, *causing anxiety.*
anxĭtūdo -ĭnis, f. *anxiousness.*
anxĭus -a -um, *anxious, uneasy.* Transf., *causing anxiety.* Adv. **anxĭē.**
Anxŭr -ŭris, n. *an old town of the Volsci.*
Ăŏnes -um, *the Boeotians*; **Ăŏnĭa** -ae, f. *part of Boeotia, resort of the Muses*; hence **Ăŏnĭdĕs** -um, f. *the Muses*; adj. **Ăŏnĭus** -a -um.
Ăornos -i, m., *the lake of Avernus.*
ăpăgĕ, interj. *away! be off!*
Ăpellēs -is, m., *a Greek painter, friend of Alexander the Great.* Adj. **Ăpellēus** -a -um.
ăper apri, m. *a wild boar.*
ăpĕrĭo ăpĕrire ăpĕrŭi ăpertum. (1) *to uncover, lay bare*; hence in gen. *to reveal.* (2) *to open what was shut, open up*; ludum, *to open a school*; annum, *to begin the year.*

Hence partic. **ăpertus** -a -um. (1) *uncovered, clear, unconcealed, manifest*; of speech, *clear, intelligible, frank*; of character, *frank, straightforward, open.* (2) *unclosed, accessible, exposed.* N. as subst., *an open space.* Adv. **ăpertē,** *openly, frankly.*

ăpex -ĭcis, m. *the top*; esp. *the top of the conical cap of the Roman* flamines, or *the cap itself*; hence any *crown, tiara, helmet*; fig., *highest honour, crown*; gram., *the long mark over a vowel.*
aphractus -i, f. *a long undecked boat.*
ăpĭcātus -a -um, *wearing the priest's cap.*
ăpĭnae -arum, f. pl. *trifles.*
ăpis or **ăpes** -is, f. *a bee.*
Ăpis -is, m., *Apis, the ox-god of the Egyptians.*
ăpiscor apisci aptus, dep., *to attain, come to, come by.*
ăpĭum -i, n. *parsley* or *celery.*
aplustrĕ -is, n. generally plur. aplustrĭa -ĭum, and aplustra -orum, *the carved stern of a ship.*
ăpŏdȳtērĭum -i, n. *the undressing-room in a bath.*
Ăpollo -ĭnis, m. *Apollo, god of the sun, born at Delos*; ad Apollinis (sc. aedem), *to the temple of Apollo.* Adj. **Ăpollĭnāris** -e, and **Ăpollĭnĕus** -a -um.
ăpŏlŏgus -i, m. *a narrative, fable.*
ăpŏphŏrēta -orum, n. *presents given to guests.*
ăpŏthēca -ae, f. *store-room.*
appărātē, adv. from apparo; q.v.
appărātĭo -ōnis, f. *preparation.*
appărātus -ūs, m.: abstr., *preparation, preparing*; concr., *provision, equipment, apparatus*, esp. on a pretentious scale; hence *splendour, magnificence, pomp, parade.*
appārĕo -ēre -ŭi -ĭtum, *to become visible, appear, be manifest*; apparet, *it is clear*; sometimes *to appear as a servant, to serve* (with dat.).
appărĭo -ĕre, *to get, obtain.*
appārĭtĭo -ōnis, f. *waiting upon, serving*; meton., plur. *servants.*
appārĭtor -ōris, m. *a servant*; esp. *a public servant*, e.g. lictor.
appăro -are, *to prepare, get ready, provide.*

Hence partic. **appărātus** -a -um, *prepared, well supplied* or *sumptuous.* Adv. **appărātē,** *sumptuously.*

appellātĭo -ōnis, f. *addressing, speech*; legal, *an appeal*; *a naming, name, title; pronunciation.*
appellātor -ōris, m. *an appellant.*
appellĭto -are, *to be accustomed to name.*
[1]**appello** -are. (1) *to address, accost, speak to*; esp. *of asking* favours, *to approach, entreat, sue*; legal, *to appeal to.* (2) *to name, entitle*; hence, *to mention by name, make known.* (3) *to pronounce.*
[2]**appello** -pellĕre -pŭli -pulsum, *to drive to, bring to, apply*; nautical, *to bring to land*; huc appelle, *put in here.*
appendix -ĭcis, f. *appendage, addition.*
appendo -pendĕre -pendi -pensum, *to weigh to, deal out by weight.*
Appennīnus -i, m. *the chain of the Appennines.*
appĕtentĭa -ae, f. and **appĕtītĭo** -ōnis, f. *desire, longing.*
appĕtītus -ūs, m. *longing, appetite*; plur., *the passions.*
appĕto -ĕre -ivi or -ii -ītum, *to make for, grasp at, seek*; of places, *to make for or go to*; in hostile sense, *to attack*: intransit., of time, *to draw near.*

Hence partic. **appĕtens** -entis, *eager, desirous, avaricious.* Adv. **appĕtenter, greedily.**

appingo -pingĕre -pinxi -pictum, *to paint to*, or *upon; to write in addition.*
Appĭus -i, m., **Appĭa** -ae, f. *a Roman* praenomen *common in the* gens Claudia; as adj. **Appĭus** -a -um, *Appian*: via, *the Appian Way, a road from Rome to Capua, afterwards extended to Brundisium*; also adj. **Appĭanus** -a -um, *belonging to an Appius, Appian.*
applaudo -plaudĕre -plausi -plausum. *to strike upon, clap.*
applĭcātĭo -ōnis, f. *attachment, application.*
applĭco -are -avi -atum, and -ŭi -ĭtum, *to apply to, place to* or *near*; corpora corporibus, *to close up the ranks*; naut., *to lay* a ship *to* or *beside;*

absol., *to land*. Transf. in gen., *to attach, connect*; with reflex. *to attach oneself, devote oneself*. Perf. partic. pass. **applĭcātus** -a -um, *situated near, built near*.

applōro -are, *to lament, deplore*.

appōno -pōnĕre -pŏsŭi -pŏsĭtum, *to place near, put to*; esp. *to serve, put on table*; *to appoint* a person, *to add* a thing; appone lucro, *reckon as gain*. Hence partic. **appŏsĭtus** -a -um, *placed near, lying near; approaching, near to; fit appropriate, apposite*; adv. **appŏsĭtē,** *appropriately*.

apporrectus -a -um, *extended near*.

apporto -are, *to carry, bring to*.

apposco -ĕre, *to ask in addition*.

apprecor -ari, dep. *to worship, pray to*.

apprĕhendo -prehendĕre -prĕhendi -prehensum, and poet. **apprendo,** *to seize, lay hold of*.

apprimē, *above all, exceedingly*.

apprĭmo -prĭmĕre -pressi -pressum, *to press to*.

apprŏbātĭo -ōnis, f. *approval, assent*; in philosophy, *proof*.

apprŏbātor -ōris, m. *one who approves* or *assents*.

apprŏbo -are, *to approve of, assent to; to prove, establish; to make acceptable to* another.

apprōmitto -mittĕre -mīsi -missum, *to promise in addition*.

apprŏpĕro -are, *to hasten, hasten on*.

apprŏpinquātĭo -ōnis, f. *approach*.

apprŏpinquo -are, *to approach, draw near*.

appugno -are, *to assault, fight against*.

Appulia v. Apulia.

appulsus -ūs, m. *a driving towards*; hence *approach, influence*; naut. *landing*.

aprīcātĭo -ōnis, f. *sun-bathing*.

aprīcor -ari, dep. *to sun oneself*.

aprīcus -a -um, adj. *open to the sun, sunny; loving the sun*.

Aprīlis -e *of April*; m. as subst. *the month of April*.

apto -are, *to fit, adapt, adjust; to make ready* or *fit*.

aptus -a -um. (1) as partic. *fitted, fastened, connected*. Transf., *depending on*; also *prepared, fitted out; fitted up with, equipped with*, with abl. (2) as adj. *suitable, appropriate, fitting*. Adv. **aptē**.

ăpŭd, prep. with acc. *at, near, by, with*; apud me, *at my house*. Of other relations; apud se, *in one's senses*; apud me valet, *it weighs with me*; apud patres *in our fathers' time*; apud Ciceronem, *in the works of Cicero*.

Āpūlĭa or **Appūlĭa** -ae, f. *Apulia, a region in S. Italy*. Adj. **Āpūlĭcus** and **Āpŭlus** -a -um.

ăqua -ae, f. *water*; aqua et ignis, *the necessaries of life*; aqua et igni interdicere homini, *to banish a person*; aquam terramque poscere, *to demand submission*. Esp. *the water of the sea, a lake, a river*, or *rain*; in plur. (*medicinal*) *springs*; often *water in the water-clock*.

aquaeductus -ūs, m. *an aqueduct; the right of conveying water*.

ăquārius -a -um, *belonging to water*; m. as subst. *a water-carrier* or *an inspector of conduits*.

ăquātĭcus -a -um, *living in water*, or *full of water, watery*.

ăquātĭlis -e, *living in water*.

ăqūatĭo -ōnis, f. *a fetching of water*; meton., *a watering-place*.

ăquātor -ōris, m. *a water-carrier*.

ăquĭla -ae, f. *an eagle*; milit., *an eagle as the standard of a Roman legion*; architect, *gable* or *pediment*.

ăquĭlĭfer -fĕri m. *an eagle-* or *standard-bearer*.

ăquĭlo -ōnis, m. *the north wind; the north*.

ăquĭlōnĭus -a -um, *northern*.

ăquĭlus -a -um, *dark-coloured, blackish*.

Ăquītānĭa -ae, f. *Aquitania, the south-west part of Gaul*. Adj. **Ăquĭtānus** -a -um.

ăquor -ari, dep. *to fetch water*.

ăquōsus -a -um, *full of water, watery*.

ăquŭla -ae, f. *a little water, small stream*.

āra -ae, f. *altar*; hence *refuge, protection*; arae, plur., *name of certain rocks at sea*.

Ărăbiă -ae, f. *Arabia*. Adj. **Ărăbĭus** and **Ărăbĭcus** -a -um, *Arabian*; adj. and subst. **Ărabs** -ăbis and **Ărăbus** -a -um *Arabian, an Arabian*.

Ărachnē -ēs, f. *a Lydian maiden turned into a spider by Minerva*.

ărānĕa -ae, f. *a spider*; menton., *the spider's web*.

ărānĕŏla -ae, f. and **ărānĕŏlus** -i, m. *a little spider*.

ărānĕōsus -a -um, *full of cobwebs*.

[1]**ărānĕus** -i, m. *a spider*.

[2]**ărānĕus** -a -um, *of a spider*; n. as subst. *a cobweb*.

ărātĭo -ōnis, f. *ploughing, agriculture*; meton., *a ploughed field*.

ărātor -ōris, m. *ploughman, husbandman*.

ăratrum -i, n. *plough*.

arbĭter -tri, m. *a witness, spectator*, legal, *an umpire, arbitrator*; hence *any judge, ruler, master*.

arbitra -ae, f. *a female witness*.

arbitrārĭus -a -um, *arbitrary, uncertain*.

arbitrātus, -ūs, m. *will, choice, decision*.

arbitrĭum -i, n. (1) *the presence of witnesses*. (2) *the decision of an umpire*; hence *any decision, judgment, authority*; arbitrio suo, *under his own control*.

arbitro -are, and **arbitror** -ari, dep. (1) *to witness; to bear witness*. (2) *to arbitrate, judge, decide*.

arbŏr (arbōs) -ŏris, f. *a tree*; also any wooden object, such as an *oar, mast, ship*; arbor infelix, *the gallows*.

arbŏrĕus -a -um, *relating to trees; treelike*.

arbustus -a -um, *planted with trees*.

N. as subst. **arbustum** -i, *a plantation, vineyard planted with trees.*
arbŭtĕus -a -um, *of the arbutus.*
arbŭtum -i, n. *the fruit, leaves,* etc., *of the wild strawberry* or *arbutus tree.*
arbŭtus -i, f. *the wild strawberry* or *arbutus tree.*
arca -ae, f. *a chest, box*; esp. *a money-box* or *coffin*; also *a cell.*
Arcădĭa -ae, f. *part of the Peloponnesus.* adj. **Arcădĭus** and **Arcădĭcus** -a -um.
arcānus -a -um, *shut, closed*; hence *silent, secret.* N. as subst. *a secret.* Adv. **arcāno,** *secretly.*
Arcăs -ădis, m. adj. and subst., *Arcadian, an Arcadian.*
arcĕo -ēre -ŭi. (1) *to shut in.* (2) *to keep at a distance, hinder, prevent, keep away.*
arcessītor -ōris, m. *a summoner.*
arcessītū abl. sing. m. *at the summons* (of a person).
arcesso (accerso) -ĕre -īvi -ītum, *to fetch, call, summon*; legal, *to summon, bring before a court of justice*; in gen., *to fetch, derive, obtain.*
Hence partic. **arcessītus**, *strained, far-fetched.*
archĕtȳpus -a -um *original.*
Archĭās -ae, m., Aulus Licinius, *a Greek poet defended by Cicero.*
archĭmăgīrus -i, m. *head cook.*
Archĭmēdes -is, m. *a mathematician and inventor, killed at the capture of Syracuse* (212 B.C.).
archĭpīrāta -ae, m. *chief pirate.*
archĭtectōn -ŏnis, m. *master-builder.*
archĭtector -ari, dep. *to build, devise.*
archĭtectūra -ae, f. *architecture.*
archĭtectus -i, m. *an architect, master-builder, inventor, maker.*
archōn -ontis, m. *an archon, an Athenian magistrate.*
arcĭtĕnens -entis, *holding the bow.*
Arctŏs -i, f. *the Great and Little Bear*; hence *the north.*
arctōus -a -um, *belonging to the Bear*; hence, *northern.*
Arctūrus -i, m. *the brightest star of Bootes.*
arcŭla -ae, f. *a casket.* Transf., *rhetorical ornament.*
arcŭo -are, *to bend* or *shape like a bow.*
arcus -ūs, m. *a bow, arch, arc*; esp. *the rainbow.*
ardĕa -ae, f. *a heron.*
ardĕlĭo -ōnis, m. *a busybody.*
ardĕo ardēre arsi, *to burn, glow, be on fire*; of bright objects, *to gleam*; of feeling (esp. of love), *to burn, smart*; of political disorder, *to be ablaze.*
Hence partic. **ardens** -entis, *hot, glowing, burning, fiery, eager*; adv. **ardenter.**
ardesco -ĕre *to take fire*; of bright objects, *to glitter*; of passions, *to become inflamed*: of strife, *to blaze up.*
ardor -ōris, m. *flame, burning, heat*; of bright objects, *gleam*; of feelings (esp. of love), *heat, eagerness*; meton., *an object of love, loved one.*
ardŭus -a -um, *steep, towering, lofty.* Transf., *difficult to undertake* or *reach*; n. as subst., *difficulty.*
ārĕa -ae, f. *a level* or *open space, site, court-yard, threshing floor*; esp. *a playground*; hence, in gen., *play, scope.*
ārĕfăcĭo -făcĕre -fēci -factum, *to make dry.*
ărēna = harena; q.v.
ārĕo -ēre, *to be dry*; partic. **ārens** -entis, *dry, thirsty.*
Ărēŏpăgus -i, m. *Mars' hill at Athens, where a court sat.* Hence **Ărēŏpăgītes** -ae, m. *a member of the court.*
Ărēs -is, m. *the Greek god of war,* Latin *Mars.*
āresco -ĕre *to become dry.*
ărĕtālŏgus -i, m. *a babbler about virtue.*
Ărĕthūsa -ae, f. *a fountain at Syracuse*; myth. *a nymph chased by the river Alpheus under the sea to Sicily.*
argentārĭus -a -um *relating to silver* or *money*; taberna, *a banker's stall.* M. as subst. *a money-changer, banker*; f. as subst., *the office* or *trade of a banker*; also *a silver mine.*
argentātus -a -um *ornamented with silver.*
argentĕus -a -um, *of silver.* Transf., *ornamented with silver; of the colour of silver; belonging to the Silver Age.*
argentum -i, n. *silver*; esp. *silver plate* or *silver coin*; hence, in gen., *money.*
Argīlētum -i, n. *the booksellers' district in Rome.*
argilla -ae, f. *white clay, potter's clay.*
Argō, Argūs, f. *the ship Argo.*
Argŏnautae -arum, m. pl. *the Argonauts, the heroes who sailed in the Argo.*
Argŏs, n. and **Argi** -orum, m. pl. *Argos, capital of Argolis in the Peloponnese.* Adj. **Argēus** and **Argīvus** -a -um: plur. subst. **Argivi,** m. *the Argives* or *Greeks.* Hence f. subst. **Argŏlis** -ĭdis, *the district Argolis*; adj. **Argŏlĭcus** -a -um.
argūmentātĭo -ōnis, f. *the bringing forward of a proof.*
argūmentor -ari, dep. *to bring forward a proof, allege as a proof.*
argūmentum -i, n. *argument, proof; subject, contents, matter.*
argŭo -ŭĕre -ŭi -ūtum, *to put in clear light; to declare, prove; to accuse, blame, expose, convict.*
Hence partic. **argūtus** -a -um: to the eye, *expressive, lively*; to the ear, *piercing, shrill, noisy*; of omens, *clear, significant*; of persons, *sagacious, cunning.* Adv. **argūtē,** *sagaciously.*
Argus -i, m. *the hundred-eyed guardian of Io.*
argūtĭae -arum, f. pl. *liveliness, animation*; of the mind, *cleverness, sagacity, cunning.*
argūtŭlus -a -um, *somewhat acute.*
Ărĭadna -ae and **Ărĭadnē** -ēs, f. *daughter of Minos of Crete.*
ārĭdŭlus -a -um *somewhat dry.*
ārĭdus -a -um, adj. *dry, arid, thirsty;*

febris, *parching*; crura, *shrivelled*; of living conditions, *meagre*; intellectually *dry, jejune*; of character, *avaricious*. N. as subst., *dry ground*.
ăriēs -iĕtis, m. *a ram; a battering ram; a prop, beam*.
ărĭĕto -are, *to butt like a ram*.
Ărīōn -ŏnis, m. *a cithara player, saved from drowning by a dolphin*.
Ariovistus -i, m. *a Germanic prince*.
ărista -ae, f. *the beard of an ear of grain*; hence *the ear itself; also a harvest*.
Ăristŏphănēs -is, m. *the Athenian comic dramatist*. Adj. **Ăristŏphănēus** -a -um.
Ăristŏtĕlēs -is and -i, m. *the Greek philosopher, pupil of Plato, founder of the Peripatetic school*. Adj. **Ăristŏtĕlēus** and **Ăristŏtĕlīus** -a -um.
ărithmētĭca -ae and **-e** -ēs, f.; also **ărithmētĭca** -orum, n. pl.; *arithmetic*.
arma -orum, n. pl. *defensive arms, armour, weapons of war*; hence *war; soldiers, military power; protection, defence*; in gen., *tools, equipment*.
armāmenta -orum, n. pl. *implements, tackle*, esp. of a ship.
armāmentārĭum -i, n. *an armoury*.
armārĭum -i, n. *a cupboard, chest*.
armātū, abl. sing. m. *with armour*; gravi armatu, *with heavy-armed troops*.
armātūra -ae, f. *equipment, armour*; meton., *armed soldiers*.
armentālis -e, *belonging to a herd*.
armentārĭus -i, m. *herdsman*.
armentum -i, n. *cattle for ploughing*; coll., *a herd*.
armĭfer -fĕra -fĕrum *bearing arms, warlike*.
armĭger -gĕra -gĕrum *bearing arms*; as subst., m. or f., an *armour-bearer*.
armilla -ae, f. *bracelet*.
armillātus -a -um *adorned with a bracelet*.
armĭpŏtens -entis *mighty in arms, warlike*.
armĭsŏnus -a -um *resounding with arms*.
armo -are, *to provide with arms, arm, equip, fit out*.
armus -i, m. *shoulder* or *shoulder-blade*; also, of an animal, *the side*.
Arnus -i, m. *chief river of Etruria* (now *Arno*).
ăro -are, *to plough, farm, cultivate*. Transf., *to furrow, wrinkle*; of ships, *to plough* the sea.
Arpīnum -i, n. *a Volscian hill-town, birthplace of Cicero*; adj. and subst. **Arpīnas** -atis; adj. **Arpīnus** -a -um.
arquātus -a -um, *relating to jaundice*; m. as subst., *a sufferer from jaundice*.
arr -; see also adr-.
arrha -ae, f. and **arrhăbo** -ōnis, m. earnest money.
ars -tis, f. (**1**) *skill, method, technique*; ex arte, *according to the rules of art*. (**2**) *an occupation, profession*. (**3**) *concrete*, in pl., *works of art*. (**4**) *conduct, character, method of acting*; bonae artes, *good qualities*.
Artaxerxēs -is, m. *name of several Persian kings*.
artērĭa -ae, f. *the wind-pipe; an artery*.
arthrītĭcus -a -um *gouty*.
artĭcŭlāris -e *of the joints*; morbus, *gout*.
artĭcŭlātim, *piecemeal, joint by joint, distinctly*.
artĭcŭlo -are, *to articulate, speak distinctly*.
artĭcŭlus -i, m.: in the body, *a small joint*; in plants, *a knob, knot*; of time, *a moment, crisis*; in gen., *a part, division, point*.
artĭfex -fĭcis, m. As adj.: act., *skilled, clever*; pass., *skilfully made*. As subst., *worker, craftsman, maker, creator, expert*.
artĭfĭcĭōsus -a -um. *skilful, accomplished; skilfully made*; hence *artificial*. Adv. **artĭfĭcĭōsē,** *skilfully*.
artĭfĭcĭum -i, n. *occupation, craft, art*; also *the theory, system of an art*; concr., *work of art*; in gen., *cleverness, skill, cunning*.
arto -are *to press together, reduce, abridge*.
artŏlăgănus -i, m. *a cake made of meal, wine, milk*, etc.
artopta -ae, m. *a baker; a bread pan*.
[1]**artus (arctus)** -a -um, *narrow, tight, close*; somnus, *fast, sound*; of supplies, *small, meagre*; of circumstances, *difficult, distressing*. N. as subst. *a narrow space*; in gen., *difficulty, constraint*. Adv. **artē,** *narrowly, tightly, closely*; dormire, *soundly, fast*: artius appellare, *to cut a name short*.
[2]**artus** -ūs, m. normally plur., *the joints*; dolor artuum, *gout*: poet., *limbs*.
ārŭla -ae, f. *a little altar*.
ărund-; see harund-.
Aruns, *an Etruscan name for a younger son*.
arvīna -ae, f. *fat, lard*.
arvus -a -um, *ploughed*. N. as subst. **arvum** -i, *ploughed land, a field*; in gen., *a region*.
arx -cis, f. *fortress, citadel, stronghold, height*; fig., *bulwark, protection, headquarters*.
as, assis, m. *a whole, a unit*, divided into 12 parts (unciae); heres ex asse, *sole heir*; as a small coin, *the as*; as a weight, *a pound*.
Ascănĭus -i, m. *son of Aeneas*.
ascendo -scendĕre -scendi -scensum *to mount, ascend, rise*.
ascensĭo -ōnis, f. *ascent*; oratorum *lofty flight*.
ascensus -ūs, m. *a going up, ascent; meton., a way up*.
ascĭa -ae, f. *a carpenter's axe; a mason's trowel*.
ascĭo -scire, *to take to oneself, adopt as one's own*.
ascisco asciscĕre ascīvi ascītum, *to receive, admit*; of persons, *to adopt*; of things, *to take up, to approve*.

Hence partic. **ascītus** -a -um, *foreign, acquired.*

Ascra -ae, f. *town in Boeotia, home of Hesiod*; adj. **Ascraeus** -a -um.

ascrībo -scrīběre -scripsi -scriptum: of things, *to write in, add in writing*; hence *to attribute, impute*; of persons, *to enrol, include, put on a list.*

ascriptīcius -a -um, *enrolled as member of a community.*

ascriptĭo -ōnis, f. *addition in writing.*

ascriptor -ōris, m. *one who approves.*

ăsella -ae, f. *she-ass.*

ăsellus -i, m. *ass.*

Āsĭa -ae, f. (1) *a town and district in Lydia.* (2) *the continent of Asia.* (3) *the peninsula of Asia Minor.* (4) *the Roman province of Asia, formed in* 133 B.C. Hence adj. **Asiānus, Asiātĭcus** and **Asĭus** -a -um; subst. **Asĭs** -ĭdis, f., poet., *Asia.*

ăsīlus -i, m. *gad-fly.*

ăsĭna -ae, f. *she-ass.*

ăsĭnus -i, m. *ass.*

ăsōtus -i, m. *sensualist, libertine.*

aspărăgus -i, m. *asparagus.*

aspargo, v. aspergo.

aspectābĭlis -e, *visible.*

aspecto -are, *to look at earnestly, look towards, observe, attend to.*

aspectus -ūs, m.: act., *looking, sight, range* or *power of vision*; pass., *sight, power of being seen, look, aspect, appearance.*

aspello -ěre, *to drive away.*

asper -ěra -ěrum, *rough, uneven*; to the taste, *pungent, sour*; to the hearing, *harsh, grating*; of weather, *rough, stormy*; of character or circumstances, *rough, wild, harsh, difficult, severe.* N. as subst. *roughness, a rough place.* Adv. **aspěrē,** roughly.

[1]**aspergo (aspargo)** -spergěre -spersi -spersum, *to sprinkle upon* or *besprinkle with.*

[2]**aspergo (aspargo)** -ĭnis, f. *sprinkling, spray.*

aspěrĭtās -ātis, f. *roughness, unevenness*; to the taste, *sourness*; to the ear, *harshness*; of character or circumstances, *harshness, fierceness, severity, difficulty.*

aspernātĭo -ōnis, f. *contempt.*

aspernor -ari, dep. *to despise, reject, spurn.*

aspěro -are, *to make rough* or *sharp; to excite, arouse.*

aspersĭo -ōnis, f. *sprinkling.*

aspĭcĭo -spĭcěre -spexi -spectum, *to look at, behold, survey, inspect, confront.* Transf., mentally, *to investigate, consider*; of places, *to look towards, face.*

aspīrātĭo -ōnis, f. *breathing, exhalation*; in speech, *pronunciation of the letter H, aspiration.*

aspīro -are: intransit., *to breathe, blow, exhale*: fig. *to be favourable, assist*; also *to climb up, reach towards* a thing; transit., *to blow* air; fig. to *infuse* spirit, etc.

aspis -ĭdis, f. *an adder, asp.*

asportātĭo -ōnis, f. *a taking away carrying off.*

asporto -are, *to carry off, take away.*

asprēta -orum, n. pl. *rough, uneven places.*

asser -ěris, m. *a stake, pole.*

assŭla -ae, f. *a shaving, chip.*

assus -a -um *dried, roasted*; n. pl. as subst. *a sweating bath.*

ast = at; q. v.

ast -; see also adst -.

astrŏlŏgĭa -ae, f. *astronomy.*

astrŏlŏgus -i, m. *an astronomer* or *astrologer.*

astrum -i, n. *a star,* or *constellation.* Transf., esp. plur., *the heights, glory, immortality.*

astu, n. *a city,* esp. *Athens.*

astus -ūs, m. *cleverness, cunning.*

astūtĭa -ae, f. *adroitness, craft*; in pl. *tricks.*

astūtus -a -um, *adroit, clever, crafty*: adv. **astutē.**

ăsylum -i, n. *a sanctuary, place of refuge.*

ăsymbŏlus -a -um, *contributing nothing to the cost of an entertainment.*

at (ast), *but, yet, moreover*; sometimes introducing an imaginary objection, *but, you may say.*

ătăt, attat, attatae, attattatae, etc. interj. *oh! ah! alas!*

ătăvus -i, m. *a great-great-great-grandfather*; in gen., *an ancestor.*

Ātella -ae, f. *a city in Campania*; adj. **Ātellānus** -a -um; f. as subst. (sc. fabella) *a kind of popular farce*; m. as subst., *a player in these farces*; adj. **Ātellānĭus** or **Ātellānĭcus** -a -um, *of Atellane farces.*

āter atra atrum, *dead black, dark*; poet. *clothed in black.* Transf., *dark, gloomy, sad; malicious, poisonous.*

Ăthēnae -arum, f. pl. *Athens*; meton., *leaning.* Adj. **Ăthēnaeus** -a -um, *Athenian*; adj. and subst. **Ăthēnĭensis** -e, *Athenian, an Athenian.*

ăthěos and **ăthěus** -i, m. *an atheist.*

athlēta -ae, m. *wrestler, athlete.*

athlētĭcus -a -um, *relating to an athlete*; adv. **athlētĭcē,** *athletically.*

Atlās -antis, m. (1) *a mountain in Mauretania.* (2) *a mythical king and giant, changed into Mount Atlas.* Hence **Atlantĭădes** -ae, m. *a male descendant of Atlas*; **Atlantis** -ĭdis, f. *a female descendant of Atlas*; adj. **Atlantĭcus, Atlantēus** -a -um.

ătŏmus -i, f. *an atom.*

atque and **ac,** *and, and also, and indeed* In comparisons: of similarity, with such words as aequus or idem, *as*; of difference, with such words as alius or secus, *than, from.*

atquī, *nevertheless, but in fact*; sometimes confirmatory, *indeed, certainly.*

ātrāmentum -i, n. *black fluid,* such as *ink* or *shoemaker's black.*

ātrātus -a -um, *clothed in black, in mourning.*

Atreus -ei, m. *son of Pelops, father of*

Agamemnon and Menelaus. Hence **Atrīdēs** or **Atrīda** -ae, m. *a son of Atreus.*

ātrĭensis -is, m. *head slave, steward.*

ātrĭŏlum -i, n. *a little* atrium, *an antechamber.*

ātrĭum -i, n. *the hall* or *entrance room in a Roman house temple* or *public building.*

atrōcĭtās -ātis, f. *frightfulness, cruelty, harshness, barbarity.*

Atrŏpŏs -i, f. *one of the three Parcae* or *Fates.*

atrox -ōcis, *terrible cruel, horrible*; of human character, *harsh, fierce, severe.* Adv. **atrōcĭtĕr.**

attactū abl. sing. m., *by touch, by contact.*

attăgēn -ēnis, m. and **attăgēna** -ae, f. *the black partridge.*

Attălus -i, m. *name of several kings of Pergamum*: adj. **Attălĭcus** -a -um.

attămen or **at tămen,** *but yet.*

attempĕro -are *to fit, adjust to*; adv. from partic., **attempĕrātē,** *appropriately.*

attendo -tendĕre -tendi -tentum, *to stretch to*; usually with animum (animos), or absol., *to direct the attention towards, attend to.*

Hence partic. **attentus,** *attentive, careful*: adv. **attentē.**

attentĭo -ōnis, f. *attentiveness, attention.*

attento or **attempto** -are, *to try, test, essay; to tamper with, try to corrupt,* or *to attack.*

attĕnŭo -are, *to make thin, reduce, weaken.*

Hence partic. **attĕnŭātus,** *made weak*; of style, *abbreviated, over-refined,* or *unadorned*; adv. **attĕnŭātē,** *simply, without ornament.*

attĕro -tĕrĕre -trīvi (-tĕrŭi) -trītum, *to rub against, rub away*; in gen., *to weaken, ruin.*

Hence partic. **attrītus** -a -um, *rubbed away, worn out*; fig., frons, *shameless.*

attestor -ari, dep. *to attest, bear witness to.*

attexo -texĕre -texŭi -textum, *to weave* or *plait on* or *to*; hence, in gen., *to add.*

Atthis -ĭdis, f. adj., *Attic, Athenian.*

Attĭca -ae, f. *Attica, the district of Greece containing Athens.*

[1]**Attĭcus** -a -um, *belonging to Attica* or *Athens, Attic, Athenian*; adv. **Attĭcē,** *in the Attic* or *Athenian manner.*

[2]**Attĭcus,** T. Pomponius, *the friend of Cicero.*

attĭnĕo -tĭnēre -tĭnŭi -tentum: transit., *to hold, keep, detain*; intransit., *to pertain to,* or *concern,* only in third person: quod ad me attinet, *as far as I am concerned*; nihil attinet, *it is pointless.*

attingo -tingĕre -tĭgi -tactum, *to touch, to reach*; of places, *to border upon*; of enemies, *to attack, to strike.* Transf., *to handle, manage, be concerned* or *connected with*; of feelings, *to affect* a person; in writing or speech, *to touch upon, to mention.*

attollo -tollĕre, *to raise, lift up.* Transf., *to elevate, excite. exalt.*

attondĕo -tondēre -tondi -tonsum, *to cut, clip, prune*; in gen., *to diminish.*

attŏno -tŏnare -tŏnŭi -tŏnĭtum, *to strike with thunder, stun.*

Hence partic. **attŏnĭtus** -a -um, *struck by thunder; stunned, senseless; inspired, frantic.*

attorquĕo -ēre, *to whirl, swing upward.*

attrăho -trăhĕre -traxi -tractum, *to draw, drag, attract.*

attrecto -are, *to touch, handle, lay hands on.*

attrĭbŭo -ŭĕre -ŭi -ūtum, *to allot, assign, hand over.* Transf., in gen., *to give, ascribe, add*; of taxes, *to impose.* N. of partic. as subst. **attrĭbūtum** -i, a *predicate, attribute.*

attrĭbūtĭo -ōnis, f. *the assignment of a debt*; rhet. *an attribute.*

attrītus -a -um, partic. from attero; q.v.

au, interj., *oh!*

auceps -cŭpis, m. *a fowler, bird-catcher; a spy, eavesdropper,* or *caviller.*

auctĭfĭcus -a -um, *increasing.*

auctĭo -ōnis, f. *an increasing*; hence, from the bidding, *an auction.*

auctĭōnārĭus -a -um, *relating to an auction.*

auctĭōnor -ari, dep. *to hold an auction.*

auctĭto -are and **aucto** -are, *to increase very much.*

auctŏr -ōris, m. *one that gives increase.* Hence (1) *an originator, causer, doer; founder* of a family; *architect* of a building; *author* of a book; *originator of* or *leader in* an enterprise; *source of* or *warrant for* a piece of information. (2) *a backer, supporter, approver, surety.*

auctōrāmentum -i, n. *a contract; wages.*

auctōrĭtās -ātis, f. (1) *support, backing, lead, warrant* ; polit., *sanction* (esp. of the senate). (2) *power conferred, rights, command*; legal *title.* (3) in gen., *influence, authority, prestige*; meton., *an influential person.*

auctōro -are, *to bind* or *hire for money.*

auctumnus = autumnus; q.v.

auctus -ūs m. *increase, enlargement, growth.*

aucŭpātĭo -ōnis, f. *fowling, bird-catching.*

aucŭpĭum -i, n. *bird-catching, fowling*; hence, in gen., *hunting, watching, eavesdropping*; aucupia verborum, *cavilling, quibbling.*

aucŭpor -ari, dep. *to catch* birds; in gen., *to watch out for, lie in wait for.*

audācĭa -ae, f. *courage, daring*; in bad sense, *audacity, impudence, temerity*; in plur., *audacious deeds.*

audax -ācis, *bold* (in good or bad sense); adv. **audactĕr** or **audācĭtĕr.**

audentĭa -ae, f. *boldness, courage.*

audĕo audēre ausus sum, *to be daring to dare, venture, bring oneself to.*

Hence partic. **audens** -entis, *daring, bold*; compar. adv. **audentĭus.**

audĭentĭa -ae, f. *hearing, attention.*

audĭo -ire, *to hear, listen; to learn* a thing *by hearing*; sometimes *to listen to and believe* (or *obey*); rarely *to be called*; bene audire, *to be well spoken of.*

Hence partic. **audĭens** -entis, as adj., *obedient*; as subst., *a hearer.*

audītĭo -ōnis, f. *hearing, listening*; concr., *hearsay report.*

audītŏr -ōris, m. *a hearer, auditor, scholar.*

audītōrĭum -i, n. *a place of audience, lecture-room, court of justice,* etc.

audītus -ūs, m. *hearing, sense of hearing*; concr., *a report.*

aufĕro auferre abstŭli ablātum, *to carry away, remove*: in bad sense, *to make away with, carry off, steal.*

Aufĭdus -i, m. *a river in Apulia.*

aufŭgĭo fŭgĕre -fūgi, *to flee, escape.*

augĕo augēre auxi auctum, *to enlarge, increase*; of rivers, in pass., *to be swollen*; in speech, *to extol, set forth*; with abl., *to enrich with, furnish with*; in transit. (rare), *to grow.*

Hence partic. **auctus** -a -um, *increased, enriched.*

augesco -ĕre, *to increase, begin to grow.*

augmĕn -ĭnis, n. *increase, growth.*

augur -ŭris, c. *augur, soothsayer, seer.*

augŭrālis -e, *relating to an augur* or *augury*; n. as subst. **augŭrāle** -is, *part of the Roman camp, where auspices were taken.*

augŭrātĭo -ōnis, f. *divining, soothsaying.*

augŭrātus -ūs, m. *the office of augur.*

augŭrĭum -i, n., *the office and work of an augur, observation and interpretation of omens, augury*; in gen., *an omen, prophecy, presentiment.*

augŭrĭus -a -um, *relating to an augur.*

augŭro -are, *to act as an augur, take auguries*; locus auguratur, *the place is consecrated by auguries*; in gen., *to have a foreboding* or *presentiment.*

augŭror -ari, dep. *to act as an augur, foretell by auguries*; hence, in gen., *to foretell* or *to guess.*

Augusta -ae, f. *a name for any female elative of the Roman emperor,* or *town named after him.*

Augustālis -e, *belonging to* or *in honour of the Emperor Augustus.*

[1]**augustus** -a -um, *consecrated, holy; majestic, dignified.* Adv. **augustē,** *reverently.*

[2]**Augustus** -i, m. *a name assumed by all Roman emperors.*

[3]**Augustus** -a -um, *relating to Augustus*; mensis, *August.*

aula -ae, f. *fore-court, court-yard*; poet = atrium, *an inner court.* Transf., *a palace, royal court*; meton., *courtiers.*

aula = olla; q.v.

aulaeum -i, n. usually plur., *embroidered work, tapestry curtains* (esp. of a theatre).

aulĭcus -a -um, of *the court, princely.*

auloedus -i, m. *one who sings to the flute.*

aura -ae, *air,* esp. *air breathed* or *blowing, breath, wind*; poet., esp. plur., *upper air, heaven*; superas ad auras, *to the light of day*; ferre sub auras, *to make known*; poet. (rarely), *smell, glitter* or *echo.*

aurārĭus -a -um, *golden, of gold*; f. as subst., *a gold-mine.*

aurātus -a -um, *golden* or *adorned with gold.*

Aurēlĭus -a -um, *name of a Roman plebeian* gens.

aurĕŏlus -a -um, *golden, glittering, splendid.*

aurĕus -a -um, *golden, made of gold* or *adorned with gold*; poet., *of the colour of gold,* and, in gen., *excellent, beautiful.*

aurichalchum = orichalchum; q.v.

aurĭcŏmus -a -um, *with golden hair* or *leaves.*

aurĭcŭla -ae, f. *the lobe of the ear*; in gen., *the ear.*

aurĭfer -fĕra -fĕrum, *gold-bearing, gold-producing.*

aurĭfex -fĭcis, m. *a goldsmith.*

aurīga -ae, c. *charioteer, driver*; of a ship, *helmsman*; as a constellation *the Waggoner.*

aurĭger -gĕra -gĕrum, *gold-bearing.*

aurīgo -are, *to drive a chariot.*

auris -is, f. *the car*; hence *hearing*; of a plough, *the earth-* or *mouldboard.*

aurītus -a -um, *long-eared*; hence *attentive.*

aurōra -ae, f. *dawn, break of day*; personified, *Aurora, goddess of morning*; meton., *the east.*

aurum -i, n. *gold; anything made of gold, gold plate, coin, a cup, ring, etc.; the golden age.*

Aurunca -ae, f. *a town in Campania.*

auscultātŏr -ōris, m. *a listener.*

ausculto -are, *to hear attentively, listen to*; sometimes also *to obey*; of servants, *to attend, wait.*

ausim, as subjunctive of audeo; q.v.

Ausŏnĭa -ae, f. *Ausonia, Lower Italy,* and in gen., *Italy*; adj. **Ăusŏnĭus** -a -um.

auspex -ĭcis, c. *one who watches birds and divines from them*; esp. *an official witness of marriage contracts*; poet., in gen., *a leader.*

auspĭcĭum -i, n. *divination by means of birds, the taking of* or *right to take auspices.* Transf., any *omen* or *sign*; poet. *leadership, guidance.*

auspĭco -are, *to take the auspices.*

Hence partic. **auspĭcātus** -a -um, *consecrated by auguries*; as adj., *favourable, auspicious.* Abl. abs. **auspĭcāto,** *after taking auspices*; hence *in a fortunate hour.*

auspĭcor -ari, dep., *to take the auspices*; hence *to begin favourably.*

auster -stri, m. *the south wind*; meton. *the south.*

austērĭtās -ātis, f., *harshness, strictness, severity.*

austērus -a -um, *sour, harsh, strict, severe, gloomy.* Adv. **austērē.**
austrālis -e, *southern.*
austrīnus -a -um, *southern.*
ausum -i, n. *a daring deed, undertaking.*
aut, *or, or else*; repeated, aut . . . aut . . ., *either . . . or . . .*
autem, *but, on the other hand, however, moreover, now.*
authepsa -ae, f. *a cooking-stove.*
Autŏmĕdōn -ontis, m. *charioteer of Achilles.*
autumnālis -e, *autumnal.*
[1]**autumnus** -i, m. *autumn.*
[2]**autumnus** -a -um, adj., *autumnal.*
autŭmo -are, *to say, assert.*
auxĭlĭāris -e, *giving help, assisting*: m. pl. as subst., *auxiliary* or *allied troops.*
auxĭlĭārĭus -a -um, *helping*; milites, *auxiliary troops.*
auxĭlĭātŏr -ōris, m. *a helper.*
auxĭlĭātus -ūs, m. *help, assistance.*
auxĭlĭor -ari, dep., *to help, assist, support.*
auxĭlĭum -i, n. *help, aid, assistance*; milit., often plur., *auxiliary troops,* or in gen., *military power.*
ăvārĭtĭa -ae and **ăvārĭtĭēs** -ēi f. *avarice, covetousness.*
ăvārus -a -um, *covetous, greedy*; adv. **ăvārē** and **ăvārĭtĕr.**
āvĕho -vĕhĕre -vexi -vectum, *to carry off, bear away*; pass., *to ride* or *sail off.*
āvello -vellĕre -velli and -vulsi (-volsi) -vulsum (-volsum), *to tear away, pluck away* (esp. with violence).
ăvēna -ae, f. *oats* or *wild oats*; hence *oaten pipe, shepherd's pipe*; in gen., *any stalk, straw.*
Ăventīnum -i, n. and **Ăventīnus** -i, m. *the Aventine, one of the seven hills of Rome.*
[1]**ăvĕo** -ēre, *to long for, desire.*
[2]**ăvĕo (hăvĕo)** -ēre, *to be well*; found only in imperat. and infin.; ave, *hail!* or *farewell!*
Ăvernus -i, m. *a lake near Puteoli, said to be an entrance to the infernal regions*; meton., *the infernal regions*; adj **Ăvernus** -a -um, **Ăvernālis** -e.
āverrunco -are, *to turn away, avert.*
āversābĭlis, *from which one must turn away, horrible.*
[1]**āversor** -ari, dep. *to turn away* (in shame, disgust, etc.); with acc., *to turn away from, avoid, shun.*
[2]**aversŏr** -ōris, m. *an embezzler.*
averto (avorto) -vertĕre -verti (-vorti) -versum (-vorsum), *to turn away, remove*: flumina, *to divert*; of feelings, *to estrange*; of property, *to carry off, appropriate embezzle*; poet., intransit., *to retire.*
Hence partic. **āversus** -a -um, *turned away, backward, behind*; of feeling, *disinclined, unfavourable, hostile.*
ăvĭa -ae. f. *a grandmother.*
ăvĭārĭum -i, *an aviary*; also *the haunts of wild birds.*
ăvĭdĭtās -ātis, f. *desire, longing*; esp. *desire for money, avarice.*
ăvĭdus -a -um, *desiring, longing for*; esp. *greedy for money, avaricious*; adv. **ăvĭdē.**
ăvis -is, f. *a bird*; often *a bird of omen,* and in gen., *an omen.*
ăvītus -a -um, *of a grandfather, ancestral.*
āvĭus -a -um: of places, *out of the way, untrodden*; of persons, *wandering, astray, lost.*
āvŏcātĭo -ōnis, f. *a calling away, diversion.*
āvŏco -are, *to call away,* or *off, to withdraw, remove, divert.*
āvŏlo -are, *to fly away, hasten away.*
ăvuncŭlus -i, m. *a mother's brother, uncle.*
ăvus -i, m. *a grandfather*; poet., in gen., *an ancestor.*
axis (or **assis**) -is, m. *an axle.* Hence (1) *a wheel*; meton., *a chariot, waggon.* (2) *the axis of the earth*; meton. *the north pole* or *the heavens*; sub axe, *in the open air.* (3) *a board, plank.*

B

B, b, the second letter of the Latin Alphabet.
băbae or **păpae,** interj. *wonderful!*
Băbȳlōn -ōnis, f. *a city on the Euphrates*; **Băbȳlōnĭa** -ae, f. *Babylonia, between the Euphrates and the Tigris*; adj. **Băbȳlōnĭcus** and **Băbȳlōnĭus** -a -um.
băca (bacca) -ae, f. *a berry, fruit*; *a pearl.*
băcātus -a -um, *set with pearls.*
baccar (bacchar) -āris, n. and **baccaris** -is, f. *a plant,* perhaps *sowbread.*
Baccha -ae, f. *a Bacchante, female worshipper of Bacchus.*
Bacchānal -is, n. *the place where Bacchus was worshipped*; plur. **Bacchānālĭa** -ium, *the (Greek) festival of Dionysus* or *Bacchus.*
bacchātĭo -ōnis, f. *revelling in Bacchanalian fashion.*
bacchor -ari, dep. *to celebrate the festival of Bacchus*: as passive, of places, *to be made the scene of Bacchic revels*; in gen., *to rage, rave like a Bacchante.* Partic. **bacchantes** = Bacchae; see Baccha.
Bacchus -i, m. *the god of wine*: meton., *the vine.,* or *wine,* or *the Bacchic cry* (Io Bacche). Adj. **Bacchēus, Bacchĭcus,** and **Bacchĭus** -a -um.
bacĭfer -fĕra -fĕrum, *bearing berries.*
băcillum -i, n. *a little staff*; esp. *the lictor's staff.*
băcŭlum -i, n. and **băcŭlus** -i, m. *a staff, walking-stick.*
Baetis -is, m. *a river in Spain*; adj. **Baetĭcus** -a -um, *relating to the Baetis*; f. subst. **Baetĭca** -ae, f. *the*

Roman province of Baetica on the Baetis.
Baiae -arum, f. pl. *a holiday-resort on the coast of Campania*; adj. **Baiānus** -a -um.
bāiŭlo -are, *to carry a burden.*
bāiŭlus -i, m. *a porter.*
bālaena -ae, f. *a whale.*
bălănus -i, f. rarely m. *an acorn, ben-nut, chestnut* or *date.*
bălatro -ōnis, m. *buffoon, jester.*
bālātus -ūs, m. *the bleating of sheep or goats.*
balbus -a -um, *stammering*; adv. **balbē.**
balbūtĭo -ire, *to stammer, stutter*; hence in gen., *to speak obscurely.*
Bălĭāres (Bălĕāres) -ium, f. pl. *the Balearic Islands*; adj. **Bălĭāris** -e, **Bălĭārĭcūs** -a -um.
bălĭnĕum or **balnĕum** -i, n. esp. in pl.; also heteroclite pl. **bălĭnĕae** or **balnĕae** -arum; *a bath, bathing place.*
ballista -ae, f. *a military engine for throwing large stones.*
balnĕae, v. balineum.
balnĕārĭus -a -um, *belonging to the bath*; n. pl. as subst. *baths, bathing-rooms.*
balnĕātor -ōris, m. *the keeper of a bath.*
balnĕŏlum -i, n. *a little bathroom.*
balnĕum, v. balineum.
bālo -are, *to bleat.*
balsămum -i, n. *the balsam-tree,* or *its gum.*
baltĕus -i, m. and **baltĕum** -i, n. *a girdle.*
bărathrum -i, n. *a pit, abyss*; esp. *of the lower world.*
barba -ae, f. *beard*; promittere barbam, *to let the beard grow.*
barbărĭa -ae and **barbărĭēs,** f. *a foreign country,* as opposed to Greece and Rome; *want of culture, rudeness, savagery.*
barbărĭcus -a -um, *foreign,* i.e., not Greek or Roman.
barbărus -a -um, *foreign, strange*; *uncultivated, rough, savage*; as subst., *a foreigner.* Adv. **barbărē,** *like a foreigner; roughly, barbarously.*
barbātŭlus -a -um, *with a slight beard.*
barbātus -a -um, *bearded.*
barbĭger -gĕra -gĕrum, *wearing a beard.*
barbĭtŏs, m. and f. *a lyre.*
barbŭla -ae, f. *a little beard.*
bardŏcŭcullus -i, m. *a Gallic overcoat.*
bardus -a -um, *stupid, slow, dull.*
bāris -ĭdos, f. *an Egyptian barge.*
barītus (barrītus) -ūs, m. *a German war-cry.*
bāro -ōnis, m. *a blockhead, simpleton.*
barrus -i, m. *elephant.*
bascauda -ae, f. *a basket.*
bāsĭātĭo -ōnis, f. *kissing, a kiss.*
bāsĭātor -ōris, m. *a kisser.*
băsĭlĭcus -a -um, *royal, kingly, princely.* M. as subst., *the best cast of the dice*; n. as subst., *a royal robe*; f. as subst., **băsĭlĭca** -ae, *a basilica, a building with double colonnades, where merchants met and courts were held.* Adv. **băsĭlĭcē,** *royally.*
bāsĭo -are, *to kiss.*
băsis -is and ĕos, f. *a pedestal, base*; villae, *foundation-wall*; trianguli, *base.*
bāsĭum -i, n. *a kiss.*
Bassăreus -ei, m. *a name of Bacchus.*
bătillum (or **vătillum**) -i, n. *a chafing-dish* or *shovel.*
battŭo (bātŭo) -ĕre, *to beat, knock.*
baubor -ari, dep., *to bark gently.*
bĕātĭtās -ātis, f. and **bĕātĭtūdo** -ĭnis, f. *happiness, blessedness.*
bĕātus -a -um, partic. from beo; q.v.
Belgae -arum, m. *the Belgae, a warlike people in the north of Gaul.*
bellārĭa -orum, n. pl. *dessert.*
bellātor -ōris, m. and **bellatrix** -īcis, f., *a warrior*; as adj. *warlike, courageous.*
bellātōrĭus -a -um, *warlike.*
bellĭcōsus -a -um, *warlike.*
bellĭcus -a -um, *of war, warlike.* N. as subst. **bellĭcum** -i, *the signal for march* or *attack.*
bellĭger -gĕra -gĕrum, *waging war, warlike.*
bellĭgĕro -are, *to wage war.*
bellĭpŏtens -entis, *mighty in war.*
bello -are and **bellor** -ari, dep. *to wage war, fight.*
Bellōna -ae, f. *the goddess of war.*
bellŭa, v. belua.
bellŭlus -a -um, *pretty, elegant.*
bellum -i, n. (old form, **duellum),** *war, fighting*; in bello, or loc., belli, *in time of war.*
bellus -a -um, colloq., *pretty, handsome*; adv. **bellē.**
bēlŭa -ae, f. *a beast, large animal*; as a term of reproach, *monster, brute, beast.*
bēlŭōsus -a -um, *full of monsters.*
Bēlus -j, m. *a king, founder of Babylon.* Hence f. pl. subst., **Bēlĭdes** -um, *the granddaughters of Belus, the Danaides.*
bĕnĕ, adv.; comp. **mĕlĭus**; superl. **optĭmē**; *well, rightly, properly*; bene rem gerere, *to succeed*; with adj. or adv., *thoroughly, very*; as an exclamation, *good, excellent*; bene facis, *I am obliged to you*; bene facta (or **benefacta),** *good deeds, benefits.*
bĕnĕfĭcentĭa -ae, f. *kindness.*
bĕnĕfĭcĭārĭus -a -um, *of a favour*; m. pl. as subst., *privileged soldiers.*
bĕnĕfĭcĭum -i, n. *a kindness, favour, service*; in political life, *favour, distinction, promotion,* also *privilege, exemption.*
bĕnĕfĭcus -a -um, comp. -entior, superl. -entissimus, *kind, generous, obliging.*
Bĕnĕventum -i, n. *a town in Samnium.*
bĕnĕvŏlens -entis, *well-wishing, obliging.*
bĕnĕvŏlentĭa -ae, f. *good-will, kindness.*
bĕnĕvŏlus -a -um, *kind, obliging, well disposed*; adv. **bĕnĕvŏlē.**
bĕnignĭtās -ātis, f. *kindness, generosity.*
bĕnignus -a -um, *kind, friendly, generous*; of things, *abundant, fruitful.* Adv. **bĕnignē,** *kindly, generously*; colloq., benigne dicis, *or* benigne, *much obliged* (accepting or refusing an offer).

bĕo -are, *to bless, enrich, make happy.* Hence partic. **bĕātus** -a -um, *happy, blessed, prosperous; well off*; n. as subst. *happiness.* Adv. **bĕātē,** *happily.*
bĕryllus -i, c. *a beryl.*
bēs bessis, m. *two-thirds.*
bestĭa -ae, f. *an animal without reason, a brute, beast.*
bestĭārĭus -a -um, *belonging to animals*; m. as subst., *one who fought with wild beasts at the public shows.*
bestĭŏla -ae, f. *a small animal.*
[1]**bēta** -ae, f. *a vegetable, beet.*
[2]**bēta,** n. indecl. *beta, the second letter in the Greek alphabet.*
bibliŏpōla -ae, m. *a book-seller.*
bibliŏthēca -ae, f. and **bibliŏthēcē** -es, f. *a collection of books, library.*
bĭbo bĭbĕre bĭbi bĭbĭtum, *to drink, drink in.*
Bibracte -is, n. *a town in Gaul.*
bĭbŭlus -a -um, *fond of drinking, thirsty*; charta, *blotting paper.*
bĭceps -cĭpĭtis, *two-headed.*
bĭcŏlor -ōris, *of two colours.*
bĭcornĭger -gĕri, m. *two-horned.*
bĭcornis -e, *two-horned, two-pronged*; luna, *the new moon*; Rhenus, *with two mouths.*
bĭcorpor -ŏris, *having two bodies.*
bĭdens -entis, *having two teeth.* As subst.: m., *a hoe with two crooked teeth*; f., *a sheep.*
bĭdental -ālis, n. *a sacred enclosure.*
bĭdŭum -i, n. *a space of two days*; abl., biduo, *in the course of two days.*
bĭennĭum -i, n. *a space of two years.*
bĭfārĭam, *in two parts.*
bĭfer -fĕra -fĕrum, of a tree, *bearing fruit twice a year.*
bĭfĭdus -a -um, *split into two parts.*
bĭfŏris -e, *having two doors* or *openings.*
bĭformātus -a -um and **bĭformis** -e, *of double form.*
bifrons -frontis, *with double forehead* or *countenance.*
bĭfurcus -a -um, *having two prongs* or *forks.*
bīgae -arum, f. pl. (and sing. **bīga** -ae) *a pair of horses,* or *a chariot drawn by a pair.*
bīgātus -a -um, *stamped with the effigy of a pair of horses*; m. as subst., *a silver coin so marked.*
bĭiugis -e and **bĭiugus** -a -um, *yoked two together*; m. pl. as subst., *a pair of horses* or *a chariot drawn by a pair.*
bĭlībra -ae, f. *two pounds weight.*
bĭlībris -e, *weighing* or *containing two pounds.*
bĭlinguis -e, *having two tongues,* or *speaking two languages*; hence *double-tongued, treacherous.*
bīlis -is, f. *gall, bile, anger, displeasure*; atra (or nigra) bilis, *black bile,* i.e. *melancholy, madness.*
bĭlix -īcis, *having a double thread.*
bĭlustris -e, *lasting ten years.*
bĭmăris -e, *lying on two seas.*
bĭmărītus, m. *the husband of two wives.*
bĭmātris -e, *having two mothers.*
bĭmembris -e, *having two kinds of limbs*; m. pl. as subst., *Centaurs.*
bĭmestris -e, *lasting two months*: porcus, *a pig two months old.*
bīmŭlus -a -um, *two years old.*
bīmus -a -um, *two years old* or *lasting two years.*
bīni -ae, -a, *twofold.* Hence *two apiece,* sometimes simply *two*; of things that match, *a pair*; findi in bina, *to be cleft in twain*; bis bina, *twice two.*
bĭnoctĭum -i, n. *a space of two nights.*
bĭnōmĭnis -e, *having two names.*
bĭpalmis -e, *two palms* or *spans long* or *broad.*
bĭpartītus or **bĭpertītus** -a -um, *divided in two*; abl. as adv., bipartito or bipertito, *in two parts, in two ways.*
bĭpătens -entis, *doubly open, open in two directions.*
bĭpĕdālis -e, *two feet long, broad, thick* or *high.*
bĭpennĭfer -fĕra -fĕrum, *armed with a two-edged axe.*
bĭpennis -e, *having two wings* or *edges*; f. as subst., *a double-edged axe.*
bĭpēs -ĕdis, *having two feet*; as subst. *biped.*
bĭrēmis -e, *two-oared*; f. as subst., *a boat with two oars* or *a ship with two banks of oars.*
bis, *twice.*
Bistŏnes -um, m. *a Thracian people*; adj. **Bistŏnius** -a -um, *Bistonian* or *Thracian.*
bĭsulcus -a -um, *split into two parts, forked.*
Bīthȳnĭa -ae, f. *a country in north-west Asia Minor.*
bīto -ĕre, *to go.*
bĭtūmen -ĭnis, n. *asphalt, bitumen.*
bĭtūmĭnĕus -a -um, *bituminous.*
bĭvĭus -a -um, *having two ways* or *passages*; n. as subst. **bĭvĭum,** *a place where two roads meet.*
blaesus -a -um, *lisping, indistinct.*
blandīmentum -i, n. *flattery, allurement.*
blandĭor -iri, dep. *to flatter, caress, coax,* with dat.
Hence partic. **blandītus** -a -um, *charming.*
blandĭtĭa -ae, f. *flattery, allurement, attraction, charm.*
blandus -a -um, adj. *flattering, caressing, alluring, tempting.* Adv. **blandē** and **blandĭtĕr,** *flatteringly.*
blătĕro -are, *to chatter, babble.*
blatta -ae, f. *a cockroach.*
bŏārĭus and **bŏvārĭus** -a -um, *relating to cattle.*
Boeōti -orum or -um, and **Boeōtii,** m. *the inhabitants of Boeotia, a district in Greece to the west of Attica.*
Bōii -orum, m. pl. *a Celtic people of north Italy, Germany and Gaul.*
bōlētus -i, m. *a mushroom.*
bŏlus -i, m. *a throw*; hence *the haul* or *catch* of a fishing net.
bombus -i, m. *a boom, deep hollow noise.*
bombȳcĭnus -a -um, *silken.*

bombyx -ȳcis, m. and f. *the silkworm, or silk.*

bŏnĭtās -ātis, f. *goodness, excellence*; esp. *moral goodness, kindness, integrity.*

bŏnus -a -um; compar. **mĕlĭor** -ius; superl. **optĭmus** -a -um; *good*: in gen., *good of its kind*; nummi boni, *genuine coin*; bona aetas, *youth*; bona verba, *words of good omen*; bona pars, *a good* (i.e. *considerable*) *proportion*; in a particular respect of tools, workmen, etc. *useful, efficient*; morally *good, virtuous, honest, kind*; polit., *patriotic, loyal.* N. as subst. **bŏnum** -i, *good*; in gen., *profit, advantage*; bonum publicum, *the common weal*; cui bono fuisset, *for whose advantage*; materially, usually pl., *goods, property*; morally, *the good*: summum bonum, *the supreme good.*

bŏo -are, *to shout, roar, echo.*

Bŏōtēs -ae, m. *a constellation in the northern hemisphere.*

Bŏrĕās -ae, m. *the north wind*; meton., *the north.* Adj. **Bŏrēus** -a -um, *northern.*

bōs, bŏvis, c. (1) *ox, bullock, cow*; bos Lucas, *elephant.* (2) *a kind of flat fish.*

Bospŏrus (**Bosphŏrus**), -i, m. *name of various straits*, esp. *those between Thrace and Asia Minor.*

bŏtŭlus -i, m. *a sausage.*

bŏvīle = bubile; q.v.

Bŏvillae -ārum, f. pl. *a town in Latium.*

bŏvillus -a -um, *relating to oxen.*

brăbeuta -ae, m. *a judge, umpire.*

brācae (**braccae**) -arum, f. pl. *breeches, trousers.*

brācātus (**braccātus**) -a -um, *wearing breeches*; Gallia Bracata, *Gaul on the north side of the Alps.*

brācchĭum -i, n. *the forearm, arm from elbow to wrist*; *any limb of a living creature*; *any other thing like an arm*, e.g. *branch, spur, yard, outwork of a fortification, mole.*

bractĕa (**brattĕa**) -ae, f. *a thin plate of metal*; *gold leaf.*

brassĭca -ae, f. *cabbage.*

brĕvĭārĭum -i, n. *a summary, epitome.*

brĕvĭlŏquens -entis, *brief in speech.*

brĕvĭlŏquentĭa -ae f. *brevity of speech.*

brĕvis -e, *short*, in space or time; of water, *shallow*; of living things, conditions, etc., *short-lived*; of style, *concise*; n. abl. **brĕvī,** *shortly, soon, briefly*; n. pl. as subst. **brĕvĭa** -ium, *shallows, shoals.* Adv. **brĕvĭtĕr,** *shortly, briefly.*

brĕvĭtās ātis, f. *shortness*, in space or time; of style, *brevity, conciseness.*

Brĭărēūs -ei, m. *a giant with a hundred arms.*

Brĭtanni -orum, m. pl. *the Britons*; **Brĭtannĭa** -ae, f. *Britain*; adj. **Brĭtannĭcus** -a -um, *British*; m. sing. as *a title commemorating successes in Britain.*

Brŏmĭus -i, m. *a surname of Bacchus.*

brūma -ae, f. *the winter solstice*; in gen., *winter, wintry cold.*

brūmālis -e, *relating to the shortest day*; in gen., *wintry.*

Brundĭsĭum -i, n. *a seaport in Calabria*; adj. **Brundĭsīnus** -a -um.

Bruttii (**Brūtii, Brittii**) -orum, m. *the inhabitants of the southern extremity of Italy.*

[1]**brūtus** -a -um, *heavy, immoveable*; *dull, without feeling or reason.*

[2]**Brūtus** -i, m. *a cognomen of the Roman* Gens Iunia.

bŭbīle -is, n. *an ox-stall.*

būbo -ōnis, m., *the owl.*

bŭbulcus -i m. *one who ploughs with oxen.*

būbŭlus -a -um, *relating to cows or oxen*; f. as subst. (sc. caro), *beef.*

bucca -ae, f. *the cheek*, esp. when puffed out. Transf., *a declaimer, bawler*; *a parasite*; *a mouthful.*

buccĭna, buccĭnātor, etc.; v. bucina, etc.

buccŭla -ae, f. *a small cheek*; of a helmet, *beaver, visor.*

būcĕrus and **būcĕrĭus** -a -um, *having ox's horns.*

būcĭna -ae, f. *a crooked trumpet* or *horn.*

būcĭnātor -ōris, m. *a trumpeter.*

būcŏlĭca -orum, n. pl. *pastoral poems.*

būcŭla -ae, f. *a heifer.*

būfo -ōnis, m. *a toad.*

bulbus -i, m. *an onion.*

būleutērĭon -i, n. *the place of meeting of a Greek council.*

bulla -ae, f. *a round swelling*; in water, *a bubble*; on furniture or equipment, *a boss, stud*; bulla aurea, *a golden ornament, an amulet.*

bullātus -a -um. (1) *inflated, bombastic*, or perhaps *transitory.* (2) *wearing the* bulla (q.v.).

būmastus -i, f. *a kind of vine.*

būris, -is, m. *the crooked hinder part of the plough.*

bustŭārĭus -a -um, *belonging to the place where corpses were burned.*

bustum -i, n. *the place where corpses were burned and buried*; hence *grave, sepulchre.*

buxĭfer -fĕra -fĕrum, *producing the box-tree.*

buxus -i, f. and **buxum** -i, n. *the evergreen box-tree*; *box-wood*; an *article made of box-wood.*

Byzantĭum -i, n. *Byzantium, a Greek city on the Bosphorus.*

C

C, c, the third letter of the Latin Alphabet.

căballus -i, m. *pack-horse, nag, hack.*

căchinnātĭo -ōnis, f. *violent laughter.*

[1]**căchinno** -are, *to laugh aloud.*

[2]**căchinno** -ōnis, m. *jester, scoffer.*

căchinnus -i m. *loud laughter.*

căcŏēthĕs -is, n. *an obstinate disease.*

căcūmen -ĭnis, n. *the extreme point, top, tip, zenith.*

căcūmĭno -are, *to point, make pointed.*

cădāver -ĕris, n. *dead body, carcass.*
cădāvĕrōsus -a -um, *corpse-like.*
Cadmus -i, m. *the founder of Thebes*; adj. **Cadmēus** -a -um, *Theban.*
cădo cădĕre cĕcīdi, *to fall, sink, drop*; vela cadunt, *are furled*; iuxta solem cadentem, *in the west*; of living beings, often *to fall in death, die*; hence *to be destroyed, to subside, sink, flag, fail*; cadere animis, *to lose heart*; with in or sub, *to come under, be subject to*; with in, *to agree with, be consistent with*; of events, *to fall out, happen*; of payments, *to fall due.*
cādūcĕātor -ōris, m. *herald.*
cādūcĕus -i, m. and **cādūcĕum** -i, n. *a herald's staff.*
cādūcĭfer -fĕra -fĕrum, *bearing the caduceus* (of Mercury).
cădūcus -a -um. (1) *fallen* or *falling.* (2) *inclined* or *ready to fall*; esp. *destined to die, devoted to death*; in gen., *frail, perishable, transitory.*
cādus -i, m. *jar* or *urn.*
caecĭgĕnus -a -um, *born blind.*
Caecĭlĭus -a -um, *name of a plebeian* gens.
caecĭtās -ātis, f. *blindness.*
caeco -are, *to make blind* or *dark.*
Caecŭbum -i, n. and **Caecŭbus ager,** *a marshy district in Latium, famous for its wine*; (vinum) Caecubum, *Caecuban wine.*
caecus -a -um: act., *blind, not seeing*; *intellectually* or *morally blind*; *uncertain, objectless*; pass., *unseen, hidden, obscure, dark.*
caedēs -is, f. *cutting down, killing, slaughter.* Transf., *persons slain*; *blood shed in slaughter.*
caedo caedĕre cĕcīdi caesum. (1) *to cut.* (2) *to beat, knock about.* (3) *to kill, slay.*
caelāmen -īnis, n. *bas-relief.*
caelātor -ōris, m. *chaser, graver, carver.*
caelātūra -ae, f. *the art of engraving* or *chasing*; *an engraving.*
caelebs -libis, *unmarried, single* (of men); of trees, *to which no vine is trained.*
caelĕs -ĭtis, *heavenly*; as subst., *a dweller in heaven, god.*
caelestis -e, *belonging to heaven, coming from heaven*; n. pl. as subst. *things in heaven, heavenly bodies.* Transf., *belonging to the gods, celestial, divine, superhuman*; as subst., esp. plur., *the gods.*
caelĭcŏla -ae, *dwelling in heaven*; as subst. *a god.*
caelĭfer -fĕra -fĕrum, *bearing the heavens.*
Caelĭus -a -um. *name of a Roman plebeian* gens; Caelius Mons, *a hill in Rome.*
caelo -are, *to engrave* or *chase, to carve in bas-relief, to fashion.*
[1]**caelum** -i, n. *the burin* or *engraving tool.*
[2]**caelum** -i, n. *the heavens, sky, air, climate.* Esp. *heaven* as the home of the gods; fig., *heaven* as the height of joy, renown, etc.
caementum -i, n. *rough stone from the quarry.*
caenōsus -a -um, *muddy.*
caenum -i, n. *mud, dirt, filth.*
caepa (**cēpa**) -ae, f. and **caepe** (**cēpe**) -is, n. *onion.*
Caerĕ, n. *a very old city of Etruria*; adj. **Caerēs** -ītis and -ētis.
caerīmōnĭa -ae, f. *holiness, sanctity; holy awe, reverence; religious usage, sacred ceremony.*
caerŭlĕus (poet. also **caerŭlus**) -a -um, *blue, dark blue* (esp. of the sea or sky).
Caesar -ăris, m. *a Roman family name of the* gens Iulia; esp. of C. Iulius Caesar, *the general and dictator, and later of all the emperors.*
caesărĭēs -ēi, f. *hair, a head of hair.*
caesim, *with cutting*; fig. of style, *in short sentences.*
caesĭus -a -um, *bluish grey* (esp. of eyes).
caespĕs (**cespĕs**) -ĭtis, m. *a turf, sod.* Transf., *a hut* or *altar of turf.*
caestus -ūs, m. *gauntlet for boxers.*
caetra (**cetra**) -ae, f. *short Spanish shield.*
caetrātus -a -um, *armed with the* caetra.
Caius = Gaius; q.v.
Călabrĭa -ae, f. *the peninsula at the south-east extremity of Italy*; adj. and subst. **Călăber** -bra -brum, *Calabrian, a Calabrian.*
călămister -tri, m. and **călămistrum** -tri, n. *a curling-iron for the hair.* Transf., *excessive ornament* or *flourish in style.*
călămistrātus -a -um, *curled with the curling-iron.*
călămĭtās -ātis, f. *loss, failure, misfortune, damage, a reverse.*
călămĭtōsus -a -um: act., *causing loss, destructive*; pass., *suffering loss, miserable.* Adv. **călămĭtōsē,** *disastrously.*
călămus -i, m. *reed*; hence *anything made of reed,* e.g. *a pen, a reed pipe, an arrow.*
călăthiscus -i, m. *a small wicker basket.*
călăthus -i, m. *a wicker basket*; and of other containers, e.g. *a milk-pai' wine-bowl.*
călātor -ōris, m. *attendant.*
calcar -āris, n. *spur.*
calcĕāmentum -i, n. *covering for th foot.*
calcĕo -are, *to shoe, provide with shoes.*
calcĕus -i, m. *shoe.*
calcitro -are, *to kick; to resist obstinately.*
calco -are, *to tread, trample on.*
calcŭlus -i, m. *a little stone, pebble.* Esp. *a piece used in the Roman game of draughts; a voting pebble; a counter for reckoning*; hence *a calculation.*
caldus = calidus; q.v.
Călēdŏnĭa -ae, f. *the highlands of Scotland*; adj. **Călēdŏnĭus** -a -um,
călĕfăcĭo (**calfăcĭo**) -făcĕre -fēci -factum, pass. călĕfio, etc., *to make warm, heat; to disturb, excite.*
călĕfacto -are, *to make warm, heat.*

Călendae = Kalendae; q.v.
călĕo -ēre -ŭi, *to be warm, to glow*; of feeling, etc. *to be inflamed, aroused, excited.*
călesco -ĕre, *to become warm, grow hot.*
călĭdus (caldus) -a -um, *warm, hot; fiery, passionate.* F. sing. as subst., **călĭda (calda)** -ae, *warm water*; n. sing. **călĭdum** -i, *warm wine and water.*
călĭendrum -i, n. *a lady's wig.*
călĭga -ae, f. *a stout shoe* or *boot* (esp. a soldier's).
călĭgātus -a -um, *wearing heavy boots*; m. as subst., *a private soldier.*
cālīgĭnōsus -a -um, *foggy, misty, dark.*
[1]**cālīgo** -ĭnis, f. *fog, mist, darkness.* Transf., *mental darkness, dullness; calamity, affliction, gloom.*
[2]**cālīgo** -are: transit., *to spread a dark mist around, to make dizzy*; intransit., *to be dark, misty.*
Călĭgŭla -ae, m. *a little soldier's shoe; nickname given by the soldiers to the emperor Gaius.*
călix -ĭcis, m. *a drinking* or *cooking vessel.*
callĕo -ēre, *to be thick-skinned.* Transf.: intransit., *to be practised, experienced*; transit., *to know by experience, understand.*
callĭdĭtās -ātis, f. *expertness, cleverness*; in bad sense, *cunning, craft, artifice.*
callĭdus -a -um, *experienced, clever, dexterous, skilful*; in bad sense, *cunning, subtle, sly.* Adv. **callĭdē.**
Callĭŏpē -ēs and **Callĭŏpēa** -ae, f. *Calliope, the Muse of epic poetry.*
callis -is, m. or f. *narrow track, footpath, cattle track.*
callōsus -a -um, *hard-skinned, solid.*
callum -i, n. *hard skin* or *flesh; toughness, insensibility.*
[1]**călo (kălo)** -are, *to call, summon.*
[2]**cālo** -ōnis, m. *a soldier's servant*; in gen., *a drudge.*
călor -ōris, m. *warmth, heat, glow; passion, excitement.*
Calpurnĭus -a -um, *name of a Roman plebeian* gens.
caltha -ae, f. *a plant*, prob. *marigold.*
călumnĭa -ae, f. *trick, artifice, chicanery, craft*; at law, *a false accusation*, or *an action for false accusation.*
călumnĭātor -ōris, m. *a false accuser, pettifogger.*
călumnĭor -ari, dep. *to accuse falsely, misrepresent*; in gen., *to practise trickery.*
calva -ae, f. *the bald scalp of the head.*
calvĭtĭēs -ēi, f. and **calvĭtĭum** -i, n. *baldness.*
calvus -a -um, *bald, without hair.*
[1]**calx** -cis, f. *the heel.*
[2]**calx** -cis, f. rarely m. *a stone, pebble*; collectively, *lime, chalk*; meton., *a goal* (marked with chalk), *an end.*
Călypsō -ūs, *a nymph who entertained Ulysses.*
cămella -ae, f. *a goblet.*
cămēlus -i, m. and f. *a camel* or *dromedary.*
Cămēna -ae, f. usually pl., *Latin goddesses of poetry*, identified with the Greek *Muses.*
cămĕra (cămăra) -ae, f. *a vaulted chamber, vault; a flat covered boat.*
Cămillus -i, m. *cognomen of several members of the* gens Furia.
cămīnus -i, m. *a forge, fire-place, fire.*
cammărus -i, m. *a crustacean*, perhaps *crayfish.*
Campānĭa -ae, f. *a district of Central Italy.*
campester -tris -tre: in gen., *on level ground, flat*; esp. *relating to the Campus Martius and its exercises and elections.* N. sing. as subst., *a loin-cloth worn by wrestlers*; n. pl. as subst., *a plain.*
campus -i, m. *a level space, plain, field*; esp. of *the Campus Martius at Rome, as a place for various exercises, and for meetings of the* comitia. Transf., *any free space, field*, or *theatre of action; any level surface*; poet., *the sea.*
Camulŏdūnum -i n. *a town in Britain* (now *Colchester*).
cămūr -a -um, *hooked, curved.*
cănālis -is, m. *waterpipe, channel canal.*
cancelli -orum, m. pl. *lattice, railing, grating.* Transf., *bounds, limits.*
cancer -cri, m. *crab; a sign of the Zodiac*; meton., *the south*, or *summer heat; the disease cancer.*
candēla -ae, f. *a wax* or *tallow candle, taper; a cord coated with wax.*
candēlābrum -i, n. *a candle-stick.*
candēo -ēre -ŭi, *to shine, white, glitter* or *glow with heat.*
candesco -ĕre -ŭi, *to begin to shine* or *glow.*
candĭdātōrĭus -a -um, *relating to a candidate.*
candĭdātus -a -um, *clothed in white*; as subst. *a candidate for office.*
candĭdŭlus -a -um, *shining, dazzling.*
candĭdus -a -um, *shining white*; of persons, with the suggestion of beauty, *fair.* Transf., of time or fortune, *happy*; of writing, *clear, lucid*; of character, *honest, straight-forward*; of dress, *clothed in white*; sententia candida, *a vote for acquittal.* N. as subst. **candĭdum** -i, *white colour.* Adv. **candĭdē,** *in white; clearly candidly.*
candor -ōris, m. *shining whiteness, lustre*; of character, *sincerity, candour*; of writing, *clarity, simplicity.*
cānĕo -ēre -ŭi, *to be white*, or *hoary.*
cānesco -ĕre, *to become white* or *hoary*; hence *to become old.*
cănīcŭla -ae, f. *little bitch*; sometimes a term of abuse. Transf., *Dog-star, Sirius; the worst throw at dice.*
cănīnus -a -um, *of a dog, canine.* Transf., *snarling, spiteful*; littera, *the letter R.*
cănis -is, c. *dog, hound*; of persons, as a term of abuse; in dice, *the worst throw.*
cănistra -orum, n. pl. *baskets.*

cānĭtĭēs, acc. -em. *whitish-grey colour,* esp. of the hair; meton., *grey hair, old age.*
canna -ae, f. *reed.* Transf., *a reed-pipe; a small boat.*
cannăbis -is, and **cannăbum** -i, n. *hemp.*
Cannae -arum, f. pl. *town in Apulia, where Hannibal defeated the Romans* (216 B.C.). Adj. **Cannensis** -e.
căno cănĕre cĕcĭni cantum, *to sing* or *play.* Intransit. *to sing*; of cocks, *to crow*; of frogs, *to croak*; also (with abl.), *to play on an instrument*; canere receptui, *to sound the signal for retreat*; of instruments, *to sound.* Transit.: (1) *to sing with the voice.* (2) *to sing of, celebrate in song.* (3) *to sound* or *play an instrument.* (4) *to prophesy.*
cănor -ōris, m. *melody, song, sound.*
cănōrus -a -um, *melodious, harmonious, sweet-sounding*; n. as subst., *harmonious sound.*
Cantabrĭa -ae, f. *a region in north-west Spain.*
cantāmen -ĭnis, n. *incantation.*
canthăris -ĭdis, f. *a beetle*: esp. *the Spanish fly.*
canthărus -i, m. *a tankard; a sea-fish, the black bream.*
canthērĭus -i, m. *a gelding, nag.*
canthus -i, m. *the tire of a wheel.*
cantĭcum -i, n. *a scene in Roman comedy, accompanied by music and dancing; a song; sing-song delivery in an orator.*
cantĭlēna -ae, f. *an old song, twaddle, chatter.*
cantĭo -ōnis, f. *a song*; *an incantation, enchantment.*
cantĭto -are, *to sing* or *play often.*
Cantĭum -i, n. *a district in Britain* (now Kent).
cantĭuncŭla -ae, f. *a flattering song.*
canto -are -avi -atum, *to sing* or *play.* Intransit., of persons, *to sing*; of cocks, *to crow*; also *to play on an instrument*; of instruments, *to sound.* Transit. (1) *to sing.* (2) *to sing of, celebrate, continually mention.* (3) *to predict.*
cantor -ōris, m. *a singer, poet, musician; an actor.*
cantus -ūs, m. *song, melody music, poetry; prophecy; incantation.*
cānus -a -um, *whitish-grey*; hence *aged*; m. pl. as subst., *grey hair.*
căpācĭtās -ātis, f. *breadth, capacity.*
căpax -ăcis, *able to hold, broad, wide, roomy.* Transf., *receptive, able to grasp, capable, fit for.*
căpēdo -ĭnis, f. *a bowl used in sacrifices.*
căpella -ae, f. *a she-goat; a star in the constellation Auriga.*
Căpēna -ae, f. *a town in Etruria*; adj. **Căpēnus** -a -um; porta Capena, *a gate in Rome at the beginning of the Via Appia.*
căper -ri, m. *he-goat.*
căpesso -ĕre -īvi and -ii -itum, *to seize, grasp eagerly*; of places, *to strive to reach, to make for*; of business, etc., *to take up, undertake*; rempublicam *to enter public life.*
căpillātus -a -um, *hairy, having hair.*
căpillus -i, m. *a hair*; usually pl., or collect. sing., *the hair of the head* or *beard.*
căpĭo căpĕre cēpi captum, *to take.* (1) in gen. *to take, seize*; of places, *to choose, reach,* or *take possession of*; of business, opportunities, etc. *to take up, take in hand, adopt*; of persons, *to choose.* (2) *to catch, take in a violent or hostile manner*; hence, *to attack, injure*; pass. capi, *to be injured* or *diseased*; oculis et auribus captus, *blind and deaf*; also *to charm, captivate, take in*; at law, *to convict.* (3) *to receive,* esp. of money; in gen., *to suffer, undergo, take on.* (4) *to take in, hold, contain, keep in*; mentally, *to grasp, comprehend.*
căpis -ĭdis, f. *a one-handled vessel.*
căpistro -are, *to fasten with a halter.*
căpistrum -i, n. *a halter.*
căpĭtālis -e, *relating to the head,* or *to life.* Transf., *deadly, mortal; first, chief, distinguished.* N. as subst. **căpĭtal** and **căpĭtālĕ,** *a capital crime.*
căpĭto -onis, m. *a man with a large head.*
Căpĭtōlĭum -i, n. *the temple of Jupiter at Rome, the Capitol*; adj. **Căpĭtōlīnus** -a -um; m. pl. as subst., *superintendents of games in honour of Jupiter Capitolinus.*
căpĭtŭlum -i, n. *a little head.*
Cappădŏcĭa -ae, f. *a district in Asia Minor.*
capra -ae, f. *a she-goat*; also *a star in the constellation Auriga.*
caprĕa -ae, f. *a roe.*
Caprĕae -arum, f. *small island off the Campanian coast* (now *Capri*).
caprĕŏlus -i, m. *a roebuck*; in **plur.,** *props, supports.*
Caprĭcornus -i, m. *Capricorn, a sign of the Zodiac.*
caprĭfīcus -i, f. *the wild fig-tree,* and *its fruit.*
caprĭgĕnus -a -um, *born of goats.*
caprĭmulgus -i, m. *goat-milker*—i.e. *a countryman.*
caprīnus -a -um, *relating to a goat.*
caprĭpēs -pĕdis, *goat-footed.*
capsa -ae, f. *a box* or *case,* esp. *for books.*
capsārĭus -i, m. *a slave who carried his young master's satchel.*
capsŭla -ae, f. *a little chest.*
captātĭo -ōnis, f. *an eager seizing*; verborum, *quibbling.*
captātor -ōris, m. *one who eagerly seizes*; esp. *a legacy-hunter.*
captĭo -ōnis, f. (1) *a cheat, deception.* (2) *harm, loss.* (3) *a fallacy, sophism.*
captĭōsus -a -um, *deceitful; captious*; n. pl. as subst. *sophistries.* Adv. **captĭōsē.**
captĭuncŭla -ae, f. *fallacy, quibble.*
captīvĭtās -ātis, f. *captivity, capture*; collectively, *a number of captives.*
captīvus -a -um, *captured, taken,* esp. *in war.* Transf., *of a prisoner.*

M. and f. as subst., *a prisoner, captive.*
capto -are, *to seize, catch at*; in gen., *to strive after, desire, seek.*
captus -ūs, m. *catching, taking*; hence *power* or *manner of comprehension, idea.*
Capŭa -ae, f. *chief town of Campania.*
căpŭlus -i, m. (1) *a coffin.* (2) *a handle*; esp. *the hilt of a sword.*
căput -ĭtis, n. *the head*; meton., *a living individual*, esp. of human beings, *a person*; also of a person's *life, existence*, esp., in Rome, *a man's political and social rights.* Transf., of lifeless things, *the top, summit, extremity*; of rivers, etc., *the source*; of persons and things, *the head, leader, chief, headquarters, chief point*; of places, *the capital.*
carbăsĕus -a -um, *made of canvas.*
carbăsus -i, f.; heteroclite pl. **carbăsa** -orum, n.; *flax*; meton., *anything made of flax*, e.g. *garments, curtains, sails.*
carbo -ōnis, m. *burning* or *burnt wood.*
carbōnārĭus -i, m. *a charcoal burner.*
carcer -ĕris, m. *prison, cell*; in plur., carceres, *the starting-place of a race-course.*
carchēsĭum -i, n. *a goblet with handles.* Transf., *the top of a mast, scuttle.*
cardĭăcus -a -um, *pertaining to the stomach*; m. as subst., *one who suffers from a disease of the stomach.*
cardo -ĭnis, m. *a hinge*; *any pole* or *pivot*: cardo duplex, *the ends of the earth's axis; a cardinal point, main consideration.*
cardŭus -i, m. *thistle.*
cārectum -i, n. *a sedgy spot.*
cărĕo -ēre -ŭi, *to be without* (with abl); of a place, *to absent oneself from.*
cārex -icis, f. *rush, sedge.*
cărĭēs, acc. -em. abl. -e, f. *rottenness, decay.*
cărīna -ae, f. *the keel of a ship*; meton., *a ship, vessel.*
cărĭōsus -a -um, *rotten, decayed.*
cāris -ĭdis, f. *a kind of crab.*
cārĭtās -atis, f. *dearness, high price*; esp. *high cost of living.* Transf., *affection, love, esteem.*
carmen -ĭnis, n. *a song, tune*, vocal or instrumental; *a poem, poetry, verse; a prediction; an incantation; a religious* or *legal formula.*
Carmentis -is, and **Carmenta** -ae, f. *a prophetess, mother of Evander*; adj. **Carmentālis** -e.
carnĭfex -fĭcis, m. *an executioner, hangman.*
carnĭfĭcīna -ae, f. *the work of a hang-man; execution, torture.*
carnĭfĭco -are, *to behead*, or *mangle.*
[1]**cāro** -ĕre, *to card.*
[2]**căro** carnis, f. *flesh.*
carpentum -i, n. *a two-wheeled carriage.*
carpo carpĕre carpsi carptum, *to pluck, pull off, select, choose out*; and so *to enjoy*; of animals, *to graze.* Transf., *to proceed on* a journey; *to pass over* a place; *to carp at, slander* a person; *to weaken, annoy, harass* an enemy; *to break up, separate, divide* forces.
carptim, *in pieces, in small parts; in different places; at different times.*
carptor -ōris, m. *one who carves food.*
carrūca -ae, f. *a four-wheeled carriage.*
carrus -i, m. *a four-wheeled baggage-waggon.*
Carthāgo (Karthāgo) -ĭnis, f. (1) *the city of Carthage in N. Africa.* (2) Carthago (Nova), *a colony of the Carthaginians in Spain* (now *Cartagena*). Adj. **Carthāgĭnĭensis** -e.
căruncŭla -ae, f. *a small piece of flesh.*
cārus -a -um, adj. *high-priced, dear costly.* Transf., *dear, beloved.*
căsa -ae, f. *hut, cottage, cabin.*
cāsĕŏlus -i, m. *a little cheese.*
cāsĕus -i, m. *cheese.*
căsĭa -ae, f. (1) *a tree with an aromatic bark, like cinnamon.* (2) *the sweet-smelling mezereon.*
Cassandra -ae, f. *a prophetess, daughter of Priam.*
cassēs -ĭum, m. pl. *a net; a trap snare*; also *a spider's web.*
cassĭda -ae, f. = cassis; q.v.
Cassĭŏpē -ēs, f. *mother of Andromeda.*
cassis -ĭdis and **cassĭda** -ae, f. *a metal helmet.*
Cassĭus -a -um, *name of a Roman* gens; adj. **Cassĭānus** -a -um.
cassus -a -um, *empty, hollow*; with abl., *devoid of.* Transf., *worthless, useless, vain*; **in cassum** or **incassum** as adv., *in vain.*
Castălĭa -ae, f. *a spring on Mount Parnassus, sacred to Apollo and the Muses.*
castănĕa -ae f. *a chestnut* or *chestnut-tree.*
castellānus -a -um, *relating to a fortress*; m. pl. as subst., *the garrison of a fortress.*
castellātim, *in single fortresses.*
castellum -i, n. *a castle, fortress, fort; a shelter, refuge.*
castīgātio -ōnis, f. *punishment, reproof.*
castīgātor -ōris, m. *one who reproves* or *corrects.*
castīgo -are, *to reprove, chasten, punish; to check, restrain.*
Hence partic. **castīgātus** -a -um, *restrained, orderly, neat.*
castĭmōnĭa -ae, f. *purity.*
castĭtās -ātis, f. *chastity.*
[1]**castor** -ŏris, m. *the beaver.*
[2]**Castor** -ŏris, m. *twin-brother of Pollux.* Hence **ecastor** and **mecastor,** *By Castor!*
castŏrĕum -i, n. *an aromatic secretion obtained from the beaver.*
castrensis -e, *pertaining to a camp.*
castro -are, *to castrate, enervate, weaken.*
castrum -i, n.: sing., *a castle, fort, fortress*; plur. **castra** -orum, *a camp, encampment*; aestiva, *summer quarters*; hiberna, *winter quarters.* Transf.: *a day's march; martial service; a party, faction.*
castus -a -um, *clean, pure, chaste*; with reference to religion, *pious,*

religious, holy. Adv. **castē,** *purely piously, religiously.*
căsŭla -ae, f. *a little hut, cottage.*
cāsus -ūs, m. *a falling, fall.* Transf.: (1) *what befalls, an accident, event, occurrence.* (2) *occasion, opportunity.* (3) *destruction, downfall, collapse*; and, in gen., *end.* (4) in grammar, *a case.*
cătaphractēs -ae, m. *a breastplate of iron scales.*
cătaphractus -a -um, *mail-clad.*
cătaplūs -i, m. *the arrival of a ship; a ship that is arriving.*
cătăpulta -ae, f. *an engine of war, a catapult.*
cătăracta (cătarracta) -ae, f. and **cătăractēs** -ae, m. *a waterfall; a sluice* or *flood-gate; a portcullis.*
cătasta -ae, f. *a stage upon which slaves were exposed in the market.*
cătēia -ae, f. *a kind of spear.*
[1]**cătellus** -i, m. and **cătella** -ae, f. *a little dog, puppy.*
[2]**cătellus** -i, m. and **cătella** -ae f. *a little chain.*
cătēna -ae, f. *a chain, fetter.* Transf., (1) *restraint.* (2) *a series.*
cătēnātus -a -um, *chained, bound, linked together*; labores, *continuous.*
căterva -ae, f. *crowd, troop, flock.*
cătervātim, *in troops, in masses.*
căthedra -ae, *a chair*; esp. a soft one for ladies, or one occupied by a professor.
Cătĭlīna -ae, m. L. Sergius, *a Roman noble, killed at the head of a conspiracy in* 62 B.C. Hence adj. **Cătĭlīnārĭus** -a -um.
cătillus -i, m. *a small dish* or *plate.*
cătīnus -i, m. *a deep dish* or *bowl.*
Căto -ōnis, m. *a cognomen belonging to members of the* gens Porcia; adj. **Cătōnĭānus** -a -um; subst. **Cătōnīni** -orum, m. *the party of* M. Porcius Cato Uticensis, *the younger Cato.*
Cătōnĭum -i, n. *the lower world* (with a play on the word Cato).
Cătullus -i, m. C. Valerius (c. 85-55 B.C.) *the Roman lyric and epigrammatic poet.*
cătŭlus -i, m. *a young animal,* esp. *a whelp, puppy.*
cătus -a -um, *sharp, cunning*; adv. **cătē.**
cauda (cōda) -ae, f. *the tail of an animal.*
caudex = codex; q.v.
Caudium -i, n. *an old city in Samnium, near the pass of the Caudine Forks.* Adj. **Caudīnus** -a -um.
caulae -arum, f. pl. *a hole, opening; a sheep-fold.*
caulis -is, m. *the stalk of a plant*; esp. of a cabbage.
caupo -ōnis, m. *a small shopkeeper* or *inn-keeper.*
caupōna -ae, f. *a tavern, inn.*
caupōnor -ari, dep. *to trade*
caupōnŭla -ae, f. *a little inn.*
Caurus (Cōrus) -i, m. *the north-west wind.*
causa (caussa) -ae, f. *a cause,* in all senses of the English word. (1) *a reason, motive, pretext.* (2) *interest*; abl., causā, *on account of, for the sake of,* with genit., meā, etc. (3) *a case at law, law-suit, claim, contention*; causam dicere, *to plead.* (4) *situation, condition, case.*
causārius -a -um, *sickly, diseased*; m. pl., milit., *men invalided out of the army.*
causĭdĭcus -i, m. *an advocate, barrister* (often used contemptuously).
causor -ari, dep. *to give as a reason,* or *pretext; to plead, pretend.*
causŭla -ae, f. *a little cause* or *case.*
cautēs -is, f. *a rough sharp rock.*
cautĭo -ōnis, f. *caution, care, fore-sight, precaution*; legal, *security, bail, bond.*
cautor -ōris, m. *one who is on his guard,* or *who gives bail for another.*
cautus -a -um, partic. from caveo; q.v.
căvaedĭum -i, n. *an inner quadrangle.*
căvĕa -ae, f. *a hollow place, cavity.* Esp. *an enclosure, den, cage; the seats in a theatre.*
cavĕo căvēre cāvi cautum, *to be on one's guard*; with acc. *to be on one's guard against*: cave ignoscas, *take care not to forgive*; with ut and the subj., *to take care that*; with dat. of person, *to take care for, provide for.* Commercial and legal, *to give security* or *to get security*; also *to provide, order,* in a will, treaty or law.

Hence partic. **cautus** -a -um: of persons, etc., *cautious, wary, careful*; of property, *made safe, secured.* Adv. **cautē, cautim,** *cautiously* or *with security.*
căverna -ae, f. *a hollow place, cavern*: navis, *the hold*; caeli, *the vault of heaven.*
căvillātĭo -ōnis, f. *raillery, jesting, irony.* Transf., *sophistry.*
căvillātor -ōris, m. *a jester* [illegible]*oker.* Transf., *a quibbler.*
căvillor -ari, dep. *to jest, joke, satirize.* Transf., *to quibble.*
căvo -are, *to hollow out, excavate, pierce.*
căvum -i, n. and **căvus** -i, m. *a hollow, hole, cavity.*
căvus -a -um, *hollow, concave.*
-cĕ, a demonstrative particle joined on to pronouns and adverbs—e.g. hisce.
Cecrops -ŏpis, m. *the mythical first king of Athens*; adj. **Cecrŏpius** -a -um, *Cecropian, Athenian.*
[1]**cēdo** cēdĕre cessi cessum, *to go, proceed*: of things, *to turn out, happen; to fall to the lot of* a person; *to change* into something else; *to go away, withdraw, retire*; with dat., *to give ground to, submit to,* hence *to be inferior to*; transit., *to grant, yield.*
[2]**cĕdŏ** and plur. **cettĕ,** colloquial imperat., *give, hand over, out with it!*
cedrus -i, f. *the cedar*; meton. *cedar-wood* or *cedar oil.*
cēlātor -ōris, m. *a concealer.*
cĕlĕber -bris -bre, *filled, crowded*; of places, *frequented*; of occasions, *well attended*; of sayings, *often repeated;*

of persons and things, *celebrated, famous, renowned.*
cĕlebrātĭo -ōnis, f. *a numerous assembly* or *attendance.*
cĕlebrātor -ōris, m. *one who praises.*
cĕlebrĭtās -ātis, f. *a crowd, multitude, numerous attendance*; of a festival, *celebration*; in gen., *fame, renown.*
cĕlebro -are, *to visit frequently*, or *in large numbers; to fill; to celebrate, solemnize; to publish, make known; to sing the praises of, to honour; to practise often, repeat, exercise.*
Hence partic. **cĕlebrātus** -a -um: of places, *much frequented*: of festivals, *kept solemn, festive*; in gen., *famous, celebrated.*
cĕler -ĕris -ĕre, *swift, quick, rapid*; in a bad sense, *hasty, rash.* Adv. **cĕlĕrĕ** and **cĕlĕrĭtĕr.**
Cĕlĕres -um, m. *early name for Roman nobles*, esp. *the body-guard of the kings.*
cĕlĕrĭpēs -pĕdis, *swift-footed.*
cĕlĕrĭtās -ātis, f. *quickness, swiftness.*
cĕlĕro -are: transit., *to make quick, accelerate*; intransit., *to hasten.*
cella -ae, f. *a room*: esp. *a store-room* or *a garret, mean apartment*; in a temple, *the shrine of the god's image.*
cellārĭus -a -um, *of a store-room*; as subst. *a cellarer.*
cēlo -are, *to hide, conceal, keep secret.*
cĕlōx -ōcis, *swift, quick*; f. as subst. *a swift vessel, yacht.*
celsus -a -um, *upraised, high, lofty, elevated*; in bad sense, *proud, haughty.*
Celtae -arum, m. pl. *the Celts*, esp. those of Central Gaul. Adj. **Celtĭcus** -a -um.
Celtĭbēri -orum, m. *the Celtiberians, a people in the middle of Spain.*
cēna -ae, f. *dinner, the main Roman meal*; meton., *a dish* or *course at a dinner.*
cēnācŭlum -i, n. *a garret, attic.*
cēnātĭo -ōnis, f. *a dining-hall.*
cēnātōrĭus -a -um, *relating to dinner*; n. pl. as subst. *clothes to dine in.*
cēnĭto -are, *to dine often.*
cēno -are: intransit., *to dine, sup*; transit, *to dine on, to eat.* Perf. partic., with middle meaning, **cēnātus,** *having dined, after dinner.*
censĕo censēre censŭi censum, *to estimate, to form* or *express an opinion* or *valuation* of a person or thing; esp. of the censor at Rome, *to take an account of the names and property of Roman citizens.* In gen., *to express an opinion, be of opinion, vote, advise, recommend*; of the senate, *to resolve.*
censor -ōris, m. *the sensor, a Roman magistrate.* Transf., *a severe judge, rigid moralist.*
censōrĭus -a -um, *relating to the censor*; homo, *an ex-censor*; tabulae, *the censor's lists.* Transf., *rigid, severe.*
censūra -ae, f. *the censor's office, censorship.* Transf., *judgment.*
census -ūs, m. *the census, an enrolment of names and assessment of property.* Transf., *the censor's list; the amount of property necessary for enrolment in a certain rank*; in gen., *property, wealth.*
centaurēum and **centaurĭum** -i, n. *the plant centaury.*
Centaurus -i, m. *a centaur*, i.e. *a monster of Thessaly, half man and half horse.*
centēni -ae -a (poet. also sing.), *a hundred together, a hundred each.*
centēsĭmus -a -um, *the hundredth.* F. sing. as subst. *the hundredth part*; hence *a tax of one per cent*, or as interest on money, *one per cent*, (reckoned at Rome by the month, therefore = 12 *per cent. per annum*).
centĭceps -cĭpĭtis, *hundred-headed.*
centĭens or **centĭēs,** *a hundred times.*
centĭmănus -a -um, *hundred-handed.*
cento -ōnis, m. *patchwork*; in war, *coverings to ward off missiles* or *extinguish fires.*
centum, *a hundred*; also *any indefinitely large number.*
centumgĕmĭnus -a -um, *hundred-fold.*
centumvĭrālis -e, *relating to the* centumviri.
centum vĭri or **centumvĭri** -orum, *a bench of judges dealing with civil suits.*
centuncŭlus -i, m. *a little piece of patchwork* or *a saddle-cloth.*
centuplex -ĭcis, *a hundred-fold.*
centŭrĭa -ae, f. *a division of* 100; *a company of soldiers; a century, a part of the Roman people, as divided by Servius Tullius.*
centŭrĭātim, *by centuries* or *companies.*
centŭrĭātus -ūs, m. *a division into companies* or *centuries; the centurion's office.*
[1]**centŭrĭo** -are, *to divide into centuries*; comitia centuriata, *the assembly in which the whole Roman people voted in their centuries.*
[2]**centŭrĭo** -ōnis, m. *commander of a century, centurion.*
centŭrĭōnātus -ūs, m. *an election of centurions.*
cēnŭla -ae, f. *a little meal.*
cenum, see caenum.
cēra -ae, f. *wax; a waxen writing-tablet, wax seal*, or *waxen image.*
cērārĭum -i, n. *a fee for sealing a document.*
cĕrastēs -ae, m. *the horned snake.*
cĕrăsus -i, f. *a cherry-tree* or *a cherry.*
Cerbĕrus -i, m. *the dog guarding Hades.*
cercŏpĭthēcus -i, m. *a kind of ape.*
cercūrus -i, m. *a species of vessel peculiar to Cyprus; a sea-fish.*
cerdo -ōnis, m. *a workman, artisan.*
cĕrebrōsus -a -um, *hot-tempered.*
cĕrebrum -i, n. *the brain; the understanding; hot temper.*
Cĕrēs -ĕris, *the Roman goddess of agriculture.* Transf., *bread, grain, corn.* Adj. **Cĕrĕālis** -e; n. pl. as subst. *the festival of Ceres on April* 10.
cērĕus -a -um, *waxen*, or *resembling wax*; m. as subst., *a wax taper.*
cērintha -ae, f. *the wax flower.*

cērĭnus -a -um, *wax-coloured*: n. pl. as subst. *wax-coloured garments.*
cerno cerněre crēvi crētum, *to separate, sift.* Transf., *to distinguish,* with the senses or with the mind; *to decide, resolve, determine.*
cernŭus -a -um, *falling headlong.*
cēro -are, *to smear* or *cover with wax.*
cērōma -ătis, n. *an ointment of oil and wax used by wrestlers.*
cērōmătĭcus -a -um, *anointed with the* ceroma.
cerrītus -a -um, *frantic, mad.*
certāmen -ĭnis, n. *contest, struggle.*
certātim, adv. *emulously, eagerly.*
certātĭo -onis, f. *contest, rivalry.*
certē and **certō,** adv. from certus; q.v.
certo -are, *to settle by contest*; hence *to contend, struggle, dispute.*
certus -a -um, adj. *settled, resolved, decided,* of projects and persons; *definite, certain, fixed; sure, to be depended on*; of things as known, *undoubted, sure*; certum scio, *I know for certain*; pro certo habeo, *I feel sure*; of persons knowing, *sure, certain*; certiorem facere, *to inform.* Adv. **certē** and **certō,** *certainly, assuredly.*
cērŭla -ae, f. *a little piece of wax.*
cērussa -ae, f. *white lead.*
cērussātus -a -um, *painted with white lead.*
cerva -ae, f. *hind*; poet., *deer.*
cervīcal -ālis, n. *cushion, pillow.*
cervīcŭla -ae, f. *a little neck.*
cervīnus -a -um, *relating to a stag.*
cervix -īcis, f. *the nape of the neck, the neck*; dare cervices, *to submit to the executioner.*
cervus -i, m. *stag, deer*; pl., milit., *stakes stuck in the ground as a palisade.*
cespes; see caespes.
cessātĭo -ōnis, f. *delaying, inactivity, laziness.*
cessātor -ōris, m. *one who loiters.*
cessĭo -ōnis, f. *a giving up, a cession.*
cesso -are, *to leave off, cease work, be idle, rest*; of things, *to be left alone, do nothing*; so of land, *to lie fallow.*
cestrosphendŏnē -ēs, f. *engine for hurling stones.*
[1]**cestus** and **cestos** -i, m. *a girdle.*
[2]**cēstus** -us, m; see caestus.
cētārĭum -i, n. *a fish-pond.*
cētārĭus -i, m. *a fishmonger.*
cētĕrōquī or **cētĕrōquīn,** *otherwise, else.*
cētĕrus -a -um, *the other, the rest*; usually plur., **cētĕri** -ae, -a; et cetera, *and so on.* Acc. n. sing. as adv. **cētĕrum,** *otherwise, moreover, but.*
Cĕthēgus -i, m. C. Cornelius, *a conspirator with Catiline, put to death by Cicero in* 63 B.C.
cētra; see caetra.
cette; see cedo.
cētus -i, m. and **cētos** n.; plur. cete; *any large sea-creature,* such as *whale, seal, dolphin.*
ceu, adv., *as, like as*; sometimes *as if.*
Chalcis -ĭdis or -ĭdos, f. *the chief city of Euboea.*
Chaldaei -orum, m. pl. *the Chaldaeans, famous as astrologers.*
chălўbēĭus -a -um, *of steel.*
chălybs -ўbis, m. *steel*; an article made of steel, such as *a sword, a horse's bit, the tip of an arrow.*
chānē or **channē** -ēs, f. *the sea perch.*
Chăos, acc. Chaos, abl. Chao, n. *boundless empty space.* Hence *the lower world*; personified, *Chaos, the father of Night and Erebus; the shapeless mass out of which the universe was made.*
chara -ae, f. *an edible root.*
Chărĭtes -um, f. pl. *the Graces,* i.e. *Aglaia, Euphrosyne, and Thalia.*
Chăron -ontis, m. *Charon, who ferried souls over the Styx.*
charta -ae, f. *a leaf of Egyptian papyrus, paper; anything written on paper, a letter, poem,* etc.
chartŭla -ae, f. *a little paper, small piece of writing.*
Chărybdis -is, f. *a whirlpool opposite the rock Scylla.*
Chatti (Catti) -orum, m. *a Germanic people.*
Chauci -orum. m. *a Germanic people on the coast of the North Sea.*
chĕlўdrus -i, m. *an amphibious snake.*
chĕlys, acc. -yn, f. *the tortoise*; hence, *the lyre made of its shell.*
chĕragra and **chiragra** -ae, f. *the gout in the hands.*
Cherrŏnēsus and **Chersŏnēsus** -i, f. *a peninsula*; esp. *of Gallipoli* or the *Crimea.*
chīlĭarchēs -ae, and **chīlĭarchus** -i, m. *a commander of* 1,000 *soldiers*; among Persians, *chancellor,* or *prime minister.*
Chĭmaera -ae, f. *a monster killed by Bellerophon.*
chĭmaerĭfer -fĕra -fĕrum, *producing the Chimaera.*
Chĭos or **Chĭus** -i, f. *an island in the Aegean Sea, famous for wine and marble.*
chīrogrăphum -i, n. *an autograph, a person's own handwriting.*
chīrŏnŏmos -i, and **chīrŏnŏmōn** -ontis, m. *a gesticulator, a mime.*
chīrurgĭa -ae, f. *surgery.*
chlămўdātus -a -um, *dressed in a* chlamys.
chlămys -ўdis, f. *a large upper garment of wool.*
chŏrāgĭum -i, n. *the training and production of a chorus.*
chŏrāgus -i, m. *he who pays for a chorus.*
chŏraulēs -ae, m. *a flute-player, accompanying the chorus.*
chorda -ae, f. *cat-gut*; usually as the *string* of a musical instrument.
chŏrēa -ae, f. *a dance in a ring.*
chŏrēus and **chŏrĭus** -i, m. *the metrical foot afterwards called a trochee.*
chŏrus -i, m. *dance in a circle, choral dance.* Transf., *the persons singing*

and dancing, the chorus; hence *a crowd, troop.*
Christus -i, m. *Christ*; **Christiānus** -i, m. *a Christian.*
chrŏmis -is, c. *a sea-fish.*
chrȳsanthus -i, m. *a flower*, perhaps *marigold.*
chrȳsŏlīthos -i, m. and f. *chrysolite*, or *topaz.*
chrȳsophrys, acc. -yn. f. *a sea-fish.*
cībārius -a -um, *relating to food*; n. pl. as subst., *food, rations.* Transf. (from the food of slaves), *ordinary, common.*
cībātus -ūs, m. *food, nourishment.*
cībōrium -i, n. *a large drinking-vessel.*
cībus -i, m. *food, fodder, nourishment, sustenance.*
cĭcāda -ae, f. *a cicada*, or *tree cricket.*
cĭcatrix -īcis, f. *a scar*; on plants, *a mark of incision*; also a *patch on an old shoe.*
cĭcer -eris, n. *a chick-pea.*
Cĭcĕro -onis, M. Tullius, *Roman Statesman, orator, and writer* (106-43 B.C.); adj. **Cĭcĕrōnĭānus** -a -um.
cĭchŏrēum -i, n. *succory* or *endive.*
cĭcōnia -ae, f. *a stork.*
cĭcur -ŭris, *tame.*
cĭcūta -ae, f. *hemlock; poison extracted from the hemlock; a shepherd's pipe, made of hemlock stalk.*
cĭĕo cĭēre cīvi cĭtum, *to move, stir, agitate.* Transf., *to give rise to, excite, arouse; to summon; to call by name.*
Hence partic. **cĭtus** -a -um, *quick, speedy.* Adv. **cĭtŏ,** *quickly*; citius quam, *sooner than, rather than.*
Cĭlĭcia -ae, f. *a region in Asia Minor.*
Cimber -bri, m.; usually pl. **Cimbri,** *the Cimbrians, a German tribe*; adj. **Cimbrĭcus** -a -um.
cīmex -ĭcis, m. a bug.
Cimmĕrii -orum, m. pl. (1) *a Thracian people, living on the Dnieper.* (2) *a mythical people, living in eternal darkness.*
cĭnaedus -i, m. *a wanton* or *shameless person.*
[1]**cincinnatus** -a -um, *having curled hair.*
[2]**Cincinnatus** -i, m. *a cognomen in the* gens Quinctia.
cincinnus -i, m. *curled hair, a lock of hair.* Transf., *artificial rhetorical ornament.*
Cincĭus -a -um, *name of a Roman* gens.
cinctūra -ae, f. *a girdle.*
cinctus -ūs, m. *a girding, a way of wearing the toga.* Transf., *a girdle.*
cinctūtus -a -um, *girded.*
cĭnĕfactus -a -um, *turned to ashes.*
cingo cingĕre cinxi cinctum, *to surround* or *equip the head* or *body*; pass., cingi, *to gird oneself*; in gen., *to surround*; esp. *to surround* with hostile intent, or for protection; of persons, *to escort, accompany.*
cingŭla -ae, f. *a girdle.*
cingŭlum -i, n. *a girdle, sword-belt.*
cingŭlus -i, m. a *girdle of the earth, zone.*
cĭniflo -onis, m. = cinerarius.
cĭnis -ĕris, m. rarely f. *ashes.*
Cinna -ae, m. *a Roman cognomen*, esp. of L. Cornelius Cinna, *supporter of Marius, noted for his cruelty.* Adj. **Cinnānus** -a -um.
cinnămōmum or **cinnămum** -i, n. *cinnamon.*
cippus -i, m. *a pale, stake*; esp. *a tombstone*; plur., milit., *palisades.*
circā. Adv., *around, round about.* Prep. with acc.: of space, *around, near*; of persons, *around* or *with*; of time or number, *about.*
circāmoerium -i, n. = pomerium; q.v.
Circē -ēs and -ae, f. *an enchantress, daughter of the Sun*; adj. **Circaeus** -a -um.
Circēii -orum, m. pl. *a town in Latium.*
circensis -e, *belonging to the circus*; m. pl. as subst. (sc. ludi), *the circus games.*
circĭno -are, *to form into a circle* hence *to fly round.*
circĭnus -i, m. *a pair of compasses.*
circĭtĕr, adv., and prep. with acc., *about.*
circlus = circulus; q.v.
circŭeo; see circumeo.
circŭĭtio and **circŭmĭtio** -ōnis, f. *a going round, patrol.* Transf., *a roundabout way of speaking.*
circŭĭtus -ūs, m. *a going round in a circle, circuit.* Hence *a roundabout way, circuitous course*; also *compass, circumference, extent*; rhet., *a period.*
circŭlor -ari, dep. *to gather in groups,* or *collect a group around oneself.*
circŭlus (**circlus**) -i, m. *a circle, circular figure, circuit; any circular body; a circle* or *group for conversation.*
circum. Adv. *roundabout, around.* Prep. with acc. *round, around, round about, near.*
circŭmăgo -ăgĕre -ēgi -actum. (1) *to turn round*; esp. in the ceremonial manumission of a slave; of time, circumagi or circumagere se, *to pass away, be spent*; of the feelings, *to influence, bring round.* (2) *to drive about from one place to another; to distract.*
circumăro -are, *to plough round.*
circumcaesūra -ae, f. *the external outline of a body.*
circumcīdo -cīdĕre cīdi -cīsum, *to cut round, to cut, trim.* Transf., *to make less, by cutting, diminish.*
Hence partic. **circumcīsus** -a -um, of places, *abrupt, steep, inaccessible*; of style, *abridged, brief.*
circumcircā, *all round about.*
circumclūdo -clūdĕre -clūsi -clūsum, *to shut in, enlcose, surround.*
circumcŏlo -ere, *to dwell around, dwell near.*
circumcurso -are, *to run round.*
circumdo -dăre -dĕdi -dătum, *surround.* (1) *to put something round,* with acc. of the thing placed, and dat. of that round which it is placed. (2)

to surround with something, with acc. and abl. (rarely double acc.).

circumdūco -dūcĕre -duxi -ductum, *to lead round, move* or *drive round.* Transf., *to cheat; to extend, amplify.*

circŭmĕo (circŭĕo) -ire, -ĭi or -īvi, circŭĭtum, *to go round*; milit., *to surround; to go the rounds of, to visit*; hence *to canvass* or *solicit.* Transf., *to cheat, circumvent.*

circumĕquĭto -are, *to ride round.*

circumfĕro -ferre -tŭli -lātum, *to carry round, take round*; esp. of the eyes, *to turn all round*; in religion, *to lustrate, purify*, by carrying round consecrated objects. Transf., *to spread*, esp. *to spread news.*

circumflecto -flectĕre -flexi -flexum, *to bend round, turn about.*

circumflo -are, *to blow round.*

circumflŭo -flŭĕre -fluxi -fluxum, *to flow round.* Transf., *to overflow, abound*; with abl., *to abound in.*

circumflŭus -a -um: act., *flowing round, circumfluent*; pass., *flowed round, surrounded by water.*

circumfŏrānĕus -a -um. (1) *round the forum*: aes, *money borrowed from bankers.* (2) *attending at markets.*

circumfundo -fundĕre -fūdi -fūsum. (1) *to pour around*; in pass., or with reflexive, *to be poured round* = *to surround.* (2) act., *to surround, encompass*, and pass., *to be surrounded*; usually with instrumental abl.

circumgĕmo -ĕre, *to growl round.*

circumgesto -are, *to carry round.*

circumgrĕdĭor -grĕdi -gressus, dep., *to go round, travel round.*

circumiăcĕo -ēre, *to lie round about, adjoin.*

circumicĭo -icĕre -iēci -iectum. (1) *to throw round, put round.* (2) *to surround* one thing with another.

Hence partic. **circumiectus** -a -um, *thrown round*, so *surrounding adjacent.*

circumiectus -ūs, m. *a surrounding, enclosing.*

circumĭtĭo = circuitio; q.v.

circumlĭgo -are. (1) *to bind round, bind to.* (2) *to bind round with* something.

circumlĭno -lĭnĕre -lĭtum. (1) *to smear one thing over another.* (2) *to besmear with, bedaub*; hence poet., *to cover.*

circumlŭo -lŭĕre, *to wash round, flow round.*

circumlŭvĭo -ōnis, f. *alluvial land.*

circummitto -mittĕre -mīsi -missum, *to send round.*

circummūnĭo -ire, *to wall round, to shut in by lines of circumvallation.*

circummūnĭtĭo -ōnis, f. *circumvallation.*

circumpădānus -a -um, *near the river Po.*

circumplector -plecti -plexus, dep. *to embrace, enclose, surround.*

circumplĭco -are, *to fold round, wind round.*

circumpono -pōnĕre -pŏsŭi -pŏsĭtum, *to place* or *put round.*

circumrētĭo -ire, *to enclose in a net, ensnare.*

circumrōdo -rōdĕre -rōsi, *to gnaw round.* Transf., *to slander.*

circumsaepĭo -saepire -saeptum, *to hedge round, enclose.*

circumscindo -ĕre, *to tear off, round, to strip.*

circumscrībo -scrībĕre -scripsi -scriptum, *to describe a circle round, to enclose in a circular line.* Transf., (1) *to confine, define, limit, restrict.* (2) *to set aside, exclude.* (3) *to take in, ensnare, defraud*; vectigalia, *to embezzle.*

Hence partic. **circumscriptus** -a -um, as rhet. t. t. *rounded, periodic*; also *concise.* Adv. **circumscriptē.** *in rhetorical periods, fully.*

circumscriptĭo -ōnis, f. *an encircling*; hence *circumference.* Transf., (1) *outline, boundary, limit*; in rhetoric, *a period.* (2) *swindling, defrauding.*

circumscriptor -ōris, m. *a cheat, swindler.*

circumsĕco -sĕcare -sectum *to cut round.*

circumsĕdĕo -sĕdēre -sēdi -sessum, *to sit round*; esp. *to besiege, beleaguer.*

circumsessĭo -ōnis, f. *encircling, beleaguering.*

circumsīdo -ĕre, *to besiege.*

circumsĭlĭo -ire, *to leap* or *jump round.*

circumsisto -sistĕre -stĕti or -stĭti, *to stand round, surround.*

circumsŏno -sonare -sonui: transit., *to sound all around* or *to make to resound*; intransit., *to resound, to echo.*

circumsŏnus -a -um, *sounding all around.*

circumspectĭo -ōnis, f. *looking about, circumspection, caution.*

circumspecto -are: intransit., *to look round repeatedly*; transit., *to look round at* or *for.*

[1]**circumspectus** -a -um; see circumspicio.

[2]**circumspectus** -ūs, m. *looking round at*; hence *attention to; prospect, view all round.*

circumspĭcĭo -spĭcĕre -spexi -spectum: intransit., *to look round*, esp. *anxiously*; hence *to consider*; transit., *to look round at, survey*; hence *to consider carefully*; also *to look about for, seek for.*

Hence partic. **circumspectus** -a -um: pass., of things, *deliberate, well considered*; act., of persons, *circumspect, cautious.*

circumsto -stare -stĕti: intransit, *to stand round* or *in a circle*; partic. as subst., circumstantes, *the bystanders;* transit., *to surround, beleaguer.*

circumstrĕpo -ĕre, *to make a loud noise around.*

circumsurgens -entis, *rising round.*

circumtĕro -tĕrĕre, *to rub against on all sides.*

circumtextus -a -um, *woven all round.*

circumtŏno -tŏnare -tŏnŭi, *to thunder round.*
circumtonsus -a -um, *shorn all round*; of discourse, *artificial.*
circumvādo -vāděre -vāsi, *to attack from every side, to surround.*
circumvăgus -a -um, *wandering round, flowing round.*
circumvallo -are, *to blockade, beleaguer.*
circumvectĭo -ōnis, f. *a carrying round of merchandise*: portorium circumvectionis, *transit dues*; in gen., *circuit, revolution.*
circumvector -ari, *to ride* or *sail round*; poet, *to go through, describe.*
circumvĕhor -vĕhi -vectus, *to ride* or *sail round*; poet., *to describe.*
circumvēlo -are, *to veil round, envelop.*
circumvĕnĭo -vĕnire -vēni -ventum, *to come round, surround, encircle.* Transf., *to beset, assail; to cheat, defraud.*
circumvertor (**-vortor**) -verti, *to turn oneself round.*
circumvestĭo -ire, *to clothe all round.*
circumvŏlĭto -are, *to fly round, rove about.*
circumvŏlo -are, *to fly round.*
circumvolvo -volvĕre -volvi -vŏlūtum, *to roll round*; usually pass., *to revolve.*
circus -i, m. *a ring, circle, orbit*: candens, *the milky way*; also *an oval course for races.*
cīris -is, f. *a bird, into which Scylla was transformed.*
cirrātus -a -um, *curly-haired.*
Cirrha -ae, f. *a city near Delphi, sacred to Apollo*; adj. **Cirrhaeus** -a -um.
cirrus -i, m. *a lock,* or *ringlet of hair; the fringe of a garment.*
cis, prep., with acc., *on this side of, within.*
Cĭsalpīnus -a -um, *on this* (*the Roman*) *side of the Alps.*
cĭsĭum -i, n. *a light two-wheeled vehicle.*
Cisrhenānus -a -um, *on this* (*the Roman*) *side of the Rhine.*
cista -ae, f. *a chest, box.*
cistella -ae, f. *a little chest* or *box.*
cisterna -ae, f. *reservoir, cistern.*
cistŏphŏrus -i, m. *an Asiatic coin.*
cistŭla -ae, f. *a little chest* or *box.*
cĭtātus -a -um, partic. from [2]cito; q.v.
cĭtĕr -tra -trum, *on this side*; usually compar., **cĭtĕrĭor** -us, genit. -oris, *on this side, nearer*; superl. **cĭtĭmus** -a -um, *nearest.*
cĭthăra -ae, f. *a stringed instrument, lyre, lute.*
cĭthărista -ae, m. *a player on the* cithara.
cĭthăristrĭa -ae, f. *a female player on the* cithara.
cĭthărizo -are, *to play the* cithara.
cĭthăroedus -i, m. *one who plays the* cithara *with voice accompanying.*
[1]**cĭtŏ,** adv. from cieo; q.v.
[2]**cito** -are (1) *to put in motion, excite, start up.* (2) *to summon, call forward*; esp. for legal, political or military purposes; hence *to appeal to, point to* authorities, etc.
Hence partic. **cĭtātus** -a -um, *quick, speedy*: citato equo, *at full gallop.* Adv. **cĭtātim.**
citrā (abl. f. from citer). Adv. *on this side, nearer.* Prep. with acc., *on this side of, nearer than*; of time, *since*; hence, in gen., *short of, without.*
citrĕus -a -um, *belonging to the citrus-tree* or *citron-tree.*
citrō, adv. found only with ultro: ultro (et) citro, *up and down, hither and thither.*
citrus -i, m. (1) *the citrus, a kind of African cypress.* (2) *the citron-tree.*
cĭtus -a -um, partic. from cieo; q.v.
cīvĭcus -a -um, *relating to a citizen, civic*; civica (corona), *the civic crown, awarded to one who had saved the life of a Roman in war.*
cīvīlis -e, *relating to a citizen, civic, civil*; esp. ius civile, *the Roman civil law* or *civil rights; befitting a citizen*; hence, *popular, affable, courteous; relating to public life* or *the state.* Adv. **cīvīlĭter,** *like a citizen; politely.*
cīvīlĭtās -ātis, f. (1) *the science of politics.* (2) *politeness, civility.*
cīvis -is, c. *citizen*; also *a fellow citizen*: under a king, *a subject.*
cīvĭtās -ātis, f.: abstr., *citizenship*; concr., *a union of citizens, state, commonwealth; the inhabitants of a city, townsfolk*; (rarely) *a city, town.*
clādēs -is, f. *destruction*; in gen., *disaster, injury, defeat.*
clam. Adv., *secretly, in secret*: esse, *to remain unknown.* Prep. with acc. or abl., *unknown to, without the knowledge of.*
clāmātor -ōris, m. *a shouter, noisy speaker.*
clāmĭto -are, *to cry aloud, shout violently.*
clāmo -are, *to call, shout, cry aloud*; with object, *to call to* or *upon* a person, *to shout* something; sometimes *to proclaim, declare.*
clāmor -ōris, m. *a loud shouting, cry*; poet., of lifeless things, *echo, reverberation.*
clāmōsus -a -um: act., *noisy, clamorous* pass., *filled with noise.*
clancŭlum. Adv. *secretly, in secret.* Prep. with acc., *unknown to.*
clandestīnus -a -um, *secret, clandestine*; Adv. **clandestīnō.**
clangor -ōris, m. *sound, clang, noise.*
clārĕo -ēre, *to be bright, to shine.* Transf., *to be evident; to be distinguished.*
clāresco clārescĕre clārŭi, *to become clear to the senses.* Transf., *to become evident; to become illustrious.*
clārĭgo -are, *to demand satisfaction,* used of the Fetialis.
clārĭsŏnus -a -um, *clearly sounding.*
clārĭtās -ātis, f. *clearness, brightness.* Transf., *clearness to the mind, plainness; fame, celebrity.*
clārĭtūdo -ĭnis, f. *clearness, brilliancy.* Transf., *fame, celebrity.*
clāro -are, *to make bright* or *clear.* Transf., *to make plain to the mind; to make illustrious.*

clārus -a -um, *bright, clear, distinct*; poet., of the wind, *making clear, bringing fair weather.* Transf., to the understanding, *clear, evident, plain*; of reputation, *illustrious, distinguished*; in bad sense, *notorious.* Hence adj. **clārē,** *clearly, brightly, distinctly; illustriously.*

classĭārĭus -a -um, *of the fleet*; m. pl. as subst., *marines.*

classĭcus -a -um. (1) *relating to the different classes of Roman citizens.* (2) *relating to the armed forces,* esp. to the fleet: m. pl. as subst., *marines*: n. sing. as subst., *the signal for battle* or *the trumpet giving this.*

classis -is, f. *a group as summoned, a division, class.* (1) *one of the classes into which Servius Tullius divided the Roman people.* (2) *the armed forces,* esp. *the fleet.* (3) in gen., *a class, group.*

clatri -orum, m. pl., *trellis, grating.*

claudĕo -ēre and **claudo** -ĕre, *to limp, halt, be lame.*

claudĭcātĭo -ōnis, f. *a limping.*

claudĭco -are, *to limp, be lame.* Transf., *to incline, be deflected; to halt, waver.*

Claudĭus (Clōdĭus) -a -um, *the name of two Roman* gentes; esp. of *the emperor Claudius* (10 B.C.-A.D. 54). Adj. **Claudĭānus** -a -um, **Claudĭālis** -e.

[1]**claudo** claudĕre clausi clausum (and **clūdo**) *to close, shut up, make inaccessible*; of military positions, *to blockade, invest*; of prisoners, etc., to *shut in, confine.* Transf., *to conclude*; agmen, *to bring up the rear.*

Hence partic. **clausus** -a -um, of character, *close, reserved*; n. as subst., *an enclosed place.*

[2]**claudo** = claudeo; q.v.

claudus -a -um, *limping, lame.* Transf., *crippled, defective*; poet. carmina alterno versu, *elegiac verse.*

claustrum -i, n., gen. plur., *a means of closing or shutting in: a bolt, bar; an enclosure, prison, den; a barricade, dam, fortress*; milit., *the key to a position.*

clausŭla -ae, f. *end, conclusion*: in rhetoric, *the close of a period.*

clāva -ae, f. *staff* or *cudgel.*

clāvārĭum -i, n. *an allowance to soldiers for buying shoe-nails.*

clāvĭcŭla -ae, f. *the tendril by which the vine clings to its prop.*

[1]**clāvĭger** -gĕri, m. *the club-bearer,* of Hercules.

[2]**clāvĭger** -gĕri, m. *the key-bearer,* of Janus.

clāvis -is, f. *a key*: claves adimere uxori, *to separate from one's wife.* Transf., *a stick for trundling a hoop.*

clāvus -i, m. (1) *a nail, spike.* (2) *a tiller, helm, rudder.* (3) *a stripe of purple on the tunic, worn broad by senators, narrow by knights.*

clēmens -entis, *mild, kind, merciful*; adv. **clēmenter,** *gentle.*

clēmentĭa -ae, f. *mildness, gentleness, mercy.*

Clĕŏpatra -ae, f. *the queen of Egypt and mistress of Antony, defeated with him at Actium.*

clĕpo clĕpere clepsi cleptum, *to steal*; se, *to conceal oneself.*

clepsydra -ae, f. *a water clock,* esp. as used to measure the time allotted to orators.

clĭens -entis, m. *a client, dependent on a* patronus (q.v.); in gen., *a vassal* or *ally.*

clĭenta -ae, f. *a female client.*

clĭentēla -ae, f. *clientship, the relation between client and patron*; hence, in gen., *dependence.* Transf. (gen. plur.) *clients.*

clīnāmen -ĭnis, n. *inclination, swerving aside.*

clīnātus -a -um, *inclined, leaning.*

Clīō -ūs, f. *the Muse of history.*

clĭpĕātus -a -um, *armed with a shield*; m. pl. as subst., *soldiers with shields.*

clĭpĕus -i, m. and **clĭpĕum** -i, n. *a (round) shield.* Transf., *the disk of the sun; a medallion portrait.*

clītellae -arum, f. pl. *a pack-saddle, pair of panniers.*

clīvōsus -a -um, *hilly, steep.*

clīvus -i, m. *a slope, rise, gradient.*

clŏāca -ae, f. *a sewer, drain.*

Clŏācīna -ae, f. *the cleanser, surname of Venus.*

Clōdius = Claudius; q.v.

Clōthō, f. *the spinner, one of the* Parcae.

clŭĕo -ēre, *I hear myself called, am named.*

clūnis -is, m. and f. *the buttocks.*

Clūsĭum -i, n. a town of Etruria; adj. **Clūsīnus** -a -um.

Clȳtaemnestra -ae, f. *wife of Agamemnon who killed her husband, and was killed by her son Orestes.*

Cnĭdus (-os), or **Gnĭdus** (-os), -i, f. *a town in Caria, famous for the worship of Venus*; adj. **Cnĭdĭus** -a -um.

Cnossus = Gnossus; q.v.

cŏăcervātĭo -ōnis, f. *a heaping up.*

coăcervo -are, *to heap up, accumulate.*

coăcesco -ăcescĕre -ăcŭi, *to become sour.*

cŏacto -are, *to compel.*

cŏactor -ōris, m. *a collector of money*; coactores agminis, *the rear-guard.*

cŏactū, abl. sing. m. *by force, under compulsion.*

cŏactum -i, n. subst. from cogo; q.v.

cŏaedĭfĭco -are, *to build on.*

cŏaequo -are, *to level, make even.*

cŏagmentātĭo -ōnis, *a connexion, binding together.*

cŏagmento -are, *to join together*; pacem, *to conclude.*

cŏagmentum -i, n. *a joining joint.*

cŏāgŭlum -i, n. *rennet* or *curds.*

cŏălesco -ălescĕre -ălŭi -ălĭtum, *to grow together; to take root, grow*; hence *to become established* or *firm.*

cŏangusto -are, *to limit, confine.*

cŏarcto, etc. = coarto, etc.; q.v.

cŏargŭo -ŭĕre -ŭi, *to show clearly,*

demonstrate fully; esp. *to prove wrong* or *guilty*.
cŏartātĭo -ōnis, f. *a confining in a small space*.
cŏarto -are, *to confine, draw together*; of discourse, *to compress*; of time, *to shorten*.
coccĭnātus -a -um, *clad in scarlet*.
coccĭnus -a -um, *scarlet-coloured*; n. pl. as subst., *scarlet clothes*.
coccum -i, n. *the berry of the scarlet oak*; hence *scarlet dye*; sometimes *scarlet cloth* or *garments*.
coclĕa (cochlĕa) -ae, f. *a snail* or *snail-shell*.
coclĕāre (cochlĕāre) -is, n. and **coclĕārĭum** -i, n. *a spoon*.
Cocles, *Roman cognomen*, esp. *of Horatius Cocles, the Roman who defended the bridge over the Tiber against Porsenna*.
coctĭlis -a, *baked*; muri, *made of burnt brick*.
Cōcȳtŏs and **-us,** -i, m. *a river of the lower world*.
cōda = cauda; q.v.
cōdex (older **caudex**) -dĭcis, m. *the trunk of a tree*; as a term of abuse, *dolt, blockhead*. Transf., *a book* (*made up of wooden tablets, covered with wax*); esp. *an account-book, ledger*.
cōdĭcārĭus (caudĭcārĭus) -a -um, *made of tree trunks*.
cōdĭcilli -orum, m. *little trunks, logs*. Transf., *small tablets for memoranda*; hence *a letter, petition, codicil, rescript*.
coel-; see cael-.
cŏĕmo -ĕmĕre -ēmi -emptum, *to buy up*.
cŏemptĭo -ōnis, f. *a form of marriage; a fictitious sale of an estate*.
coen-; see caen-.
cŏĕo -ire -ii -ivi -ĭtum, *to go* or *come together, assemble*; of enemies, *to engage*; of friends, etc., *to unite, combine*; transit., societatem coire, *to form an alliance*; of things, *to unite, come together*; of blood, *to curdle*; of water, *to freeze*.
coepio coepĕre, coepi coeptum (only the perfect-stem tenses are class.; see incipio), *to begin, commence*. N. of partic. as subst. **coeptum** -i, *a thing begun or undertaken*.
coepto -are, *to begin* or *undertake* (*eagerly*).
coeptus -ūs, m. (only in plur.), *a beginning*.
cŏerceo -cēre -cŭi -cĭtum, *to enclose, shut in, confine, restrain*; vitem, *to prune*.
cŏercĭtĭo -ōnis, f. *confining, restraint*; hence *punishment*.
coerŭlĕus = caeruleus; q.v.
coetus (cŏĭtus) -ūs, m. *meeting together, union, assemblage*.
cōgĭtātĭo -ōnis, f. *thinking, conception, reflection, reasoning*: sometimes a particular *thought, idea* or *intention*.
cōgĭto -are, *to turn over in the mind, to think, reflect*; sometimes *to intend, plan*.

Hence partic. **cōgĭtātus** -a -um, *considered, deliberate*: n. pl. as subst. *thoughts, reflections, ideas*. Adv. **cōgĭtātē,** *thoughtfully*.
cognātĭo -ōnis, f. *relationship, connexion by blood*; meton., *persons related, kindred, family*: in gen., *connexion, agreement, resemblance*.
cognātus -a -um, *related, connected by blood*; m. and f. as subst. *a relation either on the father's or mother's side*. Transf., *akin, similar*.
cognĭtĭo -ōnis, f. *getting to know, study, knowledge, acquaintance; recognition; legal inquiry, investigation*; in plur., *ideas, conceptions*.
cognĭtor -ōris, m. *a knower*; legal, *a witness* or *an attorney*; in gen., *a supporter*.
cognōmĕn -ĭnis, n. *a surname, family name*.
cognōmentum -i, n. *a surname, a name*.
cognōmĭnātus -a -um, *of the same meaning*; verba, *synonyms*.
cognōmĭnis -e, *having the same name*.
cognosco -gnoscĕre -gnōvi -gnĭtum, *to become acquainted with, get to know, learn*; in perf. tenses, *to know; to know again, recognize*; of judges, *to examine, hear, decide*.

Hence partic. **cognĭtus** -a -um, *known, proved*.
cōgo cōgĕre cŏēgi cŏactum, *to bring, drive*, or *draw to one point, to collect; to bring close together, compress*: of liquids, etc. *to thicken, curdle*; milit., agmen cogere, *to bring up the rear*. Transf., *to restrict, confine; to compel*.

Hence partic., **cŏactus,** *constrained*: n. as subst., *thick cloth, felt*.
cŏhaerentĭa -ae, f. *coherence*.
cŏhaerĕo -haerēre -haesi -haesum: of a whole, *to cohere, hold together*; of one thing (or person), *to cling, adhere, be connected to* another.
cŏhaeresco -haerescĕre -haesi, *to hang together*.
cŏhērēs -ēdis, m. *a coheir*.
cŏhĭbĕo -ēre -ŭi -ĭtum, *to hold in, hold together*: hence *to confine, restrain, hold back, repress*.
cŏhŏnesto -are, *to do honour to*.
cŏhorresco -horrescĕre -horrŭi, *to shudder* or *shiver*.
cŏhors -tis, f. *an enclosure, yard*. Transf., *a troop, company, throng*; milit., *a cohort, the tenth part of a legion*; praetoria cohors, *the retinue of the governor of a province*.
cŏhortātĭo -ōnis, f. *exhortation, encouragement*.
cŏhortor -ari, dep. *to encourage, incite, exhort*.
cŏĭtĭo -ōnis, f. *a coming together, meeting; a faction, coalition, conspiracy*.
cŏĭtus -us, *see* coetus.
cŏlăphus -i, m. *a cuff, box on the ear*.
Colchis -ĭdis, f. *Colchis, a country on the Black Sea*; adj. **Colchĭcus** and

Colchus -a -um; f. adj. **Colchis** -ĭdis.
cōlĕus -i; see culeus.
cōlīphĭa (cōlȳphĭa) -orum, n. *a food used by athletes.*
cōlis = caulis; q.v.
coll-; see also conl-.
Collātĭa -ae, f. *a town in Latium*; adj. **Collatīnus** -a -um.
collīnus -a -um, *hilly, relating to a hill*: porta Collina, *a gate of Rome near the Quirinal Hill.*
collis -is, m. *hill, high ground.*
collum -i, n. (**collus** -i, m.) *neck.*
collȳbus -i, m. *exchange of money*, or *rate of exchange.*
collȳrĭum -i, n. *eye-salve.*
cŏlo cŏlĕre cŏlŭi cultum, *to cultivate, till, tend; to dwell in, inhabit* a place; in gen., *to take care of, attend to. foster, honour, worship, court.*
Hence partic. **cultus** -a -um, *cultivated, tilled, planted*; n. pl. as subst., *cultivated land.* Transf., physically, *tidy, well-dressed, smart*; mentally, *refined.* Adv. **cultē,** *elegantly.*
cŏlŏcāsĭa -orum, n. pl. *the Egyptian bean.*
cŏlōna -ae, f. *a country-woman.*
cŏlōnĭa -ae, f. *a farm, estate; a colony*; meton., *colonists.*
cŏlōnĭcus -a -um, *relating to agriculture* or *to a colony.*
cŏlōnus -i, m. *a farmer, sometimes a tenant farmer; a colonist, inhabitant of a colony.*
cŏlor (cŏlos) -ōris, m. *colour, tint, hue*; esp. *complexion*; sometimes *beautiful complexion, beauty.* Transf., *outward show, external appearance; cast, character, tone; an artful excuse.*
cŏlōro -are, *to colour*; partic. **cŏlōrātus** -a -um, *coloured*: of complexion, *tanned, dark.*
cŏlossēus and **cŏlossĭcus** -a -um, *colossal, gigantic.*
cŏlossus -i, m. *a colossus, statue larger than life*; esp. that of Apollo at Rhodes.
cŏlŭber -bri, m. *serpent, snake.*
cŏlubra -ae, f. *female serpent.*
cŏlubrĭfer -fĕra -fĕrum, *snake-bearing, snaky-haired* (of Medusa).
cōlum -i, n. *colander, sieve, strainer.*
cŏlumba -ae, f. *a pigeon, dove.*
cŏlumbīnus -a -um, *belonging to a pigeon.*
cŏlumbus -i, m. *a male dove* or *pigeon.*
cŏlŭmella -ae, f. *a little column.*
cŏlŭmen -ĭnis, n. *a height, summit, ridge*; of buildings, *roof, gable.* Transf., *chief, summit, crown; support, pillar.*
cŏlumna -ae, f. *a pillar, column*; columnae, *pillars as signs of booksellers' shops in Rome*; columnae Herculis, *the pillars of Hercules.* Transf., *a support, pillar of the state; a water-spout.*
cŏlumnārĭum -i, n. *a tax on pillars.*
cŏlumnārĭus, *a rascal, thief.*
cŏlurnus -a -um, *of hazel-wood.*
cŏlus -i and -ūs, f. or m., *a distaff.*
cŏma -ae, f. *the hair of the head.* Transf., *leaves; rays* of light.
cŏmans -antis, *hairy*; galea, *crested*; stella, *a comet.*
cŏmātus -a -um, *hairy*; Gallia Comata, a name for *Transalpine Gaul*: comata silva, *in full leaf.*
[1]**combĭbo** -bĭbĕre -bĭbi, *to drink in, suck up.*
[2]**combĭbo** -ōnis, m. *a comrade in drinking.*
combūro -ūrĕre -ussi -ustum, *to burn up*; hence *to ruin* or *consume.*
cŏmĕdo -esse -ēdi -ēsum or -estum, *to eat up, consume*; of property, *to waste, squander.*
cŏmĕs -ĭtis, c. *a fellow-traveller*; hence *a companion, comrade*; sometimes *attendant*; in plur., comites, *retinue.*
cŏmētēs -ae, m. *a comet.*
cōmĭcus -a -um, *of comedy, comic*; esp. *represented in comedy.* M. as subst. *an actor in comedy* or *writer of comedy.* Adv. **cōmĭcē,** *in the manner of comedy.*
cominus=comminus; q.v.
cōmis -e, *courteous, kind, friendly, obliging*; adv. **cōmĭter.**
cōmissābundus -a -um, *revelling, rioting.*
cōmissatĭo -ōnis, f. *a revel, riotous procession.*
cōmissātor -ōris, m. *a reveller.*
cōmissor -ari, dep. *to revel.*
cōmĭtās -ātis, f. *courtesy, friendliness, civility.*
cŏmĭtātus -ūs, m. *train, retinue, following.*
cōmĭter, adv. from comis; q.v.
cŏmĭtĭa; see comitium.
cŏmĭtĭālis -e, *relating to the* comitia.
cŏmĭtĭātus -ūs, m. *the assembly of the people in the* comitia.
cŏmĭtĭum -i, n. *a place of assembly*, esp. *one in the forum at Rome*; plur. **cŏmĭtĭa,** *the assembly of the Roman people for the election of magistrates*, etc.; hence *elections.*
cŏmĭto -are, *to accompany*: esp. as partic. **cŏmĭtātus** -a -um, *accompanied.*
cŏmĭtor -ari, dep. *to attend, accompany, follow.*
commăcŭlo -are, *to pollute.*
commănĭpŭlāris -is, m. *a soldier belonging to the same company.*
commĕātus -ūs, m., *free passage, going and coming*; milit., *leave of absence, furlough*; also (often plur.) *supply of provisions, food, forage.*
commĕdĭtor -ari, dep. *to practise, represent.*
commĕmĭni -isse, *to remember fully.*
commĕmŏrābĭlis -e, *worthy of mention, memorable.*
commĕmŏrātĭo -ōnis, f. *reminding, mention.*
commĕmŏro -are, *to call to mind, recollect; to remind another*, so *to mention, relate, recount.*
commendābĭlis -e, *commendable, praiseworthy.*

commendātīcĭus -a -um, *giving recommendation.*
commendātĭo -ōnis, f. *recommendation; that which recommends, excellence.*
commendātor -ōris, m. and **commendātrix** -īcis, f., *one that commends.*
commendo -are, *to commit to the care* or *protection of anyone.* Hence, in gen., *to commit; to recommend; to set off, render agreeable.*
commensus, partic. of commetior; q.v.
commentārĭŏlum -i, n. *a short treatise.*
commentārĭus -i, m. and **commentārĭum** -i, n. *a memorandum, note-book*; as the title of a book, *a memoir* (usually plur.); legal, *a brief.*
commentātĭo -ōnis, f. *reflection, careful consideration; practice.*
commentīcĭus -a -um, *invented, fictitious.*
[1]**commentor** -ari, dep. *to consider thoroughly; to practise, prepare; to invent, compose, write.*
[2]**commentor** -ōris, m. *an inventor.*
commĕo -are, *to go up and down, come and go.*
commercĭum -i, n. *trade, commerce*; meton. *the right to trade,* or *an article of traffic, merchandise,* or *a place of trade, depot.* Hence in gen., *intercourse, communication.*
commercor -ari, dep. *to buy up.*
commĕrĕo -ēre (also **commereor,** dep.) *to deserve fully; to commit a fault.*
commētĭor -mētiri -mensus, dep. *to measure*: sometimes *to measure one thing against another, compare.*
commēto -are, *to go frequently.*
commigro -are, *to move in a body, migrate.*
commīlĭtĭum -i, n. *companionship in war* or *military service*; in gen., *fellowship.*
commīlĭto -ōnis, m. *a fellow-soldier.*
commĭnātĭo -ōnis, f. *threatening, threat.*
commingo -mingĕre -minxi -mictum, *to make water on, defile.*
commĭniscor -mĭnisci -mentus, dep. *to think out, contrive, invent.* Perf. partic. in passive sense, **commentus** -a -um, *feigned, invented*; n. as subst. **commentum** -i, n. *a fiction, invention, contrivance.*
commĭnor -ari, dep. *to threaten.*
commĭnŭo -ŭĕre -ŭi -ūtum, *to make small, break up, diminish, weaken.*
comminus, *hand to hand,* esp. *in close combat*; in gen., *close up, close at hand.*
commiscĕo -miscēre -miscŭi -mixtum, *to mix together, mix up.*
commĭsĕrātĭo -ōnis, f. *pity*; rhet. *the exciting of pity.*
commĭsĕresco -ĕre, *to pity.*
commĭsĕror -ari, dep. *to pity, bewail*; of a speaker, *to excite pity.*
commissĭo -ōnis, f. *a setting together*: hence *the start of games, contests,* etc.
commissūra -ae, f. *a joining together, connexion, joint*

committo -mittĕre -mīsi -um.miss (1) *to unite, connect, combine*; esp. *to bring together in a contest, to match*: hence *to compare.* (2) *to begin, set on foot, initiate*: with ut and the subj., *to bring it about that*; esp. of crimes, etc., *to commit, perpetrate,* and of penalties, *to incur.* (3) *to entrust, commit,* esp. with reflex. N. of partic. as subst. **commissum** -i. *an undertaking; a crime, fault; a trust, secret.*
commŏdĭtās -ātis, f. *proportion, fitness*; hence *a fit occasion,* also *convenience, advantage*; of persons, *kindness.*
commŏdo -are, *to make fit, adapt*; hence *to adapt oneself to a person, to please, oblige, serve*; with acc. *to furnish, lend, give.*
commŏdus -a -um, *to measure, in full, complete*; hence *proper, fit, appropriate*; of persons, character, etc., *friendly, obliging, pleasant.* N. as subst. **commŏdum** -i, *suitable time, opportunity, convenience; use, advantage, interest; remuneration; loan.* N. acc. as adv. **commŏdum,** *at the right time, opportunely; just then.* Adv. **commŏde,** *rightly, properly, fitly; pleasantly, comfortably, kindly*
commōlĭor -iri, dep. *to set in motion.*
commŏnĕfăcĭo -făcĕre -fēci -factum, *to remind, warn* a person, or *to call to mind* a thing.
commŏnĕo -ēre, *to remind, warn* a person, or *to call to mind* a thing.
commonstro -are, *to show fully.*
commŏrātĭo -ōnis, f. *delaying, lingering.*
commŏror -ari, dep. *to linger, stay*; transit., *to delay.*
commōtĭo -ōnis, *violent movement excitement.*
commŏvĕo -mŏvēre -mōvi -mōtum, *to move violently, shake, disturb, carry about* or *away*; nummum, *to employ in commerce*; esp. of the mind or passions, *to excite, influence, upset*; of abstract things, *to start up, produce cause.*

Hence partic. **commōtus** -a -um, *insecure, unsteady; excited, upset.*
commūnĭcātĭo -ōnis, f. *communicating, imparting.*
commūnĭco -are (1) *to share out, give a share in*; hence *to communicate, impart* a matter; without object, *to take counsel, confer with* a person. (2) *to join, unite.* (3) *to take a share participate.*
[1]**commūnĭo** -ire, *to fortify thoroughly.*
[2]**commūnĭo** -ōnis, f. *sharing, mutual participation.*
commūnis -e, *shared, common, universal, public*; loca, *public places*; loci, *commonplaces*; of persons, *approachable, affable.* N. as subst. **commūnĕ,** *common property,* esp. in plur.; *state, commonwealth*; **in commūne,** *for the public good,* also *in general.* Adv. **commūnĭter,** *jointly, generally.*
commūnĭtās -ātis, f. *community, fellowship; sense of fellowship, affability.*

commurmŭror -ari, dep. *to mutter, murmur.*
commūtābĭlis -e, *changeable.*
commūtātus -ūs, m. *change, alteration.*
commūto -are, *to change, alter; to exchange, barter, interchange.*
cōmo cōmĕre compsi comptum, *to put together, make tidy, arrange, adorn*; esp. of the hair.
Hence partic. **comptus** -a -um, *formed, framed; adorned, neat.*
cōmoedia -ae, f. *comedy.*
cōmoedus, *comic*; m. as subst., *a comic actor.*
cŏmōsus -a -um, *hairy*; of plants, *leafy.*
compactĭo -ōnis, f. *joining together.*
compactum or **compectum** -i, n. *an agreement.*
compāgēs -is, f. *a joining together, connexion*: hence either *something that joins, a joint, seam,* or *something joined together, a structure.*
compāgo -ĭnis, f. *a joining together.*
compār -păris: as subst., *an equal, companion, mate*; as adj. *like, similar.*
compărābĭlis -e, *capable of comparison, comparable.*
[1]**compărātĭo** -onis, f. *preparing, providing.*
[2]**compărātĭo** -onis, f. *a putting together*; hence, *comparison.*
compărātīvus -a -um, *relating to comparison, comparative.*
comparco (comperco) -parcĕre -parsi or -persi, *to scrape together, save up.*
compārĕo -pārēre -pārŭi *to appear, be visible; to be present, be in existence.*
[1]**compăro** -are, *to prepare, get ready, provide*; hence *to arrange, settle.*
[2]**compăro** -are, *to couple together,* esp. for a contest, *to match.* Transf., *to liken, compare.*
compasco -pascĕre -pastum, *to feed* (cattle) *together.*
compascŭus -a -um, *of common pasturage.*
compellātĭo -ōnis, f. *accosting, rebuking.*
[1]**compello** -pellĕre -pŭli -pulsum, *to drive together, collect; to force, compel.*
[2]**compello** -are, *to address, accost*; esp. *to reproach, rebuke*; legal, *to accuse before a court.*
compendĭārĭus -a -um *short*; f. and n. as subst., *a short cut.*
compendĭum -i, n. *saving, profit, advantage; shortening, abbreviation*; compendi facere, *to make short*; in plur. *short ways, short cuts.*
compensātĭo -ōnis, f. *balancing, compensation.*
compenso -are, *to weight together, balance.*
comperco = comparco; q.v.
compĕrendĭnātĭo -ōnis, f. and **compĕrendĭnātus** -ūs, m. *a putting off to the next day but one.*
compĕrendĭno -are, *to remand to the next day but one.*
complector -plecti -plexus, dep. *to embrace, surround, encompass.* Transf., *to hold fast, master; to attach oneself to, esteem;* of the mind, *to embrace, grasp, comprehend; to unite in oneself, to include.*
complementum -i, n. *a complement.*
compleo -plēre -plēvi -plētum, *to fill up*; milit., *to man,* or *to bring up to strength*; of a sum, *to make up*; of fate, etc., *to fulfil*; of a task, *to finish.*
Hence partic. **complētus** -a -um, *perfect, complete.*
complexĭo -ōnis, f. *connexion, combination*; in rhetoric, *a summary* or *a period*; in logic, *the statement of a syllogism* or *a dilemma.*
complexus -ūs, m. of persons, *embrace, grasp,* either in love or in combat; of things, *compass* or *connexion.*
complĭco -are *to fold together*; complicata notio, *confused, intricate.*
complōrātĭo -ōnis, f. and **complōrātus** -ūs, m. *lamentation.*
complōro -are, *to bewail, lament.*
complūres, -ĭum, *several.*
complŭvĭum -i, n. *roofless space in the centre of a Roman house.*
compōno -pōnĕre -pŏsŭi -pŏsĭtum. (1) *to put together*; esp. of unlike persons or things, either *to match as opponents,* or *to compare.* (2) *to make up a whole, compose.* (3) *to put in place, arrange, settle*; of enemies, *to reconcile.*
Hence partic. **compŏsĭtus** -a -um. *constructed, put together; arranged in order, settled*; hence *adapted* to a purpose. Adv. **compŏsĭtē**, *in an orderly way.*
comporto -are, *to bring together, collect.*
compŏs -pŏtis, *having control of, possessed of, sharing in.*
compŏsĭtĭo -ōnis, f. *putting together*; of opponents, *matching; composing, compounding; orderly arrangement, settlement.*
compŏsĭtor -ōris, m. *an arranger, adjuster.*
compŏsĭtūra -ae, f. *connexion, joining.*
compŏsĭtus -a -um, partic. from compono; q.v.
compōtātĭo -ōnis, f. *drinking party.*
compōtor -ōris, m. and **compōtrix** -īcis, f. *a drinking-companion.*
compransor -ōris, m. *a dinner companion.*
comprĕcātĭo -ōnis, f. (*common*) *supplication.*
comprĕcor -ari, dep. *to pray to* or *for, supplicate.*
comprĕhendo -prĕhendere -prĕhendi -prĕhensum and **comprendo** -prendĕre -prendi -prensum, *to grasp; to take together, unite*, hence *to embrace, include; to take firmly, seize;* ignem, *to catch fire*; often of persons, *to capture, arrest*; of criminals, *to catch red-handed.* Transf., *to comprehend, perceive.*
comprĕhensĭbĭlis -e, *comprehensible.*
comprĕhensĭo -ōnis, f. (1) *a taking together, uniting*; rhet., *a period.* (2) *seizing, arrest.* Transf., *comprehending, comprehension.*
comprendo = comprehendo; q.v.

compressĭo -ōnis, f. *an embrace; compression of style, conciseness.*

compressū, abl. sing. m. *by pressing together; by embracing.*

comprĭmo -prĭmĕre -pressi -pressum, *to press together; to press tightly*; hence *to embrace*; to *check, restrain, suppress.* Hence compar. adv. **compressĭus,** *more* (*or rather*) *concisely.*

comprŏbātĭo -ōnis, f. *approval.*

comprŏbātor -ōris, m. *one who approves.*

comprŏbo -are (1) *to approve fully.* (2) *to confirm, prove, establish.*

comprōmissum -i, n. *reference to arbitrator.*

comprōmitto -mittĕre -mīsi -missum, *to agree to refer a cause to arbitration.*

[1]**comptus** -a -um, partic. from como; q.v.

[2]**comptus** -ūs, m. *a head-dress; a band, tie.*

compungo -pungĕre -punxi -punctum, *to prick, puncture*; hence *to tattoo.*

compŭto -are, *to reckon togetker, calculate, compute.*

computresco -ĕre, *to rot, putrefy.*

Cōmum -i, n. *a lake-side town in Cisalpine Gaul* (now Como).

cōnāmen -mĭnis, n. *effort, endeavour*; concr., *a support.*

cōnātum -i, n. *an undertaking.*

cōnātus -ūs, m. *an exertion, effort*; sometimes *impulse, inclination; an undertaking.*

concaedēs -ium, f. pl. *a barricade of trees.*

concălĕfăcĭo -făcĕre -fēci -factum (pass. **concălĕfīo**) *to warm thoroughly.*

concălesco -călescĕre -călŭi, *to become thoroughly warm.*

concallesco -callescĕre -callŭi, *to become thoroughly hard*; hence *to become practised* or *callous.*

concăvo -are, *to hollow out, make concave.*

concăvus -a -um, *hollow, vaulted, arched, concave*; aqua, *swelling.*

concēdo -cēdĕre -cessi -cessum: intransit., *to retire, withdraw*; concedere vita, *to die*; hence *to yield, submit, give way to,* with dat.; concedere naturae, *to die a natural death*; transit., *to yield, grant, give up*; of faults, *to pardon, overlook*; of actions, *to permit, allow.*

concĕlebro -are. *to visit often,* or *in large companies; to pursue an* occupation *eagerly; to celebrate* a festivity; also *to praise, extol* a person or thing.

concēnātĭo -ōnis, f. *supping together.*

concentĭo -ōnis, f. *signing together, harmony.*

concentus -ūs, m. *singing together, harmony*; hence *agreement, unity, concord.*

conceptĭo -ōnis, f. *conception, becoming pregnant; drawing up of legal formulae.*

conceptus -ūs, m. *conceiving, pregnancy; collecting,* or *a collection.*

concerpo -cerpĕre -cerpsi -cerptum, *to tear in pieces.* Transf., *to abuse.*

concertātĭo -ōnis, f. *contest, strife, dispute.*

concertātor -ōris, m. *a rival.*

concertātōrĭus -a -um, *relating to a contest.*

concerto -are, *to strive eagerly.*

concessĭo -ōnis, f. *yielding, granting.*

concessū, abl. sing. m. *by permission, with leave.*

concha -ae, f. *a sea-shell*; hence *a shell-fish,* esp. *mussel* or *pearl-oyster* or *the fish yielding purple dye*; poet., *a pearl* or *purple dye.* Transf., *a vessel like a shell,* e.g. *a salt-cellar* or *trumpet.*

conchȳlĭātus -a -um, *dyed with purple* or *dressed in purple.*

conchȳlĭum -i, n. *a shell-fish* esp. *a mussel* or *oyster,* or *the shell-fish which yielded the purple dye*: meton., *purple dye* or *a purple garment.*

[1]**concĭdo** -cĭdĕre -cĭdi, *to fall down.* Transf., *to sink, perish*; of winds, *to subside*; of persons, *to be ruined, to fail,* esp. at law.

[2]**concīdo** -cidere -cidi, -cisum, *to cut up, cut down, destroy.* Transf., *to ruin, strike down.*

Hence partic. **concīsus** -a -um, *cut up small, brief, concise.* Adv. **concīsē.**

concĭĕo -cĭēre -cīvi -cĭtum and **concĭo** -ire. (1) *to collect, bring together.* (2) *to move violently, excite, arouse, stir up.*

concĭlĭābŭlum -i, n. *a place of assembly.*

concĭlĭātĭo -ōnis, f. *a bringing together, uniting, conciliating, causing of goodwill*; sometimes *inclination.*

concĭlĭātor -ōris, m. *one who brings about a result.*

concĭlĭātrix -īcis, f. *she who unites*; hence *a match-maker.*

concĭlĭātū, abl. sing. m., *by union, by connexion.*

concĭlĭo -are, *to bring together, unite, reconcile, win over*; hence of results, *to bring about, cause.*

Hence partic. **concĭlĭātus** -a -um, *won over, inclined, favourable.*

concĭlĭum -i, n. *bringing together, connexion, assembling, union*; esp. *an assembly for deliberation, a council.*

concinnĭtās -ātis, and **concinnĭtūdo** ĭnis, f. *elegance, harmony,* esp. of style.

concinno -are, *to put together carefully, to arrange*: hence *to produce, cause.*

concinnus -a -um, *well put together*; hence *pleasing, elegant, neat,* esp. of style. Adv. **concinnē,** *elegantly.*

concĭno -cĭnĕre -cĭnŭi: intransit., *to sing in chorus, play together*; hence *to agree in saying* and in gen. *to agree*; transit., of songs, *to sing together*; of festivals, *to celebrate*; of the future, *to prophesy.*

[1]**concĭo** = concieo; q.v.

[2]**concĭo** -ōnis = contio; q.v.

concĭpĭo -cĭpĕre -cēpi -ceptum. (1) *to take together, contain, hold*; of ideas, *to express in a certain form of* *words.* (2) *to take completely in, absorb*; of fluids, *to suck in*; of fire, *to catch*; of air, *to draw in*; often also *to conceive.* Transf., *to take in, grasp* by senses or intellect; *to conceive, imagine*; of passions, *to begin to feel*; of action, *to devise*, esp. in bad sense.

concīsĭo -ōnis, f. *the breaking up of a clause into divisions.*

concīsus -a -um, partic. from [2]concido; q.v.

concĭtātĭo -ōnis, f. *violent movement.* Hence *tumult, sedition*; also *disturbance of mind, passion.*

concĭtātor -ōris, m. *one who stirs up.*

concĭto -are, *to move violently, stir up, excite*; equum calcaribus, *to spur to a gallop*; aciem, *to move forward the army.* Hence in gen., *to stir up, incite*; of results, *to cause, produce.*

Hence partic. **concĭtātus** -a -um, *quick, rapid*; *excited, violent, passionate.* Adv. **concĭtātē,** *excitedly.*

concĭtor -ōris, m. *one who stirs up.*

conclāmātĭo -ōnis, f. *loud* or *combined shouting.*

conclāmo -are. (1) *to shout together* or *loudly*; with ut, *to demand loudly that*; with acc. of a dead person, *to bewail.* (2) *to call together.*

conclāve -is, n. *a room, chamber.*

conclūdo -clūdĕre -clūsi -clūsum *to shut up, enclose, confine.* Hence *to include, comprise*; *to bring to an end*; in logic, *to argue, infer.* Adv. from partic., **conclūsē,** *with well-turned periods.*

conclūsĭo -ōnis, f. *a shutting, closing*; milit, *a blockade.* Transf., *a close, conclusion*; rhet., *the conclusion of a speech, peroration,* or *a period*; in logic, *a conclusion, consequence.*

conclūsĭuncŭla -ae, f. *a foolish inference.*

concŏlor -ōris, *similar in colour.*

concŏquo -cŏquĕre -coxi -coctum. *to boil* or *cook thoroughly*; hence *to digest.* Transf., *to bear, endure, stomach; to consider well, deliberate upon.*

concordĭa -ae, f. *agreement, union, harmony.*

concordĭter, adv. from concors; q.v.

concordo -are, *to agree, be in harmony.*

concors -dis, *of one mind* or *opinion, agreeing, harmonious.* Adv. **concordĭter.**

concrēbresco -brescĕre -brŭi *to increase.*

concrēdo -crēdĕre -crēdĭdi -crēdĭtum, *to entrust, commit.*

concrĕmo -are, *to burn down, burn entirely.*

concrĕpo -are -ŭi -ĭtum: intransit., *to rattle, creak, clash*; digitis concrepare, *to snap the fingers*; transit., *to rattle, strike upon.*

concresco -crescĕre -crēvi -crētum. *to grow, collect, be formed; to become stiff, congeal, harden.*

Hence perf. partic. **concrētus** -a -um, *compounded; congealed, stiff.*

concrētĭo -ōnis, f. *a growing together, congealing; matter.*

concrŭcĭo -are, *to torture violently.*

concŭbīna -ae, f. *a concubine.*

concŭbīnus -i, m. *a man living with a concubine.*

concŭbĭtus -ūs, m. *lying* or *reclining together*; hence *copulation.*

concŭbĭus -a -um, in the phrase concubia nocte, *at the time of first sleep, at dead of night.*

conculco -are, *to tread down, trample under foot.*

concumbo -cumbĕre -cŭbŭi -cŭbĭtum, *to lie* or *recline together* (at table); *to lie with, have intercourse with.*

concŭpisco -piscere -pīvi or -pĭi -pītum, *to desire eagerly, covet, aim at.*

concurro -currĕre -curri (or -cŭcurri) -cursum, *to assemble hurriedly, flock to one spot; to rush together, clash,* esp. *to meet in conflict, engage.*

concursātĭo -ōnis, f. *running together, concourse*; hence *coincidence*; in gen., *running about*; milit. *skirmishing.*

concursātor -ōris, m. *a skirmisher.*

concursĭo -ōnis, f. *running together, concourse*; rhet., *frequent repetition of a word.*

concurso -are, *to run about, rush to and fro*; milit., *to skirmish.*

concursus -ūs, m. *running together, concourse, union; a rushing together, clashing; a hostile encounter.*

concussū, abl. sing. m. *by shaking, by concussion.*

concŭtĭo -cŭtĕre -cussi -cussum *to shake together, agitate, disturb.* Hence, physically, *to shatter, impair*; of persons, *to shake the clothes of,* and so *to examine*; mentally, *to alarm, trouble, excite.*

condĕcŏro -are, *to adorn carefully.*

condemnātor -ōris, m. *one who causes condemnation, an accuser.*

condemno -are, *to condemn*; of an accuser, *to urge* or *effect the condemnation of a person*; in gen., *to blame, disapprove.*

condenso -are and **condensĕo** -ēre, *to make thick, press close together.*

condensus -a -um, *dense, thick.*

condĭcĭo -ōnis, f. *an arrangement, agreement.* Hence (1) *a condition, stipulation, provision*; esp. *conditions of marriage, marriage contract.* (2) *state, condition, place, circumstances.*

condīco -dīcĕre -dixi -dictum, *to make arrangement, agree, fix, settle*; esp. *to agree to dine with* a person.

condignus -a -um, *very worthy*; adv. **condignē.**

condīmentum -i, n. *spice, seasoning, sauce, condiment.*

condĭo -ire; of fruits, etc., *to pickle, preserve*; of corpses, *to embalm*; in gen., *to season, temper.*

Hence partic. **condītus** -a -um, *seasoned, savoury.*

condiscĭpŭlus -i, m. and **condiscĭpŭla** -ae, f. *a schoolfellow.*

condisco -discĕre -dĭdĭci, *to learn thoroughly.*

[1]**condĭtio** = condicio; q.v.

[2]**condĭtio** -ōnis, f. *pickling* or *seasoning.*

condĭtor -ōris, m. *a founder*; hence, in gen., *contriver, composer, author.*

condĭtōrĭum -i, n. *the place in which a corpse* or *its ashes are preserved.*

condo -dĕre -dĭdi -dĭtum. (1) *to build, found; form, establish*; of literary work, *to compose, write* a poem, etc., and also *to write of* a subject. (2) *to put up, put away safely, store, to hide, withdraw*; of corpses, *to bury*; of time, *to pass, dispose of.*

condŏcĕfăcĭo -făcĕre -fēci -factum, *to train, instruct, teach.*

condŏlesco -dŏlescĕre -dŏlŭi, *to suffer severely, feel much pain.*

condōnātĭo -ōnis, f. *a giving away.*

condōno -are, *to give away, present, give up, sacrifice*; of debts, *to excuse*; of faults, *to overlook, forgive*; sometimes *to forgive* an injury *for the sake of a third party* (dat.).

condūco -dūcĕre -duxi -ductum: transit., *to bring* or *lead together, collect, unite, connect*; as commercial term, *to hire*, also *to contract for, farm*; intransit. (3rd person only), *to be of use, to profit, serve*, with dat.

conductĭcĭus -a -um, *hired.*

conductĭo -ōnis, f. *a bringing together, uniting*; commerc., *hiring, farming.*

conductor -ōris, m. *one who hires: a contractor.*

condupl̄ico -are, *to double.*

condūro -are, *to harden.*

cōnecto -nectĕre -nexŭi -nexum, *to fasten, tie together, connect, join, unite.*

Hence partic. **cōnexus** -a -um, *joined, connected*; n. as subst. *logical connexion.*

cōnexĭo -ōnis, f. *binding together; logical sequence.*

cōnexus -ūs, m. *connexion, union.*

confābŭlor -ari, dep. *to talk, converse.*

confarrĕātĭo -ōnis, f. *a Roman form of marriage.*

confarrĕo -are, *to marry by the ceremony of* confarreatio.

confātālis -e, *determined by the same fate.*

confectĭo -ōnis, f. (1) *production, completion*; tributi, *complete exaction.* (2) *consumption.*

confector -ōris, m. *one who produces* or *completes; a destroyer, consumer.*

confercĭo -fercire -fertum, *to press close together, compress, cram together*; usually in perf. partic. **confertus** -a -um, *compressed, dense*; of troops, *in close formation*; with abl., *stuffed with, full of*; adv. **confertim,** *compactly.*

confĕro -ferre -tŭli -lātum. (1) *to bring or put together, collect, concentrate*; of money, etc. *to contribute*; milit., *to bring into contact* or *collision*; pedem (cum pede), *to fight foot to foot*; signa conferre, *to engage*; of speech and ideas, *to interchange, discuss*; of diverse things, *to compare* (2) *to bring to* a particular place, sphere, task, etc.; se conferre, *to betake oneself*, or *to devote oneself*; in time, *to put off, postpone*; of responsibility, *to impute, attribute.*

confertus; see confercio.

confervĕfăcĭo -făcĕre, *to make very hot, melt.*

confervesco -fervescĕre -ferbŭi, *to begin to boil* or *glow.*

confessĭo -ōnis, f., *a confession, acknowledgment.*

confessus -a -um, partic. from confiteor; q.v.

confestim, *immediately, without delay.*

confĭcĭo -fĭcĕre -fēci -fectum. (1) *to finish, make ready, bring about, accomplish*; of arrangements, *to conclude, settle*; of time or space, *to complete, pass through*; of results, *to produce, cause.* (2) *to get together, obtain, win over.* (3) *to use up, exhause, consume*: of food, *to chew, eat* and also *to digest*; of property, *to waste*; of living creatures, *to destroy, kill*; in gen., *to weaken, wear out,* esp. of persons.

Hence partic. **confĭcĭens** -entis *productive, efficient.*

confictĭo -ōnis, f. *a fabrication, invention.*

confīdens, confīdenter; see confido.

confīdentĭa -ae, f. *confidence*; in bad sense, *impudence, boldness.*

confīdo -fīdĕre -fīsus sum, *to have complete trust in, be assured.*

Hence partic. **confīdens** -entis, *confident, self-reliant*; in bad sense *bold, self-assured*; adv. **confīdenter.**

confīgo -fīgĕre -fixi -fixum, *to fasten together; to pierce through, transfix, pin down.*

confingo -fingĕre -finxi -fictum, *construct, fashion, fabricate.*

confīnis -e. *having the same boundary, adjacent*; m. as subst. *a neighbour.* Transf., *closely allied, similar.*

confīnĭum -i, n. *a confine, boundary border.*

confirmātĭo -ōnis, f. *a thorough strengthening*; of an institution, *a securing, making firm*; of a person, *consolation, encouragement, support*; of a fact or statement, *confirmation, verification.*

confirmātor -ōris, m. *one who confirms.*

confirmo -are, *to make firm, strengthen, support*; se confirmare, *to recover strength*; polit. *to ratify*; of persons, *to strengthen in mind, encourage*; of assertions, either *to corroborate, establish* or *to affirm, state positively.*

Hence partic. **confirmātus** -a -um *encouraged, emboldened*; of things, *certain.*

confisco -are, *to lay up, preserve in a chest; to appropriate to the imperial treasury, to confiscate.*

confīsĭo -ōnis, f. *confidence, assurance.*

confĭtĕor -fĭtēri -fessus sum, dep. *to confess, admit, acknowledge; to reveal, make known.*

Hence partic. **confessus** -a -um: in act. sense, *having confessed;* pass., *undoubted, acknowledged, certain.*

conflagro -are, *to blaze up, be well alight.*

conflictio -ōnis, f. *collision, conflict.*

conflicto -are, pass. or intransit., *to collide, contend*; transit., *to harass*; pass. *to be harassed* or *tormented.*

conflictū, abl. sing. m. *by striking together.*

confligo -flīgĕre -flixi, flictum: transit., *to strike* or *throw together; to bring together in order to compare*; intransit., *to collide, clash, come into conflict.*

conflo -are, *to blow up; blow into flame*; of metals, *to melt* or *forge*; of money, *to coin.* Transf., *to excite; to forge, fabricate, put together.*

conflŭo -flŭĕre -fluxi, *to flow, stream* or *flock together.* Partic. **conflŭens** -entis, *flowing together*; m. sing. or pl. as subst. *the confluence of two rivers*; as a place-name **Conflŭentes,** f. pl. *Coblenz.*

confŏdio -fŏdĕre -fōdi -fossum, *to dig thoroughly; to stab, pierce through.*

conformātio -ōnis, f. *form, shape*; vocis, *expression*; verborum, *arrangement*; philosoph., *an idea*; rhet., *a figure of speech.*

conformo -are, *to form, to put together, to adapt one thing to another.*

confrăgōsus -a -um, *rugged, uneven*; n. pl. as subst., *uneven places.*

confrăgus -a -um = confragosus; q.v.

confrĕmo -frĕmĕre -frĕmŭi, *to murmur, make a noise.*

confrĭco -frĭcare -frĭcŭi -frĭcatum, *to rub hard.*

confringo -fringĕre -frēgi -fractum, *to break in pieces; to destroy.*

confŭgio -fŭgĕre -fūgi, *to fly, take refuge; to have recourse to.*

confŭgium -i, n. *a place of refuge.*

confulcio -fulcire -fultus, *to prop up.*

confundo -fundĕre -fūdi -fūsum, *to pour; to pour together, mingle, mix, join*; hence *to confuse, throw into disorder, trouble, disturb, upset.*

Hence partic. **confūsus** -a -um, *disorderly, confused*; mentally, *embarrassed, troubled.* Adv. **confūsē.**

confūsio -ōnis, f. *blending, union; confusion, disorder.*

confūto -are, *to check, repress;* by speech, *to put down, silence.*

congĕlo -are: transit., *to freeze, harden, thicken*; intransit., *to freeze up, become inert.*

congĕmĭno -are, *to redouble.*

congĕmo -gĕmĕre -gĕmŭi: intransit., *to sigh* or *groan loudly*; transit., *to bewail, lament.*

conger -gri, m. *a sea* or *conger eel.*

congĕrĭēs -ēi, f. *a heap, mass,* esp. *of wood*; rhet., *accumulation.*

congĕro -gĕrĕre -gessi -gestum, *to bring together, collect, pile up, accumulate*; esp. *to build up*; in discourse, *to bring together, comprise*; of benefits, abuse, etc., *to heap upon* a person.

congestīcius -a -um, *heaped up.*

congestus -ūs, m. *a heaping together*; of birds, *the building of nests.* **Transf.,** *a heap, mass.*

congĭārium -i, n. *a donation* (originally of wine, oil, etc.).

congĭus -i, m. *a Roman liquid measure* (= *six* sextarii).

conglăcio -are; intransit., *to freeze, be inert*; transit. *to turn to ice.*

conglŏbātio -ōnis, f. *a heaping* or *crowding together.*

conglŏbo -are, *to form into a ball, press tightly together.*

conglŏmĕro -are, *to roll, twist, entangle.*

conglūtĭnātio -ōnis, f. *cementing together, connexion.*

conglūtĭno -are, *to cement together, connect, bind closely.*

congrātŭlor -ari, dep. *to wish joy to, congratulate.*

congrĕdior -grĕdi -gressus, dep. *to meet,* esp. in conflict; in words, *to dispute, argue.*

congrĕgābilis -e, *sociable, inclined to collect.*

congrĕgātio -ōnis, f. *an assembling, society, union.*

congrĕgo -are, *to collect into a flock* or *swarm*; of men, *to gather together*; with reflex., or in pass., *to swarm, assemble.*

congressio -ōnis, f. *meeting, intercourse, association.*

congressus -ūs, m. *a meeting*; either *a friendly meeting, social intercourse,* or *a hostile encounter, combat.*

congrŭentia -ae, f. *agreement, symmetry, proportion.*

congrŭo -ŭĕre, -ŭi, *to run together, come together, meet*; in time, *to coincide*; in gen., *to be suited to, correspond with, agree.*

Hence partic. **congrŭens** -entis, *agreeing, fit, appropriate, suitable*; concentus, *harmonious, uniform*; clamor, *unanimous.* Adv. **congrŭentĕr**, *agreeably, suitably.*

congrŭus -a -um, *agreeing, fit, suitable.*

conicio -icĕre -iēci -ectum, *to throw together; to cast lots*; mentally, *to put two and two together, conjecture, guess; to interpret* dreams, etc.; in gen., *to throw, hurl*; se conicere, *to betake oneself, flee*; of abstract things, *to bring up, bring in*; of money, *to throw away.*

coniectio -ōnis, f. *hurling, throwing; conjectural interpretation.*

coniecto -are, *to throw together*; hence *to put two and two together; conclude, infer, guess.*

coniector -ōris, m. *an interpreter.*

coniectūra -ae, f. *a guess, conjecture, inference; interpretation of dreams and omens, divination.*

coniectūrālis -e, *conjectural.*

coniectus -ūs, m. *a throwing* or *throwing together.*

cōnifĕr -fĕra -fĕrum and **cōnigĕr,** *cone-bearing.*

cōnītor -nīti -nīsus or -nixus, dep. *to lean* or *press hard; to make a great* *effort, physical* or *mental*; transit., of offspring, *to bring forth with difficulty.*

coniŭgālis -e, *of marriage, conjugal.*

coniŭgātĭo -ōnis, f. *etymological connexion of words.*

coniŭgātor -ōris, m., *one who connects.*

coniŭgĭālis -e, *of marriage, conjugal.*

coniŭgĭum -i, n., *a close connexion, union*; esp. *marriage, wedlock*; meton. *a husband* or *wife.*

coniŭgo -are, *to bind together, connect.*

coniunctĭo -ōnis, f. *uniting, joining together, connexion*; grammat., *a connecting particle, conjunction*; of persons, *union, association, connexion* (esp. by blood or marriage).

coniungo -iungĕre -iunxi -iunctum, *to join together, connect, unite*; amicitias, *to form*; esp. *to unite* persons *by marriage, friendship, alliance,* etc.

Hence partic. **coniunctus** -a -um, *connected, joined, agreeing, allied*; of place, with dat. *bordering on, near*; of time, *contemporary*; of persons, *connected* by blood or marriage or friendship. N. as subst., *an inherent property* or *quality*; rhet., *connexion.* Adv. **coniunctē,** *conjointly, in connexion; intimately, on friendly terms*; **coniunctim,** *conjointly, in common.*

coniunx (**coniux**) -iŭgis, c. *a husband* or *wife*; poet. *a betrothed virgin, bride.*

coniūrātĭo -ōnis, f. *a union confirmed by an oath*; in bad sense, *conspiracy, plot*; meton., *conspirators.*

coniūro -are, *to take an oath together*; in bad sense, *to plot, conspire*; perf. partic. (in act. sense) **coniūrātus** -a -um, *sworn, united by oath*; m. pl. as subst. *conspirators.*

coniux = coniunx; q.v.

cōnīvĕo -nīvēre -nīvi or -nixi, *to close the eyes, wink, blink.* Transf. *to wink at, let pass.*

conlăbĕfacto -are, *to cause to totter, to soften up.*

conlăbĕfīo -fĭĕri -factus, *to be made to totter, to be softened* or *broken.*

conlābor -lābi -lapsus, dep. *to fall* or *sink down, collapse; to fall down in a swoon* or *death.*

conlăcĕrātus -a -um, *much lacerated* or *torn.*

conlacrĭmātĭo -ōnis, f. *a weeping together.*

conlacrĭmo -are, *to weep together* or *weep much*; transit., *to weep for.*

conlactĕus -i, m., and **-a** -ae, f., *a foster-brother* or *sister.*

conlātĭo -ōnis, f. *a bringing together*; signorum, *a battle*; of money, *a contribution, collection.* Transf., *a comparison, simile, analogy.*

conlātus -a -um, partic. from confero; q.v.

conlaudātĭo -ōnis, f. *strong praise.*

conlaudo -are, *to praise very much.*

conlaxo -are, *to widen, extend.*

conlecta -ae, f. *a contribution in money*

conlectīcĭus -a -um, *gathered together*; exercitus, *quickly levied.*

conlectĭo -ōnis, f. *a gathering together, collection*; rhet. *a brief recapitulation*; in logic, *a conclusion, inference.*

conlēga -ae, m. *a colleague, partner in office*; in gen., *an associate.*

conlēgĭum -i, n.; abstr., *colleagueship*; concr., *persons united as colleagues, a body, guild, corporation, college.*

conlībertus -i, m. *a fellow-freedman.*

conlĭbet or **conlŭbet** -bēre -bŭit or -bĭtum est, impers., *it pleases, is agreeable.*

conlīdo līdĕre -līsi -līsum, *to strike* or *dash together, to bring into hostile collision.*

conlĭgātĭo -ōnis, f. *a binding together connexion.*

[1]**conlĭgo** -lĭgĕre -lēgi -lectum, *to gather* or *bring together, collect*; poet., *to gather into a smaller space, contract*; conligere se, *or* animum, *or* mentem, *to compose onesel , gain courage*; in the mind, *to put together,* hence *to infer, conclude.*

[2]**conlĭgo** -are, *to bind, tie, fasten together, connect*; sometimes *to detain, hinder, tie down.*

conlīnĕo are, *to direct in a straight line.*

conlĭno -lĭnĕre -lēvi -lĭtum, *to besmear, daub.*

conlĭquĕfactus -a -um, *liquefied melted.*

conlŏcātĭo -ōnis, f. *a placing, arrangement*; esp. *a giving in marriage.*

conlŏco -are, *to place, lay, set, arrange*; of time, money, etc. *to lay out, employ, spend*; of persons, *to settle, place*; of troops, *to billet, quarter*; of women, *to settle in marriage.*

conlŏcuplēto -are, *to enrich.*

conlŏcūtĭo -ōnis, f. *conversation.*

conlŏquĭum, -i, n., *talk, conversation, conference.*

conlŏquor -lŏqui -lŏcūtus, dep. *to speak to, converse with, to treat* or *negotiate with.*

conlūcĕo -ēre, *to shine on all sides, be completely illuminated.*

conlūdo -lūdĕre -lūsi -lūsum, *to play with; to have a secret understanding with, to act in collusion.*

conlŭo -lŭĕre -lŭi -lūtum, *to wash thoroughly, rinse.*

conlūsĭo -ōnis, f. *secret understanding.*

conlūsor -ōris, m. *a play-fellow; a fellow-gambler.*

conlustro -are, *to illuminate on all sides; to survey, look at on all sides.*

conlŭvĭo -ōnis and **conlŭvĭēs** -ēi *collection of impurities, filth*; of people, *scum, rabble.*

conm-; see comm-.

conn-; see con-.

cōnōpēum or **cōnōpĭum** -i, n. *a mosquito net.*

cōnor -ari, dep. *to undertake, try, strive.*

conp-; see comp-.

conquassātĭo -ōnis, f., *a violent shaking.*

conquasso -are, *to shake thoroughly, shatter.*

conquĕror -quĕri -questus, dep. *to complain loudly* (*of*).

conquestĭo -ōnis, f. *a loud complaint.*

conquestū, abl. sing. m. *by loud complaint.*

conquīesco -quiescĕre -quiēvi -quiētum, *to take rest, repose, be still, stop.*

conquīro -quirĕre -quisīvi -quisītum, *to seek out, get together.*
Hence partic. **conquīsītus** -a -um, *carefully sought out, chosen, costly.*

conquīsītio -ōnis, f. *search, collection*; of soldiers, *levying, conscription.*

conquīsītor -ōris, m., *a recruiting officer.*

conr-: see corr-.

consaepĭo -saepire -saepsi -saeptum, *to fence round, hedge in*; n. of partic. as subst. **consaeptum** -i, *an enclosure.*

consălūtātĭo -ōnis, f., *mutual salutation.*

consălūto -are, *to greet (mutually), hail, salute.*

consānesco -sānescĕre -sānŭi, *to become healthy, get well.*

consanguĭnĕus -a -um, *related by blood, brotherly, sisterly*; m. as subst., *brother*; f., *sister*; m. plur., *relations.*

consanguĭnĭtās -ātis, f., *relationship by blood, consanguinity.*

conscĕlĕro -are, *to defile with crime*; partic. **conscĕlĕrātus** -a -um, *villainous, depraved.*

conscendo -scendĕre -scendi -scensum, *to ascend, mount, go up*; equum, *to mount on horseback*; naut. (with or without navem, etc.), *to go on board ship, embark.*

conscensĭo -ōnis, f. *embarkation.*

conscĭentĭa -ae, f., *knowledge shared* with others, "*being in the know*", *joint knowledge; knowledge shared with oneself*, i.e. *consciousness*, esp. *of right* or *wrong, a good* or *a bad conscience.*

conscindo -scindĕre -scĭdi -scissum, *to tear in pieces.*

conscĭo -ire, *to be conscious of guilt.*

conscisco -sciscĕre -scīvi and -scĭi -scītum, *to agree on, resolve, decree; to inflict upon oneself* (with or without sibi).

conscĭus -a -um. *sharing knowledge with others, privy to* a thing, *cognizant of*; m. or f. as subst., *an accomplice, fellow-conspirator; sharing knowledge with oneself*, i.e. *conscious*, esp. *of right* or *wrong.*

conscrībo -scrībĕre -scripsi -scriptum, *to enter on a list, enroll*; of troops, *to levy;* patres conscripti (patres et conscripti), *senators; to write, compose*; of physicians, *to prescribe; to write all over* an object.

conscriptĭo -ōnis, f. *writing, composition.*

consĕco -sĕcare -sĕcŭi -sectum, *to cut up, dismember.*

consecrātĭo -ōnis, f. *dedication, consecration*; of dead emperors, *apotheosis.*

consecro -are, *to consecrate*; sometimes *to dedicate to the gods below, to curse;* of persons, *to deify*; in gen., *to make holy* or *immortal.*

consectārĭus -a -um, *following logically, consequent*; n. pl. as subst., *logical conclusions, inferences.*

consectātĭo -ōnis, f. *eager pursuit, striving after.*

consectātrix -īcis, f., *an eager pursuer, devoted friend.*

consectĭo -ōnis, f., *cutting to pieces.*

consector -ari, dep. *to follow, pursue eagerly; to make for, try to join, imitate, attain*; in hostile sense, *to chase, hunt.*

consĕcūtĭo -ōnis, f.: philosoph., *an effect, consequence*; rhet., *order, connexion, arrangement.*

consĕnesco -sĕnescĕre -sĕnŭi, *to become old, lose one's strength, decay.*

consensĭo -ōnis, f., *agreement, harmony, consent*; in bad sense, *plot, conspiracy.*

consensus -ūs m. *agreement, concord*; abl. consensu, *unanimously*; in bad sense, *secret agreement, conspiracy.*

consentānĕus -a -um, *agreeing, fit, suitable*; consentaneum est, *it is reasonable* or *suitable.*

consentĭo -sentire -sensi -sensum; of physical sensation, *to feel together*; of thought or sentiment, *to agree, assent, resolve unanimously*; with acc., bellum, *to resolve upon war*; in bad sense, *to plot, conspire*; of things, *to agree, harmonize.*
Hence partic. **consentĭens** -entis, *harmonious.*

consēpĭo=consaepio; q.v.

consĕquentĭa -ae, f., *a consequence, succession.*

consĕquĭa -ae, f. = consequentia; q.v.

consĕquor -sĕqui -sĕcūtus, dep. (1) *to follow, go after*; in hostile sense, *to pursue; to follow* in time, *follow logically, result.* (2) *to follow right up, reach, obtain, catch, get*; of states and events, *to befall, happen to* a person; in speech or thought, *to understand, grasp.*
Hence partic. **consĕquens** -entis, *appropriate, consequent*; n. as subst. *a logical consequence.*

[1]**consĕro** -sĕrĕre -sēvi -sītum, *to sow, plant.* Transf., *to cover.*

[2]**consĕro** -sĕrĕre -sĕrŭi -sertum, *to connect, join, twine together*; milit., *to join in* conflict, esp. manum (*or* manus) conserere, *to engage.*
Hence, from partic., adv. **consertē,** *connectedly.*

conserva -ae, f. *fellow slave.*

conservātĭo -ōnis, f. *preservation, keeping, laying up.*

conservātor -ōris, m., *preserver.*

conservo -are, *to keep, preserve, maintain.* Pres. partic. as adj. **conservans** antis, *preserving.*

conservus -i, m. *fellow slave.*

consessor ōris, m., *one who sits near, a neighbour*; in court, *an assessor.*

consessus -ūs, m. *assembly.*

consīdĕrātĭo -ōnis, f., *consideration, contemplation.*

consīdĕro -are, *to look at, regard carefully, contemplate*; mentally, *to consider, reflect upon.*

Hence partic. **consīdĕrātus** -a -um; pass., *well weighed, deliberate*; act., of persons, *cautious, circumspect*. Adv. **consīdĕrātē**, *thoughtfully, carefully*.

consīdo -sīdĕre -sēdi -sessum, *to sit down, to settle*; esp. *to sit down in an assembly* or *court*; milit., *to take up one's position* or *encamp*. Transf.: of things, *to settle, sink, subside; to be overcome* or *neglected*; of ideas, *to sink in*; of feelings, *to subside*.

consigno -are, *to seal; to vouch for, authenticate; to record*.

consĭlĭārĭus -a -um, *deliberating*; m. as subst. *an adviser, assessor, interpreter*.

consĭlĭātor -ōris, m., *counsellor, adviser*.

consĭlĭor -ari, dep. *to consult, take counsel; to give counsel, advise*.

consĭlĭum -i, n. (1) *deliberation, consultation*; meton., *persons in consultation, an assembly, council*; as a quality, *judgment, understanding*. (2) *a resolution, plan*; abl., consilio, *intentionally, designedly*. (3) *advice, suggestion*.

consĭmĭlis -e, *exactly similar*.

consĭpĭo -sĭpĕre, *to be in one's right mind*.

consisto -sistĕre -stĭti -stĭtum, *to take one's stand, place oneself; to stand still, stop; to be posted* or *to halt*. Transf., of things, *to fall to, come upon, rest on; to stop, stay; to stand firm;* with abl. etc., *to consist, be formed of*.

consĭtĭo -ōnis, and **consĭtūra** -ae, f., *sowing, planting*.

consĭtor -ōris, m., *sower, planter*.

consōbrīnus -i, m. and **consōbrīna** -ae, f., *cousin* (*on the mother's side*).

consŏcĭātĭo -ōnis, f., *union, connexion*.

consŏcĭo -are, *to unite, connect, share, make common*.

Hence partic. **consŏcĭātus** -a -um, *united, harmonious*.

consōlābĭlis -e, *consolable*.

consōlātĭo -ōnis, f., *consolation, encouragement, alleviation*; *consoling words*.

consōlātor -ōris, m., *consoler*.

consōlātōrĭus -a -um, *consolatory*.

consōlor -ari, dep.: of persons, *to console, comfort, encourage*; of things, *to alleviate, lighten*.

consŏno -sŏnare -sŏnŭi. (1) *to sound together*; hence *to harmonize, agree*. (2) *to resound, echo*.

consŏnus -a -um, *sounding together, harmonious, accordant, suitable*.

consōpĭo -ire, *to lull to sleep, stupefy*.

consors -sortis: act., *sharing in, partaking of;* as subst., *brother* or *sister*; as adj., *brotherly, sisterly*; pass., *shared*.

consortĭo -ōnis, f., *companionship, partnership*.

consortĭum -i, n., *partnership, participation*.

[1]**conspectus** -a -um, partic. from conspicio; q.v.

[2]**conspectus** -ūs m.: act., *seeing, look, sight, view*; hence *mental view, survey;* pass., *appearance*.

conspergo -spergĕre -spersi -spersum, *to sprinkle* or *moisten by sprinkling*.

conspĭcĭo -spĭcĕre -spexi -spectum, *to catch sight of, behold, perceive; to look at with attention, watch*; pass., conspici, *to attract notice, be gazed at*. Transf., *to see mentally, understand*.

Hence partic. **conspectus** -a -um, *visible; striking, remarkable, conspicuous*. Gerundive **conspĭcĭendus** -a -um, *worth looking at, notable*.

conspĭcor -ari, dep. *to catch sight of perceive*.

conspĭcŭus -a -um, *visible*; *remarkable, striking, conspicuous*.

conspīrātĭo -ōnis, f., *blowing* or *breathing together*; *harmony, agreement, union*; in bad sense, *conspiracy, plot*.

conspīro -are, *to blow* or *breathe together*; of instruments, *to blow together, sound together*. Transf., *to agree, harmonize in opinion and feeling*; in bad sense, *to conspire*.

Hence partic. **conspīrātus** -a -um, *sworn together, united by oath;* m. as subst., *a conspirator*.

consponsor -ōris, m. *a joint surety*.

conspŭo -spŭĕre, *to spit upon*.

conspurco -are, *to cover with dirt, defile*.

consputo -are, *to spit upon*.

constans -antis, partic. from consto; q.v.

constantĭa -ae, f., *steadiness, firmness*.

consternātĭo -ōnis, f., *fear, alarm, dismay, confusion; mutiny, tumult*.

[1]**consterno** -sternĕre -strāvi -strātum, *to strew, scatter, cover by strewing*.

Hence partic. **constrātus** -a -um; esp. constrata navis, *a decked ship*; n. as subst., *flooring, deck*.

[2]**consterno** -are, *to throw into confusion, alarm, frighten; to stampede*.

constīpo -are, *to press, crowd together*.

constĭtŭo -stĭtŭĕre -stĭtŭi -stĭtūtum, *to cause to stand, set up, place, establish, settle*; milit., *to post, station, arrange, bring to a halt; to settle* people in homes or quarters; *to found, set up* buildings, etc. Transf., *to appoint* a person *to an office; to settle, fix upon* an amount, time, etc.; *to decide* about a fact, *decide that; to decide* on a course of action, *decide to*.

Hence partic. **constĭtūtus** -a -um, *arranged, settled;* n. as subst., *anything arranged, settled* or *agreed upon*.

constĭtūtĭo -ōnis, f., *the act of settling; settled condition, disposition; a regulation, order, ordinance*; rhet., *the issue, point in dispute*.

consto -stare -stĭti -stātum. (1) to *stand together*; hence *to be composed, consist; to depend upon, rest upon; to correspond, be consistent* (with dat.); with abl., *to cost*. (2) *to stand firm, stand still; to remain the same, be unaltered*; of resolves, *to be fixed, firm;* of evidence, facts, etc., *to be* *established, sure, well-known*; impers. constat, *it is agreed*; in gen., *to exist.*

Hence partic. **constans** -antis, *steady, firm, unchanging, constant, consistent, resolute*; adv. **constantĕr,** *steadily, firmly.*

constringo -stringĕre -strinxi -strictum, *to bind together, bind fast, confine, restrain*; in speech, *to compress, abbreviate.*

constructĭo -ōnis, f., *putting together, building, construction.*

constrŭo -strŭĕre -struxi -structum, *to heap up together; to construct, build up; to arrange.*

constuprātor -ōris, m. *ravisher, debaucher.*

constupro -are *to debauch, ravish, corrupt.*

consuāsor -ōris, m. *an adviser.*

consuēfăcĭo -făcĕre -fēci -factum, *to accustom, habituate.*

consuesco -suescĕre -suēvi -suētum: transit., *to accustom, habituate*; intransit., *to accustom oneself*; in perf., consuevi, *I am accustomed*; cum homine, *to cohabit with a person.*

Hence partic. **consuetus** -a -um: of persons, *accustomed to*; of things, *accustomed, usual.*

consuētūdo -ĭnis, f., *custom, usage, habit*; of relations with persons, *intimacy, familiar acquaintance*; of lovers, *intrigue.*

consuētus -a -um, partic. from consuesco; q.v.

consul -sŭlis, m., *a consul*; plur., consules, *the consuls, the two chief magistrates at Rome under the Republic*; consul designatus, *consul elect*; pro consule, *an officer in the place of the consul, a proconsul,* e.g. *a governor of a province.*

consŭlāris -e. (1) *relating to a consul, consular.* (2) *having been a consul*; m. as subst., *an ex-consul*, or *provincial governor of consular rank.* Adv. **consŭlārĭtĕr**, *in a manner worthy of a consul.*

consŭlātus -ūs, m. *the office of consul, consulship.*

consŭlo -sŭlĕre -sŭlŭi -sultum. (1) *to reflect, consult, consider*; with dat., *to look to the interests of*; as a result of deliberation, *to come to a conclusion, to take measures;* boni (or optimi) consulere, *to take in good part.* (2) *to ask the advice of, consult.*

Hence partic. **consultus** -a -um: of things, *well considered, deliberated upon*; of persons, *experienced* (with genit). N. as subst. **consultum** -i: the act of deliberation, *reflection, consideration*; the result of deliberation, *a resolution, plan, decision*; esp. *a decree* of the senate at Rome. Abl. as adv. **consulto**, *deliberately, designedly*. Adv. **consultē**, *advisedly, after consideration.*

consultātĭo -ōnis, f., *a full consideration, deliberation; an asking for advice, inquiry.*

consulto -are. (1) *to consider maturely, weigh, ponder*; with dat., *to look to the interests of.* (2) *to consult, ask advice of.*

consultor -ōris, m. (1) *an adviser.* (2) *one who asks advice,* esp. legal advice; *a client.*

consummātĭo -ōnis, f. *a summing up, adding up; a finishing, completion.*

consummo -are, *to add together, sum up; to form a whole, complete, perfect.*

Hence partic. **consummātus** -a -um, *complete, perfect.*

consūmo -sūmĕre -sumpsi -sumptum, *to spend, employ* on a purpose; in gen., *to use up, finish, waste away, destroy.*

consŭo -sŭĕre -sŭi -sūtum, *to stitch* or *put together; to form.*

consurgo -surgĕre -surrexi -surrectum, *to rise up, stand up,* esp. to speak, or as a mark of respect. Transf.: of persons, *to be roused to action*; of things, *to arise, break out.*

consurrectĭo -ōnis, f., *a general standing up.*

contābesco -tābescĕre -tābŭi, *to waste away gradually.*

contăbŭlātĭo -ōnis, f., *planking, floor, storey.*

contăbŭlo -are, *to cover with boards, equip with floors* or *storeys.*

contactus -ūs, m., *contact, touching; contagion.*

contāgēs -is, f., *touch, contact.*

contāgĭo -ōnis, f., and **contāgĭum** -i, n., *touching, contact*; hence *contagion, infection.*

contāmĭno -are, *to pollute, infect*; of authors, *to blend* (*and so spoil*) Greek plays.

contĕgo -tĕgĕre -texi -tectum, *to cover, shield.*

contemno -temnĕre -tempsi -temptum, *to think meanly of, despise, contemn.*

Hence partic. **contemptus** -a -um, *despised; despicable, contemptible.*

contemplātĭo -ōnis, f., *surveying, contemplation.*

contemplor -ari, dep., *to mark out*; hence *to look at attentively, survey, regard; to consider carefully.*

contemptim, *contemptuously.*

contemptĭo -ōnis, f., *contempt, scorn, disdain.*

contemptor -ōris, m., **contemptrix** -rīcis, f., adj. and subst., *a despiser, contemptuous.*

[1]**contemptus** -a -um, partic. from contemno; q.v.

[2]**contemptus** -ūs, m., *contempt, disdain.*

contendo -tendĕre -tendi -tentum, *to strain, stretch, exert*; of missiles, *to shoot, cast*; intransit., *to strive, strain, exert oneself, hasten*; of statements, *to assert with confidence, maintain.* In relation to another: transit., *to compare, contrast*; intransit., *to compete.*

Hence partic. **contentus** -a -um, *strained, stretched, tense; eager, zealous.* Adv. **contentē**, *eagerly, earnestly.*

[1]**contentē,** adv. from contendo; q.v.
[2]**contentē,** adv. from contineo; q.v.
contentĭo -ōnis, f., *exertion, effort, straining, striving.* In relation to another, *contrast, comparison*; or *combat, contest, strife.*
[1]**contentus** -a -um, partic. from contendo; q.v.
[2]**contentus** -a -um, *contented,* partic. from contineo; q.v.
contermĭnus -a -um, *bordering upon, adjacent, near.*
contĕro -tĕrĕre -trīvi -trītum, *to rub away, grind, pound*; in gen., *to wear away, destroy, obliterate*; of time, *to consume, spend.*
conterrĕo -ēre, *to terrify, frighten much.*
contestor -ari, dep. *to call to witness*; litem, *to start an action by calling witnesses*; partic. **contestātus** -a -um, in pass. sense, *witnessed to, approved.*
contexo -texĕre -texŭi -textum, *to weave* or *twine together, connect, unite, construct, form.*
Hence partic. **contextus** -a -um, *interwoven, connected, united.* adv. **contextē,** *in close connexion.*
[1]**contextus** -a -um, partic. from contexo; q.v.
[2]**contextus** -ūs, m., *uniting, connexion.*
contĭcesco (**contĭcisco**) -tĭcescĕre -tĭcŭi, *to become silent, be stilled, abate.*
contignātĭo -ōnis, f., *floor of planks.*
contigno -are, *to floor with planks.*
contĭgŭus -a -um, *touching, contiguous, near*; with dat., *within reach of.*
contĭnens -entis, partic. from contineo; q.v.
contĭnentĭa -ae, f., *self-control, moderation, temperance.*
contĭnĕo -tĭnēre -tĭnŭi -tentum. (1) *to hold together, keep together*; hence *to connect, join.* (2) *to keep in, surround, contain, confine*; hence *to include, comprise.* (3) *to hold back, restrain.* Hence pres. partic. **continens** -entis. (1) *lying near, adjacent.* (2) *hanging together, unbroken, continuous*; f. as subst., *a continent*; n. as subst., rhet., *a main point.* (3) *self-controlled, temperate, continent.* Adv. **continenter,** *without break, continuously*; *continently, temperately.* Partic. **contentus** -a -um, *contented, satisfied* (with abl.).
contingo -tingĕre -tĭgi -tactum: transit., *to touch, reach, grasp*; *to touch with* something, *smear* or *sprinkle* with; hence *to affect, infect* (esp. in perf. partic.); geograph. *to border on*; intransit., *to happen, befall,* usually of good luck (with dat.).
contĭnŭātĭo -ōnis, f., *unbroken continuance* or *succession*; rhet., *a period.*
contĭnŭĭtās -ātis, f., *continuity, unbroken succession.*
[1]**contĭnŭō,** adv. from continuus; q.v.
[2]**contĭnŭo** -are, *to connect up, unite, make continuous, form into a series*; verba, *to make into a sentence*; magistratum, *to prolong.*
contĭnŭus -a -um, *connected up, hanging together, continuous, uninterrupted.* N. abl. as adv. **contĭnŭō,** *immediately, at once*; in argument, *necessarily, as an immediate consequence.*
contĭo -ōnis, f., *an assembly, public meeting.* Transf. *a speech made in such an assembly,* or *the speaker's platform.*
contĭōnābundus -a -um, *haranguing, speaking in public.*
contĭōnālis -e and **contĭōnārĭus** -a -um, *relating to a public assembly.*
contĭōnātor -ōris, m., *a popular orator, demagogue.*
contĭōnor -ari, dep., *to attend an assembly*; esp. *to speak in public before an assembly.*
contĭuncŭla -ae, f., *a short harangue.*
contorquĕo -torquēre -torsi -tortum *to twist, whirl, turn violently, contort; to whirl* a spear, etc., in throwing, and so *to hurl.*
Hence partic. **contortus** -a -um. (1) *intricate, confused, complicated.* (2) *whirling*; so *powerful, vigorous.* Adv. **contortē,** *intricately.*
contortĭo -ōnis, f., *whirling, twisting, intricacy.*
contra. Adv., *opposite, over against, on the opposite side*; of equivalence, *in return, back*; of difference, *otherwise*; of opposition, *against.* Prep., with acc., *opposite to, over against; against, in opposition to.*
contractĭo -ōnis, f., *drawing together, contraction*; orationis, *abbreviation*; animi, *anxiety, depression.*
contractus -a -um, partic. from contraho; q.v.
contrādīco -dīcĕre -dixi -dictum, *to gainsay, contradict.*
contrādictĭo -ōnis, f., *a speaking against, contradiction.*
contrăho -trăhĕre -traxi -tractum. (1) *to draw together, collect, unite; to conclude* or *complete* any arrangement; in gen., *to cause, bring on, bring about*; aes alienum, *to contract debt.* (2) *to shorten, narrow, contract, reduce*; frontem, *to frown*; vela, *to furl one's sails*; of the spirits, *to depress.*
Hence partic. **contractus** -a -um, *contracted, narrow, straitened*; of persons, *retired quiet.*
contrārĭus -a -um, *opposite, opposed, contrary*; vulnera, *wounds in front*; with genit, or dat., *opposed to*; in gen., *hostile, injurious.* N. as subst. **contrārĭum** -i, *the opposite*; ex contrario, *on the other side.* Adv. **contrārĭē,** *in an opposite direction* or *manner.*
contrectātĭo -ōnis, f., *touching, handling.*
contrecto -are, *to touch, feel, handle*; of familiar handling, *to violate*; mentally, *to consider.*
contrĕmisco -trĕmiscĕre -trĕmŭi: intransit., *to tremble, quake*; transit., *to tremble before, be afraid of.*

contrĕmo -ĕre, *to tremble, quake.*
contrĭbŭo -trĭbŭĕre -trĭbŭi -trĭbūtum, *to brigade with, incorporate, unite*; of contributions, *to bring in.*
contristo -are, *to make sad* or *gloomy.*
contrītus -a -um, partic. from contero; q.v.
contrōversĭa -ae, f., *a dispute* (esp. at law); sine controversia, *indisputably.*
contrōversĭōsus -a -um, *strongly disputed.*
contrōversus -a -um, *disputed, controverted.*
contrŭcīdo -are, *to cut in pieces, hew down, slay.*
contrūdo -trūdĕre -trūsi -trūsum, *to thrust, push together.*
contrunco -are, *to cut in pieces.*
contŭbernālis -is, c. (1) *a messmate, comrade.* (2) *a young staff-officer.*
contŭbernĭum -i, n. Concrete, *a soldiers' tent; the common dwelling of a male and female slave.* Abstract, *comradeship, companionship, intimacy; concubinage; junior staff duties.*
contŭĕor -tŭēri -tŭĭtus, dep. *to see, survey, look at attentively*; mentally, *to consider, reflect upon.*
contŭĭtū (contūtū), abl. sing. m., *by surveying.*
contŭmācĭa -ae, f., *firmness, stubbornness, obstinacy.*
contŭmax -ācis, *firm, stubborn, obstinate*; adv. **contŭmācĭtĕr.**
contŭmēlĭa -ae, f. *outrage, physical violence*; of speech, *insult, affront.*
contŭmēlĭōsus -a -um, adj. *outrageous, insulting, abusive*; adv. **contŭmēlĭōsē.**
contŭmŭlo -are, *to bury, inter.*
contundo -tundĕre -tŭdi -tūsum, *to bruise, crush, pound, beat up, break up, demolish.*
contŭor -i = contueor; q.v.
conturbātĭo -ōnis f., *disorder, confusion.*
conturbo -are, *to throw into disorder, disturb, distress; to ruin, make bankrupt.*
contus -i, m. *a pole used in boating; a long spear or pike.*
cōnus -i, m., *a cone; the apex of a helmet.*
convălesco -vălescĕre -vălŭi, *to become strong, establish oneself*; esp. *to recover from a disease, get well.*
convallis -is, f., *an enclosed valley.*
convāso -are, *to pack up baggage.*
convecto -are, *to bring together, collect.*
convector -ōris, m. *a fellow-traveller.*
convĕho -vĕhĕre -vexi -vectum, *to bring together, carry into one place.*
convello -vellĕre -velli -vulsum, *to pluck up, pull away, wrench off*; milit., convellere signa, *to decamp*; in gen., *to weaken, overthrow, destroy.*
convĕna -ae, c.: adj., *coming together*; as subst., in plur., *a concourse, assembled multitude.*
convĕnĭentĭa -ae, f., *agreement, harmony, conformity.*
convĕnĭo -vĕnīre -vēni -ventum. (1) *to meet*: intransit., *to come together, assemble*; legal, convenire in manum, of the wife, *to come into the power of her husband*; transit., *to visit, meet, call upon.* (2) *to fit, be suitable, be congenial*; impers. convenit, *it is fitting.* (3) *to agree*; usually in pass. sense, *to be agreed upon;* impers., convenit, *it is agreed.*
Hence partic. **convĕnĭens** -entis, *agreeing, unanimous, concordant*; *fit, appropriate, suitable*; adv. **convenienter,** *agreeably, suitably.* N. of perf. partic. as subst., **conventum** -i, *an agreement, compact.*
conventĭcŭlum -i, n., *a coming together, assembly, association; a place of meeting.*
conventĭo -ōnis, f. *assembly; agreement, compact.*
conventum; see convenio.
conventus -ūs, m. *coming together, assembly, union, congress*; conventus agere, *to hold assizes*; in gen., *agreement.*
converro -verrĕre -verri -versum, *to sweep together, brush up; to beat thoroughly; to scrape together.*
conversātĭo -ōnis, f., *frequent use*; esp. *frequent sojourn in a place,* or *regular dealings with persons.*
conversĭo -ōnis, f. *a turning round, alteration,* or *periodical return*; rhet. *rounding off of a period,* or *repetition of word at the end of a clause.*
converso -are, *to turn round often*; pass. in middle sense, *to live, consort, have dealings.*
converto -vertĕre -verti -versum. (1) to *turn round, whirl round*; se convertere, *to revolve, to turn back*; milit., signa convertere, *to wheel round*; terga, or se, convertere, *to flee.* Transf., *to change, alter*; of books, *to translate.* (2) *to turn in any direction, direct*; conversus ad, *facing.* Transf., *to direct, devote* (esp. with reflex.; rarely intransit.); pecuniam publicam domum, *to embezzle.*
convestĭo -ire, *to clothe; to cover, surround.*
convexus -a -um. (1) *vaulted, arched, convex*; n. as subst., *arch.* (2) *sloping downwards.*
convīcĭātor -ōris, m., *a railer, reviler.*
convīcĭor -ari, dep., *to rail, revile.*
convīcĭum n. *a loud cry, shout, clamour*; esp. *abuse, reproach, insult*; hence, in gen., *censure, reproof*
convictĭo -ōnis, f. *intercourse, familiarity*; meton., *familiar friends.*
convictor -ōris, m., *a constant associate.*
convictus -ūs, m. *living together, intercourse; entertainment, feast.*
convinco -vincĕre -vīci -victum, *to convict of a crime; to prove mistaken*; of things, esp. crimes or mistakes, *to prove conclusively, demonstrate.*
convīso -ere, *to examine carefully*; poet. *to beam upon.*
convīva -ae, m. *guest.*
convīvālis -e, *of a feast.*
convīvātor -ōris, m. *a host.*

convīvĭum -i, n. *a feast, entertainment, banquet*; meton., *the company assembled, guests.*
convīvo -vīvĕre -vixi -victum, *to live with, to feast with.*
convīvor -ari, dep. *to feast* (as a guest).
convŏcātĭo -ōnis, f. *calling together.*
convŏco -are, *to call together, assemble, convoke.*
convŏlo -are, *to fly together, run together.*
convolvo -volvĕre -volvi -vŏlūtum, *to roll together* or *roll round; to intertwine.*
convŏmo -ere, *to vomit all over.*
convulsus -a -um, partic. of convello; q.v.
cŏŏpĕrĭo -ŏpĕrīre -ŏpĕrŭi -ŏpertum, *to cover up, envelop, overwhelm;* lapidibus *to stone to death.*
cŏoptātĭo -ōnis, f., *election of a colleague, co-optation*; censoria, *filling up of the senate by the censors.*
cŏopto -are, *to choose, elect, co-opt.*
cŏŏrĭor -ŏriri -ortus, dep., *to arise, come forth together*; of things, *to appear, to break out*; of people, *to rise for insurrection* or *fight.*
cŏortus -ūs, m., *arising, breaking forth.*
Cŏos (Cŏus) = Cos; q.v.
cŏphĭnus -i, m., *basket, hamper.*
cōpĭa -ae, f., *plenty, abundance* (of persons or things); milit., *supplies, provisions*; also *troops, forces* (esp. plur.). Transf., *means, opportunity*; with genit. of person, *access to.*
cōpĭōsus -a -um, *richly provided, wealthy; plentiful, abundant*; of speech, *copious, eloquent.* Adv. **cōpĭōsē,** *abundantly, plentifully, copiously.*
cōpo, cōpōna = caupo, caupona; q.v.
cōpŭla -ae, f., *a link, bond, tie, connexion; a rope, a leash*; plur. *grapnels.*
cōpŭlātĭo -ōnis, f., *union, connexion.*
cōpŭlo -are, *to join together, connect, unite.*
Hence partic. **cōpŭlātus** -a -um, *connected, united, coupled.*
cŏquo cŏquĕre coxi coctum, *to cook, prepare food; to burn, ripen; to digest*; mentally: *to think of, meditate, contrive* a thing; *to harass* a person.
cŏquus (cŏcus) -i, m. and **cŏqua** -ae, f., *a cook.*
cŏr, cordis, n., *the heart*; often as seat of emotions or thought, *heart, mind, judgment*; meton., *a person.*
cōram. Adv., *personally, openly, face to face.* Prep., with abl., *in presence of.*
corbis -is, m. and f. *a wicker basket.*
corbīta -ae, f., *a slow-sailing merchant vessel.*
corcŭlum -i, n., *little heart.*
Corcȳra -ae, f., *Corcyra, an island in the Ionian Sea.*
cordātus -a -um, *prudent, wise*; adv. **cordātē.**
Cordŭba -ae, f. *a town in Hispania Baetica* (now *Cordova*).
Cŏrinthus -i, f. *Corinth, a city of Greece.*
Cŏrĭŏli -orum, m. pl. *a town of the Volsci in Latium*; adj. **Cŏrĭŏlānus** -a -um.
cŏrĭum -i, n. *hide, skin, leather; a leathern thong, strap.*
Cornēlĭus -a -um, *name of a Roman* gens, *including the Scipios.* Adj. **Cornēlĭānus** -a -um.
cornĕŏlus -a -um, *horny.*
[1]**cornĕus** -a -um, *horny, made of horn; like horn, hard.*
[2]**cornĕus** -a -um, *of cornel-tree*; or *cornel-wood.*
cornĭcĕn -cĭnis, m., *a horn-blower.*
cornĭcŭlum -i, n. *a little horn; a horn-shaped decoration for soldiers.*
cornĭger -gĕra -gĕrum, *horned.*
cornĭpēs -pĕdis, *horn-footed, hoofed.*
cornix -īcis, f. *crow.*
cornū -ūs, n. *a horn*; fig., *strength, courage; anything made of horn,* esp. *a bow, trumpet, lantern; anything resembling a horn,* esp. *a hoof, beak, tip of a helmet, end of a stick* or *spar, end of a promontory, wing of an army.*
Cornūcōpĭa -ae, *the horn of Amalthea, symbol of plenty.*
cornum -i, n. *the cornel-cherry*; meton. *a spear of cornel-wood.*
cornus -i (and -ūs), f. *the cornel-tree*; hence *the wood of the cornel-tree, a spear of cornel-wood.*
cornūtus -a -um, *horned.*
cŏrolla -ae, f., *a little crown.*
cŏrollārĭum -i, n. *a garland of flowers; a present, gratuity.*
cŏrōna -ae, f. *garland, chaplet, crown*; sub corona vendere, *to sell into slavery prisoners of war* (*wearing chaplets*). Transf., *anything resembling a crown; a constellation; a circle of people, audience*; milit. *besiegers* (or *defenders*) *of a city.*
cŏrōnārĭus -a -um, *of a garland.*
cŏrōno -are, *to wreath, crown with a garland; to surround, enclose in a circle.*
corpŏrĕus -a -um, *of the body, bodily of flesh.*
corpŭlentus -a -um, *fat, stout.*
corpus -pŏris, n. *body, substance, matter*; esp. *the body* of men and animals; *flesh, the trunk*; sometimes *a corpse.* Transf., *a person,* "*a body*"; the "*body politic*"; in gen., *the main mass* of a thing.
corpuscŭlum -i, n. *a little particle, atom; a small body.*
corrādo -rādĕre -rāsi -rāsum, *to scrape* or *rake together.*
correctĭo -ōnis, f., *straightening out, improvement, amendment.*
corrector -ōris, m. *improver, amender, corrector.*
corrēpo -rēpere -repsi -reptum, *to creep, slink, crawl.*
correptĭus, compar. adv. from corripio; q.v.
corrĭgĭa -ae, f. *a shoe-string, boot-lace.*
corrĭgo -rĭgĕre -rexi -rectum, *to put straight, set right, reform, amend.*
corrĭpĭo -rĭpĕre -rĭpŭi -reptum, *to seize, snatch up*; **pecuniam,** *to steal*;

viam, *to hasten on a journey*; se, *to hurry off*. Transf., of disease, etc., *to attack*; of the passions, *to overcome*; of persons, *to blame, rebuke, accuse, bring to trial*; in time, *to shorten*; hence, from partic., compar. adv. **correptius,** *more shortly*.

corrōbŏro -are, *to strengthen, invigorate*.

corrōdo -rōdere -rōsi, -rōsum, *to gnaw away*.

corrŏgo -are, *to get together, collect by begging*.

corrūgo -are, *to wrinkle up*.

corrumpo -rumpĕre -rūpi -ruptum. (1) *to break up, destroy, annihilate*. (2) *to spoil, make worse, weaken*; of documents, *to falsify*; of characters, *to corrupt*; corrumpere pecuniā, *to bribe*.

Hence partic. **corruptus** -a -um, *spoilt, damaged, corrupt*; adv. **corruptē,** *corruptly, incorrectly*.

corrŭo -rŭere -rŭi: intransit. *to fall to the ground, sink down, be ruined*; transit., *to throw down, overthrow*.

corruptēla -ae, f., *corruption, bribery, seduction*; meton., *a corrupter*.

corruptĭo -ōnis, f. *corrupting; a corrupt state*.

corruptor -ōris, m. *corrupter, seducer, briber*.

corruptus -a -um, partic. from corrumpo; q.v.

cors = cohors; q.v.

Corsĭca -ae, f. *the island of Corsica*; adj. **Corsus** and **Corsĭcus** -a -um.

cortex -tĭcis, m. and f. *bark, rind, shell*; esp. *the bark of the cork tree, cork*.

cortīna -ae, f. *a round kettle or cauldron*; esp. *the cauldron-shaped Delphic tripod*: cortina Phoebi, *the oracle of Apollo*.

cŏrŭlus = corylus; q.v.

cōrus = caurus; q.v.

cŏrusco -are: transit., *to move quickly, swing, shake*; intransit., *to tremble, flutter*; of light, *to twinkle, flash*.

cŏruscus -a -um, *shaking, trembling*: of light, *twinkling, flashing*.

corvus -i, m. *a raven*; perhaps also *a rook*.

Cŏrўbantes -ium, m. pl. *the priests of Cybele*.

cōrўcus -i, m. *a sand-bag, a punch-ball*.

cŏrўlētum -i, n. *a hazel copse*.

cŏrўlus -i, f. *a hazel tree*.

cŏrymbus -i, m. *a bunch of flowers* or *fruit*, esp. *a cluster of ivy berries*.

cŏrўphaeus -i, m. *a leader, chief*.

cōrўtus or **cōrўtos** -i, m. *a quiver*.

[1]**cōs** cōtis, f. *any hard, flinty stone*; esp. *a whetstone, grindstone*.

[2]**Cōs** or **Cōus** (**Cŏos**) Coi, f. *a small island in the Aegean Sea*; adj. **Cōus** -a -um; n. sing. as subst., *Coan wine*; n. plur., *Coan garments*.

cosmēta -ae, m. *a woman's valet*.

cosmĭcos -a -um, *of the world*; m. as subst. *a citizen of the world*.

costa -ae, f. *a rib* or *side*.

costum -i, n. *an eastern aromatic plant*.

cŏthurnātus -a -um, *in buskins*; hence *tragic, elevated*.

cŏthurnus -i, m. *a large hunting boot; a boot* or *buskin worn by tragic actors*; hence *tragedy, elevated style*.

cotid. = cottid.; q.v.

cottăna (**cotŏna, coctŏna, coctăna**) -orum, n. *a kind of small fig*.

cŏturnix -īcis, f. *a quail*.

cŏvinnārĭus -i, m. *a soldier in a war chariot*.

cŏvinnus -i, m. *a war-chariot; a travelling-chariot*.

coxa -ae, f. *the hip-bone*.

coxendix -īcis, f. *the hip*.

crabro -ōnis, m. *a hornet*.

crambē -ēs, f. *cabbage*.

crāpŭla -ae, f. *drunkenness*; its *after-effects*, "*hangover*".

crās, *tomorrow*.

crassĭtūdo -ĭnis, f. *thickness, density*.

[1]**crassus** -a -um, *thick, dense, solid*; aer, *misty, heavy*; of intellect, *dull* or *uneducated*. Adv. **crassē,** *roughly, rudely*.

[2]**Crassus** -i, m. *name of a family in the* gens Licinia; q.v.

crastĭnus -a -um, *of tomorrow*; n. as subst. *the morrow*.

crātēra -ae, f. and **crātēr** -ēris, m. *a bowl*, esp. *for mixing wine with water; the crater of a volcano; a constellation, the Bowl*.

crātis -is, *a wicker frame, hurdle, a harrow*; milit. *fascines*; favorum, *honeycomb*; spinae, *the joints of the backbone*.

crĕātĭo -ōnis, f., *choice, election*.

crĕātor -ōris, m. and **crĕātrix** -īcis, f. *maker, founder; parent*.

crēber -bra -brum; of space, *thick, crowded together, close, numerous*; with abl., *crowded with, full of*; of time, *repeated, numerous, frequent*; of persons, to signify *repeated* action, e.g. creber pulsat, *he beats repeatedly*. Adv. **crēbrō,** *repeatedly, often*.

crēbresco (**crēbesco**) -escĕre -ŭi, *to become frequent, increase, gather strength*.

crēbrĭtās -ātis, f. *frequency*.

crēbrō, adv. from creber; q.v.

crēdĭbĭlis -e, *credible, worthy of belief*; adv. **crēdĭbĭlĭter,** *credibly*.

crēdĭtor -ōris, m., *a creditor*.

crēdo -dĕre -dĭdi -dĭtum, *to trust*: with acc. and dat., *to entrust, commit*, esp. of secrets and money; n. of perf. partic. as subst., creditum, a loan; with dat., *to trust in, rely upon*; also with dat., *to believe, give credence to*; with acc., *to believe as a fact, to accept as true*; in gen., *to believe, think, be of opinion*.

crēdŭlĭtās -ātis, f., *credulity*.

crēdŭlus -a -um, *believing easily, credulous, confiding*.

crĕmo -are, *to burn, consume with fire*.

crĕmor -ōris, m. *juice, pulp, cream*.

crĕo -are, *to make, create, produce; to elect* to an office; of parents, *to beget, bear*.

crĕpĭda -ae, f. *sandal*.

crĕpĭdātus -a -um, *wearing sandals*.

crĕpīdo -ĭnis, f., *a base, foundation, pedestal; a quay, pier, dam.*
crĕpĭtācŭlum and **crĕpĭtācillum** -i, n. *a rattle.*
crĕpĭto -are, *to rattle, creak, crackle, rustle.*
crĕpĭtus -ūs, m. *rattling, creaking, rustling, clattering*: digitorum, *snapping of the fingers.*
crĕpo -are -ŭi -ĭtum: intransit., *to creak, rattle, rustle, crackle*; digiti crepantis signa, *a snapping of the fingers*; transit., *to make resound; to chatter about.*
crĕpundĭa -orum, n. pl. *a child's plaything; a rattle* or *amulet.*
crĕpuscŭlum -i, n. *twilight.*
cresco crescĕre crēvi crētum. (1) *to come into existence, spring forth, arise*; past partic. cretus, *sprung* (*from*). (2) of what exists, *to grow, grow up, increase in size, height*, etc.; luna crescens, *waxing*; fig., *to increase in fame, power*, etc.
[1]**Crēta** -ae, f. and **Crētē** -ēs, f. *Crete.* Hence m. adj. and subst. **Crēs** -ētis; f. adj. and subst. **Cressa** -ae; adj. **Crētensis** -e, and **Crētĭcus** -a -um, *Cretan.*
[2]**crēta** -ae, f. *chalk*, or *fuller's earth.*
crētātus -a -um, *chalked*; hence *in white.*
crētĭo -ōnis, f. *a declaration by an heir accepting an inheritance.*
crētōsus -a -um, *abounding in chalk.*
crētŭla -ae, f. *white clay for sealing.*
Crĕūsa -ae, f. *wife of Aeneas.*
crībrum -i, n. *a sieve.*
crīmen -ĭnis, n. (1) *an accusation, charge*: esse in crimine, *to be accused*; meton., *an object of reproach.* (2) *fault, guilt, crime*; meton., *cause of crime.*
crīmĭnātĭo -ōnis, f. *accusation, calumny, charge.*
crīmĭnātor -ōris, m. *accuser, calumniator.*
crīmĭnor -ari, dep: with acc. of person, *to accuse, charge*; esp. *to calumniate*; with acc. of offence, *to complain of, bring up.*
crīmĭnōsus -a -um, *reproachful, calumnious, slanderous*; adv. **crīmĭnōsē**, *by way of accusation, reproachfully.*
crīnālis -e, *of* or *for the hair*; n. as subst. a *hair-band.*
crīnis -is, m. *hair*; esp. in pl.; of a comet, *the tail.*
crīnītus -a -um, *hairy, with long hair*; stella crinita, *a comet*; galea, *crested.*
crispĭsulcans -antis, *forked, wavy.*
crispo -are, *to curl; to move rapidly, brandish*; intransit. partic. **crispans** -antis, *curled, wavy.*
crispŭlus -a -um, *curly-haired, curly.*
crispus -a -um, *curly, curly-headed; trembling, quivering.*
crista -ae, f., *the crest, plume*; of a cock, *the comb.*
cristātus -a -um, *with a crest, plume* or *comb.*
crŏcĕus -a -um, *of saffron; saffron-coloured, golden, yellow.*
crŏcĭnus -a -um, *of saffron, saffron-coloured, yellow*; n. as subst. *saffron oil.*
crŏcŏdīlus -i, m. *crocodile.*
crŏcōtŭla -ae, f., *a saffron-coloured robe.*
crŏcus -i, m. and **crŏcum** -i n. *the crocus*; *saffron*, prepared from crocus; hence *the colour of saffron, yellow.*
Croesus -i, m., *a king of Lydia, famous for his wealth.*
crŏtălĭa -orum, n. *ear-rings.*
crŏtălistrĭa -ae, f. *a castanet-dancer*
crŏtălum -i, n. *a castanet.*
Crŏtōn -ōnis, c. *a Greek town near the "toe" of Italy.*
crŭcĭāmentum -i, n. *torture.*
crŭcĭātus -ūs, m., *torture, torment.*
crŭcĭo -are, *to torture, torment.*
crūdēlis -e, adj. *unfeeling, cruel*; adv. **crūdēlĭter.**
crūdēlĭtās -ātis, f., *cruelty, inhumanity.*
crūdesco -escĕre -ŭi, *to become hard* or *violent.*
crūdĭtās -ātis, f., *overloading of the stomach, indigestion.*
crūdus -a -um, adj. (1) *bleeding.* (2) *uncooked, raw*; of material, *fresh, not prepared*; of fruit *unripe*, in gen. *green, fresh, immature, untimely*; of food, *undigested*; of persons, *stuffed, dyspeptic*; of feeling, etc., *hard, cruel*; of the voice, *harsh.*
crŭento -are, *to make bloody, stain with blood.*
crŭentus -a -um, *bloody, bloodthirsty; blood-red.*
crŭmēna -ae, f. *a pouch, purse; store of money, funds.*
crŭor -ōris, m. *blood shed, gore; murder, slaughter.*
crūs crūris, n. *the shin, shin-bone, leg*; of a bridge, *pier, support.*
crusta -ae, f. (1) *crust, rind, shell, bark.* (2) *inlaid work, bas-relief, embossing.*
crustŭlum -i, n. *a little cake.*
crustum -i, n. *bread, cake.*
crux crŭcis, f. *a cross*; hence *torment, trouble*; as a term of abuse, *gallows bird.*
crypta -ae, f. *covered gallery, vault. grotto.*
crystallĭnus -a -um, *of crystal*; pl. as subst., *crystal vases.*
crystallus -i, f. and **crystallum** -i, n. *crystal; a crystal drinking vessel; a precious stone looking like crystal.*
cŭbĭcŭlāris -e, *of a bedchamber.*
cŭbĭcŭlārĭus -a -um, *of a bedchamber*; m. as subst. *a chamber-servant.*
cŭbĭcŭlum -i, n. *bedroom.*
cŭbīle -is, n. *bed*; esp. *marriage-bed*; of animals, *lair, den, nest*; of bees, *hives*; in. gen., *seat, resting-place.*
cŭbĭtal -tālis, n., *an elbow cushion.*
cŭbĭtālis -e, *one cubit long.*
cŭbĭto -are, *to lie down often.*
cŭbĭtum -i, n. *the elbow; a cubit.*
cŭbĭtus -ūs, m. *lying down.*
cŭbo -are -ŭi -ĭtum, *to lie down, recline*; esp. at table or in bed; *to be ill in bed*; cubitum ire, *to go to bed*; of things, *to lie*; partic. cubans, *sloping.*

cŭcullus -i, m. *a hood, cowl.*
cŭcūlus -i, m. *cuckoo.*
cŭcŭmis -mĕris, m. *cucumber.*
cŭcurbĭta -ae, f. *a gourd; a cupping-glass.*
cūdo -ĕre, *to beat, pound, thresh*; of metals, *to forge, stamp, coin.*
cūiās -ātis, *of what country?*
cuicuimŏdi *of whatever kind.*
cūius (quoius) -a -um: interrog., *whose?*; relat., *whose*; quoia causa, *wherefore.*
cūiuscĕmŏdi, *of whatever kind.*
cūiusdammŏdi, *of a certain kind.*
cūiusmŏdi, *of what kind?*
cūiusquĕmŏdi, *of every kind.*
culcĭta -ae, f. *bolster, pillow.*
cūlĕus = culleus; q.v.
cŭlex -ĭcis, m. *gnat, midge.*
cŭlīna -ae, f. *kitchen*; meton., *food, fare.*
cullĕus (cūlĕus) -i, m. *a leather sack.*
culmen -ĭnis, n. *top, summit; the ridge of a roof; a stalk.*
culmus -i, m. *stalk, haulm, thatch.*
culpa -ae, f. *fault, blame*; esp. *the fault of unchastity*; meton., *a cause of error* or *sin.*
culpo -are, *to blame, find fault with, disapprove.*
cultellus -i, m. *a little knife.*
culter -tri, m. *a knife; a ploughshare, coulter.*
cultĭo -ōnis, f. *cultivation, agriculture.*
cultor -ōris, m., *a cultivator, planter, husbandman*; with genit., *an inhabitant, occupier* of a place; *a friend, supporter* of a person; *a worshipper* of gods.
cultrix -īcis f. *she who tends* or *takes care*; *an inhabitant.*
cultūra -ae, f. *tilling, culture, cultivation, husbandry;* animi, *mental culture, cultivation*; potentis amici, *courting of.*
[1]**cultus** -a -um, partic. from colo; q.v.
[2]**cultus** -ūs, m. *tilling, cultivation, tending*; in gen., *care, careful treatment*; deorum, *reverence*, animi, *training, education*; hence *refinement, culture, civilization.*
cŭlullus -i, m. *a drinking-vessel.*
[1]**cum** (older form quom) conj., *when; whenever; since; although*; cum . . . tum . . ., *both . . . and. . . .*
[2]**cum,** prep., with abl., *with, together with; at the same time as*; cum eo quod, ut, or ne, *on condition that.*
Cūmae -arum, f. *a city of Campania*; adj. **Cūmānus** and **Cūmaeus** -a -um.
cumba (cymba) -ae, f. *small boat, skiff.*
cŭmĕra -ae, f. a *corn-bin.*
cŭmīnum -i, n. *a herb, cummin.*
cumprimis, see primus.
cumque (cunque, quomque), adverb, usually found added to a relative, with the force of *-ever, -soever.*
cŭmŭlo -are, *to heap up, pile up, increase, heighten; to fill up, overload*; cumulatus laude, *loaded with praise*; also *to crown, bring to perfection.*
Hence partic. **cŭmŭlātus** -a -um: *heaped up, increased, enlarged; crowned perfected.* Adv. **cŭmŭlātē,** *abundantly, fully.*
cŭmŭlus -i, m. *heap, pile, mass; addition, increase, finishing touch.*
cūnābŭla -orum, n. pl. *cradle.*
cūnae -arum, f. pl., *cradle*, of young birds, *nest.*
cunctābundus -a -um, *loitering, dilatory.*
cunctātĭo -ōnis, f. *delay, lingering hesitation.*
cunctātor -ōris, m. *one who delays.*
cunctor -ari, dep. *to delay, linger, hesitate*; of things, *to move slowly.*
Hence partic. **cunctans** -antis, *lingering, slow*; adv. **cunctanter.**
cunctus -a -um, *all, all collectively, the whole.*
cŭnĕātim, *in wedge formation.*
cŭnĕo -are, to *secure with wedges; to shape like a wedge.*
Hence partic. **cŭnĕātŭs** -a -um, *pointed like a wedge.*
cŭnĕus -i, m. *a wedge; troops in wedge formation; any triangular figure;* often of *the wedge-shaped compartments into which the seats of a theatre were divided.*
cŭnīcŭlōsus -a -um, *full of rabbits* (or *of caverns*).
cŭnīcŭlus -i, m. (1) *a rabbit, cony.* (2) *an underground passage*; milit. *a mine.*
cūpa -ae, f. *cask, butt.*
cŭpĭdĭtās -ātis, f. *eager desire, passionate longing.* Esp. *ambition; avarice, factiousness, party spirit.*
cŭpīdo -ĭnis, f. and poet. m., *longing, desire.* Esp. *desire for power, ambition; avarice*; physical *desire, love.* Personified, **Cŭpīdo** -ĭnis, m. *Cupid*, god of love; plur. **Cŭpīdĭnes,** *Cupids*; adj. **Cŭpīdĭnĕus** -a -um.
cŭpĭdus -a -um, *desirous, eager, keen.* Esp. *eager for power, ambitious; avaricious*; physically, *desirous, passionate*; towards persons, *attached, partial.* Adv. **cŭpĭdē,** *eagerly, passionately.*
cŭpĭo cŭpĕre cŭpīvi or -ĭi -ītum, *to desire, long for, wish for.*
Hence partic. **cŭpĭens** -entis *longing, eager*; as adj., with genit.; adv. **cŭpĭenter.**
cŭpītor -ōris, m. *one who desires.*
[1]**cuppēdĭa** -ae, f. *taste for delicacies.*
[2]**cuppēdĭa** -orum, n. pl. *delicacies, tit-bits.*
cuppēdĭnārius -i, m. *a confectioner.*
cuppēdo = cupido; q.v.
cupressētum -i, n. *a cypress wood.*
cupressĕus -a -um, *made of cypress wood.*
cupressĭfer -fĕra -fĕrum, *cypress-bearing.*
cupressus -i (-ūs), f. *the cypress; a casket of cypress wood.*
cūr (quor) *why? wherefore?*
cūra -ae, f. *care*: (1) *care taken, carefulness, pains, attention, minding* of things or persons; of business, *management, administration*; meton., *an object of care*, or *a guardian, care-*

taker. (2) *care felt, anxiety, worry, disquiet.*

cūrălium -i, n. *coral*, esp. *red coral.*

cūrātio -ōnis, f. *care, attention*; esp. *medical attention, healing, curing*; of business *management, administration*; frumenti, *commission to buy corn*; agraria, *commission to divide land.*

cūrātor -ōris, m. *guardian, overseer.*

cūrātus, partic. from curo; q.v.

curcŭlio -onis, m. *a weevil, corn-worm.*

Cŭrēs -ium, f. *a town of the Sabines*; adj. **Cŭrensis** -e.

Cūrētes -um, m. *ancient inhabitants of Crete*; adj. **Cūrētis** -ĭdis = *Cretan.*

cūrĭa -ae, f. (1) *a curia, a division of the Roman patricians*; meton., *the meeting-place of a* curia. (2) *the meeting-place of the senate, senate-house*; at Athens, *the Areopagus.*

cūrĭālis -e, *belonging to the same* curia.

cūrĭātim, *by* curiae.

cūrĭātus -a -um, *relating to* curiae; comitia curiata, *the original assembly of the Roman people.*

cūrĭo -ōnis, m. *the priest of a* curia; *a herald, crier.*

cūrĭōsĭtās -atis, *inquisitiveness.*

cūrĭōsus -a -um. (1) *careful, attentive.* (2) *inquisitive.* (3) *wasted by cares.* Adv. **cūrĭōsē,** *carefully; inquisitively.*

cŭris or **quĭris,** f. *a spear.*

cūro -are, *to care for, pay attention to, trouble about*; with gerundive *to see to* a thing being done; of business, *to manage, administer*; physically, *to minister to, cure, rest*; in business *to provide* or *procure* money; curare Romae, *to be in charge at Rome.*

Hence partic. **cūrātus** -a -um, *cared for; showing care.* Compar. adv. **cūrātĭus,** *more carefully.*

currĭcŭlum -i, n. *running; a contest in running, race; raceground, course lap; a racing chariot.*

curro currĕre cŭcurri cursum, *to run, hasten*; esp. *to run in a race*; at sea, *to sail*; of time, *to pass.*

currus -ūs, m. *a chariot, car*; esp. one used in racing, or war, or at a triumph; meton., *a triumph.* Transf., *a plough with wheels; a ship.*

cursim, *hastily, quickly.*

cursĭto -are, *to run up and down.*

curso -are, *to run hither and thither.*

cursor -ōris, m. *a runner; a courier, messenger; a running footman.*

cursus -ūs, m. *running, rapid motion; course, direction, movement, journey.*

curto -are, *to shorten, abbreviate.*

curtus -a -um, *shortened, mutilated, defective*; esp. *gelded.*

cŭrūlis -e, *relating to a chariot*; equi, *horses provided for the Circus*; (sella) curulis, *the curule chair*, official seat of consuls, praetors, and curule aediles.

curvāmen -ĭnis, n. and **curvātūra** -ae, f. *curving, arching.*

curvo -are, *to bend, arch, curve; to influence.*

curvus -a -um, *bent, bowed, arched, curved, winding*; morally, *crooked.*

cuspis -ĭdis, f. *point*, esp. *of a spear*; hence *a spear, lance; a trident; a spit.*

custōdĭa -ae, f. *watching, guarding, custody, care*; milit., *keeping guard, watch*; of prisoners, *custody, safe-keeping*; custodia libera, *house-arrest.* Transf., *persons guarding, guards, sentinels; the station of the guard, post, prison; persons guarded, prisoners.*

custōdĭo -ire, *to guard, watch, keep, take care of; to keep in sight, observe; to keep in prison, hold captive.*

custōs -ōdis, c. *guardian, watchman, keeper, attendant; a gaoler, sentinel guard, spy.*

cŭtīcŭla -ae, f. *skin, cuticle.*

cŭtis -is, f. *skin, hide, leather.*

cy̆ăthus -i, m. *a ladle for filling goblets with wine*; as *measure of capacity* = one-twelfth of a sextarius.

cy̆baea -ae, f. (with or without navis), *a merchantman.*

Cy̆bĕlē or **Cy̆bēbē** -ēs f. *a Phrygian goddess, worshipped at Rome.*

[2]**cyclas** -ădis, f., *a female robe of state.*

[1]**Cyclas** -ădis, f., gen. plur., **Cyclădes**, *a group of islands in the Aegean Sea.*

cyclĭcus -a -um, *cyclic.*

Cyclops -clōpis, m. *a Cyclops*, gen. plur., **Cyclōpes**, *the Cyclopes, a gigantic one-eyed race*; adj. **Cyclōpĭus** -a -um.

cycnēus or **cygnēus** -a -um, *belonging to the swan.*

cycnus or **cygnus** -i, m. *the swan.*

cy̆lindrus -dri, m. *a cylinder; a roller.*

Cyllēnē -ēs and -ae, f. *a mountain in Arcadia, where Mercury was born.* Adj. **Cyllēnēus** and **Cyllēnĭus** -a -um.

cymba -ae, f. = cumba; q.v.

cymbălum -i, n. *a cymbal.*

cymbĭum -i, n., *a small drinking-vessel.*

Cy̆nĭcus -a -um *Cynic, of the Cynic school.*

cy̆nŏcĕphălus -i m. *the dog-faced baboon.*

Cy̆nŏsūra -ae, f., *the constellation Ursa Minor.*

Cynthus -i, m. *a mountain in Delos, birth-place of Apollo and Diana*; hence adj. as subst., m. **Cynthius** -i, *Apollo*, f. **Cynthia** -ae, *Diana.*

Cy̆părissus, f. = cupressus; q.v.

Cyprus or **Cypros** -i, f., *the island of Cyprus*; adj. **Cyprĭus** -a -um, *Cyprian*; f. as subst. *Venus.*

Cy̆rēne -es and **Cy̆rēnae** -arum, f. *a city of north-eastern Africa*; adj. **Cy̆rēnaeus and Cy̆rēnăĭcus** -a -um, *Cyrenaic*; m. pl. as subst., *the Cyrenaic philosophers.*

Cy̆thēra -orum, n., *the island Cythera, sacred to Venus*; adj. **Cy̆thĕrēus** and **Cy̆thĕrēĭus** -a -um, *Cytherean*; f. as subst. = *Venus.*

cy̆tĭsus -i, c. *clover* or *lucerne.*

D

D, d the fourth letter of the Latin alphabet.

Dāci -orum, m. *the Dacians, a warlike people on the Lower Danube.* **Dācĭa** -ae, f. *their country.*

dactȳlĭcus -a -um, *dactylic.*

dactȳlĭŏthēca -ae, f. *a casket for rings.*

dactȳlŭs -i, m. *a metrical foot, a dactyl* (— ˘ ˘).

daedălus -a -um: act., *skilful;* (natura) daedala rerum, *quaint artificer;* pass., *curiously wrought, variegated.*

[2]**Daedălus** -i. m., *mythical Athenian, builder of the Cretan labyrinth;* adj. **Daedălēus** and **Daedălĭus** -a -um.

Dalmătae (Delmătae) -arum, m. pl., *the Dalmatians, inhabitants of Dalmatia.*

Dămascus -i, f. *Damascus, capital of Syria;* adj. **Dămascēnus** -a -um. *Damascene;* pruna, *damsons.*

damma (older **dāma**) -ae, f. or m. *a fallow-deer, chamois, antelope:* as meat *venison.*

damnātĭo -ōnis, f. *condemnation.*

damnātōrĭus -a -um, *condemnatory.*

damno -are, *to cause loss* or *injury to;* at law, *to condemn, sentence, punish* (offence usually genit., punishment genit. or abl.); damnari inter sicarios, *to be condemned as an assassin;* in gen., *to condemn, disapprove of;* of deities, damnare voti *or* voto, *to grant a person's wish, and compel him to discharge his vow;* also *to assign, devote, make over.*

damnōsus -a -um: act., *causing loss* or *damage, detrimental;* pass., *damaged, injured;* middle sense, *self-injuring.* Adv. **damnōsē,** *ruinously.*

damnum -i, n. *loss, damage, injury;* at law, *a fine.*

Dănăē -ēs, f. *mother of Perseus.*

Dănăus -i, m. *son of Belus, who left Egypt for Argos;* adj. **Dănăus** -a -um, *Argive, Greek;* m. pl. **Dănăi** -orum, *the Greeks;* **Dănăĭdes** -um, f. *the fifty daughters of Danaus.*

dănīsta -ae, m. *money-lender.*

dăno = old form of do; q.v.

Dānŭvĭus -i, m. *the Danube.*

Daphnē -ēs, f. *daughter of Peneus, changed into a laurel-tree.*

daphnōn -ōnis, m. *a grove of laurels.*

daps, dăpis, f. *a sacrificial feast, religious banquet;* in gen., *meal, feast, banquet.*

dapsĭlis -e, *sumptuous, plentiful.*

Dardăni -orum, m. pl. *a warlike Illyrian people.*

Dardănus -i, m. *son of Jupiter, mythical ancestor of the royal family of Troy;* adj. **Dardănus** and **Dardănĭus** -a -um, *Trojan;* subst. **Dardănĭa** -ae, f. = *Troy;* **Dardănĭdes** -ae, m. *a male descendant of Dardanus;* **Dardănis** -ĭdis, *a Trojan woman.*

Dārēus -i, m. *name of several Persian kings.*

dătĭo -ōnis, f. *a giving;* legal, *right of alienation.*

dătīvus -a -um, *to do with giving;* (casus) dativus, *the dative case.*

dăto -are, *to give away.*

dător -ōris, m. *giver.*

Daunus -i, m. *a mythical king of Apulia, ancestor of Turnus;* adj. **Daunĭus** -a -um, *Daunian;* f. subst., **Daunĭas** -ădis, *Apulia.*

dē, prep., with abl. (1) in space, *down from, away from.* Transf., *coming from* an origin; *taken from* a class or stock, *made from* a material, *changed from* a previous state; of information, *from* a source. (2) in time; *following from, after; in the course of, during.* (3) *about* a subject; *on account of* a cause; *according to* a standard.

dĕa -ae, f. *goddess.*

dĕalbo -are, *to whitewash, plaster.*

dĕambŭlo -are, *to take a walk.*

dĕarmo -are, *to disarm.*

dēbacchor -ari, dep. *to rave, revel furiously.*

dēbellātor -ōris, m., *a conqueror.*

dēbello -are: intransit., *to fight to the end, finish a war;* transit. *to fight out* a fight; *to conquer* an enemy.

dēbĕo -ēre -ŭi -itum, *to owe.* Lit. of money, etc.; n. of perf. partic. pass. as subst., debitum -i, *a debt.* Transf., *to be indebted* to somebody for anything; with infin., *to be due to* do a thing, *be morally bound to* or *be bound by logic* or *necessity* or *law to; to have to pay* because of fate, *to be destined to give.*

dēbĭlis -e, *feeble, weak.*

dēbĭlĭtās -ātis, f. *weakness, feebleness.*

dēbĭlĭtātĭo -ōnis, f. *weakening, disabling.*

dēbĭlĭto -are, *to weaken, enfeeble, disable; to enervate, break down.*

dēbĭtĭo -ōnis, f. *owing, debt.*

dēbĭtor -ōris, m. *one who owes, a debtor.*

dēbĭtum -i, subst. from debeo; q.v.

dēcanto -are: transit., *to sing* or *say repeatedly;* intransit., *to leave off singing.*

dēcēdo -cēdĕre -cessi -cessum. (1) *to move away, withdraw, retire;* milit. *to march away.* Transf., *to retire, give up;* with dat., *to yield to, retire in favour of,* esp. *to depart from life, to die.* (2) of things, *to retire, abate, cease;* sol decedens, *setting.* (3) *to go astray, deviate.*

dĕcem, indecl. *ten.*

Dĕcember -bris, adj. *of December* (originally the tenth Roman month); December (mensis), *December.*

dĕcempĕda -ae, f. *a ten-foot rule.*

dĕcempĕdātor -ōris, m. *a land-surveyor.*

dĕcemprīmi -orum, m. pl. *the ten chief men in the senate of a municipium* or *colonia.*

dĕcemvir -i, m.; usually plur., *a board of ten commissioners at Rome* for various purposes.

dĕcemvĭrālis -e *relating to the decemvirs.*

dĕcemvĭratus -ūs, m. *the office of decemvir.*

dĕcennis -e, *of ten years.*
dĕcens -entis, partic. from decet; q.v.
dĕcentĭa -ae, f., *propriety, comeliness*
dēcerno -cernĕre -crēvi -crētum, *to decide, determine; to settle that* a thing is so; and of action, *to decide to do* or *to give* a thing; of a body, *to decide, decree*; as a member of a body, *to move, propose*; of combatants, *to settle by fighting.*
Hence partic. **dēcrētus** -a -um; n. as subst. **dēcrētum** -i, *a resolve, decree*; philosoph. *doctrine, principle.*
dēcerpo -cerpĕre -cerpsi -cerptum, *to pluck off, pluck away.* Transf., *to gather; to derive; to take away.*
dēcertātĭo -onis, f. *contest.*
dēcerto -are, *to contend, fight to a finish.*
dēcessĭo -ōnis, f., *a withdrawing, departure*; esp. *of a governor retiring from his province.* Transf., *deduction, diminution.*
dēcessor -ōris, m., *one who retires from an office, a predecessor.*
dēcessus -ūs, m. *withdrawal, departure.* Esp. *the retirement of an official; death*; of water, *ebb.*
dĕcet -ēre -ŭit, *it is proper, it is fitting* (physically or morally).
Hence partic. **dĕcens** -entis, *proper, fit*; adv. **dĕcenter.**
[1]**dēcĭdo** -cĭdĕre -cĭdi, *to fall down, to fall dead, die*; in gen., *to sink, fall.*
[2]**dēcīdo** -cīdĕre -cīdi -cīsum, *to cut down, cut off; to cut short, to settle, to arrange.*
dĕcĭens and **dĕcĭēs,** *ten times.*
decim-; see also decum-.
dĕcĭmus (older **dĕcŭmus**) -a -um, *tenth*; decimum, *for the tenth time.*
dēcĭpĭo -cĭpĕre -cēpi -ceptum, *to catch*; hence *to cheat, deceive, beguile* (esp. of time).
dēcīsĭo -onis, f. *a settlement, decision.*
Dĕcĭus -a -um, *name of a Roman* gens; adj. **Dĕcĭānus** -a -um.
dēclāmātĭo -ōnis, f., *loud, violent speaking, declamation; practice in oratory,* or *a theme* for such practice.
dēclāmātor -ōris, m. *a declaimer.*
dēclāmātōrĭus -a -um, *of declamation, rhetorical.*
dēclāmĭto -are, *to speak loudly, declaim*; esp. *to practise public speaking*; causas, *to plead for practice.*
dēclāmo -are, *to speak loudly*; esp. *to practise speaking in public*; with object, *to declaim.*
dēclārātĭo -ōnis, f. *making clear, open expression.*
dēclāro -are, *to make clear, explain, reveal, declare*; of appointments, *to proclaim* a person as chosen.
dēclīnātĭo -ōnis, f. *bending away, turning aside.* Transf., *an avoiding, declining*; rhet. *a digression*; grammat. *inflexion, declension.*
dēclīno -are: transit., *to bend aside, turn away, deflect.* Transf., *to avoid, to shun*; intransit., *to deviate, swerve, digress.*
dēclīvis -e, *inclined downwards, sloping*; n. as subst. **dēclīvĕ** -is, *a slope declivity.*
dēclīvĭtās -ātis, f., *a declivity.*
dēcocta -ae, f. subst. from decoquo; q.v.
dēcoctor -ōris, m., *spendthrift, bankrupt.*
dēcollo -are, *to behead.*
dēcōlo -are, *to trickle away.*
dēcŏlor -ōris, *off-colour, pale.*
dēcŏlōrātĭo -ōnis, f. *discolouring.*
dēcŏlōro -are, *to discolour.*
dēcŏquo -cŏquĕre -coxi -coctum, *to boil thoroughly; to boil down, boil away*; of metals, *to melt away*; of property, *to waste*; commerc., *to ruin oneself, become bankrupt.*
Hence partic. **dēcoctus** -a -um, *boiled down*; of style, *insipid*; f. as subst. *a cold drink.*
dĕcor -ōris, m. *grace, comeliness beauty.*
dĕcŏro -are, *to embellish, beautify, adorn.*
dĕcōrus -a -um, physically, *graceful, beautiful comely*; morally, *proper, fit, becoming.* N. as subst. **dĕcōrum** -i, *propriety, grace.* Adv. **dĕcōrē,** *fitly, becomingly.*
dēcrĕpĭtus -a -um, *infirm, decrepit.*
dēcresco -crescĕre -crēvi -crētum, *to grow down, become smaller, decrease.*
dēcrētum -i, subst. from decerno; q.v.
dĕcŭma (**dĕcĭma**) -ae, f. *a tenth part tithe* (as an offering, tax or largess).
dĕcŭmānus (**dĕcĭmānus**) -a -um, *of the tenth.* (1) *relating to the provincial tax of a tenth*; m. as subst. *the farmer of such a tax.* (2) *belonging to the tenth legion*; m. pl. as subst. *its members.* (3) *belonging to the tenth cohort.*
dĕcŭmātes -ĭum, pl. adj. *relating to tithes.*
dēcumbo -cumbĕre -cŭbŭi, *to lie down, fall, fall down.*
dĕcŭmo (**dĕcĭmo**) -are, *to take a tithe*; milit. *to decimate troops.*
dĕcŭrĭa -ae, f. *a body of ten men; a class, division,* esp. of jurors; *a party, club.*
dĕcŭrĭātĭo -ōnis, f. and **dĕcŭrĭātus** -ūs, m., *a dividing into* decuriae.
[1]**dĕcŭrĭo** -are, *to divide into bodies of ten,* or *into classes* in gen.
[2]**dĕcŭrĭo** -ōnis, m., *head of a body of ten*; milit. *company-commander* in the cavalry; polit., *a senator of a* municipium *or* colonia.
dēcurro -currĕre -cŭcurri or -curri -cursum., *to run down, hasten down*; milit. *to move down* or *to manoeuvre.* Transf., *to run in a race*; transit. to *run through, traverse* a set course; *to have recourse to, take refuge in*; of ships, *to sail downstream* or *to land*; of water, *to run down.*
dēcursĭo -ōnis, f., milit., *a manoeuvre* or *charge.*
dēcursus -ūs, m. *a running down*; milit, *a manoeuvre, a charge, attack.* Transf., *the completion of a course*; rhet., *rhythmical movement.*

dēcurtatus -a -um., *mutilated* (of style).
dĕcŭs -ŏris, n. *distinction, honour, glory, grace*; moral *dignity, virtue*; of persons, *pride, glory*; plur., decora, *distinguished acts.*
dĕcŭtĭo -cŭtĕre -cussi -cussum, *to shake down, shake off, knock off.*
dēdĕcet -dĕcēre -dĕcŭit, *it is unbecoming, unsuitable, unfitting.*
dēdĕcŏro -are, *to dishonour bring shame upon.*
dēdĕcōrus -a -um, *shameful, dishonourable.*
dēdĕcŭs -ŏris, n. *shame, dishonour, disgrace; a dishonourable action, crime, vice.*
dēdĭcātĭo -ōnis, f., *consecration.*
dēdĭco -are, *to dedicate, consecrate; to specify, indicate.*
dēdignor -ari, dep. *to think unworthy, scorn, reject.*
dēdisco -discĕre -dĭdĭci, *to unlearn, forget.*
dēdĭtĭcĭus -a -um, *relating to surrender*; m. plur., dediticii, *subjects of Rome without rights.*
dēdĭtĭo -ōnis, *unconditional surrender, capitulation.*
dēdo dēdĕre -dĭdi -dĭtum, *to give up, surrender*; esp. of the conquered, *to give up, surrender.* Transf., *to give up to, dedicate, devote.*
Hence partic. **dēdĭtus** -a -um, *devoted to, addicted to*; deditā operā, *intentionally.*
dēdŏceo -ēre, *to cause to unlearn, to unteach; teach not to.*
dēdŏlĕo -dŏlēre -dŏlŭi, *to make an end of grieving.*
dēdūco -dūcĕre -duxi -ductum, *to lead* or *bring down*; in time, from the past, *to trace downwards* to the present; in amount, *to reduce*, or, from an amount, *to subtract*; in gen., *to lead* or *draw away; to lead forth colonists, to found a colony; to escort* a person to a place; of persons and things, to *bring* out of one state, opinion, etc. into another; in weaving, *to draw* threads; hence, *to draw out, spin out* in speech or writing.
dēdūctĭo -ōnis, f. *a leading down; a reduction; a leading away* of colonists, etc.
deerro -are, *to wander from the right path, go astray.*
dēfătīgātĭo -ōnis, f. *exhaustion, fatigue.*
dēfătīgo -are, *to weary, fatigue.*
dēfătiscor = defetiscor; q.v.
dēfectĭo -ōnis, f. *failure.* Hence *defection, rebellion; weakening, failing, vanishing.* Partic. **dēfectus** -a -um, *failing, deficient.*
dēfector -ōris, m. *rebel, deserter.*
[1]**dēfectus** -a -um, partic. of deficio; q.v.
[2]**dēfectus** -ūs, m., *a failing, disappearing;* esp. *a failing of light, eclipse.*
dēfendo -fendĕre -fendi -fensum. (**1**) *to repel, repulse, ward off, drive away.* (**2**) *to defend, protect*; esp. *to defend in court;* in argument, *to maintain a proposition* or *statement; to sustain* a part.
dēfensĭo -ōnis, f. (**1**) *a warding off.* (**2**) *defence.*
defensĭto -are, *to defend frequently.*
defenso -are, *to defend vigorously.*
dēfensor -ōris, m. (**1**) *one who wards off* or *averts.* (**2**) *a defender, protector,* esp. in court.
dēfero -ferre -tŭli -lātum, *to bring down, carry down*; in gen., *to bring* or *carry away,* esp. to a particular place; deferre rationes, *to hand in accounts*; fig., *to offer, hand over, refer*; of news, *to communicate, report,* esp. to authority; legal, deferre nomen *to inform against* a person, *indict*: deferre crimen, *to bring a charge.*
dēfervesco -fervescĕre -fervi or ferbŭi, *to cease boiling*; of passion, *to cease to rage.*
dēfĕtiscor (dēfătiscor) -fĕtisci -fessus, dep. *to become tired, grow weary*: esp. in perf. partic. **dēfessus** -a -um, *weary, tired.*
dēfĭcĭo -fĭcĕre -fēci -fectum: intransit. *to do less than one might, to fail*; hence, *to desert, rebel, revolt*; of things, *to fail, run short*; of sun or moon, *to become eclipsed*; of fire, *to go out*; of water, *to ebb*; of strength, etc., *to fail, become weak*; animo deficere, *to lose heart*; transit., *to abandon, leave, fail*; rarely pass. defici, *to be failed.*
Hence partic. **dēfectus** -a -um, *feeble,* esp. because of age.
dēfīgo -figĕre -fixi, -fixum, *to fasten down, fix in*; in gen., *to secure, plant firmly;* of sight or thought, *to concentrate, fix upon*; of persons, *to fix, make motionless,* with astonishment, etc.; partic. defixus, *astounded*; of enchantment, *to bind by a spell.*
dēfingo -fingere -finxi, *to form, mould.*
dēfīnĭo -ire, *to limit, bound, mark out; to set limits* to a thing, *confine*; *to set as a limit, appoint, assign; to interpret* ideas or words in terms of each other, *to understand* one thing by another; in logic, *to define.*
Hence partic. **dēfīnītus** -a -um, *definite, distinct*; adv. **dēfīnītē.**
dēfīnītĭo -ōnis, f., *limiting, prescribing*; in logic, *a definition.*
dēfīnītīvus -a -um, *definitive. explanatory.*
dēfit (as from defio), *fails.*
dēflagrātĭo -ōnis, f. *burning, destruction by fire.*
dēflagro -are, *to be burnt down, destroyed by fire*; in gen., *to be destroyed*; of passions, *to cease burning, abate, cool.* Partic. in pass. sense, **dēflagrātus** -a -um, *burnt down, destroyed.*
dēflecto -flectĕre -flexi -flexum: transit., *to bend down* or *aside*; intransit., *to turn aside, turn away*; in speech, *to digress.*
dēflĕo -flēre -flēvi -flētum, *to bewail, weep for.*

dēfloccatus -a -um, *bald.*
dēflōresco -flōrescĕre -flōrŭi, *to shed blossom, fade, wither.*
dēflŭo -flŭĕre -fluxi. (1) *to flow down, slip down, descend*; abstr., *to come down*, esp. of the gifts of heaven. (2) *to flow away, disappear, be lost.*
dēfŏdĭo -fŏdĕre fōdi -fossum, *to dig down into;* to *form by digging, excavate; to dig in, cover, bury, conceal.*
dēformātĭo -ōnis, f. *deforming, disfiguring; degradation.*
dēformis -e. (1) *deformed, misshapen, ugly, disgusting.* Transf., *foul, shameful.* (2) *formless, shapeless.* Adv. **dēformĭter,** *in an ugly fashion.*
dēfōrmĭtās -ātis, f. *deformity, ugliness; disgrace, dishonour.*
dēformo -are. (1) *to form, fashion; to delineate.* (2) *to put out of shape, disfigure; to disgrace, dishonour.*
dēfraudo (dēfrudo) -are, *to deceive, cheat*; genium suum, *to deprive oneself of pleasure.*
dēfrēnātus -a -um, *unbridled, unrestrained.*
dēfrĭco -frĭcare -frĭcŭi -frictum, *to rub down*; fig. *to satirize, lash.*
dēfringo -fringĕre -frēgi -fractum, *to break down, break off.*
dēfrŭtum -i, n. *new wine boiled down.*
dēfŭgĭo -fŭgĕre -fūgi: intransit., *to flee away*; transit., *to fly from, avoid.*
dēfundo -fundĕre -fūdi -fūsum, *to pour down, pour out.*
dēfungor -fungi -functus, dep. *to perform, discharge, have done with*; (vita) defungi, *to die.*
dēgĕner -ĕris, *fallen away from one's origin, unworthy of one's race, degenerate, unworthy, ignoble.*
dēgĕnĕro -are: intransit., *to become unlike one's kind, to fall off, degenerate*; transit., *to cause to degenerate*, or *disgrace by degeneracy.*
dēgĕro -ĕre, *to carry off.*
dēgo dēgĕre dēgi, *to pass time*; absol., *to live.*
dēgrandĭnat, impers., *it hails violently*, or (perhaps) *it ceases to hail.*
dēgrăvo -are, *to weigh down, bring down, lower.*
dēgrĕdĭor -grĕdī -gressus, dep., *to step down, march down.*
dēgusto -are, *to take a taste from, taste*; of fire, *to lick*; of a weapon, *to graze*; in gen., *to try, make a trial of, sound.*
dĕhinc, *from here, hence; from this time, henceforth, immediately after that time, thereupon.*
dĕhisco -ĕre, *to gape, open, split down.*
dehŏnestāmentum -i, n. *blemish, deformity disgrace.*
dehŏnesto -are, *to dishonour, disgrace.*
dehortor -ari, dep. *to discourage, dissuade.*
dēicĭo -icĕre -iēci -iectum, *to throw, cast, hurl down*; with reflex., *to rush down*; of upright things, *to throw to the ground, fell*; of persons, *to kill, bring down.* In gen., *to fling away* or *aside*; naut., deici, *to be thrown off course*; milit. *to dislodge; to eject, dispossess; to shift* a person from an opinion, attitude; *to disappoint.*
Hence partic. **dēiectus** -a -um *low-lying; dispirited, dejected.*
dēiectĭo -ōnis, f. *throwing down; eviction* from property.
[1]**dēiectus** -a -um, partic. from deicio; q.v.
[2]**dēiectus** -ūs, m. *a throwing down; a declivity, steep slope.*
dēiero -are, *to swear.*
dein; see deinde.
dĕinceps, *one after another, successively.*
dĕinde, and abbrev. **dĕin:** of space, *from that place*; of time, *thereafter, thereupon, then, afterwards*; in enumerations, *next, and then.*
Dēiŏtărus -i, m. *a king of Galatia, defended by Cicero.*
dēiungo -ĕre, *to disconnect.*
dēlābor -labi -lapsus, dep. *to glide down, fall down, sink*; of liquids, *to flow down.* Transf., *to sink to, come down to* circumstances, etc.; *to proceed from, be derived from* an origin; *to fall unawares* among people.
dēlăcĕro -are, *to tear to pieces.*
dēlāmentor -ari, dep. *to bewail, lament.*
dēlasso -are, *to weary, tire out.*
dēlātĭo -ōnis, f. *reporting, giving information against, denunciation.*
dēlātor -ōris, m., *an informer, denouncer.*
dēlectābĭlis -e, *delightful, pleasant.*
dēlectāmentum -i, n. *delight, amusement.*
dēlectātĭo -ōnis, f. *delight, pleasure.*
delecto -are, *to divert, attract, delight*; in pass., with abl. *to take delight in*: in pass. with infin., *to delight to.*
dēlectus -ūs, m. *choosing, choice.*
dēlēgātĭo -ōnis, f. *assignment of a debt.*
dēlēgo -are, *to transfer, commit, assign; to impute, attribute, ascribe.*
dēlēnīmentum -i, n. *what soothes* or *charms.*
dēlēnĭo (dēlīnĭo) -ire, *to soften down; to soothe* or *charm.*
dēlēnītor -ōris, m. *one who soothes* or *cajoles.*
dēlĕo -lēre -lēvi -lētum, *to blot out, efface*; in gen., *to destroy, annihilate.*
dēlīberābundus -a -um, *carefully considering, deliberating.*
dēlīberātĭo -ōnis, f. *consideration, consultation.*
dēlīberātīvus -a -um, *relating to deliberation.*
dēlīberātor -ōris, m., *one who deliberates.*
dēlībĕro -are, *to weigh carefully, consider, consult about; to ask advice*, esp. of an oracle; as a result of deliberation, *to resolve.*
Hence partic. **dēlībĕratus** -a -um. *resolved, determined.*
dēlībo -are, *to take a little from, to taste*; in gen., *to extract, derive; to take from* so as to *enjoy; to take from* so as to *lessen* or *spoil.*

dēlībro -are, *to peel the bark off.*
dēlībūtus -a -um, *steeped.*
dēlĭcātus -a -um, *soft, tender*; in bad sense, *luxurious* of things, *spoilt, effeminate* of persons; of tastes, *fastidious, dainty, nice.* Adv. **dēlĭcātē,** *luxuriously.*
dēlĭcĭae -arum, f. pl. *allurements, charms, delights, fancies*; esse in deliciis, *to be a favourite*; concr., *darling, sweetheart.*
dēlĭcĭŏlae -arum, f. pl. *a darling.*
dēlictum -i, n. *a fault, crime.*
[1]**dēlĭgo** -lĭgĕre -lēgi -lectum *to pick, pluck; to choose, select.*
[2]**dēlĭgo** -are, *to fasten, bind up.*
dēlingo -ere, *to lick off, lick up.*
dēlinquo -linquĕre -līqui -lictum, *to fail, be wanting,* esp. *to fail in duty, commit a crime.*
dēlĭquesco -lĭquescĕre -lĭcŭi, *to melt, dissolve; to vanish, disappear.*
dēlĭquo and **dēlĭco** -are, *to clarify; to explain.*
dēlīrātĭo -ōnis, f. *folly, silliness, dotage.*
dēlīro -are, "*to go off the rails*" *act crazily, rave.*
dēlīrus -a -um, *silly, crazy doting.*
dēlĭtesco -lĭtescĕre -lĭtŭi, *to conceal oneself, lie hid, take refuge.*
dēlītĭgo -are, *to scold furiously.*
Dēlos -i, f., *a small island in the Aegean Sea, birth-place of Apollo and Diana*; adj. **Dēlĭăcus** and **Dēlĭus** -a -um, *of Delos*; as subst. **Dēlĭus** -i, m. = *Apollo*; **Dēlĭa** -ae, f. = *Diana.*
Delphi -orum, m. *a town in Phocis, famous for its oracle of Apollo*; adj. **Delphĭcus** -a -um.
delphīnus -i and **delphīn** -īnis, m. *dolphin.*
dēlūbrum -i, n. *a shrine, temple.*
dēluctor -ari, dep. and **dēlucto** -are, *to wrestle.*
dēlūdo -lūdĕre -lūsi -lūsum, *to mock, cheat.*
dēlumbo -are, *to lame, enervate, weaken.*
dēmădesco -mădescĕre -mădŭi, *to become wet through.*
dēmando -are, *to entrust, commit.*
dēmens -mentis, *out of one's mind, insane, senseless*; adv. **dēmenter.**
dēmentĭa -ae, f., *senselessness, insanity*; in plur., *mad actions.*
dēmentĭo -ire, *to be mad, rave.*
dēmĕrĕo -ēre and **dēmĕrĕor** -ēri, dep. *to earn thoroughly; to deserve well of* a person, *to oblige.*
dēmergo -mergĕre -mersi -mersum, *to sink, plunge into, dip under*; aere alieno demersus, *over head and ears in debt.*
dēmētĭor -mētīri -mensus, dep. *to measure out*; partic. **dēmensus** -a -um, in pass. sense, with n. as subst., *an allowance.*
dēmĕto -mĕtĕre -messŭi -messum, *to mow, reap, cut down* or *off.*
dēmigro -are, *to emigrate, depart.* Transf., *to die.*
dēmĭnŭo -mĭnŭĕre -mĭnŭi -mĭnūtum, *to take away from, diminish, lessen*; capite se deminuere, *to suffer a loss of civil rights.*
dēmĭnūtĭo -ōnis, f. *lessening, diminution*; sui, *loss of prestige*; capitis, *loss of civil rights; right of alienation.*
dēmīror -ari, dep. *to wonder* (*at*).
dēmissĭo -ōnis, f., *sinking, lowering*; animi, *dejection.*
dēmītĭgo -ari, *to make mild, soften.*
dēmitto -mittĕre -mīsi -missum, *to send down, lower, put down*; tunica demissa, *hanging loosely*; demissi capilli, *growing long;* milit., *to lead down;* naut., *to lower* gear or *bring* a vessel *downstream* or *to land.* Transf., *to sink, bury, plunge*; of spirits, *to lower.*

Hence partic. **dēmissus** -a -um, *hanging down*; of dress and hair, *long, loose*; of places, *low-lying.* Transf., *feeble, weak; unassuming, modest; down-cast, dispirited.* Adv. **dēmissē,** *low, near the ground.* Transf., *modestly, humbly meanly.*
dēmo dēmĕre dempsi demptum, *to take away, subtract.*
Dēmocrĭtus -i, m. *a philosopher of Abdera* (c. 460-370 B.C.). Hence adj. **Dēmocrĭtĭcus** -a -um.
dēmōlĭor -iri, dep. *to throw down, demolish.*
dēmōlītĭo -ōnis, f. *throwing down, demolition.*
dēmonstrātĭo -ōnis, f. *pointing out, indication, explanation, description*; rhet., *oratory concerned with praise and censure.*
dēmonstrātīvus -a -um, *demonstrative*; rhet., of oratory, *concerned with praise and censure.*
dēmonstrātor -ōris, m., *one who points out* or *indicates.*
dēmonstro -are *to indicate, explain, describe.*
dēmŏrĭor -mŏri -mortŭus, dep. *to die, die off*; with acc. of person, *to die for love of.*
dēmŏror -ari, dep.: intransit., *to delay, loiter*; transit., *to stop, delay, retard.*
Dēmosthĕnēs -is (also -i), *the Athenian orator* (384-322 B.C.).
dēmŏvĕo -mŏvēre -mōvi -mōtum, *to move away, remove*; hominem de sententia, *to make a person change his opinion.*
dēmūgītus -a -um, *filled with the noise of lowing.*
dēmulcĕo -mulcēre -mulsi, *to stroke down, caress by stroking.*
dēmum, of time, *at length, at last*; in enumerations, *finally, in short*; id demum, *that and that alone.*
dēmurmŭro -are, *to murmur* or *mutter over.*
dēmūtātĭo -ōnis, f., *change, alteration,* esp. for the worse.
dēmūto -are: transit., *to change, alter* a thing, esp. for the worse; intransit. *to change one's mind* or *become different.*

dēnārĭus -a -um, *containing ten*; denarius nummus, or denarius alone, *a Roman silver coin.*
dēnarro -are, *to narrate, tell, relate.*
dēnăto -are, *to swim down.*
dēnĕgo -are, *to deny, say no; to deny, refuse, reject a request.*
dēni -ae, -a, *ten by ten, ten at a time, by tens.*
dēnĭcālis -e, *releasing from death*; feriae, *a funeral ceremony.*
dēnĭquĕ: in time, *at last, finally*; in enumerations, *again, further* or *finally; in short, in fine.*
dēnōmĭno -are, *to name.*
dēnormo -are, *to make crooked.*
dēnŏto -are, *to mark out for another, designate precisely; to take note of.*
dens dentis, m. *a tooth.* Transf., of things resembling a tooth, e.g., *a mattock* or *sickle*; abstr., of anything sharp, biting, destructive.
denso -are, and **densĕo** -ēre, *to make thick, condense, press together.*
densus -a -um, *thick, close, dense*; in time, *frequent*; in degree, *intense, vehement*; in style, of work or author, *condensed.* Adv. **densē**, *densely*; of time, *frequently.*
dentālĭa -ĭum, n. pl. *the share-beam of a plough.*
dentātus -a -um, *provided with teeth, toothed; polished by teeth.*
dentĭo -ire, *to cut teeth*; of teeth, *to grow.*
dēnūbo -nūbĕre -nupsi -nuptum, *to be married off, to marry* (of the woman), esp. *beneath her.*
dēnūdo -are, *to lay bare, uncover, reveal.* Transf., *to rob, plunder.*
dēnuntĭātĭo -ōnis, f. *announcement, declaration, threat.*
dēnuntĭo -are, *to announce, give notice, declare, threaten*; bellum denuntiare, *to declare war*; legal, *to give notice, serve a summons.*
dēnŭō, *anew, again; a second time.*
deŏnĕro -are, *to unload, disburden.*
dĕorsum or **dĕorsus**, *downwards*; sursum deorsum, *up and down, backwards and forwards.*
dēpăciscor = depeciscor; q.v.
dēpactus -a -um, *fastened down, firmly fixed.*
dēpasco -pascĕre -pāvi -pastum and **dēpascor** -pasci, dep. *to feed off*; in gen., *to eat up, consume, reduce.*
dēpĕciscor -pĕcisci -pectus, dep. *to make a bargain for* or *about; to settle for, accept* a condition.
dēpecto -pectĕre -pexum, *to comb down*; in comedy, *to beat soundly.*
dēpĕcūlātor -ōris, m. *plunderer embezzler.*
dēpĕcūlor -ari, dep. *to rob, plunder.*
dēpello -pellĕre -pŭli -pulsum, *to drive down,* or *away, expel, remove*; milit., *to dislodge*; naut., *to drive off course*; in gen., *to drive away, avert*; of persons, *to dissuade.*
dēpendĕo -ēre, *to hang down; to depend upon; to be derived from.*
dēpendo -pendĕre -pendi -pensum, *to weigh out and pay over.*
dēperdo -perdĕre -perdĭdi -perdĭtum, *to lose, waste, destroy*; esp. of the effects of love.
dēpĕrĕo -pĕrire -pĕrii, *to perish* or *be ruined utterly; to be desperately in love.*
dēpĭlo -are, *to strip of hair* or *feathers.*
dēpingo -pingĕre -pinxi -pictum, *to paint, depict, portray.*
dēplango -plangĕre -planxi, *to bewail, lament.*
dēplexus -a -um, *clasping.*
dēplōro -are: intransit., *to weep bitterly, lament*; transit., *to lament. bewail; to regard as lost, give up.*
dēplŭit -plŭere, *rains down.*
dēpōno -pōnĕre -pŏsŭi -pŏsĭtum. (1) *to lay down, put down*; esp. *to lay as wager* or *prize.* (2) for safe-keeping, *to put down, deposit; to commit, entrust.* (3) *to lay aside, have done with.*

Hence partic. **dēpŏsĭtus** -a -um. (1) *laid out; dying, despaired of, dead* (2) *entrusted*; n. as subst. *a deposit.*
dēpŏpŭlātĭo -ōnis, f., *laying waste ravaging.*
dēpŏpŭlātor -ōris, m. *a ravager.*
dēpŏpŭlor -ari, dep.; also **dēpŏpŭlo** -are, *to lay waste, ravage, destroy.*
dēporto -are, *to carry down, carry off, take away; to bring home; to banish for life* (with loss of rights and property).
dēposco -poscĕre -pŏposci, *to demand,* usually for a purpose, esp. for punishment.
dēprāvātĭo -ōnis, f. *perverting, distorting*; animi *depravity.*
dēprāvo -are, *to make crooked, pervert, disfigure*; verbally, *to distort, misrepresent*; morally, *to spoil, corrupt.* Adv. from partic., **dēprāvātē**, *perversely.*
dēprĕcābundus -a -um. *earnestly entreating.*
dēprĕcātĭo -ōnis, f. (1) *an attempt to avert by entreaty, deprecating.* (2) *an entreaty against a person,* for his punishment.
dēprĕcātor -ōris, m. (1) *one that begs off, an intercessor.* (2) *one that pleads for.*
dēprĕcor -ari, dep. (1) *to try to avert by entreaty, to deprecate; to allege in excuse* (so as to avoid punishment). (2) *to entreat against a person, to curse.* (3) *to entreat for, beg for, intercede.*
dēprĕhendo and **dēprendo** -endĕre -endi -ensum, *to seize upon, catch hold of*; esp. *to surprise, catch, detect* a person in a crime or fault; *to discover, detect, observe* a thing.
dēprĕhensĭo -ōnis, f. *detection.*
dēprĭmo -prĭmĕre -pressi -pressum, *to press down, depress*; esp. *to plant deep in the ground, dig deep*; of ships, *to sink.*

Hence partic. **depressus** -a -um, *low-lying.*

dēproelĭans -antis, *struggling violently.*
dēprōmo -prōmĕre -prompsi -promptum, *to take down produce, fetch out.*
dēprŏpĕro: intransit, *to hasten*; transit., *to hasten over, produce in haste.*
dēpŭdet -pŭdēre -pŭdŭit, *ceases to be ashamed, loses all sense of shame.*
dēpugno -are, *to fight hard, fight it out.*
dēpulsĭo -ōnis, f. *driving away*; rhet. *defence.*
dēpulsor -ōris, m. *an averter.*
dēpŭto -are. (1) *to prune, cut off.* (2) *to count, estimate.*
deque; see susque deque.
dērĕlinquo -linquĕre -līqui -lictum, *to forsake, desert, abandon.*
dērĕpentĕ, *suddenly.*
dērēpo -rēpĕre -repsi, *to creep, crawl down.*
dērīdĕo -rīdēre -rīsi -rīsum, *to laugh at, mock, deride.*
dērīdĭcŭlus -a -um, *very laughable*; n. as subst. *ridicule*; esse deridiculo, *to be an object of ridicule.*
dērĭgo -rĭgĕre -rexi -rectum, *to set straight, direct*; of placing (also in form dirigo), *to order, dispose*; milit. *to draw up.* Transf., *to direct, aim, guide* abstr. things.
dērĭgŭi, perf., *grew quite stiff.*
dērĭpĭo -rĭpĕre -rĭpŭi -reptum, *to tear down, snatch away.*
dērīsor -ōris, m. *a mocker.*
dērīsus -ūs, m. *mockery, derision.*
dērīvātĭo -ōnis, f. *turning away* or *diversion of water.*
dērīvo -are, *to turn into another channel, to divert.*
dērŏgo -are, *to modify a law*; in gen., *to diminish, detract from.*
dērōsus -a -um, *gnawed away.*
dēruncĭno -are, *to cheat, fleece.*
dērŭo -rŭĕre -rŭi -rŭtum, *to cast down, make to fall.*
dēruptus -a -um, *broken off*; hence *precipitous, steep*; n. pl. as subst., *precipices.*
dēsaevĭo -ire -ĭi -ītum, *to rage violently.*
dēscendo -scendĕre -scendi -scensum, *to climb down, come down, descend*; milit., *to march down*; of things, *to sink, pierce, penetrate*; of mountains, *to slope down*; of the voice, *to sink.* Transf., of persons, *to lower oneself, stoop*; of things, *to sink in, penetrate.*
dēscensĭo -ōnis, f. *going down, descent*; Tiberina, *voyage down the Tiber.*
dēscensus -ūs, m. *going down, descent; way down.*
dēscisco -sciscĕre -scīvi or -scĭi -scītum, *to break away, revolt, withdraw, diverge.*
dēscrībo -scrībĕre -scripsi -scriptum. (1) *to transcribe, copy.* (2) *to describe, delineate, represent, portray.*
dēscriptĭo -ōnis, f. (1) *a copy.* (2) *a representation, figure, description.*
dēsĕco -sĕcare -sĕcŭi -sectum, *to hew off, cut off.*
dēsĕro -sĕrĕre -sĕrŭi -sertum, *to forsake, abandon, leave; to neglect, disregard.*
Hence partic. **dēsertus** -a -um, *forsaken, abandoned*; n. pl. as subst., *deserts, wildernesses.*
dēsertor -ōris, m. *one who forsakes,* milit., *deserter.*
dēservĭo -ire, *to serve zealously, be a slave to.*
dēsĕs -sĭdis, m. (nom. sing. not found), *idle, lazy, inactive.*
dēsĭdĕo -sĭdēre -sēdi -sessum, *to sit idle, be slothful.*
dēsīdĕrābĭlis -e, *desirable.*
dēsīdĕrātĭo -ōnis, f. *desire, longing.*
dēsīdĕrĭum -i, n. *desire* or *longing, grief for the absence* or *loss of* a person or thing; in gen., *a desire* or *request.*
dēsīdĕro -are, *to long for what is absent* or *lost, to wish for; to miss, find a lack of*; milit., *to lose.*
dēsĭdĭa -ae, f. *idleness, inactivity, apathy.*
dēsĭdĭōsus -a -um, *slothful, idle, lazy*; adv. **dēsĭdĭōsē.**
dēsīdo -sīdĕre -sēdi, *to sink down, subside, settle.* Transf., *to deteriorate.*
dēsignātĭo -ōnis, f. *marking out, designation: appointment to an office.*
dēsignātor -ōris, m. = dissignator; q.v.
dēsignātor -ōris, m. = dissignator; q.v.
dēsigno -are, *to mark out, trace, plan*; in gen., *to point out, indicate, signify; to portray, delineate*; polit., *to nominate, elect*; partic. **dēsignātus,** *elected, designate.*
dēsĭlĭo -sĭlire -sĭlŭi -sultum, *to leap down*; ad pedes, *dismount.*
dēsĭno -sĭnĕre -sĭi -sĭtum: transit., *to cease, desist from*; intransit., *to cease, stop, end*; with in and acc., *to end in.*
dēsĭpĭentĭa -ae, f. *foolishness.*
dēsĭpĭo -sĭpĕre *to be foolish, act foolishly.*
dēsisto -sistĕre -stĭti -stĭtum, *to stand away*: from a person, *to withdraw*; from action, etc., *to desist, leave off, cease.*
dēsōlo -are, *to leave solitary, forsake.*
dēspecto -are, *to regard from above, look down upon; to despise.*
[1]**dēspectus** -a -um, partic. from despicio; q.v.
[2]**dēspectus** -ūs, m. *a looking down, downward view; an object of contempt.*
dēspērātĭo -ōnis, f. *hopelessness, despair.*
dēspēro -are: intransit., *to be without hope, despair*; transit., *to despair of, give up.* Adv. from pres. partic., **dēspēranter,** *despairingly, hopelessly.* Perf. partic. **dēspērātus** -a -um; in pass. sense, *despaired of*; in middle sense, *desperate.*
dēspĭcātĭo -ōnis, f. and **dēspĭcātus** -ūs, m. *contempt.*
dēspĭcĭentĭa -ae, f., *looking down upon; contempt.*
dēspĭcĭo -spĭcĕre -spexi -spectum, *to look down, regard from above; to look down upon, despise.* Pres. partic. act. **dēspĭcĭens,** *contemptuous.* Perf. partic. pass. **dēspectus** -a -um, *despised, contemptible.*

dēspĭcor -ari, *to look down upon, despise.* Perf. partic. in pass. sense **despĭcātus** -a -um, *despised, contemptible.*

dēspŏlĭo -are, *to plunder, despoil.*

dēspondĕo -spondēre -spondi -sponsum, *to pledge, to promise,* esp. *to promise in marriage, betroth*; in gen., *to pledge, devote*; with animum *or* animos, *to lose heart, despair.*

dēspūmo -are. (1) *to skim off.* Transf., *to digest.* (2) *to drop foam.*

dēspŭo -spŭĕre, *to spit down, spit on the ground.* Transf., *to reject.*

dēsquāmo -are, *to take off the scales, to scale.*

dēsterto -stertĕre -stertŭi, *to finish snoring* or *dreaming.*

dēstillo -are, *to drip down, distil.*

dēstĭnātĭo -ōnis, f. *fixing, determining, appointment.*

dēstĭno -are, *to make fast, fix down; to fix, determine, settle, appoint*; with infin., *to resolve to do*; of persons, *to appoint* to an office; of things *to fix upon, intend to buy.*

Hence partic. **dēstĭnātus** -a -um, *fixed, determined*; n. as subst., *an objective* or *intention*; (ex) destinato, *intentionally.*

dēstĭtŭo -stĭtŭĕre -stĭtŭi -stĭtūtum, *to set down, place*; esp. *to leave in the lurch, forsake, desert.*

dēstĭtūtĭo -ōnis, f. *forsaking, abandoning.*

dēstringo -stringĕre -strinxi -strictum. (1) *to strip*; esp. *to draw* or *bare* a sword. Transf., *to satirize, censure.* (2) *to touch lightly, graze.*

Hence partic. **dēstrictus** -a -um, *severe.*

dēstrŭo -strŭĕre -struxi -structum, *to pull down, dismantle, destroy, ruin.*

dēsŭbĭtō (or **dē sŭbĭtō**), *suddenly.*

dēsūdo -are, *to sweat violently, exert oneself hard.*

dēsuēfĭo -fĭĕri -factus sum, pass., *to be made unaccustomed.*

dēsuesco -suescĕre -suēvi -suētum, *to become unaccustomed*; esp. partic. **dēsuētus** -a -um: in pass. sense, *disused*; in middle sense, *unaccustomed, unused to.*

dēsuētūdo -ĭnis, f. *disuse.*

dēsultor -oris, m. *a leaper, acrobat.* Transf., *an inconstant person.*

dēsultōrĭus -a -um, *relating to a* desultor.

dēsum -esse -fŭi, *to be down, fall short, fail, be missing* or *remiss.*

dēsūmo -sūmĕre -sumpsi -sumptum, *to take out, choose, select.*

dēsŭpĕr, *from above.*

dēsurgo -surgĕre -surrexi -surrectum, *to rise and go down* or *out.*

dētĕgo -tĕgĕre -texi -tectum, *to uncover, lay bare, disclose.*

dētendo -tendĕre -tensum, *to unstretch*; tabernacula, *to strike tents.*

dētergĕo -tergēre -tersi -tersum. (1) *to wipe off, clear away, brush off.* (2) *to cleanse by wiping.*

dētĕrĭor -ĭus, genit. -ōris, compar. (superl. deterrimus), *lower, inferior, poorer, worse.* Adv. **dētĕrĭus,** *worse.*

dētermĭnātĭo -ōnis, f., *boundary, end.*

dētermĭno -are, *to bound, fix the limits of, determine.*

dētĕro -tĕrĕre trīvi -trītum, *to rub away, wear out; to detract from, weaken.*

dēterrĕo -terrēre -terrŭi -terrĭtum, *to frighten away, deter, discourage.*

dētestābĭlis -e, *abominable, horrible.*

dētestātĭo -ōnis, f. (1) *a cursing, execration.* (2) *a warding off, averting.*

dētestor -ari, dep. (1) *to pray against: to pray for deliverance from* a person or thing, or *to curse, execrate.* (2) of the gods' action, *to avert, remove.*

dētexo -texĕre -texŭi -textum, *to make by plaiting; to finish, complete.*

dētĭnĕo -tĭnēre -tĭnŭi -tentum, *to hold back, detain; to prevent; to engage, occupy exclusively.*

dētondĕo -tondēre -tŏtondi and -tondi -tonsum, *to shear, clip.*

dētŏno -tŏnare -tŏnŭi *to cease to thunder* or *rage.*

dētorquĕo -torquēre -torsi -tortum. (1) *to turn away, bend aside.* (2) *to twist out of shape, distort.*

dētractĭo -ōnis, f. *drawing off, withdrawal, taking away*; rhet., *ellipsis.*

dētracto = detrecto; q.v.

dētractor -ōris, m., *detractor, disparager.*

dētrăho -trăhĕre -traxi -tractum. (1) *to draw down, drag down*; *to lower, humiliate.* (2) *to draw off, drag away, remove*; numerically, *to subtract*; in speech, *to detract from* a person, *disparage, slander.*

dētrectātĭo -ōnis, f. *refusal.*

dētrectātor -ōris, m. *disparager, detractor.*

dētrecto -are. (1) *to decline, refuse, shirk.* (2) *to disparage, detract from depreciate.*

dētrīmentōsus -a -um, *detrimental, hurtful.*

dētrīmentum -i, n. *loss, damage, injury*; milit., *loss, defeat.*

dētrītus -a -um, partic. from detero; q.v.

dētrūdo -trūdĕre -trūsi -trūsum, *to push down, thrust down;* milit., *to dislodge*; legal, *to dispossess, eject.* Transf., of persons, *to force, compel*; of functions, *to put off, postpone.*

dētrunco -are, *to lop* or *cut off; to mutilate.*

dēturbo -are, *to force away, dash down*; milit., *to dislodge*; legal, *to eject dispossess.*

Deucălĭōn -ōnis, m. *son of Prometheus, saved in an ark from a great flood, with his wife Pyrrha.*

deunx -uncis, m. *eleven-twelfths of a unit.*

deūro -ūrĕre -ussi -ustum, *to burn down*; of cold, *to destroy, nip.*

dĕus -i, m. *a god, a deity*; di meliora (ferant), *God forbid.*

dēvasto -are, *to lay waste, devastate.*

dēvĕho -vĕhĕre -vexi -vectum, *to carry away* or *down*; pass. devehi (sc. navi), *to sail*.

dēvello -vellere -velli -vulsum, *to pluck, tear away*.

dēvēlo -are, *to unveil, uncover*.

dēvĕnĕror -ari, dep. (1) *to worship, revere*. (2) *to avert by prayers*.

dēvĕnĭo -vĕnīre -vēni -ventum, *to come to, arrive at, reach*.

dēverbĕro -are, *to thrash soundly*.

[1]**dēversor** -ari, dep., *to lodge as a guest*.

[2]**dēversor** -ōris, m., *a guest*.

dēversōrĭŏlum -i, n. *a small lodging*.

dēversōrĭus -a -um, *fit to lodge in*; n. as subst. *an inn, lodging, refuge*.

dēvertĭcŭlum (**dēvort-**) -i, n. (1) *a by-way, by-path*; hence *digression*. (2) *an inn, lodging, refuge, resort*.

dēverto (**dēvorto**) -vertĕre -verti -versum; *to turn aside*; esp. *to turn aside to a lodging, to put up at, stay with*. Transf., *to digress*.

dēvexus -a -um, *moving downwards, descending, sinking*; of position, *sloping down, shelving, steep*; of tendency, *inclining to*.

dēvincio -vincire -vinxi -vinctum, *to bind, tie fast, attach, connect*.

Hence partic. **dēvinctus** -a -um, *attached, devoted*.

dēvinco -vincĕre -vīci -victum, *to conquer thoroughly, subjugate, overcome*.

dēvītātĭo -ōnis, f. *avoiding*.

dēvīto -are, *to avoid*.

dēvĭus -a -um, *off the beaten track, out of the way, solitary, retired*; in mind, *erroneous, unreasonable*.

dēvóco -are, *to call down* or *away*; devocare in dubium, *to bring into danger*.

dēvŏlo -are, *to fly down, hasten down*.

dēvolvo -volvĕre -volvi -vŏlūtum, *to roll down*; pass., *to roll down, fall headlong, sink back*.

dēvŏro -are, *to swallow, devour, seize upon*; of words, *to articulate badly, mispronounce*; of property, *to consume, waste*; of disagreeable things, *to swallow, accept, put up with*.

dēvortĭcŭlum; see deverticulum.

dēvortĭum -i, n., *a by-way, by-path*.

dēvōtĭo -ōnis, f. (1) *consecrating, devoting*. (2) *cursing*. (3) *enchantment, incantation*.

dēvōto -are, *to consecrate* or *devote to death*.

dēvŏvĕo -vŏvēre -vōvi -vōtum, *to consecrate, devote*, esp. to a god, or to death; *to curse, execrate; to bewitch, enchant*; in gen., *to devote, give up*.

Hence partic. **dēvōtus** -a -um, *devoted; accursed; attached* to a person; m. pl. as subst. *faithful followers*.

dextella -ae, f., *a little right hand*.

dextĕr -tĕra -tĕrum, or -tra -trum; compar. **dextĕrĭor** -ĭus, superl. **dextĭmus** -a -um; *right, on the right hand, on the right side*. Transf., *dexterous, skilful; propitious, favourable, opportune*. F. as subst., **dextĕra** or **dextra** -ae, *the right hand*; (a) dextra, *on the right*; esp. *the right hand* as pledge of faith; sometimes, in gen. *the hand*. Adv. **dextĕrē** or **dextrē**; compar. **dextĕrĭus**; *dexterously, skilfully*.

dextĕrĭtās -ātis, f., *skilfulness, readiness*.

dextrorsum and **dextrorsus**, *on the right, towards the right*.

Dīa -ae, f. *mother of Mercury*.

dĭădēma -ătis, n., *a royal headband, diadem*.

dĭaeta -ae, f. (1) *a way of living prescribed by a physician, regimen, diet*. (2) *a living-room*.

dĭălectĭcus -a -um, *of discussion, dialectical*; m. as subst., **dĭălectĭcus** -i, *a dialectician, logician*; f. **dĭălectĭca** -ae, and **dĭălectĭcē** -es, *the art of dialectic, logic*; n. pl. **dĭălectĭca** -orum, *dialectical discussion*; adv. **dĭălectĭcē**, *dialectically*.

dĭālis -e, *relating to Jupiter*; (flamen) dialis, *the priest of Jupiter*.

dĭălŏgus -i, m., *a philosophical conversation*.

Dĭāna (older **Dīāna**) -ae, f. *the virgin goddess of the moon and of hunting*; adj. **Dĭānĭus** -a -um, *belonging to Diana*.

dĭārĭa -orum, n. pl. *a day's allowance of food* or *pay*.

dĭbăphus (-a) -um, *double-dyed*; as f. subst. **dĭbăphus** -i, *the purple-striped robe of the higher magistrates in Rome*.

dĭca -ae, f., *law-suit, action* in a Greek court.

dĭcācĭtās -ātis, f. *wit, satire, raillery*.

dĭcātĭo -ōnis, f. *settling as a citizen*.

dĭcax -ācis, *ready of speech; witty, satirical, sarcastic*.

dĭchŏrēus -i, m. *a double trochee*.

dĭcĭō -ōnis, f. *power, sovereignty, authority*.

dĭcis (genit.); dicis causa, dicis gratia, *for form's sake, for the sake of appearances*.

[1]**dĭco** -are, *to consecrate, dedicate, devote to the gods; to deify, place among the gods; to inaugurate*. Transf., *to devote, give up, set apart*; se civitati, or in civitatem, *to become a citizen*.

[2]**dīco** -dīcĕre dixi dictum, *to indicate; to appoint;* most commonly, *to say, speak, tell, mention*; in pass. with infin., *to be said to*; impersonally, dicitur, *it is said that*; of ideas, *to express, put into words*; ius, *to administer law, give rulings*; of persons or things, *to mention, speak of, tell of, relate; to name, call; to mean, refer to*. N. of partic. as subst. **dictum** -i, *a word, saying, speech; a witty saying, a bon-mot; a prediction; an order, command*.

dicrŏtum -i, n. *a vessel with two banks of oars*.

dictamnus -i, f. *dittany, a plant*.

dictātor -ōris, m. *a dictator*; in Rome, *an extraordinary magistrate, elected* *in emergency and granted absolute power*; elsewhere, *a chief magistrate.*

dictātōrĭus -a -um, *belonging to a dictator, dictatorial.*

dictātūra -ae, f., *the office of dictator, dictatorship.*

dictĭo -ōnis, f. *saying, speaking, talk, oratory.*

dictĭto -are, *to say often, reiterate, assert repeatedly*; dictitare causas, *to plead frequently.*

dicto -are, *to say often; to say over, dictate a* thing to be written; hence *to get written down.*

dictum -i, n. subst. from [2]dico; q.v.

[1]**Dīdō** -ūs, f., *the founder of Carthage,* also called Elisa or Elissa.

[2]**dīdo** dīdĕre dīdĭdi dīdĭtum, *to divide, distribute, spread round.*

dīdūco -dūcĕre -duxi -ductum, *to draw apart, separate*; milit., *to divide, distribute,* also *to scatter, disperse.*

dĭēcŭla -ae, f. *a little day, a short time.*

dĭērectus -a -um, an abusive expression, like *go and be hanged!*

dĭēs -ēi, m. or f., *daytime, day; a day, period of twenty-four hours*; diem ex die, *from day to day*; in dies, *daily,* esp. of a continuing process of change; in diem vivere, *to live for the day*; meton., *the business* or *events of the day*; in gen., *time.* Esp. *a particular day, fixed date; a historic day; day of death; anniversary,* esp. *birthday.*

Dĭespĭter -tris, m. *a name for Jupiter.*

diffāmo -are, *to spread evil reports about, to defame.*

diffĕrentĭa -ae, f., *difference, distinction.*

diffĕrĭtās -ātis, f. *difference.*

diffĕro differre distŭli dīlātum. Transit., *to carry in different directions, spread abroad, scatter; to spread news; to harass, disturb, discredit* a person; in time, *to delay, postpone* business, *to put off* persons. Intransit., *to differ, be different*; nihil differt, *there is no difference.*

differtus -a -um, *stuffed full, crammed.*

diffĭcĭlis -e, *difficult*; of character, *hard to deal with, morose, obstinate.* Adv. **diffĭcĭlĭtĕr** and **diffĭcultĕr,** *with difficulty.*

diffĭcultās -ātis, f., *difficulty, need, trouble, distress*; of character, *obstinacy, moroseness.*

diffīdentĭa -ae, f., *want of confidence, distrust, despair.*

diffīdo -fīdĕre -fīsus sum, *to have no confidence, mistrust, despair*; partic. **diffīdens** -entis, *distrustful, diffident*; adv. **diffīdentĕr.**

diffindo -findĕre -fĭdi -fissum, *to split, cleave, open*; legal, diem, *to postpone business.*

diffingo -ĕre, *to form again, forge anew*; fig., *to change.*

diffĭtĕor -ēri, dep. *to deny, disavow.*

difflo -are, *to blow apart.*

difflŭo -flŭĕre -fluxi -fluxum, *to flow in different directions, to dissolve, melt away.*

diffringo -fringĕre -fractum, *to shatter.*

diffŭgio -fŭgĕre -fūgi -fŭgĭtum, *to fly in different directions, to disperse.*

diffŭgĭum -i, n. *dispersion.*

diffundĭto -are, *to scatter.*

diffundo -fundĕre -fūdi -fūsum, *to pour in different directions, to spread out, diffuse, extend*; esp. *to make relax, brighten up, gladden.*

Hence partic. **diffūsus** -a -um, *spread out, extensive, wide*; adv. **diffūsē**, *copiously, diffusely.*

diffūsĭlis -e, *capable of spreading, elastic.*

dīgĕro -gĕrĕre -gessi -gestum, *to carry in different directions, to separate, spread*; esp. in orderly fashion, *to arrange.*

dīgestĭo -ōnis, f. *arrangement, distribution.*

dīgestus -a -um, partic. from digero; q.v.

dĭgĭtŭlus -i, m. *a little finger; the touch of a finger.*

dĭgĭtus -i, m. (1) *a finger*; digitus pollex, *the thumb*; index, *the forefinger*; as a measure, *a finger's breadth, an inch.* (2) *a toe.*

dīglădĭor -ari, dep. *to flourish the sword; to fight, struggle fiercely*; in words, *to dispute.*

dignātĭo -ōnis, f. *esteem; dignity, reputation, honour.*

dignĭtās -ātis, f. *worth, worthiness, merit.* Transf., *dignified appearance* or *style; dignified position, esteem, honour*; esp. *official rank*; plur. dignitates, *persons of rank.*

digno -are, and **dignor** -ari, dep. *to consider worthy*; with infin., *to deign to.*

dignosco (**dīnosco**) -noscĕre -nōvi, *to recognize as different, to distinguish.*

dignus -a -um. (1) *worthy, deserving*; esp. of persons, usually with abl. or genit. (2) of things, *worth having, deserved, suitable, fittings*; dignum est. foll. by infin., *it is proper.* Adv. **dignē.**

dīgrĕdĭor -grĕdi -gressus, dep. *to go apart, depart, deviate*; in speech, *to digress.*

dīgressĭo -ōnis, f. and **dīgressus** -ūs, m. *separation, departure*; in speech, *digression.*

dĭiūdĭcātĭo -ōnis, f. *judging, decision.*

dĭiūdĭco -are. (1) *to judge between parties, to decide, determine.* (2) *to distinguish, find a difference between.*

dĭiun-; see disiun-.

dīlābor -lābi -lapsus, dep., *to glide apart*: of solids, *to fall to pieces, fall down, melt, dissolve*; of liquids, gases, etc., *to flow apart, run away*; of persons in groups, *to break up, slip away*; in gen., *to break up, vanish* of time, *to go by.*

dīlăcĕro -are, *to tear in pieces.*

dīlămĭno -are, *to split in two.*

dīlănĭo -are, *to tear in pieces.*

dīlăpĭdo -are, *to demolish.*

dīlargior -īri, dep. *to hand round, give liberally.*

dīlātĭo -ōnis, f. *putting off, postponing.*

dīlāto -are, *to spread out, extend;* litteras, *to pronounce broadly.*

dīlātor -ōris, m., *a dilatory person, loiterer.*

dīlātus, partic. from differo; q.v.

dīlaudo -are, *to praise highly.*

[1]**dīlectus** -a -um, partic. from diligo; q.v.

[2]**dīlectus** -ūs, m.: in gen., *choosing, choice, selection;* milit., *a levy, recruiting of troops, conscription;* meton., *troops* so raised.

dīlĭgens -entis partic. from diligo; q.v.

dīlĭgentĭa -ae, f., *carefulness, attentiveness, accuracy;* esp. *care in management, economy.*

dīlĭgo -lĭgĕre -lexi -lectum, *to choose out; to prize, love, esteem highly.* Hence pres. partic. **dīlĭgens** -entis, *attentive, careful;* esp. *careful in housekeeping, economical, saving;* adv. **dīlĭgentĕr,** *attentively, carefully.*

dīlōrīco -are, *to tear open.*

dīlūcĕo -ēre, *to be clear, evident.*

dīlūcesco -lūcescĕre -luxi, *to grow light, become day; to become clear.*

dīlūcĭdus -a -um, *clear, lucid, plain;* adv. **dīlūcĭdē.**

dīlūcŭlum -i, n., *the break of day, dawn.*

dīlūdĭum -i, n., *an interval, breathing-space.*

dīlŭo -lŭĕre -lŭi -lūtum. (1) *to wash apart, separate, dissolve;* of troubles, *to remove, resolve;* of puzzles, *to clear up.* (2) *to dilute, temper; to weaken, lessen, impair.*

dīlŭvĭēs -ēi, f. *washing away, inundation.*

dīlŭvĭo -are, *to flood, inundate.*

dīlŭvĭum -i, n. *flood, deluge, inundation.*

dīmāno -are, *to flow in different directions, spread abroad.*

dīmensĭo -ōnis, f. *measuring.*

dīmētĭor -mētīri -mensus, dep. *to measure out.*

dīmēto -are and dep. **dīmētor** -ari, *to measure out.*

dīmĭcātĭo -ōnis, f., *a fight, struggle, battle.*

dīmĭco -are, -avi, *to brandish weapons;* hence *to fight, contend, struggle.*

dīmĭdĭātus -a -um, *halved, divided, half.*

dīmĭdĭus -a -um, *halved, divided in half;* dimidia pars, *half.* N. as subst. **dīmĭdĭum** -i, *half:* dimidio minus, *less by half.*

dīmĭnūtĭo; see deminutio.

dīmissĭo -ōnis, f. (1) *a sending out.* (2) *a dismissing, discharging.*

dīmitto -mittĕre -mīsi -missum. (1) *to send forth, send in different directions;* without object, *to send (word) round.* (2) *to send away, let go, let fall;* milit. *to disband* or *to detach;* of a gathering, *to break up, dismiss;* of places, *to give up, leave;* of abstr. things, *to give up, renounce, abandon.*

dimmĭnŭo -ĕre, *to dash to pieces.*

dīmŏvĕo -mŏvēre -mōvi -mōtum. (1) *to move asunder, part, divide.* (2) *to separate, remove, take away.*

dīnosco = dignosco; q.v.

dīnŭmĕrātĭo -ōnis, f. *enumeration.*

dīnŭmĕro -are, *to count,* esp. *to count money, to pay.*

dĭoecēsis -ĕos and -is, f., *a district* under a governor.

dĭoecētes -ae, m., *a revenue official* or *treasurer.*

Dĭŏmēdēs -is, m. (1) *a hero of the Trojan War, son of Tydeus.* (2) *king of the Bistones in Thrace.*

Dĭōnē -ēs, f. and **Dĭōna** -ae, f. (1) *the mother of Venus.* (2) *Venus.* Adj. **Dĭōnaeus** -a -um.

Dĭŏnȳsus (-os) -i, m., *the Greek name of Bacchus.* Hence **Dĭŏnȳsĭa** -orum, n. pl. *the feast of Dionysus.*

dĭōta -ae, f. *a two-handled wine-jar.*

diplōma -ătis, n. (1) *a letter of introduction given to travellers.* (2) *a government document conferring privileges.*

dīremptus -ūs, m. *a separation.*

dīreptĭo -ōnis, f. *plundering, pillaging.*

dīreptor -ōris, m., *plunderer, pillager.*

dĭrĭbĕo -ēre -ĭtum, *to sort tablets when taken out of the ballot-box.*

dĭrĭbĭtĭo -ōnis, f. *sorting of voting tablets.*

dĭrĭbĭtor -ōris, m., *the officer who sorted voting tablets.*

dīrĭgo -rĭgĕre -rexi -rectum, *to arrange, direct.*

Hence partic. **dīrectus** -a -um, *straight, direct; straightforward, plain, simple.* Abl. as adv. **dīrectō** and adv. **dīrectē,** *straight, directly.* See also derigo.

dĭrĭmo -ĭmĕre -ēmi -emptum, *to part, separate, divide.* Transf., *to break off, interrupt, stop* temporarily or permanently.

dīrĭpĭo -rĭpĕre -rĭpŭi -reptum, *to snatch apart, tear to pieces;* of spoil, *to divide,* hence, milit., *to pillage, lay waste; to tear away.*

dīrĭtās -ātis, f. *misfortune, disaster; cruelty, fierceness.*

dīrumpo -rumpĕre -rūpi -ruptum, *to break apart* or *to pieces, shatter;* of friendship, etc., *to sever, break up;* in pass., dirumpi, *to burst with envy, grief, anger.*

dīrŭo -rŭĕre -ŭi -ŭtum, *to pull apart, demolish, destroy, break up;* financially, *to ruin.*

dīrus -a -um, *fearful, horrible, frightful, cruel.* N. pl. **dīra** -orum, and f. pl. **dīrae** -arum, as subst., *unlucky omens, curses;* **Dīrae** -arum, as name for the *Furies.*

[1]**Dīs,** Dītis, m. *a name of Pluto, god of the Lower World.*

[2]**dīs,** dītis (contracted from dives), *rich; having* or *containing* or *bringing wealth.*

discēdo -cēdĕre -cessi -cessum. (1) *to*

go asunder, part, separate. (2) *to depart, go away*; milit., *to march away*; discedere ab signis, *to break the ranks*; ab armis, *to lay down arms; to come out of a contest, to come off*; in gen., *to depart, pass away; to deviate, swerve, digress*; polit., of the senate, in sententiam discedere, *to support a resolution.*

disceptātĭo -ōnis, f. *debate, discussion, controversy.*

disceptātor -ōris, m. and **disceptātrix** -trīcis, f. *an arbitrator.*

discepto -are. (1) *to decide, settle, determine.* (2) *to dispute, debate, discuss.*

discerno -cernĕre -crēvi -crētum, *to sever, separate, set apart.* Transf., *to distinguish, discern.*

discerpo -cerpĕre -cerpsi -cerptum, *to pluck to pieces, dismember.*

discessĭo -ōnis, f. (1) *going separate ways, separation*; polit., *voting, a division in the senate.* (2) *a going away, departure.*

discessus -ūs, m. (1) *parting, separation.* (2) *departure, going away*; milit., *marching off; banishment.*

discĭdĭum -i, n. *tearing apart; separation, division; separation in feelings, disagreement.*

discīdo -ĕre, *to cut in pieces.*

discindo -ĕre -scĭdi -scissum, *to cleave asunder, split.*

discingo -cingĕre -cinxi -cinctum, *to take off the girdle, ungird.* Partic. **discinctus** -a -um, *ungirt; at ease, careless, dissolute.*

disciplīna -ae, f., *instruction, teaching; training, education*; esp. *military training.* Transf., *results of training, discipline, ordered way of life; that which is taught, learning, body of knowledge, science; a rhetorical* or *philosophical school* or *system.*

discĭpŭla -ae, f., *a female pupil.*

discĭpŭlus -i, m. *a pupil, apprentice.*

disclūdo -clūdĕre -clūsi -clūsum, *to shut away, separate, divide.*

disco discĕre dĭdĭci, *to learn, get to know*; discere fidibus, *to learn to play on the lyre;* in gen., *to receive information, find out; to become acquainted with, learn to recognize.*

discŏlor -ōris, *of different colours*; in gen., *different.*

disconvĕnĭo -ire, *to disagree, not to harmonize.*

discordābĭlis -e, *disagreeing.*

discordĭa -ae, f. *dissension, disagreement*; milit., *mutiny, sedition.*

discordĭōsus -a -um, *full of discord, mutinous.*

discordo -are, *to be at discord, disagree, be opposed*; milit., *to be mutinous.*

discors -cordis, *disagreeing, inharmonious, opposed, different.*

discrĕpantĭa -ae, f. *disagreement, difference.*

discrĕpātĭo -ōnis, f. *disagreement, disunion.*

discrĕpĭto -are, *to be quite unlike.*

discrĕpo -are -ŭi, *to differ in sound, be discordant; to disagree, be different.* Res discrepat, or impers., discrepat, *people are not agreed*; with acc. and infin., *it is inconsistent that.*

discrībo -scrībĕre -scripsi -scriptum, *to mark out, arrange, classify, define; to allot, fix, appoint.*

Hence partic. **discriptus** -a -um, *classified, arranged*; adv. **discripte.**

discrīmen -ĭnis, n. (1) *dividing line, distinction, difference, interval.* (2) *turning-point, critical moment; crisis, hazard, danger.*

discrīmĭno -are, *to separate, sunder, divide.*

discriptĭo -ōnis, f. *an arrangement definition, distribution.*

discrŭcĭo -are, *to torture, torment,* esp. mentally.

discumbo -cumbĕre -cŭbŭi -cŭbĭtum. (1) *to recline at table.* (2) *to go to bed.*

discŭpĭo -cupĕre (colloq.), *to long.*

discurro -currĕre -cŭcurri and -curri -cursum, *to run about, run to and fro.*

discursus -ūs, m. *a running about, running to and fro.*

discus -i, m., *a quoit.*

discŭtĭo -cŭtĕre -cussi -cussum, *to shatter.* Transf., *to disperse, scatter, break up.*

dĭsertus -a -um, *eloquent, expressive*; adv. **dĭserte** and **dĭsertim.**

disĭcĭo disĭcĕre disiēci disiectum, *to throw in different directions, cast asunder;* of buildings, etc., *to throw down*; of military formations, *to break up, disperse*; of abstr. things, *to break up, frustrate.*

disiecto -are, *to toss about.*

[1]**disiectus** -a -um, partic. from disicio; q.v.

[2]**disiectus** -us, m., *scattering, dispersing.*

disiunctĭo -ōnis, f. *separation, estrangement;* in logic, *a disjunctive proposition.*

disiungo (**dĭiungo**) -iungĕre -iunxi -iunctum, *to unbind, loosen, separate, remove, distinguish.*

Hence partic. **disiunctus** -a -um, *separated, apart, distant, remote*; of speech, *disconnected*; in logic, *disjunctive.* Compar. adv. **disiunctĭus,** *rather in disjunctive fashion.*

dispando -pandĕre -pandi -pansum, or -pessum, *to expand, stretch out.*

dispār -păris, *unlike, dissimilar, unequal.*

dispărĭlis -e, *unlike, dissimilar, unequal.*

dispăro -are, *to separate, part, divide*; n. of partic. as subst. **dispărātum** -i, rhet., *the contradictory proposition.*

dispartĭo = dispertio; q.v.

dispello -pellĕre -pŭli -pulsum, *to drive in different directions, to scatter.*

dispendĭum -i, n. *expenditure, expense loss.*

dispenno = dispando; q.v.

dispensātĭo -ōnis, f., *weighing out; management, administration; the office of a treasurer.*

dispensātor -ōris, m. *steward, bailiff treasurer.*

dispenso -are, *to weigh out* or *pay out;* in gen., *to distribute, to arrange.*

disperdo -dĕre -dĭdi -dĭtum, *to squander, ruin, spoil.*
dispĕrĕo -ire -ĭi, *to perish utterly, be squandered, ruined.*
dispergo -spergĕre -spersi -spersum, *to scatter, disperse.* Adv. from perf. partic. **dispersē,** *dispersedly, here and there.*
dispertĭo -ire, and dep. **dispertĭor** -iri, *to separate, divide, distribute.*
dispĭcĭo -spĭcĕre -spexi -spectum, *to see clearly,* esp. by an effort; *to make out, discern, perceive; to reflect upon, consider.*
displĭcĕo -ēre, *to displease*; displicere sibi, *to be dissatisfied with oneself, be out of spirits.*
displōdo -plōdĕre -plōsi -plōsum, *to burst noisily.*
dispōno -pōnĕre -pŏsŭi -pŏsĭtum, *to put in different places, to distribute, put in order*; milit., *to station at intervals.*
Hence partic. **dispŏsĭtus** -a -um, *arranged, orderly;* adv. **dispŏsĭtē,** *in order, methodically.*
dispŏsĭtĭo -ōnis, f. *regular arrangement* or *order in a speech.*
dispŏsĭtū abl. sing. m., *in* or *by arranging.*
dispŏsĭtūra -ae, f., *arrangement, order.*
dispŭdet -ēre -ŭit, *it is a great shame.*
dispŭtātĭo -ōnis, f. *arguing, debate.*
dispŭtātor -ōris, m. *debater, disputant.*
dispŭto -are, *to reckon up; to debate, discuss, argue.*
disquīro -ĕre, *to inquire into, investigate.*
disquīsītĭo -ōnis, f. *inquiry, investigation.*
dissaepĭo -saepire -saepsi -saeptum, *to hedge off, separate, divide*; n. of perf. partic. as subst. **dissaeptum** -i, *barrier, partition.*
dissĕco -sĕcare -sĕcŭi -sectum, *to cut up.*
dissēmĭno -are, *to spread abroad, disseminate.*
dissensĭo -ōnis, f. *difference in feeling* or *opinion; disagreement, variance, conflict, opposition.*
dissensus -ūs, m. *disunion, disagreement.*
dissentānĕus -a -um, *disagreeing, different.*
dissentĭo -sentire -sensi -sensum, *to be of different feeling* or *opinion, to be opposed, not to agree.*
dissĕrēnat -are, impers., *it is clearing up all round,* of the weather.
[1]**dissĕro** -sĕrĕre -sēvi -sĭtum, *to scatter seed, sow; to spread.*
[2]**dissĕro** -sĕrĕre -sĕrŭi -sertum, *to set in order*; hence *to examine, treat of, discuss.*
disserpo -ere, *to creep about, spread.*
dissertĭo -ōnis, f. *a severance.*
disserto -are, *to treat of, discuss, argue.*
dissĭdĕo -sĭdēre -sēdi -sessum, *to sit apart, be distant, disagree, be opposed*; of clothes, *to sit unevenly.*
dissīdo -sīdĕre -sēdi, *to fall apart, disagree.*
dissignātĭo -ōnis, f. *arrangement.*
dissignātor -ōris, m. *one that arranges, a supervisor.*
dissigno -are, *to arrange, regulote, manage.*
dissĭlĭo -sĭlire -sĭlŭi, *to eap apart, break asunder.*
dissĭmĭlis -e, *unlike, dissimilar*; adv. **dissĭmĭlĭtĕr,** *differently.*
dissĭmĭlĭtūdo -ĭnis, f. *unlikeness, difference.*
dissĭmŭlātĭo -ōnis, f. *a concealing, dissembling,* esp. *of irony.*
dissĭmŭlātor -ōris, m. *dissembler, concealer.*
dissĭmŭlo -are. (1) *to dissemble, disguise, keep secret*; pass. with middle force, dissimulata deam, *concealing her divinity.* (2) *to ignore, leave unnoticed.* Adv. from pres. partic. **dissĭmŭlantĕr,** *in a dissembling manner.*
dissĭpābĭlis -e, *that can be scattered.*
dissĭpātĭo -ōnis, f. *scattering.*
dissĭpo or **dissŭpo** -are, *to scatter, disperse*; milit. *to break up, rout; to break up, destroy, squander.*
Hence partic. **dissĭpātus** -a -um, *disconnected.*
dissĭtus, partic. from dissero; q.v.
dissŏcĭābĭlis -e: act., *separating*; pass. *unable to be united.*
dissŏcĭātĭo -ōnis, f. *separation, parting.*
dissŏcĭo -are, *to separate, sever, divide*; in feeling, *to estrange.*
dissŏlūbĭlis -e, *dissoluble, separable.*
dissŏlūtĭo -ōnis, f. *breaking up, dissolution, destruction*; naturae, *death*; navigii, *shipwreck*; criminum, *refutation*; rhet., *want of connexion.*
dissolvo -solvĕre -solvi -sŏlūtum, *to loosen, break up, undo, destroy*; glaciem, *to melt*; animam, *to die*; criminationem, *to refute*; of debts, *to pay, discharge; to release* a person from difficulties, *to unravel, explain* a difficulty.
Hence partic. **dissŏlūtus** -a -um, *loose*; navigium, *leaky*; of style, *disconnected*; of character, *wanting in energy, lax; profligate, dissolute.* Adv. **dissŏlūtē,** *disconnectedly, loosely; carelessly, negligently, without energy.*
dissŏnus -a -um, *discordant, different, disagreeing.*
dissors -sortis, *having a different lot* or *fate.*
dissuādĕo suādēre -suāsi -suāsum, *to advise against, oppose by argument.*
dissuāsĭo -ōnis, f. *advising to the contrary, speaking against.*
dissuāsor -ōris, m. *one who advises to the contrary, one who speaks against.*
dissulto -are, *to leap apart, burst asunder.*
dissŭo -sŭĕre -sŭi -sūtum, *to unstitch, undo.*
distaedet -ēre, *causes boredom* or *disgust.*
distantĭa -ae, f. *distance, difference, diversity.*
distendo (distenno) -tendĕre -tendi -tentum, *to stretch apart, expand,* esp.

to fill full, distend. Transf., *to distract, perplex.*

Hence partic. **distentus** -a -um, *distended, full.*

distermĭno -are, *to separate by a boundary, divide.*

distĭchon distichi, n., *a poem of two lines, distich.*

distinctĭo -ōnis, f. *a distinction, difference; the finding of a difference, the act of distinguishing, discriminating*; rhet., *a division* in a speech; *a pause, stop.*

[1]**distinctus** -a -um, partic. from distinguo; q.v.

[2]**distinctus** -ūs, m. *difference, distinction.*

distĭnĕo -tĭnēre -tinŭi -tentum, *to hold asunder, keep apart, separate.* Transf., *to divide in feeling; to distract; to keep away, prevent* a thing from happening.

Hence partic. **distentus** -a -um, *distracted, occupied.*

distinguo -stinguĕre -stinxi -stinctum, *to mark off, distinguish, divide.* Transf., *to separate, distinguish*; gram., *to punctuate; to set off, decorate, adorn.*

Hence partic. **distinctus** -a -um, *separate, distinct; set off, diversified, adorned.* Adv. **distinctē,** *clearly, distinctly.*

disto -are, *to be apart, be distant; to differ, be distinct*; impers., distat, *there is a difference.*

distorquĕo torquēre -torsi -tortum, *to twist apart, distort; to torture.*

Hence partic. **distortus** -a -um, *distorted, deformed*; of speech, *perverse.*

distortĭo -ōnis, f. *distortion.*

distractĭo -ōnis, f. *pulling apart, separation, disunion.*

distrăho -trăhĕre -traxi -tractum, *to pull apart* or *pull to pieces*; of associations, *to break up, dissolve*; of persons, *to draw away, estrange,* also *to distract*; of property, *to sell up*; gram., *to leave a hiatus in a verse.*

distrĭbŭo -ŭĕre -ŭi -ūtum, *to distribute, divide.* Adv. from partic. **distrĭbūtē,** *methodically, with logical arrangement.*

distrĭbūtĭo -ōnis, f. *division, distribution.*

distringo -stringĕre -strinxi -strictum, *to draw apart, stretch out, to engage at different points, divert, occupy.*

Hence partic. **districtus** -a -um, *busy, occupied, engaged.*

disturbātĭo -onis, f. *destruction.*

disturbo -are, *to drive apart in confusion; to destroy, raze to the ground; to bring to naught, frustrate, ruin.*

dītesco -ere, *to become rich.*

dīthy̆rambĭcus -a -um, *dithyrambic.*

dīthy̆rambus -i, m. *a dithyrambic poem* (originally in honour of Bacchus).

dĭtĭo, better **dicio;** q.v.

dītĭor, dītissĭmus; see dis.

dīto -are, *to enrich, make wealthy.*

dĭū, adv. (1) *by day.* (2) *for a long time.* (3) *a long time ago.* Compar. **diūtĭus,** *longer; too long.* Superl. **dĭūtissĭmē.**

dĭurnus -a -um, *belonging to a day* or *lasting for a day*; n. as subst. *a journal, account-book* or *a daily allowance.*

dīus -a -um, *divine, god-like*; hence *fine, noble*; also (apparently) *out of doors, in the open air.*

dĭūtĭnus -a -um, *lasting a long time, long*; adv. **dĭūtĭnē.**

dĭūtĭus, dĭūtissĭmē; see diu.

dĭŭturnĭtās -ātis, f. *long duration.*

dĭŭturnus -a -um, adj., *lasting a long time, of long duration.*

dīvārĭco -are, *to stretch apart, spread out.*

dīvello -vellĕre -velli -vulsum (-volsum), *to pluck apart, tear asunder, break up, destroy, interrupt; to distract, pull away, remove, separate.*

dīvendo -vendĕre -vendĭtum, *to sell in separate lots.*

dīverbĕro -are, *to strike apart, cleave, divide.*

dīverbĭum -i, n. *dialogue on the stage.*

dīversĭtās -ātis, f. *contrariety, contradiction; difference, diversity.*

dīversōrĭum; see deversorium.

dīverto (**dīvorto**) -vertĕre -verti -versum, *to turn different ways*; hence *to differ.*

Hence partic. **dīversus** -a -um, *turned away, turned in different directions*; of places, *out of the way, remote*; of character, *fluctuating, irresolute*; in gen., *different, unlike, opposed, hostile.* Adv. **dīversē,** *differently, diversely.*

dīves -vĭtis, *rich, wealthy*; with abl. or genit., *rich in.*

dīvexo -are, *to tear asunder*; hence *to destroy, plunder, to distract.*

dīvĭdĭa -ae, f. *division, trouble.*

dīvĭdo -vĭdĕre -vīsi -vīsum. (1) *to divide up, separate into parts*; esp. *to divide among persons, distribute, allot*; polit., sententiam, *to divide a resolution into parts so that each part can be voted on*; in music, *to accompany.* (2) *to separate from one another; to distinguish; to set off, to adorn.*

Hence partic. **dīvīsus** -a -um, *separate.*

dīvĭdŭus -a -um, *divisible; divided, parted*; fig., *distracted.*

dīvīnātĭo -ōnis, f. *the gift of prophecy, divination*; legal, *the selection of a prosecutor.*

dīvīnĭtās -ātis, f. *divine nature, divinity; the power of prophecy* or *divination; excellence, surpassing merit.*

dīvīnĭtŭs, *divinely, by divine influence; by inspiration, by means of divination; admirably, nobly.*

dīvīno -are, *to foretell, prophesy, forebode.*

dīvīnus -a -um. (1) *belonging* or *relating to a deity, divine*; res divina, *the service of the gods*; n. as subst. *a sacrifice,* in plur. *divine things* or *attributes.* (2) *divinely inspired, prophetic*; vates, *a poet*; m. as subst., *a seer.* (3) *noble, admirable.* Adv. **dīvīnē,** *divinely, by divine* *power; by divine inspiration, prophetically; admirably, excellently.*

dīvīsĭo -ōnis, f. *division, distribution.*

dīvīsor -ōris, m. *a divider; a distributor,* esp. of lands; *a hired bribery agent.*

dīvīsŭī, dat. sing. m., *for division.*

dīvĭtĭae -arum, f. pl. *riches, wealth; ornaments, rich offerings*; of soil, *richness.*

dīvortĭum -i, n. *divergence, separation*; of things, *a boundary, parting of the ways*; of persons, *separation, divorce.*

dīvorto; see diverto.

dīvulgo -are, *to make common, publish, spread abroad.*
Hence partic. **dīvulgātus** -a -um, *spread abroad, made common.*

dīvus -a -um: as adj., *divine* or *deified*; as subst., m. *a god* and f. *a goddess* (often as epithet of dead and deified emperors); sub divo (neuter), *in the open air.*

do dăre dĕdi dătum. (1) *to offer, give, grant, lend, bestow; to hand over, commit, devote*; of letters, *to give for dispatch*; vela dare ventis, *to sail*; poenas, *to pay a penalty*; verba, *to give words only,* i.e., *to cheat*; of news, *to tell, communicate.* (2) *to cause, bring about, put.*

dŏcĕo dŏcēre dŏcŭi doctum, *to teach, instruct* (with acc. of person and/or of thing); with clause, *to inform that* or *how*; docere fabulam *to teach a play to the actors, to bring out, exhibit.*
Hence partic. **doctus** -a -um, *taught; learned, instructed, well-informed; experienced, clever, shrewd.* Adv. **doctē,** *learnedly, skilfully; cleverly, shrewdly.*

dochmĭus -i, m. *a metrical foot, the dochmiac.*

dŏcĭlis -e, *teachable, docile.*

dŏcĭlĭtās -ātis, f. *teachableness, docility.*

doctor -ōris, m. *a teacher.*

doctrīna -ae, f. *teaching, instruction; knowledge, learning.*

doctus -a -um, partic. from doceo; q.v.

dŏcŭmen -ĭnis, n. and **dŏcŭmentum** -i, n., *example, pattern, warning, proof.*

dodrans -antis, m. *three fourths*; as a measure of length, *nine inches.*

dogma -ătis, n. *a philosophical doctrine.*

Dolabella -ae, m. *a Roman family name in the* gens Cornelia.

dŏlabra -ae, f. *a pick-axe.*

dŏlĕo dŏlēre dŏlŭi, *to suffer pain,* physical or mental, *to be pained, to grieve*; of things, *to cause pain.*
Hence partic. **dŏlens,** *painful*; adv. **dŏlentĕr,** *painfully, sorrowfully.*

dŏlĭum -i, n. *a wine-jar, cask.*

[1]**dŏlo** -are, *to hew with an axe, to work roughly*; caput fuste, *to cudgel.*

[2]**dŏlo** or **dŏlon** -ōnis, m. (1) *a pike, sword-stick.* (2) *a small foresail.*

dŏlor -ōris, m., *pain,* physical or mental; esp. *disappointment, resentment.* Transf., *cause of sorrow*; rhet., *pathos.*

dŏlōsus -a -um, *crafty, deceitful, cunning*; adv. **dŏlōse.**

dŏlus -i, m. *a device, artifice; fraud, deceit, guile; a trap.*

dŏmābilis -e, *tameable.*

dŏmestĭcus -a -um. (1) *belonging to house* or *family, domestic*; m. as subst., esp. plur., *members of one's family.* (2) *native*; crudelitas, *towards citizens*; bellum, *civil war.*

dŏmĭcĭlĭum -i, n. *place of residence, dwelling.*

dŏmĭna -ae, f. *mistress of a household; wife, mistress, lady*; of abstr. things, *ruler, controller.*

dŏmĭnātĭo -ōnis, f. *mastery, control, irresponsible power, despotism.*

dŏmĭnātor -ōris, m. *ruler, governor.*

dŏmĭnātrix -īcis, f. *a female ruler, mistress.*

dŏmĭnātus -ūs, m. *mastery, absolute power.*

dŏmĭnĭum -i, n. (1) *rule, power, ownership.* (2) *a feast, banquet.*

dŏmĭnor -ari, dep., *to rule, be supreme, domineer.*

dŏmĭnus -i, m. *master of a house, lord, master.* Transf. *husband* or *lover; a master, owner, possessor; employer; ruler, lord, controller.*

dŏmĭporta -ae, f. *one with her house on her back, the snail.*

Dŏmĭtĭānus -i, m. *son of Vespasian, brother of Titus, Emperor from* 81 to 96 A.D.

Dŏmĭtĭus -a -um, *name of a plebeian* gens *in Rome.*

dŏmĭto -are, *to tame, subdue, break in.*

dŏmĭtor -ōris, m, *tamer, conqueror, victor.*

dŏmĭtrix -īcis, f. *she who tames.*

dŏmĭtus -ūs, m. *taming.*

dŏmo dŏmare dŏmŭi dŏmĭtum, *to tame, break in, conquer, subdue.*

dŏmus -ūs, f. *a house, home*; locative domi, *at home, in the house*; domi habere, *to have at home, to possess*; domum, *home, homewards*; domo, *from home.* Transf., *dwelling, abode; native country; household; philosophical school* or *sect.*

dōnārĭum -i, n. (1) *a temple, shrine, altar.* (2) *a votive offering.*

dōnātĭo -ōnis, f. *giving, donation.*

dōnātīvum -i, n. *an imperial largess.*

dōnĕc (older **donĭcum**). (1) *up to the time when, until.* (2) *so long as, while.*

dōno -are. (1) rem homini, *to give as a present, to present, grant, bestow, give up*; esp. *to remit a debt* or *obligation*; *to forgive, pardon.* (2) hominem re, *to present with.*

dōnum -i, n. *a gift, present*; dono dare, *to give as a present*; esp. *a votive offering.*

dorcas -ădis, f. *gazelle, antelope.*

Dōres -um, m., *the Dorians, one of the Hellenic tribes*; adj. **Dōrĭcus** and **Dōrĭus** -a -um, *Dorian, Greek.* F. **Dōris** -ĭdis: as adj., *Dorian*; as subst., *the country of the Dorians; the wife of Nereus*; meton., *the sea.*

dormĭo -ire, *to sleep; to rest, be inactive.*

dormīto -are, *to be sleepy, begin to sleep, nod; to dream, be lazy*; of a lamp, iam dormitante lucerna, *just going out.*
dormītōrĭus -a -um, *for sleeping.*
dorsum -i, n. *the back*, of men, animals or things; immane dorsum mari summo, *a reef; a mountain ridge, ' hog's back '.*
dōs dōtis, f., *a dowry, marriage portion; a gift, quality, endowment.*
dōtālis -e, *belonging to* or *forming a dowry.*
dōto -are, *to provide with a dowry, endow*; partic. **dōtātus** -a -um, *richly endowed.*
drachma (**drachŭma**) -ae, f., *a drachma, a small Greek coin.*
drăco -ōnis, m., *a kind of snake, dragon.*
drăcōnĭgĕna -ae, c. *dragon-born.*
drāpĕta -ae, m. *a runaway slave.*
Drĕpănum -i, n. and **Drĕpăna** -orum, plur., *a town on the west coast of Sicily.*
drŏmas -ădis, m. *a dromedary.*
Drŭentĭa -ae, f. *a river in Gaul* (now *Durance*).
Drŭĭdēs -um and **Drŭĭdae** -arum, m. *the Druids.*
Drūsus -i, m. *a cognomen of the* gens Livia; hence adj. **Drūsĭanus** and **Drūsīnus** -a -um, *of Drusus*: subst. **Drūsilla** -ae, f. *name of several females of the* gens Livia.
Drȳăs -ădis, f. *a wood nymph, Dryad.*
dŭbĭtābĭlis -e, *doubtful, uncertain.*
dŭbĭtātĭo -ōnis, f., *doubt, uncertainty; hesitation, irresolution.*
dŭbĭto -are. (1) *to doubt, waver in opinion, be uncertain.* (2) *to waver as to action, be irresolute, hesitate.* Adv. from partic., **dŭbĭtantĕr,** *doubtingly, hesitatingly.*
dŭbĭus -a -um, *doubtful.* (1) act., *wavering*: in opinion, *doubting; uncertain*; as to action, *hesitating, irresolute.* (2) pass., *uncertain, doubted, doubtful*; n. as subst.; in dubium vocare, *to call in question*; procul dubio, *without doubt.* (3) fig., *doubtful, dangerous, critical.* Adv. **dŭbĭē,** *doubtfully*; haud dubie, *certainly.*
dŭcēni -ae, -a, *a group of two hundred,* or *two hundred each.*
dŭcentēsĭma -ae, f. *the two hundredth part, one-half per cent.*
dŭcenti -ae, -a, *two hundred.*
dŭcentĭe(n)s, *two hundred times.*
dūco dūcĕre duxi ductum. (1) *to draw; to draw along* or *away*; hence *to shape* anything long, *to construct*; carmina, *to make verses*; of time, either *to spend* or *to delay, protract.* Transf., *to charm, influence, mislead; to derive.* (2) *to draw in*; aera spiritu, *to inhale*; pocula, *to quaff.* (3) *to lead*; in marriage, *to marry a wife*; milit., either *to lead on the march,* or *to command.* (4) *to calculate, count, reckon; to esteem, consider.*
ductim, *by drawing; in a stream.*
ductĭto and **ducto** -are, *to lead,* esp. *to lead home* a wife. Transf., *to cheat.*
ductor -ōris, m. *a leader, commander; a guide.*
ductus -ūs, m. (1) *drawing, drawing off.* (2) *shaping, shape*; oris, *the lineaments of the face*; muri, *line of a wall.* (3) *leading, command, leadership.*
dūdum, *some time ago; a little while ago, not long since; a long while ago* or *for a long time.*
dŭellum, dŭellĭcus, dŭellātor = bellum, bellicus, bellator; q.v.
Dŭīlĭus -a -um, *name of a Roman* gens.
dulcēdo -ĭnis, f., *sweetness, pleasantness, charm.*
dulcesco -ĕre, *to become sweet.*
dulcĭcŭlus -a -um, *somewhat sweet.*
dulcis -e, *sweet*; unda, *fresh water*; in gen., *pleasant, delightful, agreeable*; of persons, *friendly, dear.* N. acc. **dulcĕ** and adv. **dulcĭter,** *sweetly.*
dulcĭtūdo -ĭnis, f. *sweetness.*
dum. (1) adv., joined as an enclitic with other words; nondum, *not yet*; vixdum, *scarcely yet*; nedum, *not to say*; age dum, *come now.* (2) conj.: *while, during the time that; while, throughout the time that; so long as, provided that; until.*
dūmētum -i, n. *a thorn brake, thicket.*
dummŏdo, *provided that, so long as.*
dūmōsus -a -um, *covered with thorn bushes, bushy.*
dumtaxat. (1) *at least, not less than.* (2) *at most, not more than.*
dūmus -i, m. *a thorn bush, bramble.*
dŭŏ -ae, -ŏ, *two.*
dŭŏdĕcĭe(n)s, *twelve times.*
dŭŏdĕcim, *twelve.*
dŭŏdĕcĭmus -a -um, *twelfth.*
dŭŏdēni -ae, -a, *twelve at a time* or *twelve each.*
dŭŏdēquādrāgēsĭmus, *thirty-eighth.*
dŭŏdēquādrāgĭnta, *thirty-eight.*
dŭŏdēquinquāgēsĭmus -a -um, *forty-eighth.*
dŭŏdētrīcĭe(n)s, *twenty-eight times.*
dŭŏdētrīgĭnta, *twenty-eight.*
dŭŏdevīcēni -ae -a, *eighteen each.*
dŭŏdevīginti, *eighteen.*
dŭŏetvīcēsĭmāni -orum, m. *soldiers of the 22nd legion.*
dŭŏetvīcēsĭmus -a -um, *twenty-second.*
duplex -plĭcis, *double, doubled, twofold.* Transf. (1) plur., *both.* (2) *two-faced, deceitful, equivocal.* Adv. **duplĭcĭtĕr,** *doubly.*
duplĭcārĭus -a -um: miles, *a soldier who gets double pay.*
duplĭco -are, *to double*; of words, *to repeat*; also *to form compound words.* Transf., *to bend double*; in gen., *to lengthen, increase.*
duplus -a -um, *twice as much, double*; n. as subst. *double,* esp. *a double penalty.*
dŭpondĭus -i, m., *a coin of two asses.*
dūrābĭlis -e, *lasting, durable.*
dūrāmen -ĭnis, n. *hardness.*
dūrătĕus -a -um, *wooden.*

duresco dūrescĕre dūrŭi, *to grow hard*; of water, *to freeze*.
dūrĭtās -ātis, f., *harshness, unfriendliness*.
dūrĭtĭa -ae, and **dūrĭtĭēs** -ēi, f., *hardness*; fig., *austerity, harshness, severity*.
dūro -are: transit., *to make hard* or *hardy, to inure*; intransit., *to become hard* or *dry; to be hard* or *callous; to endure, hold out; to last, remain, continue*.
dūrus -a -um, *hard, harsh; tough, strong, enduring*; in demeanour or tastes, *rough, rude, uncouth*; in character, *hard, austere*, sometimes *brazen, shameless*; of things, *hard, awkward, difficult, adverse*. Adv. **dūrē** and **dūrĭtĕr**, *hardly, hardily; roughly, rudely; harshly, unpleasantly, severely*.
dŭumvir and **dŭŏvir** -vĭri, m. usually pl., *a pair of magistrates, a commission of two*.
dux dŭcis, c. (1) *a guide, conductor*. (2) *a leader, ruler, commander*.
dy̆nastēs -is, m. *ruler, prince*.
Dyrrhăchĭum -i, n. *a port in Illyria*.

E

E, e, the fifth letter of the Latin alphabet.
e, prep. = ex; q.v.
ĕā, adv. = abl. of is; q.v.
ĕādem, *by the same way, likewise*.
ĕātĕnus, *so far*.
ĕbĕnus -i, m. = hebenus; q.v.
ēbĭbo -bĭbĕre -bĭbi, *to drink up*.
ēblandĭor -iri, dep. *to obtain by flattery*.
ēbrĭĕtās -atis, f. *drunkenness*.
ēbrĭŏlus -a -um, *tipsy*.
ēbrĭōsĭtās -ātis, f. *love of drink, drunkenness*.
ēbrĭōsus -a -um, *drink-loving*.
ēbrĭus -a -um, *drunk, intoxicated*.
ēbullĭo -ire, *to boil up; to boast of*.
ēbŭlum -i, n. (or **-us** -i, m.), *the dwarf elder*.
ĕbur -ŏris, n. *ivory*. Transf. (1) of things made of ivory. (2) *the elephant*.
ĕburnĕŏlus -a -um, *made of ivory*.
ĕburnĕus or **ĕburnus** -a -um, *made of ivory, white as ivory*.
ēcastor; see Castor.
eccĕ, *behold! lo! see!*
eccĕrē, *there you are!*
ecclēsĭa -ae, f., *an assembly of the (Greek) people*.
ecdĭcus -i, m. *a solicitor for a community*.
Ĕcētra -ae, f. *capital of the Volsci*.
ecf-; see eff-.
ĕchĕnēis -ĭdis, f., *a sucking fish, the remora*.
ĕchīnus -i, m. (1) *an edible sea-urchin*. (2) *a copper dish*.
ēchō -ūs, f. *an echo*; personif., *Echo, a wood-nymph*.
eclŏgārĭi -orum, m. pl. *select passages* or *extracts*.
ecquando, adv., *ever? at any time?*
ecqui, ecquae or ecqua, ecquod, interrog. adj., *is there any . . . that? does any . . .?*
ecquis, ecquid, interrog. pron., *is there any that? does anyone?* Hence **ecquid** or **ecqui,** *at all?* or *whether?* **ecquō,** *whither?*
ĕcŭlĕus i, m. *a little horse, colt; a rack, instrument of torture*.
ĕdācĭtās -ātis, f. *greediness, gluttony*.
ĕdax -ācis, f. *greedy, gluttonous; destructive, consuming*.
ĕdĕpol; see Pollux.
ēdīco -dīcĕre -dixi -dictum, *to announce, declare*; esp. of a magistrate, *to decree, ordain by proclamation*. Hence n. of partic. as subst. **ēdictum** -i, *a decree, edict*.
ēdictĭo -ōnis, f. *an edict*.
ēdicto -are, *to proclaim*.
ēdisco -discĕre -dĭdĭci, *to learn thoroughly*.
ēdissĕro -sĕrĕre -sĕrŭi -sertum, *to explain, set forth, relate fully*.
ēdisserto -are, *to explain exactly*.
ēdĭtĭcĭus -a -um, *announced, proposed*: iudices, *jurors chosen by a plaintiff*.
ēdĭtĭo -ōnis, f. *the publishing of a book; a statement*; editio tribuum, *a proposal by a plaintiff for the choice of a jury*.
[1]**ĕdo** ĕdĕre or esse ēdi ēsum, *to eat, devour, consume, waste*.
[2]**ēdo** -dĕre -dĭdi -dĭtum, *to put forth, give out*; animam, *to breathe one's last, die*; clamorem, *to utter*. Esp. (1) *to bring into the world, to bring forth, give birth to*; of things, *to produce*. (2) *to make known*: of writings, *to publish*; of ideas and information, *to divulge, spread*; officially, *to proclaim*; as legal t. t., *to fix, determine, nominate*. (3) *to bring about, cause, produce*; of magistrates, *to provide games for the people*.

Hence partic. **ēdĭtus** -a -um, *raised, high, lofty*; n. as subst. *a high place, eminence*.
ēdŏcĕo -dŏcēre -dŏcŭi -doctum, *to instruct thoroughly, inform fully*.
ēdŏmo -dŏmare -dŏmŭi -dŏmĭtum, *to tame thoroughly, entirely subdue*.
Ēdōni -orum, *a Thracian people, famed for the worship of Bacchus*; adj. **Ēdōnus** -a -um, and **Ēdōnis** -nĭdis, f. *Thracian*.
ēdormĭo -ire, *to have one's sleep out*; transit., *to sleep off*.
ēdormisco -ĕre, *to sleep off*.
ēdŭcātĭo -ōnis, f. *bringing up, training, education*.
ēdŭcātor -ōris, m. *one who brings up; a foster-father* or *a tutor*.
ēdŭcātrix -īcis, f. *a foster-mother, nurse*.
[1]**ēdŭco** -are, *to bring up, raise, rear, educate*.
[2]**ēdūco** -dūcĕre -duxi -ductum. (1) *to draw out, lead out*; of time, *to spend*; milit., *to march troops out*; legal, *to bring before a court of law*; naut., *to take a ship out of port*. (2) *to raise up* (of persons and buildings); in

astra, *to praise sky-high.* (3) *to bring up, rear.*
ĕdūlis -e, *eatable.*
ēdūro -are, *to last, endure.*
ēdūrus -a -um, *very hard.*
effarcio = effercio; q.v.
effātum -i, n. from partic. of effor; q.v.
effectĭo -ōnis, f. *practising.* Transf., *an efficient cause.*
effector -ōris, m. *one who produces, causes, originates.*
effectrix -trīcis, f. *she that causes or produces.*
[1]**effectus** -a -um, partic. of efficio; q.v.
[2]**effectus** -ūs, m. *doing, execution, performance; effect, result.*
effēmĭno -are, *to make into a woman;* in character, *to make effeminate.*
Hence partic. **effēmĭnātus** -a -um, *effeminate, womanish*; adv. **effēmĭnātē.**
effercio or **effarcĭo** -fercire, -fertum, *to stuff full*; partic. **effertus,** *stuffed.*
effĕrĭtās -ātis, f., *wildness, savagery.*
[1]**effĕro** -are, *to make wild, make savage*; partic. **effĕrātus** -a -um, *wild, savage.*
[2]**effĕro** (**ecfero**) efferre extŭli ēlātum. (1) *to carry out, bring out*; efferre signa, *to march out.* Esp. *to carry to the grave, bury*; pass., efferri, *to be borne out, buried*; of the earth, *to bring forth, bear; to utter, express, publish* words or ideas. (2) *to carry off* or *away*; pass., efferri *to be carried away* by feelings. (3) *to raise up, lift up; to praise, extol*; efferri or se efferre, *to pride oneself, be puffed up.* (4) *to endure to the end.*
Hence partic. **ēlātus** -a -um, *elevated, exalted*; adv. **ēlātē,** *loftily.*
effertus -a -um, partic. from effercio; q.v.
effĕrus -a -um, *wild, savage.*
effervesco -fervescĕre -fervi, *to boil up, effervesce*; of an orator, *to be passionate.*
effervo -ĕre, *to boil up* or *over; to swarm forth.*
effētus -a -um, *weakened* (by giving birth); *effete.*
effĭcācĭtās -ātis, f. *efficacy.*
effĭcax -ācis, *effective, efficient, efficacious*; adv. **effĭcācĭtĕr.**
effĭcĭens -entis, partic. from efficio; q.v.
effĭcĭentĭa -ae, f. *efficiency.*
effĭcĭo -fĭcĕre -fēci -fectum, *to do, produce, effect, make*; of results, *to bring about, cause* (esp. with ut and subj.); of numbers, *to make up, amount to*; philosoph. *to prove, show*; of appointments and changes, *to make.*
Hence partic. **effĭcĭens** -entis, *effective*: causa, *efficient cause*; adv. **effĭcĭentĕr,** *efficiently, powerfully.*
effĭgĭēs -ēi, or **effĭgĭa** -ae, f. *an image, likeness, effigy; a shade, ghost; an ideal.*
effingo -fingĕre -finxi -fictum. (1) *to wipe.* (2) *to mould, form, fashion*; esp. *to form one thing like another,* and so *to copy, represent, express* in words, *conceive* in thought.
effĭo (**ecf-**) -fĭĕri, old pass. of efficio; q.v.
efflāgĭtātĭo -ōnis, f., *an urgent demand.*
efflāgĭtātū abl. sing. m., at *an urgent request.*
efflāgĭto -are, *to ask earnestly, demand, entreat.*
efflīgo -ĕre -flixi -flictum, *to destroy.*
efflo -are, *to blow out, breathe out*: animam, *to die.*
efflōresco -flōrescĕre -flōrŭi, *to blossom, break into bloom.*
efflŭo (**ecflŭo**) -flŭĕre -fluxi, *to flow out.* Transf. (1) *to vanish, drop off.* (2) *to pass out of mind, be forgotten.* (3) *to come to light, become known.*
efflŭvĭum -i, n., *flowing out, outlet.*
effŏdĭo -fŏdĕre -fōdi -fossum. (1) *to dig out, gouge out.* (2) *to make by digging, to excavate.* (3) *to gut, to rummage.*
effor (**ecfor**) -fari -fatus, dep. *to speak out, express, speak*: in logic, *to state a proposition*; in religion, *formally to dedicate* a place.
Hence partic. (in pass. sense) **effātus** -a -um, *pronounced; dedicated.*
effrēnātĭo -ōnis, f. *unbridled impetuosity.*
effrēno -are, *to unbridle, let loose*; partic. **effrēnātus** -a -um, *unbridled, unrestrained, violent*; adv. **effrēnātē.**
effrēnus -a -um, *unbridled, unrestrained.*
effringo -fringĕre -frēgi -fractum, *to break open.*
effŭgĭo -fŭgĕre -fūgi -fŭgĭtum: intransit., *to flee, fly away, escape, get off*; transit., *to escape from, avoid, shun.*
effŭgĭum -i, n. *a flying away, flight; means* or *opportunity of flight.*
effulgĕo -fulgēre -fulsi, *to shine out, glitter; to be distinguished, conspicuous.*
effultus -a -um, *resting upon, supported by.*
effundo (**ecf-**) -fundĕre -fūdi -fūsum, *to pour out, pour forth, shed;* of solids, *to fling out, empty out*; with violence, *to throw off, fling down*; esp. of horses, *to throw their riders*; of weapons, *to discharge*; spiritum extremum, *to die*; se effundere, and effundi, *to stream forth, pour forth,* also *to give oneself up to, indulge in*: of sounds, *to utter*; with ideas of generosity, waste, etc. *to pour out freely, squander*; habenas, *to slacken.*
Hence partic. **effūsus** -a -um, *poured out*; hence *widespread, extensive; extravagant, wasteful; unrestrained*; adv. **effūsē.**
effūsĭo -ōnis, f. *a pouring forth; violent movement; extravagance, prodigality; exuberance of spirits.*
effūsus, partic. from effundo; q.v.
effūtĭo -ire, *to blab out, chatter.*
ēgĕlĭdus -a -um, *with the chill off; lukewarm, tepid.*
ĕgens -entis, partic. from egeo; q.v.

ĕgēnus -a -um, *needy, destitute*; with genit. or abl., *in need of.*

ĕgĕo -ēre -ŭi, *to want, be in need*; with genit, or abl. *to be in want of, to be without, not to have*; also *to desire, wish for, want.*

Hence partic. **ĕgens** -entis, *needy, destitute*; with genit., *in need of.*

Ēgĕrĭa -ae, f. *a nymph, instructress of Numa Pompilius.*

ēgĕro -gĕrĕre -gessi -gestum, *carry out* or *off.*

ĕgestās -ātis, f. *poverty, indigence, need*; with genit., *want of.*

ēgestĭo -ōnis, f. *wasting.*

ĕgŏ, I; plur. nos. *we* (often used for sing.); alter ego, *my second self*; ad me, *to my house*; apud me, *at my house,* also *in my senses.*

ēgrĕdĭor -grĕdi -gressus, dep.: intransit., *to go out, pass out*; milit., *to march out*; naut., egredi (ex) navi, *to disembark*; in speech, *to digress*; sometimes *to go up, ascend*; transit., *to go out of, pass beyond, overstep, pass.*

ēgrĕgĭus -a -um, *not of the common herd; excellent, extraordinary, distinguished*; adv. **ēgrĕgĭē.**

ēgressus -ūs, m. *going out, departure*; esp. *landing from a ship, disembarkation.* Transf., *a passage out; the mouth of a river*; in speech, *digression.*

ehem, *oho!*

ēheu, *alas! woe!*

ĕhŏ, *hi!*

ei (hei), *ah! woe!*

eĭă and **heĭă:** expressing joy or surprise, *well!*; in exhortation, *come on!*

ēiăcŭlor -ari, dep. *to throw out, hurl out.*

ēicĭo -ĭcĕre -iēci -iectum, *to throw out, cast out, eject*; vocem, *to utter*; armum, *to dislocate*; se eicere, *to rush out*; naut., *to bring to shore*; pass., *to be cast ashore, stranded*; eiectus, *a shipwrecked person.* Transf., *to drive out, expel, dispossess*; domo, *to divorce*; ex patria, *to banish*; of feelings *to cast out, put aside.*

ēiectāmentum -i, n. *that which is thrown up.*

ēiectĭo -ōnis, f. *banishment, exile.*

ēiecto -are, *to hurl out, eject.*

ēiectus -ūs, m. *casting out.*

ēiŭlātĭo -ōnis, f., and **ēiŭlātus** -ūs, m. *wailing, lamenting.*

ēiŭlo are, *to wail, lament.*

ēiūro and **ēiĕro** -are, *to refuse* or *deny on oath*; bonam copiam, *to swear that one is insolvent*; forum sibi iniquum, *to declare that a court is partial*; magistratum, imperium, *to resign, abdicate*; in gen., *to give up, disown.*

ēiusdemmŏdi, *of the same kind.*

ēiusmŏdi, *of this kind, such, so.*

ēlābor -lābi -lapsus, dep. *to glide out, slip away, escape, disappear.*

ēlăbōro -are; intransit., *to labour hard, strive, take pains*; transit., *to labour on, work out, elaborate,* esp. in partic.

ēlăbōrātus, -a -um, *elaborate, artificial.*

ēlāmentābĭlis -e, *very lamentable.*

ēlanguesco -guescĕre -gŭi, *to become weak, be relaxed.*

ēlātĭo -onis, f. a *lifting up*; fig., *exaltation.*

ēlātro -are, *to bark out, cry out.*

ēlātus -a -um, partic. from effero; q.v.

Ĕlĕa or **Vĕlĭa** -ae, f. *town in Lucania, birth-place of Parmenides and Zeno, the founders of the Eleatic school of philosophy*; subst. **Ĕlĕātes** -ae, m. *Zeno*; adj. **Ĕlĕātĭcus** -a -um, *Eleatic.*

ēlectĭo -ōnis, f. *choice, selection.*

ēlectrum -i, n. *amber*; plur. *amber balls; an alloy of gold and silver, resembling amber.*

[1]**ēlectus** -a -um, partic. from eligo; q.v.

[2]**ēlectus** -ūs, m. *choosing, choice.*

ēlĕgans -antis, *choice, fine, neat, tasteful*; in bad sense, *fastidious, fussy*; adv. **ēlĕgantĕr.**

ēlĕgantĭa -ae, f. *taste, refinement, grace*; in bad sense, *fastidiousness.*

ĕlĕgi -orum, m. pl. *elegiac verses.*

ĕlĕgīa and **ĕlĕgēa** -ae, f. *an elegy.*

ēlĕmentum -i, n. *an element, first principle*; in plur., *physical elements; letters of the alphabet, beginnings, the elements of any science* or *art.*

ĕlenchus -i, m. *a pearl pendant worn as an ear-ring.*

ĕlĕphantus -i, c. *an elephant; ivory.*

ĕlĕphās (-ans) -phantis, m. *an elephant; the disease elephantiasis.*

ēlĕvo -are, *to lift up, raise, elevate; to weaken, impair, disparage; to alleviate, lighten.*

ēlĭcĭo -lĭcĕre -lĭcŭi -lĭcĭtum, *to lure out, entice, call forth*; inferorum animas, *to conjure up.*

ēlīdo -līdĕre -līsi -līsum. (1) *to strike, knock, thrust out, expel.* (2) *to dash to pieces, shatter.*

ēlĭgo -lĭgĕre -lēgi -lectum, *to pick out, choose, select*; fig., *to root out.*

Hence partic. **ēlectus** -a -um, *chosen, select*; adv., **ēlectē,** *choicely.*

ēlīmĭno -are, *to carry out of doors*; dicta, *to blab.*

ēlīmo -are, *to file off, polish, elaborate, perfect.*

ēlinguis -e, *speechless* or *without eloquence.*

Ĕlissa (Ĕlīsa) -ae, f. *another name of Dido.*

ēlixus -a -um, *boiled, sodden.*

ellĕbŏrus (hell-) -i, m. and **ellĕbŏrum (hell-)** -i, n. *hellebore,* a plant considered a remedy for madness.

ēlŏco -are, *to let, hire out.*

ēlŏcūtĭo -ōnis, f. *oratorical delivery, elocution.*

ēlŏgĭum -i, n. *a short saying, maxim; an inscription*; esp. on a gravestone, *epitaph; a clause in a will, codicil; a record of a case.*

ēlŏquentĭa -ae, f. and **ēlŏquĭum** -i, n., *eloquence.*

ēlŏquor -lŏqui -lŏcūtus, dep. *to speak out, express*; esp. *to speak eloquently*; partic. **ēlŏquens** -entis, *eloquent*; adv. **ēlŏquentĕr.**

ēlūcĕo -lūcēre -luxi, *to beam forth, shine out, glitter.*

ēluctor -ari, dep: intransit., *to struggle out*; transit., *to struggle out of, surmount a dfficulty.*

ēlūcubro -are, and **ēlūcubror** -ari, dep. *to compose by lamplight.*

ēlūdo -lūdĕre -lūsi -lūsum: intransit., *to finish playing*, esp. of the waves of the sea; transit., *to parry a blow; to ward off, evade; to beat* an opponent in play; *to delude, mock.*

ēlūgĕo -lūgēre -luxi, *to mourn for the prescribed period.*

ēlumbis -e, *weak, feeble.*

ēlŭo -lŭĕre -lŭi -lūtum, *to wash out, wash clean, rinse, cleanse.* Transf., *to squander; to wash away, efface, remove.*

Hence partic. **ēlūtus** -a -um, *washed out, watery, insipid.*

ēlŭvĭēs -ēi, f. *a flowing out, discharge; a flowing over, flood.*

ēlŭvĭo -ōnis, f., *an inundation.*

Ēlȳsĭum -i, n., *Elysium, the abode of the blessed*; adj. **Ēlȳsĭus** -a -um; m. plur. as subst. *the Elysian fields.*

[1]**em** = hem; q.v.

[2]**em,** interj. *here! hi!*

ĕmācĭtās -ātis, f. *fondness for buying.*

ēmancĭpātĭo -ōnis, f. *emancipation* or *transfer.*

ēmancĭpo (-cŭpo) -are, *to release* or *emancipate a son from the* patria potestas; *to transfer* or *make over* property; *to give up* persons.

ēmāno -are, *to flow out; to arise, spring, emanate, spread abroad.*

Ēmăthĭa -ae, f. *a district of Macedonia*; adj. **Ēmăthĭus** -a -um, and f. **Ēmăthĭs** -ĭdis, *Macedonian*; Emathides, *the Muses.*

ēmātūresco -tūrescĕre -tūrŭi, *to become mature, to ripen; to become mild, be softened.*

ĕmax -ācis, *fond of buying.*

emblēma -ătis, n. *inlaid* or *mosaic work.*

embŏlĭum -i, n. *a dramatic interlude.*

ēmendābĭlis -e, *that may be amended.*

ēmendātĭo -ōnis, f. *improvement, emendation, amendment.*

ēmendātor -ōris, m. and **ēmendātrix** -īcis, f. *amender, corrector.*

ēmendo -are, *to free from errors, correct, improve*; partic. **ēmendātus** -a -um, *free from mistakes, correct, faultless*; adv. **ēmendātē.**

ēmentĭor -iri -ītus, dep. *to devise falsely, feign, counterfeit*; absol., *to make false statements.*

ēmercor -ari, dep. *to buy up.*

ēmĕrĕo -ēre -ŭi -ĭtum and **emĕrĕor** -ēri -ĭtus, dep. *to obtain by service, earn completely; to deserve well of a person*; milit., *to earn pay, to serve, finish one's time.*

Hence partic. **ēmĕrĭtus** -a -um: m. as subst., *a soldier that has served his time, a veteran*; as adj. *worn out, finished with.*

ēmergo -mergĕre -mersi -mersum: transit., *to cause to rise up*; emergere se *or* emergi, *to rise up, emerge, free oneself*; intransit., *to come forth, come up, emerge, free oneself, get clear*; also *to rise, come to the top; to come to light, appear.*

ēmĕrĭtus -a -um, partic. from emereo; q.v.

ēmētĭor -iri -mensus, dep., *to measure out.* Transf., *to pass over, traverse a distance;* partic. emensus -a -um in pass. sense, *traversed; to pass through, live through a period of time.*

ēmĕto -ere, *to reap away.*

ēmĭco -mĭcare -mĭcŭi -mĭcatum. (1) *to spring out, leap forth.* (2) *to gleam, shine forth, be conspicuous.*

ēmīgro -are, *to move from a place, migrate*; e vita, *to die.*

ēmĭnentĭa -ae, f. *standing out, prominence; the lights* of a picture.

ēmĭnĕo -mĭnēre -mĭnŭi, *to project, stand out, be conspicuous, be remarkable.*

Hence partic. **ēmĭnens** -entis, *outstanding, projecting; distinguished, eminent.*

ēmĭnor -ari, *to threaten.*

ēmĭnus, *at a distance, from a distance.*

ēmīror -ari, dep. *to wonder exceedingly, be astonished at.*

ēmissārĭum -i, n. *an outlet for water.*

ēmissārĭus -i, m. *an emissary, spy.*

ēmissĭo -ōnis, f. *sending forth, letting loose.*

ēmissus -ūs, m. *sending forth.*

ēmitto -mittĕre -mīsi -missum, *to send forth, send out.* Hence (1) *to dispatch, send on a chosen course*; of books, *to publish.* (2) *to let go, let loose, free, let slip.*

ĕmo ĕmĕre ēmi emptum, *to buy, purchase*; male or magno, *dear*; bene or parvo *cheap.* Transf., *to bribe, buy.*

ēmŏdĕror -ari, dep., *to moderate.*

ēmŏdŭlor -ari, dep., *to put to music.*

ēmōlĭor -iri, dep., *to achieve by effort.*

ēmollĭo -ire -īvi -ītum, *to soften, make mild* or *effeminate.*

ēmŏlo -ĕre, *to grind away.*

ēmŏlŭmentum, -i, *n. result of effort; gain, advantage.*

ēmŏnĕo -ēre, *to warn, admonish.*

ēmŏrĭor -mŏri -mortuus, dep. *to die off, perish.*

ēmŏvĕo -mŏvēre -mōvi -mōtum, *to move out* or *away, remove.*

Empĕdŏcles -is, m. *a poet and philosopher of Agrigentum, of the fifth century* B.C.; adj. **Empĕdŏclēus** -a -um; n. pl. as subst. *the doctrines of Empedocles.*

empīrĭcus -i, m. *an unscientific physician, empiric.*

empŏrĭum -i, n. *a place of trade, market.*

emptĭo -ōnis, f. *buying, purchasing; a purchase.*

emptĭto -are, *to buy up.*
emptor -ōris, m. *buyer, purchaser.*
ēmūgĭo -ire, *to bellow.*
ēmulgĕo -mulgēre -mulsum, *to drain out, exhaust.*
ēmungo -mungĕre -munxi -munctum, *to clean a nose*; with reflex. or in pass., *to wipe one's nose.* Transf. *to cheat a person.*
Hence partic. **ēmunctus** -a -um: emunctae naris, *with a clean nose,* i.e. *shrewd, discerning.*
ēmūnĭo -ire, *to fortify, make safe; to build up*; paludes, *to clear up.*
ēn (sometimes **ēm**) *lo! behold! see!* Interrog., *look, say*; with imperat., *come!*
ēnarrābĭlis -e, *that can be narrated* or *told.*
ēnarrātĭo -onis, f. *exposition; scansion.*
ēnarro -are, *to narrate* or *explain.*
ēnascor -nasci -nātus, dep. *to grow out, spring forth, arise.*
ēnăto -are, *to swim away, escape by swimming, to extricate oneself.*
ēnāvĭgo -are, *to sail away*; undam, *over the waves.*
endo; archaic = in.
endrŏmis -ĭdis, f. *a rough cloak worn after exercise.*
Endȳmĭōn -ōnis, m. *a beautiful young man, loved by the Moon.*
ēnĕco (**ēnĭco**) -nĕcare -nĕcŭi -nectum, *to kill off; to wear out, exhaust, torture.*
ēnervis -e, *powerless, weak.*
ēnervo -are, *to remove the sinews from; to weaken.*
Hence partic. **ēnervātus** -a -um, *weakened, powerless.*
ēnĭco = eneco; q.v.
ĕnim, conj. *for; namely, for instance; indeed, truly, certainly*; at enim, *but you may object . . .*; sed enim, *but indeed.*
ĕnimvēro, *to be sure, certainly.*
ēnitĕo -ēre -ŭi, *to shine out, shine forth, be conspicuous.*
ēnitesco -ĕre, *to gleam, shine forth.*
ēnītor -nīti -nīsus or -nixus, dep. *to work one's way up, struggle up, ascend*; with acc., *to climb*; in gen., *to strive, struggle, make an effort*; also transit., *to bring forth, bear.*
Hence partic. **ēnixus** -a -um, *strenuous, eager*; adv. **ēnixē.**
Enna = Henna; q.v.
Ennĭus -i, m., Q. (239-169 B.C.), *the 'father of Roman poetry'.*
ēno -are, *to swim out, escape by swimming, flee.*
ēnōdātĭo -ōnis, f. *untying*; hence *explanation.*
ēnōdis -e, *without knots; clear, plain.*
ēnōdo -are, *to free from knots; to make clear, explain*; adv. from partic., **ēnōdātē,** *clearly, plainly.*
ēnormis -e, *irregular, unusual; very large, immense, enormous.*
ēnormĭtās -ātis, *irregular shape.*
ēnōtesco -nōtescĕre -nōtŭi, *to become known, be made public.*
ensĭfĕr -fĕra -fĕrum and **ensĭgĕr** -gĕra -gĕrum, *sword-bearing.*
ensis -is, m. *sword.*
enthȳmēma -ătis, n., *a thought, line of thought, argument*; esp. *a kind of syllogism.*
ēnūbo -nūbĕre -nupsi -nuptum, of a woman, *to marry out of her rank.*
ēnuclĕo -are, *to take out the kernel*; hence *to explain in detail*; partic. **ēnuclĕātus** -a -um, *straightforward, simple, clear*; adv. **ēnuclĕātē.**
ēnŭmĕrātĭo -ōnis, f. *counting up, enumeration; recapitulation.*
ēnŭmĕro -are, *to reckon, count up, enumerate*; esp. *to pay out*; also *to recount, recapitulate.*
ēnuntĭātĭo -ōnis, f. *an enunciation, proposition.*
ēnuntĭo -are, *to tell, divulge, announce, express in words*; in logic, *to state a proposition*; also *to pronounce clearly.* N. of partic. as subst., **ēnuntĭātum** -i, *a proposition.*
ēnuptĭo -ōnis, f.: gentis, a woman's *marrying out of her* gens.
ēnūtrĭo -ire, *to nourish, rear, bring up.*
[1]**ĕo** īre īvi and ĭi ĭtum, *to go*; cubitum ire, *to go to bed*; milit., ire ad arma, *to fly to arms*; polit. (pedibus) ire in sententiam, *to support a motion.* Transf., *to pass, proceed*; in exclamations, i, *go to*; melius ire, *to go better*; ire in, with acc., *to be changed to.*
[2]**ĕō.** (1) old dat., *thither, to that point*; of degree, *so far, to such a pitch.* (2) locative, *there*; esp. with loci (partitive genit.). (3) abl., *for that, on that account.*
ĕōdem. (1) old dat., *to the same place; to the same point* or *person.* (2) locative, *in the same place*; *in the same condition.*
Ēōs, f. dawn; adj. **Ēōus** and **Ĕōus** -a -um, *belonging to the morning,* or *eastern.*
ēpastus -a -um, *eaten up.*
ĕphēbus -i, m. *a young man between eighteen and twenty.*
ĕphēmĕris -ĭdis, f. *a journal, diary.*
ĕphippĭātus -a -um, *provided with a saddle.*
ĕphippĭum -i, n., *a horse-cloth, saddle.*
ĕphŏrus -i, m., *an ephor, a Spartan magistrate.*
ĕpĭcōpus -a -um, *provided with oars.*
ĕpĭcrŏcus -a -um, *transparent, fine.*
Ĕpĭcūrus -i, m. *an Athenian philosopher, founder of the Epicurean school* (342-270 B.C.): adj. and subst. **Ĕpĭcūrēus** -a -um, *Epicurean, an Epicurean.*
ĕpĭcus -a -um, *epic.*
ĕpĭdīctĭcus -a -um, *for display.*
ĕpĭdīpnis -ĭdis, f., *dessert.*
ĕpigramma -ătis, n. *an inscription; an epigram.*
ĕpĭlŏgus -i, m. *a conclusion, peroration, epilogue.*
ĕpĭmēnĭa -orum, n. pl. *a month's rations.*
ĕpĭrēdĭum -i, n., *the strap by which a horse was fastened to a vehicle; a trace.*

Ēpīrus -i, f., *a region in north-west Greece*; adj. **Ēpīrensis** -e, *of Epirus*; subst. **Ēpīrōtes** -ae, m., *an Epirote.*
ĕpistŏlĭum -i, n. *a little letter, note.*
ĕpistŭla (or **ĕpistŏla**) -ae, f., *a written communication, letter, epistle* ; ab epistulis, *to do with correspondence*, of secretaries. Transf., *sending of letters, post.*
ĕpĭtaphium -i, m. *a funeral oration.*
ĕpĭthălămĭum -i, n. *a nuptial song.*
ĕpĭthēca -ae, f. *addition.*
ĕpĭtŏma -ae and **ĕpĭtŏmē** -ēs, f. *abridgment, epitome.*
ĕpops -opis, m. *the hoopoe.*
ĕpos, n. *an epic poem.*
ēpōtus -a -um, *drunk up, drained.* Transf. (1) *spent on drink.* (2) *swallowed up.*
ĕpŭlae -arum, f. *food, dishes, a banquet, feast.*
ĕpŭlāris -e, *belonging to a banquet.*
ĕpŭlo -ōnis, m. *feaster*; Tresviri (later Septemviri) epulones, *a college of priests who had charge of sacrificial feasts.*
ĕpŭlor -ari, dep. *to feast, feast on.*
ĕpŭlum -i, n. *a banquet, feast*, esp. on public occasions.
ĕqua -ae, f. *a mare.*
ĕquĕs -ĭtis, m. *a horseman, rider, cavalryman*; polit., equites, *the knights, order between senate and plebs*; also collectively in sing.
ĕquester -stris -stre, *relating to horsemen, equestrian; relating to cavalry*; polit., *relating to the knights.*
ĕquĭdem *indeed, truly, for my part*; concessive, *of course, certainly, admittedly.*
ĕquinus -a -um, *relating to horses.*
ĕquĭtātus -ūs, m. *cavalry.*
ĕquĭto -are, *to ride on horseback*; of winds, *to rush.*
ĕquŭlĕus = eculeus; q.v.
ĕquus -i, m. (older forms **ĕquos** and **ĕcus**) *a horse*; equus bellator, *a war-horse*; equis virisque, *with horse and foot, with all one's might*; ad equum rescribere, to make a person *a knight.*
ĕra -ae, f. *mistress, lady.*
ērādīco -are, *to root out.*
ērādo -rādĕre -rāsi -rāsum, *to scratch out; to destroy, get rid of.*
Ĕrătō, f. *the Muse of lyric and love-poetry.*
ercisco, erctum = hercisco, herctum; q.v.
Ĕrĕbus -i, m. *a god of the lower world*; hence *the lower world.* Adj. **Ĕrĕbēus** -a -um.
Ĕrechtheus -ĕi, m. a mythical king of Athens; adj. **Ĕrechthēus** -a -um, m. *Athenian*; subst. **Ĕrechthīdae** -arum, m. pl. *the Athenians.*
ērectus, partic. from erigo; q.v.
ērēpo -rēpĕre -repsi -reptum, *to creep out; to creep up* or *over.*
ēreptĭo -ōnis, f. *taking by force, seizure.*
ēreptor -ōris, m., *one who takes by force, a robber.*
ergā, prep. with acc., *towards*, esp. of personal relations; more generally, *about.*
ergastŭlum -i, n. *a workhouse for debtors* or *slaves*; in plur., *the inmates of an* ergastulum.
ērgŏ: prep., preceded by genit., *because of, on account of*; adv., *therefore, accordingly, then.*
Ĕrichthŏnĭus -i, m. *a mythical king of Athens*; also *a mythical king of Troy*; adj. **Ĕrichthŏnĭus** -a -um, *Athenian* or *Trojan.*
ērĭcĭus -i, m. *hedgehog*; milit. *chevaux de frise.*
ērĭgo -rĭgĕre -rexi -rectum, *to set up, place upright, erect, raise*; milit., *to march a body of soldiers up a height.* Transf., *to arouse, excite; encourage, cheer.*
Hence partic. **ērectus** -a -um, *raised, upright, erect; high, elevated, proud; alert, anxious, intent, with minds on the stretch; resolute, cheerful.*
ĕrīlis -e, *of a master or mistress.*
Ĕrīnȳs -ȳos, f., *one of the Furies*; plur. Erinyes, *the Furies.* Transf., *scourge, curse.*
ērĭpĭo -rĭpĕre -rĭpŭi -reptum, *to snatch away, tear out*; in good sense, *to free, rescue.*
Hence partic. **ēreptus** -a -um, *snatched away* or *rescued.*
ērŏgātĭo -ōnis, f., *payment, expenditure.*
ērŏgo -are, *to ask for and obtain*; used in the sense *to pay out* money, esp. from public funds.
errābundus -a -um, *wandering.*
errātĭcus -a -um, *wandering, erratic.*
errātĭo -ōnis, f. and **errātus** -ūs m. *wandering, straying.*
[1]**erro** -are, *to wander, stray, rove*; transit., *to wander over.* Transf., *to waver; to err, be mistaken.* N. of partic. as subst. **errātum** -i, *a fault, error*, technically or morally.
[2]**erro** -ōnis, m. *a wanderer, vagabond.*
error -ōris, m. *wandering about.* Transf., *wavering, uncertainty, error, mistake; source of error, deception.*
ērŭbesco -rŭbescĕre -rŭbŭi, *to grow red, blush*; with infin., *to blush to*; with acc., *to blush for, to respect*; gerundive **ērŭbescendus** -a -um, *of which one should be ashamed.*
ērūca -ae, f. *a colewort.*
ēructo -are, *to belch forth, throw up, vomit.* Transf. (1) *to talk drunkenly about.* (2) *to cast out, eject.*
ērŭdĭo -ire, *to free from roughness; to instruct, teach, educate.*
Hence partic. **ērŭdītus** -a -um, *instructed, educated*; adv. **ērŭdītē,** *learnedly.*
ērŭdītĭo -ōnis, f. *teaching, instruction; knowledge, learning.*
ērumpo -rumpĕre -rūpi -ruptum: transit., *to break open, cause to burst forth; to vent, discharge*; intransit., *to break out, burst forth*; milit., *to rush forth.*
ērŭo -rŭĕre -rŭi -rŭtum, *to tear out, dig up*; of buildings, *to raze, demolish.*

ērup̆tio -ōnis, f. *a bursting* or *breaking forth*; milit., *sally, attack.*
ĕrus -i, m. *master, owner, lord.*
ervum -i, n. *bitter vetch.*
Ĕryx -rȳcis or **Ĕrȳcus** -i, m., *a mountain and city on the west coast of Sicily, with a famous temple of Venus.* Adj. **Ĕrȳcīnus** -a -um; f. as subst. *Venus.*
esca -ae, f. *food, victuals,* esp. *as bait.*
escārĭus -a -um, *relating to food* or *bait.*
ēscendo -scendĕre -scendi -scensum: intransit., *to climb up, ascend; to go up from the sea-coast inland*; transit., *to ascend.*
ēscensĭo -ōnis, f., *a movement inland,* esp. hostile.
escŭlentus -a -um, *edible, esculent.*
escŭletum, escŭlus; see aesc-.
ēsĭto -are, *to keep eating.*
Esquĭlĭae -arum, f. *one of the seven hills of Rome, the Esquiline.* Hence adj. **Esquĭlĭus** and **Esquĭlīnus** -a -um, *Esquiline;* f. as subst. **Esquĭlīna** -ae, *the Esquiline gate.*
essĕdārĭus -i, m. *a fighter in a British* or *Gallic war-chariot.*
essĕdum -i, n. *a war-chariot used by Gauls and Britons.*
ēsū, abl. sing. m., *in the eating.*
ēsŭrĭo -ire, *to be hungry, desire food*: in gen., *to long for.*
ēsŭrītĭo -ōnis, f. *hunger.*
et; as adv., *also, even*; as conj., *and; and indeed*; in narrative, *and then*; occasionally adversative, *and yet*; after alius, idem, par, *as* or *than*; repeated et . . . et . . ., *both* . . . *and* . . .; so -que . . . et . . .; nec (neque) . . . et, *not only not* . . . *but.*
ĕtĕnim, *for indeed.*
ĕtēsĭae -arum, m. pl. *winds which blow about the dogdays, Etesian winds.*
ēthŏlŏgus i, m. *a mimic.*
ĕtĭam. (1) as yet, still; etiam atque etiam, *again and again.* (2) *also, besides, even*; non solum (*or* modo) . . . sed (*or* verum) etiam, *not only* . . . *but also*; with comparatives, *still.* (3) in answers, *yes, certainly.* (4) in questions, expressing incredulity, *actually? really?*
ĕtĭamnum and **ĕtĭamnunc,** *yet, still, till now.*
ĕtĭam-si, *even if, although.*
ĕtĭam-tum and **ĕtĭam-tunc,** *even then, till that time, till then.*
Etrūrĭa -ae, f. *a district in north-west Italy*; hence adj. and subst. **Etruscus** -a -um, *Etruscan,* an *Etruscan.*
et-si, *even if, although*; elliptically, *and yet, notwithstanding.*
ĕtȳmŏlŏgĭa -ae, f., *etymology.*
eu, *good! well done!*
Euan or **Euhan,** m. *a name of Bacchus.*
euans or **euhans** -antis, *shouting Euan,* of Bacchanals.
euge and **eugĕpae,** *well done!*
Euĭas or **Euhĭas** -adis, f., *a Bacchante.*
Euĭus or **Euhĭus** -i, m., *a name of Bacchus.*
Eumĕnĭdes -um, f., *Eumenides, the gracious ones,* euphem. for the Furies.
eunūchus -i, m., *a eunuch.*
euoe, euhoe, interj., *shout of the Bacchantes.*
Eurīpĭdes -is, m., *the Athenian tragic poet* (c. 485-406 B.C.); adj. **Eurīpĭdēus** -a -um.
Eurīpus -i, m. *a channel, strait,* esp. *the strait between Euboea and Boeotia; a canal* or *water-course.*
Eurōpa -ae, f. and **Eurōpē** -ēs, f.: myth., *daughter of Agenor, whom Jupiter, in the form of a bull, carried off to Crete*; geograph., *the continent of Europe.* Adj. **Eurōpaeus** -a -um, *belonging to Europa or to Europe.*
Eurus -i, m., *the south-east* or *east wind*; adj. **Eurōus** -a -um, *eastern.*
Euterpē -ēs, f. *Muse of harmony.*
Euxīnus -a -um, *an epithet of the Black Sea.*
evādo -vādĕre -vāsi -vāsum. Intransit., *to go out, go forth*; esp. *to climb up* or *out; to escape, get off.* Transf., *to turn out, result.* Transit., *to go out through, pass over; to climb up; to escape.*
ēvăgor -ari, dep.: intransit., *to wander out, stray away*; milit. *to wheel right and left, manoeuvre*; transit., *to overstep.*
ēvălesco -vălēscĕre -vălŭi, *to grow strong, prevail, come into vogue*; in perf., *to have power, be able.*
ēvānesco -vānescĕre -vānŭi, *to vanish, disappear, pass away.*
ēvānĭdus -a -um, *vanishing, passing away.*
ēvasto -are, *to devastate, lay waste utterly.*
ēvĕho -vĕhĕre -vexi -vectum, *to carry out* or *up*; with reflex., or pass., of ships, *to sail away*; of riders, *to ride away.*
ēvello -vellĕre -velli -vulsum, *to tear out, pluck out.*
ēvĕnĭo -vĕnire -vēni -ventum, *to come out.* Transf., *to turn out, result; to befall, happen, occur.* Hence n. of partic. as subst. **ēventum** -i, *issue, consequence, result; event, occurrence, experience.*
ēventus -ūs, m. *consequence, issue, result; event, occurrence, experience.*
ēverbĕro -are, *to strike violently.*
ēverrĭcŭlum -i, n., *a fishing-net, drag-net*; fig., *a clean sweep.*
ēverro -verrĕre -verri -versum, *to sweep out; to plunder.*
ēversĭo -ōnis, f. *overturning, destruction, ruin.*
ēversor -ōris, m. *overturner, destroyer.*
ēverto -vertĕre -verti -versum, *to turn out, dislodge, eject; to turn up, stir; to overturn, throw down, demolish destroy, ruin.*
ēvestīgātus -a -um, *tracked out, discovered.*

ēvĭdens -entis, *visible, clear, plain, evident*; adv. **ēvĭdentĕr.**
ēvĭdentĭa -ae, f., *distinctness of language.*
ēvĭgĭlo -are: intransit. *to wake up; to be awake, be vigilant*; transit., *to watch through, pass in watching; to work hard at, to elaborate.*
ēvīlesco -vīlescĕre -vīlŭi, *to become, contemptible.*
ēvincĭo -vincire -vinxi -vinctum, *to bind, bind round.*
ēvinco -vincĕre -vīci -victum, *to conquer entirely, utterly subdue*; in gen., *to prevail over, get through, get over*; of results *to bring about*; of conclusions, *to prove irresistibly.*
ēviscĕro -are, *to disembowel, tear in pieces.*
ēvītābĭlis -e, *that can be avoided.*
ēvīto -are, *to avoid, shun.*
ēvŏcātor -ōris, m., *one who calls to arms.*
ēvŏco -are, *to call out*; esp. *to summon the spirits of the dead*, or *a deity*; milit. and polit. *to call out, call up, summon.* Transf., *to draw out, draw on; to call forth, produce.* M. pl. of partic. as subst. **ēvŏcāti** -orum, *veteran soldiers recalled to the colours.*
ēvoe; see euoe.
ēvŏlo -are, *to fly out, fly away; to come out quickly, rush forth, escape.*
ēvŏlūtĭo -ōnis, f., *the unrolling* and *reading of a book.*
ēvolvo -volvĕre -volvi -vŏlūtum. (1) *to roll out, roll forth*; of news, evolvi, *to spread.* (2) *to unroll, roll open*; esp. *to unroll a book to read it.* Transf., *to extricate, disentangle, detach; to unravel, disclose, explain.*
ēvŏmo -ĕre -ŭi -ĭtum, *to vomit forth, disgorge.*
ēvulgo -are, *to publish, make known.*
ēvulsĭo -ōnis, f. *pulling out.*
ex or **ē,** prep. with abl. (1) in space: *from* or *out of*; ex equo pugnare, *to fight on horseback* (operating *from* it); ex adverso *opposite.* (2) in time, *since*, esp. ex quo, *from which time, since*; also *immediately after*; aliud ex alio, *one thing after another.* (3) in other relations: to denote origin, *from, away from, out of, of*; ex animo, *heartily*; ex industria, *on purpose*; unus ex, *one of*; pocula ex auro, *gold cups*; to denote cause or occasion, *from, on account of, by reason of*; e vulnere mori, *to die of a wound*; to denote correspondence, *in accordance with*; ex re et ex tempore, *according to time and circumstance*; to denote advantage, e.g. e republica, *for the benefit of the state*; in gen., *in regard to, with respect to*; ex parte, *in part.*
exăcerbo -are, *to provoke, exasperate, embitter.*
exactĭo -ōnis, f. *driving out, expulsion; demanding, exacting,* esp. *collecting of debts, tribute,* etc.; in gen., *management, direction.*
exactor -ōris, m. *one who drives out; one who demands* or *exacts,* esp. *a collector of taxes*; in gen., *superintendent, overseer.*
exactus -a -um, partic. from exigo; q.v.
exăcŭo -ŭĕre -ŭi -ūtum, *to sharpen to a point, make sharp, intensify, stimulate.*
exadversum or **exadversus,** *opposite.*
exaedĭfĭcātĭo -ōnis, f. *building up.*
exaedĭfĭco -are *to build up, erect, finish.*
exaequātĭo -ōnis, f. *making equal, equality.*
exaequo -are. (1) *to make level* or *equal, level up, relate.* (2) *to equal, be like.*
exaestŭo -are, *to be hot, boil up, foam up.*
exaggĕrātĭo -ōnis, f., *heaping up*; hence *elevation, exaltation.*
exaggĕro -are, *to heap up; to enlarge, increase; to heighten, exalt, magnify.*
exăgĭtātor -ōris, m. *a censurer.*
exăgĭto -are, *to chase about; to harass, disquiet, disturb; to scold, blame, censure, criticize; to excite, irritate.*
exalbesco -bescĕre -bŭi, *to grow white, turn pale.*
exāmen -ĭnis, n. (1) *a swarm; a throng, crowd, shoal.* (2) *the tongue of a balance*; *testing, consideration.*
exămĭno -are, *to weigh; to consider.*
exămussim, *according to rule, exactly.*
exanclo -are, *to drain, exhaust; to bear to the end, endure.*
exănĭmālis -e, *dead; deadly.*
exănĭmātĭo -ōnis, f. *want of breath,* esp. from fright.
exănĭmis -e and **exănĭmus** -a -um, *lifeless, dead*; also (exanimis only), *breathless,* esp. from fright.
exănĭmo -are. (1) *to take away the breath of, to wind, stun, weaken.* (2) *to deprive of life, to kill.*
exantlo = exanclo; q.v.
exardesco -ardescĕre -arsi -arsum, *to blaze up, to become hot,* or *inflamed*; of disturbances, *to break out.*
exāresco -ārescĕre -ārŭi, *to dry, become dry* or *exhausted.*
exarmo -are, *to disarm, deprive of arms.*
exăro -are, *to plough up, dig up; to produce by ploughing*; hence *to write on waxen tablets.*
exaspĕro -are, *to make rough, to irritate.*
exauctōro -are, *to dismiss from military service, discharge, cashier.*
exaudĭo -ire, *to hear plainly; to hear favourably, listen to.*
exaugĕo -ēre, *to increase much.*
exaugŭrātĭo -ōnis, f. *profanation, desecration.*
exaugŭro -are, *to desecrate, profane.*
exauspĭco -are, *to take an augury from.*
excaeco -are, *to make quite blind; to stop up a* channel.
excalcĕo -are, *to take the shoes from;* in drama, *to take the tragic* cothurnus *from* an actor.
excandescentĭa -ae, f., *heat, irascibility.*

excandesco -descĕre -dŭi, *to become hot, to glow.*
excanto -are, *to charm out, bring forth by incantations.*
excarnĭfĭco -are, *to tear to pieces.*
excăvo -are, *to hollow out.*
excēdo -cēdĕre -cessi -cessum: intransit., *to go out, go away, pass out*; e vita, *to die; to go beyond* a point or limit; *to attain to, result in*; transit., *to leave, pass beyond, exceed.*
excellentĭa -ae, f. *eminence, distinction.*
excello -ĕre, *to stand out, excel, be distinguished*; partic. **excellens,** *high, lofty, eminent, remarkable*; adv. **excellentĕr,** *eminently.*
excelsĭtās -ātis, f., *height, elevation.*
excelsus -a -um, adj., *lofty, high, elevated, eminent.* N. as subst. **excelsum** -i, *a height, eminence.* Adv. **excelsē,** *loftily.*
exceptĭo -ōnis, f. *exception, restriction, limitation*; esp. *an exception by the defendant to the plaintiff's statement of a case.*
excepto -are. (1) *to take up, catch*; auras, *to snuff up.* (2) *to take in succession.*
excerno -cernĕre -crēvi -crētum, *to separate, sift, sort.*
excerpo -cerpĕre -cerpsi -cerptum, *to pick out; to gather out, choose; to put on one side, separate.* N. of partic. as subst. **excerptum** -i, *an extract.*
excessus -ūs, m. *departure; from life,* i.e. *death; from subject,* i.e. *digression.*
excetra -ae, f. *a snake, viper.*
excĭdĭum -i, n. *overthrow, destruction.*
[1]**excĭdo** -cĭdĕre -cĭdi, *to fall out, fall away, be lost*; of words, *to slip out unawares, escape*; of ideas, *to pass from memory* or *thought, be forgotten.*
[2]**excīdo** -cīdĕre -cīdi -cīsum, *to cut out*; lapides e terra, *to quarry.* Transf. (1) *to destroy, demolish*; portas, *to force open.* (2) *to root out, banish.*
excĭĕo and **excĭo** -cīre -cīvi and -cĭi -cĭtum and cĭtum, *to call out, arouse*; esp. *to awaken from sleep* or *to summon to help*; in gen., of persons, *to excite, arouse*; of feelings, *to call forth, excite, produce*; of material things, *to stir, shake.*
excĭpĭo -cĭpĕre -cēpi -ceptum. (1) *to take out*; hence *to rescue; to except.* (2) *to take up, catch; to greet, welcome* a person; *to pick up* news or ideas by listening; of events, *to take* people, *come upon them.* (3) passively, *to receive; to take over from, follow, succeed, come later.*
excīsĭo -ōnis, *destruction.*
excĭto -are, *to arouse, rouse up*; of things, *to provoke, call forth, cause*; of persons, *to console, cheer, inspire*; of buildings, *to raise, erect*; of fire, *to kindle, inflame.*
Hence partic. **excĭtātus** -a -um, *lively, vigorous, loud.*
exclāmātĭo -ōnis, f. *exclamation.*
exclāmo -are, *to shout, cry aloud; to exclaim; to call* somebody *by name.*
exclūdo -clūdĕre -clūsi -clūsum, *to shut out, exclude, keep away*; of things, *to knock out*; of birds, *to hatch.*
exclūsĭo -ōnis, f. *shutting out, exclusion.*
excōgĭtātĭo -ōnis, f. *contriving, devising.*
excōgĭto -are, *to think out, devise, contrive, invent.*
excŏlo -cŏlĕre -cŏlŭi -cultum, *to tend* or *cultivate carefully; to adorn, polish, refine; to serve, honour* a deity or person.
excŏquo -cŏquĕre -coxi -coctum, *to boil down, boil away; to cook, bake, make hard*; fig., *to cook up.*
excors -cordis, *foolish, silly, without intelligence.*
excrēmentum -i, n. *excrement*; oris, *spittle.*
excresco -crescĕre -crēvi -crētum, *to grow up, spring up.*
excrētus -a -um, partic. of excerno, or of excresco.
excrŭcĭo -are, *to torture, torment.*
excŭbĭae -arum, f. pl. *lying out*; milit., *keeping watch, keeping guard.* Transf., *watchfires; watchmen, guard.*
excŭbĭtor -ōris, m. *sentinel, watchman, guard.*
excŭbo -bare -bŭi -bĭtum, *to lie* or *sleep out of doors*; milit., *to keep watch; to be watchful, vigilant.*
excūdo -cūdĕre -cūdi -cūsum, *to strike out, beat out*; esp. *to hammer, forge*; of birds, *to hatch.* Transf., of bees, *to mould*; of writers, *to compose.*
exculco -are, *to trample firm, tread hard.*
excurātus -a -um, *carefully seen to.*
excurro -currĕre -cŭcurri and -curri -cursum *to run out, hasten forth*; milit., *to attack, make a sortie*; with acc., *to run over*; fig., *to run out, move freely*; of places, *to run out, to project.*
excursĭo -ōnis, f. *running out; movement forwards*; fig., *outset* of a speech; milit., *attack, assault, sally.*
excursor -ōris, m. *scout, skirmisher.*
excursus -ūs, m. *running out*; rhet., *digression*; milit., *attack, sally, assault.*
excūsābĭlis -e, *excusable.*
excūsātĭo -ōnis, *an excuse, plea, defence.*
excūso -are, *to exempt from blame* or *accusation; to excuse* a person, *to make excuses for* a thing; *to allege in excuse, to plead.*
Hence partic. **excūsātus** -a -um, *free from blame*; adv. **excūsātē,** *excusably.*
excŭtĭo -cŭtĕre -cussi -cussum. (1) *to shake out*; esp. *to shake out* clothes to find anything hidden; hence *to search, examine* a person; fig., *to investigate.* (2) *to strike off, throw out, knock away, shake off.*
exec-; see exsec-.

exĕdo -esse -ēdi -ēsum, *to eat up, devour, consume; to wear down, exhaust, destroy.*
exedra -ae, f. *a hall for conversation* or *debate.*
exemplāris -e, *serving as a copy*; n. as subst. **exemplar** -āris, *a copy, transcript; a likeness; a pattern, ideal.*
exemplum -i, n. (1) *a sample, example*; exempli causa (*or* gratia), *for instance; general character, manner, fashion* (as shown by examples); *an example to be followed, model; a precedent; an example of what may happen, warning, object-lesson*; hence *a punishment intended to deter.* (2) *a copy, transcript.*
exemptus -a -um, partic. of eximo; q.v.
exentĕro -are, *to torture, exhaust.*
exĕo -ire -ii (-īvi) -itum: intransit., *to go out, go away, go forth; to pass from* state to state; *to get out, to become known*; of time, *to come to an end, pass away*; transit., *to pass over*; also *to ward off.*
exeq-; see **exseq-**.
exercĕo -ēre -ŭi -ĭtum, *to keep at work, exercise, train, cultivate*; of abstr. things, *to employ, exploit*; of feelings, arts, and processes, *to practise, exercise*; of the mind, *to train*; hence *to overwork, harass, trouble.*
Hence partic. **exercĭtātus** -a -um, *trained, schooled; harassed; severe, vexatious.*
exercĭtātĭo -ōnis, f. *practice, exercise; experience.*
exercĭtĭum -i, n. *practice, exercise.*
exercĭto -are, *to train hard, keep at work.*
Hence partic. **exercĭtatus** -a -um, *trained, practised, exercised; troubled, harassed.*
[1]**exercĭtus** -a -um, partic. of exerceo; q.v.
[2]**exercitus** -ūs, m. *training; a trained body of soldiers, army*; esp. *the infantry*; poet. in gen., *crowd, swarm.*
exēsor -ōris, m. *one who gnaws* or *eats away.*
exhālātĭo -ōnis, f. *exhalation, vapour.*
exhālo -are: transit., *to exhale, breathe out*; intransit., of things, *to steam*; of persons, *to expire.*
exhaurĭo -haurire -hausi -haustum. (1) *to draw out*; in gen., *to remove, take out, take away.* (2) *to drain dry, empty out, impoverish; to finish, bring to an end; to endure, suffer.*
exhērēdo -are, *to disinherit.*
exhērēs -ēdis, *disinherited.*
exhĭbĕo -hĭbēre -hĭbŭi -hĭbĭtum, *to produce, show, display, exhibit, present; to offer, allow; to produce* by making, *to cause.*
exhĭlăro -are, *to make cheerful.*
exhorresco -horrescĕre -horrŭi, *to shudder exceedingly, be terrified*; transit., *to tremble at, to dread.*
exhortātĭo -ōnis, f. *exhortation, encouragement.*
exhortātīvus -a -um, *of exhortation.*
exhortor -ari, dep. *to exhort, encourage.*
exĭgo -ĭgĕre -ēgi -actum. (1) *to drive out* or *away; to force out, exact, demand; to sell.* (2) *to drive through*; hence *to complete, finish; to determine, settle, adjust, regulate; to ascertain, decide.*
Hence partic. **exactus** -a -um, *accurate, precise, exact.*
exĭgŭĭtās -ātis, f. *littleness, smallness.*
exĭgŭus -a -um, *small, little, scanty*: of quantity, in size, *small*; in number, *scanty*; in time, *short*; of quality, *meagre.* N. as subst. **exĭgŭum** -i, *small extent.* Adv. **exĭgŭē,** *sparingly, scantily, scarcely.*
exīlis -e, *thin, slender, meagre*; in possessions, *poor*; with genit., *without*; of style, *dry, dreary.* Adv. **exīlĭtĕr,** *thinly, poorly, meagrely.*
exīlĭtās -ātis, f. *thinness, meagreness, weakness.*
exĭmĭus -a -um, *excepted*; hence *selected; exceptional, distinguished.* Adv. **exĭmĭē,** *uncommonly, exceptionally.*
exĭmo -ĭmĕre -ēmi -emptum, *to take out, take away*, esp. off a list or out of a group; *to free, release; to take away, remove* an abstr. thing; of time, *to waste.*
exin = exinde; q.v.
exĭnānĭo -ire, *to empty*; gentes, *to plunder.*
exinde (**exin, exim**): in space, *thence, next*; in time, *thereupon, after that, then*; in logic, *consequently, accordingly.*
existĭmātĭo -ōnis, f. *the opinion that a man has, judgement; the opinion that others 'have of a man*, esp. morally, *reputation, good name, honour, character*; in finance, *credit.*
existĭmātor -ōris, m., *one who forms* or *gives an opinion, a critic.*
existĭmo (**-ŭmo**) -are, *to judge a thing according to its value*; in gen., *to judge, consider, regard.*
exĭtĭābĭlis -e, *deadly, destructive.*
exĭtĭālis -e, *destructive, fatal, deadly.*
exĭtĭo -ōnis, f. *going out.*
exĭtĭōsus -a -um, *destructive, fatal, deadly.*
exĭtĭum -i, n. *going out* or *away*; hence *destruction, ruin*; also *a cause of destruction.*
exĭtus -ūs, m. *going out, going forth; a means of going out, exit; end, finish; issue, result.*
exlex -lēgis, *bound by no law, lawless, reckless.*
exmŏvĕo = emoveo; q.v.
exobsecro -are, *to entreat earnestly.*
exŏcŭlo -are, *to deprive of eyes.*
exŏdĭum -i, n., *a comic afterpiece.*
exŏlesco -ŏlescĕre -ŏlēvi -ŏlētum, *to grow old and weak, decay, fade out*; partic. **exŏlētus** -a -um, *worn out*; m. as subst. *a dissolute person.*
exŏnĕro -are, *to unload, disburden*; in gen., *to free, release, relieve.*
exopto -are, *to desire eagerly, long for;*

partic. **exoptātus** -a -um, *desired, longed for.*

exōrābĭlis -e, *able to be entreated, placable.*

exōrātor -ōris, m., *one who entreats successfully.*

exordĭor -ordiri -orsus, dep. *to begin to weave*; in gen., *to begin.* Partic. in pass. sense **exorsus** -a -um, *begun.*

exordĭum -i, n., *the warp of a web*; in gen., *a beginning*; esp. *the beginning of a speech.*

exŏrĭor -ŏriri -ortus, dep. *to rise, spring up, issue, appear, come forward.*

exornātĭo -ōnis, f., *adorning, ornament.*

exornātor -ōris, m., *one who adorns, an embellisher.*

exorno -are, *to furnish, provide plentifully*; also *to ornament, adorn.*

exōro -are, *to entreat successfully, obtain* a thing *by entreaty, prevail upon* a person.

[1]**exorsus** -a -um, partic. of exordior; q.v.

[2]**exorsus** -ūs, m., *a beginning.*

exortus -ūs, m., *a rising; the East.*

exŏs -ossis, *without bones.*

exoscŭlor -ari, dep. *to kiss.*

exosso -are, *to bone, take out the bones.*

exostra -ae, f. *a theatrical machine, revealing the inside of a house to the spectators.*

exōsus -a -um, *hating exceedingly.*

exōtĭcus -a -um, *foreign, outlandish, exotic.*

expallesco -pallescĕre -pallŭi, *to become very pale*; with acc., *to dread.*

expalpo -are, *to coax out.*

expando -ĕre, *to stretch out, expand, spread out.* Transf., *to explain.*

expăvesco -păvescĕre -pavi, *to grow very frightened*; with acc. *to dread exceedingly.*

expĕdĭo -ire -īvi and -ĭi -ītum, *to free from a snare, disengage, disentangle, set free; to get things ready for action*; fig., *to release, clear, set free, set straight*; in speech, *to clear up* a point, *explain*; res expedit, or impers. expedit, *it is expedient, useful, advantageous.*

Hence partic. **expĕdītus** -a -um, *unshackled, unimpeded*; milit., *lightly equipped*; in gen., *free, ready*; n. as subst. *clear ground*; of abstr. things, *clear, settled, ready.* Adv. **expĕdītē,** *freely, easily.*

expĕdītĭo -ōnis, f., *a military operation, expedition.*

expello -pellĕre -pŭli -pulsum, *to drive out, expel, thrust away.*

expendo -pendĕre -pendi -pensum, *to weigh out*; esp. *to weigh out in payment, pay out, put down*; sometimes *to pay* a penalty. Transf., *to value, rate*; in gen., *to weigh up, consider.*

Hence partic. **expensus** -a -um, *weighed out,* hence *paid out*; ferre homini expensum, *to note* a thing *as paid* to a person, *charge* to. N. as subst. **expensum** -i, *payment.*

expergēfăcĭo -făcĕre -fēci -factum, *to awaken, rouse, excite.*

expergiscor -pergisci -perrectus, dep. *to wake up, arouse oneself.*

expergo -pergĕre -pergi -pergĭtum, *to awaken.*

expĕrĭentĭa -ae, f., *trial, testing, attempt; knowledge gained by experience.*

expĕrīmentum -i, n. *experience; proof from experience.*

expĕrĭor -pĕriri -pertus, dep. *to try, test, prove, put to the test*; experiri ius, *to go to law*; in perf., *to know by having tried, know by experience; to try to do* a thing. Pres. partic. **expĕrĭens** -entis, *enterprising, venturesome.* Perf. partic. **expertus** -a -um: pass., *tested, tried, approved*; act., with *experience, experienced.*

experrectus -a -um, partic. of expergiscor; q.v.

expers -pertis, *having no part in, not sharing in; wanting in, destitute of.*

expertus -a -um, partic. from experior q.v.

expĕtesso -ere, *to desire, wish for.*

expĕto -ĕre -ĭi and -īvi -ītum: transit., *to desire, strive after, make for*; of things due, *to demand, require*; with infin., *to seek to do;* intransit., *to fall upon.*

expĭātĭo -onis, f. *atonement, expiation.*

expīlātĭo -ōnis, f. *plundering, robbing.*

expīlator -ōris, m., *plunderer, robber.*

expīlo -are, *to plunder, rob.*

expingo -pingĕre -pinxi -pictum, *to paint over*; fig., *to describe, depict in writing.*

expĭo -are, *to propitiate, appease* an offended or threatening power; *to purify* what is defiled; *to atone for* an offence.

expiscor -ari, dep. *to fish out; to search out, find out.*

explānātĭo -ōnis, f. *making clear, explanation*; rhet., *illustration,* also *clear articulation.*

explānātor -ōris, m., *one who explains; an interpreter.*

explāno -are, *to make level, smooth out*; hence *to explain, make clear: to set out clearly,* or *articulate clearly.*

explaudo = explodo; q.v.

explēmentum -i, n., *filling, stuffing.*

explĕo -plēre -plēvi -plētum, *to fill, fill up; to complete* a required amount; *to make good* losses, etc.; in quality, *to complete, perfect*; of time, *to complete, finish*; of duties, *to fulfil, discharge*; of wants, *to satisfy, quench, appease.*

Hence partic. **explētus** -a -um, *perfect, complete.*

explētĭo -ōnis, f., *satisfying.*

explĭcātĭo -ōnis, f. *unfolding, uncoiling.* Transf., *explanation, interpretation.*

explĭcātor -ōris, m. and **explicātrix** -īcis, f. *interpreter, explainer.*

[1]**explĭcātus** -a -um, partic. from explico; q.v.

[2]**explĭcātus** -ūs, m. *explanation, exposition.*

explĭco -are -avi -atum and -ŭi -ĭtum, *to unfold, unroll, disentangle*; in gen.

to spread out, extend, expand; milit., *to extend ranks, deploy*. Transf., *to disentangle, put in order*; of a debt, *to pay off; to explain, expound, interpret*; *to set free*.
Hence partic. **explĭcātus** -a -um, *ordered, arranged; made plain, clear*; also **explĭcĭtus** -a -um, *straightforward, easy*; adv. **explĭcātē,** *plainly*.
explōdo (**-plaudo**) -plōdĕre -plōsi -plōsum, *to hiss* an actor *off the stage*; in gen., *to scare off, reject*.
explōrātĭo -ōnis, f. *investigation*.
explōrātor -ōris, m. *explorer, scout, spy*.
explōro -are, *to search out, investigate, explore*; milit., *to spy out, reconnoitre; to test, try, put to proof*.
Hence partic. **explōrātus** -a -um, *established, confirmed, certain*; exploratum habeo, *I am sure*; adv. **explōrātē,** *certainly, surely, definitely*.
expŏlĭo -ire -ii and -īvi -ītum, *to smooth, polish, refine*; partic. **expŏlītus** -a -um, *smooth, polished*.
expŏlītĭo -ōnis, f. *smoothing, polishing*.
expōno -pōnĕre -pŏsŭi, pŏsĭtum. (1) *to put outside, cast out; to expose* a child; naut. *to land, disembark*. (2) *to put on view, display, show*; in words, *to set forth, exhibit, explain*.
Hence partic. **expŏsĭtus** (**expostus**) -a -um, *exposed, open, accessible*; of persons, *affable*; in bad sense, *vulgar*.
exporrĭgo -rĭgĕre -rexi -rectum, *to stretch out, expand, smooth out*.
exportātĭo -ōnis, f., *exportation*.
exporto -are, *to carry out*; esp. *to export*.
exposco -poscĕre -pŏposci, *to implore, entreat earnestly*; esp. *to demand the surrender* of a person.
expŏsĭtĭo -ōnis, f. *putting out*; hence *statement, exposition, narration*.
expostŭlātĭo -ōnis, f. *complaint, expostulation*.
expostŭlo -are. (1) *to demand earnestly*, esp. *to demand the surrender of* a person. (2) *to make a claim* or *complaint, to expostulate*.
expōtus = epotus; q.v.
exprĭmo -prĭmĕre -pressi -pressum. (1) *to press out, force out; to extort*. (2) *to mould* or *form* one thing in imitation of another; hence *to copy, express, portray, represent*; esp. *to express in words, describe; to translate; to articulate*. (3) *to raise up*.
Hence partic. **expressus** -a -um, *made clear, prominent, distinct*.
exprobrātĭo -ōnis, f. *reproach, upbraiding*.
exprobro -are, *to reproach; to bring up* a thing *against* a person.
exprōmo -prōmĕre -prompsi -promptum, *to bring forth, produce, exhibit, display; to disclose, set forth, state, utter*.
expugnābĭlis -e, *that may be taken by storm*.
expugnātĭo -ōnis, f., *the taking of a place by storm*.
expugnātor -ōris, m. *taker, capturer*; pudicitiae, *violator*.
expugno -are, *to take by storm, capture*; hence *to overcome, subdue; to gain forcibly, extort*: with ut and the subj., *bring it about that*.
expulsĭo -ōnis, f., *driving out, expulsion*.
expulsor -ōris, m. and **expultrix** -trīcis, f. *one who drives out*.
expungo -pungĕre -punxi -punctum, *to prick out*; hence *to cancel, expunge*.
expurgātĭo -ōnis, f. *vindication, justification*.
expurgo -are, *to cleanse, purify*. Hence *to cure; to purify; to justify, defend*.
expūtesco -ĕre, *to rot away*.
expŭto -are, *to lop away*; hence *to consider; to comprehend*.
exquīro (**-quaero**) -quīrĕre -quīsīvi -quīsītum. (1) *to search for, look for, ask for*. (2) *to search through, examine*.
Hence partic. **exquīsītus** -a -um, *carefully sought* or *worked out, choice, exquisite, artificial*. Adv. **exquīsītē,** *accurately, carefully*.
exsaevĭo -ire, *to rage to an end, cease to rage*.
exsanguis -e, *bloodless, without blood; deathly pale*; act., *making pale*.
exsarcĭo -sarcire -sartum, *to patch up, make good, repair*.
exsătĭo -are, *to satisfy thoroughly, satiate*.
exsătŭrābĭlis -e, *that can be satiated*.
exsătŭro -are, *to satisfy, satiate*.
exscen-; see escen-.
exscindo -scindĕre -scĭdi -scissum, *to tear out; to destroy utterly*.
exscrĕo -are, *to cough out*.
exscrībo -scrībĕre -scripsi -scriptum, *to write out; to copy; to note down, register*.
exsculpo -sculpĕre -sculpsi -sculptum, *to scratch out, erase; to carve* or *scoop out*.
exsĕco -sĕcare -sĕcŭi -sectum, *to cut out, cut away*.
exsecrābĭlis -e, *cursing, execrating*.
exsecrātĭo -ōnis, f. *curse, execration; an oath containing an imprecation*.
exsecror -ari, dep. *to curse, execrate; to swear with an imprecation*; partic. in pass. sense, **exsecrātus** -a -um, *cursed, execrated*.
exsectĭo -ōnis, f. *cutting out*.
exsĕcūtĭo -ōnis, f. *performance, accomplishment*; exsecutio Syriae, *administration*; of speech, *a discussion*.
exsĕquĭae -arum, f. pl. *a funeral procession*.
exsĕquĭālis -e, *belonging to a funeral procession*.
exsĕquor -sĕqui -sĕcūtus, dep. *to follow to the grave*; in gen., *to follow to the end; to maintain, keep up, to carry out, accomplish, execute; to avenge, punish; to relate, describe explain* a matter; *to suffer, endure*.
exsĕro -sĕrĕre -sĕrŭi -sertum, *to stretch out, thrust out*; hence *to put*

forth, assert. Perf. partic. **exsertus** -a -um, *bared, protruding.*
exserto -are, *to stretch out.*
exsībĭlo -are, *to hiss out*; esp. *to hiss* an actor *off the stage.*
exsicco -are, *to dry thoroughly; to drain dry, to empty* by drinking.
Hence partic. **exsiccātus** -a -um, of style, *dry, jejune.*
exsigno -are, *to mark out.*
exsĭlĭo -sĭlire -sĭlŭi, *to leap out* or *up.*
exsĭlĭum -i, n. *banishment, exile.* Transf., *place of exile*; plur. = exsules, *exiles.*
exsisto (**existo**) -sistĕre -stĭti -stĭtum, *to stand forth, appear; to spring forth, arise, come into existence.*
exsolvo -solvĕre -solvi -sŏlūtum. (1) *to loosen, untie, unbind, open*; glaciem, *to dissolve*; of persons, *to disentangle, free*; of things, *to explain.* (2) *to pay off; to discharge* any obligation, *perform* anything due.
exsomnis -e, *sleepless, wakeful.*
exsorbĕo -ēre, *to suck up, suck dry.*
exsors -sortis, *without lot; for which no lot has been cast, specially chosen; having no share in, deprived of,* with genit.
exspătĭor -ari, dep. *to deviate from the course*; fig., *to digress.*
exspectābĭlis -e, *that is to be expected, probable.*
exspectātĭo -ōnis, f. *waiting, looking for, expectation* (with objective genit.).
exspecto -are, *to look out for, wait for, await, wait to see*; esp. *with longing, fear, desire,* etc., *to hope for, dread.*
Hence partic. (with compar. and superl.) **exspectātus** -a -um, *awaited, wished for, welcome.*
exspergo -spergĕre -spersum, *to sprinkle, scatter.*
exspēs, *without hope, hopeless.*
exspīrātĭo -ōnis, f. *exhalation.*
exspiro -are: transit., *to breathe out, exhale, emit*; intransit., *to blow forth, rush forth; to give up the ghost, to die.*
exspŏlĭo -are, *to plunder, rob, despoil.*
exspŭo -spŭĕre -spŭi -spūtum, *to spit out; to get rid of, cast away.*
exsterno -ĕre, *to frighten, terrify.*
exstillo -are, *to drop moisture, drip, trickle.*
exstĭmŭlātor -ōris, m. *inciter, instigator.*
exstĭmŭlo -are, *to goad, excite, instigate.*
exstinctĭo -ōnis, f. *annihilation, extinction.*
exstinctor -ōris, m. *one who extinguishes, destroys, annihilates.*
exstinguo -stinguĕre -stinxi -stinctum, *to put out, extinguish*; of persons, *to kill*; in gen., *to abolish, destroy, annihilate.*
exstirpo -are, *to root out, extirpate*
exsto (**exto**) -are, *to stand out, project; to be visible, show itself, appear; to be still in existence, be extant.*
exstructĭo -ōnis, f. *building up, erection.*
exstrŭo -strŭĕre -struxi -structum, *to heap up, pile up, build up.*
exsuctus -a -um, partic. of exsugo; q.v.
exsūdo -are; intransit., *to come out in sweat, exude*; transit., *to sweat out, sweat through, perform with great labour.*
exsūgo -sūgĕre -suxi -suctum, *to suck out, suck dry.*
exsul -sŭlis, c., *a banished person, an exile.*
exsŭlo (**exŭlo**) -are, *to be banished, live in exile.*
exsultātĭo -ōnis, f. *leaping up; exultation, excessive rejoicing.*
exsultim, adv. *friskingly.*
exsulto (**exulto**) -are, *to leap up frequently* or *violently.* Transf., *to rejoice exceedingly, exult, triumph*; of orators, etc., *to run riot, range freely.*
exsŭpĕrābĭlis -e, *that can be overcome.*
exsŭpĕrantĭa -ae, f., *superiority, pre-eminence.*
exsŭpĕro -are: intransit., *to mount up, appear above; to be prominent, excel*; transit., *to surmount; to surpass, exceed, overcome.*
exsurdo -are, *to deafen*; of taste, *to make dull* or *blunt.*
exsurgo -surgĕre -surrexi, *to rise up, lift oneself up, stand up; to regain strength.*
exsuscĭto -are, *to awaken from sleep*; of fire, *to kindle* or *fan*; mentally, *to excite, arouse*; se exsuscitare, *to make an effort.*
exta -orum, n. pl. *entrails of animals,* esp. *the heart, lungs, liver,* used by Romans for divination.
extābesco -tābescĕre -tābŭi, *to waste away entirely; to vanish, disappear.*
extāris -e, *used for cooking.*
extemplo (**-tempŭlo**), *immediately, forthwith.*
extempŏrālis -e, *extemporary, unrehearsed.*
extendo -tendere -tendi -tensum and -tentum, *to stretch out, expand, extend*; milit., *to extend in order of battle*; in gen., *to increase, extend*; in time, *to extend, prolong; to strain, exert.*
Hence partic. **extentus** -a -um, *wide, extensive.*
extento -are, *to stretch out, strain.*
extĕnŭātĭo -ōnis, f. *thinning*; as a figure of speech, *diminution, lessening.*
extĕnŭo -are, *to make thin* or *small, to reduce, diminish*; milit., *to extend*; in gen., *to lessen, weaken, diminish*; in speech, *to disparage, depreciate.*
Hence partic. **extĕnŭātus** -a -um, *weak, poor, slight.*
exter and **extĕrus** -a -um, *outward, foreign, strange*; compar. **extĕrĭor** -ĭus, genit. -ōris, *outer*; superl. **extrēmus** -a -um, *outermost*; n. as subst. *outer edge, extreme*; in time, *last*; n. as subst. *an end*; extremum, acc., *for the last time*; ad extremum, *to the end* or *at the end;* in degree or quality, *extreme*; esp. *lowest, worst*; extremum bonorum, malorum, *the*

highest good, evil; superl. **extĭmus** -a -um, *outermost.*

extĕrebro -are, *to bore out, extract by boring.*

extergĕo -tergēre -tersi -tersum, *to wipe off, wipe clean; to strip clean, plunder.*

extĕrĭor, exterius; see exter.

extermino -are, *to drive out, expel, banish; to put aside, remove.*

externus -a -um, *outside, external, foreign, strange*; m. as subst. *a foreigner, stranger*; n. pl. as subst. *outward* or *foreign things.*

extĕro -tĕrĕre -trīvi -trītum, *to rub out; to wear away.*

exterrĕo -terrēre -terrŭi -territum, *to frighten badly, scare, terrify.*

extĕrus; see exter.

extexo -ĕre, *to unweave; to cheat.*

extĭmesco -tĭmescĕre -tĭmŭi: intransit. *to be terrified*; transit., *to be greatly afraid of, to dread.*

extĭmus; see exter.

extispex -spĭcis, m., *a soothsayer predicting from the entrails of victims.*

extollo -ĕre, *to lift up, raise up*; of buildings, *to raise, erect*; of spirits, etc., *to elevate, exalt*; in words, *to praise* or *exaggerate*; sometimes *to adorn; to defer, postpone.*

extorquĕo -torquēre -torsi -tortum, *to twist out, wrest away, wrench out, dislocate.* Transf., *to obtain by force, extort.*

extorris -e, *driven from the country, exiled, banished.*

extrā: adv. *outside*; extra quam, extra quam si, *except, unless*; prep., with acc., *beyond, outside of, without; except for*; extra iocum, *joking apart.*

extrăho -trăhĕre -traxi -tractum, *to draw out, drag out, extract, remove, extricate*; sometimes *to bring forward*; in time, *to draw out, prolong, protract.*

extrānĕus -a -um, *outside, extraneous; foreign, strange*; m. as subst. *a foreigner, stranger.*

extrāordĭnārĭus -a -um, *extraordinary, anomalous, irregular, unnatural*; milit. equites, cohortes, *picked troops of the auxiliary forces.*

extrārĭus -a -um, *outward, external, extrinsic; strange, unrelated, foreign.*

extrēmĭtās -ātis, f. *end, farthest portion, extremity.*

extrēmus -a -um; see exter.

extrĭco -are, *to disentangle, extricate; to clear up, unravel.*

extrinsĕcus, *from without, from the outside; on the outside, outwardly.*

extrūdo -trūdĕre -trūsi -trūsum, *to push out, thrust forth*; merces, *to get sold.*

extundo -tundĕre -tŭdi -tūsum. (1) *to form by beating with a hammer; to invent, devise.* (2) *to beat out violently, drive away; to extort.*

exturbo -are, *to drive away, thrust out*; mentem, *to agitate.*

exūbĕro -are, *to grow thickly, abound.*

exul; see exsul.

exulcĕro -are, *to make worse, aggravate; to irritate, embitter.*

exŭlŭlo -are, *to howl out, howl loudly*; partic. **exŭlŭlātus** -a -um, *invoked with howlings.*

exundo -are, *to overflow, to flow out* or *over, to abound.*

exŭo -ŭĕre -ŭi -ūtum. (1) *to lay aside, put off, put away.* (2) *to strip, deprive* of a thing.

exūro -ūrĕre -ussi -ustum, *to burn out, burn up, consume*; also *to dry up, warm, heat.*

exustĭo -ōnis, f. *burning up, conflagration.*

exŭvĭae -arum, f. pl. *that which is taken off*; of men *dress; spoils taken from the enemy, arms,* etc.; *the skin, slough,* or *hide* of animals.

F

F, f, the sixth letter of the Latin Alphabet.

făba -ae, f. *the broad bean.*

făbālis -e, *of beans.*

fābella -ae, f. *a little story, fable* or *drama.*

făber -bra -brum, *ingenious, skilful.* M. as subst. **făber** -bri, *a worker, craftsman*; faber tignarius, *a carpenter*; ferrarius, *a blacksmith*; milit. fabri, *the engineers*; also *a fish,* perhaps *dory.* Adv. **fabrē,** *skilfully.*

Făbĭus -a -um, *name of a Roman gens.*

fabrēfăcĭo -făcĕre -fēci -factum, *to make* or *fashion skilfully.*

fabrĭca -ae, f. *the art of a* faber; *a device, trick, a workshop.*

fabrĭcātĭo -ōnis, f., *making, framing, construction.*

fabrĭcātor -ōris, m. *maker, artificer.*

Fabrĭcius -a, -um, *name of a Roman gens.*

fabrĭco -are, and **fabrĭcor** -ari, dep., *to form, make, forge.*

fabrīlis -e, *relating to an artificer*; n.pl. as subst., *tools.*

fābŭla -e, f. (1) *talk, conversation*: fabulam fieri, *to get talked about.* (2) *a tale, story, fable, drama, myth*; fabulae! *nonsense!*

fābŭlor -ari, dep. (1) *to talk, converse, chatter.* (2) *to tell an untruth.*

fābŭlōsus -a -um, *renowned in story, fabled.*

făcesso făcessĕre făcessi făcessītum: transit., *to do eagerly, perform, fulfil, accomplish*; homini negotium, *to give trouble to*; intransit., *to make off, go away, depart.*

făcētĭa -ae, f.; sing., *wit*; plur., *wit, drollery, humour.*

făcētus -a -um, *fine, elegant; witty, facetious.* Adv. **făcētē,** *elegantly; wittily, humorously.*

făcĭēs -ēi, *shape, form, figure, outwar appearance*; esp. *face, countenance.* Transf., *character, nature; seeming, pretence.*

făcĭlis -e, *easy to do; easy to manage,*

convenient, favourable; of movements, *easy, mobile*; of persons, *facile, dexterous, clever*; of character, *affable, easy, good-natured*. N. acc. as adv. **făcĭlĕ,** *easily, without difficulty; indisputably, certainly*; haud facile, *not easily, hardly*; facile pati, *to bear willingly*.

făcĭlĭtās -ātis, f. *easiness, ease*; of character, *willingness, friendliness, affability, good-nature*.

făcĭnŏrōsus -a -um, *wicked, criminal*.

făcĭnus -ŏris, n., *a deed, action*; esp. *a bad deed, crime, villainy*; hence *instrument of crime*; in plur., *criminals*.

făcĭo făcĕre fēci factum (the pass. is fio; q.v.). Transit., *to make, form, do, perform*; of feelings and circumstances, *to cause, bring about*; esp. copiam *or* potestatem, *to give a chance, grant permission*; with clause as object, esp. with subj., e.g. fac sciam, *let me know*; facere non possum quin, *I cannot but*; of troubles, *to experience, suffer*; with double acc., *to make, appoint, change into*; with genit., *to make something the property of* a person or thing, *to bring into the power of*, or mentally *to put into a category, to regard, to esteem, value*; with acc. and infin., *to take it, assume* or *to make out, represent* that a thing is so. Intransit., *to act*; with adverbs, *to behave*; facere cum, or ab, homine, *to act on the side of, support; to sacrifice; to be serviceable, to suit, help, be of service*; used instead of repeating another verb, *to do so*.

Hence partic. **factus** -a -um, *done, wrought*; n. of compar., factius, *nearer to achievement*; n. of positive as subst. **factum** -i, *a deed, act, exploit*.

factĭo -ōnis, f. (1) *a making, doing*; also *the right of making* or *doing*. (2) *a party, group*; esp. *a political party, faction, side*.

factĭōsus -a -um, *busy; factious, associated with a faction*.

factĭto -are. (1) *to practise, be accustomed to make* or *do*. (2) *to appoint openly*.

factus -a -um, partic. from facio; q.v.

făcŭla -ae, f., *a little torch*.

făcultās -ātis, f. *feasibility, opportunity, power, means; capacity, ability; resources, stock, abundance*.

fācundĭa -ae, f., *eloquence, readiness of speech*.

fācundus -a -um, *eloquent, fluent, ready of speech*; adv. **fācundē.**

faecŭla -ae, f. *lees of wine*.

faenebris -e, *relating to interest*.

faenĕrātĭo -ōnis, f. *lending at interest, usury*.

faenĕrātor -ōris, m. *money-lender, usurer*.

faenĕror -ari, dep. and **faenĕro** **(fenĕro)** -are, *to lend at interest*; provincias, *to despoil by usury*; beneficium *to trade in benefits*.

faenĕus -a -um, *of hay*; homines, *men of straw*.

faenīlĭa -ĭum, n. pl. *hay-loft*.

faenĭsĕca -ae, m., *a mower; a countryman*.

faenum (fēnum) -i, n. *hay*.

faenus (fēnus) -ŏris, n. *interest on money*; pecuniam dare faenore, *to lend at interest*; accipere faenore, *to borrow*. Transf., *debt, indebtedness; capital, usury*.

Faesŭlae -arum, f. *town in Etruria*, (now *Fiesole*); adj. **Faesŭlanus** -a -um.

faex faecis, f. *the dregs* or *lees of liquid*, esp. *of wine*; fig. socially, *the dregs, the lower orders*.

fāgĭnĕus and **fāgĭnus** -a -um, *of beech*.

fāgus -i, f. *beech-tree*.

făla (phăla) -ae, f. *a wooden tower* or *pillar*.

fălārĭca (phălārĭca) -ae, f. *a missile covered with tow and pitch*.

falcārĭus -i, m., *a sickle-maker*.

falcātus -a -um, *furnished with sickles; sickle-shaped*.

falcĭfer -fĕra -fĕrum, *carrying a scythe* or *sickle*.

Fălernus ăger, *the Falernian country, in Campania*; n. of adj. as subst. **Fălernum** -i, *Falernian wine*.

fallācĭa -ae, f. *deceit, trick, fraud*.

fallax -ācis, *deceitful, treacherous, false*; adv. **fallācĭter.**

fallo fallĕre fĕfelli falsum, *to deceive, lead astray, cause to be mistaken*; nisi fallor, *unless I am mistaken*; of abstr. things, *to disappoint, fail in*; poet., *to beguile, wile away; to escape the notice of, be concealed from*; impers. non fallit me, *I am not unaware*.

Hence partic. **falsus** -a -um. (1) *wrong, mistaken, misled*; n. as subst., a mistake; abl. as adv., falso, *falsely, mistakenly*. (2) *false, untrue, spurious*. (3) *deceitful, lying*; n. as subst. *a lie*; abl. as adv., falso, *falsely, fraudulently*. Adv. **falsē.**

falsĭdĭcus -a -um, and **falsĭlŏquus** -a -um, *lying*.

falsus -a -um, partic. from fallo; q.v.

falx falcis, f. *a sickle, bill-hook, pruning-hook*; *a sickle-shaped implement of war*.

fāma -ae, f. *talk, report, rumour, tradition*; fama est, *there is a rumour; public opinion; standing in public opinion, repute*, good or bad.

fămēlĭcus -a -um, *hungry, famished*.

fămes -is, f. *hunger, famine; insatiable desire; poverty of expression*.

fāmĭgĕrātor -ōris, m. *rumour-monger*.

fămĭlĭa -ae, *a household* (*of slaves*), *establishment*; pater familias or paterfamilias, *the head of the household*; materfamilias, *a married woman* or *an unmarried woman whose father was dead*; filiusfamilias, *a son still under his father's power*. Transf., *a family estate; a family*, as a subdivision of a gens; any *fraternity, group, sect*.

fămĭlĭāris -e. (1) *belonging to the*

slaves of a house; as subst. **fămĭlĭārĭs** -is, m. *a servant, slave.* (2) *belonging to a family* or *household; known in the house* or *family, intimate, friendly*; m. and f. as subst. *a familiar friend.* (3) in augury, fissum familiare, *or* pars familiaris, *the part of the entrails relating to the persons sacrificing.* Adv. **fămĭlĭārĭter,** *familiarly, intimately.*

fămĭlĭārĭtās -ātis, f. *confidential friendship, intimacy*; meton., *familiar friends.*

fāmōsus -a -um: pass., *much spoken of, renowned*; in bad sense, *infamous, notorious*; act., *libellous, defamatory.*

fămul, fămŭla; see famulus.

fămŭlāris -e, *relating to servants* or *slaves.*

fămŭlātus -ūs, m. *servitude, slavery, service*; meton., *an establishment of slaves.*

fămŭlor -ari, dep. *to be a servant, to serve.*

fămŭlus -a -um, *serving, servile*; as subst. m. **fămŭlus** (**fămul**) -i, *a servant, slave, attendant*; f. **fămŭla** -ae, *a female slave, handmaid.*

fānātĭcus -a -um, *inspired*; *enthusiastic*; *frenzied.*

fānum -i, n. *a temple with the land round it, a holy place.*

fār farris, n. *spelt, grain, meal.*

farcio farcire farsi fartum, *to fill full, stuff full.*

fărīna -ae, f., *meal, flour.*

farrāgo -ĭnis, f. *mixed fodder for cattle, mash; a medley, mixture.*

farrātus -a -um, *provided with grain; made of corn.*

farrĕus -a -um, *made of spelt* or *corn.*

fartim (**fartem**), acc. sing., *stuffing, minced meat.*

fartor -ōris, m. *a fattener of fowls.*

fās, n. indecl. *divine command* or *law*; sometimes *fate, destiny*; in gen. *right, that which is allowed, lawful*; fas est, *it is allowed, is lawful.*

fascĭa -ae, f. *a bandage, band, girdle, girth.*

fascĭcŭlus -i, m., *a little bundle* or *packet*; florum, *a nosegay.*

fascĭno -are, *to bewitch; to envy.*

fascĭŏla -ae, f., *a little bandage.*

fascis -is, m. *a bundle, packet*; plur., fasces, *bundles of sticks with an axe projecting, carried by lictors before the chief Roman magistrates*; hence *high office,* esp. *the consulate.*

fasti -orum, m.; see fastus -a -um.

fastīdĭo -ire, *to loathe, feel distaste for, dislike.*

fastīdĭōsus -a -um, *squeamish, nice, dainty, fastidious*; with genit., *sick of, disgusted with, impatient of*; in act. sense, *disgusting, loathsome.* Adv. **fastīdĭōsē,** *fastidiously, with disgust.*

fastīdĭum -i, n. *loathing, squeamishness, disgust, dislike*; hence *scorn, haughtiness, disdain.*

fastīgātus -a -um, *pointed* or *sloping down*; adv. **fastīgātē,** *slantingly.*

fastīgĭum -i, n. *the gable end, pediment* of a roof; hence *a slope,* either up or down; of measurements looking up, *height*; looking down, *depth*; abstract, *high rank, dignity; principal point* in a subject.

[1]**fastus** -ūs, m. *pride, haughtiness, arrogance.*

[2]**fastus** -a -um: dies fastus, plur. dies fasti, *or* simply fasti, *days on which the praetor could administer justice, court-days.* Transf., *a list of these days, with festivals,* etc., *the Roman calendar; a register, record; a list of magistrates.*

fātālis -e, *relating to destiny* or *fate; fated, destined by fate*; in bad sense, *deadly, fatal.* Adv. **fātālĭter,** *according to fate.*

fătĕor fătēri fassus, dep., *to confess, admit, allow; to reveal, make known.*

fātĭcănus and **-cĭnus** -a -um, *prophetic.*

fātĭdĭcus -a -um, *announcing fate, prophetic*; m. as subst. *a prophet.*

fātĭfer -fĕra -fĕrum, *deadly, fatal.*

fătīgātĭo -ōnis, f. *weariness, fatigue.*

fătīgo -are, *to weary, fatigue; to vex, harass; to tease, importune, worry.*

fātĭlŏqua -ae, f. *a prophetess.*

fătisco -ere and **fătiscor** -i, dep., *to gape, crack, open; to become weak, droop.*

fătŭĭtās -ātis, f. *foolishness, silliness.*

fātum -i, n., *an utterance,* esp. *a divine utterance*; hence *destiny, fate; the will of a god*; personif. Fata, *the Parcae* or *Fates; doom, fate, natural death, misfortune, ruin, calamity.*

fătŭus -a -um, *foolish, idiotic, silly.*

Faunus -i, m. *a mythic deity of the forests.*

faustĭtās -ātis, f., *prosperity.*

faustus -a -um, *favourable, lucky, auspicious*; adv. **faustē.**

fautor -ōris, m. *patron, promoter, partisan.*

fautrix -trīcis, f., *a patroness.*

faux, f.; usually plur. **fauces** -ĭum, *gullet, throat, jaws.* Transf., *a chasm, gorge, defile; an isthmus, neck of land; straits.*

făvĕo făvēre fāvi fautum, *to favour, be favourable to, help, support,* with dat.; with infin., *to be inclined to do.* Esp. as religious t. t., *to speak no words of bad omen*; hence *to be silent.*

făvilla -ae, f. *glowing ashes,* esp. *of the dead; a spark.*

făvĭtor -ōris, m. = fautor; q.v.

Făvōnĭus -i, m. = Zephyrus, *the west wind.*

făvor -ōris, m., *favour, good-will, support, inclinaton*; esp. *applause at the theatre, acclamation.*

făvōrābĭlis -e, *in favour, popular.*

făvus -i, m. *honeycomb.*

fax făcis, f. (1) *a torch,* esp. as carried at weddings and funerals. (2) *a fire-brand*; of persons, *instigator*; of things, *stimulus.* (3) *light, flame,* esp. of heavenly bodies; fig., *brilliance* or *passion.*

fĕbrĭcŭla -ae, f., *a slight fever, feverishness.*
febris -is, f. *fever.*
Fĕbrŭārĭus -i, m. or **Fĕbrŭārĭus Mensis,** *the cleansing month, February*; Kalendae Februariae, *the 1st of February.*
fĕbrŭum -i, n. *religious purification*; **Fĕbrŭa** -orum, pl. *the Roman feast of purification on the 15th of February.*
fētiālis = fetialis; q.v.
fēcundĭtās -ātis, f. *fruitfulness, fecundity.*
fēcundo -are, *to fructify, fertilize.*
fēcundus -a -um, *fruitful, prolific; abundant, full, plentiful*; with genit., *rich in, abounding in*; act., *making fruitful.*
fel fellis, n. *the gall-bladder, gall, bile; poison, venom; bitterness.*
fēles -is, f. *a cat*; hence *a thief.*
fēlīcĭtās -ātis, f. *happiness, good fortune, success*; personif., *Good Fortune as a goddess.*
felix -īcis, *fruitful, fertile.* Transf., *of good omen, favourable, bringing good luck; fortunate, lucky, successful*; Felix, *the Lucky One, surname of Sulla.* Adv. **fēlīcĭter,** *fruitfully; auspiciously, favourably; luckily, successfully.*
fĕmella -ae, f. *young woman, girl.*
fĕmen = femur; q.v.
fēmĭna -ae, f. *a female, woman*; of animals, *the female.*
fēmĭnĕus -a -um, *female, feminine; womanish, effeminate.*
fĕmur -ŏris or -ĭnis, n. *the thigh.*
fĕnestra -ae, f. *a window; a breach, loophole.*
fĕra -ae, f.; see ferus.
fērālis -e, *relating to the dead, funereal; deadly, fatal; mournful*; n. pl. as subst. *the festival of the dead, in February.*
fĕrax -ācis, *fruitful, fertile, prolific*; compar. adv. **fĕrācĭus,** *more fruitfully.*
fercŭlum -i, n. *a frame, litter, bier, tray*; of food, *a course* or *dish.*
fĕrē. (1) *almost, nearly*; with negatives, *scarcely, hardly.* (2) *just, exactly.* (3) *as a rule, generally, usually.*
fĕrentārĭus -i, m. *a light-armed soldier.*
fĕretrum -i, n., *a bier for carrying a corpse.*
fērĭae -arum, f. pl. *festivals, holidays.*
fērĭātus -a -um, *keeping holiday, idle, at leisure.*
fĕrīnus -a -um, *relating to a wild beast, wild*; f. as subst. *flesh of wild animals, game.*
fĕrĭo -ire, *to strike, knock, smite, hit*; esp. *to strike dead, slay, kill*; colloq., *to cheat.*
fĕrĭtās -ātis, f. *wildness, savageness.*
fermē. (1) *almost, nearly*; with negatives, *hardly, scarcely.* (2) *usually.*
fermentum -i, n. *leaven, yeast; a kind of beer.* Transf., *anger, passion.*
fĕro ferre, with perf. tŭli, supine latum. (1) *to bear, bring, carry*; prae se ferre, *to display, make public*; often *to endure, submit to*; esp. with adv.; ferre aegre, *to take ill, be vexed at.* (2) *to bring orth, produce.* (3) *to bring to* a place or person, *fetch, offer*; suffragium, sententiam, *to vote*; legem, *to propose a law*; ferre ut, *to propose that*; commercial, expensum ferre, *to set down in an account-book as paid; to cause, bring about; to report to others, spread abroad, speak of*; fama fert, *the story goes*; esp. *to publish* a person's *praises.* (4) *to bear away, carry off*; ferre et agere, *to plunder.* Transf., *to win, get*; centuriam, tribus, *to gain the votes of.* (5) *to bear along, move forward, put in motion*; milit., signa ferre, *to march.* Transf., *to move, impel, carry away*; without object, *to lead, tend.*
fĕrōcĭa -ae, f. *high spirit, courage*; in bad sense, *arrogance, ferocity.*
fĕrōcĭtās -ātis, f. *courage, untamed spirit*; in bad sense, *arrogance.*
fĕrox -ōcis, *courageous, high-spirited, warlike*; in bad sense, *wild, unbridled, arrogant*; adv. **fĕrōcĭter.**
ferrāmenta -orum, n. pl. *tools made of,* or *shod with, iron.*
ferrārĭus -a -um, *of iron*; m. as subst. *a blacksmith*; f. pl. as subst., *iron-mines.*
ferrātĭlis -e, *in irons*; of slaves.
ferrātus -a -um, *furnished* or *covered with iron*; servi, *in irons*; m. pl. as subst. *soldiers in armour.*
ferrĕus -a -um, *of iron; made of iron* or *like iron; hard, unfeeling, cruel; immovable, firm.*
ferrĭtĕrĭum -i, n. = ergastulum; q.v.
ferrūgĭnĕus and **ferrūgĭnus** -a -um, *rust-coloured, dusky.*
ferrūgo -ĭnis, f. *iron rust; the colour of rust.*
ferrum -i, n. *iron*; hence *any iron instrument; plough, axe, scissors,* and esp. *sword.*
fertĭlis -e, *fruitful, fertile, productive; fertilizing, making fruitful.*
fertĭlĭtās -ātis, f. *fruitfulness, fertility*
fertum (ferctum) -i, n. *a sacrificial cake.*
fĕrŭla -ae, f. (1) *the herb fennel.* (2) *a stick, cane,* esp. *to punish slaves and children.*
fĕrus -a -um, *wild, uncultivated, uncivilized, rough, cruel*; m. and f. as subst., *a wild animal.*
fervēfăcĭo -făcĕre -fēci -factum *to make hot, boil, melt.*
fervĕo fervēre ferbŭi (and **fervo** fervĕre fervi) *to be boiling hot, to boil, seethe, glow.* Transf., *to be in quick movement, to seethe; to be excited by passion, rage.*

Hence partic. **fervens** -entis, *glowing, hot, heated*; of character or feeling, *heated, fiery.* Adv. **ferventer,** *hotly, warmly.*
fervesco -ĕre, *to become hot, begin to glow* or *boil.*
fervĭdus -a -um, *boiling, seething*

foaming; of character or feelings, *fiery, passionate, excited.*
fervo = ferveo; q.v.
fervor -ōris, m. *boiling heat, seething, foaming; ardour, passion.*
Fescennĭa -ae, f. *a town in Etruria famous for verse dialogues.* Adj. **Fescennīnus** -a -um.
fessus -a -um, *weary, tired, exhausted*; fessa aetas, *old age*; res fessae, *distress.*
festīnātĭo -ōnis, f. *haste, speed, hurry.*
festīno -are: intransit., *to hasten, hurry*; transit., *to hasten, accelerate.* Hence adv. **festīnanter** and **festīnātō,** *hastily.*
festīnus -a -um, *hastening, hasty.*
festīvĭtās -ātis, f. *gaiety, jollity*; of speech or writing, *cheerfulness, humour.*
festīvus -a -um, *of a holiday, festive; merry, good-humoured, cheerful*; adv. **festīvē.**
festūca -ae, f. *a stalk, straw, stem.* Transf., *a rod used in the manumission of slaves.*
festus -a -um, *of a holiday, festive*; of people, *keeping holiday*; n. as subst. *a feast.*
fētĭālis -s, m. *one of a college of priests responsible for formally making peace* or *declaring war*; as adj. = *belonging to the* fetiales.
fētūra -ae, f. *the bringing forth of young, breeding*; meton. *brood, offspring.*
[1]**fētus** -a -um. (1) *pregnant; fruitful, fertile: teeming with, full of.* (2) *that has brought forth, newly delivered.*
[2]**fētus** -ūs, m. *the bringing forth* or *hatching of young*; of the soil, *bearing, producing.* Transf., *that which is brought forth: offspring, brood*; of plants *fruit, produce, shoot.*
fibra -ae, f. *a fibre, filament; the entrails of an animal.*
fībŭla -ae, f. *a buckle, brooch, clasp; an iron clamp.*
fīcēdŭla -ae, f. *a small bird, the becafico.*
fictĭlis -e, *shaped*; hence *earthen, made of clay*; n. as subst., esp. pl., *earthenware, earthen vessels.*
fictĭo -ōnis, f. *forming, feigning; assumption.*
fictor -ōris, m. *an image-maker, a moulder*; in gen., *maker, contriver.*
fictrix -īcis, f. *she that forms or fashions.*
fictūra -ae, f. *forming, fashioning.*
fictus, partic. from fingo; q.v.
fīculnus and **fīculnĕus** -a -um, *of the fig-tree.*
fīcus -i, and -ūs, f. *a fig-tree; a fig.*
fĭdĕĭcommissum -i, n. legal, *a trust.*
fĭdēlĭa -ae, f. *an eathenware pot* or *vase.*
fĭdēlis -e, *trusty, steadfast, faithful*; m. as subst., esp. pl., *confidants, faithful friends.* Adv. **fĭdēlĭter,** *faithfully; securely, without danger.*
fĭdēlĭtās -ātis, f., *faithfulness, trust, fidelity.*
Fīdēnae -arum, and **Fīdēna** -ae, f. *a town in Latium*; adj. **Fīdēnas** -ātis.
fīdens -entis, partic. from fido; q.v.
fīdentia -ae, f. *confidence, boldness.*
[1]**fĭdes** -ei, f., *trust, confidence, reliance, belief, faith*; fidem facere, *to create confidence, cause belief*; as mercantile t. t., *credit.* Transf., *that which produces confidence; faithfulness, conscientiousness*; fidem praestare, *to be loyal*; (ex) bona fide, *in good faith, sincerely*; of things, *credibility, actuality, fulfilment; a promise, assurance, word of honour, engagement;* fidem fallere, *to break a promise*; servare, *to keep a promise*; fide mea, *on my word of honour*; fides (or fides publica) *a promise of protection, safe-conduct*; hence, in gen., *faithful protection, constant help.*
[2]**fĭdes** -is, f., usually plur. *a gut-string for a musical instrument*; hence *a lyre, lute, harp.*
fĭdĭcĕn -cĭnis, m., *a player on the harp, lyre, lute;* poet., *a lyric poet.*
fĭdĭcina -ae, f. *a female player on the lute* or *harp.*
fĭdĭcĭnus -a -um, *of lute-playing.*
fĭdĭcŭla -ae, f., usually plur. *a little lyre* or *lute; an instrument for torturing slaves.*
Fĭdĭus -i, m., *a surname of Jupiter*; esp. in phrase, medius fidius! *So help me God!*
fīdo fīdĕre fīsus sum, *to trust, believe, confide in*; with dat. or abl.

Hence partic. **fīdens** -entis, *without fear, confident, courageous*; adv. **fīdenter.**

fīdūcĭa -ae, f. (1) *confidence, trust, assurance*; with sui, or absol., *self-confidence, self-reliance, courage.* (2) *fidelity.*
fīdūcĭārĭus -a -um, *entrusted, committed.*
fīdus -a -um, *trusty, true, faithful, sure*; superl. adv. **fīdissĭme.**
fīgo fīgĕre fixi fixum. (1) *to fix, fasten, make fast, attach, affix*; esp. with oculos, *to fix the gaze.* (2) *to thrust home* a weapon, etc. so as to stick fast. (3) *to transfix.*

Hence partic. **fixus** -a -um, *fixed, firm, immovable.*

fĭgŭlāris -e, *of a potter.*
fĭgŭlus -i, m., *a worker in clay, potter.*
fĭgūra -ae, f. *form, shape, figure, size; an atom; shade of a dead person*; the abstr., *kind, nature, species*; rhet., *a figure of speech.*
fĭgūro -are, *to form, mould, shape*; rhet., *to adorn with figures.*
fīlātim, *thread by thread.*
fīlĭa -ae, f. *daughter.*
fīlĭcātus -a -um, *adorned with ferns; embossed with fern leaves.*
fīlĭŏla -ae, f. *little daughter.*
fīlĭŏlus -i, m. *little son.*
fīlĭus -i, m. *son.*
fīlix -ĭcis, f. *fern.*
fīlum -i, n. *a thread,* pendere filo (tenui), *to hang by a thread; a woollen fillet.* Transf., *form, shape*; of speech or writing, *texture, thread.*
fimbrĭae -arum, f. pl., *fringe, border edge.*

fimbrĭātus -a -um, *fringed.*
fīmus -i, m. and **fīmum** -i, n. *dung, dirt.*
findo findĕre fĭdi fissum, *to split, cleave, divide, halve.*
Hence partic. **fissus** -a -um, *split, cloven*; n. as subst., *a split, cleft*; in augury, *a divided liver.*
fingo fingĕre finxi fictum, *to shape, fashion, form, mould*; also *to arrange, put in order; to represent, imagine, conceive; to feign, fabricate, devise*; fingere vultum, *to put on an artificial expression.*
Hence partic. **fictus** -a -um, *feigned, false*; n. as subst. *a falsehood.*
finĭo -ire, *to bound, limit, enclose, restrain; to define, determine, appoint; to put an end to, conclude, finish*; esp. *to finish speaking*, or *to die*; pass., *to end, cease.* Perf. partic. **fīnītus** -a -um; of a phrase, *well-rounded*; adv. **fīnītē,** *moderately, within bounds.*
fīnis -is, m. (sometimes f.) *boundary, limit, border; summit, end; object, aim;* in pl. *enclosed area, territory.*
fīnĭtĭmus and **fīnĭtŭmus** -a -um, *neighbouring, adjacent; related to, resembling, similar.* M. pl. as subst. *neighbours.*
fīnĭtor -ōris, m., *one who determines boundaries, a land surveyor.* Transf., *the horizon.*
fīo fĭĕri factus sum, used as pass. of facio. (1) of persons and things, *to be made, come into existence*; with predicate, *to become, be appointed*; with genit., *to be valued at.* (2) of actions, *to be done*; of events, *to happen*; with abl., quid illo fiet? *what will happen to him?* fieri ut, *to come about that*; fieri non potest quin, *it must be that.*
firmāmen -ĭnis, n. *support, prop.*
firmāmentum -i, n., *a means of support, prop; the main point* in an argument.
firmātor -ōris, m., *one who makes firm* or *establishes.*
firmĭtās -ātis and **firmĭtūdo** -dĭnis, f., *firmness, stability; strength of mind, constancy.*
firmo -are, *to make firm, strengthen; to make durable, make secure*; of spirits, *to encourage, cheer, animate*; of ideas, *to prove establish,* also *to assert, maintain.*
firmus -a -um, *firm, strong, stout; lasting, valid; morally strong.* Adv. **firmē** and **firmĭter,** *firmly, strongly, steadfastly.*
fiscella and **fiscĭna** -ae, f., *a small basket.*
fiscus -i, m. *a basket;* hence *a money-bag, purse; the state treasury*; under the empire, *the emperor's privy purse* (opp. aerarium, *the state treasury*).
fissĭlis -e, *that can be split*; also *split.*
fissĭo -ōnis, f. *splitting, cleaving, dividing.*
fistūca -ae, f. *a rammer, mallet.*
fistŭla -ae, f. *a water-pipe*; *a reed-pipe, shepherd's pipe*; eburneola, *a pitch-pipe of ivory.*
fistŭlātor -ōris, m., *one who plays the reed-pipe.*
fixus -a -um, partic. from figo; q.v.
flābellum -i, n. *a small fan.*
flābĭlis -e, *airy.*
flābra -orum, n. pl. *blasts of wind, breezes.*
flaccĕo -ēre, *to be flabby; to fail* or *flag.*
flaccesco flaccescĕre flaccŭi, *to begin to flag, become flabby.*
flaccĭdus -a -um *flabby; weak, languid.*
flaccus -a -um, *flabby*; of men, *flap-eared.*
Flaccus; see Horatius, and Valerius.
flăgello -are, *to whip, scourge, beat.*
flăgellum -i, n. *a whip, scourge; the thong of a javelin; a young sprout, vine-shoot*; plur. *the arms of a polypus;* fig., *the sting* of conscience.
flāgĭtātĭo -ōnis, f., *an earnest demand* or *entreaty.*
flāgĭtātor -ōris, m., *one who earnestly demands* or *entreats.*
flāgĭtĭōsus -a -um, *shameful, disgraceful, infamous*; adv. **flāgĭtĭōsē.**
flāgĭtĭum -i, n. *a disgraceful action, shameful crime; shame, disgrace*; meton., *scoundrel, rascal.*
flāgĭto -are, *to entreat, ask, demand earnestly; to demand to know; to summon before a court of justice.*
flagrantĭa -ae, f. *burning, blazing, glittering.*
flagritrība -ae, m., *one that wears out whips, whipping boy.*
flagro -are, *to blaze, burn, glow, flame,* also *to glitter.* Transf., *to glow* or *burn with passion; to suffer from,* with abl.
Hence partic. **flagrans** -antis, *blazing, burning, glittering.* Transf., *passionate, ardent.* Adv. **flagranter.**
flagrum -i, n. *scourge, whip.*
[1]**flāmen** -ĭnis, m. *the priest of some particular god.*
[2]**flāmen** -ĭnis, n. *a blowing, blast.*
flāmĭnĭca -ae, f. *the wife of a flamen.*
Flāmĭnīnus, *a surname in the patrician* Gens Quinctia; see Quinctius.
flāmĭnĭum -i, n., *the office of a flamen.*
Flāmĭnĭus -a -um, *name of a Roman* gens.
flamma -ae, f., *a flame, blazing fire.* Transf., *a source of light, torch, star, lightning; lustre, glitter; the fire* or *glow of passion; devouring flame, destruction.*
flammĕŏlum -i, n., *a small bridal veil.*
flammesco -ĕre, *to become inflamed.*
flammĕus -a -um, *fiery, flaming; flashing, fiery-red*; n. as subst. **flammĕum** -i, *a (flame-coloured) bridal veil.*
flammĭfer -fĕra -fĕrum, *flaming, fiery.*
flammo -are: intransit., *to flame, blaze, burn*; transit., *to set on fire inflame.*
flammŭla -ae, f. *little flame.*
flātus -ūs, m. *blowing, blast, breathing.*

Transf., *haughtiness, arrogance*, gen. plur.
flāvens -entis, *yellow* or *gold-coloured.*
flāvesco -ĕre, *to become yellow or gold-coloured.*
Flāvĭus -a -um, *name of a Roman* gens *to which the emperors Vespasian, Titus, and Domitian belonged.*
flāvus -a -um, *gold-coloured, yellow.*
flēbĭlis -e: pass., *lamentable, wretched, deserving tears;* act., *tearful, doleful.* Adv. **flēbĭlĭter.**
flecto flectĕre flexi flexum, *to bend.* (1) *to alter the shape of, to bow, twist, curve.* Transf., *to change, alter, influence.* (2) *to alter the direction of, to turn, wheel*; vocem, *to modulate.*
flĕo flēre flēvi flētum: intransit., *to weep; to drip, trickle*; transit., *to weep for, lament, bewail*; flendus, *to be lamented.*
[1]**flētus** -a -um, partic. of fleo; q.v.
[2]**flētus** -ūs, m. *weeping, bewailing.*
flexĭbĭlis -e, *that can be bent, flexible*; of speech or the voice, *adaptable*; in bad sense, *fickle, changeable.*
flexĭlis -e, *flexible, pliant, supple.*
flexĭlŏquus -a -um, *equivocal, ambiguous.*
flexĭo -ōnis, f. *bending*; vocis, or modorum, *modulation of the voice*; deverticula flexionesque, *twists and turns.*
flexipēs -pĕdis, *crooked-footed, twining.*
flexŭōsus -a -um, *full of windings and turnings, crooked.*
flexūra -ae, f. *bending.*
[1]**flexus** -a -um, partic. of flecto; q.v.
[2]**flexus** -ūs, m. *bending, turning*; of the voice, *modulation.* Transf., *change, alteration.*
flictus -ūs, m. *striking together, dashing against.*
flīgo -ere, *to beat* or *dash down.*
flo flare flavi flatum, *to blow*; intransit., of winds, persons and instruments; transit., *to blow, blow forth; to blow on* an instrument; *to cast metals, to coin.*
floccus -i, m. *a flock of wool*; flocci non facere, *to think nothing of.*
Flōra -ae, f., *the goddess of flowers, and Spring;* adj. **Flōrālis** -e, *belonging to Flora*; n. pl. as subst. *the festival of Flora.*
Flōrentĭa -ae, f. *a town in Etruria* (now *Florence*); adj. **Flōrentīnus** -a -um.
florĕo -ēre -ŭi, *to bloom, flower.* Transf., *to be in one's prime, to prosper, flourish, be in repute;* with abl., *to abound in, swarm with.*

Hence partic. **flōrens** -entis, *blooming, flourishing.*
flōresco -ĕre, *to begin to blossom* or *flourish.*
florĕus -a -um, *made of flowers; rich in flowers, flowery.*
flōrĭdus -a -um, *flowery, blossoming; made of* or *rich in flowers*; of age, *fresh, blooming*; of speech, *flowery, florid.*
flōrĭfer -fĕra fĕrum, *flower-bearing.*
flōrĭlĕgus -a -um, *culling flowers.*
flōs flōris, m. *a flower, blossom.* Transf., *the prime, flower of* anything, *the best, the pride*; on the face, *first beard, down*; vini *bouquet*; of speech, *ornament.*
floscŭlus -i, m., *a little flower.* Transf., *best part, pride*; of speech, *ornament.*
fluctĭfrăgus -a -um, *wave-breaking.*
fluctŭātĭo -ōnis, f. *moving backwards and forwards, fluctuation*; *indecision.*
fluctŭo -are, *to be wave-like, move up and down*; sometimes of a *glittering effect*; of persons and passions, *to be tossed about, to waver.*
fluctŭor -ari -atus, dep. *to toss about, waver.*
fluctŭōsus -a -um, *full of waves, stormy.*
fluctus -ūs, m. *a streaming, flowing.* Transf., *commotion, disturbance.*
flŭentum -i, n., *running water, a stream.*
flŭĭdus -a -um, *flowing, fluid.* Transf., *lax, languid; relaxing.*
flŭĭto -are, *to flow hither and thither, to float, swim, sail, move up and down, be tossed about.* Transf. *to flutter; to waver, vacillate.*
flūmen -ĭnis, n. *flowing*; hence *a river, stream*; flumine secundo, *downstream*; flumine adverso, *upstream*; fig., *a stream of* blood, tears, words, etc.
flūmĭnĕus -a -um, *of a river.*
flŭo flŭĕre fluxi fluxum: of fluids, *to flow*; of a solid object, *to flow, drip with any liquid.* Transf., in gen., *to flow, stream, pour*; of abstr. things, *to proceed, issue, spread*; of circumstances, *to tend*; of language, *to flow; to sink, droop.*

Hence pres. partic. **flŭens** -entis, *flowing*; hence *lax*; of speech, *fluent* or *diffuse*; adv. **flŭenter,** *in a flowing manner.* Past partic. **fluxus** -a -um, *flowing*; hence *leaky*; of solid objects, *waving, fluttering, loose*; of character, *lax, loose, weak*; of abstr. things, *fleeting, unstable.*
flŭto -are, *to flow, float, swim.*
flŭvĭālis and **flŭvĭātĭlis** -e, *of a river.*
flŭvĭdus -a -um, *flowing, fluid.*
flŭvĭus -ĭi, m., *flowing water; a stream, river.*
fluxus -a -um, partic. from flŭo; q.v.
fōcāle -is, n. *a wrapper for the neck.*
fōcillo -are, *to warm up, refresh by warmth.*
fŏcŭla -orum, n pl. *stoves.*
fŏcŭlus -i, m. *a brazier.*
fŏcus -i, m. *a fireplace, hearth;* meton., *house, family, home*; sometimes *altar-fire* or *funeral pyre.*
fŏdĭco -are, *to dig, jog*; latus, *to dig in the ribs.*
fŏdĭo fŏdĕre fōdi fossum, *to dig*; also *to dig out; to excavate.* Transf., *to prick, prod, jog.*
foecundus, foecundo = fecundus, fecundo; q.v.
foedĕrātus -a -um, *confederate, allied.*
foedifrăgus -a -um, *treaty-breaking.*
foedĭtās -ātis, f. *foulness, filthiness.*
foedo -are, *to make foul, make filthy, defile, disfigure*; morally, *to dishonour, disgrace.*
[1]**foedus** -a -um, *foul, filthy, horrible, disgusting*; adv. **foedē.**

[2]**foedus** -ĕris, n. *a league* between states; *a compact, covenant, agreement.* Transf., *a law.*
foen-; see faen-.
foetĕo -ēre, *to have a bad smell.*
foetĭdus -a -um, *having a bad smell, stinking.*
foetor -ōris, m. *a bad smell, stink.*
foetus; see fetus.
fŏlĭātus -a -um, *leafy*; n. as subst. *a salve* or *oil of spikenard leaves.*
fŏlĭum -i, n. *a leaf.*
follĭcŭlus -i, m. *a little sack* or *bag.*
follis -is, m. *a leather bag; a pair of bellows; a purse; a puffed-out cheek.*
fōmentum -i, n. *poultice, fomentation.* Transf., *alleviation.*
fōmĕs -ĭtis, m. *touchwood, tinder.*
fons fontis, m. *a spring, fountain; fresh* or *spring water.* Transf., *spring, origin, source.*
fontānus -a -um, *of a spring* or *fountain.*
Fontēius -a -um, *name of a Roman gens.*
fontĭcŭlus -i, m. *a little fountain* or *spring.*
for fāri fātus, dep. *to speak, say*; also *to speak of.*
fŏrābĭlis -e, *that can be bored through, penetrable.*
fŏrāmen -ĭnis, n. *hole, opening, aperture.*
fŏras, *out of doors, forth, out*; (scripta) foras dare, *to publish.*
forceps -cĭpis, m. and f. *a pair of tongs, pincers.*
forda -ae, *a cow in calf.*
fŏre, fŏrem, used as fut. infin. and imperf. subj. of sum; q.v.
fŏrensis -e, *relating to the market* or *forum;* hence *of the business of the Roman forum,* esp. *legal.*
forfex -fĭcis, f. *a pair of shears* or *scissors.*
[1]**fŏris** -is, f. *a door*; plur. fores, *folding-doors.* Transf., *any opening, entrance.*
[2]**fŏris**, adv. (1) (situated) *out of doors, outside, without*; sometimes, *abroad, outside Rome.* (2) *from without, from abroad.*
forma -ae, f. *form, figure, shape; beautiful shape, beauty; image, likeness; a shape serving as model,* e.g. *a shoemaker's last; a mould, stamp;* abstr., *form, manner, type*; in logic, *species; outline, general notion.*
formālis -e, *formal, having a set form.*
formāmentum -i, n. *conformation.*
formātor -ōris, m. *a fashioner.*
formātūra -ae, f. *forming, shaping.*
Formiae -arum, f. *town on the coast of Latium*; adj. **Formĭānus** -a -um.
formīca -ae, f. *an ant.*
formīdābĭlis -e, *fearful, formidable.*
[1]**formīdo** -are, *to be terrified, to dread.*
[2]**formīdo** -ĭnis, f. *dread, terror*; meton., *source of fear, dreadfulness, awfulness; a scarecrow.*
formīdŏlōsus -a -um: act., *causing dread, terrible, fearful*; pass. *fearful, timid.* Adv., **formīdŏlōsē**, *dreadfully, terribly.*
formo -are, *to form, shape, fashion; to arrange, order, regulate, dispose.*
formōsĭtās -ātis, f. *beauty.*
formōsus -a -um, *beautifully formed, beautiful*; adv. **formōsē.**
formŭla -ae, f. *physical beauty*; legal, *set form, formula*; esp. *the form of an alliance*; in gen., *rule, principle.*
fornācālis -e, *of an oven.*
fornācŭla -ae, f., *a little oven.*
fornax -ācis, f. *oven, furnace, kiln*; Aetnae, *the crater.*
fornĭcātus -a -um, *arched, vaulted.*
fornix -ĭcis, m. *arch, vault; arcade;* milit. *an arched sallyport.*
fornus = furnus; q.v.
fŏro -are, *to bore, pierce.*
fors, *chance, luck*; in nom. **fors,** also **forsit** (fors sit), **forsăn** (fors an), and **forsĭtăn** (fors sit an), *perhaps, perchance*; abl. **fortĕ,** *by chance, accidentally, as it happened.*
fortassĕ (**fortassis**), *perhaps.*
fortĕ; see fors.
fortĭcŭlus -a -um, *fairly bold.*
fortis -e, physically, *strong, powerful, robust*; morally, *brave, courageous, steadfast*; fortes fortuna adiuvat, *fortune favours the brave*; in bad sense, *bold, audacious.* Adv. **fortĭter,** *strongly, bravely.*
fortĭtūdo -ĭnis, f. *physical strength, moral bravery, courage*; plur., *deeds of bravery.*
fortŭītus -a -um, *accidental, casual, fortuitous, unpremeditated*; n. pl. as subst. *chance occurrences.* Abl. sing. as adv. **fortŭīto,** *by chance, fortuitously.*
fortūna -ae, f. *chance, fate, lot, luck, fortune*; fortuna prospera, secunda, *good fortune*; adversa, *misfortune.* Transf., *lot, condition, state, mode of life; property, possessions.*
fortūno -are, *to make happy, bless, prosper.*

Hence partic. **fortūnātus** -a -um, *blessed, lucky, fortunate; well off, wealthy, rich.* Adv. **fortūnātē,** *happily, fortunately.*
fŏrŭli -orum, m., *a bookcase.*
fŏrum -i, n. *an open square, market-place*; forum bovarium, or boarium, *the cattle-market*; forum holitorium, *vegetable-market*; forum piscarium, or piscatorium, *fish-market*; in gen., *a place of public business,* commercial, political and judicial esp. in Rome. Transf., of the business transacted in a forum; forum agere, *to hold an assize*; forum attingere, *to apply oneself to public business.*
forus -i, m. *the gangway of a ship; a block of seats in the theatre*; plur., *tiers of cells* in a beehive.
fossa -ae, f. *ditch, trench, channel.*
fossĭo -ōnis, f. *digging, excavation.*
fossor -ōris, m. *a digger, delver; a boor, clown.*
fossūra -ae, f. *digging.*
fōtus, partic. of foveo; q.v.
fŏvĕa -ae, f. *a pit,* esp. *as a trap for game, a pitfall.*
fŏvĕo fŏvēre fōvi fōtum, *to warm,*

keep warm, caress: fig., *to stay constantly in* a place; in gen., *to foster, cherish, support, encourage*.

fractus -a -um, partic. from frango; q.v.

frāga -orum, n. pl. *strawberries*.

frăgĭlis -e, *crackling; easily broken, fragile*. Transf., *fleeting, transitory; weak, feeble*.

frăgĭlĭtās -ātis, f., *frailty, weakness*.

fragmen -mĭnis, n. *a breaking*; hence, usually plur., *fragments, remains, ruins*.

fragmentum -i, n. *a piece broken off, fragment*.

frăgor -ōris, m., *a breaking; a noise of breaking, crack, crash*.

frăgōsus -a -um, *crashing, roaring; fragile; broken, rough*.

fragro -are, *to emit a smell*, esp. *a sweet smell*; pres. partic. **fragrans** -antis, *sweet-smelling, fragrant*.

frāgum; see fraga.

frango frangĕre frēgi fractum, *to break, break in pieces, shatter*; gulam laqueo, *to strangle*; fruges saxo, *to grind*; diem morantem mero, *to shorten*; of persons, passions, etc., *to master, subdue, humble*; frangi animo, *to be discouraged*.

Hence partic. **fractus** -a -um, *broken, humbled, enfeebled*.

frāter -tris, m. *a brother*; frater germanus, *own brother*; fratres, *brothers and sisters*; also *a cousin* or *a brother-in-law*. Transf., *a comrade, compatriot, ally*.

frātercŭlus -i, m. *little brother*.

frāternĭtās -ātis, f. *brotherhood, fraternity*.

frāternus -a -um, *of a brother, brotherly, fraternal*; sometimes *of a cousin*. Transf., *of a related person; of some thing related to another*. Adv. **frāternē,** *in a brotherly manner, like a brother*.

frātrĭcīda -ae, m. *one who kills a brother, a fratricide*.

fraudātĭo -ōnis, f. *deceit, fraud, swindling*.

fraudātor -ōris, m. *deceiver, swindler*.

fraudo -are, *to cheat, defraud, swindle; to steal, embezzle*.

fraudŭlentĭa -ae, f. *deceitfulness*.

fraudŭlentus -a -um, *deceitful, fraudulent*.

fraus, fraudis, f.: act., *deceit, fraud*; sine fraude, *honourably*; in gen., *a crime, offence; delusion, error; damage, harm*; sine fraude, *without harm*.

fraxĭnĕus and **fraxĭnus** -a -um, *of ashwood, ashen*.

fraxĭnus -i, f. *an ash-tree*; meton., *a spear* or *javelin, with a shaft of ashwood*.

Frĕgellae -arum, f. *town of Volsci, in Latium*.

frĕmĕbundus -a -um, *roaring, murmuring*.

frĕmĭtus -ūs, m. *roaring, murmuring, growling*.

frĕmo -ĕre -ŭi -ĭtum, *to roar, murmur, growl;* with acc. *to murmur out something, grumble, complain*.

frĕmor -ōris, m. *roaring, murmuring*.

frendo -ĕre: intransit., *to gnash the teeth*; transit., *to crush, bruise, grind*.

frēni -orum, m.; see frenum.

frēno -are, *to bridle, curb, restrain, check*.

frēnum -i, n., usually plur. **frēna** -orum, n.; also **frēni** -orum, m. *bridle, reins, bit, curb*. Transf., *restraint*.

frĕquens -entis, *crowded*, numerous, *full*; of places, *full, frequented, populous*; of time, *repeated, frequent, constant*; of persons, *often doing* a thing; of things, *often done* or *used*. Adv. **frĕquenter,** *in large numbers; frequently, often*.

frĕquentātĭo -ōnis, f., *frequency, crowding*.

frĕquentĭa -ae, f.: of persons, *a large concourse, numerous assembly, population*; of things, *a large number, abundance*.

frĕquento -are, *to crowd*; of number *to collect in large numbers; to fill* a place with people or things; *to do* a thing *in crowds* or *with a crowd*; of time, *to do* or *use* a thing *frequently*: domum, *to visit often*; Hymenaee! frequentant, *they repeat*.

frĕtum -i; n. *a strait, sound, estuary firth, channel*; fretum Siciliae, fretum Siciliense, or fretum, *the Straits of Messina; the sea* in gen., usually plur.: fig., *disturbance, turmoil*.

[1]**frētus** -a -um, *relying on, confiding in*, with abl.

[2]**frĕtus** -ūs, m. *a strait; an interval, difference*.

frĭco frĭcare frĭcŭi frictum and frĭcātum, *to rub, rub down*.

frīgĕo -ēre, *to be cold; to be inactive, lifeless, dull*; colloq., *to be coldly received, fall flat*.

frīgesco -ĕre, *to become cold* or *dull*.

frīgĭdŭlus -a -um, *somewhat cold* or *faint*.

frīgĭdus -a -um, *cold, cool, chilly*; f. sing. as subst. *cold water*. Transf., in act. sense, *chilling, causing cold*; fig., *cold, dull, lifeless*; of speech, *flat*. Adv. **frīgĭdē,** *coldly; languidly, feebly*.

frīgo frīgĕre frixi frictum, *to roast, parch*.

frīgus -ŏris n. *cold, coolness; the cold of winter; a cold place; the cold of death* or *fright*. Transf., *coldness in action, dullness, indolence; a cold reception, coolness, disfavour*.

frĭguttĭo -ire, *to stammer*.

frĭo -are, *to rub, crumble*.

frĭtillus -i, m. *a dice-box*.

frīvŏlus -a -um, *trifling, worthless*; n. pl. as subst. *sticks of furniture*.

frondātor -ōris, m. *a pruner of trees*.

frondĕo -ēre, *to be in leaf, be leafy*.

frondesco ĕre, *to come into leaf, put forth leaves*.

frondĕus -a -um, *leafy*.

frondĭfer -fĕra -fĕrum, *leaf-bearing, leafy*.

frondōsus -a -um, *full of leaves, leafy*.

[1]**frons** frondis, f. *a leaf, foliage*; meton., *a chaplet* or *crown of leaves*.
[2]**frons** frontis, f. *the forehead, brow*; frontem contrahere, *to frown*. Transf., in gen., *the front, forepart*; milit., *the van; the outside end of a book roll; frontage* (in measuring land).
frontālĭa -ĭum, n. pl. *the frontlet of a horse*.
fronto -ōnis, m., *a man with a broad forehead*.
fructŭarĭus -a -um, *fruit-bearing, fruitful*.
fructŭōsus -a -um, *fruitful, fertile*.
fructus -ūs, m.: abstr., *enjoyment, enjoying*; concr., *proceeds, profit, produce, income*; esp. *the fruits of the earth*.
frūgālis -e, *frugal, economical, honest*; adv. **frūgālĭter**.
frūgālĭtās -ātis, f., *frugality, economy, honesty*; of style, *restraint*.
frūgi; see frux.
frūgĭfer -fĕra -fĕrum, *fruitful, fertile; profitable, advantageous*.
frūgĭfĕrens -entis, *fruitful, fertile*.
frūgĭlĕgus -a -um, *collecting grain*.
frūgĭpărus -a -um, *fruitful, prolific*.
frūmentārĭus -a -um, *of grain* or *corn*; res, *the supply of corn*; m. as subst. *a corn-merchant*.
frūmentātĭo -ōnis, f. *a foraging; a distribution of corn*.
frūmentātor -ōris, m. *a forager* or *a provider of corn*.
frūmentor -ari, dep., *to forage, fetch corn*.
frūmentum -i, n., *corn, grain*.
frŭor frŭi fructus and frŭĭtus, dep., *to have the benefit of, to enjoy*, usually with abl.: votis, *to obtain one's wishes*; as legal t. t., *to have the use and enjoyment of*.
frustillātim, *bit by bit*.
frustrā, *in error*: frustra esse, *to be deceived, mistaken*. Transf., *in vain, without effect; wantonly, without reason*.
frustrāmen -ĭnis, n. *deception*.
frustrātĭo -ōnis, f. *deception, disappointment, frustration*.
frustro -are, and **frustror** -ari, dep. *to disappoint, deceive, trick*.
frustum -i, n. *a bit, piece, morsel*.
frŭtex -tĭcis, m. *a shrub, bush*; as a term of reproach, *blockhead*.
frŭtĭcētum -i, n., *a thicket*.
frŭtĭco -are and **frŭtĭcor** -ari, dep. *to shoot out, become bushy*.
frŭtĭcōsus -a -um, *bushy* or *full of bushes*.
frux frūgis, f., usually plur. **frūges** -um, *fruits of the earth*; in gen., *fruits, success*; ad bonam frugem se recipere, *to improve oneself*. Dat. sing. **frūgī,** used as adj., *useful, honest, discreet, moderate*.
fūco -are, *to colour, paint, dye*; fig., *to colour, embellish*.
Hence partic. **fūcātus** -a -um, *painted; counterfeited, simulated*.
fūcōsus -a -um, *painted; simulated, counterfeited*.
[1]**fūcus** -i, m., *red* or *purple dye; red* or *purple colour; rouge*; in gen., *paint, dye* of any colour; *bee-glue*. Transf., *deceit, pretence*.
[2]**fucus** -i, m. *a drone bee*.
Fūfĭus -a -um, *name of a Roman* gens.
fŭga -ae, f. *flight, running away*; esp. *flight from one's country, exile, banishment*. Transf., *swift course, speed; avoiding*, with genit.
fŭgax -ācis, *ready to flee, flying; speeding, fleeting, transitory*; with genit., *avoiding*. Hence compar. adv. **fŭgācĭus.**
fŭgĭo fŭgĕre fūgi fŭgĭtum, *to flee*. Intransit., *to take to flight, run away; to pass away, disappear*. Transit., *to flee from, run away from, avoid*; with infin., fuge quaerere, *do not seek*; of things, *to escape the notice of* a person.
Hence partic., **fŭgĭens** -entis, *fleeing*; *avoiding*, with genit.; *fleeting, deteriorating*.
fŭgĭtīvus -a -um, *flying, fugitive*; m. as subst., *a fugitive*, esp. *a runaway slave*.
fŭgĭto -are, *to flee*; transit., *to fly from, avoid, shun*.
Hence partic., **fŭgĭtans** -antis, *fleeing*; with genit., *avoiding*.
fŭgo -are, *to put to flight, chase away; to drive into exile, to dismiss, avert*.
fulcīmen -ĭnis, n., *a prop, support, pillar*.
fulcĭo fulcire fulsi fultum, *to prop up, support; to strengthen, secure*; morally *to support, stay, uphold*.
fulcrum -i, n., *the post* or *foot of a couch*.
fulgĕo fulgēre fulsi, *to flash, to lighten*; in gen., *to shine, gleam, glitter*; fig., *to be distinguished, to shine*.
fulgĭdus -a -um, *shining, gleaming, glittering*.
fulgo -ĕre = fulgeo; q.v.
fulgor -ōris, m., *lightning*; in gen., *glitter, brightness*; fig., *brightness, glory*.
fulgur -ŭris, n. *a flash* or *stroke of lightning*; sometimes *an object struck by lightning*; in gen., *brightness*.
fulgŭrālis -e, *relating to lightning*.
fulgŭrātor -ōris, m., *a priest who interpreted omens from lightning*.
fulgŭrītus -a -um, *struck by lightning*.
fulgŭro -are, *to lighten; to shine, be brilliant*.
fŭlĭca -ae, f. *a coot*.
fūlĭgo -ĭnis, f. *soot; powder for darkening the eyebrows*.
fullo -ōnis, m. *a cloth-fuller*.
fullōnĭca -ae, f. *the art of fulling*.
fulmen -ĭnis, n. *a stroke of lightning, a thunderbolt*. Transf. *a crushing calamity; mighty* or *irresistible power*.
fulmĭnĕus -a -um, *of lightning; like lightning, rapid* or *destructive*.
fulmĭno -are, *to lighten*.
fultūra -ae, f., *support, prop, stay*.
Fulvĭus -a -um, *name of a Roman* gens.
fulvus -a -um, *tawny, yellowish brown*,

fūmĕus and **fumĭdus** -a -um, *smoky, full of smoke.*
fūmĭfer -fĕra -fĕrum, *smoky.*
fūmĭfĭcus -a -um, *causing smoke.*
fūmo -are, *to smoke, steam, reek.*
fūmōsus -a -um, *smoked.*
fūmus -i, m. *smoke, steam, vapour.*
fūnālis -e, *attached to a rope.* N. as subst. **fūnāle** -is, *the thong of a sling; a wax-torch.*
fūnambŭlus -i, m. *a rope-dancer.*
functĭo -ōnis, f. *performance, execution.*
funda -ae, *a sling; a sling-stone; a casting-net.*
fundāmen -ĭnis, n. and **fundāmentum** -i, n. usually plur., *a foundation, basis.*
fundātor -ōris, m. *founder.*
fundĭto -are, *to sling.*
fundĭtor -ōris, m. *a soldier with a sling, a slinger.*
fundĭtus, *from the bottom; completely, entirely; at the bottom, below.*
[1]**fundo** -are, *to lay the foundation of, to found*; also *to make firm, to strengthen.*
Hence partic. **fundātus** -a -um, *founded, firm.*
[2]**fundo** fundĕre fūdi fūsum: of liquids, *to pour, pour out*; of metals, *to melt, cast.* Transf., *to pour out, shower, give abundantly; to squander*; se fundere, *to rush, stream*; of sounds, *to utter*; with emphasis on distribution, *to spread, extend, scatter*; milit. *to rout, defeat, scatter, put to flight.*
Hence partic. **fūsus** -a -um, *spread out, extended*; crines, *flowing free*; of speech, *diffuse*; adv. **fūsē,** *widely, copiously.*
fundus -i, m. *ground; the bottom* or *base of anything; a farm, estate.*
fūnebris -e, *of a funeral funereal; deadly, destructive.*
fūnĕrĕus -a -um, *of a funeral, funereal; fatal, ill-omened.*
fūnĕro -are, *to bury solemnly, inter with funeral rites*; partic. **fūnĕrātus** -a -um, *done to death.*
fūnesto -are, *to defile* or *pollute with death.*
fūnestus -a -um: pass., *filled with mourning, defiled by death*; act., *fatal, disastrous, deadly.*
fungīnus -a -um, *of a mushroom.*
fungor fungi functus, dep. *to occupy oneself with* anything, *to perform, execute, undergo,* usually with abl.; absol. in special sense, *to be affected, suffer.*
fungus -i, m. *a mushroom, fungus; a dull, stupid fellow; a ' thief ' in the wick of a candle, a candlesnuff.*
fūnĭcŭlus -i, m. *thin rope, cord, string.*
fūnis -is, m. *rope, cord, line.*
fūnus -ĕris, n. *a funeral, burial.* Transf., *the corpse; death; destruction, ruin; a cause of ruin.*
fŭo fŭi fŭtūrus, etc.; see sum.
fūr fūris, c. *a thief.*
fūrax -ācis, *inclined to steal, thievish.* Hence superl. adv. **fūrācissĭmē,** *most thievishly.*

furca -ae, f., *a (two-pronged) fork, a pitch-fork; a fork-shaped prop* or *pole; an instrument of punishment, with two prongs to which the arms were tied*; geograph., *a narrow pass.*
furcĭfer -fĕra -fĕrum, *carrying the* furca *as a punishment*; applied to slaves, *gallows-bird.*
furcilla -ae, f., *a little fork.*
furcillo -are, *to support.*
furcŭla -ae, f. *a little fork; a fork-shaped prop*; geograph., *a narrow pass,* esp. of *the Caudine forks.*
furfur -ŭris, m. *bran; scales, scurf on the skin.*
fŭrĭa -ae, f., usually plur. *rage, frenzy, madness, passion*; personif., of *the mythological Furies, avenging deities*; fig., of persons.
fŭrĭālis -e, *furious, raging, frenzied; belonging to the Furies*; **fŭrĭālĭter,** *furiously, madly.*
fŭrĭbundus -a -um, *raging, furious; inspired.*
fŭrĭo -are, *to make furious, madden*; partic., fŭrĭātus -a -um, *raging.*
fŭrĭōsus -a -um, *raging, raving, mad, furious*; adv. **fŭrĭōsē.**
Fŭrĭus -a -um, *name of a Roman* gens.
furnus -i, m. *an oven, bakehouse.*
fŭro -ĕre, *to rage, rave, be mad*; often of impassioned persons, *to rave, be frantic*; furere aliquā, *to be madly in love with.* Adv. from partic., **fŭrenter,** *furiously.*
[1]**fūror** -ari, dep., *to steal, pilfer*; fig., *to steal away, withdraw; to counterfeit, personate.*
[2]**fŭror** -ōris, m. *madness, raving, insanity; furious anger, martial rage; passionate love; inspiration, poetic* or *prophetic frenzy*; meton., *an object of passion.*
furtĭfĭcus -a -um, *thievish.*
furtim, adv. *by stealth, stealthily.*
furtīvus -a -um, *stolen; secret, concealed, furtive.* Adv. **furtīvē.**
furtum -i, n. *theft, robbery*; in plur., *stolen property*; fig., *underhand methods, trick, deceit,* esp. *secret* or *stolen love.*
fūruncŭlus -i, m. *a sneak thief, pilferer.*
furvus -a -um, *dark-coloured, black.*
fuscĭna -ae, f. *a three-pronged fork, trident.*
fusco -are, *to darken, blacken.*
fuscus -a -um, *dark-coloured*; of the voice, *indistinct.*
fūsĭlis -e, *molten, liquid, soft.*
fūsĭo -ōnis, f. *pouring-out, out-pouring.*
fustis -is, m. *a stick, cudgel, club.*
fustŭārĭum -i, n. *cudgelling to death.*
[1]**fūsus** -a -um, partic. from fundo; q.v.
[2]**fūsus** -i, m. *a spindle.*
fūtātim, *abundantly.*
futtĭlis and **fūtĭlis** -e, *brittle; vain, worthless, good for nothing.*
futtĭlĭtās and **fūtĭlĭtās** -ātis, f. *worthlessness, folly, silliness.*
fŭtūrus -a -um used as future partic. of sum; q.v.

G

G, g, the seventh letter of the Latin alphabet, originally represented by C.
Găbĭi -orum, m. *an ancient city of Latium*; adj. **Găbīnus** -a -um.
Găbīnĭus -a -um, *name of a Roman* gens.
Gādēs -ium, f. *a town in Hispania Baetica* (now *Cadiz*); adj. **Gādītānus** -a -um.
gaesum -i, n. *a long heavy javelin.*
Gaetūli -orum, m. pl. *a people in north-west Africa.*
Gāĭus, abbrev. C., *a Roman* praenomen; fem. Gāĭa.
Gălătae -arum, m. *a Celtic people settled in Asia Minor, the Galatians.*
Galba -ae, m. *a cognomen of the Sulpician* gens; esp. of Ser. Sulpicius, *Roman emperor* A.D. 68-69.
galbănĕus -a -um, *of galbanum*; q.v.
galbănum -i, n., *the resinous sap of a Syrian plant.*
galbīnus -a -um, *greenish-yellow.*
gălĕa -ae, f. *helmet.*
gălĕo -are, *to cover with a helmet*; partic., **gălĕātus** -a -um, *helmeted.*
gălērĭcŭlum -i, n. *skull-cap; wig.*
gălērītus -a -um, *wearing a hood* or *skull-cap.*
gălērum -i, n. and **gălērus** -i, m. *skull-cap; wig.*
galla -ae, f. *oakapple.*
Galli -orum, m. pl. *the Gauls, a Celtic people, to the west of the Rhine and in the north of Italy*; **Gallĭa** -ae, f. *Gaul, the land of the Gauls*; Cisalpina = *Northern Italy*; Transalpina = *France*; adj. **Gallĭcānus** and **Gallĭcus** -a -um, *Gaulish*; f. as subst., gallĭca, *a slipper.*
gallĭambus -i, m. *a song of the priests of Cybele.*
gallĭca; see **Galli.**
gallīna -ae, f. *hen.*
gallīnācĕus -a -um, *of poultry*; gallus, *a poultry-cock.*
gallīnārĭus -a -um, *of poultry*; m. as subst., *poultry-farmer.*
[1]**gallus** -i, m. *cock.*
[2]**Gallus,** *a Gaul*; see Galli.
[3]**Gallus** -i, m. usually plur. **Galli** -orum, m. *a priest of Cybele.*
gānĕa -ae, f. and **gānĕum** -i, n. *a brothel* or *a low eating-house.*
gānĕo -ōnis, m. *a debauchee.*
Gangēs -is, m., *the river Ganges in India.* Adj. **Gangētĭcus** -a -um; f. adj. **Gangētis** -ĭdis = *Indian.*
gannĭo -ire, *to yelp, snarl, growl.*
gannītus -ūs, m. *yelping, snarling.*
Gănȳmēdēs -is, m. *the cup-bearer of Jove.*
garrĭo -ire, *to chatter, prate, babble.*
garrŭlĭtās -ātis, f. *chattering.*
garrŭlus -a -um, *talkative, chattering, babbling, noisy.*
gărum -i, n. *fish-sauce.*
Gărumna -ae, f. *a river in Gaul* (now *Garonne*); **Gărumni** -orum, m.pl. *a people living on the Garonne.*
gaudĕo gaudēre gāvīsus sum, *to rejoice, be glad*; with abl. of cause, *to delight in*; in sinu gaudere, *to rejoice in secret.*
gaudĭum -i, n. *joy, gladness, delight; a source of delight.*
gausăpĕ -is, and **gausăpum** -i, n. *woollen cloth with a long nap, frieze.*
gāza -ae, f. *the royal treasure of Persia*; in gen., *treasure, riches, wealth.*
gĕlăsīnus -i, m. *dimple.*
gĕlĭdus -a -um, *cold, frosty, icy*; in act. sense, *chilling*; f. as subst. **gĕlĭda** -ae, *cold water.* Adv. **gĕlĭdē,** *coldly, feebly.*
gĕlo -are, transit., *to cause to freeze*; intransit., *to freeze.*
gĕlu -ūs, n. (earlier **gĕlus** -ūs, m. and **gĕlum** -i, n.), *frost, chill.*
gĕmĕbundus -a -um, *groaning, sighing.*
gĕmellĭpăra -ae, f. adj. *twin-bearing.*
gĕmellus -a -um, *twin, paired, double*; m. as subst., *a twin.*
gĕmĭnātĭo -ōnis, f. *doubling.*
gĕmĭno -are: transit., *to double; to join together, strike together, repeat*; partic. gĕmĭnātus -a -um, *doubled*; intransit., *to be double.*
gĕmĭnus -a -um, *twin, double; paired* or *half-and-half; similar, like*; m. pl. as subst. **gĕmĭni** -orum, *twins,* esp. *Castor and Pollux.*
gĕmĭtus -ūs, m., *a sigh, groan*; of things, *groaning, roaring.*
gemma -ae, f. *a bud* or *eye of a plant.* Transf., *a jewel, gem, precious stone; a jewelled goblet; a seal-ring, seal; a literary gem.*
gemmātus -a -um, *set* or *adorned with jewels.*
gemmĕus -a -um, *made of* or *set with jewels; bright.*
gemmĭfer -fĕra -fĕrum, *bearing* or *producing jewels.*
gemmo -are, *to bud*; pres. partic. **gemmans** -antis, *set with jewels, glittering like jewels.*
gĕmo gĕmĕre gĕmŭi gĕmĭtum: intransit., *to sigh, groan*; of lions, *to roar*; of doves, *to coo*; of things, *to creak*; transit., *to sigh over, lament, bemoan.*
gĕna -ae, f. usually plur., *cheek, cheeks and chin.* Transf., *eye-socket, eye.*
Genāva -ae, f. *a town of the Allobroges* (now *Geneva*).
gĕnĕālŏgus -i, m. *a genealogist.*
gĕner -eri, m. *a son-in-law; a grand-daughter's husband; a brother-in-law.*
gĕnĕrālis -e. (1) *belonging to a kind, generic.* (2) *universal, general.* Adv. **gĕnĕrālĭter,** *in general, generally.*
gĕnĕrasco -ĕre, *to be produced, come to birth.*
gĕnĕrātim. (1) *according to kinds* or *classes.* (2) *in general, generally.*
gĕnĕrātor -ōris, m. *begetter, producer*
gĕnĕro -are, *to beget, produce, bring to life.*
gĕnĕrōsus -a -um, *of noble birth, noble, well-bred*; of a place, *producing well.* Transf., of character, *noble, magnanimous.* Adv. **gĕnĕrōsē,** *nobly.*

gĕnĕsis -is, f. *the constellation which presides over one's birth.*
gĕnĕtīvus -a -um, *inborn, innate*; nomina, *family names*; casus, *the genitive case.*
gĕnetrix -trīcis f. *one who brings forth, a mother.*
gĕnĭālis -e. (1) *relating to marriage.* (2) *relating to enjoyment; joyful, gay.* Adv. **gĕnĭālĭter,** *jovially, gaily.*
gĕnĭcŭlātus -a -um, *knotty, full of knots.*
gĕnista (gĕnesta) -ae, f. *the plant broom.*
gĕnĭtābĭlis -e, *fruitful, productive.*
gĕnĭtālis -e, *creative, fruitful*; dies, *birthday*; of Diana, *presiding over births.* Adv. **gĕnĭtālĭter,** *in a fruitful manner.*
gĕnĭtīvus; see genetivus.
gĕnĭtor -ōris, m. *a begetter, father, producer.*
gĕnĭtūra -ae, f. *begetting, engendering*; in astrology, *nativity.*
gĕnĭus -i, m. *the guardian spirit of a man* or *place, a genius*; esp. *as a spirit of enjoyment, one's taste, inclination*; genium curare, *to enjoy oneself.* Transf., *talent, genius.*
gĕno = gigno; q.v.
gens gentis, f. *a clan, stock, people, tribe, nation.* Transf., *an offspring, descendant; a district, country*; esp. in partitive genit.: ubi gentium? *where in the world?*; plur., gentes, *foreigners.*
gentĭcus -a -um, *a nation, national.*
gentīlĭcĭus -a -um, *of a particular* gens.
gentīlis -e, *of a* gens; *of a country, national.*
gentīlĭtās -ātis, f. *the relationship between the members of a* gens.
gĕnu -ūs, n. *the knee.*
Gĕnŭa -ae, f. *coast-town in Liguria* (now *Genoa*).
gĕnŭālĭa -ium, n. pl. *garters.*
[1]**gĕnŭīnus** -a -um, *natural, innate.*
[2]**gĕnŭīnus** -a -um, *belonging to the cheek* or *jaw*: dentes, *the jaw-teeth*; m. as subst. *a jaw-tooth.*
[1]**gĕnus** -ĕris, n. *birth, descent, origin; race, stock, family, house*; hence *offspring, descendant(s); sex*; in gen., *class, kind, variety, sort*; in logic, *genus*; of action, etc., *fashion, manner, way.*
[2]**genus** -ūs = genu; q.v.
gĕōgrăphĭa -ae, f. *geography.*
gĕōmetres -ae, m. a *geometer.*
gĕōmetrĭa -ae, f. *geometry.*
gĕōmetrĭcus -a -um, *geometrical*; m. as subst., **gĕōmetrĭcus** -i, *a geometer*; n. pl. **gĕōmetrĭca,** *geometry.*
gĕorgĭcus -a -um, *agricultural*; n. pl. as subst. **Gĕorgica** -orum, *the Georgics of Vergil.*
Germāni -orum, m. pl., *the Germans*; adj. **Germānus** -a -um, *German*; f. subst. **Germānĭa** -ae, *Germany*; adj. **Germānĭcus** -a -um, *German*; m. as subst. **Germānĭcus** -i, a surname assumed after victories in Germany.
germānĭtās -ātis, f. *the relationship between brothers or sisters; brotherhood, sisterhood.*
[1]**germānus** -a -um, *having the same parents*; m. or f. as subst. *own brother, own sister.* Transf., *brotherly, sisterly; genuine, real, true.* Adv. **germāne,** *faithfully, honestly.*
[2]**Germānus** -a -um; see Germani.
germen -ĭnis, n. *an embryo; a bud, shoot* or *graft*; fig., *germ.*
germĭno -are, *to sprout forth.*
[1]**gĕro** gĕrĕre gessi gestum. Lit. (1) *to carry, bear*; esp. *to wear.* (2) *to bear, give birth to.* Transf., *to carry about, display* an appearance; personam gerere, *to act a part*; se gerere, *to conduct oneself* (with adv.); *to carry about, entertain a feeling; to carry on conduct, manage* business; res gestae, *exploits*, esp., *warlike exploits.*
[2]**gĕro** -ōnis, m., *a carrier.*
gerrae -arum, f. pl. *wattled twigs.* Transf., *trifles, nonsense.*
gerro -ōnis, m. *a trifler, idler.*
gĕrŭlus -i, m. *porter, carrier.*
Gēryŏn -ŏnis, and **Gēryŏnēs** -ae, m. myth., *a king in Spain with three bodies, killed by Hercules.*
gestāmen -ĭnis, n. *that which is carried; that by which anything is carried, a carriage* or *litter.*
gestĭcŭlātĭo -ōnis, f. *pantomime, gesticulation.*
gestĭcŭlor -ari, dep. *gesticulate.*
gestĭo -ōnis, f., *management, performance.*
gestĭto -are, *to carry often, wear often.*
gesto -are, *to carry, bear about*; pass. *to ride about.*
gestor -ōris, m. *a tale-bearer, gossip.*
gestus -ūs, m. *carriage of the body, posture*; esp. *the gestures of an actor* or *orator.*
Gĕtae -arum, m. pl. *a people of Thrace living near the Danube.* Adj. **Gĕtĭcus** -a -um, *Thracian*; adv. **Gĕtĭcē,** *after the Getic fashion.*
Gētŭlus, etc. = Gaetulus, etc.; q.v.
gibba -ae, f. *hump, hunch.*
gibber -ĕra, -ĕrum, *hump-backed.*
gibbus -i, m. *hump, hunch.*
Gĭgas -gantis, m. *a giant*; adj. **Gĭganteus** -a -um.
gigno gignĕre gĕnŭi gĕnĭtum, *to beget, bear, bring forth; to cause.*
gilvus -a -um, *pale yellow.*
gingīva -ae, f. *gum* (*of the mouth*).
glăber -bra -brum, *bald*; m. as subst., *a page.*
glăcĭālis -e, *icy.*
glăcĭes -ēi, f. *ice.* Transf., *hardness.*
glăcĭo -are, *to freeze.*
glădĭātor -ōris, m. *one hired to fight at public shows, a gladiator*; hence *bandit, brigand*; gladiatoribus, *at a show of gladiators.*
glădĭātōrĭus -a -um, *of gladiators, gladiatorial*; n. as subst., *gladiators' pay.*
glădĭātūra -ae, f. *the profession of gladiator.*

glădĭus -i, *sword.*
glaeba = gleba; q.v.
glaesum (glesum) -i, n. *amber.*
glandĭfer -fĕra -fĕrum, *acorn-bearing.*
glandĭum -i, n. *a delicate glandule* in meat.
glans glandis, f. *mast; an acorn, chestnut,* etc. Transf., *a bullet.*
glārĕa -ae, f. *gravel.*
glārĕōsus -a -um, *gravelly full of gravel.*
glaucōma -atis, n. (also -ae, f.) *a disease of the eye, cataract.*
glaucus -a -um *bluish-* or *greenish-grey.*
glēba (glaeba) -ae, f. *a lump* or *clod of earth*; hence *land, soil; a piece, lump* of anything.
glēbŭla -ae, f., *a little clod* or *lump*; *a little farm* or *estate.*
glēsum = glaesum; q.v.
glīs glīris, m. *dormouse.*
glisco -ĕre, *to grow up, swell up, blaze up.*
glŏbo -are, *to form into a ball* or *mass.*
glŏbōsus -a -um, *spherical.*
glŏbus -i, m. *a ball, globe, sphere; a troop, crowd, mass of people.*
glŏmĕrāmen -ĭnis, n. *a round mass, globe.*
glŏmĕro -are, *to form into a sphere,* or *rounded heap*; in gen., *to gather together, collect, amass.*
glŏmus -ĕris, n. *clue, skein, ball of thread.*
glōrĭa -ae, f. *fame, renown, glory.* Transf., of a member of a group, *the pride, the glory; desire of glory, ambition, boastfulness*; plur., *glorious deeds.*
glōrĭātĭo -ōnis, f. *glorying, boasting.*
glōrĭŏla -ae, f. *a little glory.*
glōrĭor -ari, dep. *to glory, boast, pride oneself.*
glōrĭōsus -a -um, *famous, glorious; ambitious, pretentious, boastful.* Adv. **glōrĭōsē,** *gloriously; vauntingly, boastingly.*
glūbo -ĕre, *to peel.* Transf., *to rob.*
glūtĕn -tĭnis, n. *glue.*
glūtĭnātor -ōris, m., *one who glues books, a bookbinder.*
glūtĭo (gluttĭo) -ire, *to swallow, gulp down.*
glūto (glutto) -onis, m. *glutton.*
Gnaeus -i, m. *a Roman* praenomen, shortened Cn.
gnārĭtās -ātis, f. *knowledge.*
gnārus -a -um; act., *knowing, aquainted with, expert*; pass., *known.*
Gnātho -ōnis, m. *a parasite in the Eunuchus of Terence*; in gen. *parasite.*
Gnātĭa = Egnatia; q.v.
gnātus, gnāvus = natus, navus; q.v.
Gnĭdus = Cnidus; q.v.
Gnossus (Gnōsus) -i, f., *an ancient city of Crete, the residence of Minos*; adj. **Gnōsĭus** and **Gnōsĭăcus** -a -um, *Gnosian; Cretan*; f. adj. **Gnōsĭas** -ădis, and **Gnōsis** -ĭdis, *Cretan* and, as subst., *Ariadne.*
gōbĭus (cōbĭus) -i, and **gōbĭo** -ōnis, m. *a gudgeon.*
gonger; see conger.
Gorgō -gŏnis, f. *also called* Medusa, *slain by Perseus*; adj. **Gorgŏnĕus** -a -um.
Gortȳna -ae, f. *an ancient city in Crete.*
grăbātus -i, m. *a low couch, camp-bed.*
Gracchus -i, m. a cognomen *in the* Gens Sempronia, esp. of Tiberius and Gaius, the 'Gracchi'. Adj. **Gracchānus** -a -um.
grăcĭlis -e, *slender, thin, slim*; of style, etc., *simple, without ornament.*
grăcĭlĭtās -ātis, f. *thinness, slenderness.*
grăcŭlus -i, m. *jackdaw.*
grădārĭus -a -um, *going step by step.*
grădātim, adv. *step by step, by degrees.*
grădātĭo -ōnis, f., in rhetoric, *climax.*
grădĭor grădi gressus, dep. *to step, walk.*
Grădīvus -i, m. *a surname of Mars.*
grădus -ūs, m. *a step.* (1) *a step as made, a pace*; suspenso gradu, *on tiptoe*; gradum facere, *to step*; gradum inferre, *to advance*; hence in gen., *an approach.* (2) *a step as climbed, a stair*; hence any *tier, gradation; a braid of hair*; abstr., *degree, stage; rank, position*; milit. *station, post.*
Graeci -orum, m. *the Greeks*; sing. **Graecus** -i, m. *a Greek*; as adj. **Graecus** -a -um, *Greek*; adv. **Graecē,** *in the Greek language*; f. subst. **Graecĭa** -ae, f. *Greece*; Magna Graecia, *the Greek colonies in the south of Italy*; dim. **Graecŭlus** -i, m. *a little Greek.*
graecisso -are, and **graecor** -ari, dep. *to imitate the Greeks.*
Grāii -orum, m. = Graeci, *the Greeks*; adj. **Grāius** -a -um, *Greek.*
Grāiŭgĕna -ae, m. *a Greek by birth.*
grallātor -ōris, m. *one that walks on stilts.*
grāmen -ĭnis, n. *grass, turf*; any *plant* or *herb.*
grāmĭnĕus -a -um, *grassy, of grass*; also *of cane* or *bamboo.*
grammătĭcus -a -um, *literary, grammatical*; as subst., m. *a philologist, grammarian*; f. sing. and n. pl. *grammar, philology.*
grammătista -ae, f. *a teacher of grammar* or *languages.*
grānārĭum -i, n. *granary.*
grandaevus -a -um, *very old.*
grandesco -ĕre, *to become great, grow.*
grandĭcŭlus -a -um, *rather large.*
grandĭfer -fĕra -fĕrum, *producing great profits.*
grandĭlŏquus -a -um, *speaking grandly; boastful.*
grandĭnat -are, impers. *it hails.*
grandĭo -ire, *to increase.*
grandis -e, *full-grown, great, large*; in stature, *tall*; in years, *old.* Transf., *great, important*; of style, *lofty, grand, sublime.*
grandĭtās -ātis, f. of style, *loftiness. sublimity.*
grando -ĭnis, f. *hail, hail-storm.*
grānĭfer -fĕra -fĕrum, *grain-carrying.*

grānum -i, n. *grain, seed.*
grăphĭcus -a -um, *concerned with painting*; hence *masterly, skilful*; adv. **grăphĭcē.**
grăphĭum -i, n. *a stilus, a pointed instrument for writing on wax.*
grassātor -ōris, m. *an idler; a footpad.*
grassor -ari, dep. *to walk about, to loiter; to go about* an undertaking; *to proceed against* somebody.
grātes, f. pl. *thanks*; grates agere, *to express thanks*; habere, *to feel gratitude.*
grātĭa -ae, f. (1) *charm, attraction, pleasantness*; personif., of *the three Graces* (Euphrosyne, Aglaia, Thalia). (2) *favour* with others; *esteem, regard, popularity.* (3) *a favour done, service, kindness*; abl. gratiā, *on account of*; meā gratiā, *for my sake.* (4) *thankfulness, thanks*; in sing. and plur.: gratias agere, with dat., *to express thanks*; gratias habere, *to feel grateful*; abl. plur. **grātĭis** or **grātīs,** *without recompense, for nothing, gratis.*
grātĭfĭcātĭo -ōnis, f. *complaisance, obligingness.*
grātĭfĭcor -ari, dep. *to oblige, gratify, do a favour to.*
grātĭōsus -a -um, *favoured, beloved; showing favour, complaisant.*
grātīs; see gratia.
grātor -ari, dep. *to wish joy, to congratulate; to give thanks.*
grātŭītus -a -um, *not paid for* or *not provoked, gratuitous, spontaneous*; abl. sing. n. as adv. **grātŭīto,** *gratuitously.*
grātŭlābundus -a -um, *congratulating.*
grātŭlātĭo -ōnis, f. *wishing joy, congratulation;* a *thanksgiving festival.*
grātŭlor -ari, dep. *to wish a person joy, congratulate* (with dat.); *to give solemn thanks,* esp. to the gods.
grātus -a -um, adj. (1) *pleasing, welcome, agreeable*; gratum facere, *to do a favour.* (2) *thankful, grateful.* Adv. **grātē,** *willingly, with pleasure; thankfully.*
grăvanter and **grăvātē;** from gravo.
grăvātim, *reluctantly.*
grăvēdĭnōsus -a -um, *subject to colds.*
grăvēdo -ĭnis, f. *cold in the head, catarrh.*
grăvĕŏlens -lentis, *strong-smelling, rank.*
grăvesco -ĕre, *to become heavy; to grow worse.*
grăvĭdĭtās -ātis, f. *pregnancy.*
grăvĭdo -are, *to load, burden; to impregnate.*
grăvĭdus -a -um, *heavy; laden, filled, full; pregnant.*
grăvis -e. (1) *heavy*; of sound, *low, deep;* fig., *weighty, important*; of character, *dignified, serious*; of style, *elevated, dignified.* (2) *burdened laden, weighed down*; esp. *pregnant.* (3) *burdensome, oppressive; grievous, painful, unpleasant.* Adv. **grăvĭter,** *heavily, weightily, reluctantly; grievously, painfully.*
grăvĭtās -ātis, f. (1) *weight;* fig., *consequence, importance*; of character, *dignity, authority, seriousness.* (2) *heaviness; pregnancy; dullness, faintness.* (3) *pressure*; fig., *unpleasantness.*
grăvo -are, *to load, burden; to heighten, exaggerate, increase; to oppress, burden, trouble*; pass., *to feel burdened* or *troubled* by a thing, or *to make heavy weather of* doing it. Adv. **grăvanter,** and **grăvātē,** *reluctantly.*
grĕgālis -e, *of a herd* or *flock; common, ordinary;* m. pl. as subst. *companions, associates, accomplices.*
grĕgārĭus -a -um, *of a herd* or *flock;* miles, *a private soldier.*
grĕgātim, *in troops* or *crowds.*
grĕmĭum -i, n. *lap, bosom; womb.*
gressus -ūs, m. *a step*; of a ship, *course.*
grex grĕgis, m. *a herd, flock, drove*; of people, *a troop, band,* esp. *a philosophical sect* or *troop of soldiers*; grege facto, *in close order.*
grunnĭo (grundĭo) -ire, *to grunt like a pig.*
grunnītus -ūs, m., *the grunting of a pig.*
grus grŭis, m. and f. *a crane.*
grȳ, n. indecl. *scrap, crumb.*
gryllus -i, m. *cricket, grasshopper.*
gryps, grȳpis, m. *griffin.*
gŭbernācŭlum (-āclum) -i, n. *rudder, helm*; hence *direction, management, government.*
gŭbernātĭo -ōnis, f. *steering; direction, government.*
gŭbernātor -ōris, m. *helmsman, steersman, pilot; director, governor.*
gŭbernātrix -īcis, f. *she that directs.*
gŭberno -are, *to steer a ship, be at the helm*; in gen., *to steer, direct, govern.*
gŭbernum -i, n. = gubernaculum; q.v.
gŭla -ae, f. *gullet, throat; hence greediness, gluttony.*
gŭlōsus -a -um, *gluttonous.*
gurges -ĭtis, m. *whirlpool, eddy*; in gen., *troubled water, a stream, flood, sea*; fig., *abyss, depth.*
[1]**gurgŭlĭo** -ōnis, f. *windpipe.*
[2]**gurgŭlĭo** -ōnis, m.; see curculio.
gurgustĭum -i, n. *hut, hovel.*
gustātus -ūs, m. *taste; appetite, flavour.*
gusto -are, *to taste, take a little of; to partake of, enjoy.*
gustus -ūs, m. *tasting; taste, flavour, a whet* or *relish.*
gutta -ae, f. *a drop; a spot* or *mark.*
guttātim, *drop by drop.*
guttŭla -ae, f. *a little drop.*
guttur -ŭris, n. *the windpipe, throat; gluttony.*
guttus -i, m. *a jug.*
Gўăros -i, f. and **Gўăra** -orum, n. *a barren island in the Aegean, used as a place of exile under the empire.*
Gȳgēs -is and -ae, m. *a king of Lydia, famous for his ring*; adj. **Gȳgaeus** -a -um.
gymnăsĭarchus -i, m. *the master of a gymnasium.*
gymnăsĭum -i, n. *school of gymnastics, gymnasium*; also *a place for philosophical discussion.*

gymnastĭcus and **gymnĭcus** -a -um, *gymnastic.*
gÿnaecēum (and **-īum**) -i, n. *the women's apartments in a Greek house.*
gypso -are, *to cover with gypsum*; partic. **gypsātus** -a -um, *covered with gypsum, whitened.*
gypsum -i, n. *gypsum*; meton. *a plaster figure.*
gÿrus -i, m .*a circle, ring*; esp. *a course* for training horses; in gen., *orbit, circuit.*

H

H, h, the eighth letter of the Latin Alphabet.
ha! hahae! hahahae! exclamations of joy or amusement.
hăbēna -ae, f. *a strap; a bridle, reins* (esp. in plur.); habenas dare, *to loosen the rein*; adducere, *to tighten it.*
hăbĕo -ēre -ŭi -ĭtum, *to have, hold; to have about one, carry, wear; to contain*; more generally, *to possess, have power over*; absol., *to possess property, be wealthy*; of places, *to own, inhabit,* or *rule over*; of persons, *to keep,* esp. in a certain state, or relation. Transf., habere in animo, *to have in mind, intend*; habes consilia nostra, *you know of*; habeo dicere, *I have it in my power to say*; bonum animum habere, *to be of good courage*; odium, *to cherish hatred*; invidiam, *to experience ill-will*; misericordiam, *to involve* or *cause pity*; concilium, *to hold a council*; orationem, *to make a speech*; with reflex., *to keep oneself, be,* in a condition; graviter se habere, *to be ill*; ut nunc res se habet, *as things now are*; intransit., bene habet, *all right*; with adv., rarely, *to use, manage, treat*; with double acc., or dat., or pro and abl., *to hold, consider, regard* in a certain light. Perf. partic. **hăbĭtus** -a -um, *disposed; in a certain condition* (physical or mental).
hăbĭlis -e, *easily managed, handy; suitable, fit, convenient.*
hăbĭlĭtās -ātis, f. *aptitude, suitability.*
hăbĭtābĭlis -e, *habitable.*
hăbĭtātĭo -ōnis, f. *dwelling, habitation.*
hăbĭtātor -ōris, m. *inhabitant.*
hăbĭto -are: transit., *to inhabit*; intransit., *to dwell.*
hăbĭtūdo -ĭnis, f. *condition.*
[1]**hăbĭtus** -a -um, partic. from habeo; q.v.
[2]**hăbĭtus** -ūs, m. *condition, habit, bearing*; of dress, *style*; of places, *lie of the land*; abstr., *nature, character, disposition, attitude.*
hāc, adv. from hic; q.v.
hactĕnus, *as far as this, so far (and no farther); hitherto; up to this point.*
Hadrĭa -ae; f. *a town in the north of Italy;* m. *the Adriatic Sea.* Adj. **Hadrĭăcus** and **Hadrĭātĭcus** -a -um, *Adriatic.*
Hadrĭānus -i, m., P. Aelius, Roman emperor from A.D. 117 to 138.
haedĭlĭa -ae, f. and **haedillus** -i, m., *a little kid.*
haedīnus -a -um, *of a kid.*
haedŭlus -i, m. *a little kid.*
haedus -i, m. *a kid, young goat.*
Haemŏnĭa -ae, f. *an old name of Thessaly*; adj. **Haemŏnius** -a -um, *Thessalian;* f. subst. **Haemŏnis** -nĭdis, *a Thessalian woman.*
haerĕo haerēre haesi haesum. (1) *to stick, cleave, adhere, hang on to* a person or thing. (2) *to come to a standstill, get stuck; be embarrassed.*
haeresco -ĕre, *to adhere, stick.*
haesĭtantĭa -ae, f. *faltering*; linguae, *stammering.*
haesĭtātĭo -ōnis, f.: in speech, *hesitation, stammering*; mentally, *hesitation, indecision.*
haesĭto -are, *to stick fast, to hesitate*; in speech, *to stammer*; mentally, *to be undecided, be at a loss.*
hālec; see alec.
hălĭaeĕtos -i, m. *sea-eagle, osprey.*
hālĭtus -ūs, m., *breath, vapour.*
hallex -ĭcis, m. *thumb* or *big toe.*
hālo -are, *to breathe out, exhale.*
hālūc-; see aluc-.
hăma (**ăma**) -ae, f. *bucket,* esp. *fireman's bucket.*
Hămādrÿas -ădis, f., *a wood-nymph, hamadryad.*
hāmātus -a -um, *provided with hooks, hooked; curved like a hook, crooked.*
Hămilcăr -căris, m. *father of Hannibal.*
hāmĭōta -ae, m., *an angler.*
Hammon; see Ammon.
hāmus -i, m. *a hook,* esp. *a fish-hook; a talon; a thorn.*
Hannĭbăl -bălis, m. *leader of the Carthaginians in the second Punic war.*
hăra -ae, f. *a pen* or *coop; a pig-sty.*
hărĭŏlor -ari, dep. *to utter prophecies.* Transf., *to talk nonsense.*
hărĭŏlus -i, m. and **hărĭŏla** -ae f. *a soothsayer, prophet.*
harmŏnĭa -ae, f. *melody, concord, harmony.*
harpăgo -ōnis, m., *a large hook, drag, grappling-iron.*
harpē -es, f. *a curved sword, scimitar.*
Harpÿiae (trisyll.) -arum, f. pl., *the Harpies, mythical monsters.*
hăruspex -spĭcis, m. *soothsayer; a seer, prophet.*
hăruspĭcīnus -a -um, *concerned with divination*; f. as subst. *divination.*
hăruspĭcĭum -i, n. *inspection of entrails, divination.*
Hasdrŭbăl (**Asdrŭbăl**) -bălis, m. *the brother of Hannibal.*
hasta -ae, f. *a spear, pike, javelin*; milit., and in ceremonial use, at public auctions and weddings.
hastātus -a -um, *armed with a spear* m pl. as subst. **hastāti** -orum, *the front rank of a Roman army when drawn up for battle.*
hastīle -is, n., *the shaft of a spear; a spear; a prop for vines,* etc.
hau, *oh!*

haud (**haut**), *not, not at all, by no means.*
hauddum, *not yet.*
haudquāquam, *by no means, not at all.*
haurĭo haurire hausi haustum, *to draw up, draw out* or *in; to drink up, absorb, swallow; to shed* blood; *to drain, empty* a receptacle; in gen., *to derive, take in*; also *to exhaust, weaken, waste.*
haustrum -i, n. *a pump.*
haustus -ūs, m. *drawing of water*; legal, *the right to draw water*; of air, *inhaling*; of drink, *drinking, a draught*; of solids, *a handful.*
haut = haud; q.v.
hăvĕo; see aveo.
hebdŏmas -ădis, f. *seventh day of a disease* (supposed critical).
Hēbē -ēs, f. *the cup-bearer of the gods.*
hĕbĕnus -i, f. *the ebon-tree; ebony.*
hĕbĕo -ēre, *to be blunt, dull, heavy, inactive.*
hĕbĕs -ĕtis, *blunt, dull; faint, sluggish, weak*; mentally, *dull, heavy, stupid.*
hĕbesco -ĕre, *to become dull, blunt, dim.*
hĕbĕto -are, *to make blunt* or *dull, to deaden, dim.*
Hebraeus -a -um, *Hebrew, Jewish.*
Hebrus -i, m., *the chief river of Thrace.*
Hĕcătē -ēs, f. *goddess of magic and enchantment,* adj. **Hĕcătēĭus** -a -um and f. **Hĕcătēĭs** -ĭdis, *Hecatean, magical.*
hĕcătombē -ēs, f. *a hecatomb.*
Hector -tŏris, m. *son of Priam, husband of Andromache*; adj. **Hectŏrĕus** -a -um.
Hĕcŭba -ae, and **Hĕcŭbē** -ēs, f. *wife of Priam.*
hĕdĕra -ae, f. *ivy.*
hēdychrum -i, n. *a fragrant ointment.*
hei, interj. = ei; q.v.
Hĕlĕna -ae, and **Hĕlĕnē** -ēs, f. *wife o Menelaus, carried off by Paris to Troy.*
Hĕlĭce -ēs, f. *a constellation, the Great Bear.*
Hĕlĭcon -ōnis, m., *a hill in Boeotia, sacred to Apollo and the Muses*; adj. **Hĕlĭcōnĭus** -a -um; subst. **Hĕlĭcōnĭădes** and **Hĕlĭcōnĭdes** -um, f. *the Muses.*
Hellē -ēs, f. *a girl drowned in the Hellespont, so named after her.*
hellĕborus; see elleborus.
Hellespontus -i, m., *the Hellespont, Dardanelles.*
hellŭo (**hēlŭo**) -ōnis, *glutton, squanderer.*
hellŭor (**hēlŭor**) -ari, dep. *to guzzle, gormandize.*
hĕlops (**ĕlops, ellops**) -ŏpis, m. *a fish,* perhaps *sturgeon.*
helvella -ae, f. *a small pot-herb.*
Helvētii -orum, m. *the Helvetii, a people in what is now Switzerland.*
hem, interj. *well! just look!*
hēmĕrodrŏmus -i, m. *a special courier, express.*
hēmĭcillus -i, m. *mule.*
hēmĭcyclĭum -i, n. *a semi-circle* (of seats).
hēmīna -ae, f. *a measure of capacity,* about half a pint.
hendĕcăsyllăbi -orum, m. pl. *verses of eleven syllables, hendecasyllables.*
Henna (**Enna**) -ae, f. *city of Sicily, with a temple of Ceres*; adj. **Hennensis** -e and **Hennaeus** -a -um.
heptēris -is, f. *a galley with seven banks of oars.*
hĕra = ĕra; q.v.
Hēra -ae, f., *the Greek goddess identified with the Roman Juno;* **Hēraea** -orum, n. pl., *her festival.*
herba -ae, f. *vegetation; a green plant; a blade* or *stalk,* esp. of corn or grass.
herbesco ĕre, *to grow into blades* or *stalks.*
herbĭdus -a -um, and **herbĭfer** -fĕra -fĕrum, *grassy.*
herbōsus -a -um, *grassy.*
herbŭla -ae, f. *a little herb.*
hercisco (**ercisco**) -ĕre, *to divide an inheritance.*
Hercle; see Hercules.
herctum -i, n. *an inheritance*; herctum ciere, *to divide an inheritance.*
Hercŭlanĕum -i, n. *town in Campania destroyed by an eruption of Vesuvius.*
Hercŭles -is and -i, m. *the son of Jupiter and Alcmena*; voc. **Hercŭles** or **Hercŭle** or **Hercle**, used as an oath, *by Hercules*; so also **Mĕhercŭles, Mĕhercŭle, Mĕhercle**; adj. **Hercŭlĕus** and **Hercŭlānĕus** -a -um.
Hercȳnĭa silva -ae, f. *the Hercynian forest, in central Germany.*
hĕrĕ = heri; q.v.
hērēdĭtārĭus -a -um, *of an inheritance; inherited, hereditary.*
hērēdĭtās -ātis, f. *inheritance.*
hērēdĭum -i, n. *patrimony.*
hērēs (**haerēs**) -ēdis, c. *an heir, heiress, successor; an owner.*
hĕrī (**hĕrĕ**), *yesterday.*
hĕrĭfŭga = erifuga; q.v.
hĕrĭlis -e = erilis; q.v.
hermaphrŏdītus -i, m. *hermaphrodite.*
Hermes or **Herma** -ae, m. *the god Hermes, identified with the Roman Mercury.*
Hērō -ūs, f., *a priestess at Sestos, loved by Leander.*
Hērōdes -is, m. *Herod*; esp. *Herod the Great.*
Hērŏdŏtus -i, m. *the Greek historian, born* 484 B.C.
hērōĭcus -a -um, *relating to the heroes, heroic.*
hērōīna -ae and **hērōĭs** -ĭdis, f. *a demigoddess, heroine.*
hērōs -ōis, m. *a demigod, hero.*
hērōus -a -um, *a hero, heroic*; m. as subst. *a hexameter.*
hĕrus = ĕrus; q.v.
Hēsĭŏdus -i, m. *an early Greek poet of Boeotia.*
Hespĕrus or **-os** -i, m. *the Evening Star*; adj. **Hespĕrĭus** -a -um, *western*; f. as subst. **Hespĕrĭa** -ae, *the western land*; *Italy* or *Spain*; f. adj. **Hespĕrĭs** -ĭdis, *western*; f. subst. **Hespĕrĭdes** -um, *daughters of Hesperus, living in the extreme west.*
hesternus -a -um, *of yesterday.*

hĕtairĭa -ae, f. *a secret society.*
heu! *oh! alas!*
heus! *hallo! ho, there! hark!*
hexămĕter -tri, m.: adj., *with six feet* (of metre); as subst., *a hexameter.*
hexēris -is, f. *a galley with six banks of oars.*
hĭātus -ūs, m. *a cleft, opening; the opening of the mouth, open jaws;* hence *gaping after, desire for;* gram. *hiatus.*
Hībēr -ēris, m. *an Iberian, Spaniard;* plur. **Hībēres** -ērum, and **Hībēri** -orum, m. *Spaniards;* **Hībērus** -i, m. *the river Ebro;* **Hībērĭa** -ae, *Spain;* adj. **Hībērĭcus** -a -um and **Hībērus** -a -um, *Spanish.*
hībērna -orum, n.; see hibernus.
hībernācŭlum -i, n.: in pl., *tents* or *huts for winter quarters.*
Hībernĭa -ae, f. *Ireland.*
hīberno -are, *to winter, spend the winter.*
hībernus -a -um, *wintry, of winter; like winter, cold* or *stormy, wintering, for the winter;* n. pl. as subst. *winter quarters.*
hĭbiscum -i, n. *marsh-mallow.*
hibrĭda (**hybrĭda**) -ae, *a hybrid.*
[1]**hīc, haec, hōc,** *this, this one; this present;* in court, *my client;* strengthened form **hīce, haece, hōce;** interrog. **hīcĭnĕ, haecĭnĕ, hōcĭnĕ.**
[2]**hīc** (and **heic**) *here; in this place, in this matter; hereupon;* strengthened **hīce** and interrog. **hīcĭnĕ.**
hĭĕmālis -e, *of winter; wintry, stormy.*
hĭĕmo -are. (1) *to winter, spend the winter.* (2) *to be stormy.*
hĭems (**hĭemps**) -ĕmis, f. *winter; the cold of winter; stormy weather, storm.*
Hĭĕrŏsŏlȳma -orum, n. pl. *Jerusalem.*
hĭlăris -e and **hĭlărus** -a -um, *cheerful, merry, gay;* n. acc. sing. as adv. **hĭlărĕ,** *cheerfully.*
hĭlărĭtās -ātis, f. *cheerfulness, gaiety.*
hĭlăro -are, *to make joyful, to cheer up.*
hĭlărŭlus -a -um, *gay, cheerful.*
hillae -arum, f. pl. *intestines of animals; a kind of sausage.*
Hīlōtae and **Īlōtae** -arum, m. pl., *the Helots, slaves of the Spartans.*
hīlum -i, n. *a trifle;* with neg. *not a whit, not in the least.*
hinc, adv., *from here, hence;* hinc atque illinc, *on this side and on that;* of causation, *hence, from this cause;* of time, *henceforth,* or *thereupon.*
hinnĭo -ire, *to neigh, whinny.*
hinnītus -ūs, m. *neighing.*
hinnŭlĕus -i, m. *a young roebuck, fawn.*
hinnus -i, m. *a mule.*
hĭo -are, *to open, stand open; to gape,* esp. in astonishment or longing; of speech, *to hang together badly;* with acc. object, *to pour forth.*
hippăgōgi -orum, f. pl. *transports for cavalry.*
Hippĭas -ae, m. *son of Pisistratus, tyrant of Athens.*
hippŏcentaurus -i, m. *a centaur.*
Hippocrătēs -is, m. *a physician of Cos* (flourishing about 430 B.C.).
Hippocrēnē -ēs, f. *a fountain on Mount Helicon.*
hippodrŏmos -i, m., *a hippodrome racecourse.*
Hippŏlȳtus -i, m. *son of Theseus.*
hippŏtoxŏta -ae, m. *a mounted archer.*
hippūrus -i, m. *a fish,* perhaps *goldfish.*
hircīnus and **hircōsus** -a -um, *of a goat; goatlike.*
hircus -i, m. *a he-goat.*
hirnĕa -ae, f. *a can* or *jug.*
hirsūtus -a -um, *hairy, shaggy, rough; unadorned.*
Hirtĭus -a -um, *name of a Roman* gens.
hirtus -a -um, *hairy, shaggy, rough, uncultivated.*
hĭrūdo -ĭnis, f. *leech.*
hĭrundo -ĭnis, f. *swallow.*
hisco -ĕre, *to open, split open, gape; to open the mouth.*
Hispāni -orum, m. pl. *the Spaniards;* **Hispānĭa** -ae, f. *the whole of the Spanish peninsula;* adj. **Hispānĭensis** -e and **Hispānus** -a -um.
hispĭdus -a -um, *rough, hairy, bristly.*
[1]**hister** = histrio; q.v.
[2]**Hister** (**Ister**) -tri, m. *name of the lower part of the Danube.*
histŏrĭa -ae, f. *inquiry; the results of inquiry; learning; historical narrative, history;* in gen., *narrative, a story.*
histŏrĭcus -a -um, *of history, historical;* m. as subst., *a historian.*
histrĭcus -a -um, *of actors.*
histrĭo -ōnis, m. *an actor.*
histrĭōnālis -e, *of actors.*
hĭulco -are, *to cause to gape, to split.*
hĭulcus -a -um, *gaping, cleft, open; gaping with desire, longing;* of speech, *badly put together;* adv. **hĭulcē,** *with hiatus.*
hŏdĭē, *today; at present, still, even now; at once.*
hŏdĭernus -a -um, *of today.*
hŏlĭtor -ōris, m. *a kitchen-gardener.*
hŏlĭtōrĭus -a -um, *of herbs;* forum, *vegetable-market.*
hŏlus (**ŏlus**) -ĕris, n. *vegetable, potherb.*
Hŏmērus -i, m. *Homer, the Greek epic poet;* adj. **Hŏmērĭcus** -a -um.
hŏmĭcīda -ae, c. *a murderer, murderess, homicide.*
hŏmĭcīdĭum -i, n. *murder, homicide.*
hŏmo -ĭnis, *a human being, man, mortal;* in pl., *men, people, the world;* used like a pronoun, *he, him;* milit. in pl., *infantry.*
hŏmullus -i, and **hŏmuncĭo** -ōnis, and **hŏmuncŭlus** -i, m. *a little man, manikin.*
hŏnestās -ātis, f. (1) *honour, repute, respectability;* in pl., *notabilities.* (2) *worth, virtue, probity.* (3) *beauty.*
hŏnesto -are, *to honour, adorn, dignify.*
hŏnestus -a -um. (1) *honoured, in good repute, respectable.* (2) *honourable, proper, virtuous;* n. as subst., *morality, virtue.* (3) *fine, beautiful.* Adv. **hŏnestē,** *respectably; honourably; properly.*
hŏnor = honos; q.v.
hŏnōrābĭlis -e, *respectful*

hŏnōrārĭus -a -um, *done* or *given as an honour.*

hŏnōrĭfĭcus -a -um, *causing honour, honouring*; adv. **hŏnōrĭfĭcē.**

hŏnōro -are, *to honour, show honour to, adorn, dignify;* partic. **hŏnōrātus** -a -um, *honoured, distinguished, respected,* or in act. sense, *conferring honour*; adv. **hŏnōrātē.**

hŏnōrus -a -um, *honourable.*

hŏnŏs and **hŏnŏr** -ōris, m. *honour, a mark of honour* or *respect, distinction;* honoris causa, *with due respect,* or *to honour,* or *for the sake of*; personif., *Honour*; frequently, *an office of dignity, a public office*; also *an offering* to the gods, *sacrifice*; poet., *beauty, grace.*

hoplŏmăchus -i, *a gladiator.*

hōra -ae, f. *an hour, the twelfth part of a day or night*; hora quota est? *what's o'clock?* in horam vivere, *to live for the moment*; in gen., *time, season*; in plur. *a clock, dial*; personif. *the Hours, goddesses who presided over the seasons.*

Hŏrātĭus -a -um, *name of a Roman* gens.

hordĕum -i, n. *barley.*

hŏrĭa -ae, f. *a small fishing-boat.*

hornōtĭnus and **hornus** -a -um, *of this year, this year's*; adv. **hornō,** *this year.*

hōrŏlŏgĭum -i, n. *a clock; a sundial* or *water-clock.*

horrĕo -ēre, *to bristle, be rough*; of the hair, *to stand on end*; of persons, *to shudder, dread.* Gerundive as adj. **horrendus** -a -um, *horrible, dreadful; awful, worthy of reverence.*

horresco horrescĕre horrŭi, *to stand on end, bristle, be rough*; of persons, *to tremble, shudder, begin to dread.*

horrĕum -i, n. *a barn, granary, store-house.*

horrĭbĭlis -e, *horrible, frightful, dreadful*; colloq., *astonishing, wonderful.*

horrĭdŭlus -a -um, *somewhat rough, unadorned.*

horrĭdus -a -um, *rough, shaggy, bristly; shivering with cold.* Transf., *wild, savage; unpolished, uncouth; frightful, horrible.* Adv. **horrĭdē,** *roughly.*

horrĭfer -fĕra -fĕrum, *causing shudders of cold* or *fear.*

horrĭfĭco -are, *to make rough; to terrify.*

horrĭfĭcus -a -um, *causing terror, dreadful;* adv. **horrĭfĭcē.**

horrĭsŏnus -a -um, *sounding dreadfully.*

horror -ōris, m. *bristling, shuddering; roughness of speech; dread, fright,* esp. *religious dread, awe*; meton., *object of dread, a terror.*

horsum, *in this direction.*

hortāmen -ĭnis, n. and **hortāmentum** -i, n. and **hortātĭo** -ōnis, f. *exhortation, encouragement, incitement.*

hortātīvus -a -um, *of encouragement.*

hortātor -ōris, m. *an inciter, encourager.*

hortātus -ūs, m. *incitement, encouragement.*

Hortensĭus -a -um, *name of a Roman* gens.

hortor -ari, dep. *to exhort, incite, encourage*; esp *to harangue troops.*

hortŭlus -i, m. *a little garden*: plur. *grounds, a small park.*

hortus -i, m. *a garden*; in plur. *grounds, park.*

hospĕs -pĭtis, m. and **hospĭta** -ae, f. (1) *a host, hostess.* (2) *a guest.* (3) *a guest-friend, friend.* (4) *a stranger*; used also like adj. *foreign.*

hospĭtālis -e, *of a guest* or *host; friendly, hospitable*; adv. **hospĭtālĭter.**

hospĭtālĭtās -ātis, f. *hospitality.*

hospĭtĭum -i, n. *hospitality*;] meton., *a guest-chamber, inn, quarters.*

hostĭa -ae, f. *an animal slain in sacrifice, a victim.*

hostĭcus -a -um, *foreign*; but usually of *the enemy, hostile*; n, as subst. *enemy territory.*

hostīlis -e, *of, by* or *for the enemy; like an enemy, unfriendly, hostile*; adv. **hostīlĭtĕr.**

Hostīlĭus -a -um, *name of a Roman* gens.

hostīmentum -i, n. *compensation, requital.*

hostĭo -ire, *to requite, recompense.*

hostis -is, c. *a stranger*; but esp. *an enemy, foe, opponent.*

hūc, *hither, to this place*; huc (atque) illuc, *hither and thither.* Transf., *in addition to this; to this pitch,* or *degree*; interrog. **hūcĭnĕ?**

hŭi, exclamation of surprise, *eh! hallo!*

hūiusmŏdi or **hūiuscĕmŏdi,** *of this kind.*

hum-; see also um-.

hūmānĭtās -ātis, f. *humanity, human nature, human feeling; kindness; refinement, education, culture.*

hūmānĭtŭs, *after the manner of men;* also *kindly.*

hūmānus -a -um, *human, of human beings*; m. as subst. *a human being;* of good qualities, *humane, kind, educated, civilized, refined.* Adv. **hūmānē** and **hūmānĭtĕr,** *humanly, politely, courteously, kindly.*

hŭmātĭo -ōnis, f. *burying, interment.*

hŭmĭlis -e, *on* or *near the ground, low, shallow.* Transf., of rank, etc., *humble, poor, insignificant*; of character, *abject* or *submissive*; of language, *mean, without elevation.* Adv. **hŭmĭlĭtĕr,** *humbly, meanly, abjectly.*

hŭmĭlĭtās -ātis, f. *nearness to the ground; lowness; shallowness.* Transf., *insignificance, obscurity; submissiveness, abjectness.*

hŭmo -are, *to cover with earth, bury; to perform any funeral rites over* a corpse.

hŭmus -i, f. *ground, earth, soil*; humi, *on the ground*; meton., *land, country.*

[1]**Hўăcinthus** (-os) -i, m., *a beautiful youth, accidentally killed by Apollo.*

[2]**hȳăcinthus** -i, m. *a flower*, perhaps *the martagon lily*.
Hȳădes -um, f. *the Hyades, seven stars in the constellation Taurus*.
hȳaena -ae, f. *hyena*.
hȳălus -i, m. *glass*; colour *glassgreen*.
Hydra -e, f. *many-headed water-snake, slain by Hercules*; also *a constellation*.
hydraulus -i, m. *a water organ*.
hydrĭa -ae, f. *an urn, jug*.
hydrōpĭcus -a -um, *dropsical*.
hydrops -ōpis, m. *the dropsy*.
hydrus -i, m. *a water-snake*.
Hȳlās -ae, m. *companion of Hercules*.
Hȳmēn -ĕnis and **Hȳmĕnaeos** or **-us** -i, m. *Hymen, the god of marriage; the marriage song; a wedding* (esp. in plur).
hȳperbătŏn -i, n. *transposition of words*.
hȳperbŏlē -ēs, f. *exaggeration*.
Hȳperbŏrĕi -ōrum, m. pl. *a people in the extreme north*; adj. **Hȳperbŏrĕus** -a -um = *northern*.
hȳpŏdĭdascălus -i, m. *an under-teacher*.
hȳpomnēma -mătis, n. *a memorandum, note*.

I

i, the ninth letter of the Latin alphabet, used both as a vowel and as a consonant, formerly written j.
Iacchus -i, m. *name of Bacchus*; meton., *wine*.
iacĕo iacēre iacŭi, *to lie, be situated; to lie low, be flat; to lie sick* or *overthrown* or *killed*; of hair or clothes, to *hang loosely*; fig., *to be neglected*, or *despised; to be overthrown; to be cast down, dejected*.
iăcĭo iăcĕre iēci iactum. (1) *to lay*. (2) *to throw, cast, hurl; to fling away, shed; to scatter, diffuse; to let fall in speaking, utter*.
iactantĭa -ae, f. *boasting, bragging*.
iactātĭo -ōnis, f. *a tossing, shaking*. Transf., *violent emotion; boasting, ostentation*.
iactātor -ōris, m. *boaster, braggart*.
iactātus -ūs, m. *shaking, quick movement*.
iactĭto -are, *to toss about; to bandy*.
iacto -are, *to throw, cast, toss, fling away* or *about; to diffuse, spread, scatter; to harass, disturb* a person; *to broadcast* words; *to bring up, discuss* a *subject; to keep bringing up, to boast of*. With reflex, or in pass., *to gesticulate*; also *to* " *throw one's weight about* ", *make oneself conspicuous*. Pres. partic. **iactans** -antis, *boastful*; adv. **iactanter.**
iactūra -ae, f. *throwing away; loss, sacrifice*.
iactus -ūs, m. *cast, throw*; intra iactum, *within range*.
iăcŭlābĭls -e, *able to be thrown*.
iăcŭlātor -ōris, m. *a thrower*; esp. *a javelin-man, light-armed soldier*.
iăcŭlatrix -īcis, f. *the huntress* (*Diana*).
iăcŭlor -ari, dep. *to throw a javelin; to shoot at a target; to throw, cast, hurl* a missile. Transf., *to make a verbal attack; to aim at, strive after; to utter*.
iăcŭlum -i, n. (1) *a dart, javelin*. (2) *a casting-net*.
iăcŭlus -a -um, *thrown, darting*.
iam, adv. *now, by now, already;* of future time, *immediately, presently, soon; henceforth; further, moreover; just, indeed;* iam diu, iam dudum, iam pridem, *now for a long time*.
ĭambēus -a -um, *iambic*.
ĭambus -i, m. *an iambus, a metrical foot* (˘ ¯); *an iambic poem*.
iamdūdum, iamprīdem; see iam.
Iānĭcŭlum -i, n. *a hill west of Rome*.
iānĭtor -ōris, m. *door-keeper, porter*.
iānitrix -īcis, f. *portress*.
ĭanthĭnus -a um, *violet-coloured*.
iānŭa ae, f. *door; entrance, approach*.
iānus -i, m. *a covered passage, arcade*; personif., **Iānus,** *Janus, an old Italian deity with two faces*; adj. **Iānālis** and **Iānŭālis** -e; hence also adj. **Iānŭārius** -a -um, *of Janus* or of *January*; Ianuarius (mensis), *January*.
Iāpyx -pȳgis, m. *a west-north-west wind*.
Iāsōn -ōnis, m. *leader of the Argonauts*; adj. **Iāsŏnĭus** -a -um.
ĭaspis -ĭdis, f. *jasper*.
ībēr-; see **hiber-**.
ĭbĭ, adv. *there, at that place; then, thereupon; therein, in that matter* or *person*.
ĭbīdem, adv. *in the same place; at that moment; in that matter*.
ībis, genit. ībis and ībĭdis, f. *the ibis*.
ībiscum=hibiscum; q.v.
Īcărus -i, m. *son of Daedalus, drowned whilst flying with wings made by his father*; adj. **Īcărĭus** -a -um, *of Icarus*.
iccirco=idcirco; q.v.
Icēni -orum, m. *a British people in East Anglia*.
ichneumon -ŏnis, m. *the ichneumon*.
īcĭo or **īco** īci ictum, *to strike, hit, smite*; esp., *to strike* a bargain.
ictĕrĭcus -a -um, *jaundiced*.
ictus -ūs, m. *a blow, stroke*; in music, *beat*.
Īda -ae and **Īdē** -ēs, f. *name of two mountains, one in Crete, one in Phrygia, near Troy*; adj. **Īdaeus** -a -um.
idcirco (**iccirco**), *on that account; for that reason or purpose*.
īdem, ĕădem, ĭdem, *the same*; with dat., or ac, et, etc., *the same as*; by way of addition, *also*; of contrast, *yet;* alter idem, *a second self*.
ĭdentidem, *repeatedly, again and again*.
ĭdĕo, adv. *on that account, therefore; for that reason* or *purpose*.
ĭdĭōta -ae, m. *an ignorant, uneducated man*.
īdōlon -i, n. *a spectre*.
ĭdōnĕus -a -um, *fit, appropriate, suitable*; adv. **ĭdōnĕē.**
Īdūmaea -ae, f. *a district in Palestine*.

Īdūs -ŭum, f. pl. *the Ides, a day in the Roman month; the fifteenth day in March, May, July, October; the thirteenth in other months.*

iĕcur, iĕcŏris and iŏcĭnĕris, n. *the liver; supposed seat of the passions.*

iĕcuscŭlum -i, n. *a little liver.*

iēiūnĭtās -ātis, f. *hungriness, emptiness*; of style, etc., *poverty, meagreness.*

iēiūnĭum -i, n. *fast, abstinence, hunger*; hence, *leanness.*

iēiūnus -a -um, *fasting, hungry, thirsty*; of objects, *poor, scanty*; of spirit, *poor, mean*: of style, *meagre, weak.* Adv. **iēiūnē,** of style, *meagrely.*

ientācŭlum -i, n. *breakfast.*

iento -are, *to breakfast.*

ĭgĭtur, *therefore, then*; *so, as I was saying*; to emphasize, *I say.*

ignārus -a -um: act., *ignorant, inexperienced in* (with genit.); pass., *unknown.*

ignāvĭa -ae, f. *idleness, listlessness; cowardice.*

ignāvus -a -um. (1) *idle, listless, inactive, inert, sluggish.* (2) *cowardly*; m. as subst. *a coward.* Adv. **ignāvē** and **ignāvĭtĕr,** *lazily, without spirit.*

ignesco -ĕre, *to kindle, catch fire; to glow with passion.*

ignĕus -a -um, *fiery, burning, glowing, ardent.*

ignĭcŭlus -i, m. *a little fire, flame, spark.*

ignĭfĕr -fĕra -fĕrum, *fire-bearing, fiery.*

ignĭgĕna -ae, m. *born of fire.*

ignĭpēs -pĕdis, *fiery-footed.*

ignĭpŏtens -entis, *ruler of fire.*

ignis is, m. *fire, conflagration; a watch-fire, beacon; a firebrand; lightning*; in gen., *glow, glitter.* Transf., *a fire-brand* (of war); *glow of passion; the beloved.*

ignōbĭlis -e, *unknown, obscure; of humble birth.*

ignōbĭlĭtās -ātis, f. *obscurity; humble birth.*

ignōmĭnĭa -ae, f. *degradation, disgrace, dishonour.*

ignōmĭnĭōsus -a -um: of persons, *disgraced*; of things, *ignominious, disgraceful.*

ignōrābĭlis -e, *unknown.*

ignōrantia -ae, and **ignōrātĭo** -ōnis, f. *ignorance.*

ignōro -are, *to be ignorant of, not to know*; rarely, *to neglect, ignore.*

ignosco -noscĕre -nōvi -nōtum, *to overlook, forgive, pardon.*

ignōtus -a -um: pass., *unknown; ignoble, obscure*; act., *ignorant.*

īlĕ -is, n., plur. **īlĭa** -ium, *intestines, guts; loin, flank*; ilia ducere, *to become broken-winded.*

Ĭlerda -ae, f. *a town in Spain* (now *Lerida*).

īlex -ĭcis, f. *holm-oak.*

Īlĭa -ae, f. *mother of Romulus and Remus.*

Īlĭăcus; see **Ilion.**

īlĭcet. (1) a formula, *it is all over.* (2) *immediately, forthwith.*

īlĭcētum -i, n. *ilex-grove.*

īlĭco (illĭco), *on the spot; immediately.*

īlignus -a -um, *of ilex or holm-oak.*

Īlĭŏn or **Īlĭum** -i, n. and **Īlĭŏs** -i, f. *Troy*; adj. **Īlĭus** and **Īlĭăcus** -a -um, *Trojan*; **Īlĭensēs** -ĭum, m. pl., *Trojans*; **Īlĭădēs** -ae, *a son of Troy*; **Īlĭăs** -adis, f. *a Trojan woman*, or *the Iliad of Homer.*

ill-, for words compounded from in/l . . ., see in-.

illā, *by that way.*

illāc, *by that way, there*; illac facere, *to belong to that party.*

illĕ, illa, illŭd (older forms **olle** and **ollus**), pron., *that, that yonder, that one*; emphatically, *that well-known*; in contrast with hic, *the former* (sometimes *the latter*); ille qui, *he who, the one who.*

[1]**illīc, illaec, illūc,** *that one*; interrog. illicine?

[2]**illīc** or **illī,** *there, at that place; therein, in that matter.*

illim, *from that place* or *person.*

illinc, *from that place; on that side.*

illō, *thither, to that place; to that matter* or *point.*

illūc, *thither, to that place; to that matter* or *person.*

Illyrii -ōrum, m. pl. *a people on the Adriatic.*

ĭmāgĭnārĭus -a -um *imaginary.*

ĭmāgĭnātĭo -ōnis, f. *imagination, fancy.*

ĭmāgĭnor -ari, *to imagine, conceive, picture to oneself.*

ĭmāgo -ĭnis, f. *an image, copy, likeness; any representation, portrait, statue*; in plur. *waxen figures, portraits of ancestors; the shade or ghost* of the dead; *an echo; a mental picture, idea, conception*; rhet., *metaphor, simile, image*; abstr., *mere form, appearance, pretence.*

imbēcillĭtās -ātis, f. *weakness, feebleness.*

imbēcillus -a -um, *weak, feeble.* Compar. adv. **imbēcillĭus,** *somewhat weakly.*

imbellis -e, *unwarlike, not fighting, indisposed* or *unable to fight*; hence *feeble, peaceful, quiet.*

imber -bris, m. *a shower* or *storm of rain, pelting rain; a rain-cloud; water* or *any fluid; a shower* of missiles.

imberbis -e and **imberbus** -a -um *beardless.*

imbĭbo -bĭbĕre -bĭbi, *to drink in*; mentally, *to conceive; to resolve, determine.*

imbrex -ĭcis, c. *a hollow tile used in roofing.*

imbrĭfĕr -fĕra -fĕrum, *rain-bringing.*

imbŭo -ŭĕre -ŭi -ūtum, *to wet, steep, saturate*; fig., *to stain, taint*; mentally, *to accustom, initiate, instruct.*

ĭmĭtābĭlis -e, *that can be imitated.*

ĭmĭtāmĕn -ĭnis, n. *an imitation*; plur., *an image.*

ĭmĭtāmentum -i, n. *imitating, imitation.*

ĭmĭtātĭo -ōnis, f. *imitation; pretence.*

ĭmĭtātor -ōris, m. and **ĭmĭtātrix** -īcis, f. *an imitator.*

imĭtor -ari, dep. *to imitate, copy; to depict; to be like, act like.*
immădŭi, infin. -isse, *to have become moist.*
immānis -e, *enormous, immense, monstrous*; of character, *savage, horrible, inhuman.*
immānĭtās -ātis, f. *savagery, frightfulness.*
immansuētus -a -um, *untamed, wild.*
immātūrĭtās -ātis, f. *immaturity; untimely haste.*
immātūrus -a -um, *unripe, immature; untimely.*
immĕdĭcābĭlis -e, *incurable.*
immĕmŏr -mŏris, *unmindful, forgetful, heedless.*
immĕmŏrābĭlis -e, *indescribable; unworthy of mention; silent, uncommunicative.*
immĕmŏrāta -orum, n. pl. *things not related.*
immensĭtās -ātis, f. *immensity.*
immensus -a -um, *immense, vast, boundless*; n. as subst., *immense size, immensity.*
immĕrens -entis, *not deserving, innocent.*
immergo -mergĕre -mersi -mersum, *to dip in, plunge in, immerse.*
immĕrĭtus -a -um: act., *not deserving (punishment), innocent*; pass., *undeserved*; adv. **immĕrĭtō,** *undeservedly.*
immersābĭlis -e, *that cannot be sunk.*
immētātus -a -um, *unmeasured.*
immigro -are, *to move away into*
immĭnĕo -ēre, *to project, overhang*; in time, *to be imminent, hang over; to threaten; to be on the watch* or *look out.*
immĭnŭo -ŭĕre -ŭi -ūtum, *to lessen, diminish; to weaken, infringe.*
immĭnūtĭo -ōnis, f. *diminishing, weakening*; rhet. *meiosis.*
immiscĕo -miscēre -miscŭi mixtum, *to mix in, intermingle; to join with, unite.*
immĭsĕrābĭlis -e, *unpitied.*
immĭsĕrĭcors -cordis, *unmerciful*; adv. **immĭsĕricordĭtĕr.**
immissĭo -ōnis, n. *letting grow.*
immītis -e, *unripe, sour; harsh, cruel, stern.*
immitto -mittĕre -mīsi -missum. (1) *to send in, put in, work in; to engraft.* (2) *to let loose*; esp. *to let grow.* (3) *to let go against, launch against*; se in hostes, *to attack;* of feelings, *to instil.*
immixus, partic. from immisceo; q.v.
immo, *on the contrary; yes indeed, no indeed; say rather.*
immōbĭlis -e, *immovable* or *hard to move; inexorable.*
immŏdĕrātĭo -ōnis, f. *excess.*
immŏdĕrātus -a -um, *immeasurable, endless; immoderate, unrestrained;* adv. **immŏdĕrātē.**
immŏdestĭa -ae, f. *want of restraint.*
immŏdestus -a -um, *unrestrained, extravagant*; adv. **immŏdestē.**
immŏdĭcus -a -um, *immoderate, excessive; unrestrained, unbridled;* adv. **immŏdĭcē.**
immŏdŭlātus -a -um, *inharmonious.*
immoenis; see immunis.
immŏlātĭo -ōnis, f. *sacrificer.*
immŏlātor -ōris, m. *a sacrifice.*
immōlītus -a -um, *built up, erected.*
immŏlo -are, *to sacrifice; to devote to death, to slay.*
immŏrĭor -mŏri -mortuus, *to die in* or *over.*
immŏror -ari, *to remain in; to dwell on* a subject.
immorsus -a -um, *bitten; stimulated.*
immortālis -e, *deathless, immortal, imperishable.* Adv. **immortālĭter,** *infinitely.*
immortālĭtās -ātis, f., *immortality; everlasting renown; extreme happiness.*
immōtus -a -um, *unmoved, motionless; undisturbed, calm; firm, steadfast.*
immūgĭo -ire, *to bellow in* or *on.*
immulgĕo -ēre, *to milk into.*
immundus -a -um, *impure, foul.*
immūnĭo -ire, *to fortify.*
immūnis -e, *without duty free, exempt;* in gen., *not working* or *not contributing; not sharing in, devoid of; stainless.*
immūnĭtās -ātis, f. *exemption from offices* or *burdens; immunity.*
immūnītus -a -um, *unfortified; unpaved.*
immurmŭro -are, *to murmur at.*
immūtābĭlis, -e *unchangeable.*
immūtābĭlĭtās -ātis, f., *immutability.*
immūtātĭo -ōnis, f. *change, alteration*; rhet., *metonymy.*
[1]**immūtātus** -a -um, *unchanged.*
[2]**immutatus** -a -um, partic. from immuto; q.v.
immūto -are, *to change, alter*; immutata oratio, *allegory.*
impācātus -a um, *restless.*
impallesco -pallescĕre -pallŭi *to turn pale.*
impār -păris, *unequal, uneven; unlike, discordant; ill-matched*; of numbers, *odd*; modi impares, *hexameter and pentameter.* Adv. **impărĭtĕr,** *unevenly, unequally.*
impărātus -a -um *unprepared, unprovided.*
impart-; see impert-.
impastus -a -um, *unfed, hungry.*
impătĭbĭlis = impetibilis; q.v.
impătĭens -entis *unable to endure, impatient*; adv. **impătĭenter.**
impătĭentĭa -ae, f. *impatience, inability to endure.*
impăvĭdus -a -um, *fearless, undaunted*; adv. **impăvĭdē.**
impĕdīmentum -i, n. *hindrance, impediment*; in plur., *the baggage of an army* or *traveller.*
impĕdĭo -ire, *to entangle, ensnare, obstruct, surround; to embarrass, hinder, prevent.*

Hence partic, **impĕdītus** -a -um, *entangled, hindered*; milit., *hindered by baggage*; of places, *impassable, blocked*; in gen., *embarrassed, obstructed; awkward, complicated.*

impĕdītĭo -ōnis, f. *hindrance.*

impello -pellĕre -pŭli -pulsum. (1) *to drive against, strike upon.* (2) *to set in motion; to incite, urge on, impel;* esp. *to push over one already slipping.*

impendĕo -ēre, *to hang over, overhang; to threaten, be close at hand.*

impendĭum -i, n. *expenditure, outlay, cost; interest on money.* Abl. as adv. **impendĭō,** colloq., *by much, very much.*

impendo -pendĕre -pendi -pensum, *to weigh out;* hence *to expand, lay out;* partic. **impensus** -a -um, of price, *considerable, great;* in gen., *strong, vehement.* Adv. **impensē,** *at great cost; urgently, eagerly.*

impĕnetrābĭlis -e, *impenetrable.*

impensa -ac, f. *expense, outlay.*

impĕrātor -ōris, m. *commander, leader;* milit., *the commander-in-chief;* also of the Roman emperors.

impĕrātōrĭus -a -um, *of a general; imperial.*

impĕrātrix -īcis, f. *a female commander.*

imperceptus -a -um *unperceived, unknown.*

impercussus -a -um, *not struck.*

imperdĭtus -a -um, *not lain, undestroyed.*

imperfectus -a -um, *incomplete, unfinished.*

imperfossus -a -um *unstabbed, unpierced.*

impĕrĭōsus -a -um, *commanding;* sibi, *master of oneself;* in bad sense, *imperious, tyrannical.*

impĕrītĭa -ae, f. *inexperience, ignorance.*

impĕrĭto -are, *to command, be in command, give an order.*

impĕrītus -a -um, *unskilled, inexperienced, ignorant;* adv. **impĕrītē.**

impĕrĭum -i, n. *an order, a command; the right to order, power, mastery, command;* esp. *political power, authority, sovereignty;* in imperio esse, *to hold office;* meton. *empire,* and in plur., *persons in authority.*

imperiūrātus -a -um, *by which no one swears falsely.*

impermissus -a -un, *forbidden.*

impĕro -are, *to impose;* hence *to requisition, order* a thing; *to order* an action *to be done, give orders to* a person; *to rule over, govern, command.*

imperterrĭtus -um, *undaunted, fearless.*

impertĭo -ire, *to give a person a share in; to share* a thing *with* a person, *to impart, bestow.*

imperturbātus -a -um, *undisturbed, calm.*

impervĭus -a -um, *impassable.*

impĕtĭbĭlis -e, *insufferable.*

impĕto -ĕre, *to make for, attack.*

impetrābĭlis -e: pass., *obtainable;* act., *successful.*

impetrātĭo -ōnis, f *obtaining by request.*

impetrĭo -ire, *to seek by favourable omens.*

impetro -are, *to get, accomplish, effect;* esp. *to obtain by asking.*

impĕtus -ūs, m. *an attack, onset;* any *rapid motion;* mental *impulse, passion, force.*

impexus -a -um *uncombed; rude, uncouth.*

impĭĕtās -ātis, f. *undutifulness; impiety unfilial conduct, disloyalty.*

impĭgĕr -gra -grum, *diligent, active,* adv. **impigrē.**

impigrĭtās -ātis, f. *activity.*

impingo -pingĕre -pēgi -pactum, *to thrust, dash, drive against;* fig., *to press upon, bring upon* a person.

impĭus -a -um, *undutiful, disloyal; godless, unfilial, unpatriotic;* adv. **impĭē.**

implăcābĭlis -e, *implacable;* compar. adv. **implăcābĭlĭus.**

implăcātus -a -um, *unappeased, unsatisfied.*

implĕo -plēre -plēvi -plētum, *to fill in, fill up, complete; to satisfy, content* a person; *to fulfil, perform; to contaminate.*

implexus -a -um *involved, entwined.*

implĭcātĭo -ōnis, f. *entwining, interweaving; embarrassment.*

implĭco -are, -āvi -ātum and -ŭi -ĭtum, *to enfold, entwine, entangle, involve; to associate, unite;* partic. **implĭcātus** -a -um, *confused, entangled;* adv. **implĭcĭtē,** *confusedly.*

implōrātĭo -ōnis, f. *an imploring for help.*

implōro -are, *to call upon with tears, to beseech, implore; to call for, beg for.*

implūmis -e, *unfledged.*

implŭo -plŭĕre -plŭi, *to rain upon.*

implŭvĭum -i, n. *an opening in the roof of a Roman house,* or *the basin for rain-water below it.*

impŏlītus -a -um, *rough, unpolished;* adv. **impŏlītē.**

impollūtus -a -um, *undefiled.*

impōno -pōnĕre -pŏsŭi -pŏsĭtum, *to put, lay, place in* or *upon;* naut. *to put on board ship, to embark;* fig., *to lay* or *put upon, impose; to put over as master; to impose upon, cheat, deceive* (with dat.).

importo -are, *to bring in, import. introduce; to bring upon, cause.*

importūnĭtās -ātis, f. *self-assertion, inconsiderateness, insolence.*

importūnus -a -um, *unsuitable, ill-adapted, unfavourable; troublesome, tiresome;* of character, *assertive, inconsiderate.*

importŭōsus -a -um, *without harbours.*

impŏs -pŏtis, *having no power over.*

impŏsĭtus -a -um, partic. from impono; q.v.

impŏtens -entis, *feeble, powerless;* with genit., *not master of;* esp. *unable to command oneself, violent, unrestrained.* Adv. **impŏtentĕr,** *weakly; intemperately, passionately.*

impŏtentĭa -ae, f. *poverty; lack of self-restraint, violent passion.*

impraesentĭārum, *in present circumstances, for the present.*

impransus -a -um, *without breakfast, fasting.*

imprĕcor -ari, dep. *to invoke harm upon, to call down upon.*
impressĭo -ōnis, f. *physical pressure an attack, assault*; rhet., *distinct expression, emphasis*; philos., *sense-data, the impressions of the senses.*
imprīmīs, *especially, first of all.*
imprĭmo -prĭmĕre -pressi -pressum, *to press upon* or *into; to seal, chase, emboss; to make by pressing, imprint.*
imprŏbātĭo -ōnis, f. *disapproval, blame.*
imprŏbĭtās -ātis, f. *badness, depravity.*
imprŏbo -are, *to disapprove, blame, reject.*
imprŏbŭlus -a -um, *somewhat wicked.*
imprŏbus -a -um, *inferior, bad; morally bad, perverse, wilful; bold, persistent, mischievous*; m.pl. as subst., *the unpatriotic.* Adv. **imprŏbē,** *badly, wickedly; impudently, boldly.*
imprōcērus -a -um, *small, low of stature.*
imprōdictus -a -um, *not postponed.*
impromptus -a -um, *not ready.*
imprŏpĕrātus -a -um, *unhurried, slow.*
improspĕr -ĕra -ĕrum, *unfortunate*; adv. **improspĕrē.**
imprōvĭdus -a -um, *without forethought, improvident*; adv. **imprōvĭdē.**
imprōvīsus -a -um, *unforeseen, unexpected*; (ex) improviso, *unexpectedly.*
imprūdens -entis, *not foreseeing, not expecting; not knowing, unaware; unwise, rash, imprudent.* Adv. **imprūdentĕr,** *without forethought; unawares; unwisely.*
imprūdentĭa -ae, f., *lack of foresight* or *knowledge; ignorance; lack of wisdom, imprudence.*
impūbēs -bĕris and -bis. (1) *youthful*; genae, *beardless*; plur. as subst. *boys.* (2) *unmarried.*
impŭdens -entis, *shameless, impudent*; adv. **impŭdentĕr.**
impŭdentĭa -ae, f. *shamelessness, impudence.*
impŭdīcĭtĭa -ae, f. *incontinence, unchastity.*
impŭdīcus -a -um *shameless*; esp. *unchaste.*
impugnātĭo -ōnis, f. *assault, attack.*
impugno -are, *to attack, assail.*
impulsĭo -ōnis, f. *pressure*; fig., *impulse, instigation.*
impulsor -ōris, m. *instigator.*
impulsus -ūs, m. *pressure, impulse; incitement, instigation.*
impūnĕ, *with impunity, unpunished, safely.*
impūnĭtās -ātis, f. *impunity, exemption from punishment.*
impūnītus -a -um, *unpunished, exempt from punishment; unrestrained*; adv. **impūnītē.**
impūrātus -a -um, *vile, infamous.*
impūrĭtās -ātis, f. *moral impurity.*
impūrus -a -um, *unclean, foul*; morally, *impure, vile, infamous.* Adv. **impūrē.**
[1]**impŭtātus** -a -um, *unpruned, untrimmed.*
[2]**impŭtātus** -a -um, partic. from imputo; q.v.
impŭto -are, *to lay to a charge, enter in an account; to reckon as a merit* or *fault* in someone, *to impute to; to reckon as a service done* or *gift given* to someone.
imus -a -um, superl. from inferus; q.v.
[1]**ĭn,** prep. (1) with acc., *into, on to, towards, against*; of time, *until*; in omne tempus, *for ever*; in diem vivere, *to live for the moment*; of tendency or purpose, *for*; in adverbial phrases, indicating manner or extent: in universum, *in general*; in vicem, in vices, *in turn.* (2) with abl., *in, on, among*; of time, *in, at, within; in relation to* a person, *in the case of.*
[2]**in-,** inseparable particle, *without, not.*
ĭnaccessus -a -um, *inaccessible.*
ĭnăcesco -ăcescĕre -ăcŭi, *to become sour.*
Ĭnăchus (**Ĭnăchŏs**) -i, m. *mythical king of Argos, father of Io, after whom the river Inachus in Argolis was named.*
ĭnadfectātus -a -um, *natural, unaffected.*
ĭnadsuētus -a -um, *unaccustomed.*
ĭnădustus -a -um, *unsinged.*
ĭnaedĭfĭco -are *to build in* or *upon; to build up, block up, barricade.*
ĭnaequābĭlis -e, *uneven, unequal*; adv. **ĭnaequābĭlĭter.**
ĭnaequālis -e. *uneven, unequal, various; making unequal, disturbing.* Adv. **ĭnaequālĭtĕr,** *unevenly.*
ĭnaequālĭtās -ātis, f. *unevenness.*
ĭnaequo -are, *to make even, level up.*
ĭnaestĭmābĭlis -e, *that cannot be estimated*; hence *priceless, inestimable*; also *having no value.*
ĭnaestŭo -are, *to boil, rage (in).*
ĭnaffectātus, see inadf-.
ĭnămābĭlis -e, *unlovely, hateful.*
ĭnămāresco -ĕre, *to become bitter.*
ĭnambĭtĭōsus -a -um, *unpretentious.*
ĭnambŭlātĭo -ōnis, f. *walking up and down.*
ĭnambŭlo -are, *to walk up and down.*
ĭnămoenus -a -um, *unlovely, dismal.*
ĭnănĭmus -a -um, *lifeless, inanimate.*
ĭnānĭo -ire, *to empty, make void.*
ĭnānis -e, *empty, void*; equus, *riderless*; navis, *unloaded*; corpus, *soulless*; with genit, or abl., *empty of*; of persons, *empty-handed, poor*; fig., *vain, hollow, idle.* N. as subst., *empty space, emptiness, vanity.* Adv. **ĭnānĭtĕr,** *vainly, uselessly.*
ĭnānĭtās -ātis, f. *emptiness, empty space; uselessness.*
ĭnărātus -a -um, *unploughed, fallow.*
ĭnardesco -ardescĕre -arsi, *to catch fire, burn, glow.*
ĭnāresco -ārescĕre -ārŭi, *to become dry.*
ĭnassuētus; see inadsuetus.
ĭnattĕnŭātus, *undiminished, unimpaired.*
ĭnaudax -ācis, *timid, fearful.*
ĭnaudĭo -ire, *to hear*; esp. *to hear as a secret.*
ĭnaudītus -a -um, *unheard* (esp. of accused persons); *unheard of, unusual.*
ĭnaugŭro -are: intransit., *to take the auguries*; transit., *to consecrate,*

install, inaugurate; **īnaugŭrātō,** *after taking the auguries.*
īnaures -ĭum, f. pl. *earrings.*
īnauro -are, *to cover with gold, gild, enrich.*
ĭnauspĭcātus -a -um, *without auspices*; **īnauspĭcātō,** *without consulting the auspices.*
īnausus -a -um, *not dared, not attempted.*
incaedŭus -a -um, *not cut, unfelled.*
incălesco -călescĕre -călŭi, *to glow, become warm or passionate.*
incalfăcĭo -făcĕre, *to heat, warm.*
incallĭdus -a -um, *ingenuous, unskilful*; adv. **incallĭdē.**
incandesco -candescĕre -candŭi, *to begin to whiten*, esp. *with heat.*
incānesco -cānescĕre -cānŭi, *to become grey.*
incanto -are, *to enchant.*
incānus -a -um, *quite grey.*
incassum, *in vain.*
incastīgātus -a -um, *unchastised.*
incautus -a -um, adj. *incautious, careless, unwary; unguarded; not guarded against, unforeseen.* Adv. **incautē.**
incēdo -cēdĕre -cessi -cessum, *to walk, step, march; to proceed, come on*; of feelings, with dat., *to come over.*
incĕlebrātus -a -um, *not spread abroad.*
incēnātus -a -um, *without dinner.*
incendĭārĭus -a -um, *fire-raising, incendiary.*
incendĭum -i, n. *a conflagration, fire; a torch, firebrand*; of passion, *fire, glow, heat*: in gen., *destruction ruin.*
incendo -cendĕre -cendi -censum, *to kindle, set fire to, burn; to make bright, illumine; to fire with passion, excite, incense.*
incensĭo -ōnis, f. *burning.*
incensus -a -um, *not enrolled by the censor, unassessed.*
incensus, partic. from incendo; q.v.
inceptĭo -ōnis, f. *a beginning; an enterprise.*
incepto -are, *to begin; to attempt, undertake.*
inceptor -ōris, m. *a beginner.*
inceptum -i, n. of partic. of incipio; q.v.
incerno -cernĕre -crēvi -crētum, *to sift.*
incēro -are, *to cover with wax.*
incertus -a -um, *uncertain, doubtful, not sure.* (1) *as to fact*: act., of persons, *not knowing, doubting*; pass., of things, *not known, obscure*; n. as subst. *uncertainty.* (2) as to action, *hesitating, irresolute, undecided*; incertam securim, *not surely aimed.*
incesso -cessĕre -cessīvi, *to attack, assail.*
incessus -ūs, m. *march, walk; manner of walking, gait; attack, assault; entrance, approach.*
incesto -are, *to defile, pollute, dishonour.*
[1]**incestus** -a -um, *impure, defiled; sinful, unchaste*; n. as subst. *unchastity, incest.* Adv. **incestē.**
[2]**incestus** -ūs, m. *unchastity, incest.*
inchŏo; see incoho.
[1]**incĭdo** -cĭdĕre -cĭdi -casum, *to fall in or upon; to fall in with*; in hostem, *to attack*; in aes alienum, *to run into debt;* in mentionem, *to happen to mention*; of abstr. things, *to occur, happen,* " *crop up.*"
[2]**incīdo** -cīdĕre -cīdi cīsum, *to cut into, cut open; to inscribe, engrave an inscription; to make by cutting; to cut through*; fig., *to cut short, bring to an end, break off.*
Hence, from partic., n. subst. **incīsum** -i, = incisio, q.v.; adv. **incīsē,** = incisim, q.v.
incīlĕ -is, n. *a ditch, trench.*
incīlo -are, *to blame, scold.*
incingo -cingĕre -cinxi -cinctum, *to surround.*
incĭno -ĕre, *to sing.*
incĭpĭo -cĭpĕre -cēpi -ceptum (cf. coepi), *to take in hand, begin, commence; sometimes, to begin to speak.* N. of partic. as subst. **inceptum** -i, *a beginning; an attempt, enterprise.*
incīsim, *in short clauses.*
incīsĭo -ōnis, f. *a clause of a sentence.*
incĭtāmentum, -i, n. *inducement, incentive.*
incĭtātĭo -ōnis, f.: act., *inciting, instigating*; pass., *violent motion excitement, vehemence.*
incĭto -are, *to put into rapid motion, urge on, hasten*; in pass., or with reflex., *to quicken one's pace, hasten.* Transf., *to excite, spur, inspire; to incite against, stir up; to increase.*
Hence partic. **incĭtātus** -a -um, *rapid, vehement*; equo incitato, *at full gallop;* compar. adv. **incĭtātĭus.** *more violently.*
[1]**incĭtus** -a -um, *in rapid motion.*
[2]**incĭtus** -a -um, *unmoved.*
inclāmo -are, *to call upon loudly*; esp., *to scold.*
inclāresco -clārescĕre -clārŭi, *to become famous.*
inclēmens -entis, *unmerciful, harsh, rough*; adv. **inclēmentĕr.**
inclēmentĭa -ae, f. *unmercifulness, harshness.*
inclīnātĭo -ōnis, f. *leaning, bending, inclination*; in gen., *movement, tendency, change; good-will, liking.*
inclīno -are: transit., *to bend, incline, turn, change,* sometimes *for the worse*; in pass., *to fall back, waver*; intransit., *to take a turn, verge, incline, change;* milit., *to waver, yield.*
Hence partic. **inclīnātus** -a -um, *inclined, prone; sinking;* of the voice, *low, deep.*
inclūdo -clūdĕre -clūsi -clūsum, *to shut in, enclose*; esp. *to block, obstruct, confine.*
inclūsĭo -ōnis, f. *shutting up, confinement.*
inclŭtus, inclĭtus -a -um, *celebrated famous, renowned.*
[1]**incoctus** -a -um, *uncooked, raw.*
[2]**incoctus** -a -um, partic. from incoquo; q.v.
incōgĭtābĭlis -e, and **incōgĭtans** -antis, *inconsiderate, thoughtless.*

incōgĭtantĭa -ae, f. *thoughtlessness.*
incōgĭtātus -a -um: pass., *unstudied*; act., *inconsiderate.*
incōgĭto -are, *to contrive, plan.*
incognĭtus -a -um, *unexamined, unknown; unrecognized,* so *unclaimed.*
incŏho -are, *to take in hand, begin.* Hence partic. **incŏhātus** -a -um, *only begun, not finished.*
incŏla -ae, c. *an inhabitant, native*; sometimes *a foreign resident.*
incŏlo -cŏlĕre -cŏlŭi, *to inhabit, dwell (in).*
incŏlŭmis -e, *uninjured, safe and sound.*
incŏlŭmĭtās -ātis, f., *safety, preservation.*
incŏmĭtātus -a -um, *unaccompanied, without retinue.*
incommendātus -a -um, *not entrusted*; hence *without protector.*
incommŏdĭtās -atis, f. *inconvenience, disadvantage, unseasonableness.*
incommŏdo -are, *to be unpleasant* or *troublesome.*
incommŏdus -a -um, *inconvenient, troublesome, disagreeable, annoying*; n. as subst., *inconvenience, disadvantage;* incommodo tuo, *to your disadvantage*; adv. **incommŏdē,** *inconveniently.*
incommūtābĭlis -e, *unchangeable.*
incompărābĭlis -e, *incomparable.*
incompertus -a -um, *unknown.*
incompŏsĭtus -a -um, *not in order, irregular*; adv. **incompŏsĭtē.**
incomprĕhensĭbĭlis -e, *impossible to catch; incomprehensible.*
incomptus -a -um, *unkempt, untrimmed; rude, rough.*
inconcessus -a -um, *not allowed, forbidden.*
inconcinnus -a -um, *awkward, inelegant, absurd.*
inconcussus -a -um, *unshaken, firm.*
incondĭtus -a -um, *not arranged, disorderly, confused*; adv. **incondĭtē.**
incongrŭens -entis, *not agreeing, inconsistent.*
inconsīdĕrātus -a -um, *thoughtless, inconsiderate;* pass. *unadvised, reckless.* Adv. **inconsīdĕrātē,** *without consideration.*
inconsōlābĭlis -e, *inconsolable; incurable.*
inconstans -stantis, *changeable, inconsistent*; adv. **inconstantĕr.**
inconstantĭa -ae, f. *changeableness, inconsistency.*
inconsultus -a -um: pass., *not consulted*; act., *without asking advice, unadvised*; hence *inconsiderate, imprudent.* Adv. **inconsultē,** *indiscreetly.*
inconsumptus -a -um, *unconsumed, undiminished.*
incontāmĭnātus -a -um, *unpolluted.*
incontentus -a -um, *not stretched*; fides, *untuned.*
incontĭnens -entis, *incontinent*; adv. **incontĭnenter.**
incontĭnentĭa -ae, f. *incontinence.*
inconvĕnĭens -entis, *not suiting, dissimilar.*
incŏquo -cŏquĕre -coxi -coctum, *to boil in* or *with; to dye.*
incorrectus -a -um, *unamended, unimproved.*
incorruptus -a -um, *not corrupted, untainted, unspoilt, unimpaired*; adv. **incorruptē.**
incrēbresco -ĕre -crebrŭi and **incrēbesco** -ĕre -crebŭi, *to become strong* or *frequent; to increase, prevail.*
incrēdĭbĭlis -e, *not to be believed, incredible*; adv. **incrēdĭbĭlĭtĕr.**
incrēdŭlus -a -um, *incredulous.*
incrēmentum -i, n. *growth, increase*; meton, *the makings of anything,* also *offspring.*
incrĕpĭto -are, *to call loudly to; to reproach, chide.*
incrĕpo -are -ŭi (-āvi) -ĭtum (ātum), *to rustle, make a noise; to be noised abroad*; transit., *to cause to sound.* Of persons, *to chide, rebuke.*
incresco -crescĕre -crēvi, *to grow* (*in* or *on*).
incrētus -a -um, partic. from incerno; q.v.
incrŭentātus and **incrŭentus** -a -um, *bloodless.*
incrusto -are, *to cover with rind, encrust.*
incŭbo -are -ŭi -ĭtum, *to lie in* or *on* or *over; to watch over; to hang over, lie heavily upon; to dwell in.*
inculco -are, *to trample in, press in, force upon, impress upon.*
inculpātus -a -um, *unblamed, blameless.*
[1]**incultus** -a -um, *uncultivated, untilled;* n. pl. as subst. *wastes, deserts*; of dress, etc., *neglected, untidy*; in gen., *unpolished, rude.* Adv. **incultē.**
[2]**incultus** -ūs, m. *neglect, want of cultivation.*
incumbo -cumbĕre -cŭbŭi -cŭbĭtum, *to lie upon, put weight on, lean over, overhang; to apply oneself to, concentrate upon* a thing; *to incline to favour, further* a cause or movement.
incūnābŭla -orum, n. pl. *swaddling-clothes*; hence *infancy; birthplace*; in gen., *source, origin.*
incūrātus -a -um, *uncared-for, unhealed.*
incūrĭa -ae, f. *carelessness, neglect.*
incūrĭōsus -a -um: act., *careless, negligent*; pass., *neglected.* Adv. **incūrĭōsē,** *carelessly.*
incurro -currĕre -curri (cŭcurri) -cursum, *to run into*; milit., *to assail, attack, make a raid into.* Transf., *to attack* with words, *inveigh against; to come upon, fall in with*; in space, *to extend into*; in time, *to coincide with.*
incursĭo -ōnis, f. a *clash, onset; collision*; milit., *attack, raid, invasion.*
incurso -are, *to run against, strike against, attack.*
incursus -ūs, m. *an attack, assault*; of the mind, *efforts, impulses.*
incurvo -are, *to bend, curve, make crooked.*

incurvus -a -um, *bent, curved, crooked.*
incūs -cūdis, f. *anvil.*
incūsātĭo -ōnis, f. *blame, reproach, accusations.*
incūso -are, *to accuse, blame, find fault with.*
incussū, abl. sing. m., *by a clash.*
incustōdītus -a -um: pass., *unwatched, unguarded*; act., *incautious, imprudent.*
incūsus -a -um, *forged, fabricated.*
incŭtĭo -cŭtĕre -cussi -cussum, *to dash, beat against; to strike into* the mind, *inspire with.*
indāgātĭo -ōnis, f. *investigation.*
indāgātor -ōris, m. and **indāgātrix** -trīcis, f. *investigator, explorer.*
[1]**indāgo** -are, *to track down,* as hounds hunting; *to explore, investigate.*
[2]**indāgo** -ĭnis, f. *surrounding and driving of game.*
indĕ, *thence, from there*; hinc . . . inde, *on this side . . . on that; from that cause, for that reason; from that time, thereafter; thereupon, then.*
indēbĭtus -a -um, *not owed, not due.*
indĕcens -centis, *unbecoming, unseemly, unsightly*; adv. **indĕcenter.**
indēclīnātus -a -um, *unchanged, firm.*
indĕcor -ris or **indĕcŏris** -e, *unbecoming, shameful,*
indĕcŏro -are, *to disgrace, dishonour.*
indĕcōrus -a -um, *unbecoming; unseemly, unsightly*; *disgraceful.* Adv. **indĕcōrē.**
indēfensus -a -um, *undefended, unprotected.*
indēfessus -a -um, *unwearied, indefatigable.*
indēflētus -a -um, *unwept.*
indēiectus -a -um, *not thrown down.*
indēlēbĭlis -e, *imperishable.*
indēlībātus -a -um, *uninjured, undiminished.*
indemnātus -a -um, *uncondemned.*
indēplōrātus -a -um, *unwept, unlamented.*
indēprensus -a -um, *undiscovered.*
indēsertus -a -um, *not forsaken.*
indēstrictus -a -um, *untouched, unhurt.*
indētonsus -a -um, *unshorn.*
indēvītātus -a -um, *unavoided.*
index -dĭcis, m. *an informer; a sign, token; the forefinger; a title; a touchstone.*
Indi -orum, m. pl. *the Indians*; sing. **Indus** -i, m. *an Indian,* or *Ethiopian; an elephant-driver, mahout.* Adj. **Indus** and **Indĭcus** -a -um, *Indian*; subst. **India** -ae, f. *India.*
indīcentĕ, abl. sing., *not saying*: me indicente, *without my saying a word.*
indĭcĭum -i, n. (1) *information, evidence; leave to give evidence; a reward for giving evidence.* (2) *any mark, sign, token.*
[1]**indĭco** -are, *to make known, show, indicate*; esp. *to inform against, give evidence about; to put a price on, value.*
[2]**indīco** -dīcĕre -dixi -dictum, *to make publicly known, proclaim*; bellum, *to declare war.*
[1]**indictus** -a -um, *not said, unsaid*: indictā causā, *without a hearing.*
[2]**indictus** -a -um, partic. from [2]indico; q.v.
indĭdem, *from the same place or matter.*
indiffĕrens -entis, *indifferent; neither good nor bad; unconcerned.* Adv. **indiffĕrentĕr.**
indĭgĕna -ae, *native.*
indĭgentĭa -ae, f. *want, need; desire.*
indĭgĕo -ēre -ŭi, *to want, need, require*; also *to long for.* Hence partic. **indĭgens** -entis, *in need.*
indĭges -gĕtis, m. *native, indigenous.*
indīgestus -a -um, *disordered, confused, unarranged.*
indignābundus -a -um, *filled with indignation.*
indignātĭo -ōnis, f. *indignation; matter* for *indignation*; rhet., *the exciting of indignation.*
indignĭtās -ātis, f. *unworthiness, vileness; unworthy behaviour* or *treatment of others, indignity; indignation at unworthy treatment.*
indignor -ari, dep. *to consider unworthy, take as an indignity, be offended.* Hence partic. **indignans** -antis, *offended.*
indignus -a -um: of persons, *unworthy, not deserving* (with abl. or genit.); of things, *unworthy*; hence *disgraceful, shameful.* Adj. **indignē,** *unworthily, dishonourably; impatiently, indignantly.*
indĭgus -a -um, *needing, in want of.*
indīlĭgens -entis, *negligent*; adv. **indīlĭgentĕr.**
indīlĭgentĭa -ae, f. *carelessness, negligence.*
indĭpiscor -dĭpisci -deptus, dep., and **indĭpisco** -ĕre, *to reach, obtain; to attain, get.*
indīreptus -a -um, *unpillaged.*
indiscrētus -a -um, *unsevered, undivided; undistinguished; indistinguishable.*
indĭsertus -a -um, *not eloquent*; adv. **indĭsertē.**
indispŏsĭtus -a -um, *disorderly, confused.*
indissŏlūbĭlis -e, *indissoluble.*
indissŏlūtus -a -um, *undissolved.*
indistinctus -a -um, *not separated; indistinct, obscure; unpretentious.*
indīvĭdŭus -a -um, *indivisible, inseparable*; n. as subst. *an atom.*
indo -dĕre -dĭdi -dĭtum, *to put in* or *on*; of names, *to give, confer*; of abstr. things, *to introduce, cause, occasion.*
indŏcĭlis -e, *unteachable, untaught; ignorant, rude, artless*; of subjects, *unable to be learned.*
indoctus -a -um, *untaught, untrained, unskilled*; adv. **indoctē.**
indŏlentĭa -ae, f. *freedom from pain.*
indŏlēs -is, f. *native constitution* or *quality; nature, disposition, character, talents.*
indŏlesco -dŏlescĕre -dŏlŭi, *to be pained* or *grieved* (*at*).
indŏmĭtus -a -um, *untamed, wild.*

indormĭo -ire -īvi -itum, *to sleep on* or *over; to be negligent about*, with dat. or in.
indōtātus -a -um, *without dowry*; corpora, *without funeral honours*; ars, *unadorned, poor.*
indŭ, archaic form of in; q.v.
indŭbĭtātus -a -um, *undoubted, certain.*
indŭbĭto -are, *to feel doubt of*, with dat.
indŭbĭus -a -um, *not doubtful, certain.*
indūcĭae = indutiae; q.v.
indūco -dūcĕre -duxi -ductum. (1) *to draw over, spread over* so as to cover; also *to cover* one thing with another; *to put on* clothing or arms; *to erase* writing, and hence *to revoke, make invalid.* (2) *to lead* or *bring in, to introduce; to enter in an account-book; to lead on, induce, persuade*; with animum, or in animum, *to decide* to do, or *decide that* a thing is so.
inductĭo -ōnis, f. *leading* or *bringing in, introduction*; animi, *resolve, intention*; erroris, *misleading*; in logic, *induction.*
inductū, abl. sing. m., *by instigation.*
indulgentĭa -ae, f. *tenderness, indulgence.*
indulgĕo -dulgēre -dulsi: intransit., *to be forbearing, patient, indulgent*; fig., *to give oneself up to, indulge in*; transit. *to grant, allow, concede.*
Hence partic. **indulgens** -entis, *kind, tender, indulgent*; adv. **indulgentĕr.**
indŭo -dŭĕre -dŭi -dūtum, *to put on*, esp. of dress. Transf., *to clothe, surround, cover; to put on, assume, take up, engage in*; se, with dat. or in, *to fall into, fall on; to entangle.*
indūresco -dūrescĕre -dūrŭi, *to become hard or firm.*
indūro -are, *to make hard* or *firm.*
industrĭa -ae, f. *industry, diligence*; de (or ex) industria, *on purpose, intentionally.*
industrĭus -a -um, *diligent, painstaking, industrious*; adv. **industrĭē.**
indūtĭae -arum, f. pl. *truce, armistice, suspension of hostilities.*
indūtus -ūs, m. *a putting on, clothing.*
ĭnēbrĭo -are, *to intoxicate; to saturate.*
ĭnēdĭa -ae, f. *fasting, abstinence from food.*
ĭnēdĭtus -a -um, *not published, unknown.*
ĭnēlĕgans -antis, *not choice, tasteless*; adv. **ĭnēlĕgantĕr.**
ĭnēlūctābĭlis -e, *from which one cannot struggle free.*
ĭnēmŏrĭor -emori, dep. *to die in* or *at.*
ĭnemptus -a -um, *unbought.*
ĭnēnarrābĭlis -e, *indescribable, inexpressible*; adv. **ĭnēnarrābĭlĭtĕr.**
inēnōdābĭlis -e, *inextricable; inexplicable.*
inĕo -ire -ĭi -ĭtum: intransit., *to go* or *come in, to enter*; of time, *to begin, commence*; transit., *to go* or *come into; to enter upon, start, begin*; consilium, *to form a plan*; numerum, or rationem, *to go into figures, make a calculation.*
ĭneptĭa -ae, f. *foolish behaviour, silliness, absurdity.*
ĭneptĭo -ire, *to talk foolishly.*
ĭneptus -a -um, *unsuitable, tasteless, silly*; adv. **ĭnepté.**
ĭnermis -e and **ĭnermus** -a -um, *unarmed, defenceless, helpless.*
ĭnerrans -antis, *not wandering, fixed.*
ĭnerro -are, *to rove about in.*
ĭners -ertis, *untrained, unskilful; inactive, lazy, idle, calm; cowardly; ineffective, dull, insipid.*
ĭnertĭa -ae, f. *unskilfulness; idleness.*
ĭnērŭdītus -a -um, *illiterate, ignorant.*
ĭnesco -are, *to allure, entice, deceive.*
ĭnēvītābĭlis -e, *unavoidable.*
ĭnexcĭtus -a -um, *unmoved, quiet.*
ĭnexcūsābĭlis -e, *without excuse; inexcusable.*
ĭnexercĭtātus -a -um, *untrained, unpractised.*
ĭnexhaustus -a -um, *unexhausted.*
ĭnexōrābĭlis -e, *not to be moved by entreaty, stern, severe.*
ĭnexperrectus -a -um, *not awakened.*
ĭnexpertus -a -um: act., *inexperienced in, unacquainted with*; pass., *untried, untested, unattempted.*
ĭnexpĭābĭlis -e, *inexpiable; implacable irreconcilable.*
ĭnexplēbĭlis -e, *insatiable.*
ĭnexplētus -a -um, *unfilled, insatiate.*
ĭnexplĭcābĭlis -e, *that cannot be untied; intricate, difficult; inexplicable, beyond explanation; inconclusive, without result.*
ĭnexplōrātus -a -um, *unexplored, uninvestigated*; abl., **inexplōrātō**, *without reconnoitring.*
ĭnexpugnābĭlis -e, *unconquerable, impregnable.*
ĭnexspectātus -a -um, *unlooked-for, unexpected.*
ĭnexstinctus -a -um, *unextinguished, inextinguishable.*
ĭnexsŭpĕrābĭlis -e, *insurmountable.*
ĭnextrĭcābĭlis -e, *that cannot be disentangled* or *unravelled.*
infabrē, *unskilfully.*
infabrĭcātus -a -um, *unwrought, unfashioned.*
infăcētĭae (**infĭc-**) -arum, f. pl. *crudity.*
infăcētus and **infĭcētus** -a -um, *dull, crude, without humour* or *wit*; adv. **infăcētē** (**infic-**).
infācundus -a -um, *not eloquent.*
infāmĭa -ae, f. *dishonour, disgrace*; also *a cause of disgrace.*
infāmis -e, *disgraced, disreputable.*
infāmo -are, *to put to shame, disgrace.*
infandus -a -um, *unutterable, abominable.*
infans -fantis, *speechless, unable to speak*; esp. of children; as subst., *a little child.* Transf., *tongue-tied, embarrassed; youthful, fresh; childish, silly.*
infantĭa -ae, f. *inability to speak; slowness of speech; infancy.*
infarcĭo (**infercĭo**) -ire, *to stuff in, cram in.*
infătŭo -are *to make a fool of.*
infaustus -a -um, *unlucky, unfortunate,*

infector -ōris, m. *a dyer.*

¹infectus -a -um, *unworked, unwrought; not done, unfinished, incomplete;* reddere infectum, *to make void, revoke; impracticable, impossible.*

²infectus, partic. from inficio; q.v.

infēcundĭtās -ātis, f. *barrenness, sterility.*

infēcundus -a -um, *barren, sterile.*

infēlīcĭtās -ātis, f. *ill-luck, misfortune.*

infēlix -īcis, *unfruitful, barren;* arbor, *the gallows.* Transf., *unhappy, unlucky;* act. sense, *causing unhappiness.* Adv. **infēlīcĭtĕr,** *unluckily.*

infenso -are, *to attack, ravage.*

infensus -a -um, *hostile, aggressive;* of weapons, *aimed, ready;* in spirit, *embittered, dangerous.* Adv. **infensē.**

infĕr -a -um, **infĕri** -orum; see inferus.

infĕrĭae -arum, f. *offerings in honour of the dead.*

infercĭo; see infarcio.

infĕrĭor, infĕrĭus; see infra and inferus.

infernē, *on the lower side, beneath.*

infernus -a -um, *below, coming from below; of the lower world, infernal.* As subst., m. pl. **inferni,** *the shades;* n. pl. **infernă,** *the lower world.*

infĕro inferre intŭli inlātum, *to carry in, to put* or *place on;* templis ignes inferre, *to set fire to;* milit., signa in hostem, *to attack, charge;* bellum, with dat., *to make war on;* se inferre, and pass. inferri, *to betake oneself, to go;* of abstract things, *to bring on, introduce, occasion;* in accounts, *to enter;* in logic, *to infer, conclude.*

infĕrus -a -um, *below, lower, southern; o the lower world.* M. pl. as subst., **infĕri** -orum, *the dead, the lower world.* Compar. **infĕrĭor** -ius, *lower,* ex inferiore loco dicere *to speak from the body of the court;* of time, *later, junior;* of number, rank, etc. *lower, inferior.* Superl. (1) **infĭmus** (**infŭmus**) -a -um, lowest; ab infima ara, from the *bottom of the altar;* of rank, etc., *lowest, meanest.* Superl. (2) **īmus** -a -um, *lowest;* n. as subst., *the bottom;* of tone, *deepest, lowest;* of time, *last;* n. as subst., *the end.*

infervesco -fervescĕre -ferbŭi, *to begin to boil, grow hot.*

infesto -are, *to attack, disquiet.*

infestus -a -um; act., *aggressive, hostile, dangerous;* pass., *infested, beset, unsafe.* Adv. **infestē,** *in a hostile manner.*

infĭcētus, infĭcētē = infacetus, infacete; q.v.

infĭcĭo -fĭcĕre -fēci -fectum. (1) *to tinge, dye, stain; to steep, imbue.* (2) *to poison, taint, corrupt.*

infĭdēlis -e, *untrue, disloyal, faithless;* adv. **infĭdēlĭtĕr.**

infĭdēlĭtās -ātis, f. *disloyalty.*

infĭdus -a -um, *untrue, disloyal.*

infīgo -fīgĕre -fixi -fixum, *to fix, fasten* or *thrust in; to imprint, impress.*

infĭmus -a -um, superl. of inferus; q.v.

infindo -findĕre -fĭdi -fissum, *to cut into.*

infīnĭtās -ātis, f. *infinity, endlessness.*

infīnītĭo, -ōnis, *infinity.*

infīnītus -a -um, *infinite, unbounded, immense;* n. as subst., *infinite space;* of time, *endless, unceasing;* of number, *countless;* also *indefinite, general.* Adv. **infīnītē,** *infinitely, endlessly.*

infirmātĭo -ōnis, f. *weakening; refuting, invalidating.*

infirmĭtās -ātis, f. *weakness, feebleness; instability, fickleness.*

infirmo -are, *to weaken, impair, shake; to refute; to annul.*

infirmus -a -um, *weak, feeble; timorous.* Adv. **infirmē,** *weakly, faintly.*

infit, defective, *he* (or *she*) *begins;* esp. *begins to speak.*

infĭtĭālis -e, *negative, containing a denial.*

infĭtĭās īre, *to deny.*

infĭtĭātĭo -ōnis, f. *denying.*

infĭtĭātor -ōris, m. *a denier;* esp. *one who denies a debt* or *deposit.*

infĭtĭor -ari, *to deny;* esp. *to deny a debt, refuse to restore a deposit.*

inflammātĭo -ōnis, f. *setting fire;* animorum, *inspiration.*

inflammo -are, *to kindle, set fire to; to inflame, excite.*

inflātĭo -ōnis, f. *inflation, flatulence.*

inflātus -ūs, m. *a blowing into, blast; inspiration.*

inflecto -flectĕre -flexi -flexum, *to bend, bow, curve.* Transf., *to warp, change; to sway, affect; to modulate* the voice.

inflētus -a -um, *unwept, unlamented.*

inflexĭo -ōnis, f. *bending, swaying.*

inflexus -ūs, m. *bending, curving.*

inflīgo -flīgĕre -flixi -flictum, *to strike, knock, dash against; to inflict a blow, cause damage.*

inflo -are, *to blow into; to play on wind instruments; to give a blast; to blow out, puff out.* Transf., *to inspire; to puff up, elate.*

Hence partic., **inflātus** -a -um, *inflated, swollen; puffed up, pompous;* of style, *turgid.* Compar. adv. **inflātĭus,** *too pompously; on a grander scale.*

inflŭo -flŭĕre -fluxi -fluxum, *to flow in.* Transf., *to steal in, to stream in, rush in.*

infŏdĭo -fŏdĕre -fōdi -fossum, *to dig in, bury.*

informātĭo -ōnis, f. *conception, idea.*

informis -e, *formless, shapeless; deformed, hideous.*

informo -are, *to give form to, to shape, fashion;* mentally, *to form, dispose; to form an idea* or *conception of.*

infortūnātus -a -um, *unfortunate, miserable.*

infortūnĭum -i, n. *misfortune, ill luck: punishment.*

infrā. Prep., with acc., *below, under,* in position, size, rank; in time, *later than.* Adv., *below, underneath; in the lower world; to the south;* in rank, *lower.* Compar., **infĕrĭus,** *lower down.*

infractĭo -ōnis, f. *breaking*; animi, *dejection*.
infrăgĭlis -e, *unbreakable, strong*.
infrĕmo -frĕmĕre -frĕmŭi, *to growl*.
infrēnātus -a -um, *without bridle*, see also infreno.
infrendĕo -ēre, *to gnash with the teeth*.
infrēnis -e and **infrēnus** -a -um, *without bridle, unbridled*.
infrēno -are, *to bridle, rein in, to restrain, check*.
infrĕquens -entis, *scanty, thin, not crowded*; of places, *not full, scantily populated*; of time, *infrequent*; of persons, *not doing a thing often*.
infrĕquentĭa -ae, f. *fewness, scantiness thinness*; of places, *emptiness, loneliness*.
infringo -fringĕre -frēgi -fractum, *to break; to weaken, impair, discourage*. Hence partic. **infractus** -a -um, *broken, weakened, impaired*.
infrons -frondis, *leafless*.
infructŭōsus -a -um, *unfruitful, unproductive*.
infūcātus -a -um, *coloured*.
infŭla -ae, f. *a band, bandage*; esp. *a fillet, a headband worn by priests, suppliants*, etc.
infundo -fundĕre -fūdi -fūsum, *to pour in* or *on;* with dat., *to pour out for*, hence *to administer*; se infundere, or pass. infundi, *to pour over*.
infusco -are, *to make dark, blacken; to disfigure, stain*.
ingĕmĭno -are: transit., *to redouble, repeat*; intransit., *to be redoubled, to increase*.
ingĕmisco -gĕmiscĕre (-escĕre) -gĕmŭi, *to sigh* or *groan over*.
ingĕmo -ĕre, *to sigh, groan over* (with dat.).
ingĕnĕro -are, *to implant, generate*.
ingĕnĭōsus -a -um, *talented, able*, of things, *requiring talent* or *naturally fit, adapted*. Adv. **ingĕnĭōsē,** *cleverly*.
ingĕnĭum -i, n. *nature, natural quality, constitution, character*, esp. *mental power, ability, genius*; meton., *a man of genius*, or *a clever invention*.
ingens -entis, *monstrous, vast, enormous*.
ingenŭĭtās -ātis, f. *free birth; noble-mindedness, uprightness, frankness*.
ingĕnŭus -a -um, *native, natural, innate; free-born, of free birth, worthy of a free man, noble, honourable, frank*. Adv. **ingĕnŭē**.
ingĕro -gĕrĕre -gessi gestum, *to carry* or *put in* or *upon; to press upon, force upon*; of *abuse, to heap on a person*.
ingigno only in perf. indic. **ingĕnŭi,** *I implanted*, and perf. partic. **ingĕnĭtus** -a -um, *implanted*.
inglōrĭus -a -um, *without fame, inglorious, undistinguished*.
inglŭvĭēs -ēi, f. *crop, maw*; meton., *gluttony*.
ingrātĭīs or **ingrātīs,** *unwillingly*.
ingrātus -a -um. (1) *unpleasant, unpleasing*. (2) *unthankful, unrewarding*. Adv. **ingrātē,** *unwillingly; ungratefully*.
ingrăvesco -ĕre, *to become heavy; to become a burden*, or *become weary*; poet., *to become pregnant*.
ingrăvo -are, *to weigh down; to aggravate*.
ingrĕdĭor -grĕdī -gressus, dep. *to step in, enter, go in; to walk*. Transf., *to enter upon, begin on*; with infin., *to begin to*.
ingressĭo -ōnis, f. *an entering, going in; walking, gait, pace*. Transf., *beginning*.
ingressus -ūs, m. *going in, entering, entry*; milit., *an inroad; walking, stepping, movement*. Transf., *beginning*.
ingrŭo -ŭĕre -ŭi, *to fall upon, assail, attack*.
inguĕn -guĭnis, n. *the groin*.
ingurgĭto -are, with reflex., *to plunge oneself*, or *to glut, gorge oneself, gormandize*.
ingustātus -a -um, *untasted*.
ĭnhăbĭlis -e, *unmanageable; unfit, ill-adapted*.
ĭnhăbĭtābĭlis -e, *uninhabitable*.
ĭnhăbĭto -are, *to inhabit*.
ĭnhaerĕo -haerēre -haesi -haesum, *to stick in, cling to, cleave to*.
ĭnhaeresco -haerescĕre -haesi -haesum, *to adhere to, begin to cling to*.
ĭnhālo -are, *to breathe upon*.
ĭnhĭbĕo -ēre -ŭi -ĭtum. (1) *to hold in, check, restrain*; naut., inhibere remis, navem retro inhibere, *to back water*. (2) *to practise, use, employ*.
ĭnhĭbĭtĭo -ōnis, f. *restraining*; remigum, *backing water*.
ĭnhĭo -are, *to gape*; hence *to covet, desire, long for*.
ĭnhŏnesto -are, *to disgrace*.
ĭnhŏnestus -a -um: morally, *degraded, dishonoured*; of things, *dishonourable, shameful*; physically, *ugly, unsightly*. Adv. **ĭnhŏnestē,** *dishonourably*.
ĭnhŏnōrātus -a -um, *not honoured; unrewarded*.
ĭnhŏnōrus -a -um, *dishonoured*.
ĭnhorrĕo -ēre, *to bristle*.
ĭnhorresco -horrescĕre -horrŭi, *to begin to bristle, to bristle up; to shudder, quiver*, esp. from fright.
ĭnhospĭtālis -e, *inhospitable*.
ĭnhospĭtālĭtās -ātis, f. *want of hospitality*.
ĭnhospĭtus -a -um, *inhospitable*.
ĭnhumānĭtās -ātis, f. *cruelty, inhumanity; incivility, discourtesy; stinginess, niggardliness*.
ĭnhūmānus -a -um, *cruel, barbarous, inhuman; rude, uncivil; uncivilized*. Adv. **ĭnhūmānē,** *inhumanly;* **ĭnhūmānĭtĕr,** *uncivilly*.
ĭnhŭmātus -a -um, *unburied*.
ĭnĭbī, adv., *therein, in that place*; of time, *near at hand*.
ĭnĭcĭo -ĭcĕre -ĭēci -iectum. (1) *to throw in, put in* or *into*. Transf., *to cause, inspire, occasion*; in conversation, *to throw in*. (2) *to throw on* or *over;*

manum inicere, *to lay hands on, appropriate, take possession of.* Transf., *to impose, lay on.*
iniectĭo -ōnis, f. *laying on.*
iniectus -ūs, m. *throwing on* or *over.*
ĭnĭmīcĭtĭa -ae, f. *enmity.*
ĭnĭmīco -are, *to make hostile, set at variance.*
ĭnĭmīcus -a -um, *unfriendly, adverse, hostile*; of things, *hurtful, prejudicial*; m. or f. as subst., *enemy, foe.* Adv. **ĭnĭmīcē,** *in an unfriendly manner.*
ĭnīquĭtās -ātis, f. *unevenness; unfavourableness, difficulty; unfairness, injustice, unreasonableness.*
ĭnīquus -a -um, *uneven, unequal.* Transf., of things, *excessive, unbalanced, adverse, disadvantageous*; of contests, *ill-matched*; of terms, *unfair*; of persons, etc. *unfair, unfavourable; perverse, disgruntled*; animo iniquo ferre, *to take badly*; m. pl. as subst. *enemies.* Adv. **ĭnīque,** *unequally; unfairly, adversely.*
ĭnĭtĭo -are, *to initiate.*
ĭnĭtĭum -i, n. *a beginning*; ab initio, *from the start*; initio, *at the start.* Transf., in plur. *elements, first principles; auspices; the beginning of a reign; a secret worship, mysteries.*
ĭnĭtus -ūs, m. *an entrance; a beginning.*
iniūcundĭtās -ātis, f. *unpleasantness.*
iniūcundus -a -um, *unpleasant.* Compar. adv. **iniūcundĭus.**
iniūdĭcātus -a -um, *undecided.*
iniungo -iungĕre -iunxi -iunctum, *to join, attach, fasten to; to inflict upon, bring upon.*
iniūrātus -a -um, *unsworn.*
iniūrĭa -ae, f. *injury, injustice, wrong*; iniuriā, *wrongly.* Transf., *a possession wrongfully obtained; revenge for an affront.*
iniūrĭōsus -a -um, *doing wrong, unjust; harmful.* Adv. **iniūrĭōsē,** *wrongfully.*
iniūrĭus -a -um, *wrongful, unjust.*
iniussū, abl. sing. m. *without orders.*
iniussus -a -um, *unbidden, spontaneous.*
iniustĭtĭa -ae, f. *injustice; severity.*
iniustus -a -um, *unfair, unjust; harsh, oppressive*; n. as subst. *injustice.* Adv. **iniustē.**
inlăbĕfactus -a -um, *unshaken, firm.*
inlābor -lābi -lapsus, dep. *to glide into, fall into* or *upon.*
inlăbōro -are, *to labour at.*
inlăcessītus -a -um, *unattacked, unprovoked.*
inlacrĭmābĭlis -e, *unwept; not to be moved by tears, pitiless.*
inlacrĭmo -are, and **inlacrĭmor** -ari, dep. *to weep over, bewail.*
inlaesus -a -um, *unhurt, uninjured.*
inlaetābĭlis -e, *gloomy, cheerless.*
inlăquĕo -are, *to entrap, ensnare.*
inlaudātus -a -um, *unpraised, obscure; not to be praised, bad.*
inlautus = inlotus; q.v.
inlĕcebra -ae, f. *allurement, attraction, charm; a decoy bird.*
inlĕcebrōsus -a -um, *attractive, enticing*; adv. **inlĕcebrōsē.**
[1]**inlectus** -a -um, *unread.*
[2]**inlectus** -ūs, m. *enticement.*
[3]**inlectus** -a -um, partic. of inlicio; q.v.
inlĕpĭdus -a -um, *inelegant, rude unmannerly*; adv. **inlĕpĭdē.**
[1]**inlex** -lĭcis, c. *a decoy, lure.*
[2]**inlex** -lēgis, *lawless.*
inlībātus -a -um, *undiminished, unimpaired.*
inlībĕrālis -e, *unworthy of a free man, ungenerous, sordid, mean*; adv. **inlībĕrālĭtĕr.**
inlībĕrālĭtās -ātis, f. *stinginess, meanness.*
inlĭcĭo -lĭcĕre -lexi -lectum, *to entice, allure, decoy.*
inlĭcĭtātor -ōris, m. *a sham bidder at an auction, puffer.*
inlĭcĭtus -a -um, *not allowed, illegal.*
inlīdo -līdĕre -līsi -līsum, *to strike beat, dash against.*
inlĭgo -are, *to bind, tie, fasten, attach connect; to entangle, impede.*
inlĭmis -e, *free from mud, clean.*
inlĭno -lĭnĕre -lēvi -lĭtum, *to smear, daub; to spread* something *on* a surface or *to spread* a surface *with* something.
inlĭquĕfactus -a -um, *molten, liquefied.*
inlittĕrātus -a -um, *ignorant, illiterate.*
inlōtus (**-lautus, -lūtus**) -a -um, *unwashed, unclean.*
inlūcesco (**-isco**) -lūcescĕre -luxi, *to become light, begin to shine*; inlucescit, *it grows light, is daylight.*
inlūdo -lūdĕre -lūsi -lūsum, *to play with, sport with; to mock, laugh at, ridicule; to maltreat.*
inlūmĭno -are, *to light up, illuminate; to make clear, set off, adorn.* Adv. from perf. partic. **inlūmĭnātē,** *luminously, clearly.*
inlūsĭo -ōnis, f. *irony.*
inlustris -e, *light, bright, brilliant; clear, plain, evident; distinguished, famous.* Compar. adv. **inlustrĭus,** *more clearly, more distinctly.*
inlustro -are, *to light up, make bright; to bring to light, make clear; to make illustrious, do honour to.*
inlŭvĭēs -ēi, f. *inundation, flood; mud, dirt.*
inm-; see imm-.
innābĭlis -e, *that cannot be swum in.*
innascor -nasci -nātus, dep. *to be born in, arise in* or *upon.*
Hence partic. **innātus** -a -um, *innate, inborn.*
innăto -are, *to swim into; to swim* or *float in* or *upon.*
innecto -nectĕre -nexŭi -nexum, *to tie in, fasten, weave together*; fig., *to put together, connect, entangle, implicate.*
innītor -nīti -nixus dep., *to lean upon, support oneself by.*
inno -nare, *to swin in* or *on; to flow over; to sail over, navigate.*
innŏcens -entis, *harmless, inoffensive, blameless*; adv. **innŏcentĕr.**
innŏcentĭa -ae f. *harmlessness, innocence, integrity.*

innŏcŭus -a -um: act., *innocuous, harmless, blameless*; pass., *unhurt, unharmed.* Adv. **innŏcŭē,** *harmlessly.*
innōtesco -nōtescĕre -nōtŭi *to become known* or *noted.*
innŏvo -are, *to renew.*
innoxĭus -a -um: act., *harmless, innocent*; pass., *unhurt, unharmed.*
innŭba -ae, *unmarried, without a husband.*
innūbĭlus -a -um, *unclouded, clear.*
innūbo -nūbĕre -nupsi -nuptum, *to marry into.*
innŭmĕrābĭlis -e, *countless, innumerable*; adv. **innŭmĕrābĭlĭtĕr.**
innŭmĕrābĭlĭtās -ātis, f. an *infinite number.*
innŭmĕrālis -e, and **innŭmĕrus** -a -um, *countless, innumerable.*
innŭo -nŭĕre -nŭi -nūtum, *to give a nod to, make a sign to.*
innupta -ae, *unmarried*; as subst., *a maiden.*
innūtrĭo -ire, *to bring up in* or *among.*
ĭnoblītus -a -um, *mindful.*
ĭnobrŭtus -a, -um, *not overwhelmed.*
ĭnobservābĭlis -e, *imperceptible.*
ĭnobservantĭa -ae, f. *negligence, carelessness.*
ĭnobservātus -a -um, *unperceived.*
ĭnoccĭdŭus -a -um, *never setting.*
ĭnoffensus -a -im, *not struck, not stumbling; unhindered, unobstructed.*
ĭnoffĭcĭōsus -a -um, *undutiful, disobliging.*
ĭnŏlens -entis, *without smell.*
ĭnŏlesco -ŏlescĕre -ŏlēvi, *to grow in* or *on.*
ĭnōmĭnātus -a -um, *inauspicious, unlucky.*
ĭnŏpĭa -ae, f. *want of means, need, poverty; helplessness.*
ĭnŏpīnans -antis, *not expecting, unawares*; adv. **ĭnŏpīnantĕr.**
ĭnŏpīnātus -a -um; pass., *unexpected, unlooked for*; (ex) inopinato, *unexpectedly*; act., *not expecting.*
ĭnŏpīnus -a -um, *unexpected, unlooked for.*
ĭnops -ŏpis, *poor, helpless, in need*; of language, *weak, poor.*
ĭnōrātus -a -um, *not brought forward and heard.*
ĭnordĭnātus -a -um, *disorderly, in confusion*: n. as subst. *disorder.*
ĭnornātus -a -um, *unadorned, plain; unpraised, uncelebrated.*
inp-; see imp-.
inquam, inquis, inquit, etc.; perf., inquĭi; *say.*
inquĭēs -ētis, *unquiet, restless.*
inquĭēto -are, *to disturb.*
inquĭētus -a -um, *unquiet, restless.*
inquĭlīnus -i, m. *tenant, lodger.*
inquĭno -are, *to befoul, pollute, stain, corrupt.* Hence partic. **inquĭnātus** -a -um, *dirty, foul, polluted*; adv. **inquĭnātē.**
inquiro -quīrĕre -quīsīvi -quīsītum, *to search for; to investigate, inquire into*; legal, *to search for evidence* against anyone.
inquīsītĭo -ōnis, f. *looking for, search*; esp. *search for evidence against*; *a looking into, investigation, inquiry.*
inquīsītor -ōris, m. *an inquirer; investigator*; legal, *one who searches for evidence to support an accusation.*
inrāsus -a -um, *unshaved.*
inraucescō -raucescĕre -rausi, *to become hoarse.*
inrĕlĭgātus -a -um, *unbound.*
inrelĭgĭōsus -a -um, *irreligious, impious*; adv. **inrelĭgĭōsē.**
inrĕmĕābĭlis -e, *from which there is no return.*
inrĕpărābĭlis -e, *that cannot be restored, irrecoverable.*
inrĕpertus -a -um, *not discovered.*
inrēpo -rēpĕre -repsi -reptum, *to creep, crawl in; to insinuate oneself.*
inreprĕhensus -a -um, *unblamed, blameless.*
inrĕquĭētus -a -um, *restless, troubled.*
inrĕsectus -a -um, *uncut.*
inrĕsŏlūtus -a -um, *not loosed, not slackened.*
inrĕtĭo -ire, *to catch in a net, entangle.*
inrĕtortus -a -um, *not turned* or *twisted back.*
inrĕvĕrens -entis, *disrespectful*; adv. **inrĕvĕrentĕr.**
inrĕvĕrentĭa -ae, f. *want of respect, irreverence.*
inrĕvŏcābĭlis -e, *that cannot be called back, irrevocable; unalterable, implacable.*
inrĕvŏcātus -a -um, *not called back.*
inrīdĕo -rīdēre -rīsi -rīsum, *to laugh at, mock, ridicule.*
inrīdĭcŭlē, *without wit* or *humour.*
inrīdĭcŭlo, predicative dat., *for a laughing-stock.*
inrĭgātĭo -ōnis, f. *watering, irrigation.*
inrĭgo -are, *to conduct* any liquid, *to diffuse; to water, irrigate, inundate, flood over.*
inrĭgŭus -a -um: act., *watering, irrigating; refreshing*; pass., *watered, soaked.*
inrīsĭo -ōnis, f. *laughing at, mocking, derision.*
inrīsor -ōris, m. *a laugher, mocker, derider.*
inrīsus -ūs, m. *laughter, mockery, derision*; dat. inrisui, *for a laughing-stock.*
inrītābĭlis -e, *irritable, easily roused.*
inrītāmen -ĭnis, n. *incitement, inducement.*
inrītāmentum -i, m. *incitement, incentive.*
inrītātĭo -ōnis, f. *stirring up, provoking, incitement.*
inrīto -are, *to stir up, stimulate, incite, excite.*
inrĭtus -a -um, *void, invalid; vain, ineffectual, useless.*
inrŏgātĭo -ōnis, f. *the imposing* of fine or penalty.
inrŏgo -are, *to propose a measure* against anyone; *to inflict, impose.*
inrōro -ae, *to moisten (with dew)*; *to trickle down upon.*
inrumpo -rumpĕre -rūpi -ruptum, *to break in, burst in, rush in.*

inrŭo -rŭĕre -rŭi: transit., *to fling in*; intransit., *to rush in.*
inruptĭo -ōnis, f. *bursting in irruption.*
inruptus -a -um, *unbroken, unsevered.*
insălūbris -e, *unhealthy.*
insălūtātus -a -um, *ungreeted*
insānābĭlis -e, *incurable.*
insānĭa -ae, f. *madness, frenzy, senseless excess, extravagance; poetical rapture* or *inspiration.*
insānĭo -ire, *to be made, rage, rave; to be inspired.*
insānĭtās -ātis, f. *disease, unsoundness.*
insānus -a -um, *of unsound mind, mad, raving, senseless*; of poets, *inspired*; of things, *raging stormy.* Adv. **insānē,** *madly.*
insătĭābĭlis -e: pass., *insatiable*: act., *that does not satiate, uncloying.* Adv. **insătĭābĭlĭtĕr,** *insatiably.*
insătŭrābĭlis -e, *insatiable*; adv. **insătŭrābĭlĭtĕr.**
inscendo -scendĕre -scendi -scensum, *to climb on, ascend, mount.*
inscĭens -entis, *not knowing fact, unaware*; in gen., *ignorant.* Adv. **inscĭentĕr.**
inscĭentĭa -ae f. *ignorance, inexperience.*
inscītĭa -ae, f. *inexperience, want of skill, ignorance.*
inscītus -a -um, *ignorant unskilful, stupid*; adv. **inscītē.**
inscĭus -a -um, *ignorant, not knowing.*
inscrībo -scrībĕre -scripsi -scriptum, *to write in* or *on, inscribe; to mark, impress; to entitle, mark as* something; *to ascribe, mark as belonging to.*
inscriptĭo -ōnis, f. *writing in* or *upon.*
[1]**inscriptus** -a -um, *unwritten.*
[2]**inscriptus** -a -um, partic. from inscribo; q.v.
insculpo -sculpĕre -sculpsi -sculptum, *to cut* or *carve in, engrave.* Transf., *to impress.*
insĕco -sĕcare -sĕcŭi -sectum, *to cut into, notch.*
insectātĭo -ōnis, f. *close following, hot pursuit.* Transf., *abuse.*
insectātor -oris, m. *pursuer, persecutor.*
insecto -are and **insector** -ari, dep. *to follow closely, pursue, harry; to harry with abuse, rail at, reproach.*
insēdābĭlĭtĕr, *incessantly.*
insĕnesco -sĕnescĕre -sĕnŭi, *to grow old at* or *among.*
insensĭlis -e, *without sensation.*
insĕpultus -a -um, *unburied.*
insĕquor -sĕqui -sĕcūtus, dep., *to follow after, follow on*; in time, *to succeed; to pursue a subject; to pursue a person, to censure, reproach*; in gen., *to attack, assail.*
[1]**insĕro** -sĕrĕre -sēvi -sĭtum, *to graft in, implant.* Hence partic. **insĭtus** -a -um, *implanted, innate; incorporated.*
[2]**insĕro** -sĕrĕre -sĕrŭi -sertum, *to let in, introduce, insert*; in gen., *to connect, put in* or *among.*
inserto -are, *to insert, put into.*
inservĭo -ire, *to be a slave, to serve; to be devoted to.*
insībĭlo -are. *to hiss, whistle in.*
insĭdĕo -ēre, *to sit in* or *on; to dwell, remain.*
insĭdĭae -arum, f. pl. *an ambush; a trap, plot.*
insĭdĭātor -oris, m. *a man in ambush; a spy, waylayer.*
insĭdĭor -ari, dep., *to lie in ambush, lie in wait; to plot against, watch for.*
insĭdĭōsus -a -um, *deceitful treacherous*; adv. **insĭdĭōsē.**
insīdo -sīdĕre -sēdi -sessum, *to sit, settle, perch upon*; milit., *to occupy, beset*; of ideas, etc., *to sink in.*
insignĕ -is, n. *a distinguishing mark, token; badge, decoration, medal*; pl. as abstr., *distinctions, beauties.*
insignĭo -ire, *to mark, distinguish.*
Hence partic. **insignītus** -a -um, *marked; conspicuous, clear*; adv. **insignītē,** *remarkably.*
insignis -e, *distinguished, remarkable, extraordinary*; adv. **insignĭtĕr.**
insĭlĭa n. pl. *the treadles* of a loom, or perhaps *leash-rods.*
insĭlĭo -sĭlire -sĭlŭi, *to leap, spring, jump in* or *on.*
insĭmŭlātĭo -ōnis, f. *accusation, charge.*
insĭmŭlo -are, *to charge, accuse,* esp. falsely.
insincērus -a -um, *tainted.*
insĭnŭātĭo -ōnis, f., rhet. t. t., *gaining the favour of the audience.*
insĭnŭo -are, *to introduce by turning, to insinuate*; with (and occasionally without) reflex., *to penetrate, work one's way in.*
insĭpĭens -entis, *foolish*; adv. **insipienter.**
insĭpĭentĭa -ae, f. *foolishness.*
insisto -sistĕre -stĭti. (1) *to set foot on, tread on; to enter on* a journey, road, etc., *to set about* a task; with dat., *to follow hard upon, pursue.* (2) *to stand still in* or *on; to halt, stop, pause; to hesitate, doubt; to dwell upon* a subject; *to persist in* a course.
insĭtĭo -ōnis, f. *grafting.*
insĭtīvus -a -um, *grafted; spurious.*
insĭtor -oris, m. *a grafter.*
insĭtus -a -um, partic. from insero; q.v.
insŏcĭābĭlis -e, *unable to combine.*
insōlābĭlĭtĕr, *inconsolably.*
insŏlens -entis, *contrary to custom.* Hence (1) *unaccustomed, unused.* (2) *unusual, excessive, extravagant; arrogant, insolent.* Adv. **insŏlentĕr,** *unusually, contrary to custom; excessively, extravagantly; haughtily, arrogantly.*
insŏlentĭa -ae, f. (1) *inexperience.* (2) *unusual character, novelty, extravagance, excess; pride, arrogance.*
insŏlesco -escĕre, *to become haughty* or *insolent.*
insŏlĭdus -a -um, *soft, tender.*
insŏlĭtus -a -um. (1) *unaccustomed.* (2) *unusual, strange, uncommon.*
insomnĭa -ae, f. *sleeplessness, loss of sleep.*
insomnis -e, *sleepless.*
insomnĭum -i, n. *a bad dream.*

insŏno -sŏnare -sŏnŭi, *to make a noise in* or *with; to sound, resound.*
insons -sontis, *innocent, guiltless, harmless.*
insōpītus -a -um, *unsleeping, watchful.*
inspectĭo -ōnis, f. *scrutiny, consideration.*
inspecto -are, *to look at, observe.*
inspērans -antis, *not hoping, not expecting.*
inspērātus -a -um, *unhoped-for, unexpected.*
inspergo spergĕre -spersi -spersum, *to sprinkle in* or *on.*
inspĭcĭo -spĭcĕre -spexi -spectum. (1) *to look into, see into.* (2) *to view, examine, inspect; to consider.*
inspīco -are, *to sharpen to a point.*
inspīro -are, *to breathe upon, blow upon, inspire.*
inspŏlĭātus -a -um, *not plundered.*
instăbĭlis -e. (1) *unstable, unsteady, inconstant.* (2) *not supporting, insecure.*
instans -antis, and **instantĕr**; from insto; q.v.
instantĭa -ae, f. *presence; perseverance.*
instăr, n. (only nom. and acc. sing.), *an image, likeness;* usually with genit., in the sense *corresponding to, like.*
instaurātĭo -ōnis, f. *repetition, renewal.*
instaurātīvus -a -um, *renewed, repeated.*
instauro -are. (1) *to set up, establish.* (2) *to renew, restore;* hence *to repay, requite.*
insterno -sternĕre -strāvi -strātum, *to spread over, cover over;* equus instratus, *saddled.*
instīgātor -oris, m. and **instīgātrix** -tricis, f. *an instigator.*
instīgo -are, *to goad, incite, stimulate.*
instillo -are, *to drop in, pour in by drops, instil.*
instĭmŭlātor -ōris m. *an instigator*
instĭmŭlo -are, *to incite.*
instinctor -ōris, m. *an instigator.*
instinctū, abl. sing. m. *by instigation.*
instinctus -a -um, *instigated, incited, impelled.*
instĭta -ae, f. *border* or *flounce on a robe.*
instĭtĭo -ōnis, f. *standing still.*
instĭtor -ōris, m. *a hawker, pedlar.*
instĭtŭo -ŭĕre -ŭi -ūtum, *to put in place, set in order; to set up, make ready, build, construct;* abstr. *to establish, introduce, arrange; to settle on* a course, *to undertake, resolve, determine; to appoint* a person; *to instruct educate, train.*
instĭtūtĭo -ōnis, f. *arrangement; regular method; education, instruction.*
instĭtūtum -i, n. *an undertaking, purpose; an arrangement, institution, plan; an instruction, precept.*
insto -stare -stĭti. (1) *to stand in* or *on.* (2) *to be close to, follow closely, pursue eagerly; to devote oneself, persist, persevere; to insist, ask pressingly;* of time or events, *to approach, impend.*
Hence partic. **instans** -antis, *present; pressing, urgent;* adv. **instanter,** *urgently.*
instrēnŭus -a -um, *inactive, lazy.*
instrĕpo -ere -ŭi -ĭtum, *to rattle, clatter, creak.*
instructĭo -ōnis, f. *drawing up in order.*
instructor -ōris, m. *a preparer.*
instructus -ūs, m. *provision; matter* (in a speech).
instrūmentum -i, n. *equipment, tool, implement; dress; store, stock: any means to an end.*
instrŭo -strŭĕre -struxi -structum, *to build in* or *into; to set up, construct; furnish,* hence *to train* a person; *to prepare, provide;* milit., *to draw up in order of battle.*
Hence partic. **instructus** -a -um, *equipped, supplied;* of persons, *trained, instructed.*
insuāvis -e, *unpleasant, disagreeable.*
Insubres -ium, *the Insubrians, a people in Cisalpine Gaul;* as adj. **Insŭbĕr** -bris -bre, *Insubrian.*
insūdo -are, *to sweat in* or *at.*
insuēfactus -a -um, *accustomed to.*
insuesco -suescĕre -suēvi -suētum; intransit., *to become used to;* transit., *to accustom, habituate anyone to.*
[1]**insuētus** -a -um: of persons, *unaccustomed, unused to;* of things, *unaccustomed, unusual.*
[2]**insuētus** -a -um, partic. from insuesco; q.v.
insŭla -ae, f. *an island.* Transf., *a detached house* or *block of flats.*
insŭlānus -i, m. *an islander.*
insulsĭtās -ātis, f. *tastelessness, absurdity.*
insulsus -a -um, *unsalted, insipid; tasteless, foolish;* adv. **insulsē.**
insulto -are, *to leap, prance in* or *on; to triumph over, insult.*
insum -esse -fŭi, *to be in* or *on; to be contained in, belong to.*
insūmo -sūmĕre -sumpsi -sumptum, *to take for a purpose, to expend.*
insŭo -sŭĕre -sutum, *to sew in, sew up.*
insŭpĕr: adv. *above, overhead; over and above, in addition, besides;* prep., with abl., *besides.*
insŭpĕrābĭlis -e, *insurmountable, impassable; unconquerable.*
insurgo -surgĕre -surrexi -surrectum, *to rise up, raise oneself up; to increase in power* or *force;* with dat., *to rise up against.*
insŭsurro -are, *to whisper, whisper in the ear.*
intābesco -tābescĕre -tābŭi, *to melt* or *wither away gradually.*
intactĭlis -e, *that cannot be touched.*
[1]**intactus** -a -um, *untouched; untried unspoilt, unhurt, virgin.*
[2]**intactus** -ūs, m. *intangibility.*
intāmĭnātus -a -um, *unstained.*
[1]**intectus** -a -um, *uncovered, unclothed; open, frank.*
[2]**intectus** -a -um, partic. from intego; q.v.
intĕgellus -a -um, *more or less pure, undamaged.*
intĕger -gra -grum. (1) *complete,*

whole, entire, intact; fresh, sound, unexhausted; in integrum restituere, *to restore to its former condition.* (2) in quality, *unspoilt, pure, fresh*; morally, *innocent, uncorrupted*: in thought or feeling, *balanced, unbiased, impartial*; of matters for discussion or action, *unprejudiced, undecided*; integrum est mihi, *I am at liberty.* (3) *renewed, begun afresh.* Hence adv. **integrē** *wholly; honestly, uprightly, impartially*; of style, *purely, correctly.*

intĕgo -tĕgĕre -texi -tectum, *to cover, protect.*

integrasco -ĕre, *to break out afresh.*

integrātĭo -ōnis, f. *renewing.*

integrĭtās -ātis, f. *unimpaired condition, soundness, health; uprightness, integrity*; of style, *purity, correctness.*

integro -are, *to make whole, heal, refresh; to renew, begin afresh.*

intĕgŭmentum -i, n. *a covering, cloak, disguise.*

intellectus -ūs, m. *understanding, comprehension.*

intellĕgentĭa -ae, f. *perception; understanding, knowledge, taste; capacity for understanding, intelligence.*

intellĕgo -lĕgĕre -lexi -lectum, *to discern, perceive; to understand, grasp; to understand* character, *judge, appreciate; to understand by* a term, *take as its meaning.*

Hence partic. **intellĕgens** -entis, *intelligent, understanding; having good sense* or *taste.* Adv. **intellĕgentĕr.**

intĕmĕrātus -a -um, *unspotted, undefiled.*

intempĕrans -antis, *extravagant, unrestrained, intemperate*; adv. **intempĕrantĕr.**

intempĕrantĭa -ae, f. *want of restraint, extravagance, excess.*

intempĕrātus -a -um, *intemperate, immoderate*; adv. **intempĕrātē.**

intempĕrĭēs -ēi, f. *wildness, lack of restraint, excess.*

intempestīvus -a -um, *unseasonable, untimely; immoderate.* Adv. **intempestīvē,** *unseasonably.*

intempestus -a -um, *unwholesome, unhealthy*: intempesta nox, *the dead of night.*

intemptātus -a -um, *untried.*

intendo -tendĕre -tendi -tentum. (1) *to stretch, strain*; abstr., *to maintain, try to prove.* (2) *to extend, aim, direct*; esp. *to direct one's course; to apply the mind, direct the thoughts; to intend, aim at.*

Hence partic. **intentus** -a -um, *stretched, tense, taut;* of thought or feeling, *anxious, intent*; of speech, *earnest*; in gen, *thorough, strict, rigorous.* Adv. **intentē,** *earnestly, attentively.*

[1]**intentātus** -a -um; = intemptatus; q.v.

[2]**intentatus** -a -um, partic., from intento; q.v.

intentĭo -ōnis, f. *stretching, straining*; of the mind, *effort, exertion, attention; an attack, accusation.*

intento -are, *to stretch towards* or *against*, esp. *threateningly.*

[1]**intentus** -ūs, m. *stretching out.*

[2]**intentus** -a -um, partic. from intendo; q.v.

intĕpesco -tĕpescĕre -tĕpui, *to become lukewarm.*

inter, prep. with acc. *between, among, amid; during, in the course of* a period; with pronouns, inter se, inter nos, etc., *between one another, mutually.*

intĕrāmenta -orum, n. pl. *woodwork of a ship.*

intĕrāresco -ĕre, *to become dry, decay.*

intercălāris -e and **intercălārĭus** -a -um, *inserted, intercalary.*

intercălo -are, *to insert*; esp. *to intercalate a day* or *month in the calendar.*

intercăpēdo -īnis, f. *interval, pause, respite.*

intercēdo -cēdĕre -cessi -cessum, *to go between, come between, intervene*; legal, *to interpose, stand surety; to step between, withstand, protest against.*

interceptĭo -ōnis, f. *taking away.*

interceptor -ōris, m. *one who takes away, an embezzler.*

intercessĭo -ōnis, f. legal, *becoming surety, going bail*; polit., *an exercise by the tribunes of their veto.*

intercessor -ōris, m. legal, *surety, bail*; polit., *one who opposes, an obstructor.*

[1]**intercīdo** -cīdĕre -cīdi -cīsum, *to cut asunder, to demolish,* Hence adv. **intercisē,** *piecemeal.*

[2]**intercĭdo** -cĭdĕre -cĭdi. (1) *to fall between, intervene.* (2) *to drop out be lost, be forgotten, perish.*

intercĭno -ere, *to sing between.*

intercĭpĭo -cĭpĕre -cēpi -ceptum, *to take by the way, intercept; to embezzle, appropriate;* through death, *to cut off, carry off prematurely*; of roads, *to block.*

interclūdo -clūdĕre -clūsi -clūsum, *to shut off, block, hinder; to enclose, shut in.*

interclūsĭo -ōnis, f. *stopping* or *blocking up; parenthesis.*

intercŏlumnĭum -i, n. *the space between two columns.*

intercurro -currĕre -cŭcurri -cursum, *to run between, to run through; to intercede; to be among, mingle with; to hasten in the meanwhile.*

intercurso -are, *to run between, run among.*

intercursū, abl. sing. m. *by running between, by the interposition.*

intercŭs -cŭtis, *under the skin*: aqua, *the dropsy.*

interdīco -dīcĕre -dixi -dictum. (1) *to stop by interposition, forbid, prohibit*; interdicĕre aqua et igni, with dat., *to outlaw.* (2) *to make an injunction to order.*

interdictĭo -ōnis, f. *forbidding, prohibition*: aquae et ignis, *outlawing.*

interdictum -i, n. *a prohibition; a praetor's interdict* or *provisional order.*

interdĭū (interdĭus), *in the daytime, by day.*
interdo -dăre -dătum, *to put between* or *among, distribute.*
interductus -ū, m. *interpunctuation.*
interdum, *sometimes, now and then.*
interdŭo = interdo; q.v.
intĕrĕā, *meanwhile*; sometimes *nevertheless, notwithstanding.*
intĕremptor -ōris, m. *a murderer.*
intĕrĕo -īre -ĭi -ĭtum, *to be lost, to perish.*
intĕrĕquĭto -are, *to ride between.*
interfātĭo -onis, f. *speaking between, interruption.*
interfātur -fāri -fātus, dep. forms, *to speak between, interrupt.*
interfectĭo -ōnis, f. *slaying.*
interfector -ōris, m. *murderer.*
interfectrix -trīcis, f. *murderess.*
interfĭcĭo -fĭcĕre -fēci -fectum, *to do away with, destroy, put an end to, kill.*
interfĭo -fĭĕri, *to perish.*
interflŭo -flŭĕre -fluxi -fluxum, *to flow between.*
interfŏdĭo -fŏdĕre -fōdi -fossum, *to dig into, pierce.*
interfor; see interfatur.
interfŭgĭo -fŭgĕre, *to flee between.*
interfulgens -entis, *shining* or *gleaming among.*
interfūsus -a -um, *poured between, flowing between*; maculis interfusa, *stained here and there.*
interiăcĕo -ēre, *to lie between* or *among.*
interiăcĭo = intericio; q.v.
intĕrĭbi, *meanwhile.*
interĭcĭo -icere -ieci -iectum, *to throw, cast, put, among* or *between*; anno interiecto, *after an interval of a year.*
interiectĭo -ōnis, f. *interjection* or *parenthesis.*
interiectus -ūs, m. *throwing between*; of time, *an interval.*
intĕrim, *meanwhile;* sometimes *however.*
intĕrĭmo -ĭmĕre -ēmi -emptum, *to take away, destroy, make an end of; to put out of the way, kill.*
intĕrĭor -ĭus, genit. -ōris, *inner, interior; remote from the sea, inland, nearer*; in racing, *on the inside.* Transf., *more secret, more intimate.* Superl. **intĭmus** -a -um; q.v. Adv. **interĭus,** *more inwardly; short, not far enough.*
intĕrĭtĭo -ōnis, f. *destruction, ruin.*
intĕrĭtus -ūs, m. *destruction, ruin.*
interiungo -iungĕre -iunxi -iunctum, *to join together, connect*; also *to unyoke.*
intĕrĭus; see interior.
interlābor -lābi -lapsus, dep. *to glide, flow between.*
interlĕgo -ĕre, *to pluck here and there.*
interlĭno -lĭnĕre -lēvi -lĭtum, *to daub between; to erase, falsify by erasure.*
interlŏquor -lŏqui -iŏcūtus, dep. *to interrupt a person speaking.*
interlūcĕo -lūcēre -luxi, *to shine* or *gleam between; to be transparent, let light through gaps.*
interlunĭum -i, n. *change of moon, time of new moon.*
interlŭo -lŭĕre, *to wash between.*
intermenstrŭus -a -um, *between two months*; n. as subst. *the time of the new moon.*
[1]**intermĭnātus** -a -um, *unbounded, boundless.*
[2]**intermĭnātus** -a -um, partic. from interminor; q.v.
intermĭnor -ari, dep. *to threaten, forbid with threats*; perf. partic. in pass. sense, *forbidden with threats.*
intermiscĕo -miscēre, -miscŭi -mixtum, *to mix with, intermix.*
intermissĭo -ōnis, f. *leaving off, interruption.*
intermitto -mittĕre -mīsi -missum: transit., *to leave a space between, leave free*; in space, *to separate, break off*; in time, *to let pass*; in gen., *to discontinue, interrupt*; vento intermisso, *the wind having dropped*; intransit., *to cease, leave off.*
intermŏrĭor -mŏri -mortuus, dep. *to die off, perish suddenly*; partic. **intermortŭus** -a -um, *swooning, half-dead*; fig., *lifeless.*
intermundĭa -ōrum, n. pl. *spaces between the worlds.*
intermūrālis -e, *between walls.*
internascor -nasci -natus, dep. *to grow between* or *among.*
internĕcĭo -ōnis, f. *extermination, massacre.*
internĕcīvus (-nĕcīnus) -a -um, *murderous, deadly.*
internĕco -are, *to exterminate.*
internecto -ĕre, *to bind together, bind up.*
internōdĭum -i, n. *the space between two knots* or *joints.*
internosco -noscĕre -nōvi -nōtum, *to distinguish between.*
internuntĭa -ae, f. *a female messenger* or *go-between.*
internuntĭo -are, *to send messengers between parties.*
internuntĭus -i, m. *a messenger, mediator, go-between.*
internus -a, -im., *inward, internal; domestic, civil.*
interpellātĭo -ōnis, f. *interruption.*
interpellātor -ōris, m. *interrupter, disturber.*
interpello -are, *to interrupt, disturb, impede, obstruct.*
interpŏlo -are, *to furbish, vamp up; to falsify.*
interpōno -pōnĕre -pŏsŭi -pŏsĭtum, *to place between* or *among, interpose*; spatio interposito, *after an interval*; fidem, *to pledge one's word*; rarely, *to falsify*; with reflex., *to engage in, interfere with.*
interpŏsĭtĭo -ōnis, f. *putting in, insertion, introduction*; rhet. *parenthesis.*
interpŏsĭtū, abl. sing. m. *by putting between, by interposition.*
interprĕs -prĕtis, c. (1) *a negotiator, mediator, messenger.* (2) *an expounder, explainer; prophet, prophetess; interpreter; translator.*
interprĕtātĭo -ōnis, f., *explanation, interpretation; translation.* Transf., *meaning, signification.*

interprĕtor -ari, dep. (1) *to put an interpretation upon, understand in a certain sense.* (2) *to translate.*
interpunctĭo -ōnis, f. *punctuation.*
interpungo -pungĕre -punxi -punctum, *to punctuate*; partic. **interpunctus** -a -um, *well-divided.*
interquĭesco -quĭescĕre -quĭēvi -quĭētum, *to pause between.*
interregnum -i, n. *a period between two reigns, interregnum.*
interrex -rēgis m. *a regent, temporary king* or *chief magistrate.*
interrītus -a -um, *undaunted.*
interrŏgātĭo -ōnis, f. *questioning, interrogation*: esp. legal, *examination of witnesses*; in logic, *an argument, syllogism*; gram., *interrogation.*
interrŏgo -are, *to ask, question, interrogate*; esp. *to examine* a witness, or *to accuse, bring an action against.*
interrumpo -rumpĕre -rūpi -ruptum, *to break in the middle, sever, interrupt, disturb.* Adv. from partic. **interruptē,** *interruptedly, disconnectedly.*
intersaepĭo -saepire -saepsi -saeptum, *to enclose, hem in, block up.*
interscindo -scindĕre -scĭdi -scissum, *to cut open, cut off, tear apart.*
interscribo -ĕre, *to write between.*
[1]**intersĕro** -sĕrĕre -sēvi -sĭtum, *to sow* or *plant between.*
[2]**intersĕro** -sĕrĕre -sĕrŭi, *to put* or *place between.*
interspīrātĭo -ōnis, f. *breathing between, taking breath.*
interstinctus -a -um, *spotted, speckled.*
interstinguo -ĕre, *to extinguish.*
interstringo -ĕre, *to squeeze tight.*
intersum -esse -fŭi, *to be between; to be among, be present at, take part in* (with dat.); in time, *to intervene*; abstr., *to be between as a difference*; rarely *to differ, be different.* Hence impers. **intĕrest,** *it makes a difference, it concerns*; magni (or multum) meā interest, *it makes a great difference to me.*
intertextus -a -um, *interwoven.*
intertrīmentum -i, n. *loss, damage.*
interturbātĭo -ōnis, f. *disturbance, disquiet.*
intervallum -i, n. *distance between, interval* (of time or space); *difference, unlikeness.*
intervĕnĭo -vĕnire -vēni -ventum, *to come between, intervene; to interrupt* (with dat.) *to delay* (with acc.).
interventor -ōris, m. *an interrupting visitor.*
interventus -ūs, m. *intervention, interference.*
interverto (**-vorto**) -vertĕre -verti -versum, *to intercept; to embezzle, purloin; to cheat, rob.*
intervīso -vīsĕre -vīsi -visum, *to look in at, visit from time to time.*
intestābĭlis -e, *disqualified, dishonoured, infamous.*
intestātus -a -um, *having made no will, intestate*; n. abl. as adv. intestato, *intestate.*
intestīnus -a -um, *inward, internal*; n. as subst., sing. and plur. *the intestines.*
intexo -texĕre -texŭi -textum, *to weave in, plait in, interweave; to weave around, wind around.*
intĭbum -i, n. *endive, succory.*
intĭmus (**intŭmus**) -a -um, superl. (compar. interior; q.v.), *innermost, inmost; most profound, most secret, intimate*; m. as subst., *an intimate friend.* Adv. **intĭmē.** *intimately; cordially, strongly.*
intingo (**-tinguo**) -tingĕre -tinxi -tinctum, *to dip in.*
intŏlĕrābĭlis -e, *unbearable, intolerable.*
intŏlĕrandus -a -um, *unbearable, unendurable.*
intŏlĕrans -antis: act. *impatient, unable to bear*; pass., *unbearable, intolerable.* Adv. **intŏlĕrantĕr,** *immoderately, impatiently.*
intŏlĕrantĭa -ae, f. *insufferable conduct, insolence.*
intŏno -tŏnare -tŏnŭi, *to thunder, thunder forth* (esp. of speakers).
intonsus -a -um, *unshorn, with long hair* or *beard*; hence of persons *rude, rough*; of country, *wooded, not cleared.*
intorquĕo -torquēre -torsi -tortum, *to twist* or *turn round*; of weapons, *to hurl*; partic. **intortus** -a -um, *twisted, tangled.*
intrā: adv. *inside*; prep., with acc. *inside, within, less than, short of.*
intrābĭlis -e, *that can be entered, accessible.*
intractābĭlis -e, *unmanageable, intractable.*
intractātus -a -um, *not handled; unattempted.*
intrĕmisco -trĕmiscĕre -trĕmŭi, *to begin to tremble.*
intrĕmo -ere, *to tremble, quake.*
intrĕpĭdus -a -um, *unconfused, calm*; adv. **intrĕpĭdē,** *calmly.*
intrīco -are, *to confuse, entangle.*
intrinsĕcus, *inside, inwardly, inwards.*
[1]**intrītus** -a -um, *not worn away, unexhausted.*
[2]**intrītus** -a -um, partic. from intero; q.v.
[1]**intrō,** *inwards, within.*
[2]**intro** -are, *to go into, enter.*
intrōdūco -dūcĕre -duxi -ductum, *to introduce, bring in, bring forward, present, suggest.*
intrōductĭo -onis, f. *bringing in, introduction.*
intrŏĕo -ire -ĭi -ĭtum, *to go into, enter.*
intrōfĕro -ferre -tŭli -lātum, *to carry in.*
intrōgrĕdĭor -grĕdi -gressus, dep. *to enter.*
intrŏĭtus -ūs, m. *an entrance; means of entrance; passage*; in gen., *beginning, introduction.*
intrōmitto -mittĕre -mīsi -missum, *to send in, allow to enter.*
introrsŭs (**-orsum**), *inwards, inwardly internally.*
intrōrumpo -rumpĕre -rūpi -ruptum, *to break into, enter by force.*
introspĭcĭo -spĭcĕre -spexi -spectum,

to look into, look inside, observe, examine.
intŭbum -i, n., see intibum.
intŭĕor -tŭēri -tŭĭtus, dep. *to look at attentively, gaze at; to consider, contemplate, look to.*
intŭmesco -tŭmescĕre -tŭmŭi, *to swell, swell up; to increase; to swell with anger.*
intŭmŭlātus -a -um, *unburied.*
intŭor -i, dep. = intueor; q.v.
inturbĭdus -a -um, *undisturbed, quiet.*
intŭs, adv. *within, inside; to* or *from the inside; inwardly.*
intūtus -a -um. (1) *unprotected.* (2) *unsafe, dangerous.*
ĭnŭla -ae, f. *the plant elecampane.*
ĭnultus -a -um. (1) *unavenged.* (2) *unpunished.*
ĭnumbro -are, *to shade, overshadow.*
ĭnundātĭo -ōnis, f. *inundation, flood.*
ĭnundo -are: transit., *to overflow, inundate, stream over*; intransit., *to overflow with.*
ĭnungo -ungĕre -unxi -unctum, *to anoint.*
ĭnurbānus -a -um, *rude, unpolished*; adv. **ĭnurbānē.**
ĭnurgĕo -urgēre -ursi, *to push, thrust against.*
ĭnūro -ūrĕre -ussi -ustum, *to burn in* or *on, brand, imprint; to inflict; to crimp, curl, adorn.*
ĭnūsĭtātus -a -um, *unusual, strange, uncommon*; adv. **ĭnūsĭtātē.**
ĭnūtĭlis -e, *useless, unserviceable, unprofitable; injurious, harmful.* Adv. **ĭnūtĭlĭtĕr.**
ĭnūtĭlĭtās -ātis, f. *uselessness, unprofitableness; harmfulness.*
invādo -vādĕre -vāsi -vāsum. (1) *to go in, enter, get in; to undertake.* (2) *to attack, fall upon, assail, usurp, seize.*
invălesco -vălescĕre -vălŭi, *to gather strength, become strong.*
invălĭdus -a -um, *weak, powerless.*
invectĭo -ōnis, f. (1) *importation.* (2) *invective.*
invĕho -vĕhĕre -vexi -vectum, *to carry in, introduce*; pass., or with reflex., *to drive, ride* or *travel*, esp. *to advance against, attack*; of verbal attack, *to inveigh.*
invĕnĭo -vĕnire -vēni -ventum, *to come upon, find, meet with, discover; to invent, devise; to procure, get, earn*; pass., or with reflex., *to show oneself.*
Hence partic., **inventus** -a -um, *discovered*; n. as subst. *an invention, discovery.*
inventĭo -ōnis, f. *inventing, invention; the inventive faculty.*
inventor -ōris, m. and **inventrix** -trīcis, f. *inventor.*
invĕnustus -a -um, *not charming, unattractive; unhappy in love.*
invĕrēcundus -a -um, *shameless, impudent.*
invergo -ĕre, *to tip* or *pour upon.*
inversĭo -ōnis, f. *irony; transposition; allegory.*
inverto -vertĕre -verti -versum *to turn over, turn about; to transpose, alter, pervert.* Hence partic. **inversus** -a -um, *overturned, upside down.*
invespĕrascit -ĕre, impers. *it grows dark.*
investīgātĭo -ōnis, f. *inquiry, investigation.*
investīgātor -ōris, m. *inquirer, investigator.*
investīgo -are, *to search out, track out.*
invĕtĕrasco -ascĕre -avi, *to become old; to become obsolete; to become established, fixed, rooted.*
invĕtĕrātĭo -ōnis, f. *inveterateness, permanence.*
invĕtĕrātus -a -um, *of long standing, established.*
invĭcem, *in turn, alternately; mutually, reciprocally.*
invictus -a -um, *unconquered, unsubdued; unconquerable, invincible.*
invĭdentĭa -ae, f. *envying, envy.*
invĭdĕo -vĭdēre -vīdi -vīsum, *to envy, grudge, be envious of.*
Hence partic. **invīsus** -a -um: pass., *hated*; act., *hostile.*
invĭdĭa -ae, f.: act., *envy, jealously, ill-will*; pass., *odium, unpopularity.* Transf., *a source of ill-will.*
invĭdĭōsus -a -um, *envious; causing envy, envied; hateful.* Adv. **invĭdĭōsē,** *jealously, bitterly.*
invĭdus -a -um, *envious, grudging.*
invĭgĭlo -are, *to watch over* (with dat.).
invĭŏlābĭlis -e, *unassailable.*
invĭŏlātus -a -um, *uninjured, unhurt; inviolable.* Adv. **invĭŏlātē,** *inviolately.*
invīsĭtātus -a -um, *not seen; unusual, strange.*
invīso -vīsĕre -vīsi -vīsum, *to go to see, visit; to inspect, look at.*
[1]**invīsus** -a -um, *unseen, secret.*
[2]**invīsus** -a -um, partic. from invideo; q.v.
invītāmentum -i, n. *invitation, attraction.*
invītātĭo -ōnis, f. *invitation, inducement.*
invītātū, abl. sing. m. *by invitation.*
invīto -are, *to invite, summon; to receive, entertain; to induce, allure*; with reflex., *to treat oneself.*
invītus -a -um, *unwilling, against one's will*; abl. absol., me invito, *against my will.* Adv. **invītē,** *unwillingly, against one's will.*
invĭus -a -um, *impassable, impenetrable*; n. pl. as subst., *trackless places.*
invŏcātĭo -ōnis, f. *calling upon, invocation.*
[1]**invŏcātus** -a -um, *uncalled, uninvited.*
[2]**invŏcātus** -a -um, partic. from invoco; q.v.
invŏco -are, *to call in, call upon for help, invoke.*
invŏlātū, abl. sing. m., *by the flight.*
invŏlĭto -are, *to float* or *wave over.*
invŏlo -are, *to fly at, seize* or *pounce upon.*
invŏlūcrum -i, n. *a wrap, cover.*
involvo -volvĕre -volvi -vŏlūtum, *to roll in* or *on; to envelop, wrap up, cover.* Hence partic. **invŏlūtus** -a -um, *rolled up; involved.*

invulgo -are, *to give information.*
invulnĕrātus -a -um, *unwounded.*
[1]**īō,** interj., *hurrah! hi!*
[2]**Īō (Īōn)** -ūs (-ōnis), f. *an Argive girl, loved by Jupiter and changed into a cow*; adj. **Īōnĭus** -a -um, *Ionian, of the sea between Italy and Greece, across which Io swam.*
iŏcātĭo -ōnis, f. *joke, jest.*
iŏco -are and **iŏcor** -ari, dep. *to joke, jest.*
iŏcōsus -a -um, *humorous, merry, facetious*; adv. **iŏcōsē.**
iŏcŭlāris -e, *jocular, laughable*; adv. **iŏcŭlārĭtĕr.**
iŏcŭlārĭus -a -um, *laughable, droll.*
iŏcŭlātor -ōris, m. *joker.*
iŏcŭlor -ari, dep. *to joke, jest.*
iŏcus -i, m. (plur. iŏci and iŏca), *a joke, jest.*
Īōnes -um, m. *the Ionians*; **Īōnĭa** -ae, f. *their country in Asia Minor*; adj. **Īōnĭăcus** and **Īōnĭcus** -a -um, *Ionian.*
Īphĭgĕnīa -ae, f. *daughter of Agamemnon.*
ipse -a -um, *self*; ego ipse, *I myself; the very, actual*; with numbers, etc., *just, exactly*; of action, *by oneself, of one's own accord.*
īra -ae, f. *wrath, anger, rage*; meton., *cause of anger.*
īrācundĭa -ae, f. (1) *angry disposition, irascibility.* (2) *state of anger, fury, wrath.*
īrācundus -a -um, *inclined to anger, irascible*; adv. **īrācundē,** *wrathfully.*
īrascor -i, dep. *to grow angry* (with dat.); partic. **īrātus** -a -um, *angry.*
Īrĭs -rĭdis, f. *messenger of the gods, and goddess of the rainbow.*
īrōnĭa -ae, f. *irony.*
irr-; see in-.
ĭs, ĕa, ĭd, *he, she, it; this* or *that* (*person* or *thing*); with qui (or ut), *one* (*of those*) *who, such . . . as*; with et, -que, etc., *and that too, and what is more*; n. sing. id, *on that account*; id temporis, *at that time*; in eo est, *the position is such,* or, *it depends on this*; id est, *that is,* in explanation.
Īsis -is and -ĭdis, f., *the Egyptian goddess Isis.*
istāc, *by that way.*
iste ista istŭd, demonstr. pron. or adj. *that of yours, that beside you*; in speeches, referring to parties opposed to the speaker (opp. to hic, *my client*); often contemptuous.
Ister = Hister; q.v.
Isthmus (-os) -i, m., *the Isthmus of Corinth.*
[1]**istĭc** istaec istŏc or istŭc, *that of yours.*
[2]**istīc,** adv. *over there, there by you; therein, in that.*
istinc, *from over there, thence.*
istĭusmŏdī or **istĭus mŏdī** or **istīmŏdī,** *of that kind, such.*
istō, adv., *thither, to that place* or *thing.*
istōc and **istūc,** *thither.*
Istri; see Histri.
ĭtă, *so, thus*; interrog., itane? *really?* in answers, *certainly*; in narration, *and so*; with adj. or adv., *so, so very*; ita . . . ut, with subjunc., *in such a way that,* or *only to the extent that, only on condition that.*
Ĭtăli -orum and -um, m. *the Italians*; **Ĭtălĭa** -ae, f. *Italy*; adj. **Ĭtălĭcus** and **Ĭtălus** -a -um, *Italian*; f. adj. **Ĭtălis** -idis.
ĭtăquĕ, *and so; therefore, for that reason.*
ĭtem, *also, likewise.*
ĭtĕr, ĭtĭnĕris, n. *going, way, direction; journey, march; right of way, permission to march*; concr., *way, road*; fig., *way, course, method.*
ĭtĕrātĭo -ōnis, f. *repetition, iteration.*
ĭtĕro -are, *to do a second time, repeat, renew.*
ĭtĕrum, *again, a second time*; iterum atque interum, *again and again.*
Ĭthăca -ae and **Ĭthăcē** -ēs, f., *an island in the Ionian Sea, home of Ulysses.*
ĭtĭdem, *likewise.*
ĭtĭo -ōnis, f. *going, travelling.*
ĭto -are, *to go.*
ĭtus -ūs, m. *movement, going, departure.*
[1]**iŭba** -ae, f. *mane, crest.*
[2]**Iŭba** -ae, m. *name of two Numidian kings.*
iŭbăr -ăris, n. *beaming light, radiance; a heavenly body,* esp. *the sun.*
iŭbātus -a -um, *having a mane, crested.*
iŭbĕo iŭbēre iussi iussum, *to order, command, bid*; salvere iubere, *to greet*; polit. *to ratify* an order. Hence, from perf. partic. **iussum** -i, n., *an order, command.*
iūcundĭtās -ātis, f., *pleasantness, delightfulness, pleasure.*
iūcundus -a -um, *pleasant, agreeable, delightful*; adv. **iūcundē.**
Iūdaea -ae, f *Judea* or *Palestine*; adj. and subst. **Iūdaeus** -a -um, *Jewish* or *a Jew.*
iūdex -ĭcis, m. *a judge*; in plur., *a panel of jurors.*
iūdĭcātĭo -onis, f. *judicial investigation; judgment, opinion.*
iūdĭcātus -ūs, m., *the office* or *business of a judge.*
iūdĭcĭālis -e and **iūdĭcĭārĭus** -a -um, *of a court of justice, judicial.*
iūdĭcĭum -i, n., *a trial, legal investigation; a law-court; jurisdiction; judgment, considered opinion, decision; power of judging, discernment, understanding, good judgment.*
iūdĭco -are, *to be a judge, judge, decide, declare*; perf. partic. iūdĭcātus -a -um, of persons, *condemned*; of things, *decided.*
iŭgālis -e, *yoked together*; m. pl. as subst. *a team of horses.* Transf., *matrimonial, nuptial.*
iŭgātĭo -ōnis, f. *the training of vines on a trellis.*
iūgĕrum -i, n. *a measure of land,* about two-thirds of an English acre.
iūgis -e, *perpetual, continuous,* esp. of water.
iūglans -glandis, f., *a walnut* or *walnut-tree.*

iŭgo -are, *to bind together, connect, couple.*

iŭgōsus -a -um, *mountainous.*

iŭgŭlo -are, *to cut the throat of, to butcher; to ruin, destroy.*

iŭgŭlum -i, n. and **iŭgŭlus** -i, m. *the throat.*

iŭgum -i, n. (1) *a yoke or collar.* Transf., *a team of oxen* or *horses; a pair, couple; a chariot*; any *bond, union; the bond of love, marriage-tie; the yoke of slavery.* (2) *a cross-bar*; esp. *the yoke under which the vanquished were sent; the beam of a pair of scales; a ridge* between mountains; plur., poet., *mountain heights.*

Iŭgurtha -ae, m. *a king of Numidia*; adj. **Iŭgurthīnus** -a -um.

Iūlĭus -a -um, *name of a Roman* gens; including the family of the Caesars; mensis Iulius *or* Iulius, *the month of July.*

Īūlus -i, m., *son of Aeneas.*

iūmentum -i n. *a beast of burden.*

iuncĕus -a -um, *made of rushes; like a rush.*

iuncōsus -a -um, *full of rushes, rushy.*

iunctĭo -ōnis, f. *joining, connexion.*

iunctūra -ae, f., *a joining, joint; relationship; combination, putting together.*

iuncus -i, m. *a rush.*

iungo iungĕre iunxi iunctum, *to join, unite, connect; to yoke, harness; to mate*; amicitiam, *to form.*

Hence partic. **iunctus** -a -um, *connected, united, associated.*

iūnĭor; see iuvenis.

iūnĭpĕrus -i, f. *the juniper-tree.*

Iūnĭus -a -um, *the name of a Roman* gens; mensis Iunius *or* Iunius, *the month of June.*

Iūnō -ōnis, f. *the goddess Juno, Greek Hera, sister and wife of Jupiter*; adj. **Iūnōnĭus** -a -um, *Junonian.*

Iuppĭter, Iŏvis, m. *Jupiter, the Roman supreme god*; sub Iove, *in the open air.*

iūrātor -ōris, m. *a sworn assessor.*

iūrĕiūro -are, *to swear an oath.*

iūrĕpĕrītus = iurisperitus; q.v.

iurgĭum -i, n., *altercation, quarrel, brawl.*

iurgo -are: intransit., *to quarrel, brawl*; transit., *to scold.*

iūrĭdĭcĭālis -e, *relating to right* or *justice.*

iūrisconsultus -i, m. *one learned in law, a lawyer.*

iūrisdictĭo -onis, f. *the administration of justice; judicial authority.*

iūrispĕrītus or **iūrĕpĕrītus** -i, m. *skilled* or *experienced in the law.*

iūro -are, *to swear, take an oath,* in verba, *to swear after a prescribed formula*; perf. partic. in act. sense **iūrātus** -a -um, *having sworn, under oath*; also *having been sworn.*

[1]**iūs** iūris, n. *broth, soup.*

[2]**iūs** iūris, n. *right, law; a court of justice; jurisdiction; right* as conferred by law; iure, *rightly.*

iusiūrandum iūrisiūrandi (or in two words), n. *an oath.*

iussū, abl. sing m., *by order, by command.*

iussum -i, n. subst. from iubeo; q.v.

iustĭtĭa -ae, f. *justice, airness, equity.*

iustĭtĭum -i, n. *a suspension of legal business*; in gen., *pause, cessation.*

iustus -a -um, *just, equitable, fair; lawful, justified, proper; regular, perfect, complete, suitable.* N. as subst., sing. **iustum** -i, *justice, what is right*; plur. **iusta** -orum, *due forms and observances,* esp. *funeral rites.* Adv. **iustē,** *justly, rightly.*

[1]**iŭvĕnālis** -e, *youthful.*

[2]**Iŭvĕnālis** -is, m., D. Iunius, *a Roman writer of satires.*

iŭvencus -a -um, *young*; m. as subst., **iŭvencus** -i, *a young man,* or *young bullock*; f. **iŭvenca** -ae, *a young woman,* or *young cow, heifer.*

iŭvĕnesco iŭvĕnescĕre iŭvĕnŭi, *to come* (or *come back*) *to the prime of life.*

iŭvĕnīlis -e, *youthful*; adv. **iŭvĕnīlĭtĕr,** *youthfully.*

iŭvĕnis -is, adj., *young, youthful*; as subst. *a young man, young woman.*

iŭvĕnor -ari, dep. *to act like a youth, be impetuous.*

iŭventa -ae, f. *youth.*

iŭventās -ātis, f. *youth.*

iŭventūs -ūtis, f. *youth, the prime of life* (between the ages of 20 and 45); meton., *young men.*

iŭvo -are iūvi iūtum. (1) *to help, assist, aid.* (2) *to delight, please, gratify.*

iuxtā: adv. *close by, near; in like manner, equally*; prep., with acc., *close to, near to*; in time, *just before*; in gen., *near to, just short of.*

iuxtim, *near, close by; equally.*

Ixīōn -ŏnis, m. *king of the Lapithae in Thessaly, bound to a perpetually revolving wheel in Tartarus.*

J

Unknown in classical Latin; invented by Italian humanists to represent the consonantal **i,** but now rarely used in classical texts.

K

The letter **K, k,** corresponding to Greek kappa (κ) belonged to the Latin Alphabet, but in some words was replaced by C.

Kălendae (Călendae) -arum, f. *the first day of a Roman month.*

Karthāgo = Carthāgo; q.v.

L

L, l, the eleventh letter of the Latin Alphabet.

lăbasco -ĕre, *to totter; to give way.*

lābēcŭla -ae, f., *a little stain, slight disgrace.*

lăbĕfăcĭo -făcĕre -fēci -factum, pass. lăbĕfīo -fĭĕrī -factus sum, *to shake, loosen, impair.*

lăbĕfacto -are, *to shake violently, weaken, disturb.*

[1]**lăbellum** -i, n., *a little lip.*

[2]**lābellum** -i, n. *a small washing-vessel.*

lābēs -is, f. *a stain, blemish; infamy, disgrace.*

lăbĭa -ae, f., and **lăbĭum** -i, n., *a lip.*

Lăbĭenus -i, m., T. *an officer of Julius Caesar, who went over to Pompey.*

lăbĭōsus -a -um, *with large lips.*

lăbĭum -i, n. = labia; q.v.

lăbo -are, *to totter, waver, be about to fall, begin to sink.*

[1]**lābor** lābi lapsus, dep. *to glide, slide, flow; to slip, fall down, fall away, decline; to make a mistake.*

[2]**lăbor (lăbos)** -ōris, m. (1) *work, toil, effort, industry, capacity for work; feat, work, result of labour.* (2) *hardship, fatigue, distress*; labores solis, *eclipse of the sun.*

lăbōrĭfer -fĕra -fĕrum, *bearing toil.*

lăbōrĭōsus -a -um: of things, *toilsome, laborious*; of persons, *industrious, toiling.* Adv. **lăbōrĭōsē,** *laboriously, with toil.*

lăbōro -are: intransit., *to work, toil, strive: to be troubled* or *anxious, to care; to suffer, be distressed* or *afflicted*; luna laborat, *is eclipsed*; transit., *to work out, elaborate, prepare, form.*

lăbos -ōris, m. = labor; q.v.

[1]**labrum** -i, n. *lip; edge, rim.*

[2]**labrum** -i, n. *basin, tub; a bathing-place.*

lābrusca -ae, f. *the wild vine.*

lābruscum -i, n. *the wild grape.*

lăbўrinthus -i, m. *a labyrinth.*

lăc lactis, n. *milk; milky sap; milk-white colour.*

Lăcaena -ae, f. adj. (*female*) *Spartan.*

Lăcĕdaemon -ŏnis, f. *the city Lacedaemon* or *Sparta*; adj. **Lăcĕdaemŏnĭus** -a -um, *Lacedaemonian.*

lăcer -cĕra -cĕrum, *torn, mangled*; act., *tearing to pieces.*

lăcĕrātĭo -ōnis, f. *tearing, mangling.*

lăcerna -ae, f. *a mantle worn over the* toga.

lăcĕro -are, *to tear to pieces, maim, mangle; to squander* money; *to slander, pull to pieces* a character.

lăcerta -ae, f. *a lizard*; also *a sea-fish.*

lăcertōsus -a -um, *muscular, powerful.*

[1]**lăcertus** -i, m., *the upper arm* with its muscles; in gen., *vigour.*

[2]**lăcertus** -i, m. = lacerta; q.v.

lăcesso -ĕre -īvi and -ĭi -ītum, *to provoke, exasperate, excite, induce.*

Lăchĕsis -is, f., *one of the three* Parcae *or Fates.*

lăcĭnĭa -ae, f. *the flap of a garment.*

Lăcō (Lăcōn) -ōnis, m., *a Spartan, Lacedaemonian*; adj. **Lăcōnĭcus** -a -um and f. adj. **Lăcōnis** -ĭdis, *Spartan.*

lacrĭma (lacrŭma) -ae, f. *a tear; exudation from certain plants*; Heliadum, *amber.*

lacrĭmābĭlis -e, *deplorable, woeful.*

lacrĭmābundus -a -um, *breaking into tears, weeping.*

lacrĭmo (lacrŭmo) -are, *to weep, shed tears; to exude, to drip.*

lacrĭmōsus -a -um: *tearful, shedding tears; causing tears, mournful, piteous.*

lacrĭmŭla -ae, f., *a little tear.*

lacrŭma, etc.; see lacrima, etc.

lactans -antis, *giving milk.*

lactātĭo -ōnis, f. *enticement.*

lactens -entis. (1) *sucking milk*; plur. as subst., *sucklings, unweaned animals.* (2) *milky, juicy, full of sap.*

lactesco -ĕre, *to be changed into milk.*

lactĕus -a -um, *milky, of milk; milk-white.*

lacto -are, *to allure, wheedle.*

lactūca -ae, f. *lettuce.*

lăcūna -ae, f. *a cavity, hollow, dip*; esp. *a pool, pond.* Transf., *gap, deficiency, loss.*

lăcūnăr -āris, n. *a panelled ceiling.*

lăcūno -are, *to work in panels, to panel.*

lăcūnōsus -a -um, *full of hollows* or *gaps.*

lăcus -ūs, m. *a hollow*; hence *a lake, pool, trough, tank, tub.*

laedo laedĕre laesi laesum, *to strike, knock*; hence *to hurt, injure, damage; to offend, annoy; to violate, outrage.*

laena -ae, f. *cloak.*

Lāertēs -ae, m. *father of Ulysses.*

laesĭo -ōnis, f. *an oratorical attack.*

laetābĭlis -e, *joyful, glad.*

laetātĭo -ōnis, f. *rejoicing, joy.*

laetĭfĭco -are, *to fertilize; to cheer, gladden, delight.*

laetĭfĭcus -a -um, *gladdening, joyous.*

laetĭtĭa -ae, f. (1) *fertility*; hence *richness, grace.* (2) *joy, delight.*

laetor -ari, dep. *to rejoice, be joyful.*

laetus -a -um, *fat, rich, fertile; glad, joyful, happy*; of style, *rich, copious, fluent.* Adv. **laetē.**

laevus -a -um, *left*; f. as subst., *the left hand, the left*; n. as subst., *the left side.* Transf., *left-handed, foolish, silly; unlucky, unpropitious*; but in augury, *favourable.* Adv. **laevē,** *on the left hand; awkwardly.*

lăgănum -i, n., *a cake.*

lăgēos -ei, f., *a Greek kind of vine.*

lăgoena *a large earthen jar with handles.*

lăgōis -ĭdis, f. *a bird,* perhaps *heathcock* or *grouse.*

lăguncŭla -ae, f. *a little bottle.*

Lāĭus -i, m. *father of Oedipus.*

lāma -ae, f. *a bog, slough.*

lambo lambĕre lambi, *to lick*; of rivers, *to wash.*

lāmenta -orum, n. pl. *wailing, weeping.*

lāmentābĭlis -e *lamentable, deplorable; expressing sorrow, mournful.*

lāmentātĭo -ōnis, f. *weeping, wailing.*

lāmentor -ari, dep. *to weep, wail, lament*; transit., *to bewail.*

lămĭa -ae, f. *a witch, vampire.*

lāmĭna, lammĭna, and **lamna** -ae, f. *a plate or thin piece of metal, marble,* etc.; *knife-blade; coin; nutshell.*

lampăs -pădis, f. *a torch*; hence *brightness*, esp. of the sun; also *a meteor*.
lāna -ae, f., *wool*; also *the down on leaves, fruit*, etc.
lānātus -a -um, *wool-bearing, woolly*.
lancĕa -ae, f. *a light spear* or *lance*.
lancĭno -are, *to tear to pieces; to squander*.
lānĕus -a -um, *of wool, woollen; soft as wool*.
languĕfăcĭo -făcĕre, *to make weak* or *faint*.
languĕo -ēre, *to be faint, weak, weary; to droop, flag*; partic. **languens** -entis, *faint, languid*.
languesco languescĕre langŭi, *to become faint, soft* or *listless*.
languĭdŭlus -a -um, *somewhat faint, limp*.
languĭdus -a -um, *faint, weak, limp*; of wine, *mild, mellow*; adv. **languĭdē**.
languor -ōris, m. *faintness, weariness, inactivity*.
lănĭātus -ūs, m. *mangling, tearing*.
lănĭēna -ae, f. *a butcher's shop*.
lānĭfĭcus -a -um, *working in wool*.
lānĭger -gĕra -gĕrum, *wool-bearing; woollen*; m. as subst. *a ram*; f., *a sheep*.
lănĭo -are, *to tear to pieces, mangle, lacerate*.
lănista -ae, m. *a trainer of gladiators; an instigator to violence, inciter*.
lānĭtĭum -i, n. *wool*.
lănĭus -i, m. *butcher*.
lanterna -ae, f. *lantern, lamp*.
lanternārĭus -i, m. *lantern-bearer*.
lānūgo -ĭnis, f. *down, of plants* or *on the cheeks*.
Lānŭvĭum -i, n. *a town in Latium*.
lanx lancis, f. *a plate, platter; the scale of a balance*.
Lāŏcŏōn -ontis, m. *a Trojan priest*.
Lāŏmĕdōn -ontis, m. *a king of Troy, father of Priam*.
lăpăthum -i, n. and **lăpăthus** -i, f. *sorrel*.
lăpĭcīdīnae -arum, f. *stone quarries*.
lăpĭdātĭo -ōnis, f. *throwing of stones*.
lăpĭdātor -ōris, m. *thrower of stones*.
lăpĭdĕus -a -um, *of stone*.
lăpĭdo -are, *to throw stones at*; impers. lapidat, *it rains stones*.
lăpĭdōsus -a -um, *full of stones, stony*.
lăpillus -i, m. *a little stone, pebble; a precious stone, gem*.
lăpis -ĭdis, m. a *stone*.
Lăpĭthae -arum, m. pl. *the Lapithae, a mountain race in Thessaly, famous for their fight with the Centaurs*.
lappa -ae, f. *a burr*.
lapsĭo -ōnis, f. *gliding; inclination, tendency*.
lapso -are, *to slip, stumble*.
lapsus -ūs, m. *gradual movement; gliding, sliding, fall; a fault, error*.
lăquĕārĕ -is, n., esp. plur., *a panelled ceiling*.
lăquĕātus -a -um, *with a panelled ceiling*.
lăquĕus -i, m. *a noose, halter, snare, trap*.
Lār Lăris, m., usually plur. **Lăres,** *Roman tutelary deities*, esp. *household deities*; meton., *hearth, dwelling, home*.
lardum (**lārĭdum**) -i, n. *bacon fat, lard*.
Lārentĭa -ae, f., or **Acca Lārentĭa,** *the wife of Faustulus, who brought up Romulus and Remus*.
Lăres; see Lar.
largĭfĭcus -a -um, *bountiful, liberal*.
largiflŭus -a -um, *flowing freely*.
largĭor -iri, dep. *to give abundantly, lavish, bestow, grant; to condone*.
largĭtās -ātis, f. *liberality*.
largĭtĭo -ōnis, f. *free giving* or *spending, lavishing; granting, bestowing*.
largĭtor -ōris, m. *a liberal giver* or *spender; a briber; a waster*.
largus -a -um, of things, *abundant, plentiful, numerous*; with genit., *rich in*; of persons, *liberal, bountiful*. Adv. **largē**, *plentifully, liberally*; **largĭtĕr,** *abundantly, much*.
lārĭdum -i, n. = lardum; q.v.
larva (**lārŭa**) -ae, f. *a ghost, spectre; a mask*.
lascīvĭa -ae, f. *playfulness, sportiveness; wantonness, licentiousness, insolence*.
lascīvĭo -ire, *to sport, play; to wanton, run riot*.
lascīvus -a -um, *playful, wanton, licentious, insolent*. Adv. **lascīvē**.
lăserpīcĭum -i, n. *a plant from which asafoetida was obtained*.
lassĭtūdo -ĭnis, f., *weariness, exhaustion*.
lasso -are, *to make weary, exhaust*.
lassŭlus -a -um, *rather tired*.
lassus -a -um, *weary, tired, exhausted*.
lătebra -ae, f. *a hiding-place, retreat; a subterfuge, loophole*.
lătebrōsus -a -um, *full of hiding-places, secret*; pumex, *porous*. Adv. **lătebrōsē,** *secretly*.
lătĕo -ēre, *to lie hid, be concealed; to live in obscurity* or *safety*; *to be unknown*.
Hence partic. **lătens** -entis, *concealed, hidden*; adv. **lătentĕr,** *secretly*.
lăter -tĕris, m. *a brick, tile*.
lătĕrāmen -inis, n. *pottery*.
lătercŭlus -i m. *a small brick* or *tile; a biscuit*.
lătĕrīcĭus -a -um, *built of brick*.
lāterna; see lanterna.
lătesco -ĕre, *to hide oneself*.
lătex -tĭcis, m. *fluid, liquid*.
lătĭbŭlum -i, n., *a hiding-place*.
lāticlāvĭus -a -um, *having a broad purple stripe* (as a distinction).
lātĭfundĭum -i, n. *a large landed estate*.
Lătīnĭtās -ātis, f. *pure Latin style; Latin rights*.
[1]**Lătīnus** -a -um; see Latium.
[2]**Lătīnus** -i, m. *king of the Laurentians, host of Aeneas*.
lātĭo -ōnis, f. *bringing*; legis, *proposing, bringing forward*.
lătĭto -are, *to lie hid, be concealed*.
lātĭtūdo -ĭnis, f. *breadth, extent*; verborum, *broad pronunciation, brogue*.
Lătĭum -i, n. *a district of Italy, in which Rome was situated*; adj. **Lătĭus** and **Lătīnus** -a -um, *Latin;* adv. **Lătīnē,** *in Latin*.

Lātō -ūs, f. and **Lātōna** -ae, f. *the mother of Apollo and Diana.*
lātor -ōris, m. *the proposer* of a law.
lātrātor -ōris, m. *a barker.*
lātrātus -ūs, m. *barking.*
[1]**lātro** -are, *to bark, bay; to rant, rumble, roar*; transit., *to bark at* or *for.*
[2]**latro** -ōnis, m. *a hired servant* or *mercenary soldier; a robber, bandit, brigand; a hunter; a piece on a draught-board.*
latrōcinium -i, n. *mercenary service; highway robbery, brigandage, villainy, roguery*; meton., *a band of robbers.*
latrōcinor -ari, dep. *to serve as a mercenary; to practise robbery.*
latruncŭlus -i, m. *a highwayman, bandit; a piece on a draught-board.*
[1]**lātus** -a -um, partic. from fero; q.v.
[2]**lātus** -a -um, *broad, wide, extensive*; of style, *diffuse, full, rich.* Hence adv. **lātē,** *broadly, widely, extensively*; longe lateque, *far and wide.*
[3]**lătus** -ĕris, n. *the side, flank*; of persons, in pl., *the lungs*; milit., a latere, *on the flank.*
lătuscŭlum -i, n. *a little side.*
laudābĭlis -e, *praiseworthy, laudable*; adv. **laudābĭlĭtĕr.**
laudātĭo -ōnis, f. *praise, commendation; a testimonial; a funeral oration.*
laudātor -ōris, m. *a praiser*; esp. *one who delivers a testimonial* or *funeral oration.*
laudātrix -īcis, f. *a (female) praiser.*
laudo -are, *to praise, extol, commend; to name, mention, cite, quote*; partic. **laudātus** -a -um, *praiseworthy, esteemed.*
laurĕātus -a -um, *crowned with laurel*; litterae, *bringing news of victory.*
laurĕŏla -ae, f. *a laurel branch, laurel crown*; meton., *a triumph, victory.*
laurĕus -a -um, *of laurel*; f. as subst., **laurĕa,** *laurel tree* or *laurel crown.*
laurĭcŏmus -a -um, *covered with laurel-trees.*
laurĭfer -fĕra -fĕrum, and **laurĭger** -gĕra -gĕrum, *crowned with laurels.*
laurus -i, f. *the laurel* or *bay-tree*; meton., *triumph, victory.*
laus laudis, f. *praise, fame, glory, commendation.* Transf., *a praiseworthy action* or *quality.*
lautĭa -orum, n. pl., *entertainment given to foreign ambassadors at Rome.*
lautĭtĭa -ae, f. *splendour, elegance, sumptuous living.*
lautŭmĭae (**lātŏmĭae**) -arum, f. *a stone-quarry.*
lautus -a -um, partic. from lavo; q.v.
lăvabrum -i, n. *a bath.*
lăvātĭo -ōnis, f. *washing, bathing; bathing apparatus.*
Lāvīnĭa -ae, f. *daughter of Latinus, wife of Aeneas.*
lăvo lăvare *or* lăvĕre lāvi lautum *or* lōtum *or* lăvatum, *to wash, bathe; to moisten, wet; to wash away.*

Hence partic. **lautus** -a -um, *washed*; hence *fine, elegant, sumptuous, refined*; adv. **lautē.**

laxāmentum -i, n. *widening, extending; relaxing, mitigation, respite.*
laxĭtās -ātis, f. *wideness, roominess.*
laxo -are, *to widen, loosen, extend, enlarge; to undo, slacken, relax, relieve; to release, set free.*
laxus -a -um, *wide, loose, spacious*; of time, *later, postponed; loose, lax, relaxed.* Adv. **laxē,** *widely, loosely, without restraint.*
lĕa -ae, and **lĕaena** -ae, f. *a lioness.*
Lēander -dri, m. *a youth who swam nightly across the Hellespont to visit Hero, till drowned in a storm.*
lĕbēs -ētis, m. *a bronze pan, cauldron,* or *basin.*
lectīca -ae, f. *a litter; a bier.*
lectīcārĭus -i, m. *litter-bearer.*
lectīcŭla -ae, f. *a small litter* or *bier; a settee.*
lectĭo -ōnis, f. *a picking out, selection, reading, perusal*; lectio senatus, *a calling over of the names of the senators.*
lectisternĭum -i, n. *a feast offered to the gods.*
lectĭto -are, *to read often* or *eagerly.*
lector -ōris, m. *a reader.*
lectŭlus -i, m. *a small bed, couch.*
[1]**lectus** -a -um, partic. from lego; q.v.
[2]**lectus** -i, m. *a bed, couch.*
Lēda -ae, and **Lēdē** -es, f. *mother of Castor, Pollux, Helen, and Clytemnestra.*
lēgātārĭus -i, m. *a legatee.*
lēgātĭo -ōnis, f. *delegated authority*; polit., *the office of an ambassador, an embassy, legation*; milit., *the post of subordinate commander*; esp. *the command of a legion.*
lēgātor -ōris, m. *testator.*
lēgātum -i, n. and **lēgātus** -i, m., from lego; q.v.
lēgĭfer -fĕra -fĕrum, *law-giving.*
lĕgĭo -ōnis, f. *a choosing; a chosen body*; esp. *a legion, a division of the Roman army.*
lĕgĭōnārĭus -a -um, *belonging to a legion.*
lēgĭtĭmus (**lēgĭtŭmus**) -a -um, *lawful, legitimate; right, proper, appropriate.* Adv. **lēgĭtĭmē,** *lawfully, properly.*
lĕgĭuncŭla -ae, f. *a small legion.*
[1]**lēgo** -are, *to ordain, appoint*; of persons, *to make a deputy, delegate authority to*; of property, *to bequeath, leave as a legacy.* M. of partic. as subst. **lēgātus** -i, *a deputy*; polit., *an ambassador, envoy,* or *the deputy of a magistrate*; milit., *a subordinate commander,* esp. *commander of a legion.* N. **lēgātum** -i, *a legacy, bequest.*
[2]**lĕgo** lĕgĕre lēgi lectum, *to collect, gather, pick, pick up*; fila, *to wind up, spin*; vela, *to furl*; of places, *to pass through, traverse, coast along*; with the eyes, *to survey, scan, read, peruse*; out of a number, *to pick out, choose, select.*

Hence partic. **lectus** -a -um, *chosen, selected; choice, excellent.*

lēgŭlēius -i, m. *a pettifogging lawyer.*
lĕgūmen -ĭnis, n. *pulse; the bean.*
Lĕmannus -i, m. *the Lake of Geneva.*

lembus -i, m. *a boat, cutter, pinnace.*
lemma -ătis, n. *theme, title; an epigram.*
lemniscātus -a -um, *ribboned.*
lemniscus -i, m. *a ribbon.*
Lemnos (-us) -i, f. *the island of Lemnos in the Aegean Sea*; adj. **Lemnĭus** -a -um, *Lemnian.*
lĕmŭrēs -um, m. pl. *ghosts, spectres*; **Lĕmūrĭa** -orum, n. pl. *a festival held in May to expel ghosts.*
lēna -ae, f. *a procuress, bawd.*
Lēnaeus -a -um, *Bacchic.*
lēnīmen -īnis, n. *means of alleviation.*
lēnīmentum -i, n. *mitigation, alleviation.*
lēnĭo -ire, *to make mild, mitigate, relieve.*
lēnis -e, *smooth, mild, gentle*; vinum, *mellow*; n. acc. as adv. **lēnĕ,** *gently*; adv. **lēnĭtĕr**, *smoothly, gently, mildly.*
lēnĭtās -ātis, f. and **lēnĭtūdo** -inis, f. *gentleness, mildness, smoothness.*
lēno -ōnis, m. *a procurer, a go-between.*
lēnōcĭnĭum -i, n. *the trade of a procurer; enticement, allurement*; of dress, *finery*; of style, '*purple patch*'.
lēnōcĭnor -ari, dep. *to work as a procurer; to make up to, to flatter: to advance, promote.*
lens lentis, f. *lentil.*
lentesco -ĕre, *to become pliant, soft, sticky; to weaken, slacken.*
lentiscus -i, f. and **lentiscum** -i, n. *the mastic-tree.*
lentĭtūdo ĭnis, f. *slowness, sluggishness, apathy.*
lento -are, *to bend.*
[1]**lentŭlus** -a -um, *somewhat slow.*
[2]**Lentŭlus** -i, m. *the name of a family in the patrician* gens Cornelia.
lentus -a -um, *tough, resistant, inert; sticky, tenacious; supple, pliant; inactive, apathetic; slow, lingering;* in dicendo, *drawling.* Adv. **lentē,** *slowly, calmly, coolly, deliberately.*
[1]**lēnuncŭlus** -i, m. *a little procurer.*
[2]**lēnuncŭlus** -i, m. *a small boat* or *skiff.*
lĕo -ōnis, m. *lion.*
lĕōnīnus -a -um, *of a lion, leonine.*
Lĕontīni -orum, m. *a town on the east coast of Sicily.*
lĕpăs -ădis, f. *a limpet.*
[1]**lĕpĭdus** -a -um, *pleasant, charming, elegant, witty*; adv. **lĕpĭdē.**
[2]**Lĕpĭdus** -i, m. *name of a family in the patrician* gens Aemilia.
lĕpor and **lĕpos** -ōris, m. *pleasantness, charm, wit.*
lĕpus -ŏris, m. *hare.*
lĕpuscŭlus -i, m. *a young hare.*
Lesbos (-us) -i, f. *an island in the Aegean Sea, birth-place of Alcaeus and Sappho.*
lētālis -e, *deadly, mortal.*
lēthargĭcus -i, m. *a drowsy, lethargic person.*
lēthargus -i, m. *drowsiness, lethargy, coma.*
Lēthē -ēs, f. *the river of forgetfulness in the underworld.*
lētĭfer -fĕra -fĕrum, *deadly.*
lēto -are, *to kill, slay.*
lētum -i, n. *death; ruin, annihilation.*
leucaspis -ĭdis, f. *having white shields.*
lĕvāmen -ĭnis, n. and **lĕvāmentum** -i, n. *alleviation, mitigation, solace.*
lĕvātĭo -ōnis, f. *alleviation, mitigation; diminution.*
lĕvĭcŭlus -a -um, *rather vain, light-headed.*
lĕvĭdensis -e, *thin, slight, poor.*
[1]**lĕvis** -e, *light*; milit., *light-armed*; in movement, *rapid, swift*; in value, *light, trifling, unimportant*; in character, *fickle, capricious, unstable.* Adv. **lĕvĭtĕr,** *lightly, softly, slightly.*
[2]**lēvis** -e, *smooth, polished, slippery; beardless, bald.*
lĕvĭsomnus -a -um, *lightly sleeping.*
[1]**lĕvĭtās** -ātis, f. *lightness; levity, fickleness, inconstancy; groundlessness.*
[2]**lēvĭtās** -ātis, f. *smoothness, polish.*
[1]**lĕvo** -are, *to raise, lift up; to make light, relieve, ease; to diminish, weaken, impair.*
[2]**lēvo** -are, *to make smooth, polish.*
lēvor -ōris, m. *smoothness.*
lex lēgis, f. *a set form of words, contract, covenant, agreement*; leges pacis, *conditions of peace*; esp. *a law, proposed by a magistrate as a bill,* or *passed and statutory*; legem ferre, rogare, *to propose a bill*; legem iubere, *to accept* or *pass a bill*; in gen., *a precept, rule.*
lībāmen -ĭnis, n. *a libation, offering to the gods; a sample, specimen.*
lībāmentum -i, n. *a libation, offering to the gods.*
lībātĭo -ōnis, f. *a libation.*
lībella -ae, f. (1) *a small coin, a tenth of a* denarius; *a farthing, mite.* (2) *a carpenter's level, plummet-line.*
lībellus -i, m. *a little book, note-book, diary; a memorial, petition; programme, placard; letter.*
lĭbens and **lŭbens** -entis, partic. from libet; q.v.
[1]**līber** -ĕra -ĕrum, *free, independent, unrestrained; free from, exempt.* Adv. **lībĕrē,** *freely, without restraint, frankly, openly, boldly.*
[2]**lĭber** -bri, m. *the inner bark of a tree*; from the use of this in writing, *a book, volume, catalogue, letter.*
[3]**Līber** -ĕri, m. *an Italian deity, identified with Bacchus.*
lībĕrālis -e, *of freedom; worthy of a free man, gentlemanlike, courteous, generous*; adv. **lībĕrālĭtĕr.**
lībĕrālĭtās -ātis, f. *courtesy, kindness, generosity.* Transf. *a grant.*
lībĕrātĭo -ōnis, f. *setting free, release, acquittal.*
lībĕrātor -ōris, m. *a liberator.*
lībĕri -ĕrōrum and -ĕrum, m. pl. *children.*
lībĕro -are, *to set free, liberate, release, exempt*; of obstacles, *to lift, raise.*
līberta -ae, f.; see libertus.
lībertās -ātis, f. *freedom, liberty, independence; freedom of speech, frankness, candour.*

lībertīnus -a -um, *of the class of freedman*; as subst. m. **lībertīnus** *a freedman*, f. **lībertīna,** *a freedwoman.*
lībertus -i, m. *a freedman*; **līberta** -ae, f. *a freedwoman.*
lĭbet (lŭbet) -bēre -bŭit or -bĭtum est, impers., *it pleases, is agreeable* (with dat. of person).
Hence partic. **lĭbens (lŭbens)** -entis, *willing, with pleasure, pleased*; me libente, *with my good-will*; adv. **lĭbenter (lŭbenter),** *willingly, with pleasure.*
lĭbīdĭnōsus -a -um, *wilful, arbitrary, capricious; passionate, lustful.* Adv. **lĭbīdĭnōsē,** *wilfully, arbitrarily.*
lĭbīdo (lŭbīdo) -ĭnis, f. *violent desire, longing*; esp. irrational *whim, caprice*; or immoderate *passion, lust.*
Lĭbĭtīna -ae, f. *goddess of the dead.*
lībo -are, *to take away from, remove, derive; to taste, touch, impair, diminish; to give a taste of, offer to the gods.*
lībra -ae, f. (1) *a balance, pair of scales*; aes et libra, *a fictitious form of sale.* (2) *the Roman pound of 12 oz.*
lībrāmentum -i, n. (1) *weight as a source of power* or *for balancing.* (2) *a horizontal plane.*
lībrārĭa -ae, f *a female who weighed out wool to slaves.*
librārĭus -a -um, *of books*; m. as subst., *a transcriber of books, a copyist*, or *a bookseller;* n. as subst., *a bookcase.*
lībrīlis -e, *of a pound weight.*
lībrĭtor -ōris, m. *an artilleryman.*
lībro -are, *to balance, hold up, poise*; of weapons, *to swing, level, brandish*; hence, *to hurl.*
lībum -i, n. *a cake, offered to the gods.*
Lĭburni -orum, m. *the Liburnians, a people of Illyria*; f. of adj. as subst. **Lĭburna** -ae, *a light vessel, galley.*
Lĭbўa -ae and **Lĭbўē** -ēs, f. *Libya*
lĭcens -centis, and **lĭcentĕr** from licet; q.v.
lĭcentĭa -ae, f. *freedom, leave, liberty; licentiousness.*
lĭcĕo -ēre -ŭi -ĭtum, *to be on sale, be valued at.*
lĭcĕor -ēri, dep. *to bid* or *bid for, offer a price.*
lĭcet lĭcēre lĭcŭit or lĭcĭtum est, impers., *it is allowed, one can* or *may*; as conjunction, *granted that, although.* Hence pres. partic. **lĭcens** -entis, *free, unrestrained, unbridled*; adv. **lĭcentĕr;** perf. partic. **lĭcĭtus** -a -um, *allowed, permitted.*
Lĭcĭnĭus -a -um, *name of a Roman* gens.
lĭcĭtātĭo -onis, f. *bidding at a sale* or *auction.*
lĭcĭtus -a -um, partic. from licet; q.v.
lĭcĭum -i, n.: in weaving, *the thrum* or perhaps *a leash*; in gen., *a thread.*
lictor -ōris, m. *a lictor, attending the chief Roman magistrates.*
lĭgāmen -ĭnis, n. *string tie, bandage.*
lĭgāmentum -i, n. *bandage.*
Lĭgĕr -gĕris, m. *a river* (now the *Loire*).
lignārĭus -i, m. *a carpenter.*
lignātĭo -ōnis, f. *wood-cutting.*
lignātor -ōris, m. *wood-cutter.*
lignĕŏlus -a -um, *wooden.*
lignĕus -a -um, *made of wood, wooden.*
lignor -ari, dep. *to cut* or *get wood.*
lignum -i, n. *wood, timber*; esp. *firewood.*
[1]**lĭgo** -are, *to bind, bandage, harness; to bind together, connect, unite.*
[2]**lĭgo** -ōnis, m. *a mattock.*
lĭgŭla (lingŭla) ae, f. *a tongue of land, promontory; a shoe-strap.*
Lĭgŭrēs -um, m. pl. *the Ligurians, a people on the north-west coast of Italy.*
lĭgūrĭo (lĭgurrĭo) -ire, *to lick lick up; to gloat over; long for.*
lĭgūrītĭo (ligurr-) -ōnis, f. *daintiness.*
lĭgustrum -i, n. *privet.*
līlĭum -i, n. *a lily*; milit. *a fortification consisting of pits and stakes.*
Lĭlўbaeon (-baeum) -i, n. *a promontory and town at the western end of Sicily.*
līma -ae, f. *a file; polishing, revision* of a composition.
līmātŭlus -a -um *rather polished, refined.*
limbus -i, m. *a border, hem, fringe.*
līmen -ĭnis, n. *threshold, doorway, entrance; home, house, dwelling; any entrance or border* or *beginning*; esp. *the starting-point in a race-course.*
līmĕs -ĭtis, m. *a by-way, path; a course, track*; esp. *a boundary-path, a boundary-line; a distinction, difference.*
līmo -are, *to file, polish, finish off; to investigate accurately; to file down, pare down, to diminish.* Partic. **līmātus** -a -um, *refined elegant*; compar. adv. **līmātĭus.**
līmōsus -a -um, *slimy, miry, muddy.*
limpĭdus -a -um, *clear, limpid.*
[1]**līmus** -a -um, of the eyes, *sidelong, looking sideways.*
[2]**līmus** -i, m. *slime, mud, mire.*
[3]**līmus** -i, m. *a priest's apron.*
līnĕa -ae, f. *a linen thread, string*; *a fishing-line, plumb-line*; ad lineam, *perpendicularly.* Transf., *a geometrical line; a boundary-line, goal.*
līnĕāmentum -i, n. *a line drawn with pen* or *pencil*; plur., *drawing, sketch, outline*; in gen., *a feature, lineament.*
līnĕo -are, *to make straight.*
līnĕus -a -um, *of flax or linen.*
lingo lingĕre linxi linctum, *to lick.*
lingua -ae, f. *a tongue; speech, language: a tongue of land, promontory.*
lingŭlāca -ae, f. *a chatterbox.*
līnĭger -gĕra -gĕrum, *clothed in linen.*
līno lĭnĕre līvi and lēvi lĭtum, *to smear* one thing *upon* another; or *to besmear* one thing *with* another; *to rub out* writing; to *befoul, dirty.*
linquo linquĕre līqui, *to leave, abandon, forsake*; pass., linqui, *to faint.*
lintĕātus -a -um, *clothed in linen.*
lintĕo -ōnis, m. *a linen-weaver.*
linter -tris, f. *a boat, skiff*; *a trough, tub, vat.*
lintĕus -a -um, *of linen*; n. as subst. *linen cloth, linen*, esp. *a sail.*

līnum -i, n. *flax, linen; a thread, line; a rope, cable.*
lippĭo -ire, *to have sore eyes, be blear-eyed.*
lippĭtūdo -ĭnis, f. *inflammation of the eyes.*
lippus -a -um, *blear-eyed; half-blind.*
lĭquĕfăcĭo -făcĕre -fēci -factum, pass. **lĭquĕfīo** -fĭĕri -factus sum, *to melt, dissolve; to decompose; to make weak, enervate.*
lĭquesco -ĕre -lĭcŭi, *to become fluid, melt, melt away, to putrefy; to become effeminate.*
lĭquĭdus -a -um. (1) *fluid, flowing, liquid*; n. as subst. *a liquid.* (2) *clear, bright, serene, calm, pure, evident, certain*; n. as subst. *certainty*; abl. sing. **lĭquĭdō** and adv. **lĭquĭdē,** *clearly, plainly.*
lĭquo -are, *to make liquid, melt; to strain, clarify.*
[1]**lĭquor** -i, dep. *to be fluid, flow, melt: to melt away*; partic. **lĭquens** -entis, *flowing.*
[2]**lĭquor** -ōris, m. *fluidity; a liquid, fluid.*
lis, lītis, f. *a legal controversy, action, suit*; in gen., *contention, strife, quarrel.*
lĭtātĭo -onis, f. *successful sacrifice.*
lĭtĭgātor -ōris, m. *a party in a law-suit, litigant.*
lĭtĭgĭōsus -a -um, of persons, *fond of dispute, litigious*; of things, *full of dispute, contested at law.*
lĭtĭgo -are, *to go to law*; in gen., *to quarrel, dispute.*
lĭto -are: intransit., *to bring an acceptable offering,* and so *to obtain favourable omens*; transit., *to sacrifice successfully.*
lĭtŏrālis -e, and **lĭtŏrĕus** -a -um, *of the shore.*
littĕra (lītĕra) ae, f. *a letter of the alphabet; a letter, dispatch, epistle;* plur., *written records, documents, deeds; literature, letters, scholarship.*
littĕrārĭus -a -um, *of reading and writing.*
littĕrātor -ōris, m. *a philologist, grammarian, critic.*
littĕrātūra -ae, f. *the alphabet, grammar.*
littĕrātus -a -um, *lettered, inscribed with letters; learned, liberally educated.* Adv. **littĕrātē,** *in clear letters, legibly; literally, word for word; learnedly.*
littĕrŭla -ae, f. *a letter* (of the alphabet) *written small*; plur., *a little letter, a note, a smattering of literature.*
littus, etc.; see **litus,** etc.
lĭtūra -ae, f. *an erasure, correction; a passage erased; a blot.*
lītus -ŏris, n. *sea-shore, beach, strand, coast; the shore of a lake* or *river.*
lĭtŭus -i, m. *an augur's curved staff; a curved cavalry trumpet, clarion.*
līvĕo -ēre, *to be bluish in colour; to be envious, envy*; partic. **līvens** -entis, *bluish, livid; envious.*
līvesco -ĕre, *to become bluish.*
līvĭdŭlus -a -um, *rather envious.*
līvĭdus -a -um, *bluish, livid, black and blue; envious, spiteful.*
Līvĭus -a -um, *name of a Roman gens.*
līvor -ōris, m. *bluish colour, a livid spot; envy, spite.*
lixa -ae, m. *a sutler, camp-follower.*
lŏcātĭo -ōnis, f. *placing*; hence *a leasing, contract, lease.*
lŏcātōrĭus -a -um, *concerned with leases.*
lŏco -are, *to place, put, set*; esp. *to give in marriage;* commerc., *to let out on hire, farm out, lease, invest; to contract for* work to be done. N. of partic. as subst. **lŏcātum** -i, *a lease, contract.*
lŏcŭlus -i, m. *a little place*; plur., loculi, *a money-box; a school satchel.*
lŏcuplēs -plētis, *with landed property, wealthy, rich*; also *trusty, sufficient, satisfactory.*
lŏcuplēto -are, *to enrich.*
lŏcus -i, m. (plur., loci, *single places*; loca, *region*), *a place*; milit., *position, ground, post*; in time, *a period,* or *moment; position, situation, rank; occasion, cause; passage in a book.*
[1]**lōcusta** -ae, f. *a locust; a kind of lobster.*
[2]**Lōcusta** -ae, f. *a notorious poisoner, accomplice of Nero.*
lŏcūtĭo -ōnis, f. *speech; pronunciation.*
lōdix -dīcis, f. *blanket, rug.*
lŏgĭcus -a -um, *logical*; n. pl. as subst. *logic.*
lŏgŏs (-us) -i, m. *a word; a joke, jest, bon mot.*
lŏlĭum -i, n. *darnel.*
lollīgo -ĭgĭnis, f. *cuttle-fish.*
lōmentum -i, n. *face-cream.*
Londĭnĭum -i, n. *London.*
longaevus -a -um, *aged, old.*
longinquĭtās -ātis, f. *length, distance, remoteness*; of time, *duration.*
longinquus -a -um, *long, distant, far, remote, foreign*; of time, *long, distant.*
longĭtūdo -īnis, f. *length.*
longŭlus -a -um, *rather long*; adv. **longŭlē,** *rather far, at a little distance.*
longŭrĭus -i, m. *a pole, rod, rail.*
longus -a -um, *long*; navis, *a man-of-war*; poet., *spacious*; of time, *long, of long duration*: esp. *too long, tedious*; of persons, *prolix, tedious.* Adv. **longē,** *a long way off, far, at a distance; by far*; in time, *long, at length*; adv. **longĭtĕr,** *far.*
lŏquācĭtās -ātis, f. *talkativeness.*
lŏquācŭlus -a -um, *rather talkative.*
lŏquax -quācis, *talkative, garrulous, babbling, noisy*; adv. **lŏquācĭtĕr.**
lŏquella (lŏquēla) -ae, f. *speech, language.*
lŏquor lŏqui lŏcūtus, dep. *to speak* (in conversation); *to tell, say, talk of.*
lōrātus -a -um, *bound with thongs.*
lōrīca -ae, f. *cuirass, corselet, breast plate; breastwork, parapet.*
lōrīcātus -a -um, *wearing a cuirass.*
lōrĭpēs -pĕdis, *bandy-legged.*
lōrum -i, n. *a strap* or *thong of leather*; plur., *reins, bridle; scourge, whip.*

lōtŏs (**-us**) -i, f. *the name of several plants*; esp. *of an African tree and its fruit.*
[1]**lōtus** -a -um, partic. from lavo; q.v.
[2]**lōtus** -i, f. = lotos; q.v.
lŭbet, lŭbīdo, etc. = libet, libido, etc.; q.v.
lūbrĭco -are, *to make slippery.*
lūbrĭcus -a -um, *slippery, smooth; quickly moving, uncertain, insecure, perilous, deceitful.*
Lūcāni -orum, m. pl. *a people in Southern Italy.*
Lūcānus -i, m., M. Annaeus, *author of the poem* Pharsalia.
lūcar -āris, n. *a forest-tax,* used for paying actors.
lŭcellum -i, n. *little profit, small gain.*
lūcĕo lūcēre luxi, *to be bright, shine, glitter; to be clear, evident*; impers., lucet, *it is light, it is day.*
Lucĕrēs -um, m. *one of the three patrician tribes.*
lŭcerna -ae, f. *lamp.*
lūcesco (**lūcisco**) lūcescĕre luxi, *to begin to shine*; impers., lucescit, *it grows light, day is breaking.*
lūcĭdus -a -um, *shining, bright; clear, lucid*; adv. **lūcĭdē.**
lūcĭfer -fĕra -fĕrum, *light-bearing, light-bringing*; m. as subst., *the morning star.*
lūcĭfŭgus -a -um, *shunning the light.*
Lūcīlĭus -a -um, *name of a Roman* gens.
Lūcīna -ae, f. *the goddess of births.*
lūcisco = lucesco; q.v.
Lūcĭus -i, m. *Roman* praenomen (abbreviated to L.).
Lucrētĭus -a -um, *name of a Roman* gens.
lucrĭfăcĭo -făcĕre, *to gain, receive as profit.*
Lucrīnus -i, m. *a lake on the coast of Campania, near Baiae, famous for oysters.*
lucror -ari, dep. *to gain, profit, win.*
lucrōsus -a -um, *gainful, profitable.*
lucrum -i, n. *gain, profit, advantage; love of gain, avarice.*
luctāmen -ĭnis, n. *effort, toil.*
luctātĭo -ōnis, f. *wrestling; a struggle contest.*
luctātor -ōris, m. *wrestler.*
luctĭfĭcus -a -um, *causing grief, baleful.*
luctĭsŏnus -a -um, *sad-sounding.*
luctor -ari, dep (and **lucto** -are), *to wrestle, struggle, strive, contend.*
luctŭōsus -a -um. (1) *causing sorrow, doleful.* (2) *feeling* or *showing sorrow, mourning.* Compar. adv. **luctŭōsĭus.**
luctus -ūs, m. *sorrow expressed, lamentation, mourning; mourning clothes.*
lūcubrātĭo -ōnis, f. *work done by night* or *lamp-light, nocturnal study.*
lūcubro -are, *to work by night*; in perf. partic. **lūcubrātus** -a -um, *done at night* or *spent in work.*
lūcŭlentus -a -um, *shining, bright, brilliant, splendid*; adv. **lūcŭlentē** and **lūcŭlentĕr,** *splendidly.*
Lūcullus -i, m. *name of a family in the* gens Licinia.
Lŭcŭmo (**Lŭcŏmo, Lucmo**) -ōnis, m. *title given to Etruscan princes and priests.*
lūcus -i, m. *a* (*sacred*) *grove* or *wood.*
lūdĭa -ae, f. *an actress* or *female gladiator.*
lūdĭbrĭum -i, n. *derision, mockery; an object of derision, laughing-stock, plaything.*
lūdĭbundus -a -um, *playful, sportive.*
lūdĭcer -cra -crum, *sportive, done for sport*; esp. *of the stage.* N. as subst. **lūdicrum** -i, *a trifle, plaything; a theatrical performance.*
lūdĭfĭcātĭo -onis, f. *deriding, deceiving.*
lūdĭfĭco -are and **lūdĭfĭcor** -ari, dep. *to make game of, deride, delude, cheat, frustrate.*
lūdĭo -ōnis, m. and **lūdĭus** -i, m. *an actor.*
lūdo lūdĕre lūsi lūsum, *to play, sport; to play at* or *with*; *to imitate, banter, deceive, delude.*
lūdus -i, m. *play, game, sport, pastime*; plur., ludi, *public games* or *spectacles.* Transf., *a trifle, jest, joke*; ludum dare, *to give free play to; a training establishment, school.*
lŭella -ae, f. *expiation.*
lŭēs -is, f. *plague, pestilence, calamity.*
Lugdūnum -i, n. *a city in Gaul* (now *Lyons*). Adj. **Lugdūnensis** -e.
lūgĕo lūgēre luxi: intransit., *to mourn, be in mourning*; transit., *to bewail, lament, wear mourning for.*
lūgubris -e, *of mourning, mournful; plaintive; grievous.* N. pl. as subst., *mourning clothes.*
lumbus -i, m. *loin.*
lūmen -ĭnis, n. *light; a light, lamp; the light of day, day; the light of life; the light of the eye, the eye; an opening, a light* in a building; fig., *clearness, insight; a shining light, glory, ornament.*
lūmĭnārĕ -āris, n. *a window-shutter window.*
lūmĭnōsus -a -um, *bright.*
lūna -ae, f. *the moon; night, a month; a crescent-shaped ornament.*
lūnāris -e, *of the moon, lunar.*
lūno -are, *to bend into a crescent*; perf. partic. **lūnātus** -a -um, *crescent-shaped.*
lŭo lŭĕre lŭi lŭitūrus, *to loose; to expiate, atone for, make good;* luere poenam, *to pay a penalty*; of trouble, *to avert.*
lŭpa -ae, f. *a she-wolf; a prostitute.*
lŭpātus -a -um, *provided with iron spikes*; m. or n. pl. as subst., *a curb with jagged spikes.*
Lŭpercus -i, m. *an Italian pastoral deity, or one of his priests*; subst. **Lŭpercal** -cālis, n. *a grotto, sacred to Lupercus:* **Lŭpercālĭa** -ium and -iorum, n. pl., *the festival of Lupercus, celebrated in February.*
[1]**lŭpīnus** -a -um, *of a wolf, wolfish.*
[2]**lŭpīnus** -i, m. and **lŭpīnum** -i, n., *the lupin.*
lŭpus -i, m. *a wolf; a voracious fish,*

the pike; a horse's bit with jagged points; a hook.

lūrĭdus -a -um, *pale yellow, lurid, ghastly.*

lūror -ōris, m. *ghastliness, paleness.*

luscĭnĭa -ae, f. *nightingale.*

luscĭōsus and **luscĭtĭōsus** -a -um, *purblind, dim-sighted.*

luscus -a -um, *one-eyed.*

lūsĭo -ōnis, f. *play, game.*

Lūsĭtānĭa -ae, f. *the modern Portugal, with part of Spain.*

lūsor -ōris, m. *a player; a playful writer; a mocker.*

lustrālis -e, *relating to expiation* or *to a period of five years.*

lustrātĭo -ōnis, f. *purification by sacrifice; a going round, traversing.*

[1]**lustro** -are, *to brighten, illumine.*

[2]**lustro** -are, *to purify, cleanse* by sacrifices; *to go round, go over, traverse; to review, observe, examine.*

[1]**lustrum** -i, n., usually plur., *the den of a wild beast, woodlands; brothels, debauchery.*

[2]**lustrum** -i, n. *an expiatory sacrifice; a period of five years.*

lūsus -ūs, m. *playing, game, sport; dalliance.*

lūtĕŏlus -a -um, *yellow.*

Lūtētĭa -ae, f. *a town in Gallia* (now *Paris*).

[1]**lūtĕus** -a -um, *saffron-yellow.*

[2]**lŭtĕus** -a -um, *of mud* or *clay; dirty.*

lŭto -are, *to smear with mud.*

lŭtŭlentus -a -um, *muddy, dirty, filthy, impure.*

[1]**lūtum** -i, n. *a plant used for dyeing yellow; yellow colour.*

[2]**lŭtum** -i, n. *mud, mire, dirt; clay.*

lux, lūcis, f. *light*; esp. *daylight, day; a day; the light of life* or *of day; the eye, eyesight; illustration, elucidation; hope, encouragement; ornament.*

luxŭrĭa -ae and **luxŭrĭēs** -ēi, f. *rankness, exuberant growth; excess, dissipation, extravagance.*

luxŭrĭo -are and **luxŭrĭor** -ari, dep., *to be luxuriant, rank, grow fast; to frisk, sport, run riot.*

luxŭrĭōsus -a -um, *luxuriant, rank; immoderate, excessive; luxurious, dissolute, extravagant.* Adv. **luxŭrĭōsē,** *luxuriously.*

luxus -ūs, m. *luxury, excess, extravagance.*

Lўaeus -i, m. *surname of Bacchus; wine.*

lychnūchus -i, m. *lamp-stand, candelabrum.*

lychnus -i, m. *lamp.*

Lўcĭa -ae, f. *a country of Asia Minor.*

Lўdĭa -ae, f. *a country of Asia Minor*; ad. **Lўdĭus** and **Lўdus** -a -um, *Lydian.*

lympha -ae, f. *water*, esp. *clear spring* or *river water.*

lymphātĭcus and **lymphātus** -a -um, *raving, mad, frantic.*

lynx -cis, c. *lynx.*

lўra -ae, f. *the lyre* or *lute, a stringed instrument; lyric poetry, song.*

lўrĭcus -a -um, *of the lyre, lyric.*

M

M, m. the twelfth letter of the Latin Alphabet.

Măcĕdō (-ōn) -ŏnis, m. *a Macedonian*; subst. **Măcĕdŏnĭa** -ae, f.; adj. **Măcĕdŏnĭcus, Măcĕdŏnĭus** -a -um.

măcellum, -i, n. *a provision-market.*

măcer -cra -crum, *lean; thin, poor.*

mācĕrĭa -ae, f. *a wall*, esp. *garden-wall.*

mācĕro -are, *to soften; to make weak, reduce; to torment, tease, vex.*

măchaera -ae, f. *a sword.*

māchĭna -ae, f. *a machine, contrivance; a crane, windlass, catapult, ballista.* Transf., *fabric; a device, trick, stratagem.*

māchĭnāmentum -i, n. *machine, instrument.*

māchĭnātĭo -ōnis, f. *contrivance, machinery, mechanism; device, machination.*

māchĭnātor -ōris, m. *a maker of machines, engineer; a deviser, contriver.*

māchĭnor -ari, dep. *to contrive, invent, devise.*

măcĭēs -ēi, f. *leanness, thinness, poverty, barrenness.*

macresco -ĕre, *to grow lean, become thin.*

macrŏcollum -i, n. *paper of the largest size.*

mactābĭlis -e, *deadly.*

mactātū, abl. sing. m. *by a sacrificial stroke.*

macte; see [1]mactus.

[1]**macto** -are, *to magnify, honour, glorify.*

[2]**macto** -are, *to slay, smite; to afflict, punish.*

[1]**mactus** -a -um, *glorified, honoured*; used only in voc. m. **mactĕ,** *well done! bravo! good luck!*

[2]**mactus** -a -um, *smitten.*

măcŭla -ae, f. *a spot, mark, stain*; sometimes *the mesh of a net; a moral stain, blemish, fault.*

măcŭlo -are, *to spot, stain, defile, pollute.*

măcŭlōsus -a -um, *spotted, speckled, stained, polluted.*

mădĕfăcĭo -făcĕre -fēci -factum, and pass. **mădĕfīo** -fĭĕri, *to mak wet, moisten, soak.*

mădĕo -ēre, *to be wet, to stream; to be drunk; to be boiled.* Transf., *to be steeped in, abound in.*

mădesco mădescĕre mădŭi, *to become wet.*

mădĭdus -a -um, *moist, wet; drunk; boiled soft; dyed, steeped.* Adv. **mădĭdē,** *drunkenly.*

mădor -ōris, m. *moisture, wetness.*

Maeandĕr and **Maeandrŏs (-us)** -dri, m. *a river of Asia Minor, proverbial for its winding course; a winding.*

Maecēnās -ātis, m. C. Cilnius, *the patron of Horace and Vergil.*

maena (mena) -ae, f. *a small sea-fish.*

Maenăs -ădis, f. *a bacchante; a prophetess.*

maerĕo -ēre: intransit., *to grieve,*

mourn, lament; transit., *to lament, bewail*.

maeror -ōris, m. *mourning, grief, sorrow*.

maestĭtĭa -ae, f. *sadness, dejection, gloom*.

maestus -a -um, *sad, dejected, gloomy*; adv. **maestĭtĕr.**

māgālĭa -ium, n. pl. *huts*.

măgĕ; see magis.

măgĭcus -a -um, *magical*.

măgĭs (or **măgĕ**), *more, to a greater extent; rather, for preference*; non magis . . . quam, *not more . . . than, just as much . . . as*; quo magis . . . eo magis, *the more . . . the more*. Superl. **maxĭmē (maxŭmē)**, *in the highest degree, most of all, especially, very much so*; quam maxime, *as much as possible*; with tum, cum, *just, precisely*.

măgister -tri, m. *master, chief, head, director*; populi, *dictator*; equitum, *master of the horse, the dictator's lieutenant*; magister (ludi), *a schoolmaster, teacher*; societatis, *director of a company*; elephanti, *driver*; navis, *master* or *helmsman*. Transf., *instigator, adviser, guide*.

măgistĕrĭum -i, n. *directorship, magistracy; direction, guidance*.

măgistra -ae, f. *a mistress, directress*.

măgistrātus -ūs, m. *a magistracy, official dignity, office*. Transf., *a magistrate, state official*.

magnănĭmĭtās -ātis, f. *greatness of soul, magnanimity*.

magnănĭmus -a -um, *high-minded, magnanimous*.

magnĭfĭcentĭa -ae, f. *loftiness* of thought and action; *grandeur, magnificence, splendour*; in bad sense, *boasting, pomposity*.

magnĭfĭco -are, *to prize highly, esteem*.

magnĭfĭcus -a -um; compar. **magnĭfĭcentĭor**; superl. **magnĭfĭcentissĭmus**; *grand, splendid, fine*; in bad sense, *boastful, pompous*. Adv. **magnĭfĭcē.**

magnĭlŏquentĭa -ae, f. *lofty* or *elevated language; pompous, boastful language*.

magnĭlŏquus -a -um, *lofty* or *elevated in language; pompous* or *boastful*.

magnĭtudō -ĭnis, f. *greatness*; animi, *magnanimity*.

magnŏpĕrĕ and separately **magnō ŏpĕrĕ**, *greatly, very much*.

magnus -a -um; compar. **māior,** maius; superl. **maxĭmus (maxŭmus)** -a -um; *great, large*; of sound, *loud*; of price or value, *high*; magno, and magni, *at a high price, dear, highly*. Transf., of time, *long, old*; of standing, *great, mighty, powerful, important*; m. pl. of compar. as subst. **māiōres,** *ancestors*; in maius, *to a higher degree*; **magnō ŏpĕrĕ**, see magnopere; for **maxĭmē,** see magis.

Māgō (-ōn) -ōnis, m. *brother of Hannibal*.

[1]**măgus** -i, m. *a learned Persian; a magician*.

[2]**măgus** -a -um, *magical*.

Māia -ae, f. *the daughter of Atlas, mother of Mercury*, adj. **Māius** -a -um, *of Maia*: (mensis) Maius, *the month of May*.

māiestās -ātis, f. *greatness, grandeur, dignity, majesty*; crimen maiestatis, *treason*.

māior, māiōres; see magnus.

Māius -a -um, adj. from Maia; q.v.

māiuscŭlus -a -um, *somewhat greater* or *older*.

māla -ae, f. *cheek-bone, jaw-bone; jaw, cheek*.

mălăcĭa -ae, f. *a calm at sea*.

mălăcus -a -um, *soft, pliable; effeminate, delicate*.

mălĕdīco -dīcĕre -dixi -dictum (sometimes separately, male dico), *to speak ill, abuse*; pres. partic., **mălĕdīcens** -entis, *abusive*; n. of perf. partic. as subst. **mălĕdictum** -i, *cursing, abusive language*.

mălĕdictĭo -ōnis, f. *reviling, abuse*.

mălĕdīcus -a -um, *abusive, scurrilous*; adv. **mălĕdīcē.**

mălĕfăcĭo -făcĕre -fēci -factum (sometimes separately, male facio), *to injure*; n. of perf. partic. as subst. **mălĕfactum** -i, *an ill deed, injury*.

mălĕfactor -ōris, m. *an evil-doer*.

mălĕfĭcĭum -i, n. *wrongdoing*; *mischief*.

mălĕfĭcus -a -um, *evil-doing, mischievous*; adv. **mălĕfĭcē.**

mălĕsuādus -a -um, *ill-advising, seductive*.

mălĕvŏlens -entis, *spiteful, ill-disposed*.

mălĕvŏlentĭa -ae, f. *ill-will, spite, malice*.

mălĕvŏlus -a -um, *ill-disposed, spiteful, malicious*.

mālĭfer -fĕra -fĕrum, *apple-bearing*.

mălignĭtās -ātis, f. *ill-nature, malignity, spite; stinginess*.

mălignus -a -um, *ill-disposed, wicked*; esp. *stingy, niggardly*; *barren, unfruitful; stinted, scanty*. Adv. **mălignē.**

mălĭtĭa -ae, f. *badness, wickedness, vice*; esp. *craft, cunning, malice*.

mălĭtĭōsus -a -um, *wicked; crafty, roguish, knavish*; adv. **mălĭtĭōsē.**

mallĕŏlus -i, m. *a little hammer; a kind of fire-dart*.

mallĕus -i. m. *a hammer, mallet, pole-axe*.

mālo malle mālŭi, *to wish rather, prefer*; with dative of person, *to be more favourable to*.

mālŏbathrum -i, n. *a plant, from which ointment was prepared*.

[1]**mălum** -i, n.; see [1]malus.

[2]**mālum** -i, n. *an apple*, or other similar fruit.

[1]**mălus** -a -um; comp. **pēior** -us; superl. **pessĭmus** -a -um; *bad, evil* (physically or morally); *unfavourable, unsuccessful, ugly*. N. as subst. **mălum** -i, *an evil; harm, disaster; punishment;* as a term of abuse, *scoundrel*. Adv. **mălĕ**, compar. **pēius**; superl. **pessĭmē,** *badly, ill;* male audire, *to be ill spoken of*; *unsuccessfully, unfortunately*; with

words bad in sense, *bitterly, excessively*; with words of favourable sense, with negative force, e.g., male gratus, *unthankful*.
[2]**mālus** -i, f. *an apple-tree*.
[3]**mālus** -i, m. *the mast of a ship; an upright, pole*.
malva -ae, f. *the mallow*.
Māmers -mertis, m. *the Oscan name of Mars*; hence **Māmertīni** -orum, m. *the name assumed by certain mercenary troops*.
mămilla -ae, f. *breast, teat*.
mamma -ae, f. *breast*.
mānābĭlis -e, *flowing, penetrating*.
manceps -cĭpis, m. *a purchaser, farmer, contractor*.
mancĭpĭum (**mancŭpĭum**) -i, n. *a formal purchase of anything*. Transf., *a slave acquired by* mancipium.
mancĭpo (**mancŭpo**) -are, *to sell formally; to give up*.
mancus -a -um, *maimed, crippled, imperfect, defective*.
mandātū abl. sing. m. *by order*.
mandātum -i, n. subst. from mando; q.v.
[1]**mando** -are, *to commit, entrust*; of actions, *to order, command, commission*. N. of partic. as subst., **mandātum** -i, *a commission charge, order*.
[2]**mando** mandĕre mandi mansum, *to chew, masticate, champ; to eat, consume*.
mandra -ae, f. *a stall, cattle-pen; a herd of cattle; a draughtboard*.
mānĕ, indecl. n.: as subst., *morning*; adv., *in the morning, early*.
mănĕo mănēre mansi mansum: intransit., *to remain, stay; to stay the night; to endure, last*; promissis, *to abide by*; transit., in gen., *to wait for, await*.
mānēs -ĭum, m. pl. *the shades of the departed, spirits of the dead*; poet., *the lower world, infernal regions; corpse, ashes, remains*.
mango -ōnis, m. *a salesman*, esp., *slave dealer*.
mănĭca -ae, f. *a sleeve, serving as a glove; handcuffs, manacles*.
mănĭcātus -a -um, *having long sleeves*.
mănĭcŭla -ae, f. *a little hand*.
mănĭfesto -are, *to show clearly, reveal*.
mănĭfestus -a -um, *palpable, clear, visible, evident; caught out, detected*. Abl. sing. n. as adv. **mănĭfestō,** *clearly*; compar. **mănĭfestĭus.**
Mānīlĭus -a -um, *name of a Roman* gens.
mănĭpŭlāris (**mănĭplāris**) *belonging to a maniple*; m. as subst. *a private soldier; a fellow-soldier*.
mănĭpŭlātim, *in bundles; in maniples*.
mănĭpŭlus (poet, **mănĭplus**) -i, m. *a handful, bundle*; milit. *a company of infantry, a division of the Roman army*.
Manlĭus -a -um, *name of a Roman* gens.
mannŭlus -i, m. *a pony*.
mannus -i, m. *a pony, cob*.
māno -are, *to flow, drip, spread*; with abl., *to drip with*; with acc., *to exude*.
mansĭo -ōnis, f. *stay, sojourn; station, stage*.
mansĭto -are, *to abide, stay*.
mansuēfăcĭo -făcĕre -fēci -factum, pass. **mansuēfīo** -fĭĕri -factus sum, *to tame; to soften, pacify, civilize*.
mansuēs -is or -ētis, *tame*.
mansuesco -suescĕre -suēvi -suētum: transit., *to tame*; intransit., *to grow tame* or *soft*.
Hence partic. **mansuētus** -a -um, *tame, mild, soft*; adv. **mansuētē.**
mansuētūdo -ĭnis, f. *tameness: mildness, gentleness*.
mantēlĕ -is, n. *towel, napkin*.
mantēlum -i, n. *covering, cloak*.
mantĭca -ae, f. *wallet, knapsack*.
manto -are, *to remain, wait, wait for*.
Mantŭa -ae, f. *a town in north Italy*.
mănŭālis -e, *fitted to the hand*.
mănŭbĭae -arum, f. *money from the sale of booty*, esp. *the general's share; spoils, profits*.
mănubrium -i, n. *haft, handle*.
mănŭf-; see manif-.
mănŭlĕus -i, m. and **mănŭlĕa** -ae, f. *a long sleeve*.
mănūmissĭo -ōnis, f. *the emancipation of a slave*.
mănūmitto -mittĕre -mīsi -missum (or as two words, manu mitto), *to manumit, emancipate a slave*.
mănuprĕtĭum (**mănipr-**) -i, n. *wages, hire, reward*.
mănus -ūs, f. *hand;* manus dare, *to surrender*; in manibus, *on hand, in preparation*; servus ad manum, *a secretary*; abl. manu, *by hand, artificially*. Transf., *the strong arm, fist, force, effort; power, jurisdiction; the hand* or *touch of artist* or *craftsman; a band* or *body of men; an elephant's trunk*; manus ferrea, *grappling-iron*.
măpālĭa -ium, n. *huts, hovels*.
mappa -ae, f. *a table-napkin*.
Marcellus -i, m. *the cognomen of a family of the* gens Claudia.
marcĕo -ēre, *to wither, droop, be feeble*.
marcesco -ĕre, *to begin to droop, grow feeble*.
marcĭdus -a -um, *withering, drooping, enfeebled*.
marcor -ōris, m. *rottenness, decay*.
marcŭlus -i, m. *a small hammer*.
Marcus -i, *a Roman praenomen*, abbreviated M.
mărĕ -is, n. *the sea*; mare nostrum, *the Mediterranean*; superum, *the Adriatic*; inferum, *the Tyrrhenian Sea*.
margărīta -ae f. and **margărītum** -i n. *a pearl*.
margĭno -are, *to border*.
margo -ĭnis, m. and f. *a border, edge, boundary*.
mărīnus -a -um, *of the sea, marine*: ros, *rosemary*.
mărītālis -e, *conjugal, matrimonial*.
mărĭtĭmus (**mărĭtŭmus**) -a -um, *of*

or *on the sea, marine*; praedo, *a pirate*; n. pl. as subst. *the sea-coast.*
mărīto -are, *to marry, give in marriage*; of vines, *to bind* to a tree, *to train.*
mărītus -a -um, *matrimonial, nuptial*; of plants, *tied* or *trained together*, As subst. **mărītus** -i, m. *husband. lover, suitor*; **mărīta** -ae, f. *wife.*
Mărĭus -a -um, *the name of a Roman* gens.
marmor -ŏris, n. *marble statue; stone; the white foamy surface of the sea.*
marmŏrĕus -a -um, *of marble, like marble.*
Măro -ōnis, m. *the cognomen of the poet P. Vergilius.*
marra -ae, f. *a hoe.*
Mars Martis, m. (old form, Māvors), *Mars, god of agriculture and of war.* Transf., *war, battle, fight.* Adj. **Martĭus** and poet. **Māvortĭus** -a -um, *of Mars*; Martius (mensis), *the month of March; warlike.* Adj. **Martĭālis** -e, *of Mars*; m. as subst. *a priest of Mars* or *soldier of the Legio Martia.*
Marsi -ōrum, m. *an ancient people of Latium*; adj. **Marsĭcus** and **Marsus** -a -um; Marsicum bellum, *the Social War.*
marsuppĭum -i, n. *purse, pouch.*
[1]**Martĭālis** -e, adj. from Mars; q.v.
[2]**Martĭālis** -is, m. M. Valerius, *Martial, the writer of epigrams.*
Martĭgĕna -ae, m. *offspring of Mars.*
Martĭus -a -um, adj. from Mars; q.v.
mas măris, m. *the male; manly, vigorous.*
mascŭlus -a -um, *male; manly, bold.*
Măsĭnissa -ae, m. *king of Numidia.*
massa -ae, f. *a lump, mass.*
massĭcum -i, n. *Massic wine.*
Massĭlĭa -ae, f. *a town in Gallia Narbonensis* (now *Marseilles*); adj. **Massĭlĭensis** -e.
mastīgĭa -ae, m. *a scoundrel.*
mastrūca -ae, f. *a sheepskin.*
matăra -ae, and **matăris** -is, f. *a pike, lance.*
mătellĭo -ōnis, m. *a small pot, vessel.*
māter, mātris, f. *mother; source, origin.*
mātercŭla -ae, f. *little mother.*
mātĕrĭa -ae, and **mātĕrĭēs** -ēi, f. *matter, material, stuff; timber.* Transf., *subject-matter; occasion, cause; natural disposition.*
mātĕrĭo -are, *to construct of wood.*
mātĕrĭor -ari, dep. *to fell wood.*
matĕris = matara; q.v.
māternus -a -um, *of a mother, maternal.*
mātertĕra -ae, f. *maternal aunt.*
măthēmătĭcus -a -um, *mathematical*; m. as subst. *a mathematician* or *astrologer*; f. **măthēmătĭca** -ae, *mathematics* or *astrology.*
mātrĭcīda -ae, c. *a matricide.*
mātrĭcīdĭum -i, n. *slaying of a mother, matricide.*
mātrĭmōnĭum -i, n. *marriage.*
mātrīmus -a -um, *having a mother still living.*
[1]**mātrōna** -ae, f. *a married woman, matron.*
[2]**Mātrŏna** -ae, m. *a river in Gaul* (now the *Marne*).
mātrōnālis -e, *of a married woman, matronly*; n. pl. as subst. **Mātrōnālĭa** -ĭum, *a festival held by Roman matrons.*
matta -ae, f. *a mat of rushes.*
mattĕa (**mattўa**) -ae, f. *a dainty dish.*
mātūresco mātūrescĕre mātūrŭi, *to ripen, become ripe.*
mātūrĭtās -ātis, f. *ripeness, maturity; the right moment, fullness of time.*
mātūro -are: transit., *to make ripe, ripen; to quicken, hasten, accelerate; to anticipate, do too soon*; intransit., *to hasten, make haste.*
mātūrus -a -um, *ripe, mature, grown up, developed, perfect; timely, quick, speedy, early.* Adv. **mātūrē** *at the right time, seasonably, opportunely: in good time, betimes, early; too soon, prematurely.*
mātūtīnus -a -um, *early in the morning, of morning.*
Mauri -orum, m. *the Moors*; adj. **Maurus** -a -um; subst. **Maurĭtānĭa** -ae, f. *Mauritania.*
māvŏlo = malo; q.v.
Māvors -vortis, m. archaic and poet. for Mars; adj. **Māvortĭus** -a -um.
maxilla -ae, f. *jaw-bone, jaw.*
maxĭmĭtās -ātis, f. *greatness, size.*
maxĭmus, superl. of magnus; q.v.
māzŏnŏmus -i, m. or **māzŏnŏmon** -i, n. *a charger, large dish.*
mĕātus -ūs, m. *a going, motion; a way, path.*
Mēcastor; see Castor.
meddix -ĭcis, m. *an Oscan magistrate.*
Mēdēa -ae, f. *an enchantress, who helped Jason to obtain the golden fleece.*
mĕdĕor -ēri, dep. *to heal, to cure, assist, alleviate*; pres. partic. as subst. **mĕdens** -entis, m. *a physician.*
Mēdi -orum, m. *the Medes*; poet. = *the Persians.*
mĕdĭastīnus -i, m. *a drudge.*
mēdĭca -ae, f. *lucerne, clover.*
mĕdĭcābĭlis -e, *curable.*
mĕdĭcāmen -ĭnis, n. *a drug, medicine, remedy; poison: dye, rouge.*
mĕdĭcāmentum -i, n. *a drug, medicine, remedy; a magic potion; poison; embellishment.*
mĕdĭcātus -ūs, m. *means of enchantment, charm.*
mĕdĭcīnus -a -um, *of the art of healing*; f. as subst. **mĕdĭcīna** -ae, *the art of healing; medicine; cure.*
mĕdĭco -are, *to drug; to dye*; partic. **mĕdĭcātus** -a -um, *steeped, drugged.*
mĕdĭcor -ari, dep., *to heal, cure.*
mĕdĭcus -a -um, *healing, medicinal*; m. as subst. **mĕdĭcus** -i, *a doctor, physician.*
mĕdimnum -i, n. and **mĕdimnus** -i, m. *a Greek measure of capacity.*
mĕdĭocris -e, *moderate, middling, ordinary*; adv. **mĕdĭocrĭter** *moderately, tolerably; with moderation.*
mĕdĭocrĭtās -ātis, f. *moderation,*

medium, the mean; mediocrity, insignificance.
Mĕdĭŏlānum and **-lānĭum** -i, n. *a town in Cisalpine Gaul* (now *Milan*).
mĕdĭtāmentum -i, n. *preparation, practice.*
mĕdĭtātĭo -ōnis, f. (1) *a thinking over, contemplation.* (2) *practice, exercise, preparation.*
mĕdĭterrānĕus -a -um, *inland*: n. pl. as subst., *inland country.*
mĕdĭtor -ari, dep. (1) *to think over, consider*; esp. *to think about doing, to meditate, intend.* (2) *to practise.* Perf. partic. in pass. sense **mĕdĭtātus** -a -um, *meditated, considered, prepared*; adv. **mĕdĭtātē,** *thoughtfully, thoroughly.*
mĕdĭus -a -um, *middle, midmost, mid; intervening, central, neutral, intermediate.* N. as subst. **mĕdĭum** -i, *the middle; the public eye, everyday life; the community, common good.* Adv. **mĕdĭē,** *moderately.*
mĕdĭus fĭdĭus; see fidius.
mĕdulla -ae, f. *the marrow of the bones.*
Mēdus; see Medi.
Mĕdūsa -ae, f. *one of the Gorgons, slain by Perseus.*
Mĕgăra -ae, f. (and -orum, n. pl.). (1) *a town in Greece.* (2) *a town in Sicily.*
mĕgistānes -um, m. *grandees, magnates.*
mēhercŭle, mēhercle; see Hercules.
mĕl mellis, n. *honey; sweetness, pleasantness.*
mĕlanchŏlĭcus -a -um, *having black bile, melancholy.*
mĕlānūrus -i, m. *small edible sea-fish.*
mĕlĭcus -a -um, *musical; lyrical, lyric.*
mĕlĭlōtŏs -i, f. *a species of clover.*
mĕlĭmēla -orum, n. pl. *honey-apples.*
mĕlĭor -us, compar. of bonus; q.v.
mĕlisphyllum and **mĕlissŏphyllŏn** -i, n. *balm.*
Mĕlĭta -ae, f. *the island of Malta*; adj. **Mĕlĭtensis** -e, *of Malta.*
mĕlĭuscŭlus -a -um, *somewhat better*; adv. **mĕlĭuscŭlē,** *somewhat better, pretty well* (in health).
mellĭfer -fĕra -fĕrum, *producing honey.*
mellītus -a -um, *honeyed; sweet as honey.*
[1]**mĕlŏs,** n. *a tune, song.*
[2]**Mēlŏs** -i, f. *an island in the Aegean Sea.*
Melpŏmĕnē -ēs, f. *the Muse of tragic poetry.*
membrāna -ae, f. *a thin skin, film, membrane; prepared skin, parchment.*
membrātim, *limb by limb; piecemeal, singly; in short sentences.*
membrum -i, n. *a limb, member, part (of the body); a clause in a sentence.*
mĕmĭni -nisse, perf. with sense of present, *to remember, recollect.* Transf. *to make mention of, to mention.*
mĕmor -ŏris, *mindful, remembering; with a good memory; grateful, thoughtful, prudent; reminiscent, reminding.*
mĕmŏrābĭlis -e, *remarkable, worthy of mention, memorable.*
mĕmŏrandus -a -um, gerundive from memoro; q.v.
mĕmŏrātor -ōris, m. *a narrator.*
mĕmŏrātus -ūs, m. *mention.*
mĕmŏrĭa -ae, *memory, the capacity for remembering, remembrance; record of the past, tradition, history.*
mĕmŏrĭŏla -ae, f. *memory.*
mĕmŏrĭter, *by heart, from memory.*
mĕmŏro -are, *to mention, call to mind, relate*; gerundive **mĕmŏrandus** -a -um, *notable, memorable.*
Memphis -is and -ĭdos, f. *a city of Egypt.*
Mĕnander -dri, m. *a Greek comic poet.*
menda -ae, f.; see mendum.
mendācĭum -i, n. *lie, falsehood.*
mendax -ācis, *lying, mendacious, false.*
mendīcĭtās -atis, f. *beggary.*
mendīco -are and **mendīcor** -ari, dep. *to beg, go begging; beg for.*
mendīcus -a -um, adj. *poor as a beggar, beggarly; paltry, pitiful;* m. as subst. **mendīcus** -i, *a beggar.*
mendōsus -a -um, *full of faults, inaccurate, making mistakes*; adv. **mendōsē,** *faultily.*
mendum -i, n. and **menda** -ae, f. *a fault, defect, blemish, mistake.*
Mĕnĕlāus -i, m. *brother of Agamemnon, husband of Helen.*
mens mentis, f. *mind, understanding, intellect, judgment; feelings, disposition; courage; opinion, thoughts; intention, resolve.*
mensa -ae, f. *a table, counter, altar; a course at a meal.*
mensārĭus -i, m. *a financial commissioner.*
mensĭo -ōnis, f. *measuring.*
mensis -is, m., *a month.*
mensor -ōris, m., *a measurer, surveyor; an architect.*
menstrŭus -a -um, *monthly; lasting a month*; n. as subst. *rations for a month, a month in office.*
mensūra -ae, f. *measuring; measure, standard, capacity; amount, proportion.*
menta (mentha) -ae, f. *the herb mint.*
mentĭo -ōnis, f. *mention.*
mentĭor -iri, dep. *to lie; to deceive, mislead, disappoint; to say falsely, invent; fabricate; to counterfeit, put on, assume.* Hence pres. partic. **mentĭens** -entis, *lying*; m. as subst. *a fallacy, sophism*; perf. partic. **mentītus** -a -um, *lying, fictitious.*
mentum -i, n. *the chin.*
mĕo mĕare, *to go, pass.*
mĕphītis -is, f. *a noxious exhalation, malaria*; personif., *the goddess who protects against malaria.*
mĕrācus -a -um, *pure, unmixed.*
mercābĭlis -e, *that can be bought.*
mercātor -ōris, m. *a merchant, wholesale trader.*
mercātōrĭus -a -um, *relating to trade.*
mercātūra -ae, f. *trade, traffic; merchandise.*
mercātus -ūs, m. *trade, traffic, business; a market, fair, place of business.*
mercēdŭla -ae, f. *low wages* or *rent.*

mercennārĭus (mercēnārĭus) -a -um, *hired, paid*; m. as subst. *a hired servant.*

mercēs -ēdis, *hire, pay, wages; a bribe; cost, punishment; interest, rent, income.*

mercĭmōnĭum -i, n. *goods, merchandise.*

mercor -ari, dep. *to carry on trade, to traffic; to buy.*

Mercŭrĭus -a -m. *Mercury, messenger of the gods*; adj. **Mercŭrĭālis** -e, *of Mercury*; m. pl. as subst. *a corporation of traders at Rome.*

merda -ae, f. *excrement.*

mĕrenda -ae, f. *a luncheon.*

mĕrĕo -ēre -ŭi, ĭtum, and **merĕor** ēri -ĭtus, dep. *to deserve, earn, obtain*; esp., *to earn pay as a soldier, serve as a soldier.* Hence perf. partic. **mĕrĭtus** -a -um., *deserving*; in pass. sense, *deserved.* N. as subst. **mĕrĭtum** -i, *desert, merit; a good action, benefit, service; blame, fault, grounds, reason.* Abl. as adv. **mĕrĭtō,** *deservedly, rightly.*

mĕretrīcĭus -a -um, *of a harlot*; adv. **mĕretrīcĭē.**

mĕretrīcŭla -ae, f. *a little harlot.*

mĕretrix -īcis, f. *a harlot.*

mergae -arum, f. *a two-pronged fork.*

mergĕs -gĭtis, f. *a sheaf of corn.*

mergo mergĕre mersi mersum, *to dip, plunge into liquid, immerse, sink, overwhelm.*

mergus -i, m. *a sea-bird,* esp. *a gull.*

mĕrīdĭānus -a -um, *of midday, meridian; southern.*

mĕrīdĭātĭo -ōnis, f. *midday sleep, siesta.*

mĕrīdĭēs -ēi, m., *midday, noon; the south.*

mĕrīdĭo -are, *to take a siesta.*

[1]**mĕrĭto** -are, *to earn regularly.*

[2]**mĕrĭto,** adv. from mereo; q.v.

mĕrĭtōrĭus -a -um, *hired*; n. pl. as subst., *lodgings.*

mĕrĭtum -i, n., subst. from mereo; q.v.

mĕrops -ŏpis, f., *a bird, the bee-eater.*

merso -are, *to dip in, immerse.*

mĕrŭla -ae, f. *a blackbird; a fish, the sea-carp.*

mĕrus -a -um, *pure, unmixed; complete, sheer*; esp. of wine, *undiluted*; n. as subst. **mĕrum** -i, *wine unmixed with water.*

merx (mers) mercis, f. *merchandise, goods, wares.*

Mĕsŏpŏtămĭa -ae, f. *the country between the Euphrates and the Tigris.*

Messāna -ae, f. *a town in Sicily on the straits between Italy and Sicily.*

messis -is, f. *harvest, crop; time of harvest, harvest-tide.*

messor -ōris, m. *a reaper, mower.*

messōrĭus -a -um, *of a reaper.*

mēta -ae, f. *a pyramidal column* used as a turning-post or winning-post; *any turning-point; a goal, end, boundary.*

mĕtallum -i, n. *a metal; a mine, quarry* (esp. plur.).

mĕtămorphōsis -is, f. *transformation*; plur. **Mĕtămorphōsēs** -ēōn, *the title of a poem by Ovid.*

mĕtăphŏra -ae, f. *metaphor.*

mētātor -ōris, m. *a measurer, one who marks out.*

Mĕtaurus -i, m. *a river in Umbria.*

mētĭor mētiri mensus, dep., *to measure; to traverse, pass over; to estimate, judge.*

mĕto mĕtĕre messŭi messum, *to reap, mow, gather harvest; to mow down, cut off.*

mētor -ari, dep. (and **mēto** -are) *to measure off, lay out.*

metrēta -ae, f. *a Greek liquid measure.*

metrum -i, n. *a measure; metre.*

mĕtŭcŭlōsus -a -um, *timid; frightful.*

mĕtŭo -ŭĕre -ŭi -ūtum, *to fear, be afraid.*

mĕtus -ūs, m. *fear, dread; reverence, awe.*

mĕus -a -um, *my, mine*; Nero meus, *my friend Nero.*

mīca -ae, f. *a crumb, morsel, grain.*

mĭco -are -ŭi, *to move rapidly to and fro, vibrate, flicker; to shine, glitter, sparkle.*

Mĭdās (Mĭda) -ae, m. *a king of Phrygia, who turned to gold everything that he touched.*

migrātĭo -ōnis, f. *removal, change of home.*

migrātū, abl. sing. m., *in transport.*

migro -are: intransit., *to migrate, depart; to change*; transit., *to move, transport; to transgress.*

mīlĕs -ĭtis, c. *a soldier; a private soldier, infantryman;* coll. *soldiery.*

mīlĭtāris -e, of a *soldier, military*; m. as subst. *a soldier*; adv. **mīlĭtārĭtĕr,** *in a soldierly manner.*

mīlĭtĭa -ae, f. *military service, warfare*; domi militiaeque, *at home and abroad, at peace and in war*; meton., *the military, soldiery.*

mīlĭto -are, *to serve as a soldier, be a soldier.*

milĭum -i, n. *millet.*

millĕ, *a thousand*; plur. **mīlĭa (millĭa)** -ĭum, *thousands*; mille passuum, *a thousand paces, a Roman mile.*

mille(n)sĭmus -a -um, *thousandth.*

millĭārĭum (mīlĭārĭum) -i, n. *a mile-stone.*

millĭārĭus (mīlĭārĭus) -a -um, *containing a thousand.*

millĭe(n)s, *a thousand times.*

mīlŭīnus (milvīnus) -a -um, *of a kite; kite-like.*

mīlŭus (milvus) -i, m. *a kite; a fish, the gurnard.*

mīma -ae, f. *an actress.*

mīmĭcus -a -um, *farcical*; adv. **mīmĭcē.**

mīmŭla -ae, f., *a little actress.*

mīmus -i, m. *a mimic actor; a mime, farce.*

[1]**mīna,** f. *smooth, hairless.*

[2]**mīna** -ae, f. *a Greek weight*; also *a Greek coin.*

mĭnae -arum, f. *battlements, parapets.* Transf., *threats, menaces.*

mĭnātĭo -ōnis, f. *threatening, menace.*

mĭnax -ācis, f. *projecting, overhanging.* Transf., *threatening.* Adv. **mĭnācĭtĕr,** *threateningly.*
mĭnĕo -ēre, *to project, overhang.*
Mĭnerva -ae, f. *goddess of wisdom and patroness of arts and sciences.* Transf., *wit, skill, art*; esp. *working in wool.*
mĭnĭātus -a -um, *coloured with red lead, painted vermilion.*
mĭnĭmē; see parum.
mĭnĭmus; see parvus.
mĭnister -tri, m. and **mĭnistra** -ae, f. *servant, attendant, assistant.*
mĭnistĕrium -i, n. *service, attendance, employment*; in plur., *attendants, retinue.*
mĭnistra -ae, f.; see minister.
mĭnistrātor -ōris, m., **mĭnistrātrix** -icis, f. *a servant, attendant, assistant.*
mĭnistro -are, *to serve, wait,* esp. *at table; to attend to, take care of, direct; to serve, supply, provide.*
mĭnĭtābundus -a -um, *threatening.*
mĭnĭto -are and **mĭnĭtor** -ari dep. *to threaten.*
mĭnĭum -i, n. *native cinnabar; red-lead, vermilion.*
[1]**mĭnor** -ari, dep. *to jut out, project.* Transf., *to threaten, menace* (with dat.). Adv. from partic. **mĭnantĕr,** *threateningly.*
[2]**mĭnor** -ōris, compar. of parvus; q.v.
Mīnōs -ōis and -ōnis, *king of Crete; after his death, a judge in Tartarus.*
Mīnōtaurus -i, m. *a monster, half-bull, half-man slain by Theseus.*
mĭnŭmē and **mĭnŭmus**; see minim-.
mĭnŭo -ŭĕre -ŭi -ūtum, *to make smaller, lessen, diminish; to cut to pieces.* Hence partic. **mĭnūtus** -a -um, *small, petty, insignificant*; adv. **mĭnūtē.**
minus; see parvus.
mĭnuscŭlus -a -um, *rather small.*
mĭnūtal -ālis, n. *a dish of minced meat.*
mĭnūtātim, *bit by bit, gradually.*
mĭnūtĭa -ae, f. *smallness.*
mĭnūtus -a -um, partic. from minuo; q.v.
mīrābĭlis -e *wonderful, extraordinary, unusual*; adv. **mīrābĭlĭtĕr.**
mīrābundus -a -um, *wondering.*
mīrācŭlum -i, n. *a wonderful thing, prodigy, miracle; wonder, surprise.*
mīrātĭo -ōnis, f. *wonder, astonishment.*
mīrātor -ōris, m. *an admirer.*
mīrātrix -icis, f. adj. *wondering.*
mīrĭfĭcus -a -um *causing wonder, wonderful, astonishing*; adv. **mīrĭfĭcē.**
mirmillo (murm-) -ōnis, m. *a kind of gladiator.*
mīror -ari, dep. *to wonder, be astonished (at); to admire, look on with admiration*; gerundive **mīrandus** -a -um, *wonderful.*
mīrus -a -um, *wonderful, astonishing, extraordinary*; adv. **mīrē.**
miscellānĕa -ōrum, n. pl., *a hash, hotchpotch.*
miscĕo miscēre miscŭi mixtum, *to mix, mingle; to combine, unite; to prepare by mixing; to confuse, confound.*
mĭsellus -a -um, *miserable, wretched, little.*
Mīsēnus -i, m. *the trumpeter of Aeneas*; **Mīsēnum** -i, n. *a promontory and town in Campania.*
mĭser -ĕra -ĕrum, *wretched, unhappy, sad*; adv. **mĭsĕrē.**
mĭsĕrābĭlis -e, *sad, wretched, mournful, plaintive*; adv. **mĭsĕrābĭlĭtĕr.**
mĭsĕrātĭo -ōnis, f. *pity, compassion; a pathetic speech* or *tone.*
mĭsĕrĕo -ēre and **mĭsĕrĕor** -ēri, dep. *to pity* (with genit.); impers. **mĭsĕret** and dep. **mĭsĕrētur,** *it excites pity, one pities.*
mĭsĕresco -ĕre, *to pity, have compassion on* (with genit.).
mĭsĕrĭa -ae, f. *wretchedness, unhappiness, distress.*
mĭsĕrĭcordĭa -ae, f. *pity, compassion, mercy; an appeal to pity.*
mĭsĕrĭcors -cordis, *pitiful, compassionate.*
mĭsĕror -ari, dep. *to bewail, deplore; to pity, have compassion on*; gerundive **mĭsĕrandus** -a -um, *pitiable, lamentable.*
missĭcĭus -a -um, *discharged from military service.*
missĭlis -e, *that can be thrown*; n. as subst., *a missile.*
missĭo -ōnis, f. *a sending off, letting go, releasing, discharge; cessation, termination.*
missĭto -are, *to send repeatedly.*
[1]**missus** -ūs, m. *a letting go, sending, throwing; a shot, the distance shot*; in races, *a course, heat.*
[2]**missus** -a -um, partic. from mitto; q.v.
mītesco -ĕre, *to become mild, soft,* or *ripe; to be allayed, to subside.*
Mithrĭdātes -is, m. *name of several kings of Pontus.*
mītĭgātĭo -onis, f. *assuaging, appeasing.*
mītĭgo -are, *to make mild,* or *ripe; to soothe, appease, pacify.*
mītis -e, *mild, soft, ripe; gentle*; of style, *mellow*; compar. adv. **mītĭus;** superl. **mītissĭmē.**
mitra -ae, f. *a head-dress, turban.*
mitrātus -a -um, *wearing the mitra.*
mitto mittĕre mīsi missum, *to send, dispatch; to send as a gift; to fling; to shed; to utter; to let go, release, give up; to dismiss, discharge; to pass over* a subject.
mītŭlus (mўtŭlus, mūtŭlus) -i, m. *an edible mussel.*
mixtūra -ae, f. *a mixing, mixture.*
mna = [2]mina; q.v.
Mnemŏnĭdĕs -um, f. pl. *the Muses.*
Mnēmŏsўnē -ēs, f. *Mnemosyne, mother of the Muses.*
mnēmŏsўnum -i, n. *a souvenir, memorial.*
mōbĭlis -e, *movable, easy to move; pliable, flexible; active, rapid; changeable, inconstant.* Adv. **mōbĭlĭtĕr,** *quickly, easily.*
mōbĭlĭtās -ātis f. *mobility; inconstancy, changeableness.*
mōbĭlĭto -are, *to set in motion.*

mŏdĕrābĭlis -e, *moderate, restrained.*
mŏdĕrāmen -ĭnis, n. *means of guiding*; rerum, *management, government.*
mŏdĕrātim, *moderately, gradually.*
mŏdĕrātĭo -ōnis, f. *moderating, restraining; moderation, restraint.*
mŏdĕrātor -ōris, m. *a governor, controller, manager*; equorum, *a driver.*
mŏdĕrātrix -īcis, f. *she that governs* or *controls.*
mŏdĕror -ari, dep. (and **mŏdĕro** -are), *to keep within bounds; to regulate, restrain; to control, govern, direct.* Hence, from pres. partic. adv. **mŏdĕrantĕr,** *with controlling force*; perf. partic. **mŏdĕrātus** -a -um, *restrained, controlled*; adv. **mŏdĕrātē,** *with restraint.*
mŏdestĭa -ae, f. *moderation; restraint, propriety, orderliness; respect, obedience to authority.*
mŏdestus -a -um, *moderate, within bounds; orderly, restrained*; adv. **mŏdestē.**
mŏdĭcus -a -um, *moderate, within bounds, limited; temperate; ordinary, undistinguished.* Adv. **mŏdĭcē,** *moderately; to a limited extent; temperately, with restraint.*
mŏdĭfĭcātus -a -um, *measured.*
mŏdĭus -i, m. *a Roman corn-measure*; pleno modio, *in full measure, abundantly.*
mŏdŏ, *by measure*; hence *only, merely, but, just*; si modo, modo si, or modo alone with subj., *provided that, if only*; modo ne, *provided that . . . not;* modo non, *all but, nearly*; non modo . . . sed etiam, *not only . . . but also.* Of time, *just, lately; soon, directly*; modo . . . modo . . ., *at one time . . . at another. . . .*
mŏdŭlātĭo -ōnis, f. *rhythmical measure.*
mŏdŭlātor -ōris, m. *a musician.*
mŏdŭlor -ari, dep. *to measure*; in music, *to modulate, to sing to the accompaniment of* an instrument; *to play* an instrument. Adv. from partic. **mŏdŭlātē,** *in time* (of music).
mŏdŭlus -i, m. *a little measure.*
mŏdus -i, m. *a measure, standard of measurement*; in music, *rhythm, measure, time*; in plur., *strains, numbers.* Transf., *limit, boundary; rule; manner, mode, way, method*; servorum modo, *after the manner of slaves*; eius modi, *in that manner, of that kind.*
moecha -ae, f. *an adulteress.*
moechor -ari, dep. *to commit adultery.*
moechus -i, m. *an adulterer.*
moenĕra=munera; *see* munus.
moenĭa -ĭum, n. pl. *the walls* or *fortifications of a city, ramparts, bulwarks*; poet., *castle, dwelling.*
Moesi -ōrum, m. pl. *a people between Thrace and the Danube*; **Moesĭa** -ae f., *their country.*
mŏla -ae, f. *a mill-stone*; plur., *a mill.* Transf., *grits, coarse meal* or *flour.*
mŏlāris -e, *of a mill, to do with grinding*; m. as subst. *a millstone; a molar tooth, grinder.*
mōlēs -is, f. *a shapeless mass,* e.g. *of rock; a massive construction,* e.g. *dam, mole, large building*; moles belli, *large military machines.* Transf., *a mass of men; greatness, might, power; trouble, difficulty.*
mŏlestĭa -ae, f. *annoyance, troublesomeness*; of style, *affectation, stiffness.*
mŏlestus -a -um, *burdensome, troublesome, irksome*; of style, *affected, laboured.* Adv. **mŏlestē,** *with annoyance*; moleste fero, *I take it badly, am annoyed*; of style, *affectedly.*
mōlīmen -ĭnis, n. and **mōlīmentum** -i, n. *great effort, exertion, endeavour.*
mōlĭor -iri, dep.: transit., *to stir, displace, work at; to construct laboriously, build, erect, contrive; to strive after; to destroy laboriously, undermine*; intransit., *to toil, struggle, exert oneself.*
mōlītĭo -onis, f. *effort, laborious undertaking; demolition.*
mōlītor -ōris, m. *a builder, contriver.*
mollesco -ĕre, *to become soft* or *gentle.*
mollĭcŭlus -a -um, *soft, tender; effeminate.*
mollĭo -ire, *to make soft, pliable, supple; to make gentle* or *effeminate; to alleviate* trouble; *to ease* a gradient.
mollĭpēs -pĕdis, *soft-footed.*
mollis -e, *soft, tender, pliant, supple*; of weather, *mild*; of gradients, *easy*; of character, *tender, gentle, sensitive,* or *effeminate*; of circumstances, *easy, mild, pleasant*; of speech, *tender, moving.* Adv. **mollĭtĕr,** *softly, easily, gently, mildly; effeminately.*
mollĭtĭa -ae, and **mollĭtĭes** -ei, f. *softness, flexibility; tenderness, mildness, sensibility; effeminacy.*
mollĭtūdo -ĭnis, f. *softness, pliability; tenderness, sensibility.*
mŏlo -ĕre -ŭi -ĭtum, *to grind in a mill.*
Mŏlossi -orum, m. *a people in Epirus.* Adj. **Mŏlossus** -a -um, pes, *a metrical foot, consisting of three long syllables*; m. as subst. *a Molossian hound.*
mōly -y̆os, n. *the herb moly.*
mōmen -ĭnis, n. *movement; a moving mass; momentum, impulse.*
mōmentum -i, n. *movement, motion; change, alteration; a cause of motion, impulse;* mental *impulse, influence; weight, importance*; of time, *a turning-point, minute, moment.*
Mŏna -ae, f. *the Isle of Man*; also *the Isle of Anglesey.*
mŏnēdŭla -ae, f. *jackdaw.*
mŏnĕo -ēre, *to remind, admonish, warn, advise, instruct.* N. pl. of partic. as subst. **mŏnĭta** -ōrum, *warnings; prophecies.*
mŏnēris -is, f. *a vessel with one bank of oars.*
Mŏnēta -ae, f. (1) *the mother of the Muses.* (2) *a surname of Juno.* (3) *the mint; money.*
mŏnētālis -e, *of the mint.*
mŏnīlĕ -is, n. *necklace, collar.*
mŏnĭmentum = monumentum; q.v.
mŏnĭtĭo -ōnis, f. *reminding, warning.*

mŏnĭtor -ōris, m. *one who reminds* or *prompts; an adviser, instructor.*
mŏnĭtus -ūs, m. *warning, admonition.*
mŏnogrammos or **-us** -i, m. adj. *sketched, shadowy.*
mŏnŏpŏdĭum -i, n. *a table with one foot.*
mons, montis, m. *a mountain; a mass; a great rock.*
monstrātor -ōris m. *a pointer-out; an inventor.*
monstro -are, *to show, point out; to ordain, appoint; to inform against, denounce.*
monstrum -i, n. *a wonder, portent.*
monstrŭōsus (monstrōsus) -a -um, *strange, wonderful*; adv. **monstrŭōsē.**
montānus -a -um, *of a mountain,* or *mountainous*; m. as subst. *a mountaineer*; n. pl. as subst. *mountainous country.*
montĭcŏla -ae, c. *a highlander.*
montĭvăgus -a -um, *wandering over mountains.*
montŭōsus (montōsus) -a -um, *mountainous.*
mŏnŭmentum (mŏnĭmentum) -i, n. *a memorial, monument; a commemorative building; written memorials, annals, memoirs.*
[1]**mŏra** -ae, f. *delay, hindrance; any space of time.*
[2]**mŏra** -ae, f. *a division of the Spartan army.*
mōrālis -e, *moral, ethical.*
mŏrātor -ōris, m. *a delayer, retarder; an advocate who talks against time.*
[1]**mŏrātus,** partic. from moror; q.v.
[2]**mōrātus** -a -um, *having certain manners* or *morals; adapted to a character, in character, characteristic.*
morbĭdus -a -um, *sickly, diseased, unwholesome.*
morbus -i, m. *disease, sickness.*
mordax -ācis, *biting, snappish; stinging, pungent; satirical.* Compar. adv. **mordācĭus,** *more bitingly.*
mordĕo mordēre mŏmordi morsum, *to bite; to cut into; to nip, sting; to vex, hurt, pain.*
mordĭcus, *with the teeth, by biting.*
mŏrētum -i, n. *a salad.*
mŏrĭbundus -a -um, *dying, expiring; subject to death, mortal; causing death, deadly.*
mōrĭgĕror -ari, dep. (and **mōrĭgĕro** -are) *to comply with, gratify.*
mōrĭgĕrus -a -um, *compliant, accommodating.*
mŏrĭor mŏri mortŭus mŏrĭtūrus, dep. *to die; to die away, wither away, decay.* Hence partic. **mortŭus** -a -um, *dead; decayed, extinct; half-dead*; m. as subst. *a corpse.*
mōrŏlŏgus -a -um, *talking like a fool.*
[1]**mŏror** -ari, dep. *to delay*: intransit., *to linger, loiter, stay*; transit., *to retard, detain, hinder;* nihil (nil) morari, *to care nothing for.*
[2]**mōror** -ari, dep. *to be foolish.*
mōrōsĭtās -ātis, f. *peevishness, fretfulness.*
mōrōsus -a -um, *peevish, captious, fretful*; adv. **mōrōsē.**
Morphĕūs -ĕos, m. *god of dreams.*
mors mortis, f. *death; a corpse; a cause of death* or *destruction.*
morsus -ūs, m. *a bite, biting; pungency; a verbal attack*; in gen. *pain, vexation.*
mortālis -e, *subject to death, mortal; transitory, perishable; human, earthly*; m. as subst. *a mortal man.*
mortālĭtās -ātis, f. *liability to death.*
mortĭfer or **mortĭfĕrus** -fĕra -fĕrum, *causing death, fatal, deadly*; adv. **mortĭfĕrē.**
mortŭālĭa -ium, n. *funeral songs, dirges.*
mortŭus -a -um, partic. from morior; q.v.
mōrum -i, n. *a mulberry; a blackberry.*
[1]**mōrus** -i, f. *a mulberry tree.*
[2]**mōrus** -a -um, *silly, foolish.*
mōs, mōris, *the will, inclination*; morem homini gerere, *to humour* a person; *custom, usage, wont, rule*; in plur., *ways, conduct, character, morals.*
Mŏsa -ae, f. *a river in Gaul* (now Meuse).
Mŏsella -ae, f. *a river in Gaul* (now Moselle).
mōtĭo -ōnis, f. *movement.*
mōto -are, *to move about.*
[1]**mōtus** -a -um, partic. from moveo; q.v.
[2]**mōtus** -ūs, m. *motion, movement*; terrae, *an earthquake; mental activity, emotion; political movement, rebellion, rising, riot.*
mŏvĕo mŏvēre mōvi mōtum, *to move, set in motion, stir; to remove, dispossess, dislodge*; se movere, and in middle sense, moveri, *to move* (oneself): milit., movere signa, movere castra, *to march away; to move mentally, influence, affect, excite; to cause* a result; *to change, shake*; politically, *to arouse, disturb.*
mox, *soon, presently; then, thereupon.*
mūcĭdus -a -um, *snivelling; mouldy, musty.*
Mūcĭus -a -um, *name of a Roman* gens; adj. **Mūcĭānus** -a -um.
mucro -ōnis, m. *a sharp point* or *edge; a sword.*
mūcus -i, m. *mucous matter.*
mūgil (mūgĭlis) -is, m. *a fish,* perhaps *mullet.*
mūgĭnor -ari, dep. *to loiter, dally.*
mūgĭo -ire, *to bellow, low, roar, rumble, groan.*
mūgītus -ūs, m. *lowing, bellowing, rumbling, groaning.*
mūla -ae, f. *a female mule.*
mulcĕo mulcēre mulsi mulsum, *to stroke; to soothe, appease, charm.*
Mulcĭber -ĕris and -ĕri, m. *surname of Vulcan*; meton., *fire.*
mulco -are, *to thrash; to handle roughly.*
mulctra -ae, f., **mulctrārĭum** -i, n., and **mulctrum** -i, n. *milk-pail.*
mulgĕo mulgēre mulsi, *to milk.*
mŭlĭēbris -e, *of a woman, feminine; effeminate*; adv. **mŭlĭēbrĭtĕr.**

mŭlĭer -ĕris, f. *a woman; a wife, matron.*
mŭlĭĕrārĭus -a -um, *womanish.*
mŭlĭercŭla -ae, f. *a little woman.*
mŭlĭĕrōsĭtās -ātis, f. *love of women.*
mŭlĭĕrōsus -a -um, *fond of women.*
mūlīnus -a -um, *of a mule, mulish.*
mūlĭo -ōnis, m. *a mule-keeper, mule-driver.*
mūlĭōnĭus -a -um, *of a muleteer.*
mullus -i, m. *the red mullet.*
mulsus -a -um, *honeyed; as sweet as honey*; n. as subst. *wine sweetened with honey, mead.*
multa -ae, f. *a fine, mulct.*
multangŭlus -a -um, *many-cornered.*
multātīcĭus -a -um, *relating to a fine.*
multātĭo -onis, f. *fining.*
multēsĭmus -a -um, *very small.*
multĭcăvus -a -um, *porous.*
multĭcĭa -orum, n. pl. *finely woven garments.*
multĭfārĭam, *on many sides, in many places.*
multĭfĭdus -a -um, *cloven into many parts.*
multĭformis -e, *having many shapes.*
multĭfŏrus -a -um, *pierced with many holes.*
multĭgĕnĕris -e and **multĭgĕnus** -a -um, *of many kinds.*
multĭiŭgus -a -um, and **multĭiŭgis** -e, *yoked many together; manifold, of many sorts.*
multĭlŏquax -ācis, *talkative.*
multĭmŏdis, *in many ways, variously.*
multiplex -plĭcis, *having many folds, winds* or *turnings; having many parts, manifold, many-sided, versatile; many times as large.*
multiplĭco -are, *to increase many times, multiply.*
multĭtūdo -ĭnis, f. *a large number, multitude, crowd; common people, mob.*
multo -are, *to punish.*
multus -a -um: sing., *much, great*; plur., *many, numerous*; multi, *the common herd*; ne multa, *briefly, in brief*; ad multum diem, *till late in the day*; in re multus, *prolix on a subject, busy in a matter*; occ., in sing., *many a*; n. acc. sing. as adv. **multum,** *much, greatly*; abl. **multo,** *by much, by far* Compar. **plus:** in sing. n. only, *more*; genit. of value **plūris,** at a *higher price, of more value*; in plur. **plūres, plūra,** *more numerous, several, many.* Superl. **plūrĭmus,** *most, very many*: in sing., of a large number, like the English *full many a*; of energy, etc., *strong*; genit. of value **plūrĭmi,** *at the highest price* or *value.*
mūlus -i, m. *a mule.*
Mulvĭus pons, *a bridge across the Tiber.*
Mummĭus -a -um, *name of a Roman gens.*
Munda -ae, f. *town in Hispania Baetica.*
mundānus -i, m. *a citizen of the world.*
mundĭtĭa -ae, and **mundĭtĭēs** -ēi, f. *cleanness, neatness, spruceness, elegance.*
[1]**mundus** -a -um, *clean, neat, elegant.*
[2]**mundus** -i, m. (1) *toilet-things, adornment.* (2) *the universe, world; mankind.*
mūnĕro -are and **mūnĕror** -ari, dep. *to give, present.*
mūnĭa -ĭōrum, n. pl., *duties, functions*; esp. *official.*
mūnĭceps -cĭpis, c. *the citizen of a* municipium; *a fellow-citizen, fellow-countryman.*
mūnĭcĭpālis -e, *belonging to a* municipium, *municipal.*
mūnĭcĭpĭum -i, n. *a borough, free town, municipal town.*
mūnĭfĭcentĭa -ae, f. *generosity.*
mūnĭfĭco -are, *to present generously.*
mūnĭfĭcus -a -um, *generous, liberal*; of wealth, *splendid*; adv. **mūnĭfĭcē.**
mūnĭmen -ĭnis, n. *a protection, defence.*
mūnĭmentum -i, n. *a fortification, defence, protection.*
mūnĭo (moenĭo) -ire, *to build*, esp. *to build a wall*; also *to surround with a wall; to fortify; to secure, defend, protect.*
Hence partic. **mūnītus** -a -um, *fortified, secured.*
mūnītĭo -ōnis, f. *fortifying, building up, paving, bridging*; concr., *a fortification.*
mūnīto -are, *to pave, make passable.*
mūnītor -ōris, m. *a builder of fortifications, sapper, engineer.*
mūnus (moenus) -ĕris, n. *an office, function, duty; a charge, tax; a service, favour, gift, present; a public show,* esp. of gladiators: *a public building.*
mūnuscŭlum -i, n. *a small gift.*
mūrālis -e, *of a wall, mural*; corona, *the crown given to the first man over the wall of a besieged city.*
[1]**mūrēna (muraena)** -ae, f. *a sea-fish, the murry* or *lamprey.*
[2]**Mūrēna** -ae, m. *a cognomen in the* gens Licinia.
mūrex -ĭcis, m. *the purple-fish; purple dye; a sharp stone, projecting rock.*
mŭrĭa -ae, f. *brine, pickle.*
murmillo = mirmillo; q.v.
murmur -ŭris, n. *a murmur, humming, roaring, rumbling, crashing.*
murmŭro -are, *to murmur, roar, crash.*
[1]**murra (myrrha)** -ae, f. *the myrrh-tree; myrrh.*
[2]**murra (myrrha)** -ae, f. *a mineral,* perhaps *fluorspar.*
[1]**murrĕus (myrrhĕus)** -a -um, *perfumed with myrrh; myrrh-coloured.*
[2]**murrĕus (myrrhĕus)** -a -um, *made of fluorspar.*
mūrus -i, m. *a wall, bank* or *dyke*; fig., *protection, defence.*
mūs, mūris, c. *a mouse* or *rat.*
Mūsa -ae, f. *a muse; a goddess of music literature and the arts.*
mūsaeus -a -um, *poetical, musical.*
musca -ae, f. *a fly.*
muscārĭum -i, n. *a fly-trap.*
muscĭpŭla -ae, f. and **muscĭpŭlum** -i, n. *a mouse-trap.*
muscōsus -a -um, *mossy.*

muscŭlus -i, m. *a little mouse; a sea-mussel*; milit., *a shed, mantelet.*
muscus -i, m. *moss.*
mūsēus -a -um = musaeus; q.v.
mūsĭcus -a -um, *belonging to poetry* or *music, musical*; m. as subst. *a musician*; f. sing. **mūsĭca** -ae and **mūsĭcē** -ēs, *music, poetry, learned studies*; adv. **mūsĭcē.**
mussĭto -are: intransit., *to grumble, mutter*; transit., *to keep quiet about* a thing.
musso -are, *to murmur, mutter, whisper; to keep quiet about* a thing; *to be at a loss.*
mustācĕum -i, n. and **mustācĕus** -i, m., *a must-cake, a sort of wedding-*cake.
mustēla (mustella) -ae, f. *a weasel.*
mustus -a -um, *young, new, fresh*; n. as subst. *new wine, must.*
mūtābĭlis -e, *changeable, variable, inconstant.*
mūtābĭlĭtās -ātis, f. *changeableness.*
mūtātĭo -ōnis, *changing, change, alteration; mutual change, exchange.*
mŭtĭlo -are, *to maim, mutilate, cut off; to curtail, diminish.*
mŭtĭlus -a -um, *maimed, mutilated.*
Mŭtĭna -ae, f. *town in Cisalpine Gaul* (now *Modena*).
mūtĭo (muttĭo) -ire, *to mutter, mumble.*
mūto -are: transit., *to move, shift; to change, alter; to exchange, barter*; with abl., *to give* or *to get* one thing *in exchange* for another; intransit., *to change, alter.*
mūtŭātĭo -ōnis, f. *borrowing.*
mūtŭor -ari dep. *to borrow.*
mūtus -a -um, *inarticulate, dumb, mute, silent, still, quiet.*
mūtŭus -a -um. (1) *interchanged, mutual, reciprocal*; n. as subst. *reciprocity, equal return*; abl. as adv. **mūtŭō,** *mutually, reciprocally.* (2) *borrowed, lent*: pecuniam dare mutuam, *to lend*; n. as subst., *a loan.*
mȳŏpăro -ōnis, m. *a small piratical galley.*
mȳrīcē -ēs, f. and **mȳrīca** -ae, f. *the tamarisk.*
myrtētum (murtētum) -i n. *a grove of myrtle-trees.*
myrtĕus (murtĕus) -a -um, *of myrtle; adorned with myrtle.*
myrtum -i, n. *myrtle-berry.*
myrtus -i and -ūs, f. *the myrtle-tree*; also *a myrtle shaft.*
mystăgōgus -i, m. *a priest who showed sacred places to strangers.*
mystērĭa -orum, n. pl. *mysteries, secrets,* esp. of worship.
mystēs or **mysta** -ae, m. *a priest at the mysteries.*
mystĭcus -a -um, *secret, mystic.*

N

N, n, the thirteenth letter of the Latin Alphabet.
nablĭum -i, n. *a kind of harp* or *lyre.*
nae = [1]nē; q.v.
naenĭa = nenia; q.v.
Naevĭus -a -um, *name of a Roman* gens; esp. of Cn. Naevius, *a poet of the third century* B.C.
naevus -i, m. *a mole on the body.*
Nāĭăs -ădis and **Nāïs** -ĭdis (-ĭdos); f. *a water-nymph, Naiad*; adj. **Nāĭcus** -a -um.
nam and **namquĕ,** conj., *for.*
nanciscor nancisci nactus *and* nanctus, dep. *to light upon, obtain, meet.*
nānus -i, m. *a dwarf.*
Narbo -ōnis, m. *town in southern Gau* (now *Narbonne*); adj. **Narbōnensis** -e.
Narcissus -i, m. *Narcissus, a beautiful young man changed into the flower of the same name.*
nardus -i, f. and **nardum,** -i, n. *nard.*
nāris -is, f. usually plur. **nāres** -ĭum, *the nostrils, nose.*
narrābĭlis -e, *able to be told.*
narrātĭo -ōnis, f. *telling, relating; a narrative.*
narrātĭuncŭla -ae, f. *a short narrative.*
narrātor -ōris, m. *a relater, narrator.*
narrātus -ūs, m. *narration, narrative.*
narro -are, *to make known; to say speak.*
narthēcĭum -i, n. *a box for perfumes* and *medicines.*
nārus = gnarus; q.v.
nascor -i, natus (and gnatus), dep. *to be born; to come into existence, arise, be produced.*
Hence partic. **nātus** -a -um, *born, naturally fitted* or *constituted*; pro re nata, *under present circumstances*; annos prope xc natus, *almost ninety years old.* As subst., m. *a son*; f. *a daughter.*
Nāsīca -ae, m. *name of a family of the Scipios.*
Nāso -ōnis, m. *cognomen of the poet* P. Ovidius.
nassa -ae, f. *a basket for catching fish; a trap, snare.*
nasturcĭum -i, n. *a kind of cress.*
nāsus -i, m. *the nose*; naso suspendere adunco, *to turn up the nose at, ridicule, mock.*
nāsūtus -a -um, *having a large nose; acute, sagacious, satirical.*
nātālĭcĭus -a -um, *relating to birth*; n. pl. as subst. *a birthday party.*
nātālis -e, *relating to birth, natal*; m. as subst., *a birthday*; plur. *birth, origin.*
nătātĭo -ōnis, f. *swimming.*
nătātor -ōris, m. *swimmer.*
nātĭo -ōnis, f. *being born, birth; a tribe, race, people,* esp. *uncivilized; a species, stock, class.*
nătis -is, f., usually plur. **nătēs** -ĭum, *the rump, buttocks.*
nātīvus -a -um, *born; native, natural; inborn, innate.*
năto -are, *to swim, float; to stream, flow; to swim with, be full of* (with abl.); f. pl. of partic. as subst. natantes, *fishes.*
nātrix -ĭcis, f. *a water-snake.*

nātū, abl. sing. m. *by birth*; maior natu, *older.*
nātūra -ae, f. *birth; nature, natura qualities* or *disposition, character; an element, substance, essence*; rerum natura, *nature, the world* or *universe.*
nātūrālis -e, *natural, relating to nature*; adv. **nātūrālĭtĕr,** *naturally, by nature.*
nātus -a -um, partic. from nascor; q.v
nauarchus -i, m. *captain of a ship.*
nauclērus -i, m. *the master of a ship.*
naucum -i, n. *a trifle*; in genit. non nauci habere, *to think nothing of.*
naufrăgĭum -i, n. *shipwreck; wreckage; ruin, loss*; naufragium facere, *to suffer shipwreck.*
naufrăgus -a -um, pass., *shipwrecked*; act., *causing shipwreck.*
naulum -i, n. *fare, passage-money.*
naumăchĭa, ae, f. *a naval battle performed as a show.*
nausĕa -ae, f. *sea-sickness, nausea.*
nausĕo -are, *to be sea-sick; to cause disgust, nauseate.*
nausĕŏla -ae, f. *squeamishness.*
nauta and **nāvĭta** -ae, m. *sailor, mariner.*
nautĭcus -a -um, *of a sailor, nautical*; m. pl. as subst. *sailors.*
nāvālis -e, *of ships, naval, nautical*; n. as subst. **nāvālĕ** -is, *a station for ships*; plur. *a dockyard,* or *materials for ship-building.*
nāvĭcŭla -ae, f. *a little ship, boat.*
nāvĭcŭlārĭus -a -um, *of (small) ships*; f. as subst. *the business of a ship-owner*; m. as subst. *a ship-owner.*
nāvĭfrăgus -a -um, *causing shipwreck.*
nāvĭgābĭlis -e, *navigable.*
nāvĭgātĭo -ōnis, f. *sailing, voyage.*
nāvĭger -gĕra -gĕrum, *ship-bearing, navigable.*
nāvĭgĭum -i, n. *a vessel, ship.*
nāvĭgo -are: intransit., *to sail, voyage, go by sea; to swim*; transit., *to sail over, sail through, navigate.*
nāvis -is, f. *a ship, vessel*; navis longa, *a man-of-war*; oneraria, *a transport*; praetoria, *flag-ship.*
nāvĭta = nauta; q.v.
nāvĭtās (gnāvĭtās) -atis, f. *energy, zeal.*
nāvo -are, *to do energetically.*
nāvus (gnāvus) -a -um, *zealous, energetic.* Adv. **nāvĭtĕr (gnāvĭtĕr),** *energetically; completely.*
[1]**nē (nae),** used before pronouns, *indeed, truly.*
[2]**nē,** *not, that not, lest;* ne . . . quidem, *not even, not . . . either.*
[3]**-nĕ** (sometimes **n'**) interrog., enclitic particle.
Nĕāpŏlis -polis, f. (1) *part of Syracuse.* (2) *a sea-port* (now *Naples*).
nĕbŭla -ae, f. *vapour, fog, mist, cloud.*
nĕbŭlo -ōnis, m. *a good-for-nothing fellow.*
nĕbŭlōsus -a -um, *misty, foggy.*
nĕc and **nĕquĕ,** *not; and not, nor*; rarely *not even*; neque enim, *for . . . not*; nec non, *and also*; nec tamen, *and yet . . . not*; nec . . . nec, neque . . . neque, *neither . . . nor.*
necdum (nĕquĕ dum), *and not yet.*
nĕcessārĭus -a -um, *necessary, unavoidable, inevitable; pressing, urgent; closely connected*; as subst. *an intimate friend* or *relative*; n. abl. **nĕcessārĭō,** and adv. **nĕcessārĭē,** *necessarily, unavoidably.*
nĕcessĕ, indecl. adj. n., used with esse and habere; *necessary, unavoidable, inevitable, indispensable.*
nĕcessĭtās -ātis, f. *inevitability, necessity, urgency*; plur. *requirements, necessary expenses.* Transf., *intimate connexion, friendship, relationship.*
nĕcessĭtūdo -ĭnis, f. *necessity, inevitableness; need, want.* Transf., *close connexion, intimate friendship*; plur., *intimate friends, near relations.*
nĕcessum = necesse; q.v.
necnĕ, *or not.*
necnōn (nĕquĕ nōn); see nec.
nĕco -are, *to kill, slay, put to death.*
nĕcŏpīnans -antis, *not expecting unaware.*
nĕcŏpīnātus (nĕc ŏpīnātus) -a -um *unexpected*; adv. **nĕcŏpīnātō.**
nĕcŏpīnus -a -um; pass., *unexpected*; act., *not expecting.*
nectar -ăris, n. *nectar, the drink of the gods; honey, milk, wine.*
nectărĕus -a -um, *of nectar.*
necto nectĕre nexŭi *and* nexi nexum, *to tie, bind, fasten; to fetter, enslave; to affix, attach; to put together, devise.*
nēcŭbi, *lest anywhere, that nowhere.*
nēcundĕ, *lest from any quarter, that from no direction.*
nēdum, *not to say*; after (implied) negative, *much less, still less*; after affirmative, *much more.*
nĕfandus -a -um, *not to be spoken of; abominable.*
nĕfārĭus -a -um, *impious, abominable*; adv. **nĕfārĭē.**
nĕfās, n. indecl., *what is contrary to divine command; sin, crime, abomination*; per fas et nefas, *by fair means or foul*; as interj. *monstrous! dreadful!*
nĕfastus -a -um, *forbidden, unholy; unlucky; sinful*; dies nefasti, *days on which no public business could be transacted.*
nĕgātĭo -ōnis, f. *denying.*
nĕgĭto -are, *to persist in denying.*
neglectĭo -ōnis, f. *neglect.*
neglectus -ūs, m. *neglect, disregard.*
neglĕgentĭa -ae, f. *carelessness, negligence.*
neglĕgo -lĕgĕre -lexi -lectum, *to neglect, disregard; to make light of, overlook, omit.*
Hence partic. **neglĕgens** -entis, *careless*; adv. **neglĕgentĕr.**
nĕgo -are, *to say no; to deny, say that . . . not; to deny a request, refuse to give* or *do.*
nĕgōtĭālis -e, *relating to business.*
nĕgōtĭātĭo -ōnis, f. *bankers' business.*
nĕgōtĭātor -ōris, m. *a business-man*; esp. *banker.*
nĕgōtĭŏlum -i, n. *a little business.*
nĕgōtĭor -ari, dep. *to carry on business*;

esp. as *a banker*; m. of partic. as subst. **nĕgōtians** -antis, *a businessman.*

nĕgōtiōsus -a -um, *full of business, busy.*

nĕgōtium -i, n. *business, occupation, employment, task; pains, trouble, difficulty; a matter, piece of business.*

Nĕmĕa -ae, and **Nĕmĕē** -ēs, f. *a valley in Argolis*; adj. **Nĕmĕaeus** -a -um, subst. **Nĕmĕa** -orum, n. pl., *the Nemean games.*

nēmo -inis, c., *no one, nobody*: nemo non, *everyone*; non nemo, *some* or *many.*

nĕmŏrālis -e and **nĕmŏrensis** -e, *of woods* or *groves; sylvan.*

nĕmŏrōsus -a -um, *full of groves; thickly leaved, full of foliage.*

nempĕ, *truly, certainly, to be sure.*

nĕmus -ŏris, n. *a wood, grove.*

nēnia -ae, f. *a funeral song, dirge; an incantation; nursery ditty, lullaby.*

nĕo nēre nēvi nētum, *to spin; to interweave.*

nĕpa -ae, f. *a scorpion*; *a crab.*

[1]**nĕpōs** -ōtis, m. *a grandson, a nephew; a descendant; a spendthrift.*

[2]**Nĕpos** -pōtis, m., C. Cornelius, *a Roman historian, friend of Cicero.*

neptis -is, f. *a grand-daughter.*

Neptūnus -i, m. *Neptune, god of the sea*; adj. **Neptūnius** -a -um.

nēquam, indecl.; compar. **nēquior,** superl. **nēquissimus;** *worthless, good for nothing, bad*; adv. **nēquitĕr.**

nēquāquam, *by no means, not at all.*

nĕquĕ = nec; q.v.

nĕquĕdum = necdum; q.v.

nĕquĕo -ire, ivi and -ii -itum, *to be unable.*

nēquīquam (**nēquicquam**), *in vain to no purpose; without good reason.*

nēquitia -ae, and **nēquitiēs** -ēi, f. *worthlessness, badness*; esp. *extravagance.*

Nereūs -ĕos and -ĕi, m. *a sea-god.*

Nĕro -ōnis, m. *a cognomen in the* gens Claudia; esp. C. Claudius Nero, *fifth Roman emperor* (54–68).

nervōsus -a -um *sinewy, nervous, strong, vigorous*; adv. **nervōsē.**

nervŭlus -i, m., *nerve, strength.*

nervus -i, m. (usually plur.), *sinew, tendon*; fig. *strength, vigour, energy; a string,* esp. of an instrument; *a strap, thong, fetter.*

nescio -ire -īvi and -ii -itum, *not to know, to be ignorant; to fail to recognise*; with infin. *to be unable to do*; nescio quis, quid, etc., *I know not who* or *what, somebody, something.*

nescius -a -um: act., *not knowing, ignorant, unaware; not knowing how, unable,* with infin.; pass., *unknown.*

Nestŏr -ŏris, m. *the most experienced of the Greek heroes at Troy.*

neu = neve; q.v.

neuter -tra -trum, *neither.* Transf., *of neither sex, neuter.* Adv. **neutrō,** *in neither direction, towards neither side.*

neutiquam (**ne ŭtiquam**), *by no means, not at all.*

nēvĕ or **neu,** *and not, or not, nor* (esp. following ut or ne).

nēvīs, nēvult = nonvis, nonvult; see nolo.

nex, nĕcis, f. *death*; usually *violent death, murder.*

nexilis -e, *tied together, plainted.*

nexum -i, n. *an arrangement by which a debtor pledged his liberty as security for debt.*

nexus -ūs, m. *a tying together, connecting, restraining*; also in the sense of nexum, q.v.

nī (**nei**) and **nīvĕ,** *if not, unless*; also in the sense of ne, q.v.; quid ni? *why not?*

nīcētērium -i, n. *reward of victory, prize.*

nicto -are, *to wink.*

nīdor -ōris, m. *vapour, reek.*

nīdŭlus -i, m. *a little nest.*

nīdus -i, m. *a nest.*

niger -gra -grum, *black, dark-coloured; blackening; bad, unlucky*; n. as subst. *a black spot.*

nigresco nigrescĕre nigrŭi, *to become black, grow dark.*

nigro -are, *to be black*; partic. **nigrans** -antis, *black, dark.*

nigror -ōris, *m. blackness.*

nihĭl and contr. **nīl,** *nothing*; nihil non, *everything*; non nihil, *something*; nihil, as internal acc., or **adv.,** *not at all.*

nĭhildum, *nothing as yet.*

nihĭlum (**nīlum**), *nothing*; as adv., *not at all*; nihilominus, *nevertheless.*

nil = nihil; q.v.

Nīlus -i, m. *the river Nile*; adj. **Nīliăcus** -a -um.

nimbĭfer -fĕra -fĕrum, *stormy.*

nimbōsus -a -um, *rainy, stormy.*

nimbus -i, m. *cloud, mist*; esp. *a black rain-cloud; a storm, shower.*

nīmīrum, *undoubtedly, certainly, of course* (often ironical).

nĭmis, *very much; too much, excessively.*

nĭmius -a -um, *very great; too great, excessive; intemperate, immoderate.* N. as subst. *a great deal, much*; also *excess, too much.*

ningo (**ninguo**) ningĕre ninxi, *to snow*; impers., ningit, *it snows.*

ninguēs -ium, f. pl. *snow.*

Nĭŏbē -es, f. and **Nĭŏba** -ae, f. *daughter of Tantalus, wife of Amphion.*

nĭsi, *if not, unless*; after negatives and questions, *except*; nisi quod, *except that.*

[1]**nīsus** (**nixus**) -ūs, m. *pressing, straining, effort.*

[2]**nīsus** -a -um, partic. from nitor; q.v.

nītēdŭla -ae, f. *dormouse.*

nĭtĕo -ēre, *to shine, glitter, be bright; to glow, be sleek, flourish.*

Hence partic. **nĭtens** -entis, *shining, bright, sleek, blooming.*

nĭtesco -ĕre, *to begin to shine; to grow sleek.*

nĭtĭdus -a -um, *bright, shining; sleek, fat; flourishing, blooming.* **Transf.,**

spruce, elegant; refined, polished. Adv. **nĭtĭdē.**

[1]**nītor** nīti nīsus or nixus, dep. (1) *to rest, lean, support oneself (on); to trust (in), depend (on).* (2) *to strive, exert oneself, make an effort*; of movement, *to press on, climb up.*

[2]**nĭtor** -ōris, m. *brilliance, brightness, splendour, glow, elegance.*

nĭvālis -e, *of snow, snowy.*

nīvĕ = ni, q.v., or neve, q.v.

nĭvĕus -a -um, *of snow, snowy.*

nĭvōsus -a -um, *snowy.*

nix, nĭvis, f. *snow.*

nixor -ari, dep. *to lean upon; to strive, strain.*

[1]**nixus** = [1]nisus; q.v.

[2]**nixus;** see [1]nitor.

no nāre nāvi, *to swim.* Transf., *to sail, flow, fly.*

nōbĭlis -e, *known; celebrated, renowned, infamous, notorious; of noble birth, highly bred*; of things, *fine.*

nōbĭlĭtās -ātis, f. *fame, celebrity; noble birth, nobility*; meton., *the aristocrats, the nobility*; in gen., *excellence, worth.*

nōbĭlĭto -are, *to make known, make famous* or *notorious.*

nŏcĕo -ēre, *to hurt, injure, harm* (with dat.); partic. **nŏcens** -entis, *hurtful, injurious, guilty, wicked*; as subst., *a guilty person.*

noctĭlūca -ae, f. *the moon.*

noctĭvăgus -a -um, *wandering by night.*

noctū, abl. from nox; q.v.

noctŭa -ae, f. *owl.*

noctŭābundus -a -um, *travelling by night.*

nocturnus -a -um, *by night, nightly, nocturnal.*

nŏcŭus -a -um, *hurtful, injurious.*

nōdo -are, *to knot, tie in a knot.*

nōdōsus -a -um, *full of knots, knotty.*

nōdus -i, m. *a knot; a girdle; any tie, bond, connexion, obligation; a knotty point, difficulty.*

nōlo nolle nōlŭi, *to be unwilling, wish not to, refuse.*

nŏmăs -ădis, c. *a nomad,* esp. *a Numidian.*

nōmen -ĭnis, n. *a name*; nomen dare, *to go for a soldier, enlist*; nomen (hominis) deferre, *to give information against, accuse*; nomina solvere, *to pay debts*; nomen Romanum, *the Roman power*; nomine meo, *in my name, on my behalf.*

nōmenclātor -ōris, m. *a slave who reminded his master of names.*

nōmĭnātim, *by name, expressly.*

nōmĭnātĭo -ōnis, f. *nomination to a public office.*

nōmĭnĭto -are, *to call regularly by name.*

nōmĭno -are, *to name, give a name to, call; to mention, speak about; to make famous; to appoint, nominate to an office; to denounce, give information against.*

Hence partic. **nōmĭnātus** -a -um, *well-known, celebrated.*

nŏmisma -mătis, n. *a coin.*

nōn (old forms **noenum, noenu**), *not*; non nihil, *something*; nihil non, *everything*; non quod, non quo, *not that, not because*; non ita, *not very, not particularly*; in questions = nonne? q.v.; in commands = ne; in answers, *no.*

nōnae -arum, f. *the nones; the fifth day in all months, except March, May, July and October, when it was the seventh.*

nōnāgēsĭmus (-ensĭmus) -a -um, *ninetieth.*

nōnāgiēs (-iens), *ninety times.*

nōnāgintā, *ninety.*

nōnānus -a -um, *belonging to the ninth legion.*

nondum, *not yet.*

nongenti -ae -a, *nine hundred.*

nonnĕ, interrog. adv., asks a question to which an affirmative answer is expected.

nonnēmo, nonnĭhil; see nemo, nihil.

nonnullus (nōn nullus) -a -um, *some*; in plur., *several.*

nonnumquam (nōn numquam), *sometimes.*

nōnus -a -um, *ninth*; f. as subst., *the ninth hour* (roughly 3 p.m.).

nōnusdĕcĭmus -a -um, *nineteenth.*

Nōrĭcum -i, n. *Noricum, a country between the Alps and the Danube*; adj. **Nōrĭcus** -a -um.

norma -ae, f. *a rule, standard.*

nōs, plur. of ego; q.v.

noscĭto -are, *to get to know, investigate, observe, perceive; to recognize.*

nosco noscĕre nōvi nōtum, *to become acquainted with, get to know*; hence, in perfect tenses, *to be acquainted with, know.* Transf., *to inquire into, investigate; to recognize; to approve, acknowledge.*

Hence partic. **nōtus** -a -um, *known; famous; notorious, familiar, customary*; m. pl. as subst. *friends, acquaintances.*

noster -tra -trum, *our, ours; of us, to us, for us*; m. pl. nostri, *our people.*

nostrās -ātis, adj. *of our country, native.*

nŏta -ae, f. *a mark, token, note, sign*; in writing, *a letter, character; a distinguishing mark, brand*; hence *sort, quality;* also *mark of disgrace, stigma* (esp. as imposed by the censor).

nŏtābĭlis -e, *remarkable, striking*; adv. **nŏtābĭlĭtĕr.**

nŏtārĭus -i, m. *secretary* or *shorthand writer.*

nŏtātĭo -ōnis, f. *marking, noting, choice; the stigma of the censor.*

nōtesco nōtescĕre nōtŭi, *to become known.*

nŏthus -a -um, *illegitimate, bastard; hybrid, mongrel*; in gen., *spurious.*

nōtĭo -ōnis, f. *an examination, investigation; an idea, notion, conception.*

nōtĭtia -ae, and **nōtĭtĭēs** -ēi, f.: pass., *being known, fame, celebrity*; act., *knowledge, acquaintance*; hence *idea, notion, conception.*

nŏto -are, *to mark, mark out, distinguish, denote; to observe; to write; to stigmatize* (esp. of the censor).

[1]**nōtus** -a -um, partic. from nosco; q.v.
[2]**nŏtus (-ŏs)** -i, m. *the south wind.*
nŏvācŭla -ae, f. *a sharp knife* or *razor.*
nŏvālis -is, f. and **nŏvālĕ** -is, n. *fallow land; a cultivated field; crops.*
nŏvātrix -icis, f. *she that renews.*
nŏvellus -a -um, *new, young; fresh, unfamiliar.*
nŏvem, *nine.*
Nŏvember and **Nŏvembris** -bris, m. *of the ninth month of the Roman year, of November*; m. as subst., *November.*
nŏvendĕcim, nŏvemdĕcim, *nineteen.*
nŏvendĭālis -e, *of nine days; happening on the ninth day; lasting nine days.*
nŏvēni -ae -a, *nine each, nine at a time*; poet., *nine.*
Nŏvensĭles dīvi, *gods whose worship had been introduced from foreign countries.*
nŏverca -ae, f. *step-mother.*
nŏvercālis -e, *of* or *like a step-mother.*
nŏvīcĭus -a -um, *new, fresh*; esp. *of persons new to slavery.*
nŏvĭēs (-ĭens), *nine times.*
nŏvĭtās -ātis, f. *newness, novelty, strangeness; the condition of a* novus homo (see novus), *newness of nobility*; in pl. *new acquaintances.*
nŏvo -are, *to make new, renew, revive; to change, alter; to invent*; novare res, *to make a revolution.*
nŏvus -a -um, *new, fresh, young; fresh, inexperienced; revived, refreshed; novel, unusual, extraordinary*; novus homo, *the first of a family to hold curule office*; novae res, *political changes, a revolution*; novae tabulae, *new account-books* (i.e. *a cancellation of debts*). N. as subst., *a new thing, news, a novelty.* Adv. **nŏvē,** *in a new* or *unusual way.* Superl., **nŏvissĭmus** -a -um, *latest, last, extreme*; agmen, *the rear*; adv. **nŏvissĭmē,** *lately, lastly, in the last place.*
nox noctis, f. *night*; meton., *sleep, darkness, gloom, death.* Abl. form as adv. **noctū,** by night.
noxa -ae, f. *harm, injury, damage; a fault, offence; punishment.*
noxĭa -ae, f. *fault, offence, crime.*
noxĭus -a -um, *hurtful, injurious; culpable, guilty.*
nūbēcŭla -ae, f. *a little cloud; a troubled expression.*
nūbes -is, f. *a cloud*; fig., *any dense mass; gloom; veil, concealment.*
nūbĭfer -fĕra -fĕrum, *cloud-bearing.*
nūbĭgĕna -ae, c. *born of a cloud.*
nūbĭlis -e, *marriageable.*
nūbĭlus -a -um, *cloudy, overcast; dark, gloomy*; n. sing. as subst., *cloudy weather*; n. pl., *clouds.*
nūbo nūbĕre nupsi nuptum, *to cover, veil*; of a bride, *to be married to, to marry* (with dat.); f. of partic. **nupta,** *married*, or, as subst., *a bride.*
nuclĕus -i, m. *the kernel of a nut, the stone of fruits.*
nŭdĭus, *it is now the . . . day since* (always with ordinal numerals); nudius tertius, *the day before yesterday.*
nūdo -are, *to make bare, strip, uncover*; milit. *to leave undefended*; *to strip, spoil, divest, deprive.*
nūdus -a -um, *naked, bare, uncovered; defenceless, deprived; unadorned, plain; bare, mere, alone, only.*
nūgae -arum, f. pl., *trifles, nonsense, stuff.*
nūgātor -ōris, m. *a trifler, humbug.*
nūgātōrĭus -a -um, *trifling, frivolous, futile.*
nūgax -ācis, *trifling, frivolous.*
nūgor -ari, dep. *to trifle, talk nonsense; to trick, cheat.*
nullus -a -um, *no, none, not any; non-existent, ruined*; nullo modo, nullo pacto, *by no means*; as a strong negative, *not at all*; as subst., esp. genit. and abl., *no one.*
num, interrog. particle, introducing a direct question, to which a negative answer is expected, or an indirect question, in the sense *whether.*
Nŭma -ae, m., Pompilius, *the second king of Rome.*
Nŭmantĭa -ae, f. *a town in Spain.*
nūmen -inis, n. *nodding, a nod; as an expression of will, command, consent*; of a deity, *divine will, divine command;* hence, in gen., *divine majesty, divinity, deity.*
nŭmĕrābĭlis, -e, *able to be counted.*
nŭmĕro -are, *to count*; esp. *to count out money, to pay; to count over* possessions, i.e. *to own; to reckon, consider.*

Hence partic. **nŭmĕrātus** -a -um, *counted out; in hard cash, in ready money*; n. as subst. *hard cash, money down.*
nŭmĕrōsus -a -um. (1) *numerous.* (2) *rhythmical, metrical, melodious.* Adv. **nŭmĕrōsē.**
nŭmĕrus -i, m. (1) *a number, reckoning, total; a mass; a mere number, cypher; a category, band, class; rank, position, regard, consideration.* (2) *measure, part, respect*; in music, *metre, number, time.* Abl. sing. as adv. **nŭmĕrō,** *exactly, at the right time; too quickly, too soon.*
Nŭmĭda -ae, m. *a Numidian.*
Nŭmĭtor -ōris, m. *king of Alba, grandfather of Romulus and Remus.*
nummārĭus -a -um, *belonging to money; bribed with money, venal.*
nummātus -a -um, *provided with money, rich.*
nummŭlārĭus -i, m. *a money-changer.*
nummŭlus -i, m. *a little piece* or *sum of money.*
nummus -i, m. *a piece of money, coin*; esp. *the sesterce, a coin of small value.*
numquam = nunquam; q.v.
nunc, *now, at present, as things are*; of past or future time, *then, already.*
nuncŭpātĭo -ōnis, f. *naming, pronouncement.*
nuncŭpo -are, *to name, call by name to pronounce solemnly.*
nundĭnae -arum, f. pl. *market-day; the market-place; traffic, trade, business.*

nundĭnātĭo -ōnis, f. *the holding of a market, trade, business.*
nundĭnor -ari, dep. *to transact business, trade, traffic; to buy*, esp. corruptly; *to be present in great numbers.*
nundĭnum -i, n. *market-time.*
nunquam (numquam), *never*; numquam non, *always*; non numquam, *sometimes.*
nuntĭātĭo -ōnis, f. *a declaration made by the augur.*
nuntĭo -are, *to announce, give notice.*
nuntĭus -a -um, *announcing, bringing news.* M. as subst. **nuntĭus** -i: (1) *a messenger.* (2) *a message, news*; esp. *an official notice.*
nūper, *lately, not long ago.*
nupta -ae, f. subst. from nubo; q.v.
nuptĭae -arum, f. pl. *marriage, a wedding.*
nuptĭālis -e, *of marriage.*
nŭrus -us, f. *a daughter-in-law; any young married woman.*
nusquam, *nowhere, at* (or *to*) *no place; in nothing, on no occasion; to* or *for nothing*; nusquam esse, *not to exist.*
nūto -are, *to nod, keep nodding; to sway, waver.*
nūtrīcius -i, m. *a tutor, guardian.*
nūtrīco -are and **nūtrīcor** -ari, dep. *to suckle, nourish; to support, sustain.*
nūtrīcŭla -ae, f. *nurse, nanny.*
nūtrīmen -īnis, n. *nourishment.*
nūtrīmentum -i, n. *nourishment; support, training.*
nūtrio -ire and **nūtrior** -iri, dep. *to suckle, nourish, bring up; to make good, support, sustain.*
nūtrix -īcis, f. *a nurse, foster-mother.*
nūtus -ūs, m. *a nod; command, will; gravitation, downward movement.*
nux nŭcis, f. *a nut; a nut-tree.*
nympha -ae, and **nymphē** -es, f. *a bride*; Nymphae, *the Nymphs.*

O

O, o, the fourteenth letter of the Latin Alphabet.
o! interj. *oh!*
ob, prep. with acc., *in front of, before; in return for; because of, on account of*; ob rem, *to the purpose, with advantage.*
ŏbaerātus -a -um, *in debt*; as subst., *a debtor.*
ŏbambŭlo -are, *to walk up and down, walk about near.*
ŏbarmo -are, *to arm.*
ŏbăro -are, *to plough up.*
obbrūtesco -ĕre, *to become stupid* or *dull.*
obc-; see occ-.
obdo -dĕre -dĭdi -dĭtum, *to place before, put against*; fores, *to shut the door.*
obdormisco -dormiscĕre -dormīvi, *to go to sleep.*
obdūco -dūcĕre -duxi -ductum. (1) *to draw over, draw in front*; of persons, *to bring forward.* (2) *to cover, close over*; venenum, *to swallow*; frontem, *to wrinkle*; of time, *to pass, spend.*
obductĭo -ōnis, f. *covering, veiling.*
obdūresco -ĕre, *to become hard, harden.*
obdūro -are, *to be hard (against); to stand out, hold out, persist.*
ŏbēdĭo = oboedio; q.v.
ŏbĕo -ire -īvi and -ĭi -ĭtum. Intransit., *to go to, go to meet, go against*; of heavenly bodies, *to set*; of the living, *to die.* Transit., *to go to, go over, traverse; to go over, encompass,* by looking or speaking; *to enter upon, engage in, perform, execute* a task; with diem or mortem, *to die.*
ŏbĕquĭto -are, *to ride up to.*
ŏberro -are, *to wander about, go astray.*
ŏbēsus -a -um, *fat, plump; swollen; coarse.*
ōbex -ĭcis, m. and f. *bolt, bar, barrier, barricade.*
obf-; see off-.
obg-; see ogg-.
ŏbhaeresco -haerescĕre -haesi -haesum, *to stick fast, adhere to.*
obiăcĕo -ēre, *to lie at, lie against.*
obicĭo -icĕre -iēci -iectum, *to throw in the way, to expose; to inspire, cause, produce; to put before, hold before, as protection* or *obstacle; to bring up* anything as a reproach, *to throw in a person's teeth.*
Hence partic. **obiectus** -a -um, *lying near, opposite to; exposed to; brought up against* a person; n. pl. as subst., *charges.*
obiectātĭo -ōnis, f. *a reproach.*
obiecto -are, *to throw in the way, expose; to set against; to bring up* anything as a reproach, *to throw in a person's teeth.*
[1]**obiectus** -a -um, partic. from obicio; q.v.
[2]**obiectus** -ūs, m. *placing against, putting opposite.*
ŏbīrascor -īrasci -īrātus, dep. *to grow angry at.*
ŏbĭtĕr, *on the way, by the way, in passing.*
ŏbĭtus -ūs, m. *an approach*; of heavenly bodies, *setting*; of the living, *death, downfall, destruction.*
obiurgātĭo -ōnis, f. *scolding, reproving.*
obiurgātor -ōris, m. *a scolder, reprover.*
obiurgātōrĭus -a -um, *reproachful, scolding.*
obiurgo -are, *to scold, reprove, blame, chastise.*
oblanguesco -languescĕre -langŭi, *to become weary.*
oblatro -are, *to bark at; to scold.*
oblectāmen -īnis, n. *delight, pleasure.*
oblectāmentum -i, n. *delight, amusement, pastime.*
oblectātĭo -ōnis, f. *delighting, amusing.*
oblecto -are, *to please, amuse; to pass* time *pleasantly, while away* time.
oblīdo -līdĕre -līsi -līsum, *to crush.*
oblĭgātĭo -ōnis, f. *a bond, tie.*
oblĭgo -are, *to tie, bind up, bandage.* Transf., *to bind, make liable, oblige; to make liable to punishment, make guilty.* Hence partic. **oblĭgātus** -a -um, *bound, under an obligation.*
oblīmo -are, *to cover with slime* or *mud.*
oblĭno -lĭnĕre -lēvi -lĭtum, *to smear, daub, besmear; to stain, defile*; perf. partic. oblĭtus -a -um, *overloaded.*

oblīquo -are, *to turn sideways, turn aside.*
oblīquus -a -um, *slanting, sideways, on one side*; of speech, *indirect, covert; looking askance, envious.* Adv. **oblīquē,** *sideways, aslant; indirectly, by implication.*
oblītesco -lĭtescĕre -lĭtŭi, *to conceal oneself.*
oblittĕro -are, *to cancel, blot out.*
oblīvĭo -ōnis, f. *forgetfulness, oblivion.*
oblīvĭōsus -a -um, *oblivious, forgetful; causing forgetfulness.*
oblīviscor oblīvisci oblītus, dep. *to forget.*
oblīvĭum -i, n., usually plur., *oblivion, forgetfulness.*
oblongus -a -um, *oblong.*
oblŏquor -lŏqui -lŏcūtus, dep. *to speak against, answer back, contradict, abuse, interrupt*; in music, *to accompany.*
obluctor -ari, dep. *to struggle against.*
obmōlĭor -iri, dep. *to build against* (as barrier or defence).
obmurmŭro -are, *to roar against.*
obmūtesco -mūtescĕre -mūtŭi, *to become dumb; to cease.*
obnātus -a -um, *growing on.*
obnītor -nīti -nixus, dep. *to press against, strive against; to take up a stand, maintain a firm position*; adv. from partic., **obnixē,** *firmly, vigorously.*
obnoxĭōsus -a -um, *submissive, compliant.*
obnoxĭus -a -um, with dat., *liable, addicted to, guilty of; indebted, obliged, dependent on; subject to, exposed to.*
obnūbo -nūbĕre -nupsi -nuptum, *to cover.*
obnuntĭātĭo -ōnis, f. *the announcement of an unfavourable omen.*
obnuntĭo -are, *to report an unfavourable omen.*
ŏboedĭentĭa -ae, f. *obedience, compliance.*
ŏboedĭo -ire, *to obey, comply with, listen to* (with dat.); partic. **ŏboedĭens** -entis, *obedient, compliant*; adv. **ŏboedĭentĕr.**
ŏbŏrĭor -ŏrīri -ortus, dep. *to arise, appear.*
obrēpo -rēpĕre -repsi -reptum, *to creep up to; to steal upon, come on by surprise.*
obrētĭo -ire, *to catch in a net.*
obrĭgesco -rĭgescĕre -rĭgŭi, *to become stiff*, esp. *to freeze.*
obrŏgo -are, *to amend* or *repeal a law by introducing another.*
obrŭo -rŭĕre -rŭi -rŭtum; fut. partic. -rŭĭtūrus. Intransit., *to fall, collapse.* Transit., *to cover, bury, swamp, drown; to overwhelm, destroy, obliterate.*
obrussa -ae, f. *assay; test.*
obsaepio -saepire -saepsi -saeptum, *to fence in, block up, render inaccessible.*
obsătŭro -are, *to stuff, choke.*
obscēnĭtās (**obscaen-**) -ātis, f. *impurity, indecency.*
obscēnus (**obscaenus**) -a -um, *foul, filthy*; morally, *impure, indecent; ill-omened.* Adv. **obscēnē.**
obscūrātĭo -ōnis, f. *darkening; disappearance.*
obscūrĭtās -ātis, f. *darkness*; of language, *obscurity*; of condition, *obscurity, low birth.*
obscūro -are, *to cover, darken, obscure; to veil, conceal, suppress.*
obscūrus -a -um, *covered, dark, obscure*; n. as subst., *darkness*; of language, *obscure, unintelligible*; of origin, etc., *unknown, obscure*; of character, *secret, reserved, close.* Hence adv. **obscūrē,** *darkly; unintelligibly; secretly.*
obsecrātĭo -ōnis, f. *earnest entreaty, supplication; public prayer to the gods.*
obsecro -are, *to beseech, implore, entreat.*
obsĕcundo -are, *to comply with.*
obsēpio = obsaepio; q.v.
obsĕquella -ae, f. *compliance.*
obsĕquens -entis, partic. from obsequor; q.v.
obsĕquentĭa -ae, f. *complaisance.*
obsĕquĭum -i, n. *compliance, submission; indulgence, pliancy.*
obsĕquor -sĕqui -sĕcūtus, dep. *to comply with, yield to, obey*; partic. **obsĕquens** -entis, *compliant, obedient*; *favourable*; adv. **obsĕquentĕr.**
[1]**obsĕro** -are, *to bolt, bar.*
[2]**obsĕro** -sĕrĕre -sēvi -sĭtum, *to sow thickly, cover* with seeds, etc.; partic. **obsĭtus** -a -um, *full of, covered with, beset by* (with abl.).
observantĭa -ae, f. *respect, attention.*
observātĭo -ōnis, f. *observing, watching; care, accuracy, circumspection.*
observātor -ōris, m. *observer, watcher.*
observĭto -are, *to watch carefully.*
observo -are, *to watch, regard, attend to*; of rules, *to keep, regard*; of persons, *to respect.*

Hence partic. **observans** -antis, *attentive, respectful.*
obses -sĭdis, c. *a hostage; a surety, security, pledge.*
obsessĭo -ōnis, f. *blockade.*
obsessor -ōris, m. *one who besets, haunts,* or *besieges.*
obsĭdĕo -sĭdēre -sēdi -sessum: intransit., *to sit down near*; transit., *to beset, haunt, frequent*; esp. *to blockade, besiege; to watch over, be on the look-out for.*
obsĭdĭo -ōnis, f. *blockade, siege.*
[1]**obsĭdĭum** -i, n. *blockade, siege.*
[2]**obsĭdĭum** -i, n. *the condition of a hostage.*
obsīdo -sīdĕre -sēdi -sessum, *to blockade, besiege, invest.*
obsignātor -ōris, m. *one who seals; a witness to a will.*
obsigno -are, *to seal*; of a witness, *to sign and seal; to stamp, impress.*
obsisto -sistĕre -stĭti -stĭtum, *to place oneself before* or *in the way of; to oppose, withstand, resist.*
obsĭtus -a -um, partic. from [2]obsero; q.v.
obsŏlēfĭo -fĭĕri -factus, *to become worn out; to be degraded.*

obsŏlesco -escĕre -ēvi, -ētum, *to go out of use, decay, wear out*; partic. **obsŏlētus** -a -um, *worn out, decayed; obsolete; threadbare, poor*; compar. adv. **obsŏlētius**, *more shabbily*.

obsōnātor -ōris, m. *a caterer*.

obsōnium -i, n. *what is eaten with bread*; e.g., *vegetables, fruit, fish*.

[1]**obsōno** -are and **obsōnor** -ari, dep., *to buy food, cater, provide a meal*.

[2]**obsŏno** -are, *to interrupt by noise*.

obsorbĕo -ēre -ŭi, *to swallow, gulp down*.

obstetrix -īcis, f. *midwife*.

obstĭnātio -onis, f. *persistence, firmness, obstinacy*.

obstĭno -are, *to persist, be resolved*.

Hence partic. **obstĭnātus** -a -um, *persistent, firm, obstinate*; adv. **obstĭnātē**.

obstĭpesco = obstupesco; q.v.

obstīpus -a -um, *leaning to one side; bent back* or *down*.

obsto -stare -stĭti -stātūrus, *to stand before* or *in the way; to oppose, resist, obstruct* (with dat.); n. pl. of partic. as subst. **obstantia,** *hindrances, obstacles, impediments*.

obstrĕpo -strĕpĕre -strĕpŭi -strĕpĭtum, *to make a noise, clamour at, disturb, interrupt* (with dat.); in pass., *to be drowned by noise* or *filled with noise*.

obstringo -stringĕre -strinxi -strictum, *to bind up, tie fast; to entangle, involve, put under an obligation*.

obstructio -ōnis, f. *hindrance, obstruction*.

obstrūdo = obtrudo; q.v.

obstrŭo -strŭĕre -struxi -structum, *to build against; to block up, close, stop*.

obstŭpĕfăcio -făcĕre -fēci -factum, *to astound, stupefy, render senseless*; pass. **obstŭpĕfīo** -fĭĕri -factus.

obstŭpesco (**obstĭp-**) -stŭpescĕre -stŭpŭi, *to become senseless, be astounded*.

obsum ŏbesse obfŭi, *to be in the way, be prejudicial to* (with dat.).

obsŭo -sŭĕre -sŭi -sūtum, *to sew on; to sew up, close up*.

obsurdesco -descĕre -dŭi, *to become deaf; to turn a deaf ear*.

obtĕgo -tĕgĕre, -texi -tectum, *to cover up; to protect; to conceal*; partic. **obtĕgens** -entis, *concealing*.

obtempĕrātio -ōnis, f. *compliance, obedience*.

obtempĕro -are, *to comply with, submit to* (with dat.).

obtendo -tendĕre -tendi -tentum. (1) *to stretch before, spread before*. Transf., *to put forward as an excuse, plead, allege*. (2) *to cover, conceal*.

[1]**obtentus** -ūs, m. *stretching* or *spreading before*. Transf., *pretext, pretence, excuse*.

[2]**obtentus** -a -um, partic. from obtineo; q.v.

[3]**obtentus** -a -um, partic. from obtendo; q.v.

obtĕro -tĕrĕre -trīvi -trītum, *to trample, crush, destroy*.

obtestātio -ōnis, f. *a calling of gods to witness; an entreaty in the name of the gods*.

obtestor -ari, dep. *to call as witness; to adjure, implore, entreat in the name of the gods*.

obtexo -texĕre -texŭi, *to cover*.

obtĭcĕo -ēre, *to be silent*.

obtĭcesco -tĭcescĕre -tĭcŭi, *to become silent*.

obtĭnĕo -tĭnēre -tĭnŭi -tentum: transit., *to hold, possess, keep, maintain*; esp. *to maintain an assertion*; also *to take hold of, grasp*; intransit., *to hold, obtain, continue*.

obtingo -tingĕre -tĭgi, *to happen, befall*.

obtorpesco -torpescĕre -torpŭi, *to become stiff, numb, insensible*.

obtorquĕo -torquēre -torsi -tortum, *to wrench, twist round*.

obtrectātio -ōnis, f. *disparagement, detraction*.

obtrectātor -ōris, m. *detractor, disparager*.

obtrecto -are, *to disparage, detract from*.

obtrūdo (**obstrūdo**) -trūdĕre -trūsi -trūsum. (1) *to gulp down, swallow down*. (2) *to force, obtrude*.

obtrunco -are, *to cut down*.

obtundo -tundĕre -tŭdi -tūsum and tunsum, *to beat upon, thump; to make blunt, dull, weaken, weary*.

Partic. **obtūsus** and **obtunsus** -a -um, *dull, blunt, blurred, insensible*.

obturbo -are, *to disturb, confuse, distract, harass*.

obturgesco -ĕre, *to swell up*.

obturo -are, *to stop up*.

obtūsus -a -um, partic. from obtundo; q.v.

obtūtus -ūs, m. *gaze, contemplation*.

ŏbumbro -are, *to overshadow, obscure; to conceal, protect, cover*.

ŏbuncus -a -um, *bent inwards, hooked*.

ŏbustus -a -um, *burnt, hardened in the fire*.

obvallo -are, *to surround with a wall, wall round*.

obvĕnio -vĕnire -vēni -ventum, *to come in the way of, to meet; to occur, happen, fall to* a person's lot.

obversor -ari, dep. *to move before, appear before*.

obverto (**-vorto**) -vertĕre -verti -versum, *to turn towards, direct against*. Partic. **obversus** -a -um, *turned towards*; m. pl. as subst., *opponents*.

obvĭam, *in the way, on the way*; hence, with dat., *towards, against, to meet*; obviam ire, with dat., *to go to meet, to oppose*; also *to help, remedy*.

obvĭus -a -um, *in the way, meeting* (with dat.); *exposed; ready at hand; affable, easy of access*.

obvolvo -volvĕre -volvi -vŏlūtum, *to wrap up, cover all round*.

occaeco -are, *to make blind, to blind, to darken; to conceal, make invisible, to make dull* or *numb*.

occallesco -callescĕre -callŭi, *to become thick-skinned, hard* or *unfeeling*.

occăno -cănĕre -cănŭi, *to sound*.

occāsĭo -ōnis, f. *a favourable moment, opportunity.*
occāsus -ūs, m. *the setting of heavenly bodies*; hence, *the west*; in gen., *fall, destruction.*
occātĭo -onis, f. *harrowing.*
occēdo -cēdĕre -cessi -cessum, *to go towards, meet.*
occento -are, *to sing a serenade to; to sing a lampoon against.*
occepto -are, *to begin.*
occĭdens -entis, m.; subst. from ²occido; q.v.
occīdĭo -ōnis, f. *slaughter, destruction, extermination.*
¹**occīdo** -cīdĕre -cīdi -cīsum, *to strike down, beat to the ground; to kill, slay; to plague to death, torment.*
²**occĭdo** -cĭdĕre -cĭdi -cāsum, *to fall, fall down*; of heavenly bodies, *to set*; of the living, *to die, perish, be ruined.* Hence pres. partic. **occĭdens** -entis, *setting*; m. as subst. (sc. sol), *the setting sun, the west.*
occĭdŭus -a -um, *setting, sinking*; hence, *western, westerly.*
occĭno -cĭnĕre -cĕcĭni and -cĭnŭi, *to sing inauspiciously.*
occĭpĭo -cĭpĕre -cēpi -ceptum, *to begin.*
occĭpĭtĭum -i, n. and **occĭput** -ĭtis, n. *the back of the head, occiput.*
occīsĭo -ōnis, f. *killing, slaughter.*
occīsor -ōris, m. *slayer, murderer.*
occlūdo -clūdĕre -clūsi -clūsum, *to shut up, close up.*
occo -are, *to harrow.*
occŭbo -are, *to lie down*, esp. *to rest in the grave.*
occulco -are, *to trample, tread down.*
occŭlo -cŭlĕre -cŭlŭi -cultum, *to cover, hide.*
Hence partic. **occultus** -a -um, *hidden, concealed, private;* of persons, *close, reserved.* N. as subst., *concealment, secrecy, a secret.* Adv. **occultē,** *secretly, obscurely.*
occultātĭo -ōnis, f. *hiding, concealment.*
occultātor -ōris, m. *hider, concealer.*
occulto -are, *to hide, conceal.*
occultus -a -um, partic. from occulo; q.v.
occumbo -cumbĕre -cŭbŭi -cŭbĭtum, *to fall down, sink down*; esp. *to fall down dead.*
occŭpātĭo -ōnis, f. *seizing, taking possession; anticipation; business, employment, occupation.*
occŭpo -are, *to take possession of, seize, occupy, master; to fall upon, attack; to take up, employ; to invest money; to anticipate, get a start on* a person, *be first to do* a thing.
Hence partic. **occŭpātus** -a -um, *busy, engaged, occupied.*
occurro -currĕre -curri -cursum, *to run to meet; to fall upon, attack; to work against, oppose, counteract*; of things, *to crop up, occur, come to mind.*
occursātĭo -ōnis, f. *attention, officiousness.*
occurso -are, *to run to meet; to oppose*; of things, *to occur, come to mind.*
occursus -ūs, m. *meeting, falling in.*

Ōcĕănus -i, m. *the ocean, the sea which encompasses the earth*; personif., *the father of the Nymphs.*
ŏcellus -i, m. *a (little) eye; a darling.*
ōcĭor, ōcĭus, compar. adj., *swifter, quicker*; adv. **ōcĭus,** *more swiftly*; serius, ocius, *sooner or later*; sometimes = *swiftly* only.
ocrĕa -ae, f. *a greave.*
ocrĕātus -a -um, *wearing greaves.*
Octāvĭus -a -um, *name of a Roman gens*; esp. of *C. Octavius*, the *Emperor Augustus*; adj. **Octāvĭānus** -a -um.
octāvus -a -um, *eighth*; octavum, *for the eighth time*; f. as subst. **octāva** -ae, *the eighth hour.*
octāvusdĕcĭmus -a -um, *eighteenth.*
octĭēs (-ĭens), *eight times.*
octingentēsĭmus -a -um, *eight hundredth.*
octingenti -ae -a, *eight hundred.*
octĭpēs -pĕdis, *having eight feet.*
octō, *eight.*
Octōber -bris, *belonging to the eighth month of the Roman year,* reckoning from March; *of October*; m. as subst., *October.*
octōdĕcim, *eighteen.*
octōgēnārĭus -a -um, *consisting of eighty.*
octōgēni -ae -a, *eighty each, eighty at a time.*
octōgēsĭmus -a -um, *eightieth.*
octōgĭēs (-ĭens), *eighty times.*
octōgintā, *eighty.*
octōiŭgis -e, *yoked eight together.*
octōnārĭus -a -um, *consisting of eight together.*
octōni -ae -a, *eight each, eight at a time, eight together.*
octōphŏros -on, *borne by eight*; n. as subst. **octōphŏron** -i, *a litter carried by eight bearers.*
octuplĭcātus -a -um, *increased eightfold.*
octuplus -a -um, *eight-fold*; n. as subst. *an eight-fold penalty.*
octussis -is, m. *a sum of eight* asses.
ŏcŭlātus -a -um, *having eyes; catching the eye, conspicuous.*
ŏcŭlus -i, m. *the eye*; esse in oculis, *to be visible; an ornament, treasure; a bud* or *eye* of a plant.
ōdi odisse; fut. partic. ōsūrus, *to hate, detest, dislike.*
ŏdĭōsus -a -um, *hateful, troublesome, annoying*; adv. **ŏdĭōsē.**
ŏdĭum -i, n. *hatred; an object of hatred*; esse odio, with dat., *to be hated by.*
ŏdor (older **ŏdōs**) -ōris, m. *a smell, odour, scent; a scent, suspicion, inkling, presentiment*; in plur., *perfumery, spices.*
ŏdōrātĭo -ōnis, f. *smelling, smell.*
¹**ŏdōrātus** -ūs, m. *smelling; the sense of smell.*
²**ŏdōrātus** -a -um, partic. from odoro; q.v.
odōrĭfer, -fĕra -fĕrum, *having a pleasant smell; producing perfumes.*
ŏdōro -are, *to make odorous*; partic. **ŏdōrātus** -a -um, *sweet-smelling.*

ŏdōror -ari, dep. *to smell; to smell out, snuff at*; hence *to aim at, aspire to; to search into, investigate; to get an inkling* or *smattering of.*

ŏdōrus -a -um. (1) *sweet-smelling.* (2) *keen-scented, tracking by smell.*

ŏdōs = odor; q.v.

Ŏdyssēa -ae, f. *the Odyssey.*

oecŏnŏmĭa -ae, f. *arrangement, division.*

oecŏnŏmĭcus -a -um, *relating to domestic economy; orderly, methodical.*

Oedĭpūs -pŏdis and -i, m. *king of Thebes, son of Laius and Jocasta, fated to kill his father and marry his mother.*

Oenōnē -ēs, f. *a Phrygian nymph, loved and deserted by Paris.*

oenŏphŏrum -i, n. *a basket for wine.*

oenus = unus; q.v.

oestrus -i, m. *the gad-fly, horse-fly; inspiration, frenzy.*

oesus = usus; q.v.

oesȳpum -i, n. *a cosmetic.*

ŏfella -ae, f. *a bit, morsel.*

offa -ae, f. *a pellet, mass, lump; a swelling.*

offendo -fendĕre -fendi -fensum: transit., *to strike against, knock; to hit upon, fall in with; to shock, offend, displease*; intransit., *to knock, strike; to run aground; to stumble, make a mistake, to give offence* (with dat.); also *to take offence.*

Hence partic. **offensus** -a -um, *injured, hurt; offensive.*

offensa -ae, f. *a striking, knocking against; injury; displeasure, offence.*

offensĭo -ōnis, f. *a striking, knocking, hitting against*; pedis, *a stumbling.* Transf., *a misfortune, setback, indisposition; displeasure, disfavour, aversion, offence.*

offensĭuncŭla -ae, f. *a slight displeasure* or *check.*

offenso -are, *to strike, knock, stumble.*

[1]**offensus** -a -um, partic. from offensus; q.v.

[2]**offensus** -ūs, m. *shock, collision; offence, dislike.*

offĕro offerre obtŭli oblātum, *to bring forward, place before, present, offer, expose; to inflict, occasion* trouble; se offerre, and pass., offerri, *to present oneself, appear.*

offĭcīna -ae, f. *a workshop, factory.*

offĭcĭo -fĭcĕre -fēci -fectum, *to act against; to get in the way of, impede, hinder, injure* (with dat.).

offĭcĭōsus -a -um, *obliging, courteous, attentive; dutiful*; adv. **offĭcĭōsē.**

offĭcĭum -i, n. *dutiful* or *respectful action; attendance, service, duty; sense of duty, respect, courtesy; submission, allegiance.*

offīgo -ĕre, *to fix in, fasten.*

offirmo -are, *to make firm, to fasten*; with reflex. or intransit., *to be determined, persevere;* partic. **offirmātus** -a -um, *firm, resolute.*

offūcĭa -ae, f. *paint, rouge; deceit.*

offulgĕo -fulgēre -fulsi, *to shine upon.*

offundo -fundĕre -fūdi -fūsum, *to pour over, spread round; to overspread, cover, conceal; to overwhelm; to bring* trouble, etc., *upon* a person.

oggannĭo -ire, *to growl at.*

oh, interj. *oh! ah!*

ōhē, interj. *ho! hi!*

oi, interj. *oh!*

ŏlĕa -ae, f. *olive, olive-tree.*

ŏlĕāgĭnus -a -um, *of the olive-tree.*

ŏlĕārĭus -a -um, *of* or *for oil.*

ŏlĕaster -tri, m. *the wild olive-tree.*

ŏlĕo -ēre, *to emit an odour; to smell of, smack of*; partic. **ŏlens** -entis, *smelling; fragrant* or *stinking.*

ŏlĕum -i, n. *olive-oil, oil.*

olfăcĭo -făcĕre -fēci -factum, *to smell; to scent out, detect.*

ŏlĭdus -a -um, *smelling.*

ōlim, *at that time*; of the past, *formerly, once*; of the future, *hereafter, one day*; with a present, *for a long time now; at times, often.*

ŏlĭt-; see holit-.

ŏlīva -ae, f. *olive; olive-tree; olive-wreath; staff of olive-wood.*

ŏlīvētum -i, n. *an olive-grove.*

ŏlīvĭfer -fĕra -fĕrum, *olive-bearing.*

ŏlīvum -i, n. *olive-oil, oil.*

olla -ae, f. *jar, pot.*

ollus, olle, obsolete form of ille; q.v.

ŏlo = oleo; q.v.

ŏlor -ōris, m. *swan.*

ŏlōrīnus -a -um, *of a swan.*

ŏlus; see holus.

Ŏlympĭa -ae, f. *a city in Elis, where the Olympic games were held.*

Ŏlympus -i, m. *a mountain range between Macedonia and Thessaly, supposed to be the abode of the gods.*

ŏmāsum -i, n. *bullocks' tripe.*

ōmen -ĭnis, n. *an omen, sign, prognostication.*

ōmentum -i, n. *fat; entrails, bowels.*

ōmĭnor -ari, dep. *to presage, prophesy, predict.*

ōmĭnōsus -a -um, *foreboding, ominous.*

ŏmitto -mittĕre -mīsi -missum, *to let go, let fall; to give up, lay aside; to disregard*; in speaking, *to leave out, omit*; with infin., *to cease.* Hence partic. **ŏmissus** -a -um, *negligent, remiss.*

omnĭfer -fĕra -fĕrum, *bearing everything.*

omnĭgĕnus -a -um, *of all kinds.*

omnĭmŏdīs, *in every way, entirely.*

omnīnō, *altogether, entirely, wholly; in general, in all; certainly, admittedly.*

omnĭpărens -entis, *all-producing.*

omnĭpŏtens -entis, *almighty.*

omnis -e, *all, every, whole; of all kinds*; in sing., *each*, or *the whole of* one person or thing.

omnĭtŭens -entis, *all-seeing.*

omnĭvăgus -a -um, *wandering everywhere.*

ŏnăger and **ŏnagrus** -i, m. *wild ass.*

ŏnĕrārĭus -a -um, *of burden, freight*; iumenta, *beasts of burden*; (navis) oneraria, *a merchant* or *transport ship.*

ŏnĕro -are, *to load, burden; to fill, weigh down; to oppress, overwhelm; to make worse, aggravate.*

ŏnĕrōsus -a -um, *heavy, burdensome; troublesome.*

ŏnus -ĕris, n. *a load, burden, weight; a trouble, charge; a public burden, tax.*

ŏnustus -a -um, *laden, loaded; full.*

ŏnyx -ychis, m. and f. *onyx; a casket of onyx.*

ŏpācĭtās -ātis, f. *shadiness.*

ŏpāco -are, *to shade, overshadow.*

ŏpācus -a -um, *shaded, shady; dark, shadowy, obscure.*

ŏpella -ae, f. *a little labour* or *trouble.*

ŏpĕra -ae, f. *trouble, pains, exertion*; operam dare, with dat., *to work hard at*; est operae pretium, *it is worth while*; opera mea, *thanks to me.* Transf., *time for work; work done*; in pl., *labourers, workmen,* also *mobsmen, gangsters.*

ŏpĕrārĭus -a -um, *relating to work*; m. **ŏpĕrārĭus** -i, *a labourer, workman.*

ŏpercŭlum -i, n. *a lid, cover.*

ŏpĕrīmentum -i, n. *a cover, covering.*

ŏpĕrĭo -pĕrire -ĕrŭi -pertum, *to cover, bury, conceal; to close, shut up; to overwhelm*; n. of partic. as subst. **ŏpertum** -i, *a secret place,* or *secret.*

ŏpĕror -ari, dep. *to work, labour, be busy*; esp. in perf. partic. **ŏpĕrātus** -a -um, *engaged, busy* (esp. *engaged in worship*).

ŏpĕrōsus -a -um: act., *laborious, painstaking, industrious*; pass., *toilsome, difficult.* Adv. **ŏpĕrōsē,** *laboriously.*

ŏpertum -i, subst. from operio; q.v.

ŏpes; see ops.

Ŏpĭcus -a -um, *Oscan.* Transf., *stupid, philistine.*

ŏpĭfer -fĕra -fĕrum, *helpful.*

ŏpĭfex -fĭcis, c. *a maker, framer; a workman, artisan.*

ŏpĭfĭcīna = officina; q.v.

ōpĭlĭo and **ūpĭlĭo** -ōnis, m. *shepherd.*

ŏpīmus -a -um, *rich, fruitful, fertile; lucrative; wealthy; sumptuous, abundant, copious*; of speech, *overloaded*; spolia opima, *spoils taken by a general from the enemy's general in single combat.*

ŏpīnābĭlis -e, *conjectural.*

ŏpīnātĭo -ōnis, f. *supposition, conjecture.*

ŏpīnātor -ōris, m. *one who supposes* or *conjectures.*

[1]**ŏpīnatus** -a -um, partic. from opinor; q.v.

[2]**ŏpīnātus** -ūs, m. *conjecture, supposition.*

ŏpīnĭo -ōnis, f. *opinion, conjecture, supposition; repute, rumour, report.*

ŏpīnĭōsus -a -um, *set in opinion.*

ŏpīnor -ari, dep. and **ŏpīno** -are, *to be of opinion, suppose, conjecture.* Partic. **ŏpīnātus** -a -um, in pass. sense, *supposed, fancied.*

ŏpĭpărus -a -um, *splendid, rich, sumptuous*; adv. **ŏpĭpărē.**

ŏpĭtŭlor -ari, dep. *to help, aid* (with dat.).

ŏportet -tēre -tŭit, impers., *it is proper, one should, one ought.*

oppēdo -ĕre, *to mock, insult.*

oppĕrĭor -pĕriri -pertus, dep. *to wait* or *wait for.*

oppĕto -ĕre -īvi and -ĭi -ītum, *to go to meet, encounter*; esp. *to encounter death, to die.*

oppĭdānus -a -um, *of a town*; sometimes *provincial, 'small-town'*; m. pl. as subst., *the inhabitants of a town.*

oppĭdo, *quite, very much*; in answers, *certainly.*

oppĭdŭlum -i, n. *a little town.*

oppĭdum -i, n. *a town*; in Britain, *a fortified wood.*

oppignĕro -are, *to pledge, pawn, give in pledge.*

oppīlo -are, *to stop up, block up.*

opplĕo -plēre -plēvi -plētum, *to fill up, block.*

oppōno -pōnĕre -pŏsŭi -pŏsĭtum, *to put opposite* or *before; to pledge against, mortgage for; to set against, oppose, interpose; to allege as an objection; to contrast.*

Hence partic. **oppŏsĭtus** -a -um, *standing against, opposite.*

opportūnĭtās -ātis, f. *convenience, fitness; a fit time, opportunity; advantage.*

opportūnus -a -um, *opportune, fit, suitable, convenient*; of time, *favourable*; with dat., sometimes, *exposed, liable to.* Adv. **opportūnē,** *seasonably, conveniently.*

oppŏsĭtĭo -ōnis, f. *opposing, opposition.*

[1]**oppŏsĭtus** -a -um, partic. from oppono; q.v.

[2]**oppŏsĭtus** -ūs, m. *placing against, opposing, interposition.*

oppressĭo -ōnis, f. *pressing down, oppression; suppression; seizure.*

[1]**oppressus** -ūs, m. *pressing down, pressure.*

[2]**oppressus** -a -um, partic. from opprimo; q.v.

opprĭmo -prĭmĕre -pressi -pressum. (1) *to press upon, press down; to crush, smother, stamp out.* (2) *to catch, take by surprise, occupy forcibly.*

opprobrĭum -i, n. *reproach, scandal, disgrace; a verbal reproach, taunt; a cause of disgrace.*

opprobro -are, *to taunt, reproach.*

oppugnātĭo -ōnis, f. *an assault* on a town; in gen., *an attack.*

oppugnātor -ōris, m. *an assailant, attacker.*

oppugno -are, *to attack, assault.*

Ops ŏpis, f.: in nom. sing., *the goddess of abundance*; other cases **ŏpem, ŏpis, ŏpĕ,** *might, power,* esp. *power to aid; help, support*; plur. **ŏpēs,** *resources, means, wealth.*

ops-; see obs-.

optābĭlis -e, *desirable, to be wished for.*

optātĭo -ōnis, f. *a wish.*

optĭmās -ātis, *one of the best, aristocratic*; m. pl. as subst. **optĭmātēs,** *the aristocratic party, the aristocrats.*

optĭmus (**optŭmus**) -a -um, superl. of bonus; q.v.

[1]**optĭo** -ōnis, f. *choice, option.*

[2]**optĭo** -ōnis, m. *a helper, assistant.*

optīvus -a -um, *chosen.*

opto -are, *to choose, select; to wish for, desire.* Hence partic. **optātus** -a

-um, *wished for, desired, welcome*; n. as subst. **optātum,** *a wish*; abl. **optātō,** *according to one's wish.*

ŏpŭlens, -entis; see opulentus.

ŏpŭlentĭa -ae, f. *wealth, riches, opulence; the power, greatness* of a state.

ŏpŭlento -are, *to make wealthy, enrich.*

ŏpŭlentus -a -um, also **ŏpŭlens** -entis, adj. *rich, wealthy; powerful, mighty; splendid, sumptuous; lucrative.* Adv. **ŏpŭlentē** and **ŏpŭlentĕr,** *richly, splendidly.*

ŏpus -ĕris, n. *work, labour; work done, a finished work; a building; a literary work* or *a work of art*; plur. milit. *works, lines, siege-engines.*

ŏpus est (or **sunt**), *there is work, there is need; one needs, it is necessary* (with nom., abl., or genit. of what is needed).

ŏpuscŭlum -i, n. *a little work.*

ōra -ae, f. *edge, rim, boundary*; esp. *coast-line, coast*; in gen., *region, clime, country; the people of a district; a hawser, cable* reaching to shore.

ōrācŭlum (ōrāclum) -i, n. *a solemn utterance, oracle, divine response, prophecy*; also *the place where an oracle is given.*

ōrātĭo -ōnis, f. *speaking, speech; language, style*; esp. *a set speech; eloquence; prose; an imperial message.*

ōrātĭuncŭla -ae, f. *a little speech, short oration.*

ōrātor -ōris, m. *speaker; spokesman, envoy; orator.*

ōrātōrĭus -a -um, *of an orator, oratorical*; f. as subst. *oratory*; adv. **ōrātōrĭē.**

ōrātrix -īcis, f. *a female suppliant.*

ōrātū, abl. sing. m. *by request.*

orbātor -ōris, m. *one who deprives another of children* or *parents.*

orbis -is, m. *a circle, ring, disk; orbit, coil*; orbis signifer, *the Zodiac*; orbis lacteus, *the Milky Way*; orbis terrae, terrarum, *the world.* Transf., *rotation, round*; of style, *roundness.*

orbĭta -ae, f. *a wheel-rut.*

orbĭtās -ātis, f. *bereavement, loss of children* or *parents.*

orbo -are, *to bereave, deprive of parents* or *children.*

orbus -a -um, *deprived of parents* or *children*; as subst. *an orphan*; in gen., *deprived, destitute.*

orca -ae, f. *a pot* or *jar with a large belly.*

orchăs -ădis, f. *a species of olive.*

orchestra -ae, f. *the part of a Roman theatre reserved for senators*; meton., *the senate.*

Orcus i-, m. *Orcus, the infernal regions.* Transf., *the god of the lower world; death.*

orděum = hordeum; q.v.

ordĭa prīma = primordia; q.v.

ordĭnārĭus -a -um, *according to order, regular, ordinary.*

ordĭnātim, *in good order, regularly, properly.*

ordĭnātĭo -ōnis, f. *setting in order, arrangement.*

ordĭno -are, *to set in order, settle, arrange, appoint; to govern* a country. Hence partic. **ordĭnātus** -a -um, *arranged, orderly.*

ordĭor ordīri orsus, dep. *to begin*; esp. *to begin speaking.* N. pl. of partic. as subst. **orsa** -orum, *beginnings, undertaking*; esp. *words uttered, speech.*

ordo -ĭnis, m. *a series, line, row, order*; milit., *a line, rank, file*; ordinem ducere, *to be a centurion*; polit. and socially, *an order, rank, class*; in gen., *order, arrangement*; ordine, *in turn, in due order, regularly*; extra ordinem, *in an unusual, irregular manner.*

Ŏrēăs -ădis, f. *a mountain-nymph.*

Ŏrestes -ae and -is, m. *son of Agamemnon and Clytemnestra, who killed his mother to avenge his father.*

ŏrexis -is, f. *desire, appetite.*

orgănĭcus -i, m. *a musician.*

orgănum -i, n. *an instrument*; esp., *a musical instrument.*

orgĭa -orum, n. pl. *a secret festival; mysteries; orgies.*

ŏrĭchalcum -i, n. *yellow copper ore; brass.*

ōrĭcŭla = auricula; q.v.

ŏrĭens -entis, m. partic. from orior; q.v.

ŏrīgo -ĭnis, f. *origin, source, beginning; an ancestor.*

Ŏrīōn -ōnis, m. *the constellation Orion.*

ŏrĭor ŏrīri ortus, dep. *to rise; to spring up, be born, proceed from a source* or *cause.* Hence partic. **ŏrĭens** -entis, *rising.* M. as subst. *the rising sun; the east; the morning.*

ŏrĭundus -a -um, *arising from, springing from.*

ornāmentum -i, n. *equipment, trappings, furniture; ornament, decoration; honour, distinction.*

ornātrix -īcis, f. *a female hairdresser, tire-woman.*

[1]**ornātus** -ūs, m. *dress, attire, equipment; embellishment, ornament.*

[2]**ornatus** -a -um, partic. from orno; q.v.

orno -are, *to equip, furnish, fit out*; also *to adorn, decorate, embellish; to honour, distinguish.*

Hence partic. **ornātus** -a -um, *furnished, equipped, provided; adorned, decorated, embellished.* Adv. **ornātē,** *splendidly, elegantly.*

ornus -i, f. *the mountain-ash.*

ōro -are, *to speak*; esp. *to speak as an orator*; with acc., *to treat, argue, plead; to beg, pray, entreat, beseech.*

Ŏrontēs -is and -ae, m. *chief river of Syria.*

Orphēūs -ĕi and -ĕos, *a mythical minstrel, husband of Eurydice.*

orsa -orum, from ordior; q.v.

orsus -ūs, m. *a beginning, undertaking.*

[1]**ortus** -ūs, m.: of heavenly bodies, *rising*; of persons, *origin, birth*; in gen., *origin, source.*

[2]**ortus** -a -um, partic. from orior; q.v.

ŏryx -ȳgis, m. *a wild goat* or *gazelle.*

ŏrȳza -ae, f. *rice.*

[1]**ōs** ōris, n. (1) *the mouth;* hence *voice, talk*; uno ore, *unanimously*; in gen., *mouth, opening, source.* (2) *the face, countenance; presence, sight; ex-*

pression; boldness of expression, impudence; a mask.
[2]**ŏs** ossis, n. *a bone.*
oscen -ĭnis, m. *a bird from whose note auguries were taken* (e.g., raven, owl, crow).
Osci -orum, *an ancient people of Italy.*
oscillum -i, n. *a little mask.*
oscĭtātĭo -ōnis, f. *gaping, yawning.*
oscĭto -are, *to gape, yawn*; partic. **oscĭtans** -antis, *yawning, sleepy, listless*; adv. **oscĭtantĕr.**
oscŭlātĭo -ōnis, f. *kissing.*
oscŭlor -ari, dep. *to kiss; to caress, make much of.*
oscŭlum -i, n. *a little mouth; a kiss.*
ōsor -ōris, m. *a hater.*
Ossa -ae, m. and f. *a mountain range in Thessaly.*
ossĕus -a -um, *bony.*
ossifrăgus -i, m. and **ossifrăga** -ae, f. *the sea-eagle, osprey.*
ostendo -tendĕre -tendi -tentum and -tensum, *to hold out, show, reveal, present*; in speech, *to make plain, declare.* N. of partic. as subst. **ostentum** -i, *a prodigy, portent.*
ostentātĭo -ōnis, f. *showing, revealing; showing off, display; deceitful show, pretence.*
ostentātor -ōris, m. *one who shows*; esp., *a boaster.*
ostento -are, *to hold out, present, offer; to show, reveal; to show off, display*; in speech, *to declare, make known.*
ostentŭi, dat. sing. m. *for a show; merely for show; as a sign* or *proof.*
ostentum -i, n., subst. from ostendo; q.v.
Ostĭa -ae, f. and **Ostĭa** -orum, n. *the harbour and port of Rome, at the mouth of the Tiber*; adj. **Ostĭensis** -e.
ostĭārĭum -i, n. *a door-tax.*
ostĭātim, *from door to door.*
ostĭum -i, n. *door*; in gen., *entrance*; fluminis, *mouth.*
ostrĕa -ae, f. and **ostrĕum** -i, n. *an oyster.*
ostrĭfer -fĕra -fĕrum, *producing oysters.*
ostrīnus -a -um, *purple.*
ostrum -i, n. *purple dye prepared from a shell-fish; a purple dress.*
Ŏtho -ōnis, m. *a Roman* cognomen.
ōtĭor -ari, dep. *to be at leisure.*
ōtĭōsus -a -um, *at leisure*, esp. *free from public duties; calm, quiet, undisturbed, neutral.* Adv. **ōtĭōsē,** *at leisure; quietly, easily.*
ōtĭum -i, n. *free time, leisure, ease; peace, repose.*
ŏvans -antis, partic. *rejoicing, exulting*; esp. *celebrating the minor triumph* (the ovatio).
ŏvātĭo -ōnis, f. *an ovation, a kind of lesser triumph.*
Ŏvĭdĭus -a, *name of a Roman gens*; esp. of the poet P. Ovidius Naso (43 B.C.-17 A.D.).
ŏvīle -is, n. *a sheepfold, an enclosure.*
ŏvillus -a -um, *of sheep.*
ŏvis -is, f. *a sheep.*
ōvum -i, n. *an egg.*

P

P, p, the fifteenth letter of the Latin Alphabet.
pābŭlātĭo -ōnis, f. *procuring fodder, foraging.*
pābŭlātor -ōris, m. *a forager.*
pābŭlor -ari, dep. *to forage, seek fodder.*
pābŭlum -i, n. *food, nourishment, fodder.*
pācālis -e, *peaceful.*
pācĭfer -fĕra -fĕrum, *peace-bringing.*
pācĭfĭcātĭo -ōnis, f. *making of peace, pacification.*
pācĭfĭcātor -ōris, m. *a peacemaker.*
pācĭfĭcātōrĭus -a -um, *peacemaking, pacific.*
pācĭfĭco -are, *to make peace; to appease, pacify.*
pācĭfĭcus -a -um, *peacemaking, pacific.*
păciscor păcisci pactus, dep. *to make a bargain* or *agreement, to covenant, contract*; transit., *to stipulate for, bargain for*; also *to give in exchange.* Perf. partic. in pass. sense, **pactus** -a -um, *agreed upon, stipulated; betrothed.* N. as subst. **pactum** -i, *an agreement, treaty, pact*; quo pacto? *how?* alio pacto, *in another way.*
pāco -are, *to pacify, make peaceful*; poet., *to make fruitful.*

Hence partic. **pācātus** -a -um, *peaceful, quiet*; n. as subst. *a peaceful country.*
pactĭo -ōnis, f. *a bargain, contract, agreement, treaty.*
pactor -ōris, m. *one who makes a contract* or *treaty, negotiator.*
pactum -i, n., and **pactus** -a -um, from paciscor; q.v.
Pācŭvĭus -i, m. *a Roman tragic poet.*
Pădus -i, m. *the river Po.*
paeān -ānis, m. (1) *the Healer, a surname of Apollo.* (2) *a hymn, paean.*
paedăgōgus -i, m. *a slave who accompanied children to and from school.*
paedor -ōris, m. *dirt, filth.*
paelex (pellex) -lĭcis, f. *a mistress, concubine.*
paelĭcātus -ūs, m. *concubinage.*
Paeligni -orum, m. pl. *an Italian tribe.*
paenĕ, *nearly, almost.*
paeninsŭla -ae, f. *a peninsula.*
paenĭtentĭa -ae, f. *repentance, regret.*
paenĭtĕo -ēre, *to repent, regret, be sorry*; impers. **paenĭtet** hominem, *a person feels regret, is sorry*; gerundive **paenĭtendus** -a -um, *regrettable, unsatisfactory.*
paenŭla -ae, f. *a travelling-cloak, greatcoat.*
paenŭlātus -a -um, *wearing the* paenula; q.v.
paeōn -ōnis, m. *a metrical foot, consisting of three short syllables and one long.*
Paestum -i, n. *a town in Lucania famous for roses.*
paetŭlus -a -um, *with a slight cast in the eye.*
paetus -a -um, *with a cast in the eyes, squinting.*
pāgānus -a -um, *belonging to a village,*

rural; rustic; m. as subst. *a villager, countryman.*
pāgātim, *in villages, by villages.*
pāgella -ae, f. *a little page.*
pāgĭna -ae, f. *a page* of a letter, book, etc.
pāgĭnŭla -ae, f. *a little page.*
pāgus -i, m. *a village* or *country district; a canton.*
pāla -ae, f. *a spade; the bezel of a ring.*
Pălaestīna -ae, and **Pălaestīnē** -ēs, f. *Palestine.*
pălaestra -ae, f. *a gymnasium* or *wrestling school; wrestling.* Transf., *training in rhetoric.*
pălaestrĭcus -a -um, *of the palaestra, gymnastic*; adv. **pălaestrĭcē.**
pălaestrīta -ae, m. *the superintendent of a* palaestra (q.v.).
pălam: adv. *openly, publicly*; prep., with abl., *in the presence of.*
Pălātĭum -i, n. *the Palatine Hill in Rome*: in plur., *a palace*; adj. **Pălātīnus** -a -um.
pălātum -i, n. and **pălātus** -i, m. *the roof of the mouth, palate; taste; critical judgment.*
pălĕa -ae, f. *chaff.*
pălĕar -āris, n. *the dewlap of an ox.*
Pălēs -is, f. *tutelary goddess of herds and shepherds*; adj. **Pălīlis** -e; n. pl. as subst. **Pălīlĭa** -ĭum, *the feast of Pales on the 21st of April.*
pălimpsestus -i, m. *a palimpsest.*
Pălīnūrus -i, m. *the pilot of Aeneas; a promontory on the coast of Lucania.*
pălĭūrus -i, m. *a plant, Christ's thorn.*
palla -ae, f. *a long outer garment*, esp. *as worn by women and actors.*
Pallas -ădis and -ădos, f. *Athene, the Greek goddess of wisdom, identified with Minerva*; adj. **Pallădĭus** -a -um; n. as subst. **Pallădĭum** -i *an image of Pallas.*
pallĕo -ēre, *to be pale* or *yellow*; partic. **pallens** -entis, *pale, wan, yellow, pale green; causing paleness; drooping, weak.*
pallesco pallescĕre pallui, *to grow pale* or *yellow*; with acc., *to turn pale at.*
pallĭātus -a -um, *clad in a* pallium, i.e. *as a Greek* (opp. togatus).
pallĭdŭlus -a -um, *somewhat pale.*
pallĭdus -a -um, *pale, wan; causing paleness.*
pallĭŏlum -i, n. *a little Greek cloak; a hood.*
pallĭum -i, n. *a coverlet; a Greek mantle.*
pallor -ōris, m. *paleness; fading.*
palma -ae, f. (1) *the palm of the hand; a hand; the blade of an oar.* (2) *the palm-tree; a date; a palm broom; a palm-branch* as token of victory; hence, *victory, honour, glory.*
palmāris -e, *deserving the palm* or *prize, excellent.*
palmārĭum -i, n. *a masterpiece.*
palmātus -a -um, *embroidered with palm-branches.*
palmĕs -ĭtis, m. *a young branch* esp. *of a vine.*
palmētum -i, n. *a palm-grove.*
palmĭfer -fĕra -fĕrum, *abounding in palm-trees.*
palmōsus -a -um, *full of palms.*
palmŭla -ae, f. *the blade of an oar.*
pālor -ari, dep. *to wander, stray.*
palpebra -ae, f. *eyelid.*
palpĭto -are, *to move quickly, tremble, throb.*
palpo -are and **palpor** -ari, dep. *to stroke; to coax, flatter, wheedle.*
pălūdāmentum -i, n. *the military cloak.*
pălūdātus -a -um, *clad in the military cloak.*
pălūdōsus -a -um, *marshy, boggy.*
pălumbes -is, m. and f. *a wood-pigeon, ring-dove.*
[1]**pālus** -i, m. *a pale, stake.*
[2]**pălūs** -ūdis, f. *a swamp, marsh, bog.*
păluster -tris -tre, *marshy, boggy.*
pampĭnĕus -a -um, *attached to* or *consisting of vine-tendrils.*
pampĭnus -i, m. and f. *a vine-tendril* or *vine-leaf.*
Pān Pānos, m. *the god of flocks, woods,* and *shepherds.*
pănăcēa -ae, f. and **pănăcēs** -is, n. *a plant, supposed to heal all diseases; panacea, heal-all.*
pānārĭum -i, n. *a bread-basket.*
panchrestus (**panchristus**) -a -um, *good for everything.*
pancrătĭum (**-ŏn**) -i, n. *a gymnastic contest.*
pando pandĕre pandi pansum and passum. (1) *to stretch out, spread out, extend*; crines passi, *dishevelled hair.* (2) *to throw open, lay open, reveal, disclose.*
Hence partic. **passus** -a -um, *spread out*, esp. *spread out to dry*; n. as subst. *raisin-wine.*
pandus -a -um, *bent, curved, crooked.*
pango pangĕre panxi, *to fasten, fix, drive in.* Transf., *to compose, write.* In perf. **pĕpĭgi** and supine **pactum,** *to fix, settle, agree upon* (cf. paciscor).
pānĭcum -i, n. *a kind of wild millet.*
pānis -is, m. *bread*; in plur., *loaves.*
pannĭcŭlus -i, m. *a little garment.*
Pannŏnia -ae, f. *Pannonia, a district on the middle Danube.*
pannōsus -a -um, *ragged, tattered.*
pannūcĕus (**-ĭus**) -a -um, *ragged; wrinkled, shrivelled.*
pannus -i, m. *a piece of cloth; garment; rag.*
Pănormus -i, f. and **Pănormum** -i, n. *a town in Sicily* (modern *Palermo*).
pansa -ae, *splay-footed.*
panthēra -ae, f. *a panther* or *leopard.*
pantŏmīmus -i, m. and **pantŏmīma** -ae, f. *a dancer, mime.*
păpae, interj. *wonderful! indeed!*
pāpās -ae and -ātis, m. *a tutor.*
păpāver -ĕris, n. *poppy.*
păpāvĕrĕus -a -um, *of the poppy.*
pāpĭlio -ōnis, m. *butterfly.*
păpilla -ae, f. *nipple, teat, breast.*
Păpīrĭus -a -um, *name of a Roman* gens.
pappo -are, *to eat.*
pappus -i, m. *the woolly seed of certain plants.*

păpŭla -ae, f. *a pimple.*
păpȳrĭfer -fĕra -fĕrum, *producing papyrus.*
păpȳrus -i, m. and f. and **păpȳrum** -i, n. *the plant papyrus; clothing* or *paper made from papyrus.*
pār păris, *equal, like, a match*; m. and f. as subst., *a companion*; n. as subst., *the like, the equivalent,* or *a pair*; par impar ludere, *to play at odd and even*; par est, *it is appropriate.* Hence adv. **părĭtĕr,** *equally, alike; together, at the same time.*
părābĭlis -e, *easily procured.*
părăbŏla -ae and **părăbŏlē** -ēs, f. *a comparison.*
părăsītus -i, m. and **părăsīta** -ae, f. *a guest*; in bad sense, *a toady, parasite.*
părātĭo -ōnis, f. *preparing, preparation.*
[1]**părātus** -a -um, partic. from paro; q.v.
[2]**părātus** -ūs, m. *preparation, fitting out, equipment.*
Parca -ae, f. *a goddess of fate*; pl. Parcae, *the three Fates.*
parco parcĕre pĕperci (and parci) parsum, *to be sparing, economize; to spare, refrain from injuring* (with dat.); *to refrain from, keep oneself from*; with infin., *to forbear to.*
parcus -a -um, *sparing, thrifty, economical; moderate, sparing*; of things, *scanty, small, meagre.* Adv. **parcē,** *sparingly, economically, moderately.*
pardus -i, m. *a panther* or *leopard.*
[1]**pārens** -entis, partic. from pareo; q.v.
[2]**părens** -entis, c. *a parent*; sometimes *grandfather* or *ancestor; author, cause, origin.*
părentālis -e, *parental, of parents* (or *ancestors*); n. pl. as subst. **părentālĭa** -ĭum, *a festival in honour of the dead.*
părento -are, *to celebrate the* parentalia. Transf., *to avenge the dead.*
pārĕo -ere, *to appear, become evident.* Transf., *to obey, give way to; to be subject to, serve* (with dat.); partic. **pārens** -entis, *obedient.*
părĭēs -ĕtis, m. *a wall, properly the wall of a house.*
părĭĕtĭnae -arum, f. pl. *old walls, ruins.*
Părīlĭa = Palilia; see Pales.
părĭlis -e, *similar, like, equal.*
părĭo părĕre pĕpĕri partum; fut. partic. părĭtūrus; *to bring forth, bear, produce.* Transf., *to occasion, create, make, get.*
Părĭs -ĭdis, m. *a Trojan prince who carried off Helen.*
parma -ae, f. *a small round shield, a buckler.*
parmātus -a -um, *armed with the parma.*
parmŭla -ae, f. *a small round shield, buckler.*
Parnāsus (-ŏs) -i, m. *a mountain in Phocis, sacred to Apollo and the Muses*; f. adj. **Parnāsis** -ĭdis, and adj. **Parnāsĭus** -a -um.
păro -are, *to set, put; to prepare, provide, furnish, obtain; to buy.*
Hence partic. **părātus** -a -um, *prepared, ready; provided, equipped*; of persons, *skilled.* Adv. **părātē,** *with preparation, readily.*
părŏcha -ae, f. *a supplying of necessaries.*
părŏchus -i, m. *an officer who looked after travelling ambassadors and magistrates.* Transf., *a host.*
păropsis -ĭdis, f. *a dessert-dish.*
Părus (-ŏs) -i, f. *an island in the Aegean Sea, famous for marble*; adj. **Părĭus** -a -um.
parra -ae, f. *a bird of ill omen,* perhaps *owl.*
parrĭcīda -ae, f. *a parricide, one who murders a parent* or *near relative*; polit., *an assassin, traitor.*
parrĭcīdĭum -i, n. *the murder of a parent* or *any near relative*; polit., *assassination, treason.*
pars partis, *a part, piece, share; a direction, region; a side, party; an actor's role*; in gen., usually plur., *office, function, duty*; pars . . . pars, *some . . . others*; pro (sua) parte, pro virile parte, *to the best of one's ability*; magna ex parte, *to a great extent*; multis partibus, *many times, much.* Adv. **partim,** *partly*; used like a noun, *some.*
parsĭmōnĭa -ae, f. *thrift, economy.*
Parthi -orum, m. pl. *the Parthians*; adj. **Parthĭcus** and **Parthus** -a -um; subst. **Parthĭa** -ae, *Parthia.*
partĭceps -cĭpis, *sharing, participating in* (with genit.); as subst., *partner, comrade.*
partĭcĭpo -are, *to share* with a person; *to cause* a person *to share.*
partĭcŭla -ae, f. *a small part, particle.*
partim, adv. from pars; q.v.
partĭo -ire and **partĭor** -iri, dep. *to share out, distribute, divide*; perf. partic. in pass. sense **partītus** -a -um, *divided*; adv. **partītē,** *with proper divisions.*
partītĭo -ōnis, f. *division, sharing, distribution.*
partŭrĭo -ire, *to desire to bring forth, have the pains of labour; to teem with* anything, *be full of.*
[1]**partus** -a -um, partic. from pario; q.v.
[2]**partus** -ūs, m. *bearing, bringing forth, birth.* Transf., *young, offspring.*
părum, *too little, not enough* (as adv. or subst.); parum habere, *to think too little, be dissatisfied with.* Compar. **mĭnus,** *less*; sometimes = *not, not at all*; sin minus, *but if not.* Superl. **mĭnĭmē** (**mĭnŭmē**), *in the least degree, very little, least of all*; sometimes *not at all, by no means.*
părumper, *for a little while.*
Părus = Paros; q.v.
parvĭtās -ātis, f. *littleness, smallness.*
parvŭlus -a um, *very small*; of age, *young, little.*
parvus -a -um, *little, small; slight, weak*; of time, *short*; of age, *young*; of value, *poor, insignificant*; n. as subst. *a little.* Compar. **mĭnor,** *smaller, less*; of time, *shorter*; of age, minor (natu), *younger*; of value, *inferior.* Superl. **mĭnĭmus.** *smallest, least;*

n. as adv., minimum, *very little.* Rare superl. **parvissĭmus** -a -um.

pasco pascĕre pāvi pastum. (1) transit., *to feed, lead to pasture; to keep, support; to nourish*; also *to give as pasture.* Transf., *to feast, gratify.* Pass. as middle, *to graze on*; also *to feast upon, delight in.* (2) intransit., of animals, *to graze, browse.*

pascŭus -a -um, *for pasture* or *grazing*; n. as subst. *a pasture.*

Pāsĭthĕa -ae and **Pāsĭthĕē** -ēs, f. *one of the three Graces.*

passer -ĕris, m. *a sparrow* or other *small bird; a sea-fish, a plaice* or *flounder.*

passercŭlus -i, m. *a little sparrow.*

passim, *here and there, far and wide; indiscriminately.*

passum -i, n., subst. from pando; q.v.

[1]**passus** -a -um, partic. from pando; q.v.

[2]**passus** -a -um, partic. from patior; q.v.

[3]**passus** -ūs, m. *a step, stride, pace*; esp. as a measure of length = five Roman feet. Transf., *footstep, track.*

pastillus -i, m. *a lozenge.*

pastĭo -ōnis, f. *pasture, pasturing.*

pastor -ōris, m. *a herd*; esp. *a shepherd.*

pastōrālis -e, **pastōrĭcĭus** -a -um and **pastōrĭus** -a -um, *of shepherds, pastoral.*

[1]**pastus** -a -um, partic. from pasco; q.v.

[2]**pastus** -ūs, m. *pasture, feeding; food, sustenance.*

Pătăvĭum -i, n. *a town in North Italy, birthplace of Livy* (now *Padua*); adj. **Pătăvīnus** -a -um.

pătĕfăcĭo -făcĕre -fēci -factum; pass. **pătĕfīo** -fĭĕri -factus sum; *to open, throw open, open up, make accessible; to bring to light, disclose, reveal.*

pătĕfactĭo -ōnis, f. *throwing open, disclosing.*

pătella -ae, f. *a dish, platter, plate.*

pătĕo -ēre, *to be open, stand open, be accessible* or *exposed; to be revealed, disclosed, clear; to stretch out, extend.* Hence partic. **pătens** -entis, *open, unobstructed, accessible, exposed*; also *evident.* Compar. adv. **pătentĭus,** *more openly.*

păter -tris, m. *father, sire; founder, head*; pater familias, *or* familiae, *head of a household*; plur., patres, *forefathers*; also as a title of the senators, patres, *or* patres conscripti; pater patriae, *father of his country, a national hero.*

pătĕra -ae, f. *a shallow dish, saucer.*

păternus -a -um, *of a father, paternal; native.*

pătesco pătescĕre pătŭi, *to be opened, lie open; to be revealed; to spread out.*

pătĭbĭlis -e: pass, *endurable, bearable*; act., *sensitive.*

pătĭbŭlum -i, n. *a yoke as an instrument of punishment, a pillory.*

pătĭentĭa -ae, f. *endurance, resignation*; in bad sense, *want of spirit.*

pătĭna -ae, f. *a dish.*

pătĭor păti passus, dep. *to suffer, undergo, experience; to permit, allow.* Hence partic. **pătĭens** -entis, *enduring, capable of enduring,* with genit.; *patient*; in bad sense, *stubborn.* Adv. **pătĭentĕr.**

patrātor -oris, m. *accomplisher, achiever.*

patrĭa -ae, f. *fatherland*; see patrius.

patrĭcĭus -a -um. *of the* patres, *patrician, noble*; m. as subst., *a patrician.*

patrĭmōnĭum -i, n. *property inherited from a father, patrimony.*

patrĭmus -a -um, *having a father still living.*

patrītus -a -um, *inherited from one's father.*

patrĭus -a -um, *of a father, fatherly, paternal; hereditary; ancestral; native.* F. as subst. **patrĭa** -ae, f. (sc. terra), *fatherland, native land.*

patro -are, *to accomplish, execute, achieve.*

patrōcĭnĭum -i, n. *the services of a patron*; esp. *defence in a court of law*; in gen., *defence, protection*; plur., **patrōcĭnĭa,** *clients.*

patrōcĭnor -ari, dep. *to protect, defend.*

patrōna -ae, f. *a protectress, patroness.*

patrōnus -i, m. *a protector, defender, patron*; esp. *an advocate in a court of law.*

patrŭēlis -e, *descended from a father's brother*; as subst., *a cousin.*

[1]**patrŭus** -i, m. *a father's brother, paternal uncle.*

[2]**patrŭus** -a -um, adj. *of an uncle.*

pătŭlus -a -um, *open, standing open, spreading, extended.*

paucĭtās -ātis, f. *fewness, scarcity.*

paucŭlus -a -um, *very small*; plur., *very few.*

paucus -a -um, oftener plur. **pauci** -ae -a, *few, little*; as subst., m. pl. **pauci,** *a few, the select few, the oligarchs*; n. pl. **paucă,** *a few words.*

paulātim (paullātim), *gradually, little by little.*

paulispĕr (paullispĕr), *for a little while.*

paulŭlus (paullŭlus) -a -um, *very little*; n. as subst. **paulŭlum** -i, *a very little*; acc. and abl., as adv., *a little.*

[1]**paulus (paullus)** -a -um, *little, small*; as subst., **paulum,** *a little*; acc., and abl. **paulo,** like adv., *a little.*

[2]**Paulus (Paullus)** -i, m. *the name of a family of the* gens Aemilia.

pauper -ĕris, *poor*; of things, *scanty, meagre.*

paupercŭlus -a -um, *poor.*

paupĕrĭēs -ēi, f. *poverty.*

paupĕro -are, *to make poor, to deprive.*

paupertās -ātis, f. *poverty.*

pausa -ae, f. *cessation, end.*

pausĭa -ae, f. *a species of olive.*

pauxillŭlus -a -um, *very little, very small.*

pauxillus -a -um, *small, little*: n. as subst. *a little.*

păvĕfactus -a -um, *frightened, terrified.*

păvĕo păvēre pāvi: intransit., *to quake with fear, panic*; transit., *to quake at.*

păvesco -ĕre: intransit., *to begin to quake, take fright*; transit., *to be alarmed by.*

păvĭdus -a -um, *trembling, quaking, fearful; causing fear.* Adv. **păvĭdē,** *fearfully.*

păvīmento -are, *to pave.*

păvīmentum -i, n. *a pavement* of tiles, brick, stone, etc.

păvĭo -ire, *to beat.*

păvĭto -are: intransit., *to shiver, tremble, quake with fear*; transit., *to quake at.*

păvo -ōnis, m. *peacock.*

păvor -ōris, m. *trembling, quaking; fear, panic.*

pax pācis, f. *peace; calm, quiet*; of the gods, *grace, favour*; pace tua, *with your good leave.*

pecco -are, *to make a mistake, go wrong, err* or *sin*; n. of partic. as subst. **peccātum** -i, *an error, fault, sin.*

pĕcŏrōsus -a -um, *rich in cattle.*

pectĕn -ĭnis, m. *a comb; a weaver's comb; a rake; clasped hands; a quill,* for striking the strings of the lyre; *a shell-fish, the scallop.*

pecto pectĕre pexi pexum, *to comb; to card; to thrash*; partic. **pexus** -a -um, *with the nap on, woolly.*

pectus -ŏris, n. *breast; heart, soul; mind.*

pĕcu, n. plur. pĕcŭa, *sheep, flocks*; also *pastures.*

pĕcŭārĭus -a -um *of sheep* or *cattle*; as subst., m. *a breeder of cattle, grazier*; n. pl. *herds of sheep* or *cattle.*

pĕcūlātor -ōris, m. *one who embezzles public money.*

pĕcūlātus -ūs, m. *embezzlement of public money.*

pĕcūlĭāris -e, *of one's private property; one's own, special, peculiar*; adv. **pĕcūlĭārĭtĕr,** *specially.*

pĕcūlĭum -i, n. *small property, savings*; esp. *the savings of slaves* or *sons.*

pĕcūnĭa -ae, f. *property, wealth*; esp. *money, cash.*

pĕcūnĭārĭus -a -um, *of money, pecuniary.*

pĕcūnĭōsus -a -um, *wealthy, rich; lucrative.*

[1]**pĕcus** -ŏris, n. *cattle, a herd, flock,* esp. *of sheep.*

[2]**pĕcus** -ŭdis, f. *a single head of cattle; a beast, animal*; esp. *a sheep.*

pĕdālis -e, *a foot long* (or *wide*).

pĕdārĭus -a -um, *of a foot*; (senatores) pedarii, *senators of inferior rank.*

pĕdĕs -ĭtis, m.: adj., *going on foot*; subst., *a foot soldier*; coll., *infantry.*

pĕdester -tris -tre, *on foot, pedestrian*; copiae, *infantry*; sometimes, *on land.* Transf., *simple, ordinary, prosaic*: of style, *written in prose.*

pĕdĕtemptim, *feeling one's way; gradually, cautiously.*

pĕdĭca -ae, f. *a fetter; a trap, snare.*

pĕdĭcŭlōsus -a -um, *lousy.*

pĕdis, -is, c. *a louse.*

pĕdĭsĕquus -i, m. and **pĕdĭsĕqua** -ae, f. *a follower, attendant, lackey.*

pĕdĭtātus -ūs, m. *infantry.*

pĕdum -i, n. *a shepherd's crook.*

Pēgăsus (**-os**) -i, m. *the winged horse which produced the fountain Hippocrene*; adj. **Pēgăsēĭus** and **Pēgăsēus** -a -um; **Pēgăsĭdes,** *the Muses.*

pegma -ătis, n. *a bookcase; a stage, scaffolding.*

pēiĕro and **periūro** -are, *to commit perjury, forswear oneself*; with acc., *to swear falsely by.*

pēior, compar. of malus; q.v.

pĕlăgus -i, n., Greek plur. pelage, *the open sea, the main.*

pēlămȳs -ȳdis, f. *the young tunnyfish.*

Pĕlasgi -orum, m. pl. *the Greeks.*

Pēlēūs -ĕi and -ĕos, m. *king of Thessaly, husband of Thetis, father of Achilles*; **Pēlīdēs** -ae, m. *son* or *grandson of Peleus.*

Pēlĭon -i, n. *mountain range in Thessaly*; adj. **Pēlĭăcus** and **Pēlĭus** -a -um.

pellăcĭa -ae, f. *enticing, allurement.*

pellax -ācis, *deceitful, seductive.*

pellĕgo = perlego; q.v.

pellex = paelex; q.v.

pellĭcĭo -lĭcĕre -lexi -lectum, *to entice, decoy, seduce.*

pellĭcŭla -ae, f. *a little skin* or *hide.*

pellĭo -ōnis, m. *a furrier.*

pellis -is, f. *a hide, skin; dressed hide, leather, felt*; milit., *a hut covered with skins.*

pellītus -a -um, *clothed in skins.*

pello pellĕre pĕpŭli pulsum, *to strike, knock, beat; to impel, propel, move, affect; to drive away, dislodge, banish.*

pellūcĕo = perluceo; q.v.

Pĕlŏponnesus -i, f. *the Peloponnese.*

Pĕlops -ŏpis, m. *the father of Atreus and Thyestes.*

pĕlōris -ĭdis, f. *an edible shell-fish, a clam.*

pelta -ae, f. *a small shield.*

peltastes or **-a** -ae, m. *a soldier armed with the* pelta.

peltātus -a -um, *armed with the* pelta.

pelvis -is, f. *a basin.*

pĕnārĭus -a -um, *of* or *for provisions.*

Pĕnātes -ĭum, m. pl., *the Penates, Latin deities of the household and family.* Transf., *home, dwelling.*

pĕnātĭger -gĕra -gĕrum, *carrying the* Penates.

pendĕo pendēre pĕpendi, *to hang; to hang upon, depend on; to hang loose, hover; to be suspended, discontinued; to be in suspense, uncertain, undecided.*

pendo pendĕre pĕpendi pensum: transit., *to cause to hang down; to weigh; to pay out money; to weigh, consider, judge, value, esteem*; poenas, supplicia, *to pay a penalty, suffer punishment*; intransit., *to weigh.*

Hence partic. **pensus** -a -um, *weighed; esteemed, valued, prized*; nihil pensi habere, *to put no value upon, be indifferent about.* N. as subst. **pensum** -i, *wool weighed out to a spinner*; hence, *a day's work, task, duty.*

pendŭlus -a -um, *hanging; in suspense, undecided.*

Pēnĕlŏpa -ae, and **Pēnĕlŏpē** -ēs, f. *the wife of Ulysses.*

pĕnĕs, prep. with acc. *in the possession*

of, in the power of, belonging to; penes se esse, *to be in one's senses.*
pĕnetrābĭlis -e: pass., *that can be passed through, penetrable*; act., *penetrating, piercing.*
pĕnetrālis -e. (1) *passing through, penetrating.* (2) *inward, internal.* N. as subst. *inner chambers, interior,* esp. of a temple.
pĕnetro -are: transit., *to put into; to pass through* or *into, to penetrate*; intransit., *to make one's way in, to penetrate.*
pēnĭcillus -i, m. *a painter's brush* or *pencil; style.*
pēnĭcŭlus -i, m. *a brush; a sponge.*
pēnis -is, m. *a tail.*
[1]**pĕnĭtus** -a -um, adj. *inward, internal.*
[2]**pĕnĭtus,** adv. *internally, inwardly, inside; deeply, through and through; widely.*
penna -ae, f. *a feather; a wing.*
pennātus -a -um, *feathered, winged.*
pennĭger -gĕra -gĕrum, *feathered, winged.*
pennĭpēs -pĕdis, *wing-footed.*
pennĭpŏtens -entis, *able to fly, winged*; plur. as subst., *birds.*
pennŭla -ae, f. *a little wing.*
pensĭlis -e, *hanging, pendent.*
pensĭo -ōnis, f. *a weighing out*; hence *paying, payment, day of payment; rent.*
pensĭto -are, *to weigh carefully, weigh out*; hence, *to pay; to ponder, consider.*
penso -are, *to weigh carefully; to estimate, ponder, consider; to counterbalance, requite; to pay for, purchase* one thing *with* another.
pensum -i, n. subst., from pendo; q.v.
Penthēūs -ĕi and -ĕos, *a king of Thebes.*
pēnūrĭa -ae, f. *lack, want, penury.*
pĕnus -ūs and -i, c., **pĕnum** -i, n., **pĕnus** -ŏris, n. *provisions, victuals.*
peplum -i, n. and **peplus** -i, m. *a robe of state.*
per, prep. with acc.: of space, *through, along, over*; sometimes *before, in the presence of*; of time, *throughout, during; in the course of, in a time of*; of means or instrument, *through, by, by means of, with, by way of*; of cause, *because of, on account of*; per me licet, *you may as far as I am concerned*; in entreaties, oaths, etc., *in the name of.*
pēra -ae, *bag, wallet.*
pĕrabsurdus -a -um, *excessively absurd.*
pĕraccommŏdatus -a -um, *very convenient.*
pĕrācer -cris -cre, *very sharp.*
pĕrăcerbus -a -um, *very sour, very harsh.*
pĕractĭo -ōnis, f. *finishing, completion.*
pĕrăcūtus -a -um, *very sharp; very shrill; very sharp-witted.* Adv. **pĕrăcūtē.**
pĕrădŭlescens -entis, *very young.*
pĕraequē, *quite equally.*
pĕrăgĭto -are, *to drive about violently, harass.*
pĕrăgo -ăgĕrĕ -ēgi -actum. (1) *to pass through*; in words, *to go over, mention.* (2) *to drive about, harass, disturb.* (3) *to carry through, complete, accomplish*; legal, *to prosecute* till conviction.
pĕragrātĭo -ōnis, f. *wandering through.*
pĕragro -are, *to wander through, travel through.*
pĕrămans -antis, *very loving*; adv. **pĕrămantĕr.**
pĕrambŭlo -are, *to walk through, pass through.*
pĕrămoenus -a -um, *very pleasant.*
pĕramplus -a -um, *very large.*
pĕrangustus -a -um, *very narrow*; adv. **pĕrangustē.**
pĕrantīquus -a -um, *very old.*
pĕrappŏsĭtus -a -um, *very suitable.*
pĕrardŭus -a -um, *very difficult.*
pĕrargūtus -a -um, *very witty.*
pĕrăro -are, *to plough through; to furrow the brow; to scratch* letters, *to write, write on.*
pĕrattentus -a -um, *very attentive*; adv. **pĕrattentē.**
perbacchor -ari, dep. *to revel throughout.*
perbĕātus -a -um, *very happy.*
perbellē, *very prettily.*
perbĕnĕ, *very well.*
perbĕnĕvŏlus -a -um, *very wel disposed.*
perbĕnignē, *very kindly.*
perbĭbo -bĭbĕre -bĭbi, *to drink up, absorb*; mentally, *to imbibe, take in.*
perblandus -a -um, *very charming.*
perbŏnus -a -um, *very good.*
perbrĕvis -e, *very short*; perbrevi, *in a very short time*; adv. **perbrĕvĭtĕr.**
perca -ae, f. *a fish, the perch.*
percălĕfactus -a -um, *thoroughly heated.*
percălesco -călescĕre -călŭi, *to become very warm.*
percallesco -callescĕre -callŭi: intransit., *to lose sensibility, become callous*; transit., *to get a good knowledge of.*
percārus -a -um. (1) *very dear, very costly.* (2) *very dear, much loved.*
percautus -a -um, *very cautious.*
percĕlebro -are, *to speak of commonly*; pass., *to be much mentioned.*
percĕler -is -e, *very swiftly;* adv. **percĕlĕrĭtĕr.**
percello -cellĕre -cŭli -culsum, *to strike, push; to beat down, overturn, shatter, ruin*; mentally, *to daunt, unnerve.*
percensĕo -censēre -censŭi, *to count over, reckon; to survey, review; to travel through.*
perceptĭo -ōnis, f. *a receiving, grasping, gathering together.*
perceptus -a -um, partic. from percipio; q.v.
percĭo -cire -cīvi -cĭtum and **percĭĕo** -cĭēre, *to stir up, set in motion*; partic. **percĭtus** -a -um, *aroused, excited*; of character, *excitable.*
percĭpĭo -cĭpĕre -cēpi -ceptum, *to lay hold of, seize; to collect, gather, harvest, gain*; with the senses, *to feel, take in*; mentally, *to learn,*

grasp, understand. N. pl. of partic. as subst. **percepta** -orum, *principles, rules.*
percĭtus -a -um, partic. from percio; q.v.
[1]**percōlo** -are, *to strain, as through a sieve.*
[2]**percŏlo** -cŏlĕre -cŏlŭi -cultum, *to adorn, decorate; to honour a* person, *revere greatly; to complete.*
percōmis -e, *very friendly.*
percommŏdus -a -um, *very fit*; adv. **percommŏdē.**
percontātĭo (percunct-) -ōnis, f. *inquiry, interrogation.*
percontātor (percunct-) -ōris, m. *an inquirer, asker of questions.*
percontor (percunctor) -ari, dep. *to sound*; hence *to inquire, interrogate, investigate.*
percŏquo -cŏquĕre -coxi -coctum, *to cook* or *heat thoroughly; to ripen; to scorch, blacken.*
percrēbresco -brescĕre -brŭi and **percrēbesco** -bescĕre -bŭi, *to become prevalent, get well known.*
percrĕpo -crĕpare -crĕpŭi -crĕpĭtum, *to resound, ring.*
percunct-; see **percont-.**
percŭpĭdus -a -um, *very fond.*
percŭpĭo -cŭpĕre, *to desire exceedingly.*
percūrĭōsus -a -um, *very inquisitive.*
percūro -are, *to cure, heal thoroughly.*
percurro -currĕre -cŭcurri or -curri -cursum, *to run through, hasten through, travel through*; in words, *to run over, mention in passing; to run over in the mind* or *with the eye; to pass through* stages.
percursātĭo -ōnis, f. *travelling through.*
percursĭo -ōnis, f. *running through; rapid consideration.*
percurso -are, *to ramble over, rove about.*
percussĭo -ōnis, f. *striking, beating*; esp. *beating time*; hence *time, rhythm.*
percussor -ōris, m. *a striker*; esp. *a murderer, assassin.*
percussus -ūs, m. *beating, knocking, striking.*
percŭtĭo -cŭtĕre -cussi -cussum, *to strike hard; to strike through, pierce, transfix; to strike down, cut down;* mentally, *to strike, shock*; colloq., *to deceive.*
perdĕcōrus -a -um, *very comely.*
perdēlirus -a -um, *senseless.*
perdiffĭcĭlis -e, *very difficult*; adv. **perdiffĭcĭlĭtĕr.**
perdignus -a -um, *very worthy.*
perdīlĭgens -entis, *very diligent*; adv. **perdīlĭgentĕr.**
perdisco -discĕre -dĭdĭci, *to learn thoroughly.*
perdĭsertē, *very eloquently.*
perdĭtor -ōris, m. *destroyer.*
perdĭtus -a -um, partic. from perdo; q.v.
perdĭū, *for a very long time.*
perdĭŭturnus -a -um, *lasting a very long time.*
perdīvĕs -vĭtis, *very rich.*
perdix -dīcis, c. *partridge.*
perdo -dĕre -dĭdi -dĭtum (in pass., usually pereo, perire), *to destroy, do away with, ruin; to lose; to waste, squander.*

Hence partic. **perdĭtus** -a -um, *miserable, ruined; morally lost, abandoned, profligate.* Adv. **perdĭtē,** *desperately, immoderately; in an abandoned manner.*
perdŏcĕo -dŏcēre -dŏcŭi -doctum, *to teach* or *instruct thoroughly*; partic. **perdoctus** -a -um, *very learned, very skilful*; adv. **perdoctē.**
perdŏmo -dŏmare -dŏmŭi -dŏmĭtum, *to tame* or *subdue thoroughly.*
perdūco -dūcĕre -duxi -ductum, *to lead through, bring along; conduct; to carry* or *construct buildings,* from one point to another; *to bring over* to an opinion, *to induce*; in time, *to continue, prolong; to smear over* with a substance.
perductor -ōris, m. *a guide; a pimp, pander.*
perdūdum, *a long time ago.*
perdŭellĭo -ōnis, f. *treason.*
perdŭellis -is, m. *a public enemy.*
perdŭim -is -it, alternative pres. subj. of perdo; q.v.
perdūro -are, *to last long, endure.*
pĕrĕdo -esse -ēdi -ēsum, *to eat up, devour; to consume, destroy.*
pĕregrē, adv. *in, to* or *from a foreign country; abroad, from abroad.*
pĕregrīnābundus -a -um, *travelling about.*
pĕregrīnātĭo -ōnis, f. *travelling* or *staying in foreign countries; roaming.*
pĕregrīnātor -ōris, m. *one who travels about.*
pĕregrīnĭtās -ātis, f. *the condition of a foreigner* or *alien; foreign manners.*
pĕregrīnor -ari, dep. *to stay* or *to travel in foreign countries; to roam, wander, ramble; to be strange, foreign.*
pĕregrīnus -a -um, *foreign, of a foreigner, strange*; m. and f. as subst., *a foreigner, stranger,* esp. *a foreigner resident in Rome.* Transf., *inexperienced.*
pĕrēlĕgans -antis *very elegant*; adv. **pĕrēlĕgantĕr.**
pĕrēlŏquens -entis, *very eloquent.*
pĕremnĭa, n. pl. *the auspices taken on crossing any running water.*
pĕrendĭē, *the day after tomorrow.*
pĕrendĭnus -a -um, *relating to the day after tomorrow.*
pĕrennis -e, *lasting throughout the year; durable, perennial.*
pĕrennĭtās -ātis, f. *duration, perpetuity.*
pĕrenno -are, *to last many years.*
pĕrĕo -ire -ĭi and -īvi -ĭtum, (often as pass. of perdo), *to go to waste, be ruined* or *lost, pass away, perish, die.*
pĕrĕquĭto -are, *to ride through, ride round.*
pĕrerro -are, *to wander through, ramble over; to look over, scan.*
pĕrērŭdĭtus -a -um, *very learned.*
pĕrexĭgŭus -a -um, *very small, very scanty*; of time, *very short.* Adv.

pĕrexĭgŭē, *very scantily very sparingly.*
perfăcētus -a -um, *very witty, brilliant*; adv. **perfăcētē.**
perfăcĭlis -e, *very easy; very courteous.* N. acc. as adv. **perfăcĭle,** *very easily; very readily.*
perfămĭlĭāris -e *very familiar, intimate*; m. as subst. *a very great friend.*
perfectĭo -ōnis f. *completion; perfection.*
perfector -ōris, m. *a perfecter, finisher.*
perfectus -a -um, partic. from perficio; q.v.
perfĕro -ferre -tŭli -lātum, *to carry through, bear to the end*; se perferre, *to betake oneself*; of news, etc., *to deliver, convey*; of tasks, *to bring to an end*; of trouble, *to bear, suffer, endure.*
Hence partic. **perfĕrens** -entis, *enduring, patient.*
perfĭca -ae, f. adj *accomplishing, perfecting.*
perfĭcĭo -fĭcĕre -fēci -fectum, *to bring to an end, complete, finish, achieve*; of time, *to live through*; of a pupil, *to make perfect.*
Hence partic. **perfectus** -a -um, *perfect, complete, finished*: adv. **perfectē.**
perfĭdēlis -e, *very faithful.*
perfĭdĭa -ae, f. *faithlessness, treachery, falsehood.*
perfĭdĭōsus -a -um, *faithless treacherous*; adv. **perfĭdĭōsē.**
perfĭdus -a -um, *faithless treacherous, false.*
perfīgo -fīgĕre -fixi -fixum, *to pierce through, stab.*
perflābĭlis -e, *able to be blown through.*
perflāgĭtĭōsus -a -um, *very shameful.*
perflo -are, *to blow through, blow over.*
perfluctŭo -are, *to surge over.*
perflŭo -flŭĕre -fluxi -fluxum, *to stream through, run away.*
perfŏdĭo -fŏdĕre -fōdi -fossum, *to dig through, pierce through; to excavate, make by digging.*
perfŏro -are, *to pierce through; to form by boring.*
perfrĕquens -entis, *much visited.*
perfrĭco -frĭcare -frĭcŭi -fricatum and -frictum, *to rub over*; os, frontem, etc., *to put on a bold face.*
perfrīgesco -frīgescĕre -frixi, *to catch a chill.*
perfrīgĭdus -a -um, *very cold.*
perfringo -fringĕre -frēgi -fractum, *to break through; to break in pieces, shatter.*
perfrŭor -frŭi -fructus, dep. *to enjoy to the full; to execute completely.*
perfŭga -ae, m. *a deserter.*
perfŭgĭo -fŭgĕre -fūgi -fŭgĭtum, *to flee away, take refuge*; esp. *to desert to the enemy.*
perfŭgĭum -i, n. *a place of refuge, shelter.*
perfunctĭo -ōnis, f. *performing, discharging.*
perfundo -fundĕre -fūdi -fūsum, *to pour over; to steep in a fluid, to dye*; in gen., *to steep in, fill with.*
perfungor -fungi -functus, dep. *to perform fully, execute, discharge; to go through, endure.*
perfŭro -ere, *to rage furiously.*
Pergămum -i, n. and **Pergămus** -i, f., also plur. **Pergăma** -orum, n. *the citadel of Troy; Troy.*
pergaudĕo -ēre, *to rejoice exceedingly.*
pergo pergĕre perrexi perrectum, *to continue, proceed, go on with.*
pergrandis -e, *very large, very great.*
pergrātus -a -um, *very pleasant.*
pergrăvis -e, *very weighty, very important*; adv. **pergrăvĭtĕr.**
pergŭla -ae, f., *a balcony, outhouse; a shop, workshop; a school.*
pĕrhĭbĕo -ēre -ŭi -ĭtum, *to bring forward, cite; to maintain, assert, hold, say.*
pĕrhīlum, *a very little.*
pĕrhŏnōrĭfĭcus -a -um, *very honourable; very respectful*; adv. **pĕrhŏnōrĭfĭcē,** *very respectfully.*
pĕrhorresco -horrescĕre -horrŭi, *to begin to shudder* or *tremble*, esp. with fear; transit., *to shudder at.*
pĕrhorrĭdus -a -um, *very dreadful.*
pĕrhūmānus -a -um, *very friendly, very civil*; adv. **pĕrhūmānĭtĕr.**
Pĕriclēs -is, m. *Athenian statesman.*
pĕrīclĭtātĭo -ōnis, f. *trial, experiment.*
pĕrīclĭtor -ari, dep.: intransit., *to try, make a trial, venture; to take a risk, be in danger*; transit., *to try, test, prove; to endanger, risk.*
pĕrīcŭlōsus -a -um, *dangerous, perilous*; adv. **pĕrīcŭlōsē.**
pĕrīcŭlum (pĕrīclum) -i, n. *a trial, proof, test, attempt; danger, peril, hazard*; at law, *a trial, action, suit*; hence, *a legal record* or *register.*
pĕrĭdōnĕus -a -um, *very suitable.*
pĕrillustris -e *very evident; very distinguished.*
pĕrimbēcillus -a -um, *very weak.*
pĕrĭmo (pĕrĕmo) -ĭmĕre -ēmi -emptum, *to do away with, destroy, kill, annihilate.* Transf., *to thwart, frustrate.*
pĕrincommŏdus -a -um, *very inconvenient*; adv. **pĕrincommŏdē.**
pĕrindĕ, adv. *in like manner*; perinde ac, ut, *or* quam, *just as*; perinde ac si, *just as if.*
pĕrindulgens -entis, *very indulgent, very tender.*
pĕrinfirmus -a -um, *very weak.*
pĕringĕnĭōsus -a -um, *very clever.*
pĕrĭnīquus -a -um, *very unfair; very discontented* or *unwilling.*
pĕrinsignis -e, *very remarkable.*
pĕrinvītus -a -um, *very unwilling.*
pĕrĭŏdus -i, m. *a sentence, period.*
Pĕrĭpătētĭcus -a -um, *belonging to the Peripatetic* or *Aristotelian school of philosophy.*
pĕrĭpĕtasma -ătis, n. *curtain, hanging.*
pĕrīrātus -a -um, *very angry.*
pĕriscĕlis -ĭdis, f. *garter* or *anklet.*
pĕristrōma -ătis, n. *curtain, coverlet, carpet, hanging.*

pĕristȳlĭum -i, n. *a court with a colonnade round it.*
pĕristȳlum -i, n. *a peristyle, a colonnade round a building.*
pĕrītĭa -ae, f. *experience, skill.*
pĕrītus -a -um, *experienced, skilful, practised, expert*; adv. **pĕrītē.**
periūcundus -a -um, *very pleasant*; adv. **periūcundē.**
periūrĭum i-, n. *false swearing, perjury.*
periūro = peiero; q.v.
periūrus -a -um, *perjured; lying.*
perlābor -lābi -lapsus, dep. *to glide through, glide along.*
perlaetus -a -um, *very joyful.*
perlātē, adv. *very widely.*
perlectĭo -ōnis, f. *perusal.*
perlĕgo (pellĕgo) -lĕgĕre -lēgi -lectum, *to survey thoroughly, scan; to read through*; senatum, *to call over the roll of senators.*
perlĕvis -e, *slight*; adv. **perlĕvĭtĕr.**
perlĭbens (perlŭbens) -entis, from perlibet; q.v.
perlībĕrālis -e, *well-bred, very liberal*; adv. **perlībĕrālĭtĕr.**
perlĭbet (perlŭbet) -ere, *it is very pleasing*; partic. **perlĭbens (perlŭb-)** -entis, *very willing*; adv. **perlĭbentĕr (perlub-).**
perlĭcĭo = pellicio; q.v.
perlĭto -are, *to offer an auspicious sacrifice.*
perlongus -a -um, *very long, tedious*; adv. **perlongē,** *very far.*
perlŭbet, etc. = perlibet, etc.; q.v.
perlūcĕo (pellūcĕo) -lūcēre -luxi, *to shine through; to be transparent.*
perlūcĭdŭlus -a -um, *transparent.*
perlūcĭdus (pellūcĭdus) -a -um, *shining, bright; transparent.*
perluctŭōsus -a -um, *very mournful.*
perlŭo -lŭĕre -lŭi -lūtum, *to wash, bathe.*
perlustro -are, *to traverse, pass through; to survey, examine.*
permagnus -a -um, *very great very large.*
permănĕo -mănēre -mansi -mansum, *to remain, stay, last, continue.*
permāno -are, *to flow through, trickle through; to penetrate, extend.* Adv. from partic. **permanantĕr,** *by flowing through.*
permansĭo -ōnis, f. *a remaining, abiding.*
permărīnus -a -um, *going over the sea.*
permātūresco -mātūrescĕre -mātūrŭi, *to become thoroughly ripe.*
permĕdĭocris -e, *very moderate.*
permĕo -are, *to go through, traverse.*
permētĭor -mētiri -mensus, dep. *to measure out; to traverse.*
permīrus -a -um, *very wonderful.*
permiscĕo -miscēre -miscŭi -mixtum, *to mix together, mingle thoroughly to confuse, throw into confusion.*
Hence partic. **permixtus** -a -um, *mixed; promiscuous*; adv. **permixtē.**
permissĭo -ōnis, f. *yielding, surrender; permission, leave.*
permissū, abl. sing. m. *by permission.*
permĭtĭālis -e, *destructive, annihilating.*
permĭtĭēs -ēi, f. *destruction, annihilation.*
permitto -mittĕre -mīsi -missum, *to let go*; esp. of weapons, *to hurl; to give up, yield, surrender, concede, sacrifice; to make allowance for; to allow, permit.*
permixtē, adv. from permisceo; q.v.
permixtĭo -onis, f. *mixture; confusion.*
permŏdestus -a -um, *very modest, very moderate.*
permŏlestus -a -um, *very troublesome*; adv. **permŏlestē,** *with much difficulty.*
permŏlo -ĕre, *to grind thoroughly.*
permōtĭo -onis, f. *movement, agitation.*
permŏvĕo -mŏvēre -mōvi -mōtum, *to move* or *stir up thoroughly; excite, agitate; to persuade, induce, influence* a person.
permulcĕo -mulcēre -mulsi -mulsum, *to stroke; to charm, soothe, soften.*
permultus -a -um, sing., *very much*; plur., *very many*; n. sing. as subst. *very much.*
permūnĭo -īre -īvi -ītum, *to fortify completely,* or *finish fortifying.*
permūtātĭo -ōnis, f. *complete change; exchange, interchange.*
permūto -are, *to change completely; to exchange, interchange.*
perna -ae, f. *ham.*
pernĕcessārĭus -a -um, *very necessary; very intimate.*
pernĕcessĕ, indecl. adj. *very necessary.*
pernĕgo -are, *to deny flatly; to persist in denying* or *refusing.*
pernĭcĭābĭlis -e, *deadly, destructive.*
pernĭcĭēs -ēi, *destruction, disaster, ruin, bane.*
pernĭcĭōsus -a -um, *destructive, ruinous*; adv. **pernĭcĭōsē.**
pernīcĭtās -ātis, f. *swiftness, agility.*
pernix -nīcis, *swift, nimble, agile*; adv. **pernīcĭtĕr.**
pernōbĭlis -e, *very famous.*
pernocto -are, *to pass the night.*
pernosco -noscĕre -nōvi -nōtum, *to investigate* or *find out thoroughly*; in perf., *to know thoroughly.*
pernōtŭit -uisse, *it has become well known.*
pernox -noctis, adj. *all-night.*
pernŭmĕro -are, *to count out, reckon up.*
pēro -ōnis, m. *a boot of untanned hide.*
pĕrobscūrus -a -um, *very obscure.*
pĕrŏdĭōsus -a -um, *very troublesome.*
pĕroffĭcĭōsē, *very attentively.*
pĕrŏlĕo -ēre, *to emit a strong smell.*
pērōnatus -a -um, *wearing leather boots.*
pĕropportūnus -a -um, *very convenient*; adv. **pĕropportūnē.**
pĕroptāto, abl. sing. n. *just as one would wish.*
pĕrōrātĭo -ōnis, f. *conclusion of a speech, peroration.*
pĕrornātus -a -um, *very ornate.*
pĕrorno -are, *to adorn greatly.*
pĕrōro -are, *to speak from beginning to end, to plead a cause throughout, explain* or *state thoroughly; to conclude a speech, wind up, close.*
pĕrōsus -a -um, *hating, detesting.*

perpăco -are, *to pacify thoroughly.*
perparvŭlus and **perparvus** -a -um, *very little.*
perpaucŭli and **perpauci** -ae, -a, *very few.*
perpaulum (perpaullum) i, -n. *a very little.*
perpauper -ĕris, *very poor.*
perpello -pellĕre -pŭli -pulsum, *to push hard, drive along; to urge, compel, constrain.*
perpendĭcŭlum -i, n. *plumbline, plummet*; ad perpendiculum, *in a straight line.*
perpendo -pendĕre -pendi -pensum, *to weigh carefully; to consider, examine.*
perpĕram, *wrongly, falsely.*
perpĕs -pĕtis, *continuous, unbroken.*
perpessĭo -ōnis, f. *suffering, endurance.*
perpessū, alb. sing. m. *in the enduring.*
perpĕtĭor -pĕti -pessus, dep. *to bear to the end, endure.*
perpetro -are, *to complete, accomplish, perform.*
perpĕtŭĭtās -ātis, f. *uninterrupted succession, continuity*; ad perpetuitatem, *for ever.*
[1]**perpĕtŭō**, adv. from perpetuus; q.v.
[2]**perpĕtŭo** -are, *to make continual, continue, perpetuate.*
perpĕtŭus -a -um, *continuous, uninterrupted* (in space or time). Transf., *universal, general.* Abl. as adv. **perpĕtŭō**, *uninterruptedly.*
perplăcĕo -ēre, *to please greatly.*
perplexābĭlis -e, *intricate, obscure.*
perplexor -ari, dep. *to perplex.*
perplexus -a -um, *confused, intricate; obscure, ambiguous.* Adv. **perplexē** and **perplexim.**
perplĭcātus -a -um, *entangled, involved.*
perplŭit -ĕre, *to let the rain through; to run away* or *pour in like rain.*
perpŏlĭo -ire, *to polish thoroughly; perfect, complete.*
Hence partic. **perpŏlītus** -a -um, *polished, accomplished, refined.*
perpŏpŭlor -ari, dep. *to lay waste, devastate completely.*
perpōtātĭo -ōnis, f. *continued drinking, drinking-bout.*
perpōto -are, *to continue drinking; to drink up.*
perprĭmo -prĭmĕre -pressi -pressum, *to press hard.*
perpugnax -ācis, *very pugnacious.*
perpurgo (perpūrĭgo) -are, *to clean thoroughly.* Transf., *to explain thoroughly, clear up.*
perpŭsillus -a -um, *very small.*
perpŭto -are, *to explain fully.*
perquam, *very much, extremely.*
perquīro -quīrĕre -quīsīvi -quīsītum, *to search for eagerly; to inquire carefully into.* Compar. adv. from perf. partic. **perquīsītĭus** *more accurately.*
perrārus -a -um, *very uncommon*; abl. as adv. **perrārō.**
perrĕcondĭtus -a -um, *very abstruse.*
perrēpo -rēpĕre -repsi -reptum, *to crawl through, creep over.*
perrepto -are, *to crawl through, crawl about.*
perrīdĭcŭlus -a -um, *very laughable*; adv. **perrīdĭcŭle.**
perrŏgo -are, *to ask in succession, to ask one after another.*
perrumpo -rumpĕre -rūpi -ruptum, *to break through, burst through; to shatter, burst.*
Persae -arum, m. pl. *the Persians*; sing. **Persa** and **Persēs** -ae, m. *a Persian*; **Persĭa** -ae, f. *Persia*; **Persis** -ĭdis, f., as adj., *Persian*, as subst., *Persia*; adj. **Persĭcus** -a -um.
persaepĕ, *very often.*
persalsus -a -um, *very witty*; adv. **persalsē.**
persălūtātĭo -ōnis, f. *a general greeting.*
persălūto -are, *to greet in succession, greet all round.*
persăpĭens -entis, *very wise*; adv. **persăpĭentĕr.**
perscĭentĕr, *very discreetly.*
perscindo -scindĕre -scĭdi -scissum, *to tear to pieces.*
perscītus -a -um, *very clever.*
perscrībo -scrībĕre -scripsi -scriptum, *to write in full; to note down officially, enter; to make over* or *assign in writing.*
perscriptĭo -ōnis, f. *entry, noting down; assigning by written document.*
perscriptor -ōris, m. *one who makes an entry.*
perscrūto -are and **perscrūtor** -ari, dep. *to search through, look through, examine, investigate.*
persĕco -sĕcare -sĕcŭi -sectum, *to cut through, cut away, dissect.*
persector -ari, dep. *to pursue eagerly; to investigate.*
persĕcūtĭo -ōnis, f. *prosecution.*
persĕdĕo (persīdĕo) -sĕdēre -sēdi -sessum, *to remain sitting.*
persegnis -e, *very languid.*
persentĭo -sentire -sensi -sensum, *to perceive distinctly, feel deeply.*
persentisco -ĕre, *to begin to perceive distinctly* or *feel deeply.*
Persĕphŏnē -ēs, f. *Greek name of Proserpina*; q.v.
persĕquor -sĕqui -sĕcūtus, dep. *to follow constantly, pursue to the end, hunt out, overtake; to strive after; to imitate; to proceed against* an offender, *punish, avenge; to accomplish* an action, *perform, execute; to treat* a subject, *expound, describe.*
[1]**Persēs** -ae and **Persĕūs** -ĕi, m. *the last king of Macedonia, defeated by the Roman general Aemilius Paulus in* 169 B.C.; adj. **Persĭcus -a -um.**
[2]**Persēs** -ae, m. *a Persian*; see Persae.
Persēūs -ĕi and -ĕos, m. *Perseus, who killed Medusa, and rescued Andromeda.*
persĕvērantĭa -ae, f. *persistence.*
persĕvēro -are, *to persist, persevere, continue.*
Hence partic. **persĕvērans** -antis, *enduring, persistent*; adv. **persĕvērantĕr.**
persĕvērus -a -um, *very strict.*
Persĭa; see Persae.
Persĭcus; see Persae and Perses.

persīdo -sīdĕre -sēdi -sessum, *to sink in, settle down.*
persigno -are, *to note down, record.*
persĭmĭlis -e, *very like.*
persimplex -ĭcis, *very simple.*
persisto -ĕre, *to remain constant, persist.*
Persĭus -i, m. A. Persius Flaccus, *a satirist in the reign of Nero.*
persolvo -solvĕre -solvi -sŏlūtum, *to unloose*; hence *to explain, expound; to pay, pay off, deal out.*
persōna -ae, f. *a mask,* esp. *as worn by actors*; hence *role, part, character, personality.*
persōnātus -a -um, *masked; disguised, counterfeit.*
persŏno -sŏnare -sŏnŭi -sŏnĭtum: intransit., *to resound, sound forth; to shout*; *to perform upon a musical instrument*; transit., *to make, resound; to proclaim loudly.*
perspergo -ĕre, *to sprinkle, moisten.*
perspĭcax -ācis, *sharp-sighted.*
perspĭcĭentĭa -ae, f. *full awareness* or *knowledge.*
perspĭcĭo -spĭcĕre -spexi, -spectum, *to see through, look through; to look at attentively, survey, examine*; mentally, to *regard, investigate, ascertain.*
Hence partic. **perspectus** -a -um, *ascertained, fully known.*
perspĭcŭĭtās -ātis, f. *clearness, perspicuity.*
perspĭcŭus -a -um, *transparent, bright; clear, evident.* Adv. **perspĭcŭē.**
persterno -sternĕre -strāvi -strātum, *to pave thoroughly.*
perstĭmŭlo -are, *to goad on violently.*
persto -stare -stĭti -stātum, *to stand firm, remain standing; to remain unchanged, last, endure; to stand firm, persist, persevere.*
perstringo -stringĕre -strinxi -strictum. (1) *to press tight, bind tight; to deaden, dull* the senses. (2) *to graze, scratch; to touch upon* a subject; *to scold, blame, reproach* a person.
perstŭdĭōsus -a -um, *very eager*; adv. **perstŭdĭōsē.**
persuādĕo -suādēre -suāsi -suāsum, *to persuade.* (1) *to convince* of a fact; sibi persuadere, *to satisfy oneself, be convinced.* (2) *to persuade, prevail upon* a person to do a thing.
persuāsĭo -ōnis, f. *persuasion; a conviction, belief.*
persuāsū, abl. sing. m. *by persuasion.*
persubtīlis -e, *very fine; very subtle.*
persulto -are, *to leap, gambol, skip about, skip over.*
pertaedet -taedēre -taesum est, *to cause weariness* or *disgust*; cf. taedet.
pertempto -are, *to prove, test, try; to weigh, consider, examine; to assail.*
pertendo -tendĕre -tendi, *to push on, proceed, continue.*
pertĕnŭis -e, *very slight.*
pertĕrebro -are, *to bore through.*
pertergĕo -tergēre -tersi -tersum *to wipe over; to brush.*
perterrĕo -ēre, *to terrify.*
perterricrĕpus -a -um, *rattling terribly.*
pertexo -texĕre -texŭi -textum, *to weave throughout; to complete, accomplish.*
pertĭca -ae, f. *a long pole* or *rod.*
pertĭmesco -tĭmescĕre -tĭmŭi, *to become very much afraid.*
pertĭnācĭa -ae, f. *firmness, obstinacy, stubbornness.*
pertĭnax -ācis, adj., *tenacious; tight-fisted, mean; firm, persistent, stubborn, obstinate.* Adv. **pertĭnācĭtĕr.**
pertĭnĕo -tĭnēre -tĭnŭi, *to reach to, extend to; to tend towards, have as object* or *result; to relate to, belong to, apply to, attach to.*
pertingo -ĕre, *to stretch out, extend.*
pertŏlĕro -are, *to endure to the end.*
pertorquĕo -ēre, *to twist, distort.*
pertractātĭo -ōnis, f. *thorough handling, detailed treatment.*
pertracto -are, *to handle, feel; to treat, study, work upon.*
pertrăho -trăhĕre -traxi -tractum, *to drag, forcibly conduct; to entice, allure.*
pertrecto = pertracto; q.v.
pertristis -e, *very sorrowful* or *austere.*
pertŭmultŭōsē, *in an agitated manner.*
pertundo -tundĕre -tŭdi -tūsum, *to bore through, perforate.*
perturbātĭo -ōnis, f. *confusion, disorder, disturbance*; philosoph. *a passion, emotion.*
perturbātrix -icis, f. *she that disturbs.*
perturbo -are, *to disturb thoroughly, confuse, disquiet, upset.*
Hence partic. **perturbātus** -a -um, *confused, disturbed*; adv. **perturbātē.**
perturpis -e, *very disgraceful.*
pertūsus -a -um, partic. from pertundo; q.v.
pĕrungo -ungĕre -unxi -unctum, *to anoint thoroughly, besmear.*
pĕrurbānus -a -um, *very polite* or *witty; over-sophisticated.*
pĕruro -urĕre -ussi -ustum, *to burn up, consume, inflame; to gall, chafe; to pinch, nip with cold.*
pĕrūtĭlis -e, *very useful.*
pervādo -vādĕre -vāsi -vāsum. (1) *to go through, pass through, pervade.* (2) *to reach, arrive at.*
pervăgor -ari, dep. *to wander through, to rove about; to be widely spread, pervade.* Hence partic. **pervăgātus** -a -um, *widespread, well known; common, general.*
pervăgus -a -um, *wandering everywhere.*
pervărĭē, *very variously.*
pervasto -are, *to lay waste completely.*
pervĕho -vĕhĕre -vexi -vectum, *to carry, lead, conduct, bring* (*to* or *through* a place); pass. pervehi, *to travel to* or *through.*
pervello -vellĕre -velli, *to pluck, pull, twitch; to stimulate; to pain, to disparage.*
pervĕnĭo -vĕnire -vēni -ventum, *to come through to, arrive at, reach, attain to, be passed to.*
perversĭtās -ātis, f. *perversity.*
perverto (**pervorto**) -vertĕre -verti -versum, *to turn upside down, overturn,*

overthrow; to undermine, subvert, pervert; in speech, *to trip up*. Hence partic. **perversus** -a -um, *crooked, awry, askew; distorted, perverse*. Adv. **perversē**.
pervespĕrī, *very late in the evening.*
pervestīgātĭo -ōnis, f. *examination, investigation.*
pervestīgo -are, *to track out, investigate, search into.*
pervĕtus -ĕris, *very old.*
pervĕtustus -a -um, *very old.*
pervīcācĭa -ae, f. *firmness, persistence; stubbornness, obstinacy.*
pervīcax -ācis, *firm, persistent; stubborn, obstinate*; compar. adv. **pervīcācĭus**, *more stubbornly.*
pervīdĕo -vĭdēre -vīdi -vīsum, *to look over, survey; to see through, discern, distinguish.*
pervĭgĕo -ēre, *to flourish, bloom continually.*
pervĭgil -ĭlis, *always watchful.*
pervĭgĭlātĭo -ōnis, f. and **pervĭgĭlĭum** -i, n. *a vigil, religious watching.*
pervĭgĭlo -are, *to remain awake all night.*
pervīlis -e, *very cheap.*
pervinco -vincĕre -vīci -victum, *to conquer completely; to surpass, outdo; to induce, prevail upon; to carry one's point; to achieve, effect; to prove, demonstrate.*
pervĭus -a -um, *passable, accessible*; as subst., *a passage.*
pervolgo = pervulgo; q.v.
pervŏlĭto -are, *to fly round, flit about.*
[1]**pervŏlo** -are, *to fly through, fly round.*
[2]**pervŏlo** -velle -vŏlŭi, *to wish greatly.*
pervŏlūto -are, *to roll round*; esp. *to unroll* and *read* a book.
pervolvo -volvĕre -volvi -volutum, *to roll about; to unroll and read* a book.
pervorsē, etc., = perverse, etc.; q.v.
pervulgo (pervolgo) -are, *to publish, make publicly known; to make generally available; to frequent, haunt* a place. Hence partic. **pervulgātus** -a -um, *very usual* or *well known.*
pēs pĕdis, m. *the foot*; pedem referre, *to return*; pedibus, *on foot*, also *by land*; servus a pedibus, *an attendant, lackey*; pedibus ire in sententiam, *to support a proposal*; milit., pedibus merere, *to serve in the infantry*; pedem conferre, *to fight hand to hand.* Transf., *a foot of a table, chair*, etc.; *a metrical foot*; a measure of length; pes (veli), *a rope* or *sheet, attached to the lower edge of a sail.*
pessĭmus, pessime; see malus.
pessŭlus -i, m. *a bolt.*
pessum, *to the ground, to the bottom, downwards*; pessum ire, *to sink, be ruined, perish*; pessum dare, *to destroy, ruin, put an end to.*
pestĭfer -fĕra, -fĕrum, *pestilential, destructive, injurious*; adv. **pestĭfĕrē**.
pestĭlens -entis, *unhealthy, fatal, noxious.*
pestĭlentĭa -ae, f. *an unhealthy condition; a plague, infectious disease, pest.*
pestĭlĭtās -ātis, f. = pestilentia; q.v.
pestis -is, f. *pest, pestilence, plague; destruction, ruin; curse, bane.*
pĕtăsātus -a -um, *wearing the* petasus; hence, *equipped for a journey.*
pĕtăso -ōnis, m. *a fore-quarter of pork.*
pĕtăsus -i, m. *a broad-brimmed felt hat, used by travellers.*
pĕtaurum -i, n. *a spring-board.*
pĕtesso (pĕtisso) -ĕre, *to long for, strive after.*
pĕtītĭo -ōnis, f. *an attack, thrust, blow; a request, application; standing for office, candidature*; at law, *a suit, a right of claim, right to bring an action.*
pĕtītor -ōris, m. *a seeker*; polit., *a candidate*; legal, *a plaintiff.*
pĕtītŭrĭo -ire, *to desire to stand for election.*
pĕtītus -ūs, m. *an inclining towards.*
pĕto -ĕre -īvi and -ĭi -ītum, *to make for, go to; to attack, assail; to seek, strive after; to ask for, beg, request, demand*; polit., *to stand for, canvas for*; legal, *to sue for*; sometimes *to fetch, derive.*
pĕtorrĭtum (petōrĭtum) -i, n. *an open four-wheeled carriage.*
Petrōnĭus -i, m. *name of a Roman* gens; esp. *of a satirist under Nero.*
pĕtŭlans -antis, *impudent, pert, wanton*; adv. **pĕtŭlantĕr**.
pĕtŭlantĭa -ae, f. *impudence, pertness, wantonness.*
pĕtulcus -a -um, *butting with the head.*
pexātus -a -um, *wearing a garment with the nap on.*
Phaedra -ae, f. *daughter of Minos, wife of Theseus.*
Phaedrus -i, m. *a freedman of Augustus, author of Latin fables.*
Phăĕthōn -ontis, m. *the son of Helios, killed trying to drive the chariot of his father.*
phălangae (pălangae) -arum, f. pl. *rollers.*
phălangītae -arum, m. pl. *soldiers belonging to a phalanx.*
phălanx -angis, f. *an array of soldiers in close formation.*
Phălăris -ĭdis, m. *a tyrant of Agrigentum.*
phălĕrae -arum, f. pl. *metal bosses; military decorations; horses' trappings.*
phălĕratus -a -um, *wearing* phalerae; q.v.
Phălērum -i, n. *the oldest port of Athens.*
phantasma -ătis, n. *an apparition.*
phăretra -ae, f. *a quiver.*
phăretrātus -a -um, *wearing a quiver.*
pharmăceutrĭa -ae, f. *sorceress.*
pharmăcŏpōla (-es) -ae, m. *a seller of drugs; a quack.*
Pharsālus (-ŏs) -i, f. *a town in Thessaly, where Pompey was defeated by Caesar in 48 B.C.*
Phărus (-ŏs) -i, f., rarely m., *an island off Alexandria, with a lighthouse*; hence in gen. *a lighthouse.*
phăsēlus -i, m. and f. *the kidney-bean* or *French bean; a light bean-shaped boat.*
Phāsis -ĭdis and -ĭdos, m. *a river in Colchis, flowing into the Black Sea*;

f. adj. **Phāsis** -ĭdis, and **Phāsĭānus** -a -um, *Colchian.*

phasma -ătis, n. *a ghost, spectre.*

phĭăla -ae, f. *a drinking-vessel; a bowl, saucer.*

Phīdĭās -ae, m. *an Athenian sculptor.*

Phĭlippi -orum, m. pl. *a city in Macedonia, where Octavian and Antony defeated Brutus and Cassius.*

Phĭlippus -i, m. *the name of several kings of Macedon*; adj. **Phĭlippēus** and **Phĭlippĭcus** -a -um; f. as subst. **Phĭlippĭca** -ae, *one of the speeches of Demosthenes against Philip,* or *of Cicero against Antony.*

phĭlŏlŏgĭa -ae, f. *love of learning, study of literature.*

phĭlŏlŏgus -a -um, *learned, literary*; m. as subst. *a scholar.*

Phĭlŏmēla -ae, f. *the daughter of Pandion, turned into a nightingale.*

phĭlŏsŏphĭa -ae, f. *philosophy.*

phĭlŏsŏphor -ari, dep. *to philosophize, apply oneself to philosophy.*

phĭlŏsŏphus -a -um, *philosophical*; m. and f. as subst. *a philosopher.*

philtrum -i, n. *a love-potion, philtre.*

phĭly̆ra -ae, f. *the inner bark of the linden-tree.*

phīmus -i, m. *a dice-box.*

Phlĕgĕthōn -ontis, m. *a river in the infernal regions.*

phōca -ae, f. and **phōcē** -ēs, f. *a seal.*

Phōcis -ĭdis, f. *a district in the north of Greece*; adj. **Phōcēus** -a -um.

Phoebē -ēs, f. *the sister of Phoebus, the Moon-goddess, Diana.*

Phoebĭgĕna -ae, m. *the son of Phoebus, Aesculapius.*

Phoebus -i, m. *Apollo, the Sun-god*; hence subst. **Phoebăs** -ădis, f. *a priestess of Phoebus, a prophetess*; adj. **Phoebēĭus** and **Phoebēus** -a -um, *of Phoebus.*

Phoenīcē -ēs, f. *Phoenicia*; m. subst. **Phoenīces** -um, *the Phoenicians*; f. subst. **Phoenissa** -ae, f. *a Phoenician woman.*

phoenīcoptĕros -i, m. *the flamingo.*

phoenix -īcis, m. *the phoenix, a fabulous bird of Arabia.*

phōnascus -i, m. *a teacher of music.*

phrĕnēsis -is, f. *madness, frenzy.*

phrĕnētĭcus -a -um, *mad, frantic.*

Phrixus -i, m. *brother of Helle.*

Phry̆ges -um, m. pl. *the Phrygians*; sing. **Phryx** -y̆gis; **Phry̆gĭa** -ae, f. *the country of Phrygia in Asia Minor*; adj. **Phry̆gĭus** -a -um, *Phrygian*; poet. = *Trojan.*

phthĭsis -is, f. *consumption.*

phy, interj. *pish! tush!*

phy̆larchus -i, m. *the head of a tribe, an emir.*

phy̆sĭca -ae, and **phy̆sĭcē** -ēs, f. *physics, natural science.*

phy̆sĭcus -a -um, *relating to physics, physical*; m. as subst. *a scientist*; n. pl. **phy̆sĭca** -orum, *physics*; adv. **phy̆sĭcē,** *in the manner of the scientists.*

phy̆sĭognōmōn -onis, m. *a physiognomist.*

phy̆sĭŏlŏgĭa -ae, f. *natural science.*

pĭābĭlis -e, *able to be atoned for.*

pĭăcŭlāris -e, *atoning, expiating*; n. pl. as subst. *expiatory sacrifices.*

pĭăcŭlum -i, n. *a means of expiating* or *appeasing; sacrifice; remedy; punishment; a victim; an act needing expiation, a sin, crime.*

pĭāmen -ĭnis, n. *means of atonement* or *expiation.*

pīca -ae, f. *a jay* or *magpie.*

pĭcārĭa -ae, f. *a place where pitch is made.*

pĭcĕa -ae, f. *the spruce-fir.*

Pīcēnum -i, n. *a district in central Italy.*

pĭcĕus -a -um, *of pitch; pitch-black.*

pĭco -are, *to smear with pitch.*

pictor -ōris, m. *a painter.*

pictūra -ae, f. *the art of painting; a painting, picture*; pictura textilis, *embroidery.*

pictūrātus -a -um, *painted;* vestes, *embroidered.*

pīcus -i, m. *a woodpecker.*

Pīĕris -ĭdis or -ĭdos, f. *a Muse*; plur. **Pīĕrĭdes,** *the Muses*; adj. **Pīĕrĭus** -a -um, *Pierian, poetic.*

pĭĕtās -ātis, f. *dutifulness, dutiful conduct; piety; patriotism; devotion; kindness.*

pĭger -gra -grum, *sluggish, unwilling, slow*; campus, *unfruitful.* Adv. **pigrē.**

pĭget -gēre -gŭit -gĭtum est, impers., *it causes annoyance* (or *regret* or *shame*); *it disgusts*; piget me, with genit., *I am disgusted with.*

pigmentārĭus -i, m. *a seller of paints and unguents.*

pigmentum -i, n. *paint, pigment*; of style, *ornament, decoration.*

pignĕrātor -ōris, m. *a mortgagee.*

pignĕro -are, *to give as a pledge, pawn, mortgage.*

pignĕror -ari, dep. *to take as a pledge; to claim.*

pignus -nŏris and -nĕris, n. *a pledge, pawn, security; a wager, bet, stake; a token, assurance, proof*; in plur., *persons as pledges of love.*

pigrĭtĭa -ae, and **pigrĭtĭes** -ēi, f. *sluggishness, indolence.*

pigro -are and **pigror** -ari, dep. *to be sluggish.*

[1]**pīla** -ae, f. *a mortar.*

[2]**pīla** -ae, f. *a pillar, pier; a bookstall.*

[3]**pĭla** -ae, f. *a ball; a game of ball.*

pīlanus -i, m. = triarius; q.v.

pīlātus -a -um, *armed with the* pilum or *javelin.*

pīlentum -i, n. *a carriage, coach.*

pillĕātus (**pīlĕ-**) -a -um, *wearing the felt cap.*

pillĕŏlus (**pīlĕ-**) -i, m. *a little cap, skull-cap.*

pillĕus (**pīlĕus**) -i, m. and **pillĕum** -i, n. *a felt cap,* esp. as worn by manumitted slaves.

pĭlo -are, *to deprive of hair.*

pĭlōsus -a -um, *covered with hair, hairy.*

pīlum -i, n. *the heavy javelin of the Roman infantry.*

[1]**pĭlus** -i, m. *a single hair; a trifle.*

[2]**pīlus** -i, m. *a division of the* triarii *in the Roman army*; primus pilus, *the*

chief centurion of the triarii *and of the legion.*
Pindărus -i, m. *a lyric poet of Thebes.*
pīnētum -i, n. *a pine-wood.*
pīnĕus -a -um, *made of pine-wood* or *deal.*
pingo pingĕre pinxi pictum, *to paint, to draw; to embroider; to stain, dye; to decorate, adorn*; in speech or writing, *to embellish, depict.*
pinguesco -ĕre, *to become fat, grow fertile.*
pinguis -e, *fat; oily; rich, fertile*; n. as subst. *fatness, fat.* Transf., *thick, dense; heavy, stupid; easy, quiet.*
pinguĭtūdo -ĭnis, f. *fatness, broadness.*
pīnĭfer -fĕra -fĕrum and **pīnĭgĕr** -gĕra -gĕrum, *producing pines.*
[1]**pinna** -ae, f. *a feather; a feathered arrow; a wing; a battlement along the top of a wall.*
[2]**pinna** (**pīna**) -ae, f. *a species of mussel.*
pinnātus -a -um, *feathered, winged.*
pinnĭger -gĕra -gĕrum, *feathered, winged*; piscis, *having fins.*
pinnĭrăpus -i, m. *a crestsnatcher,* i.e. *a kind of gladiator.*
pinnŭla -ae, f. *a small feather* or *wing.*
pinso, pinsĕre; pinsi and pinsŭi; pinsum pinsĭtum and pistum, *to stamp, pound, crush.*
pīnus -i and -ūs, f. *a fir* or *pine; anything made of pine-wood,* e.g. *a torch, oar, ship.*
pĭo -are, *to appease, propitiate; to venerate; to make good, atone for.*
pĭper pĭpĕris, n. *pepper.*
pīpĭlo -are, *to twitter, chirp.*
pīpŭlus -i, m. and **pīpŭlum** -i, n. *outcry.*
Pīraeēūs and **Pīraeus** -i, m. *the Piraeus, the main port of Athens.*
pīrāta -ae, m. *pirate.*
pīrātĭcus -a -um, *piratical*; f. as subst. *piracy.*
pĭrum -i, n. *a pear.*
pĭrus -i, f. *a pear-tree.*
piscātor -ōris, m. *a fisherman; a fishmonger.*
piscātōrĭus -a -um, *of fishermen* or *fishing.*
piscātus -ūs, m. *fishes; fishing, a catch.*
piscĭcŭlus -i, m. *a little fish.*
piscīna -ae, f. *a fish-pond; a swimming-bath.*
piscīnārĭus -i, m. *one fond of fish-ponds.*
piscis -is, m. *a fish.*
piscor -ari, dep. *to fish.*
piscōsus -a -um, *abounding in fish.*
pistillum -i, n. *a pestle.*
pistor -ōris, m. *a grinder, miller; a baker.*
pistrīnum -i, n. *a mill; a bakery.*
pistris -is, and **pistrix** -trīcis, f. *a sea monster; a whale, shark, saw-fish.* Transf., *a small fast ship.*
pītŭīta -ae, f. *phlegm, rheum.*
pītŭītōsus -a -um, *full of phlegm.*
pĭus -a -um, *dutiful; godly, holy; patriotic; devoted, affectionate*; in gen., *honest, upright, kind.*
pix pĭcis, f. *pitch.*
plācābĭlis -e; pass., *easy to appease*; act., *appeasing.*
plācābĭlĭtās -ātis, f. *placability.*
plācāmen -ĭnis, and **plācāmentum** -i, n. *means of appeasing.*
plācātĭo -ōnis, f. *soothing, appeasing.*
plăcĕo -ēre -ŭi and -itus sum, -itum, *to please, be agreeable to*; impers. **plăcet,** *it seems good, it is agreed* or *resolved.*
Hence partic. **plăcĭtus** -a -um, *pleasing, agreeable; agreed upon.* N. as subst. *what is agreeable*; plur., *opinions, teaching.*
plăcĭdus -a -um, *quiet, still, gentle*; adv. **plăcĭdē.**
plăcĭtus -a -um, partic. from placeo; q.v.
plāco -are, *to soothe, calm; to reconcile, appease.*
Hence partic. **plācātus** -a -um, *soothed, appeased; calm, gentle, quiet*; adv. **plācātē.**
[1]**plāga** -ae, f. *a blow, stroke; a wound.*
[2]**plăga** -ae, f. *a district, zone, region.*
[3]**plăga** -ae, f. *a net for hunting; a trap, snare.*
plăgĭārĭus -i, m. *a kidnapper; a plagiarist.*
plāgōsus -a -um, *fond of flogging.*
plăgŭla -ae, f. *a bed-curtain.*
planctus -ūs, m. *beating*; esp. *beating of the breast, lamentations.*
plango plangĕre planxi planctum, *to beat, strike,* esp. *noisily; to strike the breast, head,* etc., as a sign of grief; hence plangere and pass. plangi, *to bewail.*
plangor -ōris, m. *loud striking* or *beating*; esp. *beating of the head and breast, loud lamentations.*
plānĭpēs -pĕdis, m. *an actor who wore no shoes.*
plānĭtās -ātis, f. *plainness, distinctness.*
plānĭtĭa -ae, and **plānĭtĭēs** -ēi, f. *a level surface, a plain.*
planta -ae, f. (1) *a green twig, cutting, graft; a plant.* (2) *the sole of the foot.*
plantārĭa -ĭum, n. pl. *young trees, slips.*
[1]**plānus** -a -um, *even, flat*; n. as subst. *a plain, level ground;* de plano, *off-hand, easily.* Transf., *plain, clear, intelligible.* Adv. **plānē,** *distinctly, intelligibly; wholly, quite, thoroughly*; in answers, *certainly.*
[2]**plănus** -i, m. *a vagabond, a charlatan.*
plătălĕa -ae, f. *a water-bird, the spoonbill.*
plătănus -i, f. *the plane-tree.*
plătĕa -ae, f. *a street.*
Plătō (-ōn) -ōnis, m. *the Greek philosopher, disciple of Socrates.*
plaudo (**plōdo**) plaudĕre plausi plausum, *to strike, beat, clap together; to make a clapping noise, clap, applaud.*
plausĭbĭlis -e, *worthy of applause.*
plausor -ōris, m. *an applauder at the theatre.*
plaustrum (**plostrum**) -i, n. *a waggon, cart; Charles's Wain.*
plausus -ūs, m. *a noise of clapping; approbation, applause.*

Plautus -i, m., T. Maccius, *the Roman comic poet, born about* 254 B.C. Adj. **Plautīnus** -a -um.

plēbēcŭla -ae, f. *the common people, mob, rabble.*

plēbēĭus -a -um, *of the plebs* or *people, plebeian; common, low, mean.*

plēbēs -ēi and -i, f. = plebs; q.v.

plēbĭcŏla -ae, m. *a friend of the common people.*

plēbiscītum -i, n. *a decree of the people.*

plebs plēbis, f. *the plebeians, the common people, lower orders.*

[1]**plecto**; see plexus.

[2]**plecto** -ĕre, *to punish*; usually pass., **plector** -i, *to be punished* (with blows).

plectrum -i, n. *a stick with which the strings of a stringed instrument were struck; a quill.* Transf., *the lyre; lyric poetry.*

Plēĭăs -ădis, f. *a Pleiad*; usually plur. **Plēĭădes** -ădum, f. *the Pleiads, the Seven Stars.*

plēnus -a -um, *full, full of* (with genit. or abl.); *complete; plump, thick; pregnant; filled, satisfied; well-stocked, rich*; of age, *mature*: of the voice, *strong, loud*; of style, *full, copious.* Adv. **plēnē**, *fully, completely.*

plērusquĕ -raque -rumque and plur. **plērīquĕ** -raeque -raque, *very many, a large part, the most part*; n. sing. as subst., *the greater part*; acc. as adv. *for the most part, mostly, commonly.*

plexus -a -um, partic. as from plecto, *braided, plaited.*

Plīas = Pleias; q.v.

plĭco -are, -ŭi and -avi, -atum and ĭtum, *to fold.*

Plīnĭus -a -um, *name of a Roman* gens; esp. of C. Plinius Secundus (Maior, *the Elder*), *author of a Natural History, and* C. Plinius Caecilius Secundus (Iunior, *the Younger*), *author of letters*, etc.

plōdo = plaudo; q.v.

plōrābĭlis -e, *deplorable.*

plōrātor -ōris, m. *a lamenter.*

plōrātus -ūs, m. *weeping, lamenting.*

plōro -are, *to lament, wail;* transit., *to weep over, deplore.*

plostellum -i, n. *a little waggon.*

plostrum = plaustrum; q.v.

plŭit plŭĕre, plŭit or plūvit, *it rains, a shower falls.*

plūma -ae, f. *a small, soft feather; down* (esp. in pl.); meton. *bolster, featherbed; the first down on the chin.*

plūmātus -a -um, *covered with feathers.*

plumbĕus -a -um, *leaden, of lead.* Transf., *dull, stupid; heavy, oppressive; bad.*

plumbum -i, n. *lead*; *a bullet; a leaden pipe*; plumbum album, *tin.*

plūmĕus -a -um, *downy, of fine feathers.*

plūmōsus -a -um, *feathered, downy.*

plŭo; see pluit.

plūrĭmus and **plūs**; see multus.

plusculus -a -um, *somewhat more, rather more.*

plŭtĕus -i, m. and **plŭtĕum** -i, n. *a shelter*; milit., *penthouse, shed, mantlet; breastwork, battlement.* Transf., *a board, couch, bookshelf.*

Plūtō (-ōn) -ōnis, m. *the king of the lower world*; adj. **Plūtōnĭus** -a -um.

plŭvĭālis -e, *of* or *from rain; bringing rain.*

plŭvĭus -a -um, *of* or *from rain, bringing rain*; as subst. **plŭvĭa** -ae, *rain.*

pōcillum -i, n. *a little cup.*

pōcŭlum -i, n. *a drinking-cup, goblet; a drink, draught.*

pŏdagra -ae, f. *gout in the feet.*

pōdex -icis, m. *fundament, anus.*

pŏdĭum -i, n. *a balcony*, esp. *in the amphitheatre.*

pŏēma -ătis, n. *a poem.*

poena -ae, f. *money paid as atonement, a fine*; in gen., *punishment, penalty; loss, hardship*; poenas dare, *to be punished.*

Poeni -orum, m. pl. *the Carthaginians*; sing. **Poenus** -i, m. adj. **Poenus, Pūnĭcus, Poenĭcĕus** -a -um, *Punic, Carthaginian.*

poenĭo = punio; q.v.

poenĭtet; see **paenitet.**

pŏēsis -is, acc. -in, f. *poetry.*

pŏēta -ae, m. a maker; esp. *a poet.*

pŏētĭcus -a -um, *poetical*; f. as subst. **pŏētĭca** -ae and **pŏētĭcē** -ēs, *the art of poetry*; adv. **pŏētĭcē.**

pŏētrĭa -ae, f. *a poetess.*

pŏl! interj. *by Pollux! truly! really!*

pŏlenta -ae, f. *pearl-barley, barley-groats.*

pŏlĭo -ire, *to polish, file, make smooth*; esp. *to cover with white, whiten*; *to adorn, to finish off.*

Hence partic. **pŏlītus** -a -um, *polished, refined, accomplished*; adv. **pŏlītē.**

pŏlītĭa -ae, acc. -an. f. *the Republic* (Plato's work).

pŏlītĭcus -a -um *of the state, political.*

pŏlītus -a -um, partic. from polio; q.v.

pollen -ĭnis, n. and **pollis** -ĭnis, c. *fine flour, meal.*

pollentĭa -ae, f. *power, might.*

pollĕo -ēre, *to be strong, powerful, able*; partic. **pollens** -entis, *powerful, mighty.*

pollex -ĭcis, m. *the thumb*; also *the big toe.*

pollĭcĕor -cēri -cĭtus, dep. *to offer, promise*; perf. partic. in pass. sense, **pollĭcĭtus** -a -um, *promised.* N. as subst. *a promise.*

pollĭcĭtātĭo -ōnis, f. *an offer, promise.*

pollĭcĭtor -ari, dep. *to keep promising.*

pollinctor -ōris, m. *an undertaker.*

pollūcĕo -lūcēre -luxi -luctum, *to offer, serve up.*

pollŭo -ŭĕre -ŭi -ūtum, *to defile, pollute, dishonour*; partic. **pollūtus** -a -um, *defiled, polluted; unchaste.*

Pollux -ūcis, m. *the twin-brother of Castor.*

pŏlus -i, m. *the end of an axis, a pole; the sky, heaven.*

Pŏlyhymnĭa -ae, f. *one of the Muses*

pōlypus -i, m. *polypus.*

pōmārĭus -a -um, *of fruit*; m. as subst., *a fruiterer*; n. as subst., *a fruit-garden, orchard.*
pōmĕrīdĭānus = postmeridianus; q.v.
pōmērĭum or **pōmoerĭum** -i, n. *a clear space beside the walls of a town.*
pōmĭfer -fĕra -fĕrum, *fruit-bearing.*
pōmōsus -a -um, *abounding in fruit.*
pompa -ae, f. *a solemn procession; a suite, retinue; display, parade, ostentation.*
Pompēii -orum, m. pl. *a town in Campania, destroyed by an eruption of Vesuvius*; adj. **Pompēiānus** -a -um.
Pompēius (trisyl.) or **Pompēĭus** -a -um, *name of a Roman* gens; esp. of Cn. Pompeius, *Pompey the Great* (106-48 B.C.); adj. **Pompēiānus** -a -um, *belonging to Pompey.*
Pompĭlĭus -a -um, *name of a Roman* gens; esp. *of* Numa Pompilius, *second king of Rome.*
pompĭlus -i, m. *the pilot-fish.*
Pomptīnus -a -um, *Pomptine* or *Pontine*: palus *or* paludes, *a marshy district in Latium.*
pōmum -i, n. *any kind of fruit; a fruit-tree.*
pōmus -i, f. *a fruit-tree.*
pondĕro -are, *to weigh, consider, ponder.*
pondĕrōsus -a -um, *heavy, weighty; significant.*
pondo (abl.) *in weight*; as indecl. subst. *a pound, pounds.*
pondus -ĕris, n. *weight; a weight, burden, mass; balance; authority, influence.*
pōnĕ: adv. *behind, at the back*; prep. with acc., *behind.*
pōno pōnĕre pŏsŭi (pŏsīvi) pŏsĭtum (postum), *to lay, put, place, set; to put in place, settle; to put aside, lay down, discard; to lay to rest, lay out for burial*; milit., *to post, station*; of money, etc., *to store, deposit, invest; to stake, wager*; of food, *to put on table, to serve*; of buildings, *to found, set up*; of laws, etc. *to establish, ordain*; of persons, *to appoint*; of an artist, *to represent, picture; to reckon, count, regard; to lay down, assert, cite.*
Hence partic. **pŏsĭtus** -a -um, *in place*; nix, *fallen snow*; of places, *situated.*
pons pontis, m. *a bridge, gangway; the deck of a ship.*
pontĭcŭlus -i, m. *a little bridge.*
pontĭfex -fĭcis, m. *a pontiff, member of a Roman guild of priests.*
pontĭfĭcālis -e, *pontifical.*
pontĭfĭcātus -ūs, m. *the office of pontiff.*
pontĭfĭcus -a -um, *pontifical.*
Pontĭus -a -um, *name of a Roman* (originally Samnite) gens.
ponto -ōnis, m. *a flat-bottomed boat, punt.*
[1]**pontus** -i, n. *the sea.*
[2]**Pontus** -i, m. *the Black Sea*; also *the country on the shores of the Black Sea*; adj. **Pontĭcus** -a -um.
pŏpa -ae, m. *a junior priest* or *temple-servant.*
pŏpănum -i, n. *a sacrificial cake.*
pŏpellus -i, m. *common people, rabble.*
pŏpīna -ae, f. *a cook-shop, eating-house; the food sold there.*
pŏpīno -ōnis, m. *a glutton.*
poplĕs -ĭtis, m. *the ham, hough; the knee.*
pŏpŭlābĭlis -e, *that can be laid waste, destructible.*
pŏpŭlābundus -a -um, *laying waste, devastating.*
pŏpŭlāris -e. (1) *belonging to the same people* or *country, native*; as subst. *fellow-countryman, adherent, partner.* (2) *of the people* or *state; popular; democratic*; m. pl. as subst. *the popular party, the democrats.* Adv. **pŏpŭlārĭtĕr,** *after the manner of the people, vulgarly; in a popular manner, like a demagogue.*
pŏpŭlārĭtās -ātis, f. *fellow-citizenship; an attempt to please the people.*
pŏpŭlātĭo -ōnis, f. *laying waste, devastating, plundering.*
pŏpŭlātor -ōris, m. *a devastator, plunderer.*
pōpŭlĕus -a -um, *of the poplar.*
pōpŭlĭfer -fĕra -fĕrum, *producing poplars.*
pŏpŭlo -are and **pŏpŭlor** -ari, dep. *to lay waste, devastate, plunder; to ruin, spoil, rob.*
[1]**pŏpŭlus** -i, m. *a people, political community, nation*; as a section of the community, *the people*; in gen., *the people, the public*; hence *any crowd, host, multitude.*
[2]**pōpŭlus** -i, f. *a poplar-tree.*
porca -ae, f. *a sow.*
porcīnus -a -um, *of a swine* or *hog.*
Porcĭus -a -um, *name of a Roman* gens.
porcus -i, m. *a pig, hog.*
porgo = porrigo; q.v.
porrectĭo -ōnis, f. *stretching out, extension.*
porrĭcĭo -rĭcĕre -rectum, *to offer as a sacrifice.*
[1]**porrĭgo** -rĭgĕre -rexi -rectum, *to stretch out, extend; to offer, grant*; pass., porrigi, *to lie stretched out*; partic. **porrectus** -a -um, *stretched out, extended, long.*
[2]**porrīgo** -gĭnis, f. *scurf, dandruff.*
porro, *forward, further; next, again, in turn*; in time, *far back, long ago,* or *in future.*
porrus -i, m. and **porrum** -i, n. *a leek.*
porta -ae, f. *a gate.*
portātĭo -ōnis, f. *carrying, conveying.*
portendo -tendĕre -tendi -tentum, *to indicate, predict, presage.*
portentĭfĭcus -a -um, *marvellous, miraculous.*
portentōsus -a -um, *extraordinary, monstrous, unnatural.*
portentum -i, n. subst. from portendo; q.v.
porthmēŭs, acc. -ĕă, m. *ferryman.*
portĭcŭla -ae, f. *a little gallery* or *portico.*
portĭcus -ūs, f. *a portico, colonnade, arcade, gallery.* Transf., *the Stoic school* of philosophers.

portĭo -ōnis, f. *a part, section*; pro portione, *in proportion.*
[1]**portĭtor** -ōris, m. *a customs-officer.*
[2]**portĭtor** -ōris, m. *a carrier*; usually *a boatman, ferryman.*
porto -are, *to bear, carry, convey, bring.*
portōrĭum i, n. *customs, harbour-dues*; any *toll, tax.*
portŭla -ae, f. *a little gate, postern.*
portŭōsus -a -um, *having many harbours.*
portus -ūs, m. *harbour, port; haven, refuge.*
posco poscĕre pŏposci, *to ask earnestly, request, call upon*; poscimur, *we are asked to sing*; esp. *to demand for punishment*, or *challenge to fight*; of things, *to demand, require.*
pŏsĭtĭo -ōnis, f. *placing, putting, posture*; caeli, *situation, climate.*
pŏsĭtor -ōris, m. *founder, builder.*
pŏsĭtūra -ae, f. *placing; situation, posture; ordering, formation.*
pŏsĭtus -ūs, m. *position, place, arrangement.*
possessĭo -ōnis, f. *a getting possession* or *possessing; occupation, enjoyment.* Transf., *a thing possessed, possession, property.*
possessĭuncŭla -ae, f. *a small property.*
possessor -ōris, m. *a possessor, occupier.*
possĭdĕo -sĭdēre -sēdi -sessum, *to possess, have, hold.*
possīdo -sīdĕre -sēdi sessum, *to take possession of, occupy.*
possum posse pŏtŭi, *to be able; one may, one can; to avail, have influence.*
Hence partic. **pŏtens** -entis, *able, powerful, capable; influential, efficacious*; with genit., *master of.* Adv. **pŏtentĕr,** *strongly, efficaciously; according to one's power.*
post (older **postĕ**). Adv. *behind, in the rear*; of time, *afterwards*; multo post, *much later.* Prep., with acc., *behind*; of time, *after*; in rank, etc., *next after.*
postĕā, *thereafter, afterwards, next.*
postĕāquam, conj. *after.*
postĕrĭtas -ātis, f. *future generations, posterity.*
postĕrus (**postĕr**) -a -um, *subsequent, following, next, future*; in posterum, *for the next day* or *for the future*; m. pl. as subst. *posterity.* Compar. **postĕrĭor** -us, *next, later; inferior, worse*; n. acc. as adv., posterius, *later.* Superl. **postrēmus** -a -um, *hindmost, last; lowest, worst.* N. abl. as adv., postremo, *at last*; n. acc. postremum, *for the last time*; ad postremum, *at last.* Superl. **postŭmus** -a -um, *the last, last-born* (esp. of children born after the father's will or death).
postfĕro -ferre, *to consider of less account.*
postgĕnĭti -ōrum, m. pl. *posterity, descendants.*
posthăbĕo -ēre -ŭi -ĭtum, *to consider of less account, put after.*
posthăc, *hereafter, in future, afterwards.*
posthinc, *next.*
posthōc, *afterwards.*
postĭcus -a -um, *hinder, back*; n. as subst. **postĭcum** -i, *a back-door.*
postĭlēna -ae, f. *a crupper.*
postillā, *afterwards.*
postis -is, m. *a door-post*; plur., *a door, doorway.*
postlīmĭnĭum -i, n. *the right to return home.*
postmĕrĭdĭānus -a -um, *of the afternoon.*
postmŏdŏ and **postmŏdum,** *presently, soon.*
postpartor -ōris, m. *heir.*
postpōno -pōnĕre -pŏsŭi -pŏsĭtum, *to consider of less account, put after.*
postquam (or **post quam**), conj. *after, when.*
postrēmo, etc.; see posterus.
postrīdĭē, *the day after, on the next day.*
postscaenĭum -i, n. *the theatre behind the scenes.*
postscrībo -scrībĕre -scripsi -scriptum, *to write after.*
postŭlātĭo -ōnis, f. *a claim, demand, application; a complaint.*
postŭlātum -i, n. subst. from postulo; q.v.
postŭlātus -ūs, m. *a legal complaint, accusation, suit.*
postŭlo -are, *to claim, demand, request*; legal, *to demand a writ*, or *to impeach, accuse* a person; of things, *to demand, require.* N. of partic. as subst. **postŭlātum** -i, *a demand.*
postŭmus -a -um, superl. of posterus; q.v.
pōtātĭo -ōnis, f. *a drinking-bout.*
pŏtĕ; see potis.
pŏtens -entis, partic. from possum; q.v.
pŏtentātus -ūs, m. *political power, supremacy.*
pŏtentĭa -ae, f. *power, might, ability; efficacy, potency*; esp. (*unofficial*) *political power.*
pŏtestās -ātis, f. *power, ability, control.* Esp. *political supremacy, dominion; the authority of a magistrate, office command*; concr., *an officer, magistrate.* Transf., *opportunity, possibility, occasion*; facere potestatem, *to give opportunity* or *permission*; potestas est, *it is possible.*
[1]**pōtĭo** -ōnis, f. *drinking; a drink, a draught*; esp. *a love-draught, philtre.*
[2]**pŏtĭo** -ire, *to put in the power of.*
[1]**pŏtĭor** -iri, dep., *to get possession of, to obtain; to possess, be master of.*
[2]**pŏtĭor**; see potis.
pŏtis, pŏtĕ; *able, capable*; potis (or pote) est, *can, is able* (or *possible*). Compar. **pŏtĭor** -us, *preferable, better*; n. acc. as adv. **pŏtĭus,** *rather, preferably.* Superl. **pŏtissĭmus** -a -um, *best of all, chief, principal*; n. as adv. **pŏtissĭmum,** *chiefly, above all.*
pōto pōtare pōtāvi pōtātum and pōtum, *to drink*; esp. *to drink heavily*; of things, *to absorb.*
Hence partic. **pōtus** -a -um: pass., *drunk, drained*; act., *having drunk, drunken.*

pōtor -ōris m. *a drinker*; esp. *a tippler, drunkard.*
pōtŭlentus (**pōcŭlentus**) -a -um, *drinkable; drunk, intoxicated.*
[1]**pōtŭs,** partic. from poto; q.v.
[2]**pōtus** -ūs, m. *a drinking, draught.*
prae. Adv. *before, in front*; prae quam, *in comparison with.* Prep. with abl., *before*; prae se ferre, *to show, exhibit; in comparison with; on account of, because of.*
praeăcūtus -a -um, *sharpened to a point, pointed.*
praealtus -a -um, *very high* or *deep.*
praebĕo -bēre -bŭi -bĭtum, *to offer, hold out; to provide, supply, allow*; with reflex., *to present* or *show oneself* in a certain character, *behave as.*
praebĭbo -bĭbĕre -bĭbi, *to drink before, drink to.*
praebĭtor -ōris, m. *a furnisher, supplier.*
praecălĭdus -a -um, *very hot.*
praecantrix -īcis, f. *a witch.*
praecānus -a -um, *prematurely grey.*
praecăvĕo -căvēre -cāvi -cautum: intransit., *to take precautions, be on one's guard*; transit., *to beware of, guard against beforehand.*
praecēdo -cēdĕre -cessi -cessum, *to go before, precede,* in space or time; in rank, etc., *to surpass, excel.*
praecello -ĕre, *to surpass, excel*; genti, *to rule over*; partic. **praecellens** -entis, *excellent, distinguished, surpassing.*
praecelsus -a -um, *very high.*
praecentĭo -ōnis, f. *a musical prelude.*
praeceps -cĭpĭtis: of motion, *headlong, fast-falling, quick*; of character, *hasty, rash, blind*; of places, *steep, precipitous*; hence *dangerous.* N. as subst., *a steep place, precipice; danger*; as adv., *headlong.*
praeceptĭo -ōnis, f. *a pre-conception; a precept; the right to receive in advance.*
praeceptor -ōris, m. and **praeceptrix** -trĭcis, f. *a teacher, instructor.*
praeceptum -i, n. subst. from praecipio; q.v.
praecerpo -cerpĕre -cerpsi -cerptum, *to pluck prematurely; to intercept.*
praecīdo -cīdĕre -cīdi -cīsum, *to cut short, lop, mutilate*; ancoras, *to cut the cables*; of speech, brevi praecidam, *I will put it briefly.*

Hence partic. **praecīsus** -a -um, *broken off*; of places, *steep, precipitous*; of speech, *brief.* Adv. **praecīsē,** *briefly, in few words; absolutely, decidedly.*
praecingo -cingĕre -cinxi -cinctum, *to gird in front, surround with a girdle.*
praecĭno -cĭnĕre -cĭnŭi -centum: intransit. *to sing* or *play before; to sing an incantation*; transit. *to prophesy, predict.*
praecipes -is = praeceps; q.v.
praecĭpĭo -cĭpĕre -cēpi -ceptum, *to take before, receive in advance*; iter, *to get the start*; mentally, *to anticipate; to instruct, advise, warn.* N. of partic. as subst. **praeceptum** -i, *a command, rule, injunction.*
praecĭpĭto -are: transit., *to cast headlong down; to hurry along*; intransit. *to fall headlong, rush down.* Adv. from pres. partic., **praecĭpĭtantĕr,** *headlong.*
praecĭpŭus -a -um, *peculiar, special; excellent, distinguished, extraordinary,* as legal term *received beforehand.* N. as subst. **praecĭpŭum** -i, *pre-eminence, superiority.* Adv. **praecĭpŭē,** *especially, chiefly, particularly.*
praecīsus -a -um, partic. from praecido; q.v.
praeclārus -a -um, *very bright, very clear; striking, beautiful; remarkable, excellent, famous*; in bad sense, *notorious.* Adv. **praeclārē,** *very clearly; admirably, excellently.*
praeclūdo -clūdĕre -clūsi -clūsum, *to close in front, shut up, make inaccessible.*
praeco -ōnis, m. *a public crier, herald.*
praecōgĭto -are, *to consider carefully beforehand.*
praecognosco -cognoscĕre -cognĭtum, *to learn beforehand.*
praecŏlo -cŏlĕre -cultum, *to cultivate before*; partic. **praecultus** -a -um, *cultivated, adorned.*
praecompŏsĭtus -a -um, *composed beforehand, studied.*
praecōnĭus -a -um, *belonging to a* praeco or *crier.* N. as subst. **praecōnĭum** -i, *the office of a crier*; hence, *publishing, making known; a public commendation.*
praeconsūmo -sūmĕre -sumptum, *to use up beforehand.*
praecontrecto -are, *to handle beforehand.*
praecordĭa -ōrum, n. pl. *the midriff, diaphragm; the stomach; the breast, heart* (as seat of passions).
praecorrumpo -rumpĕre -ruptum, *to bribe beforehand.*
praecox -cŏcis and **praecŏquis** -e, *ripe before the time, premature.*
praecultus -a -um, partic. from praecolo; q.v.
praecurro -currĕre -cŭcurri and -curri -cursum, *to run before, go on ahead*; in time, *to precede*; in quality, *to surpass.* N. pl. of partic. as subst. **praecurrentĭa** -ĭum, *antecedents.*
praecursĭo -ōnis, f. *going before, running ahead*; rhet., *preparation of the hearer.*
praecursor -ōris, m. *a forerunner*; milit., *vanguard, advance-guard; spy, scout.*
praecursōrĭus -a -um, *sent in advance.*
praecŭtĭo -cŭtĕre -cussi -cussum, *to shake before, brandish before.*
praeda -ae, f. *spoils of war, plunder, booty*; of animals, *prey*; in gen., *plunder, gain.*
praedābundus -a -um, *plundering.*
praedamno -are, *to condemn before*; spem, *to give up hope.*
praedātĭo -ōnis, f. *plundering, pillaging.*
praedātor -ōris, m. *plunderer, robber*; poet, *hunter.*

praedātōrĭus -a -um, *plundering, predatory.*
praedēlasso -are, *to weary beforehand.*
praedestĭno -are, *to appoint beforehand.*
praedĭātor -ōris, m. *a buyer of landed estates.*
praedĭātōrĭus -a -um, *relating to the sale of land.*
praedĭcābĭlis -e, *praiseworthy.*
praedĭcātĭo -ōnis, f. *making publicly known, proclamation; praising, commending.*
praedĭcātor -ōris, m. *a praiser, commender, public eulogist.*
[1]**praedĭco** -are, *to make publicly known, publish, proclaim, declare; to praise, commend; to boast.*
[2]**praedīco** -dīcĕre -dixi -dictum, *to say* or *name beforehand; to predict, foretell, prophesy; to warn, admonish, instruct.* Hence n. of partic. as subst. **praedictum** -i, *a prophecy, prediction; an order, command; a previous agreement.*
praedictĭo -ōnis, f. *prophesying, predicting*; rhet. *premising.*
praedictum -i, n. subst. from praedico; q.v.
praedĭŏlum -i, n. *a small estate, little farm.*
praedisco -ĕre, *to learn before.*
praedispŏsĭtus -a -um, *arranged at intervals beforehand.*
praedĭtus -a -um, *endowed, furnished, provided.*
praedĭum -i, n. *a farm, landed estate.*
praedīvĕs -ĭtis, *very rich.*
praedo -ōnis, m. *robber, plunderer.*
praedŏcĕo -dŏcēre -doctum *to teach before.*
praedor -ari, dep. *to plunder, rob; to carry off.*
praedūco -dūcĕre -duxi -ductum *to lead forward, bring in front.*
praedulcis -e, *very sweet.*
praedūrus -a -um, *very hard, very strong.*
praeēmĭnĕo -ēre, *to project; to excel.*
praeĕo -īre -īvi and -ĭi -ĭtum, *to go before, precede*; hence *to go over beforehand* verbally, *say in advance, dictate; to order, command.*
praefātĭo -ōnis, f. *saying beforehand; a religious* or *legal form of words, formula; a preface, introduction.*
praefectūra -ae, f. *the office of superintendent*; esp. *a subordinate provincial command.* Transf., *a town* or *district governed by a* praefectus.
praefectus -a -um, partic. from praeficio; q.v.
praefĕro -ferre -tŭli -lātum. (1) *carry in front; to show, display; to prefer; to anticipate.* (2) *to carry by*; praeferri, *to ride by.*
praefĕrox -ōcis, *very bold, impetuous.*
praeferrātus -a -um, *tipped with iron.*
praefervĭdus -a -um, *burning hot, very hot.*
praefestĭno -are, *to hasten prematurely; to hasten by.*
praefĭcĭo -fĭcĕre -fēci -fectum, *to set over, appoint as superintendent.* M. of partic. as subst. **praefectus** -i, *an overseer, superintendent, civil* or *military officer*; praefectus urbis, *governor of the city (Rome).*
praefīdens -entis, *over-confident.*
praefīgo -fīgĕre -fixi -fixum, *to fix in front, fasten before; to tip, point with; to pierce through, transfix.*
praefīnĭo -ire, *to fix, prescribe, appoint beforehand.*
praeflōro -are, *to deprive of blossom*; fig., *to diminish, lessen.*
praeflŭo -flŭĕre, *to flow past.*
praefōco -are, *to choke, suffocate.*
praefŏdĭo -fŏdĕre -fōdi -fossum, *to dig in front of; to bury previously.*
praefor -fāri -fātus, dep. *to speak before, to say beforehand*, esp. of prayers; divos, *to invoke.*
praefrīgĭdus -a -um, *very cold.*
praefringo -fringĕre -frēgi -fractum, *to break off in front*; partic. **praefractus** -a -um, of style, *abrupt, disconnected*; of character, *stern, harsh*; adv. **praefractē.**
praefulcĭo -fulcire -fulsi -fultum, *to support, prop up; to use as a prop.*
praefulgĕo -fulgēre -fulsi, *to gleam, shine forth*; with dat., *to outshine.*
praegĕlĭdus -a -um, *very cold.*
praegestĭo -ire, *to desire exceedingly.*
praegnans -antis, *pregnant; full.*
praegrăcĭlis -e, *very slim, lank.*
praegrăvis -e, *very heavy; unwieldy, wearisome; stupefied.*
praegrăvo -are, *to press heavily upon, to weigh down, oppress; to outweigh.*
praegrĕdĭor -grĕdi -gressus, dep. *to go before, precede; to outstrip; to pass by, march by.*
praegressĭo -ōnis, f. *going before, precedence.*
praegustātor -ōris, m. *one who tastes before, a taster.*
praegusto -are, *to taste before.*
praeiăcĕo -ēre, *to lie before.*
praeiūdĭcĭum -i, n. *a previous judgment, preliminary decision* or *examination; a premature decision; an example, precedent.*
praeiūdĭco -are, *to decide beforehand, give a preliminary judgment.*
Hence partic. **praeiūdĭcātus** -a -um, *previously decided*; opinio praeiudicata, *a prejudice.*
praeiŭvo -iŭvare -iūvi, *to assist before.*
praelābor -lābi -lapsus, dep. *to glide past, before* or *along.*
praelambo -ĕre, *to lick before, taste before.*
praelĕgo -lĕgĕre -lēgi -lectum. (1) *to read out* as a teacher, *to lecture upon.* (2) *to sail past, coast along.*
praelĭgo -are, *to bind in front; to bind up.*
praelongus -a -um, *very long.*
praelŏquor -lŏqui -lŏcūtus, dep. *to speak beforehand* or *first.*
praelūcĕo -lūcēre -luxi, *to shine* or *carry a light before*; with dat., *to outshine, surpass.*
praelūsĭo -ōnis, f. *prelude.*
praelustris -e, *very fine.*

praemando -are, *to order beforehand*; n. pl. of partic. as subst. **praemandāta** -orum, *a warrant of arrest.*

praemātūrus -a -um, *too early, premature.*

praemĕdĭcātus -a -um, *protected by medicine* or *charms.*

praemĕdĭtātĭo -ōnis, f. *considering beforehand.*

praemĕdĭtor -ari, dep. *to practise* or *consider beforehand*; perf. partic., in pass. sense, **praemĕdĭtātus** -a -um, *considered beforehand.*

praemĕtŭo -ĕre, *to fear beforehand, be apprehensive*; adv. from partic. **praemĕtŭentĕr,** *apprehensively, anxiously.*

praemitto -mittĕre -mīsi -missum, *to send before, send on ahead.*

praemĭum -i, n. *that which is taken first, the pick; a gift, award, reward, recompense*; poet., *notable exploit.*

praemŏlestĭa -ae, f. *trouble beforehand.*

praemōlĭor -iri, dep. *to prepare beforehand.*

praemŏnĕo -ēre, *to warn, advise beforehand; to foretell, presage.*

praemŏnĭtus -ūs, m. *prediction, warning.*

praemonstro -are, *to point out the way; to prophesy, predict.*

praemordĕo -mordēre -mordi -morsum, *to bite off; to pilfer.*

praemŏrĭor -mŏri -mortŭus, dep. *to die prematurely.*

praemūnĭo -ire, *to fortify in front; to secure, make safe.*

praemūnĭtĭo -ōnis, f. *fortifying beforehand*; rhet., *preparation of one's hearers.*

praenăto -are, *to swim before* or *past.*

praenĭtĕo -ēre, *to outshine.*

praenōmen -ĭnis, n. *the first name, usually standing before the gentile name* (e.g., Marcus, in M. T. Cicero).

praenosco -ĕre, *to get to know beforehand.*

praenōtĭo -ōnis, f. *a preconception, innate idea.*

praenūbĭlus -a -um, *very cloudy* or *dark.*

praenuntĭo -are, *to announce beforehand, foretell.*

praenuntĭus -a -um, *foretelling*; as subst. *a harbinger, token, omen.*

praeoccŭpo -are, *to seize beforehand, to preoccupy; to anticipate, prevent.*

praeopto -are, *to choose before, to prefer.*

praepando -ĕre, *to open wide in front, extend before.*

praepărātĭo -ōnis, f. *preparation.*

praepăro -are, *to make ready, prepare*; ex praeparato, *by arrangement.*

praepĕdĭo -ire, *to entangle, shackle, fetter; to hinder, impede, obstruct.*

praependĕo -ēre, intransit., *to hang before, hang in front.*

praepĕs -pĕtis, *rapidly flying, swift*; m. and f. as subst., *a bird,* esp. *a bird of good omen.*

praepĭlātus -a -um, *having a button in front* (of foils, etc.).

praepinguis -e, *very fat* or *rich.*

praepollĕo -ēre, *to be very* or *more powerful.*

praepondĕro -are, *to outweigh, to turn the scale.*

praepōno -pōnĕre -pŏsŭi -pŏsĭtum, *to put before; to put over, set over as commander,* etc.; *to prefer.* Hence m. of partic., as subst. **praepŏsĭtus** -i, *a commander.*

praeporto -are, *to carry before.*

praepŏsĭtĭo -ōnis, f. *placing before; preferring, preference*; gram., *a preposition.*

praepossum -posse -pŏtŭi, *to have the chief power.*

praepostĕrus -a -um, *having the last first, inverted, perverse*; adv. **praepostĕrē.**

praepŏtens -entis, *very powerful.*

praeprŏpĕrantĕr, *very hastily.*

praeprŏpĕrus -a -um, *over-hasty, precipitate*; adv. **praeprŏpĕrē.**

praequam; see prae.

praequĕror -quĕri -questus, dep. *to complain beforehand.*

praerădĭo -are, *to outshine.*

praerăpĭdus -a -um, *very rapid.*

praerĭgesco -rĭgescĕre -rĭgŭi, *to grow very stiff.*

praerĭpĭo -rĭpĕre -rĭpŭi -reptum, *to snatch before* somebody else; *to carry off before the time; to anticipate, forestall.*

praerōdo -rōdĕre -rōdi -rōsum, *to gnaw off, bite through.*

praerŏgātīvus -a -um, *asked before others* (for vote, opinion, etc.); f. as subst. **praerŏgātīva** -ae, f. *the tribe* or *century voting first in the* comitia; hence *the first century's vote*; in gen., *a previous choice; a sure sign, indication.*

praerumpo -rumpĕre -rūpi -ruptum, *to break off in front.*

Hence partic. **praeruptus** -a -um, *broken off*; of places, *steep, precipitous*; of character, *headstrong, hasty.*

[1]**praes** praedis, m. *a surety, security, one who stands bail.*

[2]**praes,** adv. *at hand.*

praesaepes (**praesaepis**) -is, f. **praesaepe** -is, n. and **praesaepĭum** -i, n. *an enclosure; a crib, manger, stall; a hive; a haunt, lodging, tavern.*

praesaepĭo, *to block up in front.*

praesăgĭo -ire, *to presage, forebode, have a presentiment of.*

praesăgĭtĭo -ōnis, f. *foreboding, presentiment.*

praesăgĭum -i, n. *presage, presentiment, foreboding; prediction.*

praesăgus -a -um, *foreboding; predicting.*

praescisco -ĕre, *to find out beforehand.*

praescĭus -a -um, *knowing beforehand, prescient.*

praescrībo -scrībĕre -scripsi -scriptum, *to write before, set out in writing; to put forward* or *use as a pretext; to outline; dictate; to prescribe, ordain, direct beforehand.* Hence n. partic. as subst. **praescriptum** -i, *a prescribed limit, regulation, rule.*

praescrīptĭo -ōnis, f. *a title, inscription, introduction; a precept, rule; a pretext*; legal, *an objection, demurrer.*

praesĕco -sĕcare -sĕcŭi -sectum, *to cut in front, cut short.*

praesens -entis, partic. from praesum; q.v.

praesensĭo -ōnis, f. *a presentiment, foreboding; preconception.*

praesentĭa -ae, f. *presence*; animi, *presence of mind*; in praesentia, *for the present*; sometimes *power, effect.*

praesentĭo -sentire -sensi -sensum, *to feel beforehand, have a presentiment of.*

praesertim, *especially, chiefly.*

praesĕs -sĭdis, *sitting before, protecting.* As subst. *a protector*; also *a chief, ruler, president.*

praesĭdĕo -sĭdēre -sēdi -sessum, *to sit before; to watch over, protect, guard; to preside over, manage, direct.* M. of partic. as subst. **praesĭdens** -entis, *a president, ruler.*

praesĭdĭārĭus -a -um, *on guard.*

praesĭdĭum -i, n. *sitting before; protection, help, support.* Milit., *guard, escort; a garrison; a post.*

praesignĭfico -are, *to indicate beforehand.*

praesignis -e, *distinguished, remarkable.*

praesŏno -sŏnare -sŏnŭi, *to sound forth.*

praespargo -ĕre, *to scatter in front.*

praestābĭlis -e, *distinguished, preeminent*; in compar., *preferable.*

praestans -antis, partic. from praesto; q.v.

praestantĭa -ae, f. *superiority, excellence.*

praestĕs -stĭtis, *protecting.*

praestĭgĭae -ārum, f. pl. *deception, illusion, juggling.*

praestĭtŭo -stĭtŭĕre -stĭtŭi -stĭtūtum, *to prescribe, appoint beforehand.*

[1]**praestō,** adv. *present, at hand ready*; with esse, *to be at hand, be ready to help.*

[2]**praesto** -stare -stĭti -stĭtum. (1) *to stand before; to be outstanding, surpass, excel*; impers., praestat, *it is better, preferable.* (2) transit., *to become surety for, answer for, be responsible for.* Transf., *to perform, execute, fulfil; to show, manifest, exhibit; to offer, present*; with se and acc. *to show oneself, behave as.*

Hence partic. **praestans** -antis, *excellent, distinguished, eminent.*

praestōlor -ari, dep., *to wait for, expect.*

praestringo -stringĕre -strinxi -strictum, *to bind up, in front.* Transf., *to make blunt* or *dull.*

praestrŭo -strŭĕre -struxi -structum. (1) *to build in front; to block up, make impassable.* (2) *to build beforehand, to prepare.*

praesŭl -sŭlis, c. and **praesultātor** -ōris, m. *a dancer.*

praesulto -are, *to leap* or *dance before.*

praesum -esse -fŭi, *to be before; to be over, preside over; to take the lead.*

Hence partic. (with compar.) **praesens** -entis, *present, at hand,* in space or time; in praesens (tempus), *for the present time*; esp. *immediate, ready; effective, powerful, helpful, resolute, determined.*

praesūmo -sūmĕre -sumpsi -sumptum, *to take beforehand; to anticipate; to take for granted.*

Hence partic. **praesumptus** -a -um, *taken for granted, presumed.*

praesūtus -a -um, *sewn over in front.*

praetempto -are, *to try, test beforehand.*

praetendo -tendĕre -tendi -tentum, *to stretch or hold out*; pass., praetendi, of places, *to lie before* or *in front.* Transf., *to hold out as a pretext, allege in excuse.*

praetento = praetempto; q.v.

praetĕpesco -tĕpescĕre -tĕpŭi, *to glow beforehand.*

praeter. Adv., *except.* Prep. with acc., *beyond, past; beside, contrary to, beside; more than; except; in addition to.*

praetĕrăgo -ĕre, *to drive past, drive by.*

praetĕrĕā, *besides, further; after this, hereafter.*

praetĕrĕo -īre -īvi and oftener -ĭi -ĭtum, *to go by, pass by.* Transf., *to escape the notice of* a person; *to pass by, pass over, omit; to surpass, outstrip; to transgress.*

Hence partic. **praetĕrĭtus** -a -um, *past, gone by.*

praetĕrĕquĭto -are, *to ride past, ride by.*

praeterfĕro -ferre -tŭli -lātum, *to carry past.*

praeterflŭo -flŭĕre, *to flow past, flow by.*

praetergrĕdĭor -grĕdi -gressus, dep. *to pass by, go beyond.*

praetĕrĭtus -a -um, partic. from praetereo; q.v.

praeterlābor -lābi -lapsus, dep. *to glide by, flow by, slip away.*

praetermĕo -are, *to pass by.*

praetermissĭo -ōnis, f. *leaving out, omission; passing over, neglecting.*

praetermitto -mittĕre -mīsi -missum, *to let pass, let go by; to neglect, omit; to pass over, overlook.*

praeterquam or **praeter quam,** *more than, beyond*; after neg., *except*; with quod, *apart from the fact that.*

praetervectĭo -ōnis, f. *a passing place.*

praetervĕhor -vĕhi -vectus sum, *to ride by, be carried past, march past, pass by.*

praetervŏlo -are, *to fly past; to slip by, escape.*

praetexo -texĕre -texŭi -textum, *to weave in front, form a border; to adorn; to cover, conceal; to put forward as a pretext.*

Hence partic. **praetextus** -a -um, *bordered,* esp. of the toga. F. as subst. **praetexta** -ae, f. *a toga bordered with purple,* worn by magistrates and boys; also praetexta (fabula), *a tragedy with Roman characters.* N. as subst. **praetextum** -i, *a pretence, pretext.*

praetextātus -a -um, *wearing the* toga praetexta; *veiled; licentious.*

praetextū, abl. sing. m. *in outward appearance; under a pretext.*

praetinctus -a -um, *moistened beforehand.*

praetor -ōris, m. *leader, chief; a magistrate*, esp. one who helped the consuls by administering justice, commanding armies, etc.

praetōrĭānus -a -um, *belonging to the imperial body-guard, praetorian.*

praetōrĭus -a -um. (1) *relating to the* praetor, *praetorian.* (2) *relating to any general* or *commander*; praetoria navis, *flagship*; cohors, *the general's body-guard.* As subst.: m. **praetōrĭus** -i, *an ex-praetor* or *man of praetorian rank*; n. **praetōrĭum** -i, *the official residence of the* praetor or propraetor; *a palace*; also *the headquarters in a Roman camp.*

praetrĕpĭdo -are, *to be hasty* or *impatient.*

praetūra -ae, f. *the office of* praetor.

praeumbro -are, *to overshadow; to obscure.*

praeustus -a -um, *burnt at the end* or *tip; frost-bitten.*

praevălĕo -vălēre -vălŭi, *to be very strong; to prevail, get the upper hand.*

praevălĭdus -a -um, *very strong;* terra, *too productive.*

praevārĭcātĭo -ōnis, f. *collusion.*

praevārĭcātor -ōris, m. *an advocate guilty of collusion.*

praevārĭcor -ari, dep. of an advocate, *to have a secret understanding with the other side, to be guilty of collusion.*

praevĕhor -vĕhi -vectus sum, *to ride* (or *run*) *before* or *past.*

praevĕnĭo -vĕnire -vēni -ventum, *to come before, anticipate, get the start of.*

praeverro -ĕre, *to sweep before.*

praeverto (praevorto) -vertĕre -verti -versum, and **praevertor** -verti -versus sum; of preference, *to put first, take first, turn first to*; of early action, *to anticipate, outstrip, forestall; to surprise, preoccupy.*

praevĭdĕo -vĭdēre -vīdi -vīsum, *to see before, foresee.*

praevĭtĭo -are, *to corrupt beforehand.*

praevĭus -a -um, *going before, preceding.*

praevŏlo -are, *to fly before.*

pragmătĭcus -a -um, *skilled in business*; m. as subst. *a person who supplied speakers with material.*

prandĕo prandēre prandi pransum, *to take lunch; to lunch upon*; perf. partic. in act. sense **pransus** -a -um, *having lunched; well-fed.*

prandĭum -i, n. *a late breakfast* or *lunch.*

pransus -a -um, partic. from prandeo; q.v.

prăsĭnus -a -um, *leek-green.*

prātensis -e, *of a meadow.*

prātŭlum -i, n. *a little meadow.*

prātum -i, n. *a meadow; meadow-grass.*

prāvĭtās -ātis, f. *crookedness, deformity; perversity, depravity.*

prāvus -a -um, adj. *crooked, deformed; perverse; depraved.* Adv. **prāvē.**

Praxĭtĕlēs -is and -i, m. *a sculptor of Athens.*

prĕcārĭus -a -um, *begged for*, or *got by entreaty; uncertain, precarious.* N. abl. as adv. **prĕcārĭo,** *by entreaty.*

prĕcātĭo -ōnis, f. *begging, request prayer.*

prĕces; see prex.

prĕcĭae -arum, f. *a kind of vine.*

prĕcor -ari, dep. *to beg, entreat, pray, invoke.*

prĕhendo prĕhendĕre prĕhendi prehensum and prendo prendĕre prendi prensum, *to lay hold of, seize, grasp; to catch, detain, arrest; to take in*, mentally or by the senses.

prĕhenso and **prenso** -are, *to lay hold of, clutch at.* Transf., *to canvass for votes.*

prēlum -i, n. *a wine or olive-press.*

prĕmo prĕmĕre pressi pressum, *to press; to step on, lie on; to hug, keep close to; to press hard, squeeze; to pursue closely, press upon; to press down, strike down; to disparage, slander; to press together, close; to check, curb.*

Hence partic. **pressus** -a -um, *subdued, measured*; of style, *compressed, concise.* Adv. **pressē,** *accurately, precisely, distinctly*; of style, *briefly, concisely.*

prendo = prehendo; q.v.

prensātĭo -ōnis, f. *canvassing for office.*

prenso = prehenso; q.v.

pressĭo -ōnis, f. *leverage* or *means of leverage.*

presso -are, *to press.*

[1]**pressus** -a -um, partic. from premo; q.v.

[2]**pressus** -ūs, m. *pressing, pressure.*

prestēr -ēris, m. *a fiery whirlwind* or *a waterspout.*

prĕtĭōsus -a -um, *costly, precious, dear*; of persons, *extravagant.* Adv. **prĕtĭōsē.**

prĕtĭum -i, n. *worth, value, price*; esse in pretio, *to be prized*; operae pretium, *worth while.* Transf., *prize, reward; a ransom; a bribe; punishment.*

prex prĕcis (usually plur.) f. *request, entreaty*; esp. *prayer to a god*; sometimes *a curse, execration.*

Prĭămus -i, m. *the last king of Troy*; adj. **Prĭămēĭus** -a -um.

Prĭāpus -i, m. *the god of gardens and vineyards.*

prīdem, *long ago, long since.*

prīdĭē, *on the day before.*

prīmaevus -a -um, *young, youthful.*

prīmāni -orum, m. pl. *soldiers of the first legion.*

prīmārĭus -a -um, *in the first rank, distinguished.*

prīmĭgĕnus -a -um, *original, primitive.*

prīmĭpīlāris -is, m. *the centurion of the first maniple of the* triarii, *the chief centurion of a legion.*

prīmĭpīlus; see pilus.

prīmĭtĭae -arum, f. *first-fruits.*

prīmĭtŭs, *first, for the first time.*

prīmordĭum -i, n. *first beginning, origin*; plur. often = *atoms.*

prīmōris -e, *first, foremost; at the tip*; primoribus labris, *superficially*; of rank, *first, most distinguished.*

prīmus; see prior.

princeps -cĭpis, adj. *first, foremost.* As subst., *leader*; polit., often as a title of the Roman emperor; milit., plur., principes, *the second line in a Roman army, between* hastati *and* triarii.

princĭpālis -e. (1) *first*, in time or rank. (2) *of a prince.* (3) *of the* principia *in a Roman camp.*

princĭpātus -ūs, m. (1) *first place, pre-eminence; rule, dominion.* (2) *beginning, origin.*

princĭpĭālis -e, *original.*

princĭpĭum -i, n. *beginning, origin; groundwork, foundation*; in plur., *elements, first principles*; polit., *the tribe* or *curia which voted first*; milit., in plur., *the front ranks* or *the headquarters in a camp.*

prĭŏr prĭus, genit. -ōris, compar. adj., *fore, former*, of place or time; *higher in importance*; m. pl. as subst., *ancestors.* N. acc. as adv. **prĭus,** *before, previously; formerly; sooner, rather*; **prĭus quam,** or **prĭusquam,** conj., *before.* Superl. **prīmus** -a -um, *first, foremost*, of place or time; of rank, etc., *first, most distinguished*; (partes) primae, *the leading part*; in primis, *especially.* N. acc. as adv. **prīmum,** *at first* or *for the first time.* N. abl. **prīmō,** *at first.*

priscus -a -um, *ancient, antique; of the old school, venerable; former, previous.* Adv. **priscē,** *in the old-fashioned way.*

pristĭnus -a -um, *former, previous, earlier.*

prĭus; see prior.

prīvātim, *privately, as a private person, in private life; at home.*

prīvātĭo -ōnis, f. *freeing, release.*

prīvigna -ae, f. *stepdaughter.*

prīvignus -i, m. *stepson.*

prīvĭlēgĭum i, n. *a special law, private law.*

prīvo -are, *to strip, deprive; to free, release.*

Hence partic. **prīvātus** -a -um, as adj., *private, unofficial*; in privato, *in private*; (vir) privatus, *a private person.*

prīvus -a -um, *single, every;* distributively, *one each; particular, special, one's own;* with genit., *deprived of.*

[1]**prō,** prep., with abl., *before, in front of; for, on behalf of, in favour of; in place of; like, as good as;* se pro cive gerere, *to behave as a citizen; as a reward for; in proportion to, according to, by virtue of;* pro virili parte, *to the best of one's abilities;* pro eo quantum, *in proportion as.*

[2]**pro! (proh!),** interj. *oh! ah!*

prŏăvĭa -ae, f. *a great-grandmother.*

prŏăvītus -a -um, *ancestral.*

prŏăvus -i, m. *a great-grandfather; an ancestor, forefather.*

prŏbābĭlis -e, (1) *probable, credible.* (2) *acceptable, good.* Adv. **prŏbābĭlĭtĕr,** *probably, credibly.*

prŏbābĭlĭtās -ātis, f. *probability, credibility.*

prŏbātĭo -ōnis, f. *proving, trial, examination; approval, proof, demonstration.*

prŏbātor -ōris, m. *one who approves, an approver.*

prŏbĭtās -ātis, f. *honesty, uprightness.*

prŏbo -are, *to make* or *find good; to approve, pronounce good*; with dat., *to recommend to*; with abl., *to judge by* a standard; in gen., *to show, prove, demonstrate.*

Hence partic. **prŏbātus** -a -um, *found good, approved; acceptable.*

probrōsus -a -um, *shameful, disgraceful, infamous.*

probrum -i, n. *abuse, reproach; ground for reproach, disgrace; infamous conduct*, esp. *unchastity.*

prŏbus -a -um, *good, excellent, fine; morally good, upright, virtuous.* Adv. **prŏbē,** *well, rightly, properly.*

prŏcācĭtās -ātis, f. *shamelessness, impudence.*

prŏcax -cācis, *shameless, bold, impudent*; adv. **prŏcācĭtĕr.**

prōcēdo -cēdĕre -cessi -cessum, *to go ahead, proceed, advance, continue; to come out, go out*; of actions, etc., *to turn out, result*; sometimes *to turn out well, prosper.*

prŏcella -ae, f. *a storm, tempest, gale*; in fighting, *charge, onset, wave.*

prŏcellōsus -a -um, *stormy, tempestuous.*

prŏcer -ĕris, m. *a chief noble, prince.*

prōcērĭtās -ātis, f. *height, length.*

prōcērus -a -um, *tall, long;* compar. adv. **prōcērĭus,** *farther forward.*

prōcessĭo -ōnis, f. *a (military) advance.*

prōcessus -ūs, m. *advance, progress.*

prōcĭdo -cĭdĕre -cĭdi, *to fall forwards.*

prōcinctū, abl. sing. m. *being girded* or *equipped; readiness for battle.*

proclāmātor -ōris, m. *a bawler.*

proclāmo -are, *to call out, cry out.*

prōclīno -are, *to bend over, incline forwards.*

prōclīvis -e and **prōclīvus** -a -um, *inclined forwards, sloping downwards*; proclive, or per proclive, *downwards.* Transf., *inclined, ready, prone; easy to do.*

prōclīvĭtās -ātis, f. *a slope.* Transf., *inclination, tendency.*

prōclīvus = proclivis; q.v.

Procnē (Prognē) -ēs, f. *wife of Tereus; changed into a swallow.*

prŏco -are and **prŏcor** -ari, dep. *to ask, demand.*

prōconsul -sŭlis, m. (also **prō consŭlĕ),** a proconsul, *one who serves as a consul*, in command of any army, or as governor of a province.

prōconsŭlāris -e, *proconsular.*

prōconsŭlātus -ūs, m. *the office of proconsul.*

prōcrastĭnātĭo -ōnis, f. *procrastination.*

prōcrastĭno -are, *to put off till tomorrow, defer.*
prōcrĕātĭo -ōnis, f. *begetting, procreation.*
prōcrĕātor -ōris, m. *begetter, creator.*
prōcrĕātrix -īcis, f. *mother.*
prōcrĕo -are, *to beget; to produce, cause make.*
prōcresco -ĕre, *to come forth, arise; to increase.*
Procrustēs -ae, m. *a robber killed by Theseus.*
prōcŭbo -are, *to lie stretched out.*
prōcūdo -cūdĕre -cūdi -cūsum, *to hammer out, forge; to form, produce.*
prŏcŭl, *far; at, to,* or *from a distance.*
prŏculco -are, *to tread on, trample down.*
prōcumbo -cumbĕre -cŭbŭi -cŭbĭtum, *to lean* or *bend forward; to fall down, sink down, be laid low.*
prōcūrātĭo -ōnis, f. *taking care, management, administration.* Esp. (1) *the office of imperial procurator.* (2) *an attempt to propitiate a deity.*
procūrātor -ōris, m. *a manager, bailiff, agent, factor*; regni, *a viceroy*; under the empire, *a financial agent* or *under-governor.*
procūrātrix -trīcis, f. *she that governs.*
procūro -are, *to take care of, look after; to manage, administer; to be a* procurator; *to sacrifice in order to avert evil.*
prōcurro -currĕre -curri and -cŭcurri -cursum, *to run forward*; of places, *to project, jut out.*
prōcursātĭo -ōnis, f. *running forward, skirmishing.*
prōcursātor -ōris, m. *a skirmisher.*
prōcurso -are, *to run forward*; milit. *to skirmish.*
prōcursus -ūs, m. *running forward*; milit., *advance, charge.*
prōcurvus -a -um, *bent forward.*
[1]**prŏcus** -i, m. = procer; q.v.
[2]**prŏcus** -i, m. *a wooer, suitor; a canvasser.*
prōdĕo -ire -ĭi -ĭtum, *to advance, go forward; to project; to come out, appear.*
prōdīco -dīcĕre -dixi -dictum, *to put off.*
prōdictātor -ōris, m. *one who acts as dictator.*
prōdĭgentĭa -ae, f. *profusion, prodigality.*
prōdĭgĭālis -e, *dealing in wonders*; adv. **prōdĭgĭālĭtĕr,** *wonderfully.*
prōdĭgĭōsus -a -um, *unnatural, wonderful.*
prōdĭgĭum -i, n. *a prodigy, portent; an enormity, an unnatural thing; a monster.*
prōdĭgo -ĭgĕre -ēgi -actum, *to drive forth; to spend, waste.*
prōdĭgus -a -um, *profuse, extravagant; rich, abound in.* Adv. **prōdĭgē.**
prōdĭtĭo -ōnis, f. *betrayal, treason.*
prōdĭtor -ōris, m. *a betrayer, traitor.*
prōdo -dĕre -dĭdi -dĭtum. (1) *to put forth, bring forth; to show, publish; to appoint.* (2) *to forsake, betray.* (3) *to hand over, deliver, transmit.*
prōdŏcĕo -ēre, *to teach, inculcate.*
prodrŏmus -i, m. *forerunner.*
prōdūco -dūcĕre -duxi -ductum, *to bring forward, bring out, extend; to produce, bring up, advance, promote; to divulge, bring to light*; in pronunciation, *to lengthen out, make long*; in time, *to prolong, continue*; also *to put off, postpone.*

Hence partic. **prōductus** -a -um, *extended, lengthened, prolonged*; of syllables, *pronounced long*; n. pl. as subst. *preferable things* (in the Stoic philosophy). Adv. **prōductē,** *long* (of pronunciation).

prōductĭo -ōnis, f. *extending, lengthening, prolonging.*
proelĭātor -ōris, m. *warrior.*
proelĭor -ari, dep. *to give battle, fight, strive.*
proelĭum -i, n. *battle, fight, strife.*
prŏfāno -are, *to profane, desecrate.*
prŏfānus -a -um, *not sacred; uninitiated; ordinary, common, profane; impious.*
prŏfectĭo -ōnis, f. *departure; source, origin.*
prŏfecto, *truly, really, indeed.*
prŏfĕro -ferre -tŭli -lātum. (1) *to bring forth, bring forward, offer to publish, bring to light, reveal; to produce, cite, mention.* (2) *to advance, bring forward, impel.* (3) *to enlarge, extend*; in time, *to lengthen*; also *to put off, postpone.*
prŏfessĭo -ōnis, f. *declaration, profession.* Transf., *a register of persons and property; an occupation, art, profession.*
prŏfessor -ōris, m. *an authority, expert.*
prŏfessōrĭus -a -um, *authoritative.*
prŏfestus -a -um, *not kept as a festival, common.*
prōfĭcĭo -fĭcĕre -fēci -fectum: of persons, *to make progress, advance*; of things, *to be of use, assist, help.*
prŏfĭciscor -fĭcisci -fectus, dep. *to start forward, set out, depart; to arise* or *spring* from an origin.
prŏfĭtĕor -fĭtēri -fessus, dep. *to acknowledge, confess; to profess* or *declare* oneself anything; *to profess* a science, art, etc.; *to make any public statement; to offer, promise.*
prōflīgātor -ōris, m. *a spendthrift.*
prōflīgo -are, *to overthrow, overcome, ruin; to lower, debase; to bring almost to an end, nearly finish.*

Hence partic. **prōflīgātus** -a -um, *ruined, degraded.*

prōflo -are, *to blow forth, breathe forth.*
prōflŭentĭa -ae, f. *fluency.*
prōflŭo -flŭĕre -fluxi fluxum, *to flow forth; to proceed.*

Hence partic. **prōflŭens** -entis, *flowing*; f. as subst. (sc. aqua), *running water*; of style, *flowing, fluent.* Adv. **prōflŭentĕr.**

prōflŭvium -i, n. *flowing forth.*
prŏfor -fari -fatus, dep. *to say, speak, declare.*
prŏfŭgĭo -fŭgĕre -fūgi: intransit., *to flee away, escape*; transit., *to flee away from.*

prŏfŭgus -a -um, *fleeing, fugitive; banished; migratory.*
prŏfundo -fundĕre -fūdi -fūsum, *to pour forth, shed, cause to flow;* pass., profundi, *to stream forth.* Transf., *to stretch at full length; to release, discharge; to utter; to spend, sacrifice, give up; to lavish, squander.*
Hence partic. **prŏfūsus** -a -um, *lavish, extravagant.* Adv. **prŏfūsē,** *in disorder; lavishly, extravagantly.*
prŏfundus -a -um, *deep, profound; high; thick, dense; boundless.* N. as subst. **prŏfundum** -i, *depth, abyss;* poet., *the sea.*
prŏfūsus -a -um, partic. from profundo; q.v.
prōgĕner -i, *a grand-daughter's husband.*
prōgĕnĕro -are, *to engender, produce.*
prōgĕnĭes -ēi, f. *descent, lineage; progeny, offspring, descendants.*
prōgĕnĭtor -ōris, m. *founder of a family, ancestor.*
prōgigno -gignĕre -gĕnŭi -gĕnĭtum, *to engender, bring forth.*
prognātus -a -um, *born, sprung from;* m. as subst., *a son.*
Prognē = Procne; q.v.
prōgrĕdĭor -grĕdi -gressus, dep., *to go forth, go out; to go forwards, advance, proceed.*
prōgressĭo -ōnis, f. *advance, progress; increase;* rhet., *climax.*
prōgressus -ūs, m. *going forwards, advance, progress; increase.*
proh! = pro!; q.v.
prŏhĭbĕo -ēre, *to hold back, restrain, hinder; to forbid, prohibit; to preserve, defend, protect.*
prŏhĭbĭtĭo -ōnis, f. *hindering, prohibition.*
prōĭcĭo -icĕre -iēci -iectum, *to throw forth; to fling forward; to put forward, cause to project* (pass., *to project*)*; to fling out, throw away, abandon; to defer, put off.*
Hence partic. **prōiectus** -a -um, *jutting forward, prominent; stretched out, prostrate;* hence *abject, contemptible, downcast;* with ad, *addicted to.*
prōiectĭo -ōnis, f., *throwing forward, stretching out.*
prōiectū, abl. sing. m. *by jutting out.*
prŏinde and **prŏin** (o and i sometimes scanned as one syllable), *consequently, therefore;* foll. by ut or quam, *just as;* foll. by quasi, ac, ac si, *just as if.*
prōlābor -lābi -lapsus dep. (1) *to glide forward, slip along* or *out.* (2) *to fall forward, fall down.*
prōlapsĭo -ōnis, f. *slipping, sliding.*
prōlātĭo -ōnis, f. *bringing forward, mentioning; an extension; putting off, deferring.*
prōlāto -are, *to extend, enlarge, lengthen; to put off, defer.*
prōlecto -are, *to entice, allure.*
prōlēs -is, f. *offspring, descendants, posterity; the young men* of a race; of plants, *fruit.*
prōlētārĭus -i, m. *a citizen of the lowest class, serving the state only by begetting children.*
prōlĭcĭo -lĭcĕre -lixi, *to lure forth, entice.*
prōlixus -a -um, *wide, broad, long.* Transf., *willing, obliging; favourable.* Adv. **prōlixē,** *freely; willingly.*
prōlŏgus -i, m. *prologue.*
prōlŏquor -lŏqui -lŏcūtus, dep. *to speak out, say openly.*
prōlūdo -lūdĕre -lūsi -lūsum, *to play beforehand, to prelude.*
prōlŭo -lŭĕre -lŭi -lūtum, *to wash away* or *off; to wash clean.*
prōlūsĭo -ōnis, f. *a prelude, preliminary exercise.*
prōlŭvĭēs -ēi, f. *an inundation; scourings, discharge.*
prōmĕrĕo -ēre -ŭi -ĭtum and **prōmĕrĕor** -ēri -ĭtus, dep. *to deserve;* n. of partic. as subst. **prōmĕrĭtum** -i, *deserts, merit.*
Prŏmēthēūs -ĕi and -ĕos, m. *Prometheus, punished for stealing fire from heaven and giving it to mankind;* adj. **Prŏmēthēus** -a -um.
prōmĭnĕo -ēre -ŭi, *to stand out, jut out, project, extend;* partic. **prōmĭnens** -entis, *jutting out, projecting;* n. as subst. *a projection.*
prōmiscus and **prōmiscŭus** -a -um, *mixed, indiscriminate, promiscuous; commonplace, usual.* Adv. **prōmiscē** and **prōmiscŭē.**
prōmissĭo -ōnis, f. *a promise.*
prōmissor -ōris, m. *a promiser.*
prōmitto -mittĕre -mīsi -missum, *to let go forward, send forth; to let grow; to promise, undertake.*
Hence partic. **prōmissus** -a -um, *let grow, long, hanging down.* N. of partic. as subst. **prōmissum** -i, *a promise.*
prōmo prōmĕre prompsi promptum, *to bring out, produce; to bring forward, disclose, express.*
Hence partic. **promptus** -a -um, *ready, at hand; easy; visible, apparent;* of persons, *prepared, resolute, prompt.* Adv. **promptē.**
prōmontorĭum -i, n. *a mountain ridge; a promontory.*
prōmŏvĕo -mŏvēre -mōvi -mōtum, *to move forwards, push onwards, make to advance; to extend; to postpone.*
promptū, abl. sing. m.: in promptu esse, *to be ready, easy,* or *manifest;* in promptu ponere, *to make manifest;* in promptu habere, *to have ready* or *have on show.*
promptus -a -um, partic. from promo; q.v.
prōmulgātĭo -ōnis, f. *publication, promulgation* (of a proposed law).
prōmulgo -are, *to publish, promulgate* (esp. a proposed law).
prōmulsĭs -ĭdis, f. *hors d'oeuvres.*
prōmuntūrĭum = promontorium; q.v.
prōmus -i, m. *a steward, butler.*
prōmūtŭus -a -um, *advanced, paid beforehand.*
prŏnĕpōs -pōtis, m. *great-grandson.*

prŏneptis -is, f. *great-granddaughter.*
prŏnoea -ae, f. *providence.*
prōnŭba -ae, f. (1) *a matron attending a bride.* (2) *epithet of Juno, as the goddess presiding over marriage.*
prōnuntĭātĭo -ōnis, f. *public declaration; the decision of a judge, a judgment*; in logic, *a proposition*; in rhetoric, *delivery.*
prōnuntĭātor -ōris, m. *a relater.*
prōnuntĭo -are, *to make publicly known, declare*; in the senate, *to announce a resolution*; at a sale, *to make a statement as to defects*; rhet. *to declaim, recite, deliver.* N. of partic. as subst. **prōnuntĭātum** -i, in logic, *a proposition.*
prōnŭrus -us, f. *a grandson's wife.*
prōnus -a -um, *inclined forward, stooping forward; rushing down* or *past; precipitous, steep.* Transf., *inclined, well-disposed, favourable; easy.* Adv. **prōnē**, *on a slope.*
prŏoemĭum -i, n. *preface, introduction, prelude.*
prŏpāgātĭo -ōnis, f. *spreading, propagation; extension, enlargement.*
prŏpāgātor -ōris, m. *an extender, enlarger.*
[1]**prŏpāgo** -are, *to spread, propagate plants; to extend, enlarge, prolong.*
[2]**prŏpāgo** -ĭnis, f. *a layer, slip* or *shoot* (esp. of the vine); of men and animals, *offspring, race, posterity.*
prōpălam, *publicly, in public.*
prōpătŭlus -a -um, *open, uncovered*; n. as subst. *an open place, unroofed space*; in propatulo, *publicly.*
prŏpĕ, adv. and prep; compar. **prŏpĭus;** superl. **prōximē.** Adv. *near,* in space or time; *nearly*; propius, *more nearly, more closely*; proxime, of time, *just now.* Prep. with acc. *near to,* in space or time; in gen., *approximating to, not far from.*
prŏpĕdĭem, *at an early date, very soon.*
prōpello -pellĕre -pŭli -pulsum, *to drive before one, drive forth* or *away.*
prŏpĕmŏdŏ and **prŏpĕmŏdum,** *almost, nearly.*
prōpendĕo -pendēre -pendi -pensum *to hang down; to preponderate; to incline, be favourable.*
Hence partic. **prōpensus** -a -um, *weighty; tending, inclined, disposed*; esp. *favourably disposed.* Adv. **prōpensē,** *readily, willingly.*
prōpensĭo -ōnis, f. *inclination, propensity.*
prŏpĕrantĕr, adv. from propero; q.v.
prŏpĕrantĭa -ae, f. *haste, rapidity.*
prŏpĕrātĭo -ōnis, f. *haste.*
prŏpĕro -are: intransit., *to hasten*; transit., *to hasten something, to accelerate, complete quickly.* Adv. from pres. partic. **prŏpĕrantĕr,** *hastily.* Past. partic. **prŏpĕrātus** -a -um, *hasty*; n. as subst. **prŏpĕrātum** -i, *haste*; abl. **prŏpĕrātō,** *in haste.*
Prŏpertĭus -i, m., Sex. Aurelius, *a poet of the Augustan age.*
prŏpĕrus -a -um, *quick, rapid, hasty*; adv. **prŏpĕrē**.
prōpexus -a -um, *combed forwards, hanging down.*
prŏpīno -are, *to drink to anyone.*
prŏpinquĭtās -ātis, f. *nearness, proximity; friendship* or *relationship.*
prŏpinquo -are: intransit., *to come near, draw near, approach*; transit. *to bring near, hasten on.*
prŏpinquus -a -um, *near, close, neighbouring; similar; nearly related, closely connected*; as subst., *a kinsman.* Adv. **prŏpinquē.**
prŏpĭor -us, genit. -ōris, *nearer,* in space or time (cf. prope); *more like; more closely connected; more suitable.* Superl. **proxĭmus (proxŭmus)** -a -um, *very near, nearest*; in time, *next, following,* or *most recent*; in rank, etc., *next, next best; most like; most nearly connected*; m. pl. as subst. *near relations* or *close friends.*
prŏpĭtĭo -are, *to soothe, appease.*
prŏpĭtĭus -a -um, *favourable, gracious.*
prŏpĭus, compar. of prope; q.v.
prŏpōla -ae, m. *a retailer, huckster.*
prōpollŭo -ŭĕre, *to pollute worse.*
prōpōno -pōnĕre -pŏsŭi -pŏsĭtum, *to put on view, expose, display; to publish, relate, tell; to propose, promise, offer as a reward* or *hold over as a threat; to imagine, put before the mind; to propose to oneself, purpose, intend.* N. of partic. as subst. **prōpŏsĭtum** -i, *a design, purpose; the subject* or *theme of a discourse; the first premiss of a syllogism.*
prŏporrō, adv. *further, moreover,* or *altogether.*
prŏportĭo -ōnis, f. *proportion, analogy, similarity.*
prōpŏsĭtĭo -ōnis, f. *a purpose; the subject of a discourse*; in logic, *the first proposition of a syllogism.*
prōpŏsĭtum -i, n. subst. from propono; q.v.
prōpraetor -ōris, m. (and **prō praetōre**) *a praetor's deputy; an ex-praetor,* sent as governor to a province or given a military command.
proprĭĕtās -ātis, f. *a property, peculiarity; ownership.*
proprĭtim, *peculiarly, specially.*
proprĭus -a -um, *one's own, special, peculiar characteristic; lasting, permanent.* Hence adv. **proprĭē,** *exclusively, peculiarly, characteristically; in a proper sense.*
propter. Adv., *near, close by.* Prep. with acc. *near; on account of, because of.*
proptĕrĕā, adv. *on that account, therefore.*
prōpŭdĭum -i, n. *a shameful action; a wretch, villain.*
prōpugnācŭlum -i, n. *a fortification rampart, defence.*
prōpugnātĭo -ōnis, f. *defence.*
prōpugnātor -ōris, m. *a defender.*
prōpugno -are, *to skirmish in front; fight in defence, defend.*

prōpulso -are, *to drive back, repel, ward off.*
prō-quaestōre, *an ex-quaestor who helped to govern a province.*
prōquam (or **prō quam**), *in proportion as, according as.*
prōra -ae, f. *the prow, bow of a ship*; poet., *a ship.*
prōrēpo -rēpěre -repsi, *to creep forward, crawl forth.*
prōrēta -ae, and **prōrēus** -i, m. *a look-out man.*
prōrĭpĭo -rĭpěre -rĭpŭi -reptum, *to snatch, tear, drag forth*; se proripere, *to rush forward.*
prōrŏgātĭo -ōnis, f. *prolongation of a term of office; deferring.*
prōrŏgo -are, *to prolong; to defer, put off.*
prorsum and **prorsŭs,** *forwards, straight ahead.* Transf., *utterly, wholly; in a word, to sum up.*
prorsus (**prōsus**) -a -um, *straightforward*; of style, *in prose.*
prōrumpo -rumpěre -rūpi -ruptum: transit., *to cause to break out, to thrust out*; prorupta audacia, *unbridled*; intransit., *to burst forth, break out.*
prōrŭo -rŭěre -rŭi -rŭtum: intransit., *to rush forth, to fall down*; transit., *to fling forward* or *down, overthrow, destroy.*
prōsāpĭa -ae, f. *family, race, stock.*
proscaenĭum -i, n. *the stage of a theatre.*
proscindo -scinděre -scĭdi -scissum, *to tear up; to break up fallow land, plough up.* Transf., *to censure, defame, satirize.*
proscrībo -scrīběre -scripsi -scriptum, *to make publicly known, publish; to offer publicly for sale* or *hire, advertise; to confiscate; to proscribe, outlaw.*
proscriptĭo -ōnis, f. *an advertisement of sale; a proscription, outlawry.*
proscriptŭrĭo -ire, *to desire a proscription.*
prōsěco -sěcare -sěcŭi -sectum, *to cut off; to plough up.* N. of partic. as subst. **prōsectum** -i, *part of a victim cut out to be offered to a god; the entrails.*
prōsěda -ae, f. *a prostitute.*
prōsēmĭno -are, *to sow* or *scatter as seed; to disseminate.*
prōsěquor -sěqui -sěcūtus, dep. *to follow* or *accompany out, to 'see off'*; in hostile sense, *to attack, pursue*; in gen., *to attend; to go on with, continue; to imitate.*
Prŏserpĭna -ae, f. *the daughter of Ceres, carried off by Pluto to the lower world.*
prŏseucha -ae, f. *a (Jewish) house of prayer, a conventicle.*
prōsĭlĭo -ire -ŭi (-īvi or -ĭi), *to spring up, leap forth.*
prōsŏcer -ěri, m. *a wife's grandfather.*
prospecto -are, *to look forward, look out upon, survey; to look forward to, expect.*
prospectus -ūs, m. *outlook, view, prospect; sight, gaze.*
prospěcŭlor -ari, dep. intransit., *to explore, reconnoitre*; transit., *to look out for, wait for.*
prosper (**prospěrus**) -a -um, *fortunate, favourable, lucky, prosperous*; n. pl. as subst. *prosperity, good fortune.* Adv. **prospěrē.**
prospěrĭtās -ātis, f. *prosperity, good fortune.*
prospěro -are, *to make fortunate, cause to succeed.*
prospěrus = prosper; q.v.
prospĭcĭentĭa -ae, f. *foresight, precaution.*
prospĭcĭo -spĭcěre -spexi -spectum: intransit., *to look forward, look out; to take care, exercise foresight*; transit., *to see ahead, make out in the distance; to look towards; to foresee; to look out for, provide, procure.*
prosterno -sterněre -strāvi -strātum, *to cast down; to debase; to overthrow, destroy, ruin.*
prostĭtŭo -stĭtŭěre -stĭtŭi -stĭtūtum, *to prostitute.*
prosto -stare -stĭti, *to stand out, project; to be exposed for sale; to prostitute oneself.*
prōsŭbĭgō -ěre, *to dig up, root up.*
prōsum prōdesse prōfŭi, *to be useful, do good, benefit* (with dat.).
prōtěgo -těgěre -texi -tectum, *to cover in front; to cover over, protect; to furnish with a roof.*
prōtēlum -i, n. *a team of oxen; a series, succession.*
prōtendo -tenděre -tendi -tentum, *to stretch forward, stretch out.*
prōtěnŭs = protinus; q.v.
prōtěro -těrěre -trīvi -trītum, *to trample under foot, tread down; to overthrow, rout, defeat; to drive away, push aside.*
prōterrěo -ēre, *to scare away.*
prŏtervĭtās -ātis, f. *boldness, impudence; pertness.*
prŏtervus -a -um, *bold, impudent*; in milder sense, *pert*; of things, *violent.* Adv. **prŏtervē.**
Prōtěus -ěi and -ěos, m. *a god of the sea, with the power of changing himself into different shapes.*
prōtĭnam, *immediately, at once.*
prōtĭnŭs (**prōtěnŭs**), adv. *forward, further on*; of time, *continuously* or *immediately.*
prōtollo -ěre, *to put forward; to lengthen, prolong.*
prōtrăho -trăhěre -traxi -tractum, *to draw, forward, drag out; to bring to light, reveal, make known; to compel, force; to protract, defer.*
prōtrūdo -trūděre -trūsi -trūsum, *to push forward, thrust out; to put off, defer.*
prōturbo -are, *to drive forward, drive away; to throw down, overcome.*
prŏŭt, *just as, according as.*
prōvěho -věhěre -vexi -vectum, *to carry forward; to carry on; to advance, promote*; pass., provehi, *to ride forward, drive, sail,* and fig. *to be carried away.*
Hence partic. **prōvectus** -a -um, *advanced,* esp. *in age.*

prōvĕnĭo -vĕnire -vēni -ventum, *to come on, appear*; of corn, *to come up, grow*; of events, *to result, come about*; esp. *to turn out well, succeed.*
prōventus -ūs, m. *coming forth, growing; product, crop; result, issue, success.*
prōverbĭum -i, n. *a proverb.*
prōvĭdentĭa -ae, f. *foresight, foreknowledge; forethought, providence.*
prōvĭdĕo -vĭdēre -vīdi -vīsum, *to look forward to, see at a distance; to see beforehand, foresee; to take precautions for* or *against, provide for, make preparation for.*
Hence partic. **prōvĭdens** -entis, *provident, prudent*; adv. **prōvĭdentĕr.** N. abl. of perf. partic. **prōvīsō,** *with forethought.*
prōvĭdus -a -um, *foreseeing; providing, taking measures for*; in gen., *cautious, prudent.*
prōvincĭa -ae, f. *employment, sphere of duty, office*, esp. that of a magistrate. Transf., *a country governed by a Roman magistrate, a province.*
prōvincĭālis -e, *of a province*; m. as subst., esp. plur., *inhabitants of provinces, provincials.*
prōvīsĭo -ōnis, f. *foresight*; hence *provision, planning.*
prōvīso -ĕre, *to look out for, go to see.*
prōvīsor -ōris, m. *one who provides for* or *against.*
prōvīsū, abl. sing. m. *by foreseeing; by providing for* or *against.*
provixisse, perf. infin. *to have lived on.*
prōvŏcātĭo -ōnis, f. *a challenge*; esp. *an appeal to a higher court.*
prōvŏcātor -ōris, m. *a challenger; a kind of gladiator.*
prōvŏco -are, *to call out; to excite, rouse, provoke; to challenge to a contest*; legal, *to appeal to a higher court.*
prōvŏlo -are, *to fly forth, to rush out.*
prōvolvo -volvĕre -volvi -vŏlūtum, *to roll forward, roll over and over*; provolvere se, and provolvi, *to throw oneself down*, hence *to abase oneself.*
prōvŏmo -ĕre, *to vomit forth.*
prōxĭmĭtās -atis, f. *nearness, close connexion; similarity.*
proxĭmus -a -um, superl.; see propior.
prūdens -entis, *foreseeing, aware; skilled, experienced, practised; prudent, discreet, judicious.* Adv. **prūdentĕr.**
prūdentĭa -ae, f. *foresight; knowledge; sagacity, discretion.*
prŭīna -ae, f. *hoar-frost, rime.*
prŭīnōsus -a -um, *frosty.*
prūna -ae, f. *a live coal.*
prunĭtĭus -a -um, *of plum-tree wood.*
prūnum -i, n. *a plum.*
prūnus -i, f. *plum-tree.*
prūrīgo -ĭnis, f. *the itch.*
prūrĭo -ire, *to itch.*
prȳtănēum -i, n. *the town-hall in a Greek city.*
prȳtănis -is, acc. -in, m. *chief magistrate in a Greek state.*
psallo psallĕre psalli, *to play on* or *sing to a stringed instrument.*
psaltērĭum -i, n. *a stringed instrument.*
psaltrĭa -ae, f. *a female player on the* cithara.
psĕcăs -ădis, f. *an anointer of hair.*
pseudŏthȳrum -i, n. *a secret door.*
psīthĭa (vitis) -ae, f. *a kind of Greek vine.*
psittăcus -i, m. *parrot.*
psȳchŏmantīum or **-ēum** -i n. *a place of necromancy*
-ptĕ, suffix, *self, own.*
ptĭsănārĭum -i, n. *a decoction of crushed barley* or *rice.*
pūbens -entis, of plants, *in full growth, luxuriant.*
pūbĕr -bĕris = pubes; q.v.
pūbertās -ātis, f. *puberty, the age of maturity; signs of puberty, growth of hair*, etc.
[1]**pūbēs** -is, f. *the signs of puberty, growth of hair*, etc.; *the youth, adult male population.*
[2]**pūbēs** and **pūbĕr** -ĕris, *arrived at the age of puberty, adult, ripe*; m. pl. as subst. **pūbĕres** -um, *the men, the adult male population.*
pūbesco -bescĕre -bŭi, *to grow up, arrive at maturity.*
publĭcānus -a -um, *of the farming of the public taxes*; m. as subst. *a farmer of the Roman taxes.*
publĭcātĭo -ōnis, f. *confiscation.*
publĭcĭtŭs, *at the public expense, in the public service; publicly.*
publĭco -are, *to confiscate; to make public, throw open, publish.*
publĭcus -a -um, *belonging to the people, public*; res publica, or respublica, *the state.* Transf., *universal, general; common, ordinary.* M. as subst. **publĭcus** -i, *a state official*; N. **publĭcum** -i, *public territory; the public revenue, the treasury; an open place, the open street.* Adv. **publĭcē,** *for the people, publicly, at the public expense; all together.*
Publĭus -i, m. *a Roman praenomen*, abbrev. P.
pŭdĕo -ēre, *to be ashamed*; usually 3rd person, *to cause shame, fill with shame*; often impers., **pŭdet;** te huius templi pudet, *you are ashamed of.* Hence gerundive **pŭdendus** -a -um, *shameful, disgraceful.* Partic. **pŭdens** -entis, *modest, shamefaced*; adv. **pŭdentĕr,** *modestly, bashfully.*
pŭdĭbundus -a -um, *modest, bashful.*
pŭdīcĭtĭa -ae, f. *modesty, chastity, virtue.*
pŭdīcus -a -um, *modest, chaste, virtuous*; adv. **pŭdīcē.**
pŭdor -ōris, m. *feeling of shame, bashfulness, decency, honour; chastity, purity; that which causes shame, a disgrace.*
pŭella -ae, f. *a girl, maiden; a young woman, young wife*, or *sweetheart.*
pŭellāris -e, *girlish, maidenly.* Adv. **pŭellārĭtĕr.**
pŭellŭla -ae, f. *a little girl.*
pŭellus -i, m. *a little boy.*

pŭer -i, m. *a child*; in plur., *children*; esp. *a boy, lad*; a puero, a pueris, *from boyhood.* Transf., *a serving-lad, page, slave.*
pŭĕrīlis -e, *youthful, boyish; puerile, silly, childish.* Adv. **pŭĕrīlĭtĕr,** *boyishly; childishly.*
pŭĕrĭtĭa -ae, f. *boyhood.*
pŭerpĕrĭum -i, n. *childbirth, labour.*
pŭerpĕrus -a -um, *of childbirth;* f. as subst. *a woman in labour.*
pŭertĭa = pueritia; q.v.
pŭĕrŭlus -i, m. *a little boy, young slave.*
pūga (pȳga) -ae, f. *the rump, buttocks.*
pŭgil -ĭlis, m. *a boxer, fighter with the* caestus.
pŭgĭlātĭo -ōnis, f. *fighting with the* caestus; *boxing.*
pŭgillāris -e, *that can be grasped with the fist*; m. pl. as subst. **pŭgillāres** -ĭum (sc. libelli), *writing-tablets.*
pūgĭo -ōnis, m. *a dagger, dirk, poniard.*
pūgĭuncŭlus -i, m. *a little dagger.*
pugna -ae, f. *a fight, battle; battle-line, array*; in gen., *contest.*
pugnācĭtās -ātis, f. *desire to fight, pugnacity.*
pugnācŭlum -i, n. *a fortress.*
pugnātor -ōris, m. *a fighter, combatant.*
pugnax -ācis, *fond of fighting, combative; obstinate, contentious.* Adv. **pugnācĭtĕr.**
pugno -are, *to fight, give battle; to struggle, contend, fight, to strive, exert oneself.*
pugnus -i m. *the fist.*
pulchellus -a -um, *pretty.*
pulcher -chra -chrum and **pulcer** -cra -crum, *beautiful, lovely*; morally *excellent, fine.* Adv. **pulchrē (pulcrē)**, *beautifully, finely*; as exclamation, *bravo! well done!*
pulchrĭtūdo -ĭnis, f. *beauty, excellence.*
pūlēium (pūlēgĭum) -i, n *fleabane, penny-royal.*
pūlex -ĭcis, m. *a flea.*
pullārĭus -i, m. *feeder of sacred chickens.*
pullātus -a -um, *clad in dirty or black garments.*
pullŭlo -are, *to shoot up, sprout, burgeon, luxuriate.*
[1]**pullus** -i, m. *a young animal*; esp. *a chicken, chick.*
[2]**pullus** -a -um, *dark-coloured, blackish*; poet., *sad, gloomy.* N. as subst. *a dark garment.*
pulmentārĭum -i, n. *a relish.*
pulmentum -i. n. *a relish*; in gen., *food, victuals.*
pulmo -ōnis, m. *the lung* (usually plur.).
pulpa -ae, f. *flesh.*
pulpāmentum -i, n. *flesh*, esp. *tit-bits.*
pulpĭtum -i, n. *a platform* or *stage.*
puls pultis, f. *porridge, pulse.*
pulsātĭo -ōnis, f. *knocking, beating.*
pulso -are, *to strike, beat, knock; to stir, move, affect.*
pulsus -ūs, m. *beating, blow, push; influence, impulse.*
pulto -are, to *knock, strike.*
pulvĕrĕus -a -um, *full of dust, dusty.*
pulvĕrŭlentus -a -um, *full of dust, dusty.*
pulvillus -i, m. *a little pillow.*
pulvīnar -aris, n. *a couch*, esp. *one carrying images of the gods at the* Lectisternium (q.v.).
pulvīnārĭum -i, n. *anchorage.*
pulvīnus -i, m. *pillow, cushion; a seat of honour.*
pulvis -ĕris, m. (rarely f.) *dust, powder.* Transf., *arena, scene of action*; sine pulvere palmae, *prize without effort.*
pūmex -ĭcis, m. *pumice-stone; any soft, porous stone.*
pūmĭcĕus -a -um, *made of pumice-stone.*
pūmĭco -are, *to polish with pumice-stone.*
pūmĭlĭo -ōnis, c. and **pūmĭlus** -i, m. *a dwarf.*
punctim, *by stabbing, by thrusting* (opp. caesim).
pungo pungĕre pŭpŭgi punctum, *to prick, puncture, stab; to touch, move, penetrate; to sting, vex, annoy.* N. of partic. as subst. **punctum** -i, *a prick, a little hole, small puncture; a point, spot.* Hence *a vote; a moment of time*; in speech, etc., *a short clause, section.*
pūnĭcĕus -a -um, *purple, red.*
Pūnĭcus; see Poeni.
pūnĭo (poenĭo) -ire and **pūnior** -iri dep. *to punish; to avenge.*
pūnītor -ōris, m. *punisher, avenger.*
pūpa -ae, f. *a little girl; a doll.*
pūpilla -ae, f. (1) *an orphan girl, ward, minor.* (2) *the pupil of the eye.*
pūpillāris -e, *of an orphan* or *ward.*
pūpillus -i, m. *an orphan* or *ward.*
puppis -is, f. *the poop* or *stern of a vessel*; poet., *the whole ship.*
pūpŭla -ae, f. *the pupil of the eye.*
purgāmen -ĭnis, n. (1) *sweepings, filth.* (2) *a means of purgation.*
purgāmentum -i, n. *sweepings, rubbish, filth.*
purgātĭo -ōnis, f. *cleaning out, cleansing; excusing, justification.*
purgo -are. (1) *to clean, cleanse, purify.* Hence *to excuse, defend, justify; to allege in defence.* (2) *to clear away wash off.*
purpŭra -ae, f. *the purple-fish.* Transf., *purple dye; purple cloth;* '*the purple*', = *high rank,* etc.
purpŭrātus -a -um, *clad in purple.* M. as subst., *a man of high rank, a courtier.*
purpŭrĕus -a -um, *purple-coloured; dark-red, dark-brown.* Transf., *clad in purple*; in gen., *gleaming, bright, beautiful.*
pūrus -a -um, *clean, pure, cleared.* Transf., *without addition, simple. plain*; morally, *upright, pure*; of style, *pure, faultless*; legally, *without conditions, absolute.* N. as subst. *the clear sky.* Adv **pūrē** and poet. **pūrĭtĕr,** *purely, cleanly*; of style *faultlessly.*
pūs pūris, n. *corrupt matter; bitterness.*

pŭsillus -a -um, *tiny; puny; petty, mean.*
pūsĭo -onis, m. *little boy.*
pŭtāmen -ĭnis, n. *cutting, paring, shell*
pŭtātor -ōris, m. *pruner.*
pŭtĕal -ālis, n. *stone curb round the mouth of a well* or *sacred place.*
pŭtĕālis -e, *of a well.*
pūtĕo -ēre, *to stink.*
pūter -tris -tre and **putris** -e, *rotten, putrid; loose, crumbling, friable, flabby.*
pūtesco pūtescĕre, *to decay.*
pŭtĕus -i, m. *a well, pit.*
pūtĭdus -a -um, *rotten, stinking, foul*; of style, *affected, in bad taste*; adv. **pūtĭdē,** *affectedly.*
pŭto -are, *to cleanse, clear*; of trees, *to lop.* Transf., *to clear up, settle,* esp. of accounts; hence *to weigh up, ponder, reckon, estimate; to consider, believe, think*; parenthetically, puto or ut puto, *I suppose.*
putrĕfăcĭo -făcĕre -fēci -factum *to make rotten* or *soft.*
putresco -ĕre, *to become rotten.*
putrĭdus -a -um, *rotten, decayed.*
pŭtus -a -um, *pure, unmixed, unadulterated.*
pȳga = puga; q.v.
Pygmaei -orum, m. *the Pygmies, a race of dwarfs in Africa.*
pȳra -ae, f. *funeral pyre.*
pȳrămis -ĭdis, f. *pyramid*; hence *a cone.*
pȳrōpus -i, m. *bronze.*
Pyrrhus -i, m. (1) *son of Achilles.* (2) *a king of Epirus, enemy of the Romans.*
Pȳthăgŏras -ae, m. *Greek philosopher of Samos* (about 540 B.C.).
Pȳtho -ūs, f. *the old name of Delphi*; adj. **Pȳthĭcus, Pȳthĭus** -a -um, *Delphic, relating to Apollo*; f. as subst., *the priestess of Apollo*; n. pl., *the Pythian games, celebrated every fourth year in honour of Apollo.*
pyxis -ĭdis, f. *a little box, casket.*

Q

Q, q, the sixteenth letter of the Latin Alphabet, only used before u and another vowel.
quā, abl. f. of qui, as adv.: relat., *by which way, where*; also *whereby,* or *as far as*; qua . . . qua, *partly . . . partly*; interrog., *by what way? how?*; indef., *in any way, at all.*
quăcumque (-cunque), *wherever; by whatever way.*
quădamtĕnŭs, *to a certain point.*
quadra -ae, f. *a square*; used of any square object or square piece.
quadrāgēni -ae -a, *forty at a time, forty each.*
quadrāgēsĭmus (-ensĭmus) -a -um, *fortieth*; f. as subst. *the fortieth part,* esp. *as a tax.*
quadrāgĭēs (-ĭens), *forty times.*
quadrāgintā, *forty.*
quadrans -antis, m. *a fourth part, quarter*; as a coin, *the fourth part of an* as.
quadrantārĭus -a -um, *of a quarter*; of price, *costing a quarter of an* as.
quadrīdŭum (quatrīdŭum) -i, n. *a space of four days.*
quadrĭennĭum -i, n. *a period of four years.*
quadrĭfārĭam, *in four parts.*
quadrĭfĭdus -a -um, *split into four.*
quadrīgae -arum, f. *a team of four horses abreast,* esp. drawing a chariot.
quadrīgārĭus -a -um, *of a racing charioteer.*
quadrīgātus -a -um, *stamped with the figure of a four-horse chariot.*
quadrīgŭlae -arum, f. *a little team of four horses.*
quadrĭiŭgis -e, *in a team of four.*
quadrĭiŭgus -a -um, *in* or *with a team of four.*
quadrīmus -a -um, *four years old.*
quadringēnārĭus -a -um, *of four hundred each.*
quadringēni -ae -a, *four hundred at a time, four hundred each.*
quadringentēsĭmus (-ensĭmus) -a -um, *four hundredth.*
quadringenti -ae -a, *four hundred.*
quadringentĭens (-ĭēs), *four hundred times.*
quadrĭpertītus -a -um, *divided into four parts, fourfold.*
quadrĭrēmis -e, *with four banks of oars*; f. as subst., *a quadrireme.*
quadrĭvĭum -i, n. *a crossroads, place where four roads meet.*
quadro -are: transit., *to make square; to join properly together;* intransit., *to be square; to fit exactly, to suit*; esp. of accounts, *to agree.* Partic. **quadrātus** -a -um, *squared, square*; n. as subst., *a square.*
quadrum -i, n. *a square.*
quadrŭpĕdans -antis, *going on four feet, galloping*; plur. as subst., *horses.*
quadrŭpēs -pĕdis, *four-footed, on four feet*; as subst., *a quadruped.*
quadruplātor -ōris, m. *a multiplier by four; an exaggerator; an informer.*
quadruplēx -plĭcis, *fourfold, quadruple.*
quadruplor -ari, dep. *to be an informer.*
quadruplus -a -um, *fourfold*; n. as subst., *four times the amount.*
quaerĭto -are, *to seek* or *enquire about eagerly.*
quaero quaerĕre quaesĭi *or* quaesīvi quaesītum, *to seek, search for*; sometimes *to obtain, get; to miss, want; to seek to know, ask, enquire into* a matter. Partic. **quaesītus** -a -um, *sought out; unusual, select*; in bad sense, *far-fetched, affected*; n. as subst., *a question* or *a gain.*
quaesītĭo -ōnis, f. *an interrogation.*
quaesītor -ōris, m. *investigator, inquirer,* esp. judicial.
quaeso -ĕre, *to seek for, ask for*; first person, quaeso, *I beg.*
quaestĭo -ōnis, f. *seeking, searching; inquiry, investigation*; esp. *judicial inquiry*; quaestiones perpetuae, *standing courts of justice.*
quaestĭuncŭla -ae, f. *a little question.*
quaestor -ōris, m. *one of the quaestors, magistrates in Rome, occupied with matters of law and finance.*

quaestōrĭus -a -um, *belonging to a* quaestor. N. as subst., *the quaestor's tent in camp,* or *residence in a province.* M. as subst., *an ex-quaestor.*

quaestŭōsus -a -um, *profitable; fond of gain; having gained much, rich.*

quaestūra -ae, f. *the office of quaestor, quaestorship.*

quaestus -ūs, m. *gaining, getting, profit; a source of profit, occupation, business.*

quālĭbĕt (quālŭbĕt) *wherever you like; in any way you please.*

quālis -e: interrog., *of what kind?*; relat. (with or without antecedent talis), *of the kind that, such as*; indef., *having some quality or other.* Adv. **quālĭtĕr,** *as, just as.*

quāliscumque (-cunque) qualecumque: relat., *of whatever kind*; indef., *any whatever.*

quālislĭbĕt, quālĕlĭbĕt, *of what sort you will.*

quālĭtās -ātis, f. *quality, property.*

quālus -i, m. and **quālum** -i, n. *wicker-basket.*

quam, adv. *how, in what way*: interrog., *how much? how?*; exclam., *how!*; relat., of correspondence, *as* (often with tam); with superl. adj. or adv., *as . . . as possible* (with or without possum); quam primum, *as soon as possible*; of comparison, *than, as.*

quamlĭbĕt (quamlŭbĕt), *as much as you please.*

quamobrem (quam ob rem): interrog., *wherefore? why?*; relat., *for which reason, wherefore.*

quamquam (quanquam), *although, though;* at the beginning of a sentence, *nevertheless, and yet.*

quamvīs, *as much as you please, ever so much*; as conj., *however much, although.*

quānam, *by what way?*

quandō, *when*: interrog., *when?*; indef., *at any time, ever*; relat., *at the time when*; sometimes causal, *since, because.*

quandōcumque (-cunque): relat., *whenever, as often as*; indef., *at some time or other.*

quandōquĕ: relat., *whenever, as often as*; indef., *at some time or other.*

quandŏquĭdem, *since, because.*

quantŏpĕrĕ (quantō ŏpĕrĕ), *with what great trouble; how much.*

quantŭlus -a -um, *how little, how small.*

quantŭluscumque -ăcumque -umcumque, *however small.*

quantus -a -um; interrog., *how great?*; exclam., *how great!*; relat. (with or without tantus), *(as great) as*; quantus quantus, *however great.* N. as subst. **quantum**: interrog., *how much?*; exclam., *how much!*; relat., *as much as*; quantum in me est, *as far as in me lies.* Neuter in genit. (or locative) of price, **quantī,** *for how much, at what price*; in abl., **quantō,** *(by) how much,* with compar. adj. or adv.

quantuscumque -acumque -umcumque, *however great.*

quantuslĭbĕt -tălĭbĕt -tumlĭbĕt, *as great as you will, however great.*

quantusvīs -ăvīs -umvīs, *as great as you please, however great.*

quāpropter, *wherefore.*

quārē (quā rē), *wherefore.*

quartădĕcŭmāni -orum, m. *soldiers of the fourteenth legion.*

quartānus -a -um, *of the fourth*; f. as subst. (sc. febris) *a quartan fever*; m. pl. as subst., *the soldiers of the fourth legion.*

quartārĭus -i, m. *the fourth part of a sextarius.*

quartus -a -um, *the fourth*; f. as subst., *the fourth hour*; n. acc. or abl. **quartum, quartō,** *for the fourth time.*

quartusdĕcĭmus -a -um, *fourteenth.*

quăsĭ, *as if, just as,* esp. in hypothetical comparisons; also with descriptions, *as it were, a sort of*; with numerals, *about.*

quăsillus -i, m. and **quăsillum** -i, n. *little basket.*

quassātĭo -ōnis, *f. a shaking.*

quasso -are: transit., *to shake violently; to shatter, break in pieces;* intransit., *to shake.*

quătĕfăcĭo -făcĕre -fēci, *to shake, weaken.*

quātĕnŭs, *how far, to what extent; in so far as, since.*

quătĕr, *four times*; hence *again and again.*

quăterni -ae -a, *four at a time, four each.*

quătĭo quătĕre quassi quassum, *to shake, brandish, agitate*; sometimes *to shatter.*

quattŭor, *four.*

quattŭordĕcim, *fourteen.*

quattŭorvĭrātus -ūs, m. *the office of the* quattuorviri.

quattŭorvĭri -ōrum, m. *a board of four magistrates.*

-quĕ, enclitic conj., *and*; repeated, -que . . . -que, *both . . . and . . .*

queis = quibus; *see* qui.

quĕmadmŏdum (quem ad mŏdum), *in what manner, how* (interrog. or relat.); esp. corresponding with sic, ita, item, etc., *as, just as.*

quĕo quīre quīvi and quĭi quĭtum, *to be able.*

quercētum -i, n. *an oak-wood.*

quercĕus -a -um, *oaken.*

quercus -ūs, f. *the oak*; sometimes *a crown of oak leaves.*

quĕrēla (quĕrella) -ae, f. *a complaint, complaining.*

quĕrĭbundus -a -um, *complaining, plaintive.*

quĕrĭmōnĭa -ae, f. *a complaining, complaint.*

quĕrĭtor -ari, dep., *to complain excessively.*

quernus -a -um, *of oak, oaken.*

quĕror quĕri questus, dep. *to complain, lament, bewail*; of animals, *to make a plaintive sound.*

querquētŭlānus -a -um, *of an oak-wood.*

quĕrŭlus -a -um, *complaining, plaintive.*

questus -ūs, m. *complaint, lament.*

[1]**quī** quae quod: interrog. adj., *which? what? what kind of?*; exclam., *what!*; indef., (with f. quae or qua) *any, some*; relat., *who, which, what, that.* Acc. n. sing., **quod,** as adv.: quod sciam, *as far as I know.* Abl. **quō,** with comparatives: quo celerius, eo melius, *the faster the better.*

[2]**quī** (old abl. of [1]qui): interrog., *in what manner? how?*; relat., *wherewith, wherefrom*; indef., *somehow.*

quiă, *because.*

quiănam, quiănĕ, *why?*

quīcum, *with whom, with which.*

quīcumque (**-cunque**) quaecumque quodcumque: relat., *whoever, whichever, whatever*; indef., *any available.*

quīdam quaedam quoddam (subst. quiddam), *a certain person* or *thing* (known but not necessarily named). Transf., *a kind of.*

quĭdem, *indeed*; ne . . . quidem *not, even . . .*

quidnī? *why not?*

quĭēs -ētis, f. *rest, quiet; peace; sleep; a dream; a resting-place.*

quĭesco -escĕre -ēvi -ētum, *to rest; to be at peace; to sleep; to cease* from action.

quietus -a -um, *resting; sleeping; at peace, undisturbed, neutral*; of character, *quiet, calm.* Adv. **quĭētē.**

quīlĭbĕt quaelĭbĕt quodlĭbĕt (subst. **quidlibet**), *any you will, anyone, anything.*

quīn: in questions, *why not?*; in commands, to encourage, *but come now*; in statements, *rather, but indeed*; in subordinate clauses, with subjunctive, *but that, without, that not, who not.*

quīnam quaenam quodnam, *which, what?*

quincunx -cuncis, *five-twelfths.*

quindĕcĭens (**-ĭēs**), *fifteen times.*

quindĕcim, *fifteen.*

quindĕcimprīmi -orum, m. *the fifteen chief senators of a* municipium.

quindĕcimvir -i, m. *one of a board of fifteen magistrates.*

quindĕcimvĭrālis -e, *of the* quindecimviri.

quindēni or **quīni dēni** -ae -a, *fifteen at a time, fifteen each.*

quingēni -ae -a, *five hundred at a time, five hundred each.*

quingentēsĭmus (**-ēnsĭmus**) -a -um, *five hundredth.*

quingenti -ae -a, *five hundred.*

quingentĭens (**-ĭēs**), *five hundred times.*

quīni -ae -a, *five at a time, five each.*

quīnīvīcēni -ae -a, *twenty-five each.*

quinquāgēni -ae -a, *fifty at a time, fifty each.*

quinquāgēsĭmus (**-ensĭmus**) -a -um, *fiftieth*; f. as subst. *(a tax of) a fiftieth part.*

quinquāgintā, *fifty.*

quinquātrūs -ŭum, f. pl., and **quinquātrĭa** -ōrum and -ĭum, n. pl. *a festival of Minerva.*

quinquĕ, *five.*

quinquennālis -e, *happening every five years,* or *lasting for five years.*

quinquennis -e, *of five years; five years old.*

quinquennĭum -i, n. *a period of five years.*

quinquĕpertītus -a -um, *in five portions, fivefold.*

quinquĕprīmi -orum, m. *the five chief senators in a* municipium.

quinquĕrēmis -e, *having five banks of oars*; f. as subst., *a quinquereme.*

quinquĕvir -i, m., *one of a board of five.*

quinquĕvĭrātus -ūs, m. *the office of* quinquevir.

quinquĭēs (**-ĭens**), *five times.*

quinquiplĭco -are, *to multiply by five.*

quintădĕcĭmāni -ōrum, m. *soldiers of the fifteenth legion.*

quintānus -a -um, *of the fifth*; f. as subst. (sc. via), *a road in a Roman camp*; m. pl., *soldiers of the fifth legion.*

Quintĭlĭānus (**Quinct-**) -i, m. M. Fabius Quintilianus, *head of a school of rhetoric at Rome.*

Quintīlis (**Quinctīlis**) -is, m. (with or without mensis), *the fifth month afterwards called Iulius.*

[1]**quintus** -a -um, *fifth*; quintum, quinto, *for the fifth time.*

[2]**Quintus** (abbrev. Q.) and f. **Quinta,** *a Roman* praenomen.

quintusdĕcĭmus -a -um, *fifteenth.*

quippĕ, *certainly, indeed, to be sure of course.*

quippĭnī, *why not?*

Quĭrīnus -i, m. *the name of Romulus after his apotheosis*; adj. **Quĭrīnus** -a -um, and **Quĭrīnālis** -e, *of Romulus*: collis, *the Quirinal Hill* at Rome; n. pl. **Quĭrīnālĭa** -ium, *a festival in honour of Romulus.*

[1]**Quĭrīs** -itis and pl. **Quĭrītēs** -ĭum and -um, m. *the inhabitants of the Sabine town Cures*; also used of *the citizens of Rome* in their civil capacity.

[2]**quĭris** or **cŭris,** *a spear.*

quĭrītātĭo -ōnis, f. *a shriek, scream.*

quĭrīto -are, *to shriek, scream, cry out.*

[1]**quĭs** quĭd, pron.: interrog., *who? what? which?*; indef., *anyone, anybody, anything.* N. nom. and acc. **quĭd?** *what?*; with genit., *how much? how many?* sometimes *why?*; quid ita? *why so?*

[2]**quīs** = quibus; *see* qui.

quisnam quaenam quidnam, pron. *who? what?*

quispĭam quaepĭam quodpĭam (subst. quidpĭam, quippĭam), *anyone, anything; someone, something*; n. acc. as adv. *at all.*

quisquam quaequam quidquam (quicquam), *anybody, anyone, anything,* esp. in negative sentences and questions.

quisque quaeque quidque (adj. quodque), *each, every, everyone, everything,*

quisquĭlĭae -arum, f. pl. *rubbish, sweepings, refuse.*

quisquis quaequae quidquid (quicquid), and adj. quodquod: relat., *whoever, whatever, whichever*; indef., *anyone, anything.*

quīvīs quaevīs quidvīs (adj. quodvīs), *whoever* or *whatever you will, anyone, anything.*

quīviscumque quaeviscumque quodviscumque, *whosoever, whatsoever.*

[1]**quō**: interrog., *where? to what place? whither? how far? to what extent? to what end?*; indef., *to any place, anywhither*; relat., *to the end that, in order that.*

[2]**quō,** *because, whereby*; see also quominus.

quoad, *how far; as far as, as long as*; also *until.*

quōcircā, *wherefore, on which account.*

quōcumque, *whithersoever*

quod, conj.; *the fact that, the point that; as to the fact that, whereas; because, on the ground that; why, on which account;* with temporal clause, *since; as far as, to the extent that*; introducing a fresh sentence, *and, but, now,* esp. foll. by si.

quōdammŏdo, *in a certain way in a certain measure.*

quōiās = cuias; q.v.

quōlĭbĕt, *whithersoever you please.*

quōmĭnŭs, *by which the less, so that not.*

quōmŏdo, *in what manner, how.*

quōmŏdocumquĕ, *in whatever way; somehow.*

quōmŏdonam, *how then?*

quōnam, *whither then?*

quondam, in the past, *formerly, once*; in the future, *sometime*; in gen., *at times, sometimes.*

quŏnĭam, *since, whereas, because.*

quōpĭam, and **quōquam,** *to any place at all.*

quŏquĕ, placed after the word which it emphasizes, *also, too.*

quōquō or **quō quō,** *whithersoever, to whatever place.*

quōquōversŭs (**-versum, -vorsum**), *in every direction.*

quorsum (**quorsŭs**), *whither? to what place? to what purpose?*

quŏt, indecl., *how many* (interrog. and exclam.); relat. (often with tot) *as many*; quot annis, *every year.*

quŏtannīs = quot annis; *see* quot.

quotcumquĕ, *as many as, however many.*

quŏtēni -ae -a, *how many each.*

quŏtīdĭānus (**cottīdĭānus, cŏtīd-**), *daily, of every day; everyday, common, ordinary.*

quŏtīdĭē (**cottīdĭē, cŏtīd-**), *daily, every day.*

quŏtĭēs (**quŏtĭens**), *how often* (interrog. and exclam.); relat. (often with toties), *as often as.*

quŏtĭescumquĕ (**-cunquĕ**), *however often.*

quotquŏt, indecl., *however many.*

quŏtus -a -um, *which in number?* quota pars, *how small a fraction?*; quotus quisque, *one in how many? how rare?*

quŏtuscumquĕ (**-cunquĕ**) -ăcumquĕ -umcumquĕ, *whatever in number*; pars quotacumque, *however small a fraction.*

quŏtusquisquĕ; *see* quotus.

quŏusquĕ (**quō usquĕ**), *how long? how far?*

quōvīs, *to whatever place you will.*

quum = [2]cum; q.v.

R

R, r, seventeenth letter of the Latin Alphabet.

răbĭdus -a -um, *raging, mad, savage;* adv. **răbĭdē.**

răbĭēs -ēi, f. *madness, rage, fury, frenzy.*

răbĭōsŭlus -a -um, *rather furious.*

răbĭōsus -a -um, *raging, mad, savage;* adv. **răbĭōsē.**

Răbīrĭus -a -um, *name of a Roman* gens.

răbŭla -ae, m. *a bawling advocate.*

răcēmĭfer -fĕra -fĕrum, *bearing clusters.*

răcēmus -i, m. *a cluster,* esp. *of grapes.*

rădĭātus -a -um, *provided with spokes* or *rays.*

rādīcĭtŭs, *with* or *by the root; utterly.*

rādīcŭla -ae, f. *a little root.*

rădĭo -are and **rădĭor** -ari, dep. *to gleam, radiate.*

rădĭus -i, m. *a staff, rod; the spoke of a wheel; the radius of a circle*; in weaving, *a shuttle*; in botany, a *kind of long olive.* Transf., *a ray, beam of light.*

rādix -īcis, f. *a root; the foot of a mountain*; in gen., *foundation, basis, origin.*

rādo rādĕre rāsi rāsum, *to scrape, shave graze; to erase; to hurt, offend.*

raeda -ae, f. *a travelling carriage.*

raedārĭus -i, m. *coachman.*

rāmālĕ -is, n. usually plur., *sticks, brushwood.*

rāmentum -i, n., usually plur., *shavings, splinters, chips.*

rāmĕus -a -um, *of branches.*

rāmex -ĭcis, m. *a rupture*; plur., *the lungs.*

Ramnes and **Ramnenses** -ĭum, m. pl. *one of the three tribes into which the early Roman citizens were divided.*

rāmōsus -a -um, *full of boughs, branching.*

rāmŭlus -i, m. *a little branch, twig.*

rāmus -i, m. *a bough, branch, twig.*

rāna -ae, f. *a frog.*

rancens -entis, *stinking, putrid.*

rancĭdŭlus -a -um, *rather putrid.*

rancĭdus -a -um, *stinking, rank, offensive.*

rānuncŭlus -i, m. *a little frog, tadpole.*

răpācĭtās -ātis, f. *greediness.*

răpax -ācis, *snatching, grasping, greedy.*

răpĭdĭtās -ātis, f. *rapid flow, rapidity.*

răpĭdus -a -um, *rushing, swift, violent*; adv. **răpĭdē.**

răpīna -ae, f. *robbery, pillage; booty, plunder.*

răpĭo răpĕre răpŭi raptum, *to seize, snatch, tear away; to plunder* a place, *to hurry along* a person or thing; se rapere, *to rush off.* Transf., *to pervert, lead astray.* N. of partic. as subst. **raptum -i,** *plunder.*

raptim, *violently, hastily, hurriedly.*
raptĭo -ōnis, f. *carrying off, abduction.*
rapto -are, *to seize and carry off, to hurry away; to rob, plunder* a place
raptor -ōris, m. *a robber, plunderer.*
raptus -ūs, m. *tearing off, rending away; carrying off, abduction, rape; plundering.*
rāpŭlum -i, n. *a little turnip.*
rārēfăcĭo -făcĕre -fēci -factum *to make thin, rarefy.*
rāresco -ĕre, *to become thin, to lose density; to widen out; to grow less.*
rārĭtās -ātis, f. *thinness, looseness of texture; fewness, rarity.*
rārus -a -um, *loose, thin; scattered, scanty, far apart*; milit., *in loose order*; in gen., *rare, infrequent*; sometimes *extraordinary, distinguished.* Adv. **rārō, rārē,** *seldom, rarely*
rāsĭlis -e, *scraped, smooth.*
rastrum -i, n., plur. gen. rastri -orum, *a hoe, rake, mattock.*
rătĭo -onis, f. *a reckoning, account, consideration, calculation*; rationem ducere, *to compute*; any *transaction, affair, business; a reason, motive, ground; a plan, scheme, system; reasonableness, method, order; a theory, doctrine, science; the reasoning faculty.*
rătĭōcĭnātĭo -ōnis, f. *reasoning*; esp. *a form of argument, syllogism.*
rătĭōcĭnātīvus -a -um, *argumentative; syllogistic.*
rătĭōcĭnātor -ōris, m. *a calculator, accountant.*
rătĭōcĭnor -ari, dep. *to compute calculate; to argue, infer, conclude.*
rătĭōnālis -e, *reasonable, rational.*
rătĭōnārĭum -i, n. *a statistical account*
rătis -is, f. *a raft*; poet., *a ship, boat.*
rătĭuncŭla -ae, f. *a little reckoning, account; a poor reason; a petty syllogism.*
rătus -a -um, partic. from reor; q.v.
raucĭsŏnus -a -um, *hoarsely sounding.*
raucus -a -um, *hoarse, harsh-sounding.*
raudus (rōdus, rūdus) -ĕris, n. *a rough mass, lump*, esp. of copper money.
rauduscŭlum -i, n. *a small sum of money.*
Răvenna -ae, f. *a town in Gallia Cispadana, near the Adriatic.*
rāvus -a -um, *tawny* or *greyish.*
rĕa; *see* reus.
rĕapsĕ, *in truth, really.*
rĕbellātĭo = rebellio; q.v.
rĕbellātrix -īcis, f. *renewing war, rebellious.*
rĕbellĭo -ōnis, f. *a renewal of war*, esp. by the conquered; *a revolt.*
rĕbellis -e, *renewing war, insurgent.*
rĕbellĭum = rebellio; q.v.
rĕbello -are, *to renew war, revolt, fight back.*
rĕbŏo -are, *to echo, resound; to make to resound.*
rĕcalcitro -are, *to kick back*; fig., *to deny access.*
rĕcălĕo -ēre, *to be warm again.*
rĕcălesco -ĕre, *to become warm again.*
rĕcalfăcĭo -făcĕre -fēci -factum, *to make warm again.*
rĕcandesco -candescĕre -candŭi, *to grow white; to become hot, begin to glow.*
rĕcanto -are: intransit., *to resound echo*; transit., *to recall, recant; to charm away.*
rĕcēdo -cēdĕre -cessi -cessum, *to go back, retreat, retire; to disappear.*
rĕcello -ere, *to spring back, fly back.*
rĕcens -entis, *new, fresh, young, recent; vigorous.* As adv. **rĕcens,** *lately, recently.*
rĕcensĕo -censēre -censŭi -censum, *to review, muster, examine; to recount.*
rĕcensĭo -ōnis, f. *reviewing, mustering.*
rĕceptācŭlum -i, n. *a reservoir, receptacle; a place of refuge, shelter, retreat.*
rĕcepto -are, *to draw back, receive back take in; to receive frequently, harbour.*
rĕceptor -ōris, m. and **receptrix** -trīcis, f. *a receiver, harbourer.*
rĕceptus -ūs, m. *drawing back; withdrawal, recantation; retiring, retreat, return*; poet., *a place of retreat.*
rĕcessim, *backwards.*
rĕcessus -ūs, m. *going back, retreat, withdrawal; a place of retreat, quiet place.*
rĕcĭdīvus -a -um, *returning, repeated.*
[1]**rĕcĭdo** -cĭdĕre -ccĭdi -cāsūrus, *to fall back; to relapse, recoil, descend, sink, fall.*
[2]**rĕcīdo** -cīdĕre -cīdi -cīsum, *to cut back, lop away.*
rĕcingo -cingĕre -cinxi -cinctum, *to ungird, loosen.*
rĕcĭno -ĕre, *to resound, echo*; transit., *to cause to resound.*
rĕcĭpĭo -cĭpĕre -cēpi -ceptum, *to hold back, retain; to take back, fetch back*; se recipere, *to withdraw, retreat; to regain, recover; to receive, accept, take to oneself; to receive hospitably.* Transf., *to accept, admit, allow; to accept an obligation*; hence *to guarantee, promise, be responsible for.* N. of partic. as subst., receptum -i, *an engagement, guarantee.*
rĕcĭprŏco -are, *to move backwards and forwards*; animam, *to breathe.*
rĕcĭprŏcus -a -um, *going backwards and forwards*; mare, *ebbing.*
rĕcĭtātĭo -ōnis, f. *a reading aloud.*
rĕcĭtātor -ōris, m. *a reader aloud.*
rĕcĭto -are, *to read aloud, read out, recite.*
reclāmātĭo -ōnis, f. *loud disapprobation.*
reclāmĭto -are, *to cry out against.*
reclāmo -are, *to cry out against, contradict loudly*; poet., *to re-echo, resound.*
reclīnis -e, *leaning backwards.*
reclīno -are, *to bend back, cause to lean back.*
reclūdo -clūdĕre -clūsi -clūsum, *to open; to reveal*; fata, *to relax.*
rĕcōgĭto -are, *to think again, reconsider.*
rĕcognĭtĭo -ōnis, f. *inspection, examination.*

rĕcognosco -noscĕre -nōvi -nĭtum, *to recognize, know again, recall; to review, inspect, investigate.*
rĕcŏlo -cŏlĕre -cŏlŭi -cultum, *to cultivate* or *work again; to resume; to set up again, rehabilitate; to reflect upon, to recall.*
rĕcompōno -pōnĕre -pŏsĭtum, *to readjust.*
rĕconcĭlĭātĭo -ōnis, f. *winning back, restoration.*
rĕconcĭlĭātor -ōris, m. *a restorer.*
rĕconcĭlĭo -are, *to restore, repair*; of persons, *to reunite, reconcile.*
rĕconcinno -are, *to restore, renovate, repair.*
rĕcondo -dĕre -dĭdi -dĭtum *to put away, put back, store, hide.*
Hence partic. **rĕcondĭtus** -a -um, *put away, concealed; abstruse, profound*; of character, *reserved, mysterious.*
rĕconflo -are, *to rekindle.*
rĕconlĭgo -lĭgĕre -lēgi -lectum, *to collect again, recover.*
rĕcŏquo -cŏquĕre -coxi -coctum, *to boil again, heat up again, remould.*
rĕcordātĭo -ōnis, f. *recollection, remembrance.*
rĕcordor -ari, dep. *to remember, recollect; to think of, ponder over.*
recrĕo -are, *to restore, refresh, invigorate, revive.*
recrĕpo -are, *to echo, resound.*
recresco -crescĕre -crēvi -crētum, *to grow again.*
recrūdesco -crūdescĕre -crūdŭi, *to become raw again, break out afresh.*
rectĭo -ōnis, f. *ruling, direction.*
rector -ōris, m. *ruler, governor, director, guide*; navis, *steersman*; of animals, *driver* or *rider.*
rectus; *see* rego.
rĕcŭbo -are, *to lie back, recline.*
rĕcumbo -cumbĕre -cŭbŭi, *to lie back, recline* (esp. at table); in gen., *to sink down, fall down.*
rĕcŭpĕrātĭo -ōnis, f. *recovery.*
rĕcŭpĕrātor (**rĕcĭpĕrātor**) -ōris, m. *a recoverer*; pl., recuperatores, a *board of arbiters appointed by the* praetor.
rĕcŭpĕrātōrĭus -a -um, *of the* recuperatores (q.v.).
rĕcŭpĕro (**rĕcĭpĕro**) -are, *to regain, recover.*
rĕcūro -are, *to restore, refresh.*
rĕcurro -currĕre -curri -cursum, *to run back; to revert, return.*
rĕcurso -are, *to run back, return.*
rĕcursus -ūs, m. *return, retreat.*
rĕcurvo -are, *to bend* or *curve backwards.*
rĕcurvus -a -um, *bent* or *curved backwards; winding.*
rĕcūsātĭo -ōnis, f. *refusal*; legal, *a protest, counter-plea.*
rĕcūso -are, *to object to, protest against, refuse*; legal, *to take exception, plead in defence.*
rĕcŭtĭo -cŭtĕre -cussi -cussum, *to strike back, cause to rebound.*
rēda -ae, f. = raeda; q.v.
rĕdămo -are, *to love in return.*
rĕdargŭo -gŭĕre -gŭi, *to refute, disprove, contradict.*
reddo -dĕre -dĭdi -dĭtum. (1) *to give back, restore*; reddi, or se reddere, *to return*; in words, *to repeat, recite; to reproduce* by imitation, *to represent, reflect.* (2) *to give in return*; hence *to answer; to translate, render interpret; to make, render, cause to be.* (3) *to give as due; to pay up, deliver; fulfil*; reddere ius, *to administer justice.*
rĕdemptĭo -ōnis, f. *a buying up, bribing; farming of taxes; buying back, ransoming, redemption.*
rĕdempto -are, *to ransom, redeem.*
rĕdemptor -ōris, m. *buyer, contractor, farmer* (of taxes).
rĕdemptūra -ae, f. *contracting, farming* (of taxes, etc.).
rĕdĕo -īre -ĭi (-īvi) -ĭtum. (1) *to go back, come back, return*; ad se, *to come to one's senses*; redit, *the matter comes up again.* (2) of revenue, income, etc., *to come in.* (3) *to fall back upon, be reduced* or *brought to.*
rĕdhālo -are, *to breathe out again.*
rĕdhĭbĕo -ēre -ŭi -ĭtum, *to take back.*
rĕdĭgo -ĭgĕre -ēgi -actum, *to drive back, bring back*; of money, etc., *to draw in, call in*; in gen., *to bring* or *reduce* to a condition; *to reduce* in number, value, etc.; *to lessen, bring down.*
rĕdĭmīcŭlum -i, n. *a fillet, chaplet.*
rĕdĭmĭo -īre -ĭi -ītum, *to bind round, wreathe, crown.*
rĕdĭmo -ĭmĕre -ēmi -emptum, *to buy back, redeem; to ransom, recover*; in gen., *to buy up, contract for, farm, hire, procure*
rĕdintegro -are, *to restore, renew, repair.*
rĕdĭpiscor -i, dep. *to get back.*
rĕdĭtĭo -ōnis, f. *going back, return.*
rĕdĭtus -ūs, m. *going back, return*; in gratiam, *reconciliation*; of money, etc., *returns, income, revenue.*
rĕdĭvĭa = reduvia; q.v.
rĕdĭvīvus -a -um, *renewed, renovated*; n. as subst., *old building materials used again.*
rĕdŏlĕo -ēre -ŭi, *to emit an odour, smell of.*
rĕdŏmĭtus -a -um, *tamed again.*
rĕdōno -are, *to give back; to give up.*
rĕdūco -dūcĕre -duxi -ductum, *to draw backwards, bring back, lead home*; also *to bring* to a state or condition.
Hence partic. **rĕductus** -a -um, *drawn back; withdrawn, retired, remote, sequestered.*
rĕductĭo -ōnis, f. *bringing back, restoration.*
rĕductor -ōris, *one who brings back.*
rĕduncus -a -um, *bent back, curved.*
rĕdundantĭa -ae, f. *overflowing; redundancy.*
rĕdundo -are, *to overflow, stream over; to be in excess, be copious. diffuse, to abound in* (with abl.); *to be left over, overflow, spread.*

rĕdŭvĭa (rĕdĭvĭa) -ae, f. *a hangnail, whitlow.*
rĕdux -dŭcis, adj.: act., *bringing back, restoring*; pass., *brought back, returned.*
rĕfectĭo -ōnis, f. *repairing, restoring.*
rĕfello -fellĕre -felli, *to refute, disprove.*
rĕfercĭo -fercire -fersi -fertum, *to stuff, to cram*; partic. **rĕfertus** -a -um, *stuffed, crammed, filled.*
rĕfĕrĭo -ire, *to strike back, strike again.* Transf., *to reflect.*
rĕfĕro rĕferre rettŭli rĕlātum. (1) *to carry back, bring back*; referre pedem, *or* se, *or* pass., referri, *to return, go back.* (2) *to bring again, restore, repeat; to echo; to reproduce, recall.* (3) *to say back, answer.* (4) *to bring as expected, pay up, deliver; to bring back a message, report; to refer a matter to authority; to enter in a record,* etc., *register, put down, enter; to assign* to a cause.
rēfert rēferre rētŭlit, impers., *it matters, it concerns, it makes a difference*; meā, illorum refert, *it matters to me, to them.*
rĕfertus -a -um, partic. from refercio; q.v.
rĕfervĕo -ēre, *to boil over.*
rĕfervesco -ĕre, *to boil up, bubble up.*
rĕfĭcĭo -fĭcĕre -fēci -fectum. (1) *to make again, restore, repair, re-establish, refresh, revive.* (2) *to get back, receive, get.*
rĕfīgo -fīgĕre -fixi -fixum, *to unfasten, demolish, remove*; of laws, *to repeal, abrogate.*
rĕfingo -ĕre, *to form anew.*
reflāgĭto -are, *to ask back, demand again.*
reflātū, abl. sing. m. *by a contrary wind.*
reflecto -flectĕre -flexi -flexum, *to bend back, turn back, divert*; intransit., *to yield, retreat.*
reflo -are: intransit., *to blow back, blow contrary*; transit., *to blow out.*
reflŭo -flŭĕre -fluxi -fluxum, *to flow back; to overflow.*
reflŭus -a -um, *flowing back.*
rĕformātor -ōris, m. *a reviver.*
rĕformīdātĭo -ōnis, f. *dread, terror.*
rĕformīdo -are, *to dread, fear, shun, avoid.*
rĕformo -are, *to form again, mould anew.*
rĕfŏvĕo -fŏvēre -fōvi -fōtum, *to warm again, revive, restore, refresh.*
refractārĭŏlus -a -um, *somewhat contentious, stubborn.*
refrāgor -ari, dep. *to oppose, withstand, thwart.*
refrēno -are, *to rein back, hold in, restrain, curb.*
refrĭco -frĭcare -frĭcŭi -frĭcatum, *to rub again; to excite again, renew.*
refrīgĕrātĭo -ōnis, f. *cooling, coolness.*
refrīgĕro -are, *to cool off*; pass., refrigerari, *to cool oneself, grow cool, grow languid.*
refrīgesco -frīgescĕre -frixi, *to grow cold, cool down; to flag, fail, grow stale.*
refringo -fringĕre -frēgi -fractum, *to break up, break open; to curb check.*
rĕfŭgĭo -fŭgĕre -fūgi: intransit., *to flee back, run away; to shrink;* of places, *to recede*; transit., *to fly from, avoid.*
rĕfŭgĭum -i, n. *refuge.*
rĕfŭgus -a -um, *fugitive, receding, recoiling.*
rĕfulgĕo -fulgēre -fulsi, *to gleam back, shine brightly, glitter.*
rĕfundo -fundĕre -fūdi -fūsum, *to pour back, to make overflow.*
rĕfūtātĭo -ōnis, f. *refutation.*
rĕfūtātū, abl. sing. m. *by refutation.*
rĕfūto -are, *to drive back, check, repress; to refute, disprove.*
rēgālis -e, *of a king, royal, regal*; adv. **rēgālĭtĕr**, *regally, tyrannically.*
rĕgĕlo -are, *to thaw, warm.*
rĕgĕro -gĕrĕre -gessi -gestum, *to carry back, throw back.*
rēgia; *see* regius.
rēgĭfĭcus -a -um, *princely, splendid.*
rĕgigno -ĕre, *to bring forth again.*
Rēgillus -i, m. *a lake in Latium, scene of a victory of the Romans over the Latins,* 496 B.C.
rĕgĭmen -ĭnis, n. *control, guidance, rule, direction, government; a ruler, governor*; poet., *rudder.*
rēgīna -ae, f. *queen; princess; lady, mistress, sovereign.*
rĕgĭo -ōnis, f. (1) *a direction, line*; esp. *a boundary line, boundary*; e regione, *in a straight line,* also *opposite, over against* (with genit. or dat.). (2) *a region, district, province.* Transf., *sphere, department.*
rĕgĭōnātim, *according to districts.*
Rēgĭum (Rhēgĭum) -i, n. (1) *a town in Gallia Cispadana.* (2) *a town in Calabria.*
rēgĭus -a -um, *of a king, royal, regal; splendid, magnificent.* F. as subst. **rēgĭa** -ae, *palace, court, the royal family; capital city.* Adv. **rēgĭē**. *royally; tyrannically.*
regnātor -ōris, m. *ruler, king.*
regnātrix -trīcis, f. adj., *ruling.*
regno -are; intransit., *to be a king, reign; to be master, be a tyrant; to prevail*; transit., in pass., regnari, *to be ruled by a king.*
regnum -i, n. (1) *royal power, monarchy, supremacy; tyranny.* (2) *a realm, kingdom, estate.*
rĕgo rĕgĕre rexi rectum, *to guide, direct, to rule, govern, administer.*
Hence partic. **rectus** -a -um, *ruled*; as adj. *straight; upright.* Transf., *right, correct, proper; honest, upright; natural, plain, straightforward*; n. as subst., *right.* Adv. **rectē**, *in a straight line; rightly properly*; recte est, *all is well.*
regrĕdĭor -grĕdi -gressus, dep. *to step back, go back*; milit., *to retire, retreat.*
regressus -ūs, m. *a going back, return; retreat; refuge, recourse.*
rēgŭla -ae, f. *a ruler, a plank.* Transf., *a rule, pattern, model.*
[1]**rēgŭlus** -i, m. *a petty king,* or *king's son, prince.*

[2]**Rēgŭlus,** *a surname in the* gens Atilia.
rĕgusto -are, *to taste again* or *repeatedly.*
rĕicĭo -icĕre -iēci -iectum, *to throw back, throw behind, throw away; to drive off*; of a storm, *to drive back, cast up.* Transf., *to throw off, reject; to refer*; in time, *to put off*; legal, *to challenge* a juror.
rĕiectĭo -ōnis, f. *throwing back, rejection*; legal, *the challenging of a juror.*
rēiecto -are, *to throw back.*
rĕlābor -lābi -lapsus, dep. *to glide back, fall back.*
rĕlanguesco -languescĕre -langŭi, *to become faint; to slacken.*
rĕlātĭo -ōnis, f. *carrying back, bringing back*; polit., *a report*; gram., *repetition.*
rĕlātor -ōris, m. *one who makes a report.*
rĕlātus -ūs, m. *a narrative; a report.*
rĕlaxātĭo -ōnis, f. *relaxation, easing.*
rĕlaxo -are, *to loosen, enlarge; to ease, lighten, relax.*
rĕlēgātĭo -ōnis, f. *banishment.*
[1]**rĕlēgo** -are, *to send away; to put aside, reject; to banish.*
[2]**rĕlĕgo** -lĕgĕre -lēgi -lectum, *to gather up again*; of places, *to pass again*; of topics, *to go over again.*
rĕlentesco -ĕre, *to become languid again.*
rĕlĕvo -are, *to lift again*; *to lighten; to relieve, alleviate.*
rĕlictĭo -ōnis, f. *leaving, deserting.*
rĕlĭcŭos and **rĕlĭcus** = reliquus; q.v.
rĕlĭgātĭo -ōnis, f. *tying up.*
rĕlĭgĭo (rellĭgĭo) -ōnis, f. of persons, *scrupulousness, conscientious exactness*; esp. *religious scruple, awe, superstition, strict observance*; in gen., *moral scruples, conscientiousness*; of gods, etc., *sanctity; an object of worship, holy thing* or *place.*
rĕlĭgĭōsus (rellĭgĭōsus) -a -um, of persons, *scrupulous, conscientious; holy, strict, superstitious*; of actions, either *required* or *forbidden by religion*; of gods, etc., *holy, sacred.* Adv. **rĕlĭgĭōsē,** *conscientiously, scrupulously; religiously.*
rĕlĭgo -are, *to tie on, fasten behind.*
rĕlĭno -lĭnĕre -lēvi -lĭtum, *to unseal.*
rĕlinquo -linquĕre -līqui -lictum, *to leave behind*; at death, *to bequeath; to leave unchanged*; pass., *to remain; to omit, leave out, pass over; to desert, abandon, forsake.*
rĕlĭquĭae (rellĭquĭae) -ārum, f. pl. *remains, relics, remnant.*
rĕlĭquus (rĕlĭcus) -a -um, *left behind, remaining,* other; of a debt, *outstanding*; of time, *remaining, future.* N. as subst., sing. and plur., *the rest; the remainder*; in reliquum, *for the future.*
relli-; see **reli-.**
rĕlūcĕo -lūcēre -luxi, *to glitter.*
rĕlūcesco -lūcēscĕre -luxi, *to become bright again.*
rĕluctor -ari, dep. *to struggle against, resist.*
rĕmănĕo -mănēre -mansi -mansum, *to remain behind, stay, continue.*
rĕmāno -are, *to flow back.*
rĕmansĭo -ōnis, f. *remaining in a place.*
rĕmĕdĭum -i, n. *means of healing, cure, remedy, medicine.*
rĕmĕo -are, *to go back, return.*
rĕmētĭor -mētīri -mensus, dep. *to measure again, go back over*; perf. partic. sometimes pass. in meaning.
rēmex -mĭgis, m. *a rower.*
rēmĭgātĭo -ōnis, f. *rowing.*
rēmĭgĭum -i, n. *rowing.* Transf. *oars; crew.*
rēmĭgo -are, *to row.*
rĕmigro -are, *to wander back, come back, return.*
rĕmĭniscor -i, dep. *to call to mind, recollect, remember.*
rĕmiscĕo -miscēre -mixtum, *to mix up, mingle.*
rĕmissĭo -ōnis, f. *letting go back, letting fall, lowering; breaking off, interrupting; remitting*; animi, *relaxation, quiet.*
rĕmitto -mittĕre -mīsi -missum. (1) *to send back, send again; throw back; echo.* (2) *to let go back, relax, loosen; to relieve, abate*; with infin., *to give up doing*; intransit., *to ease off.* (3) *to give up, yield; abandon, sacrifice; to forgive* an offence, *remit* punishment.

Hence partic. **rĕmissus** -a -um, *relaxed, mild, gentle*; in bad sense, *negligent, remiss.* Adv. **rĕmissē.**
rĕmōlĭor -iri, dep. *to push back.*
rĕmollesco -ĕre, *to become soft again.*
rĕmollĭo -ire, *to make soft again, to weaken.*
rĕmŏra -ae, f. *delay, hindrance.*
rĕmŏrāmen -ĭnis, n. *delay.*
rĕmordĕo -mordēre -morsum, *to worry, harass.*
rĕmŏror -ari, dep.: intransit., *to remain behind, linger, loiter*; transit., *to obstruct, hinder.*
rĕmōtĭo -ōnis, f. *putting away, removing.*
rĕmŏvĕo -mŏvēre -mōvi -mōtum, *to move back, withdraw.*

Hence partic. **rĕmōtus** -a -um, *removed, withdrawn, distant, far off, remote*; adv. **rĕmōtē,** *far off, at a distance.*
rĕmūgĭo -ire, *to bellow again, bellow back.*
rĕmulcĕo -mulcēre -mulsi *to stroke back.*
rĕmulcum -i, n. *a tow-rope.*
rĕmūnĕrātĭo -ōnis, f. *a recompense, return.*
rĕmūnĕror -ari, dep. *to repay, reward.*
rĕmurmŭro -are, *to murmur back.*
[1]**rēmus** -i, m. *an oar.*
[2]**Rēmus** -i, m. *twin brother of Romulus.*
rĕnarro -are, *to relate again.*
rĕnascor -nasci -nātus, dep. *to be born again, grow again.*
rĕnāvĭgo -are, *to sail back.*
rĕnĕo -nēre, *to unravel.*
rēnes -um, m. pl. *the kidneys.*
rĕnīdĕo -ēre, *to shine back, glitter; to beam with joy, laugh, smile.*
rĕnītor -i, dep. *to oppose, withstand, resist.*
[1]**rĕno** -nare, *to swim back.*

[2]**rēno** (**rhēno**) -onis, m. *a garment made of fur.*
rĕnōdo -are, *to tie back.*
rĕnŏvāmen -ĭnis, n. *renewal.*
rĕnŏvātĭo -ōnis, f. *renewal, renovation*; renovatio singulorum annorum, *compound interest.*
rĕnŏvo -are, *to renew, restore, repair; to repeat.*
rĕnŭmĕro -are, *to count over again; to pay back.*
rĕnuntĭātĭo -ōnis, f. *a formal report, public announcement.*
rĕnuntĭo -are. (1) *to bring back word, report, announce.* (2) *to disclaim, refuse, renounce.*
rĕnŭo -nŭĕre -nŭi, *to deny, refuse, reject.*
rĕnūto -are, *to refuse, decline.*
rĕor rēri rătus, dep. *to think suppose, judge*; partic., in pass. sense, **rătus** -a -um, *determined, settled;* ratum facere, *to ratify, confirm, make valid;* pro rata, *in proportion.*
rĕpāgŭla -orum, n. pl. *bars* or *bolts; restraints, limits.*
rĕpandus -a -um, *bent backwards, turned up.*
rĕpărābĭlis -e, *that can be restored.*
rĕparco = reperco; q.v.
rĕpăro -are, *to restore, renew, make good; to get in exchange, purchase.*
rĕpastĭnātio -ōnis, f. *digging up again.*
rĕpecto -pectĕre -pexum, *to comb back.*
rĕpello rĕpellĕre reppŭli, rĕpulsum, *to drive back, drive away; to banish, repel;* a spe, *to disappoint;* criminationes, *to refute.*
rĕpendo -pendĕre -pendi -pensum, *to weigh back again; to ransom; to repay, requite.*
rĕpens -entis, *sudden, unexpected; fresh, recent.* Adv. **rĕpentĕ,** *suddenly, unexpectedly.*
rĕpentīnus -a -um, *sudden, unexpected*; n. abl. as adv. **rĕpentīnō,** *suddenly.*
rĕperco (**rĕparco**) -percĕre -persi or -pĕperci, *to spare, be sparing, abstain.*
rĕpercussus -ūs, m. *reverberation; echo, reflection.*
rĕpercŭtĭo -cŭtĕre -cussi -cussum, *to strike back, make rebound*; perf. partic. **rĕpercussus** -a -um, *rebounding, reflected.*
rĕpĕrĭo rĕpĕrire reppĕri rĕpertum, *to get again; to find, discover, ascertain, invent.*
rĕpertor -ōris, m. *discoverer, inventor.*
rĕpĕtentĭa -ae, f. *recollection, remembrance.*
rĕpĕtītĭo -ōnis, f. *repetition.*
rĕpĕtītor -ōris, m. *one who demands back.*
rĕpĕto -ĕre -īvi *and* -ĭi -ītum, *to seek again, go back for* or *to; to ask back*; res repetere, *to demand satisfaction*; (pecuniae) repetundae, *money claimed back, as having been extorted; to return to, renew, begin again; to trace back, deduce; to recollect, recall.*
rĕpĕtundae; see repeto.

replĕo -plēre -plēvi -plētum *to fill again, fill up; to make full, fill, satisfy.* Hence partic. **replētus** -a -um, *filled, full.*
replĭcātĭo -ōnis, f. *rolling again, folding round.*
replĭco -are, *to unroll; to turn over, review.*
rēpo rēpĕre repsi reptum, *to creep, crawl.*
rĕpōno -pōnĕre -pŏsŭi -pŏsĭtum, *to lay back; to put aside, lay up, deposit, store; mentally, to reckon, place; to replace, restore; to replace by a substitute; to requite.*
rĕporto -are, *to bring back, carry back*; of reports, *to deliver.*
rĕposco -ĕre, *to ask back again; to demand as a right, claim.*
rĕpostor -ōris, m. *a restorer.*
rĕpōtĭa -ōrum, n. *an after-party, second entertainment.*
repraesentātĭo -ōnis, f. (1) *vivid presentation, lively description.* (2) *payment in cash.*
repraesento -are, *to bring back, reproduce; to perform immediately, hasten on;* pecuniam, *to pay cash.*
reprĕhendo -prĕhendĕre -prĕhendi -prĕhensum, and **reprendo** -prendĕre -prendi -prensum, *to catch, hold fast, detain, check; to blame, reprove; to refute.*
reprĕhensĭo -ōnis, f. *stopping, check; blame, censure; refutation.*
reprĕhenso -are, *to hold back, hold fast.*
reprĕhensor -ōris, m. *a censurer reprover; an improver, reformer.*
repressor -ōris, m. *a restrainer.*
reprĭmo -prĭmĕre -pressi -pressum, *to hold back, restrain, hinder, repress.*
reprōmissĭo -ōnis, f. *a counterpromise.*
reprōmitto -mittĕre -mīsi -missum, *to promise in return.*
repto -are, *to creep, crawl along.*
rĕpŭdĭātĭo -ōnis, f. *refusal, rejection.*
rĕpŭdĭo -are, *to refuse, reject, disdain; to divorce.*
rĕpŭdĭum -i, n. *divorce.*
rĕpŭĕrasco -ĕre, *to become a boy again, to frolic.*
rĕpugnantĭa -ae, f. *incompatibility.*
rĕpugno -are *to fight against, oppose, resist; to be opposed, repugnant, inconsistent, incompatible.*
Hence partic. **rĕpugnans,** *contrary, opposed*; n. pl. as subst. *contradictions*; adv. **rĕpugnantĕr,** *unwillingly.*
rĕpulsa -ae, f. *repulse, rejection; denial refusal.*
rĕpulsans -antis, partic., *beating back*; colles verba repulsantes, *echoing.*
repulsū, abl. sing. m. *by striking back, by reflection, by echoing.*
rĕpungo -ĕre, *to prick again.*
rĕpurgo -are, *to clean again; to purge away.*
rĕpŭtātĭo -ōnis, f. *re-appraisal.*
rĕpŭto -are. (1) *to reckon back, count, compute.* (2) *to think over, reconsider.*
rĕquĭēs -ētis, f. *rest, repose.*

rĕquiesco -quiescĕre -quiēvi -quiētum, *to rest, repose*; pass. partic. **rĕquiētus** -a -um, *rested, refreshed*; ager, *fallow.*
rĕquīro -quīrĕre -quisĭi *and* -quisīvi -quisitum, *to ask for, look for, enquire after; to demand, desire; to miss, feel the want of.*
rēs rĕi, f. *a thing, object, matter, affair, circumstance*; natura rerum, *the world, the universe, nature*; pro re, *according to circumstance*; esp. *the real thing, fact, truth, reality*; rē verā, *in truth; possessions, property, wealth; interest, advantage, benefit*; in rem, *to one's advantage; cause, ground, reason*; qua re, quam ob rem, *wherefore; a matter of business; a law-suit, action*; res publica or respublica, *the republic, state, commonwealth*; e republicā, *in the public interest.*
rĕsacro = resecro; q.v.
rĕsaevĭo -ire, *to rage again.*
rĕsălūto -are, *to salute back, greet in return.*
rĕsānesco -sānescĕre -sānŭi, *to become sound again.*
rĕsarcĭo -sarcire -sartum, *to patch up, mend, repair, restore.*
rescindo -scindĕre -scĭdi -scissum, *to tear back, cut away, break open*; vulnus, *to reopen*; of laws, etc., *to* rescind, repeal.
rescisco -sciscĕre -scīvi *and* -scĭi -scītum, *to find out, ascertain.*
rescrībo -scrībĕre -scripsi -scriptum, *to write again, rewrite; to enrol again, transfer; to write back, answer in writing;* in book-keeping, *to pay, repay.*
rĕsĕco -sĕcare -sĕcŭi -sectum, *to cut back, cut short.*
rĕsēmĭno -are, *to produce again.*
rĕsĕquor -sĕqui -sĕcūtus, dep. *to follow again*; dictis, *to answer.*
rĕsĕro -are, *to unbolt, open up, disclose, reveal.*
rĕservo -are, *to lay up, keep back, reserve; to save, preserve, keep.*
rĕsĕs -sĭdis, *sitting; inactive, calm, quiet.*
rĕsĭdĕo -sĭdēre -sēdi -sessum, *to remain sitting, stay, rest.*
rĕsīdo -sīdĕre -sēdi, *to sit down, settle, sink, subside, abate.*
rĕsĭdŭus -a -um, *remaining, outstanding*; pecuniae, *arrears.*
rĕsigno -are, *to unseal, open, reveal; to cancel, annul; to transfer, give back, resign.*
rĕsĭlĭo -sĭlire -sĭlŭi -sultum, *to leap back, rebound; to shrink, contract.*
rĕsīmus -a -um, *bent backwards, turned up.*
rēsīna -ae, f. *resin.*
rĕsĭpĭo -sipere, *to have a flavour* of anything.
rĕsĭpisco -sĭpiscĕre -sĭpĭi, also -sĭpīvi, *to recover one's senses; to become rational again.*
rĕsisto -sistĕre -stĭti. (1) *to stay, still, stop, continue; to recover one's footing.* (2) *to resist, oppose, withstand*; usually with dat.
rĕsolvo -solvĕre -solvi -sŏlūtum, *to untie, loosen, open; to melt; to dissipate; to dispel; to release; to reveal; to weaken.*
rĕsŏnābĭlis -e, *resounding.*
rĕsŏno -are; intransit., *to resound, echo*; transit., *to make resound.*
rĕsŏnus -a -um, *resounding, echoing.*
rĕsorbĕo -ēre, *to swallow again, suck back.*
respecto -are, *to look eagerly back (at); to have a regard for, give thought to.*
respectus -ūs, m. *looking back*; hence *care, regard, consideration; looking around one*; meton., *refuge, retreat.*
respergo -spergĕre -spersi -spersum, *to sprinkle, splash.*
respersĭo -ōnis, f. *sprinkling.*
respĭcĭo -spĭcĕre -spexi -spectum, *to look behind, look back (at); to look back upon; to look to, provide for; to look to, depend upon; to have a regard for, care for, consider.*
respīrāmen -ĭnis, n. *windpipe.*
respīrātĭo -ōnis, f. *taking breath, respiration; exhalation.*
respīrātus -ū, m. *taking breath.*
respīro -are. (1) *to breathe back, blow in a contrary direction.* (2) *to breathe again, to take breath; to recover* from fear, etc.; of things, *to abate, decline.*
resplendĕo -ēre, *to glitter back, gleam again.*
respondĕo -spondēre -spondi -sponsum: intransit., *to match, correspond to, answer to; to resemble;* legal, *to answer to one's name, appear, be present*; transit., *to give an answer to* person or thing, *to answer, reply.* N. of partic. as subst. **responsum** -i, *an answer, reply*; a lawyer's *opinion.*
responsĭo -ōnis, f. *a reply, answer.*
responsĭto -are, *to keep giving an answer* or *opinion.*
responso -are, *to keep answering; to re-echo*; with dat., *to defy, withstand.*
responsum -i, n. subst. from respondeo; q.v.
respublĭca; see res.
respŭo -spŭĕre -spŭi, *to spit out, reject, refuse, repel.*
restagno -are, *to overflow, be swamped.*
restauro -are, *to restore, rebuild.*
restĭcŭla -ae, f. *a thin rope.*
restinctĭo -ōnis, f. *slaking, quenching.*
restinguo -stinguĕre -stinxi -stinctum, *to put out again, extinguish, quench, slake, destroy.*
restĭo -ōnis, m. *a rope-maker.*
restĭpŭlātĭo -ōnis, f. *a counter-engagement.*
restĭpŭlor -ari, dep. *to obtain a promise in return.*
restis -is, *a rope, cord.*
restĭto -are, *to remain behind, linger.*
restĭtŭo -ŭĕre -ŭi -ūtum, *to put back, replace, restore; to reinstate, re-establish; to repair, make good.*
restĭtūtĭo -ōnis, f. *restoration, reinstatement.*
restĭtūtor -ōris, m. *restorer.*

resto -stare -stĭti. (1) *to make a stand, resist, oppose.* (2) *to stand still, stay behind; to be left over, survive; to remain available* or *possible*; of the future, *to await, be in store.*
restringo -stringĕre -strinxi -strictum, *to bind back, draw back; to confine, restrict, restrain.*
Hence partic. **restrictus** -a -um, *close, tight; stingy; strict, severe.* Adv. **restrictē,** *sparingly; strictly.*
rĕsulto -are *to spring back, rebound; to echo, resound*; of style, *to go jerkily.*
rĕsūmo -sūmĕre -sumpsi -sumptum, *to take again, resume; to renew, repeat.*
rĕsŭpīno -are, *to throw down, prostrate.*
rĕsŭpīnus -a -um, *bent backwards, on one's back;* also *with head thrown back.*
rĕsurgo -surgĕre -surrexi -surrectum, *to rise up again, appear again.*
rĕsuscĭto -are, *to revive, resuscitate.*
rĕtardātĭo -ōnis, f. *hindering.*
rĕtardo -are, *to slow down, retard, impede.*
rētĕ -is, n. *a net.*
rĕtĕgo -tĕgĕre -texi -tectum, *to uncover, reveal, open, disclose.*
rĕtempto -are, *to attempt again.*
rĕtendo -tendĕre -tendi -tensum *and* -tentum, *to slacken, unbend.*
rĕtentĭo -ōnis, f. *keeping back; withholding.*
[1]**rĕtento** -are, *to hold firmly; to preserve maintain.*
[2]**rĕtento** = retempto; q.v.
rĕtentus -a -um, partic. from retendo or from retineo; q.v.
rĕtexo -texĕre -texŭi -textum, *to unravel, undo, reverse; to cancel, annul; to retract; to revise.*
rētĭārĭus -i, m. *a gladiator using a net.*
rĕtĭcentĭa -ae, f. *keeping silent.*
rĕtĭcĕo -ēre: intransit., *to keep silence, say nothing:* transit., *to keep silent about.*
rētĭcŭlum -i, n. *a little net; a net-bag; a hair-net.*
rĕtĭnācŭla -ōrum, n. pl. *a rope, cable.*
rĕtĭnentĭa -ae, f. *recollection.*
rĕtĭnĕo -tĭnēre -tĭnŭi -tentum, *to hold back, detain; to restrain; to keep, reserve, maintain.*
Hence partic. **rĕtĭnens** -entis, *tenacious.*
rĕtinnĭo -ire, *to resound, ring again.*
rĕtŏno -are, *to thunder back, resound.*
rĕtorquĕo -torquēre -torsi -tortum, *to twist back, bend back.*
retractātĭo -ōnis, f. (1) *refusal, denial.* (2) *reconsideration.*
retracto (retrecto) -are. (1) *to handle again, undertake anew, reconsider.* (2) *to draw back, refuse, be reluctant;* dicta, *to withdraw.*
retrăho -trăhĕre -traxi -tractum, *to draw back; to hold back, withdraw; to draw on again, induce.*
Hence partic. **retractus** -a -um, *withdrawn; distant, remote.*
retrĭbŭo -trĭbŭĕre -trĭbŭi -trĭbūtum, *to give again* or *give as due.*
retrō, *backwards, back, behind.*
retrŏăgo -ăgĕre -ēgi -actum, *to drive back, reverse.*
retrorsum, *backwards, behind, in return, in reversed order.*
retrūdo -trūdĕre -trūsum, *to push back*; perf. partic. retrūsus, *remote, obscure.*
rĕtundo rĕtundĕre rĕtŭdi (rettŭdi) rĕtūsum (rĕtunsum), *to hammer back, blunt, dull; to check* or *weaken;* partic. **rĕtūsus (rĕtunsus)** -a -um, *dull, blunt.*
rĕus -i, m. and **rĕa** -ae, f. *a party in a law-suit, whether plaintiff* or *defendant*; esp. *a defendant, accused person*; in gen., *one bound* or *answerable.*
rĕvălesco -vălescĕre -vălŭi, *to become well again, be restored, recover.*
rĕvĕho -vĕhĕre -vexi -vectum, *to carry back*; pass., *to drive back, ride back, sail back.*
rĕvello -vellĕre -velli -vulsum, *to tear back, pull away; to remove, banish.*
rĕvēlo -are, *to unveil, lay bare.*
rĕvĕnĭo -vĕnire -vēni -ventum, *to come back, return.*
rēvērā, adv. from res; q.v.
rĕvĕrentĭa -ae, f. *respect, fear, awe.*
rĕvĕrĕor -vĕrēri -vĕrĭtus, dep. *to revere, respect, fear*; partic. **rĕvĕrens** -entis, *respectful, reverent*; adv. **rĕvĕrenter;** gerundive, **rĕvĕrendus** -a -um, *awesome, venerable.*
rĕversĭo (rĕvorsĭo) -ōnis, f. *turning back, return, recurrence.*
rĕverto (rĕvorto) -vertĕre -verti, and pass. **rĕvertor (rĕvortor)** *to return, come back, revert.*
rĕvincĭo -vincire -vinxi -vinctum, *to tie back, bind fast.*
rĕvinco -vincĕre -vīci -victum, *to beat back, subdue; to refute.*
rĕvĭresco -vĭrescĕre -vĭrŭi, *to grow green* or *strong again; to revive.*
rĕvīso -ĕre: intransit., *to pay a fresh visit, return*; transit., *to come to see again, revisit.*
rĕvīvisco -vīviscĕre -vixi, *to come to life again, revive.*
rĕvŏcābĭlis -e, *able to be called back.*
rĕvŏcāmen -ĭnis, n. *calling back, recall.*
rĕvŏcātĭo -ōnis, f. *calling back; withdrawing, revocation.*
rĕvŏco -are, *to call again* or *back; to recall; to bring* or *get back, recover; to refer; to revoke.*
rĕvŏlo -are, *to fly back.*
rĕvŏlūbĭlis -e, *able to be rolled back.*
rĕvolvo -volvĕre -volvi -vŏlūtum, *to roll backwards*; esp. *to unroll* or *open a book*; hence *to go over again*; pass., *to roll back, come round again in due course.*
rĕvŏmo -vŏmĕre -vŏmŭi, *to vomit up, disgorge.*
rĕvor-; see rever-.
rex, rēgis, m. *ruler, king, prince, chief; monarch, tyrant.*
Rhădămanthus -i, m. *brother of Minos, a judge in the lower world.*

[1]**Rhēa (Rēa) Silvĭa,** *mother of Romulus and Remus.*
[2]**Rhĕa** -ae, f. *old name of Cybele.*
rhēda = raeda; q.v.
Rhēnus -i, m. *the Rhine.*
rhētor -ŏris, m. *a teacher of rhetoric, a rhetorician.*
rhētŏrĭcus -a -um, *rhetorical*; subst., f. **rhētŏrĭca** -ae and **rhētŏrĭcē** -ēs, *the art of oratory*; m. pl. **rhētŏrĭci** -ōrum, *teachers of rhetoric*; adv. **rhētŏrĭcē,** *rhetorically.*
rhīnŏcĕrōs -ōtis, m. *a rhinoceros.*
rhō, n. indecl. *the Greek name of the letter R.*
Rhŏdănus -i, m. *the Rhone.*
Rhŏdus (**-ŏs**) -i, f. *Rhodes*; adj. **Rhŏdĭus** -a -um, and **Rhŏdĭensis** -e.
rhombus (**-ŏs**) -i, m. (1) *a magician's circle.* (2) *the turbot.*
rhomphaea (**rumpĭa**) -ae, f. *a long javelin.*
rhythmĭcus -i, m. *one who teaches rhythm.*
rhythmus (**-ŏs**) -i, m. *rhythm, time, harmony.*
rhȳtĭum -i, n. *a drinking-horn*
rīca -ae, f. *a veil.*
rīcīnum -i, n. *a small veil.*
rictus -ūs, m. and **rictum** -i, n. *the open mouth.*
rīdĕo rīdēre rīsi rīsum: intransit., *to laugh, smile, look cheerful*; with dat., *to please*; transit., *to laugh at.*
rīdĭcŭlārĭus and **rīdĭcŭlōsus** -a -um, *laughable, droll.*
rīdĭcŭlus, *exciting laughter; droll, humorous; absurd, ridiculous*; m. as subst., *a joker, jester*; n., *a joke, jest.* Adv. **rīdĭcŭlē,** *humorously; absurdly.*
rĭgĕo -ēre, *to be stiff* (esp. with cold); of hair, *to stand on end*; partic. **rĭgens** -entis, *stiff.*
rĭgesco rĭgescĕre rĭgŭi, *to grow stiff*; of hair, *to stand on end.*
rĭgĭdus -a -um, *stiff, unbending, hard; stern, inflexible.* Adv. **rĭgĭdē.**
rĭgo -are, *to lead* or *conduct water; to wet, moisten, bedew.*
rĭgor -ōris, m. *stiffness, hardness,* esp. from cold. Transf., *sternness.*
rĭgŭus -a -um; act., *watering*; pass., *well-watered, irrigated.*
rīma -ae, f. *a crack, fissure, leak.*
rīmor -ari, dep. *to cleave; to probe, pry into, examine.*
rīmōsus -a -um, *full of cracks, leaky.*
ringor -i, dep. *to show the teeth; to snarl, be angry.*
rīpa -ae, f. *bank, shore.*
rīpŭla -ae, f. *a little bank.*
riscus -i, m. *a box, trunk.*
rīsĭo -ōnis, f. *laughter.*
rīsor -ōris, m. *a laugher, mocker.*
rīsus -ūs, m. *laughing, laughter; ridicule; an object of laughter.*
rītĕ, *in due form, with proper ceremonies, properly, fitly, rightly.*
rītus -ūs, m. *usage, ceremony, rite*; abl., ritu, with genit., *after the manner of.*
rīvālis -is, m. *a rival in love.*
rīvālĭtās -ātis, f. *rivalry* (in love).
rīvŭlus -i, m. *small brook, rivulet.*
rīvus -i, m. *stream.*
rixa -ae, f. *quarrel, brawl, contention.*
rixor -ari, dep. *to quarrel brawl contend.*
rōbīgĭnōsus -a -um, *rusty.*
rōbīgo (**rūbīgo**) -ĭnis, f. *rust; blight, mildew; inaction, mental rust.* Personif. **Rōbīgo** (**Rūb-**) -ĭnis, f. or **Rōbīgus** (**Rūb-**) -i, m. *a deity invoked to preserve grain from mildew*; **Rōbīgālĭa** -ĭum, n. *the festival of Robigo.*
rōbŏrĕus -a -um, *oaken.*
rōbŏro -are, *to strengthen, make firm.*
rōbur -ŏris, n. *hard wood*; esp., *oak, oak-wood; a dungeon at Rome,* also called the Tullianum; as a quality, *hardness, strength*; in gen., *the pick flower,* of anything.
rōbustus -a -um, *of hard wood*; esp. *of oak, oaken; strong, powerful, firm.*
rōdo rōdĕre rōsi rōsum, *to gnaw, nibble at; to corrode, consume; to disparage, backbite, slander.*
rŏgālis -e *of the funeral pile.*
rŏgātĭo -ōnis, f. *asking; a question; a request; a proposed law, a bill.*
rŏgātĭuncŭla -ae, f. *a minor question* or *bill.*
rŏgātor -ōris, m. *one who asks; the proposer of a bill; a polling-clerk.*
rŏgātū, abl. sing. m. *at the request.*
rŏgĭto -are, *to ask eagerly.*
rŏgo -are, *to ask, inquire; to ask for, request;* polit., rogare aliquem sententiam, *to ask a person his opinion*; rogare populum *or* legem, *to propose a law, introduce a bill*; rogare magistratum, *to offer a person for election.*
rŏgus -i, m. *funeral pile.*
Rōma -ae, f. *Rome*; adj. **Rōmānus** -a -um.
Rōmŭlus -i, m. *son of Mars, founder and first king of Rome*; adj. **Rōmŭlĕus** and **Rōmŭlus** -a -um.
rōrārĭi -ōrum, m. pl. *light-armed troops skirmishers.*
rōrĭdus -a-um, *bedewed.*
rōrĭfer -fĕra -fĕrum, *dew-bringing.*
rōro -are: intransit., *to drop dew, drip, be moist;* transit., *to bedew, moisten, water; to drip, let fall in drops.*
rōs rōris, m. *dew, moisture*; ros marinus, rosmarinus, *rosemary.*
rōsa -ae, f. *a rose; a garland of roses; a rose-tree.*
rŏsārĭus -a -um, *of roses*; n. as subst. *a rose-garden.*
roscĭdus -a -um, *bedewed, dewy; dripping like dew; moistened.*
Roscĭus -a -um, *name of a Roman* gens.
rŏsētum -i, n. *a garden of roses.*
rŏsĕus -a -um, *of roses; rose-coloured, rosy.*
rosmărĭnus; see ros.
rostrātus -a -um, *having a beak, beaked curved*; columna rostrata, *a pillar in the forum, adorned with ships' prows.*
rostrum -i, n. *beak, snout; a ship's prow*; plur. **rostra** -ōrum, *the speaker's platform in the Forum* (ornamented with prows of ships).

rŏta -ae, f. *a wheel*; poet., *a chariot.*
rŏto -are, *to whirl round, swing, brandish*; pass. rotari, *to revolve, to roll round.*
rŏtundo -are, *to round, make round.*
rŏtundus -a -um, *round circular*; sometimes *spherical; rounded, complete, self-contained.* Adv. **rŏtundē,** of style, *elegantly, smoothly.*
rŭbĕfacio -făcĕre -fēci -factum, *to redden, make red.*
rŭbellus -a -um, *reddish.*
rŭbĕo -ēre, *to be red; to blush*; partic. **rŭbens** -entis, *red, blushing.*
rŭber -bra -brum, *red, ruddy.*
rŭbesco -bescĕre -bŭi, *to become red.*
[1]**rŭbēta** -ae, f. *a species of toad.*
[2]**rŭbēta** -ōrum, n. pl. *bramble-thickets.*
rŭbĕus -a -um, *of bramble.*
Rŭbĭco -ōnis, m. *a river, once the boundary between Italia and Gallia Cisalpina.*
rŭbĭcundus -a -um, *red, ruddy.*
rūbīgo = robigo; q.v.
rŭbor -ōris, m. *redness; a blush; modesty; shame, disgrace.*
rubrīca -ae, f. *red earth; red ochre; a law with its title written in red.*
rŭbus -i, m. *a bramble-bush; a blackberry.*
ructo -are, and **ructor** -ari, dep. *to belch.*
ructus -ūs, m. *belching.*
rŭdens -entis, m. *a rope, halyard.*
rŭdīmentum -i, n. *a trial, attempt, essay.*
[1]**rŭdis** -e, *rough, raw, uncultivated; unrefined, unskilled, awkward.*
[2]**rŭdis** -is, f. *a small stick; a foil* (given to gladiators on their discharge).
rŭdo rŭdĕre rŭdīvi rŭdītum, *to bellow, roar.*
[1]**rūdus (rōdus)** -ĕris, n. *broken fragments of stone.*
[2]**rūdus** = raudus; q.v.
rūfus -a -um, *red, ruddy.*
rūga -ae, f. *a wrinkle.*
rūgōsus -a -um, *wrinkled.*
rŭīna -ae, f. *falling down, collapse, ruin, destruction; the ruins of a building, debris.*
rŭīnōsus -a -um, *going to ruin.*
rŭmex -ĭcis, f. *sorrel.*
Rūmīna -ae, f. *a Roman goddess*; **Rūmīnālis ficus,** m. *a fig-tree under which the she-wolf had suckled Romulus and Remus.*
rūmĭnātĭo -ōnis, f. *chewing the cud; ruminating.*
rūmĭno -are, *to chew the cud, ruminate.*
rūmor -ōris, m. *report, rumour, common talk, hearsay; general opinion, popular judgment.*
rumpo rumpĕre rūpi ruptum, *to break, shatter, burst open; to cause to break forth; to destroy, violate, annul; to break off, interrupt.*
rūmuscŭlus -i, m. *trifling rumour, idle talk, gossip.*
rūna -ae, f. *a dart.*
runco -are, *to weed, thin out.*
rŭo rŭĕre rŭi rŭtum; fut. partic. rŭĭtūrus; intransit., *to rush down, fall, collapse, be ruined; to rush along; to be precipitate;* transit., *to hurl down*; also *to cast up.*
rūpēs -is, f. *rock, cliff.*
ruptor -ōris, m. *breaker, violator.*
rūrĭcŏla -ae, *inhabiting* or *cultivating the country.*
rūrĭgĕna -ae, m. *one born in the country, a rustic.*
rūro -are and **rūror** -ari, dep. *to live in the country.*
rursus and **rursum,** *backward, back; on the other hand, in return; again, afresh.*
rūs rūris, n. *the country, a country-seat, farm, estate*; acc., rus, *to the country*; locative, ruri (or rure), *in the country.*
russus -a -um, *red, russet.*
rustĭcānus -a -um, *of the country, rustic.*
rustĭcātĭo -ōnis, f. *living in the country.*
rustĭcĭtās -ātis, f. *rustic manners, rusticity.*
rustĭcor -ari, dep. *to live in the country.*
rustĭcŭlus -a -um, *countrified*; m. as subst., *a rustic.*
rustĭcus -a -um, *of the country, rural, rustic; plain, simple; awkward, boorish*; m. as subst. *a countryman, a boor.* Adv. **rustĭcē.**
rūta -ae, *the herb rue; bitterness, unpleasantness.*
rŭtĭlo -are: intransit., *to shine reddish*; transit., *to make red.*
rŭtĭlus -a -um, *red, golden, auburn.*
rutrum -i, n. *a spade, shovel.*
rŭtŭla -ae, f. *a little bit of rue.*
Rŭtŭli -ōrum, m. pl. *an ancient people of Latium.*

S

S, s, the eighteenth letter of the Latin alphabet.
Săba -ae, f. *a town in Arabia, famous for perfumes.*
sabbăta -ōrum, n. pl. *the Sabbath, the Jewish day of rest.*
Săbelli -ōrum, m. *poetic name of the Sabines.*
Săbīni -orum, m. pl. *an ancient people of Italy, northerly neighbours of the Latins.*
săbŭlum -i, n. *gravel, sand.*
săburra -ae, f. *sand used as ballast.*
sacco -are, *to strain* or *filter.*
saccŭlus -i, m. *a small bag.*
saccus -i, m. *a sack, bag*; esp. *a purse.*
săcellum -i, n. *a small shrine, chapel.*
săcer -cra -crum, *sacred, holy, consecrated*; in bad sense, *accursed, devoted to destruction, horrible.* N. sing. as subst. **sacrum** -i, *a holy thing* or *place; a sacrifice* or *victim*; n. pl. *sacred rites, worship.*
săcerdōs -dōtis, c. *a priest, priestess.*
săcerdōtālis -e, *priestly.*
săcerdōtĭum -i, n. *priesthood.*
sacrāmentum -i, n.: legal, *money deposited by the parties in a suit*; hence *a civil suit, legal process*; milit., *oath of allegiance*; hence *an oath* or *solemn promise.*

sacrārĭum -i, n. (1) *a place where sacred things are kept, sacristy.* (2) *a place of worship, chapel, shrine.*
sacrĭcŏla -ae, c. *a sacrificing priest* or *priestess.*
sacrĭfer -fĕra -fĕrum, *carrying sacred things.*
sacrĭfĭcālis -e, *of sacrifices.*
sacrĭfĭcātĭo -ōnis, f. *sacrificing.*
sacrĭfĭcĭum -i, n. *sacrifice.*
sacrĭfĭco -are, *to sacrifice.*
sacrĭfĭcŭlus -i, m. *a sacrificing priest.*
sacrĭfĭcus -a -um, *sacrificial, sacrificing.*
sacrĭlĕgĭum -i, n. *stealing of sacred things, sacrilege, profanation.*
sacrĭlĕgus -a -um, *stealing sacred things, sacrilegious, impious.*
sacro -are. (1) *to dedicate to a god, consecrate; to devote, allot; to doom, curse.* (2) *to make holy, make inviolable; to immortalize.*
Hence partic. **sacrātus** -a -um, *holy, consecrated.*
sacrōsanctus -a -um, *consecrated, holy, sacred, inviolable.*
sacrum; see sacer.
saecŭlāris -e, *relating to a* saeculum *or age*; ludi, *secular games* (celebrated at intervals of about 100 years).
saecŭlum (poet. **saeclum**) -i, n. *a generation; the spirit of the age, the times; a hundred years, a century, an age.*
saepĕ, *often, frequently*; **saepĕnŭmĕrō,** *repeatedly, again and again.*
saepes (**sēpes**) -is, f. *hedge, fence.*
saepīmentum -i, n. *hedge, enclosure.*
saepĭo saepire saepsi saeptum, *to hedge in, enclose, surround, confine*; n. of partic. as subst. **saeptum** -i, *barrier, wall, enclosure*; in plur., *the enclosure where the Romans voted* at the comitia.
saeta -ae, f. *a bristle, stiff hair; part of an angler's line.*
saetĭger -gĕra -gĕrum, *having bristles, bristly*; m. as subst. *a boar.*
saetōsus -a -um, *bristly.*
saevĭdĭcus -a -um, *angrily spoken.*
saevĭo -īre -ĭi -ītum, *to rage, be furious, take violent action.*
saevĭtĭa -ae, f. *rage, ferocity.*
saevus -a -um, *raging, fierce, furious, violent, savage, cruel*; adv. **saevē** and **saevĭtĕr.**
sāga -ae, f., *a prophetess, fortune-teller.*
săgācĭtās -ātis, f. *keenness, acuteness, shrewdness.*
săgātus -a -um, *clothed in a* sagum; q.v.
săgax -ācis, *keen, acute*; esp. *keen-scented; mentally acute, shrewd, clever.* Adv. **săgācĭtĕr.**
săgīna -ae, f. *fattening, cramming; food, nourishment.*
săgīno -are, *to fatten, cram.*
săgitta -ae, f. *arrow.*
săgittārĭus -a -um, *of an arrow*; m. as subst. *an archer.*
săgittĭfer -fĕra -fĕrum, *carrying arrows.*
săgitto -are, *to shoot arrows.*
sagmen -ĭnis, n. *a bunch of sacred herbs.*
săgŭlum -i, n. *a small military cloak.*
săgum -i, n. *a cloak of coarse wool,* as worn by servants, and esp. by soldiers, saga sumere, *to take up arms, prepare for war.*
Săguntum -i, n. and **Săguntus** (-ŏs) -i, f. *a town on the coast of Spain.*
sāl, sălis, m. *salt; brine, sea-water;* fig., sing. and plur., *wit.*
sălăco -ōnis, m. *a swaggerer, braggart.*
Sălămis -mīnis, f. (1) *an island in the Saronic Gulf.* (2) *a town in Cyprus.*
sălăpūtĭum -i, n. *a little man, manikin.*
sălārĭus -a -um, *of salt*; n. as subst. *salt money, an allowance, pay.*
sălax -ācis, *lustful, lecherous.*
sălebra -ae, f. *jolting; a rough patch of road*; of style, *ruggedness.*
sălebrōsus -a -um, *rugged, rough.*
Sălĭātus -ūs, m. *the office of a priest of Mars*; see Salii.
sălictum -i, n. *a plantation of willows.*
sălignus -a -um, *of willow-wood.*
Sălĭi -ōrum, m. *a college of 12 priests of Mars Gradivus*; adj. **Sălĭāris** -e, *relating to the Salii; splendid, magnificent.*
sălillum -i, n. *a little salt-cellar.*
sălīnae -arum, f. *salt-works, brine-pits.*
sălīnum -i, n. *a salt-cellar.*
sălĭo sălire sălŭi saltum, *to spring, leap, bound*; f. pl. of partic. as subst. **sălĭentēs** -ium, *fountains.*
sălĭunca -ae, f. *wild nard.*
sălīva -ae, f. *spittle, saliva; appetite, taste.*
sălix -ĭcis, f. *a willow.*
Sallustĭus -i, m.: C. Sallustius Crispus, *the Roman historian Sallust, contemporary of Cicero.*
salpa -ae, f. *a kind of stock-fish.*
salsāmentum -i, n. *fish-pickle, brine; salted* or *pickled fish.*
salsūra -ae, f. *salting, pickling.*
salsus -a, -um, *salted, salty*; hence *sharp, biting, witty*; adv. **salsē.**
saltātĭo -ōnis, f. *a dancing, dance.*
saltātor -ōris, m. *a dancer.*
saltātōrĭus -a -um, *of dancing.*
saltātrix -trīcis, f. *a dancing-girl.*
saltātus -ūs, m. *a dancing, dance.*
saltem, *at least, at all events.*
salto -are, *to dance,* esp. *with gesticulation*; with acc., *to represent in pantomime, to sing with gestures.*
saltŭōsus -a -um, *wooded.*
[1]**saltus** -ūs, m. *a spring, leap, bound.*
[2]**saltus** -ūs, m. *a forest* or *mountain pasture; a pass, dale, ravine, glade.*
sălūbris and **sălūber** -bris -bre, *healthful, healthy, wholesome; sound, useful; healthy, vigorous.* Adv. **sălūbrĭtĕr,** *wholesomely, advantageously.*
sălūbrĭtās -ātis, f. *wholesomeness; soundness, health.*
sălum -i, n. *the open sea.*
sălūs -ūtis, f. *health, soundness; safety, welfare, well-being, salvation; a wish for a person's welfare, salutation, greeting.*

sălūtāris -e, *healthful, wholesome, advantageous*; n. pl. as subst. *remedies, medicines.* Adv. **sălūtārĭtĕr.**
sălūtātĭo -ōnis, f. *greeting, salutation; a call, ceremonial visit*; concr., *visitors.*
sălūtātor -ōris, m. *a visitor, caller.*
sălūtātrix -trīcis, f. adj. *greeting, paying a visit.*
sălūtĭfer -fĕra -fĕrum, *health-bringing.*
sălūto -are, *to wish well, greet, call upon, pay respect to, reverence.*
salvĕo -ēre, *to be well, be in good health*; salve, salvete, as a greeting, *Good day! Good morning!*, used also in bidding farewell.
salvus -a -um, *safe, unhurt, well, all right*; salvo iure, *without infraction of law.* Adv. **salvē.**
sambūca -ae, f. *a species of harp.*
sambūcistrĭa -ae, f. *a female harpist.*
Samnĭum -i, n. *a region of central Italy*; adj. and subst. **Samnīs** -ītis, *Samnite, a Samnite.*
Sămŏs (-ŭs) -i, f. *an island in the Aegean Sea*; adj. **Sămĭus** -a -um.
Sămothrācē, -ēs, **Sămothrāca** -ae, and **Sămothrācĭa** -ae, f. *Samothrace, an island in the northern Aegean.*
sānābĭlis -e, *curable.*
sānātĭo -ōnis, f. *healing, curing.*
sancĭo sancire sanxi sanctum (sancītum), *to consecrate, hallow, make inviolable, confirm, ratify, decree*; also *to forbid on pain of punishment, provide against.*
Hence partic. **sanctus** -a -um, *consecrated, holy, sacred; pure, virtuous.* Adv. **sanctē,** *solemnly, conscientiously.*
sanctĭmōnĭa -ae, f. *sanctity, sacredness; purity, chastity, virtue.*
sanctĭo -ōnis, f. *a clause in a law defining a penalty.*
sanctĭtās -ātis, f. *inviolability, sanctity; purity, chastity.*
sanctĭtūdo -ĭnis, f., *sanctity.*
sanctor -ōris, m., *an enacter.*
sanctus -a -um, partic. from sancio; q.v.
sandălĭum -i, n. *a slipper, sandal.*
sandăpĭla -ae, f. *a bier used for poor people.*
sandyx -dȳcis, f. *vermilion.*
sanguĭnans -antis, *bloodthirsty.*
sanguĭnārĭus -a -um, *of blood; bloodthirsty, savage.*
sanguĭnĕus -a -um, *of blood, bloody; blood-red.*
sanguĭnŏlentus -a -um, *stained with blood, bloody; wounding, injuring; blood-red.*
sanguis -ĭnis, m. (and **sanguen,** n.) blood. Transf. *blood-relationship, race, family, progeny; life-blood, strength, vigour.*
sănĭēs -ēi, f. *corrupted blood, matter; slaver, venom, poison.*
sānĭtās -ātis, f. *health, soundness; good sense, sanity*; of style, *correctness, purity.*
sanna -ae,f . *a mocking grimace.*
sannĭo -ōnis, m. *a buffoon.*
sāno -are, *to heal, cure, restore, repair.*
sānus -a, -um, *sound, healthy, uninjured; of sound mind, rational, sane;* of style, *correct.* Hence adv. **sanē,** *rationally, sensibly.* Transf., *really, indeed, to be sure*; with imperatives, *then, if you will*; sane quam, *exceedingly, extremely.*
săpa -ae, f. *must* or *new wine.*
săpĭentĭa -ae, f. *wisdom, good sense, discernment*; esp. *proficiency in philosophy, science,* etc.
săpĭo săpĕre săpīvi or săpĭi. (1) *to taste*; with acc., *to taste of* or *smell of.* (2) *to have taste, be able to taste.* (3) mentally, *to discern, be sensible, be wise, think.*
Hence partic. **săpĭens** -entis, *wise, sensible, judicious*; as subst., *a sensible, judicious person*; also *wise man, philosopher, sage.* Adv. **săpĭentĕr.**
săpor -ōris, m. *taste, flavour, flavouring; sense of taste; taste in style* or *conduct.*
Sapphō -ūs, f. *a lyric poetess of Mytilene in Lesbos.*
sarcĭna -ae, f. *a bundle, pack, burden, load.*
sarcĭnārĭus -a -um, *of burdens* or *baggage.*
sarcĭnātor -ōris, m. *cobbler.*
sarcĭnŭla -ae, f. *a little bundle.*
sarcĭo sarcire sarsi sartum, *to mend, patch, repair, make good.*
Hence partic. **sartus** -a -um; sartus (et) tectus, *in good condition, well-preserved.*
sarcŏphăgus -i, m. *coffin, grave.*
sarcŭlum -i, n. *a light hoe.*
Sardēs (Sardīs) -ĭum, f. pl. *Sardis, the old capital of Lydia*; adj. **Sardĭānus** -a -um.
Sardi -ōrum, m. *the Sardinians*; adj. **Sardus, Sardŏnĭus, Sardōus** -a -um, *Sardinian*; subst. **Sardĭnĭa** ae, f. *Sardinia.*
sardŏnyx -nȳchis, m. and f. *a precious stone, sardonyx.*
sargus -i, m. *a salt-water fish, the sargue.*
sărīsa -ae, f. *the long Macedonian pike.*
sărīsŏphŏrus -i, m. *a Macedonian pikeman.*
Sarmăta -ae, m. *a Sarmatian*; subst. **Sarmătĭa** -ae, f. *Sarmatia*; adj. **Sarmătĭcus** -a -um, *Sarmatic*; adv. **Sarmătĭcē**; f. adj. **Sarmătĭs** -ĭdis.
sarmentum -i, n. *twigs, brushwood.*
sarrācum -i, n. = serracum; q.v.
sarrĭo (sărĭo) -ire -ŭi and -īvi, *to hoe, weed.*
sartāgo -ĭnis, f. *frying-pan.*
sartus -a -um, partic. from sarcio; q.v.
săt, sătăgĭto, sătăgo; see satis.
sătellĕs -ĭtis, c. *a guard, attendant; an accomplice*; plur., *escort, suite, train.*
sătĭās -ātis, f. *sufficiency, abundance; satiety.*
sătĭĕtās -ātis, f. *sufficiency, abundance; satiety.*
sătĭnĕ, sătin = satisne; see satis.
[1]**sătĭo** -are, *to satisfy, fill; to cloy, satiate.*
[2]**sătĭo** -ōnis, f. *a sowing* or *planting*; in plur. *sown fields.*
sătĭra; see satur.

sătĭs or **săt,** *enough, sufficient;* as adv., *enough, sufficiently, fairly, quite*; compar. **sătĭus,** *better, more advantageous*; **sătĭnĕ, sătĭn** = satisne, *introducing questions;* **sătĭs** (or **săt**) **ăgo** or **sătăgo** -ăgĕre, *to satisfy* or *pay a creditor; to have enough to do, have one's hands full*; **sătĭs do** dare, *to give bail* or *security*; **sătĭs accĭpĭo** accĭpĕre, *to take bail* or *security*; **sătis făcĭo** or **sătisfăcĭo** -făcĕre, *to give satisfaction, satisfy, pay up, make amends*; also *to prove sufficiently.*

sătisdătĭo -ōnis, f. *a giving bail* or *security.*

sătisfactĭo -ōnis, f. *amends, reparation, apology.*

sătĭus, compar. of satis; q.v.

sător -ōris, m. *a sower, planter, begetter, father, producer.*

satrăpes -is; plur. satrapae -arum; m., *the governor of a Persian province, viceroy.*

sătur -ŭra -ŭrum, *full, sated, rich, copious.* F. as subst. **sătŭra** -ae, *a dish of various ingredients, a medley*; per saturam, *indiscriminately*; **sătŭra** (or **sătĭra**), *'satire', as a literary form.*

sătŭrēia -ae, f., plur. **sătŭrēia** -ōrum, n.; *the herb savory.*

sătŭrĭtās -ātis, f. *satiety, abundance.*

Sāturnālĭa, etc.; see Saturnus.

Sāturnus -i, m. (1) *the planet Saturn.* (2) *a mythical king of Latium.* Hence adj. **Sāturnĭus** -a -um, and **Sāturnālis** -e; n. pl. as subst. **Sāturnālĭa** -ĭum and -ĭorum, *a festival of Saturn beginning on the 17th of December.*

sătŭro -are, *to satisfy, fill.*

[1]**sătus** -a -um, partic. from sero; q.v.

[2]**sătus** -ūs, m. *sowing, planting; begetting, origin.*

sătўrus -i, m. *a satyr.* Transf., *Greek Satyric drama.*

sauciātĭo -onis, f. *wounding.*

saucĭo -are, *to wound, hurt.*

saucĭus -a -um, *wounded, hurt, stricken, distressed.*

sāvĭor -ari, dep. *to kiss.*

sāvĭum (suāvĭum) -i, n. *a kiss.*

saxētum -i, n. *a rocky place.*

saxĕus -a -um, *of rock, stony.*

saxĭfĭcus -a -um, *petrifying.*

saxōsus -a -um, *full of rocks, rocky.*

saxŭlum -i, n. *a little rock.*

saxum -i, n. *a rock, stone*; esp. *the Tarpeian rock.*

scăbellum (scăbillum) -i, n. *footstool; a musical instrument played with the foot.*

scăber -bra -brum, *scabby; rough.*

scăbĭēs -ēi, f. *scab, mange, itch; roughness; itching desire.*

scăbĭōsus -a -um, *scabby; rough.*

scăbo scăbĕre scābi, *to scratch.*

scaena (scēna) -ae, f. *stage, scene, theatre; natural background; publicity, the public eye.*

scaenālis -e, *theatrical.*

scaenĭcus -a -um, *of the stage, theatrical*; m. as subst. *a stage-hero, an actor.*

Scaevŏla -ae, m. *the left-handed, a surname of the* gens Mucia.

scaevus -a -um, *left, on the left.* Transf., *awkward.*

scālae -arum, f. pl. *a flight of stairs, ladder*; milit., *scaling-ladders.*

scalmus -i, m. *a thole-pin, rowlock.*

scalpellum -i, n. *a lancet, scalpel.*

scalpo scalpĕre scalpsi scalptum, *to carve, scrape, scratch.*

scalprum -i, n. *a chisel; a penknife.*

scammōnĕa (-mōnĭa) -ae, f. *the plant scammony.*

scamnum -i, n. *a bench, stool.*

scando scandĕre scandi scansum, *to climb, mount, rise.*

scăpha -ae, f. *a small boat, skiff.*

scăphĭum -i, n. *a pot, bowl, drinking-vessel.*

scăpŭlae -ārum, f. pl. *the shoulder-blades; the shoulders, back.*

scāpus -i, m. *a weaver's beam,* or *perhaps leash-rod.*

scărus -i, m. *a salt-water fish; perhaps parrot-fish.*

scătebra -ae, f. *a spouting up, bubbling up.*

scătĕo -ēre and **scăto** -ĕre, *to gush, spout up; to teem, abound.*

scăturrīgo -gĭnis, f. *a bubbling spring.*

scăturrĭo -ire, *to gush, bubble over.*

scaurus -a -um, *with swollen ankles.*

scazōn -ontis, m. *an iambic trimeter with a spondee or trochee in the last foot.*

scĕlĕro -are, *to pollute with guilt.* Partic. **scĕlĕrātus** -a -um, *polluted with guilt; impious, wicked; tiresome, noxious*; adv. **scĕlĕrāte,** *impiously, wickedly.*

scĕlĕrōsus -a -um, *guilty, wicked.*

scĕlestus -a -um, *guilty, wicked, accursed*; adv. **scĕlestē.**

scĕlus -ĕris, n. *a crime.* Transf., *misfortune, calamity.* As a term of abuse, *scoundrel, rascal.*

scēn-; see scaen-.

sceptrĭfer -fĕra -fĕrum, *sceptre-bearing.*

sceptrum -i, n. *a sceptre;* poet., *dominion, kingdom.*

sceptūchus -i, m. *wand-bearer, a court official.*

schĕda and **scĭda** -ae, f. *a strip of papyrus bark; a leaf of paper.*

schēma -ae, f. and -ătis, n. *shape, figure, form.*

schoenŏbătēs -ae, m. *a rope-walker.*

schŏla -ae, f. *learned leisure; conversation, debate; a lecture, dissertation; a school; a sect.*

schŏlastĭcus -a -um, *of a school*; esp. *rhetorical*; m. as subst. *a student* or *teacher of rhetoric.*

scĭda = schida; q.v.

scĭentĭa -ae, f. *knowing, knowledge, acquaintance, skill.*

scĭlĭcĕt, *evidently, certainly, of course;* ironically, *no doubt*; in answers, *certainly*; explanatory, *namely.*

scilla (squilla) -ae, f. *a sea-leek, squill; a crayfish* or *prawn.*

scĭn = scisne; see scio.

scindo scindĕre scĭdi scissum, *to cut, rend, split; to divide, separate.* Partic. **scissus** -a -um, *torn, rent*; of the voice, *harsh.*
scintilla -ae, f. *a spark; a glimmer.*
scintillo -are, *to sparkle, glitter.*
scintillŭla -ae, f. *a little spark.*
scĭo scīre scīvi or scĭi scītum, *to know, understand*; with infin., *to know how to*; with adv., scire Graece, *to understand Greek.*
Hence partic. **scĭens** -entis, *knowing, aware; understanding; versed in, acquainted with* (with genit.); adv. **scĭentĕr;** for **scītus** -a -um, see scisco.
[1]**scīpĭo** -ōnis, m. *a staff, wand.*
[2]**Scīpĭo** -ōnis, m. *a family of the gens* Cornelia; **Scīpĭădēs** -ae, *one of the family of the Scipios, a Scipio.*
scirpĕus (sirpĕus) -a -um, *of rushes*: f. as subst. *basket-work.*
scirpĭcŭlus (sirpĭcŭlus) -a -um, *of rushes*; m. and f. as subst. *a rush-basket.*
scirpus (sirpus) -i, m. *a rush, bulrush.*
sciscĭtor -ari, dep. and **sciscĭto** -are, *to inquire, examine, interrogate.*
scisco sciscĕre scīvi scītum, *to investigate, inquire*; polit. *to vote, ordain, resolve.*
Hence partic. **scītus** -a -um, *knowing, shrewd, judicious; pretty, fine*; adv. **scītē,** *skilfully*; n. of partic. as subst., *a decree, statute*; plebis scitum, *a decree of the people of Rome.*
scissus -a -um, partic. from scindo; q.v.
scītor -ari, dep., *to seek to know, inquire, ask.*
scītū, abl. sing. m. *by a decree.*
scītus -a -um, partic. from scisco; q.v.
sciūrus -i, m. *a squirrel.*
scŏbis -is, f. *filings, chips, shavings, sawdust.*
scomber -bri, m. *a mackerel.*
scōpae -ārum, f. pl. *a besom, broom.*
scŏpŭlōsus -a -um, *rocky, craggy.*
scŏpŭlus -i, m. *a rock, crag, cliff, danger, ruin.*
scorpĭo -ōnis, and **scorpĭus (-ŏs)** -i, m. *a scorpion*; milit., *an engine for throwing missiles*; a *salt-water fish,* perhaps *the sculpin.*
scortĕus -a -um, *leathern, made of leather*; f. as subst. *a leathern garment.*
scortor -ari, dep. *to whore, go with harlots.*
scortum -i, n. *a harlot, prostitute.*
scrĕo -are, *to clear the throat, hawk, hem.*
scrība -ae, m. *a clerk, secretary, notary.*
scriblīta -ae, f. *a kind of pastry.*
scrībo scrībĕre scripsi scriptum, *to engrave, draw lines, write, write on, write about*; polit., *to draw up* laws, etc.; legal, dicam scribere, *to bring an action*; with double acc., *to appoint in writing*; milit., *to enrol.* N. of partic. as subst. **scriptum** -i *a mark* or *line; a composition, piece of writing*; esp. *a decree, law.*
scrīnĭum -i, n. *a case for books or papers.*
scriptĭo -ōnis, f. *the act of writing; authorship, composition; wording.*
scriptĭto -are, *to write often.*
scriptor -ōris, m. *a scribe, clerk, secretary; a writer, author, composer.*
scriptŭla -ōrum, n. *the lines on a draught-board.*
scriptum -i, n., subst. from scribo; q.v.
scriptūra -ae, f. *a piece of writing, composition; a testamentary disposition; a rent paid on public pastures.*
scrīpŭlum (scrūpŭlum, scriptŭlum) -i, m. *a small weight* or *measure.*
scrŏbis -is, c. *a ditch; a grave.*
scrōfa -ae, f. *a breeding sow.*
scrūpĕus and **scrūpōsus** -a -um, *of sharp stones, rugged, rough.*
scrūpŭlōsus -a -um, *full of stones, rough, rugged.* Transf., *exact, scrupulous, precise.*
scrūpŭlum = scripulum; q.v.
scrūpŭlus -i, m. *a small stone.* Transf., *an anxiety, doubt, scruple.*
scrūpus -i, m. *a sharp stone.* Transf., *a worry, anxiety.*
scrūta -ōrum, n. pl. *frippery, trash.*
scrūtor -ari, dep. *to search through, investigate, examine.*
sculpo sculpĕre sculpsi sculptum, *to carve, cut, chisel.*
sculptĭlis -e, *carved.*
sculptor -ōris, m. *sculptor.*
scurra -ae, m. *a dandy, man-about-town; a jester, buffoon.*
scurrīlis -e, *like a buffoon; mocking, jeering.*
scurrīlĭtās -ātis, f. *buffoonery.*
scurror -ari, dep. *to play the buffoon.*
scūtāle -is, n. *the thong of a sling.*
scūtātus -a -um, *armed with a shield.*
scŭtella -ae, f. *a flat dish, saucer.*
scŭtĭca -ae, f. *a whip.*
[1]**scŭtŭla** -ae, f. *a little square-shaped dish.*
[2]**scŭtŭla** -ae, f. *a roller, cylinder.*
scŭtŭlāta -ōrum, n. pl. *checked cloths, checks.*
scūtŭlum -i, n. *a little shield.*
scūtum -i, n. *a large quadrangular shield.*
Scylla -ae, f. *a rock at the straits between Sicily and Italy,* opposite to Charybdis; adj. **Scyllaeus** -a -um.
scymnus -i, m. *cub, whelp.*
scȳphus -i, m. *a drinking-cup, goblet.*
scȳtăla -ae and **scȳtălē** ēs, f. = scutula; q.v.
Scȳthēs (Scȳthă) -ae, m. *a Scythian*; **Scȳthĭa** -ae, f. *Scythia.*
sē or **sēsē,** acc. sing. and plur.; **sŭī,** genit.; **sĭbĭ,** dat.; **se** or **sēsē,** abl.; strengthened forms, sēpse, sēmet; reflexive pronoun of third person, *himself, herself, itself, themselves*; sibi velle, to mean; secum = cum se; inter se, *reciprocally.*

sēbum -i, n. *tallow, fat.*
sēcēdo -cēděre -cessi -cessum, *to go apart, withdraw.*
sēcerno -cerněre -crēvi -crētum, *to separate, part, sunder; to distinguish; to set aside, reject.*
Hence partic. **sēcrētus** -a -um, *separate, alone, special; retired, solitary; hidden, secret*; with abl., *deprived of.* N. as subst. **sēcrētum** -i, *retirement, solitude; a secret, mystery.* Abl. as adv. **sēcrētō,** *apart, separately.*
sēcessĭo -ōnis, f. *a going apart, withdrawal, secession.*
sēcessus -ūs, m. *a going apart, withdrawal, retirement; a retreat, recess.*
sēcius; see secus.
sēclūdo -clūděre -clūsi -clūsum, *to shut off; to confine, to separate from others.*
sěco sěcare sěcŭi sectum, *to cut, amputate, to wound, hurt; to divide, part*; hence *to settle* disputes; *to cut out, make by cutting.*
sēcretus -a -um, partic. from secerno; q.v.
secta -ae, f. *a way, mode of life, procedure; a school of thought.*
sectātor -ōris, m. *a follower, hanger-on*; plur., *train, retinue.*
sectĭlis -e, *cut; able to be cut.*
sectĭo -ōnis, f. *cutting.* Transf., *the buying up of state property*; concr., *auctioned property, a lot.*
[1]**sector** -ōris, m. *a cutter.* Transf., *a buyer of state property.*
[2]**sector** -ari, dep. *to follow eagerly; to accompany, attend*; of enemies, *to run after, chase*; in gen., *to strive after, try to get* or *find.*
sectūra -ae, f. *cutting*; aerariae secturae, *copper-mines.*
sēcŭbĭtus -ūs, m. *lying alone.*
sēcŭbo -are, -ui, *to sleep alone.*
sēcŭl-; see saecul-.
sēcum = cum se; see se.
sěcundāni -ōrum, m. pl. *soldiers of the second legion.*
sěcundārĭus -a -um, *second-rate.*
sěcundo -are, *to favour, assist.*
sěcundum: adv., *after, behind*; prep., with acc., *following, after, along beside; during; in addition to; next after, next to; according to; in favour of.*
sěcundus -a -um. (1) *going after, second, following; inferior, second-rate.* (2) *going the same way, attending, favouring*; secundo flumine, *downstream*; res secundae, *prosperity, success.* As subst.: n. abl. sing. **sěcundō,** *secondly*; f. pl. **sěcundae** -ārum, *the second role, second fiddle*; n. pl. **sěcundă** -ōrum, *prosperity, success.*
sěcūrĭfer -fěra -fěrum, and **sěcūrĭger** -gěra -gěrum, *carrying an axe.*
sěcūris -is, f. *an axe, hatchet*; esp. *the headsman's axe*; hence *supreme power, Roman supremacy.*
sēcūrĭtās -ātis, f. *freedom from care; peace of mind, composure; carelessness, false confidence.* Transf., *freedom from danger, security.*
sēcūrus -a -um, *free from care, unconcerned, fearless, tranquil; careless*; objectively, *safe, secure.* Adv. **sēcūrē.**
[1]**sěcus,** n. indecl., *sex.*
[2]**sěcŭs,** adv. *otherwise, not so*; foll. by atque (ac), or quam, *otherwise than, differently from*; non secus, haud secus, *just so.* Transf., *not as one would wish,* i.e. *wrongly, badly.* Compar. **sěquĭŭs** or **sētĭŭs,** *otherwise, not so; less; rather badly.*
sěcūtor -ōris, m. *a gladiator armed with sword and shield.*
sěd (sět), *but, however*; sed enim, *but in fact*; confirming, *and indeed, and what is more.*
sēdātĭo -ōnis, f. *allaying, soothing.*
sēděcim, *sixteen.*
sēdēcŭla -ae, f. *a low seat, stool.*
sěděo sěděre sēdi sessum, *to sit; to sit in council* or *judgment; to sit about, be inactive*; milit. *to remain encamped*; of things, *to be settled, stay fixed*; of resolves, *to be firmly determined.*
sēdēs -is, f. *a seat; a chair, throne; an abode, home*; of things, *place, seat, base, foundation.*
sědīle -is, n. *a seat, bench.*
sēdĭtĭo -ōnis, f. *insurrection, rising, mutiny; dissension, quarrel.*
sēdĭtĭōsus -a -um, *quarrelsome, turbulent, restless*; adv. **sēdĭtĭōsē.**
sēdo -are, *to settle, soothe, calm, allay*; partic. **sēdātus** -a -um, *calm, composed*; adv. **sēdātē.**
sēdūco -dūcěre -duxi -ductum, *to lead apart, turn aside, separate*; partic. **sēductus** -a -um, *remote, distant.*
sēductĭo -ōnis, f. *leading aside.*
sēdŭlĭtās -ātis, f. *zeal, application.*
sēdŭlus -a -um, *busy, diligent*; in bad sense, *officious.* N. abl. as adv. **sēdŭlō,** *busily; purposely, designedly.*
sěgěs -ětis, f. *a cornfield; standing corn, a crop*; in gen., *field, ground, soil; source, origin; profit.*
segmentātus -a -um, *adorned with borders or patches.*
segmentum -i, n. *a cutting, shred*; plur., *borders* or *patches of purple* or *gold.*
segnĭpēs -pědis, *slow-footed.*
segnis -e, *slow, tardy, sluggish, lingering.* N. acc. as adv. **segně,** and adv. **segnĭtěr,** *slowly, sluggishly.*
segnĭtĭa -ae, and **segnĭtĭēs** -ēi, f. *sluggishness, slowness.*
segrěgo -are, *to segregate, separate, remove.*
sēiŭgātus -a -um, *separated.*
sēiŭgis -is, m. *a chariot drawn by six horses.*
sēiunctim, *separately.*
sēiunctĭo -ōnis, f. *separation.*
sēiungo -iungěre -iunxi -iunctum, *to separate, sever, disjoin.*
sēlectĭo -ōnis, f. *choosing out, selection.*
Sěleucus -i, m. *name of several kings of Syria.*

sēlībra -ae, f. *half a pound.*
sēlĭgo -lĭgĕre -lēgi -lectum, *to choose, select.*
sella -ae, f. *a seat, chair, stool*; sella (curulis), *a magistrate's seat*; sella (gestatoria), *a sedan-chair.*
sellisternĭa -ōrum, n. pl. *religious banquets in honour of goddesses.*
sellŭla -ae, f. *a little chair.*
sellŭlārĭus -i, m. *a sedentary worker.*
sĕmĕl, *once, a single time; for the first time; once for all*; indef., *once, ever, at any time.*
Sĕmĕla -ae, and **Sĕmĕlē** -ēs, f. *mother of Bacchus.*
sēmen -ĭnis, n. *seed; a seedling, scion, shoot; a stock, race; an element; a cause, origin; an author, instigator.*
sēmentĭfer -fĕra -fĕrum, *seed-bearing, fruitful.*
sēmentis -is, *a sowing* or *planting*; plur., sementes, *young growing corn.*
sĕmentīvus -a -um, *of seed-time.*
sēmestris (**sēmenstris**) -e, *of six months, lasting six months.*
sēmēsus -a -um, *half-eaten.*
sēmiădăpertus -a -um, *half-open.*
sēmiănĭmis -e and **sēmiănĭmus** -a -um, *half-alive, half-dead.*
sēmiăpertus -a -um, *half-open.*
sēmĭbōs -bŏvis, m. *half-ox.*
sēmĭcăper -pri, m. *half-goat.*
sēmĭcrĕmātus and **sēmĭcrĕmus** -a -um, *half-burnt.*
sēmĭcŭbĭtālis -e, *half a cubit long.*
sēmĭdĕus -a -um, *half-divine*; as subst., *a demigod.*
sēmĭdoctus -a -um, *half-taught.*
sēmĭermis (**sēmermis**) -e and **sēmĭermus** (**sēmermus**) -a -um, *half-armed, half-equipped.*
sēmĭēsus = semesus; q.v.
sēmĭfactus -a -um, *half-done, half-finished.*
sēmĭfer -fĕra -fĕrum, *half-animal; half-savage.*
sēmĭgermānus -a -um, *half-German.*
sēmĭgrăvis -e, *half-overcome.*
sēmigro -are, *to go away, depart.*
sēmihĭans -antis, *half-open.*
sēmihŏmo -hŏmĭnis, m. *half-man; half-wild.*
sēmihora -ae, f. *half an hour.*
sēmĭlăcer -cĕra -cĕrum, *half-mangled.*
sēmĭlīber -bĕra -bĕrum, *half-free.*
sēmĭlixa -ae, m. *half a sutler.*
sēmĭmărīnus -a -um, *half in the sea.*
sēmĭmas -măris, m. *half-male, hermaphrodite; castrated.*
sēmĭnārĭum -i, n. *a plantation, nursery.*
sēmĭnātor -oris, m. *begetter, author.*
sēmĭnex -nĕcis, *half-dead.*
sēmĭnĭum -i, n. *a begetting; a race* or *breed.*
sēmĭno -are, *to sow, plant; to beget, produce.*
sēmĭnūdus -a -um, *half-naked; ill-protected.*
sēmĭplēnus -a -um, *half-full, half-manned.*
sēmĭpŭtātus -a -um, *half-pruned.*
sēmĭrĕductus -a -um, *half bent back.*
sēmĭrĕfectus -a -um, *half-repaired.*
sēmĭrŭtus -a -um, *half-ruined, half pulled down.*
sēmis -issis, m. *the half of anything*, e.g. of an as or iuger; as a rate of interest = 6 *per cent per annum.*
sēmĭsĕpultus -a -um, *half-buried.*
sēmĭsomnus -a -um and **sēmĭsomnis** -e, *half-asleep, drowsy.*
sēmĭsŭpīnus -a -um, *half on the back.*
sēmĭta -ae, f. *a narrow way, footpath.*
sēmĭtālis -e, and **sēmĭtārĭus** -a -um *of the footpaths.*
sēmĭustŭlātus = semustulatus; q.v.
sēmĭustus (**sēmustus**) -a -um, *half-burnt.*
sēmĭvir -vĭri, m. adj., *half-man half-animal; hermaphrodite; castrated, effeminate.*
sēmĭvīvus -a -um, *half-dead, very faint.*
sēmŏdĭus -i, m. *half a* modius.
sēmŏvĕo -mŏvēre -mōvi -mōtum, *to move away, set aside, separate*; partic. **sēmōtus** -a -um, *remote, distant.*
sempĕr, *always, at all times.*
sempĭternus -a -um, *continual, everlasting.*
Semprōnĭus -a -um, *name of a Roman* gens.
sēmuncĭa -ae, f. *half an* uncia.
sēmuncĭārĭus -a- um, *of the fraction* 1/24: faenus, 1/24 *per cent monthly*, i.e. ½ *per cent per annum.*
sēmustŭlātus (**sēmĭustŭlātus**) -a -um *half-burnt.*
sĕnācŭlum -i, n. *an open space in the Forum, used by the Senate.*
sēnārĭŏlus -i, m. *a trifling* senarius.
sēnārĭus -a -um, *composed of six in a group*; senarius (versus), m. a senarius, *a verse of six feet.*
sĕnātor -ōris, m. *a member of the senate, a senator.*
sĕnātōrĭus -a -um, *of a senator, senatorial.*
sĕnātus -ūs, (or -i), m *a council of elders, the Senate*; senatus (senati) consultum, *a formal resolution of the senate.*
Sĕnĕca -ae, m. M. Annaeus Seneca, *a rhetorician from Corduba in Spain*; L. Annaeus Seneca, *his son, a Stoic philosopher, tutor of Nero.*
[1]**sĕnectus** -a -um, *old, aged*; f. as subst. **sĕnecta** -ae, *old age.*
[2]**sĕnectūs** -ūtis, f. *old age*; concr., *old men.*
sĕnĕo -ēre, *to be old.*
sĕnesco senescĕre sĕnŭi, *to grow old; to flag, wane.*
sĕnex sĕnis; compar. **sĕnĭor**: adj., *old, aged*; subst., *an old person.*
sēni -ae -a, *six at a time, or six each.*
sĕnīlis -e, *of an old man, senile*; adv. **sĕnīlĭtĕr.**
sēnĭo -ōnis, m. *the number six upon dice.*
sĕnĭor, compar. of senex; q.v.
sĕnĭum -i, n. *old age; decline, decay; gloom, grief.*
sensĭcŭlus -i, m. *a little sentence.*

sensĭfer -fĕra -fĕrum, *producing sensation.*
sensĭlis -e, *having sensation, sensitive.*
sensim, *just perceptibly, gradually, by degrees.*
sensus -ūs, m. *sense, sensation; feeling, attitude; judgment, perception, understanding; sense, meaning* of words, etc.; a *sentence.*
sententĭa -ae, f. *a way of thinking, opinion, thought, meaning, purpose; a decision, vote; meaning, sense* of words, etc.; *a sentence, period*; esp., *a maxim, aphorism.*
sententĭŏla -ae, f. *a short sentence, maxim, aphorism.*
sententĭōsus -a -um, *pithy, sententious*; adv. **sententĭōsē.**
sentĭcētum -i, n. *a thorn-brake.*
sentīna -ae, f. *bilge-water; rabble, dregs of the population.*
sentĭo sentire sensi sensum, *to feel, perceive; to experience, feel the force of* a thing; *to realize* a truth; *to hold* an opinion, *judge, suppose*; legal, *to decide, to vote.* N. pl. of partic. as subst. **sensa** -ōrum, *thoughts, sentiments.*
sentis -is, c. *a thorn-bush, briar.*
sentisco -ĕre, *to begin to perceive*
sentus -a -um, *neglected, rough.*
sĕorsum, sorsum, sorsus, *apart, separately.*
sēpărātim, *apart, separately, differently.*
sēpărātĭo -ōnis, f. *separation, severance.*
sēpăro -are, *to sever, separate; to consider* or *treat separately.*
Hence partic. **sēpărātus** -a -um, *separate, distinct*; compar. adv. **sēpărātĭŭs,** *less closely.*
sĕpĕlĭo -pĕlīre -pĕlīvi and -pĕlĭi -pultum, *to bury; to ruin, destroy*; partic. sĕpultus, *buried, sunk, immersed.*
sēp-; see also saep-.
sēpĭa -ae, f. *cuttle-fish.*
sēpōno -pōnĕre -pŏsŭi -pŏsĭtum, *to put on one side, place apart, reserve; to put out of the way, banish; to distinguish, divide.* Partic. **sēpŏsĭtus** -a -um, *distant, remote; choice, select.*
sepse = se ipse; see ipse.
septem, *seven.*
September -bris, *of September*; (mensis) *September, the seventh month of the Roman year, September.*
septemdĕcim, *seventeen.*
septemflŭus -a -um, *with seven mouths.*
septemgĕmĭnus -a -um, *sevenfold.*
septemplex -plĭcis, *sevenfold.*
septemtrĭōnālis -e, *northern.*
septemtrĭōnēs (septen-) -um, m. pl. *the seven stars of either the Great Bear or the Little Bear*; in gen., *the north; the north wind.*
septemvir -vĭri, m. *one of the* septemviri, *a college* or *guild of seven persons*; adj. **septemvĭrālis** -e, *of* septemviri; subst. **septemvĭrātus** -ūs, m. *the office of a* septemvir.
septēnārĭus -a -um, *containing seven*; m. pl. as subst. **septēnārĭi,** *verses containing seven feet, heptameters.*
septendĕcim = septemdecim; q.v.
septēni -ae, -a, *seven at a time or seven each.*
septentrĭo = septemtrio; q.v.
septĭes (-ĭens), *seven times.*
septĭmānus -a -um, *of the seventh*; m. pl. as subst. *soldiers of the seventh legion.*
septĭmus (septŭmus) -a -um, *seventh*; **septĭmum,** *for the seventh time.*
septĭmus dĕcĭmus -a -um, *seventeenth.*
septingentēsĭmus (-ensĭmus) -a -um, *seven hundredth.*
septingenti -ae -a, *seven hundred.*
septŭāgēsĭmus (-ensĭmus) -a -um, *seventieth.*
septŭāgintā, *seventy.*
septŭennis -e, *of seven years.*
septum = **saeptum**; q.v.
septunx -uncis, m. *seven-twelfths.*
sĕpulcrālis -e, *of a tomb, sepulchral.*
sĕpulcrētum -i, n. *a burial-place, cemetery.*
sĕpulcrum -i, n., *a place of burial, grave, tomb.*
sĕpultūra -ae, f. *burial, interment*; also *the burning of a dead body.*
Sēquăna -ae, m. *a river of Gaul* (now *the Seine*).
sĕquax -ācis, *following, attending, pursuing.*
sĕquester -tri or -tris, m. *a depositary; a go-between, agent, mediator.*
sĕquestra -ae, f. *a mediator.*
sĕquius = secius, compar. of secus; q.v.
sĕquor sĕqui sĕcūtus, dep. *to follow, accompany, attend; to pursue, chase*; in time, *to follow, ensue; to follow logically, follow as a consequence*; of property, *to go to, fall to; to conform to; to strive after, aim at.*
sĕra -ae, f. *a bar* or *bolt.*
sĕrēnĭtās -ātis, f. *clear weather.*
sĕrēno -are, *to make clear, make bright.*
sĕrēnus -a -um, *clear, bright, fair*; n. as subst. *fair weather.*
Sērĕs -um, m. *the Chinese, famous for their silks*; adj. **Sērĭcus** -a -um, *Chinese; silken.*
sĕresco -ere, *to become dry.*
sērĭa -ae, f. *a large jar.*
sĕrĭes, acc. -em, abl. -e, f. *a row, chain, series; a line of descent, lineage.*
sērĭus -a -um, *serious, earnest*; n. as subst. *earnest, seriousness;* abl. as adv. **sērĭō,** *in earnest, seriously.*
sermo -ōnis, m. *talk, conversation; discussion; common talk, report, rumour; a subject of conversation; a conversational style,* or *prose; any manner of speaking, style, expression, diction, language, dialect.*
sermōcĭnor -ari, dep. *to converse, talk, discuss.*
sermuncŭlus -i, m. *rumour, tittle-tattle.*
[1]**sĕro** sĕrĕre sēvi sătum, *to sow, set, plant*; n. pl. of partic. as subst., săta -ōrum, *standing corn, crops; to beget, engender, bring forth*; partic. sătus -a -um, *sprung, born*; in gen., *to produce, give rise to.*

[2]**sěro** sĕrĕre sĕrŭi sertum, *to join together, put in a row, connect*, partic. **sertus** -a -um, *linked, connected*; n. as subst. **sertum** -i, and plur. **serta** -orum, *a garland, wreath*; also f. **serta** -ae.
serpens -entis, c. *a snake, serpent*.
serpentĭgĕna -ae, m. *sprung from a serpent*.
serpentĭpēs -pĕdis, *snake-footed*.
serpĕrastra -orum, n. *bandages* or *knee-splints*.
serpo serpĕre serpsi serptum, *to creep, crawl, advance slowly*.
serpyllum (-pillum, -pullum) -i, n. *wild thyme*.
serra -ae, f. *a saw*.
serrācum (sarr-) -i, n. *a kind of waggon*.
serrātus -a -um, *toothed like a saw, serrated*; m. pl. as subst. (sc. nummi), *milled coins*.
serrŭla -ae, f. *a little saw*.
sertum; see sero.
sĕrum -i, n. *whey*.
sērus -a -um, *late, too late*; n. as subst. **serum** -i, *a late hour*; n. abl. sing. as adv. **sērō,** *late, too late*.
serva -ae, f. see servus.
servābĭlis -e, *able to be saved*.
servātor -ōris, m. and **servātrix** -icis, f., *a preserver, saviour; a watcher*.
servīlis -e, *of a slave, servile*; adv. **servīlĭtĕr.**
Servīlĭus -a -um, *name of Roman* gens.
servĭo -ire, (with dat.), *to be a slave, to serve, help, gratify*; legal, of buildings, etc., *to be subject to certain rights*, e.g. *to be mortgaged*.
servĭtĭum -i, n. *slavery, servitude, subjection*; concr., *slaves, servants*, a *household*.
servĭtūdo -ĭnis, f. *slavery, servitude*.
servĭtūs -ūtis, f. *slavery, servitude*; in gen., *subjection, obedience*; legal, of houses, etc., *liability to certain burdens*, e.g. *a right of way*; concr., *slaves*.
servo -are, *to watch over, observe; to keep, protect, save; to lay up, reserve; to keep, retain* a promise, etc.; *to keep to, stay* in a place. Partic., in superl., **servantissĭmus** -i, *most careful, most observant*.
servŭlus (servŏlus) -i, m. and **servŭla (servŏla)** -ae, f. *a young slave*.
servus, -a -um, adj., *serving, servile, subject*; legal, of lands, etc., *subject to other rights*; m. and f. as subst., *a slave, servant*.
sescēnāris -e, *a year and a half old*.
sescēnārĭus -a -um, *consisting of six hundred*.
sescēni -ae -a, *six hundred at a time or six hundred each*.
sescentēsĭmus (-ensĭmus) -a -um, *six hundredth*.
sescenti -ae -a, *six hundred*; in gen., *countless*.
sescentĭēs (-ĭens), *six hundred times*.
sĕsĕlis -is, f. *a plant, hartwort*.
sesquĭ, *one half more, half as much again*.
sesquĭalter -altĕra -altĕrum, *one and a half*.
sesquĭhōra -ae, f. *an hour and a half*.
sesquĭmŏdĭus -i, m. *a* modius *and a half*.
sesquĭoctāvus -a -um, *containing* 9/8 *of a thing*.
sesquĭpĕdālis -e, *a foot and a half long*.
sesquĭpēs -pĕdis, m. *a foot and a half long, wide*, etc.
sesquiplāga -ae, f. *a blow and a half*.
sesquiplex -plĭcis, *one and a half times as much*.
sesquĭtertĭus -a -um, *containing* 4/3 of *anything*.
sessĭbŭlum -i, n. *a seat, stool, chair*.
sessĭlis -e, *fit for sitting*; of plants, *low, dwarf*.
sessĭo -ōnis, f. *the act of sitting; loitering, idling; a session; a place for sitting, seat*.
sessĭto -are, *to sit much, sit often*.
sessĭuncŭla -ae, f. *a little company* or *assembly*.
sessor -ōris, m. *a sitter; an inhabitant*.
sestertĭus -a -um, *consisting of two and a half*; m. as subst. **sestertĭus** -i, *a sesterce, a silver coin*, = ¼ denarius, = 2½ asses.
Sestĭus -a -um, *name of a Roman* gens.
sĕt = sed; q.v.
sēta = saeta; q.v.
seu; see sive.
sĕvērĭtās -ātis, and **sĕvērĭtūdo** -ĭnis, f. *gravity, sternness*.
sĕvērus -a -um, *grave, serious, strict, stern, hard*; adv. **sĕvērē.**
sēvŏco -are, *to call aside, withdraw, separate*.
sēvum = sebum; q.v.
sex, *six*.
sexāgēnārĭus -a -um, *containing sixty; sixty years old*.
sexāgēni -ae -a, *sixty at a time*, or *sixty each*.
sexāgēsĭmus (-ensĭmus) -a -um, *sixtieth*.
sexāgĭēs (-ĭens), *sixty times*.
sexāgintā, *sixty*.
sexangŭlus -a -um, *hexagonal*.
sexcen-; see sescen-.
sexdĕcim = sedecim; q.v.
sexennis -e, *six years old*.
sexennĭum -i, n. *a period of six years*.
sexĭēs (-ĭens), *six times*.
sexprīmi -ōrum, m. *a board of six magistrates in a provincial town*.
sextādĕcĭmāni -orum, m. pl. *soldiers of the 16th legion*.
sextans -antis, m. *one sixth*.
sextārĭus -i, m. *one sixth*, esp. of a congius (about a pint).
Sextīlis -e, *of the sixth month of the old Roman year*; sextilis (mensis), *the sixth month*, afterwards called *Augustus*.
sextŭla -ae, f. 1/72.
sextus -a -um, *sixth*; **sextum,** *for the sixth time*.
sextusdĕcĭmus -a -um, *sixteenth*.
sexus -ūs, m. *sex*.

sī, *if, supposing that*; quod si, *and if, but if*; si modo, *if only*; si quis, *if anybody;* si non, si minus, nisi, *if not, unless.*

sībĭla -ōrum, n. pl.: as adj., *hissing*; as subst., = plur. of sibilus (q.v.).

sībĭlo -are,: intransit., *to hiss, whistle*; transit., *to hiss at.*

sībĭlus -i, m. (poet. plur. sibila; q.v.), *a hissing, whistling.*

Sĭbylla -ae, f. *a prophetess of Apollo, a Sibyl*; adj. **Sĭbyllīnus** -a -um, *of the Sibyl, Sibylline.*

sīc, *so, thus, in this way; like this, as follows; in that case, with this limitation*; leading up to consecutive clause, *so much, to such a degree*; interrog. **sīcĭnĕ**, *is it thus that?*

sīca -ae, f. *dagger, dirk, poniard.*

Sĭcāni -ōrum, m. pl. *an ancient people of Sicily*; adj. **Sĭcānus** and **Sĭcānĭus** -a -um, *Sicanian*; subst. **Sĭcānĭa** -ae, f. *Sicania = Sicily.*

sīcārĭus -i, m. *an assassin, murderer.*

siccĭtās -ātis, f. *dryness, drought; sound health*; of style *plainness, simplicity.*

sicco -are, *to make dry, to dry; to stanch; to drain.*

siccus -a -um, *dry; thirsting, thirsty*; of health, *sound; sober, temperate*; of style *plain, simple*; adv. **siccē**

Sĭcĭlĭa -ae, f.; see Siculi.

sīcĭnĕ ; see sic.

sīcŭbī, *if anywhere.*

Sĭcŭli -ōrum, m. pl., *the Sicilians*; adj. **Sĭcŭlus** -a -um, *Sicilian*; subst. **Sĭcĭlĭa** -ae, f. *Sicily.*

sīcundĕ, *if from anywhere.*

sīcŭt and **sīcŭtī**, *as, just as; as for example; as it were*; with verb in subj., *just as if.*

Sĭcўōn -ōnis, f. *a city in the Peloponnese*; adj. **Sĭcўōnĭus** -a -um, *Sicyonian*; n. pl. as subst. *a kind of soft shoes from Sicyon.*

sīdĕrĕus -a -um, *of the stars starry; gleaming.*

sīdo sīdere sīdi and sēdi sessum, *to sit* or *sink down, settle, alight; to remain lying* or *fixed*; naut. *to stick fast, be stranded*; of feelings, *to subside.*

Sīdōn -onis, f. *a city of Phoenicia*; adj. **Sīdōnĭus** -a -um; f. adj. **Sīdŏnis** -ĭdis.

sīdus -ĕris, n. *a constellation,* or *a single star; any luminary, heavenly body; time of year, season, weather*; in astrology, *star, destiny*; plur., *the heavens.* Transf., *pride, glory.*

sĭgilla -ōrum, n. pl. *small figures, images; a seal.*

sĭgillātus -a -um, *adorned with small figures.*

sigma -ătis, n. *the Greek letter sigma; a semicircular dining-couch.*

signātor -ōris, m. *one who seals; a witness.*

signĭfer -fĕra -fĕrum, *bearing signs* or *figures; covered with constellations.* M. as subst. **signĭfer** -fĕri *a standard-bearer; a leader.*

signĭfĭcātĭo -ōnis, f. *indication, sign, token; sign of assent, approbation; emphasis; meaning, signification.*

signĭfĭco -are, *to indicate, show; to foreshow; to mean, signify*; partic. **signĭfĭcans** -antis, *distinct, clear*; adv. **signĭfĭcantĕr.**

signo -are, *to mark, inscribe; to seal, seal up; to coin, stamp* money. Transf., *to impress, indicate; to observe, notice.*

signum -i, n. *a sign, mark, token; a warning, symptom*; milit., *a standard, banner, ensign,* or *a signal, order, command,* or *a watchword, password; a figure, image, statute; a seal, signet; a group of stars, constellation.*

sĭlānus -i, m. *a fountain.*

sĭlentĭum -i, n. *silence, stillness, quiet; repose; obscurity.*

sĭlĕo -ēre -ŭi, *to be still, silent*; with acc., *to be silent about; to be still, rest, be inactive*; partic. **sĭlens** -entis, *silent, still*; pl. as subst. *the dead.*

sĭler -ĕris, n. *the brook-willow.*

sĭlesco -ere, *to become silent, grow still.*

sĭlex -ĭcis, m. (rarely f.), *any hard stone, such as flint; crag, rock, cliff.*

sĭlĭcernĭum -i, n. *a funeral feast.*

sĭlīgo -ĭnis, f. *wheat; wheaten flour.*

sĭlĭqua -ae, f. *a husk, pod, shell*; in plur., *pulse.*

Sĭlĭus -a -um, *name of Roman gens.*

Sĭlŭres -um, pl. *a British people.*

sīlus -a -um, *snub-nosed, pug-nosed.*

silva, *a wood, forest; bush; a plantation, grove; a mass, plenty, abundance.*

Silvānus -i, m. *god of woods and forests.*

silvesco -ĕre, of a vine, *to run wild, run to wood.*

silvestris -e, *of woods; wooded; wild, rural.*

silvĭcŏla -ae, m. and f. and **silvĭcultrix** -trĭcis, f. *inhabiting woods.*

silvifrăgus -a -um, *shattering the woods.*

silvōsus -a -um *well wooded.*

sīmĭa -ae, f. *ape, monkey.*

sĭmĭlis -e; compar. similior, superl. simillimus; *like, resembling, similar* (with genit. or dat.); veri similis, *probable*; n. as subst. *a resemblance* or *comparison*; adv. **sĭmĭlĭtĕr**, *similarly.*

sĭmĭlĭtūdo -ĭnis, f. *likeness, resemblance*; veri similitudo, *probability; intended likeness, imitation; a metaphor, simile· uniformity, monotony.*

sĭmĭlo = simulo; q.v.

sīmĭŏlus -i, m. *little ape.*

sĭmĭtū, *together.*

sīmĭus -i, m. *ape, monkey.*

simplex -plĭcis; *simple, single; unmixed, pure, plain, absolute; morally simple, straightforward.* Adv. **simplĭcĭtĕr**, *simply, plainly; artlessly; frankly.*

simplĭcĭtās -ātis, f. *simplicity; straightforwardness, honesty, candour.*

simplum -i, m. *the simple sum* or *number* (opp. double, etc.).

simpŭlum -i, n. *a ladle.*

simpŭvĭum -i, n. *a sacrificial bowl.*

sĭmul, *at once, at the same time, together*; simul atque (ac), *as soon as.*
sĭmŭlacrum -i, n. *an image, likeness, portrait; effigy, a shade, ghost, imitation, phantom, appearance.*
sĭmŭlāmen -ĭnis, n. *an imitation.*
sĭmŭlātĭo -ōnis, f. *assumed appearance, pretence, feint.*
sĭmŭlātor -ōris, m. *an imitator; a pretender, feigner.*
sĭmŭlo -are, *to make like, cause to resemble; to make a copy of, to represent; to play the part of; to pretend* a thing is so, *simulate, feign*; partic. **sĭmŭlans** -antis, *imitating, imitative*; adv. from perf. partic. **sĭmŭlātē,** *feignedly.*
sĭmultās -ātis, f. *a clash, rivalry, feud.*
sīmŭlus -a -um, *rather snub-nosed.*
sīmus -a -um, *snub-nosed.*
sīn, conj. *but if, if however.*
sĭnāpi -is, n. and **sĭnāpis** -is, f. *mustard.*
sincērĭtās -ātis, f. *purity, soundness, integrity.*
sincērus -a -um, *pure, whole, sound, genuine, uncorrupt*; adv. **sincērē,** *honestly, frankly.*
sincĭput -pĭtis, n. *half a head; the smoked chap of a pig.*
sindōn -ŏnis, f. *fine cotton cloth, muslin.*
sĭnĕ, prep. with abl., *without.*
singillātim, *singly, one by one.*
singŭlāris -e, *alone, single individual, singular; unique, extraordinary.* Adv. **singŭlārĭtĕr,** *singly; in the singular number; particularly, extraordinarily.*
singŭli; see singulus.
singultim, *with sobs.*
singulto -are: intransit., *to gasp, sob*; transit., *to sob out, gasp out.*
singultus -ūs, m. *a sobbing, gasping.*
singŭlus -a -um, more freq. plur. **singŭli** -ae, -a, *single, separate, one at a time*; distributive, *one each.*
sĭnister -tra -trum, *left, on the left hand; wrong, perverse; unfavourable, adverse*; sometimes, in augury, *favourable.* F. as subst. **sĭnistra** -ae, *the left hand*; also *the left side.* Adv. **sĭnistre,** *wrongly, unfavourably.*
sĭnistrorsus (-orsum), *to the left.*
sĭno sĭnĕre sīvi sĭtum, *to let alone, leave; to let, allow, permit;* partic. **sĭtus** -a -um, *placed, laid down; lying, situated.*
Sĭnōpa -ae, and **Sĭnōpē** -ēs, f. *a town on the Black Sea.*
sīnum; see [1]sinus.
sĭnŭo -are, *to bend, curve.*
sĭnŭōsus -a -um, *winding, sinuous.* Transf., *roundabout, diffuse.*
[1]**sīnus** -i, m. and **sīnum** -i, n. *a large bowl.*
[2]**sĭnus** -ūs, m. *a curve, fold, winding*; of dress, *a fold, pocket, lap*; in a coastline, *a bay, gulf.* Transf., *heart, secret feelings.*
sīpărĭum -i, n. *a curtain; a drop-scene at a theatre.*
sīpho (sīfo) -ōnis, m. *a siphon; a fire-engine.*
sīquando, *if ever.*
sīquĭdem, *if indeed*; sometimes *since, because.*
Sīrēn -ēnis, f., usually plur. **Sīrēnes** -um, *the Sirens, nymphs who by their song lured mariners to destruction.*
Sīrĭus -i, m. *the Dog-Star Sirius.*
sīs = (1) si vis; see volo. (2) second sing. of pres. subj. of sum; q.v. (3) dat. or abl. plur. of suus; q.v.
sisto sistĕre stĭti stătum: transit., *to cause to stand, set, place*; legal, *to cause to appear in court*; vadimonium sistere, *to appear on the appointed day; to stop, check; to establish firmly*; intransit., *to place oneself, stand*; legal, *to present oneself in court; to stand still to halt; to stand firm.*

Hence partic. **stătus** -a -um, *fixed, determined, regular.*
sistrum -i, n. *a sort of rattle used in the worship of Isis.*
sĭsymbrĭum -i, n. *an aromatic herb, perhaps mint.*
Sīsÿphus -i, m. *a robber, condemned in the lower world to roll a stone uphill for ever.*
sĭtella -ae, f. *an urn for drawing lots.*
sĭtĭcŭlōsus -a -um, *very dry, parched.*
sĭtĭo -ire: intransit., *to thirst, to be thirsty, dry, parched;* transit., *to thirst for, thirst after*; partic. **sĭtĭens** -entis, *thirsty, dry, parched; eager, desirous*; adv. **sĭtĭentĕr.**
sĭtis -is, f. *thirst; dryness, drought*; *eager desire.*
sĭtĭtor -ōris, m. *a thirster.*
sittÿbus -i, m. *a strip of parchment showing the title of a book.*
sĭtŭla -ae, f. *a jar.*
[1]**sĭtus** -a -um, partic. from sino; q v.
[2]**sĭtus** -ūs, m. (1) *layout, site, position, situation.* (2) *being left; neglect, dirt, decay*; mental *rusting, dullness.*
sīvĕ and **sēŭ,** *or if*; sive (seu) . . . sive (seu), *whether . . . or.*
smărăgdus -i, m. and f. *emerald.*
sŏbŏles, sŏbŏlesco = suboles, subolesco; q.v.
sōbrīnus -i, m. and **sōbrīna** -ae, f. *a cousin on the mother's side.*
sōbrĭus -a -um, *sober; without wine; moderate, frugal; sober-minded, reasonable, sensible.* Adv. **sōbrĭē.**
soccŭlus -i, m. *a little* soccus: q.v.
soccus -i, m. *a light shoe* or *slipper,* esp. *as worn by comic actors.*
sŏcer -ĕri, m. *father-in-law*; plur., soceri, *father- and mother-in-law.*
sŏcĭa -ae, f., *see* socius.
sŏcĭābĭlis -e, *easily united, compatible.*
sŏcĭālis -e, *of partners* or *allies; conjugal; sociable.* Adv. **sŏcĭālĭtĕr,** *sociably.*
sŏcĭĕtās -ātis, f. *partnership, fellowship, association, alliance.*
sŏcĭo -are, *to unite, combine, associate.*
sŏcĭus -a -um, *sharing, associated, allied.* M. and f. as subst. *a partner comrade, associate, ally.*
sōcordĭa (sēcordĭa) -ae, f. *folly, stupidity; negligence, indolence.*

sōcors -cordis, *weak-minded, stupid; negligent, slothful, careless*; compar. adv. **sōcordĭus,** *too feebly.*
Sōcrătēs -is, m. *the Athenian philosopher, put to death in* 399 B.C. Adj. **Sōcrătĭcus** -a -um, *Socratic*; m. pl. as subst., *followers of Socrates.*
socrus -ūs, f. *mother-in-law.*
sŏdālĭcium -i, n. *an association*; esp. *a secret society*; in gen., *comradeship.*
sŏdālĭcius -a -um, *of companionship.*
sŏdālis -is, c. *member of an association,* esp. *of a priesthood* or *a secret society*; in gen., *a comrade*; of things, *companion, attendant on.*
sŏdālĭtās -ātis, f. *an association; comradeship, intimacy.*
sōdēs, *if you please, with your leave.*
sōl sōlis, m. *the sun*; poet., *a day*; personif., *the Sun-god.*
sōlācĭŏlum -i, n. *a small consolation.*
sōlācium -i, n. *consolation, comfort, relief.*
sōlāmen -ĭnis, n. *consolation comfort.*
sōlāris -e, *of the sun, solar.*
sōlārium -i, n. *a sundial; a terrace exposed to the sun.*
sōlātor ōris, m. *a consoler, comforter.*
soldŭrii -ōrum, m. pl. *retainers, vassals.*
soldus = solidus; q.v.
sŏlĕa -ae, f. *a sandal; a kind of fetter; a shoe for an animal; a fish, the sole.*
sŏlĕātus -a-um, *wearing sandals.*
sōlennis = sollemnis; q.v.
sŏlĕo sŏlēre sŏlĭtus sum, *to be accustomed*; ut solet, *as usual*; partic. **sŏlĭtus** -a -um, *accustomed, habitual, usual*; n. as subst. *that which is usual.*
sōlers = sollers; q.v.
sŏlĭdĭtās -ātis, f. *solidity.*
sŏlĭdo -are, *to make firm* or *solid.*
sŏlĭdus (soldus) -a -um, *dense, solid; whole, complete, entire; firm, enduring, real;* n. as subst., *firm ground, solid substance, entirety.* Adv. **sŏlĭdē,** *firmly*; scire, *to know for certain.*
sōlĭferrĕum -i, n. *a javelin entirely of iron.*
sōlistĭmus -a -um; *see* tripudium.
sōlĭtārĭus -a -um, *alone, lonely.*
sōlĭtūdo -ĭnis, f. *solitude, loneliness; desertion, deprivation, want.*
sŏlĭtus -a -um, partic. from soleo; q.v.
sŏlĭum -i, n. (1) *a chair of state, throne*; hence *dominion, regal power.* (2) *a bath-tub.*
sōlĭvăgus -a -um, *wandering alone; solitary, lonely.*
sollemnis -e, *yearly, annual, recurring; solemn, festive, religious; usual, customary.* N. as subst. **sollemnĕ** -is. *a solemn feast, religious rite; a custom.* Adv. **sollemnĭtĕr.**
sollers -ertis, *clever, skilful*; adv. **sollertĕr.**
sollertĭa -ae, f. *cleverness, skill.*
sollĭcĭtātĭo -ōnis, f. *inciting, instigation.*
sollĭcĭto -are, *to move violently, disturb, agitate; to rouse, vex, disquiet; to incite, instigate, tamper with.*
sollĭcĭtūdo -ĭnis, f. *uneasiness, disquiet, anxiety.*
sollĭcĭtus -a -um, *disturbed, agitated, restless; anxious, uneasy, worried*; of animals, *watchful*; in act. sense, *disquieting.* Adv. **sollĭcĭtē,** *anxiously, carefully.*
sōlo -are, *to make solitary.*
sŏloecismus -i, m. *a grammatical error.*
Sŏlōn -ōnis, m. *a famous Athenian legislator, active about* 600 B.C.
sōlor -ari, dep. *to comfort, console; to assuage, relieve troubles,* etc.
solstĭtĭālis -e, *of the summer solstice; of summer; of the sun.*
solstĭtĭum -i, n. *solstice,* esp. *the summer solstice; summer.*
sŏlum -i. n. *bottom, floor, foundation; the sole of the foot,* or *shoe; soil, ground, earth, land, country.*
sōlus -a -um, *alone, only, sole*; of places, *solitary, uninhabited.* N. acc. as adv. **sōlum,** *alone, only.*
sŏlūtĭo -ōnis, f. *a loosening; a paying, payment*; *a solution, explanation.*
solvo solvĕre solvi sŏlūtum, *to loosen; to untie, release, free; to dissolve, break up; to exempt; to break up, weaken, bring to an end; to pay off, discharge a debt;* solvendo non esse, *to be insolvent; to meet* engagements, *perform* duties; *to break down* a restraining influence; *to solve* a problem, *explain* a difficulty.
Hence partic. **sŏlūtus** -a -um, *loosened, unbound, free, unencumbered, independent*; in bad sense, *unrestrained, unbridled; lax, lazy, negligent*: of style, *fluent* or *in prose.* Adv. **sŏlūtē,** *loosely, freely; carelessly.*
somnĭcŭlōsus -a -um, *sleepy, drowsy*; adv. **somnĭcŭlōsē.**
somnĭfer -fĕra -ferum, *sleep-bringing; narcotic, deadly.*
somnĭo -are, *to dream*; with acc., *to dream of; to imagine foolishly.*
somnĭum -i, n. *a dream; a fancy, day-dream; foolishness, nonsense.*
somnus -i, m. *sleep, slumber; drowsiness, laziness, inactivity; night.*
sŏnābĭlis -e, *resounding.*
sŏnĭpēs -pĕdis, *sounding with the feet*; m. as subst., *a horse.*
sŏnĭtus -ūs, m. *a sound, noise.*
sŏnĭvĭus -a -um, *sounding*; sonivium tripudium, *the noise of the food falling from the beaks of the sacred chickens.*
sŏno sŏnare sŏnŭi sŏnĭtum, *to sound, resound, make a noise; to sing of, to celebrate*; of words, *to mean.*
sŏnor -ōris, m. *sound, noise, din.*
sŏnōrus -a -um, *sounding, resonant, loud.*
sons sontis, *guilty.*
sontĭcus -a -um, *important, serious.*
sŏnus -i, m. *noise, sound; tone, character, style.*
sŏphia -ae, f. *wisdom.*
sŏphistēs -ae, m. *a sophist.*
Sŏphoclēs -is and -i, m. *the Greek tragic poet*; adj. **Sŏphoclēus** -a -um.

[1]**sŏphŏs** (-ŭs) -i, m. *wise*; as subst., *a wise man.*
[2]**sŏphōs,** adv. *bravo! well done!*
sōpĭo -ire, *to put to sleep, lull to sleep, quieten; to stun, render senseless.*
sŏpor -ōris, m. *deep sleep; laziness; a sleeping draught.*
sŏpōrātus -a -um *full of sleep.*
sŏpōrĭfer -fĕra -fĕrum, *causing deep sleep.*
sŏpōrus -a -um, *sleep-bringing.*
Sōractĕ -is, n. *a mountain in Etruria.*
sorbĕo -ēre, *to suck in, drink, swallow.*
sorbĭlo, *by sipping; drop by drop.*
sorbum -i, n. *a service-berry.*
sordĕo -ēre, *to be dirty; to appear vile.*
sordēs -is, f. often plur. **sordēs** -ĭum, *dirt, filth; shabby* or *dirty garments; low rank; sordid conduct, meanness.*
sordesco sordescĕre sordŭi, *to become dirty.*
sordĭdātus -a -um, *wearing shabby* or *dirty clothes.*
sordĭdŭlus -a -um, *somewhat dirty* or *mean.*
sordĭdus -a -um, *dirty, filthy, shabby; low, base* in rank; *mean* in conduct. Adv. **sordĭdē,** *meanly; stingily.*
sōrex -ĭcis, m. *a shrew-mouse.*
sŏror -ōris, *a sister.*
sŏrōrĭcīda -ae, m. *one who murders a sister.*
sŏrōrĭus -a -um, *of a sister, sisterly.*
sors sortis, f. *a lot; a casting of lots; an oracular response, prophecy; official duty* as allotted; with genit., *share, part; fate, fortune, destiny; money, capital out at interest.*
sortĭlĕgus -a -um, *prophetic, oracular*; m. as subst., *a soothsayer, fortune-teller.*
sortĭor -iri, dep., and **sortĭo** -ire: instransit., *to cast lots;* transit., *to allot, cast lots for; share out*; also *to obtain by lot; to choose.*

Hence partic. **sortītus** -a -um; dep., *having obtained* (by lots) or *cast lots for*; pass. *gained by lot*; n. abl. as adv., **sortītō,** *by lot, by fate.*

sortītĭo -ōnis, f. *casting lots, deciding by lot.*
[1]**sortītus** -ūs, m. *casting lots, deciding by lot.*
[2]**sortītus** -a -um, partic. from sortior; q.v.
sospĕs -ĭtis, *safe, unhurt, uninjured; lucky, favourable.*
Sospĭta -ae, f. *the Saviour*; epithet of Juno.
sospĭto -are, *to keep safe, preserve.*
sōtēr -ēris; acc. -ēra; m. *a saviour.*
sōtērĭa -ōrum, n. pl. *presents given on recovery from sickness.*
spādix -dīcis, *chestnut-coloured*
spădo -ōnis, m. *a enuuch.*
spargo spargĕre sparsi sparsum, *to scatter, sprinkle, throw about; to spread, circulate, distribute; to disperse, dissipate*; with abl. *to besprinkle with.*

Hence partic. **sparsus** -a -um, *spread out, scattered; speckled, spotted.*

sparsĭo -ōnis, f. *a sprinkling.*
Sparta -ae, and **Spartē** -es, f. *Sparta, the capital of Laconia*; adj. **Spartānus** -a -um, *Spartan.*
spartum -i, n. *Spanish broom.*
spărŭlus -i, m. *a fish, sea-bream.*
spărus -i, m. *a spear with a curved blade.*
spătha -ae, f. *a broad two-edged sword.*
spătĭor -ari, dep. *to walk about, take a walk*; of things, *to spread out, expand.*
spătĭōsus -a -um, *ample, wide*; of time, *long*; adv. **spătĭōsē.**
spătĭum -i, n. *space, extent, room; distance, interval; dimensions, size; a tract, course,* esp. in a race; *an open space, a walk.* Transf., *a space of time, period; leisure, opportunity; metrical time, measure, quantity.*
spĕcĭālis -e, *individual, particular, special.*
spĕcĭes -ēi, f.: act., *a seeing, view;* pass., *sight, look; shape, form, outward appearance; beauty; a vision, phantom; a representation, image, statue.* Transf., *pretext, pretence; notion, idea; kind, species.*
spĕcillum -i, n. *a surgeon's probe.*
spĕcĭmen -ĭnis, n. *a visible mark, example, model; a pattern, ideal.*
spĕcĭo (**spĭcĭo**) spĕcĕre spexi, *to look at, see.*
spĕcĭōsus -a -um, *beautiful, handsome, imposing*; in bad sense, *plausible, specious.* Adv. **spĕcĭosē.**
spectābĭlis -e, *visible; worth seeing, notable.*
spectācŭlum -i, n. *sight, show, spectacle; the seats in* the *theatre* or *circus.*
spectātĭo -ōnis, f. *looking, watching, viewing; inspection of money.*
spectātor -ōris, m. and **spectātrix** -trīcis, f. *a watcher, spectator, observer; an examiner, critic.*
spectĭo -ōnis, f. *the right to observe auspices.*
specto -are, *to look at, contemplate, watch; to test, examine*; of places, *to look towards, face.* Transf., *to consider, contemplate, look for; to bear in mind, have in view*; of things, *to tend, incline.*

Hence partic. **spectatus** -a -um, *tried, approved*; hence *esteemed, respected.*

spectrum -i. n. *a spectre, apparition.*
[1]**spĕcŭla** -ae, f. *a look out, watch-tower.*
[2]**spĕcŭla** -ae, f. *a little hope, ray of hope.*
spĕcŭlābundus -a -um, *watching, on the watch.*
spĕcŭlāris -e, *like a mirror; transparent*; n. pl. **spĕcŭlārĭa** -ōrum, *window-panes.*
spĕcŭlātor -ōris, m.: milit., *scout, spy*; in gen., *observer, investigator.*
spĕcŭlātōrĭus -a -um, *of a scout*; f. as subst. *a spy-boat.*
spĕcŭlātrix -īcis, f. *a (female) observer, watcher.*
spĕcŭlor -ari, dep. *to look out, spy, watch.*
spĕcŭlum -i, n. *a mirror*; fig., *image, copy.*

spĕcus -ūs, m., f., and n. *a cave, hole, hollow.*
spēlaeum -i, n. *a cave, den.*
spēlunca -ae, f. *a cave, den.*
sperno spernĕre sprēvi sprētum, *to remove; to reject, scorn, spurn.*
spēro -are, *to look for, expect*; of good things, *to hope, hope for*; of bad, *to anticipate, forebode.*
spēs -ĕi, f. *expectation*; of good things, *hope*; of bad, *anticipation, foreboding.*
sphaera -ae, f. *a globe, sphere.*
sphaeristērium -i, n. *a place for playing ball.*
Sphinx Sphingis, f. *the Sphinx, a mythical monster at Thebes.*
spīca -ae, f. *a spike; an ear of corn; a tuft.*
spīcĕus -a -um, *of ears of corn.*
spīcĭfer -fĕra -fĕrum, *carrying ears of corn.*
spīcŭlum -i, n. *sharp point; sting; spear, dart.*
spīna -ae, f. *a thorn, prickle; a thorn-bush*; in pl., *anxieties, difficulties, perplexities.*
spīnētum -i, n. *thorn-hedge, thorn-brake.*
spīnĕus -a -um, *of thorns, thorny.*
spīnōsus -a -um, *of thorns, thorny, prickly*; of style, *crabbed, obscure*; of feeling, *anxious.*
spīnus -i, m. *blackthorn.*
spīra -ae, f. *a coil, twist.*
spīrābĭlis -e, *that may be breathed.*
spīrācŭlum -i, n. *an air-hole.*
spīrāmen -ĭnis, n. *an air-hole; a breath, puff.*
spīrāmentum -i, n. *an air-hole; a breathing-space, pause, interval.*
spīrĭtŭs -ūs, m. *breathing, breath, exhalation; a sigh, the breath of life, life; inspiration; spirit, disposition; a high spirit, pride.*
spīro -are: intransit., *to breathe, blow, draw breath; to be alive; to have inspiration, be inspired*; transit., *to breathe out, exhale.*
spissesco -ĕre, *to become thick.*
spisso -are, *to make thick, thickness.*
spissus -a -um, *close, dense, thick, crowded; slow, tardy, difficult*; adv. **spissē.**
splendĕo -ēre, *to shine, glitter, be bright.*
splendesco -ĕre, *to become bright.*
splendĭdus -a -um, *shining, bright, brilliant; distinguished, outstanding; showy, specious*; of sound, *clear.* Hence adv. **splendĭdē,** *splendidly, finely, nobly.*
splendor -ōris, m. *brilliance, brightness, lustre, distinction*; of sound, *clarity.*
splēnium -i, n. *an adhesive plaster.*
spŏlĭātĭo -ōnis, f. *plundering, stripping.*
spŏlĭātor -ōris, m. and **spŏlĭātrix** -trīcis, f. *plunderer.*
spŏlĭo -are, *to strip, despoil, plunder, rob.*
spŏlĭum -i, n. usually plur., *skin* or *hide stripped from an animal; arms, clothing,* etc., *taken from an enemy*; in gen., *spoils, plunder, booty.*
sponda -ae, f. *a bedstead, bed, sofa, bier.*
spondālĭum -i, n. *a sacrificial hymn.*
spondĕo spondēre spŏpondi sponsum, *to pledge oneself to, promise solemnly, vow; to be a security, go bail for a person.* Partic. as subst.: **sponsus** -i, m. *a betrothed man, bridegroom*; **sponsa** -ae, f. *a betrothed woman, bride*; **sponsum** -i, n. *a covenant.*
spondēus -i, m. *a spondee* (— —).
spondȳlus -i, m. *a kind of mussel.*
spongĭa (-ĕa) -ae, f. *a sponge; an open-worked cuirass.*
sponsa -ae, f. subst. from spondeo; q.v.
sponsālis -e, *of betrothal*; n. pl. as subst. **sponsālĭa** -ĭum or -iōrum, *a betrothal, betrothal feast.*
sponsĭo -ōnis, f. *a solemn promise, engagement, guarantee; a wager.*
sponsor -ōris, m. *a surety, bail.*
sponsū, abl. sing. m. *by an engagement.*
sponsus -i, m. and **sponsum** -i, n. subst. from spondeo; q.v.
spontĕ, abl. f.: of persons, *willingly, of one's own accord; unaided;* of things, *by itself, automatically; in itself, alone.*
sporta -ae, f. *a basket, hamper.*
sportella -ae, f. *a little basket.*
sportŭla -ae, f. *a little basket; a dole, given by the great to their clients.*
sprētĭo -ōnis, f. *contempt, disdain.*
sprētor -ōris, m. *a despiser.*
spūma -ae, f. *foam, froth.*
spūmesco -ĕre, *to begin to foam.*
spūmĕus -a -um, *foaming, frothy.*
spūmĭfer -fĕra -fĕrum, and **spūmĭger** -gĕra -gĕrum, *foaming.*
spūmo -are, *to foam, froth.*
spūmōsus -a -um, *foaming, frothy.*
spŭo spŭĕre spŭi spūtum, *to spit out*; n. of partic. as subst. **spūtum** -i, *spittle.*
spurcĭtĭa -ae, f. and **spurcĭtĭēs** -ēi, f. *filthiness, dirt.*
spurco -are, *to make dirty, defile*; partic. **spurcātus** -a -um, *foul.*
spurcus -a -um, *dirty, filthy, unclean*; adv. **spurcē.**
spūto -are, *to spit, spit out.*
spūtum -i, n. subst. from spuo; q.v.
squālĕo -ēre, *to be rough, stiff; to be overgrown* or *dirty from neglect; to wear mourning.*
squālĭdus -a -um, *rough, stiff, scaly; squalid, dirty; in mourning*; of style, *rough*; adv. **squālĭde.**
squālor -ōris, m. *roughness, stiffness; dirt caused by neglect; mourning;* of style, *roughness.*
squălus -i, m. *a kind of fish.*
squāma -ae, f. *a scale; scale armour; a fish.*
squāmĕus -a -um, *scaly.*
squāmĭger -gĕra -gĕrum, *scale-bearing, scaly*; m.pl. as subst. *fishes.*
squāmōsus -a -um, *covered with scales, scaly.*
st! *hush! hist!*
stăbĭlīmentum -i, n. *a stay, support.*
stăbĭlĭo -ire, *to make firm; to establish.*

stăbĭlis -e, *firm, steady, stable*; adv. **stăbĭlĭtĕr.**

stăbĭlĭtās -ātis, f. *firmness, stability; durability.*

stăbŭlo -are: transit., *to stable cattle;* intransit., *to have a stall.*

stăbŭlum -i, n. *standing-room, quarters, habitation; a pothouse, brothel.*

stacta -ae, and **stactē** -ēs, f. *oil of myrrh.*

stădĭum -i, n. *a stade, a Greek measure of length; a race-course.*

stagno -are: intransit. *to be stagnant, stagnate*; of places, *to lie under water*; transit., *to overflow, inundate.*

stagnum -i, n. *standing water; a pond, marsh, swamp; a lake, strait.*

stāmen -ĭnis, n. *the warp on a loom; the thread hanging from a distaff*; stamina ducere, *to spin; any thread* or *woven cloth.*

stāmĭnĕus -a -um, *full of threads.*

stannum -i, n. *an alloy of silver and lead.*

stătārĭus -a -um, *steady, stable, stationary*; f. as subst. **stătārĭa** -ae, *a quiet kind of comedy*; m. pl. **stătārii** -ōrum, *the actors in this.*

stătēra -ae, f. *a steelyard, a balance.*

stătim, *firmly, steadfastly; on the spot, at once.*

stătĭo -ōnis, f. *a standing still; a place of abode*; milit., *post, station,* or *picket*; naut., *roadstead, anchorage.*

Stātĭus -m.: Caecilius Statius, *a comic poet, born* 168 B.C.: P. Papinius Statius, *a poet of Domitian's time.*

stătīvus -a -um, *standing still, fixed*; n. pl. as subst. *a permanent camp.*

[1]**stător** -ōris, m. *a magistrate's attendant.*

[2]**Stător** -ōris, m. *stayer of flight, a surname of Jupiter.*

stătŭa -ae, f. *a statue, image.*

stătŭārĭus -a -um, *of statues*; f. as subst. *the art of sculpture*; m. *a statuary.*

stătūmen -ĭnis, n. *stay, support*; in pl., *the ribs of a ship.*

stătŭo -ŭĕre -ŭi -ūtum *to cause to stand, place, set up; to establish, settle* a point; *to give a ruling, make arrangements; to decide* (on a course of action or matter of fact).

stătūra -ae, f. *stature, height.*

[1]**stătus,** partic. from sisto; q.v.

[2]**stătus** -ūs, m. *a standing posture, position, condition, state*; rhet. *the answer to an action.*

stella -ae, f. *a star*; stella comans, *a comet.*

stellans -antis, *starry, set with stars, bright.*

stellātus -a -um, *set with stars, starry, bright.*

stellĭfer -fĕra -fĕrum and **stellĭger** -gĕra -gĕrum, *star-bearing, starry.*

stellĭo (**stēlĭo**) -ōnis, m. *a spotted lizard.*

stemma -ătis, n. *a garland, chaplet; a genealogical tree.*

stercŏro -are, *to dung, manure.*

stercus -ŏris, n. *dung, manure.*

stĕrĭlis -e *barren; bare, empty; fruitless, vain.*

stĕrĭlĭtās -ātis, f. *barrenness.*

sternax -ācis, *throwing to the ground.*

sterno sternĕre strāvi strātum, *to stretch out, spread*; se sternere, *to lie down; to strike down, lay down, overthrow; to make smooth; to calm, allay; to strew, spread* a thing (with something else); lectum, *to make, make up;* equos, *to saddle*; viam, *to pave.* N. of partic. as subst. **strātum** -i, *a coverlet, blanket; a bed; a saddle-cloth, saddle; a pavement.*

sternūmentum -i, n. *a sneeze.*

sternŭo -ŭĕre -ŭi, *to sneeze*; of a light, *to sputter.*

sterquĭlīnĭum -i, n. *a dung-heap.*

sterto -ĕre, *to snore.*

stĭbădĭum -i, n. *a semicircular seat.*

stigma -ătis, n. *a brand put upon slaves*; in gen., *infamy, stigma.*

stigmătĭas -ae, m. *a branded slave.*

stilla -ae, f. *a drop.*

stillĭcĭdĭum -i, n. *dripping moisture; rain-water falling from the eaves of houses.*

stillo -are.: intransit., *to drip, drop*; transit., *to drop, let drop; to instil* feelings or ideas

stĭlus, *a stake, pale; the pointed instrument with which the Romans wrote on waxen tablets*; hence *writing, composition; mode of writing, style.*

stĭmŭlātĭo -ōnis, f. *spurring on, stimulating.*

stĭmŭlo -are to *goad, prick; to vex, annoy; to incite, stir up.*

stĭmŭlus -i, m. *a goad*; *a sting, torment; spur, incentive*; milit., *a pointed stake.*

stinguo -ĕre, *to extinguish, annihilate.*

stĭpātĭo -ōnis, f. *a crowd of attendants, retinue.*

stĭpātor -ōris, m. *an attendant, follower*; in plur., *train, retinue.*

stĭpendĭārĭus -a -um. (1) *liable to taxes, tributary*; m. pl. as subst. *tributaries.* (2) of soldiers, *serving for pay.*

stĭpendĭum -i, n. (1) *a tax, tribute, contribution.* Transf., *punishment.* (2) *the pay of a soldier; military service; a year's service, campaign.*

stīpĕs -ĭtis, m. *a log, stump, tree-trunk; a branch, post, club; a blockhead.*

stīpo -are, *to press closely, compress; to crowd* a place; *to press round* a person, *accompany, attend.*

stips stĭpis, f. *a small coin, gift, ee.*

stĭpŭla -ae, f. *stalk, haulm, stubble; a reed-pipe.*

stĭpŭlātĭo -onis, f. *agreement, covenant, stipulation.*

stĭpŭlor -ari, dep. *to make demands, bargain, stipulate.*

stīrĭa -ae, f. *icicle.*

stirpĭtŭs, *root and branch, thoroughly.*

stirps (**stirpes, stirpis**), stirpis, f. rarely m., *the stock* or *stem of* a plant; *a young shoot*; of men, *stock, source, origin*; of things, *root, foundation.*

stīva -ae, f. *a plough-handle.*
stlātārĭus -a -um, *brought by sea*; hence *costly.*
stlis, archaic, = lis; q.v.
sto stāre stĕti stătum, *to stand, stand still, remain standing; to stand up stiffly*; milit., *to be stationed*, or *to stand firm*; naut., *to lie at anchor*; of abstr. things, *to remain, be fixed, stand firm, persist; to be resolved*; with ab, cum, pro, *to stand by, support, favour*; with abl. of price, *to cost*; per hominem stare, *to happen through a person's fault, be due to a person.*
Stōĭcus -a -um, *Stoic*; m. as subst., *a Stoic*; n. pl. *the Stoic philosophy*; adv. **Stōĭcē,** *like a Stoic, stoically.*
stŏla -ae, f. *a long outer garment, worn by Roman matrons and musicians.*
stŏlĭdus -a -um, *stupid, dull, obtuse*; adv. **stŏlĭdē.**
stŏmăchor -ari, dep. *to be angry.*
stŏmăchōsus -a -um, *angry, peevish, cross*; compar. adv. **stŏmăchōsĭus.**
stŏmăchus -i, m. *the gullet, oesophagus; the stomach*; stomachus bonus, *a good digestion*, hence *good humour; taste, liking; distaste, chagrin, anger.*
stŏrĕa (**stŏrĭa**) -ae, f. *a rush mat.*
străbo -ōnis, m. *a squinter.*
strāgēs -is, f. *an overthrow; debris; slaughter, massacre, carnage.*
strāgŭlus -a -um, *covering, serving as a cover*; n. as subst. **strāgŭlum** -i, *a covering, carpet, mattress.*
strāmen -ĭnis, n. *straw, litter.*
strāmentum -i, n. *straw, litter; a saddle, housing* (for mules).
strāmĭnĕus -a -um, *made of straw.*
strangŭlo -are, *to choke, strangle, throttle.*
strangūrĭa -ae, f. *strangury.*
strătēgēma -ătis, n. *a piece of generalship, a stratagem.*
strātum -i, n., subst. from sterno; q.v.
strēna -ae, f. *a favourable omen; a new year's gift.*
strēnŭĭtās -ātis, f. *briskness.*
strēnŭus -a -um, *brisk, active, vigorous*; in bad sense, *turbulent, restless*; adv. **strēnŭē.**
strĕpĭto -are, *to rustle, rattle, clatter.*
strĕpĭtus -ūs, m. *clattering, crashing, creaking, rumbling.*
strĕpo -ĕre -ŭi -ĭtum, *to clatter, creak, clash, rumble*; of persons *to cry out*; of places, *to resound.*
strictim, *so as to graze; superficially, slightly, summarily.*
strictūra -ae, f. *a mass of iron.*
strictus -a -um, partic. from stringo; q.v.
strīdĕo strīdēre strīdi and **strīdo** strīdĕre, *to make a harsh noise; to creak, grate, hiss.*
strīdor -ōris, m. *a creaking, grating* or *hissing noise.*
strīdŭlus -a -um, *creaking, hissing, grating.*
strĭgĭlis -is, f. *a scraper used at the baths.*
strĭgo -are, *to halt, stop.*
strĭgōsus -a -um, *lean, thin*; of style, *dry, meagre.*
stringo stringĕre strinxi strictum. (1) *to draw tight together, to bind, tie.* (2) *to strip off, pluck, prune*; esp. *to draw a weapon from its sheath.* (3) *to graze, touch lightly; to affect, injure*; in speech, *to touch upon.*
Hence partic. **strictus** -a -um, *close, tight; strict*; of style, *brief, concise.*
stringor -ōris, m. *a shock, a twinge.*
strix strĭgis, f. *a screech-owl.*
strŏpha -ae, f. *a trick, artifice.*
strŏphĭum -i, n. *a breast-band; a head-band, chaplet.*
structĭlis -e, *used in building.*
structor -ōris, m. (1) *a builder, mason, carpenter.* (2) *a waiter, carver.*
structūra -ae, f. *the act of building*; concr. *a building*; of style, *arrangement, putting together.*
strŭēs -is, f. *a heap.*
strūma -ae, f. *a scrofulous tumour.*
strūmōsus -a -um, *scrofulous.*
strŭo strŭĕre struxi structum, *to put together, arrange; to pile up; to build, erect, construct; to devise, contrive.*
stŭdĕo -ēre -ŭi, *to be eager, take pains, strive after* (usually with dat.); *to side with, support, favour* a person; *to study* a subject.
stŭdĭōsus -a -um, *eager, zealous, keen; favouring* a person or side, *partial, devoted*; esp. *devoted to learning, studious.* Adv. **stŭdĭōsē,** *eagerly.*
stŭdĭum -i, n. *zeal, eagerness, application, enthusiasm; devotion to, goodwill towards* a person or cause; *application to learning, study.*
stultĭtĭa -ae, f. *foolishness, silliness.*
stultus -a -um, *foolish, silly*; m. as subst., *a simpleton, fool*; adv. **stultē.**
stūpa = stuppa; q.v.
stŭpĕfăcio -făcĕre -fēci -factum, pass. **stŭpĕfīo** -fĭĕri, *to make senseless, benumb, stun.*
stŭpĕo -ēre -ŭi, *to be stunned, astounded, amazed*; of inanimate things, *to stand still, halt, cease.*
stŭpesco stŭpescĕre stŭpŭi, *to become amazed, astounded.*
stŭpĭdĭtās -ātis, f. *dullness, senselessness.*
stŭpĭdus -a -um, *senseless, stunned; stupid, dull.*
stŭpor -ōris, m. *senselessness, insensibility; astonishment; dullness, stupidity.*
stuppa (**stūpa**) -ae, f. *tow, oakum.*
stuppĕus -a -um, *of tow.*
stupro -are, *to ravish, defile, pollute.*
stuprum -i, n. *disgrace, defilement*; esp. *ravishing, violation.*
sturnus -i, m. *a starling.*
Stȳgĭālis, Stȳgĭus; see Styx.
stȳlus; see stilus.
Styx, Stȳgis and Stȳgos; acc. Stȳgem and Stȳga; f. *a river in Arcadia*; also *a river in the infernal regions*; adj. **Stȳgĭālis** -e, and **Stȳgĭus** -a -um, *Stygian, infernal.*
suādēla -ae, f. *persuasion.*

suādĕo suādēre suāsi suāsum, *to recommend, advise* (a course of action to a person).
suādus -a -um, *persuasive*; f. as subst., *persuasion.*
suāsĭo -ōnis, f. *advice, recommendation; persuasive eloquence.*
suāsor -ōris, m. *an adviser, recommender; one who advocates a law.*
suāsōrĭus -a -um, *of persuasion*; as subst. *persuasive discourse.*
suāsus -ūs, m. *persuasion.*
suāvĕŏlens -entis, *sweet-smelling.*
suāvĭdĭcus -a -um, *sweetly speaking.*
suāvĭlŏquens -entis, *sweetly speaking.*
suāvĭlŏquentĭa -ae, f. *sweetness of speech.*
suāvĭŏlum, suāvĭor; see sav-.
suāvis -e, *sweet, pleasant*; adv. **suāvĭtĕr.**
suāvĭtās -ātis, f. *sweetness, pleasantness.*
suāvium = savium; q.v.
sŭb, prep. (1) with abl.: *underneath, under; close under, at the foot of;* in time, *at, near to; in the power of, under; under cover of.* (2) with acc., *to* (or *along*) *the underside of; up under, down under, along under; close up to*; in time, *towards, just before*; also *immediately after; into the power of.*
sŭbabsurdus -a -um, *somewhat absurd*; adv. **sŭbabsurdē.**
sŭbaccūso -are, *to accuse a little.*
sŭbactĭo -ōnis, f. *preparation, discipline.*
sŭbadrŏganter, *somewhat arrogantly.*
sŭbagrestis -e, *somewhat rustic* or *boorish.*
sŭbămārus -a -um, *somewhat bitter.*
sŭbausculto -are, *to listen secretly.*
subc-; see succ-.
subdiffĭcĭlis -e, *somewhat difficult.*
subdiffīdo -ĕre, *to be somewhat distrustful.*
subdĭtīcĭus and **subdĭtīvus** -a -um, *supposititious, substituted, counterfeit.*
subdo -dĕre -dĭdi dĭtum, *to put, place* or *lay under; to subject, subdue; to put in the place of another substitute; to counterfeit.*
subdŏcĕo -ēre, *to teach as an assistant, help in teaching.*
subdŏlus -a -um, *with secret guile; sly, crafty*; adv. **subdŏlē.**
subdŭbĭto -are, *to doubt* or *hesitate a little.*
subdūco -dūcĕre -duxi -ductum, *to draw up from under, pull up, raise, remove; to take away stealthily, steal*; naut., *to draw a ship up on shore*; milit., *to withdraw*; of accounts, *to balance, cast up.*
subductĭo -ōnis, f. *the drawing up of a ship on dry land; a reckoning, computing.*
sŭbĕdo -esse -ēdi, *to eat from under, wear away.*
sŭbĕo -īre -ĭi or -īvi -ĭtum. (1) *to go under, pass under*; of a bearer, *to to under and support; to undergo, submit to, take upon oneself.* (2) *to come from under, approach, advance, mount, climb*; of thoughts, etc., *to come into,* or *come over, the mind.* (3) *to come on after, to follow*; sometimes *to come and support.*
Hence partic. **sŭbĭtus** -a -um, as adj., *sudden; coming suddenly, taking by surprise*; pass., *suddenly done, hastily contrived, improvised.* **N.** as subst. *a sudden occurrence, emergency.* N. abl. as adv. **sŭbĭtō,** *suddenly.*
sūber -ĕris, n. *cork-tree; cork.*
subf -; see suff-.
subg -; see sugg-.
sŭbhorrĭdus -a -um, *somewhat rough.*
subiăcĕo -ēre -ŭi, *to lie under; to be subject to, be connected with.*
subicĭo -icĕre -iēci -iectum. (1) *to throw* or *place under; to submit, subject*; in speech or writing, *to append, reply.* (2) *to throw up from below, raise, lift; to put into a mind, suggest.* (3) *to substitute, insert by guile, counterfeit.*
Hence partic. **subiectus** -a -um, *subjected*; of places, *lying near, adjacent*; superl. adv. **subiectissĭmē,** *most submissively.*
subiectĭo -ōnis, f. *a laying under, placing under; a counterfeiting, forging.*
subiecto -are, *to put under*; also *to throw up from below.*
subiector -ōris, m. *forger, counterfeiter.*
sŭbĭgo -ĭgĕre -ēgi -actum, *to drive under; to subject, constrain, subdue, compel; to drive up from below, to propel; to work* the soil; in gen., *to work at; to train, discipline.*
sŭbimpŭdens -entis, *somewhat impudent.*
sŭbĭnānis -e, *somewhat vain.*
sŭbindĕ, *immediately afterwards; repeatedly.*
sŭbinsulsus -a -um, *somewhat insipid.*
sŭbinvĭdĕo -ere, *to envy somewhat*; partic. **sŭbinvīsus** -a -um, *somewhat hated.*
sŭbinvīto -are, *to invite mildly.*
sŭbīrascor -īrasci -īrātus, dep. *to get a little angry.*
sŭbĭtārĭus -a -um, *hastily contrived, improvised.*
sŭbĭto, sŭbĭtus; from subeo; q.v.
subiungo -iungĕre -iunxi -iunctum, *to yoke beneath; to join on, attach; to subdue, subjugate.*
sublābor -lābi -lapsus, dep. *to glide up; to glide from beneath, slip away.*
sublatĭo -ōnis, f. *lifting up, elevation.*
sublātus -a -um, partic. from tollo; q.v.
sublĕgo -lĕgĕre -lēgi -lectum, *to gather from below, pick up; to carry off secretly; to choose in the place of another.*
sublĕvātĭo -ōnis, f. *a relieving, lightening.*
sublĕvo -are, *to raise, lift, support; to encourage* a person; *to alleviate* troubles.
sublĭca -ae, f. *a pile, stake.*
sublĭcĭus -a -um, *resting upon piles.*
sublĭgăcŭlum -i, and **sublĭgar** -āris, n. *a loincloth, kilt.*

sublĭgo -are, *to bind below, bind on.*
sublīmis -e (archaic **sublīmus** -a -um), *high, raised, lofty; elevated, sublime.* N. acc. sing. as adv. **sublīmĕ,** *on high, aloft.*
sublīmĭtās -ātis, f. *loftiness height, sublimity.*
sublīmus; see sublimis.
sublūcĕo -ēre, *to gleam faintly, glimmer.*
sublŭo -lŭĕre -lūtum, *to wash below*; of rivers, *to flow beneath.*
sublustris -e, *gleaming faintly, glimmering.*
subm -; see summ-.
subnascor -nasci -nātus, dep. *to grow up out of* or *after.*
subnecto -nectĕre -nexŭi -nexum, *to tie on, bind on beneath.*
subnĕgo -are, *to deny a little, partly refuse.*
subnixus (subnīsus) -a -um, *propped up, supported.*
subnŏto -are, *to mark beneath, write underneath; to notice secretly.*
subnŭba -ae, f. *a rival.*
subnūbĭlus -a -um, *somewhat cloudy.*
sŭbo -are, *to be in heat.*
sŭbobscēnus -a -um, *somewhat obscene.*
sŭbobscūrus -a -um, *somewhat obscure.*
sŭbŏdĭōsus -a -um, *rather unpleasant.*
sŭboffendo -ĕre, *to give some offence.*
sŭbŏlĕo -ēre (only in 3 pers.), *to emit a smell*; hence *to make itself felt.*
sŭbŏlēs -is, f. *a sprout, shoot, offspring, progeny.*
sŭbŏlesco -ĕre, *to grow up.*
sŭbŏrĭor -ŏriri, dep. *to arise after* or *in succession.*
sŭborno -are. (1) *to furnish, equip, provide.* (2) *to instigate secretly, suborn.*
sŭbortus -us, m. *an arising after* or *in succession.*
subp -; see supp-.
subrancĭdus -a -um, *somewhat putrid.*
subraucus -a -um, *somewhat hoarse.*
subrectus (surr-), partic. from subrigo; q.v.
subremigo (surr-) -are, *to row underneath.*
subrēpo (surr-) -rēpĕre -repsi, *to creep* or *crawl up to from below.*
subreptĭcĭus = surrepticius; q.v.
subrīdĕo (surr-) -rīdēre -rīsi -rīsum, *to smile.*
subrīdĭcŭlē, *somewhat laughably.*
subrĭgo (surr-) -rĭgere -rexi -rectum, *to raise, lift up.*
subringor -i, dep. *to make a wry face.*
subrĭpĭo = surripio; q.v.
subrŏgo (surr-) -are, *to suggest that a person be chosen as substitute for another.*
subrostrāni -ōrum, m. *loungers about the* rostra, *idlers.*
subrŭbĕo -ēre, *to blush slightly, be rather red.*
subrŭo -rŭĕre -rŭi -rŭtum, *to undermine, overthrow, destroy.*
subrustĭcus -a -um, *somewhat clownish.*
subscrībo -scrībĕre -scripsi -scriptum, *to write under, write beneath; to sign* a document; *to complete an indictment,* hence *to prosecute, accuse*; with dat., *to support, assent to; to note down, make a note of.*
subscriptĭo -ōnis, f. *a writing beneath, signature; the completion of an indictment; a record, register.*
subscriptor -ōris, m. *the signer of an indictment; an accuser.*
subsĕcīvus = subsĭcīvus; q.v.
subsĕco -sĕcare -sĕcŭi -sectum, *to cut away below.*
subsellĭum -i, n. *a bench, seat,* esp. *in the courts.*
subsentĭo -sentire -sensi, *to notice secretly.*
subsĕquor -sĕqui -sĕcūtus, dep. *to follow after; to support* a cause, etc.
subservĭo -ire, *to be subject to, comply with.*
subsĭcīvus (subsec-) -a -um, *left over; extra, superfluous, spare.*
subsĭdĭārĭus -a -um, *in reserve.*
subsĭdĭum -i, n.: milit., *reserve troops, auxiliary forces*; in gen., *support, help, assistance.*
subsīdo -sīdĕre -sēdi -sessum, *to crouch down, settle, sink, subside; to stay, remain; to lie in wait, lurk in ambush.*
subsignānus -a -um, *serving beneath the standard*; milites, *reserve legionaries.*
subsigno -are, *to write under, endorse; to enter on a list, to register.*
subsĭlĭo -sĭlire -sĭlŭi, *to leap up, spring up.*
subsisto -sistĕre -stĭti, *to stand; to make a stand, to withstand; to come to a stand, stop, halt, cease; to stay, remain.*
subsortĭor -iri, dep. *to choose by lot as a substitute.*
subsortītĭo -ōnis, f. *the choice of a substitute by lot.*
substantĭa -ae, f. *substance, essence; property, means of subsistence.*
substerno -sternĕre -strāvi -strātum, *to spread beneath, lay under; to set out, provide.*
substĭtŭo -ŭĕre -ŭi -ūtum, *to put next; to put under, to put in the place of another, to substitute.*
substo -stare, *to stand firm.*
substringo -stringĕre -strinxi -strictum, *to draw together, bind up;* partic. **substrictus** -a -um, *narrow, contracted, small.*
substructĭo -ōnis, f. *a base, foundation.*
substrŭo -strŭĕre -struxi -structum, *to build beneath, lay a foundation.*
subsulto -are, *to spring up, leap up.*
subsum -esse -fŭi, *to be near, be close at hand; to be under; to be subject; to be there, to exist.*
subsūtus -a -um, *fringed, edged below.*
subtēmen -ĭnis, n. *the weft* or *woof in weaving.*
subter (supter), adv. and prep., *beneath, below, underneath.*
subterfŭgĭo -fŭgĕre -fūgi, *to escape.*
subterlābor -lābi -lapsus, dep. *to glide under, flow under; to slip away, escape.*

subtĕro -tĕrĕre -trīvi -trītum, *to wear away underneath.*
subterrānĕus -a -um, *underground, subterranean.*
subtexo -texĕre -texŭi -textum, *to weave beneath; to connect, join on; to cover, darken.*
subtīlis -e, *finely woven, slender, fine*; of senses, etc., *discriminating, nice*; of style, *plain, simple, unadorned.* Hence adv. **subtīlĭtĕr,** *by fine links* or *passages*; of judgment, *with discrimination*; of style, *plainly, simply.*
subtīlĭtās -ātis, f. *fineness, minuteness*; of judgment, *discrimination*; of style, *plainness, simplicity.*
subtĭmĕo -ēre, *to be a little afraid.*
subtrăho -trăhĕre -traxi -tractum, *to draw up from beneath; to draw away secretly, remove, steal away.*
subturpĭcŭlus -a -um, *rather on the disgraceful side.*
subturpis -e, *rather disgraceful.*
subtŭs, adv. *beneath, below, underneath.*
subtūsus -a -um, *somewhat bruised.*
sŭbūcŭla -ae, f. *a shirt.*
sūbŭla -ae, f. *a shoemaker's awl.*
sŭbulcus -i, m. *a swineherd.*
Sŭbūra -ae, f. *a part of Rome, north-east of the Forum.*
sŭburbānĭtās -ātis, f. *nearness to the city.*
sŭburbānus -a -um, *near the city* (Rome), *suburban*; n. as subst. *an estate near Rome.*
sŭburbĭum -i, n. *a suburb.*
sŭburguĕo -ēre, *to drive close.*
subvectĭo -ōnis, f. *carrying up, conveyance, transport.*
subvecto -are *to carry up, convey, transport.*
subvectus -ūs, m. *a carrying up.*
subvĕho -vĕhĕre -vexi -vectum, *carry up, convey, transport.*
subvĕnĭo -vĕnire -vēni -ventum, *to come up to aid, to succour, relieve.*
subvĕrĕor -ēri, dep. *to be rather anxious.*
subversor -ōris, m. *overthrower.*
subverto (-vorto) -vertĕre -verti -versum, *to overthrow, overturn, destroy.*
subvexus -a -um, *sloping upwards.*
subvŏlo -are, *to fly up.*
subvolvo -ĕre, *to roll up.*
succăvus -a -um, *hollow underneath.*
succēdo -cēdĕre -cessi -cessum. (1) *to go under; to submit to.* (2) *to go from under, ascend, mount.* (3) *to come after; to succeed, relieve, follow*; of things, *to turn out well, prosper, succeed.*
succendo -cendĕre -cendi -censum, *to set on fire from below; to kindle, inflame.*
succensĕo = suscenseo; q.v.
[1]**succentŭrĭo** -are, *to put in the place of another, to substitute.*
[2]**succentŭrĭo** -ōnis, m. *an under-centurion.*
successĭo -ōnis, f. *succeeding, succession.*
successor -ōris, m. *a successor, follower, heir.*
successus -ūs, m. (1) *an advance uphill, approach.* (2) *success.*
succīdĭa -ae, f. *a flitch of bacon.*
[1]**succĭdo** -cĭdere -cĭdi, *to fall under; to sink, flag, fail.*
[2]**succīdo** -cīdĕre -cīdi -cīsum, *to cut from under, cut down.*
succĭdŭus -a -um, *sinking, failing.*
succingo -cingĕre -cinxi -cinctum, *to gird below, gird up; to equip, arm, provide, surround*; partic. **succinctus** -a -um, as adj., *concise, succinct.*
succingŭlum -i, n. *a girdle.*
succĭno -ĕre, *to sing to, accompany;* in speech, *to chime in.*
succlāmātĭo -ōnis, f. *shouting in reply.*
succlāmo -are, *to shout back.*
succontŭmēlĭōsē, *somewhat insolently.*
succresco -crescĕre -crēvi, *to grow up, increase; to grow up to, match.*
succrispus = subcrispus; q.v.
succumbo -cumbĕre -cŭbŭi -cŭbĭtum, *to lie down under, sink down, give way, succumb, surrender.*
succurro -currĕre -curri -cursum. (1) *to run beneath, go under; to undergo*; of ideas, *to come into the mind.* (2) *to come to aid, succour, help, assist.*
succŭtĭo -cŭtĕre -cussi -cussum, *to shake from beneath, fling aloft.*
sūcĭdus -a -um, *juicy, full of sap.*
sūcĭnus -a -um, *of amber.*
sūco -ōnis, m. *a sucker.*
sūcus (succus) -i, m. *juice, sap; a draught; flavour, taste; sap, vigour, energy.*
sūdārĭum -i, n. *handkerchief, towel.*
sūdātōrĭus -a -um, *of sweating*; n. as subst. *a sweating-room.*
sūdātrix -trīcis, f. *causing perspiration.*
sŭdis -is, f. *a stake, pile; a spike, point.*
sūdo -are: intransit., *to sweat, perspire; to make a great effort; to drip with moisture; to drip from, distil*; transit., *to sweat out, to exude; to soak with sweat.*
sūdor -ōris, m. *sweat, perspiration; great exertion; any moisture.*
sūdūs -a -um, *dry*; of weather, *bright cloudless*; n. as subst. *fine weather.*
Suēbi (Suēvi) -orum, m. *a Germanic tribe.*
suemus, 1 plur. as from sueo, *we are accustomed.*
suesco -suescĕre suēvi suētum: intransit., *to become accustomed*; transit., *to accustom.*
Hence partic. **suētus** -a -um *accustomed; customary, usual.*
Suētōnĭus -i, m. C. Suetonius Tranquillus, *author of the Lives of the Caesars.*
suētus -a -um, partic. from suesco; q.v.
Suēvi = Suebi; q.v.
sŭfes (suffes) -fĕtis, m. *the chief magistrate at Carthage.*
suffarcĭno -are, *to stuff, cram.*
suffĕro sufferre, *to hold up, support, to endure, suffer.*

suffĭcĭo -fĭcĕre -fēci -fectum: transit., *to put under*; hence, *to stain, steep, suffuse; to provide, supply; to put in place of another, to substitute, choose as a substitute*; intransit., *to be adequate, suffice*; with infin., *to be able.*
suffīgo -fīgĕre -fixi -fixum, *to fix up, fasten.*
suffīmen -ĭnis and **suffīmentum** -i, n. *incense.*
suffĭo -ire, *to fumigate, perfume; to warm.*
sufflāmen -ĭnis, n. *a brake, drag, hindrance.*
sufflo -are: intransit., *to blow*; transit., *to blow up, inflate.*
suffōco -are, *to strangle, choke, suffocate.*
suffŏdĭo -fŏdĕre -fōdi -fossum, *to pierce underneath, excavate, undermine.*
suffrāgātĭo -ōnis, f. *voting in favour, support.*
suffrāgātor -ōris, m. *a voter in favour; a (political) supporter.*
suffrāgātōrĭus -a -um, *relating to the support of a candidate.*
suffrāgĭum -i, n. *a voting tablet, a vote; the right to vote, franchise*; in gen., *judgment; approval, support.*
suffrāgor -ari, dep. *to vote for; to favour, approve, support.*
suffringo -ĕre, *to break underneath.*
suffŭgĭo -fŭgĕre -fūgi, *to flee, escape.*
suffŭgĭum -i, n. *a shelter, place of refuge.*
suffulcĭo -fulcire -fulsi -fultum, *to support beneath, undergo, underprop.*
suffundo -fundĕre -fūdi -fūsum, *to pour over, spread through, suffuse; to steep, stain, cover.*
suffuscus -a -um, *brownish, dark.*
Sŭgambri (Sȳg-, Sĭg-) -ōrum, m. pl. *a Germanic tribe.*
suggĕro -gĕrĕre -gessi -gestum, *to bring up, supply, provide; to add, attach; to place next.*
suggestum -i, n. and **suggestus** -ūs, m. *a raised place, height, elevation*; esp., *a platform.*
suggrandis -e, *somewhat large.*
suggrĕdĭor -grĕdi -gressus, dep. *to go up to, approach, attack.*
sūgillātĭo -ōnis, f. *a bruise; mockery, insult.*
sūgillo -are, *to beat, to insult.*
sūgo sūgĕre suxi suctum, *to suck.*
sŭillus -a -um, *of swine.*
sulcātor -ōris, m. *a plougher.*
sulco -are, *to furrow, plough; to wrinkle.*
sulcus -i, m. *a furrow; ploughing; a trench* or *ditch; a track, path.*
sulfur (sulpur) -ŭris, n. *sulphur; lightning.*
sulfŭrātus -a -um, *containing sulphur.*
sulfŭrĕus -a -um, *sulphurous.*
Sulla (Sylla) -ae, m. *a name of a family in the* gens Cornelia; adj. **Sullānus** -a -um; verb **sullātŭrĭo** -ire, *to wish to imitate Sulla.*
Sulmo -ōnis, m. *birth-place of Ovid*; adj. **Sulmōnensis** -e.
sulpur = sulfur; q.v.
sultis = si vultus; see volo.
sum, esse, fŭi, *to be, to exist, be there, be so*; with dat., *to be in one's possession*; copulative, *to be* so and so, with complement; fut. partic. **fŭtūrus** -a -um, *future, about to be*; n. as subst. *the future.*
sūmen -ĭnis, n. *the udder of a sow; a sow.*
summa -ae; see summus.
summātim, adv. *summarily, briefly.*
summātus -ūs, m. *supremacy, chief authority.*
summergo -mergĕre -mersi -mersum, *to plunge under, to sink.*
summĭnistro -are, *to help by supplying.*
summissĭo (subm-) -ōnis, f. *a letting down, lowering.*
summitto (subm-) -mittĕre -mīsi -missum. (1) *to let down, send under, lower; subject, subordinate*; with animum, *or* se, *to condescend, submit.* (2) *to send up from below, to raise, rear, make to grow.* (3) *to send as help.* (4) *to send secretly.*

Hence partic. **summissus (subm-)** -a -um, *let down, lowered; mild, gentle, humble*; in bad sense, *mean, abject.* Adv. **summissē,** *softly, calmly; modestly, humbly.*
summŏlestus (subm-) -a -um, *somewhat troublesome*; adv. **summŏlestē,** *with some vexation.*
summŏnĕo (subm-) -ēre, *to remind secretly.*
summŏpĕrĕ (summō ŏpĕrĕ), *very much, exceedingly.*
summōrosus (subm-) -a -um, *somewhat peevish.*
summŏvĕo (subm-) mŏvēre -mōvi -mōtum, *to move up from below; to move away, drive off, expel*; esp. of the lictor *to clear a way* for a magistrate, *to keep back the crowd; to force away from, compel, to give up*; pass. partic., **summōtus,** *lying out of the way, remote.*
summūto (subm-) -are, *to exchange.*
sūmo sūmĕre sumpsi sumptum, *to take, choose, obtain, buy*; of clothes, etc., *to put on; to exact* a punishment; *to take upon oneself, claim; to take for granted, assume.*
sumptĭo -ōnis f. *the premiss of a syllogism.*
sumptŭārĭus -a -um, *relating to expense, sumptuary.*
sumptŭōsus -a -um: of things, *costly, expensive*; of persons, *lavish, extravagant*; adv. **sumptŭōsē,** *expensively, sumptuously.*
sumptus -ūs, m. *cost, expense.*
sŭo sŭĕre sŭi sūtum, *to sew, stitch together, join together.*
sŭōmet and **sŭōpte**; see suus.
sŭŏvĕtaurīlĭa -ĭum, n. pl., *a sacrifice of a pig, sheep and bull.*
sŭpellex -lectĭlis, f. *household furniture.*
[1]**sŭper** -a -um; see superus.

[2]**sŭper.** Adv., *over, above; besides, beyond, moreover; remaining, over and above.* Prep.: with abl., of place *over, above*; of time, *at; concerning, about; besides, beyond*; with acc., of place, *over, above, upon; besides, beyond*; of time, *during*; of superiority, *above, more than.*

sŭpĕrā; see supra.

sŭpĕrābĭlis -e, *that can be surmounted; conquerable.*

sŭpĕraddo -addĕre -addĭtum, *to add as well, put on besides.*

sŭpĕrātor -ōris, m. *a conqueror.*

sŭperbĭa -ae, f. *pride; haughtiness, arrogance.*

sŭperbĭo -ire: of persons, *to be proud, pride oneself*; of things, *to be splendid, superb.*

sŭperbus -a -um, *haughty, exalted, proud; arrogant, overbearing; brilliant, splendid.* Adv. **sŭperbē,** *haughtily, proudly.*

sŭpercĭlĭum -i, n. *an eyebrow; the eyebrows; a nod* (as expression of will); *arrogance, censoriousness*; of things, *ridge, summit.*

sŭpĕrēmĭneo -ēre, to *overtop.*

sŭperfĭcĭēs -ēi, f. *top, surface.*

sŭperfĭo -fĭĕri, *to be left over.*

sŭperfixus -a -um, *fixed on the top.*

sŭperflŭo -flŭĕre, *to flow over, overflow, be superfluous.*

sŭperfundo -fundĕre -fūdi -fūsum, *to pour over, pour upon*; pass., *to overflow*; in gen., *to spread about, spread over.*

sŭpergrĕdĭor -grĕdi -gressus, dep. *to step beyond, overstep; to exceed, surpass.*

sŭperiăcĭo -iăcĕre -iēci -iectum or -iactum, *to throw over, throw upon; to overtop, exceed, go beyond.*

sŭpĕrimmĭnĕo -ēre, *to overhang.*

sŭpĕrimpendens -entis, *overhanging.*

sŭpĕrimpŏsĭtus -a -um, *laid over, placed upon.*

sŭpĕrincĭdens -entis, *falling on top.*

sŭpĕrincŭbans -antis, *lying over* or *upon.*

sŭpĕrincumbo -cumbĕre -cŭbŭi *to lie on, lie over.*

sŭpĕrinicĭo -inicĕre -iniēci -iniectum, *to throw upon.*

sŭpĕrinsterno -sternĕre -strāvi, *to spread over, lay over.*

sŭpĕrĭor -oris, compar. of superus; q.v.

sŭperlātĭo -ōnis, f. *exaggeration, hyperbole.*

sŭperlātus -a -um, *exaggerated, hyperbolical.*

sŭpernus -a -um, *above, upper, high*; adv. **sŭpernē,** *above* or *from above.*

sŭpĕro -are: intransit., *to go above, overtop, project; to prevail, conquer; to abound; to remain, be over*; esp. *to remain alive, survive; to be too much, to exceed*; transit., *to rise above, surmount, overtop, pass; to surpass, excel, exceed; to overcome, conquer.* Compar. of pres. partic. **sŭpĕrantĭor** -oris, *more dominant.*

sŭpĕrobrŭo -ŭĕre, *to overwhelm.*

sŭperpendens -entis, *overhanging.*

sŭperpōno -pōnĕre -pŏsŭi -pŏsĭtum, *to place over*, or *upon*; *to put in authority.*

sŭperscando -ĕre, *to climb over.*

sŭpersĕdĕo -sĕdēre -sēdi -sessum, *to sit above, sit out*; hence *to forbear, refrain.*

sŭperstagno -are, *to spread out into a lake.*

sŭpersterno -sternĕre -strāvi -strātum, *to spread over* or *upon.*

sŭperstĕs -stĭtis, *standing over* or *near; present, witnessing; surviving, living on.*

sŭperstĭtĭo -ōnis, f. *superstition, fanaticism.*

sŭperstĭtĭōsus -a -um, *superstitious*; adv. **sŭperstĭtĭōsē.**

sŭpersto -are, *to stand over* or *upon.*

sŭperstrŭo -strŭĕre -struxi -structum, *to build upon.*

sŭpersum -esse -fŭi -fŭtūrus, *to be over and above; to be left, remain, survive; to be plentiful, to abound; to be superfluous, be redundant.*

sŭpĕrurgĕo -ēre, *to press from above.*

sŭpĕrus (rarely **sŭper**) -a -um, *situated above; upper, higher*; m. pl. as subst. *the gods above*; also *men on earth*; n. pl. *heights* or *heavenly* bodies. Compar. **sŭpĕrĭor** -ĭus, *higher, upper*; of time, *earlier, former, past*; of rank, etc., *higher, greater.* Superl. **suprēmus** -a -um, of place, *highest, uppermost*; in time, *last, final*; of degree, *highest, greatest*; of rank, *highest*; n. sing. as subst., *the end*; n. pl., **suprēma** -ōrum, *death, funeral rites, last will and testament.* Used as another superl. **summus** -a -um, *highest, uppermost, at the top*; summa urbs, *the highest part of the city*; of the voice, *highest, loudest*; of time, *last*; of rank, etc., *greatest, highest, most distinguished.* F. as subst. **summa** -ae *the highest place, the main thing, most important point; a summary, the gist, the sum total of an amount.* N. as subst. **summum** -i, *surface, top*; acc. as adv., *at most.* Adv. **summē,** *in the highest degree, extremely.*

sŭpervăcānĕus and **sŭpervăcŭus** -a -um, *superfluous, unnecessary, extra.*

sŭpervado -ĕre, *to go over, surmount.*

sŭpervĕhor -vĕhi -vectus sum, *to ride* or *sail past.*

sŭpervĕnĭo -vĕnire -vēni -ventum, *to come upon, rise above; to arrive, come up*, esp. *unexpectedly.*

sŭperventus -ūs, m. *coming up,* (*unexpected*) *arrival.*

sŭpervīvo -ĕre, *to survive.*

sŭpervŏlĭto -are, and **sŭpervŏlo** -are, *to fly over, fly above.*

sŭpīno -are, *to put face upwards, throw on the back.*

sŭpīnus -a -um, *lying on the back, face-upwards*; manus, *with palm upwards*; of streams, *flowing up, returning*; of ground, *sloping upwards*; of character, *negligent, lazy.*

suppaenĭtet -ēre, *to cause slight regret.*
suppār -păris, *almost equal.*
suppĕdĭtātĭo -ōnis, f. *abundant provision.*
suppĕdĭto -are: intransit., *to be at hand, be ready, suffice*; transit., *to provide, supply, give.*
suppernātus -a -um, *lamed in the hip.*
suppĕtĭae -ārum, f. pl. *help, aid.*
suppĕtĭor -ari, dep. *to help, assist.*
suppĕto -ĕre, -īvi and -ĭi, -ītum, *to be in store, be at hand; to suffice, be enough.*
supplanto -are, *to trip up.*
supplēmentum -i, n. *filling up, completion*; milit., *a body of recruits, reinforcements.*
supplĕo -plēre -plēvi -plētum, *to fill up, make complete.*
supplex -plĭcis, *kneeling; entreating, suppliant*; adv. **supplĭcĭtĕr.**
supplĭcātĭo -ōnis, f. *solemn public prayer* or *thanksgiving; a religious festival* or *fast.*
supplĭcĭum -i, n. (1) *a humble entreaty, supplication, prayer.* (2) *punishment*; esp. *capital punishment.*
supplĭco -are, *to kneel, beseech, entreat*; esp. *to pray to the gods.*
supplōdo -plōdĕre -plōsi, *to stamp.*
supplōsĭo -ōnis, f. *a stamping.*
suppōno -pōnĕre -pŏsŭi -pŏsĭtum. (1) *to put under; to subject.* (2) *to put next to, to add.* (3) *to put in the place of; to substitute, counterfeit, forge.*
supporto -are, *to carry up.*
suppŏsĭtīcĭus -a -um, *substituted, spurious.*
suppressĭo -ōnis, f. *embezzlement.*
supprĭmo -prĭmĕre -pressi -pressum, *to press under; to hold down, check, restrain; to keep back, suppress, conceal;* pecuniam, nummos, *to embezzle.* Partic. **suppresssus** -a -um, *checked, restrained*; of the voice, *low, subdued.*
suppŭdet -ēre, *to cause some shame.*
suppus -a -um, *head-downwards.*
suppŭto -are, *to count up, compute.*
suprā. Adv. *over, on the top;* of time, *before, previously*; in writing, *above*; of amount, etc., *over, more, beyond*; supra quam, *more than.* Prep., with acc., *above, over*; of time, *before*; of amount, *more than, above, beyond.*
suprascando -ĕre, *to climb over, surmount.*
suprēmus, etc.; see superus.
sūra -ae, f. *the calf of the leg.*
surcŭlus -i, m. *a young shoot, sprout, twig; a slip, sucker.*
surdaster -tra -trum, *somewhat deaf.*
surdĭtās -ātis, f. *deafness.*
surdus -a -um, *deaf; unwilling to hear, insensible; not heard, still, silent*; of sounds, etc., *indistinct, faint.*
surēna -ae, m. *a Parthian grand vizier.*
surgo surgĕre surrexi surrectum, *to rise, get up; to spring up, arise.*
surpŭit, etc., forms from surripio; q.v.
surr-; see also subr-.
surreptīcĭus (subr-) -a -um, *stolen, secret, surreptitious.*
surrĭpĭo -rĭpĕre -rĭpŭi -reptum, *to take away secretly; to steal, filch.*
sursum (sursus), *upwards, on high*; sursum deorsum, *up and down, backwards, and forwards.*
sus sŭis, c. *a sow, swine, pig, hog; a kind of fish.*
suscensĕo -ēre -ŭi, *to be angry, bear a grudge.*
susceptĭo -ōnis, f. *undertaking.*
suscĭpĭo -cĭpĕre -cēpi -ceptum, *to take up, catch up; to support, raise; to accept, receive,* esp. *to acknowledge* a child *as one's own; to take upon oneself, undertake, begin; to maintain* a point, *be ready to prove.*
suscĭto -are, *to stir up, arouse, excite.*
suspecto -are, *to keep looking at, gaze upon; to look upon with suspicion, suspect.*
[1]**suspectus** -a -um, partic. from suspicio; q.v.
[2]**suspectus** -ūs, m. *looking upwards; respect, esteem.*
suspendĭum -i, n. *a hanging of oneself.*
suspendo -pendĕre -pendi -pensum, *to hang up; to prop up, support; to keep in suspense, leave undecided; to check, break off.*

Hence partic. **suspensus** -a -um, *hovering, hanging, suspended; dependent*; *ambiguous, doubtful, in suspense.*
suspĭcax -ācis: act., *suspicious, suspecting;* pass., *suspicious, suspected.*
[1]**suspĭcĭo** -spĭcĕre -spexi -spectum, *to look from below, look upwards; to look up to, esteem, respect; to look askance at, suspect.*

Hence partic. **suspectus** -a -um, *suspected.*
[2]**suspĭcĭo** -ōnis, f. *mistrust, suspicion; a faint idea, imperfect conception.*
suspĭcĭōsus -a -um, *feeling suspicion, suspecting; exciting suspicion, suspicious*; adv. **suspĭcĭōsē,** *in a suspicious manner, suspiciously.*
suspĭcor -ari, dep. *to suspect; to conjecture, suppose, surmise.*
suspīrātus -ūs, and **suspīrĭtus** -ūs, and **suspīrĭum** -i, n. *a deep breath, a sigh.*
suspīro -are: intransit., *to draw a deep breath, to sigh*; transit., *to sigh for, long for.*
susquĕ dequĕ, *up and down.*
sustentācŭlum -i, n. *a prop, support.*
sustentātĭo -ōnis, f. *forbearance.*
sustento -are, *to hold up, support, sustain; to maintain; to put off, hinder, delay.*
sustĭnĕo -tĭnēre -tĭnŭi -tentum, *to hold up, support, sustain*; with infin., *to endure to, have the heart to; to maintain; to put off, delay; to hold back, check, restrain.*
sustollo -ĕre, *to lift up, raise; to take away, remove, destroy,*
sŭsurrātor -ōris, m. *a mutterer.*
sŭsurro -are, *to murmur, mutter, whisper*; of bees, *to hum.*
[1]**sŭsurrus** -i, m. *a murmur, muttering, whisper, hum, buzz.*
[2]**sŭsurrus** -a -um, *whispering, muttering.*
sūtĭlis -e, *stitched together, fastened together.*
sūtor -ōris, m. *a shoemaker, cobbler.*

sūtōrĭus and **sūtrīnus** -a -um, *of a shoemaker.*
sūtūra -ae, f. *a seam, suture.*
sŭus -a -um, reflexive possessive pronoun of 3rd person, *his, her, its, their* (*own*); often strengthened by -pte or -met; sometimes *proper, due, suitable, favourable; independent.* As subst., *one's own people, property,* etc.
Sўbăris -ris, f. *a town in Lucania, famous for luxury.*
sycŏphanta -ae, f. *an informer, trickster.*
Sylla = Sulla; q.v.
syllăba -ae, f. *a syllable*; in plur., *verses, poems.*
syllăbātim, *syllable by syllable.*
syllŏgismus (or **-ŏs**) -i, m. *a syllogism.*
symbŏla -ae, f. *a contribution towards a common feast.*
symphōnĭa -ae, f. *a concert, musical performance.*
symphōnĭăcus -a -um, *of* or *for a concert.*
sўnedrus -i, m. *a Macedonian councillor.*
syngrăpha -ae, f. *a bond, agreement to pay.*
sўnŏdūs -ontis, m. *a fish, perhaps bream.*
synthĕsis -is, f. *a dinner-service; a suit of clothes; a dressing-gown.*
Sўrācūsae -ārum, f. pl. *the chief town of Sicily.*
Sўrĭa -ae, f. *Syria*; adj. **Sўrĭus, Sўrus, Sўrĭăcus** -a -um, *Syrian*; subst. **Sўri** -orum, *the Syrians.*
syrma -mătis, n. *a long robe, worn by tragic actors.*
syrtis -is, f. *a sandbank, quicksand*; esp. *one on the coast of Northern Africa.*

T

T, t, the nineteenth letter of the Latin Alphabet.
tăbella -ae, f. *a small flat board* or *tablet; a writing-tablet; a document, letter, record; a votive tablet; a voting-ticket, ballot; a picture.*
tăbellārĭus -a -um, *of letters* or *of voting.* M. as subst. *a letter-carrier.*
tābĕo -ere, *to waste away; to drip, run.*
tăberna -ae, f. *a booth, hut; a cottage, hovel; a stall, shop; an inn, tavern; a block of seats in the Circus.*
tăbernācŭlum -i, n. *a hut, tent.*
tăbernārĭus -i, m. *a shopkeeper.*
tābēs -is, f. *wasting away, decay, melting; disease, pestilence; demoralization; decayed matter, corruption.*
tābesco tābescĕre tābŭi, *to melt, waste away; to pine, be spoiled.*
tābĭdŭlus -a -um, *wasting, consuming.*
tābĭdus -a -um: pass., *melting, wasting, dissolving*; act., *consuming.*
tābĭfĭcus -a -um, *consuming.*
tăbŭla -ae, f. *a board, plank; a draught-board; a painted panel, a painting; a votive tablet; a map; a writing-tablet; a document*; in plur., *a record, register; a catalogue; an auction.*
tăbŭlārĭum -i, n. *archives, records.*
tăbŭlātĭo -ōnis, f. *flooring, planking; a storey.*
tăbŭlātus -a -um, *floored, boarded*; n. as subst., *a floor, storey; a row* or *layers of vines.*
tābum -i, n. *corrupt moisture, matter; a plague, pestilence.*
tăcĕo -ēre -ŭi -ĭtum, *to be silent, say nothing; to be still, quiet*; transit., *to be silent about, pass over in silence.*
Hence partic. **tăcĭtus** -a -um: pass., *passed over in silence, unmentioned; implied, tacit; secret, concealed*; act., *silent, mute, still, quiet.* Adv. **tăcĭtē.**
tăcĭturnĭtās -ātis, f., *silence, taciturnity*
tăcĭturnus -a -um, *silent, still, quiet.*
tăcĭtus -a -um, partic. from taceo; q.v.
Tăcĭtus -i, m., Cornelius, *the historian of the early Empire.*
tactĭlis -e, *able to be touched.*
tactĭo -ōnis, f. *touching, sense of touch.*
tactus -ūs, m. *touch, touching; influence, operation; the sense of touch.*
taeda -ae, f. *pine-wood; a board, a torch,* esp. as used at weddings.
taedet taedēre taedŭit, and taesum est, impers., *it causes weariness* or *boredom.*
taedĭfer -fĕra -fĕrum, *torch-bearing.*
taedĭum -i, n. *disgust, weariness, boredom.*
taenĭa -ae, f. *a fillet, head-band.*
taeter -tra -trum, *foul, hideous, offensive; disgraceful, abominable*; adv. **taetrē.**
tăgax -ācis, *thievish, given to pilfering.*
tālāris -e, *of* or *stretching to the ankles*; n. pl. as subst. *wings on the ankles, winged sandals,* or *a robe reaching to the ankles.*
tālārĭus -a -um, *of dice.*
tālĕa -ae, f. *a cutting, slip; a short stake* or *bar.*
tălentum -i, n. *a* (*Greek*) *weight*; also *a sum of money.*
tālĭo -ōnis, f. *retaliation.*
tālis -e, *of such a kind, such.*
talpa -ae, f. or m. *a mole.*
tālus -i, m. *the ankle, ankle-bone; the heel; a die* (made originally of ankle-bones of animals).
tam, *so, so far, to such a degree.*
tămărix -ĭcis, f. *the tamarisk.*
tamdĭū, *so long.*
tămĕn, *however, yet, nevertheless.*
Tămĕsis -is, m. and **Tămĕsa** -ae, *the Thames.*
tămetsi, *even if, although.*
tamquam (tanquam), *as, just as, like as; just as if.*
tandem, *at length, at last;* in questions, *after all, may I ask?*
tango tangĕre tĕtĭgi tactum, *to touch, strike, push, hit; to border on, to reach; to steal; to defile; to taste; to affect* the feelings; *to touch upon* a subject.
Tantălus i-, m. *a son of Jupiter, who offended the gods and was " tantalised " in Hades.*
tantillus -a -um, *so little, so small*
tantispĕr, *just so long.*
tantŏpĕrē, *so greatly, so much.*
tantŭlus -a -um, *so small, so little*; n. as subst. *such a trifle.*

tantum; see tantus.
tantummŏdo, *only just.*
tantus -a -um, *of such a size, so great.* N. as subst. **tantum** -i, *so much;* acc. as adv., *so far,* or *only;* tantum non, *all but;* genit. **tanti,** *for so much, worth so much;* abl. **tanto,** *by so much.*
tantusdem tantădem tantundem, *just so much, just so great.*
tăpēta -ae, m. **tăpēta** -ōrum, n. pl., and **tăpētĭa** -ĭum, n. pl., *drapery, tapestry.*
tardesco -ĕre, *to become slow.*
tardĭpēs -pĕdis, *slow-footed, limping.*
tardĭtās -ātis, f. *slowness, tardiness; dullness, stupidity.*
tardo -are: intransit., to *loiter, be slow;* transit., *to slow down, hinder, delay.*
tardus -a -um, adj. *slow, tardy; dull, stupid;* poet., *making slow;* of speech, *measured, deliberate.* Adv. **tardē,** *slowly.*
Tărentum -i, n. *a coastal town of southern Italy* (now Taranto); adj. **Tărentīnus** -a -um.
Tarpēius -a -um, *name of a Roman family;* mons Tarpeius, *the Tarpeian rock, from which criminals were thrown.*
Tarquinii -orum, m. pl. *an old town in Etruria, whence came the Tarquin family, including two kings of Rome.*
Tarrăco -ōnis, f. *a town in Spain.*
Tartărus (**-ŏs**) -i, m.; plur. **Tartără** -ōrum, n. *the infernal regions;* adj. **Tartărĕus** -a -um.
taurĕus -a -um, *of a bull;* f. as subst. *a whip of bull's hide.*
taurĭformis -e, *shaped like a bull.*
taurīnus -a -um, *of* or *like a bull.*
taurus -i, m. *a bull.*
Taurus -i, m. *a mountain range in Asia Minor.*
taxātĭo -onis, f. *rating, valuing, appraising.*
taxillus -i, m. *a small die.*
taxus -i, f. *yew-tree.*
[1]**tē**; see tu.
[2]**-tĕ,** suffix added to tu, etc.
techna -ae, f. *a cunning trick, artifice.*
tector -ōris, m. *a plasterer.*
tectōrĭŏlum -i, n. *plaster* or *stucco work.*
tectōrĭus -a -um, *used for covering, of* or *for plastering;* n. as subst. *plaster, stucco, fresco painting, cosmetic.*
tectus -a -um, partic. from tego; q.v.
tĕgĕs -ĕtis, f. *a mat, rug, covering.*
tĕgĭmen, tĕgŭmen, tegmĕn -ĭnis, n. *a cover, covering.*
tĕgĭmentum, tĕgŭmentum, tegmentum -i, n. *a covering.*
tĕgo tĕgĕre texi tectum, *to cover; to bury; to conceal; to shield, protect.*
Hence partic. as adj. **tectus** -a -um, *covered, concealed; close, reserved, cautious.* N. as subst. **tectum** -i, *a roof* or *ceiling; a shelter, dwelling.* Adv. **tectē,** *covertly.*
tegu-; see also tegi-.
tēgŭla -ae, f. *a roof-tile.*
tela -ae, f. *a web* in weaving; *a warp; a spider's web; a loom; a design.*
Tēlĕmăchus -i, m. *son of Penelope and Ulysses.*
tellūs -ūris, f. *earth, soil, land; a country; the world.*
tēlum -i, n. *a missile; a dart, javelin, spear; any weapon; a beam of light.*
tĕmĕrārĭus -a -um, *accidental; inconsiderate, thoughtless, rash.*
tĕmĕrĕ, adv. *blindly, by chance, casually, heedlessly;* non temere, *not for nothing, not lightly, not easily.*
tĕmĕrĭtās -ātis, f. *chance, accident; rashness.*
tĕmĕro -are, *to darken; to defile, dishonour.*
tēmētum -i, n. *intoxicating drink; wine,* etc.
temno temnĕre tempsi temptum, *to despise.*
tēmō -ōnis, m. *a pole; the pole of a waggon; a waggon; Charles's Wain.*
Tempē, n. pl., indecl. *a valley in Thessaly.*
tempĕrāmentum -i, n. *a right proportion, middle way, mean, moderation.*
temperantĭa -ae, f. *temperance moderation, self-control.*
temperātĭo -ōnis, f. *moderation, just proportion; an organizing principle.*
tempĕrātor -ōris, m. *one who arranges* or *governs.*
tempĕri; see tempus.
tempĕrĭēs -ēi, f. *a proper mixture, tempering;* of climate, *mildness.*
tempĕro -are: intransit., *to be moderate, control oneself;* with dat. *to control, use with moderation,* or *to spare;* with ab, or with abl., *to keep from, refrain from;* transit., *to mix properly, temper, mitigate, regulate.*
Hence partic. as adj. **tempĕrans** -antis, *moderate, temperate, restrained;* adv. **tempĕranter:** perf. partic. **tempĕrātus** -a -um, *tempered, ordered, moderate;* adv. **tempĕrātē.**
tempestās -ātis, f. *a period of time, a season; weather;* esp. *bad weather, storm, tempest;* fig., *attack, fury.*
tempestīvĭtās -ātis, f. *fit time, proper season.*
tempestīvus -a -um, *opportune, fit, appropriate; early; ripe, mature.* Adv. **tempestīvē,** *seasonably.*
templum -i, n. *a section, a part cut off; a space marked out by the augur for auspices; consecrated ground,* esp. *a sanctuary, asylum; a place dedicated to a deity, a shrine, temple; any open space, quarter, region; a rafter, cross-beam.*
tempŏrālis -e, *temporary, lasting for a time.*
tempŏrārĭus -a -um *temporary; seasonable.*
tempŏri; see tempus.
temptābundus -a -um, *trying, attempting.*
temptāmĕn -ĭnis, and **temptāmentum** -i, n. *a trial, attempt, essay.*
temptātĭo -ōnis, f. *a trial, test; an attack.*
temptātor -ōris, m. *an assailant.*

tempto -are, *to prove, try, test, attempt; to test by attack, to assail; to work upon, tamper with, excite, disturb.*
tempus -ŏris, n. *a division, section;* of *the temples* of the head; of time, *a space, period, moment; time,* in gen.; *a fit time, occasion, opportunity; the state, condition of things* (esp. bad); *time in pronouncing a syllable, quantity; time in grammar, tense.* As adv. **tempŏrĕ, tempŏrī,** and **tempĕrī,** *at the right time,* or *for the occasion;* **in tempŏrĕ,** *at the right moment;* **ex tempŏrĕ,** *on the spur of the moment.*
tēmŭlentus -a -um, *drunken, tipsy.*
tĕnācĭtās -ātis, f. *tenacity; stinginess.*
tĕnax -ācis, *holding fast, clinging, tenacious; sparing, frugal, stingy; firm, steady; obstinate.* Adv. **tĕnācĭtĕr,** *firmly, steadily.*
tendĭcŭla -ae, f. *a snare, trap.*
tendo tendĕre tĕtendi tentum and tensum: transit., *to stretch, extend, spread; to direct, present, give;* barbiton, *to string;* praetorium, *to pitch;* intransit., *to direct one's course, tend, make towards; to be inclined, aim at, strive after;* with infin., *to try, attempt;* milit., *to pitch one's tent, encamp.*
tĕnebrae -arum, f. pl. *darkness; night; blindness; obscurity.*
tĕnebrĭcōsus -a -um, *dark, gloomy, obscure.*
tĕnebrōsus -a -um, *dark, gloomy.*
tĕnĕo tĕnēre tĕnŭi tentum, *to hold; to possess, keep, preserve, maintain; to understand, grasp, know, remember; to contain, comprise;* milit. *to occupy, garrison; to master, restrain, keep back; to charm, amuse;* intransit., *to keep on, persevere, persist, endure.*
tĕner -ĕra -ĕrum, *tender, delicate, soft; young;* adv. **tĕnĕrē.**
tĕnĕrasco -ĕre, *to grow tender.*
tĕnĕrĭtās -ātis, f. *tenderness, softness.*
tĕnor -ōris, m. *course, continued movement; duration, career.*
tensa -ae, f. *a car on which images of the gods were carried.*
tento, etc.; see tempto, etc.
tentīgo -ĭnis, f. *lecherousness.*
tentōrĭum -i, n. *a tent.*
tentus -a -um, partic. from tendo and teneo; q.v.
tĕnŭĭcŭlus -a -um, *very mean, slight.*
tĕnŭis -e, *thin, slight, slender; refined, subtle; little, trivial, feeble; mean, low.* Adv. **tĕnŭĭtĕr,** *thinly; subtly; slightly, poorly.*
tĕnŭĭtās -ātis, f. *thinness; refinement, subtlety; slightness, poverty.*
tĕnŭo -are, *to make thin, attenuate; to weaken, diminish.*
tĕnŭs, prep. after noun or pronoun in abl. or genit., *up to, down to, as far as.*
tĕpĕfăcĭo -făcĕre -fēci -factum, *to make warm.*
tĕpĕo -ēre, *to be warm,* or *lukewarm.*
tĕpesco tĕpescĕre tĕpŭi, *to grow warm* or *lukewarm.*
tĕpĭdus -a -um, *warm, lukewarm, tepid;* compar. adv. **tĕpĭdĭus.**
tĕpor -ōris, m. *lukewarmness, moderate heat.*
tĕr, *three times, thrice.*
terdĕcĭēs (-ĭens) *thirteen times.*
tĕrĕbinthus -i, f. *the terebinth-tree.*
tĕrebro -are, *to bore through, pierce, perforate.*
tĕrēdo -ĭnis, f. *a worm that gnaws wood.*
Tĕrentĭus -a -um, *the name of a Roman gens;* esp. of M. Terentius Afer, *the comic dramatist.*
tĕrēs -rĕtis, *rounded, polished, well-turned, smooth; refined, elegant.*
tergĕmĭnus = trigeminus; q.v.
tergĕo -ēre and **tergo** -ĕre, tersi tersum, *to wipe, scour, clean;* partic. **tersus** -a -um, *clean, neat, correct.*
tergĭversātĭo -ōnis, f. *backwardness, reluctance, evasion.*
tergĭversor -ari, dep. *to be backward and reluctant, shuffle, find excuses, evade.*
tergo = tergeo; q.v.
tergum -i, n. *the back;* terga dare, *to flee;* a tergo, *in the rear; a hide, skin;* meton., *a thing made out of hide.*
tergus -ŏris, n. *the back; skin, hide, leather.*
termĕs -ĭtis, m. *a branch,* esp. of olive.
Termĭnālĭa -ĭum and -ĭōrum, n. *the Festival of Terminus (god of boundaries).*
termĭnātĭo -ōnis, f. *limiting, determining, termination.*
termĭno -are, *to limit, set bounds to, restrict, define, close.*
termĭnus -i, m. *a boundary-mark, limit, end;* personif., *the god of boundaries.*
terni -ae -a, *three at a time,* or *three each.*
tĕro tĕrĕre trīvi trītum, *to rub; to whet, smooth; to grind, thresh; to wear out, use up, spend.*

Hence partic. as adj. **trītus** -a -um, *worn; frequented; practised;* of words, etc., *trite, well-known.*
Terpsĭchŏrē -ēs, f. *the Muse of dancing;* in gen., *poetry.*
terra -ae, f. *earth, land, ground, soil; a country, land, region;* orbis terrarum, *the whole world.*
terrēnus -a -um, *belonging to the earth, terrestrial; made of earth, earthen;* n. as subst. *land, ground.*
terrĕo terrēre, *to frighten, terrify; scare away; to deter.*
terrestris -e, *of the earth, terrestrial.*
terrĕus -a -um, *of earth, earthly.*
terrĭbĭlis -e, *terrible, dreadful.*
terrĭcŭla -ōrum, n. pl. *a bogey.*
terrĭfĭco -are, *to frighten, terrify.*
terrĭfĭcus -a -um, *frightful, terrible.*
terrĭgĕna -ae, m. and f. *earth-born.*
terrĭlŏquus -a -um, *terror-speaking.*
terrĭto -are, *to frighten, intimidate, scare.*
terrĭtōrĭum -i, n. *land belonging to a town, district, territory.*
terror -ōris, m. *fright, fear, terror; a frightening object.*

tersus -a-um, partic. from tergeo; q.v.
tertĭādĕcĭmāni -ōrum, m. pl. *soldiers of the thirteenth legion.*
tertĭānus -a -um. (1) *of the third day*; f. as subst., *a tertian fever.* (2) *belonging to the third legion*; m. pl. as subst., *soldiers of the third legion.*
tertĭus -a -um, *third*; acc. n. sing. **tertium,** *for the third time*; abl. **tertiō,** *for the third time*, or *thirdly.*
tertĭusdĕcĭmus -a -um, *thirteenth.*
tĕruncĭus -i, m. *one quarter*; ne teruncius quidem, *not a farthing.*
tesqua (tesca) -ōrum, n. pl. *wastes, deserts.*
tessella -ae, f. *a small cube of stone.*
tessĕra -ae, f. *a cube; a piece of mosaic paving; a die* (with numbers on all six sides); *a token; a watchword.*
tessĕrārĭus -i, m. *the officer who received the watchword.*
testa -ae, f. *an earthen vessel, pot, jug, urn,* etc.; *a potsherd; a brick* or *tile; the shell of shell-fish*; any *shell, covering.*
testāmentārĭus -a -um, *relating to a will*; m. as subst., *a forger of wills.*
testāmentum -i, n. *a last will, testament.*
testātĭo -onis, f. *calling to witness*, or *bearing witness.*
testĭfĭcātĭo -onis, f. *bearing witness, testifying; evidence, proof.*
testĭfĭcor -ari, dep. *to bear witness to, give evidence of; to show, bring to light; to call to witness.*
testĭmōnĭum -i, n. *witness, evidence; proof, indication.*
[1]**testis** -is, c. *one who gives evidence, a witness; an eye-witness, spectator.*
[2]**testis** -is, m. *a testicle.*
testor -ari, dep. (1) *to bear witness to, give evidence of; to make known, publish, declare*; as pass., *to be attested, declared.* (2) *to make a will.* (3) *to call to witness.*
testūdĭnĕus -a -um, *of a tortoise; of tortoise-shell.*
testūdo -ĭnis, f. *a tortoise; tortoise-shell; a lyre, cithara,* etc.; *an arch or vault*; milit., *a shed, to protect soldiers while attacking fortifications,* also *a formation with shields held over the soldiers' heads and interlocking.*
testŭla -ae, f. *a potsherd.*
testum -i, n. with abl. testo and testu, *an earthen pot.*
teter; see taeter.
Tēthys -thy̆os; acc. -thyn; f. *a marine goddess.*
tetrachmum or **tetradrachmum** -i, n. *a Greek coin of four drachmae.*
tetrarchēs -ae, m. *ruler over one-fourth of a country, tetrarch.*
tetrarchĭa -ae, f. *a tetrarchy.*
tetrĭcus -a -um, *harsh, gloomy, severe.*
Teucer -cri, and **Teucrus** -i, m. (1) *son of Telamon,* and *brother of Ajax.* (2) *first king of Troy*; hence adj. **Teucrus** -a -um, *Trojan*; m. pl. as subst. *the Trojans*; **Teucrĭa** -ae, f. *Troy.*
Teutŏni -ōrum, and **Teutŏnes** -um, m. pl. *the Teutons, a Germanic people.*
texo texĕre texŭi textum, *to weave; to twine together, plait; to put together, construct, build*; of speech or writing, *to compose.* N. of partic. as subst. **textum** -i, *woven cloth, a web, fabric*; of composition, *style.*
textĭlis -e, *woven, textile, plaited.* N. as subst. *a woven fabric, piece of cloth.*
textor -ōris, m. and **textrix** -trīcis, f. *a weaver.*
textrīnum -i, n. *weaving.*
textum -i, n. subst. from texo; q.v.
textūra -ae, f. *a web, texture; putting together, construction.*
textus -ūs, m. *a web; texture, structure*; of speech or writing, *connexion.*
thălămus -i, m. *a room,* esp. *a woman's bedroom; a marriage-bed; any abode, dwelling.*
thălassĭnus -a -um, *sea-green.*
Thălīa -ae, f. *the Muse of comic poetry.*
thallus -i, m. *a green branch.*
Thapsus (**-ŏs**) -i, f. *a town in Africa, where Caesar conquered the Pompeians.*
thĕātrālis -e, *of a theatre, theatrical.*
thĕātrum -i, n. *a theatre.*
Thēbae -arum, f. pl. *Thebes.* (1) *a city of Upper Egypt.* (2) *the chief city of Boeotia.* Adj. **Thēbānus** -a -um, *belonging to Thebes in Boeotia.*
thēca -ae, f. *a case, envelope, covering.*
thĕma -ătis, n. *a topic, subject.*
thĕŏlŏgus -i, m. *a theologian.*
thermae -arum, f. pl. *warm springs, warm baths.*
thēsaurus -i, m. *a treasure, store, hoard; a treasury, store-house.*
Thēsēūs -ĕi and -ĕos, m. *a king of Athens, conqueror of the Minotaur*; adj. **Thēsēus** and **Thēsēĭus** -a -um, *of Theseus.*
thĕsis -is, f. *a proposition, thesis.*
Thessălĭa -ae, f. *Thessaly, a region in the north of Greece*; adj. **Thessălĭcus** and **Thessălus** -a -um, *Thessalian*; f. adj. **Thessălis** -ĭdis, *Thessalian.*
Thĕtis -ĭdis or -ĭdos, f. *a sea-nymph, mother of Achilles*; poet., *the sea.*
thĭăsus -i, m. *a Bacchic rout, band of revellers.*
Thisbē -ēs, f. *a Babylonian maiden, loved by Pyramus.*
thŏlus -i, m. *a cupola, dome.*
thōrax -ācis, m. *a breastplate, cuirass.*
Thrācĭa -ae; also **Thrāca** -ae and **Thrācē** -ēs; f. *the country of Thrace*; adj. **Thrācĭus** and **Thrēĭcĭus** -a -um, *Thracian*; **Thrax** -ācis and **Thrēx** -ēcis, m. *Thracian, a Thracian.*
Thūcȳdĭdēs -is, m. *the Athenian historian of the Peloponnesian war.*
Thūlē (**Thȳlē**) -ēs, f. *an island in the extreme north of Europe.*
thunnus (**thynnus**) -i, m. *a tunny-fish.*
thūs, thūrārĭus, etc. = tus, turarius, etc.; q.v.
Thy̆estēs -ae and -is, m. *son of Pelops, brother of Atreus.*
Thȳĭăs and **Thy̆ăs** -ădis, f. *a Bacchante.*
Thȳlē = Thule; q.v.
thymbra -ae, f. *the herb savory.*
thy̆mum -i, n. *the herb thyme.*

thynnus = thunnus; q.v.
thyrsus -i, m. *the stalk of a plant; a wand, as carried by Bacchus and his attendants.*
tĭāra -ae, f. and **tĭārus** -ae, m. *a turban.*
Tĭbĕris -bĕris, m.; also poet. **Tībris** or **Thībris** -brĭdis, m. *the river Tiber*; adj. **Tĭbĕrīnus** -a -um, *of the river Tiber*; m. as subst. *the river-god of the Tiber.*
Tĭbĕrĭus -i, m. *a Roman praenomen,* abbreviated Ti.
tībĭa -ae, f. *the shin-bone, tibia; a pipe, flute* (originally made of a hollow bone).
tībīcĕn -ĭnis, m. *a flute-player, piper; a pillar, prop.*
tībīcīna -ae, f. *a female flute-player.*
tībīcĭnĭum -i, *playing on the flute.*
Tibris = Tiberis; q.v.
Tĭbullus -i, m.; Albius, *a Roman elegiac poet.*
Tībŭr -bŭris, n. *an old town in Latium*; adj. **Tīburs** -burtis, **Tīburtīnus** and **Tīburnus** -a -um.
tĭgillum -i, n. *a small beam.*
tignārĭus -a -um, *of beams*; faber, *a carpenter.*
tignum -i, n. *a beam.*
Tigrānēs -is, m. *a king of Armenia.*
tigris -ĭdis and -is, c. *a tiger.*
tĭlĭa -ae, f. *linden* or *lime-tree.*
tĭmĕfactus -a -um, *frightened, alarmed.*
tĭmĕo -ēre, *to be afraid, fear, dread*; partic. **tĭmens** -entis, *fearing, fearful.*
tĭmĭdĭtās -ātis, f. *fearfulness, timidity.*
tĭmĭdus -a -um, *fearful, timid*; adv. **tĭmĭdē.**
tĭmor -ōris, m. *fear, dread; an object exciting fear.*
tinctĭlis -e, *in which something is dipped.*
tĭnĕa -ae, f. *a grub, larva, worm.*
tingo tingĕre tinxi tinctum, *to wet, moisten; to dye, colour, imbue.*
tinnĭo -ire, *to ring, tinkle; to talk shrilly; to make to chink*; hence *to pay money.*
tinnītus -ūs, m. *ringing, tinkle, jingle.*
tinnŭlus -a -um, *ringing, tinkling, jingling.*
tintinnābŭlum -i, n. *a bell.*
tintinno (tintĭno) -are, *to ring, tinkle.*
tīnus -i, f. *a shrub, the laurustinus.*
Tīrīdātēs -dātis, m. *name of several kings of Armenia.*
tīrō -ōnis, m. *a young soldier; a recruit, beginner, learner.*
tīrōcĭnĭum -i, n. *the state of a recruit, rawness, inexperience; beginning, apprenticeship*; concr. *a body of recruits.*
tīruncŭlus -i, m. *a young beginner.*
Tīryns -nthis or -nthos, f. *an Argive town where Hercules was brought up*; adj. **Tīrynthĭus** -a -um.
Tīsĭphŏnē -ēs, f. *one of the Furies.*
Tītān -tānis, and **Tītānus** -i, m.; usually plur. **Tītānes** -um and **Tītāni** -ōrum, *the Titans, who warred against Jupiter and were by him cast into Hades.*
Tīthōnus -i, m. *husband of Aurora.*
Tĭtĭes -ĭum and **Tĭtĭenses** -ĭum, m. pl., *one of the three original tribes at Rome.*
tītillātĭo -ōnis, f. *a tickling.*
tītillo -are, *to tickle.*
tĭtŭbātĭo -ōnis, f. *a staggering, reeling; uncertainty.*
tĭtŭbo -are, *to totter, stagger; to stammer; to falter, waver, hesitate*: adv. from partic. **tĭtŭbantĕr,** *hesitatingly, uncertainly.*
tĭtŭlus -i, m. *an inscription, label, notice; a title, honour; pretence, pretext.*
Tĭtus -i, m. *a Roman praenomen,* abbreviated T.
tŏcŭlĭo -ōnis, m. *a usurer.*
tōfus (tōphus) -i, m. *tufa.*
tŏga -ae, f. *the white woollen upper garment worn by Roman citizens.*
tŏgātŭlus -i, m. *a little client.*
tŏgātus -a -um, *wearing the* toga; m. as subst. *a Roman citizen*; f. as subst. *the national drama of the Romans.*
tŏgŭla -ae, f. *a little toga.*
tŏlĕrābĭlis -e; pass., *bearable*; act., *tolerant, patient;* compar. adv. **tŏlĕrābĭlĭus,** *rather patiently.*
tŏlĕrantĭa -ae and **tŏlĕrātĭo** -onis, f. *bearing, endurance.*
tŏlĕro -are, *to carry, bear, endure, sustain; to sustain; to support, keep up, maintain.* Hence pres. partic. **tŏlĕrans** -antis, *enduring, patient*; adv. **tŏlĕrantĕr;** perf. partic. **tŏlĕrātus** -a -um, *endurable.*
tollēno -ōnis, m. *a machine for raising weights, a crane.*
tollo tollĕre sustŭli sublātum. (1) *to lift up, raise, elevate*; in crucem, *to crucify*; tollere ancoras, *to weigh anchor;* laudibus, *to extol;* of children, *to acknowledge as one's own, to bring up.* (2) *to take away, remove, carry off, steal; to destroy, abolish.*
tŏmācŭlum (-aclum) -i, n. *a kind of sausage.*
tōmentum -i, n. *the stuffing of a pillow, mattress,* etc.
Tŏmi -ōrum, m. pl. and **Tŏmis** -is, f. *a town on the Black Sea, Ovid's place of exile.*
tŏmus -i, m. *a cutting, chip, shred.*
tondĕo tondēre tŏtondi tonsum, *to shave, shear, clip; to mow, reap, prune; to browse on, crop; to fleece* a person.
tŏnitrus -ūs, m. and **tŏnitruum** -i, n. *thunder.*
tŏno -are -ŭi -ĭtum, *to thunder.* Transf.: instransit., *to make a loud noise;* transit., *to thunder forth.*
tonsa -ae, f. *an oar.*
tonsīlis -e, *shorn, clipped, cut.*
tonsillae -arum, f. *the tonsils.*
tonsor -ōris, m. *a hair-cutter, barber.*
tonsōrĭus -a -um, *of* or *for clipping.*
tonstrīcŭla -ae, f. *a little female barber.*
tonstrīna -ae, f. *a barber's shop.*
tonstrix -īcis, f. *a female barber.*
tonsūra -ae, f. *clipping, shearing, shaving.*

tophus, etc. = tofus, etc.; q.v.
tŏpiārius -a -um, *of ornamental gardening*; m. as subst. *a landscape gardener*; f. as subst. *the art of landscape gardening.*
tŏrăl -ālis, n. *the valance of a couch.*
tŏreuma -ătis, n. *carved* or *embossed work.*
tormentum -i, n. *an instrument for twisting* or *pressing*; *a windlass; the rack; any instrument of torture*; hence *suasion, pressure; torture, torment*; milit., *a piece of artillery*, or *a missile.*
tormĭna -um, n. pl. *the colic, gripes.*
tormĭnōsus -a -um, *suffering from colic.*
torno -are, *to turn in a lathe; to round, make round.*
tornus -i, m. *a lathe.*
tŏrōsus -a -um, *muscular, brawny.*
torpēdo -ĭnis, f. (1) *lethargy, sluggishness.* (2) *a fish, the electric ray.*
torpĕo -ēre, *to be sluggish, numb, inert, inactive.*
torpesco -pescĕre -pŭi, *to become sluggish* or *numb.*
torpĭdus -a -um, *numb, sluggish.*
torpor -ōris, m. *numbness, sluggishness, dullness, inactivity.*
torquātus -a -um, *wearing a twisted collar* or *necklace.*
torquĕo torquēre torsi tortum, *to twist, wind, curl, wrench; to distort; to hurl violently, whirl; to rack, torture, torment, plague, try, test.*
Hence partic. **tortus** -a -um, *twisted, crooked, intricate*; adv. **tortē.**
torquis (**torquēs**) -is, m. and f. *a twisted collar* or *necklace; a ring, wreath, chaplet.*
torrĕo torrēre torrŭi tostum, *to burn, parch, dry up.*
Hence partic. as adj. **torrens** -entis, *burning, hot, parched; rushing, seething.* M. as subst. *a torrent.*
torresco -ĕre, *to become parched.*
torrĭdus -a -um, *parched, burnt, dry.* Transf., *pinched, nipped with cold.*
torris, is, m. *a firebrand.*
tortĭlis -e, *twisted, twined.*
torto -are, *to torture, torment.*
tortor -ōris, m. *a torturer, tormentor; a wielder.*
tortŭōsus -a -um, *tortuous, intricate, involved.*
[1]**tortus** -a -um, partic. from torqueo; q.v.
[2]**tortus** -ūs, m. *a twisting, curve.*
tŏrus -i, m. *any round protuberance; a muscle; a bed, sofa; a marriage couch; a bier; a mound*; fig., *an ornament.*
torvĭtās -ātis, f. *savageness, wildness.*
torvus -a -um, *savage, grim, fierce.*
tŏt, indecl. *so many.*
tŏtĭdem, indecl. *just as many.*
tŏtĭēs (**-iens**), *so often, so many times.*
tōtus -a -um, genit. tōtĭus, dat. tōtī; *whole, complete, entire; whole-hearted, absorbed.* N. as subst. **tōtum** -i, *the whole*; ex toto, in toto, *on the whole.*
toxĭcum -i, n. *poison* (*for arrows*).
trăbālis -e, *of beams of wood; like a beam.*
trăbĕa -ae, f. *a white robe with scarlet stripes and a purple seam,* worn by kings and knights.
trăbĕātus -a -um, *clad in the* trabea; q.v.
trabs trăbis, f. *a beam of wood; a tree-trunk; a ship; a roof; a table.*
tractābĭlis -e, *that can be handled, manageable; yielding, compliant.*
tractātĭo -ōnis, f. *handling, management.*
tractātor -ōris, m. *a masseur.*
tractātrix -īcis, f. *a masseuse.*
tractātus -ūs, m. *handling, management, treatment.*
tractim, *gradually, by degrees.*
tracto -are, *to drag along, haul, pull about; to handle, manage, treat; to behave towards* a person.
[1]**tractus** -a -um, partic. from traho; q.v.
[2]**tractus** -ūs, m. *a dragging process*; verborum, *drawling*; belli, *extension*; concr., *a track, trail; extent, position; a tract, district.*
tradĭtĭo -ōnis, f. *giving up, surrender; instruction, relation.*
trādĭtor -ōris, m. *traitor.*
trādo (**transdo**) -dĕre -dĭdi -dĭtum, *to hand over, give up, surrender, betray; to hand down to posterity*; esp. *to hand down an account of an event, to report, relate, teach*; with reflex., *to commit, surrender, devote oneself.*
trādūco (**transdūco**) -dūcĕre -duxi -ductum, *to lead over, bring over* or *across; to lead past in front of others; to transpose, transfer*; of time, *to pass, spend, lead; to show, display; to expose to ridicule, "show up".*
trāductĭo -ōnis, f. *transferring*; rhet., *metonymy*; temporis, *passage* or *lapse of time.*
trāductor -ōris, m. *a transferrer.*
trādux -ŭcis, m. *vine-layer.*
trăgĭcus -a -um, *tragic; lofty, sublime; awful, fearful.* M. as subst. *a tragic poet.* Adv. **trăgĭcē,** *tragically.*
trăgoedĭa -ae, f. *tragedy; a dramatic scene.*
trăgoedus -i, m. *tragic actor, tragedian.*
trăgŭla -ae, f. *a species of javelin.*
trăhĕa -ae, f. *sledge, drag.*
trăho trăhĕre traxi tractum, *to trail, pull along; to drag, pull violently; to draw in, take up*; of air, *to breathe; to draw out,* hence *to lengthen; to draw together, contract.* Transf., *to draw, attract; to take in* or *on, assume, derive; to prolong, spin out; to ascribe, refer, interpret.*
Hence partic. **tractus** -a -um, of speech, *fluent, flowing.* N. as subst., *a flock of wool.*
trāicĭo (transicĭo) -icĕre -iēci -iectum. (1) *to throw* a thing (or person) *across something; to convey over, transport.* (2) *to pass through* or *across* a thing (or person); *to cross, penetrate, pierce.*
trāiectĭo -ōnis, *a passing over, crossing over; transferring, transposition; hyperbole.*
trāiectus -ūs, m. *crossing over, passage.*

tralat- = translat-; q.v.
trālūcĕo = transluceo; q.v.
trāma -ae, f. *the woof in weaving.*
trāmĕo = transmeo; q.v.
trāmĕs -itis, m. *by-way, foot-path.*
trāmigro = transmigro; q.v.
trāmitto = transmitto; q.v.
trānăto (transnăto) -are, *to swim across, pass through.*
tranquillĭtās -ātis, f. *quiet, calm.*
tranquillo -are, *to calm.*
tranquillus -a -um, *quiet, calm.* N. as subst. *a calm, quietness.* Adv. **tranquillē.**
trans, prep. with acc., *over, across, on* or *to the other side of.*
transăbĕo -ire -ĭi, *to go through* or *past.*
transactor -ōris, m. *manager, accomplisher.*
transădĭgo -ĭgĕre -ēgi -actum, *to drive* a thing *through* something else; also *to pierce, penetrate.*
Transalpīnus -a -um, *beyond the Alps, transalpine.*
transcendo (transscendo) -scendĕre -scendi -scensum, *to climb over, pass over; to step over, transgress.*
transcrībo (transscribo) -scrībĕre -scripsi -scriptum, *to copy, transcribe.* Transf., *to transfer, convey, assign.*
transcurro -currĕre -cŭcurri and -curri -cursum, *to run across* or *over, hasten past.*
transcursus -ūs, m. *a running past, hastening through.*
transdo = trado; q.v.
transdūco = traduco; q.v.
transenna -ae, f. *lattice-work, grating.*
transĕo -īre -ĭi -ĭtum, *to go over, cross, pass over, go past.* Transf., *to be changed; to pass* time; *to pass beyond, transgress; to pass over, ignore,* or *touch lightly on.*
transfĕro transferre transtŭli translātum and trālātum, *to carry over* or *across; to transfer, transport, convey.* Transf., *to put off, defer; to change;* in writing, *to copy; to translate into another language; to use* a word *figuratively* or *metaphorically.*
transfīgo -fīgĕre -fixi -fixum, *to pierce through,* or *thrust through.*
transfŏdĭo -fŏdĕre -fōdi -fossum, *to stab through, transfix.*
transformis -e, *changed, transformed.*
transformo -are, *to change, transform.*
transfŭga -ae, *deserter.*
transfŭgĭo -fŭgĕre -fūgi -fŭgĭtum, *to desert to the enemy.*
transfŭgĭum -i, n. *desertion.*
transfundo -fundĕre -fūdi -fūsum, *to pour from one vessel into another, to transfer.*
transfūsĭo -ōnis, f. *a pouring out, pouring off.*
transgrĕdĭor -grĕdi -gressus, dep. *to go across, pass over.*
transgressĭo -ōnis, f. *going over, passage; transposition of words.*
transgressus -ūs, m. *going over, passage.*
transĭgo -ĭgĕre -ēgi -actum, *to stab, pierce through;* of time, *to pass, spend;* of business, *to finish, complete, accomplish, transact;* of a difference or dispute, *to settle.*
transĭlĭo (transsĭlĭo) -sĭlire -sĭlŭi, *to spring over, leap across; to pass over* a thing, or *to pass beyond, transgress.*
transĭtĭo -ōnis, f. *going across, passing over; communication, infection, contagion;* concr., *a passage.*
transĭtus -ūs, m. *passing over* or *across, transit; changing over, transition.*
translātīcĭus (trālātīcĭus) -a -um, *customary, prescriptive; common, usual.*
translātĭo (trālātĭo) -ōnis, f. *transferring, handing over;* of plants, *grafting; a translation; a metaphor, trope.*
translātīvus -a -um, *transferable.*
translātor -ōris, m. *transferrer.*
translūcĕo (trālūcĕo) -ēre, *to shine through* or *across.*
transmărīnus -a -um, *from beyond the sea, foreign.*
transmĕo (trāmĕo) -mĕare, *to go over* or *through.*
transmigro -are, *to migrate.*
transmissĭo -ōnis, f. and **transmissus** -ūs, m. *passage.*
transmitto (trāmitto) -mittĕre -mīsi -missum. (1) *to send across, send over, transmit; to convey, make over, entrust;* of time, *to let pass.* (2) *to go across, pass through* or *over; to leave unnoticed.*
transmontāni -ōrum, m. pl. *dwellers beyond the mountains.*
transmŏvĕo -mŏvēre -mōvi -mōtum, *to remove, transfer.*
transmūto -are, *to change, transmute.*
transnăto = tranato; q.v.
transpădānus -a -um, *beyond* (i.e. north of) *the Po, transpadane.*
transpectus -ūs, m. *a looking through, seeing through.*
transpicĭo (transspĭcĭo) -spĭcĕre, *to look through, see through.*
transpōno -pōnĕre -pŏsŭi -pŏsĭtum, *to put over, remove, transfer.*
transporto -are, *to convey across, transport.*
transrhēnānus -a -um, *beyond the Rhine.*
transtĭbĕrīnus -a -um, *beyond the Tiber.*
transtrum -i, n. *cross-beam; thwart.*
transulto (transsulto) -are, *to spring across.*
transŭo (transsŭo) -sŭĕre, *to sew through;* hence *to pierce through.*
transvectĭo (trāvectĭo) -ōnis, f. *a carrying across* or *past;* esp. *the riding of a Roman knight past the censor at the periodical muster.*
transvĕho (trāvĕho) -vĕhĕre -vexi -vectum, *to carry over* or *past;* pass., *to ride, sail,* etc., *across;* of a knight, *to ride past the censor at a muster;* of time, *to pass by.*
transverbĕro -are, *to pierce through, transfix.*
transversārĭus -a, -um, *lying across, transverse.*

transversus, trāversus and **transvorsus** -a -um, *transverse, oblique, athwart*; transverso itinere, *obliquely*; transversum digitum, *a finger's breadth*; de transverso, *unexpectedly.*
transvŏlito -are, *to fly across.*
transvŏlo (trāvŏlo) -are, *to fly over* or *across; to hasten through* or *past.*
trăpētus -i, m. **trăpētum** -i, n. and plur. **trăpētes** -um, m. *an oil-press.*
Trăsŭmēnus (also **Trasy-** and **Trasi-**; also with double **n**) -i, m. *the Trasimene lake, where Hannibal conquered the Romans under Flaminius* (217 B.C.).
trav- = transv-; q.v.
trĕcēni -ae, -a, *three hundred at a time* or *each.*
trĕcentēsĭmus -a -um, *three-hundredth.*
trĕcenti -ae -a, *three hundred.*
trĕcentiēs (-ĭens) *three hundred times.*
trĕchĕdipnum -i, n. *a light garment worn at table.*
trĕdĕcim, *thirteen.*
trĕmĕbundus -a -um, *trembling.*
trĕmĕfăcĭo -făcĕre -fēci -factum, *to cause to tremble.*
trĕmesco (-isco) -ĕre, *to tremble, quake*; with acc., *to tremble at.*
tremi-; see treme-.
trĕmo -ĕre -ŭi, *to tremble, quake*; with acc. *to tremble at*; gerundive as adj. **trĕmendus** -a -um, *fearful, terrible.*
trĕmor -ōris, m. *a trembling, quaking.*
trĕmŭlus -a -um, *trembling, quaking*; poet., *that causes trembling.*
trĕpĭdātĭo -ōnis, f. *agitation, anxiety.*
trĕpĭdo -are, *to be agitated, be busy, bustle about*; with acc., *to be anxious about*; with infin., *to be in a hurry to* do a thing; of flame, *to flicker.* Adv. from partic. **trĕpĭdantĕr,** *anxiously, hurriedly.*
trĕpĭdus -a -um, *agitated, restless, disturbed, in an emergency*; adv. **trĕpĭdē.**
trēs trĭa, *three.*
tresvĭri = triumviri; q.v.
Trēvĕri (Trēvĭri) -ōrum, m. pl. *a Germanic people.*
trĭangŭlus -a -um, *three-cornered, triangular.* N. as subst. *a triangle.*
trĭārii -ōrum, m. pl. *experienced Roman soldiers, drawn up in the third rank, behind the others.*
trĭbŭārĭus -a -um, *relating to a tribe.*
trĭbūlis -is, m. *a fellow-tribesman.*
trĭbŭlum -i, n. *threshing machine.*
trĭbŭlus -i, m. *a thorny plant, the caltrop.*
trĭbūnăl -ālis, n. *the tribunal,* a *raised platform* used by magistrates and generals.
trĭbūnātus -ūs, m. *tribuneship.*
trĭbūnĭcĭus -a -um, *of a tribune, tribunicial*; m. as subst. *an ex-tribune.*
trĭbūnus -i, m. *a tribune*: tribuni aerarii, *paymasters who assisted the quaestors*; tribuni militum, or militares, *military officers, of whom there were six to every legion*; tribuni plebis, *tribunes of the people, magistrates who protected the plebeians.*
trĭbŭo -ŭĕre -ŭi -ūtum, *to divide out, allot, assign; to grant, give, allow, yield, ascribe, attribute.*
trĭbus -ūs, f. *a tribe, a division of the Roman people.*
trĭbūtārĭus -a -um, *relating to tribute.*
trĭbūtim, *tribe by tribe.*
trĭbūtĭo -ōnis, f. *a distribution.*
trĭbūtum -i, n. *tax, tribute.* Transf., *a gift, present.*
trĭbūtus -a -um, *arranged according to tribes.*
trīcae -ārum, f. pl. *trifles, nonsense; vexations, troubles.*
trĭcēni -ae -a, *thirty at a time* or *each.*
trĭceps -cĭpĭtis, *three-headed.*
trĭcēsĭmus (-ensĭmus) *thirtieth.*
trĭchĭla -ae, f. *summer-house, arbour.*
trĭciēs (-ĭens), *thirty times.*
triclīnĭum -i, n. *dining-couch*; hence *dining-room.*
trīcor -ari, dep. *to make difficulties, shuffle, trifle.*
trĭcorpŏr -pŏris, *having three bodies.*
trĭcuspis -ĭdis, *having three points.*
trĭdens -entis, *having three teeth* or *prongs.* M. as subst. *a trident, a three-pronged spear.*
trĭdentĭfer and **trĭdentĭger** -ĕri, m. *the trident-bearer* (of Neptune).
trĭdŭum -i, n. *a space of three days.*
trĭennĭa -ĭum, n. pl. *a festival celebrated every three years.*
trĭennĭum -i, n. *a space of three years.*
trĭens -entis, m. *a third part, one-third.*
trĭentābŭlum -i, n. *the equivalent in land for the third part of a sum of money.*
trĭērarchus -i, m. *the commander of a trireme.*
trĭĕtērĭcus -a -um, *recurring every three years, triennial.*
trĭĕtēris -ĭdis, f. *a space of three years* or *a triennial festival.*
trĭfārĭam, *in three places, on three sides.*
trĭfaux -faucis, *having three throats.*
trĭfĭdus -a -um, *split in three parts, three-forked.*
trĭformis -e, *having three forms.*
trĭgĕmĭnus (tergĕmĭnus) -a -um, *threefold, triple.*
trīgintā, *thirty.*
trĭgon -ōnis, m. *a ball for playing.*
trĭlībris -e, *of three pounds' weight.*
trĭlinguis -e, *having three tongues.*
trĭlix -īcis, *having three threads.*
trĭmetrŏs (-us) -a -um, *containing three double feet.* M. as subst., *a trimeter.*
trīmus -a -um, *three years old.*
Trīnacrĭa -ae, f. *the triangular land,* i.e. *Sicily*; adj. **Trīnacrĭus** -a -um, and f. **Trinacris** -ĭdis, *Sicilian.*
trīni -ae, -a; *three at a time, three together.*
Trinobantes -um, m. *a people in east Britain.*
trĭnōdis -e, *having three knots.*
trĭōnēs -um, m. pl. *the ploughing oxen; the constellations Great Bear and Little Bear.*
trĭpart-; see tripert-.
trĭpectŏrus -a -um, *having three breasts.*

trĭpĕdālis -e, *of three feet in measure.*
trĭpertītus (-partītus) -a -um, *threefold, triple.* N. abl. sing. **trĭpertītō (-partītō)**, *in three parts.*
trĭpēs -pĕdis, *having three feet.*
triplex -lĭcis, *threefold, triple.* M. pl. as subst. *a writing tablet with three leaves.*
triplus -a -um, *threefold, triple.*
tripudio -are, *to beat the ground with the feet, to dance,* esp. as a religious rite.
trĭpŭdĭum -i, n. (1) *a religious dance.* (2) *a favourable omen, when the sacred chickens ate fast.*
trĭpūs -pŏdis, m. *three-legged seat, tripod,* esp. that at Delphi.
trĭquetrus -a -um, *three-cornered, triangular.*
trĭrēmis -e, *having three banks of oars;* f. as subst., *a trireme.*
triscurrĭa -ōrum, n. pl. *gross buffooneries.*
tristĭcŭlus -a -um, *somewhat sorrowful.*
tristis -e, *sad, gloomy, dismal, forbidding, harsh;* of taste or *smell, harsh, bitter.* N. acc. **tristĕ** used like adv. *harshly.*
tristĭtĭa -ae and **tristĭtĭēs** -ēi, f. *sadness, gloom, harshness.*
trĭsulcus -a -um, *three-pointed, three-pronged.*
trītĭcĕus -a -um, *wheaten.*
trītĭcum -i, n. *wheat.*
Trītōn -ōnis or -ōnos, m. (1) *Triton, son of Neptune, a god of the sea.* (2) *a lake in Africa, supposed birth-place of Minerva;* adj. **Trītōnĭăcus, Trītōnĭus** -a -um, and f. **Trītōnis** -ĭdis or -ĭdos, esp. in connexion with Minerva.
trītūra -ae, f. *threshing.*
trĭumphālis -e, *triumphal.* N. pl. as subst. *the distinctions of a triumphing general.*
trĭumpho -are, *to triumph, to have a triumph;* hence, **fig.**, *to exult;* pass., *to be triumphed over, be completely conquered.*
trĭumphus (old form **trĭumpus**) -i, m., *triumphal procession, triumph.*
trĭumvir -vĭri, m. *a triumvir;* usually plur. **trĭumvĭri** (also **trēsvĭri**), *a board or commission of three.*
trĭumvĭrālis -e, *of a triumvir.*
trĭumvĭrātus -ūs, m. *the office of a triumvir.*
trĭvĭālis -e, *ordinary, trivial.*
trĭvĭum -i, n. *a place where three roads meet, crossroads, public place.*
trĭvĭus -a -um, *of three ways, of crossroads;* esp. of deities *worshipped* at crossroads; f. as subst. **Trĭvĭa** -ae, *Diana* or *Hecate.*
Trōăs -ădis; see Tros.
trŏchaeus -i, m. *a trochee, a metrical foot* (— ⏑).
trochlĕa -ae, f. *a set of blocks and pulleys for raising weights.*
trŏchus -i, m. *child's hoop.*
Trōes; see Tros.
Trōia, Trōĭădes, Trōĭcus; see Tros.
Trōiŭgĕna -ae, *born in Troy, Trojan.*
trŏpaeum, -i, n. *a trophy, monument of victory.* Transf., *any memorial.*
Trōs Trōis, m. *a king of Phrygia, after whom Troy was named;* **Trōiă** or **Trōiă** -ae, f. *the town of Troy, besieged and finally captured by the Greeks;* adj. **Trōus, Trōĭus, Trōĭcus, Trōiānus** -a -um, *Trojan;* subst. **Trōs** Trōis, m. *a Trojan;* f. adj. and subst. **Trōăs** -ădos, *Trojan, a Trojan woman.*
trŭcīdātĭo -onis, f. *slaughtering, massacre.*
trŭcīdo -are, *to slaughter, massacre; to demolish, destroy.*
trŭcŭlentĭa -ae, f. *roughness, ferocity.*
trŭcŭlentus -a -um, *rough, ferocious, cruel, wild;* compar. adv. **trŭcŭlentĭus.**
trŭdis -is, f. *pointed staff, stake.*
trūdo trūdĕre trūsi trūsum, *to push, thrust; to press, urge on, force.*
trulla -ae, f. *ladle, pan* or *basin.*
trunco -are, *to shorten, maim, mutilate.*
truncus -a -um, *maimed, mutilated, cut short.* M. as subst. **truncus** -i, *a lopped tree, the trunk of a tree; the trunk of the human body.* Transf., *dolt, blockhead.*
trŭtĭna -ae, f. *a balance, pair of scales.*
trux trŭcis, *savage, fierce, grim.*
tū; pron. of the 2nd person; strengthened forms in -te, -met, temet; *thou, you;* plur. vos, etc. *ye, you.*
tŭba -ae, f. *the straight war-trumpet of the Romans.*
[1]**tūber** -ĕris, n. *swelling, hump.* Transf., *truffle.*
[2]**tūber** -ĕris; m. *a kind of apple-tree;* f. *the fruit of this tree.*
tŭbĭcĕn -ĭnis, m. *a trumpeter.*
tŭbĭlustrĭum -i, n. *a feast of trumpets.*
tŭdĭto -are, *to strike often.*
tŭĕor (or **tŭor**) tŭēri tŭĭtus and tūtus, dep., and tŭĕo -ēre, *to look at, regard;* esp. *to look after, watch over, guard.* Perf. partic. as pass. adj. **tūtus** -a -um, *watched over;* hence *safe, secure, out of danger; watchful, cautious.* N. as subst. **tūtum** -i, *a safe place, safety.* N. abl. **tūtō** and adv. **tūtē,** *safely.*
tŭgŭrĭum -i, n. *peasant's hut, cottage.*
tŭĭtĭo -ōnis, f. *a protecting, preservation.*
Tullĭus -a -um, *the name of a Roman gens;* esp. of Servius Tullius, *sixth king of Rome,* and of M. Tullius Cicero, *the Roman orator and statesman.* Hence adj. **Tulliānus** -a -um, *Tullian;* n. as subst. **Tulliānum,** -i, *part of a Roman state prison.*
tum, *then, at that time; next, thereupon, afterwards;* cum . . . tum, *both . . . and especially,* or *not only . . . but also.*
tŭmĕfăcĭo -făcĕre -fēci -factum, *to cause to swell; to puff up with pride.*
tŭmĕo -ēre, *to swell, be swollen, be puffed up; to swell with pride, anger* or *excitement;* of style, *to be pompous, tumid.*

tŭmesco tŭmescĕre tŭmŭi, *to begin to swell; to swell with anger* or *excitement.*
tŭmĭdus -a -um, adj. *swollen, puffed up; swollen with pride, anger* or *excitement*; of style, *pompous, tumid, bombastic.*
tŭmor -ōris, m. *swelling, protuberance; excitement of the mind,* esp. *in pride* or *anger*; in gen., *ferment, commotion*; of style, *turgidity, bombast.*
tŭmŭlo -are, *to bury.*
tŭmŭlōsus -a -um, *full of mounds, hilly.*
tŭmultŭārĭus -a -um; of troops, *hastily brought together, suddenly levied*; in gen., *sudden, hasty, improvised.*
tŭmultŭātĭo -ōnis, f. *confusion, bustle.*
tŭmultŭor -ari, dep. and **tŭmultŭo** -are, *to be confused, be in an uproar.*
tŭmultŭōsus -a -um, adj. *alarmed, disturbed, confused; disquieting, turbulent*; adv. **tŭmultŭōsē,** *confusedly, tumultuously.*
tŭmultus -ūs, m. *confusion, uproar, bustle*; esp. of *political commotion, insurrection, rebellion.* Transf., *mental disturbance, excitement.*
tŭmŭlus -i, m. *mound of earth, hillock, hill*; esp. *a sepulchral mound.*
tunc, *then, at that time; next.*
tundo tundĕre tŭtŭdi tunsum and tūsum, *to thump, pound, strike repeatedly; to deafen, importune.*
tŭnĭca -ae, f. *a sleeved garment, tunic; a jacket, coat, covering.*
tŭnĭcātus -a -um, *clothed in a tunic.*
tŭor = tueor; q.v.
turba -ae, f. *tumult, disturbance*; hence *a mob, throng, crowd.*
turbāmentum -i, n. *means of disturbance.*
turbātĭo -ōnis, f. *disturbance, confusion.*
turbātor -ōris, m. *disturber, troubler.*
turbĕn -ĭnis, n. = [2]turbo; q.v.
turbĭdus -a -um, *confused, disordered, wild*; adv. **turbĭdē.**
turbĭnĕus -a -um, *shaped like a top.*
[1]**turbo** -are, *to disturb, throw into disorder* or *confusion; to upset*; esp. *to cause political disturbance, to unsettle.*
Hence partic. as adj. **turbātus** -a -um, *disturbed, disordered, restless, troubled*; sometimes *angered, exasperated*; adv. **turbātē.**
[2]**turbo** -ĭnis, m. *an eddy, whirling round; a mental* or *political disturbance; a child's top; a reel; a spindle.*
turbŭlentus -a -um: pass., *confused, restless, stormy, boisterous*; act., *turbulent, causing disturbance*; adv. **turbŭlentē** and **turbŭlentĕr,** in *confusion, tumultuously.*
turdus -i; m. and **turda** -ae, f. *a thrush.*
tūrĕus -a -um, *of incense.*
turgĕo turgēre tursi, *to swell up, be swollen*; of style, *to be pompous, turgid.*
turgesco -ĕre, *to begin to swell, swell up; to swell with passion*; of style, *to be pompous.*
turgĭdus -a -um, *swollen*; of style, *turgid, bombastic.*
tūrĭbŭlum -i, n. *a censer for burning incense.*
tūrĭcrĕmus -a -um, *burning incense.*
tūrĭfer -fĕra -fĕrum, *producing incense.*
tūrĭlĕgus -a -um, *collecting incense.*
turma -ae, f. *a troop of cavalry, a squadron; any troop, throng.*
turmālis -e, *of a troop* or *squadron.*
turmātim, *troop by troop, in troops.*
Turnus -i, m. *a king of the Rutuli, killed by Aeneas.*
turpĭcŭlus -a -um, *somewhat ugly* or *deformed.*
turpĭfĭcātus -a -um, *corrupted.*
turpis -e, *ugly, foul;* morally *foul, disgraceful*; n. as subst. **turpĕ,** *a disgrace*; adv. **turpĭtĕr,** *foully, disgracefully.*
turpĭtūdo -inis, f. *ugliness*; moral *baseness, disgrace.*
turpo -are, *to make ugly, befoul; to disgrace, dishonour.*
turrĭger -gĕra -gĕrum, *tower-bearing.*
turris -is, f. *tower*; esp. as used in military operations; sometimes *howdah.* Transf., *dove-cote.*
turrītus -a -um, *turreted, furnished with towers; towering.*
turtur -ŭris, m. *turtle-dove.*
tūs (**thūs**) tūris, n. *incense, frankincense.*
Tusci -ōrum, m. *the Tuscans, Etruscans, inhabitants of Etruria*; adj. **Tuscus** -a -um, *Etruscan.*
tussĭo -ire, *to have a cough, to cough.*
tussis -is, f. *a cough.*
tūtāmen -ĭnis, and **tūtāmentum** -i, n. *a defence, protection.*
tūtēla -ae, f. *protection, guard, charge,* esp. of wards, etc., *guardianship, tutelage*; concr., act. *protector, guardian*; pass., *the person or thing protected.*
[1]**tūtor** -ōris, m. *a watcher, protector*; esp. *the guardian of a woman, minor,* or *imbecile.*
[2]**tūtor** -ari dep.: also **tūto** -are; *to protect, watch, keep.* Transf., *to guard against.*
tūtus -a -um, partic. from tueo; q.v.
tŭus -a -um, possess. pron. of the 2nd pers. sing., *thy, thine, your.*
Tȳdeūs -ĕi and -ĕos, m. *the son of Oeneus*; hence **Tȳdīdes** -ae, m. *son of Tydeus,* i.e. *Diomedes.*
tympănum (**tȳpănum**) -i, n. *a tambourine, kettle-drum; a drum* or *wheel for raising weights.*
Tyndărēūs -ĕi, and **Tyndărus** -i, m. *king of Sparta, father of Castor and Pollux, Helen and Clytemnestra*; adj. **Tyndărĭus** -a -um; subst. m. **Tyndărĭdēs** -ae, *a male descendant,* and f. **Tyndăris** -ĭdis, *a female descendant of Tyndareus.*
tȳpus -i, m. *a figure on a wall.*
tȳrannĭcīda -ae, m. *the slayer of a tyrant.*
tȳrannĭcus -a -um, *tyrannical*; adv. **tȳrannĭcē.**
tȳrannis -ĭdis, f. *despotism, tyranny.*

tўrannoctŏnus -i, m. *the slayer of a tyrant.*
tўrannus -i, m. *an absolute ruler, prince, lord; a usurper, despot, tyrant.*
Tўrĭus, see Tyrus.
tўrŏtărīchŏs -i, m. *a dish of cheese and salt-fish.*
Tyrrhēni -ōrum, m. pl. *a Pelasgian people*; subst. **Tyrrhēnĭa** -ae, f. *their country, Etruria*; adj. **Tyrrhēnus** -a -um, *Etruscan.*
Tўrus (-ŏs) -i, f. *Tyre, a city of Phoenicia, famous for its purple*; adj. **Tўrĭus** -a -um.

U

U, u, originally written V, v, the 20th letter of the Latin Alphabet.
[1]**ūber** -ĕris, n. *an udder, teat, breast; richness, abundance, fertility.*
[2]**ūber** -eris, adj., *rich, fertile, fruitful, copious*; adv. in compar. **ūbĕrĭus** and superl. **ūberrĭmē,** *more* and *most abundantly.*
ūbertās -ātis, f. *fruitfulness, abundance.*
ūbertim, *abundantly, copiously.*
ŭbī, *where* (interrog. and relat.); of time, *when, as soon as*; of other relations, *wherein, whereby, with whom.*
ŭbīcumquĕ (-cunquĕ): relat., *wherever*; indef., *anywhere, everywhere.*
Ubĭi -ōrum, m. *a Germanic people.*
ŭbīquĕ, *everywhere.*
ŭbīvīs, *wherever you will, anywhere.*
ūdus -a -um, *wet, moist.*
ulcĕro -are, *to make sore, ulcerate, wound.*
ulcĕrōsus -a -um, *full of sores, ulcerous, wounded.*
ulciscor ulcisci ultus, dep. (1) *to take vengeance for, to avenge.* (2) *to take vengeance on, to punish.*
ulcus -ĕris, n. *a sore, ulcer, wound.*
ūlīgo -ĭnis, f. *moisture, damp.*
Ŭlixēs -is or ei, m. *Latin name for Ulysses* or *Odysseus, husband of Penelope, king of Ithaca.*
ullus -a -um; genit. ullius, dat. ulli; *any*; as subst., *anyone, anything.*
ulmĕus -a -um, *of elm-wood.*
ulmus -i, f. *elm.*
ulna -ae, f. *elbow, arm; an ell.*
ultĕrĭor -ĭus, compar. as from ulter, *farther, more distant, more advanced, more remote.* Superl. **ultĭmus** -a -um, *most distant, farthest, extreme*; in time or succession, either *original* or *last, final*; ad ultimum, *to the last*; ultimum, *for the last time*; in rank, etc., *either highest, greatest,* or *meanest, lowest.*
ultĭo -ōnis, f. *avenging, punishment, revenge.*
ultor -ōris, m. *avenger, punisher.*
ultrā, adv. and prep. *beyond, on the far side* (*of*), *farther* (*than*), *more* (*than*).
ultrix -īcis, f. *avenging.*
ultrō, adv. *to the far side, beyond*; ultro et citro, *up and d wn.* Transf., *besides, moreover; of one's own accord, spontaneously, gratuitously.*
ŭlŭla -ae, f. *an owl.*
ŭlŭlātus -ūs, m. *howling, wailing, yelling.*
ŭlŭlo -are, *to howl, yell*; transit., *to howl to*; of places, *to resound with howling.*
ulva -ae, f. *sedge.*
umbella -ae, f. *a parasol.*
umbĭlīcus -i, m. *the navel; middle, centre; the end of the roller of a scroll; a kind of sea-snail.*
umbo -ōnis, m. *a boss, round projection*; esp. *the centre of a shield; a shield; the elbow.*
umbra -ae, f. *a shade, shadow; a shady place; protection; idleness, pleasant rest; a phantom, ghost, shade, semblance; an uninvited guest; a fish,* perhaps *grayling.*
umbrācŭlum -i, n. *a shady place, arbour; quiet, retirement; a parasol.*
umbrātĭlis -e, *retired, contemplative.*
Umbri -ōrum, m. pl. a *people of central Italy*; **Umbria** -ae, f. *Umbria.*
umbrĭfer -fĕra -fĕrum, *shady.*
umbro -are, *to shade, over-shadow.*
umbrōsus -a -um, *shady.*
ūmecto (hū-) -are, *to wet, moisten.*
ūmectus (hū-) -a -um, *moist.*
ūmĕo (hū-) -ēre, *to be moist*; partic. **ūmens** -entis, *moist.*
ŭmĕrus (hū-) -i, m. *the upper arm or shoulder.*
ūmesco (hū-) -ĕre, *to become moist.*
ūmĭdŭlus (hū-), -a -um, *moist.*
ūmĭdus (hū-) -a -um, *wet, moist, damp*; ligna, *unseasoned*; n. as subst. *a wet place.*
ūmor (hū-) -ōris, m. *moisture, fluid.*
umquam (unquam), *at any time, ever.*
ūnā, adv. from unus; q.v.
ūnănĭmĭtās -ātis, f. *concord, unanimity.*
ūnănĭmus -a -um, *of one mind, agreeing, unanimous.*
uncĭa -ae, f. *a twelfth; an ounce.*
uncĭārĭus -a -um, *of a twelfth part*; faenus, $8\frac{1}{3}\%$.
uncĭātim, *little by little.*
uncīnātus -a -um, *hooked.*
uncĭŏla -ae, f. *a mere twelfth.*
unctĭo -ōnis, f. *anointing.*
unctĭto -are, *to anoint, besmear.*
unctor -ōris, m. *an anointer.*
unctūra -ae, f. *anointing of the dead.*
unctus -a -um, partic. from ungo; q.v.
[1]**uncus** -i, m. *a hook.*
[2]**uncus** -a -um, *hooked, curved.*
unda -ae, f. *water, fluid,* esp. as *a wave*; fig. *a stream* of people, etc.
undĕ, *whence, from where* (interrog. and relat.). Transf., *how, from whom.*
undĕcĭēs (-ĭens) *eleven times.*
undĕcim, *eleven.*
undĕcĭmus -a -um, *eleventh.*
undĕcumquĕ (-cunquĕ), *from whatever place.*
undēni -ae -a, *eleven at a time* or *eleven each.*
undēnōnāgintā, *eighty-nine.*
undeoctōgintā, *seventy-nine.*
undēquadrāgintā, *thirty-nine.*

undēquinquāgēsĭmus -a -um, *forty-ninth.*
undēquinquāgintā, *forty-nine.*
undēsexāgintā, *fifty-nine.*
undētrīcēsĭmus -a -um, *twenty-ninth.*
undēvīcēsĭmus, *nineteenth.*
undēvīgintī, *nineteen.*
undĭquĕ, *from* or *on all sides, from everywhere, everywhere; altogether, in every respect.*
undĭsŏnus -a -um, *resounding with waves.*
undo -are: intransit., *to surge, wave, undulate*; transit., *to flood.*
undōsus -a -um, *surging, billowy.*
ūnetvīcēsĭmāni -ōrum, m. pl. *soldiers of the twenty-first legion.*
ūnetvīcēsĭmus -a -um, *twenty-first.*
ungo (unguo) ungĕre unxi unctum, *to anoint, besmear*; partic. **unctus** -a -um, *besmeared, anointed, greasy; rich, copious*; n. as subst. *a sumptuous repast.*
unguĕn -ĭnis, n. *fatty substance, ointment.*
unguentārĭus -a -um, *of ointment*; m. as subst. *a dealer in unguents.*
unguentātus -a -um, *anointed.*
unguentum -i, n. *salve, ointment, perfume.*
unguĭcŭlus -i, m. *a finger* or *toe-nail.*
unguis -is, m. *a finger-* or *toe-nail*; of animals, *claw, hoof*; de tenero ungui, *from childhood*; ad (or in) unguem, *to a hair, nicely, perfectly.*
ungŭla -ae, f. *a hoof, claw, talon.*
unguo = ungo; q.v.
ūnĭcŏlor -oris, *of one colour.*
ūnĭcus -a -um, *one, only, sole; singular, unique*; adv. **ūnĭcē,** *singly, especially.*
ūnĭformis -e, *having one form, simple.*
ūnĭgĕna -ae, *of the same race; only-begotten, unique.*
ūnĭmănus -a -um, *having but one hand.*
ūnio -ōnis, m. *a large pearl.*
ūnĭtās -ātis, f. *unity, oneness.*
ūnĭtĕr, *in one, together.*
ūnĭversālis -e, *general, universal.*
ūnĭversĭtās -atis, f. *the whole, total; the universe, the world.*
ūnĭversus (archaic **ūnĭvorsus**) -a -um, *combined in one, whole, entire*; plur. **ūnĭversi** -ae -a, *all together*; n. as subst. **ūnĭversum** -i, *the whole; the world, the universe*; phrase, in universum, and adv. **ūnĭversē,** *generally, in general.*
ūnus -a -um, genit. ūnĭus, dat. ūni, *one; only one; one and the same; any one*; ad unum omnes, *all to a man*; in unum, *into one place*; uno tempore, *at the same time.* Adv. **ūnā,** *in one, together.*
ūpĭlĭo (ōpĭlĭo) -ōnis, m. *a shepherd.*
Ūrănĭa -ae and **Ūrănĭē** -ēs, f. *the Muse of Astronomy.*
urbānĭtās -ātis, f. *city life,* esp. *life in Rome.* Hence *politeness, urbanity, refinement; wit, pleasantry.*
urbānus -a -um, *of a city* (esp. Rome); *urban*; hence *refined; elegant; witty, pleasant*; m. pl. as subst. *the inhabitants of a city, the townsfolk.* Adv. **urbānē,** *politely, courteously; wittily, elegantly.*
urbs -bis, f. *a walled town* or *city*; esp. *the city of Rome.*
urcĕŏlus -i, m. *a small jug* or *pitcher.*
urcĕus -i, m. *a jug, pitcher.*
ūrēdo -ĭnis, f. *a blight on plants.*
urgĕo urgēre ursi, *to push, press, drive, urge; to beset, oppress; to stress*; of work, *to press on with, ply hard, follow up.*
ūrīna -ae, f. *urine.*
ūrīnātor -ōris, m. *a diver.*
ūrīno -are and **ūrīnor** -ari, dep. *to dive.*
urna -ae, f. *a jug, pitcher, jar, pot.*
ūro ūrĕre ussi ustum, *to burn; to dry up, parch; chafe, gall; to disturb, harass.*
ursa -ae, f. *a she-bear.*
ursus -i, m. *a bear.*
urtīca -ae, f. *a nettle.* Transf., *desire.*
ūrus -i, m. *a kind of wild ox.*
ūsĭtātus -a -um, *customary, usual*; adv. **ūsĭtātē.**
uspĭam, *anywhere.*
usquam, *anywhere; at all, in any way; in any direction.*
usquĕ, *through and through, all the way, continuously; always*; usque Romam, *as far as Rome*; usque a Romulo, *ever since Romulus.*
usquĕquāquĕ, *always.*
ustor -ōris, m. *a burner of corpses.*
ustŭlo -are, *to burn, scorch, singe.*
[1]**ūsūcăpĭo** -căpĕre -cēpi -captum, *to acquire ownership by long use.*
[2]**ūsūcăpĭo** -ōnis, f. *ownership acquired by long possession* or *use.*
ūsūra -ae, f. *use, enjoyment*; esp. *use of borrowed capital; interest paid for money borrowed.*
ūsurpātĭo -ōnis, f. *using, use; undertaking.*
ūsurpo -are, *to use, bring into use; to take possession of, acquire, appropriate, usurp; to perceive, to notice; to use* a word, *to mention*; hence *to call, name.*
ūsus -ūs, m. *use, application, practice, exercise; social intercourse, familiarity*; legal, usus et fructus, ususfructus, *the use of others' property.* Transf., *practice, skill, experience; utility, usefulness, profit*; usui esse, ex usu esse, *to be useful, be of use*; usus est, *there is need of, occasion for*; usu venit, *it happens.*
ūsusfructus; see usus.
ŭt or **ŭtī.** (1) with indic. verb: *how* (interrog. and exclam.); relat., *as,* esp. with corresponding sic or ita; ut ut, *in whatever way*; explanatory, *as, as being* (sometimes without verb); temporal, *as when, while, since*; of place, *where.* (2) with subjunctive: in indirect questions, *how*; in wishes, *o that*; concessive, *granted that*; consecutive, *so that,* often preceded by ita, tam, etc.; explaining or defining, *namely that*; final, *in order that* (negat. ne or ut ne); in " indirect command " *that, to*; after verbs of fearing (= ne non), *that . . . not.*

utcumquĕ (-cunquĕ), *in whatever manner, however; whenever.*

ūtensĭlĭa -ĭum, n. pl., *useful things, utensils.*

[1]**ūter** ūtris, m. *the skin of an animal used as bag* or *bottle.*

[2]**ŭtĕr** utra utrum; genit. utrĭus, dat. utri; interrog., *which of the two?;* plur., *which side? which set?;* relat., *that* (*of two*) *which*; indef., *either of the two.*

ŭtercumquĕ (**-cunquĕ**) utrăcumquĕ utrumcumquĕ, *whichever of the two.*

ŭterlĭbet utrălĭbet utrumlĭbet, *whichever of the two you please.*

ŭterquĕ utrăquĕ utrumquĕ; genit. utrĭusquĕ, dat. utrīquĕ; *each of two*; in plur., usually, *each side, each set*; sometimes of individuals, *both.*

ŭtĕrus -i, m. and **ŭtĕrum** -i, n. *womb; belly.*

ŭtervīs utrăvīs utrumvīs; genit. utriusvīs, dat. utrīvīs; *whichever of the two you please.*

ŭtī = ut; q.v.

Ŭtĭca -ae, f. *a town in Africa where Cato the younger killed himself*; adj. **Ŭtĭcensis -e.**

ūtĭlis -e, *useful, fit, profitable*; adv. **ūtĭlĭtĕr.**

ūtĭlĭtās -ātis, f. *usefulness profit, advantage.*

ŭtĭnam, *would that! oh that!*

ŭtīquĕ, *at any rate, certainly, at least.*

ūtor ūti ūsus, dep. *to use, employ; to possess, enjoy*; of persons, *to associate with*, or, with a predicate, *to find.*

Hence partic. **ūtens** -entis, *possessing.*

utpŏtĕ, *seeing that, inasmuch as.*

utrārĭus -i, m. *a water-carrier.*

utrimquĕ (**-inquĕ**) *from* or *on both sides.*

utrō, *to which of two places? to which side?*

utrŏbīquĕ (utrŭbīquĕ), *on each of two sides; both ways.*

utrōquĕ, *to both sides, in both directions; at each point, both ways.*

utrum, *whether*; used mainly in alternative questions, direct or indirect.

ŭtŭt, *however*; see ut.

ūva -ae, f. *a bunch of grapes*; meton., *vine.* Transf., *a cluster.*

ūvesco -ĕre, *to become moist.*

ūvĭdŭlus -a -um, *moist.*

ūvĭdus -a -um, *moist, damp, wet.* Transf., *drunken.*

uxor -ōris, f. *a wife*; uxorem ducere, *to marry a wife.*

uxōrĭus -a -um. (1) *of a wife.* (2) *too devoted to one's wife, uxorious.*

V

V, v, the twenty-first letter of the Latin Alphabet.

văcātĭo -ōnis, f. *freedom, immunity, exemption.* Transf., *money paid for exemption from military duties.*

vacca -ae, f. *a cow.*

vaccīnĭum -i, n. *the blueberry, whortleberry*; according to some, *the hyacinth.*

văcēfīo -fĭĕri, *to be made empty.*

văcillātĭo -ōnis, f. *rocking, reeling.*

văcillo (vaccillo) -are, *to totter, reel stagger.*

văcīvus (**vŏcīvus**) -a -um, *empty.*

văco -are, *to be empty*; of property, *to be vacant, to have no master*; in gen., *to be free from* anything, *be without; to be free from work, be at leisure*; with dat., *to have time for*; impers., vacat, *there is time* (*for*).

văcŭēfăcĭo -făcĕre -fēci -factum, *to make empty.*

văcŭĭtās -ātis, f. *freedom, exemption, immunity; a vacancy in a public office.*

văcŭo -are, *to make void, to empty.*

văcŭus -a -um, *empty, void; empty-handed; vacant; devoid, exempt, without* (with abl. or *ab*); *free, at leisure*; with dat., *free for*; *worthless, useless, vain.* N. as subst. **văcŭum** -i, *an empty place, vacuum.*

vădĭmōnĭum -i, n. *bail, security recognizance.*

vādo -ĕre, *to go, hasten, rush.*

vădor -ari, dep. *to bind over by bail.*

vădōsus -a -um, *shallow.*

vădum -i, n. *a shallow, shoal, ford* in river or sea; in gen., *water, river, sea*; fig., *shallows*, typical either of *safety* or of *danger.*

vae, interj. *alas! woe!*

văfer vafra vafrum, *artful, sly, crafty*; adv. **vafrē.**

vāgīna -ae, f. *a scabbard, sheath, case; the husk of grain.*

vāgĭo -ire, *to whimper as a child.*

vāgītus -ūs, m. *whimpering, crying.*

vāgor -ōris, m. = vagitus; q.v.

văgor -ari, dep. *to wander, ramble, rove.*

văgus -a -um, *wandering, roaming; fickle; diffuse, aimless.* Adv. **văgē,** *dispersedly.*

vah (vaha), interj. *ah! oh!*

valdē, *intensely, very much*; in replies *certainly, very much so.*

vălĕdico -ĕre, *to say good-bye.*

vălĕo -ēre, *to be strong, vigorous, in good health, well; to have force, avail, prevail, be able; to be worth*; of words, *to mean, signify*; as a farewell greeting, vale, or valeas, *farewell, good-bye*; valere iubere, *to bid farewell, say good-bye to.*

Hence partic. **vălens** -entis, *strong, powerful, healthy*; adv. **vălentĕr.**

Vălĕrĭus -a -um, *name of a Roman gens.*

vălesco -ĕre, *to grow strong.*

vălētūdo -ĭnis, f. *state of health*; sometimes either *ill-health, weakness,* or *good health.*

vălĭdus -a -um, *strong, powerful; healthy, well; mighty, influential*; of medicines, *efficacious.* Adv. **vălĭdē,** *strongly, powerfully*; in replies, *certainly to be sure.*

vallāris -e, *relating to the* vallum; q.v.
vallēs (vallis) -is, f. *a vale, valley, hollow.*
vallo -are, *to fortify with a palisade; to strengthen.*
vallum -i, n. *a palisade of stakes; a fortification, defence.*
vallus -i, m. *a post, stake*; collectively, *a palisade, stockade.*
valvae -ārum, f. pl. *folding-doors.*
vānesco -ĕre, *to pass away, disappear.*
vānĭlŏquentĭa -ae, f. *idle talk, vaunting.*
vānĭlŏquus -a -um, *lying; boastful.*
vānĭtās -ātis, f. *emptiness; worthlessness, unreality; boasting, ostentation.*
vannus -i, f. *winnowing-fan.*
vānus -a -um, *empty, void; vain, idle, worthless, meaningless*; of persons, *ostentatious, boastful, unreliable.*
văpĭdus -a -um, *spiritless, spoiled, flat.*
văpor (văpōs) -ōris, m. *vapour, steam; warm exhalation, warmth.*
văpōrārĭum -i, n. *a steam flue.*
văpōro -are; intransit., *to steam, reek*; transit., *to fill with vapour, heat, warm.*
vappa -ae, f. *flat wine.* Transf., *a worthless fellow.*
vāpŭlo -are, *to be flogged, beaten, knocked about*; of things, *to be wasted.*
vărĭantĭa -ae, and **vărĭātĭo** -ōnis, f. *difference, variation.*
vārĭco -are, *to stand with feet apart.*
vārĭcōsus -a -um, *having varicose veins.*
vārĭcus -a -um, *straddling.*
vărĭĕtās -ātis, f. *variety, difference, diversity.*
vărĭo -are: transit., *to vary, diversify, change, alter, do* or *say differently*; pass., variari, *to waver, be divided, vary*; intransit., *to be different, vary.*
[1]**vărĭus** -a -um, *various, manifold, changeable, diverse*; of persons, in bad sense, *fickle, changeable*; adv. **vărĭē**, *diversely, variously.*
[2]**Vărĭus** -a -um, *name of a Roman* gens.
vărix -ĭcis, c. *a varicose vein.*
Varro -ōnis, m. *a surname in the* gens Terentia.
[1]**vārus** -a -um, *knock-kneed*; in gen., *crooked, bent; diverse, different.*
[2]**Vārus** -i, m. *a Roman surname.*
[1]**văs** vădis, m. *a bail, surety.*
[2]**vās** vāsis, n. *a utensil*; plur. (vāsa -ōrum) milit., *war materials, equipment.*
vāsārĭum -i, n. *an outfit allowance.*
vascŭlārĭus -i, m. *a maker of vessels*, esp. *in metal.*
vascŭlum -i, n. *a small vessel.*
vastātĭo -ōnis, f. *devastating, laying waste.*
vastātor -ōris, m. *devastator, ravager.*
vastĭfĭcus -a -um, *devastating.*
vastĭtās -ātis, f. *a waste, emptiness, desolation*; concr. in plur., *devastators.*
vasto -are, *to empty; to lay waste, ravage, devastate, prey upon.*
vastus -a -um, *empty, waste, desolate; laid waste, devastated.* Transf., *vast, enormous; rough, rude.* Adv. **vastē**, *widely, extensively; rudely, roughly.*
vātēs -is, c. *a prophet, seer; a bard, poet.*
Vātĭcānus -a -um, *Vatican*: mons, collis, *the Vatican Hill on the west side of the Tiber.*
vātĭcĭnātĭo -ōnis, f. *soothsaying, prophecy.*
vātĭcĭnātor, ōris, m. *soothsayer, prophet.*
vātĭcĭnor -ari, dep. *to prophesy; to talk wildly, to rave.*
vātĭcĭnus -a -um, *soothsaying, prophetic.*
vătillum (bắt-) -i, n. *a chafing-dish* or *shovel.*
Vătĭnĭus -a -um, *the name of a Roman* gens.
-vĕ, enclitic, *or, or perhaps.*
vēcordĭa (vae-) -ae, f. *folly, madness.*
vēcors (vae-) -cordis, *senseless, mad.*
vectīgal -gālis, n. *revenue, income*; esp. *a tax, impost, duty.*
vectīgālis -e, *relating to income* or *to taxes; liable to tax, tributary.*
vectĭo -ōnis, f. *carrying, conveyance.*
vectis -is, m. *a lever, crow-bar; a bar, bolt.*
vecto -are, *to carry, convey*; pass., *to ride* or *be driven.*
vector -ōris, m.: act., *a carrier, bearer*; pass., *a passenger, rider.*
vectōrĭus -a -um, *for carrying*; navigia, *transports.*
vectūra -ae, f. *conveying, transportation; passage-money, fare.*
vĕgĕo -ēre, *to stir up, excite.*
vĕgĕtus -a -um, *lively, vigorous, fresh.*
vēgrandis -e, *diminutive.*
vĕhĕmens (poet. **vēmens**) -entis, *violent, furious, impetuous*; adv. **vĕhĕmentĕr**, *violently; forcibly, exceedingly.*
vĕhĭcŭlum -i, n. *vehicle, conveyance.*
vĕho vĕhĕre vexi vectum, *to carry, convey*; pass., *to sail, ride, drive*, etc.; so also pres. partic., vehens, *riding.*
Vēii -ōrum, m. pl. *an old town in Etruria*; adj. **Vēiens** -entis.
vĕl: conj., singly, *or*; doubled, *either . . . or*; adv. *even, actually; for example.*
vēlāmen -ĭnis, n. *covering, garment.*
vēlāmentum -i, n. *a covering, veil*; in plur., *olive-branches wrapped in wool, carried by suppliants.*
vēlārĭum -i, n. *an awning in a theatre.*
vēlāti -ōrum, m. pl., milit. *the reserve, supernumary troops.*
vĕlĕs -ĭtis, m. usually plur., velites, *light-armed infantry, skirmishers.*
vēlĭfer -fĕra -fĕrum, *carrying sail.*
vēlĭfĭcātĭo -ōnis, f. *sailing.*
vēlĭfĭco -are and **vēlĭfĭcor** -āri, dep. *to sail.* Transf., *to work for* an end.
vēlĭtāris -e, of *light-armed troops.*
vēlĭvŏlans -antis, and **vēlĭvŏlus** -a -um, *flying with sails.*
vellĭco -are, *to pluck, twitch; to taunt, criticize.*
vello vellĕre velli (vulsi, volsi) vulsum (volsum), *to pull, twitch; to pluck out*; partic. **vulsus** -a -um, *plucked, smooth.*
vellus -ĕris, n. *a fleece; skin, hide.*
vēlo -are, *to cover, veil, hide.*

vēlōcĭtās -ātis, f. *quickness, rapidity.*
vēlox -ōcis, *quick, rapid, swift*; adv. **vēlōcĭtĕr.**
vēlum -i, *a sail*; vela dare, *to sail; a covering, awning, curtain.*
vĕlŭt (vĕlŭtī), *as, just as; even as; as for instance*; with subjunctive, velut, or velut si, *as if, just as if.*
vēmens = vehemens; q.v.
vēna -ae, f. *a blood-vessel, vein, artery; a water-course; a vein of metal; a vein of talent, disposition, natural inclination.*
vēnābŭlum -i, n. *a hunting-spear.*
Vĕnafrum -i, n. a *Samnite town in Campania.*
vēnālĭcĭus -a -um, *of the sale of slaves*; m. as subst. *a slave-dealer.*
vēnālis -e, *on sale, to be sold; venal*; m. as subst. *a slave put up for sale.*
vēnātĭcus -a -um, *of* or *for the chase.*
vēnātĭo -ōnis, f. *the chase, hunting; game.*
vēnātor -ōris, m. *a hunter, sportsman.*
vēnātōrĭus -a -um, *of* or *for the chase.*
vēnātrix -īcis, f. *huntress.*
vēnātus -ūs, m. *the chase, hunting.*
vendĭbĭlis -e, *on sale, saleable; popular, acceptable.*
vendĭtātĭo -onis, f. *a putting up for sale*; hence *boasting, vaunting.*
vendĭtātor -ōris, m. *vaunter, boaster.*
vendĭtĭo -ōnis, f. *selling, sale.*
vendĭto -are, *to offer for sale, try to sell; to praise, advertise.*
vendĭtor -ōris, m. *seller, vendor.*
vendo -dĕre -dĭdi -dĭtum (pass. usually veneo; q.v.), *to put up for sale, sell; to betray; to recommend, advertise.*
vĕnēfĭcĭum -i, n. *poisoning; magic, sorcery.*
vĕnēfĭcus -a -um, *poisonous, magical*; m. as subst., *a poisoner, sorcerer; a sorceress, witch.*
vĕnēnĭfer -fĕra -fĕrum, *poisonous.*
vĕnēno -are, *to poison, drug*; partic. **vĕnēnātus** -a -um, *poisoned, drugged, enchanted.*
vĕnēnum -i, n. *a drug; poison* (fig. *ruin, destruction*); *a love-potion; colouring matter, dye; rouge.*
vēnĕo vēnire vēnĭi vēnum, *to go for sale, to be sold* (used as pass. of vendo).
vĕnĕrābĭlis -e, *venerable, reverend.*
vĕnĕrābundus -a -um, *reverent, respectful.*
vĕnĕrātĭo -ōnis, f. *reverence, respect.*
vĕnĕrātor -ōris, m. *a venerator, reverer.*
vĕnĕrĭus; see venus.
vĕnĕror -ari, dep. *to ask reverently; to revere, respect, worship.*
vĕnĭa -ae, f. *grace, indulgence, favour, permission; pardon, forgiveness.*
vĕnĭo vĕnire vēni ventum, *to come*; in course of time, *to happen, come, arrive; to grow, arise.*
vēnor -ari, dep, *to hunt.*
venter -tris, m. *the belly, stomach; the womb.*
ventĭlo -are, *to wave, brandish, fan.*
ventĭto -are, *to come often, resort.*
ventōsus -a -um, *full of wind, windy; swift* or *light as wind; puffed up, vain; changeable, inconstant.*
ventrĭcŭlus -i, m. *the belly; a ventricle.*
ventŭlus -i, m. *a slight wind.*
ventus -i, m. *wind; rumour, favour.*
vēnŭcŭla (venn-) -ae, f. *a kind of grape.*
vēnum and **vēno**, acc. and dat. n., *for sale.*
vēnumdo (vēnundo) -dăre -dĕdi -dătum, *to offer for sale, to sell.*
vĕnus -ĕris, f. *charm, loveliness; love; a loved one*; personif., **Vĕnus,** *goddess of love; the Venus throw, highest throw of the dice*; adj. **Vĕnĕrĕus (-ĭus)** -a -um, *of Venus* or *of love.*
Vĕnŭsĭa -ae, f. *a town on the borders of Lucania and Apulia, birthplace of Horace.*
vĕnustās -ātis, f. *loveliness, charm, attractiveness.*
vĕnustus -a -um, *charming, lovely, graceful*; adv. **vĕnustē.**
vēpallĭdus -a -um, *very pale.*
veprēcŭla -ae, f. *a thorn-bush.*
veprēs -is, m. *a thorn-bush, briar-bush.*
vēr vēris, n. *spring*; primo vere, *in the beginning of spring*; ver sacrum, *an offering of the firstlings.*
vērātrum -i, n. *hellebore.*
vērax -ācis, *speaking the truth, truthful.*
verbēna -ae, f., often in pl., *sacred boughs carried by the* Fetiales.
verber -ĕris, n. *a lash; a whip, scourge, thong; a blow, stroke; whipping.*
[1]**verbĕro** -are, *to beat, whip, thrash*; with words, *to assail, lash.*
[2]**verbĕro** -ōnis, m. *a rascal.*
verbōsus -a -um, *copious, diffuse, wordy*; adv. **verbōsē.**
verbum -i, n. *a word;* verbum facere, *to speak*; uno verbo, *in a word, briefly*; ad verbum, *word for word*; verbi causa, *for example*; grammat., *a verb; an expression, saying; mere words, mere talk*; verba dare homini, *to cheat a person.*
Vercingĕtŏrix -rĭgis, m. *a Gallic chief.*
vĕrēcundĭa -ae, f. *modesty, diffidence, bashfulness*; with genit., *respect for, scruple about.*
vĕrēcundor -ari, dep. *to be bashful, ashamed, shy.*
vĕrēcundus -a -um, *bashful, modest, shy, diffident*; adv. **vĕrēcundē.**
vĕrēdus -i, *a swift horse, hunter.*
vĕrĕor -ēri -ĭtus, dep. *to be afraid, fear; to have respect for, revere*; gerundive **vĕrendus** -a -um, *venerable, reverend.*
Vergĭlĭus -i, m. P. Vergilius Maro, *author of the Aeneid, Georgics, and Eclogues.*
Vergĭnĭus -a -um, *the name of a Roman* gens.
vergo vergĕre versi: intransit., *to bend, be inclined, verge*; of time, *to draw to an end*; transit., *to bend, turn, incline.*
verĭdĭcus -a -um, *truthful.*
verĭlŏquĭum -i, n. *etymology.*
verĭsĭmĭlis -e, *probable, likely.*
verĭsĭmĭlĭtūdo ĭnis, f. *probability.*

vērĭtās -ātis, f. *the truth, reality; truthfulness, telling of truth*; in gen., *honesty.*

vermen -ĭnis, n. *a griping pain.*

vermĭcŭlus -i, m. *little worm, grub.*

vermis -is, m. *worm.*

verna -ae, c. *a slave born in the master's house; a native.*

vernācŭlus -a -um, *of a slave born in the house; native, domestic.*

vernīlis -e, *like a slave; mean, abject; pert, forward*; adv. **vernīlĭtĕr,** *like a slave.*

verno -are, *to flourish, grow green.*

vernŭla -ae, c. *a little slave born in the house*; as adj. *native, indigenous.*

vernus -a -um, *of spring, vernal.*

Vērōna -ae, f. *a town of northern Italy, birthplace of Catullus.*

[1]**verrēs** -is, m. *a boar.*

[2]**Verrēs** -is, m. C. Cornelius, *praetor in Sicily, prosecuted by Cicero*; adj. **Verrĭus** and **Verrīnus** -a -um.

verrīnus -a -um, *of a boar.*

verro verrĕre verri versum, *to drag, pull, sweep, sweep up; to sweep clean, brush, scour.*

verrūca -ae, f. *a wart; blemish.*

verrunco -are, *to turn out*; bene verruncare, *to turn out well.*

versābundus -a -um, *whirling round, revolving.*

versātĭlis -e, *turning round, revolving; versatile.*

versĭcŏlor -ōris, *of various colours.*

versĭcŭlus -i, m. *a little line; a poor little verse.*

versĭfĭcātĭo -ōnis, f. *making of verses.*

versĭfĭcātor -ōris, m. *versifier.*

versĭfĭco -are, *to write verse.*

verso (vorso) -are, *to turn about, turn this way and that; to bend, ply, twist; to influence, agitate; to turn over in the mind, think of.* Pass., *to be about, hover, resort; to be engaged, take part, be employed.*

versum = versus; q.v.

versūra -ae, f. *turning; the borrowing of money to pay a debt*; hence *a loan.*

[1]**versus (vors-)** and **versum (vors-),** *towards*; used esp. after an accusative or prep. and acc.; sursum versus, *upwards.*

[2]**versus (vors-)** -a -um, partic. from verro or verto; q.v.

[3]**versus (vors-)** -ūs, m. *a row, line; a line of writing*, esp. of poetry.

versūtĭa -ae, f. *wile, stratagem.*

versūtus -a -um, *dexterous; cunning, crafty, sly*; adv. **versūtē.**

vertex (vortex) -ĭcis, m. (1) *a whirl, eddy, whirlwind, gust.* (2) *the crown of the head*; in gen., *head, summit, elevation.* (3) *the pole* of the heavens.

vertĭcōsus (vortĭc-) -a -um, *eddying.*

vertīgo -ĭnis, f. *whirling round, revolution; giddiness, vertigo.*

verto (vorto) vertĕre verti versum, *to turn, turn round, turn up*; intransit., *to turn oneself*, milit., vertere in fugam, *to put to flight, rout*; terga vertere, *to flee*; *to interpret, construe, understand* in a certain way, *to impute; to alter, change; to translate; to change for another, exchange*; vertere solum, *to go into exile; to upset, overthrow*; pass. or intransit., of time, *to roll round*; pass., *to move in a certain sphere, to depend on, centre in.*

Vertumnus (vor-) -i, m. *god of the changing year.*

vĕrū -ūs, n. *a spit; a javelin.*

vērus -a -um, *true, real, genuine; truthful, veracious; just, reasonable.* N. as subst. *truth, reality; right, duty*; veri similis, *likely, probable.* N. nom. as adv. **vērum,** *but yet, still, however*; strengthened, **vēruntămen (vērum-),** *notwithstanding, nevertheless.* N. abl. as adv. **vērō,** *in truth, indeed, in fact*; in a climax, *even, indeed*; ironically, *to be sure*; adversative, *but indeed, but in fact.* Adv. **vērē,** *truly, really, rightly.*

vĕrutum -i, n. *javelin.*

vĕrūtus -a -um, *armed with a javelin.*

vervex -vēcis, m. *a wether; a sheep, dolt.*

vēsānĭa -ae, f. *madness, insanity.*

vēsānĭens -entis, *raging.*

vēsānus -a -um, *mad, insane*; of things, *furious, wild.*

vescor -i, dep. *to eat, feed on; to use, enjoy.*

vescus -a -um: act., *consuming*; pass., *wasted, thin.*

vēsīca -ae, f. *the bladder; a purse, a lantern* of style, *bombast.*

vēsīcŭla -ae, f. *a little bladder.*

vespa -ae, f. *wasp.*

Vespăsĭānus -i, m., T. Flavius, *Roman emperor,* A.D. 69-79.

vesper -ĕris or -ĕri, m. *evening; the west; the evening star*; vespere, vesperi, *in the evening.*

vespĕrasco -ĕre, *to become evening.*

vespertīnus -a -um, *of evening; western.*

vespillo -ōnis, m. *a corpse-bearer for the poor.*

Vesta -ae, f. *goddess of the hearth and domestic life*; adj. **Vestālis** -e, *Vestal*; f. as subst. *a Vestal virgin, priestess of Vesta.*

vester (voster) -tra -trum, *your, yours.*

vestĭbŭlum -i, n. *entrance-court, court-yard*; in gen., *entrance; beginning.*

vestīgĭum -i, n. *a foot-step, track; a trace, mark*; in plur., *the foot*; in vestigio, e vestigio, *at that moment.*

vestīgo -are, *to track, trace.*

vestīmentum -i, n. *clothing, a garment.*

vestĭo -ire, *to dress, clothe; to cover, adorn.*

vestis -is, f. *a covering* or *garment, clothing; a blanket, carpet, tapestry.*

vestītus -ūs, m. *clothing, clothes; a covering.*

Vĕsŭvĭus -i, m. *Vesuvius, the volcano in Campania.*

vĕtĕrānus -a -um, *old*; m. pl. *old soldiers, veterans.*

vĕtĕrasco -ascĕre -āvi, *to grow old.*

vĕtĕrātor -ōris, m. *an old hand, old stager.*

vĕtĕrātōrĭus -a -um, *cunning, crafty*; adv. **vĕtĕrātōrĭē.**

vĕtĕrīnus -a -um, *of draught*; bestia, *a beast of burden.*

vĕternōsus -a -um, *lethargic, sleepy, dull.*

vĕternus -i, m. *age; lethargy, inactivity, sloth.*

vĕto (vŏto) vĕtare vĕtŭi vĕtĭtum, *to forbid, prohibit*; n. of perf. partic. as subst. **vĕtĭtum** -i, *that which is forbidden; a prohibition.*

vĕtŭlus -a -um, *little old, poor little old*; as subst., *an old man* or *woman.*

vĕtus -ĕris; superl. vĕterrĭmus; *old, ancient, of long standing; experienced.* M. pl. as subst. *the ancients.*

vĕtustās -ātis, f. *age; antiquity, past time; long duration, length of time* (including future time).

vĕtustus -a -um, *old, ancient, of long standing; old-fashioned, antiquated.*

vexāmen -ĭnis, n. *shaking, upheaval.*

vexātĭo -ōnis, f. *shaking, jolting, shock; ill-treatment.*

vexātor -ōris, m. *one who shakes, harasses, disturbs.*

vexillārĭus -i, m. *a standard-bearer*; in plur. *a corps of veterans, a reserve.*

vexillum -i, n. *a standard, flag; a company, troop.*

vexo -are, *to shake, toss, jostle; to harass, annoy.*

vĭa -ae, f. *a way, passage; a highway, road, street; a course, march, journey; means, way, method*; abl. viā, *methodically.*

vĭātĭcus -a -um, *relating to a journey*; n. as subst., *journey money*; also *savings* or *prize-money.*

vĭātor -ōris, m. (1) *a traveller, wayfarer.* (2) *an apparitor, messenger.*

vibro -are: transit., *to cause to vibrate, brandish, shake; to brandish and hurl* a weapon; *to curl, frizzle* hair; intransit., *to shake, tremble, quiver, vibrate.*

vīburnum -i, n. *the wayfaring-tree.*

vīcānus -a -um, *dwelling in a village*; m. pl. as subst. *villagers.*

vĭcārĭus -a -um, *substituted, vicarious*; m. as subst., *a substitute*; esp. *an under-servant.*

vīcātim, *from street to street; in villages.*

vĭcĕ, vĭcem, ; see vicis.

vīcēni -ae -a, *twenty at a time* or *twenty each.*

vīcēsĭmāni -ōrum, m. pl. *soldiers of the twentieth legion.*

vīcēsĭmārĭus -a -um, *relating to the* vicesima.

vīcēsĭmus (vīcens-) -a -um, *twentieth*; f. as subst. **vīcēsĭma (vīcens-)** -ae, *the twentieth part, as a toll* or *tax.*

vĭcĭa -ae, f. *vetch.*

vĭcĭēs (-ĭens), *twenty times.*

vīcīnālis -e, *neighbouring, near.*

vīcīnĭa -ae, and **vīcīnĭtās** -ātis, f. *neighbourhood; vicinity; likeness*; concr., *the neighbours.*

vīcīnus -a -um, *near, neighbouring*; m. and f. as subst., *a neighbour*; n. as subst., *neighbourhood, vicinity.*

vĭcis (genit. nom. not found); *change, interchange, alternation;* per vices, in vices, *alternately, reciprocally; recompense, retaliation; the vicissitude of fate, lot, destiny; one's place, office, duty*; vicem, vice, in vicem, ad vicem, *in place of, instead of, like.*

vĭcissim, *in turn.*

vĭcissĭtūdo -ĭnis, f. *change, alteration.*

victĭma -ae, f. *an animal offered in sacrifice, victim.*

victĭmārĭus -i, m. *to live on, feed on.*

victor -ōris, m. and **victrix** -trīcis, f. *conqueror, victor*; as adj., *victorious.*

victōrĭa -ae, f. *victory, conquest.*

victōrĭātus -i, m. *a silver coin stamped with a figure of Victory.*

victōrĭŏla -ae, f. *a small statue of Victory.*

victrix -trīcis, f.; see victor.

victus -ūs, m. *living; manner of life; nourishment, food.*

vīcŭlus -i, m. *a little village, hamlet.*

vīcus -i, m. *part of a town, a street; a village, hamlet; an estate, country-seat.*

vĭdēlĭcet, *it is clear*; as adv. *clearly, plainly, manifestly; namely*; ironically, *of course, to be sure.*

vĭdĕo vĭdēre vīdi vīsum, *to see; to perceive, notice, observe; to look into* a matter, *see to, provide for.* Pass., *to be seen; to seem, appear, be thought*; also *to seem good, seem right.* N. of perf. partic. as subst. **vīsum** -i, *a sight, appearance, vision.*

vĭdŭĭtās -ātis, f. *want; widowhood.*

vĭdŭo -are, *to deprive*; f. of perf. partic. **vĭdŭāta** -ae, *widowed.*

vĭdŭus -a -um, *deprived, bereaved, widowed*; f. as subst. **vĭdŭa** -ae, *a widow,* or *an unmarried woman.*

Vĭenna -ae, f. *town in Gallia Narbonensis* (now Vienne).

vĭĕo -ēre, *to weave together*; partic. **vĭētus** -a -um, *shrivelled, shrunken.*

vĭgĕo -ēre, *to be vigorous, thrive, flourish.*

vĭgesco -ĕre, *to become vigorous, begin to thrive.*

vīgēsĭmus = vicesimus; q.v.

vĭgil -ĭlis, *wakeful, watchful*; m. as subst., *a watchman.*

vĭgĭlantĭa -ae, f. *watchfulness, vigilance.*

vĭgĭlax -ācis, *watchful, wakeful.*

vĭgĭlĭa -ae, f. *wakefulness, sleeplessness, watch; a watch of the night; the watch, sentinels*; fig. *watchfulness, vigilance, care.*

vĭgĭlo -are: intransit., *to keep awake, watch; to be vigilant, watchful, careful*; transit. in pass, *to be watched through, watched over.* Pres. partic. **vĭgĭlans** -antis, *watch ul, vigilant* adv. **vĭgĭlantĕr.**

vīginti, *twenty.*

vīgintīvĭrātus -ūs, *the office of the* vigintiviri.

vīgintīvĭri -ōrum, m. pl. *a commission of twenty.*

vĭgor -ōris, m. *force, energy.*
vīlĭco -are, *to manage an estate as bailiff.*
vīlĭcus -i, m. *a bailiff, steward, overseer of an estate*; f. **vīlĭca** -ae, *a bailiff's wife.*
vīlis -e, *cheap, worth little*; adv. **vīlĭtĕr.**
vīlĭtās -ātis, f. *cheapness, low price*; in gen., *worthlessness.*
villa -ae, f. *a country-house, estate, farm.*
villĭc-; see vilic-.
villōsus -a -um, *shaggy, hairy.*
villŭla -ae, f. *a small country-house, little farm.*
villum -i, n. *a sup of wine.*
villus -i, m. *shaggy hair.*
vīmen -ĭnis, n. *an osier, twig; a basket.*
vīmentum = vimen; q.v.
Vīmĭnālis collis, *one of the seven hills of Rome.*
vīmĭnĕus -a -um, *of osiers, wicker.*
vīn = visne; see volo.
vīnācĕus -a -um, *belonging to wine* or *a grape.*
vīnālia -ĭum and -ĭōrum, n. pl. *wine festivals, one in April, one in August.*
vīnārĭus -a -um, *of wine*; as subst. m. *a vintner*; n. *a wine-jar.*
vincĭbĭlis -e, *easily gained.*
vincĭo vincire vinxi vinctum, *to bind, tie up; to surround, encompass; to restrain, confine, secure.*
vinco vincĕre vīci victum, *to conquer, overcome, master, surpass; to prove successfully, win one's point.*
vincŭlum (vinclum) -i, n. *a band, cord, chain, fetter, tie*; plur., *imprisonment.*
Vindĕlĭci -ōrum, m. pl. *a Germanic people.*
vindēmĭa -ae, f. *vintage; grapes, wine.*
vindēmĭātor -ōris, m. *a harvester of grapes.*
vindēmĭŏla -ae, f. *a little vintage; a perquisite.*
vindex -ĭcis, c. *a claimant* or *protector; an avenger, punisher.*
vindĭcātĭo -ōnis, f. *defending, protecting; avenging.*
vindĭcĭae -ārum, f. pl. *things* or *persons claimed as property; the making of a claim.* Transf., *protection.*
vindĭco -are, *to claim; to arrogate, assume; appropriate; to claim as free*; hence *to liberate, deliver* or *protect; to avenge, punish.*
vindicta -ae, f. *a rod used in manumitting slaves.* Transf., *deliverance; vengeance, punishment.*
vīnĕa -ae, f. *a vineyard*; milit. *a mantlet, penthouse.*
vīnētum -i, n. *vineyard.*
vīnĭtor -ōris, m. *a vinedresser.*
vīnŏlentĭa -ae, f. *wine-drinking, intoxication.*
vīnŏlentus -a -um, *mixed with wine; drunk, intoxicated.*
vīnōsus -a -um, *full* or *fond of wine.*
vīnum -i, n. *wine, wine-drinking.*
vĭŏla -ae, f. *a violet* or *stock; the colour violet.*
vĭŏlābĭlis -e, *able to be injured.*
vĭŏlārĭum -i, n. *a bed of violets.*
vĭŏlātĭo -ōnis, f. *injury, violation, profanation.*
vĭŏlātor -ōris, m. *injurer, violator, profaner.*
vĭŏlens -entis, *violent, furious, impetuous*; adv. **vĭŏlentĕr.**
vĭŏlentĭa -ae, f. *violence, impetuosity.*
vĭŏlentus -a -um, *violent, vehement, furious, impetuous.*
vĭŏlo -are, *to violate, outrage, injure.*
vīpĕra -ae, f. *a viper; a snake, serpent.*
vīpĕrĕus -a -um, *of a viper* or *snake; snaky.*
vīpĕrīnus -a -um, *of a viper* or *snake.*
vĭr, vĭri, m. *a man, male person*; esp. *a grown man; a husband; a man of character* or *courage, " he-man "*; milit. *a soldier,* esp. *an infantryman; a single man, individual.*
vĭrāgo -ĭnis, f. *a female warrior, heroine.*
vĭrectum (-ētum) -i, n. *greensward, turf.*
vĭrĕo -ēre, *to be green, vigorous, healthy, fresh.*
vīres -ĭum, f. pl.; see vis.
vĭresco -ĕre, *to grow green.*
vĭrētum = virectum; q.v.
virga -ae, f. *a green twig, a slip; a rod; a wand; a broom; a streak, stripe*; in plur., virgae, *the lictors' rods.*
virgātus -a -um. (1) *made of twigs.* (2) *striped.*
virgētum -i, n. *an osier-bed.*
virgĕus -a -um, *of twigs* or *rods.*
Virgĭlĭus = Vergilius; q.v.
virgĭnālis -e, **virgĭnārĭus, virgĭnĕus** -a -um, *maidenly.*
virgĭnĭtās -ātis, f. *virginity.*
virgo -ĭnis, f. *a maiden, virgin, girl.*
virgŭla -ae, f. *a little bough, twig; a rod, staff.*
virgultum -i, n. (1) *a thicket, copse.* (2) *a slip for planting.*
virguncŭla -ae, f. *a little girl.*
vĭrĭdans -antis, *green*; hence verb **vĭrĭdor** -ari, *to become green.*
vĭrĭdārĭum -i, n. *a pleasure-garden.*
vĭrĭdis -e, *green.* Transf., *fresh, young, vigorous.*
vĭrĭdĭtās -ātis, f. *greenness; freshness, bloom.*
vĭrīlis -e, *manly, male, virile; of a grown man, adult; courageous, spirited*; pro virili parte, *to the best of one's ability.* Adv. **vĭrīlĭtĕr,** *manfully.*
vĭrīlĭtās -ātis, f. *manhood, virility.*
vĭrītim, *man by man, individually.*
vīrōsus -a -um, *stinking, fetid.*
virtūs -ūtis, f. *manliness; excellence, worth, goodness, virtue; bravery, courage.*
vīrus -i, n. *slimy liquid, slime; poison,* esp. of snakes, *venom; any harsh taste* or *smell.*
vīs, acc. vim, abl. vī; plur. **vīrēs** -ĭum, f. *force, power, strength; might, influence*; in sing. also *violence; a large number, quantity; the force,*

nature, meaning of a thing; plur., milit., *troops, forces.*

viscātus -a -um, *smeared with bird-lime.*

viscĕrātĭo -ōnis, f. *public distribution of meat.*

viscum -i, n. and **viscus** -i, m. *mistletoe; bird-lime.*

viscus -ĕris, usually plur. **viscĕra** -um, n. *flesh*; also *internal organs, entrails; inmost part* or *heart* of anything.

vīsĭo -ōnis, f. *seeing, view; appearance; notion, idea.*

vīsĭto -are, *to see often; to visit.*

vīso vīsĕre vīsi vīsum, *to look at, look into, see after; to go to see, visit, call upon*; gerundive **vīsendus** -a -um, *worth seeing, notable.*

vīsum -i, n. subst. from video; q.v.

vīsus -ūs, m. *seeing, sight; an appearance.*

vīta -ae, f. *life.*

vītābĭlis -e, *that can* or *should be avoided.*

vītābundus -a -um, *trying to avoid.*

vītālis -e, *of life, vital; living, surviving*; adv. **vītālĭtĕr,** *vitally.*

vītātĭo -ōnis, f. *avoiding, shunning.*

Vĭtellius -a -um, *the name of a Roman* gens; Aulus Vitellius, *the Roman emperor who succeeded Otho* (A.D. 69).

vĭtellus -i, m. *the yolk of an egg.*

vītĕus -a -um, *of a vine.*

vītĭcŭla -ae, f. *a little vine.*

vītĭfer -fĕra -fĕrum, *vine-bearing.*

vītĭgĕnus -a -um, *produced from the vine.*

vĭtĭo -are, *to injure, damage, corrupt; to forge, falsify.*

vĭtĭōsĭtās -ātis, f. *viciousness, corruption.*

vĭtĭōsus -a -um, *faulty, corrupt, bad, wrong*; adv. **vĭtĭōsē.**

vītis -is, f. *a vine; a centurion's staff.*

vītĭsător -ōris, m. *one who plants vines.*

vĭtĭum -i, n *a fault, defect, blemish; crime, vice;* relig., *a defect in auguries* or *auspices.*

vīto -are, *to avoid, shun.*

vitrĕus -a -um, *of glass; glassy, transparent, glittering.*

vītrĭcus -i, m. *stepfather.*

vitrum -i, n. (1) *glass.* (2) *woad.*

vitta -ae, f. *a ribbon, band, fillet.*

vittātus -a -um, *bound with a fillet.*

vĭtŭla -ae, f. *calf, heifer.*

vĭtŭlīnus -a -um, *of a calf*; assum, *roast veal*; f. as subst. *veal.*

vĭtŭlus -i, m. *a bull-calf*; also of the young of other animals.

vĭtŭpĕrābĭlis -e, *blamable.*

vĭtŭpĕrātĭo -ōnis, f. *blaming, scolding, censure*; meton., *blameworthy conduct.*

vĭtŭpĕrātor -ōris, m. *a blamer.*

vĭtŭpĕro -are, *to blame, scold, censure.*

vīvārĭum -i, n. *a warren, preserve, fish-pond.*

vīvātus -a -um, *quickened, vivid.*

vīvax -ācis, *long-lived, lasting, enduring; brisk, lively, vigorous.*

vīvesco vīvescĕre vixi, *to grow lively.*

vīvĭdus -a -um, *full of life, animated, vigorous; life-like.*

vīvĭrādix -īcis, f. *a cutting with a root, a layer.*

vīvisco = vivesco; q.v.

vīvo vīvĕre vixi victum, *to live, be alive; to live well, to enjoy life; to survive; to live on* anything; *to dwell.*

vīvus (vīvŏs) -a -um, *alive, living; lifelike*; flumen, *running water*; ros, *fresh*; sulfur, *natural.*

vix, *with difficulty, scarcely, only just*; vix dum, or vixdum, *hardly yet*

vŏcābŭlum -i, n. *name, appellation;* grammat. *a noun.*

vōcālis -e, *vocal; speaking, singing*; f. as subst. *a vowel.*

vŏcāmen -ĭnis, n. *name, appellation.*

vŏcātĭo -ōnis, f. *summons, invitation.*

vŏcātor -ōris, m. *an inviter.*

vŏcātus -ūs, m. *summons, invocation.*

vōcĭfĕrātĭo -ōnis, f. *loud calling, shouting.*

vōcĭfĕror -ari, dep. *to cry aloud, shout.*

vŏcĭto -are, *to be accustomed to name; to shout loudly* or *often.*

vŏco -are, *to call, summon, invoke, invite; to name, designate; to bring* or *put into any state* or *condition*; in dubium, *to call in question.*

vōcŭla -ae, f. *a low, weak voice; a low tone; a petty speech.*

vŏlaema pĭra, n. pl. *a kind of large pear.*

vŏlātĭcus -a -um, *winged, flying; flighty, inconstant.*

vŏlātĭlis -e, *winged, flying; swift, rapid; fleeting, transitory.*

vŏlātus -ūs, m. *flying, flight.*

Volcānus (Vulc-) -i, m. *Vulcan, the god of fire, husband of Venus.*

volgo, volgus = vulgo, vulgus; q.v.

vŏlĭto -are, *to fly about, flit, flutter, rush around.*

volnĕro = vulnero; q.v.

[1]**vŏlo** velle vŏlŭi (vīn = visne; sīs = si vis; sultis = si vultis); *to be willing, to wish, want; to will, ordain; to suppose, maintain that*; sibi velle *to mean, signify.*

Hence partic. **vŏlens** -entis, *willing, favourable.*

[2]**vŏlo** -are, *to fly; to move rapidly, rush*; f. pl. of partic. volantes, -ium = *birds.*

vŏlōnes -um, m. pl. *volunteers* (in the Second Punic War).

Volsci -ōrum, m. pl. *a people in Latium.*

volsella -ae, f. *a pair of tweezers.*

volsus -a -um, partic. from vello; q.v.

volt-; see vult-.

vŏlūbĭlis -e, *rolling, revolving, turning round; changeable, inconstant*; of speech, *rapid, fluent;* adv. **vŏlūbĭlĭtĕr,** *fluently.*

vŏlūbĭlĭtās -ātis, f. *turning, revolution; roundness; inconstancy, flow of words, fluency.*

vŏlŭcer volucris volucre, *flying, winged; fleet, swift, fleeting.* F. as subst. **vŏlucris** -is, *a bird* or *flying insect.*

vŏlūmen -ĭnis, n. *a scroll, book; a roll, wreath, fold.*

vŏluntārĭus -a -um, *voluntary, acting* or *done voluntarily*; m. pl. as subst. *volunteers.*

vŏluntās -ātis, f. *will, wish, inclination*; esp. *goodwill; last will, testament*; of words, etc., *meaning, sense.*

vŏlup, *agreeably, pleasantly.*

vŏluptārĭus -a -um, *pleasant; concerned with* or *devoted to pleasure.*

vŏluptās -ātis, f. *pleasure, delight, enjoyment*; in plur., *public shows.*

vŏluptŭōsus -a -um, *delightful.*

vŏlūtābrum -i, n. *a place for pigs, a slough.*

vŏlūtābundus -a -um, *rolling, wallowing.*

vŏlūtātĭo -ōnis, f. *rolling about, wallowing; disquiet.*

vŏlūto -are, *to roll round, tumble about*; partic. volutans, *rolling about.* Transf., *to turn over in the mind, consider*; *to busy, occupy.*

volva (vulva) -ae, f. *womb*; esp. *a sow's womb*

volvo volvĕre volvi vŏlūtum, *to wind, turn, roll, twist round*; in pass. *to roll.* Esp. *to unroll a book, to read.* Transf., of time, *to make roll by;* of persons, *to turn over in the mind, consider; to experience, go through.*

vōmer (vōmis) -ĕris, m. *ploughshare.*

vŏmĭca -ae, f. *an ulcer, sore, boil; a plague, curse.*

vŏmis -eris, m. = vomer; q.v.

vŏmĭtĭo -ōnis, f. *vomiting, throwing up.*

vŏmo -ere -ŭi -ĭtum, *to vomit*; *to vomit forth, throw up.*

vŏrāgo -ĭnis, f. *pit, chasm, abyss.*

vŏrax -ācis, *gluttonous, voracious.*

vŏro -are, *to eat greedily, swallow up, consume, devour.*

vors-; see vers-.

vort-; see vert-.

vōs, *you,* plur. of tu; q.v.

vōtīvus -a -um, *of a vow, votive, vowed.*

vōtum -i, n. *a vow, promise to the gods; a votive offering*; in gen., *prayer, wish, desire.*

vŏvĕo vŏvēre vōvi vōtum, *to vow, promise to a god; to pray for, wish.*

vox vōcis, f. *voice, cry, call; accent, language; sound, tone; a saying, utterance.*

Vulcānus = Volcanus; q.v.

vulgāris (volg-) -e, *common, ordinary, usual*; adv. **vulgārĭtĕr,** *in the ordinary way.*

vulgātus -a -um, partic. from vulgo; q.v.

vulgĭvăgus -a -um, *wandering, vagrant.*

vulgo (volgo) -are, *to make common* or *accessible, spread, publish, impart*; partic. **vulgātus** -a -um, *common, commonly known.*

vulgus (volgus) -i, n. (occ. m.) *the people, the public; a mass, crowd, rabble, mob.* Abl. as adv. **vulgō,** *commonly, generally, in public.*

vulnĕrātĭo (voln-) -ōnis, f. *wounding, a wound.*

vulnĕro (voln-) -are, *to wound, injure.*

vulnĭfĭcus (voln-) -a -um, *inflicting wounds.*

vulnus (volnus) -ĕris, n. *a wound, injury.*

vulpēcŭla (volp-) -ae, f. *a little fox.*

vulpēs (volpēs) -is, f. *a fox.*

vulsus -a -um, partic. from vello; q.v.

vultĭcŭlus -i, m. *look, aspect.*

vultŭōsus -a -um, *grimacing, affected.*

vultur (voltur) -ŭris, m. *a vulture.*

vultŭrīnus (volt-) -a -um, *of* or *like a vulture.*

vultŭrĭus (volt-) -i, m. *a vulture.* Transf., *a rapacious man.*

Vulturnus (Volt-) -i, m. *a river in Campania.*

vultus (voltus) -ūs, m. *expression of face, countenance, look, aspect.* Transf., *face.*

X

X, x, the twenty-second letter of the Latin alphabet.

xĕnĭum -i, n. *a present to a guest.*

Xĕnŏphōn -ōntis, m. *an Athenian soldier and writer.*

xērampĕlĭnae -ārum, f. pl. *dark-red garments.*

Xerxēs -is, m. *king of the Persians, defeated at Salamis.*

xĭphĭas -ae, m. *sword-fish.*

xystus -i, m. and **xystum** -i, n. *an open colonnade, a walk planted with trees.*

Y

Y, y, a letter borrowed from the Greek in order to represent the Greek upsilon.

Z

Z, z, representing the Greek zeta.

Zăma -ae, f. *a town in Numidia, where Scipio defeated Hannibal* (201 B.C.).

zēlŏtȳpus -a -um, *jealous.*

Zēno (-ōn) -ōnis, m. *name of several Greek philosophers.*

zĕphȳrus -i, m. *a warm west wind, zephyr.*

zm-; see sm-.

zōdĭăcus -i, m. *the zodiac.*

zōna -ae, f. *a girdle, money-belt*; in pl. zonae, *terrestrial zones.*

zōnārĭus -a -um, *of a girdle*; m. as subst. *girdle-maker.*

zōthēca -ae, f. *a private room.*

CASSELL'S ENGLISH-LATIN DICTIONARY

A

A, an; often not translated; sometimes *unus*; a certain, *aliquis, quidam*.
abandon, *relinquĕre, deserĕre, destituĕre*; of things, *omittĕre*.
abandoned, *perditus, nefarius*.
abase, *frangĕre, (de)minuĕre, comprimĕre*.
abasement, *demissio, deminutio*.
abash, *percellĕre, perturbare*.
abate: transit. *imminuĕre, remittĕre*: intransit. *cadĕre, imminui, decrescĕre*; of passion, *defervescĕre*.
abatement, *remissio, deminutio*.
abbreviate, *imminuĕre, contrahĕre*.
abbreviation, *compendium, contractio*.
abdicate, (*magistratu*) *se abdicare*; (*magistratum*) *eiurare*.
abdication, *abdicatio, eiuratio*.
abdomen, *abdomen*.
abduction, *raptus* (*-ūs*), *raptio*.
aberration, *error*.
abet, *adiuvare*.
abettor, *socius, adiutor*.
abeyance: to be in —, *in dubio esse, intermitti*; to leave in —, *rem integram relinquĕre*.
abhor, *abhorrēre ab, odisse, odio habēre*.
abhorrence, *odium*.
abhorrent, = inconsistent, *abhorrens, alienus, contrarius*; see also hateful.
abide: = linger, (*com*)*morari, manēre*; = last, *durare*; to abide by, *stare in*.
abiding, *diuturnus, stabilis, mansurus*.
ability, *potestas, vires, facultas*; = mental strength, *ingenium*; according to one's —, *pro sua parte, pro parte virili*.
abject, *abiectus, contemptus, humilis*.
abjure, *abiurare, recusare*.
ablative, (*casus*) *ablativus*.
able, *potens*; = mentally strong, *ingeniosus*; to be able, *posse, valēre*.
able-bodied, *firmus, robustus, validus*.
ablution, *lavatio, ablutio*.
abnegation, *temperantia*.
abnormal, *novus, inusitatus, singularis*.
aboard: to go —, (*navem*) *conscendĕre*; to be —, *in nave esse*.
abode: = sojourn, *habitatio*; see also house.
abolish, *abolēre, tollĕre, delēre, exstinguĕre*.
abolition, *dissolutio*; — of debts, *tabulae novae*.
abominable, *detestabilis, immanis*.
abominate, *odisse, detestari*.
aborigines, *indigenae, aborigines*.
abortive: of premature birth, *abortivus*; fig., = unsuccessful, *inritus*.
abound, *abundare, superesse*; — in, (*re*) *abundare*.
about; adv. of time or number, *fere, ferme, circiter*; prep., of place, *circa, circum*; of time, *circa*; of respect, = concerning, *de* with *abl*.
above, adv. of place, *supra*; from above, *desuper, superne*; prep., *super, supra*.
abreast, *pariter*; two horses yoked —, *equi biiugi* or *biiuges*.
abridge; see abbreviate.
abroad, adv.: = out of doors, *foras* (of motion), *foris* (of rest); = in a foreign land, *peregre*; to travel —, *peregrinari*; to spread —, = publish, *divulgare*.
abrogate, *abrogare, rescindĕre*.
abrupt: = steep, *abruptus, arduus, praeruptus*: of speech, *abruptus*; = sudden, *subitus, repentinus, improvisus*. Adv. *abrupte, praerupte; subito, de improviso, repente*.
abscess, *vomica*.
abscond, *delitescĕre, latēre, occultari*.
absence, *absentia*: in my —, *me absente*.
absent, adj. *absens*; to be —, *abesse*.
absent, v. to absent oneself, *se removēre, non comparēre*.
absolute, *absolutus, simplex*; absolute power, *dominatio, imperium singulare*. Adv. *plane, prorsus, omnino*; opp. to relatively, *per se, simpliciter*.
absolve, (*ab*)*solvĕre*.
absorb, (*com*)*bibĕre, absorbēre*; absorbed in a thing, *totus in re*.
abstain, (*se*) *re abstinēre*.
abstinence, *abstinentia, temperantia*. days of —, *ieiunium*.
abstinent, *abstinens, temperatus*.
abstract, subst. *epitome, epitoma*.
abstract, adj. *quod nullo sensu percipi potest*.
abstract, v. *abstrahĕre, sevocare*; see also steal.
abstracted, *omnium rerum* (or *sui*) *oblitus*.
abstraction, *oblivio*.
abstruse, *abstrusus, obscurus, reconditus*.
abstruseness, *obscuritas*.
absurd, *absurdus, ineptus, ridiculus*; adv. *absurde, inepte, ridicule*.
absurdity, *insulsitas, ineptia*.
abundance, *abundantia, ubertas, copia*.
abundant, *largus, amplus*; adv. *abunde, abundanter, large*.
abuse, subst.; = wrong use, *usus* (*-ūs*) *perversus*; = abusive language, *convicium*; a bad custom, *mos pravus*.
abuse, v.: = to misuse, (*re*) *abuti*; = to speak abusively to, (*homini*) *maledicĕre*.
abusive, *maledicus, maledicens, contumeliosus*; adv. *maledice, contumeliose*.
abut, *adiacēre, attingĕre*.
abyss, *gurges, barathrum, vorago*.
academy; at Athens, *Academia*; = school, *ludus, schola*.
accede; see agree.
accelerate, *accelerare*.
accent, *vox, sonus* (*-ūs*), *tenor*.
accept, *accipĕre, recipĕre*.
acceptable, *iucundus, acceptus, gratus*.
acceptation; = significance, *significatio*.
access, *aditus* (*-ūs*), *accessus* (*-ūs*).
accessary, = accomplice, *conscius*, (*culpae*) *socius*.

accessible, *facilis.*
accession; = increase, *accessio*; to the throne, *initium regni.*
accessory, = additional; use verb *accedo.*
accident, *casus* (-*ūs*).
accidental, *fortuitus*; adv. *forte, casu, fortuito.*
acclaim, subst., *clamor, acclamatio.*
acclaim, v. *acclamare.*
accommodate, *accommodare.*
accommodating, *obsequens, facilis.*
accommodation, *hospitium*; see also agreement.
accompaniment, *comitatus* (-*ūs*).
accompany, *comitari;* in a crowd, *stipare*; accompanied by, *cum* (with abl.); in music, *concinĕre.*
accomplice, *socius, sceleris conscius.*
accomplish, *conficĕre, perficĕre, absolvĕre, peragĕre, exsequi.*
accomplished, *politus, elegans, doctus, eruditus.*
accomplishment: = fulfilment, *confectio, perfectio, absolutio*; = skill, *ars.*
accord, subst.: of one's own —, *sponte* (*sua*), *ultro*; see also harmony.
accordance: in — with, *ex, de, pro,* with abl.; in — with circumstances, *ad tempus, pro re.*
according to; see accordance.
accordingly, *ergo, itaque.*
accost, *appellare, compellare, adoriri.*
account, subst. = reckoning, *ratio*: = account books, *tabulae* (-*arum*); to be of —, *magni habēri*; to be of no —, *nullo numero esse*; on my —, *mea de causa, meo nomine*; on — of, *propter, ob*; = narrative, *memoria, narratio.*
account, v.: = to think, *habēre, aestimare, ducĕre*; to — for, *rationem de re reddĕre.*
accountable; see responsible.
accountant, *scriba.*
accretion, *accessio, incrementum, cumulus.*
accumulate, (*co*)*acervare, exaggerare.*
accumulation, *cumulus, acervus.*
accuracy: = care taken, *cura, diligentia*: = truth, *veritas.*
accurate: = careful, *diligens, religiosus*; = carefully done, *accuratus*; = true, *verus.*
accusation, *accusatio, crimen.*
accusative, *accusativus* (*casus*).
accuse, *accusare, arguĕre, insimulare.*
accused, *reus.*
accuser: on a criminal charge, *accusator*; in a civil suit, *petitor*; = informer, *index, delator.*
accustom, *adsuefacĕre*; to grow accustomed, *adsuescĕre*; to be accustomed, *solĕre.*
accustomed, *adsuetus, solitus.*
ache, subst., *dolor.*
ache, v. *dolēre.*
achieve: = to finish, *conficĕre, efficĕre, perficĕre*; = to gain, reach, *adsequi, consequi.*
achievement: = doing, *confectio*; = deed, *facinus* (-*oris*).
acid, adj., *acidus, acerbus, acer*; in temper, *acerbus, morosus.*
acknowledge: = to accept as one's own, *agnoscĕre*; to — a child, *suscipĕre, tollĕre*; = to admit, *fateri, confiteri*; = to give thanks, *gratias agĕre*; to — a payment, (*in*) *acceptum referre.*
acknowledged, *cognitus, probatus, spectatus.*
acknowledgement: = confession, *confessio*; = thanks, *gratiae* (-*arum*).
acme, *fastigium*; or use *summus.*
acorn, *glans.*
acquaint; see inform.
acquaintance: = knowledge; of things, *scientia*; of persons, *usus, familiaritas*; = person known, *amicus, familiaris.*
acquainted, *notus, cognitus*; — with a person, *familiaris*; — with a thing, *peritus, sciens.*
acquiesce, *acquiescĕre, rem aequo animo ferre.*
acquiescence, *adsensus* (-*ūs*).
acquire; see gain.
acquirement, acquisition: = thing gained, see gain; = skill or knowledge, *ars, scientia*; the process of — *comparatio, adeptio.*
acquisitive, *lucri studiosus.*
acquit, *absolvĕre.*
acquittal, *absolutio, liberatio.*
acrid, *acer, acerbus.*
acrimonious, *mordax, acerbus, amarus, aculeatus.*
acrimony, *acerbitas.*
across: adv., use compound verb with *trans-*; prep., *trans.*
act, subst.: of a play, *actus* (-*ūs*); of Parliament, *lex*; = thing done, *factum.*
act, v.: = to behave, *agĕre, facĕre, se gerĕre*; of drugs, *efficax esse*; to act on the stage, *in scena esse*; to act the chief part, *primas partes agĕre.*
action: = doing, *actio*; = deed, *factum*; = battle, *pugna, proelium*; = part of a play, *actio*; = legal proceedings, *lis, actio*; to take (legal) —, *litem* or *actionem intendĕre, diem dicĕre, lege agĕre.*
actionable, (*res*) *cuius actio est.*
active: = quick, *celer, acer, promptus*; = industrious, *impiger,* (*g*)*navus, strenuus;* adv. actively, *impiger,* (*g*)*naviter, strenue.*
activity; = quickness, *celeritas, agilitas*; = industry, *industria,* (*g*)*navitas.*
actor, *qui agit* or *facit, actor*; on a stage, *histrio, actor*: comic —, *comoedus*; tragic —, *tragoedus.*
actress, *mima.*
actual, *verus*; adv. *vere, re vera.*
actuate, *movēre, impellĕre.*
acumen, *ingenii acies* or *acumen.*
acute: of pain, *acer, gravis, vehemens*; of intellect, *acutus, perspicax, sagax.* Adv., of feeling, *acute*; of intellect, *acriter, subtiliter.*
acuteness, *ingenii acies* or *acumen, subtilitas.*
adage, *proverbium.*
adamant, subst. *adamas* (-*antis*), m.
adamantine, adj. *adamantinus.*
adapt, *accommodare, aptare.*

adaptation, *accommodatio.*
adapted, *aptus, idoneus.*
add, *adděre, adicěre;* to — up, *computare.*
adder, *vipera.*
addict, v.; to — oneself, *se dare, deděre, traděre.*
addicted, *deditus.*
addition: = adding, *accessio;* in arithmetic, *additio.*
additional, *novus, additus, adiectus.*
address, v. = to speak to, *adloqui, adfari, appellare, compellare;* to address a letter, (*homini*) *epistulam inscribere.*
address, subst.: *speech, contio, oratio;* the — of a letter, *inscriptio;* = place, *locus;* = adroitness, *dexteritas, sollertia.*
adduce, *adducěre, proferre.*
adept, *callidus, peritus.*
adequate, *aptus, idoneus;* adv. *apte, satis.*
adhere, (*in*)*haerēre.*
adherent, *socius, fautor, cliens.*
adhesive, *tenax.*
adieu! *vale!* plur. *valete;* to bid —, (*hominem*) *valēre iubēre.*
adjacent, *contiguus, vicinus, finitimus;* to be —, *adiacēre.*
adjective, *nomen adiectivum.*
adjoin; see adjacent.
adjourn, *ampliare, rem differre.*
adjournment, *dilatio.*
adjudge, *addicěre, adiudicare.*
adjudicate; see judge.
adjunct; see addition.
adjure, = entreat, *obsecrare, obtestari.*
adjust; see arrange, adapt.
adjustment, *accommodatio.*
administer, *administrare, procurare;* to — medicine, *medicinam dare, adhibēre;* to — justice, *ius dicěre.*
administration: the act, *administratio, procuratio;* = the government, *ei qui reipublicae praesunt.*
admirable, (*ad*)*mirabilis, praeclarus;* adv. *admirabiliter, mirum in modum, praeclare.*
admiral, *praefectus classis*
admiration, *admiratio.*
admire, (*ad*)*mirari.*
admissible, *aequus;* or use verb.
admission: = leave to enter, *aditus* (*-ūs*), *accessus* (*-ūs*); = confession, *confessio;* in argument, *concessio.*
admit; to let in, *admittěre, recipěre;* in argument, *conceděre, dare;* = to confess, *fateri, confiteri;* to — of, = allow, *recipěre, pati.*
admonish, (*ad*)*monēre, commonēre.*
admonition, (*ad*)*monitio.*
ado: with much —, *vix, aegre;* see fuss.
adolescence, *adulescentia.*
adolescent, *adulescens.*
adopt, *adoptare;* = to choose, accept, *adsuměre, accipěre, recipěre;* to — a resolution, *constituěre.*
adoption, *adoptio.*
adoptive, *adoptivus.*
adorable, *sanctus, venerandus.*
adoration, *cultus* (*-ūs*), *veneratio.*
adore, *venerari, colěre;* = to love, *diligěre, amare.*
adorn, (*ex*)*ornare, decorare.*
adornment, *ornatus* (*-ūs*), *exornatio.*
adrift, to be, *fluctibus iactari.*
adroit, *callidus, sollers, dexter;* adv. *callide, dextere.*
adroitness, *dexteritas.*
adulation, *adulatio, adsentatio.*
adult, *adultus, pubes.*
adulterate, *corrumpěre, vitiare.*
adulterer, *adulter, moechus.*
adultery, *adulterium.*
adults, subst. *puberes* (plur. only).
adumbrate, *adumbrare.*
adumbration, *adumbratio.*
advance, v.: intransit., *progredi, proceděre;* to become advanced in years, *aetate provehi;* transit., *promovēre, provehěre, adiuvare, augēre.*
advance-guard, *primum agmen.*
advantage, *commodum, lucrum, fructus* (*-ūs*), *utilitas, bonum;* to be of — *expedire, prodesse, usui esse.*
advantageous, *utilis, fructuosus, opportunus;* adv. *utiliter.*
advent, *adventus* (*-ūs*).
adventitious, *adventicius, externus.*
adventure, subst.: = exploit, *facinus* (*-oris*), *inceptum;* = happening, *casus* (*-ūs*).
adventure, v. *audēre, tentare, experiri, periclitari.*
adventurous, *audax;* adv. *audacter.*
adverb, *adverbium.*
adversary, *adversarius.*
adverse, *adversus, contrarius;* adv. *contra, secus.*
adversity, *res adversae, calamitas.*
advertise; = to make known, *praedicare, pronuntiare;* of goods, *proscriběre, inscriběre.*
advertisement, = notice of sale, *proscriptio.*
advice, *consilium;* by my —, *me auctore.*
advise, *suadēre, monēre;* see also inform.
advisedly, *consulte, considerate, de industria.*
adviser, *suasor, auctor.*
advocate, subst.; legal, *patronus;* in gen., *suasor, auctor.*
advocate, v. *suadēre.*
adze, *ascia.*
aerial, *aerius, aetherius.*
afar, *procul, longe.*
affability, *comitas.*
affable, *adfabilis, comis;* adv. *comiter.*
affair, *res, negotium.*
affect, v.: = to influence, *adficěre, tangěre,* (*com*)*movēre;* = to be fond of, *diligěre, amare;* = to make a show of, *simulare, imitari.*
affectation, *simulatio.*
affected, *quaesitus, simulatus;* of style, *putidus, molestus;* adv. *putide, moleste.*
affection: in gen., *adfectio, adfectus* (*-ūs*); = friendly sentiment, *amor, caritas, studium;* dutiful —, *pietas.*
affectionate, adj. *amans;* dutifully — *pius;* adv. *amanter, pie.*

affiance, = betroth, (*de*)*spondēre*.
affidavit, *testimonium per tabulas datum*.
affinity, *propinquitas, necessitudo*; in gen., = close connexion, *cognatio, coniunctio*.
affirm, *adfirmare, confirmare*
affirmation, *adfirmatio*.
affirmative, use verb.
affix, *adfigere, adligare, adnectěre*.
afflict, *adflictare, vexare*.
affliction, *aegritudo, dolor, molestia*.
affluence, *divitiae, opes, copia*.
affluent, *dives*.
afford, = supply, *praestare praebēre, sufficěre, suppeditare*.
affray, *rixa, pugna*.
affright; see frighten.
affront, subst. *contumelia*.
affront, v. *contumeliā adficěre*.
afloat: to be —, *navigare, navi vehi*.
afoot, *pedibus*.
aforesaid, *quem* (*quod*) *supra scripsi*.
afraid, *timidus, pavidus, trepidus*; to be —, *timēre, metuěre*.
afresh; see again.
after. Prep.: of place or time, *post*, with acc.; of rank, etc., *secundum*, with acc.; of conformity, = according to, *ad*, with acc. Conj., *postquam, cum, ubi*.
afterwards, *post, postea, dein*(*de*), *inde*; = after this, *posthac*; some months —, *paucis postea mensibus, aliquot post menses*.
afternoon: in the —, *post meridiem*; adj. *postmeridianus*.
again, *rursus, rursum, denuo*; = a second time, *iterum*; again and again, *identidem*; = further, moreover, *porro, autem*.
against, *contra, adversus, in*, with acc.; — the stream, *adverso flumine*; — my will, *me invito*.
age: = time (esp. time of life), *aetas*; of the same —, *aequalis*; = old age, of persons, *senectus*, of things, *vetustas*.
aged, *aetate provectus*; an — man, *senex* (*-is*).
agency, = instrumentality, *opera*.
agent, *procurator*.
aggrandize, *amplificare, augēre*.
aggrandizement, *amplificatio*; or use verb.
aggravate: = to make worse, (*ad*)-*gravare*; = to annoy, *exasperare, lacessěre*.
aggregate, *summa*.
aggression, *impetus* (*-ūs*), *incursus* (*-ūs*), *iniuria*.
aggressive, *hostilis, infensus*.
aggressor, *qui prior oppugnat qui iniuriam facit*.
aggrieve; see grieve.
aghast, *stupefactus, perturbatus*; to stand —, *stupēre, obstupescěre*.
agile, *agilis, velox, pernix*.
agility, *agilitas, pernicitas, velocitas*.
agitate: = to shake, *agitare, quatěre, vibrare*; mentally, = to disturb, *percutěre, perturbare, sollicitare*; = to discuss, *agitare, disputare, disserěre*.
agitated, *sollicitus, trepidus*.
agitation: physical, *agitatio, iactatio*; mental, *animi motus* (*-ūs*), *commotio concitatio*.
agitator, *turbator*.
ago, *abhinc*; long —, (*iam*) *pridem, iam dudum*.
agony, *aegritudo, dolor*.
agrarian, *agrarius*.
agree, *conciněre, consentire*; it is agreed, *constat*; to — upon, = settle, *componěre, constituěre*.
agreeable: of things, *acceptus, gratus, dulcis*; of persons, *commodus, lepidus*.
agreement; = harmony, *consensus* (*-ūs*), *concordia*; = arrangement, compact *pactum, pactio, conventum*.
agricultural, *rusticus*.
agriculture, *agri cultura, agri cultio*.
agriculturist, *agricola*.
aground, to run, *siděre*.
ague, *febris*.
ah! aha! interj. *a, ah, aha*.
ahead, use compound verb with *prae-* or *pro-*.
aid, subst. *auxilium, adiumentum, subsidium, opem* (nom. *ops* not used).
aid, *adiuvare, subvenire, succurrěre, opem ferre*.
ailing, *aeger*; see sick.
aim, subst. *finis, propositum, consilium*.
aim, v. to take aim, *telum dirigěre* or *intenděre*; to aim at, *telo petěre*; fig., *adfectare, petěre, quaerěre, spectare*.
air, subst. (1), *aer, aether* (upper air), *aura* (breeze), *anima* (= breath); in the open —, *sub Iove, sub divo*. (2), = look manner, *vultus* (*-ūs*), *aspectus* (*-ūs*), *species*. (3) = tune *modus, numeri*.
air, v. *ventilare*.
airy, *aerius*.
akin: = related, *consanguineus, propinquus, agnatus, cognatus*; = similar, connected, *finitimus, vicinus*.
alacrity, *alacritas, pernicitas*.
alarm, subst.: = loud noise, *clamor, strepitus* (*-ūs*); = disturbance, *turba, tumultus* (*-ūs*); = fear, *terror, trepidatio*.
alas! *heu! eheu! vae! ei!*
alcove, *zotheca*.
alder, *alnus*; adj. *alneus*.
alert, *vigil, alacer, promptus*.
alias, *nomen alienum*.
alien, adj.: = foreign, *peregrinus, externus*; = adverse, *alienus, aversus*.
alien, subst. *peregrinus, advena, alienigena*.
alienate, (*ab*)*alienare, avertěre*.
alienation, (*ab*)*alienatio*.
alight, v. *descenděre*.
alike: adj. *par, similis*; adv. *pariter, similiter, aeque*.
alive, *vivus*; to be —, *vivěre*.
all: = every single, *omnis*; = the whole, *totus*; all together, *cunctus, universus*; in —, *omnino*; not at —, *minime*; — but, *tantum non*.
allay, *lenire, sedare, mitigare*.
allegation, *adfirmatio*; see also accusation.
allege: see assert.

allegiance, *fides*; to swear — to, *in verba hominis iurare.*
allegory, *allegoria.*
alleviate, (*ad*)*levare*; see also allay.
alleviation, *levatio, mitigatio, levamen.*
alley, *angiportus* (-*ūs*).
alliance, *societas, foedus* (-*eris*).
allot: by lot, *sortiri*; in gen., *distribuĕre, adsignare, adiudicare.*
allotment, *adsignatio*; of land, *ager adsignatus, possessio.*
allow. (1) = permit, *sinĕre, pati; permittĕre, concedĕre*; I am —ed, *licet mihi.* (2) = admit, *concedĕre, confiteri.* (3) = grant; q.v.
allowable, *concessus, licitus.*
allowance: = indulgence, *indulgentia*; to make — for, *ignoscĕre, condonare*; an — of food, *diaria, demensum.*
alloy: without —, *sincerus, purus.*
allude to, = to refer to, *significare, designare.*
allure, *adlicĕre, inlicĕre, invitare, inescare.*
allurement, *invitamentum, blanditia, inlecebra.*
alluring, *blandus.*
allusion, *significatio, mentio*; or use verb.
ally, subst. *socius.*
ally, v.: = make an alliance, *foedus facĕre* (or *ferire*), *societatem inire*; = join together as allies, *sociare.*
almanack, *fasti* (-*orum*), *ephemeris.*
almighty, *omnipotens.*
almond, *amygdala.*
almost, *prope, paene.*
alms, *stips* (-*is*, f.: nom. not used).
aloft, *sublime, alte; sublimis,* adj.
alone: adj. *solus, unus*; adv. = only; q.v.
along: adv., *porro, protinus*; prep., *secundum, praeter*; — with, *una cum.*
aloof, *procul.*
aloud, *clara* or *magna voce.*
already, *iam.*
also, *etiam, praeterea, quoque, item.*
altar, *ara, altaria* (plur.).
alter: transit., *mutare, commutare, immutare,* (*con*)*vertĕre*; intransit., use passive, e.g. *mutari.*
alterable, adj. *mutabilis.*
alteration, (*com*)*mutatio*; a sudden —, *conversio.*
altercation, *altercatio, iurgium, rixa.*
alternate, v.; transit., *alternare, variare*; intransit., *variare.*
alternate, adj. *alternus*; adv. *invicem.*
alternation, *vicissitudo.*
alternative: there is no alternative left except . . ., *nihil restat nisi ut* . . . .
although, *quamquam; etsi* (= even if); *quamvis* (= however much); *licet* (= granted that).
altitude, *altitudo.*
altogether, = wholly, *omnino.*
always, *semper.*
amalgamate, (*com*)*miscēre.*
amalgamation, *coniunctio, mixtura.*
amanuensis, *librarius, servus a manu.*
amass, (*co*)*acervare, aggerare, accumulare.*
amaze, *obstupefacĕre.*
amazed, (*ob*)*stupefactus, stupidus*; to be —, *stupēre,* (*ob*)*stupescĕre.*
amazement, *stupor.*
amazing, *mirus, admirabilis*; adj. *admirabiliter, mirum in modum.*
ambassador, *legatus.*
amber, *sucinum, electrum.*
ambiguity, *ambiguitas; ambages* (plur.; = riddle).
ambiguous, *anceps, ambiguus, dubius*; adv. *ambigue.*
ambition, *ambitio, gloria; laudis studium contentio honorum.*
ambitious, *gloriae* (or *laudis*) *cupidus.*
ambrosia, *ambrosia.*
ambush, *insidiae* (plur.).
ameliorate, *corrigĕre, emendare.*
amen! *fiat! esto!*
amenable, (*dicto*) *oboediens.*
amend, *emendare, corrigĕre.*
amendment, *correctio, emendatio.*
amends, *satisfactio, expiatio*: to make — for, *expiare, satisfacĕre.*
amenity, *amoenitas.*
amiability, *suavitas.*
amiable, *suavis, amabilis*; adv. *suaviter*
amicable; see friendly.
amidst, *inter,* with acc.
amiss, *male, perperam, prave*: to take —, *aegre ferre.*
ammunition, *apparatus* (-*ūs*) *belli, arma* (-*orum*); see also bullet.
amnesty, use *venia,* or *ignoscĕre.*
among, *inter,* with acc.; *in,* with abl.; *apud,* with acc.
amorous, *amans*; in bad sense, *libidinosus.*
amount, *summa.*
amount to, v. *efficere*: what does it — to? *quae summa est?* it —s to the same thing, *idem est, nihil interest.*
amphitheatre, *amphitheatrum.*
ample, *amplus*; adv. *ample, abunde.*
amplify, *amplificare.*
amplitude, *amplitudo.*
amputate, *praecidĕre, amputare.*
amuse, *delectare, oblectare.*
amusement, *delectatio, oblectatio, oblectamentum.*
amusing, *facetus, festivus.*
anachronism; use phrase, e.g. *tempora miscēre.*
analogous, *similis.*
analogy, *similitudo.*
analyse, *explicare; quasi in membra discerpĕre.*
analysis, *explicatio, enodatio.*
anarchy, *licentia.*
anatomy; refer to the structure of the body, = *compages* or *conformatio corporis.*
ancestor; sing. *auctor generis*; plur. *maiores.*
ancestral, *avitus, proavitus.*
ancestry, *origo, genus.*
anchor, subst. *ancora*; to cast —, *ancoram iacĕre*; to weigh —, *ancoram tollĕre.*
anchor, v. transit. (*navem*) *ad ancoras deligare.*
anchorage, *statio.*
ancient, *antiquus, vetus, vetustus, priscus*; the ancients, *veteres, antiqui.*

and, *et; -que* (enclitic); *atque, ac*; — so, *itaque*; — yet, *tamen*; — not, *et non, neque, nec.*
anecdote, *fabula, fabella.*
anew, *denuo, ab integro.*
anger, subst. *ira, iracundia, indignatio.*
anger, v. *lacessĕre, inritare.*
angle, *angulus.*
angle, v. *piscari.*
angler, *piscator.*
angry, adj. *iratus, iracundus*; to be (or become) angry, *irasci*; adv. *iracunde.*
anguish, *cruciatus* (-*ūs*), *dolor, angor.*
angular, *angulatus.*
animadvert, *animadvertĕre.*
animal, subst. *animal, animans*; = a beast, *bestia, pecus* (-*udis*, domestic), *belua* (large), *fera* (wild).
animal, adj. *animalis*; or genit. of *animal, corpus*, etc.
animate, v. *animare*; fig., *excitare, incitare.*
animate, adj. *animalis, animatus.*
animated, *animatus, animans, animalis*; = lively, *vegetus, alacer.*
animation, *alacritas, vigor.*
animosity, *odium, invidia.*
ankle, ankle-bone, *talus.*
annals, *annales* (-*ium*, plur.).
annex, v.: = add, (*ad*)*iungĕre, addĕre*; = conquer, *sibi subicĕre.*
annihilate, *delēre, exstinguĕre.*
annihilation, *exstinctio, excidium.*
anniversary, *festus dies anniversarius.*
annotate, *adnotare.*
annotation, *adnotatio.*
announce, (*re*)*nuntiare, praedicare.*
annoy, *lacessĕre, inritare, vexare.*
annoyance, *molestia, vexatio.*
annual, *annuus, anniversarius*; adv. *quotannis.*
annuity, *annua pecunia.*
annul, *tollĕre, delēre, abrogare, abolēre.*
anoint, (*in*)*unguĕre.*
anointing, subst. *unctio.*
anon, *brevi* (*tempore*), *mox.*
anonymous, *sine nomine.*
another, pron. and adj. *alius; alter* (= a second); they fear one —, *alius alium timet, inter se timent.*
answer, subst. *responsum*; to a charge, *defensio, excusatio.*
answer, v. *respondēre*; to a charge, *se defendĕre, excusare*; of an oracle, *responsum dare*; to — for, (*rem*) *praestare.*
answerable: to be — to a person, *homini rationem reddĕre.*
ant, *formica.*
antagonist, *adversarius.*
antagonistic, *contrarius, adversus, infensus.*
antecedent, adj. *antecedens, prior.*
antecedents, subst. *antecedentia* (-*ium*).
antechamber, *vestibulum, atriolum.*
antelope; see deer.
anterior, *antecedens, prior.*
anthem, *cantus* (-*ūs*).
anticipate: = to act first, forestall, *occupare, praevertĕrĕ, antevertĕre*; = to expect, *exspectare.*
anticipation: see anticipate; = expectation, *exspectatio, spes.*
antics, *ludi, ioca.*
antidote, *remedium.*
antipathy: of things, (*rerum*) *discordia, repugnantia*; of persons, *odium.*
antiquary, antiquarian, *rerum antiquarum studiosus.*
antiquated, *obsoletus, priscus.*
antique, *antiquus.*
antiquity, *antiquitas, vetustas.*
antithesis: rhet. *contentio*; = the opposite, *contrarium.*
antler, *cornu.*
anvil, *incus* (-*udis*).
anxiety, *anxietas, cura, sollicitudo.*
anxious, *anxius, sollicitus, trepidus*; adv. *anxie, sollicite.*
any, anyone: with negative, or in questions, *ullus* (adj.) *quisquam* (substantival); after *si, nisi*, or *ne*, use *qui, qua, quod* (adj.), *quis* (subst.); — you like, — you please, *quivis, quilibet.*
anywhere, *usquam; ubivis* (= anywhere you please); *quoquam* (= to any place).
apace, *celeriter.*
apart, *seorsum*; or use compound verbs with *dis-* and *se-*.
apartment; see room.
apathetic, *hebes, lentus.*
apathy, *stupor, lentitudo.*
ape, *simia, simius.*
ape, v. *imitari.*
Apennines, *Apenninus.*
aperture; see opening.
apex, *cacumen, apex.*
aphorism, *sententia, dictum, elogium.*
apiece, use distrib. num.
apologise, *excusare.*
apology: = defence, *defensio*; = excuse, *excusatio.*
apophthegm, *elogium, sententia, dictum.*
apostrophize; see address.
apothecary, *medicus.*
appal, (*ex*)*terrēre*; see frighten.
apparatus, *apparatus* (-*ūs*).
apparel, *vestis, vestimentum.*
apparent: = evident, *manifestus, apertus*; to be —, *apparēre*; = not real, *fictus, simulatus*; adv. *ut videtur.*
apparition: = appearing, *adventus*(-*ūs*); = spectre, *simulacrum, species.*
appeal, subst.: legal, *appellatio, provocatio*; = entreaty, *obsecratio, preces.*
appeal, v.: legal, to a magistrate, (*hominem*) *appellare*; to the people, *ad populum provocare*; appeal to, = entreat, *obtestari, obsecrare*; appeal to, = please, *placēre.*
appealing, *supplex.*
appear: = become visible, be evident, *apparere, conspici*; to appear in public, *in publicum prodire*; —, = be present, put in an appearance, *comparēre, adesse*; to —, = seem, *videri.*
appearance: = arrival, *adventus* (-*ūs*); or use verb; = looks, *species, facies, habitus* (-*ūs*); = semblance, *species.*
appease, *placēre*; of hunger etc., *sedare.*
appeasement, *placatio.*
appellant; see appeal.
append, *addĕre, adiungĕre.*
appendage, *appendix, accessio.*

appetite, *appetentia, appetitio*; for food, *fames.*
applaud, (*ap*)*plaudĕre.*
applause, *plausus* (*-ūs*).
apple, *malum*; — tree, *malus,* f.
appliance, *apparatus* (*-ūs*), *instrumentum.*
application: = request, *petitio*; of the mind, *animi intentio, diligentia.*
apply, v.: transit., = bring to bear, *adhibēre, admovēre*; to — oneself, *se conferre*; intransit., = refer, *pertinēre*; = make application, *adirē.*
appoint, *constituĕre, dicĕre, destinare*; of officials, *creare, facĕre*; to — to command, *praeponĕre, praeficĕre.*
appointment: = office, *munus* (*-eris*), *magistratus* (*-ūs*); = agreement to meet, *constitutum.*
apportion, *dividĕre, distribuĕre, adsignare.*
apposite, *aptus, accommodatus.*
appraise, *aestimare.*
appreciate, *aestimare; agnoscĕre.*
apprehend, *comprehendĕre*; = to grasp mentally, *comprehendĕre, complecti* (*animo* or *mente*), *intellegĕre*; = fear; q.v.
apprehension: = mental grasp, *intellegentia*; = fear, *timor.*
apprehensive; see timid.
apprentice, subst. *homo* (*homini*) *addictus.*
apprentice, v. *addicĕre.*
approach, subst. *adventus* (*-ūs*), *aditus* (*-ūs*).
approach, v. *accedĕre, appropinquare, adventare.*
approbation; see approval.
appropriate, adj. *idoneus, aptus, accommodatus*; adv. *apte, accommodate.*
appropriate, v. (*ad*)*sumĕre, sibi adrogare, sibi vindicare.*
approval, *approbatio, comprobatio*; with your approval, *pace tua.*
approve, (*ap*)*probare, comprobare.*
approved, *probatus, spectatus.*
approximate, adj. *propinquus.*
approximate, v., see approach.
April, *Aprilis* (*mensis*).
apron, *subligaculum.*
apt: = appropriate; q.v.; = prone, *pronus, propensus*; adv. *apte.*
aptitude, *habilitas.*
aquatic, *aquatilis.*
aqueduct, *aquae ductus* (*-ūs*).
aquiline, *aduncus.*
arable; see plough.
arbiter, *arbiter, disceptator.*
arbitrarily, *libidinose.*
arbitrary: = capricious, *libidinosus*; of power, use *dominari* or *dominatio.*
arbitrate, v. *disceptare, diiudicare.*
arbitration, *arbitrium.*
arbour, *umbraculum.*
arc, *arcus* (*-ūs*).
arcade, *porticus* (*-ūs*).
arch, subst. *arcus* (*-ūs*), *fornix.*
arch, adj. *petulans, improbus, malus.*
arch, v. *arcuare*; see curve.
archaeology, *rerum antiquarum scientia.*
archaism, *verbum obsoletum.*
archer, *sagittarius.*
architect, *architectus.*
architecture, *architectura.*
archives, *tabulae publicae.*
arctic, *septentrionalis, arctous.*
ardent, *ardens, fervens, acer*; adv., *ardenter, acriter.*
ardour, *ardor, fevor, studium.*
arduous, *arduus, difficilis.*
area, *area, superficies.*
arena, *harena.*
argue: = to discuss, *disserĕre, disputare*; = conclude, seek to prove, *argumentari, conligĕre.*
argument: = dispute, *disputatio*; line of —, *argumentum.*
arid, *aridus, siccus.*
aright, *recte, bene.*
arise, *surgĕre,* (*ex*)*oriri, exsistĕre.*
aristocracy: = aristocrats, *optimates, patricii, nobiles*; as a form of government, *optimatium dominatus* (*-ūs*).
aristocrat, aristocratic; see aristocracy.
arithmetic, *arithmetica* (*-orum*).
arithmetical, *arithmeticus.*
ark, = chest, *arca.*
arm, subst. *bracchium*; upper —, *lacertus*; arms, = embrace, *complexus* (*-ūs*), *manūs* (plur.); see also arms.
arm, v. transit. *armare*; intransit., *armari, arma capĕre.*
arm-chair, *sella.*
armed, *armatus.*
armistice, *indutiae* (*-arum*).
armour, *arma* (*-orum*); armour-bearer, *armiger.*
armourer, *faber armorum.*
armpit, *ala.*
arms, *arma* (*-orum*), *tela* (*-orum*), (offensive).
army, *exercitus*(*-ūs*); in marching array, *agmen*; in battle array, *acies.*
aromatic, *odorus, odoratus.*
around: adv. and prep., *circa, circum.*
arouse, *excitare, suscitare.*
arraign; see accuse.
arrange, *ordinare, componĕre, disponĕre, digerĕre*; abstr., *constituĕre, componĕre.*
arrangement, *ordo, ratio, dispositio*; or use verb.
arrant, render by superl., or *summus.*
array: of battle, *acies*; = dress, *vestis.*
array, v. = dress, *vestire.*
arrears, *pecuniae residuae.*
arrest: = put under arrest, *comprehendĕre, in custodiam dare*; = stop; q.v.
arrival, *adventus* (*-ūs*), *accessus* (*-ūs*).
arrive, *advenire, pervenire, adventare.*
arrogance, *adrogantia, superbia.*
arrogant, *adrogans, superbus*; adv. *adroganter, superbe.*
arrogate, v. *sibi adrogare,* (*ad*)*sumĕre.*
arrow, *sagitta.*
arsenal, *armamentarium*; naval —, *navalia* (*-ium*).
art, *ars, artificium, peritia* (= acquired skill); the fine —s, *artes ingenuae* or *liberales.*
artful, *astutus, callidus*; adv. *astute, callide.*
artfulness *astutia, calliditas, dolus.*

article, *res*; = clause or item, *caput, condicio.*
articulate, adj. *clarus.*
articulate, v. *dicĕre.*
artificer, *artifex, opifex.*
artificial, adj. *artificious*; adv. *arte, manu, opere.*
artillery, *tormenta* (*-orum*).
artisan, *opifex, faber.*
artist, *artifex*; or *poeta, pictor,* etc.
artistic, adj. *artifex*; adv. *artificiose, summa arte.*
artless, adj. *simplex*; adv. *simpliciter, sine arte.*
as, adv. and conj.: see while, because, since, though; as . . . as., *tam . . . quam . . .*; such . . . as . . ., *talis . . . qualis . . .*; as great as . . ., *tantus . . . quantus*; as soon as, *simul ac*; the same as, *idem ac, atque, qui*; as far as, *tenus* (prep.), *usque* (adv., = all the way); as if, as though, *quasi, tamquam, velut*; as regards . . ., *quod ad . . . attinet.*
ascend, *scandĕre, ascendĕre.*
ascendency, render by *superior* or *summus.*
ascent, *ascensus* (*-ūs*).
ascertain, *explorare, cognoscĕre, comperire.*
ascetic, render by phrase (e.g. *cibo abstinēre*).
ascribe, *ascribĕre, adiudicare, attribuĕre.*
ash (tree), *fraxinus*; adj. *fraxineus*; mountain-ash, *ornus.*
ashamed, *pudore adfectus*; I am ashamed, *pudet me.*
ashes, *cinis, favilla.*
ashore: of rest, *in litore*; of motion, *in litus*; to put —, *exponĕre.*
aside, seorsum; see apart.
ask: of questions, *rogare, interrogare, quaerĕre*; of favours, etc., *rogare, petĕre, poscĕre.*
askance: to look — at, *limis oculis adspicĕre.*
aslant, *oblique, ex transverso.*
asleep, *dormiens, in somno, per somnum.*
asp, *aspis.*
aspect, *aspectus* (*-ūs*), *forma, facies, species.*
asperity, *asperitas, acerbitas.*
asperse, *infamiā aspergĕre, calumniari.*
aspersion, *calumnia, opprobrium.*
aspirate, *aspiratio.*
aspire, (*ad rem*) *aspirare, contendĕre*; (*rem*) *adfectare.*
aspiration, *appetitio, adfectatio.*
ass, *asinus*; a little —, *asellus.*
ass-driver, *asinarius.*
assail, *oppugnare, adoriri.*
assailant, *qui oppugnat.*
assassin, *sicarius, percussor.*
assassinate, *insidiis interficĕre.*
assassination, *caedes*; to accuse of —, *accusare inter sicarios.*
assault, *impetus* (*-ūs*), *incursus* (*-ūs*), *oppugnatio*; legal, *vis.*
assay, subst. *obrussa.*
assemble, v. transit., *convocare*; intransit., *convenire, coire.*
assembly, *conventus* (*-ūs*), *concilium.*
assent, subst. *adsensio, adsensus* (*-ūs*).
assent, v. *adsentire, adnuĕre.*
assert: = to state, *dicĕre, adfirmare, confirmare*; to — a right, *ius retinēre, obtinēre.*
assertion: = statement, *adfirmatio*; = maintenance, *defensio, vindicatio.*
assess, *aestimare.*
assessment, *aestimatio, census* (*-ūs*).
assessor, *censor*; = a judge's assistant, *adsessor.*
assets, *bona* (*-orum*).
assiduity, *adsiduitas, sedulitas.*
assiduous, *adsiduus, sedulus, industrius*; adv. *adsidue, sedulo, industrie.*
assign, *adsignare,* (*at*)*tribuĕre.*
assignation, *constitutum.*
assimilate: = to make like, (*ad*) *aequare, similem facĕre*; = to digest, *concoquĕre.*
assist, (*ad*)*iuvare, auxilium ferre, auxiliari, opitulari, subvenire.*
assistance, *opem* (nom. sing. not used), *auxilium, adiumentum.*
assistant, *adiutor.*
associate, subst. *socius, sodalis.*
associate, v. transit., (*con*)*iungĕre,* (*con*)*sociare, congregare*; intransit., use pass., or reflex.
association, *societas, sodalitas, sodalicum.*
assort, *digerĕre.*
assuage, *mitigare, lenire, sedare, levare.*
assume: = take to oneself, *sibi adrogare,* (*ad*)*sumĕre, occupare*; = take for granted, *ponĕre, sumĕre.*
assurance: = strong assertion, *confirmatio*; = confidence, *fiducia.*
assure, *homini* (*pro certo*) *adfirmare, confirmare*; = to secure; q.v.
assured: of things, *certus, exploratus*; to feel assured, *credĕre, confidĕre, pro certo habēre.*
assuredly, *profecto, certe.*
astern, *in* or *a puppi.*
astonish, *obstupefacĕre.*
astonished, *attonitus*; to be —, *obstupescĕre, stupēre.*
astonishing, *mirabilis, mirus*; adv. *mire, mirum in modum, mirabiliter.*
astonishment, *stupor,* (*ad*)*miratio.*
astray, use adj. *vagus,* or verb *vagari.*
astrologer, *astrologus, mathematicus.*
astrology, *astrologia.*
astronomy; treat as astrology; q.v.
astute, *astutus, callidus.*
asunder, *seorsum*; see apart.
asylum; see refuge.
at: of place, *ad, apud, in,* or locative case; of time, *in, ad,* or abl. case.
atheism, *deum esse negare.*
athlete, *athleta.*
athwart; see across.
atmosphere, *aer, caelum.*
atmospheric, use genit. *aeris* or *caeli.*
atom, *atomus, corpusculum.*
atone, (*ex*)*piare.*
atonement, *piaculum.*
atrocious, *nefandus, nefarius, atrox*; adv. *nefarie.*
atrocity: as quality, *immanitas, atrocitas*; as deed, *res atrox, nefas.*
attach, *adfigĕre, adligare*; fig., *adiungĕre, applicare.*

attached, *aptus*; = fond, *studiosus*.
attachment, *studium, amor, caritas*.
attack, *impetus* (-*ūs*), *oppugnatio, incursus* (-*ūs*).
attack, v. *oppugnare, adoriri, adgredi* (*ap*)*petĕre*; to be —ed by disease, *morbo corripi*.
attacker, *oppugnator*.
attain, *adsequi, consequi*.
attainment, *adeptio, comparatio*; = acquired skill, *ars, doctrina, eruditio*.
attempt, subst. *conatus* (-*ūs*), *inceptum*.
attempt, v. *conari, temptare*.
attend: of physical presence, (*hominem*) *comitari, prosequi, deducĕre*; as a servant, (*homini*) *famulari, ministrare*; at a gathering, *adesse, interesse, frequentare*; mentally, = to pay attention, *operam dare, curare, animadvertĕre, animum attendĕre, hoc agĕre*; not to attend, *aliud agĕre*.
attendance, *apparitio, adsectatio*; of large numbers, *frequentia*.
attendant: = escort, (*ad*)*sectator, stipator*; = servant, *servus, minister, famulus*.
attention, *animus attentus, animi intentio*; = an attentive act, *officium*.
attentive: = paying attention, *attentus, intentus, erectus*; adv. *attente, intente*; = helpful, kind, *officiosus, observans*.
attenuate, v. *attenuare, extenuare*.
attest: = vouch for, *testari, testificari*; = call to witness, *testari, testem facĕre*.
attestation, *testificatio*; = evidence, *testimonium*.
attire; see dress.
attitude: physical, (*corporis*) *habitus* (-*ūs*), *status* (-*ūs*); mental, *animus*.
attract, *attrahĕre, allicĕre*.
attraction, *vis attrahendi*; = pleasant object, *oblectamentum*.
attractive, adj. *iucundus, suavis*.
attribute, subst.; use phrase with *natura* or *proprius*; gram., *attributio, attributum*.
attribute, v. (*at*)*tribuĕre, adsignare*.
attrition; render by verb *terĕre*.
attune; use phrase with *concinĕre* or *consonus*.
auburn, *fulvus*.
auction, *auctio*; to hold an —, *auctionari*.
auctioneer, *magister auctionis, praeco*.
audacious, *audax, protervus, confidens*.
audacity, *audacia, protervitas*.
audience: = hearing *admissio, aditus* (-*ūs*); = hearers, *audientes, corona*; a large —, *audientium frequentia*.
audit, v. *rationes dispungĕre*.
augment, v. (*ad*)*augēre, amplificare*.
augmentation, *amplificatio*.
augur, subst. *augur*.
augur, v., = foretell, *praedicĕre, vaticinari, augurari*.
augury, *augurium, omen*.
August, (*mensis*) *Sextilis*; later *Augustus*.
august, adj. *augustus, inlustris, magnificus*.
aunt, *amita* (= father's sister); *matertera* (= mother's sister).
auspices, *auspicium*.
auspicious, *felix, prosper, faustus*; adv. *feliciter, prospere, fauste*.
austere, *austerus, severus, tristis*; adv. *austere, severe*.
austerity, *austeritas, severitas*.
authentic, *certus, verus*; adv. *certo auctore*.
authenticity, *fides, auctoritas*.
author: = originator, *auctor, inventor*; = writer, *scriptor*.
authoritative, *gravis*.
authority, *auctoritas, gravitas*; an — for speech or action, *auctor*; the —s, *magistratus, potestates*.
authorize, *auctor esse, potestatem facĕre, permittĕre*.
autocrat, *dominus*.
autumn, *autumnus*.
autumnal, *autumnalis*.
auxiliaries, *auxilia*, (*milites*) *auxiliares*.
auxiliary, adj. *auxiliaris, auxiliarus*.
avail, *valēre, prodesse*; to — oneself of, *uti*.
avarice, *avaritia*.
avaricious, *avarus*.
avaunt! *abi! apage!*
avenge, *vindicare, ulcisci*.
avenger, *ultor, vindex*.
avenue, *xystus*.
aver; see affirm, assert.
averse, *aversus, alienus*.
avert, *avertĕre, prohibēre*.
aversion, *odium, animus aversus*.
avoid, *vitare, declinare, aversari*.
avow, *profitēri, confitēri*.
avowal, *confessio*.
avowed, *apertus*; adv. *aperte*.
await, *exspectare, manēre, opperiri*.
awake, adj. *vigilans*; to be —, *vigilare*.
awake, v.: transit., (*e somno*) *excitare*; intransit., *expergisci, excitari*.
award, subst. *arbitrium, addictio*.
award, v. *addicĕre, adiudicare*; see give.
aware, *gnarus*; to be —, *scire, novisse*.
away, *procul*; often rendered by compound verb with *ab-*.
awe, subst. *formido, reverentia, veneratio*.
awe, v. *terrēre; formidinem inicĕre*.
awe-inspiring, awful, *dirus, formidolosus, terribilis*.
awhile, *aliquamdiu, paulisper, parumper*.
awkward, *agrestis, rusticus, rudis, inscitus*; adv. *inscite, rustice*.
awkwardness, *rusticitas. inscitia*.
awl, *subula*.
awning, *velum*.
awry; adj. *obliquus, perversus*; adv. *oblique, perverse*.
axe, *securis, dolabra*.
axis, axle, *axis*.
ay, aye, adv. *ita, certe, sane*; I say ay, *aio*.
azure, *caeruleus*.

B

baa, v. *balare*.
babble, v. *blaterare, garrire*.
babbler, *garrulus*.
babe, baby, *infans*.

baboon: see ape.
bachelor, *caelebs.*
back, subst. *tergum*: on one's back, *supinus* (adj.).
back, v.: transit., = move backwards, *retro movēre*; = support, *favēre*; intransit., = go back, *se recipĕre, recedĕre.*
back, backwards, *retro, retrorsum*; or use compound verb with *re-*.
backbite, *rodĕre, absenti maledicĕre.*
bacon, *lardum.*
bad, *malus, pravus* (= crooked), *turpis* (= ugly, foul); *improbus, perversus, nequam*; in — health, *aeger*; adv. *male, prave, turpiter, improbe.*
badge, *signum, insigne, nota.*
badger, *meles.*
badness, *pravitas, turpitas, nequitia.*
baffle, *eludĕre, ad inritum redigĕre.*
bag, *saccus, culeus.*
baggage, *sarcinae, impedimenta* (*-orum*), *vasa* (*-orum*).
bail, subst.: = security given, *vadimonium*; = person giving security, *vas, sponsor.*
bail, v. *spondēre.*
bailiff; on an estate, *procurator, vilicus*; at law courts, *apparitor.*
bait, subst. *esca.*
bait, v. = put bait on (a hook), *escam* (*hamo*) *imponĕre*; = feed, *cibum praebēre*; = worry, *vexare, lacessĕre.*
bake, *coquĕre, torrēre.*
baker, *pistor.*
bakery, *pistrinum.*
balance, subst.: = scales, *trutina, libra*; = remainder, use adj. *reliquus.*
balance, v. *aequis ponderibus librare*; fig., *compensare*; the accounts —, *ratio constat.*
bald, *glaber, calvus*; of language, *incultus.*
baldness, *calvitium.*
bale, subst. *fascis.*
bale (out), v. *egerĕre, exhaurire.*
baleful, *perniciosus, exitiosus.*
balk, v. *frustrari, eludĕre.*
ball: = round object, *globus*; a — to play with, *pila, follis* (= football); see also bullet; —, = dance, *saltatio.*
ballad, *carmen.*
ballast, *saburra.*
ballet, *pantomimus*; — dancer, *pantomimus.*
ballot, *suffragium, tabella.*
balm, *balsamum*; fig., *solatium.*
balustrade, *cancelli* (*-orum*).
ban; see forbid.
band, subst.: for binding, *fascia, ligamen*; = company, *manus, turba, grex, caterva.*
band (together), v.; see combine.
bandage; see band and bind.
bandit, *latro.*
bandy: to — words, *altercari.*
bandy, bandy-legged, *loripes.*
bane, *venenum, virus*; fig., *pernicies, pestis.*
baneful, *perniciosus, exitiosus.*
bang, subst., *crepitus* (*-ūs*), *sonitus* (*-ūs*).
bang, v.; see strike.

banish, v. (*homini*) *aqua et igni interdicĕre;* (*hominem*) (*ex*)*pellĕre, exterminare, relegare, deportare.* Transf., *exterminare,* (*ex*)*pellĕre, amovēre.*
banishment, *interdictio aquae et ignis, relegatio, deportatio, exsilium.*
bank, subst.: of earth, *agger*; of a river, *ripa*; financial, *argentaria, mensa publica.*
banker, *argentarius.*
bankrupt, *decoctor*; to become —, (*rationes*) *conturbare, decoquĕre.*
banner, *vexillum.*
banquet, *epulae* (*-arum*), *convivium, cena.*
banter, subst. *cavillatio, ludibrium.*
banter, v. *cavillari, iocari.*
bar, subst.; = a long piece, *asser, later*; = bolt, *claustrum, obex, sera*; legal, *forum*; to practise at the —, *causas agĕre, dicĕre, orare.*
bar, v. = bolt, *occludĕre, obserare*; = hinder, *impedire, prohibēre.*
barbarian, *barbarus.*
barbaric, barbarous, *barbarus*; = savage, cruel, *immanis, saevus, crudelis*; adv. *barbare, saeve, crudeliter.*
barbarity, *immanitas.*
barbed, *hamatus.*
barber, n. *tonsor*: a —'s shop, *tonstrina.*
bard, *vates.*
bare, adj., *nudus*; = mere, *merus.*
bare, v. *nudare, aperire.*
barefaced, *impudens.*
barefoot, *pedibus nudis.*
barely, *vix, aegre.*
bargain, subst. *pactio, pactum.*
bargain, v. *pacisci.*
bark, subst.: of trees, *cortex, liber*; of dogs, *latratus.*
bark, v. *latrare.*
barley, *hordeum.*
barn, *horreum.*
barracks, *castra* (*-orum*).
barrel, *cupa, seria, dolium, orca.*
barren, *sterilis, infecundus.*
barrenness, *sterilitas.*
barricade, subst. *munimentum.*
barricade, v. *praesepire, obstruĕre, oppilare.*
barrier, *septum, cancelli* (*-orum*), *claustra* (*-orum*).
barrister; see advocate.
barrow, *ferculum.*
barter, subst. (*per*)*mutatio mercium.*
barter, v. *merces mutare.*
base, subst. *basis, fundamentum, radix.*
base, adj. *turpis*; — coin, *nummi adulterini*; — born, *ignobilis, humili loco natus.* Adv. *turpiter.*
baseness, *turpitudo.*
bashful, *pudens, pudicus, verecundus*; adv. *verecunde.*
bashfulness, *pudor, verecundia.*
basin, *pelvis, trulla.*
basis; see base.
bask, *apricari.*
basket, *corbis, qualus, sporta, calathus.*
bas-relief, *toreuma* (*-atis*, n.).
bass, (in music), *gravis.*
bastard, *nothus.*

bat: the flying creature, *vespertilio*; for games, *clava*.
batch, *numerus*.
bath, subst. *balineum, balneum, balneae* (*-arum*, plur.).
bath, bathe, v.: transit. *lavare, abluĕre, perfundĕre*; intransit., *lavari, perlui*.
bath-tub, *alveus*.
battalion, *cohors*.
batter, *pulsare, percutĕre, verberare*.
battering-ram, *aries*.
battery: = assault, *vis*; of artillery, *tormenta* (*-orum*).
battle, *proelium, pugna*.
battle-array, *acies*.
battle-axe, *bipennis, securis*.
battle-cry, *clamor*.
battle-field, *locus pugnae*; sometimes *acies*.
battlement, *pinna*.
bawl, *vociferari, clamitare*.
bay, subst.: the tree, *laurea, laurus*; of the sea, *sinus* (*-ūs*).
bay, adj. *spadix, badius*.
bay, v. *latrare*.
be, *esse; exsistĕre, exstare*.
beach, *litus*.
beacon: = lighthouse, *pharus*; = fire, *ignis*.
bead, *baca*.
beak, *rostrum*.
beaker, *poculum*.
beam, subst.: of wood, *tignum, trabs*; of light, *radius, iubar*.
beam, v. (*ad*)*fulgēre*.
bean, *faba*.
bear, subst.: the animal, *ursus, ursa*; the constellation, *arctos, septentriones*: the Great —, *ursa major*; the Little —, *ursa minor*.
bear, v.: = carry, *ferre, gestare, portare*; = endure, (*per*)*ferre, pati, sustinēre, tolerare*; = have, (feeling, etc.), *gerĕre*; = produce, bring forth, *parĕre, ferre*.
beard, subst. *barba*.
beard, v.; see defy.
bearer: = porter, *baiulus*; — of letters, *tabellarius*.
beast, *bestia* (wild); *belua; pecus* (*-udis*, tame); *fera* (wild); *iumentum* (— of burden).
beastliness, *spurcitia*.
beastly, *spurcus, immundus*.
beat, v.: = strike, *ferire, percutĕre, pulsare*; to be beaten, *vapulare*; to beat down, (*pro*)*sternĕre*; —, = overcome, *vincĕre, superare*; intransit., *palpitare, salire*.
beating, subst. *ictus* (*-ūs*), *verbera* (*-um*, plur.).
beau, *homo bellus* or *elegans*.
beautiful, *pulcher, speciosus, formosus, bellus, amoenus* (of landscapes, etc.); adv. *pulchre, belle*.
beautify, (*ex*)*ornare*.
beauty, *pulchritudo, species, forma, amoenitas* (of places).
beaver, *castor, fiber*.
becalmed, *ventis destitutus*.
because, *quod, quia, quoniam*; because of, *propter, ob*.
beck, = nod, *nutus* (*-ūs*).
beckon, *digito innuĕre*.
become, v. *fieri, evadĕre*; = to suit, *decēre, convenire*.
bed: for sleeping, *lectus*: to make a —, *lectum sternĕre*; to go to —, *cubitum ire*: of a river, *alveus*.
bedaub, (*ob*)*linĕre, perungĕre*.
bed-clothes, bedding, *stragulum, lodix*.
bedew, *inrorare*.
bedizen, (*ex*)*ornare*.
bedroom, *cubiculum*.
bee, *apis*: — hive, *alvus, alveus*; a swarm of —s, *examen apium*.
beech, *fagus*; adj. *fageus, faginus*.
beef, (*caro*) *bubula*.
beetle, subst. *scarabeaus*.
befall, *accidĕre, contingĕre*.
befit, *convenire, aptum esse, decēre*.
before. Adv.: in space, *prae*; in time, *prius, ante*. Prep.: in space, =in presence of, *coram*; = in front of, *ante*; in time, *ante*. Conj., *antequam, priusquam*.
beforehand, *antea*.
befoul, *inquinare, foedare*.
befriend, *adiuvare, favēre*.
beg, *mendicare;* = to ask earnestly, *precari, orare, rogare*.
beget, *gignĕre, generare, procreare*.
beggar, *mendicus*.
beggarly, *miser, vilis*.
beggary, *egestas, paupertas, mendicitas*.
begin, *incipĕre, ordiri, inchoare*.
beginning, *initium, principium, primordium*; — of a speech, *exordium*; the —s of a science, *elementa* (*-orum*), *rudimenta* (*-orum*).
beginner, = novice, *tiro*.
begone! *abi! apage te!*
begrudge, *invidēre*.
beguile, *decipĕre, fallĕre*.
behalf: on — of, *pro*.
behave, *se gerĕre*.
behaviour, *mores* (*-um*, plur.).
behead, *detruncare, obtruncare*; in execution, *securi ferire*.
behind: adv. *pone, post, retro, a tergo*; prep. *pone, post*.
behold, v. *adspicĕre, intueri, contemplari, spectare*.
behold! *en! ecce!*
beholden, = indebted, *obnoxius*.
behove: it behoves, *decet, convenit, oportet*.
being, *natura*; a human being, *homo*.
belated, *serus*.
beleaguer, *obsidēre*.
belie: = misrepresent, *criminari, calumniari*; = refute, *refellĕre, refutare*.
belief, *fides, opinio, persuasio*.
believe, *credĕre, fidem habēre*; = to think, *credĕre, putare, arbitari, opinari*; I firmly —, *mihi persuasum est*.
bell, *tintinnabulum*; sometimes *aes*.
bellow, subst. *mugitus* (*-ūs*).
bellow, v. *mugire*.
bellows, *follis*.
belly, *venter, alvus, abdomen*.
belong, *esse*, with genit. or possess. adj.; *attinēre, pertinēre*.

below: adv., *subter, infra*; prep., *infra, subter, sub.*
belt, *cingulum, zona, balteus.*
bench, *scamnum, subsellium*; for rowers, *transtrum.*
bend: transit., *(in)flectĕre, inclinare*; intransit., pass. or reflex.
bending, *flexus* (-*ūs*), *flexio, inclinatio.*
beneath; see below.
beneficence, *beneficentia, liberalitas.*
beneficent, *liberalis, beneficus.*
beneficial, *utilis, salutaris.*
benefit, subst. *beneficium.*
benefit, v.: transit., *prodesse*,(*ad*)*iuvare;* intransit., *proficĕre.*
benevolence, *benevolentia.*
benevolent, *benevolus.*
benign, *benignus.*
benignity, *benignitas.*
bent, subst. *animi inclinatio, voluntas.*
bent, adj. *curvus*; bent on a thing, *rei* (genit.) *studiosus, cupidus.*
benumb; to be —ed, *obtorpescĕre, torpēre.*
bequeath, *legare.*
bequest, *legatum.*
bereave, *orbare.*
bereaved, *orbus.*
bereavement, *orbitas.*
berry, *baca, bacula, acinus.*
beseech, *orare, implorare, obtestari.*
beset, *obsidēre, urgēre, premĕre.*
beside, prep.: = near, *prope, iuxta*; = except, *praeter*; — the point, *nihil ad rem*; — oneself, *sui impotens.*
besides, *praeter* (*quam*); as adv. = in addition, *praeterea, ultro.*
besiege, *obsidēre, circumsedēre.*
besmear, (*ob*)*linĕre.*
bespatter, *adspergĕre, conspergĕre.*
bespeak, *imperare.*
best, *optimus*; see good.
bestir: to bestir oneself, *se* (*com*)*movēre, excitare.*
bestow; see give.
bet, subst. *pignus* (-*oris*).
betake: to betake oneself, *se conferre.*
betimes, *mature.*
betoken, *significare.*
betray, *prodĕre.*
betrayal, *proditio.*
betrayer, *proditor.*
betroth, (*de*)*spondēre.*
betrothal, *sponsalia* (-*ium* or -*iorum*).
better, adj. *melior, potior* (= preferable); I am getting better, *convalesco.*
better, adv. *melius.*
better, v. transit. *meliorem facĕre, corrigĕre, emendare.*
between, *inter*, with acc.
beverage, *potio, potus* (-*ūs*).
bevy, *grex.*
bewail, *deplorare, deflēre,* (*con*)*queri.*
beware, v. *cavēre.*
bewilder, (*con*)*turbare.*
bewitch, *fascinare*; see also charm.
beyond: adv., *ultra, supra*; prep., *trans, ultra, extra, praeter.*
bias, subst. *inclinatio animi.*
bias, v. *inclinare* (*animum*).
bibulous, *bibulus.*
bid, subst. (at a sale), *licitatio.*
bid, v.: = command, *iubēre, imperare*; = invite, *invitare*; at a sale, *liceri.*
bide, *manēre.*
bier, *feretrum, sandapila.*
big, *magnus, grandis, vastus.*
bile, *bilis.*
bilge-water, *sentina.*
bill: of a bird, *rostrum*; = a proposed law, *rogatio*; to bring forward a —, *rogationem ferre*; to reject a —, *antiquare*; to carry a —, *perferre.*
billet, subst., = letter, *epistula.*
billet, v.: to billet troops, *milites per domos disponĕre.*
billow, *fluctus* (-*ūs*).
billowy, *fluctuosus.*
bind, v. (*ad*)*ligare, vincire*; fig., *obligare, adstringĕre*: to — together, *conligare, constringĕre*; to — over, *vadari.*
biographer; see historian.
biped, *bipes.*
birch, *betula.*
bird, *avis, volucris, ales*; — catcher, *auceps*; — lime, *viscum.*
birth, *ortus* (-*ūs*); of noble —, *nobili genere natus.*
birthday, *dies natalis.*
bishop, *episcopus.*
bit: of a horse, *frenum*; = piece, *frustum.*
bitch, *canis* (femina).
bite, subst., *morsus* (-*ūs*).
bite, v. *mordēre.*
biting, *mordens, mordax, acidus.*
bitter, *amarus, acerbus, acidus*; adv. *amare, acerbe.*
bitterness, *acerbitas.*
bivouac, subst. *excubiae* (-*arum*).
black, *ater, niger*; dressed in —, *sordidatus, pullatus, atratus*; a black man, *Aethiops.*
blackberry, *rubus.*
blackbird, *merula.*
blacken, v.: transit., *nigrum facĕre*; intransit., *nigrescĕre.*
Black Sea, *Pontus Euxinus.*
blacksmith, *faber* (*ferrarius*).
bladder, *vesica.*
blade: of grass, *herba*; of an oar, *palma*; of a knife, *lamina.*
blame, subst. *culpa, reprehensio, vituperatio.*
blame, v. *reprehendĕre, culpare, vituperare.*
blameless, *innocens, integer, sanctus.*
blamelessness, *innocentia, integritas, sanctitas.*
bland, *blandus, lenis, mitis*; adv. *blande.*
blandishment, *blanditia, blandimentum.*
blank, *vacuus.*
blanket, *lodix.*
blast, subst. *flamen, flatus* (-*ūs*).
blast, v. transit.; see blight.
blaze, subst. *flamma.*
blaze, v. *ardēre,* (*con*)*flagrare.*
bleach, *candidum facĕre.*
bleak; see cold.
blear-eyed, *lippus*; to be —, *lippire.*
bleat, subst. *balatus* (-*ūs*).
bleat, v. *balare.*
bleed, v. *sanguinem dare* or *effundĕre.*
blemish, subst. *vitium, mendum, macula.*
blemish, v. (*com*)*maculare.*

blend, (*com*)*miscēre.*
bless: in words, *bonis ominibus prosequi*: in gen., *beare, fortunare.*
blessed, *beatus, fortunatus.*
blessedness, *felicitas.*
blight, subst. *robigo.*
blight, v. *robigine adficĕre*; of hopes, *frustrari.*
blind, adj. *caecus, oculis captus*; adv., = rashly, *temere.*
blind, v. (*oc*)*caecare, oculis privare.*
blindfold, *oculis opertis.*
blindness, *caecitas.*
blink, *connivēre, nictare.*
bliss, *felicitas.*
blister, *pustula.*
blithe, *laetus, hilaris.*
bloated, *turgidus, tumidus.*
block, subst. *stipes, truncus, caudex.*
block, v. *claudĕre, occludĕre, opplēre, obstruĕre.*
blockade, subst. *obsessio, obsidio.*
blockade, v. *obsĭdēre, obsīdĕre, circumvallare.*
blockhead; see block.
blood, *sanguis, cruor*; = birth, race, *sanguis, genus.*
bloodless, *exsanguis, incruentus.*
blood-red, *cruentus, sanguineus.*
blood-relation, *consanguineus.*
bloodshed, *caedes.*
bloodshot, *sanguine suffusus.*
blood-stained, *cruentus.*
blood-thirsty, *sanguinarius.*
bloody, *cruentus, sanguineus.*
bloom, subst. *flos.*
bloom, v. *florēre, vigēre.*
blossom; see bloom.
blot, subst.; on paper, *litura*; in gen. *macula, labes.*
blot, v. (*com*)*maculare*; to — out, *delēre, exstinguĕre.*
blow, subst. *ictus* (*-ūs*), *plaga.*
blow, v. *flare*; to — into, *inflare*; to — on, *adflare.*
blowing, subst. *flatus* (*-ūs*).
bludgeon, *fustis.*
blue, *caeruleus.*
blunder, subst. *error, erratum, mendum.*
blunder, v. *errare.*
blunt, adj. *hebes*; fig., = rude, *agrestis, rusticus*; adv., of speech, *libere.*
blunt, v. transit. *hebetare, obtundĕre.*
blurt out, *effutire.*
blush, subst. *rubor.*
blush, v. *erubescĕre, rubēre.*
bluster, subst. *declamatio.*
bluster, v. *declamare, declamitare.*
boar, *verres*; a wild —, *aper.*
board, subst.: = plank, *tabula*; = food, *victus* (*-ūs*), *alimentum*; = body of officials, *conlegium.*
board, v.: to — over, *contabulare*; to — a ship, *navem conscendĕre*; to — with anyone, *apud hominem habitare.*
boast, *gloriari,* (*se*) *iactare.*
boaster, *iactator, homo gloriosus.*
boasting, subst. *gloriatio, iactatio.*
boastful, *gloriosus*; adv. *gloriose.*
boat, *linter, scapha, navicula.*
boatman, *nauta.*
bodily, *corporeus.*
body, *corpus* (*-oris*); a — of men, *manus, numerus, grex.*
bodyguard, *stipatores, satellites.*
bog, *palūs* (*-ūdis*).
boggy, *uliginosus, paluster.*
bogy, *terricula* (*-orum,* plur.).
boil, subst. *vomica.*
boil, v. transit., *coquĕre*; intransit., *fervēre,* (*ef*)*fervescĕre,* (*ex*)*aestuare.*
boisterous, *turbidus*; of weather, *turbulentus.*
bold, *audax, confidens, ferox, animosus*; adv. *audacter, confidenter, ferociter, animose.*
boldness, *audacia, confidentia.*
bole, *truncus, stirps.*
bolster, *cervical, culcita, pulvinus.*
bolt, subst.: = fastening, *obex, sera, pessulus*; = weapon, *telum.*
bolt, v. *claudĕre, occludĕre, obserare.*
bombast, (*verborum*) *tumor, inflata oratio.*
bombastic, *inflatus.*
bond, *vinculum, ligamentum, compes, catena*; = legal document, *chirographum, syngrapha.*
bondage, *servitūs* (*-ūtis*), *servitium.*
bone, *os* (*ossis*).
bony, *osseus.*
book, *liber, volumen, codex.*
bookseller, *bibliopola.*
boon, *beneficium.*
boorish, *agrestis, inurbanus, rusticus*; adv. *rustice, inurbane.*
boot, *calceus*; an army —, *caliga.*
bootless, *inutilis, inritus*; adv. *frustra.*
booty, *praeda.*
border, *margo*; of a stream, *ripa*; of a country, *finis.*
border, v.; to border on, *adiacere, attingĕre.*
bore, subst. *homo importunus* or *odiosus.*
bore, v.: = perforate, *perforare, terebrare*; = weary, *obtundere, defatigare, vexare*; I am bored, *taedet me.*
boredom, *taedium.*
born: to be —, *nasci.*
borrow, *mutuari, mutuum sumĕre.*
borrowed, *mutuus, alienus.*
bosom, *sinus* (*-ūs*), *pectus* (*-oris*), *gremium.*
boss, *umbo, bulla.*
botany, (*ars*) *herbaria.*
both, *ambo; uterque* (= each); both . . . and . . ., *et . . . et . . ., cum . . . tum . . .*
bother, subst. *molestia, incommodum.*
bother, v.; see annoy; = to take trouble, *curare.*
bottle, *lagena, ampulla.*
bottom, *fundus, solum*; the bottom of the sea, *imum mare.*
bough, *ramus.*
bounce, *resilire.*
bound, subst.: = limit, *finis, modus, terminus*; = jump, *saltus* (*-ūs*).
bound, v.: = limit, (*de*)*finire, terminare*; = jump, *salire.*
boundary, *finis, terminus, confinium.*
boundless, *infinitus, immensus.*
bountiful, *largus, liberalis*; adv. *large, liberaliter.*
bounty, *largitas, liberalitas, munificentia.*
bout, *certamen*; a drinking —, *comissatio.*

bow, subst.: the weapon, *arcus* (*-ūs*); of a ship, *prora*; = movement of the body, *corporis inclinatio.*
bow, v. *flectĕre, demittĕre, inclinare*; to bow to, *salutare*; fig., *obsequi, obtemperare.*
bowman, *sagittarius.*
bowstring, *nervus.*
bowels, *viscera* (*-um*), *alvus.*
bower, *umbraculum.*
bowl, subst. *crater, cratera, patera.*
bowl, v. *volvĕre.*
box, subst.: = receptacle, *arca, cista, pyxis*; the shrub, *buxus*; adj. *buxeus.*
box, v. intransit. *pugnis certare.*
boxer, *pugil.*
boy, *puer.*
boyhood, *aetas puerilis, pueritia.*
boyish, *puerilis*; adv. *pueriliter.*
brace, subst.: = strap, *fascia, vinculum*; = stay (rigid), *fibula*; = a pair, *par.*
brace, v. (*ad*)*ligare*; mentally, (*con*)*firmare.*
bracelet, *armilla.*
brackish, *amarus.*
brag; see boast.
braid, subst. *limbus*; of hair, *gradus.*
braid, v. *texĕre, nectĕre.*
brain, *cerebrum.*
bramble, *rubus, vepris.*
branch, subst. *ramus.*
branch, v. *dividi.*
brand, subst.: = firebrand, *torris, fax*; = a mark, *nota.*
brand, v. *notam inurĕre, notare.*
brandish, *vibrare, iactare.*
brass, *orichalcum.*
bravado, *iactatio.*
brave, *fortis, strenuus, animosus*; adv. *fortiter, strenue.*
bravery, *fortitudo.*
bravo! *euge! factum bene! macte!*
brawl, subst. *rixa, iurgium.*
brawl, v. *rixari.*
brawny, *robustus, lacertosus.*
brazen, *a*(*h*)*eneus, aereus*; fig., = shameless, *impudens*; — face, *os durum.*
breach, subst.: to make a —, *perfringĕre, discutĕre*; a — of treaty, *foedus ruptum* or *violatum.*
bread, *panis*; = subsistence, *victus* (*-ūs*).
breadth, *latitudo.*
break, subst. *intervallum*; — of day, *prima lux, diluculum.*
break, v. (1) transit. *frangĕre, confringĕre, rumpĕre*; to — open, *refringĕre*; fig., = to weaken, subdue, *domare, frangerĕ, infringĕre*; to — a treaty, *foedus violare*; — a promise, *fidem fallĕre.* (2) intransit. *frangi, confringi, rumpi*; to break in, *inrumpĕre*; to — out, *erumpĕre*, fig. *exoriri, exardescĕre, gliscĕre.*
breaker, *fluctus* (*-ūs*).
breakfast, *ientaculum.*
breakwater, *moles.*
breast, *pectus, animus* (fig.).
breast-plate, *lorica, thorax.*
breastwork, *pluteus, lorica.*
breath, *spiritus* (*-ūs*), *anima*; to put out of —, *exanimare.*
breathe, *spirare*; to — again, *respirare*; to — upon, *adflare*; to — out, *exhalare.*
breathless, *exanimatus, exanimis.*
breeches, *bracae*; wearing —, *bracatus.*
breed, subst. *genus* (*-eris*, n.).
breed, v. transit. *gignĕre, generare parĕre, procreare*; intransit., *nasci.*
breeding, *cultus* (*-ūs*).
breeze, *aura.*
brevity, *brevitas.*
brew, *coquĕre*; of trouble, *imminĕre, impendĕre.*
briar; see brier.
bribe, subst. *pretium.*
bribe, v. (*pretio, pecuniā, etc.*) *corrumpĕre.*
briber, *corruptor.*
bribery, *largitio*; or use verb.
brick, *later*; adj. *latericius.*
bridal, adj. *nuptialis.*
bride, bridegroom, (*nova*) *nupta,* (*novus*) *maritus.*
bridge, *pons.*
bridle, *frenum.*
bridle, v. (*in*)*frenare.*
brief, *brevis*; in —, *ne longus sim.* Adv. *breviter, paucis* (*verbis*).
brier, briar, *vepris, dumus, frutex.*
brigade, *legio.*
brigand, *latro.*
bright, *clarus, lucidus, splendidus, fulgens*; of weather, *serenus*; to be —, *clarēre.* Adv. *clare, lucide.*
brighten, v.: transit., *inlustrare, inluminare*; intransit., *clarescĕre.*
brightness, *candor, splendor, nitor fulgor*; of weather, *serenitas.*
brilliant, *splendidus, inlustris, luculentus, praeclarus.*
brim, *ora, margo, labrum.*
Brindisi, *Brundisium.*
brine, *muria, salsamentum.*
bring: by carrying, (*ad*)*ferre,* (*ap*)*portare*; by leading, etc., (*ad*)*ducĕre*: to — back, *referre, reducĕre*; to — together, *cogĕre*; to — about, *efficĕre* (*ut*); to — forward, *in medium proferre*; to — in, yield, *reddĕre*; to — up, *educare.*
brink, *margo, ripa.*
brisk, *alacer, vegetus.*
briskness, *alacritas.*
bristle, subst. *saeta.*
bristle, v. *horrēre.*
bristly, *saetosus.*
brittle, *fragilis.*
broach, *aperire.*
broad, *latus, amplus*; adv. *late.*
broil, subst. *rixa.*
broil, v. *torrēre.*
bronze, subst. *aes.*
bronze, adj. *a*(*h*)*eneus, aereus.*
brooch, *fibula.*
brood, subst. *fetus* (*-ūs*).
brood, v. *incubare.*
brook, subst. *rivus, rivulus.*
brook, v. *ferre, tolerare.*
broom: the plant, *genista*; for sweeping, *scopae* (*-arum*, plur.).
broth, *ius* (*iuris*).
brother, *frater.*

brotherhood, = association, *societas, sodalitas.*
brotherly, *fraternus.*
brow: = eyebrow, *supercilium*; = forehead, *frons*; of a hill, *summus collis.*
brown, *fuscus, fulvus.*
bruise, v. *contundĕre.*
bruit, v. (*di*)*vulgare.*
brush, subst. *penicillus*; see broom.
brush, v. transit. *verrĕre,* (*de*)*tergĕre.*
brush-wood, *virgultum, sarmentum.*
brutal, *ferus, inhumanus, immanis*; adv. *inhumane, immaniter.*
brutality, *immanitas.*
brute, *pecus, belua*; see beast.
bubble, subst. *bulla.*
buccaneer, *pirata, praedo.*
bucket, *situla, hama.*
buckle, *fibula.*
buckler, *scutum, clipeus, parma.*
bud, subst. *gemma, germen.*
bud, v. *gemmare.*
budge, *loco cedĕre.*
buff, *luteus.*
buffalo, *bos.*
buffet, = blow, *alapa, colaphus.*
buffoon, *sannio, scurra.*
buffoonery, *scurrilitas.*
bug, *cimex* (*-icis*).
bugbear; see bogy.
bugle, *bucina.*
build, *aedificare,* (*ex*)*struĕre.*
builder, *aedificator, structor.*
building, subst.: the process, *aedificatio, exstructio*; the thing built, *aedificium.*
bulb, *bulbus.*
bulk, *magnitudo, amplitudo, moles.*
bulky, *amplus, ingens.*
bull, *taurus.*
bullock, *iuvencus.*
bullet, *glans.*
bullion, *aurum, argentum.*
bulrush, *iuncus, scirpus.*
bulwark, *propugnaculum.*
bump, subst.: = swelling, *tumor, tuber*; = bang, *ictus* (*-ūs*).
bump, v.: to bump into, *offendĕre.*
bumper; see cup.
bunch, of fruit, *racemus, uva*; see bundle.
bundle, *fascis, manipulus, sarcina.*
bung, *obturamentum.*
buoyant, *levis.* Transf., *hilaris.*
burden, subst. *onus* (*-eris*): beast of —, *iumentum.*
burden, v. *onerare, opprimĕre.*
burdensome, *gravis, molestus.*
bureau, *scrinium.*
burgess, burgher, *municeps, civis.*
burglar, *fur.*
burglary, *furtum.*
burial, *sepultura, humatio.*
burial-ground, *sepulturae locus, sepulcrum.*
burn, v. transit., = set on fire, *incendĕre*; to burn up, *comburĕre,* (*con*)*cremare*; intransit., = to blaze, *ardēre, flagare.*
burnish, *polire.*
burrow, *cuniculus.*
burst, v. transit. (*di*)*rumpĕre.*
bury, *humare, sepelire.*
bush, *frutex, dumus.*
bushy, *fruticosus.*
bushel, *medimnus.*
business, *res, negotium.*
buskin, *cothurnus.*
bust, *effigies.*
bustle, subst. *festinatio, trepidatio.*
bustle, v. *festinare, trepidare.*
busy, *occupatus, negotiosus*; adv. *sedulo, industrie.*
busy-body, *ardelio.*
but: = except, *praeter*; all but, *tantum non*; = only, *modo, tantum, solum*; as adversat. conj., *sed, verum, at; atqui* (= and yet); *tamen* (= however); but if, *sin, quodsi.*
butcher, *lanius.*
butcher, v. *caedĕre*; of persons, *trucidare.*
butchery, *caedes.*
butler, *cellarius, promus.*
butt, = object of ridicule, *ludibrium.*
butt, v. *arietare, cornu petĕre.*
butterfly, *papilio.*
buttocks, *clunes* (*-ium*), *nates* (*-ium*), *pyga.*
buttress, v. *fulcire.*
buxom, *hilaris.*
buy, v. (*co*)*emĕre, mercari.*
buyer, *emptor.*
by: of place, *ad, apud, iuxta, prope*; to go —, *praeterire*; to stand —, *adesse*; of time, — night, *noctu, nocte*; — moonlight, *ad lunam*; of means or manner, *per* with acc.; of agency, *ab* (*homine*); in adjuration, *per* with acc.; of distribution, one — one, *singuli, singillatim.*
by-way, *trames* (*-itis*), *semita, deverticulum.*
by-word: to become a —, *contemptui esse.*

C

cabbage, *brassica, caulis.*
cabin, *casa, tugurium.*
cabinet: = room, *conclave*; = cupboard, desk, etc., *armarium, thesaurus, scrinium.*
cable, *ancorale, funis ancorarius.*
cackle, *strepĕre.*
cadaverous, *exsanguis.*
cadence, *numerus.*
cadet, *tiro.*
Cadiz, *Gades* (*-ium,* plur.).
cage, *cavea.*
cajolery, *blanditiae* (*-arum*).
cake, subst. *placenta.*
cake, v., = stick together, *concrescĕre.*
calamitous, *calamitosus, luctuosus.*
calamity, *calamitas, clades.*
calculate, *computare.*
calculated, *accommodatus, aptus, idoneus.*
calculation, *ratio.*
caldron, *a*(*h*)*enum, cortina.*
calendar, *fasti* (*-orum*).
calf, *vitulus, vitula*; — of the leg, *sura.*
call, subst.: = cry, *vox*; = visit, *salutatio.*
call, v.: = cry out, *clamare*; = name, *vocare, nominare, appellare*; = summon, (*ad*)*vocare*; to — together.

convocare; to — for, = to demand, (*de*)*poscere*, *flagitare*; to — on, = visit, *salutare*, *visěre*.
caller, = visitor, *salutator*.
callous, *callosus*. Transf., *durus*.
calm, subst. *quies*, *tranquillitas*, *otium*, *pax*; — at sea, *malacia*.
calm, adj. *quietus*, *tranquillus*, *placidus*; adv. *tranquille*, *placide; aequo animo*.
calm, v. *sedare*, *lenire*, *tranquillare*.
calumniate, *calumniari*, *criminari*.
calumniator, *obtrectator*.
calumny, *criminatio*, *calumnia*.
camel, *camelus*.
camp, *castra* (-*orum*).
campaign, *stipendium*.
can, subst.; see jug.
can, v. *posse*; see able.
canal, *fossa*.
cancel, *delēre*, *tollěre*.
candid, *liber*, *apertus*, *verus*, *simplex*; adv. *libere*, *aperte*.
candidate, *candidatus*.
candour, *libertas*, *candor*.
candle, *candela*.
candlestick, *candelabrum*.
cane, subst. *harundo*, *calamus*; for walking, *baculum*; for correction, *ferula*.
cane, v. (*ferulā*) *verberare*.
canine, *caninus*.
canker, v. *corrumpěre*.
cannon, *tormentum*.
canoe, *cymba*.
canon, = a rule, *lex*, *regula*, *norma*.
canopy, *aulaeum*.
canton, *pagus*.
canvas, in a sail, *carbasus*, *velum*.
canvass, *ambire*.
canvassing, *ambitio*, *ambitus* (-*ūs*).
cap, *pileus*, *galerus*.
capability, *facultas*.
capable, *aptus*, *idoneus*; often rendered by *posse*.
capacious, *capax*, *amplus*.
caparison, *phalerae* (-*arum*, plur.).
capital, subst.: = chief city, *caput*; or use *urbs* with adj.: of a pillar, *capitulum*; of money, *sors*, *caput*.
capital, adj., *capitalis*; see excellent, etc.
capitulate; see surrender.
caprice, *libido*, *levitas*.
capricious, *inconstans*, *levis*.
captain, *princeps*, *dux*; of a ship, *navarchus*, *magister*.
captious, *morosus*, *difficilis*.
captivate, *capěre*.
captive, *captus*, *captivus*.
captivity, *captivitas*.
capture, *capěre*, *comprehenděre*.
car, *carrus*, *cisium*, *plaustrum*, *vehiculum*.
caravan, *comitatus* (-*ūs*).
carcase, *cadaver*.
card, subst. *charta*.
card, v. *pectěre*.
care, subst.: = attention, caution, *cura*, *diligentia*; = anxiety, *cura*, *sollicitudo*; = management, *cura*, *curatio*.
care, v.; to — for, — about, *curare*.
career, *curriculum*, *cursus* (-*ūs*).
careful, *diligens*, *accuratus*, *attentus*; adv. *diligenter*, *accurate*.
careless, *neglegens*.
carelessness, *imprudentia*, *neglegentia*, *incuria*.
caress, subst. *complexus* (-*ūs*)
caress, v. *blandiri*, *permulcēre*.
caressing, *blandus*.
cargo, *onus* (-*eris*).
carnage, *caedus*, *strages*.
carnal, render by genit. *corporis*.
carnival, *feriae* (-*arum*).
carousal, *comissatio*, *potatio*.
carouse, v. *comissari*, *potare*.
carp, v.: to — at, *carpěre*, *vellicare*.
carpenter, *faber* (*tignarius*).
carpet, *tapeta* (-*ae*), *tapeta* (-*orum*), *tapetia* (-*ium*).
carriage: = act of carrying, *gestura*; = bearing, *habitus*; = vehicle, *vehiculum*.
carrier, *gerulus*; letter —, *tabellarius*.
carry, *ferre*, *portare*, *vehěre*, *gerěre*; to — out (= perform), *conficěre*, *exsequi*.
cart, *plaustrum*.
carve, *caelare*, *scalpěre*, *sculpěre*: to — meat, *scindere*, *secare*.
carver, *caelator*, *sculptor*.
carving, *caelatura*, *scalptura*, *sculptura*.
cascade, *aquae ex alto desilientes*.
case: = receptacle, *theca*, *involucrum*; gram., *casus* (-*ūs*); judicial, *causa*; = chance, *res*, *casus* (-*ūs*).
casement, *fenestra*.
cash, subst. *pecunia praesens* or *numerata*.
cash, v. *praesenti pecunia solvěre*.
cashier, v. = discharge, *exauctorare*.
cask, *dolium*, *cupa*.
casket, *arcula*, *capsula*.
casque, *galea*, *cassis*.
cast, subst., = throw, *iactus* (-*ūs*).
cast, v. *iacěre*, *conicěre*, *iactare*, *mittěre*; to — in metal, *funděre*; to be — down, *adfligi*.
castaway, *perditus*, *profligatus*; by ship-wreck, *naufragus*.
castigate; see punish.
castle, *castellum*.
casual, *fortuitus*, *forte oblatus*; adv. *forte*, *casu*, *fortuito*.
cat, *feles* (or *felis*).
catalogue, *index*.
catapult, *catapulta*.
cataract, in the eye, *glaucoma*; see also cascade.
catarrh, *gravedo*, *pituita*.
catastrophe; see disaster.
catch, *capěre*, *excipěre*, *deprehenděre*, *comprehenděre*; to — up, *adsequi*, *consequi*; to — fire, *ignem concipěre*.
categorical, *simplex*, *definitus*.
category, *genus* (-*eris*), *numerus*.
cater, *obsonare*.
caterpillar, *eruca*.
cattle, *boves*; coll., *pecus* (-*oris*); a head of —, *pecus* (-*udis*).
cauldron; see caldron.
cause, subst. *causa; materia* (= occasion, ground); *res* (= case, affair).
cause, v. transit., *facěre*, *efficěre* (*ut*); *movēre*, *excitare*.
causeway, *agger*.

caustic, *mordax, acerbus.*
cauterize, *adurĕre.*
caution, = care, *cautio, cura, prudentia.*
caution, v. *monēre.*
cautious, *providus, prudens, cautus*; adv. *prudenter, caute.*
cavalcade, *comitatus* (*-ūs*).
cavalier = horseman, *eques.*
cavalierly, *adroganter, insolenter.*
cavalry, *equitatus, equites* (*-um,* plur.).
cave, *caverna, specus, spelunca, antrum.*
cavil; see carp.
cavity; see hole.
cease, *desinĕre, desistĕre.*
ceaseless, *perpetuus, adsiduus;* adv. *perpetuo, adsidue.*
cedar, *cedrus.*
cede, *concedĕre.*
ceiling, *tectum.*
celebrate, *celebrare.*
celebrated, *celeber, clarus, inlustris.*
celebration, *celebratio.*
celebrity, *gloria, laus*; = celebrated person, *vir insignis.*
celerity, *celeritas.*
celestial, *caelestis, divinus.*
cell, *cella, cubiculum.*
cellar, *cella*; a wine — *apotheca.*
cement, subst. *gluten.*
cemetery, *sepulchra* (*-orum*).
censor, *censor.*
censorious, *severus.*
censure, subst. *reprehensio, vituperatio.*
censure, v. *reprehendĕre, vituperare.*
census, *census* (*-ūs*); to take a census, *censēre.*
centaur, *centaurus.*
centre, subst. *media pars*; or use *medius* (e.g. the — of the city, *media urbs*).
centurion, *centurio.*
century, *centum anni, saeculum.*
ceremonious, *sollemnis.*
ceremony, *ritus* (*-ūs*), *caerimonia.*
certain, *certus, stabilis, fidus* (= trustworthy); a — person, *quidam*; to know for —, *certo scire.*
certainly, *certo*; in answers, *profecto, sane*; = admittedly, *certe, quidem, sane.*
certify, *confirmare.*
cessation, *intermissio.*
chafe, v.: transit., *calefacĕre*; intransit., *stomachari, aestuare.*
chaff, *palea.*
chagrin, *aegritudo, stomachus, dolor.*
chain, subst., *catena, vinculum*; = series, *series.*
chain, v. *vincire.*
chair, *sella, sedile, cathedra.*
chalice, *calix.*
chalk, *creta.*
challenge, (*ad pugnam*) *provocare*
chamber, *cubiculum.*
champ, *mandĕre.*
champion, *propugnator, defensor.*
chance, *casus* (*-ūs*), *fors*; by —, *forte, casu.*
chance, v. *accidĕre*; see also happen, risk.
change, subst. (*com*)*mutatio, vicissitudo.*
change, v.: transit., (*com*)*mutare, convertĕre*; intransit., (*com*)*mutari.*
changeable, *mutabilis, inconstans, varius.*
changeableness, *mutabilitas, varietas.*
changeling, *puer subditus.*
channel, *fossa, canalis, fretum.*
chant, v. *canĕre, cantare.*
chaos, *chaos, confusio, perturbatio.*
chaotic, *confusus, perturbatus.*
chapel, *aedicula, sacellum.*
chapter, of a book, *caput.*
character: = symbol, letter, *littera*; = disposition, nature, *natura, ingenium, mores* (*-um*); = part played, *persona, partes* (*-ium*); = reputation, *fama, existimatio.*
characteristic, subst. *proprietas.*
characteristic, adj. *proprius*; adj. *proprie, more suo.*
characterize, *notare, designare.*
charcoal, *carbo.*
charge, subst.: = price, *pretium*; = command, *mandatum*; = care (of), *cura, custodia*; = accusation, *accusatio, crimen*; = attack, *impetus* (*-ūs*), *incursus* (*-ūs*).
charge, v. to — to a person, *homini imputare*; to — with a duty, (*homini*) *committĕre, mandare.*; = accuse, *accusare, insimulare*; = attack, *invadĕre, impetum facĕre, incurrĕre.*
charger: = dish, *lanx*; = horse, *equus.*
chariot, *currus* (*-ūs*).
charioteer, *auriga.*
charitable, *benignus, liberalis, beneficus*; adv. *benigne, liberaliter.*
charity, *benignitas*; as conduct, *beneficentia, liberalitas.*
Charles, *Carolus.*
charm, subst.: = magic formula, *carmen*; = amulet, *fascinum*; = attraction, *blandimentum, dulcedo, lepor.*
charm, v.: by magic, *fascinare*; see delight.
charming, *suavis, lepidus*; of country, *amoenus.*
chart, *tabula.*
chary, *parcus.*
chase, subst. *venatio, venatus* (*-ūs*).
chase, v. *venari*; = engrave, *caelare.*
chasm, *hiatus* (*-ūs*), *specus* (*-ūs*).
chaste, *castus, pudicus.*
chastise, *castigare*; see punish.
chastisement, *castigatio, animadversio.*
chastity, *castitas, pudicitia.*
chat, subst. *sermo.*
chat, v. *fabulari, garrire.*
chatter, *garrulitas.*
chattering, *garrulus, loquax.*
cheap, *vilis.*
cheat, subst.: = deception, *fraus, dolus*; = deceiver, *circumscriptor, fraudator.*
cheat, v. *fallĕre, decipĕre, fraudare.*
check, subst. *impedimentum, mora.*
check, v. *continēre, impedire, reprimĕre.*
cheek, *gena*; puffed out, *bucca.*
cheer, subst.: = shout, *clamor*; to be of good —, *bono animo esse.*
cheer, v. = shout, *clamare*; = gladden *exhilarare, erigĕre.*
cheerful, *hilaris, laetus*; adv. *hilare laete.*
cheering, subst. *favor.*
cheerless, *tristis, maestus.*

cheese, *caseus.*
chequered, *varius.*
cherish, *fovēre, colĕre, tuēri.*
cherry, *cerasus.*
chest, *pectus* (*-oris*); = receptacle, *arca, cista.*
Chester, *Deva.*
chestnut, *castanea.*
chew, *mandĕre.*
chicanery, *dolus, calumnia.*
chicken, *pullus* (*gallinaceus*).
chide, *obiurgare, increpare.*
chiding, *obiurgatio.*
chief, subst. *caput, princeps, dux.*
chief, adj. *primus, praecipuus*; adv. *praecipue.*
chieftain, *regulus.*
child: male, *filius*; female, *filia*: a small —, *infans*; children, *pueri, liberi.*
child-birth, *partus* (*-ūs*).
childhood, *pueritia, aetas puerilis.*
childish, *puerilis*; adv. *pueriliter.*
childless, (*liberis*) *orbus.*
chill, subst. *horror, frigus* (*-oris*).
chill, v. *refrigerare.*
chin, *mentum.*
china, use *murra*; adj. *murrinus.*
chink, *rima.*
chip, *assula.*
chirp, *pipilare.*
chisel, subst. *scalprum, caelum.*
chivalrous, *magnanimus.*
chivalry, as an institution, *ordo equester*; as a spirit, *magnanimitas.*
choice, subst. *delectus* (*-ūs*), *magnanimitas.*
choice, adj. *electus, eximius.*
choir, *chorus.*
choke, v. *suffocare, animam intercludĕre.*
choler; see anger.
choose, v. *eligĕre, diligĕre.*
chop, *abscidĕre, praecīdĕre.*
chord, *nervus.*
chorus, *chorus.*
Christ, *Christus.*
Christian, *Christianus.*
chronic, *longinquus, diuturnus.*
chronicle, subst. *annales* (*-ium*).
chronicle, v. transit., *in annales referre.*
chronicler, *annalium scriptor.*
chronology, *temporum* (or *rerum*) *ordo.*
church, *ecclesia.*
churlish, *agrestis, rusticus, inurbanus.*
cinder, *cinis.*
cipher, subst.: = a secret writing, *notae*; = a nobody, *numerus.*
cipher, v. *computare.*
circle, *orbis, circulus*; of people, *corona.*
circuit, *circuitus* (*-ūs*), *orbis, circulus.*
circular, *rotundus.*
circulate, v. transit. *circumagĕre, dispergĕre*; of news, etc., *divulgare.*
circumlocution, *circumitio verborum.*
circumnavigate, *circumvehi* (*navi*).
circumscribe, *circumscribĕre, definire.*
circumspect, *cautus, providus, prudens.*
circumspection, *cautio, prudentia.*
circumstance, *res, tempus*: according to —s, *pro re* (*natā*); in these —s, *quae cum ita sint.*
circumvallation, *circummunitio.*
circumvent, *circumvenire, circumscribĕre.*
cistern, *cisterna, lacus, puteus.*
citadel, *arx.*
cite, v. *proferre, memorare*; before a court, *citare, in ius vocare.*
citizen, *civis.*
citizenship, *civitas.*
city, *urbs.*
civic, *civilis, civicus.*
civil: = civic, *civilis, civicus*: — war, *bellum civile, intestinum, domesticum*; = polite, *urbanus*; adv. *urbane.*
civilization, *cultus* (*-ūs*), *humanitas.*
civilize, *expolire.*
civilized, *humanus.*
clad, *vestitus.*
claim, v. *postulare, vindicare*; to — back, *repetĕre.*
claimant (at law), *petitor.*
clammy, *lentus.*
clamour, subst. *vociferatio, clamor.*
clamour, v. (*con*)*clamare, vociferari.*
clan, *gens, tribus* (*-ūs*).
clandestine, *clandestinus, furtivus*; adv. *clam, furtim.*
clang, subst. *sonus* (*-ūs*), *sonitus* (*-ūs*).
clang, v. *strepĕre,* (*re*)*sonare.*
clank, subst. *crepitus* (*-ūs*), *strepitus* (*-ūs*).
clank, v. *crepare, crepitare.*
clap, subst.: of hands, *plausus* (*-ūs*); of thunder, *tonitrus* (*-ūs*).
clap, v. (*manibus*) *plaudĕre.*
clash, subst.: = collision, *concursus* (*-ūs*); = loud noise, *crepitus* (*-ūs*), *strepitus* (*-ūs*).
clash, v. *concrepare*; = disagree, *inter se* (*re*)*pugnare, dissidēre, discrepare.*
clasp, subst.: = fastener, *fibula*; see also embrace, grasp.
class, *genus* (*-eris*), *classis, ordo.*
classical, from the Roman point of view, *Graecus.*
classify, *in genera describĕre.*
clatter, subst. *crepitus* (*-ūs*), *strepitus* (*-ūs*).
clatter, v. *crepare, strepĕre.*
clause, *pars, membrum, caput.*
claw, *unguis.*
clay, *argilla.*
clean, adj. *purus, mundus.*
clean, v. *purgare.*
cleanliness, *munditia, mundities.*
clear, adj. *clarus*; of weather, *serenus, lucidus*; of style, *lucidus*; = evident, intelligible, *planus, manifestus*; it is —, *apparet, liquet.* Adv. *clare, plane, manifeste, lucide.*
clear, v. *expedire, purgare*; to — up a matter, *expedire, explicare.*
clearness, *claritas*; of weather, *serenitas.*
cleave: = split, (*dif*)*findĕre, scindĕre*; = stick, (*ad*)*haerēre.*
cleaver, *culter.*
cleft, *rima.*
clemency, *clementia, mansuetudo.*
clement, *clemens, mansuetus, indulgens, lenis.*
clench: to — the fist, *digitos comprimĕre.*

clerk, *scriba.*
clever, *sollers, callidus, astutus*; adv. *sollerter, callide, astute.*
cleverness, *sollertia, calliditas.*
client, *cliens, consultor.*
cliff, *scopulus, cautes.*
climate, *caelum.*
climax, *gradatio.*
climb, subst. *ascensus* (*-ūs*).
climb, v. *scandĕre, ascendĕre, eniti.*
cling, (*ad*)*haerēre, amplecti.*
clip, *tondēre, praecidĕre, resecare.*
cloak, subst. *amiculum, pallium*; for journeys, *lacerna*; a soldier's —, *sagum.*
cloak, v. *dissimulare, tegĕre.*
clod, *glaeba.*
clog, v. *impedire.*
cloister, *porticus* (*-ūs*).
close, subst., = end, *finis, exitus.*
close, adj.: = reserved, *taciturnus, tectus*; = niggardly, *parcus*; = near, *propinquus, vicinus, finitimus*; = closely packed, *densus, confertus, artus*; adv. *arte, dense.*
close, adv. *prope, iuxta.*
close, v.: transit., = shut, *claudĕre, occludĕre*; = finish, *finire*; intransit., = be shut, *claudi*; = come to an end, *finiri.*
closeness, = nearness, *propinquitas, vicinitas.*
closet, *cubiculum.*
clot, subst., of blood, *sanguis concretus.*
clot, v. *concrescĕre.*
cloth, *textum, textile.*
clothe, v. *vestire, amicire.*
clothes, clothing, *vestis, vestimenta* (*-orum*).
cloud, subst. *nubes, nimbus.*
cloud, v. *obscurare.*
cloudless, *serenus.*
cloudy, *nubilus.*
clownish, *rusticus, agrestis.*
cloy, *satiare, saturare.*
club, subst.: = cudgel, *clava, fustis*; = association, *circulus, sodalitas.*
clubfooted, *scaurus.*
clue, *glomus* (*-eris*), *filum*; = indication, *indicium.*
clump, *globus.*
clumsiness, *inscitia.*
clumsy, *inhabilis, ineptus, inscitus*; adv. *inepte, inscite.*
cluster, = bunch, *racemus, uva.*
clutch, *comprehendĕre, adripĕre.*
coach; see carriage.
coachman, *raedarius, auriga.*
coagulate, v. *coire, concrescĕre.*
coal, *carbo*; a live —, *pruna.*
coalesce, *coalescĕre, coire.*
coalition, *coniunctio, consociatio.*
coarse, *crassus*; of behaviour, etc., *incultus, inurbanus.* Adv. *crasse*; *inculte.*
coarseness, *crassitudo; mores inculti.*
coast, subst. *litus* (*-oris*), *ora*; on the —, adj., *maritimus.*
coast, v. *oram legĕre, praetervehi.*
coat, *toga, tunica*; = hide, *vellus* (*-eris*), *pellis.*
coax, *blandiri, permulcēre.*
cobble, (*re*)*sarcire.*
cobbler, *sutor.*
cock, *gallus* (*gallinaceus*).
code, *leges.*
coerce, *coercēre, cohibēre, cogĕre.*
coercion, *coercitio, vis.*
coffer, *cista, arca.*
coffin, *arca, capulus.*
cog, of a wheel, *dens.*
cogency, *pondus* (*-eris*), *vis.*
cogent, *firmus, validus, gravis.*
cogitate, *cogitare.*
cognizance, *cognitio.*
cognizant, *conscius.*
coheir, *coheres.*
cohere, *cohaerēre.*
coherent, *cohaerens, contextus, congruens.*
cohort, *cohors.*
coin, *nummus.*
coin, v. transit. *cudĕre, signare.*
coinage, *res nummaria.*
coincide, *congruĕre, eodem tempore fieri.*
coincidence, = chance; q.v.
Colchester, *Camulodunum.*
cold, subst. *frigus* (*-oris*), *algor*; in the head, *gravedo.*
cold, *frigidus, gelidus*: to be —, *frigēre, algēre;* adv. *frigide, gelide.*
collapse, v. *conlabi, concidĕre, corruĕre.*
collar, subst. *monile, torques.*
collate, v. transit. *conferre.*
collation: = comparison, *conlatio*; = meal, *cena.*
colleague, *conlega.*
collect, v.: transit. *conligĕre, congerĕre*; to — money, etc., *exigĕre*; intransit., *convenire, coire.*
collection, *conlatio, congeries.*
college, *conlegium, societas, sodalitas.*
collide, *confligĕre.*
collision, *concursus* (*-ūs*), *concursio.*
collocation, *conlocatio.*
colloquial; — speech, *sermo humilis.*
colloquy, *conloquium.*
collusion, *conlusio, praevaricatio.*
Cologne, *Colonia Agrippina.*
colonel, *tribunus militum, praefectus.*
colonist, *colonus.*
colonnade, *porticus* (*-ūs*).
colony, *colonia.*
colossal, *vastus, ingens.*
colour, subst. *color*; = paint, *pigmentum.*
colour, v. *colorare, tingĕre, inficĕre*; intransit., see blush.
colt, *eculeus.*
column: = pillar, *columna*; milit., *agmen.*
comb, *pecten*; of a cock, *crista.*
comb, v. (*de*)*pectĕre.*
combat, subst. *pugna, certamen.*
combat, v.: see fight.
combination (*con*)*iunctio, societas.*
combine, v. transit. (*con*)*iungĕre, consociare.*
come, *venire, pervenire, advenire, accedĕre*; to — about, *fieri;* to — back, *redire*; to — together, *convenire*; to — upon, *invenire.*
comedy, *comoedia.*
comeliness, *venustas, decor, pulchritudo.*
comely, *bellus, venustus, pulcher.*
comet, *cometes* (*-ae*).

comfort, subst.; = consolation, *solatium, consolatio*; —s, *commoda* (-*orum*).
comfort, v. (*con*)*solari, adlevare.*
comfortable, *commodus.*
comforter, *consolator.*
comic, comical: = of comedy, *comicus*; = ridiculous, *ridiculus, facetus*; adv. *ridicule, facete.*
coming, subst. *adventus* (-*ūs*).
command, subst.; = right to give orders, *imperium*; supreme —, *summa imperii*; = an order given, *imperium, iussum, mandatum*; a — of the senate, *decretum.*
command, v. (*hominem*) *iubērē*, (*homini*) *imperare*; of places, = dominate, *imminĕre, despectare.*
commander, *dux, imperator, praefectus.*
commemorate, *celebrare.*
commemoration, *celebratio.*
commence, *incipĕre*; see begin.
commend: = commit, entrust, *commendare, committĕre, credĕre*; = praise, *laudare, commendare, probare.*
commendable, *laudabilis.*
commendation, *commendatio, laus.*
commendatory, *commendaticius.*
comment, subst. *dictum.*
comment, v. *sententiam dicĕre, censēre.*
commentator, *interpres, explanator.*
commerce, *commercium, negotia* (-*orum*), *mercatura.*
commiserate, (*com*)*miserari*; see pity.
commissariat, *res frumentaria, commeatus* (-*ūs*).
commission, subst. = allotted task, *mandatum*; = position of trust, *munus* (-*eris*).
commission, v. *mandare.*
commit: = entrust, *mandare, commendare, committĕre, credĕre*; = do, perpetrate, *facĕre, committĕre, patrare*; = oblige, engage, *obligare, obstringĕre.*
committee, *consilium.*
commodious, *commodus, opportunus, aptus*; adv. *commode, opportune, apte.*
commodity, *res, merx.*
common, subst. *ager publicus.*
common, adj.: = belonging to several or all, *communis*; = belonging to people or state, *publicus*; = commonplace, ordinary, *vulgaris, quotidianus*; the — people, *plebs.* Adv., = usually, *fere, ferme, plerumque.*
commonplace, subst. *locus communis.*
commonwealth, *respublica, civitas.*
commotion, *tumultus* (-*ūs*), *motus* (-*ūs*).
commune, *conloqui.*
communicate, *communicare*; see also share, tell.
communication, *communicatio.*
communicative, *loquax.*
communion, *commercium, societas.*
community, = state, society, *civitas, respublica.*
commute; see exchange.
compact, subst. *pactio, pactum, conventus* (-*ūs*).
compact, adj. *densus, crassus, confertus*; adv. *confertim.*
companion, *comes, socius, sodalis.*
companionable, *adfabilis, facilis.*
company, *societas*; milit., *manipulus.*
comparable, *comparabilis.*
comparative, *comparativus.*
compare, *comparare, componĕre, conferre.*
comparison, *comparatio, conlatio*; **in** — with, *prae, ad.*
compass, subst.: = extent, *ambitus* (-*ūs*), *circuitus* (-*ūs*); a pair of —es, *circinus.*
compass, v.; see encompass, accomplish.
compassion, *misericordia.*
compassionate, *misericors.*
compatible, *congruens, conveniens.*
compatriot, *civis.*
compel, *cogĕre, compellĕre, adigĕre.*
compendious, *brevis.*
compensate; to — for, *compensare, rependĕre.*
compensation, *compensatio.*
compete, *contendĕre, certare.*
competent: see able: to be —, *competĕre.*
competition, *contentio, certamen, certatio.*
competitor, *competitor.*
compile, *componĕre.*
complacent, *qui sibi placet.*
complain, (*con*)*queri.*
complaint, *questus* (-*ūs*), *querimonia, querela*; = illness, *morbus.*
complaisance, *obsequium, obsequentia, indulgentia.*
complaisant, *indulgens, facilis, obsequens.*
complement, *complementum.*
complete, adj. *absolutus, perfectus, iustus*; adv. *omnino, prorsus.*
complete, v. *complēre, explēre, absolvĕre, conficĕre.*
completion, *confectio, absolutio, finis.*
complex, *multiplex.*
complexion, *color.*
compliance, *obsequium.*
complicate, *impedire.*
complicated, *involutus, impeditus.*
complication, *implicatio.*
compliment, *laus*; to pay —s, *laudare.*
complimentary, *honorificus.*
comply, v. *obsequi,* (*con*)*cedĕre, morem gerĕre.*
components, *partes* (-*ium*).
compose: = make up, constitute, *componĕre, efficĕre*; of literature, *componĕre, scribĕre.*
composed, = calm, *tranquillus.*
composer, *scriptor.*
composition: the act, *compositio*; literary, *scriptio, scriptura*; the product, *scriptum.*
composure, *tranquillitas, aequus animus.*
compound, adj. *compositus, multiplex.*
compound, v. *miscēre, confundĕre.*
comprehend: = contain, *continēre, complecti*; = understand, (*mente*) *comprehendĕre, complecti, intellegĕre.*
comprehension, *comprehensio, intellegentia.*
comprehensive, *late patens.*
compress, *comprimĕre, condensare.*
compression, of style, *compressio.*
compromise, v.: = to settle, *componĕre,*

compromittĕre; = to embarrass, *impedire*.
compulsion, *vis, necessitas*; under —, *coactus -a -um*.
compunction, *paenitentia*.
compute, *computare*.
comrade, *socius, comes, sodalis*.
comradeship, *sodalitas, contubernium*.
concave, (*con*)*cavus*.
conceal, *celare, occulĕre, occultare, abdĕre*.
concede, (*con*)*cedĕre, permittĕre*.
conceit; render by *sibi placēre*.
conceive: physically, *concipĕre*; mentally, *concipĕre, intellegĕre, comprehendĕre*.
concentrate: = bring together, *conligĕre, contrahĕre*; to — on, = attend to, (*animum*) *attendĕre*.
conception: physical, *conceptio, conceptus* (-*ūs*); mental, *notio, opinio*.
concern, subst.: = affair, *res, negotium*; = anxiety, *cura, anxietas, sollicitudo*.
concern, v. *pertinēre, attinēre*; it —s, *interest, refert*.
concerning, = about, *de*.
conciliate, *conciliare*.
conciliation, *conciliatio*.
conciliatory, *pacificus, blandus*.
concise, *brevis, pressus, adstrictus*; adv. *adstricte, breviter*.
conciseness, *brevitas*.
conclave; see assembly.
conclude: = finish, *finire, conficĕre*; = draw a conclusion, *concludĕre, conligĕre*.
conclusion, *finis, conclusio*.
conclusive, *gravis, certus*.
concoct, *miscēre*; fig., *fingĕre, excogitare, conflare*.
concoction, *potus* (-*ūs*).
concord, *concordia, consensus* (-*ūs*).
concordant, *concors*.
concourse, *concursus* (-*ūs*), *concursio*.
concrete, = solid, *solidus*.
concur, *consentire, congruĕre*.
concurrence, *consensio, consensus* (-*ūs*).
concurrently, *una, simul*.
condemn, *damnare, condemnare*.
condemnation, *damnatio, condemnatio*.
condense, v. transit., *densare, spissare*; intransit., *concrescĕre*.
condensed, *densus, spissus, concretus*; of style, *pressus, densus*.
condescend, *se submittĕre, descendĕre*.
condescending, *comis, facilis*.
condescension, *comitas, facilitas*.
condign, = due, *debitus, meritus*.
condiment, *condimentum*.
condition: = state, *condicio, status* (-*ūs*); = stipulation, *condicio, pactum, lex*.
conditioned, adj. *adfectus*.
condole, *casum* (*hominis*) *dolēre*.
conduce, *conducĕre* (*ad rem*).
conducive, *utilis*.
conduct, subst.: = behaviour, *vita, mores* (-*um*, plur.); = management, *administratio*.
conduct, v.: = lead, (*de*)*ducĕre*; = manage, *gerĕre, administrare*.
conductor, *dux*.
conduit, *canalis*.
cone, *conus, meta*.

confederacy, *foedus* (-*eris*, n.), *societas*.
confederates, *socii, foederati*.
confer: = give, *conferre, tribuĕre*; = talk, *conloqui, consultare*.
conference, *conloquium*.
confess, *fateri, confiteri*.
confession, *confessio*.
confidant, *conscius* (f. *conscia*).
confide: = entrust, *committĕre, mandare, credĕre*; to — in, (*con*)*fidere*.
confidence, *fides, fiducia, confidentia*.
confident, (*con*)*fidens*; adv. (*con*)*fidenter*.
confidential; see secret.
confiding, adj. *credulus*.
confine, subst. *finis, terminus, confinium*.
confine, v. *includĕre, coercēre, cohibēre*.
confined, adj. *artus*.
confinement, *inclusio*; = imprisonment, *custodia*.
confirm, (*con*)*firmare*; = ratify, *sancire, ratum facĕre*.
confiscate, *publicare*.
confiscation, *publicatio*.
conflagration, *incendium, ignis*.
conflict, subst. *certamen, pugna*.
conflict, v.: = fight, *pugnare, certare, contendĕre*; = differ, *dissentire, discrepare, repugnare*.
confluence, *confluens* or plur. *confluentes*.
conform, *obsequi, obtemperare*.
conformable, *accommodatus, congruens*.
conformation, *conformatio, forma, figura*.
conformity, *convenientia*; in — with, *ex, secundum*.
confound; = confuse, *confundĕre*; = astonish, *obstupefacĕre*; = frustrate, *frustrari*.
confront, v. *obviam ire, se opponĕre*.
confuse, *confundĕre,* (*per*)*miscēre,* (*per*)*turbare*.
confused, *confusus, perplexus*; adv. *confuse, perplexe*.
confusion, *confusio, perturbatio*.
confute, *refellĕre, redarguĕre, confutare*.
congeal: transit. *congelare*; intransit. *concrescĕre*.
congenial, *gratus, concors*.
congratulate, *gratulari*.
congratulation, *gratulatio*.
congregate, *congregari, convenire, confluĕre*.
congregation, *conventus* (-*ūs*), *coetus* (-*ūs*).
congress, *conventus* (-*ūs*), *concilium*.
conjecture, subst. *coniectura, opinio*.
conjecture, v. *augurari, conicĕre, coniectare*.
conjugal, adj. *coniugalis*.
conjugate, gram., *declinare*.
conjugation, gram., *declinatio*.
conjure, v.: transit., = entreat, *obtestari, obsecrare*; to — up, (*mortuorum*) *animas elicĕre*; intransit., = perform tricks, *praestigiis uti*.
conjurer, *magus, praestigiator*.
connect, *adligare,* (*con*)*iungĕre, conectĕre*.
connexion, *coniunctio*; between persons, *societas, necessitudo*; by marriage, *adfinitas*.

connive, *connivēre,* (*rem*) *dissimulare.*
connivance, *indulgentia.*
connoisseur, *iudex, existimator.*
conquer, (*de*)*vincĕre, superare.*
conqueror, *victor.*
conquest, *victoria.*
consanguinity, *consanguinitas.*
conscience, *conscientia.*
conscientious, *religiosus, sanctus*; adv. *religiose, sancte.*
conscientiousness, *religio, sanctitas, fides.*
conscious, = aware, *gnarus, conscius*; adv., render by adj. *prudens.*
consciousness, *sensus* (-*ūs*).
conscript: see recruit.
conscription, *delectus* (-*ūs*).
consecrate, *consecrare, dedicare.*
consecrated, *sacer.*
consecration, *consecratio, dedicatio.*
consecutive, *continens, continuus*; adv. *continenter.*
consent, subst. *consensus* (-*ūs*).
consent, v. *velle.*
consequence: = result, *exitus* (-*ūs*), *eventus* (-*ūs*); in — of, *ex, propter*; = importance, *momentum, auctoritas.*
consequently, *itaque, ergo, igitur.*
conserve, (*con*)*servare*; of fruit, *condire.*
conservative, polit., *qui nihil in republica immutari vult.*
consider: = think about, *considerare, expendĕre, delibare, contemplari*; = take into account, *respicĕre*; to — that, *arbitrari, ducĕre*; = to regard as, *ducĕre, habēre, existimare.*
considerable, *magnus, gravis*; adv. *aliquantum.*
considerate, *humanus, officious, benignus.*
considerateness, *humanitas, benignitas.*
consideration: = thought, *consideratio, deliberatio, contemplatio*; = proper regard, *ratio, respectus* (-*ūs*).
consign, *committĕre, credĕre, mandare.*
consist, *consistĕre, constare.*
consistent: — with, *consentaneus, congruens*; = unchanging, *constans*; adv. *constanter.*
consolation, *solatium, consolatio.*
console, (*con*)*solari.*
consoler, *consolator.*
consonant, subst., gram., *consonans.*
consonant, adj. *consentaneus, congruens.*
consort, subst. *comes, socius*; = husband or wife, *coniunx.*
consort, v.; to — with, *familiariter uti.*
conspicuous, *conspicuus, clarus, insignis*; adv. *clare.*
conspiracy, *coniuratio.*
conspirator, *coniuratus.*
conspire, *coniurare, conspirare.*
constable, *lictor.*
constancy, *constantia, fides, fidelitas.*
constant, *constans, firmus*; = incessant, *continuus, perpetuus*; = faithful, *fidelis, fidus.* Adv. *constanter; semper, perpetuo.*
constellation, *sidus* (-*eris,* n.), *signum.*
consternation, *pavor, terror.*
constitute; = to make up, *componĕre, efficĕre*; = to establish, *statuĕre, constituĕre, designare*; = to appoint, *creare, facĕre.*
constitution, *constitutio, habitus* (-*ūs*); of a state, *civitatis status* (*ūs*).
constitutional: = natural, *innatus, insitus*; = legal, *legitimus.* Adv. *naturā*; *legitime, e republica.*
constrain, *cogĕre, compellĕre.*
constraint, *vis.*
construct, *facĕre, fabricari.*
construction: as an act, *fabricatio, aedificatio*; = form, plan, *structura, figura, forma*; = interpretation, *interpretatio*; to put a good — on, *rem in bonam partem accipĕre.*
construe, *interpretari, accipĕre.*
consul, *consul*; ex-consul, *vir consularis.*
consulship, *consulatus* (-*ūs*).
consult, *consultare, deliberare*; to — a person, *hominem consulĕre.*
consume, *consumĕre, conficĕre, absumĕre.*
consummate, adj. *summus, absolutus, perfectus;* adv. *summe, absolute, perfecte.*
consummation, *absolutio, perfectio.*
contact, (*con*)*tactus* (-*ūs*).
contagion, *contagio.*
contain, *capĕre, habēre, continēre.*
contaminate, *contaminare, inquinare, polluĕre.*
contamination, *macula, labes.*
contemplate, *contemplari, intuēri.*
contemplation, *contemplatio.*
contemporary, *aequalis.*
contempt, *contemptus* (-*ūs*), *fastidium.*
contemptible, *contemptus, turpis.*
contend: = to struggle, *contendĕre,* (*de*)*certare*; = to maintain, *contendĕre, confirmare, adfirmare.*
content, subst. *animus contentus.*
content, adj. *contentus.*
content, v. *satisfacĕre* (with dat.); to — oneself with saying, *satis habēre dicĕre.*
contentedly, *aequo animo*; or use adj. *contentus.*
contentious, *pugnax.*
conterminous, *confinis.*
contest, subst. *certatio, certamen, contentio.*
contest, v. *contendĕre.*
context, *argumentum.*
contiguity, *vicinitas, propinquitas.*
contiguous, *confinis, continens.*
continence, *continentia, temperantia.*
continent, subst. *continens.*
continent, adj. *continens, castus*; adv. *continenter, caste.*
contingency, *casus* (-*ūs*).
contingent, subst. *auxilia* (-*orum*).
contingent, adj. *fortuitus, forte oblatus.*
continual, *continuus, perpetuus, adsiduus*; adv. *continenter, adsidue, perpetuo.*
continuance, continuation, *perpetuitas, adsiduitas, diuturnitas.*
continue, v.: transit. *extendĕre, producĕre, continuare*; intransit., = to persevere, *pergĕre, perseverare*; = to last, *durare,* (*per*)*manēre.*
continuity, *continuatio, perpetuitas.*
contort, *depravare, distorquēre.*
contortion, *distortio, depravatio.*
contour, *forma, figura.*

contract, subst. *pactum, conductio, locatio, redemptio.*
contract, v.: = draw in, *contrahĕre, adducĕre*; = incur, *contrahĕre*; to — for, *locare, conducĕre,* or *redimĕre*; intransit., = become smaller, *se contrahĕre, minui.*
contracted, *contractus, angustus, brevis.*
contraction, *contractio.*
contractor, *conductor, redemptor.*
contradict, *obloqui, contradicĕre*; fig., *repugnare, discrepare.*
contradictory, *contrarius, repugnans, diversus.*
contrary, subst.: on the —, *contra*; in answers, *immo.*
contrary, adj. *adversus, contrarius.*
contrary to, *contra, praeter,* with acc.
contrast, subst. *diversitas, dissimilitudo.*
contrast, v. transit. *comparare, conferre*; intransit. *discrepare.*
contravene, *violare, frangĕre.*
contribute, v.: = give, *contribuĕre, conferre*; = help, *prodesse, adiuvare.*
contrite, adj.; see penitent.
contrivance: = contriving, *inventio, excogitatio*; = thing contrived, *machina.*
contrive, *excogitare, invenire, fingĕre, efficĕre.*
control, subst. *potestas, imperium, dicio*; self —, *moderatio, temperantia.*
control, v. *moderari, temperare, coercēre.*
controversial, = disputed, *controversus.*
controversy, *controversia, contentio.*
controvert, *refellĕre, refutare.*
contumacious, *contumax, pertinax*; adv. *contumaciter, pertinaciter.*
contumacy, *pertinacia, contumacia.*
contumelious, *contumeliosus, probrosus.*
contumely, *contumelia.*
convalescent, use verb *convalescĕre.*
convene, *convocare.*
convenience, *commoditas, opportunitas.*
convenient, *commodus, opportunus, accommodatus*; adv. *commode, opportune, accommodate.*
convention: = assembly, *conventus* (-*ūs*); = agreement, *foedus* (-*eris,* n.), *pactio*; = custom, *mos.*
conventional, *translaticius, usu receptus.*
converge, *coire, in unum vergĕre.*
conversant, *versatus, exercitatus, peritus.*
conversation, *sermo, conloquium.*
converse, v. *conloqui, sermonem conferre.*
conversion, (*com*)*mutatio, conversio.*
convert, v. (*com*)*mutare, convertĕre*; — to an opinion, *ad sententiam traducĕre.*
convex, *convexus.*
convey: see carry; legal, *transcribĕre, abalienare.*
convict, v. *condemnare, convincĕre.*
conviction, *damnatio*; = belief, *opinio, sententia.*
convince, *persuadēre.*
convivial, *hilaris.*
conviviality, *hilaritas.*
convoke, *convocare.*
convoy, subst. *praesidium.*
convoy, v. *deducĕre, comitari.*
convulse, *agitare, percutĕre,* (*com*)*movēre.*
convulsion, *motus* (-*ūs*), *turba*; medical, *convulsio.*
cook, subst. *coquus.*
cook, v. *coquĕre.*
cool, subst. *frigus* (-*oris,* n.).
cool, adj. *frigidus*; of temper, etc., *lentus* (= phlegmatic), *impavidus* (= undismayed), *impudens* (= impudent). Adv. *frigide; lente.*
cool, v.: transit., *refrigerare*; intransit., *refrigerari, defervescĕre.*
co-operate, *una agĕre*; to — with, *adiuvare.*
co-operation, *opera, auxilium.*
cope, v. *resistĕre, certare*; able to —, *par.*
coping, *fastigium.*
copious, *copiosus, abundans, largus*; adv. *copiose, abundanter, large.*
copiousness, *copia, abundantia.*
copper, subst. *aes.*
copper, adj. *a*(*h*)*enus.*
coppice, copse, *silva.*
copy, subst. *exemplum, exemplar.*
copy, v. *imitari*; to — out, *transcribĕre, describĕre.*
cord, *restis, funis.*
cordial, *benignus, comis*; adv. *benigne, comiter.*
cordiality, *benignitas, comitas.*
core, *nucleus, granum.*
cork, subst. *cortex.*
corn, *frumentum*; the price of —, *annona*; — field, *seges.*
corner, *angulus.*
cornet, *cornu, buccina.*
corporal, subst. *decurio.*
corporal, corporeal, adj. *corporeus,* or genit. of *corpus.*
corporation, *municipium, conlegium.*
corps, *manus* (-*ūs*).
corpse, *cadaver.*
corpulent, *obesus, pinguis.*
correct, adj.; of conduct, *honestus, rectus*; of style, *emendatus, purus*; = true, *verus.* Adv. *recte, honeste; pure; vere.*
correct, v. *corrigĕre, emendare*; see also punish.
correction, *correctio, emendatio*; see also punishment.
correspond, v. *respondēre, congruĕre*; letter, *litteras dare et accipĕre.*
correspondence: = agreement, *congruentia, convenientia*; = letters, *litterae, epistulae.*
corresponding, *par.*
corroborate, *confirmare, comprobare.*
corroboration, *confirmatio.*
corrode, *rodĕre.*
corrupt, adj. *corruptus, impurus, pravus*; adv. *corrupte, impure, prave.*
corrupt, v. *corrumpĕre, depravare, vitiare.*
corrupter, *corruptor.*
corruptible, = venal, *venalis.*
corruption, *corruptio, depravatio, corruptela.*
corsair, *pirata.*
corslet, *thorax, lorica.*
cortege, *comitatus* (-*ūs*).
cosmetic, *fucus.*

cost, subst. *pretium, sumptus* (-*ūs*); — of living, *annona.*
cost, v. (*con*)*stare, venire.*
costly, *carus, pretiosus.*
costume, *vestitus* (-*ūs*), *habitus* (-*ūs*).
cot, *lectulus.*
cottage, *casa, tugurium.*
cottager, *rusticus.*
couch, subst. *lectus, lectulus, cubile.*
couch, v. *cubare, latēre, delitescĕre.*
cough, subst. *tussis.*
cough, v. *tussire.*
council, *concilium*; a — of war, *consilium, praetorium.*
councillor, *senator, decurio.*
counsel, = advice, *consilium, auctoritas.*
counsel, v.; see advise.
count: = to number, (*e*)*numerare, percensēre, computare*; = to consider, *habēre, ducĕre*; to — upon, *confidĕre.*
countenance, subst.: = face, *vultus* (-*ūs*), *os*; = favour, *favor.*
countenance, v.: = approve, *approbare*; = allow, *permittĕre.*
counter, subst.: for counting, *calculus*; in a shop, *mensa.*
counter, adv.: — to, *contra*; to run — to, *adversari.*
counteract, *resistĕre.*
counter-balance, (*ex*)*aequare, compensare.*
counterfeit, adj. *falsus.*
counterfeit, v. *simulare.*
counterpane, *lodix.*
countless, *innumerabilis, innumerus.*
country: opp. to town, *rus*: in the —, *ruri*; = native land, *patria*; = region, *terra, regio.*
country-house, *villa.*
countryman, (*homo*) *rusticus.*
country-town, *municipium, oppidum.*
couple, subst. *par, bini -ae -a.*
couple, v. transit. (*con*)*iungĕre, copulare.*
courage, *fortudo, virtus, animus.*
courageous, *fortis, strenuus, animosus*; adv. *fortiter, strenue.*
courier, *nuntius, tabellarius.*
course, *cursus* (-*ūs*); — of life, *vitae curriculum*; a — of action, *ratio*; of —, *scilicet, sane*; a — at dinner, *ferculum.*
court, subst.: = enclosed space, *area*; a royal —, *aula, regia*; a — of justice, *forum, basilica.*
court, v. transit., *petĕre, colĕre, captare.*
courteous, *comis, urbanus*; adv. *comiter, urbane.*
courtesy, *urbanitas, comitas.*
courtier, *aulicus.*
cousin, (*con*)*sobrinus, patruelis.*
covenant, subst. *pactio, pactum, conventio.*
covenant, v. *pacisci.*
cover, subst.: = lid, *operimentum*; = shelter, *perfugium.*
cover, v.: to — up, (*con*)*tegĕre, operire, velare*; = to protect, *protegĕre, defendĕre.*
covering, *tegmen.*
covert, subst., = thicket, *dumetum.*
covert, adj.: see secret.
covet, *adpetĕre, concupiscĕre.*
covetous, *avarus, avidus*; adv. *avare, avide.*
covetousness, *avaritia, aviditas.*
cow, subst. *vacca.*
cow, v. *domare.*
coward, *homo ignavus* or *timidus.*
cowardice, *ignavia, timiditas.*
cowardly, *ignavus, timidus.*
cowl, *cucullus.*
coy, *verecundus.*
crab, *cancer.*
crabbed: in temper, *acerbus, morosus*; of style, *implicatus, impeditus.*
crack, subst.: = noise, *crepitus* (-*ūs*), *fragor*; = fissure, *rima.*
crack, v.: transit., *frangĕre, findĕre, rumpĕre*; intransit., = break open, *dissilire, dehiscĕre*; = make a noise, *crepare.*
cradle, *cunae* (-*arum*), *cunabula* (-*orum*).
craft: = cunning, *dolus, astutia*; = skill, trade, *ars, artificium*; = boat, *cymba, scapha.*
craftsman, *artifex, opifex.*
crafty, *astutus, callidus, dolosus*; adv. *astute, callide, dolose.*
crag, *scopulus, rupes.*
cram, *farcire, refercire, stipare.*
cramp; see confine.
crane: the bird, *grus*; the machine, *trochlea, tolleno.*
crank, of a machine, *uncus.*
cranny, *rima.*
crash, subst. *fragor, strepitus* (-*ūs*).
crash, v. *strepĕre.*
crater, *crater.*
crave; see beg, need.
craving, *desiderium.*
crawl, *repĕre, serpĕre.*
crazy: = decrepit, *decrepitus, imbecillus*; = deranged, *cerritus.*
creak, v. *stridēre, crepare.*
creaking, subst. *stridor, crepitus* (-*ūs*).
crease, v. *rugare.*
crease, subst. *ruga.*
create, *creare, gignĕre, generare, facĕre.*
creator, *creator, fabricator, auctor.*
creature, *animal.*
credibility, *fides, auctoritas.*
credible, *credibilis.*
credit, subst. *fides.*
credit, v.: = to believe, *credĕre*; to — a thing (to a person), *rem acceptam* (*homini*) *referre.*
creditable, *honestus, honorificus*; adv. *honeste.*
creditor, *creditor.*
credulity, *credulitas.*
credulous, *credulus.*
creek, *sinus* (-*ūs*), *aestuarium.*
creep, see crawl.
crest, *crista, iuba.*
crested, *cristatus, iubatus.*
crestfallen, *demissus.*
crevice; see crack.
crew: on a ship, *nautae* (-*arum*); in gen., *grex.*
crib, *praesepe.*
crime, *scelus* (-*eris*), *delictum, facinus* (-*oris*).
criminal, *scelestus, sceleratus, nefarius*: adv. *nefarie.*

crimson, *coccineus.*
cringe, *adulari.*
cringing, *abiectus.*
cripple, *debilitare, frangĕre, infringĕre.*
crippled, *claudus, mancus, debilis.*
crisis, *discrimen.*
crisp: = curled, *crispus*; = brittle, *fragilis.*
criterion, *norma, obrussa.*
critic, *iudex, criticus, existimator.*
critical: = discriminating, *elegans, subtilis*; = of a crisis, *anceps, dubius.*
criticism, *iudicium.*
criticize; = to judge, *iudicare*; = to find fault with, *reprehendĕre, culpare.*
croak, v. *crocire, queri.*
crockery, *fictilia (-ium).*
crocodile, *crocodilus.*
crocus, *crocus.*
crone, *vetula, anus (-ūs), anicula.*
crook, a shepherd's, *pedum.*
crooked, *pravus*; adv. *prave.*
crookedness, *pravitas.*
crop, subst.: of corn, etc., *messis, fruges (-um)*; of birds, *ingluvies.*
crop, v.: = to browse on, *(at)tondēre*; = to cut short, *praecīdĕre, amputare.*
cross, subst. *crux.*
cross, adj.: = transverse, *transversus, obliquus*; = annoyed, *difficilis, morosus.*
cross, v.: = to go across, *transire, transgredi*; = to oppose, *obsistĕre, adversari*; to — out, *delēre.*
cross-examine, *interrogare.*
crossing, subst. *transitus (-ūs).*
crouch, *se demittĕre.*
crow, subst. *cornix.*
crow, v. *canĕre.*
crowd, subst. *turba, vulgus, multitudo.*
crowd, v.: transit., *stipare, cogĕre*; intransit., *concurrĕre, congregari.*
crown, subst.: = garland, *corona*; a king's *diadema (-atis)*; fig., = sovereignty, *regnum*; the — of the head, *vertex.*
crown, v. *coronare, diadema (regi) imponĕre.*
crucifixion, *crucis supplicium.*
crucify, *cruci adfigĕre.*
crude: = raw, unripe, *crudus*; = rough, *informis, incultus, rudis*; adv. *inculte.*
cruel, *crudelis, saevus, atrox*; adv. *crudeliter, atrociter.*
cruelty, *crudelitas, saevitia.*
cruise, v. *(per)vagari, circumvectari, navigare.*
crumb, *mica.*
crumble: transit., *comminuĕre, conterĕre*; intransit., render by pass.
crumple, *(con)rugare.*
crush, v. *opprimĕre, contundĕre, conterĕre*; fig., *adfligĕre.*
crust, *crusta.*
crutch, *baculum.*
cry, subst. *clamor, vociferatio*; of distress, *ploratus (-ūs).*
crystal: subst. *crystallus*; adj. *crystallinus.*
cub, *catulus.*
cube, *tessera, cubus.*
cuckoo, *cuculus.*
cucumber, *cucumis.*
cud: to chew the cud, *ruminare, remandĕre.*
cudgel, subst. *baculum, fustis.*
cue, = hint, *signum, indicium.*
cuff, subst.: = blow, *alapa, colaphus*; = sleeve, *manica extrema.*
cuirass, *thorax, lorica.*
culmination, *fastigium.*
culpable, *culpandus.*
culprit; see criminal.
cultivate, *(ex)colĕre, exercēre.*
cultivation, culture, *cultus (-ūs), cultura*; = education, etc., *humanitas, litterae (-arum).*
cultivator, *cultor.*
cumber, *impedire, (prae)gravare, onerare.*
cumbrous, *gravis, incommodus.*
cunning, subst. *calliditas, astutia, dolus.*
cunning, adj. *callidus, astutus, dolosus*; adv. *callide, astute.*
cup, *poculum, scyphus, calix.*
cup-bearer, *minister, servus.*
cupboard, *armarium.*
cupidity, *cupiditas, avaritia.*
curb, subst. *frenum.*
curb, v. *frenare, coercēre, cohibēre.*
curdle, v.: transit., *coagulare*; intransit., *concrescĕre.*
cure, subst. *medicina, sanatio.*
cure, v. *sanare, medēri.*
curiosity, *noscendi studium.*
curious: = inquisitive, *curiosus*; = strange, *insolitus, novus, mirus.*
curl, v. transit. *crispare.*
curling-irons, *calamister.*
curly, *crispus.*
currency, *nummi (-orum).*
current, subst.: in a river, *flumen*; at sea, *aestus (-ūs).*
current, adj.: = this, *hic*; = common, *usitatus, vulgaris*; adv. *vulgo.*
curse, subst.: of speech, *exsecratio, imprecatio*; = malign influence, *pernicies, pestis.*
curse, v. *exsecrari, detestari.*
cursory; see brief.
curt, *brevis, abruptus*; adv. *breviter, praecise.*
curtail, *(co)artare, (im)minuĕre.*
curtain, *velum, aulaeum.*
curve, subst. *flexus (-ūs), sinus (-ūs).*
curve, v. transit. *(in)curvare, (in)flectĕre.*
cushion, *pulvinus, pulvinar.*
custody, *custodia, vincula (-orum).*
custom, *consuetudo, mos, usus (-ūs).*
customary, *usitatus, quotidianus, solitus.*
custom-duty, *vectigal, portorium.*
customer, *emptor.*
cut, v. *secare, caedĕre*; to — corn, etc., *(de)metĕre*; to — down, *succīdĕre*; to — off, = destroy, *absumĕre, exstinguĕre*; to — short, *praecīdĕre, amputare.*
cutlery, *cultri (-orum).*
cut-throat, *sicarius.*
cutting, adj., of speech, *mordax.*
cuttlefish, *sepia, lolligo.*
cycle, *orbis, circulus.*
cylinder, *cylindrus.*
cymbal, *cymbalum.*
cynic, *cynicus.*

cynical, *mordax.*
cypress, *cupressus.*

D

dabble: to — in, *attingĕre.*
daffodil, *narcissus.*
dagger, *pugio, sica.*
daily: adj., *quotidianus*; adv., *quotidie.*
daintiness: = fussiness, *cuppedia*; = elegance, *venustas.*
dainty: = particular, *fastidiosus*; = elegant, *elegans, delicatus.*
dale, *vallis.*
dalliance, *lascivia, ludus.*
dally: = to linger, *morari*; = to sport, *lascivire, ludĕre.*
dam, subst.: = mother, *mater*; = breakwater, *moles, agger.*
dam, v. *obstruĕre, coercēre.*
damage, subst. *damnum, incommodum, noxa.*
damage, v. *laedĕre, nocēre.*
dame, *matrona, domina.*
damn, *damnare, condemnare.*
damp, subst. *umor.*
damp, adj. *umidus, udus.*
damp, v. *umectare*; fig., *comprimĕre, restinguĕre.*
damsel, *puella, virgo.*
dance, subst. *saltatio, saltatus* (*-ūs*).
dance, v. *saltare.*
dancer, *saltator* (f. *saltatrix*).
dandy, *homo elegans.*
danger, *periculum, discrimen.*
dangerous, *periculosus, infestus, lubricus*; adv. *periculose.*
dangle, (*de*)*pendĕre.*
dank, *umidus.*
Danube, *Danubius.*
dapper, *nitidus.*
dappled, *maculosus.*
dare, *audēre*; = to challenge, *provocare.*
daring, subst. *audacia.*
daring, adj. *audax.*
dark, subst.; see darkness.
dark, adj. *obscurus*; in colour, *fuscus, pullus.* Adv. *obscure.*
darken, v. *obscurare, occaecare.*
darkness, *obscuritas, tenebrae* (*-arum*), *caligo.*
darling, subst. *deliciae* (*-arum*).
darling, adj. *suavissimus, mellitus.*
darn, *sarcire.*
dart, subst. *telum, iaculum*; to throw —s, *iaculari.*
dart, v. = to dash, *provolare, se conicĕre.*
dash, subst., = rush, *impetus* (*-ūs*).
dash, v.: transit., to — one thing against another, *adfligĕre, offendĕre*; to — down, *proruĕre*; intransit., see dart.
dastardly, *ignavus.*
date, subst.: the fruit, *palmula*; = a particular time, *dies, tempus* (*-oris*); out of —, *obsoletus.*
date, v.; to — a letter, *diem in epistula ascribĕre.*
dative, (*casus*) *dativus.*
daub, (*ob*)*linĕre,* (*per*)*ungĕre.*
daughter, *filia*: — -in-law, *nurus* (*-ūs*).
dauntless, *impavidus.*
dawdle, *cessare.*
dawn, *diluculum, prima lux, aurora* (poet.); it is —, *lucescit.*
day, *dies*: at break of —, *prima luce*; good —, *salve*(*te*); a period of two —, *biduum*; on the — before, *pridie*; on the — after, *postridie.*
day-break; see dawn.
dazzle, *perstringĕre, caecare.*
dead, *mortuus.* Transf., = dull, *languidus*; at — of night, *nocte intempesta.*
deaden, *hebetare, enervare, debilitare.*
deadly, *mortifer, exitialis, perniciosus.*
deaf, *surdus, auribus captus.*
deafen, *exsurdare, obtundĕre.*
deafness, *surditas.*
deal, v.: to — out, *dividĕre, distribuĕre*; to — with, see treat.
dealer, *mercator, negotiator*; a retail —, *institor, propola.*
dealing, *commercium, negotium, usus* (*-ūs*).
dear: = expensive, *carus, pretiosus*; = beloved, *carus.*
dearly, = at a high price, *care, magno pretio.*
dearness, *caritas.*
dearth, *inopia, caritas, penuria.*
death, *mors, letum, obitus* (*-ūs*).
debar, *excludĕre, prohibēre.*
debase, *corrumpĕre, vitiare.*
debasement, *ignominia.*
debate, subst. *disceptatio, disputatio.*
debate, v. *disceptare, disputare.*
debauch, subst. *comissatio.*
debauch, v. *corrumpĕre, depravare, vitiare.*
debauchery, *stuprum.*
debenture, *syngrapha.*
debility, *infirmitas, imbecilitas, debilitas.*
debit, v.: to — a thing to a person, *homini rem expensam ferre.*
debt, *aes alienum.*
debtor, *debitor, obaeratus.*
decade, *decem anni.*
decamp, *discedĕre.*
decant, *diffundĕre.*
decanter, *lagena.*
decapitate; see behead.
decay, *tabes, defectio virium.*
decay, v. *marcescĕre, senescĕre, tabescĕre.*
decease, *obitus* (*-ūs*).
deceit, *fallacia, fraus, dolus.*
deceitful, *fallax, dolosus, fraudulentus*; adv. *fallaciter, dolose.*
deceive, *decipĕre, fallĕre, circumvenire.*
deceiver, *fraudator.*
December, (*mensis*) *December.*
decency, *honestas, decentia, decorum.*
decent, *honestus, decens, decorus*; adv. *honeste, decenter, decore.*
deception, *fraus, dolus, fallacia.*
decide, *statuĕre, constituĕre.*
decided, *certus*; of persons, *constans, firmus.* Adv. *firme, constanter*; in answers, *vero, plane, sane.*
decimate, *decimare.*
decipher, *explanare, explicare.*
decision: = settlement, *arbitrium,*

sententia; of character, *constantia, firmitas.*
deck, subst. *pons.*
deck, v.; see adorn; a decked ship, *navis constrata.*
declaim, *pronuntiare, declamare.*
declamation, *declamatio, pronuntiatio.*
declaration, *declaratio, praedicatio*; — of war, *belli denuntiatio.*
declare, *declarare, praedicare, pronuntiare*; to — war, *bellum denuntiare* or *indicĕre.*
declension, *declinatio.*
decline, subst. *deminutio.*
decline, v.: = refuse, *recusare, renuĕre*; to — battle, *pugnam detrectare*; = fail, *deficĕre, (de)minui, decrescĕre.*
declivity, *declivitas, clivus.*
decompose: transit., *(dis)solvĕre, resolvĕre*; intransit., *dissolvi, tabescĕre, putrescĕre.*
decomposition, *(dis)solutio, tabes.*
decorate, *(ex)ornare, decorare.*
decoration, *ornatus (-ūs), ornamentum.*
decorous, *decorus*; adv. *decore.*
decoy, subst. *inlex.*
decoy, v. *inlicĕre, adlicĕre, inescare.*
decrease, subst. *deminutio, imminutio.*
decrease, v.: transit., *(de)minuĕre, imminuĕre, extenuare*; intransit., *decrescĕre, (de)minui.*
decree, subst. *decretum, edictum.*
decree, v. *decernĕre, edicĕre, sancire.*
decrepit, *decrepitus.*
decry, *vituperare, obtrectare.*
dedicate, *(de)dicare, consecrare.*
deduce: = derive, *(de)ducĕre*; = infer, *conligĕre, concludĕre.*
deduct, *detrahĕre, deducĕre.*
deduction: = decrease, *deductio, deminutio*; = inference, render by verb.
deed: = action, *factum, res gesta*; = document, *tabula, syngrapha.*
deep, subst. *altum, pontus.*
deep, adj. *altus, profundus*; of sounds, *gravis*; fig., *summus, gravis.* Adv. *alte, penitus; graviter.*
deer, *cervus* (f. *cerva*).
deface, *deformare, foedare.*
defame, *calumniari, obtrectare.*
default: = error, *culpa, peccatum*; = lack, *defectio, inopia*; legal, to let judgment go by —, *vadimonium deserĕre.*
defeat, subst. *clades.*
defeat, v.: see conquer, baffle.
defect, *labes, vitium, mendum.*
defection, *defectio.*
defective, *imperfectus, mendosus, vitiosus*; adv. *imperfecte, mendose, vitiose.*
defence, *defensio, tutela, praesidium.*
defenceless, *inermis.*
defend, *defendĕre, tuēri.*
defendant, *reus.*
defensive: — weapons, *arma (-orum).*
defer, *differre, proferre, procrastinare*; to — to, *cedĕre, obsequi.*
deference, *observantia, obsequium.*
deferential, *submissus, observans*; adv. *submisse.*
defiance, *provocatio.*
deficiency, *defectio, inopia.*
deficient; see defective.
defile, subst. *angustiae (-arum), fauces (-ium).*
defile, v. *contaminare, maculare, foedare, pollŭere.*
defilement, *macula, labes.*
define, *(de)finire, circumscribĕre.*
definite, *certus, status, definitus*; adv. *certe, certo, definite.*
definition, *(de)finitio.*
deflect, v.: transit., *deflectĕre*; intransit., *declinare, errare.*
deform, *deformare.*
deformed, *distortus, deformatus.*
deformity, *deformitas, pravitas.*
defraud, *(de)fraudare, circumvenire.*
defray, *suppeditare, solvĕre.*
defunct, *mortuus.*
defy, = challenge, *provocare.*
degenerate, adj. *degener.*
degenerate, v. *degenerare, depravari, peior fieri.*
degradation, *ignominia, dedecus (-oris, n.).*
degrade, = lower in rank, *in ordinem cogĕre* (of soldiers), *ex loco movere*; see also disgrace.
degrading, *indignus, indecorus.*
degree: = amount, *gradus (-ūs)*; by —s, *gradatim, sensim*; = rank, *gradus, ordo.*
deify, *consecrare, in deorum numerum referre.*
deign, *dignari, velle,* with infin.
deity, *deus, numen.*
dejected, *maestus, perculsus, adflictus*; adv. *maeste.*
dejection, *maestitia, tristitia, maeror.*
delay, subst. *mora, cunctatio.*
delay, v.: transit., *(re)morari, detinēre*; intransit., *(com)morari, cunctari.*
delegate, subst. *legatus.*
delegate, v.: = to depute, *legare, adlegare*; = to entrust, *committĕre, mandare.*
deleterious, *noxius.*
deliberate, adj. *consideratus, cogitatus*; adv. *considerate, cogitate, consulto.*
deliberate, v. *deliberare, consulĕre, considerare.*
deliberation, *deliberatio, consultatio*; see also slowness.
deliberative, *deliberativus*; a — body, *consilium.*
delicacy: of taste, etc., *elegantia, subtilitas, humanitas*; of health, *suavitas.*
delicate: = tender, *tener, mollis, delicatus*; in taste, etc., *elegans, subtilis, humanus*; in health, *imbecillus, infirmus*; of tasks, *difficilis.* Adv. *molliter, delicate, eleganter, subtiliter.*
delicious, *suavis, dulcis*; adv. *suaviter.*
delight, subst. *delectatio, voluptas.*
delight, v.: transit., *delectare, oblectare*; intransit., *gaudēre, delectari, oblectari.*
delightful, *iucundus, suavis, gratus*; adv. *iucunde, suaviter, grate.*
delightfulness, *suavitas, iucunditas.*
delineate, *describĕre, adumbrare.*
delineation, *adumbratio, descriptio.*
delinquency, *delictum, scelus (-eris, n.).*
delirious, *delirus.*

delirium, *delirium, furor.*
deliver: = to hand over, *prodĕre, dedĕre, tradĕre*; = to utter, *pronuntiare;* see also free.
deliverance, *liberatio, salūs (-ūtis).*
deliverer, *liberator, vindex.*
delivery, *actio, elocutio, dictio.*
dell, *vallis.*
delude, *deludĕre.*
deluge, subst. *eluvio.*
deluge, v. transit. *inundare.*
delusion, *fraus, dolus, fallacia*; *error.*
delusive, *falsus, fallax, vanus.*
delve, *fodĕre.*
demagogue, *plebicola, plebis dux.*
demand, subst. *postulatio, flagitatio.*
demand, v. *poscĕre, postulare, flagitare.*
demarcation: a line of —, *finis, confinium.*
demean, v.; to — oneself; = to behave, *se gerĕre*; = to stoop, *descendĕre, se demittĕre.*
demeanour, *mores (-um), habitus (-ūs).*
demerit, *culpa.*
demigod, *heros.*
demise, subst. *obitus (-ūs).*
democracy, *reipublicae forma popularis.*
democrat, *plebicola, popularium fautor.*
democratic, *popularis.*
demolish, *demoliri, evertĕre.*
demolition, *demolitio, eversio.*
demonstrate, *demonstrare, docēre, probare.*
demonstration: =proof, *demonstratio*; = display, *ostentatio.*
demoralize: = corrupt, *mores corrumpĕre*; = unnerve, *percellĕre.*
demur: legal, *exceptionem facĕre*; = to hesitate, *dubitare, haesitare.*
demure, *verecundus.*
demurrer, legal, *exceptio.*
den, *specus (-ūs), latibulum.*
denial, *negatio, repudiatio.*
denizen, *incola.*
denominate, *(de)nominare.*
denotation, *significatio.*
denote, *designare, indicare, significare.*
denounce, *increpare, vituperare*; in court, *accusare, nomen deferre.*
dense, *densus, confertus, crassus*; adv. *dense, confertim.*
dent, subst. *nota, vestigium.*
denunciation, *delatio, accusatio.*
deny: = say that . . . not, *negare, infitias ire*; = refuse to give, *negare.*
depart, *abire, discedĕre, digredi.*
department: = office, *munus (-eris,* n.), *provincia*; = branch, *pars, genus (-eris,* n.).
departure, *abitus (-ūs), discessus (-ūs).*
depend: = to be dependent, *pendĕre (ex), positum* or *situm esse (in)*; = to rely on, *(con)fidĕre*; — upon it, *mihi crede.*
dependence, *clientela*; = reliance, *fiducia.*
dependent, subst. *cliens.*
dependent, adj. *obnoxius.*
depict, *depingĕre, describĕre.*
deplorable, *flebilis, miserabilis.*
deplore, *deplorare, deflēre.*
deploy, *explicare, dilatare.*
deport, = to remove, *deportare.*
deportment, *gestus (-ūs), habitus (-ūs), mores (-um).*
depose, *loco movĕre*; as a witness, *testari, testificari.*
deposit, v., *(de)ponĕre.*
deposition: = evidence, *testimonium.*
depravation, *depravatio, corruptio.*
deprave, *depravare, corrumpĕre, vitiare.*
depravity, *pravitas, mores corrupti.*
deprecate, *deprecari.*
depreciate, = disparage, *clevare, obtrectare.*
depreciation, *obtrectatio.*
depredation, *latrocinium.*
depress, *premĕre, deprimĕre*; mentally, *animum frangĕre, infringĕre.*
depression, = low spirits, *tristitia.*
deprivation, *privatio, spoliatio.*
deprive, *privare, (de)spoliare.*
deprived, *orbus.*
depth, *altitudo.*
deputation, *legatio, legati (-orum).*
depute, *(ad)legare.*
deputy, *legatus, vicarius.*
derange, *perturbare, conturbare.*
deranged, *demens, insanus.*
derangement, *perturbatio*; =insanity, *dementia, insania.*
deride, *deridēre, inridēre.*
derision, *inrisio.*
derive, *(de)ducĕre, trahĕre.*
derogate; to — from, *derogare, detrahĕre.*
descend, *descendĕre*; of property, *pervenire (ad hominem).*
descendant, *prognatus*; plur. *posteri.*
descent: = movement, *descensus (-ūs)*; = slope, *declivitas*; = origin, *origo, genus (-eris,* n.).
describe, *describĕre, depingĕre, explicare.*
description, *descriptio.*
desecrate, *profanare, polluĕre, violare.*
desecration, *violatio.*
desert, subst. *dignitas, meritum.*
desert, subst., = wilderness, *solitudo, vastitas.*
desert, adj. *desertus, solus, vastus.*
desert, v.: = abandon, *deserĕre, (de)relinquĕre, destituĕre*; = change sides, *transfugĕre.*
deserter, *desertor, transfuga.*
desertion, *(de)relictio; transitio ad hostem.*
deserve, *(com)merēre, (com)merēri; dignum esse (re).*
deservedly, *merito, pro meritis, iure.*
deserving, *(re) dignus.*
design, subst.: = outline, form, *descriptio, forma;* = purpose, *consilium.*
design, v. = delineate, *designare, describere*; = intend, *in animo habēre, cogitare.*
designate, *designare, notare, nominare.*
designedly, *consulto, de industria.*
designing, *callidus, astutus, vafer.*
desirable, *optabilis.*
desire, subst. *appetitio, cupiditas, cupido.*
desire, v. *appetĕre, cupĕre, avēre.*
desirous, *cupidus, studiosus.*
desist, *desistĕre, absistĕre.*
desk, *mensa, scrinium.*

desolate, adj. *vastus, desertus.*
desolate, v. *vastare, populari.*
despair, subst. *desperare, spem abicĕre.*
despatch, *litterae (-arum), epistula.*
despatch, v.: = send, *mittĕre*; = complete, finish, *conficĕre, perficĕre*; = hasten, haste, *maturare*; = kill, *interficĕre, interimĕre.*
desperate: = hopeless, *desperatus, exspes*; = dangerous, *periculosus.* Adv. *desperanter.*
desperation, *desperatio.*
despicable, *contemptus.*
despise, *contemnĕre, despicĕre, spernĕre.*
despite: in — of, *contra.*
despond, v. *desperare, animum demittĕre.*
despondency, *animus demissus.*
despot, *tyrannus, dominus.*
despotic, *imperiosus, superbus*; adv. *superbe, tyrannice.*
despotism, *dominatus (-ūs), tyrannis, regnum.*
dessert, *mensa secunda.*
destine, *destinare, constituĕre.*
destiny, *fatum, sors.*
destitute, *inops, egens, privatus.*
destitution, *inopia, egestas.*
destroy, *perdĕre, delēre, exstinguĕre.*
destruction, *excidium, exstinctio, pernicies.*
destructive, *perniciosus, exitiosus*; adv. *perniciose.*
desuetude, *desuetudo*; to fall into —, *obsolescĕre.*
desultory, *inconstans, levis.*
detach, *separare, seiungĕre, disiungĕre.*
detachment, of troops, *manus (-ūs).*
details, *singula (-orum).*
detail, v. *(singula) explicare, exsequi.*
detain, *tenēre, retinēre.*
detect, *invenire, deprehendĕre.*
detention, *retentio; custodia.*
deter, *deterrēre, absterrēre.*
deteriorate: transit., *depravare, corrumpĕre*; intransit., *in peius mutari.*
deterioration, *deterior condicio.*
determination: = intention, *institutum, consilium*; of character, *constantia, firmitas animi.*
determine, *statuĕre, constituĕre.*
determined, *certus*; = resolute, *constans, firmus.*
detest, *odisse, detestari.*
detestable, *detestabilis.*
detestation, *odium.*
dethrone, *regno expellĕre.*
detract; see derogate, depreciate.
detriment, *damnum, detrimentum.*
detrimental, *perniciosus, iniquus.*
devastate, *(per)vastare, (de)populari.*
devastation, *vastatio; vastitas.*
develop, v. transit., *educare, excolĕre, alĕre*; intransit., *crescĕre, adulescĕre, augeri.*
development, *auctus (-ūs), progressus (-ūs).*
deviate, *declinare, decedĕre, aberrare.*
deviation, *declinatio, digressio.*
device: = emblem, *insigne*; = plan, *machina, dolus.*
devil, *diabolus* (eccl.); go to the —! *abi in malam crucem.*
devious, *devius, vagus.*
devise, *excogitare, fingĕre, machinari*; see also bequeath.
devoid, *vacuus, liber.*
devolve, v.: transit., *deferre, permittĕre, mandare*; intransit., *(per)venire, permitti.*
devote, *devovēre. consecrare, (de)dicare*; fig., *dedĕre, conferre.*
devoted, *deditus, studiosus*; adv. *studiose.*
devotion, = zeal, *studium*; plur., see prayers.
devour, *(de)vorare, consumĕre.*
devouring, *edax.*
devout, *pius (erga deos)*; adv. *pie, sancte.*
dew, *ros.*
dewy, *roscidus.*
dexterity, *dexteritas, sollertia.*
dexterous, *dexter, sollers*; adv. *dext(e)re sollerter.*
diadem, *diadema (-atis,* n.).
diagonal, *diagonalis.*
diagram, *descriptio, forma.*
dial, *solarium,*
dialect, *lingua.*
dialectics, *dialectica.*
dialogue, *dialogus*; in plays, *diverbium*; = conversation, *sermo, conloquium.*
diamond, *adamas.*
diaphragm, *praecordia (-ium,* plur.).
diary, *commentarii diurni.*
dice, die, *talus, tessera*; — box, *fritillus.*
dictate, *dictare*; see also order.
dictator, *dictator.*
dictatorial, *dictatorius, imperiosus.*
dictatorship, *dictatura.*
diction, *dicendi* or *scribendi genus (-eris).*
die, v. *mori, (mortem) obire*; of wind, *cadĕre.*
diet, *victus (-ūs), diaeta.*
differ, *discrepare, differre.*
difference, *varietas, diversitas, dissensio.*
different, *alius, diversus, varius*; adv. *aliter, diverse, varie.*
difficult, *difficilis, arduus, impeditus.*
difficulty, *difficultas*; to be in difficulties, *laborare*; with —, *vix, aegre.*
diffidence, *verecundia, diffidentia.*
diffident, *verecundus, diffidens*; adv. *verecunde, diffidenter.*
diffuse, v.: transit., *diffundĕre*; intransit., *diffundi, permeare.*
diffuse, adj. *verbosus, fusus*; adv. *verbose, fuse.*
dig, *fodĕre*; to — up, *effodĕre.*
digest, v. *concoquĕre.*
digger, *fossor.*
dignified, *gravis, augustus.*
dignify, *honestare, honorare.*
dignity, *dignitas, amplitudo, auctoritas maiestas.*
digress, *digredi, aberrare.*
digression, *digressio.*
dike: = earthwork, *moles, agger*; = ditch, *fossa.*
dilapidated, *ruinosus.*
dilapidation, *ruina.*
dilate: = to extend, *dilatare*; in speech, *latius dicĕre.*
dilatory, *tardus, lentus.*

dilemma, in logic, *complexio.*
diligence, *diligentia, industria.*
diligent, *diligens, industrius*; adv. *diligenter, industrie.*
dilute, *aquā miscēre, diluĕre.*
dim, adj. *obscurus, hebes*; to grow —, *hebescĕre.*
dim, v. transit., *obscurare, hebetare.*
diminish, v.: transit., *(im)minuĕre, deminuĕre*; intransit., render by passive.
din, subst. *strepitus* (*-ūs*).
din, v.: to — into (a person), (*hominis*) *aures obtundĕre.*
dine, *prandĕre, cenare.*
dingy, *fuscus, sordidus.*
dining-room, *triclinium.*
dinner, *prandium* (morning), *cena* (evening).
dint: by — of, *per,* or abl.
dip, v.: transit., *tingĕre, mergĕre*; intransit., *tingi, mergi, vergĕre*; to — into a book, *librum attingĕre.*
diploma, *diploma* (*-atis,* n.).
diplomat, *legatus.*
diplomatic, = clever, *astutus, callidus.*
dire, *dirus, atrox.*
direct, adj. *rectus.* Adv. *recte*; = immediately, *statim, confestim.*
direct, v. *regĕre, dirigĕre, intendĕre; gubernare, administrare*; = to show the way, *viam monstrare*; to — a letter, *epistolam inscribĕre.*
direction: = course, *cursus* (*-ūs*), *via, regio*; = management, *cura, regimen, administratio.*
director, *magister, curator, praefectus.*
dirge, *nenia.*
dirt, *caenum, sordes.*
dirty, adj. *spurcus, sordidus, turpis*; to be —, *sordēre.* Adv. *spurce.*
dirty, v. *inquinare, polluĕre.*
disable, *enervare, debilitare.*
disadvantage, *incommodum, iniquitas.*
disadvantageous, *incommodus, iniquus*; adv. *incommode, inique.*
disaffected, (*ab*)*alienatus, aversus.*
disaffection, *animus alienus* or *aversus.*
disagree, *dissentire, dissidēre.*
disagreeable, *ingratus, gravis, molestus*; adv. *ingrate, graviter, moleste.*
disagreement, *discrepantia, dissensio, dissidium.*
disallow, *vetare.*
disappear, *e conspectu abire, evanescĕre.*
disappoint, *frustrari, spem fallĕre, spe depellĕre.*
disapproval, *improbatio.*
disapprove, *improbare, condemnare.*
disarm, *armis exuĕre.*
disarrange, (*per*)*turbare, confundĕre.*
disarrangement, *perturbatio.*
disaster, *clades, calamitas.*
disastrous, *calamitosus, funestus*; adv. *calamitose, funeste.*
disavow, *infitiari, abnuĕre.*
disavowal, *infitiatio.*
disband, *exauctorare, dimittĕre.*
disbelieve, *non credĕre.*
disburden, *exonerare liberare, expedire.*
disc, *orbis.*
discern, (*dis*)*cernĕre, dispicĕre.*
discerning, *perspicax, sagax, subtilis, prudens.*
discernment, *prudentia, iudicium, subtilitas.*
discharge, subst., (*di*)*missio*; = shooting, *emissio, coniectio, coniectus* (*-ūs*).
discharge, v.: from service, *missum facĕre, dimittĕre*; = to shoot, (*e*)*mittĕre, conicĕre*; = to perform, (*per*)*fungi.*
disciple, *discipulus, auditor.*
discipline, subst. *disciplina*; sense of —, *modestia.*
discipline, v. *instituĕre, exercēre.*
disclaim, *repudiare.*
disclose, *detegĕre, aperire, patefacĕre.*
disclosure, *patefactio, indicium.*
discolour, *decolorare.*
discomfit, *profligare, adfligĕre.*
discomfiture, *clades.*
discomfort, *incommodum.*
disconcert, *percellĕre, perturbare.*
disconsolate, *maestus.*
discontent, *molestia, taedium.*
discontinue, *interrumpĕre, intermittĕre, omittĕre.*
discord, = disagreement, *dissensio, dissidium, discordia.*
discordant: in music, *dissonus, absonus*, = disagreeing, *discors, discrepans.*
discount, subst. *deductio, decessio.*
discountenance, *improbare, condemnare.*
discourage, *animum frangĕre, infringĕre*; to — from, *deterrēre, dissuadēre.*
discourse, subst., = conversation, *sermo, conloquium*; = set speech, *oratio, contio.*
discourse, v.: = to converse, *confabulari, conloqui*; = to make a speech, *orationem habēre, contionari.*
discourteous, *inurbanus, inlepidus*; adv. *inurbane, inlepide.*
discourtesy, *inurbanitas.*
discover, v. *invenire, reperire, cognoscĕre*; see also disclose.
discoverer, *inventor.*
discovery, *inventio, investigatio*; = thing discovered, *inventum.*
discredit, subst., = disgrace, *dedecus* (*-oris,* n.), *ignominia.*
discreditable, *inhonestus, turpis.*
discreet, *prudens, cautus*; adv. *prudenter, caute.*
discretion, *prudentia, iudicium.*
discriminate, *diiudicare, discernĕre, distinguĕre.*
discrimination, *distinctio, discrimen.*
discursive, *varius, vagus.*
discuss, *disceptare, disputare, disserĕre.*
discussion, *disceptatio, disputatio.*
disdain, subst. *fastidium, contemptio.*
disdain, v. *spernĕre, fastidire, aspernari.*
disdainful, *fastidiosus.*
disease, *morbus.*
diseased, *aeger, aegrotus.*
disembark, v.: transit., *exponĕre*; intransit., *egredi.*
disembarkation, *egressus* (*-ūs*).
disengage, *solvĕre, liberare.*
disengaged, *otiosus, vacuus.*
disentangle, *expedire, explicare.*
disfavour, *invidia, offensa.*

disfigure, *deformare.*
disfranchise, *civitatem adimĕre, suffragio privare.*
disgrace, *dedecus* (*-oris,* n.), *infamia, ignominia.*
disgrace, v. *dedecorare, dehonestare.*
disgraceful, *turpis, inhonestus, flagitiosus*; adv. *turpiter, inhoneste, flagitiose.*
disguise, *vestis mutata, persona* (= mask); fig., *simulatio.*
disguise, v. *aliena veste occultare*; fig., *dissimulare.*
disgust, subst. *fastidium, taedium, satietas.*
disgust, v. *fastidium* (or *taedium*) *movēre.*
disgusting, *foedus, molestus*; adv. *foede, moleste.*
dish, subst. *patina, lanx.*
dish, v.: to — up, *adponĕre.*
dishearten, *animum frangĕre.*
dishonest, *malus, improbus*; adv. *male, improbe.*
dishonesty, *improbitas, fraus.*
dishonour: see disgrace.
dishonourable, *inhonestus.*
disinclination, *declinatio, animus aversus.*
disinclined, *aversus*; to be —, *nolle.*
disinherit, *exheredare.*
disinherited, *exheres.*
disintegrate, v. transit. *dissolvĕre.*
disinter, *effodĕre, eruĕre.*
disinterested, *suae utilitatis immemor.*
disjoin, *disiungĕre, seiungĕre.*
disjointed, *incompositus*; adv. *incomposite.*
disk, *orbis.*
dislike, subst. *odium, fastidium.*
dislike, v. *fastidire, abhorrēre.*
dislocate, *extorquēre, luxare.*
dislodge, (*de*)*pellĕre, expellĕre, deicĕre.*
disloyal, *improbus, infidus, infidelis.*
disloyalty, *infidelitas.*
dismal, *maestus, miser*; adv. *maeste, misere.*
dismantle, *nudare, diruĕre.*
dismast, *malo privare.*
dismay, *consternatio, pavor, terror.*
dismay, v. *consternare, pavefacĕre,* (*per*)*terrēre.*
dismember, *discerpĕre.*
dismiss, *dimittĕre, ablegare.*
dismissal, *dimissio.*
dismount, *ex equo desilire.*
disobedience, *contumacia.*
disobey, *non parēre.*
disoblige, *offendĕre.*
disorder, subst. *confusio, turba.*
disorder, v. (*per*)*turbare, miscēre, confundĕre.*
disordered, =sick, *aeger.*
disorderly: =confused, *confusus,* (*per*)*turbatus, perplexus, incompositus*; = insubordinate, *turbidus, turbulentus.*
disown, *repudiare, infitiari.*
disparage, *extenuare, elevare, obtrectare.*
disparagement, *obtrectatio.*
disparity, *dissimilitudo, differentia.*
dispassionate, *placidus, placatus, tranquillus.*
dispatch: see despatch.
dispel, *discutĕre, dissipare, dispellĕre.*
dispense, *distribuĕre, dividĕre*; to — with, (*di*)*mittĕre.*
dispersal, *dissipatio, diffugium.*
disperse, v.: transit., *dissipare, dispergĕre, dispellĕre*; intransit., *dilabi, diffugĕre.*
displace, *loco* (*suo*) *movēre.*
display, subst. *ostentatio.*
display, v. *ostentare, ostendĕre.*
displease, *displicēre, offendĕre.*
displeasure, *offensio, offensa.*
disposal, *arbitrium*: at the — of, *penes* (with acc.).
dispose: = to arrange, *ordinare, constituĕre*; = to incline, *inclinare*; see also sell, use, and rid.
disposed, *inclinatus, propensus, pronus.*
disposition: = arrangement, *conlocatio, ordinatio*; = character, *ingenium, indoles, natura.*
dispossess, *possessione depellĕre.*
disproportion, *dissimilitudo.*
disproportionate, *impar.*
disprove, *refellĕre, redarguĕre.*
dispute, subst. *controversia, altercatio, rixa.*
dispute, v. *ambigĕre, disputare; contendĕre, rixari.*
disqualify, = hinder, *impedire.*
disquieted, *inquietus, sollicitus.*
disregard, subst., *neglegentia, incuria.*
disregard, v. *neglegĕre, omittĕre.*
disreputable, *infamis.*
disrepute, *infamia.*
disrespect, *insolentia.*
disrespectful, *insolens.*
dissatisfaction, *molestia, offensa, offensio.*
dissatisfied: I am —, *paenitet me* (with genit.).
dissatisfy, *displicēre.*
dissect, *persecare.*
dissemble, *dissimulare.*
dissembler, *dissimulator.*
disseminate, *spargĕre, dispergĕre*
dissension, *discordia.*
dissent, subst *dissensio.*
dissent, v. *dissentire, dissidēre.*
dissimilar, *dissimilis, dispar.*
dissimulation, *dissimulatio.*
dissipate, *dissipare.*
dissipated, *dissolutus, luxuriosus.*
dissipation, *luxuria, licentia.*
dissolute; see dissipated.
dissolution, *dissolutio.*
dissolve, v.: transit., *liquefacĕre,* (*dis*)*solvĕre*; intransit., *liquescĕre,* (*dis*)*solvi.*
dissonant, *dissonus, absonus.*
dissuade, *dissuadēre, dehortari, deterrēre.*
dissuasion, *dissuasio.*
distaff, *colus.* f.
distance, subst. *spatium, intervallum*; at a —, *procul, longe*; from a —, *eminus.*
distance, v. *superare.*
distant, *remotus, longinquus*; to be —, *distare, abesse.*
distaste, *fastidium.*
distasteful, *molestus, ingratus.*
distemper, *morbus.*
distend, *distendĕre.*

distil, v. *stillare.*
distinct: = separate, *separatus, disiunctus*; = clear, *distinctus, clarus, perspicuus.* Adv. *distincte, clare, perspicue.*
distinction, *discrimen, distinctio*; honourable —, *honor, dignitas*; a mark of —, *insigne.*
distinctive, *proprius*; adv. *proprie.*
distinguish, *distinguĕre, secernĕre, diiudicare*; see also honour.
distinguished, *insignis (prae)clarus.*
distort, *detorquēre, distorquēre.*
distorted, *pravus.*
distract; = to make inattentive, *distrahĕre, distinēre*; = to agitate, *(per)turbare.*
distracted, distraught, *(per)turbatus, amens, vecors.*
distraction: see agitation, frenzy.
distrain, v. *bona vendĕre.*
distress, subst. *miseria, aerumna, labor.*
distress, v. *angĕre, vexare, sollicitare, adflictare.*
distressed, *sollicitus, anxius, adflictus*; to be —, *laborare.*
distressing, *gravis, acerbus.*
distribute, *distribuĕre, dividĕre.*
distribution, *distributio.*
district, *ager, regio, terra.*
distrust, subst. *diffidentia.*
distrust, v. *diffidĕre.*
distrustful, *suspiciosus, diffidens.*
disturb, *(per)turbare, commovēre.*
disturbance, *turba, turbatio, tumultus (-ūs).*
disturber, *turbator.*
disunion, *dissensio, dissidium, discordia.*
disunite, *seiungĕre, secernĕre, disiungĕre.*
disused, *desuetus.*
ditch, *fossa.*
ditcher, *fossor.*
ditty, *nenia, carmen.*
diurnal, *diurnus.*
dive, *urinari, se (de)mergĕre.*
diver, *urinator.*
diverge, *decedĕre, discedĕre*; of roads, *in diversas partes ferre.*
divergence, *declinatio.*
diverse, *alius, diversus, dissimilis*; adv. *aliter, diverse, dissimiliter.*
diversify, *variare, distinguĕre.*
diversion: = turning aside, *derivatio, deductio*; = distracting, *avocatio*; = recreation, *oblecatio, oblectamentum.*
diversity, *diversitas, discrepantia.*
divert: = turn aside, *avertĕre*; = amuse, *delectare, oblectare*; see also distract.
divest, *nudare, spoliare, privare*; to — oneself of a thing, *exuĕre.*
divide: transit., *dividĕre, partiri, distribuĕre*; intransit., *dividi, discedĕre.*
divination, *divinatio, vaticinatio, auguratio.*
divine, adj. *divinus, caelestis*; adv. *divine, divinitus.*
divine, v. *divinare, vaticinari, augurari, coniectare.*
diviner, *haruspex, hariolus.*
divinity, *divinitas, numen.*
divisible, *dividuus.*
vision, *partitio, divisio*; = part, *pars*; milit., *legio.*
divorce, subst. *divortium, repudium.*
divorce, v. *divortium facĕre.*
divulge, *(di)vulgare, (in medium) proferre, aperire, patefacĕre.*
dizziness, *vertigo.*
dizzy, *vertiginosus.*
do, *facĕre, efficĕre, agĕre, gerĕre*: how do you —? *quid agis?* he is done for, *de eo actum est.*
docile, *docilis.*
docility, *docilitas.*
dock, subst.: for ships, *navale*; in the —, *reus.*
dock, v.; see curtail.
doctor, subst. *medicus.*
doctor, v. *curare.*
doctrine, *dogma (-atis,* n.), *disciplina.*
document, *litterae (-arum), instrumentum.*
dodge, v. *eludĕre.*
doe, *cerva.*
doer, *actor, auctor.*
doff, *exuĕre.*
dog, subst. *canis*; of a —, *caninus.*
dog, v. *indagare, investigare.*
dogged, *pervicax, pertinax*; adv. *pertinaciter.*
dogma, *dogma, placitum.*
doing; see action.
dole, subst. *stips, diaria (-orum), sportula.*
dole, v.; see distribute.
doleful, *tristis, flebilis, maestus;* adv. *flebiliter, maeste.*
dolphin, *delphinus.*
dolt, *stipes, caudex, baro.*
domain: = kingdom, *regnum*; = estate, *possessio.*
dome, *tholus.*
domestic, subst.; see servant.
domestic, adj.; = of the home, *domesticus, familiaris, privatus*; = not foreign, *intestinus, domesticus.*
domesticate; see tame.
domicile, *domicilium, domus.*
dominate, *dominari, regnare.*
domination, *dominatio, dominatus (-ūs).*
domineer, *dominari.*
domineering, *imperiosus, superbus.*
dominion, *potestas, imperium, dicio*; of a king, *regnum.*
Don, *Tanais.*
donation, *donum.*
doom, subst. *fatum, sors.*
doom, v. *condemnare, damnare.*
door, *ostium, ianua*; back —, *posticum*; out of —-s, *foras, foris.*
doorkeeper, *ianitor* (f. *ianitrix*).
doorpost, *postis.*
dormant: to lie —, *iacēre.*
dormitory, *cubiculum.*
dormouse, *glis.*
dose, subst. *potio, medicamentum.*
dose, v. *medicamentum dare.*
dot, *punctum.*
dotage, *senium.*
dotard, *senex, delirus.*
dote, v.: to — upon, *deamare, deperire.*
double, adj. *duplex* (=twofold), *duplus* (=twice as much), *geminus* (= twin).
double, v. *duplicare*; = to sail round, *flectĕre, circumvehi.*
doublet, *tunica.*

double-tongued, *bilinguis.*
doubly, *bis, dupliciter.*
doubt, subst. *dubitatio, scrupulus.*
doubt, v. *dubitare, animi pendēre.*
doubtful, adj. *dubius, incertus*; adv. *dubie, ambigue, dubitanter* (= doubtingly).
doubtless, *sine dubio.*
dough, *farina.*
doughty, *fortis, strenuus.*
dove, *columba.*
Dover, *Portus Dubris.*
dower, dowry, *dos.*
down, subst.: of feathers, etc., *pluma, lanugo*; = hill, *collis, clivus.*
down: prep., — from, *de*; — stream, *secundo flumine*; adv. rendered by compound verb with *de* —; see downwards.
downcast, *demissus, tristis, maestus.*
downfall, (*oc*)*casus* (-*ūs*), *ruina.*
downpour, *imber.*
downright, adj.: = complete, *merus, summus*; = straight-forward, *simplex.*
downright, adv. *prorsus, omnino.*
downtrodden, *adflictus.*
downwards, *desuper, deorsum.*
downy, *plumeus.*
doze, v. *dormitare.*
dozen, *duodecim.*
drab, *ravus*; see brown.
drag, v. *trahĕre.*
dragon, *draco, serpens.*
drain, subst. *fossa, cloaca.*
drain, v. *siccare,* (*ex*)*haurire.*
drama, *fabula.*
dramatic, *scaenicus.*
draper, *qui pannos vendit.*
draught; of drink, *haustus* (-*ūs*), *potio*; of air, *spiritus* (-*ūs*), *aura.*
draw, v. (1) transit., *trahĕre, ducĕre*; of fluids, *haurire*: to — a sword, *gladium* (*de*)*stringĕre*; to — tight, *adducĕre, adstringĕre*; = to portray by drawing, *describĕre,* (*de*)*pingĕre*; = to induce, *movēre*; to — up (a document), *concipĕre*; to — up (troops) *instruĕre.* (2) intransit.: to — near, *accedĕre, appropinquare*; to — back, *recedĕre, se recipĕre.*
draw-bridge, *pons, ponticulus.*
drawer: of water, *aquarius*; chest of drawers, *armarium.*
drawing, *pictura.*
dray, *carrus, plaustrum.*
dread: see fear.
dream, subst. *somnium*; in a —, *in somno.*
dream, v. *somniare*; to — of, *vidēre in somnis.*
dreamy, *somniculosus.*
dreary, *tristis, miser*; adv. *misere.*
dregs, *faex.*
drench, *madefacĕre, perfundĕre.*
dress, subst. *vestis, vestitus* (-*ūs*), *ornatus* (-*ūs*).
dress, v. *vestire*; of food, *coquĕre*; of wounds, *curare.*
dressed, *vestitus*; — in black, *sordidatus*; — in white, *albatus.*
dressing, medic., *fomentum.*
drift, subst. = aim, *consilium, ratio.*
drift, v. *ferri, fluitare.*
drill, subst.: the tool, *terebra*; of troops, *exercitatio.*
drill, v.; = to bore, *perforare, terebrare*; = to train, *exercēre, exercitare.*
drink, subst. *potio, potus* (-*ūs*).
drink, v. *bibĕre, potare, haurire* (= drink up); to — to a person, *homini propinare.*
drinker, *potor, potator* (habitual).
drinking-bout, *potatio, comissatio.*
drip, *stillare.*
drive, subst. *gestatio.*
drive, v. (1) transit., *agĕre, pellĕre*; to — out, *expellĕre, exturbare*; = to force, *cogĕre, compellĕre.* (2) intransit.: in a carriage, etc., (*in*)*vehi, gestari*; to — at, *petĕre.*
drivel: see nonsense.
driver, *raedarius, auriga*; of animals, *agitator.*
drizzle, v. *leniter pluĕre.*
droll, *lepidus, ridiculus, facetus*; adv. *lepide, ridicule, facete.*
drone, *fucus.*
droop, v.: transit., *demittĕre*; intransit., (*de*)*pendēre*; = wither, *languescĕre, flaccescĕre.*
drop, subst. *gutta, stilla.*
drop, v.: transit., *demittĕre, deicĕre*; intransit., = fall in drops, (*de*)*stillare*; = fall to the ground, *delabi, decidĕre.*
dropsy, *hydrops.*
dross, = refuse; q.v.
drought, *siccitas.*
drove, *grex, armentum.*
drover, *pecuarius, armentarius.*
drown, (*in aquam*) *summergĕre*; with noise, *obstrepĕre.*
drowsy, *somniculosus, semisomnus.*
drudge, subst. *servus, mediastinus.*
drudge, v. *servire.*
drudgery, *opera servilis.*
drug, subst. *medicamentum*; poisonous —, *venenum.*
drum, *tympanum.*
drunk, *ebrius, temulentus.*
drunkenness, *ebrietas*; as habit, *ebriositas, vinolentia.*
dry, adj. *siccus, aridus, sitiens* (= thirsty). Transf., *exilis, ieiunus, aridus.* Adv., of style, *exiliter, ieiune.*
dry, v. transit. *siccare*; to — tears, *abstergēre lacrimas*; intransit., *siccari, arescĕre.*
dryness, *siccitas.*
dubious; see doubtful.
duck, subst. *anas.*
duck, v. (*sub*)*mergĕre*; to — the head, *caput demittĕre.*
dudgeon, *ira, stomachus.*
due, subst. *ius* (*iuris*), *debitum*; —s, *vectigal*; harbour —s, *portorium.*
due, adj. *debitus; meritus, iustus, idoneus.*
duel, *certamen.*
dulcimer, *sambuca.*
dull, adj. *hebes, obtusus, tardus*; = uninteresting, *aridus, frigidus.* Adv. *tarde, frigide.*
dull, v. *hebetare, obscurare, obtundĕre.*
dulness, of mind, (*ingenii*) *tarditas, stupor.*
dumb, *mutus*; to become —, *obmutescĕre.*

dumbfounder, *obstupefacĕre.*
dun, adj. *fucus, suffuscus.*
dunce, *stipes.*
dung, *stercus* (*-oris*), *fimus.*
dungeon, *carcer, robur.*
dunghill, *sterquilinium.*
dupe, subst. *homo credulus.*
duplicate; see copy.
duplicity, *allacia, fraus.*
durable, *firmus, stabilis, perpetuus;* adv. *firme, stabiliter.*
duration, *temporis spatium.*
during, *per* with acc.; *in* with abl.; *inter* with acc.
dusk, *crepusculum.*
dusky, *fuscus;* see dark.
dust, subst. *pulvis.*
dust, v. *detergēre.*
dusty, *pulverulentus.*
dutiful, *pius, officiosus;* adv. *pie, officiose.*
dutifulness, *pietas.*
duty, *officium, munus;* sense of —, *pietas, religio;* —tax, vectigal.
dwarf, *nanus, pumilio.*
dwarfish, *pusillus.*
dwell, *habitare,* (*in*)*colĕre.*
dweller, *incola.*
dwelling, *domicilium, sedes, domus.*
dwindle, (*de*)*minui, decrescĕre.*
dye, v. *tingĕre, inficĕre.*
dyer, *infector.*
dynasty; use phrase with *domus.*
dyspepsia, *cruditas.*
dyspeptic, *crudus.*

E

each: of two, *uterque;* of three or more, *unusquisque, quisque, omnis;* — other, *inter se, alius alium.*
eager, *cupidus, studiosus, acer;* adv. *cupide, studiose, acriter.*
eagerness, *cupiditas, studium, ardor.*
eagle, *aquila.*
ear, *auris;* of corn, *spica, arista.*
early, adj. *matutinus* (= in the morning), *novus* (= fresh), *maturus, tempestivus* (= in good time).
early, adv. *mane* (in the morning); *mature, tempestive.*
earn, *merēre* and *merēri.*
earnest, adj. *intentus, gravis, serius;* in —, *serio.* Adv. *intente, impense.*
earnestness, *studium, contentio.*
earnings, *quaestus* (*-ūs*), *lucrum.*
earth: = soil, *terra, solum;* = the globe, *terra, orbis* (*terrarum*).
earthen, *terrenus.*
earthenware; adj., *fictilis;* subst., *fictilia* (*-ium*).
earthly, *terrestris; humanus.*
earthquake, *terrae motus* (*-ūs*).
earthwork, *agger.*
ease, subst. = rest, *tranquillitas, quies, otium, pax;* to be at ease, *quiescĕre;* = readiness, *facilitas.*
ease, v. *exonerare, expedire.*
easiness, *facilitas.*
east, subst. *oriens, orientis* (*solis*) *partes.*
eastern, easterly, *orientis; ad orientem versus.*
easy, *facilis;* = tranquil. *tranquillus, quietus, otiosus.*
eat, *ĕdĕre,* (*re*)*vesci;* to — away, *rodĕre.*
eatable, *esculentus.*
eating-house, *popina.*
eaves-dropper, *auceps.*
ebb, subst. *aestūs decessus* (*-ūs*).
ebb, v. *recedĕre.*
ebony, *hebenus.*
Ebro, *Hiberus.*
ebullition: use *effervescĕre;* of passions, *impetus* (*-ūs*), *aestus* (*-ūs*).
eccentric, *inusitatus.*
echo, subst. *imago vocis.*
echo, v. *vocem reddĕre, resonare;* see also imitate.
eclipse, subst. *defectio, defectus* (*-ūs*).
eclipse, v. transit. *obscurare.*
economical, *frugi, parcus;* adv. *parce.*
economy: = management, in gen., *rei familiaris administratio;* = frugality, *parsimonia.*
ecstasy: = frenzy, *insania, furor;* = bliss, *elatio voluptaria.*
ecstatic, *fanaticus, furens, insanus.*
eddy, *vertex.*
edge, a cutting —, *acies;* = margin, *margo, ora.*
edible, *esculentus.*
edict, *edictum, decretum, iussum*
edify, *docēre.*
edit, (*librum*) *ēdĕre.*
educate, *instituĕre, erudire, educare.*
education, *educatio, disciplina, eruditio.*
eel, *anguilla.*
efface, *delēre, abolēre.*
effect, subst. (1), = consequence, *effectus* (*-ūs*), *eventus* (*-ūs*), *consecutio.* (2), = influence, *vis, effectus* (*-ūs*); without —, *frustra;* in —, *revera, reapse.* (3), —s, = property, *res, bona* (*-orum*).
effect, v. *facĕre, efficĕre, conficĕre.*
effective, effectual, *efficiens, efficax;* adv. *efficienter, efficaciter.*
effeminacy, *mollitia, mollities.*
effeminate, *mollis, effeminatus;* adv. *molliter, effeminate.*
effervesce, *effervescĕre.*
effete, *effetus, obsoletus.*
efficacy, *efficientia, vis.*
effigy, *effigies, imago, simulacrum.*
effort, *opera, labor, conatus* (*-ūs*); to make an —, *operam dare, contendĕre.*
effrontery, *impudentia, os* (*impudens*).
effulgence, *splendor, fulgor.*
egg, *ovum.*
egoism, egotism, *sui ostentatio, sui amor.*
egoist, egotist, *qui sibi soli studet.*
egregious, *singularis, praeclarus.*
egress, *egressus* (*-ūs*), *exitus* (*-ūs*).
eight, adj. *octo;* — each, *octoni;* — times, *octies.*
eighteen, *duodeviginti.*
eighteenth, *duodevicesimus.*
eighth, *octavus;* an —, *octava pars.*
eightieth, *octogesimus.*
eighty, *octoginta;* — each, *octogeni;* — times, *octogies.*
either, *alteruter, utervis, uterlibet;* either . . . or, *aut . . . aut, vel. . . . vel.*

ejaculate, *vocem emittĕre.*
ejaculation, *vox.*
eject, *expellĕre, eicĕre, deicĕre.*
ejection, *expulsio, eiectio, deiectio.*
eke, v.: to — out, *rei* (dat.) *parcĕre.*
elaborate, adj. *elaboratus, exquisitus*; adv. *exquisite.*
elaborate, v. *elaborare, expolire.*
elapse, *intercedĕre, praeterire.*
elated, *elatus.*
elation, *animus elatus; gaudium.*
Elbe, *Albis.*
elbow, *cubitum.*
elder, *maior* (*natu*).
elderly, *aetate provectus.*
elect, adj. *designatus.*
elect, v. *creare, legĕre, eligĕre.*
election, *electio*; as an occasion, *comitia* (*-orum*).
electioneering, subst. *ambitio.*
elective, *suffragiis creatus.*
elector, *qui ius suffragii habet.*
elegance, *elegantia, venustas.*
elegant, *elegans, venustus, nitidus*; adv. *eleganter, venuste, nitide.*
elegy, *elegia* (*-orum*).
element: scientific, *elementum*; =part, *membrum, pars*; the —s of a subject, *elementa* (*-orum*), *principia* (*-orum*).
elementary, *primus.*
elephant, *elephantus, elephas.*
elevate, (*at*)*tollĕre, extollĕre.*
elevated, of places, *editus, altus*; of spirits, *elatus.*
elevation: = raising, *elatio*; of spirits, *elatio, altitudo*; = rising ground, *locus editus* or *superior.*
eleven, *undecim*: — each *undeni*; — times, *undecies.*
eleventh, *undecimus.*
elicit, *elicĕre, evocare.*
eligible, *opportunus, idoneus, dignus.*
elk, *alces.*
ell, *ulna, cubitum.*
elm, *ulmus.*
elocution, *pronuntiatio.*
elongate; see lengthen.
elope, *clam fugĕre.*
eloquence, *eloquentia, facundia.*
eloquent, *eloquens, facundus*; adv. *facunde, diserte.*
else, adj. *alius.*
else, adv.: = besides, *praeterea*; = otherwise, *aliter, alioqui*(*n*).
elsewhere, *alibi.*
elucidate; see explain.
elude, (*e*)*vitare, declinare.*
elusive, *fallax.*
Elysian, *Elysius.*
Elysium, *Elysium.*
emaciate, *attenuare, macerare.*
emaciated, *macer.*
emaciation, *macies.*
emanate, *emanare, effundi.*
emancipate, *liberare;* of slaves, *manumittĕre.*
emancipation, *liberatio*; of slaves, *manumissio.*
emancipator, *liberator.*
embalm, *condire.*
embankment, *agger, moles.*
embark, v.: transit., *imponĕre in navem*; intransit. *conscendĕre* (*navem*).
embarrass, (*con*)*turbare, impedire.*
embarrassing, *difficilis.*
embarrassment, *implicatio, conturbatio*; financial —, *angustiae* (*-arum*).
embassy, *legatio, legati* (*-orum*).
embellish, (*ex*)*ornare, decorare.*
embellishment, *decus* (*-oris*, n.), *ornamentum.*
embers, *cinis, favilla.*
embezzle, *avertĕre, supprimĕre.*
embezzlement, *peculatus* (*-ūs*), *suppressio.*
embezzler, *pecuniae aversor.*
embitter, *exacerbare.*
emblem, *insigne, signum.*
embody: to — troops, *milites conscribĕre*; = to include, *includĕre.*
emboss, *caelare.*
embrace, subst. *amplexus* (*-ūs*), *complexus* (*-ūs*).
embrace, v. *amplecti, amplexari, complecti*; = to contain, *comprehendĕre*; to — an opportunity, *occasionem capĕre*; to — an opinion, *in sententiam transire.*
embrocation, *fomentum.*
embroider, (*acu*) *pingĕre.*
embroil, *conturbare*; to — in a matter, *re implicare.*
emend, *emendare, corrigĕre.*
emendation, *emendatio.*
emerald, *smaragdus.*
emerge, *emergĕre, exsistĕre.*
emergency, *casus*(*-ūs*), *discrimen.*
emigrate, (*e*)*migrare, demigrare.*
emigration, (*e*)*migratio.*
eminence: = high ground, *locus editus, tumulus*; = distinction, *praestantia, fastigium.*
eminent, *insignis,* (*prae*)*clarus, egregius.* Adv. *egregie, praecipue, imprimis.*
emissary, *legatus, emissarius.*
emit, (*e*)*mittĕre, iacĕre.*
emolument, *emolumentum, lucrum.*
emotion, *animi motus* (*-ūs*) or *adfectus* (*-ūs*).
emperor, *imperator, princeps.*
emphasis, *vis.*
emphatic, *gravis, vehemens*; adv. *graviter, vehementer.*
empire, *imperium, principatus* (*-ūs*).
employ, (*re*) *uti;* (*rem*) *usurpare, exercĕre, adhibēre*; of persons, to be —ed, *detineri, versari.*
employment: as an act, *usus* (*-ūs*), *usurpatio*; = business, *res, negotium.*
emptiness, *inanitas.*
empty, adj. *inanis, vacuus, vanus, cassus.*
empty, v. *vacuefacĕre, exinanire.*
emulate, *aemulari.*
emulation, *aemulatio.*
emulous, *aemulus*; adv. *certatim.*
enable, *homini rei* (genit.) *facultatem facĕre.*
enact, (*legem*) *sancire, iubēre, statuĕre, constituĕre.*
enactment; see law.
enamoured; see love.
encamp, v. *castra ponĕre, considĕre.*
enchant, (*ef*)*fascinare.* Transf., *capĕre, delectare.*
enchantment; see charm.
enchantress, *venefica.*

encircle, *cingĕre, circumdare.*
enclose, *includĕre, saepire, continēre.*
enclosure, *saeptum, saepimentum.*
encomium, *laus, laudatio.*
encompass; see encircle.
encounter, subst. *congressus* (*-ūs*), *concursio.*
encounter, v. *concurrĕre, congredi, obviam fieri*; = to face unwelcome things, *obire, oppetĕre.*
encourage, (*ad*)*hortari, confirmare, erigĕre.*
encouragement, *confirmatio,* (*ad*)*hortatio.*
encroach, v.: to — on, *occupare, invadĕre.*
encroachment, *iniuria.*
encumber, *onerare, praegravare, impedire.*
encumbrance, *onus* (*-eris,* n.), *impedimentum.*
end, subst.: = termination, *finis, exitus* (*-ūs*); in the —, *tandem, denique*; = aim, object, *finis, consilium, propositum.*
end, v.: transit., *finire, conficĕre, terminare*; intransit., *finem habēre, desinĕre*; to — well, *bene evenire.*
endanger, *in periculum adducĕre, periclitari.*
endear, *devincire.*
endearments, *blanditiae* (*-arum,* plur.).
endeavour, subst. *conatus* (*-ūs*), *nisus* (*-ūs*).
endeavour, v. *conari,* (*e*)*niti.*
endless, *infinitus, aeternus, perpetuus*; adv. *sine fine, perpetuo.*
endorse; see allow, sanction.
endow: to — a daughter, *dotem filiae dare*; see also give.
endowed, *ornatus, praeditus, instructus.*
endurable, *tolerabilis, patibilis.*
endurance, *patientia, perpessio.*
endure: = to bear, (*per*)*ferre, sustinēre, pati, perpeti*; = to last, (*per*)*manēre, durare.*
enemy, *hostis* (public), *inimicus* (personal or private); *adversarius.*
energetic, *acer, strenuus, impiger*; adv. *acriter, strenue, impigre.*
energy, *vis, impetus* (*-ūs*), *contentio.*
enervate, *enervare, debilitare,* (*e*)*mollire.*
enervation, *debilitatio, languor.*
enforce, *exsequi.*
enfranchise, *in civitatem adscribĕre; civitate donare.*
enfranchisement, *civitas, civitatis donatio.*
engage: = to bind, make liable, *obligare, obstringĕre*; = to promise, undertake, *spondēre, promittĕre, recipĕre*; = to join battle, *confligĕre, congredi.*
engaged: = busy, *occupatus*; — to be married, *sponsus, pactus.*
engagement: = promise, *sponsio, pactum, pactio, promissum*; an — to marry, *pactio nuptialis*; = piece of business, *negotium*; = battle *pugna, proelium.*
engaging, *blandus, suavis.*
engender, *gignĕre, generare.*
engine, *machina, machinatio, machinamentum.*
engineer, *machinator, faber.*
England, *Anglia; Britannia* (= Britain).
English, *Anglus, Anglicus; Britannus, Britannicus.*
engrave, *incīdĕre, insculpĕre, scalpĕre.*
engraver, *scalptor.*
engross, = occupy exclusively, *occupare, tenēre.*
engulf, *absorbēre,* (*de*)*vorare,* (*ex*)*haurire.*
enhance, *augēre, amplificare.*
enhancement, *amplificatio.*
enigma, *aenigma* (*-atis,* n.), *ambages* (*-um*).
enigmatic, *obscurus, ambiguus*; adv. *ambigue, per ambages.*
enjoin; see command.
enjoy, (*re*) *frui, gaudēre*; = to have, *uti, habēre.*
enjoyment, *gaudium, voluptas.*
enlarge, *amplificare, dilatare, augēre*; to — upon, *pluribus* (*verbis*) *disputare.*
enlighten, *inlustrare, inluminare.* Transf., *docēre, erudire.*
enlightenment, *humanitas.*
enlist, v.; transit., of troops, (*con*)*scribĕre*; in gen., = win over, *conciliare*; intransit., *nomen dare.*
enliven, *excitare, exhilarare.*
enmity, *inimicitia, odium, simultas.*
ennoble, *nobilium ordini adscribĕre*; *ornare, honestare.*
ennui, *taedium.*
enormity, *immanitas*; = monstrous action, *scelus* (*-eris,* n.), *flagitium.*
enormous, *ingens, immanis*; adv. *praeter modum.*
enough, *sat, satis, adfatim*; more than —, *nimis*; not —, *parum.*
enquire; see ask; to — into, *quaerĕre, inquirĕre, cognoscĕre.*
enquiry, *quaestio, inquisitio, cognitio.*
enrage, *inritare, exasperare.*
enrich, *locupletare, ditare.*
enroll, (*ad*)*scribĕre*; see enlist.
enshrine, *dedicare, consecrare.*
ensign: = banner, *signum, vexillum*; = banner-bearer, *signifer, aquilifer.*
enslave, (*hominem*) *in servitutem redigĕre.*
enslaved, *servus.* Transf., *addictus, emancipatus.*
ensnare, *capĕre, inretire, inlicĕre.*
entail, *adferre, inferre*; see cause.
entangle, *impedire, implicare.*
entanglement, *implicatio.*
enter, *intrare, introire, inire, ingredi*; to — upon an undertaking, *ingredi, inire, suscipĕre, incipĕre*; to — public life, *ad rempublicam accedĕre*; to — an alliance, *societatem facĕre.*
enterprise, *inceptum, opus* (*-eris,* n.).
enterprising, *promptus, acer, audax.*
entertain: = to have, *habēre*; = to amuse, *delectare, oblectare*; = to receive hospitably, *hospitio accipĕre, excipĕre.*
entertaining; see amusing.
entertainment: = hospitality, *hospitium*; = banquet, *epulae* (*-arum*) *convivium.*
enthusiasm, *studium, fervor, ardor.*

enthusiastic, *fanaticus, ardens, fervidus*; adv. *ardenter, acriter.*
entice, *adlicĕre, adlectare, inlicĕre.*
enticement, *inlecebrae, esca.*
enticing, *blandus.*
entire, *totus, integer, solidus.* Adv. *omnino, plane, prorsus, penitus.*
entitle: =to name, *appellare, nominare*; =to give a title to, *ius* or *potestatem dare.*
entrails, *intestina* (*-orum*), *viscera* (*-um*).
entrance, subst.: as act, *ingressio, introitus* (*-ūs*); = place of —, *aditus* (*-ūs*), *introitus* (*-ūs*), *ostium.*
entrap; see ensnare.
entreat, *precari, rogare, orare, obsecrare.*
entrench, *fossā* (*com*)*munire, vallare.*
entrenchment, *vallum, munitio, munimentum.*
entrust, (*con*)*credĕre, committĕre, mandare, commendare.*
entry; see entrance; in accounts, *nomen.*
entwine, (*in*)*nectĕre, implicare, redimire.*
enumerate, (*di*)*numerare, enumerare.*
enunciate, *edicĕre, pronuntiare, enuntiare.*
enunciation, *enuntiatio.*
envelope, subst. *involucrum.*
envelope, v. *involvĕre, obducĕre.*
envenom, *venenare, veneno imbuĕre.*
enviable, *fortunatus, beatus.*
envious, *invidus, lividus.*
environs, render by phrase with *loca* and *circum.*
envoy, *legatus.*
envy, subst. *invidia, livor.*
envy, v. *invidēre.*
ephemeral, *unius diei, caducus, brevis.*
epic, *epicus, heroicus*; an — poem, *epos.*
Epicurean, *Epicureus*; = hedonist, *voluptarius.*
epidemic, *morbus, pestilentia.*
epigram, *epigramma* (*-atis*, n.).
epigrammatic, *salsus.*
epilepsy, *morbus comitialis.*
epilogue, *epilogus.*
episode, *embolium, excursus* (*-ūs*).
epistle, *epistula, litterae* (*-arum*).
epitaph, *titulus, elogium.*
epitome, *epitome, summarium.*
epoch, *tempus* (*-oris*, n.), *aetas, saeculum.*
equability, *aequus animus, aequabilitas.*
equable, *aequus, aequabilis*; adv. *aequo animo, aequabiliter.*
equal, subst. *par, compar.*
equal, adj. *aequus, aequalis, par, compar*; adv. *aeque, aequaliter, pariter.*
equal, v. (*ad*)*aequare, aequiparare.*
equality, *aequalitas, aequabilitas.*
equalize, (*ex*)*aequare, adaequare.*
equanimity, *aequus animus, aequitas animi.*
equestrian, subst. *eques* (*-itis*).
equestrian, adj. *equester* or *equestris.*
equidistant, to be, *pari intervallo inter se distare.*
equilateral, *aequis lateribus.*
equilibrium, *aequilibrium*; to hold in —, *librare.*
equinox, *aequinoctium.*
equip, *armare, instruĕre, ornare.*
equipment, *arma* (*-orum*), *armamenta* (*-orum*), *armatura.*
equitable, adj. *aequus, iustus, meritus.*
equity, *aequitas, aequum, iustitia.*
equivalent; see equal.
equivocal, *ambiguus, anceps, dubius.*
equivocate, *tergiversari.*
equivocation, *ambiguitas.*
era, *tempus.*
eradicate, *extirpare, evellĕre, eruĕre.*
erase, *delēre, inducĕre.*
erasure, *litura.*
ere; see before.
erect, adj. (*e*)*rectus.*
erect, v. *erigĕre, tollĕre*; = build, *aedificare, exstruĕre.*
erection: as act, *aedificatio, exstructio*; = a building, *aedificium.*
erotic, *amatorius.*
err, *errare, vagari*; *falli* (=be mistaken); *peccare* or *delinquĕre* (= do wrong).
errand, *mandatum.*
erratic, *vagus, inconstans.*
erroneous, *falsus*; adv. *falso, perperam.*
error, *error, erratum; peccatum* (=sin).
erst, *quondam, olim.*
erudite, *litteratus, doctus, eruditus.*
erudition, *doctrina, eruditio.*
eruption, *eruptio.*
escape, subst. *fuga, effugium.*
escape, v. (*ef*)*fugĕre, elabi, evadĕre.*
escarpment, *vallum.*
eschew, *vitare*; see avoid.
escort, *comitatus* (*-ūs*); under a person's —, *homine comitante.*
escort, v. *comitari, deducĕre, prosequi.*
esoteric, *arcanus, occultus.*
especial, *praecipuus*; adv. *praesertim, praecipue, maxime.*
espouse; see betroth and marry.
essay, subst.: = attempt, *conatus* (*-ūs*); = treatise, *libellus.*
essay, v. *conari.*
essence, *natura, vis.*
essential, *verus, proprius*; adv. *reapse, vere, necessario.*
establish: = set up, *statuĕre, instituĕre*; = make strong, *confirmare, stabilire*; = prove, *probare, vincĕre.*
establishment, *constitutio, confirmatio*; = household, *familia.*
estate: = condition, *status* (*-ūs*), *habitus* (*-ūs*), *condicio, sors*; = property, *res, fundus, praedium.*
esteem, subst. *opinio, existimatio.*
esteem, v.: = think, *existimare, putare*; = respect, *diligĕre, vereri.*
estimable, *bonus, gravis, probus.*
estimate, subst. *aestimatio*; in gen., = judgment, *iudicium.*
estimate, v., = value, *aestimare, censēre.*
estimation; see esteem.
estrange, (*ab*)*alienare.*
estrangement, *alienatio, discidium.*
estuary, *aestuarium.*
eternal, *aeternus, sempiternus, perpetuus*; adv. *in aeternum, perpetuo.*
eternity, *aeternitas.*
ether, *aether.*
ethereal, *aetherius.*
ethical, *moralis*; or use phrase with *mores.*

ethics, *philosophia moralis*; see ethical.
etiquette, *mos, usus* (*-ūs*).
eulogy, *laudatio, laus.*
euphemism; render by phrase, such as *mitiorem in partem vertĕre dicendo.*
euphony, *sonus dulcis.*
evacuate, *vacuefacĕre,* (*de*)*relinquĕre; loco discedĕre.*
evade, (*ef*)*fugĕre, subterfugĕre.*
evaporate, *in vaporem vertĕre.*
evasion, *ambages* (*-um*), *tergiversatio.*
evasive, *ambiguus*; adv. *ambigue.*
even, adj. *aequus, planus*; of numbers, *par.* Adv. *aequaliter, pariter.*
even, adv. *etiam, vel, adeo*: not —, *ne . . . quidem*; — if, *etsi, etiamsi.*
evening, subst. *vesper* (*-eris* or *-eri*); in the —, *vesperi.*
evening, adj. *vespertinus*; the — star, *Hesperus, Vesper.*
evenness, *aequalitas*; of temper, *aequus animus.*
event: = result, *eventus* (*-ūs*), *exitus* (*-ūs*); = occurrence, *factum, casus* (*-ūs*): at all —s, *certe, saltem.*
eventful, *memorabilis.*
ever, adv.: = always, *semper*; = at any time, *umquam* (*unquam*), *quando* (after *num* and *si*); for —, *in aeternum, in perpetuum.*
everlasting; see eternal.
every, *quisque, omnis*: — one, *unusquisque*; one in — ten, *decimus quisque*; — body, *omnes* (*-ium*), *nemo non*; — day, *quotidie*; — thing, *omnia* (*-ium*); — where, *ubique, passim.*
evict, (*ex*)*pellĕre, detrudĕre.*
evidence: legal, *testimonium, indicium*; in gen., *argumentum.*
evident, *manifestus, apertus*; it is —, *apparet, liquet.* Adv. *aperte, manifesto.*
evil, subst. *malum, incommodum.*
evil, adj. *malus, pravus, improbus.*
evil-doer, *maleficus.*
evil-speaking, *maledicus.*
evince, *ostendĕre, probare, praestare.*
evoke, *evocare, elicĕre, excitare.*
evolution: — of soldiers, *decursus* (*-ūs*); in nature, *rerum progressio.*
ewe, *ovis femina*; — lamb, *agna.*
ewer, *urceus, hydria, urna.*
exact, *exactus, subtilis, diligens*; adv. *diligenter, accurate, subtiliter.*
exacting, *rapax.*
exaction, *exactio.*
exactitude, *subtilitas, diligentia.*
exaggerate, *augēre, in maius extollĕre.*
exaggeration, *superlatio, traiectio.*
exalt, *augēre, amplificare,* (*ex*)*tollĕre.*
exaltation: of feeling, *elatio*; in rank, *dignitatis accessio.*
exalted, *altus,* (*ex*)*celsus, elatus.*
examination, *investigatio, inquisitio.*
examine, *investigare, inquirĕre.*
example, *exemplum, exemplar, documentum*; for —, *verbi causa, exempli gratia, vel.*
exasperate, *inritare, exasperare.*
exasperation, *ira.*
excavate, (*ex*)*cavare, effodĕre.*
excavation, *cavum.*
exceed, *excedĕre, egredi.*
excel, *excellĕre, praestare* (with dat).
excellence, *excellentia, praestantia.*
excellent, *excellens, praestans, egregius, optimus*; adv. *excellenter, egregie, optime.*
except, prep. *praeter, extra*; except you, *te excepto.*
except, v. *excipĕre, eximĕre.*
exception, *exceptio*; all without —, *omnes ad unum.*
exceptional, *rarus*; adv. *praeter modum.*
excess: — in quantity, *nimium*; in conduct, *intemperantia, licentia.*
excessive, *nimius, immodicus*; adv. *nimis, immodice, praeter modum.*
exchange, subst. *permutatio*; of money, *collybus.*
exchange, v. (*per*)*mutare.*
exchequer, *aerarium, fiscus.*
excitable, *inritabilis, fervidus.*
excite, *excitare, concitare,* (*com*)*movēre, incendĕre.*
excited, *trepidus.*
excitement, *concitatio, commotio.*
exclaim, (*ex*)*clamare, vociferari.*
exclamation, *exclamatio, vox.*
exclude, *excludĕre, prohibēre, arcēre.*
exclusive: of persons, *rari aditūs*; of properties, = belonging to one only, *proprius.*
excrescence, *tuber.*
excruciating, *acerbissimus.*
exculpate, *excusare,* (*ex*)*purgare*
exculpation, *purgatio.*
excursion, *iter* (*-ineris*).
excuse, subst. *excusatio.*
excuse, v.: = make excuses for, *excusare,* (*ex*)*purgare*; = pardon, *ignoscĕre, veniam dare.*
execrable; see abominable.
execrate, *exsecrari, detestari, abominari.*
execute: = carry out, *exsequi, persequi, efficĕre*; = punish by death, *necare, securi ferire.*
execution: = carrying out, *effectio*; = capital punishment, *supplicium*; = slaughter, in gen., *strages, caedes.*
executioner, *carnifex.*
executive; use phrase with *administrare.*
exegesis, *explanatio, interpretatio.*
exemplary, adj.; see excellent.
exempt, adj. *immunis, liber, solutus.*
exempt, v. *excipĕre, eximĕre, liberare.*
exemption, *immunitas.*
exercise, subst. *exercitatio*; = literary task, *thema* (*-atis*).
exercise, v.: = carry on, *exercēre, facĕre, efficĕre*; = work, train, *exercēre.*
exert, v. *contendĕre, intendĕre*; to — oneself, *niti, eniti, conari.*
exertion, *contentio, conatus* (*-ūs*).
Exeter, *Isca* (*Dumnoniorum*).
exhale, (*ex*)*halare.*
exhalation, *exhalatio.*
exhaust, *exhaurire*; = wear out, *consumĕre, conficĕre.*
exhausted, *confectus, defessus, fatigatus.*
exhaustion; see fatigue.
exhibit, v. *proponĕre, exhibēre*; see show.

exhibition, *spectaculum, ludi* (*-orum*).
exhilarate, (*ex*)*hilarare, hilarem facĕre.*
exhilaration, *hilaritas.*
exhort, (*ad*)*hortari.*
exigence, *necessitas, angustiae* (*-arum*).
exile, subst.: = banishment, *exsilium, relegatio*; to be in —, *exsulare*; = person banished, *exsul.*
exile, v. *eicĕre, relegare,* (*ex*)*pellĕre.*
exist, *esse, exsistĕre, exstare.*
existence; use *esse.*
exit: = going out, *exitus* (*-ūs*); = way out, *exitus* (*-ūs*), *ostium.*
exonerate, (*culpa*) *liberare.*
exorbitant, *immodicus*; adv. *immodice.*
exordium, *exordium, prooemium.*
exotic, *peregrinus, externus.*
expand, v. transit. (*ex*)*pandĕre, extendĕre, laxare.*
expanse, *spatium.*
expatiate, *pluribus* (*verbis*) *disputare.*
expatriate; see banish.
expect, *exspectare, sperare.*
expectant, *adrectus, suspensus.*
expectation, *exspectatio, spes.*
expectorate, *exscreare, exspuĕre.*
expediency, *utilitas.*
expedient, subst. *ratio, consilium.*
expedient, adj. *commodus, utilis*: it is —, *expedit.*
expedite, *expedire, maturare.*
expedition: = speed, *celeritas*; milit., *expeditio.*
expeditious, *celer, promptus*; adv. *celeriter, prompte.*
expel, (*ex*)*pellĕre, eicĕre.*
expend, *expendĕre, impendĕre.*
expense, *impensa, impendium.*
expensive, *sumptuosus, carus, pretiosus*; adv. *sumptuose, pretiose.*
expenditure, of public money, *erogatio*; see also expense.
experience, subst. *rerum usus* (*-ūs*), *experientia*; I speak from —, *expertus dico.*
experience, v. *experiri, pati.*
experienced, (*rerum*) *peritus.*
experiment, *experimentum, periculum.*
expert, *sciens, callidus, peritus.*
expertness, expertise, *calliditas, peritia.*
expiate, *luere, expiare.*
expiation, *expiatio, poena, piaculum.*
expiatory, *piacularis.*
expire, *exspirare*; of time, *exire.*
explain, *exponĕre, explicare, interpretari.*
explanation, *explicatio, interpretatio.*
explicit, *apertus, definitus*; adv. *plane, definite.*
explode: = to discredit (a theory), *explodĕre, refellĕre, confutare*; intransit., = to burst, *dirumpi.*
export, *exportare.*
exportation, *exportatio.*
exports, *merces* (*quae exportantur*).
expose, *exponĕre*; to danger, etc., *obicĕre, offerre*; = to unmask, *detegĕre.*
exposition, *expositio.*
expound; see explain.
express, (in words), *significare, declarare*; to — oneself, *loqui, dicĕre.*
expression: = thing said, *verbum, sententia, dictum, vox*; of the features, *vultus* (*-ūs*).
expressive, *significans*; adv. *significanter.*
expressiveness, *vis.*
expulsion, *exactio, expulsio.*
expunge, *delēre, oblitterare.*
expurgate, (*ex*)*purgare.*
exquisite, *exquisitus, venustus*; adv. *exquisite, venuste.*
extant: to be —, *exstare.*
extempore, *subitus*; to speak —, *ex tempore dicĕre.*
extend, v.; transit., *extendĕre, augēre, amplificare;* intransit., *patēre, extendi.*
extensive, *magnus, amplus, latus*; adv. *late.*
extent, *ambitus* (*-ūs*), *spatium*; to this —, *hactenus*; to a certain —, *aliqua ex parte.*
extenuate, *levare, mitigare, minuĕre.*
extenuation, *imminutio.*
exterior, subst. *forma, species.*
exterior, adj.; see external.
exterminate, *ad unum interficĕre; eradicare, exstirpare.*
extermination, *internecio, occidio.*
external, *externus exter*(*us*), *exterior*; adv. *extrinsecus.*
extinct, *exstinctus, obsoletus.*
extinction, *exstinctio.*
extinguish, *exstinguĕre, restinguĕre.*
extirpate, *exstirpare, eradicare, excīdĕre.*
extol, *laudibus,* (*ef*)*ferre,* (*con*)*laudare.*
extort, *exprimĕre, extorquēre.*
extortion, *res repetundae.*
extortionate, *rapax, avarus.*
extra, adv. *praeterea.*
extract, v. *extrahĕre, evellĕre, exprimĕre*; from a book, *excerpĕre.*
extraction: as act, *evulsio*; = origin, *origo, genus* (*-eris,* n.).
extraneous; see external.
extraordinary, *inusitatus, insolitus, novus, mirus.* Adv. *extra ordinem, praeter morem, mire.*
extravagance: in expenditure, *sumptus* (*-ūs*); in gen., = excess, *intemperantia, immoderatio.*
extravagant: = lavish, *prodigus, sumptuosus*; in gen., = excessive, *nimius, immoderatus, intemperans.* Adv. *prodige, sumptuose; immoderate, intemperanter.*
extreme, subst.; see extremity.
extreme, adj. *extremus, ultimus, summus.* Adv. *summe*; often rendered by superl.
extremity: = top, *cacumen, fastigium*; = farthest part, or extreme degree, render by adj. *extremus.*
extricate, *expedire,* (*ex*)*solvĕre.*
extrude, *extrudĕre, eicĕre.*
exuberance, *ubertas, luxuria.*
exuberant, *luxuriosus, laetus*; adv. *uberrime.*
exude, (*ex*)*sudare, manare.*
exult, *exsultare, gestire, laetari.*
exultant, *laetus.*
exultation, *laetatio, exsultatio.*
eye, subst. *oculus, ocellus.*
eye, v. *adspicĕre, contemplari, intueri.*

eye-ball, *pupula.*
eye-brow, *supercilium.*
eye-lid, *palpebra* (usually plur.)
eyesight, *acies.*
eye-witness, *arbiter, spectator et testis.*

F

fable, *fabula* (*commenticia*).
fabled, fabulous, *fabulosus, fictus, commenticius.*
fabric: built, *aedificium*; woven, *textum, textile*; fig., *compages.*
fabricate, *fabricari, texĕre.*
fabrication: = making, *fabricatio*; = falsehood, *commentum, mendacium.*
fabricator, *auctor.*
face, subst. *facies, vultus* (-*ūs*), *os* (*oris*); — to —, *coram.*
face, v.: = to be opposite, (*a*)*spectare*; = to encounter, *obire, obviam ire.*
facetious, *iocosus, facetus*; adv. *iocose, facete.*
facetiousness, *facetiae* (-*arum*).
facilitate, *faciliorem reddĕre.*
facility, *facilitas.*
facing, *contra, adversus.*
facsimile, *descriptio imagoque.*
fact, *res, factum*; in —, *reapse, sane.*
faction, *factio, pars.*
factious, *factiosus, seditiosus*; adv. *per factionem, seditiose.*
factiousness, *factio, studium partium.*
factitious; see false.
factory, *fabrica, officina.*
faculty, *vis, facultas.*
fade, *pallescĕre.*
faded; see pale.
fading, = transient, *caducus, fluxus.*
fagot, *fascis, sarmenta* (-*orum*, plur.).
fail, subst.: without —, *certo, omnino.*
fail, v.: = to give out, *deficĕre, deesse*; = not to succeed, *concidĕre, cadĕre*; transit., *deficĕre, deserĕre, destituĕre.*
failing, *peccatum, vitum.*
failure, *defectio.*
fain: I would — do, *velim facĕre, libens faciam.*
faint, adj. *languidus, defessus.*
faint, v. *conlabi,* (*animo*) *linqui.*
faint-hearted, *timidus.*
faintness, *languor.*
fair, subst. *nundinae* (-*arum*).
fair, adj.: = beautiful, *pulcher, venustus, formosus*; of weather, *serenus*; = favourable, *secundus, idoneus*; morally, *aequus, iustus*; = moderately good, *mediocris.* Adv., *aeque, iuste; mediocriter.*
fairness: = beauty, *pulchritudo, forma, venustas*; = justice, *iustitia, aequitas.*
fairy, *nympha.*
faith: = fidelity, *fides, fidilitas, pietas*; = belief, *opinio, persuasio, fides*; to have — in, *credĕre, confidĕre.*
faithful, *fidelis, fidus*; adv. *fideliter.*
faithfulness, *fidelitas, fides, constantia.*
faithless, *perfidus*; adv. *perfide.*
faithlessness, *perfidia, infidelitas.*
fall, subst. *casus* (-*ūs*), *lapsūs* (-*us*); = ruin, *ruina, excidium*; = lessening, *deminutio.*
fall, v. *cadĕre, decĭdĕre, ruĕre*; to — dead, *cadĕre, concĭdĕre, occĭdĕre*; of a city, *expugnari, capi*; to — back, = retreat, *pedem referre*; to — back on, *recurrĕre* or *confugĕre ad*; to — upon, = attack, *invadĕre, incurrĕre*; to — out, = happen, *evenire*; = disagree, *dissentire, dissidēre.*
fallacious, *fallax, falsus*; adv. *fallaciter, falso.*
fallacy, *vitium, captio.*
fallible, *errori obnoxius.*
fallow: the field lies —, *ager cessat*; — ground, *novalis.*
false, *falsus; fictus, commenticius* (= made up), *subditus* (=forged), *perfidus* (=treacherous); to play —, *deesse.* Adv. *falso, perperam.*
falsehood, *mendacium, commentum.*
falsify, *vitiare, corrumpĕre.*
falter, *haesitare, haerēre, titubare.*
falteringly, *titubanter.*
fame, *laus, gloria, fama.*
familiar: = well known, *familiaris, notus*; = acquainted, *sciens, gnarus, peritus.* Adv. *familiariter.*
familiarity, *familiaritas, consuetudo.*
family, subst. *familia* (= household); *domus; gens* (= clan); *genus* (-*eris*, = race, stock); of good —, *nobilis.*
family, adj. *familiaris, domesticus; gentilis; privatus* (opp. to *publicus*).
famine, *fames, cibi inopia.*
famish, *fame enecare, conficĕre.*
famous, (*prae*)*clarus, inlustris, celeber.*
fan, subst.: for winnowing, *vannus*; for fanning oneself, *flabellum.*
fan, v. *ventilare.*
fanatical, *fanaticus.*
fancied, *opinabilis, opinatus.*
fancy, subst.: as a faculty, *inventio, cogitatio*; = idea, notion, *opinio*; = liking, preference, *libido.*
fancy, v.: = to imagine, *fingĕre*; = to think, *opinari, putare.*
fang, *dens.*
fanged, *dentatus.*
far: in space, *procul, longe*: from — off, *eminus*; farther, *longius, ultra*; as — as, *tenus* (prep.), *usque* (adv. = all the way); — and wide, *longe lateque*; in degree, — better, *longe* or *multo melior*; — from it, *minime*; so —, *hactenus.*
farce, *mimus.*
farcical, *mimicus, ridiculus*; adv. *mimice, ridicule.*
fare, subst.: = food, *cibus, victus* (-*ūs*); = money for journey, *vectura, naulum.*
fare, v. *se habēre*, with adv.
farewell! *valē! valēte!*; to bid — *valēre iubēre.*
far-fetched, *longe repetitus, arcessitus.*
farm, subst. *fundus, praedium, ager.*
farm, v.: = till, *arare, colĕre*; = hire, *redimĕre, conducĕre*; — out, = let out on contract, (*e*)*locare.*
farmer, *agricola, colonus*; a — of revenues, *publicanus.*
farming, *agricultura, res rusticae*; = hiring, *redemptio, conductio.*
farthing, *quadrans, teruncius*; I do not care a — for, *haud flocci facio.*

fascinate, *fascinare*; see charm.
fascination, *fascinum.* Transf., *blanditia, dulcedo.*
fashion, subst.: = custom, way, *mos, consuetudo, ritus* (*-ūs*); = style of dress, *habitus* (*-ūs*), *ornatus* (*-ūs*); = what is fashionable, *saeculum*; out of —, *obsoletus.*
fashion, v. *fabricari,* (*ef*)*fingĕre.*
fashionable, *elegans*; adv. *eleganter.*
fast, subst. *ieiunium.*
fast, adj.; = quick, *celer, citus, rapidus*; = fixed, firm, *firmus, stabilis*; to make —, *firmare, stabilire.*
fast, adv.: = quickly, *celeriter, rapide*; = firmly, *firme, firmiter.*
fast, v. *ieiunium servare.*
fasten, (*ad*)*figĕre,* (*ad*)*ligare, adnectĕre*; to — together, *connectĕre.*
fastening, *vinculum, claustra* (*-orum*).
fastidious, *fastidiosus, delicatus*; adv. *fastidiose, delicate.*
fat, subst. *adeps, sebum.*
fat, adj. *pinguis, obesus.*
fatal, *perniciosus, funestus.*
fatality: = power of fate, *fatum*; = accident, *casus* (*-ūs*).
fate, *fatum, necessitas, sors*; the Fates, *Parcae.*
fated, *fatalis.*
father, subst. *pater, parens;* fathers= ancestors, *maiores* (*-um*).
father, v. *ascribĕre, tribuĕre.*
father-in-law, *socer.*
fatherless, *orbus.*
fatherly, *paternus.*
fathom, subst. *ulna.*
fathom, v. *explorare.*
fatigue, subst. (*de*)*fatigatio, lassitudo.*
fatigue, v. (*de*)*fatigare.*
fatigued, (*de*)*fatigatus,* (*de*)*fessus.*
fatten: transit., *saginare*; intransit., *pinguescĕre.*
fatuity, *fatuitas, ineptia.*
fatuous, *fatuus, ineptus*; adv. *inepte.*
fault, *culpa, vitium, delictum*; to find — with, *culpare, accusare.*
faultless, *integer, innocens*; adv. *integre, innocenter.*
faulty, *mendosus, vitiosus*; adv. *mendose, vitiose.*
favour, subst.; as position, *gratia*; as disposition, goodwill, *favor, benevolentia*; an act of —, *beneficium*; to do a —, *gratificari.*
favour, v. *favēre, studēre, suffragari.*
favourable, *propitius* (of gods), *commodus, secundus*; adv. *benigne, commode.*
favourer, *fautor* (f. *fautrix*).
favourite, subst. *deliciae* (*-arum*).
favourite, adj. *carus, gratiosus.*
fawn, subst. *hinnuleus.*
fawn, v.: to — upon, *adulari.*
fawning, subst. *adulatio.*
fealty, *fides, fidelitas.*
fear, subst. *metus* (*-ūs*), *timor, pavor.*
fear, v. *metuĕre, timēre, verēri.*
fearful: = afraid, *timidus, pavidus*; = dreadful, *dirus, terribilis.* Adv. *timide, pavide; dire.*
fearless, *impavidus, intrepidus*; adv. *sine timore, impavide.*
feasible, *quod fieri potest.*
feast, subst.: = feast-day, *dies festus*; = banquet, *convivium, epulae* (*-arum*).
feast, v.: transit., *pascĕre*; intransit., *epulari, convivari.*
feat, *facinus* (*-oris,* n.), *factum.*
feather, subst. *penna* (*pinna*).
feature, of the face, *lineamentum*; the —s, *vultus* (*-ūs*).
February, (*mensis*) *Februarius.*
fecund, *fecundus.*
fecundity, *fecunditas, fertilitas.*
federal, *foederatus, foedere, sociatus.*
fee, subst. *merces.*
fee, v. *mercedem dare.*
feeble, *infirmus, invalidus, debilis*; adv. *infirme.*
feebleness, *debilitas, infirmitas.*
feed, v.: transit., *pascĕre, alĕre*; intransit., *vesci,* (*de*)*pasci.*
feel: = to touch, handle, *temptare, tangĕre*; to — an emotion, *laetitiam,* etc., *capĕre, percipĕre, sentire.*
feeler, *crinis, corniculum.*
feeling, subst. *sensus* (*-ūs*), *tactus* (*-ūs*); = emotion, *animus, animi motus* (*-ūs*) or *adfectus* (*-ūs*).
feeling, adj. *humanus, misericors.*
feign, *fingĕre, simulare.*
feigned, *fictus, simulatus*; adv. *ficte, simulate.*
feint, *simulatio.*
felicitate, *gratulari.*
felicitation, *gratulatio.*
felicitous, of style, *venustus.*
felicity: = happiness, *vita beata*; of style, *venustas.*
fell, adj. *dirus, saevus.*
fell, v. *caedere, excidĕre*; in gen., = knock down, (*con*)*sternĕre.*
fellow: = associate, *socius, comes*; = equal, *par*; = person, *homo.*
fellow-citizen, fellow-countryman, *civis.*
fellow-heir, *coheres.*
fellow-servant, *conservus.*
fellowship, *societas*; = corporation, *conlegium.*
fellow-soldier, *commilito.*
felon: see criminal.
felt, *coactum.*
female, subst. *femina, mulier.*
female, feminine, *muliebris, femineus*; gram., *femininus.*
fen, *palūs* (*-ūdis,* f.), *uligo.*
fence, subst. *saepes, saepimentum.*
fence, v.: = enclose, *saepire*; = fight with swords, *batuĕre.*
fencer, *gladiator.*
fenny, *uliginosus, paluster.*
ferment, *fermentum.* Transf., *frevor, aestus* (*-ūs*).
ferment, v. *fervēre.*
fern, *filix.*
ferocious, *ferus, saevus, atrox.*
ferocity, *saevitia, atrocitas.*
ferret, subst. *viverra.*
ferry, subst. *traiectus* (*-ūs*); — -boat, *scapha, cymba*; — -man, *portitor.*
ferry, v. *traicĕre, transmittĕre.*
fertile, *fecundus, fertilis, uber.*
fertility, *fertilitas, ubertas, fecunditas.*

fervent, fervid, *fervidus, fervens, ardens*; adv. *ardenter, ferventer.*
fervour, *ardor, fervor.*
festival, *dies festus, feriae* (*-arum*).
festive, *hilaris, festus.*
festivity: see festival; = mirth, *festivitas, hilaritas.*
festoon, subst. *serta* (*-orum*).
fetch, *adferre, adducĕre.*
fetid, *teter, foetidus, gravis.*
fetter, subst. *compes, catena, vinculum.*
fetter, v. *vincula inicĕre.* Transf., *impedire.*
feud, *simultas; inimicitia.*
fever, *febris*; to be in a — (fig.), *trepidare, aestuare.*
feverish, *febriculosus.* Transf., *trepidus*; — excitement, *summa trepidatio.*
few, *pauci, rari.*
fib, *mendaciunculum.*
fibre, *fibra.*
fickle, *inconstans, levis.*
fickleness, *inconstantia, levitas.*
fiction, *res ficta, fabula, commentum.*
fictitious, *commenticius, fictus.*
fiddle, *fides* (*-ium*).
fiddler, *fidicen.*
fidelity, *fidelitas, fides.*
fidget, v. *trepidare.*
fidgety, *inquietus.*
field: = piece of land, *ager, arvum, campus* (= plain); — of battle, *acies*; fig., = sphere, *campus, locus, area.*
fiendish, *nefandus, immanis, atrox.*
fierce, *ferox, ferus, saevus*; adv. *ferociter, saeve.*
fierceness, *ferocitas, saevitia.*
fiery, *igneus, flammeus.* Transf., *ardens, fervidus, ferox.*
fife, *tibia.*
fifteen, *quindecim*: — each, *quini deni*; — times, *quindecie(n)s.*
fifteenth, *quintus decimus.*
fifth, *quintus.*
fiftieth, *quinquagesimus.*
fifty, *quinquaginta*; — each, *quinquageni.*
fig, *ficus.*
fight, subst. *pugna, certamen.*
fight, v. (*de*)*pugnare, dimicare, proeliari.*
fighter, *pugnator, proeliator.*
figment: see fiction.
figurative, *translatus*; adv. *per translationem.*
figure, subst.: = form, shape, *figura, forma, species*; = image, representation, *signum, figura, imago*; a — of speech, *conformatio, figura.*
figure, v. *fingĕre*; see imagine.
figured, *sigillatus, caelatus.*
filament, *fibra, filum.*
file, subst.: the tool, *lima, scobina*; milit., *ordo*; rank and —, *milites.*
file, v. *limare, polire.*
filial, *pius* (*erga parentes*); adv. *pie.*
filings, *scobis.*
fill, v. *implēre, complēre.*
fillet, *vitta, infula* (religious).
film, *membrana.*
filter, subst. *colum.*
filter, v. (*per*)*colare, liquare.*
filth, *impuritas*; see dirt.
filthy, *impurus, obscenus*; adv. *impure.*
fin, *pinna.*
final, *ultimus, extremus*; adv. *ad extremum, postremo.*
finance, finances: domestic, *res familiaris*; of a state, *vectigalia* (*-ium*), *aerarium.*
find, v. *invenire, reperire*; to — out, *cognoscere, invenire.*
finder, *inventor, repertor.*
fine, subst. *multa.*
fine, adj. *praeclarus, pulcher*; the — arts, *artes liberales*; = thin, *tenuis, subtilis*; of weather, *serenus, sudus.* Adv. *praeclare; tenuiter, subtiliter.*
fine, v. *multare.*
fineness, *elegantia*; = thinness, *tenuitas, subtilitas*; of weather, *serenitas.*
finery, *munditia, apparatus* (*-ūs*).
finesse, *artificium.*
finger, subst. *digitus.*
finger, v. *tangĕre, attrectare.*
finish, subst. *absolutio, perfectio.*
finish, v.: = complete, *conficĕre, absolvĕre, peragĕre*; = put an end to, *finire, terminare.*
finished, *absolutus, perfectus.*
finite, *finitus, circumscriptus.*
fir, *abies, pinus.*
fire, subst. *ignis, flamma, incendium*; to be on —, *ardēre, flagrare;* to set on —, *incendĕre.* Transf., = ardour, (*animi*) *vis, ardor, fervor*; of missiles, *telorum coniectus* (*-ūs*).
fire, v.: transit., *incendĕre*; intransit., to — up, *exardescĕre.*
fire-brand, *fax, torris.*
fire-brigade, *vigiles.*
fire-engine, *sipho*(*n*).
fire-place, fire-side, *caminus, focus.*
fire-wood, *lignum* (usually plur.).
firm, *firmus, stabilis, solidus;* adv. *firmiter, firme, solide.*
firmness, *firmitas, stabilitas*; of mind, *constantia.*
first, adj. *primus, prior* (of two).
first, adv. *primum, primo.*
first-born, *natu maximus* (of two, *maior*).
first-fruits, *primitiae* (*-arum*).
fish, subst. *piscis.*
fish, v. *piscari*; fig., to — for, *captare.*
fisherman, *piscator.*
fishhook, *hamus.*
fishing, *piscatus* (*-ūs*); of —, adj., *piscatorius.*
fishing-line, *linum.*
fishing-net, *rete, iaculum.*
fishing-rod, *harundo.*
fishmonger, *cetarius.*
fissure, *rima.*
fist, *pugnus.*
fisticuffs, *pugilatio.*
fit, subst. *impetus* (*-ūs*).
fit, fitted, adj. *aptus, idoneus, commodus*; adv. *apte, commode.*
fit, v.: transit. *aptare, accommodare*; to — out, (*ex*)*ornare, instruĕre*; intransit. *convenire.*
fitness, *habilitas, opportunitas.*
five, *quinque*; — each, *quini*; a period of — years, *lustrum, quinquennium*; — times, *quinquie(n)s.*
fix, v. (*ad*)*figĕre.*
fixed, *certus.*

flabby, flaccid, *marcidus, fluidus.*
flag, subst. *signum, vexillum*; — ship, *navis praetoria.*
flagon, *lagena.*
flagrant, *impudens*; adv. *impudenter.*
flail, *pertica.*
flame, subst. *flamma.*
flame, v. *ardēre, flagrare.*
flaming, *flammeus.*
flank, *latus* (*-eris*, n.).
flap, subst. *lacinia.*
flap, v.: to — the wings, *alis plauděre*; in gen., *fluitare.*
flare, v. *flagrare.*
flash, subst. *fulgor.*
flash, v. *fulgēre, splendēre.*
flask, *ampulla.*
flat: = level, *planus, aequus, pronus* (= lying —); of wine, *vapidus*; of jokes, etc., *frigidus.* Adv. *plane.*
flatter, *adulari, blandiri.*
flatterer, *adsentator.*
flattering, *blandus.*
flattery, *adulatio, blandimentum.*
flaunt, *iactare, ostentare.*
flavour, subst. *sapor, sucus.*
flavour, v. *condire.*
flaw, *vitium, mendum.*
flawless, *emendatus.*
flax, *linum, carbasus.*
flaxen, *lineus*; of colour, *flavus.*
flay, *pellem detrahěre* (*corpori*).
flea, *pulex.*
fledged, *plumatus.*
flee, (*ef*)*fugěre.*
fleece, subst. *vellus* (*-eris*, n.).
fleece, v. *tondēre*; = rob, *expilare, spoliare.*
fleecy, *laniger.*
fleet, subst. *classis.*
fleet, adj. *velox, celer, pernix.*
fleeting, *fugax, caducus, fluxus.*
fleetness, *velocitas, pernicitas.*
flesh, *caro* (= meat), *viscera* (*-um*), *corpus* (*-oris*, n.).
flexible, *flexibilis, lentus, facilis.*
flicker, *trepidare, micare.*
flight: = fleeing, *effugium, fuga*; to put to —, *fugare*; = flying, *lapsus* (*-ūs*), *volatus* (*-ūs*); of stairs, *scalae* (*-arum*).
flightiness, *mobilitas, levitas.*
flighty, *mobilis, levis, inconstans.*
flimsiness, *tenuitas.*
flimsy, *tenuis.* Transf., *inanis.*
flinch, *refugěre.*
fling, *iacěre, coniceře.*
flint, *silex.*
flippancy, *petulantia.*
flippant, *petulans.*
flirt, v., perhaps *subblandiri.*
flit, *volitare.*
flitch, *succidia.*
float, *innare, fluitare*; in the air, *pendēre, volitare.*
flock, subst. *grex.*
flock, v. *adfluěre, confluěre*; to — together, *concurrěre.*
flog, *verberare*; to be flogged, *vapulare.*
flogging, *verbera* (*-um*).
flood, subst. *eluvio*; — tide, *aestūs accessus* (*-ūs*). Transf., *vis magna, flumen.*
flood, v. transit. *inundare.*
floor, *solum, pavimentum* (of stone).
floral, *floreus* (poet).
Florence, *Florentia.*
florid, *rubicundus.* Transf., *floridus.*
flounder, *fluitare.* Transf., *titubare.*
flour, *farina.*
flourish, subst., in style, *calamister.*
flourish, v.: intransit., *florēre, vigēre*; transit., *vibrare.*
flout, *ludificari, deridēre.*
flow, subst. *fluxio, lapsus* (*-ūs*); of words, *volubilitas, copia* (*verborum*).
flow, v. *fluěre, labi* (= glide), *manare* (= ooze).
flower, subst. *flos, flosculus*; = best part, *flos, robur.*
flower, v. *florēre,* (*ef*)*florescěre.*
flowery, *floreus, floridus.*
flowing, of speech, *fluens, volubilis, fusus.*
fluctuate, *fluctuare, pendēre.*
fluency, *facundia, volubilitas.*
fluent, *volubilis, disertus*; adv. *volubiliter.*
fluid, subst. *liquor, humor.*
fluid, adj. *liquidus.*
flush, subst. *rubor.*
flush, v. *rubescěre.*
fluster, *agitare, sollicitare.*
flute, *tibia, harundo.*
flute-player, *tibicen.*
fluted, *striatus.*
flutter, subst. *trepidatio.*
flutter, v. *trepidare, volitare.*
fly, subst. *musca.*
fly, v. *volare, volitare*, see also flee.
flying, *volatilis, volucer.*
foal, *eculeus, pullus equinus.*
foam, subst. *spuma.*
foam, v. *spumare,* (*ex*)*aestuare.*
foamy, *spumeus, spumosus.*
fodder, *pabulum.*
foe, *hostis* (public), *inimicus* (private).
fog, *nebula, caligo.*
foggy, *nebulosus, caliginosus.*
foible, *vitium.*
foil, subst.: a fencer's —, *rudis*; of metal, *lamina.*
foil, v. *ad inritum rediǵere, eluděre.*
foist, *supponěre, subděre.*
fold, subst.: in fabric, etc., *sinus* (*-ūs*); for animals, *ovile, stabulum.*
fold, v. (*com*)*plicare*; with -ed hands, *compressis manibus.*
folding-doors, *valvae* (*-arum*).
foliage, *frons*, plur. *frondes.*
folk; see people.
follow, (*con*)*sequi, insequi, persequi* (to the end); to — after, succeed, *succeděre.*
follower, (*ad*)*sectator.*
following, subst. *secta.*
following, (*in*)*sequens, proximus, posterus.*
folly, *stultitia, ineptia.*
foment, *fovēre.* Transf., *excitare.*
fond: = loving, *amans, studiosus*; = foolish, *stultus.* Adv. *amanter; stulte.*
fondle, (*per*)*mulcēre, amplexari.*
fondness: = love, *studium, amor, caritas*; = folly, *stultitia.*
food, *cibus, victus* (*-ūs*), *alimentum*; of animals, *pabulum.*
fool, subst. *homo stultus*; to play the —, *ineptire, desipěre.*

fool, v. *(e)luděre, ludificare.*
foolery, *ineptiae (-arum), nugae (-arum).*
foolhardy, *temerarius.*
foolish, *stultus, ineptus, insulsus*; adv. *stulte, inepte, insulse.*
foot, *pes*; on — (adj.), *pedes, pedester*; the — of the mountain, *infimus mons*; as a measure, *pes*; a — in size, *pedalis*; a metrical —, *pes.*
footing, *ratio, status (-ūs).*
footman, *pedisequus, servus a pedibus.*
footpad, *latro.*
foot-path, *semita, callis.*
foot-print, *vestigium.*
foot-soldier, *pedes.*
footstool, *scamnum, scabillum.*
for, prep.: = on behalf of, instead of, in return for, *pro*, with abl.; — this reason, *propter hoc*; — a sum of money, render by genit. or abl. of price; of time, to last for, for the purposes of, *in* with acc.: = during, render by acc., or *per* with acc.
for, conj. *nam(que), etenim enim* (second word in clause).
forage, subst. *pabulum.*
forage, v. *pabulari, frumentari.*
forager, *pabulator, frumentator.*
foraging, subst. *pabulatio, frumentatio.*
forbear, *parcěre, temperare, (se) abstiněre.*
forbearance, *abstinentia, patientia.*
forbid, *vetare, interdicěre*; it is forbidden, *non licet.*
force, subst. *vis*; to be in —, *valēre*; milit., forces, *copiae (-arum).*
force, v.; see compel.
forced, of language, *arcessitus*; a — march, *magnum iter.*
forcible: = done by force, *per vim factus*; = strong, *validus, gravis, vehemens.* Adv. *vi, per vim; valide, vehementer.*
ford, subst. *vadum.*
ford, v. *vado transire.*
forearm, subst. *bracchium.*
forebode: = to prophesy, *portenděre*; = to expect, *praesagire, praesentire.*
foreboding, subst. *praesensio.*
forecast, v. *praevidēre, prospicěre.*
forefather, *avus, proavus*; —s, *maiores (-um).*
forefinger, *digitus index.*
forego, *dimittěre, (con)ceděre.*
forehead, *frons (-ntis).*
foreign, *peregrinus, externus, adventicius*; = incompatible, *abhorrens, alienus.*
foreigner, *peregrinus, advena.*
foremost, *primus, princeps.*
forenoon, *dies antemeridianus.*
forensic, *forensis.*
forerunner, *praenuntius.*
foresee, *praevidēre, prospicěre.*
foresight, *providentia.*
forest, *silva.*
forestall, *praevenire.*
foretell, *praedicěre.*
forethought, *providentia.*
forewarn, *praemonēre.*
forfeit, subst. *poena, multa.*
forfeit, v. *amittěre; multari.*
forge, subst. *fornax, officina.*
forge, v. *procuděre, fabricari.* Transf.: = make, in gen., *fabricari, fingěre*; = counterfeit, *subicěre, supponěre.*
forged, of money, *adulterinus.*
forger, (of documents) *subiector.*
forgery, (of documents) *subiectio.*
forget, *oblivisci, dedisceře*: to be forgotten, *e memoria exciděre.*
forgetful, *obliviosus, immemor.*
forgetfulness, *oblivio.*
forgive, *ignoscěre; veniam dare.*
forgiveness, *venia.*
forgiving, *clemens, exorabilis.*
fork, (for hay-making), *furca, furcilla.*
forked, *bifurcus.*
forlorn, *relictus, destitutus.*
form, subst.: = shape, *figura, forma, facies*; in proper —, *rite*; = bench, *scamnum.*
form, v.: = shape, make, *(ef)fingěre (con)formare, fabricari*; milit., to — (up) troops, *instruěre, ordinare.*
formality, *ritus (-ūs).*
formation, *conformatio, forma.*
former, *prior, pristinus, superior*; the — . . . the latter, *ille . . . hic.* Adv. *antea, olim, quondam.*
formidable, *metuendus, terribilis, formidolosus*; adv. *formidolose.*
formless, *informis, rudis.*
formula, *formula, carmen, verba (-orum).*
forsake, *deserěre, destituěre.*
forsooth! *scilicet, sane.*
forswear, = swear falsely, *periurare.* See also abjure.
fort, *arx, castellum, castrum.*
forth, of place, *foras*; often rendered by compound verb with *e-* or *ex-* or *pro*; and so —, *et cetera.*
forthcoming, express by future tense.
forthwith, *extemplo, statim.*
fortification, *munitio, munimentum.*
fortify, *(com)munire.*
fortitude, *fortitudo, virtūs (-ūtis, f.).*
fortuitous, *fortuitus, forte oblatus*; adv. *forte, fortuito, casu.*
fortunate, *felix, fortunatus, beatus*; adv. *feliciter, fortunate.*
fortune, *fortuna, fors, casus (-ūs)*; = wealth, *divitiae (-arum), res (familiaris), bona (-orum).*
fortune-teller, *sortilegus;* female, *saga.*
forty, *quadraginta*; — each, *quadrageni*; — times, *quadragie(n)s.*
forward, adj., = pert, *protervus.*
forward, adv. *porro, ante*; to go —, *pergěre.*
forward, v.; of letters, *perferendum curare*; = help, *promote, adiuvare.*
foster, *nutrire, alěre.*
foster-child, *alumnus,* f. *alumna.*
foster-father, *nutricius.*
foster-mother, *nutrix.*
foul, *foedus, turpis. immundus*; adv., *foede, turpiter.*
foulness, *foeditas.*
found: of cities, etc., *conděre, fundare*; = cast in metal, *funděre.*
foundation, *fundamenta (-orum)*; from the —s, *funditus.*
founder, subst. *conditor, auctor.*
founder, v. *submergi, deperire*

fount, fountain, *fons, caput.* Transf., *fons, principium, origo.*
four, *quattuor*: — each, *quaterni*; — times, *quater*; a period of — years, *quadriennium*; — fold, *quadruplex.*
fourteen, *quattuordecim*: — each, *quaterni deni*; — times, *quater decie(n)s.*
fourteenth, *quartus decimus.*
fourth, *quartus*: for the — time, *quartum.*
fowl, subst. *avis, volucris, ales*; = hen, *gallina.*
fowl, v. *aucupari.*
fowler, *auceps.*
fowling, *aucupium.*
fox, *vulpes*; of a —, adj. *vulpinus.*
fraction, *pars.*
fractious, *morosus, difficilis*
fracture, v. *frangĕre.*
fragile, *fragilis.*
fragility, *fragilitas.*
fragment, *fragmentum.*
fragrance, *odor suavis.*
fragrant, *suavis; suaveolens* (poet).
frail, adj. *infirmus, debilis.*
frailty, *infirmitas.*
frame, subst. *compages*; — of mind, *animus.*
frame, v. *fingĕre, fabricari*; — draw up in words, *concipĕre, componĕre.*
framework, *compages, contignatio.*
France, *Gallia.*
franchise, *civitas, iūs* (*iūris*, n.).
frank, *candidus, apertus*; adv. *candide, aperte.*
frankincense, *tūs* (*tūris*, n.).
frankness, *simplicitas, libertas.*
frantic, *insanus, amens*; adv. *insane.*
fraternal, *fraternus*; adv. *fraterne.*
fraternity, *germanitas, fraternitas*; = society, *sodalitas, sodalicium.*
fratricide: as act, *parricidium fraternum*; as person, *fratricida.*
fraud, *fraus, dolus* (*malus*), *fallacia.*
fraudulent, *fraudulentus, dolosus*; adv. *fraudulenter, dolo malo, dolose.*
fraught, *refertus, repletus.*
fray, *pugna.*
free, adj.: = unrestricted, *liber, solutus, vacuus*; to be — from, (*re*) *carēre*; of space, = unoccupied, *patens, apertus*; = without cost, *gratuitus*; = generous, *largus, liberalis.* Adv. *libere, solute*; = generously, *large.*
free, v. *liberare, eximĕre, solvĕre*; of slaves, *manumittĕre.*
freebooter, *latro, praedo.*
free-born, *ingenuus.*
freedman, *libertus, libertinus.*
freedom, *libertas, licentia*; — of choice, *arbitrium*; — from punishment. *impunitas.*
freehold, *praedium liberum.*
freeholder, *possessor.*
freewill, *voluntas.*
freeze, transit., *glaciare,* (*con*)*gelare.*
freight, *onus* (*oneris*, n.).
French, *Gallicus*; a — man, *Gallus.*
frenzied, *furens, insanus, amens.*
frenzy, *furor, insania, amentia.*
frequency, *frequentia, crebritas.*
frequent, adj. *frequens, creber*; adv. *frequenter, crebro, saepe.*
frequent, v. *celebrare, frequentare.*
frequented, *frequens, celeber.*
fresh: = new, *recens, novus*; = refreshed, untired; *recens, integer, vegetus*; = cold, *frigidus.*
freshen, *recreare, reficere*; intransit., of wind, *increbrescere.*
freshness, *viriditas.*
fret: transit., = chafe, *atterĕre*, = distress, *sollicitare, vexare*; intransit., *dolere, macerari.*
fretful, *morosus, stomachosus*; adv. *morose, stomachose.*
fretfulness, *morositas, stomachus.*
friable, *puter* or *putris.*
friction, *tritus* (*-ūs*).
friend, *amicus* (f. *amica*), *sodalis.*
friendliness, *comitas, adfabilitas.*
friendly, *amicus, comis.*
friendship, *amicitia, familiaritas.*
frieze, (the cloth), *gausape* or *gausapum*
fright, *terror, pavor.*
frighten, (*ex*)*terrēre.*
frightful, *terribilis, formidolosus*; adv. *terribilem in modum, formidolose.*
frigid, *frigidus.*
frill, *segmenta* (*-orum*).
fringe, *fimbriae* (*-arum*), *limbus.*
frisk, *salire, lascivire.*
frisky, *lascivus.*
fritter, subst., *laganum.*
fritter, v. (*con*)*terĕre, dissipare.*
frivolity, *nugae* (*-arum*), *levitas.*
frivolous, *levis, inanis.*
fro: to and —, *huc* (*et*) *illuc, ultro citro*(*que*).
frog, *rana.*
frolic, subst. *ludus, lascivia.*
frolic, v. *ludĕre, lascivire.*
frolicsome, *lascivus, ludibundus, iocosus.*
from, *a, ab; ex* (= out of); *de* (=down from).
front, subst. *frons, pars prior*; in — of, *pro*, with abl.
front, v., = look towards, *aspectare.*
frontier, *finis, terminus, confinium.*
fronting, *adversus, oppositus.*
frost, *gelu, pruina; frigus* (*-oris*, n. = frosty weather).
frosty, *frigidus.*
froth, subst. *spuma.*
froth, v. *spumare.*
frothy, *spumosus, spumeus.*
froward, *contumax, pertinax*; adv. *contumaciter, pertinaciter.*
frowardness, *contumacia, pertinacia.*
frown, subst. *frontis contractio.*
frown, v. *frontem contrahĕre.*
frozen, *rigidus.*
frugal, *parcus, frugi* (indecl.); adv. *parce, frugaliter.*
frugality, *parsimonia, frugalitas.*
fruit, *fructus* (*-ūs*), *frux* and plur. *fruges* (esp. of grain), *pomum* (esp. = fruit of trees), *baca* (= berry).
fruitful, *fecundus, fertilis, uber*; adv. *fecunde.*
fruitfulness, *fecunditas, fertilitas.*
fruition, *fructus* (*-ūs*).

fruitless, *inutilis, cassus, inritus*; adv. *incassum, frustra, re infecta.*
fruit-tree, *pomum.*
frustrate, *ad inritum redigĕre.*
fry, v. *frigĕre.*
frying-pan, *sartago.*
fuel, *ligna* (*-orum*).
fugitive, subst. *fugitivus, profugus.*
fugitive, adj. *fugax, fugitivus.*
fulfil, *explēre, exsequi, conficĕre.*
fulfilment, *confectio.*
full: = filled, *plenus, repletus*; — of food, *satur*; = complete, *plenus, integer*; of a writer or speaker, *copiosus.* Adv. *plene; copiose, abundanter.*
fuller, *fullo.*
full-grown, *adultus.*
fulminate, *fulminare, intonare.*
fulsome, *putidus*; adv. *putide.*
fumble; see feel.
fume, subst. *vapor, halitus* (*-ūs*)
fume, v. (*ex*)*aestuare.*
fumigate, *suffire.*
fun, *iocus, ludus.*
function, *munus* (*-eris*, n.), *officium.*
fund, *pecunia.*
fundamental, *primus, principalis*; adv. *penitus.*
fundamentals, *elementa* (*-orum*), *principia* (*-orum*).
funeral, subst. *funus* (*-eris*, n.), *exsequiae* (*-arum*).
funeral, adj. *funebris*; — pile, *rogus, pyra.*
funereal, *funebris, lugubris.*
funnel, *infundibulum.*
funny, *ridiculus, iocularis*; adv. *ridicule.*
fur, *pellis.*
furbish, *interpolare, expolire.*
furious, *rabidus, furens*; adv. *rabide.*
furl, (*vela*) *contrahĕre.*
furlong, *stadium.*
furlough, *commeatus* (*-ūs*).
furnace, *fornax.*
furnish: = equip, (*ad*)*ornare, instruere*; = supply, give, *suppeditare, praebere.*
furnished, *instructus, praeditus.*
furniture, *supellex; apparatus* (*-ūs*).
furrow, subst. *sulcus.*
furrow, v. *sulcare.*
further: adj. *ulterior*; adv. *ulterius, amplius; praeterea.*
furthest, *ultimus.*
furtive, *furtivus*; adv. *furtim, furtive.*
fury, *furor, rabies.*
fuse, *liquefacĕre, fundĕre.*
fuss, subst. *trepidatio, tumultus* (*-ūs*).
fuss, v. *trepidare.*
fusty; see mouldy.
futile, *futilis, inanis, vanus.*
futility, *futilitas.*
future, subst. *futura* (*-orum*); for the —, *in futurum.*
future, adj. *futurus, posterus.*

G

gabble, *garrire, blaterare.*
gable, *fastigium.*
gadfly, *asilus, tabanus.*
gage, *pignus* (*-oris*, n.).
gaiety, *hilaritas, laetitia.*
gain, subst. *lucrum, quaestus* (*-ūs*; = profit), *commodum* (= advantage).
gain, v. *lucrari, lucri facĕre, consequi, capĕre*; to — over, *conciliare.*
gainful, *quaestuosus, lucrosus.*
gait, *incessus* (*-ūs*).
gala; see festival.
galaxy, *orbis lacteus.*
gale, *ventus, aura* (= breeze).
gall, subst. *fel, bilis.*
gall, v. *terĕre*; = annoy, *mordēre, urĕre.*
gallant, *amator.*
gallant, adj.: = brave, *fortis, animosus*; adv. *fortiter, animose*; = attentive to females, *officiosus.*
gallantry, *virtus* (*-utis*, f.), *fortitudo*; in love, *amores* (*-um*).
gallery, *porticus* (*-ūs*).
galley, *navis longa, triremis.*
gallon, *congius.*
gallop, subst. *gradus* (*-ūs*) *citatus*: at a —, *equo admisso.*
gallop, v. *equo admisso vehi* or *currĕre.*
gallows, *crux.*
gamble, v. *aleā ludĕre.*
gambler, *aleator.*
gambling, *alea.*
gambol, subst. *lusus* (*-ūs*).
gambol, v. *ludĕre, lascivire.*
game, susbt.: as played, *ludus*; a — of chance, *alea*; as hunted, *ferae* (*-arum*); on table, (*caro*) *ferina.*
gammon, *perna.*
gammon, interj. *gerrae!*
gander, *anser* (*mas* or *masculus*).
gang, *grex, caterva.*
gangway, *forus.*
gaol, *carcer*; *vincula* (*-orum*).
gaoler, *custos.*
gap, *lacuna, hiatus* (*-ūs*).
gape, (*in*)*hiare,* (*de*)*hiscĕre.*
garbage, *purgamentum, quisquiliae* (*-arum*).
garble, *corrumpĕre, vitiare.*
garden, subst. *hortus.*
garden, v. *in horto fodĕre, hortum colĕre.*
garish, *clarus, splendidus.*
garland, *corona, sertum* (usually plur.).
garlic, *alium.*
garment, *vestimentum.*
garner, subst. *horreum.*
garner, v. *condĕre.*
garnish, (*ex*)*ornare, instruĕre, decorare.*
garret, *cenaculum.*
garrison, subst. *praesidium.*
garrison, v. (*urbi*) *praesidium imponĕre.*
garrulity, *garrulitas, loquacitas.*
garrulous, *garrulus, loquax, verbosus*; adv. *loquaciter.*
gas, *spiritus* (*-ūs*), *vapor.*
gash, subst. *vulnus* (*-eris*, n.).
gash, v. *vulnerare.*
gasp, subst. *anhelitus* (*-ūs*).
gasp, v. *anhelare.*
gasping, adj. *anhelus.*
gate, *ianua, ostium*; of a city, *porta.*
gate-keeper, *ianitor.*
gate-post, *postis.*
gather, v.: transit., *legĕre, conligĕre.*

conferre; = conjecture, *conicĕre*; intransit., *convenire, congregari.*
gathering, subst.: as act, *conlectio*; = assembly, *coetus* (-*ūs*); = a sore, *suppuratio.*
gaudy, *fucatus, magnificus.*
gauge, v. *metiri.*
gaunt, *macer.*
gauntlets, *manicae* (-*arum*).
gay: of spirits, *hilaris, laetus*; adv. *hilare, laete*; of colour, etc., *splendidus, nitidus.*
gaze, subst. *obtutus* (-*ūs*).
gaze, v.: to — at, *intueri, contemplari.*
gazelle, *dorcas.*
gazette, *acta* (*diurna*).
gear, *ornatus* (-*ūs*), *supellex, apparatus* (-*ūs*).
gem, *gemma.*
gender, *genus* (-*eris*, n.).
genealogy, render by *origo* or *stirps.*
general, subst. *dux, imperator*; a lieutenant-—, *legatus*; the —'s tent, *praetorium.*
general, adj. *generalis, communis, vulgaris*; often rendered by genit. plur. *omnium.* Adv., = in —, *ad summam, in universum, generatim*; = usually, *fere, vulgo, plerumque.*
generalship, *ductus* (-*ūs*); under the — of Caesar, *Caesare duce.*
generate, *gignĕre, generare, parĕre.*
generation, *saeculum, aetas.*
generosity, *benignitas, liberalitas.*
generous, *benignus, liberalis*; of birth, *generosus, nobilis.* Adv. *benigne, liberaliter, large.*
genial, *comis, benignus*; adv. *comiter.*
geniality, *comitas.*
genitive, (*casus*) *genitivus.*
genius, = ability, *ingenium* or *indoles*, with adj. such as *praeclarus*; a man of —, *homo ingeniosus* or *praeclaro ingenio* (*praeditus*).
genteel, *elegans, urbanus*; adv. *eleganter, urbane.*
gentility, *elegantia, urbanitas.*
gentle: = well-born, *generosus, ingenuus, nobilis*; = mild, *lenis, mitis, mansuetus*; adv. *leniter, mite, mansuete.*
gentleman: by birth, see gentle; in behaviour, etc., *homo liberalis.*
gentlemanly, *liberalis, urbanus, honestus.*
gentleness, *mansuetudo, lenitas.*
gentlewoman: see lady.
gentry, *nobilitas, nobiles* (-*ium*).
genuine, *sincerus, merus, germanus*; adv. *reapse, sincere, vere.*
geography, *geographia, terrarum descriptio.*
geometrical, *geometricus.*
geometrician, *geometres* (-*ae*).
geometry, *geometria.*
George, *Georgius* (late Latin).
germ, *germen, semen.*
German, *Germanus, Germanicus.*
germane, *adfinis.*
Germany, *Germania.*
germinate, *germinare.*
germination, *germinatio.*
gesticulate, *se iactare, gestum facĕre.*
gesticulation, gesture, *iactatio, gestus* (-*ūs*).
get, v.: transit., *capĕre, adipisi,* (*com*)*parare, consequi*; to — anything done, *rem faciendam curare*; intransit., = become, *fieri*; to — along, *procedĕre*; — at, *attingĕre*; — away, *effugĕre*; — down, *descendĕre*; — in, *introire*; — out, *egredi, exire*; — up, *surgĕre.*
ghastliness, *pallor.*
ghastly, *exsanguis, pallidus.*
ghost, *manes* (-*ium*), *lemures* (-*um*); the Holy Ghost, *Spiritus Sanctus*; to give up the —, *exspirare.*
giant, *vir maior quam pro humano habitu*; myth., *gigas.*
gibe, subst. *cavillatio.*
gibe, v. *cavillari.*
giddiness, *vertigo.*
giddy, *vertiginosus.* Transf., *levis, inconstans.*
gift, *donum.*
gig, *cisium.*
gild, *inaurare.*
gills, *branchiae* (-*arum*).
gimlet, *terebra.*
gingerly, *pedetemptim, sensim.*
giraffe, *camelopardalis.*
gird, (*suc*)*cingĕre, accingĕre*: to — on, *accingĕre*; to — oneself, (*suc*)*cingi* or *accingi.*
girdle, *zona, cingulum.*
girl, *puella, virgo.*
girlhood, *aetas puellaris.*
girlish, *puellaris.*
girth, *ambitus* (-*ūs*), *circuitus* (-*ūs*); of a horse, *cingula.*
give, *dare, tribuĕre, donare*; to — back, *reddĕre*; to give up, = surrender, *tradĕre, dedĕre*; = cease, *desistĕre*; to — in, — way, *cedĕre.*
gizzard, *ingluvies, guttur.*
glad, *laetus, hilaris*; adv. *laete, libenter.*
gladden, (*ex*)*hilarare.*
glade, *silva, saltus* (-*ūs*).
gladiator, *gladiator*; a trainer of —s, *lanista.*
gladiatorial, *gladiatorius.*
gladness, *laetitia, hilaritas.*
glance, subst. *aspectus* (-*ūs*).
glance, v. *aspicĕre.*
glare, subst.: of light, *fulgor*; = fierce look, *oculi torvi.*
glare, v., of light, *fulgĕre*; = look fiercely, *torvis oculis intuēri.*
glass, subst. *vitrum*; a looking- —, *speculum.*
glass, adj., or **glassy,** *vitreus.*
gleam, subst. *fulgor.*
gleam, v. *fulgēre.*
gleaning, subst. *spicilegium.*
glee, *hilaritas, laetitia, gaudium.*
glen, (*con*)*vallis.*
glib, *loquax, volubilis*; adv. *loquaciter, volubiliter.*
glibness, *loquacitas, volubilitas.*
glide, (*pro*)*labi.*
glimmer, *sublucēre.*
glimmering, adj. *sublustris.*
glitter, subst. *fulgor.*
glitter, v. *fulgēre, nitēre, lucēre.*
glittering, *lucidus, nitidus*; — white, *candidus.*

gloat, *aspectu se delectare.*
globe, *globus, sphaera*; = the earth, *orbis terrarum.*
globular, *globosus.*
gloom, *obscuritas, caligo, tenebrae* (*-arum*); = sadness, *tristitia, maestitia.*
gloomy: = dark, *obscurus*; = sad, *tristis, maestus*; adv. *maeste.*
glorify, *laudare, celebrare.*
glorious, (*prae*)*clarus, amplus, inlustris*; adv. (*prae*)*clare, ample.*
glory, subst. *gloria, honor, decus* (*-oris*, n.).
gloss, subst.: = shine, *nitor*; = explanation, *interpretatio.*
gloss, v.: to — over, *extenuare.*
glossary, *glossarium.*
glossy, *nitidus.*
Gloucester, *Glevum.*
gloves, *manicae* (*-arum*, = long sleeves).
glow, subst. *ardor, fervor.*
glow, v. *ardēre, flagrare.*
glow-worm, *cicindela.*
glue, subst. *gluten.*
glue, v. *glutinare.*
glut, subst. *satietas.*
glut, v. *satiare, explēre.*
glutinous, *lentus, glutinosus.*
glutton, *helluo.*
gluttonous, *edax, vorax.*
gluttony, *gula, edacitas.*
gnarled; see knotty.
gnash; to — the teeth, (*dentibus*) (*in*)*frendĕre.*
gnat, *culex.*
gnaw, (*ad*)*rodĕre.*
gnawing, adj. *mordax.*
go, v. *ire, vadĕre* (esp. fast), *gradi* (=to step), *proficisci* (= set out) *discedĕre* (= depart); to — back, *redire, reverti*; — beyond, *excedĕre*; — down, *descendĕre*; — forward, *procedĕre*; — in, *inire, intrare, ingredi*; — off, *abire*; — on, = continue, *pergĕre*, = happen, *fieri, agi*; — out, *exire, egredi*; — up, *ascendĕre*; — without, *carēre*; to —, = to become, *fieri.*
goad, subst. *stimulus.*
goad, v. *stimulare, incitare.*
goal, *meta, calx.*
goat, m. *caper, hircus*; f. *capra, capella.*
gobble, (*de*)*vorare.*
go-between, *conciliator, interpres.*
goblet, *poculum, scyphus.*
god, *deus, divus, numen* (*divinum*); the —s, *di* (*dii*), *divi, numina, caelestes, superi*; —s of the household, *lares, penates*; so help me —, *ita me deus* (*ad*)*iuvet.*
goddess, *dea, diva.*
godhead, *numen.*
godless, *impius.*
godlike, *divinus.*
godliness, *pietas* (*erga deos*).
godly, *pius* (*erga deos*).
godsend, *res quasi divinitus oblata.*
gold, *aurum.*
golden, *aureus.*
gold-mine, *aurifodina.*
goldsmith, *aurifex.*
good, subst. *bonum, salus* (*-utis*, f.); to do —, *prodesse*; —s, = property, possessions, *bona* (*-orum*); = merchandise, *merx.*
good, adj. *bonus, probus*; morally —, *bonus, probus, honestus*; = kind, *bonus, benignus*; = useful, *utilis*; = convenient, *commodus*; = wholesome, *saluber, salutaris*; — day! *salve!* good!, interj., *euge! bene habet.*
goodbye, *vale* (plur. *valete*).
good-for-nothing, *nequam.*
good-humour, *comitas, facilitas.*
good-humoured, *comis, facilis.*
good-looking, *pulcher, venustus.*
good-nature, *facilitas, comitas, benignitas.*
good-natured, *facilis, comis, benignus.*
goodness, *bonitas*; moral —, *probitas, virtūs* (*-ūtis*, f.); = kindness, *benignitas, bonitas.*
good-tempered, *mitis, lenis.*
goose, *anser.*
gore, subst. *cruor.*
gore, v. (*cornibus*) *transfigĕre.*
gorge, subst.: = throat, *gula, guttur, fauces* (*-ium*); = narrow pass, *angustiae* (*-arum*), *fauces* (*-ium*).
gorge, v. (*ex*)*satiare.*
georgeous, *splendidus, magnificus*; adv. *splendide, magnifice.*
georgeousness, *splendor, magnificentia.*
gory, *cruentus, cruentatus.*
gospel, *evangelium.*
gossamer, *aranea.*
gossip, subst.; = talk, *sermo, rumor*; = talker, *garrulus* or *loquax*; = friend, *familiaris.*
gossip, v. *sermonem conferre, garrire.*
gourd, *cucurbita.*
gout, *articulorum dolor*; — in the hands, *chiragra*; — in the feet, *podagra.*
gouty, adj. *arthriticus.*
govern: politically, *gubernare, administrare, curare*; in gen., = restrain, guide, *moderari, temperare, regĕre.*
government, *administratio, gubernatio*; = supreme power, *imperium, regnum*; = those in power, render by relative clause.
governor, *gubernator, rector*; with delegated powers, *praefectus, legatus.*
governorship, *praefectura.*
gown: man's, *toga*; woman's, *stola palla.*
grace, subst.: = favour, goodwill, *gratia, favor*; by the — of god, *deo favente*; = gracefulness, charm, *lepos* (*lepor*), *venustas, elegantia*; myth., the Graces, *Gratiae* (*-arum*).
grace, v. (*ad*)*ornare, decorare.*
graceful, *venustus, elegans*; adv. *venuste, eleganter.*
gracious, *propitius*; see also kind.
grade, *gradus* (*-ūs*).
gradually, *paullatim, gradatim, sensim.*
graft, subst. *surculus.*
graft, v. *inserĕre.*
grain: = particle, *granum, mica*; = corn, *frumentum.*
grammar, *grammatica* (*-ae*, f., or *-orum*, n. pl.).

grammarian, *grammaticus.*
grammatical, *grammaticus.*
granary, *horreum, granaria* (*-orum*).
grand, *grandis, magnificus, amplus.*
granddaughter, *neptis.*
grandees, *nobiles, proceres.*
grandeur, *amplitudo, magnificentia.*
grandfather, *avus.*
grandiloquent, *grandiloquus.*
grandmother, *avia.*
grandson, *nepos.*
grant, subst. *donum*; = act of granting, *concessio.*
grant, v.: = bestow, *permittĕre, concedĕre*; = admit, *concedĕre, dare*; —ed that, *ut* with subj.
grape, *acinus*; bunch of grapes, *uva.*
graphic, *expressus.*
grapple, *luctari.*
grappling-iron, *ferrea manus* (*-ūs*), *harpago.*
grasp, subst.: physical, *complexus* (*-ūs*), *manūs* (plur.); mental, *captus* (*-ūs*).
grasp, v.: physically, (*ap*)*prehendĕre, comprehendĕre, prensare*; mentally, *intellegĕre, animo comprehendĕre*; to — at, *captare, adfectare, appetĕre.*
grasping, *avarus, appetens.*
grass, *gramen, herba.*
grasshopper, *gryllus.*
grassy, *gramineus, herbidus.*
grate, subst. *focus, caminus.*
grate, v.: = rub, (*con*)*terĕre*; = make a grating noise, *stridĕre.*
grateful: = thankful, *gratus*; adv. *grate, grato animo*; = pleasant, *gratus, acceptus.*
gratification: as act, *expletio, delectatio*; = pleasure, *voluptas.*
gratify: see please.
grating, subst.: = bars, *cancelli* (*-orum*), *clatri* (*-orum*); = harsh noise, *stridor.*
gratitude, *gratus animus.*
gratuitous, *gratuitus*; adv. *gratis, gratuito.*
gratuity; see alms, gift.
grave, subst.: = place of burial, *sepulcrum*; = place of cremation, *bustum*; = state of death, *mors.*
grave, adj. *gravis, serius, tristis.*
gravel, *glarea.*
gravity, *gravitas.*
gravy, *ius* (*iuris,* n.), *sucus.*
graze: of animals, transit. *pascĕre,* intransit. *pasci*; = to touch in passing, *radĕre, stringĕre.*
grazier, *pecuarius.*
grazing, subst. *pascua* (*-orum,* plur.).
grease, subst. *adeps, lardum.*
grease, v. *ung*(*u*)*ĕre.*
greasy, *unctus, pinguis.*
great, *magnus, grandis, amplus; clarus, summus, ingens*; as plur., the great, *nobiles* (*-ium*); greater, *maior*; greatest, *maximus*; how —, *quantus*; so —, *tantus*; too —, *nimius.* Adv., greatly, *magnopere.*
greaves, *ocreae.*
Greece, *Graecia.*
greed, *aviditas, cupiditas.*
greedy, *avidus. cupidus*; adv. *avide, cupide.*
Greek, adj. and subst. *Graecus.*
green, subst.: = greenness, *viriditas, color viridis*: = grassy space, *campus.*
green, adj. *viridis, virens*; to be — *virēre*; = fresh, *viridis, recens.*
greens, *holus* (*-eris,* n.).
greet, *salutare, salvēre iubēre.*
greeting, (*con*)*salutatio.*
grey, *canus* (= hoary); *caesius* or *glaucus* (grey-blue).
greyness, *canities.*
gridiron, *craticula.*
grief, *dolor, aegritudo, maeror, luctus* (*-ūs*; = mourning).
grievance, *iniuria*; *querimonia* (=complaint).
grieve, v.: transit., *dolore adficĕre, angĕre*; intransit., *dolēre, maerēre, lugēre.*
grievous, *acerbus, gravis*; adv. *acerbe, graviter.*
grill, v. *torrēre.*
grim, *torvus, saevus.*
grimace, subst. *os distortum.*
grimness, *saevitia, torvitas.*
grimy; see dirty.
grin, subst. *rictus* (*-ūs*).
grin, v. *ridēre.*
grind, v. *molĕre*; to — the teeth, *dentibus frendĕre.*
grinder, (of teeth) *dens genuinus.*
grindstone, *cos.*
grip; see grasp.
grisly, *foedus, horrendus.*
grist, *farina.*
groan, subst. *gemitus* (*-ūs*).
groan, v. *gemĕre.*
groin, *inguen.*
groom, subst. *agaso.*
groom, v. *curare.*
groove, *canalis.*
grope, *praetemptare.*
gross: = great, too great, *magnus, nimius*; = disgraceful, *turpis, foedus.* Adv. *nimium*; *turpiter, foede.*
grot, grotto, *antrum.*
grotesque, *mirus; ridiculus.*
ground, subst.: = earth, soil, *humus* (f.), *solum, terra*; on the —, *humi*; = place, position, *locus*; = reason, basis, *causa, ratio*: on the — that, *quod.*
ground, v. of a ship, *sidĕre.*
groundless, *vanus, falsus*; adv. *temere, falso.*
groundlessness, *vanitas.*
groundwork, *fundamentum.*
group, subst. *caterva, globus, circulus.*
group, v. *disponĕre.*
grouping, *dispositio.*
grove, *lucus, nemus* (*-oris,* n.).
grovel, *humi iacēre.*
grovelling, *abiectus, humilis, submissus.*
grow: intransit., *crescĕre, augeri*; to — up, *adolescere*; = to become, *fieri*; transit., *alĕre, colĕre.*
grower, *cultor.*
growl, subst. *fremitus* (*-ūs*).
growl, v. *fremĕre.*
grown, grown-up, *adultus, pubes.*
growth, *auctus*(*-ūs*), *incrementum.*
grub, subst. *vermiculus.*
grub, v.: to — up, *eruĕre.*
grudge, subst. *simultas, invidia.*

grudge, v. (*rem homini*) *invidēre.*
gruff, *asper*; adv. *aspere.*
grumble, *murmurare, fremĕre.*
grunt, subst. *grunnitus* (*-ūs*).
grunt, v. *grunnire.*
Guadalquivir, *Baetis.*
guarantee, subst.: as a thing, *fides, sponsio, vadimonium*; = guarantor, *vas, sponsor.*
guarantee, v. *praestare, fidem dare.*
guard, subst. *custodia, praesidium*; to mount —, *excubare, excubias* or *vigilias agĕre*; to be on one's —, (*prae*)*cavēre*; off one's —, *incautus, imprudens*; = persons on guard, *custodes* (*-um*), *custodia, praesidium.*
guard, v. *custodire, tueri.*
guarded, *cautus, circumspectus*; adv. *caute.*
guardian, *custos, defensor*; of a ward, *tutor.*
guardianship, *custodia*; of a ward, *tutela.*
guess, subst. *coniectura.*
guess, v. *conicĕre, divinare, augurari.*
guest, *hospes* (*-itis*), f. *hospita*; at a party, *conviva.*
guidance, *ductus* (*-ūs*), *consilium.*
guide, *dux.*
guide, *ducĕre.* Transf., *regĕre, gubernare, moderari.*
guild, *conlegium.*
guile, *dolus, astutia.*
guileless, *simplex, apertus*; adv. *simpliciter.*
guilelessness, *simplicitas.*
guilt, *vitium, culpa, noxia.*
guiltless, *innocens, insons.*
guilty, *sons, sceleratus, nocens*; adv. *scelerate.*
guise, *habitus* (*-ūs*), *species.*
gulf, *sinus* (*-ūs*, = bay); *gurges* (= abyss).
gullet, *gula, guttur.*
gullible, *credulus.*
gully, *alveus.*
gulp, subst. *haustus* (*-ūs*).
gulp, v. *haurire, obsorbēre.*
gum: of the mouth, *gingiva*; of plants, *gummi.*
gun: use *tormentum.*
gurgle, *murmurare.*
gush, v. *effundi.*
gust, *flabra* (*-orum*, n. plur.).
gusty, *turbidus, procellosus.*
gut, subst. *intestinum.*
gut, v. *exinanire.*
gutter, *canalis, cloaca.*
guttural, of sounds, *gravis.*
gymnasium, *gymnasium, palaestra.*
gymnastic, *gymnicus, palaestricus.*

H

ha! *ha!*
habit: = custom, *consuetudo, mos, usus* (*-ūs*); = state, *habitus* (*-ūs*).
habitable, *habitabilis.*
habitation, *domicilium, sedes, domus.*
habitual, *inveteratus, usitatus*; adv. *de* or *ex more.*
habituate, *adsuefacĕre.*
hack, v. *caedĕre.*
hackneyed, *tritus.*
haft, *manubrium.*
hag, *anus* (*-ūs*), *anicula.*
haggle, *de pretio ambigĕre.*
hail, subst. *grando.*
hail, v.: it —s, *grandinat*; = to greet, *salutare, appellare.*
hail, interj. *salve!* plur. *salvete!*
hair: single, *pilus, capillus, saeta* (= bristle); coll., use plur., or *crinis, comae* (*-arum*), *caesaries* (flowing).
hairdresser, *tonsor.*
hairpin, *crinale.*
hairsplitting, *disserendi spinae* (*-arum*).
hairy, *pilosus, capillatus.*
halcyon, subst. *alcedo,* (*h*)*alcyon.*
halcyon, adj. *serenus.*
hale, adj. *sanus, validus, robustus.*
hale, v. *rapĕre, trahĕre.*
half, subst. *dimidium.*
half, adj. *dimidius, dimidiatus.*
half-asleep, *semisomnus, semisopitus.*
half-burnt, *semiustus.*
half-hour, *semihora.*
half-open, *semiapertus.*
half-pound, *selibra.*
hall, *atrium.*
hallo! *heus! ohe!*
halloo, subst. *clamor.*
halloo, v. *clamare, vociferari.*
hallow, *consecrare, dedicare.*
hallowed, *sacer, sanctus.*
hallucination, *error.*
halm, *calamus.*
halt, adj. *claudus.*
halt, v.: = limp, *claudicare*; = stop *consistĕre.*
halter, *capistrum, laqueus* (= noose).
halve, *ex aequo dividĕre.*
halved, *dimidiatus.*
ham, *poples*; salted, smoked, etc., *perna.*
hamlet, *vicus, viculus.*
hammer, subst. *malleus.*
hammer, v. *malleo* (*con*)*tundĕre.*
hamper, subst. *corbis.*
hamper, v. *implicare, impedire.*
hamstring, v. *poplitem succidĕre.*
hand, subst. *manus* (*-ūs*, f.), *palma* (= palm); right —, (*manus*) *dextra* or *dextera*; left —, (*manus*) *sinistra* or *laeva*; to give a person one's —, *homini dextram porrigĕre*; = workman, *opera* (usually plur.); an old —, *veterator*; to be at —, *praesto esse, adesse*; in —, on —, *in manibus*; — to — (in fighting), *comminus.*
hand, v. *dare, tradĕre, porrigĕre.*
handcuffs, *manicae* (*-arum*).
handful, *manipulus.*
handicraft, *artificium.*
handiwork, *opus* (*-eris*, n.), *opificium.*
handkerchief, *sudarium.*
handle, subst. *manubrium, capulus, ansa* (lit. and fig.).
handle, v. *tractare, contrectare.*
handling, *tractatio.*
handsome, *formosus, venustus, pulcher.* Transf., *liberalis*; adv. *praeclare, liberaliter.*
handwriting, *manus* (*-ūs*, f.), *chirographum.*

handy, *habilis, promptus.*
hang, v.: intransit., *pendēre*; to — over, *imminēre*; to — back, *cessare*; transit., *suspendĕre*; to — the head, *caput demittĕre.*
hanger-on, *adsecla.*
hanging, subst. *suspendium.*
hangman, *carnifex.*
hanker; to — after, *desiderare.*
haphazard, adv. *temere.*
hapless, *miser, infelix.*
haply, *fortasse, forsitan.*
happen, *fieri, accĭdĕre, contingĕre.*
happiness, *vita beata, felicitas.*
happy, *beatus, felix, fortunatus*; of language, *aptus.* Adv. *beate, feliciter.*
harangue, *contio*; to deliver a —, *contionari.*
harass, *vexare, sollicitare.*
harbinger, *praenuntius, antecursor.*
harbour, subst. *portus* (*-ūs*); — -dues, *portorium*; full of —s, *portuosus.*
harbour, v. (*hospitio*) *excipĕre.*
hard, adj. *durus*; = difficult, *difficilis, arduus.*
hard, adv. *summa vi, enixe.*
harden, v.: transit., *durum facĕre*; intransit., *obdurescĕre.*
hard-hearted, *durus, ferreus.*
hardihood, *audacia.*
hardly, = scarcely, *vix, aegre.*
hardness, *duritia* (or *durities*); = severity, *iniquitas, crudelitas.*
hardship, *labor, incommodum, molestia.*
hardware, *ferramenta* (*-orum*).
hardy, *robustus.*
hare, *lepus* (*leporis*, m.).
hark! interj. *heus!*
harlequin, *sannio.*
harm, subst. *damnum, detrimentum.*
harm, v. *nocēre, laedĕre.*
harmful, *nocens, noxius.*
harmless, *innocens, innoxius.*
harmlessness, *innocentia.*
harmonious, *concors* (lit. and fig.); *congruens, conveniens.* Adv. *concorditer, congruenter, convenienter.*
harmonize, v.: transit. *concordes facĕre, componĕre,* (*re*)*conciliare*; intransit., *concinĕre, consentire.*
harmony, *concordia* (lit. and fig.); *consensus* (*-ūs*), *convenientia.*
harness, subst. *ornamenta equi.*
harness, v. (*equum*) *ornare.*
harp, subst. *lyra.*
harp, v. *psallĕre.*
harpist: m. *fidicen, psaltes* (*-ae*); f. *fidicina, psaltria.*
harpy, *harpyia.*
harrow, subst. (*h*)*irpex, crates.*
harrow, v. *occare*; to — the feelings, (*ex*)*cruciare.*
harrowing, *terribilis, atrox.*
harry, *vexare, cruciare.*
harsh: in sound, *raucus, asper*; in taste, *acer, asper*; in temper, *asper, morosus, durus.* Adv. *aspere.*
harshness, *asperitas.*
hart, *cervus.*
harvest, subst. *messis.*
harvester, *messor.*
haste, subst. *festinatio, celeritas*; nervous —, *trepidatio.*
haste, hasten, v.: intransit., *properare, festinare, maturare*; transit., *accelerare, maturare, properare.*
hastiness, of temper, *iracundia.*
hasty: = hurried, (*prae*)*properus, citus, praeceps*: = irritable, *iracundus, stomachosus.* Adv. *propere, properanter, raptim.*
hat, *petasus.*
hatch, v. (*ex ovis*) *excludĕre*: = to concoct, *moliri, machinari.*
hatches, *claustra* (*-orum*).
hatchet, *securis, ascia, dolabra.*
hate, hatred, *odium, invidia.*
hate, v. *odisse*; to be hated, *odio esse.*
hateful, *odiosus, invisus*; adv. *odiose.*
haughtiness, *superbia, insolentia, adrogantia.*
haughty, *superbus, insolens, adrogans*; adv. *superbe, insolenter, adroganter.*
haul, v. *trahĕre, ducĕre.*
haulm; see stalk.
haunch, *clunis.*
haunt, subst. *latebrae* (*-arum*), *latibulum, lustra* (*-orum*).
haunt, v. *frequentare,* (*con*)*celebrare*; of spirits, cares, etc., *agitare, sollicitare.*
have, *habēre, tenēre*; to — to do, *debēre facĕre.*
haven, *portus* (*-ūs*).
havoc, *vastatio, strages.*
hawk, subst. *accipiter* (*-tris*, m.).
hawk, v. = sell, *venditare.*
hay, *faenum.*
hay-fork, *furca.*
hazard, subst. *fors, casus* (*-ūs*), *periculum* (= risk), *alea* (= gambling).
hazard, v.; see dare or endanger.
hazardous, *periculosus*; adv. *periculose.*
haze, *nebula, caligo.*
hazel, *corylus.*
hazy, *nebulosus.*
he, *hic, ille, is*; = himself, *ipse.*
head, subst. *caput, vertex*; the back of the —, *occipitium*; = understanding or memory, *mens, animus, iudicium*; = chief, leader, *caput, princeps, dux*; to be at the —, *praeesse*; to put at the —, *praeficere*; = point, heading, *caput.*
head, adj. *primus, primarius, princeps.*
head, v. *ducĕre, praeesse.*
head-band, *infula, vita, redimiculum.*
head-dress, *mitra.*
headland, *promontorium.*
headlong, *praeceps.*
headquarters, *praetorium, principia* (*-orum*).
headstrong, *pervicax, temerarius.*
head-wind, *ventus adversus.*
heady, = intoxicating, *fervidus.*
heal, v.: transit., *sanare, medēri, curare*; intransit., *consanescĕre.*
healing, subst. *sanatio.*
healing, adj. *saluber, salutaris.*
health, *sanitas, valetudo.*
healthful, *saluber, salutaris.*
healthy, *sanus, salvus, saluber* (of places); adv. *salubriter.*
heap, subst. *acervus, agger.*
heap, v. *cumulare, coacervare, congerĕre.*
hear, *audire, auscultare* (= listen to). Transf., = find out, learn, *cognoscĕre, accipĕre.*

hearer, *auditor.*
hearing, subst.: as sense, *auditus* (*-ūs*); as process, *auditio*; = an audience, *audientia*; a judicial —, *cognitio.*
hearken, *auscultare.*
hearsay, *rumor, auditio.*
heart: physical, *cor*; = seat of feeling, etc. *animus, mens, pectus* (*-oris*, n.); from the —, *ex animo*; = courage, *animus*; = memory: to know by —, *memoria tenēre*; to learn by —, *ediscĕre*; dear —, (*mea*) *vita.*
heart-breaking, *miserabilis, maestus, flebilis.*
heart-broken, *animo fractus* or *adflictus.*
heartfelt, *verus.*
hearth, *focus.*
heartiness, *studium, alacritas.*
heartless, *crudelis, saevus*; adv. *crudeliter, saeve.*
heartlessness, *crudelitas, saevitia.*
heart-sick, *animo aeger.*
hearty, *verus* (= true), *alacer* (= brisk), *benignus* (=kind). Adv. *summo studio.*
heat, subst. *calor, ardor, fervor, aestus* (*-ūs*); of passion, etc., *ardor, fervor, aestus.*
heat, v. *calefacĕre, fervefacĕre.* Transf., *accendĕre.*
heath: as plant, *erice*(*-es*, f.); as a place, *loca inculta.*
heathen, adj. *paganus.*
heave, v.: transit., (*at*)*tollĕre, extollĕre*; to — a sigh, *gemitum dare*, or *ducĕre*; intransit., *aestuare, fluctuare, tumescĕre.*
heaven: = sky, *caelum*; = gods, *di* (*dei*), *superi*; the will of —, *numen divinum*; for —'s sake! *per deos immortales!* — forbid, *di meliora.*
heavenly, *caelestis, divinus.*
heaviness, *gravitas, pondus*(*-eris*, n.); of atmosphere, *crassitudo*; = sadness, *tristitia, maestitia.*
heavy, *gravis, ponderosus*; of air, *crassus*; of soil, *spissus*; of rain, *magnus*; abstr., = oppressive, *gravis, molestus*; = downcast, *tristis, adflictus, maestus.* Adv. *graviter.*
heavy-armed; — troops. *gravior armatus* (*-ūs*).
Hebrew, adj. *Hebraeus, Hebraicus.*
hectic, *febriculosus.*
hector, *se iactare.*
hedge, subst. *saepes, saepimentum*
hedge, v. *saepire.*
hedgehog, *ericus, echinus.*
heed, subst.: to take —, *cavēre.*
heed, v. *curare, observare*; = obey, *parēre, obedire.*
heedless, *neglegens, temerarius*; adv. *neglegenter, temere.*
heedlessness, *neglegentia, temeritas.*
heel, subst. *calx.*
heel, v. *in latus labi* or *inclinari.*
heifer, *iuvenca.*
height, *altitudo, proceritas*; the — of glory, *summa gloria*; = high place, *locus editus, altitudines* (*-um*, plur.).
heighten; render by *altior*; = increase, *augēre, amplificare, exaggerare.*
heinous, *foedus, nefarius, atrox*; adv. *foede, nefarie, atrociter.*
heinousness, *atrocitas.*
heir, *heres*; sole —, *heres ex asse.*
heirloom, *res hereditaria.*
Helen, *Helena.*
hell, *inferi* (*-orum*), *Tartarus*, or n. plur. *Tartara.*
hellebore, (*h*)*elleborus, veratrum.*
Hellenic, *Graecus.*
hellish, *infernus, nefandus.*
helm, *gubernaculum.*
helmet, *cassis, galea.*
helmsman, *gubernator.*
help, subst. *auxilium, subsidium.*
help, v. (*ad*)*iuvare, subvenire, succurrĕre*; so — me God, *ita me di ament*; I can't — saying, *facĕre non possum quin dicam.*
helper, *adiutor*; f. *adiutrix.*
helpful, *utilis.*
helpless, *inermis, inops.*
helplessness, *inopia.*
hem, subst. *limbus, instita.*
hem, v.: = sew, *suĕre*; to — in, *circumsedēre, obsīdēre.*
hemp, *cannabis.*
hen, *gallina.*
hence, *hinc*; as interj., *apage*; a few days —, *paucis diebus, post paucos dies.*
henceforth, *posthac.*
Henry, *Henricus.*
her, possessive, *eius, illius*; — own, *suus -a -um.*
herald, subst., *caduceator, fetialis, praeco*; = forerunner, *praenuntius.*
herald, v. *nuntiare.*
herb, *herba, olus* (*oleris*, n.).
herd, subst. *grex*; of large cattle, *armentum*; of a —, *gregalis, gregarius*; in —s, *gregatim*; of people, the common —, *vulgus* (*-i*, n.).
herd, v. intransit. *congregari.*
herdsman, *pastor, armentarius.*
here: = at this place, *hic*; to be —, *adesse*; = to this place, hither, *huc*; from — (hence), *hinc*; — and there *rarus* (adv. *raro*).
hereafter, *posthac, aliquando.*
hereditary, *hereditarius, paternus.*
herein, *in hac re.*
hereupon, *hic.*
heritage, *hereditas, patrimonium.*
hermit, *homo solitarius.*
hero: = demigod, *heros*; = brave man, *vir fortissimus*; in a play, *persona prima.*
heroic, *heroicus*; = brave, valiant, *fortis*; adv. *fortiter.*
heroine: = demi-goddess, *heroina, herois*; = brave woman, *femina fortissima.*
heroism, *eximia virtus* (*-utis*). *animus fortis.*
heron, *ardea.*
hers; see her.
herself, reflex., *se*; otherwise *ipsa.*
hesitate, *dubitare, cunctari, haesitare.*
hesitation, *dubitatio, haesitatio, cunctatio.*
heterogeneous, *diversus, dissimilis.*
hew, *caedĕre, dolare.*
hewn; hewn stone, *saxum quadratum.*
hexameter, *hexameter* (or *-trus*).
heyday, *flos aetatis.*

hiatus, *hiatus* (*-ūs*).
hibernate, *per hiemen dormire* or *quiescĕre*.
hiccough, hiccup, *singultus* (*-ūs*).
hidden, *occultus*; to lie —, *latēre*.
hide, subst. *corium, pellis*.
hide, v.: transit., *abdĕre, celare*; of feelings, etc., *dissimulare*; intransit., render by reflex.
hideous, *foedus, turpis*; adv. *foede*.
hideousness, *foeditas, deformitas*.
hiding-place, *latibulum, latebra*.
higgledy-piggledy, *confuse*.
high, adj. *altus*, (*ex*)*celsus, procerus* (= tall), *sublimis* (= raised aloft); in rank, *amplus*; of prices, *magnus*; of sound, *acutus*; of meat, *rancidus*. Adv. *alte*; to value —, *magni aestimare*.
high-born, *generosus, nobili loco ortus*.
high-flown, *tumidus*.
high-handed, *superbus, imperiosus*.
highlander, *homo montanus*.
highlands, *loca montuosa* (*-orum*).
high-minded, *magnanimus, generosus*.
high-priest, *Pontifex Maximus*.
high-spirited, *ferox, animosus*.
high-tide *plurimus aestūs accessus* (*-ūs*).
highway, *via*.
highwayman, *latro, grassator*.
hilarity, *hilaritas, laetitia*.
hill, *collis, tumulus*; up —, *adverso colle*
hilly, *montuosus, clivosus*.
hilt, *capulus*.
him; see he.
himself, reflex., *se*; otherwise *ipse*.
hind, subst.: = female stag, *cerva*; = servant, *verna, servus*; = peasant, *rusticus, agrestis*.
hind, adj. *aversus, posterior*.
hinder, *impedire, obstare, officĕre*.
hindmost, *postremus, ultimus, novissimus*.
hindrance, *impedimentum*.
hinge, subst. *cardo*.
hint, subst. *significatio*.
hint, v. *significare*.
hip, *coxendix*.
hire, subst. *merces*.
hire, v. *conducĕre*.
hired, *conductus, mercenarius*.
hireling, *mercenarius*.
hirer, *conductor*.
his, *eius, illius, huius*; — own *suus -a -um*.
hiss, subst. *sibilus* (plur. *sibila*).
hiss, v. *sibilare*; to — off the stage, *exsibilare, explodĕre*.
hist! *st!*
historian, *rerum* (*gestarum*) *scriptor*.
historic, historical, *historicus*; — writings, *libri ad historiam pertinentes*.
history, *historia, rerum gestarum memoria, annales*; ancient —, *antiquitatis memoria*.
histrionic, *scaenicus*.
hit, subst. *plaga, ictus* (*-ūs*).
hit, v. *ferire, tundĕre, percutĕre*; to — it off, = agree, *convenire*; to — upon, *offendĕre, incidĕre*.
hitch, subst. *impedimentum* (= hindrance), *mora* (= delay).
hitch, v. (*ad*)*iungĕre, adnectĕre*.
hither, adj. *citerior*.
hither, adj. *huc*; — and thither, *huc illuc*.
hitherto, *adhuc, hactenus*.
hive, *alvearium, alvus*.
ho! *heus!*
hoard, subst. *copia, acervus*.
hoard, v. *conquirĕre, coacervare*.
hoar-frost, *pruina*.
hoarse, *raucus*; adv. *rauca voce*.
hoary, *canus*.
hoax, subst. *ludificatio*.
hoax, v. *ludificari, inludĕre*.
hobble, *claudicare*.
hobby, *studium*.
hock, *poples*.
hoe, subst. *sarculum, marra*
hoe, v. *sarire*.
hog, *sus, porcus*.
hoggish, *suillus*.
hogshead, *dolium*.
hoist, *sublevare, tollĕre*.
hold, subst.: = grasp *manus* (*-ūs*); of a ship, *caverna*.
hold, v.: = to have, possess, *tenēre, obtinēre, possidēre, habēre*; = to contain, *capĕre, continēre*; = to conduct, *agĕre, habēre*; to — an opinion, — that, *censēre, ducĕre*; = to check, *cohibēre*; to — out (= endure), *durare, sustinēre*.
holding, subst. *possessio*.
hole, *cavum, foramen; rima* (= chink); *lacuna* (= pit).
holiday, *dies festus, feriae*(*-arum*).
holiness, *sanctitas, religio*.
Holland, *Batavia*.
hollow, subst., = valley, *convallis, valles* (*vallis*); see also hole.
hollow, adj. (*con*)*cavus*; of sounds, *fuscus, raucus*; = insincere, *vanus, simulatus*.
hollow, v. (*ex*)*cavare*.
holm-oak, *ilex*.
holy, *sacer, sanctus*; adv. *sancte*.
homage, *cultus* (*-ūs*), *observantia*.
home, subst. *domus, domicilium*; at — *domi*; from —, *domo*; —wards *to* one's —, *domum*.
home, adj. *domesticus, familiaris*.
homeless, *domo carens*.
homeliness, *simplicitas*.
homely, *simplex, rudis*.
homewards, *domum*.
homicide; see murder.
homily, *oratio*.
homogeneous, *eiusdem generis*.
honest, *probus, sincerus, frugi*. adv. *probe, sincere*.
honesty, *probitas, sinceritas, fides*.
honey, *mel*
honeycomb, *favus*.
honeyed, honied, *mellitus, suavis. dulcis*.
honour, subst.: = official distinction, *dignitas, honos* (*honor*); = moral integrity, *honestas, fides*; sense of — *pudor*; an — to, = a credit to, *decus*.
honour, v. *colĕre, honorare, celebrare*.
honourable: = honoured, *honoratus, amplus*; = bring honour, *honestus, honorificus*. Adv. *honeste, honorifice*.
hood, *cucullus*.
hoodwink, *ludificari, inludĕre*.

hoof, *ungula.*
hook, subst. *hamus, uncus.*
hook, v. *hamo capĕre.*
hooked, *aduncus, hamatus.*
hoop, *circulus*; a child's —, *trochus.*
hoopoe, *upupa.*
hoot, hooting, subst.: of owls, *cantus* (*-ūs*); of persons, *vociferatio.*
hoot, v.: of owls, *canĕre*; of persons, *vociferari, obstrepĕre.*
hop, v. *salire.*
hope, subst. *spes*; a gleam of —, *specula*; to have no —, *desperare.*
hope, v. *sperare.*
hopeful, hopefully; render by phrase with *spes.*
hopeless: = despairing, *spe carens*; = despaired of, *desperatus.*
hopelessness, *desperatio; res desperatae.*
horde, *grex, caterva.*
horizon, *orbis finiens*; = sky, in gen., *caelum.*
horizontal, *aequus, libratus*; adv. *ad libram.*
horn, *cornu*; as a drinking-cup, *poculum.*
horned, *corniger, cornutus.*
hornet, *crabro.*
horny, *corneus.*
horoscope, *horoscopus, genesis*; to cast a —, *sidera natalicia notare.*
horrible, horrid, *horribilis, foedus, atrox*; adv. *foede.*
horrify, (*ex*)*terrēre, obstupefacĕre.*
horror, *horror, timor, pavor*; a —, = a monster, *monstrum.*
horse, *equus*; = cavalry, *equites* (*-um*), *equitatus* (*-ūs*).
horseback; to ride on —, *in equo vehi, equitare*; to fight on — *ex equo pugnare.*
horse-fly, *tabanus.*
horse-hair, *pilus equinus.*
horseman, *eques.*
horse-race, *curriculum equorum*
horse-shoe, *solea.*
horticulture, *hortorum cultus* (*-ūs*).
hospitable, *hospitalis*; adv. *hospitaliter, comiter.*
hospitality, *hospitium, hospitalitas.*
host, *hospes*; at a feast, *convivator*; at an inn, *caupo*; = multitude; army, *exercitus* (*-ūs*).
hostage, *obses.*
hostelry, *caupona.*
hostess, *hospita.*
hostile, *hostilis, inimicus, infestus.*
hostility, *animus infestus, inimicitia, odium*; hostilities, *hostilia* (*-ium*), *bellum.*
hot, *calidus, fervidus, fervens, ardens*; to be —, *calēre, fervēre, aestuare*; to make —, *calefacĕre.* Adv. *ardenter.*
hotel, *deversorium, hospitium.*
hotheaded, *fervidus, temerarius.*
hound, subst. *canis* (*venaticus*).
hound, v. *instigare, urgēre.*
hour, *hora*; half an —, *semihora*; what — is it? *quota hora est?*
hourly, *singulis horis, in horas.*
house, subst. *domus, aedes, aedificium, domicilium*; = race, clan, *gens, genus*; at my —, *apud me, domi meae*
house, v. = store, *condĕre.*
housebreaker, *fur.*
household, subst. *domus, familia.*
household, adj. *domesticus*; —-gods, *lares* (*-um*), *penates* (*-ium*).
householder, *paterfamilias.*
house-keeper, *promus.*
house-maid, *ancilla.*
house-wife, *materfamilias, hera.*
hovel, *tugurium, gurgustium.*
hover, (*circum*)*volitare, imminēre.*
how. (1) interrog. *quomodo? quemadmodum? qui?*; with adj. or adv., *quam?*; how great? *quantus?*; how small? *quantulus?*; how many? *quot?*; how often? *quotie*(*n*)*s?*. (2) in exclamation, *ut, quam*; also *quantus, quantulus,* etc.
howbeit, (*at*)*tamen.*
however: adv. *quamvis, quamlibet*; — great, *quantuscunque, quantus quantus*; — many, *quotquot*; — often, *quotienscunque*; conj., *sed, autem,* (*at*)*tamen, nihilominus.*
howl, subst. *ululatus* (*-ūs*), *eiulatus* (*-ūs*).
howl, v. *ululare, fremĕre, eiulare.*
hubbub, *tumultus* (*-ūs*), *turba.*
huckster, *caupo, institor.*
huddled, *conferti.*
hue, *color.*
hug, subst. *complexus* (*-ūs*).
hug, v. *amplecti, complecti*; to — the shore, *litus premĕre* or *legĕre.*
huge, *immanis, ingens.*
hulk, *alveus navis.*
hum, subst. *fremitus* (*-ūs*), *murmur, susurrus.*
hum, v. *fremĕre, murmurare*; = sing softly, *secum canĕre.*
human, *humanus, hominum* (= of men); — feelings, *humanitas*; — being, *homo.* Adv. *humano modo.*
humane, *misericors, clemens*; adv. *clementer, humane.*
humanity: = nature of man, *humanitas, natura humana*; = mankind, *homines* (*-um*), *gens humana*; = kindly feeling, *clementia, misericordia.*
humble, adj.: = obscure, *humilis, obscurus*: of — origin, *humili loco natus*; = modest, unassuming, *summissus, verecundus.* Adv. *summisse.*
humble, v. *infringĕre, comprimĕre*; to — oneself, *se* or *animum summittĕre.*
humid, *humidus.*
humidity, *humor.*
humiliation, *dedecus* (*-oris,* n.).
humility, *animus summissus.*
humorous: of situations, *ridiculus*; of persons, *iocosus, lepidus, facetus.*
humour: = fluid, *humor*; = disposition, *ingenium, natura, animus*; = fancy, caprice, *voluptas, libido*; I am in the — to do, *libet mihi facere*; = sense of fun, *festivitas, facetiae*(*-arum*).
humour, v. *indulgēre, morem gerĕre* (with dat.).
hump, *gibbus, gibba.*
humpbacked, *gibber.*
hundred, adj. *centum*; a — at a time, *centeni -ae -a*; a — times, *centie*(*n*)*s*
hundred-fold, *centuplex.*
hunger, subst. *fames.*
hunger, v. *esurire.*

hungry, *esuriens, ieiunus*; adv. *avide.*
hunt, v. *venari, consectari.*
hunt, subst. *venatio, venatus* (-*ūs*).
hunter, huntsman, *venator.*
huntress, *venatrix.*
hurdle, *crates.*
hurl, *iacĕre, iaculari, conicĕre.*
hurling, subst. *coniectus* (-*ūs*).
hurrah! *io!*
hurricane, *tempestas, procella.*
hurried, *citatus, praeceps*; adv. *festinanter, propere, raptim.*
hurry, subst. *festinatio, trepidatio.*
hurry, v.: transit. *accelerare, incitare, rapĕre; maturare* (= to hurry on); instransit., *festinare, properare, maturare.*
hurt, subst. *vulnus* (-*eris*, n.).
hurt, adj.: physically, *saucius*; in feelings, *offensus.*
hurt, v. *laedĕre, nocēre*; to — a person's feelings, *hominem offendĕre*; to be — at a thing, *rem aegre ferre*; it —s, *dolet.*
hurtful, *nocens, noxius, molestus.*
husband, subst. *maritus, vir, coniunx.*
husband, v. *parcĕre.*
husbandman, *agricola, colonus.*
husbandry, *res rustica, agricultura.*
hush! interj. *st! tacē* (plur. *tacēte*).
hush, v. *comprimĕre*
husk, *folliculus.*
hustings, *suggestus* (-*ūs*), *comitium.*
hustle, v. *offendĕre, pulsare.*
hut, *casa, tugurium.*
hutch, *cavea* (= cage).
hyacinth, *hyacinthus* (*hyacinthos*).
hymeneal, *nuptialis.*
hymn, subst. *carmen, hymnus* (ecclesiastical).
hymn, v. *canĕre, cantare, celebrare.*
hyperbole, *hyperbole, veritatis superlatio.*
hyperbolical, *superlatus.*
hypercritical, *nimium severus.*
hypochondria, *atra* (or *nigra*) *bilis.*
hypochondriacal, *melancholicus.*
hypocrisy, (*dis*)*simulatio, fraus.*
hypocrite, (*dis*)*simulator.*
hypocritical, *simulatus, fictus*; adv. *simulate, ficte.*
hypothesis, *opinio, sententia, coniectura.*

I

iambic, subst. *iambus.*
iambic, adj. *iambeus.*
ice, *glacies, gelu.*
icicle, *stiria.*
icy, *glacialis, gelidus, frigidus.*
idea: = notion, conception, *notio, notitia, imago*; in gen., = thought, *cogitatio, opinio, sententia*; = purpose, *consilium.*
ideal, subst., = perfect type, *exemplar, specimen.*
ideal, adj.: = perfect, *perfectus, optimus, summus*; = existing only in the mind, *commenticius.*
identical, *idem.*
identify, = recognize, *agnoscĕre.*
identify; render by *idem* (= same), or phrase like *quis sit* (= who he is).
ides, *idūs* (-*uum*).
idiocy, *fatuitas.*
idiom, *propria loquendi ratio.*
idiotic, *fatuus.*
idle, adj.: = inactive, lazy, *otiosus, vacuus, piger, segnis*; = useless, *inutilis, vanus, inritus.* Adv. *segniter*; = in vain, *frustra, incassum.*
idle, v. *cessare, nihil agĕre.*
idleness: = inactivity, *cessatio, otium*; = laziness, *segnitia, pigritia.*
idler, *homo deses; cessator.*
idol, *idolum* (ecclesiastical); *fictus deus.*
idolize, (*tamquam deum*) *colĕre.*
idyl, *bucolica* (-*orum*, n.; = pastoral poetry).
if, *si*; and —, *quodsi*; but —, *sin*; — only, *si modo* (or *dum modo* with subj.); even —, *etsi, etiamsi*; as —, *quasi, tamquam*; in indirect questions, if (= whether) is *num.*
igneous, *igneus.*
ignite, v.: transit., *accendĕre, incendĕre*; intransit., *exardescĕre, accendi, incendi.*
ignoble: by descent, *ignobilis, obscuro loco natus*; in character, *inliberalis, abiectus, turpis*; adv. *trupiter.*
ignominious, *turpis*; adv. *turpiter, cum ignominia.*
ignominy, *ignominia, dedecus* (-*oris*).
ignorance, *inscientia, ignoratio.*
ignorant, *inscius, ignarus, imperitus* (= inexperienced), *indoctus* (= untaught); to be —, *nescire, ignorare.* Adv. *inscienter, imperite*; or render by adj.
ignore, *praeterire, neglegĕre.*
ill, subst. *malum.*
ill, adj.: = sick, *aeger, aegrotus*: to be —, *aegrotare*; = evil, *malus*; —-fame, *infamia.*
ill, adv. *male, prave.*
ill-advised, *inconsultus, temerarius.*
ill-bred, *inhumanus, inurbanus.*
ill-disposed, *malevolus.*
illegally, *contra leges.*
illegitimate: of actions, *non legitimus*; of persons, *nothus.*
ill-fated, *infelix, miser.*
ill-gotten, *male partus.*
ill-health, *valetudo infirma.*
illiberal, *inliberalis, sordidus, malignus.*
illicit, *inlicitus, vetitus*; see illegally.
illiterate, *indoctus.*
ill-matched, *impar.*
ill-natured, *malevolus, malignus.*
illness, *aegrotatio, valetudo infirma.*
illogical, *absurdus.*
ill-omened, *dirus, tristis.*
ill-starred, *infelix.*
ill-tempered, *acerbitas, morositas, iracundia.*
illume, illuminate: = throw light on, *inlustrare, inluminare*; = enlighten the mind, *docēre, erudire*; = adorn with pictures, *varie pingĕre, coloribus distinguĕre.*
illusion, *error, opinio vana.*
illusory, *vanus, falsus.*
illustrate (*librum*) *picturis ornare*; see also explain.

illustration; in a book, *pictura, tabula;* = example, *exemplum.*
illustrious, *(prae)clarus, inlustris, insignis.*
ill-will, *malevolentia.*
image, *imago, simulacrum, species.*
imaginary, *opinabilis, commenticius; fictus, falsus.*
imagination, *cogitatio.*
imagine, *animo concipěre, (cogitatione) fingěre, excogitare;* = to think, *putare, opinari.*
imbecile, *fatuus, stultus.*
imbecility, *imbecillitas animi, stultitia.*
imbibe, *(com)biběre, imbiběre.*
imbue, *inficěre, imbuěre, tingěre.*
imitable, *imitabilis.*
imitate, *imitari;* = portray, *exprimère, effingěre;* = emulate, *aemulari.*
imitation, *imitatio, aemulatio;* = a copy, *effigies, imago, simulacrum.*
imitator, *imitator* (f. *imitatrix*); *aemulus, aemulator.*
immaculate, *purus, integer;* adv. *pure.*
immaterial, *sine corpore, expers corporis;* = unimportant, *nullius momenti, levis.*
immature, *immaturus, crudus.*
immeasurable, *immensus, infinitus.*
immediate: = direct, *proximus;* = without delay, *praesens.* Adv., = directly, render by *ipse;* —before, or —after, *sub* with acc.; = at once, *statim, confestim, extemplo.*
immemorial; render by *antiquus.*
immense, *ingens, vastus, immensus* Adv. *in immensum;* = very much *maxime, valde.*
immensity, *immensitas.*
immigrate, *(im)migrare.*
immigrant, *advena.*
imminent, *praesens;* to be — *instare, imminēre, impendēre.*
immoderate, *immodicus, nimius, intemperans;* adv., *immodice, intemperanter, praeter modum, nimis.*
immodest, *impudicus, impudens;* adv. *impudenter.*
immodesty, *impudicitia.*
immolate, *immolare.*
immolation, *immolatio.*
immoral, *pravus, inhonestus, turpis;* adv. *prave, inhoneste, turpiter.*
immorality, *mores corrupti; turpitudo.*
immortal, *immortalis, aeternus, sempiternus* (of things).
mmortality, *immortalitas, aeternitas; sempiterna gloria.*
immoveable, *immobilis, stabilis.*
immune, *immunis;* see also free.
immunity, *vacatio, immunitas.*
immure, *includěre.*
immutability, *immutabilitas, constantia.*
immutable, *immutabilis, constans, stabilis;* adv. *constanter.*
impair, *(im)minuěre, debilitare, infringěre.*
impale, *(hasta* or *palo) transfigěre.*
impart, *impertire, communicare, dare.*
impartial, *aequus;* to be —, *neutri favēre.*
impartiality, *aequitas.*
impassable, *invius, impeditus.*
impassioned, *ardens, vehemens.*
impassive, *lentus.*
impassivity, *lentitudo, lentus animus.*
impatience, *festinatio.*
impatient, *impatiens morae, ardens acer;* adv. *ardenter, acriter.*
impeach, *accusare.*
impeachment, *accusatio.*
impede, *impedire.*
impediment, *impedimentum;* in speech. *haesitantia linguae.*
impel, *impellěre, urgēre.*
impend, *impendēre, imminēre.*
impenetrable, *impenetrabilis impervius, impeditus.*
impenitent, *obstinatus, offirmatus.*
imperative, gram., *imperativus* (adj.).
imperfect: gram., *imperfectus* (adj.); = unfinished, *imperfectus, rudis;* = faulty, *vitiosus, mendosus;* adv. *vitiose, mendose, male.*
imperfection, *vitium, mendum, culpa.*
imperial, render by genit., e.g. *imperatoris, principis.*
imperil, *in discrimen adducěre.*
imperious, *superbus, adrogans;* adv. *superbe, adroganter.*
imperishable, *immortalis, aeternus.*
impersonate; see imitate.
impertinence, *insolentia.*
impertinent: = rude, *insolens;* adv. *insolenter;* = not to the point, *nihil ad rem.*
imperturbable, *stabilis, firmus, gravis;* adv. *firme, graviter.*
impervious; see impenetrable.
impetuosity, *violentia, impetus* (-*ūs*).
impetuous, *violentus, rapidus, vehemens;* adv. *violenter, vehementer.*
impetus, *impetus* (-*ūs*), *vis.*
impiety, *impietas (erga deos), nefas.*
impious, *impius (erga deos) nefarius;* adv. *impie, nefarie.*
impinge, *inciděre, impingi.*
implacable, *implacabilis, inexorabilis:* adv. *atrociter, saeve.*
implant, *inserěre, ingenerare.*
implement, *instrumentum.*
implicate, *implicare, admiscēre, inligare.*
implicated, *implicatus, conscius.*
implicit: = implied, *tacitus;* = complete, *totus, summus.* Adv. *tacite:* see also altogether.
implore, *implorare, rogare, orare.*
imply: = to mean, indicate, *significare;* = to involve, *(in se) habēre;* to be implied, *(in re) inesse.*
impolite, *inurbanus;* adv. *inurbane.*
impoliteness, *inhumanitas, rusticitas.*
import, subst.; in plur., = imported goods, *res quae importantur;* = meaning, *vis, significatio.*
import, v.: = bring into a country, *invehěre, importare;* = signify, *significare, valēre.*
importance: of things, *momentum, pondus* (-*eris*), *vis;* of persons, = position, etc., *amplitudo, dignitas, auctoritas.*
important, *gravis, magnus;* to be —, *magni momenti esse, multum valēre.*

import-duty, *portorium.*
importunate, *molestus, improbus.*
importune, *fatigare; flagitare.*
importunity, *flagitatio.*
impose, *imponěre*; see also cheat.
imposing, *speciosus, magnificus.*
imposition, = deception, *fallacia, fraus.*
impossible, *quod fieri non potest.*
impost, *vectigal, tributum.*
impostor, *fraudator.*
impotence, *imbecillitas, infirmitas.*
impotent, *invalidus, infirmus, imbecillus.*
impound, = confiscate, *publicare.*
impoverish, *in egestatem redigěre.*
impoverishment, *egestas, inopia.*
impracticable, *quod fieri non potest.*
imprecate, *(im)precari*; see also curse.
imprecation, *preces (-um), exsecratio.*
impregnable, *inexpugnabilis.*
impress, *impriměre, inculcare.*
impression, *impressio*; = copy, *exemplum, imago expressa*; = footstep, *vestigium.* Transf., = effect on the mind, *animi motus (-ūs)*; to make an —, *animum (com)movēre*; = thought, idea, *opinio*; to be under an —, *putare, opinari.*
impressive, *gravis*; adv. *graviter.*
impressiveness, *gravitas.*
imprint; see impress.
imprison, *in custodiam* (or *carcerem*) *conicěre.*
imprisonment, *custodia, carcer, vincula (-orum).*
improbable, *non verisimilis.*
impromptu, *ex tempore.*
improper, *indecorus, indignus*; adv. *indecore, indigne, perperam.*
improve, v.: transit., *meliorem facěre, emendare, corrigěre*; intransit., *meliorem fieri, proficěre.*
improvement, *correctio, emendatio*: or render by *melior.*
improvidence, *imprudentia.*
improvident, *improvidus, imprudens*; adv. *improvide, imprudenter.*
improvised, *subitarius, ex tempore.*
imprudence, *imprudentia, temeritas.*
imprudent, *imprudens, temerarius*; adv. *imprudenter, temere.*
impudence, *impudentia, os impudens.*
impudent, *impudens, procax, improbus*; adv. *impudenter.*
impugn, *impugnare, improbare.*
impulse, *impulsio, impulsus (-ūs)*; or render by verb.
impulsive, *vehemens, acer.*
impunity, *impunitas*; with —, *impune.*
impure, *impurus, obscenus, foedus, turpis*; adv. *impure, obscene, foede, turpiter.*
impurity, *impuritas, obscenitas, turpitudo.*
imputation, = charge, *crimen, culpa, accusatio.*
impute, *adsignare, ascriběre, attribuěre.*
in: of place, render by locative, or *in* with abl., or plain abl.; when = into, *in* with acc.; of time, render by abl., or by *in* and abl.; in the case of, *in* with abl.; in the hands of, *penes* with acc.; in the writings of, *apud* with acc.
inability, *infirmitas, inopia*; or render by *non posse.*
inaccessible, *inaccessus*; of persons, *rari aditūs.*
inaccurate: of a person, *indiligens*; of reports, etc., *falsus.*
inaction, inactivity, *otium, quies*; = laziness, *desidia, inertia.*
inactive, *quietus, iners; segnis.*
inadequate, *impar*; adv. *parum, haud satis.*
inadmissible, *inlicitus.*
inadvertence, *imprudentia.*
inadvertent, *imprudens*; adv. *imprudenter, temere.*
inalienable, *quod abalienari non potest*
inane, *inanis.*
inanimate, *inanimus, inanimatus.*
inanition, *inanitas.*
inapplicable, to be, *non valēre.*
inapposite; see inappropriate.
inappropriate, *non idoneus.*
inaptitude, *inutilitas.*
inarticulate, *parum distinctus.*
inasmuch as, *quandoquidem.*
inattention, *neglegentia, incuria.*
inattentive, *non attentus*; to be — *aliud agěre.*
inaugurate, *inaugurare, dedicare, consecrare.*
inauguration, *dedicatio, consecratio.*
inauspicious, *infelix, nefastus*; adv. *infeliciter, malis ominibus.*
incalculable, *immensus, ingens.*
incandescent, *candens.*
incantation, *carmen, cantio.*
incapable; render by *non posse.*
incarcerate; see imposing.
incarnate, *incarnatus* (ecclesiastical); *specie humana* (or *corpore*) *indutus.*
incautious, *incautus, inconsultus*; adv. *incaute, inconsulte, temere.*
incendiary, *incendiarius, incendiorum auctor.*
incense, subst. *tus (turis).*
incense, *accenděre, incenděre.*
incentive, *stimulus, incitamentum.*
inception, *initium.*
inceptive, *incipiens.*
incessant, *perpetuus, adsiduus, continuus*; adv. *perpetuo, adsidue.*
inch, *uncia.*
inchoate, *inchoatus.*
incident, *casus (-ūs), res.*
incidental, *fortuitus, forte oblatus*; adv. *casu, forte, fortuito.*
incipient, render by *initium* or *incipio.*
incisive, *mordax*; adv. *praecise.*
incite, *incitare, stimulare, impellěre.*
incivility, *inurbanitas, inhumanitas.*
inclement: of persons, *severus, saevus*; of weather, *gravis, asper.*
inclination: physical, *inclinatio*; = slope, *fastigium, clivus*; mental, = propensity, *inclinatio, studium.*
incline, v.: transit., *inclinare*; intransit., *inclinari, (se) inclinare, propenděre.*
inclined, *inclinatus, propensus, pronus.*
inclose; see enclose.
include, *comprehenděre, complecti, adscriběre*; to — among the accused, *in reos referre.*
including, *cum* with abl.

incognito, *alieno* or *dissimulato nomine.*
incoherent, *interruptus*; adv. *interrupte*; to speak —, *haud cohaerentia dicĕre.*
income, *vectigal, reditus* (-*ūs*, = returns), *pecunia, quaestus* (-*ūs*).
incommode, *incommodum* or *molestum esse.*
incomparable, *unicus, singularis, egregius*; adv. *unice, egregie.*
incompatibility, *repugnantia, diversitas.*
incompatible, *alienus, contrarius*; to be —, *abhorrēre, repugnare.*
incompetence, *inscitia.*
incompetent, *inscitus, inhabilis*; adv. *inscite.* Legally, render by phrase with *ius* or *potestas.*
incomplete, *imperfectus*; adv. *imperfecte.*
incomprehensible, *quod comprehendi non potest.*
inconceivable, *quod* (*mente*) *comprehendi non potest*; sometimes *incredibilis.* Adv. *incredibiliter, mirum in modum.*
inconclusive, (*argumentum*) *quo nihil efficitur.*
incongruity, *repugnantia.*
incongruous, *alienus, non aptus.*
inconsiderable, *levis, tenuis, exiguus.*
inconsiderate, = unthinking, *inconsideratus, inconsultus*; adv. *inconsiderate, nullo consilio, temere.*
inconsistency, *inconstantia, repugnantia.*
inconsistent, *inconstans, contrarius, repugnans*; adv. *inconstanter.*
inconsolable, *inconsolabilis; qui nullo solacio levari potest.*
inconspicuous, *obscurus.*
inconstancy, *inconstantia, levitas, varietas.*
inconstant, *inconstans, levis, varius.*
incontinence, *incontinentia, intemperantia.*
incontinent, *incontinens, intemperans*; adv. *incontinenter*; = immediately, *statim.*
incontrovertible, *quod refutari non potest.*
inconvenience, *incommodum*; to cause —, *negotium exhibēre.*
inconvenient, *inopportunus, incommodus*; adv. *incommode.*
incorrect, *falsus, mendosus*; = morally wrong, *improbus, iniustus.* Adv. *perperam, falso, mendose.*
incorrigible, *perditus; qui corrigi non potest.*
incorruptibility, *integritas, sanctitas.*
incorruptible, *incorruptus, integer, sanctus*; adv. *incorrupte, integre, sancte.*
increase, subst. *incrementum, auctus* (-*ūs*).
increase, v.: transit., *augēre, amplificare*; intransit., *crescĕre, augēri, gliscĕre.*
incredible, *incredibilis*; adv. *incredibiliter.*
incredulous, *incredulus.*
increment, *incrementum.*
incriminate, *suspectum reddĕre*; to — oneself, *se scelere adligare.*
inculcate, *inculcare; docēre.*
incumbent; see ought, must.
incur, *suscipĕre, contrahĕre*; to — disgrace, *dedecus in se admittĕre.*
incurable, *insanabilis.*
incursion, *incursio*; see attack.
indebted: = owing money, *obaeratus*; = obliged, *obnoxius, obligatus.*
indecency, *turpitudo, obscenitas.*
indecent, *indecorus, turpis*; adv. *indecore, turpiter.*
indecision, *dubitatio, haesitatio.*
indecisive, *dubius, anceps*; adv. (of fighting), *aequo marte.*
indecorous, *indecorus.*
indeed: emphatic, *vere, profecto, sane*; and —, *atque adeo*; then —, *tum vero*; concessive, *quidem*; interrogative, *ain tu? itane est?*; ironical, *scilicet, nimirum, videlicet.*
indefatigable, *adsiduus, impiger*; adv. *adsidue, impigre.*
indefensible, *quod defendi non potest.*
indefinable, *quod* (*verbis*) *definiri non potest.*
indefinite, *incertus, dubius, anceps, ambiguus*: for an — period, *in incertum*; gram., *infinitus, indefinitus.*
indelible, *quod deleri non potest.*
indelicate, *impudicus, impurus.*
indemnify, *damnum restituĕre.*
independence, *libertas.*
independent, *liber, solutus, sui iuris.* from taxes, etc., *immunis*; adv *libere, suo arbitrio.*
indescribable, *inenarrabilis, singularis*; adv. *inenarrabiliter, singulariter.*
indestructible, *quod everti non potest; perennis, perpetuus.*
indeterminate, *incertus.*
index, *index*; of a dial, *gnomon, horarum index.*
India, *India.*
Indian: subst. *Indus*; adj. *Indicus.*
indicate, *indicare, significare.*
indication, *indicium, significatio, signum.*
indicative: render by *indicium* or *indico*; gram., the — mood, *modus indicativus.*
indict, *accusare, nomen deferre.*
indictment; bill of —, *crimen, accusatio.*
indifference: = neglect, *neglegentia, incuria*; = calmness, *aequus animus, securitas*; = apathy, *lentitudo.*
indifferent: = negligent, *neglegens, remissus*; = calm, *securus*, or render by *aequo animo*; = apathetic, *lentus*; = mediocre, *mediocris.* Adv. *neglegenter*; *lente, aequo animo*; = without discrimination, *promiscue.*
indigence, *inopia, egestas.*
indigenous, *vernaculus*; applied to persons, *indigena.*
indigent, *inops, egens.*
indigestible, *gravis.*
indigestion, *cruditas.*
indignant, *indignans,* (*sub*)*iratus.*
indignation, *indignatio, stomachus, ira.*
indignity, *ignominia, contumelia.*
indirect: physically, *non rectus, devius*; of speech, *obliquus*; gram., *obliquus*; adv. *oblique.*

indirectness; in speech, *circumitio*
indiscreet, *inconsultus.*
indiscretion, see imprudence.
indiscriminate, *promiscuus*; adv. *promiscue, sine ullo discrimine, temere.*
indispensable, *necessarius.*
indispose, *abstrahĕre, avocare.*
indisposed: = unwell, *aegrotus, infirma valetudine*; = disinclined, *aversus, alienus.*
indisputable, *certus, manifestus*; adv. *certe, haud dubie.*
indissoluble, *indissolubilis; aeternus.*
indistinct: *parum clarus, obscurus*; adv. *parum clare, obscure.*
indistinguishable, *quod discerni non potest.*
indite, *scribĕre.*
individual, subst.; see man, person.
individual, adj. *proprius, singularis*; *singuli -ae -a.*
individuality, *propria natura.*
individually, *singillatim, viritim; in singulos.*
indivisible, *individuus, quod dividi non potest.*
indoctrinate, *erudire, docēre, instituĕre.*
indolence, *ignavia, desidia, segnities.*
indolent, *ignavus, deses, segnis*; adv. *ignave, segniter.*
indomitable, *invictus, indomitus.*
indoor, adj. *umbratilis.*
indoors, *domi, intus.*
indorse; see endorse.
indubitable, *haud dubius, certus.*
induce, *inducĕre, impellĕre, inlicĕre, persuadēre.*
inducement, *incitamentum, inlecebra.*
induct, *inaugurare.*
induction, in logic, *inductio.*
indulge, v. *indulgēre, morem gerĕre, (in)servire.*
indulgence, *indulgentia, venia* (= pardon).
indulgent, *indulgens, benignus*; adv. *indulgenter, benigne.*
industrious, *industrius, sedulus, strenuus*; adv. *industrie, strenue.*
industry, *industria, sedulitas.*
indwelling, *insitus, innatus.*
inebriated, *ebrius, temulentus.*
inebriation, *ebrietas.*
ineffable, *inauditus, incredibilis*; adv. *incredibiliter.*
ineffective, *irritus, inutilis*; to be —, *effectu carēre*; adv. *frustra, nequicquam.*
inelegant, *invenustus, inelegans, inurbanus*; adv. *ineleganter, inurbane.*
ineligible, = unsuitable, *inopportunus.*
inept, *ineptus.*
inequality, *inaequalitas, dissimilitudo.*
inequitable, *iniquus, iniustus*; adv. *inique, iniuste.*
inert, *iners, tardus, segnis*; adv. *tarde, segniter.*
inestimable, *inaestimabilis, singularis, unicus*; adv. *singulariter, unice.*
inevitable, *necessarius, haud dubius, inevitabilis*; adv. *necessario.*
inexact, *haud accuratus* (of things), *indiligens* (of persons).
inexcusable, *quod nihil excusationis habet.*
inexhaustible, *quod exhauriri non potest; infinitus.*
inexorable, *inexorabilis, severus, durus.*
inexpediency, *inutilitas.*
inexpedient, *inutilis, inopportunus.*
inexperience, *imperitia, inscientila.*
inexperienced, *imperitus, ignarus, rudis.*
inexpiable, *inexpiabilis.*
inexplicable, *inexplicabilis.*
inexpressible, *inauditus, inenarrabilis.*
inextinguishable, *quod exstingui non potest.*
inextricable, *inexplicabilis, inextricabilis.*
infallible, *certus, haud dubius*; to be —, *omni errore carēre.* Adv. *certo.*
infamous, *infamis, turpis, flagitiosus*; adv. *turpiter, flagitiose.*
infamy, *infamia, dedecus, ignominia.*
infancy, *infantia, pueritia.*
infant: subst. *infans*; adj. *infans, puerilis.*
infantine, *puerilis.*
infantry, *pedites* (*-um*), *peditatus* (*-ūs*).
infatuate, *infatuare, occaecare, pellicĕre.*
infatuated, *amens, demens.*
infatuation, *amentia, dementia.*
infect, *inficĕre, contaminare.*
infection, *contagio, contactus* (*-ūs*).
infectious; an — disease, *pestilentia.*
infelicity, *infelicitas, malum.*
infer, *concludĕre, conligĕre.*
inference: as a process, *argumentatio, coniectura*; = conclusion, *conclusio, coniectura.*
inferior, adj. *inferior, deterior, minor.*
infernal, *infernus*; the — regions, *inferi* (*-orum*); = diabolical, *nefandus, nefarius.*
infertility, *sterilitas.*
infest, *infestum reddĕre.*
infested, *infestus.*
infidelity, *infidelitas, perfidia.*
infinite, *infinitus, immensus.* Adv., = very much, *incredibiliter, sane quam.*
infinitesimal, *minimus,* (*per*)*exiguus.*
infinity, *infinitas.*
infirm, *infirmus, invalidus, debilis.*
infirmity: = weakness, *infirmitas, imbecillitas, debilitas*; = a failing, *vitium.*
inflame, *inflammare, accendĕre, incendĕre.*
inflammable, *facilis ad exardescendum.*
inflammatory, *seditiosus, turbulentus.*
inflate, *inflare.*
inflated, *inflatus, tumidus, turgidus.*
inflation, *inflatio.*
inflect, gram., *declinare.*
inflection, gram., *declinatio, flexus* (*-ūs*).
inflexibility, *obstinatio, pertinacia.*
inflexible, *obstinatus, pertinax*; adv. *obstinate, pertinaciter.*
inflict, (*rem homini*) *adferre, infligĕre, imponĕre*; (*re hominem*) *adficĕre.*
infliction, = trouble, *malum, incommodum.*
influence, subst. *vis, pondus* (*-eris*), *momentum*: divine —, *adflatus* (*-ūs*) *divinus*; personal —, *auctorita* (= prestige), *potentia* (= unofficial power), *gratia* (= interest); to have — *valēre, pollēre, posse.*

influence, v. *movēre, impellĕre.*
influential, *potens, gravis, gratiosus.*
influx; render by *influere.*
inform: = to form, shape, *(ef)fingĕre, (con)formare;* = to tell, *certiorem facĕre, docēre;* to — against a person, *hominis nomen deferre.*
informality, at auspices, etc., *vitium;* otherwise phrase, e.g. *res haud sollemni more facta.*
information: = news, *nuntius;* = knowledge, *scientia, doctrina;* = accusation, *delatio, indicium.*
informer, *delator, index.*
infrequency, *raritas.*
infrequent, *rarus.*
infringe, *rumpĕre, frangĕre, violare.*
infringement, *immunitio, violatio.*
infuriate, *efferare, exasperare.*
infuriated, *furens.*
infuse, *infundĕre; inicĕre, incutĕre.*
ingenious, *sollers, callidus, artificiosus;* adv. *sollerter, callide, artificiose.*
ingenuity, *ars, sollertia, subtilitas.*
ingenuous, *apertus, simplex, liber;* adv. *aperte, simpliciter, libere.*
ingenuousness, *libertas.*
inglorious, *inglorius, inhonestus;* adv. *sine gloria, inhoneste.*
ingraft, *inserĕre.*
ingrained, *insitus, inveteratus.*
ingratiate: to — oneself, *favorem sibi conciliare.*
ingratitude, *animus ingratus.*
ingredient, *pars.*
ingress, *ingressus* (-*ūs*).
inhabit, *incolere, habitare;* thickly —ed, *frequens.*
inhabitable, *habitabilis.*
inhabitant, *incola, habitator;* of a city, *civis.*
inhale, *spiritu ducĕre.*
inharmonious, *discors, absonus, dissonus.*
inhere, *inesse, inhaerēre.*
inherent, *insitus, innatus, proprius;* adv. *naturā, per se.*
inherit, *(rem) hereditate accipĕre;* see also heir.
inheritance, *hereditas.*
inherited, *hereditarius, patrius.*
inhibit, *interdicĕre.*
inhibition, *interdictum.*
inhospitable, *inhospitalis.*
inhospitality, *inhospitalitas.*
inhuman, *inhumanus, crudelis,* adv. *inhumane, crudeliter.*
inhumanity, *inhumanitas, crudelitas.*
inimical, *inimicus;* see also hostile.
inimitable, *haud imitabilis.*
iniquitous, *iniustus, iniquus;* adv. *iniuste, inique, improbe.*
iniquity, *iniustitia, iniquitas.*
initial, adj. *primus.*
initiate, *initiare; imbuĕre, instituĕre;* see also begin.
initiative: to take the —, *occupare.*
injudicious, *inconsultus, temerarius;* adv. *inconsulte, temere.*
injunction; see command.
injure, *laedĕre, violare, nocēre.*
injurious, *noxius, damnosus, gravis, malus;* adv. *male.*
injury, *detrimentum, incommodum, damnum, malum, iniuria.*
injustice, *iniustitia;* = unjust act, *iniuria.*
ink, *atramentum.*
inkling, *odor.*
inland, *mediterraneus.*
inlay, *inserĕre, variare, distinguĕre.*
inlet, of the sea, *aestuarium.*
inmate, *deversor, inquilinus;* see inhabitant.
inmost, *intimus;* — being, *viscera* (-*um*), *medulla.*
inn, *deversorium, hospitium, caupona.*
innate, *innatus, insitus, proprius.*
inner, *interior, intestinus, domesticus.*
innkeeper, *caupo.*
innocence, *innocentia, integritas;* = simplicity, *simplicitas.*
innocent, *innocens, insons; integer, sanctus;* adv. *integre, caste.*
innocuous, *innocuus;* adv. *sine fraude.*
innovate, *(res) novare, mutare.*
innovation; political —s, *res novae* (plur.).
innumerable, *innumerabilis.*
inoffensive, adj. *innocens.*
inopportune, *inopportunus.*
inordinate, *immodicus, nimius;* adv. *praeter modum, immodice, nimis.*
inquire: = ask questions, *quaerĕre, sciscitari, percontari, rogare;* = hold an inquiry, *quaerĕre, inquirĕre, cognoscĕre*
inquiry, *percontatio, interrogatio;* a judicial —, *quaestio, inquisitio, cognitio.*
inquisitive, *audiendi cupidus, curiosus;* adv. *curiose.*
inquisitiveness, *studium audiendi, curiositas.*
inquisitor, *quaesitor.*
inroad, *incursio, incursus* (-*ūs*), *inruptio.*
insane, *insanus, amens* (= distracted), *demens* (= deranged), *furiosus* (= raving); adv. *insane, dementer, furiose.*
insanity, *insania, furor, amentia, dementia.*
insatiable, *insatiabilis inexplebilis.*
inscribe, *inscribĕre, ascribĕre.*
inscription, *inscriptio, index, titulus, epigramma* (-*atis,* n.).
inscrutable, *obscurus, occultus, tectus.*
insect, *insectum, bestiola.*
insecure, *instabilis, incertus, lubricus,* or neg. with *tutus* or *firmus.*
insensibility, *torpor.* Transf., *lentitudo.*
insensible, *sensūs expers.* Transf., *lentus.* Adv. *sensim, paulatim.*
insert, *inserĕre, includĕre, intericĕre, addĕre, adscribĕre* (in writing).
insertion, *interpositio;* or render by verb.
inside, subst. *pars interior.*
inside, adv. *intus, intro.*
inside, prep. *in* (with abl.), *intra* (with acc.).
insidious, *fallax, dolosus;* adv. *fallaciter, dolose.*
insidiousness, *fallacia, dolus, fraus.*
insight: = knowledge, *cognitio, intellegentia, perspicientia;* = intelligence, *iudicium, consilium.*

insignia, *fasces* (*-ium*), *insignia* (*-ium*).
insignificance, *exiguitas.*
insignificant, *exiguus, minutus, levis, nullius momenti.*
insincere, *falsus, simulatus*; adv. *falso, simulate.*
insincerity, *fallacia, simulatio.*
insinuate: to — oneself, *se insinuare, adrepĕre*; = to suggest, hint, *significare.*
insinuating, *blandus.*
insinuation, *significatio.*
insipid, *insulsus, ineptus, frigidus*; adv. *insulse, inepte, frigide.*
insist: = state positively, *confirmare, declarare, dictitare*; = demand, *flagitare,* (*ex*)*poscĕre.*
insolence, *insolentia, impudentia, adrogantia.*
insolent, *insolens, impudens, adrogans*; adv. *insolenter, impudenter, adroganter.*
insoluble, *quod liquefieri non potest.* Transf., *inexplicabilis.*
insolvent, to be, *non esse solvendo.*
insomuch, . . . that, *sic, ita* or *adeo . . . ut.*
inspect, *inspicĕre, intuēri, contemplari.*
inspection, *cura, custodia.*
inspector, *custos, curator.*
inspiration, = breathing in, *spiritus* (*-ūs*); divine —, *divinus adflatus* (*-ūs*); by divine —, *divinitus*; = suggestion, in gen., *monitus* (*-ūs*), *consilium.*
inspire, *inspirare*; = instil, *inicĕre, incutĕre*; = excite, *excitare, incendĕre.*
inspired, *divino spiritu inflatus.*
inspirit, *animum addĕre.*
instability, *inconstantia.*
install, *inaugurare.*
instalment, *pensio, pars, portio.*
instance, subst.: = urgent request, *preces* (*-um*); = example, *exemplum, specimen*; for —, *verbi causa, velut, vel.*
instant, subst. *punctum* or *momentum temporis*; at the very —, (*in*) *tempore ipso.*
instant, adj.; = urgent, *vehemens, intentus, impensus*; = immediate, *praesens.*
instantaneous, *subitus, praesens*; adv. *momento temporis, e vestigio.*
instantly: = immediately, *statim, confestim, extemplo*; = urgently, *intente, vehementer, impense.*
instead, adv. *potius, magis.*
instead of, prep., *pro* with abl., (*in*) *loco* with genit.; — fighting he sleeps, *non pugnat sed dormit,* or *cum possit pugnare, dormit.*
instep, *pes superior.*
instigate, *incitare, impellĕre, stimulare.*
instigation, *stimulus*; at your —, *impulsu tuo.*
instigator, *auctor, impulsor, suasor.*
instil, *instillare*; see also inspire.
instinct, subst. *natura*; = natural appetite, *appetitus* (*-ūs*).
instinct, adj. *imbutus.*
instinctive, *naturalis*; adv. *naturā, naturaliter.*
institute, institution: as act, *initium*; or render by verb; = custom, *institutum, lex, mos*; = corporation, *conlegium, sodalitas.*
institute, v. *condĕre, instituĕre, constituĕre.*
instruct: = teach, *erudire, docēre, instituĕre*; = order, *mandare, praecipĕre.*
instruction: = teaching, *institutio, eruditio, doctrina*; = direction, *praeceptum, mandatum.*
instructor, *magister, praeceptor.*
instrument, *instrumentum, machina*; steel —s, *ferramenta* (*-orum*); a stringed —, *fides* (*-ium*); legal, = deed, *instrumentum, tabula.*
instrumental, *utilis, aptus*; — music, *cantus nervorum et tibiarum.*
instrumentality, *opera, ministerium.*
insubordinate, *seditiosus, turbulentus.*
insubordination, *immodestia.*
insufferable, *intolerabilis.*
insufficient, *haud sufficiens, impar*; adv. *parum, haud satis.*
insult, subst. *contumelia, probrum.*
insult, v. *contumeliam imponĕre.*
insulting, *contumeliosus, maledicus*; adv. *contumeliose, maledice.*
insuperable, *in*(*ex*)*superabilis*; = invincible, *invictus.*
insurgent, subst. and adj., *rebellis.*
insurrection, *rebellio, seditio, motus* (*-ūs*).
intact, *integer, salvus, incolumis.*
intangible, *intactilis; quod tangi non potest.*
integral, *necessarius.*
integrity, *integritas, probitas.*
intellect, *mens, ingenium, intelligentia.*
intelligence; see intellect; = news *nuntius.*
intelligent, *mente praeditus, intellegens; sapiens, prudens.* Adv. *intellegenter, sapienter, prudenter.*
intelligible, *quod facile intellegi potest; planus, perspicuus*; adv. *perspicue, plane.*
intemperance, *intemperantia, impotentia*; in drink, *ebrietas.*
intemperate, *intemperans, impotens, immodicus*; — in drink, *ebriosus* Adv. *intemperanter, immodice.*
intend, (*facĕre*) *in animo habēre; cogitare, destinare, intendĕre.*
intense, *acer, magnus, summus, nimius*; adv. *valde, magnopere, acriter, summe.*
intensify, *maiorem reddĕre, augēre.*
intent, *intentus, attentus*; to be —, *animum intendĕre, incumbĕre, studēre.*
intention, *consilium, propositum, institum.*
intentionally, *consulto, de industria.*
inter, *sepelire, humare.*
intercalary, *intercalaris, intercalarius.*
intercede, (*de*)*precari.*
intercession, *deprecatio.*
intercessor, *deprecator.*
intercept, *intercipĕre, excipĕre*; in gen., = cut off, *intercludĕre.*
interchange, subst. *permutatio, vicissitudo.*
interchange, v. (*com*)*mutare, permutare.*
interchangeably, *invicem.*

intercourse, in gen. *usus* (*-ūs*), *commercium*; sexual, *concubitus* (*-ūs*), *consuetudo, coitus* (*-ūs*).
interdict; subst. *interdictum.*
interdict, v. *interdicĕre.*
interest, subst.: = attention, *studium*; = advantage, *bonum, utilitas, usus* (*-ūs*); it is in my —, *interest meā, refert meā, expedit mihi*; = influence, *gratia*; — on money, *faenus* (*-oris*), *usura*; compound —, *anatocismus*; simple —, *perpetuum faenus*; to lend out money on —, *faenerari.*
interest, v.: = to hold the attention, *tenēre*; sometimes *placēre*; to — oneself in, *studēre, operam dare.*
interested: = attentive, *attentus, erectus; studiosus*, with genit.; = concerned, see interest, subst.
interfere, *intervenire, se interponĕre, se immiscēre*; to — with, = to hinder, *impedire.*
interim, *temporis intervallum*; an — decree, *edictum ad tempus propositum.*
interior, subst. *pars interior.*
interior, adj. *interior, internus.*
interject, *interponĕre, intericĕre.*
interjection, *interiectio.*
interlace, *implicare.*
interlude, *embolium.*
intermarriage, *connubium.*
intermediate, *medius.*
interment, *sepultura, humatio.*
interminable, *infinitus*; adv. *infinite, sine fine.*
intermingle, (*inter*)*miscēre.*
intermission, *intermissio.*
intermittently, *aliquando, nonnumquam, interdum.*
internal; see inner; adv. *intus, penitus.*
international: — law, *ius* (*iuris*, n.) *gentium.*
internecine, *internecivus.*
interpellation, *interpellatio.*
interpolate, *addĕre, inserĕre*; = to falsify, *corrumpĕre, interpolare.*
interpose, *interponĕre, intericĕre*; = to intervene, *se interponĕre.*
interposition, *interiectus* (*-ūs*), *interventus* (*-ūs*); = mediation, intervention, *interventus* (*-ūs*).
interpret, *interpretari*; to — favourably, *in bonam partem interpretari* or *accipĕre.*
interpretation, *interpretatio, explanatio.*
interpreter, *interpres.*
interregnum, *interregnum.*
interrogate, (*inter*)*rogare, quaerĕre, exquirĕre.*
interrogation, *percontatio, quaestio, interrogatio.*
interrogative, gram., *interrogativus.*
interrupt, *interrumpĕre, interpellare, interfari.*
interruptedly, *interrupte.*
interruption: in speaking, *interpellatio, interfatio*; in gen., = pause, *intermissio, intervallum.*
intersect, *secare, scindĕre*; so as to form the figure X, *decussare.*
intersection, = the figure X, *decussatio, decussis.*
intersperse, (*in*)*miscēre.*
interstice, *rima, foramen.*
interval, *intervallum, spatium*; in the —, *interim*; at —s, *aliquando, nonnumquam.*
intervene: = be between, *interiacēre, intercedĕre*; = come between, *intercedĕre, intervenire.*
intervention, *interventus* (*-ūs*).
interview, subst. *congressio, congressus* (*-ūs*), *conloquium.*
interweave, *intexĕre.*
intestate, *intestatus*; adv. *intestato.*
intestine, adj. *intestinus.*
intestine(s), subst. *intestina, viscera, exta* (all plur.).
intimacy, *familiaritas, consuetudo, necessitudo.*
intimate, adj. *familiaris, intimus, coniunctus*; adv. *familiariter, intime, penitus.*
intimate, v. *significare, indicare.*
intimation, *significatio, nuntius.*
intimidate, (*de*)*terrēre, timorem inicĕre.*
intimidation, = threats, *minae* (*-arum*).
into, *in* with acc.
intolerable, *intolerabilis*; adv. *intoleranter.*
intolerance, *superbia, adrogantia.*
intolerant, *immitis, difficilis, superbus.*
intone, *canĕre.*
intoxicate, *ebrium reddĕre.*
intoxicated, *ebrius, temulentus.*
intoxication, *ebrietas.*
intractable, *indocilis, difficilis.*
intrepid, *intrepidus, impavidus.*
intrepidity, *animus intrepidus* or *impavidus; fortitudo.*
intricacy, *contortio.*
intricate, *contortus implicatus, perplexus, impeditus.*
intrigue, subst.; = plot, *dolus, fallacia*; = amour, *adulterium.*
intrigue, v. = plot, *dolis* or *fallacia contendĕre*; see also interest.
intrinsic, *verus, in re ipsa positus*; adv. *per se, vere.*
introduce, *introducĕre, inducĕre, invehĕre*; of persons, = make one known to another, *introducĕre, commendare.*
introduction, *introductio, inductio, invectio*; an — to a book, etc., *prooemium, exordium, praefatio.*
introspection, *ipsum se inspicĕre.*
intrude, *se interponĕre* or *offerre.*
intrusion, *importunitas.*
intrusive, *molestus, importunus*; adv. *moleste.*
intuition, *cognitio, perceptio*; as a quality, *ingenii, acumen* or *acies.*
inundation, *eluvio, diluvium.*
inure, *adsuefacĕre.*
invade, *invadĕre, incurrĕre, incursionem facĕre.*
invader, *hostis.*
invalid, subst. *aeger, aegrotus.*
invalid, adj. *inritus, infirmus, vitiosus.*
invalidate, *inritum facĕre, tollĕre, rescindĕre.*
invasion, *incursio, inruptio.*
invective, *convicium, probrum.*
inveigh, *invehi, insectari, increpare.*
inveigle; see mislead.

invent, *invenire, reperire, excogitare.*
invention, *inventio, excogitatio;* = thing invented, *inventum, reperta* (*-orum,* plur.); = falsehood, *commentum, mendacium.*
inventor, *inventor, repertor, auctor.*
inventory, *tabula, index.*
inverse, *inversus, conversus.*
inversion, *conversio.*
invert, (*con*)*vertĕre, invertĕre.*
invest: to — with an office, *magistratum mandare, deferre;* to — with a quality, *addĕre, impertire;* to — money, *pecuniam conlocare, occupare;* = to besiege, *circumsedēre, obsidēre.*
investigate, *exquirĕre,* (*per*)*scrutari, investigare;* judicially, *quaerĕre, cognoscĕre.*
investigation, *investigatio, inquisitio;* a judicial —, *quaestio, cognitio.*
investigator, *investigator, indagator.*
inveterate, *inveteratus;* to become —, *inveterascĕre.* Adv. *penitus.*
invidious, *invidiosus;* adv. *invidiose.*
invidiousness, *invidia.*
invigorate, *corroborare,* (*con*)*firmare.*
invincible, *invictus, in*(*ex*)*superabilis.*
inviolability, *sanctitas.*
inviolable, *inviolabilis, inviolatus; sanctus, sacrosanctus;* adv. *inviolate.*
inviolate, *integer; inviolatus, intactus.*
invisible, *caecus;* to be —, *sub oculos non cadĕre.*
invitation, *invitatio;* at your —, *invitatus* (or *vocatus*) *a te.*
invite, *invitare, vocare;* = to allure, *adlectare, invitare.*
inviting, *blandus, gratus, amoenus.*
invocation: of help, *imploratio;* of witnesses, *testatio.*
invoice, *libellus.*
invoke, *invocare, implorare;* as a witness, *testari, invocare testem.*
involuntary, *invitus, coactus;* adv. *non sponte,* or render by adj. *invitus.*
involve: = to envelop, *involvĕre;* = to implicate, *implicare, adligare, admiscēre;* to be —d in debt, *aere alieno laborare;* = to imply, comprise, *continēre, habēre.*
invulnerable, *invulnerabilis.*
inward, *interior;* adv. *introrsus, intus, intrinsecus.*
inweave, *intexĕre.*
inwrought, *intextus.*
irascibility, *iracundia.*
irascible, *iracundus, in iram praeceps, stomachosus.*
ire; see anger.
Ireland, *Hibernia.*
irk: it —s, *piget, taedet, molestum est.*
irksome, *gravis, molestus, odiosus.*
irksomeness, *taedium, molestia.*
iron, subst. *ferrum;* of —, adj. *ferreus;* tipped with —, *ferratus;* —s, = fetters, *vincula, compedes.*
iron, adj. *ferreus;* — tools, *ferramenta* (*-orum*).
ironically, *per ironiam.*
ironmongery, *ferramenta* (*-orum,* plur.).
irony, *ironia, dissimulatio.*
irradiate, *inlustrare, conlustrare.*
irrational, *absurdus, rationis expers, stultus;* adv. *absurde.*
irreconcilable; of persons, etc. *implacabilis, inexorabilis;* of ideas, (*res*) *inter se repugnantes, contrariae.*
irrecoverable, *inreparabilis.*
irrefragable, *certus, firmus; quod refelli non potest.*
irregular, *enormis* (= shapeless), *incompositus* (= rough), *inusitatus* (= unusual); *inaequalis* (= not uniform); gram., *anomalus;* at elections, *vitiosus;* of troops, *tumultuarius.* Adv. *enormiter, incomposite, praeter morem; vitio.*
irregularity, *enormitas;* gram., *anomalia;* of conduct, *licentia;* at an election, *vitium.*
irrelevant, *alienus;* it is —, *nihil ad rem pertinet.*
irreligion, *impietas* (*erga deos*), *deorum neglegentia.*
irreligious, *impius* (*erga deos*); adv. *impie.*
irremediable; see incurable.
irremovable, *immobilis, immutabilis.*
irreparable, *inreparabilis.*
irreproachable; see blameless.
irresistible, *invictus, in*(*ex*)*superabilis cui nulla vi resisti potest.*
irresolute, *dubius, incertus;* to be —, *dubitare, haesitare.* Adv. *dubitanter.*
irresolution, *dubitatio, haesitantia.*
irrespective, *sine ullo discrimine.*
irreverence, *impietas* (*erga deos*).
irreverent, *inverecundus, impius* (*erga deos*); adv. *impie.*
irrevocable, *inrevocabilis.*
irrigate, *inrigare.*
irrigation, *inrigatio, inductio aquarum.*
irritable, *stomachosus, iracundus;* adv. *stomachose.*
irritate: to — a wound, *inflammare;* mentally, *inritare.*
irritation, = annoyance, *stomachus.*
irruption, *inruptio, incursio.*
island, *insula.*
islander, *insulanus, insulae incola.*
isle; see island.
isolate, *secernĕre, seiungĕre, separare.*
isolated, *remotus, solus.*
isolation, *solitudo.*
issue, subst.: = outcome, *exitus* (*-ūs*), *eventus* (*-ūs*); = subject, *res, causa;* = offspring, *liberi* (*-orum*), *progenies, stirps.*
issue, v.: transit., = give out, of orders, etc. *edĕre, proponĕre, pronuntiare;* of stores, etc., *dispensare, distribuĕre;* intransit., = come out, *egredi, erumpĕre;* = end up, turn out, *evadĕre, exire, evenire.*
isthmus, *isthmus* or *isthmos.*
it, *hic, haec, hoc; is, ea, id; ille, illa, illud.*
Italian, *Italicus, Italus.*
Italy, *Italia.*
itch, subst.: as disease, *scabies;* as sensation, *prurigo, pruritus* (*-ūs*).
itch, v. *prurire;* to — to do a thing, *gestire facĕre.*
item, in a list, *pars, res.*
iterate, *iterare.*

itinerant, *circumforaneus.*
itinerary, *itineris descriptio.*
ivory, subst. *ebur.*
ivory, adj. *eburneus.*
ivy, *hedera.*

J

jabber, v. *blaterare, garrire.*
jabbering, subst. *clamor, strepitus* -*ūs*).
jackass, *asinus.*
jackdaw, *graculus.*
jacket, *tunica.*
jade: of a horse, *caballus*; of a woman, *mulier importuna.*
jaded, *fatigatus,* (*de*)*fessus.*
jagged, *serratus*; of rocks, *asper, praeruptus.*
jail, *carcer.*
jailbird, *furcifer.*
jamb, *postis.*
James, *Iacobus.*
janitor, *ianitor, ostiarius.*
January, *Ianuarius* (*mensis*).
jar, subst. *olla, cadus, urceus, urna, amphora*; on the —, of a door, *semiapertus.*
jar, v. *discrepare.*
jargon, *sermo barbarus.*
jarring, *dissonus, absonus, discors.*
jasper, subst. *iaspis.*
jaundice, *morbus regius* or *arquatus.*
jaundiced, *arquatus.* Transf., *lividus, invidus.*
jaunt, *iter, excursio;* to take a —, *excurrĕre.*
javelin, *pilum, iaculum*; to throw a —, *iaculari.*
jaw, *mala*; the —s of death, etc., *fauces* (-*ium*).
jealous, *invidus, lividus*; to be —, *aemulari, invidēre.*
jealousy, *invidia, aemulatio.*
jeer, subst. *cavillatio, ludibrium, inrisio.*
jeer, v. *cavillari, inridēre, in ludibrium vertĕre.*
jejune, *ieiunus, aridus, exilis*; adv. *ieiune.*
jeopardize, *in periculum adducĕre.*
jeopardy; see danger.
jerkin, *tunica.*
jerky, of style, *salebrosus.*
Jerusalem, *Hierosolyma* (-*orum*).
jest, subst. *iocus, ridiculum*; in —, *ioco, per iocum.*
jest, v. *iocari, ioculari, cavillari.*
jester, scurra.
jet, *gagates*; — black, *niger*; a — of water, *aqua saliens.*
jetsam, *res naufragio eiectae.*
jetty, *moles.*
Jew, *Iudaeus.*
jewel, *gemma.*
jewelled, *gemmeus, gemmatus*
jeweller, *aurifex.*
Jewish, *Iudaicus.*
jig; see dance.
jilt, *repudiare.*
jingle, *tinnire.*
jingling, subst. *tinnitus* (-*ūs*).
job, *opus* (-*eris,* n.); a put-up —, *fraus.*
jockey, *agaso* (= groom).
jocose, jocular, *iocosus, ridiculus, facetus*; adv. *iocose, per iocum, facete.*
jocularity, *iocus, facetiae* (-*arum*).
jog, subst. *impulsus* (-*ūs*).
jog, v.: transit., *fodicare, impellĕre*; intransit., to — on, — along, *lente progredi.*
John, *Ioannes.*
join, v.: transit., = connect, (*con*)*iungĕre, conectĕre, copulare*; to — battle, *proelium* or *pugnam committĕre*; intransit., (*con*)*iungi, conecti*; to — in, *interesse.*
joiner, *faber.*
joint, subst.: in a body, *commissura, articulus*; in a plant, *nodus*; in other things, *coagmentum, compages compactura.*
joint, adj. *communis*; adv. *coniuncte, coniunctim, una, communiter.*
jointed, *geniculatus.*
joint-heir, *coheres.*
joist, *tignum transversum.*
joke; see jest.
joker, *homo ridiculus.*
jollity, *hilaritas, lascivia.*
jolly, *hilaris, lascivus.*
jolt, v. *iactare, concutĕre, quassare.*
jolting, subst. *iactatio, quassatio.*
jostle, *fodicare.*
jot, subst.: not a —, *nihil, minime*; not to care a — for, *non flocci facĕre.*
jot, v.: to — down, *adnotare, scribĕre.*
journal: = diary, *ephemeris*; = newspaper, *acta diurna* (-*orum*).
journey, subst. *iter, cursus* (-*ūs*), *via*; a — abroad, *peregrinatio*; a — by sea, *navigatio.*
journey, v. *iter facĕre*; to — abroad, *peregrinari.*
journeyman, *opifex.*
Jove, *Iuppiter*; by —! *mehercle!*
jovial, *hilaris, lascivus*; adv. *hilare, lascive.*
joviality, *hilaritas, lascivia.*
joy, *gaudium, laetitia*; = pleasure, *voluptas.*
joy, v. *gaudēre, laetari, exsultare.*
joyful, *laetus, hilaris.* Adv. *laete, libenter, hilare*; often rendered by adj. *laetus* or *libens.*
jubilant, *gaudio exsultans* or *triumphans.*
judge, subst.: in court, *iudex, quaesitor, praetor*; in gen., *iudex, aestimator, existimator.*
judge, v., *iudicare; existimare, censēre*: to — between *diiudicare.*
judgment: in court, *iudicium*; to pronounce —, *ius dicĕre*; a — seat, *tribunal*; in gen., = considered opinion, *iudicium, sententia*; in my —, *meo iudicio, me iudice*; = discernment, *iudicium, consilium.*
judicature, *iurisdictio.*
judicial, *iudicialis, forensis*; a — decree, *edictum*; a — investigation, *iudicium.* Adv. *iure, lege*; to proceed —, *lege agĕre.*
judicious, *sagax, sapiens, prudens*: adv. *sagaciter, sapienter, prudenter.*
jug, *urceus, urceolus.*
juggle, *praestigias agĕre.*
juggler, *praestigiator.*

juggling, subst. *praestigiae* (*-arum*); = trickery, *dolus, fraus.*
juice, *sucus.*
July, *Quinctilis* or *Iulius* (*mensis*).
jumble, subst. *congeries, turba, farrago.*
jumble, v. (*per*)*miscēre.*
jump, subst. *saltus* (*-ūs*).
jump, v. *salire*; to — for joy, *exsultare gaudio*; to — in, *insilire*; to — over, *transilire.*
junction, (*con*)*iunctio.*
juncture, *tempus, tempestas.*
June, (*mensis*) *Iunius.*
jungle, *loca virgultis obsita.*
junior, *iunior,* (*natu*) *minor.*
juniper, *iuniperus.*
jurisconsult, *iuris* or *iure peritus.*
jurisdiction, *iurisdictio.*
jurisprudence, *iuris prudentia.*
jurist; see jurisconsult.
juror, *iudex.*
jury, *iudices* (*-um*).
just, adj. *iustus, aequus, meritus* (= deserved); adv. *iuste, iure, legitime, merito.*
just, adv.: of time, *commodum*; — now, *in praesentia*; — lately, *modo, nuperrime, recens*; in gen., = exactly, *admodum,* or render by *ipse,* esp. with numerals; — as, *ita* (or *sic*) *ut, perinde ac*; in replies, — so, *ita vero, admodum*; = only, *modo, solum, tantum.*
justice, *iustitia, aequitas*; = rights, just treatment, *ius* (*iuris,* n.).
justifiable, *iustus, legitimus*; adv. *recte, iure.*
justification, *purgatio, excusatio.*
justify, *purgare, excusare.*
jut: to — out, *exstare, eminēre*; of geographical features, *excurrĕre.*
juvenile, *puerilis, iuvenilis.*

K

keel, *carina.*
keen: physically, *acer*; of perception, *acutus, perspicax, sagax*; = enthusiastic, *acer, studiosus.* Adv. *acriter; acute, sagaciter; studiose, summo studio.*
keenness: = poignancy, *acerbitas*; = penetration, *sagacitas, perspicacitas*; — of vision, *acies*; = enthusiasm, *studium.*
keep, v. Transit., (*con*)*servare, custodire, tenēre, habēre*: of animals = to support, *alĕre*; to — in, *includĕre, continēre*; to — apart, *distinēre*; to — back, *retinēre, cohibēre*; to — off, *arcēre*; to — faith, *fidem servare*; to — watch, *custodias agĕre*; to — a secret, *rem celare* or *occultam tenēre*: Intransit.: = to remain, (*re*)*manere*: to — silent, *tacēre*; to — on doing a thing, *pergĕre, perseverare.*
keeper, *custos, curator.*
keeping, subst. *custodia, tutela*
keg, *dolium.*
ken, *conspectus* (*-ūs*).
kennel, *stabulum* (*canis*).
Kent, *Cantium.*
kerb, *crepido.*
kerchief, *sudarium.*
kernal, *nucleus.* Transf., *medulla, flos, robur.*
kettle, *cortina, lebes, a*(*h*)*enum.*
kettle-drum, *tympanum.*
key, *clavis.*
kick, subst. *pedis* or *calcis ictus* (*-ūs*).
kick, v. *calcitrare, calce petĕre*; to — back, *recalcitrare.*
kid, *haedus, haedulus.*
kidnap; see steal.
kidney, *renes* (*renum*).
kidney-bean, *phaselus.*
kill, *interficĕre, caedĕre, occidĕre, necare* (violently), *trucidare* (= butcher, massacre); to — oneself, *mortem sibi consciscĕre, se interimĕre*; to — time, *horas fallĕre.*
kiln, *fornax.*
kin; see kindred.
kind, subst. *genus* (*-eris,* n.); *modus*; of such a —, *talis*; a — of, render by *quasi* or *quidam*; every — of, *omnis* or plur., *omnes.*
kind, adj. *benignus, beneficus* (in action), *benevolus* (in disposition), *humanus, indulgens, clemens*; a — action, *beneficium, officium.* Adv. *benigne, clementer, indulgenter, humane.*
kindle, v.: transit., *accendĕre, incendĕre, inflammare*; intransit., *accendi,* (*ex*)*ardescĕre.*
kindness, *bonitas, benignitas, benevolentia, humanitas*; an act of —, *beneficium, officium.*
kindred, subst., abstr. *consanguinitas, cognatio, necessitudo*; = relatives, *consanguinei, cognati, necessarii* (*-orum*).
king, *rex*; a petty —, *regulus.*
kingdom, *regnum.*
kingfisher, n. (*h*)*alcedo,* (*h*)*alcyon.*
kingly, *regius, regalis.*
kingship, *regia potestas, regnum.*
kinsman; see relative.
kiss, subst. *osculum, suavium.*
kiss, v. *osculari, suaviari.*
kissing, subst. *osculatio.*
kitchen, *culina.*
knapsack, *mantica, sarcina.*
knave, *homo nequam* or *sceleratus*; colloquially, *scelestus, furcifer.*
knavery, *nequitia, fraus, dolus.*
knavish, *nequam, fraudulentus*; adv. *fraudulenter.*
knead, *depsĕre, subigĕre*
knee, *genu.*
kneel, *genibus niti.*
knife, *culter*; small —, *cultellus.*
knight, *eques.*
knighthood, *ordo equester; dignitas equestris.*
knit, *texĕre*; to — the brow, *frontem contrahĕre.*
knob, *bulla, nodus* (in plants).
knobbed, knobbly, *nodosus.*
knock, v. *pulsare*; to — against, *offendĕre*; to — down, *sternĕre*; to — up, = arouse, *suscitare*; -ed up, = exhausted, (*de*)*fessus.*
knocking, subst. *pulsatio.*
knock-kneed, *varus.*

knot, subst. *nodus*; = group of people, *circulus*.
knot, v. *nodare, nectĕre*.
knotty, *nodosus*. Transf., *difficilis, spinosus*; a — point, *nodus*.
know, *scire, cognitum* or *compertum habēre*; to get to —, (*cog*)*noscĕre*; not to —, *nescire, ignorare*; = be acquainted with, *novisse* (perf. of *noscere*); to — again, = recognize, *agnoscĕre, noscitare*.
knowing, adj. *sciens, prudens*; = clever, *callidus, astutus*. Adv. *consulto, de industria*; or render by adj. *sciens* or *prudens*.
knowledge, *scientia, notitia, cognitio*; as imparted and acquired, *doctrina, disciplina*; without the — of a person, *clam homine*.
known, *notus*; to make —, *declarare*.
knuckle, *articulus* (*digiti*).

L

laborious, *laboriosus, operosus*; adv. *laboriose, operose*.
labour, subst. *labor, opus* (*-eris*, n.), *opera*; in childbirth, *partus* (*-ūs*); to be in —, *parturire*.
labour, v.: = work, toil, *laborare, niti, contendĕre*; = be distressed, *laborare* (with abl.); to — under a delusion, *decipi, falli*.
laboured, *adfectatus, nimis exquisitus*.
labourer, *operarius, opera*.
labyrinth, *labyrinthus*.
labyrinthine, *perplexus, impeditus*.
lacerate, *lacerare, laniare*.
laceration, *laceratio, laniatus* (*-ūs*).
lachrymose, *lacrimabundus*.
lack, subst. *inopia, penuria, egestas*
lack, v. *carēre, egēre, indigēre*.
lackey, *pedisequus*.
lack-lustre, *decolor*.
laconic, = concise, *brevis, adstrictus*; adv. *breviter, adstricte*.
lad, *puer*.
ladder, *scalae* (*-arum*).
lade, = to load, *onerare*.
laden, *onustus, oneratus, gravis*.
lading, subst. *onus* (*-eris*, n.).
ladle, subst. *trulla, cyathus*.
ladle, v. *haurire*.
lady, in gen., *femina, mulier, matrona*; the — of the house, *domina, hera, materfamilias*.
lady-like, *liberalis; quod matronā dignum est*.
lady's-maid, *famula, ornatrix*.
lag, *cessare, morari, cunctari*.
laggard, *cessator, cunctator*.
lagoon, *lacus* (*-ūs*), *lacuna*
lair, *latibulum, cubile*.
laird, *dominus, possessor*.
lamb, *agnus*, f. *agna*; as meat, (*caro*) *agnina*.
lame, adj. *claudus*; = feeble, *debilis*; to be —, *claudicare*; a — excuse, *excusatio vana*.
lameness, *claudicatio*.
lament, lamentation, *lamentum* (usually plur.), *lamentatio, ploratus* (*-ūs*).
lament, v. *lamentari, deflēre,* (*de*)*plorare*.
lamentable, *lamentabilis, flebilis*; adv. *flebiliter*.
lamented, *flebilis*.
lamp, *lucerna, lychnus*.
lamp-black, *fuligo*.
lampoon, *carmen famosum*.
lance, subst., *lancea, hasta, sarisa*.
lance, v. *incidĕre*.
lancet, *scalpellum*.
land, subst.: opp. to sea, *terra*; — as possessed, cultivated, etc., *ager, solum, terra*; = a particular country, *terra, regio, ager, fines* (*-ium*).
land, adj. *terrestris, terrenus*.
land, v.: transit., (*in terram*) *exponĕre*; intransit., (*ex nave*) *egredi*.
landed: — property, *ager, possessio* (usually plur.); a — proprietor, *agrorum possessor*.
landing, subst. *egressus* (*-ūs*).
landlord, *agrorum possessor*; *caupo* (= innkeeper).
landmark, *lapis, terminus*.
landslide, *terrae lapsus* (*-ūs*).
lane, *angiportum*; a country — *semita*.
language, *oratio*; the — of a people, tongue, *lingua, sermo*; = diction, style, *oratio, sermo*; = things said, *verba* or *dicta* (*-orum*).
languid, *languidus*; to be —, *languēre*; adv. *languide*.
languish, *languere, languescĕre; tabescĕre*.
languor, *languor*.
lank, lanky, *prolixus*.
lantern, *lanterna*.
lap, subst. *gremium* (= bosom), *sinus* (*-ūs*; = fold of the gown); on a race-course, *spatium*.
lap, v. *lambĕre*.
lap-dog, *catellus*.
lapse, subst.: = error, *lapsus* (*-ūs*), *error, peccatum*; of time, *fuga*; after the — of a year, *interiecto anno*.
lapse, v.: = go wrong, *errare peccare*; of property, *reverti*.
lard, *adeps, lar*(*i*)*dum*.
larder, *cella penaria, carnarium*.
large, *magnus, grandis, amplus*. Adv., = to a great extent, *magna ex parte*.
large-hearted, *magnanimus, liberalis, benignus*.
largeness, *magnitudo, amplitudo*; — of mind, *magnanimitas*.
largess, *largitio, congiarium*.
lark, *alauda*.
larynx, *guttur*.
lascivious, *impudicus*; adv. *impudice*.
lash, subst.: = whip, *flagrum, flagellum, scutica*; = blow (lit. and fig.). *verber*.
lash, v.: = whip, *flagellare, verberare*; = tie, bind, (*ad*)*nectĕre,* (*ad*)*ligare*.
lassitude, *lassitudo, languor*.
last, subst.: let the cobbler stick to his —, *ne sutor supra crepidam*.
last, adj.: = final, *ultimus, extremus, postremus, novissimus*; = most recent, *proximus*. **At last,** *tandem, postremum*. Adv. **lastly,** *postremo, denique*.

last, v. *durare*, (*per*)*manēre*.
lasting, *stabilis*, *diuturnus*, *perennis*.
latch, *pessulus* (=bolt).
late, adj.: = coming —, *serus*; = recent, *recens*; the —, = the dead, *demortuus*; of an emperor, *divus*. Adv. **lately, of late,** *nuper*, *recens*, *modo*.
late, adv.: = too —, *sero*; rather —, *serius*; — at night, *multa nocte*.
lateness, render by adj.
latent, *occultus*, *abditus*.
lateral, *a latere*.
lathe, *tornus*; to work at the —, *tornare*.
Latin, adj. *Latinus*; the — tongue, *lingua Latina*, *sermo Latinus*; to translate into —, *Latine reddere*.
latinity, *latinitas*.
latitude, = freedom, *libertas*, *licentia*.
latter, *posterior*: the former . . . the —, *hic . . . ille*.
lattice, *cancelli* (*-orum*).
laud; see praise.
laudable, *laudabilis*, *laude dignus*; adv. *laudabiliter*.
laudatory, *honorificus*.
laugh, laughter, *risus* (*-ūs*), *cachinnus* (loud), *cachinnatio*; to be a —ing stock, *ludibrio* or *inrisui esse*; to raise a —, *risum movēre*.
laugh, v.: intransit., *ridēre*; loudly, *cachinnare*; to — at, transit., (*de*)-*ridēre*, *inridēre*.
laughable, *ridiculus*.
laughter; see laugh.
launch, v.: transit., of ships, *deducĕre*; intransit., to — out, *in aequor efferri*. Transf., *exspatiari*.
laurel, *laurus* (*-i* and *-us*), *laurea*; adj., of —, *laureus*; decked with —, *laureatus*.
lava, *massa ardens*, *saxa* (*-orum*, pl.) *liquefacta*.
lavish, adj. *prodigus*, *profusus*; a — giver, *largitor*. Adv. *large*, *prodige*, *effuse*.
lavishness, *effusio*, *largitas*, *munificentia*.
law, *lex*, *ius* (*iuris*, n.); *fas* (= divine —); *norma*, *regula* (= rule, standard); to carry a —, *legem perferre*; to go to —, *lege agĕre*.
lawful, *legitimus*; it is —, *licet*. Adv. *legitime*, *lege*, *per leges*.
lawgiver; see legislator.
lawless, *effrenatus*; adv. *effrenate*, *licenter*, *contra legem*.
lawlessness, (*effrenata*) *licentia*.
lawn: = fine linen, *sindon*; of grass, *pratum*, *herba*.
lawsuit, *lis*, *controversia*.
lawyer, *iurisconsultus*, *iurisperitus*.
lax, (*dis*)*solutus*, *remissus*, *neglegens*; adv. (*dis*)*solute*, *remisse*, *neglegenter*.
lay, subst.; see song.
lay, v. *ponĕre*, (*con*)*locare*; to — foundations, *fundamenta iacĕre*; to — an ambush, *insidiari*; to — siege, *obsĭdēre*; to — eggs, (*ova*) *parĕre*; to — aside, (*de*)*ponĕre*; to — before, *proponĕre*; to — down an office, *magistratu se abdicare*; to — down arms, *ab armis discedĕre*; to — up, *condĕre*, *reponĕre*; to — waste, *vastare*.
layer, of a plant, *propago*.
laziness, *ignavia*, *segnitia*.
lazy, *piger*, *ignavus*, *segnis*; adv. *pigre*, *ignave*, *segniter*.
lead, subst. *plumbum*.
lead, v.: = conduct, *ducĕre*; to — past, *traducĕre*; to — back, *reducĕre*; to — the way, *praeire*; = command, *ducĕre*, *praeesse*; = induce, *adducĕre*, *persuadēre*; = pass, spend, *agĕre*; of roads, to — in a certain direction, *ferre*, *ducere*.
leaden, *plumbeus*.
leader, *dux*, *ductor*, *auctor*.
leadership, *ductus* (*-ūs*); under my —, *me duce*.
leading, *princeps*, *primarius*, *summus*.
leaf: of a tree, *folium*, *frons*; of a book, *scheda*, *pagina*, *charta*; of metal, *bractea*, *lamina*.
leafy, *frondosus*, *frondeus*, *frondifer*.
league, subst. *foedus* (*-eris*, n.), *pactum*, *societas*.
leak, subst. *rima*; to spring a —, *rimam agĕre*.
leak, v.; to — away, *perfluĕre*.
leaky, *rimosus*, *rimarum plenus*.
lean, adj. *macer*, *exilis*; *strigosus* (of horses, etc.).
lean, v. (*se*) *inclinare*; to — upon, (*re*) (*in*)*niti*.
leanness, *macies*.
leap, subst. *saltus* (*-ūs*).
leap, v. *salire*: to — down, *desilire*; — forward, *prosilire*; — for joy, *gestire*, *exsultare*.
leap-year, *annus bisextus*.
learn, *discĕre*, *ediscĕre* (by heart), *perdiscĕre* (thoroughly); *cognoscĕre* (= get to know, in gen.).
learned, *doctus*, *eruditus*; adv. *docte*, *erudite*.
learner, *discipulus*.
learning, *doctrina*, *eruditio*.
lease, subst. *conductio*.
lease, v. *conducĕre* (= take a — of), *locare* (= give a — of).
leash, *lorum*, *copula*.
least, adj. *minimus*.
least, adv. *minime*; at —, *saltem*, *certe*; not in the —, *nihil omnino*.
leather, *corium*, *aluta* (tanned); adj., of —, *scorteus*.
leave, subst.: = permission, *permissio*, *licentia*; to give —, *potestatem facĕre*; with your —, *pace tua*; I have —, *mihi licet*; to take — of, *valēre iubēre*; — of absence, *commeatus* (*-ūs*).
leave, v.: = desert, abandon, *relinquĕre*, *deserĕre*, *destituĕre*; to — property, *relinquĕre*, *legare*; = to depart, *discedĕre*, *proficisci*; to — off, *desistĕre*; to — out, *omittĕre*, *praetermittĕre*.
leaven, subst. *fermentum*.
leaven, v. *fermentare*.
leavings, *reliquiae* (*-arum*).
lecture, *schola*, *acroasis*.
lecture-room, *schola*, *auditorium*.
ledge; — of rock, *dorsum*.
ledger, *codex* (*accepti et expensi*).
leech, *hirudo*, *sanguisuga*.
leek, *porrum*, *porrus*.
leer, *oculis limis intuēri*.

leering, *limus.*
lees, *faex.*
left, = remaining, *reliquus*; to be —, *restare.*
left, (opp. right) *sinister, laevus*; the — hand, *sinistra*; on the —, *a sinistra.*
leg, *crus* (*cruris,* n.); — of a table, *pes.*
legacy, *legatum.*
legal, *legitimus*; adv. *legitime, lege.*
legate, *legatus, nuntius.*
legation, *legatio.*
legend: on coins, etc., *inscriptio, titulus*; = myth, fable, *fabula.*
legendary, *fictus, fabulosus.*
leggings, *ocreae* (*-arum*).
legible, *quod facile legi potest.*
legion, *legio.*
legionary, *legionarius.*
legislate, *leges facĕre* or *constituĕre.*
leisure, *otium*; to be at —, *vacare, otiari, cessare*; at —, *otiosus, vacuus.*
leisurely, *lentus*; adv. *otiose.*
lend, *mutuum dare, commodare*; to — at interest, *faenerari.*
length, *longitudo*; in time, *longinquitas, diuturnitas*: at —, *tandem.*
lengthen, v. *longiorem facĕre*; in time, *producĕre, prorogare.*
length-wise, *in longitudinem.*
lengthy, in words, *verbosus, longus.*
leniency, *clementia, lenitas.*
lenient, *clemens, lenis*; adv. *clementer.*
lentil, *lens.*
less: adj. *minor*; adv. *minus*; much —, *nedum.*
lessee, *conductor.*
lessen, (*de*)*minuĕre, imminuĕre.*
lessening, *deminutio, imminutio.*
lesson: to give —s, *docēre*; = warning or example, *documentum.*
lest, conj., *ne* with subj.
let, = to allow, *sinĕre, pati, permittĕre*; — us go, *eamus;* to — alone, *omittĕre*; to — down, *demittĕre,* to — fly, *emittĕre*; to — go, (*di*)*mittĕre*; to — in, *admittĕre*; to — off, *absolvĕre*; to — slip, *omittĕre*; see also lease.
lethal, *mortifer, exitialis.*
lethargic, *torpidus*; a — person, *lethargicus.*
lethargy, *lethargus, torpor.*
letter: of the alphabet, *littera*; to the —, *ad verbum*; = epistle, *litterae* (*-arum*), *epistula.*
letter-carrier, *tabellarius.*
lettered, *litteratus.*
letters, = learning, *doctrina, litterae* (*-arum*); a man of —, *homo doctus.*
lettuce, *lactuca.*
levee, *salutatio.*
level, adj. *aequus, planus*; — ground, *planities.*
level, v.: = make even, (*ex*)*aequare*; = bring to the ground, *solo aequare, sternĕre*; to — a weapon, *librare.*
lever, *vectis.*
leveret, *lepusculus.*
levity, *inconstantia, levitas; iocus, iocatio.*
levy, subst. *dilectus* (*-ūs*); to hold a —, *dilectum habēre.*
levy, v.: to — soldiers, *milites* (*con*)*scribĕre*; to — tribute, *tributum imponĕre, vectigal exigĕre.*
lewd, *impudicus, impurus*; adv. *impure.*
liable, *obnoxius.*
liar, (*homo*) *mendax.*
libation, *libamentum*; to make a —, *libare.*
libellous, *famosus, probrosus.*
liberal, *liberalis, largus, munificus*; too —, *prodigus, profusus*; the — arts, *artes liberales* or *ingenuae.* Adv. *liberaliter, large, munifice*; to give —ly, *largiri.*
liberate, *liberare*; to — a slave, *manumittĕre.*
liberation, *liberatio*; of a slave, *manumissio.*
liberator, *liberator.*
libertine, *homo dissolutus, ganeo.*
liberty, *libertas*; excessive —, *licentia*: at —, *liber.*
library, *bibliotheca.*
licence, subst.: = permission, *copia, potestas*; = liberty, *licentia.*
license, v. *potestatem dare.*
licentious, *dissolutus, impudicus*; adv. *dissolute, impudice.*
licentiousness, *libido, impudicitia.*
lick, *lingĕre, lambĕre*; to — up, *ligur*(*r*)*ire.*
lid, *operculum, operimentum.*
lie, subst. *mendacium.*
lie, v. = tell a lie, *mentiri.*
lie, v. = be situated, *iacēre, cubare, positum esse*; to — between, *interiacēre*; to — down, *procumbĕre*; to — hid, *latēre*; to — in wait, *insidiari.*
lief; I had as —, *malim.*
lieu; in — of, *pro, loco, vice.*
lieutenant, *legatus.*
life, *vita, anima*; to come to — again, *reviviscĕre*; the necessaries of —, *victus* (*-ūs*); time of —, *aetas*; the prime of —, *flos aetatis, aetas, integra.* Transf., = liveliness, *vis, vigor, alacritas*; full of — *vividus, vegetus, alacer.*
life-guards, (*milites*) *praetoriani.*
lifeless, *exanimis*; of style, *frigidus, exilis, ieiunus*; adv. *frigide.*
life-time, *aetas*; in my —, *me vivo.*
lift, v. (*at*)*tollĕre, extollĕre,* (*sub*)*levare.*
ligament, *ligamentum, ligamen.*
light, subst. *lumen, lux*; to bring to —, *in lucem proferre, patefacĕre*; source of —, *lumen, lucerna* (= lamp), *candela* or *cereus* (= taper or torch); to work by lamp- —, *lucubrare.*
light, adj.: opp. to dark, *clarus, inlustris, candidus* (in colour); opp. to heavy, *levis*; — soil, *solum tenue*; — -hearted, *hilaris, curis vacuus.* Adv. *leviter*; — clad, *expeditus.*
light, v.: = set light to, *accendĕre*; = illuminate, *inlustrare*; to — upon, *incĭdĕre, offendĕre.*
lighten: = make less heavy, *exonerare*; = cause lightning, *fulgurare, fulgēre.*
lighthouse, *pharus.*
lightness, *levitas.*
lightning, *fulmen, fulgur*; struck by —, *fulmine ictus, de caelo tactus.*

like, adj. *similis, par.*
like, adv. *similiter; instar, modo, ritu* (all with genit.).
like, v. *amare, diligĕre*; I — this, *hoc mihi placet* or *cordi est*; I — to do it, *iuvat me facĕre.*
likelihood, *veri similitudo, probabilitas.*
likely, *veri similis, probabilis.*
like-minded, *concors.*
liken, *comparare.*
likeness: = resemblance, *similitudo*; = portrait, *effigies, imago.*
likewise, *item, itidem.*
liking, *amor, voluptas* (= pleasure), *libido* (= caprice); to one's —, *gratus, iucundus.*
lily, *lilium.*
limb, *membrum, artus* (*-uum*, plur.).
lime, subst.: the mineral, *calx*; bird- —, *viscum*; the tree, *tilia.*
lime, v. (with bird- —), *visco inlinĕre.*
lime-kilm, (*fornax*) *calcaria.*
limit, subst. *terminus, finis, modus.*
limit, v. *finire, terminare.*
limitation, *determinatio*; = exception, *exceptio.*
limited, *parvus, angustus, brevis.*
limp, adj. *languidus.*
limp, v. *claudicare, claudum esse.*
limpet, *lepas.*
limpid, *limpidus, pellucidus.*
limpness, *languor.*
Lincoln, *Lindum.*
linden-tree, *tilia.*
line, *linea*; in a straight —, *e regione, rectā lineā, ad lineam*; a — of poetry, *versus* (*-ūs*), *versiculus*; milit., — of battle, *acies*; — of march, *agmen*; the front —, *prima acies, hastati* (*-orum*); second —, *principes* (*-um*); third —, *triarii* (*-orum*); in plur., lines (= entrenchments, etc.), *munitiones* (*-um*), *munimenta* (*-orum*), *vallum*; = cord, thin rope, *funis, funiculus*; a fishing —, *linea*; plumb- —, *perpendiculum.*
line, v. *complēre.*
lineage, *stirps, genus* (*-eris*, n.), *origo.*
lineaments, *lineamenta* (*-orum*).
linen, *linum*; — cloth, *linteum*; adj., of —, *linteus.*
linger, *cessare, morari, cunctari.*
lingerer, *cunctator, cessator.*
lingering, subst. *mora, cunctatio, cessatio.*
lingering, adj. *tardus, lentus.*
liniment, *unguentum.*
link, subst.: = torch, *fax, taeda, funale*; = bond, *vinculum, necessitudo*; — of a chain, *annulus.*
link, v. *connectĕre,* (*con*)*iungĕre.*
lint, *linamentum.*
lintel, *limen superum.*
lion, *leo*; adj., of a —, *leoninus.*
lioness, *leaena.*
lion-hearted, *magnanimus.*
lip, *labrum, labia.*
liquid, subst. *liquor, umor, latex.*
liquid, adj. *liquidus*; to become —, *liquescĕre, liquefieri*; to make —, *liquefacĕre.*
Lisbon, *Olisipo.*
lisp, *balbutire.*
lisping, *blaesus.*
list, *tabula, libellus, index.*
listen; see hear.
listless, *socors, deses, languidus*; adv. *languide.*
listlessness, *languor, socordia, desiaia.*
literal: the — sense *propria vis.* Adv. *ad verbum*; to translate —ly, *ad verbum transferre.*
literary, *litteratus, litterarum studiosus*; — tastes, *studia* (*-orum*) *litterarum.*
literature, *litterae* (*-arum*), *litterarum monumenta* (*-orum*).
lithe, *mollis, flexibilis.*
litigate, *litigare, rem lite persequi.*
litigation, *lis.*
litigious, *litigiosus.*
litter, subst.: = the vehicle, *lectica*; = brood, *fetus* (*-ūs*), *suboles;* of straw, *stramentum.*
little, a little, as subst., *paulum, nonnihil, parum* (= too little); just a —, *paululum*; a — better, *paulo melior*; a — before, sub (with acc.); a — sad, *subtristis*; — by —, *sensim, gradatim*; he said —, *pauca dixit.*
little, adj. *parvus, parvulus, exiguus*; often rendered by diminutive of subst; so —, *tantulus*; how —, *quantulus*; for a — while, *parumper, paulisper.*
little, adv. *paulum*; see also little, subst.
littleness, *parvitas, exiguitas.*
live, adj = living; q.v.
live, v. *esse, spirare, vivĕre*; to — on a thing, *re vivĕre* or *vesci*; to — in a place, *locum incolĕre* or *habitare.*
livelihood, *victus* (*-ūs*).
liveliness, *alacritas.*
lively, *alacer, vegetus, vehemens.*
liver, *iecur.*
livid, *lividus*; — colour, *livor*; to be —, *livēre.*
living, adj. *vivus.*
lizard, *lacerta, lacertus, stellio.*
lo! *en, ecce.*
load, subst. *onus* (*-eris*, n.).
load, v. *onerare, onus imponĕre*; of firearms (*arma*) *parare, instruĕre.*
loaded, *onustus, oneratus.*
loaf, *panis.*
loam, *lutum.*
loan, *mutuum, res commodata;* of money, *pecunia mutua.*
loath, *invitus*: I am —, *piget me, nolo.*
loathe, v. *fastidire, odisse, aspernari.*
loathing, *fastidium,odium.*
loathsome, *teter, foedus.*
lobby, *vestibulum.*
lobster, *cancer* (= crab).
local, render by genitive *loci* or *regionis.*
locality, *locus, loci natura.*
loch, *lacus* (*-ūs*).
lock, subst.: on a door, *claustra* (*-orum*); see also hair.
lock, v. *obserĕre, occludĕre*; to — up, *concludĕre.*
locker, *armarium.*
lock-jaw, *tetanus.*
locust, *locusta.*
lodge, v.: intransit., = stay, *deversari, devertĕre*; = stick, *haerēre*; transit., *hospitio excipĕre.*

lodger, *deversor, inquilinus.*
lodgings, *deversorium, deverticulum, meritoria* (*-orum*).
loft, *cenaculum.*
loftiness, *altitudo, elatio, excelsitas.*
lofty, *altus,* (*ex*)*celsus, editus, sublimis*; of speech, *grandis.* Adv. *alte, excelse.*
log, *lignum, stipes* (= tree-trunk).
logic, *logica* (*-orum*), *dialectica* (*-ae,* f. or *-orum,* n.); *disserendi ratio.*
logical, *logicus, dialecticus*; a — consequence, *consequens.* Adv. *dialectice*; often *ratione.*
logician, *dialecticus.*
loin, *lumbus.*
Loire, *Liger.*
loiter, *cessare.*
loll, *recumbĕre, recubare.*
London, *Londinium.*
lone, lonely, *solus, solitarius.*
loneliness, *solitudo.*
long, adj.: in space, *longus, procerus* (= tall): very —, *praelongus*; — hair, *capillus promissus*; six feet —, *longus pedes sex*; a — way, *longe, procul*; in time, *longus, diuturnus*; for a — time, *diu*; a — time ago, *iam pridem.*
long, adv. of time, *diu*; how —?, *quamdiu*? so —, *tam diu*; see also long, adj.
long, v. *avēre, cupĕre, gestire.*
longer, of time, *diutius, longius, amplius*; no —, *non iam, non diutius.*
longing, *appetitus* (*-ūs*), *appetitio, cupido.*
look, subst. *aspectus* (*-ūs*), *conspectus* (*-ūs*), *obtutus* (*-ūs,* = gaze); = expression, *vultus* (*-ūs*); = appearance, in gen., *species, facies.*
look, v.: to — at, *aspicĕre, intuēri, contemplari, spectare;* to — about, *circumspicĕre*; to — back, *respicĕre*; to — down, *despicĕre*; to — up, *suspicĕre*; of position, to — in a certain direction, *spectare;* = to appear, seem, *vidēri.*
looking-glass, *speculum.*
loom, subst. *tela.*
loop, subst. *laqueus.*
loophole, *foramen, fenestra.*
loose, adj.: = slack, *laxus, fluxus, remissus*; of soil, *rarus*; at liberty, *liberatus, liber*; of morals, (*dis*)*solutus, effrenatus.* Adv. *laxe,* (*dis*)*solute.*
loose, v. (*re*)*laxare, remittĕre,* (*re*)*solvĕre.*
lop; to — off, *amputare, praecīdĕre.*
lopsided; see uneven.
loquacious, *loquax, verbosus*; adv. *loquaciter.*
loquacity, *loquacitas.*
lord, *dominus.*
lordly, = proud; q.v.
lordship, *imperium, dominatus* (*-ūs*).
lore, *eruditio, doctrina.*
lose, *amittĕre, perdĕre* (wilfully); to — a battle, *vinci*; to — colour, *pallescĕre*; to — heart, *animo cadĕre* or *deficĕre*; to — one's way, *errare*; = to be bereft of, *privari, orbari.*
losing, subst. *amissio.*
loss, *damnum, detrimentum, iactura*; I am at a —, *dubius sum, haereo dubito.*
lost, to be, *perire*; — in thought, *in cogitation defixus.*
lot, *sors*: casting of —s, *sortitio, sortitus* (*-us*); to decide by —, *sortiri.*
loth; see loath.
lottery, *sors, sortitio, alea.*
loud, *clarus, magnus*; adv. *magna voce.*
lounge, v. *nihil agĕre, desidēre.*
louse, *pediculus.*
loutish, *rusticus, agrestis.*
love, subst. *amor, caritas* (= affection), *pietas* (= devotion), *studium* (= enthusiasm); a — affair, *amor*; god of —, *Cupido, Amor*; goddess of —, *Venus*; my —! *mea voluptas! deliciae meae!*
love, v. *amare, diligĕre, studēre* (with dat.).
loved, *carus.*
loveliness, *venustas, amoenitas.*
lovely, *venustus; amoenus* (esp. of scenery).
lover, *amator, amans,* and f. *amatrix.*
loving, adj. *amans, studiosus*; adv. *amanter.*
low, adj. *humilis, demissus*; of voice, *summissus*; of price, *vilis*; of character or standing, *humilis, ignobilis, obscurus*; of spirits, *tristis, maestus.*
low, adv. *humiliter, demisse*; to speak —, *submissa voce dicĕre.*
low, v., of cattle, *mugire.*
low-born, *obscuro* (or *humili*) *loco natus.*
lower, adj. *inferior.*
lower, v. *demittĕre*; to — the voice, *vocem submittĕre*; to — oneself = condescend, *se submittĕre, descendĕre.*
lowering; see dark, threatening.
lowest, *infimus, imus.*
lowing, of cattle, *mugitus* (*-ūs*).
lowlands, *loca* (*-orum*) *plana.*
lowliness, *humilitas, obscuritas*; as a virtue, *modestia.*
lowly: of rank, *humilis, obscurus;* = unassuming, *modestus.*
lowness, *humilitas* (lit. and fig.); of price, *vilitas.*
loyal, *fidelis, fidus*; adv. *fideliter.*
loyalty, *fides, fidelitas.*
lubricate, *ung*(*u*)*ĕre.*
lucid, (*pel*)*lucidus, dilucidus, perspicuus*; adv. (*di*)*lucide, perspicue.*
lucidity, *perspicuitas.*
luck, *fortuna, fors, casus* (*-ūs*); good —, *res secundae, felicitas*; good — to it! *bene vertat!*
lucky, *felix, fortunatus, faustus*; adv. *feliciter, fauste.*
lucrative, *quaestuosus, lucrosus.*
lucre, *lucrum, quaestus* (*-ūs*).
ludicrous, *ridiculus.*
lug, *trahĕre.*
luggage, *impedimenta* (*-orum*), *vasa* (*-orum*), *sarcinae* (*-arum,* = knapsacks).
lugubrious, *lugubris, flebilis, maestus.*
lukewarm, *tepidus*; = unenthusiastic, *languidus, frigidus.*

lull, v.: transit., *sedare*; to — to sleep, *sopire*; intransit., the wind —s, *venti vis cadit*.
lullaby, *cantus* (*-ūs*).
lumber, *scruta* (*-orum*).
luminary, = heavenly body, *sidus* (*-eris*, n.).
luminous, *lucidus, inlustris*; see also lucid.
lump, *massa, glaeba* (*gleba*).
lumpy, *crassus, glebosus*.
lunar, *lunaris*.
lunatic; see mad, madman.
lunch, subst. *prandium*.
lunch, v. *prandēre*.
lung, *pulmo*; —s, *pulmones, latera*.
lurch, see roll; to leave in the —, *deserĕre, destituĕre*.
lure, subst. *inlex, inlecebra*.
lure, v. *adlicĕre, inlicĕre, pellicĕre*.
lurid, *obscurus, caliginosus*.
lurk, *latēre, latitare, delitescĕre*.
luscious, (*prae*)*dulcis*.
lust, subst. *libido, cupiditas*.
lust, v. *concupiscĕre*.
lustful, *libidinosus, impudicus*.
lustily, *valide*.
lustre: = brightness, *nitor, splendor*; = a space of five years, *lustrum*.
lusty, *validus, vegetus*.
lute, *lyra, fides* (*-ium*), *cithara* (poet.).
luxuriant, *laetus, luxuriosus*.
luxuriate, *luxuriare*.
luxurious, *luxuriosus, mollis, delicatus*; adv. *luxuriose, molliter, delicate*.
luxury, *luxus* (*-ūs*), *luxuria*.
lynx, *lynx*.
lynx-eyed, *lynceus*.
Lyons, *Lugdunum*.
lyre; see lute.
lyric, lyrical, *melicus, lyricus*.

M

Maas or **Meuse,** *Mosa*.
mace, *fasces* (*-ium*).
Macedonia, *Macedonia*; a —n, *Macedo*; —n, adj., *Macedonius, Macedonicus*.
macerate, *macerare*.
machination, *machina, dolus*.
machine, *machina, machinatio, machinamentum*.
mackerel, *scomber*.
mad, *insanus, furiosus, demens*; to be —, *furĕre, insanire*. Adv. *insane, furiose, dementer*.
madden, (*homini*) *furorem incutĕre, mentem alienare*; fig., *exacerbare, exasperare*.
madness, *insania, dementia, furor*.
magazine, = store, *horreum, receptaculum, armamentarium*; see also journal.
maggot, *vermis, vermiculus*.
magic, subst. *ars magica, magice*.
magic, adj. *magicus; mirabilis, mirus*.
magician, *magus*.
magistracy, *magistratus* (*-ūs*).
magistrate, *magistratus* (*-ūs*).
magnanimity, *magnanimitas, magnus animus*.
magnanimous, *magnanimus*.
magnet, (*lapis*) *magnes*.
magnificence, *magnificentia, splendor*.
magnificent, *magnificus, splendidus, amplus*; adv. *magnifice, splendide, ample*.
magnify, *augēre, amplificare, exaggerare*.
magniloquence, *magniloquentia*.
magniloquent, *magniloquus*.
magnitude, *magnitudo, spatium* (= extent).
magpie, *pica*.
maid: = virgin, *virgo*; = any girl, *puella*; = servant-girl, *ancilla, famula*,
maidenhood, *virginitas*.
maidenly, *virgineus, virginalis*.
mail: = *armour, arma* (*-orum*); = letters, *litterae* (*-arum*).
maim, *mutilare, truncare*.
maimed, *mancus, truncus*.
main, subst. = sea, *pelagus, altum*.
main, adj. *primus, praecipuus, princeps*; the — point, *caput, res* (*summa*). Adv. *praecipue, potissimum*.
mainland, *terra* (*continens*).
maintain: = preserve, *sustinēre, sustentare,* (*con*)*servare, retinēre*; = keep alive, *alĕre*; to — in argument, *contendĕre, confirmare, adfirmare*.
maintenance, *conservatio, salus*; = livelihood, *victus* (*-ūs*).
maize, *far*.
majestic, *augustus, sanctus, magnificus*; adv. *auguste*.
majesty, *maiestas, dignitas, amplitudo*; divine —, *numen*.
major, subst.: milit., *tribunus militum*; in law, (*homo*) *sui iuris*.
major, adj. *maior*.
majority, *maior pars, maior numerus, plures* (= more people), *plurimi* (= most).
make, subst. *figura, forma, conformatio*.
make: = form, create, *facĕre, efficĕre, fabricari, aedificare*; to — one's way, *iter facĕre*; = render, cause to be, *facĕre, reddĕre*; to — good, *reparare, resarcire*; = to appoint, *facĕre, creare, instituĕre*; in valuing, to — much of a thing, *rem magni facĕre*; = cause, compel, *facĕre* or *efficĕre* (with ut and subj.), *cogĕre* (with infin.); in arithmetic, = form, come to, *efficĕre, esse*; to — away with, *interficĕre, tollĕre*; to — for, *petĕre*; to — up a story, *fingĕre, comminisci*; to — way, *cedĕre*.
maker, *fabricator*; or use verb.
makeshift, adj. *subitarius*.
maladministration, *prava rerum administratio*.
malady; see illness.
malapropos, adv. *intempestive*.
malaria, *caelum grave et pestilens*.
malcontent, *homo rerum novarum cupidus*.
male, adj. *virilis, mas, masculus*; the — sex, *virilis sexus* (*-ūs*).
malediction, *exsecratio, dirae* (*-arum*).
malefactor, *homo maleficus* or *sceleratus*.
malevolent, *malevolus*.

malice, *malignitas, invidia, malevolentia.*
malicious, *malevolus, malignus, invidus.*
malign, v.; see slander.
maligner, *obtrectator.*
malignity, *malevolentia*; of a disease, *vis* (*morbi*).
malleable, *lentus, mollis.*
mallet, *fistuca, malleus.*
mallow, *malva, malache.*
Malta, *Melita.*
maltreat, *male tractare, vexare.*
mammal, *animal.*
man, *homo* (= human being); *vir* (i.e. not woman or child); men, plur., *mortales, homines, genus humanum*; all to a —, *omnes ad unum*; — by —, *viritim*; no —, *nemo.* Transf., in draughts, *calculus*; in chess, *latro, latrunculus*; of ships, merchant-—, *navis mercatoria*; — -of-war, *navis longa.*
man, v. = furnish with men, *complēre.*
manacle, subst. *compes, catena.*
manacle, v. *vincire.*
manage, *tractare, administrare, gerĕre,* (*pro*)*curare.*
manageable, *habilis, docilis, facilis.*
management, *administratio, tractatio, cura,* (*pro*)*curatio.*
manager, *administrator,* (*pro*)*curator.*
mandate, *iussum, mandatum.*
mandible, *maxilla.*
mane, *iuba*; with a —, *iubatus.*
mange, *scabies.*
manger, *praesepe* or *praesepis.*
mangle, v. (*di*)*laniare, lacerare.*
mangled, *truncus, lacer.*
manhood, *aetas adulta*; to reach —, *togam virilem sumĕre.*
mania, *insania.*
manifest, adj. *apertus, manifestus, perspicuus,* it is —, *patet, apparet*; adv. *aperte, manifesto.*
manifest, v. *aperire, patefacĕre, manifestum facĕre.*
manifestation, *demonstratio, indicium.*
manifesto, *edictum.*
manifold, *multiplex, varius.*
manipulate, *tractare.*
mankind, *homines* (*-um*), *genus humanum.*
manliness, *virtūs* (*-ūtis*); *animus virilis.*
manly, *virilis, fortis.*
manner, *ratio, modus, via*; = sort, kind, *genus* (*-eris,* n.); — of writing, *oratio, sermo.*
manners, *mores* (*-um*); a person of good —, *homo bene moratus.*
mannikin, *homuncio, homunculus, homullus.*
manoeuvre, *decursus* (*-ūs*), *decursio*; = trick, stratagem, *artificium, dolus.*
manoeuvre, v. (*in armis*) *decurrĕre, evagari.*
manor, *fundus, praedium.*
mansion, *aedes* (*-ium*), *domus.*
manslaughter, *hominis caedes, homicidium.*
mantelet, *vinea, pluteus, testudo.*
mantel-piece, *mensa, abacus, tabula.*
mantle, *amiculum, palla* (for women), *pallium; lacerna* or *paenula* (for travelling); *sagum* (= soldier's —).
manual, subst. *libellus.*
manual, adj., render by *manu.*
manufacture, subst. *fabrica.*
manufacture, v. *fabricari* or *fabricare.*
manufacturer, *opifex, artifex, fabricator.*
manumission, *manumissio.*
manumit, *manu mittĕre,* or *manumittĕre.*
manure, *stercus* (*-oris,* n.), *fimus.*
manure, v. *stercorare.*
manuscript, *chirographum.*
many, *multi*; a good —, *complures, plerique*; very —, *permulti, plurimi*; — times as great, *multiplex*; — a time, *saepe, saepenumero*; as — as, *tot . . . quot*; just as —, *totidem*; so — times, *totie*(*n*)*s.*
many-coloured, *variis coloribus distinctus.*
map, *tabula.*
map, v., to — out, *designare, describĕre.*
maple, *acer*; adj., of —, *acernus.*
mar, *foedare, deformare, corrumpĕre.*
marauder, *praedator, direptor.*
marauding, *praedatorius, praedabundus.*
marble, subst. *marmor.*
marble, adj. *marmoreus.*
March, (*mensis*) *Martius.*
march, subst. *iter*; a regular day's —, *iustum iter*; to make forced —es, *magnis itineribus contendĕre*; troops on the —, *agmen.*
march, v.: intransit., *iter facĕre, incedĕre*: — off, *proficisci*; — fast, *contendĕre*; — in the rear, *agmen cogĕre*; transit., *ducĕre*; to — back, *reducĕre*; to — across, *tra*(*ns*)*ducĕre.*
marches, *fines* (*-ium*), *confinium.*
mare, *equa.*
margin, *margo.*
marginal, *in margine scriptus* or *positus.*
marine, adj. *marinus, ad mare pertinens.*
mariner, *nauta.*
marines, *classiarii, classici milites.*
maritime, *maritimus.*
marjoram, *amaracus.*
mark, subst. *nota, signum, indicium*; it is the — of a wise man to do so, *est sapientis facĕre*; to make one's —, *clarum fieri.*
mark, v. (*de*)*signare, notare*; = take notice of, *observare, animadvertĕre*; to — out, *metiri, designare.*
marked, *inlustris, insignis.*
market: the place, *macellum, forum*; cattle —, *forum boarium*; the business, *mercatus* (*-ūs*), *nundinae* (*-arum*).
marketable, *venalis.*
marriage, *coniugium, matrimonium, nuptiae* (*-arum*), *conubium.*
marriageable, *nubilis, adultus.*
marriage-contract, *pactio nuptialis.*
marriage-settlement, *dos.*
marrow, *medulla.*
marry, v.; = give in marriage, *in matrimonium dare*; of a man, to — a woman, *ducĕre* (*in matrimonium*); of a woman, to — a man, *nubĕre* (with dat.); to — out of her station,

enubere; to — beneath her, *denubĕre*; of a couple, to — each other, *matrimonio* or *nuptiis* (*con*)*iungi*.
marry! interj. *medius fidius, mehercle.*
Marseilles, *Massilia.*
marsh, *palūs*, (*-ūdis*, f.).
marshal, subst. *dux.*
marshal, v. *instruĕre, disponĕre.*
marshy, *paluster, uliginosus.*
martial, *militaris, bellicosus.*
martyr: to become a — for a cause, *pro re mortem occumbĕre.*
marvel, subst. *miraculum, portentum.*
marvellous, (*per*)*mirus, mirificus,* (*ad*)*mirabilis*; adv. *mire mirifice,* (*ad*)*mirabiliter.*
masculine, *virilis, masculus.*
mask, subst., *persona, larva.* Transf., *persona, species, simulatio.*
mask, v. *tegĕre, occultare, dissimulare.*
mass, *massa, moles*; a great —, *magna copia* or *vis*; — of people, *multitudo.*
massive, *solidus, magnus, gravis.*
massacre, subst. *caedes, strages, trucidatio.*
massacre, v. *caedĕre, trucidare.*
mast: on ships, *malus*; = acorns, etc., *glans.*
master, subst.: = owner, ruler, *dominus*; — of a house, *pater familias, herus*; — of property, *possessor*; to become —, *potiri*; a school- —, *magister*; one's own —, *sui potens, sui iuris*; = expert, *artifex, homo peritus.*
master, v.: = subdue, *domare, vincĕre, superare*; to — passions, *continēre, coercēre*; to — a subject, = understand, *intellegĕre,* (*per*)*discĕre, comprehendĕre.*
masterful, *superbus, imperiosus, adrogans.*
masterly, *artificiosus, artifex* (of persons); or render by *ars.*
mastery, = victory, *victoria.*
masticate, *manducare, mandĕre.*
mat, subst. *storea* or *storia, teges.*
mat, v.; to — together, *implicare.*
match, subst.: = one's equal, *par* (with dat.); no — for, *impar*; = contest, *certamen*; = marriage, *condicio, nuptiae* (*-arum*).
match, v.: = equal, suit, *parem esse, aequare*; = bring together as opponents, *componĕre, conferre*; to — oneself with *congredi, certare.*
matchless, *singularis, unicus, egregius.*
match-maker, (*nuptiarum*) *conciliator* (f. *-trix*).
mate, subst. *socius* (= companion), *coniunx* (= husband or wife).
mate, v.: in chess, *ad incitas redigĕre*; = be united, *coniungi.*
material, subst. *materies* or *materia, copia rerum.*
material, adj., *corporeus*; see also important. Adv.; see much.
maternal, *maternus.*
mathematical, *mathematicus.*
mathematician, *mathematicus.*
mathematics, *mathematica.*
matricide, *matricidium* (the crime); *matricida* (the person).
matrimonial; see conjugal.
matrimony, *matrimonium*; see marriage.
matron, = married woman, *matrona.*
matronly, *matronalis.*
matter, subst. (1), = physical substance, *corpus, res corporeae.* (2) in discussion, etc.: — available, *materies* or *materia, silva, copia rerum*; subject- —, the — in hand, *res, propositum, institutum.* (3), = affair, in gen., *res, causa*; how do —s stand? *quo loco res est?*; a business —, *negotium.* (4), = trouble: what's the —? *quid* (*rei*) *est?* (5), = pus, *pus* (*puris*).
it matters, *interest, refert*; — to me, *meā*; — to him, *eius*; — a great deal, *magnopere* or *multum* or *magni.*
mattock, *dolabra.*
mature, *maturus, adultus.*
maturity, *maturitas.*
matutinal, *matutinus.*
maudlin; see drunken, silly.
maul; see injure.
maw, *ingluvies, venter.*
mawkish, *putidus*; adv. *putide.*
maxim, *praeceptum, regula, institutum, sententia.*
maximum, *quod maximum est.*
May, (*mensis*) *Maius.*
may, v., I may do: = I can, *possum facĕre*; = I have permission, *licet mihi facĕre*; = perhaps I will do, *fortasse faciam.*
mayor, *urbis praefectus.*
maze, *labyrinthus.*
mead, as a drink, *mulsum.*
mead, meadow, *pratum*; adj., of the —, *pratensis.*
meagre, *ieiunus, exilis, exiguus*; adv. *ieiune, exiliter.*
meagreness, *ieiunitas, exilitas.*
meal: = flour, *farina*; of food, in gen. *cibus, epulae* (*-arum*, = banquet); a morning —, *prandium*; the main — of the day, *cena.*
mean, subst. *modus, mediocritas.*
mean, adj.: = central, *medius*; = low in rank, *humilis, ignobilis, obscurus*; = morally low, *inliberalis, abiectus, sordidus.* Adv. *inliberaliter, abiecte, sordide.*
mean, v.: = intend, *in animo habēre, cogitare, velle*; = signify, indicate, *significare, sibi velle, valēre*; = refer to, allude to, *significare, dicĕre, intellegĕre.*
meaning: = signification, *significatio, vis, sententia*; see also purpose.
meanness: moral, *inliberalitas, animus abiectus, sordes* (plur.); of rank, *humilitas, obscuritas.*
means: = instrument, method, way, *via, ratio, consilium*; by all —, *omnino*; by no —, *minime, nullo modo*; by — of, render by abl. or *per*; = resources, *res familiaris, fortuna, opes* (*-um*, plur.).
meantime, in the, *interea, interim.*
measure, subst. *mensura, modus*; in full —, *pleno modio, cumulate*; according to the — of, *pro*, with abl.; beyond —, *praeter modum,*

immodice, nimis; in some —, *aliquatenus, aliqua ex parte*; = steps taken, course of action, *ratio, consilium*; in music, *modi, numeri* (*-orum*).
measure, v.: transit., (*di*)*metiri*; intransit., *esse*, with genit.
measured; see moderate.
measureless, *immensus, infinitus.*
measurement, *mensio, mensura.*
measurer, *mensor.*
measuring-rod, *decempeda.*
meat, *cibus*; = flesh, *caro.*
mechanic, *faber, opifex.*
mechanical, *mechanicus.*
mechanism, *machina, machinatio.*
medallion, *clipeus* or *clipeum.*
meddle, *se interponĕre*, (*rem*) *attingĕre.*
meddler, *ardelio, homo importunus.*
mediate, v. *se interponĕre*; to — a peace, *pacem conciliare.*
mediator, *deprecator, arbiter, conciliator.*
medical, *medicus.*
medicinal, *saluber, salutaris.*
medicine: = remedy, *medicina, medicamentum, remedium*: = medical science, *medicina, ars medendi.*
mediocre, *mediocris.*
mediocrity, *mediocritas.*
meditate, *cogitare, meditari, commentari.*
meditation, *cogitatio, commentatio, meditatio.*
meditative, *in cogitatione defixus.*
Mediterranean Sea, *Mare Internum, mare nostrum.*
medium; see mean and means.
medley, *farrago; conluvies, conluvio.*
meek, *demissus, verecundus*; adv. *verecunde.*
meekness, *animus demissus, verecundia.*
meet, adj.; see fit, proper.
meet, v.: transit., *obviam fieri, incĭdĕre, offendĕre*; to go to —, *obviam ire, occurrĕre*; to — death, *mortem obire* or *oppetĕre*; intransit., to — together, (*inter se*) *congredi, convenire, coire; confluĕre* (in large numbers), *convolare* (in haste).
meeting, *congressio, concursus* (*-ūs*); = assembly, *conventus* (*-ūs*), *coetus* (*-ūs*); a crowded —, *frequentia.*
melancholy, subst.: = hypochondria, *atra bilis*; = sorrow, *tristitia, maestitia.*
melancholy, adj. *tristis, maestus.*
melee, *pugna, proelium.*
mellow, adj. *maturus, mitis*; of wine, *lenis, mollis.*
mellow, v.: transit., *coquĕre*; intransit., *maturescĕre.*
melodious, *canorus, numerosus*; adv. *numerose.*
melody, *melos, cantus* (*-ūs*).
melt, v.: transit., *liquidum facĕre, liquefacĕre, dissolvĕre*; intransit., *liquescĕre, liquefieri, dissolvi, tabescĕre.*
member: of the body, *membrum*; a — of a nation, *civis*; of the senate, *senator*; of a corporation, *sodalis.*
membrane, *membrana.*
memoirs, *historiae* (*-arum*), *commentarii* (*-orum*).
memorable, *memorabilis, memoriā dignus.*
memorandum, *libellus, index.*
memorial, *monumentum.*
memory, *memoria, recordatio* (= recollection): to keep in —, *memoria tenēre*; from —, *ex memoria, memoriter*; to commit to —, *ediscĕre*; in the — of man, *post hominum memoriam.*
menace; see threat.
mend, v.: transit., *reficĕre, reparare, reconcinnare*, (*re*)*sarcire*; fig., *emendare, corrigĕre*; intransit., = improve; q.v.
mendacious, *mendax*; adv. *falso, per mendacium.*
mendacity, *mendacium.*
mendicancy, *mendicitas, egestas.*
mendicant, *mendicus.*
menial, adj. *servilis.*
mensuration, *ars metiendi.*
mental, render by genit. *animi, ingenii, mentis.* Adv. *mente, animo, cogitatione.*
mention, subst. *mentio, commemoratio.*
mention, v. *mentionem facĕre, commemorare*; above- —ed, render by *supra*, with *commemorare* or *dicĕre.*
mentor; see adviser.
mercenary, subst. *miles mercennarius* or *conducticius.*
mercenary, adj. *mercennarius, conductus; venalis* (= readily bribed).
merchandise, *merx, res* (*rerum*) *venales.*
merchant, *mercator, negotiator.*
merchant-ship, *navis mercatoria* or *oneraria.*
merciful, *misericors, clemens, mansuetus*; adv. *clementer, mansuete.*
merciless, *immitis, inclemens, inhumanus, crudelis*; adv. *inclementer, inhumane, crudeliter.*
mercilessness, *inclementia, inhumanitas, crudelitas.*
mercurial, *mobilis, levis.*
mercury; the god, *Mercurius*; the metal, *argentum vivum.*
mercy, *misericordia, clementia, mansuetudo.*
mere, subst. *lacus* (*-ūs*).
mere, adj. *merus, solus, unus*; often *ipse.* Adv. *tantum, modo, solum.*
meretricious, *fucatus.*
merge; see dip or mingle.
meridian, adj. *meridianus.*
merit, subst. *meritum, dignitas, virtus*; according to —, *pro merito.*
merit, v.; see deserve.
merited, *meritus, debitus.*
meritorious, *laude dignus, laudabilis*; adv. *bene, optime.*
merriment, *hilaritas, festivitas.*
merry, *hilarus, hilaris, festivus*; adv. *hilariter, festive.*
mesh, *macula.*
mess, subst.: = common meal, *convivium*; = dirt, *squalor, conluvio*; = confusion, *turba, perturbatio rerum.*
message, *nuntius, mandatum.*
messenger, *nuntius* (f. *nuntia*).
messmate, *conviva, sodalis.*

metal, *metallum.*
metaphor, *translatio, verba (-orum) translata.*
metaphorical, *translatus*; adv. *per translationem, translatis verbis.*
metaphysics; render by *philosophia.*
mete; see measure.
meteor, *fax (caelestis).*
method, *ratio, via, modus, ars.*
methodical, render by phrase; adv., *ratione et via.*
metonymy, *immutatio.*
metre, *numerus, metrum.*
metrical, *numerosus, metricus.*
metropolis, *caput.*
mettle, *animus, audacia, ferocitas.*
mettlesome, *animosus, audax, ferox.*
Meuse; see Maas.
midday, subst. *meridies, tempus meridianum.*
midday, adj. *meridianus.*
middle, subst. *medium*; the — of the road, *media via.*
middle, adj. *medius*; the — way, *mediocritas.*
middling, *mediocris.*
midland, adj. *mediterraneus.*
midnight, subst. *media nox.*
midst, render by adj. *medius*; in the — of, *inter, in.*
midsummer, *summa aestas.*
midway, render by adj. *medius.*
midwife, *obstetrix.*
midwinter, *bruma.*
mien, *habitus (-ūs), vultus (-ūs).*
might, subst. *vis, robur, nervi (-orum,* plur.); with all one's —, *summa vi, summa ope.*
mighty, *potens, validus*; adv. *magnopere, valde, summa vi.*
migrate, *abire, discedĕre, migrare.*
migration, *profectio.*
Milan, *Mediolanum.*
mild, adj. *lenis, mitis*; to make —, *mitigare, lenire*; to grow —, *mitescĕre*; of character, etc., *mitis, clemens, mansuetus.* Adv. *leniter, clementer, mansuete.*
mildew, *robigo* or *rubigo, mucor, situs (-ūs).*
mildness, of character, *lenitas, mansuetudo, clementia.*
mile (Roman), *mille,* plur. *milia (passuum).*
milestone, *miliarium.*
military, adj. *militaris, bellicus*; — service, *militia*; — stores, *apparatus (-ūs) belli*; — skill, *rei militaris peritia.*
militate, to — against, *obstare, adversari.*
milk, subst. *lac*; new —, *lac recens*; curdled —, *lac concretum.*
milk, v. *mulgēre.*
milk-pail, *mulctra, mulctrum.*
milk-white, milky, *lacteus*; the — Way, *lacteus orbis, via lactea.*
mill, *mola, pistrinum.*
miller, *pistor.*
millet, *milium.*
million, *decies centena mil(l)ia.*
mimic, v. *imitari.*
mimicry, *imitatio.*
minaret, *turris.*
mince, v. *concidĕre, consecare.*
mince, minced meat, subst. *minutal.*
mincing, *putidus.*
mind, subst. *animus, mens, ingenium* (= intellect or character); to show presence of —, *praesenti animo uti*; to be in one's right —, *sanae mentis esse*; to be out of one's —, *insanire*; to bear in —, *meminisse*; to call to —, *recordari*; to make up one's —, *statuĕre, constituĕre.*
mind, v.: = attend to, *animum (ad rem) advertĕre, (rem) animadvertĕre, curare, agĕre*; mind you come, *cura (ut) venias*; object to, *aegre ferre.*
mindful, *memor.*
mine, subst., *metallum*; milit., *cuniculus.*
mine, possess. pron., *meus.*
mine, v. *(ef)fodĕre*; milit., *cuniculos agĕre.*
mineral, subst. *metallum.*
mingle; see mix.
minimum, *minimum, pars minima.*
minion, *minister, servus.*
minister, subst., *minister, servus*; a — of state, *principis socius et administer omnium consiliorum, ille penes quem est cura administrandae reipublicae.*
minister, *conducĕre, prodesse.*
ministry, *ministerium, administratio.*
minor, subst., *filius* (f. *filia*) *familias.*
minor, adj.; see little, small.
minority, *aetas nondum adulta*; = smaller number, *pars* or *numerus minor.*
minstrel, *citharoedus.*
mint, subst.: the plant, *ment(h)a*; where money is coined, *moneta.*
mint, v.; see coin.
minute, subst., = moment, *punctum* or *momentum temporis.*
minute, adj.: = very small, *exiguus, pusillus, minutus*; = exact, *subtilis, accuratus*; adv. *subtiliter, accurate.*
minutes, plur. subst. *libellus, commentarii (-orum).*
miracle, *res mira, miraculum.*
miraculous, *mirus, mirificus, mirabilis*; in a — manner, *mirum in modum.*
mire, *lutum.*
mirror, *speculum.*
mirth, *hilaritas, laetitia, gaudium.*
mirthful, *hilaris (hilarus), laetus.*
miry, *luteus, lutulentus.*
misadventure, *casus (-ūs), incommodum.*
misanthrope, *qui genus humanum odit.*
misapply, *abuti, perverse uti.*
misapprehend; see misunderstand.
misbehave, *male se gerĕre.*
miscalculate, *male computare; errare, falli, decipi.*
miscalculation, *error.*
miscarriage, *abortus (-ūs), abortio*; a — of justice, *iudicium perversum.*
miscarry, *abortum facĕre*; in gen. = fail, *cadĕre, secus procedĕre.*
miscellaneous, *varius, diversus.*
miscellany, as a literary form, *satura.*
mischance; see misfortune.

mischief; = damage, *malum, incommodum, damnum*; = wrongdoing, *maleficium*.
mischief-maker, *mali auctor.*
mischievous; = harmful, *noxius, perniciosus*; = playful, *lascivus.*
misconceive, *perperam accipĕre.*
misconception, *opinio falsa, error.*
misconduct, *delictum, peccatum.*
misconstrue; see misinterpret.
miscreant, (*homo*) *scelestus* or *sceleratus.*
misdeed, *scelus* (-*eris*, n.), *maleficium.*
misdemeanour, *delictum.*
misdirect, (*epistulam*) *perperam inscribĕre*; = to misuse, *abuti, perperam uti.*
miser, *homo avarus.*
miserable, *miser, infelix, adflictus*; adv. *misere.*
miserliness, *avaritia, sordes* (-*ium*).
miserly, *avarus, tenax.*
misery, *miseria, aerumna, tristitia.*
misfortune, *fortuna adversa, res adversae, calamitas, incommodum*; he had the — to, *accidit ei ut.*
misgive; see distrust, doubt.
misgiving, *timor, sollicitudo, praesagium.*
misgovern, *male regĕre* or *administrare.*
misguide, *in errorem inducĕre.*
mishap; see misfortune.
misinform, *falso docēre.*
misinterpret, *male* or *perperam interpretari.*
misjudge, *male iudicare.*
mislead, *decipĕre, fallĕre, in errorem inducĕre.*
mismanage; see misgovern.
misogynist, *qui mulieres odit.*
misplace, (*in*) *alieno loco conlocare*; misplaced, fig., can be rendered by *male* or *perperam*, e.g. with —d humour, *male salsus.*
misprint, *mendum.*
mispronounce, *male pronuntiare.*
misquote, render by phrase, such as *verba* (*auctoris*) *vitiose proferre.*
misrepresent, *calumniari, depravare.*
misrule; see misgovern.
miss, subst.; render by verb.
miss, v.: = feel the loss of *desiderare, requirĕre*; = fail to meet or find, (*de*)*errare*; — out, = omit, *omittĕre, praetermittĕre.*
misshapen, *deformis, distortus.*
missile, subst. *telum,* (*telum*) *missile.*
missile, adj. *missilis.*
missing, to be, *desiderari, deesse.*
mission, *missio*; = delegation, *legatio.*
misspend, *perdĕre*; see also waste.
misstatement, *quod falsum est*; *mendacium.*
mist, *nebula, caligo.*
mistake, subst. *error, erratum*; to make a —, *errare, peccare*; a — in writing, *mendum.*
mistaken, to be, *errare, falli.*
mistakenly, *per errorem, perperam.*
mistress, *domina*; — of a house, *materfamilias, hera*; a school- —, *praeceptrix, magistra*; = sweetheart, *amica.*
misty, *nebulosus, caliginosus*; fig. *obscurus.*
misunderstand, *perperam intellegĕre.*
misunderstanding, *error*; between persons, *offensio, dissidium.*
misuse, subst. *usus* (-*ūs*) *perversus.*
misuse, v. *abuti, male uti.*
mitigate, *lenire, mitigare.*
mitigation, *mitigatio, levatio.*
mix, v.: transit., *miscēre, admiscēre, temperare*; to — up, = confuse, *confundĕre, permiscēre*; intransit., use transit. verb in pass. or with reflex.
mixed, (*per*)*mixtus, promiscuus.*
mixture, *mixtura, temperatio; permixtio*; a — of good and evil, *bona mixta malis.*
moan, subst. *gemitus* (-*ūs*).
moan, v. *gemĕre.*
moat, fossa.
mob, *turba, multitudo; vulgus, plebs.*
mobile, *mobilis.*
mobility, *mobilitas, agilitas.*
mock, adj. *simulatus, fictus, falsus.*
mock, v. *deridēre, inludĕre, ludibrio habēre*; see also disappoint.
mocker, *derisor.*
mockery, *ludibrium.*
mockingly, *per ludibrium.*
mode, *ratio, modus*; — of dress, *habitus* (-*ūs*).
model, subst. *exemplar, exemplum.*
model, adj. *optimus.*
model, v. *fingĕre, formare.*
moderate, adj.: = restrained, *moderatus, modestus, temperatus*; = middling, *modicus, mediocris.* Adv. *moderate, modeste, temperate; modice, mediocriter.*
moderate, v. *moderari, temperare, coercēre.*
moderation, *modus, modestia, temperantia.*
modern, *recens, novus; huius aetatis.*
modest, *pudens, verecundus*; = moderate, slight, *mediocris, modicus.* Adv. *pudenter, verecunde.*
modesty, *pudor, verecundia.*
modify, (*im*)*mutare*; see also change.
modulate, *modulari.*
modulation, *flexio, flexus* (-*ūs*).
moiety; see half.
moist, *humidus.*
moisten, *conspergĕre* (= sprinkle), *rigare* (= water).
moisture, *humor.*
molar, subst. *dens genuinus.*
mole: = mound, *moles, agger*; the animal, *talpa*; = mark on the body, *naevus.*
molest, *sollicitare, vexare.*
mollify, *mollire, mitigare, lenire.*
molten, *liquefactus.*
moment: of time, *punctum* or *momentum temporis*; for the —, *in praesens*; at the —, *hoc tempore, in praesentia*; = importance, *momentum.*
momentary, *brevissimus.*
momentous, adj. *magni momenti.*
momentum, *momentum, vis.*
monarch, *rex, princeps, dominus.*
monarchical, *regius*; a — form of government, *genus reipublicae regium,*

monarchy, *imperium singulare, potestas regia, regnum.*
monetary, *pecuniarius, nummarius, argentarius.*
money, *pecunia, argentum*; ready —, *pecunia praesens* or *numerata*; a piece of —, *nummus.*
money-bag; see purse.
mongrel, *hibrida.*
monk, *monachus* (eccl.).
monkey, *simia.*
monotheist, *qui unum modo deum esse credit.*
monotonous, *canorus*; or render by *idem* and *semper.*
monsoon, *ventus* (*qui certo tempore flare consuevit*).
monster, *monstrum, portentum, belua.*
monstrous, *immanis, monstruosus*; adv. *monstruose, praeter naturam.*
month, *mensis.*
monthly: adj. *menstruus*; adv. *singulis mensibus, in singulos menses.*
monument, *monumentum.*
monumental, = important, *gravis, magni momenti.*
mood, *animus*; gram., *modus.*
moody, *morosus.*
moon, *luna*; — -light, *lunae lumen*; a —light night, *nox lunā inlustris.*
moor, moorland, *loca* (*-orum*) *fruticetis obsita.*
moor, v. *religare, deligare.*
moot point; it is a —, *incertum* or *dubium est.*
mop, subst. *peniculus.*
mop, v. *detergere.*
moping, *tristis, maestus.*
moral, adj.: = relating to morals, *moralis*; — teaching, *morum praecepta* (*-orum*); = morally correct, *honestus, probus.*
morale, *animus.*
morality, morals, *mores* (*-um*).
moralize, *de moribus praecipěre.*
morass, *palūs* (*-ūdis*).
morbid, *aeger, aegrotus.*
more, subst. = a greater amount, *plus.*
more, adj.: sing., *plus* or *amplius* with genit.; plur., *plures.*
more, adv., render by compar. of adj. or adv.; otherwise by *magis* or *potius* (= rather); no — (= no longer), *non iam*; the — . . . the — . . ., *quo* (with compar.), *eo* (with compar.).
moreover, *praeterea, ultro.*
moribund, *moribundus.*
morn, morning, subst. *tempus matutinum*; in the —, *mane, matutino tempore*; early in the —, *multo mane, prima luce*; good —! *salve!*
morning, adj. *matutinus.*
morning-star, *Lucifer.*
morose, *morosus, acerbus, difficilis*; adv. *morose, acerbe.*
moroseness, *morositas, acerbitas.*
morrow, *posterus dies*; *crastinus dies* (= tomorrow).
morsel, *offa, mica, pars exigua.*
mortal, adj. *mortalis*; see also fatal.
mortality *condicio mortalis, mortalitas*; see also death.
mortar: for mixing, *pila*; for binding together, *arenatum.*
mortgage, subst. *pignus* (*-oris,* n.).
mortgage, v. *pignori dare, obligare.*
mortification, *offensio, dolor.*
mortify, v.: intransit., *putrescěre*; transit., fig., *offenděre, vexare.*
mosaic, subst. *pavimentum* or *opus tessellatum.*
mosaic; adj. *tessellatus.*
mosquito, *culex.*
moss, *muscus.*
mossy, *muscosus, musco circumlitus.*
most, adj. *plurimus*; for the — part, *plerumque, maximam partem*; at the —, *summum.*
most, adv., render by superl. of adj. or adv.; otherwise *maxime; plurimum.*
mostly, *fere, plerumque; maximam partem.*
moth, *blatta.*
mother, *mater*; of a —, adj., *maternus.*
mother-in-law, *socrus* (*-ūs*).
motherly, *maternus.*
mother-tongue, *patrius sermo.*
motion, *subst.*: = movement, *motus* (*-ūs*); to be in —, *movēri*; = proposal, *sententia, rogatio.*
motion, v. = to gesture, *adnuěre, significare.*
motionless, *immotus, immobilis.*
motive, *causa, ratio.*
mottled, *maculosus.*
motto, *sententia, dictum, praeceptum.*
mould, subst.: = shape, *forma*; = soil, *terra.*
mouldy, *mucidus.*
moult, *plumas poněre.*
mound, *tumulus, agger.*
mount, subst.; see horse.
mount, v.: intransit., see rise; transit., = ascend, *scanděre, ascenděre*; to — a horse, *conscenděre equum*; = furnish with horses, (*milites*) *equis imponěre*: —ed, *equo vectus.*
mountain, *mons*; of a —, *montanus.*
mountainous, *montuosus.*
mountebank, *circulator, planus.*
mourn, *maerēre, lugēre*; see also lament.
mournful, *tristis, maestus, flebilis*; adv. *maeste, flebiliter.*
mourning, subst. *maeror, maestitia luctus* (*-ūs*); *vestis lugubris*; in —, adj. *sordidatus.*
mouse, *mus* (*muris*).
mouse-trap, *muscipula.*
mouth, *os*; with open —, *hians.*
movable, *mobilis, agilis.*
move: transit., (*com*)*movēre*; to — rapidly, *agitare*; to — round *versare*; to — to action, *impellěre*; intransit., *movēri, se movēre, ferri.*
movement, *motus* (*-ūs*).
mow, *demetěre, secare.*
mower, *faenisex.*
much, subst. *multum* or *multa.*
much, adj. *multus*; sometimes *magnus* (= great); too —, adj. *nimius.*
much, adv. *multum, valde:* very —, *plurimum*; with compar. or superl., *multo*; too —, adv., *nimium, nimis*; — less, *nedum, ne dicam.*

mud, *lutum, caenum.*
muddle, subst. *turba, confusio.*
muddle, v. *confundĕre, (per)miscēre, turbare.*
muddy, *lutulentus, luteus.*
muffle, *velare, obvolvĕre.*
muggy, *humidus* (= damp), *calidus* (= warm).
mulberry, *morum*; — -tree, *morus.*
mulct, *multare.*
mule, *mulus.*
mull: —ed wine, *vinum fervidum.*
mullet, *mullus, mugil(is).*
multifarious, *multiplex, varius.*
multiform, *multiformis.*
multiply, *multiplicare.*
multitude, *multitudo, vis, vulgus.*
multitudinous, *creber, frequens, multus.*
munch, *manducare.*
mundane, *humanus, quotidianus.*
municipality, *municipium.*
munificence, *munificentia, liberalitas.*
munificent, *munificus, liberalis.*
munition, *belli instrumenta* (*-orum*) or *apparatus* (*-ūs*).
mural *muralis.*
murder, subst. *caedes, occisio, homicidium*; — of a near relative, *parricida.*
murderous, *sanguinarius, cruentus.*
murmur, subst. *murmur, susurrus, fremitus* (*-ūs*); = complaint, *querela.*
murmur, v. *murmurare, fremĕre, mussare*; = complain, *fremĕre, queri.*
muscle, in anatomy, *musculus, torus*; —s, = strength, *lacerti* (*-orum*), *nervi* (*-orum*).
muscular, *lacertosus.*
muse, *Musa, Camena.*
mushroom, *fungus, boletus.*
music, (*ars*) *musica*; a piece of —, *modi* (*-orum*), *cantus* (*-ūs*).
musical, *musicus, symphoniacus*; = understanding music, *artis musicae peritus*; = melodious, *canorus, numerosus.*
musician, *musicus*; or *fidicen, tibicen,* etc.
muslin, *sindon.*
must, subst. *mustum.*
must, v.: I — go, *eundum est mihi, ire debeo, ire me oportet, necesse est eam.*
mustard, *sinapi.*
muster, v.: transit., *recensēre*; = assemble, *convocare*; to — up courage, *animum sumĕre*; intransit., *congregari, coire, convenire.*
musty, *mucidus.*
mutability, *mutabilitas.*
mutable, *mutabilis, inconstans, mobilis.*
mute, adj. *mutus.*
mutilate, *mutilare, truncare.*
mutilated, *mutilus, mutilatus, truncatus.*
mutinous, *seditiosus*; adv. *seditiose.*
mutiny, subst. *seditio, motus* (*-ūs*).
mutiny, v. *seditionem facĕre.*
mutter, *mussare, mussitare, murmurare.*
muttering, subst. *murmur.*
mutton, *caro* (*ovilla*).
mutual, *mutuus*; adv. *mutuo*
my, *meus,* sometimes *noster.*
myriad, *decem millia*; = an indefinitely large number, *sescenti.*
myrmidon, *satelles, adsecula.*
myrrh, *murra*; of —, *murrinus.*
myrtle, *myrtus*; of —, adj. *myrteus*; —berry, *myrtum*; — grove, *myrtetum.*
myself; see self.
mysterious, *occultus, secretus, arcanus.*
mystery: religious, *mysteria* (*-orum*); in gen., *res occulta.*
mystic, *mysticus*; see also secret, strange.
mystification, *ambages* (*-um*).
mystify, *tenebras* (*homini*) *offundĕre.*
myth, *fabula.*
mythical, *fabulosus.*
mythology, *fabulae* (*-arum*), *historia fabularis.*

N

nail, subst.: on finger or toe, *unguis*; for hammering, *clavus.*
nail, v. (*clavis*) *adfigĕre.*
naive, *simplex.*
naked, *nudus*; adv. *aperte.*
nakedness, *nudatum corpus*; of style, *ieiunitas, exilitas.*
name, subst. *nomen, vocabulum, cognomen* (= family name); in — (only) *verbo*; good — (= reputation) *nomen, fama, existimatio.*
name, v. *nominare, appellare, dicĕre*; = mention, *nominare*; = appoint q.v.
nameless, *nominis expers.*
namely; render by simple apposition, or relative clause or *dico* (= I mean).
namesake (*homo*) *eodem nomine appellatus.*
nap, subst.: = sleep, *somnus* (*brevis*); of cloth, *villi* (*-orum*).
nap, v.; see sleep; Homer is caught —ping, *dormitat Homerus.*
napkin, *mappa, mantele.*
Naples, *Neapolis.*
narrate, (*e*)*narrare, referre, memorare.*
narration, *narratio, expositio.*
narrative, subst. *narratio, historia.*
narrator, *narrator.*
narrow, adj. *angustus, artus* (= tight), *contractus* (= narrowed); to have a — escape, *aegre periculum effugĕre.* Adv.: = scarcely, *aegre, vix*; = carefully, *accurate, diligenter.*
narrowness, *angustiae* (*-arum*); — of mind, *animus angustus.*
narrows, *augustiae* (*-arum*), *fauces* (*-ium*).
nasal, *narium* (genit.).
nastiness: = unpleasantness, *amaritudo, gravitas*; = foulness, *foeditas.*
nasty: = disagreeable, *amarus, gravis*; = foul, *foedus, spurcus.*
natal, *natalis, natalicius.*
nation, *populus, gens* (= people), *civitas* (= body of citizens), *respublica* (= state).
national, render by genit.; in the — interest, *e republica.*
native, subst. *indigena*; a — of Rome, *homo Romae natus.*
native, adj. *indigena*; — land, *patria*; — language, *patrius sermo.*

natural, *naturalis, nativus, innatus* or *insitus* (= inborn); *simplex* or *candidus* (= unaffected); — ability or disposition, *indoles, ingenium, natura*; — death, *mors necessaria*; — science or philosophy, *physica, naturae investigatio.* Adv. *secundum naturam, naturaliter; sponte* (= without compulsion); *simpliciter* (= unaffectedly).
naturalize: to — a person, *homini civitatem dare*; to — an animal or plant, *importare.*
nature, natura; the realm of —, *rerum natura*; the — of a person (or thing), natura, *ingenium, indoles.*
naught, *nihil*; to set at —, *neglegĕre.*
naughtiness, *improbitas, petulantia, malitia.*
naughty, *improbus, petulans, malus.*
nausea, *nausea, fastidium* (= disgust).
nauseous; see loathsome, disgusting.
nautical, naval, adj. *navalis, nauticus.*
navigable, *navigabilis, navium patiens.*
navigate, *navigare.*
navigation, *navigatio, res nauticae.*
navigator; see sailor.
navy, *classis.*
nay; = no, *non*; — rather . . ., *immo (vero), atque adeo.*
near, adj. *propinquus*: —er, *propior*; —est, *proximus*; *vicinus* (= neighbouring).
near, adv. *prope, iuxta, propter.*
nearly, *prope, paene, fere or ferme.*
nearness, *propinquitas.*
neat: = clean, tidy, *nitidus, mundus, concinnus;* = undiluted, *merus.* Adv. *nitide, concinne.*
neatness, *munditia, concinnitas.*
nebulous, *nebulosus.*
necessaries, *res necessariae.*
necessary, adj. *necessarius*: this is —, *hoc est necessarium, opus est hoc*; adv. *necessarie, necessario.*
necessitate, *cogĕre*; see compel.
necessity: = what must be, *necessitas, res necessaria*; = want, *necessitas, egestas.*
neck, *collum, cervix* (often plur., *cervices*).
necklace, *monile, torques.*
need, subst. *necessitas*: there is — of, *opus est* (with nom. or abl.).
need, v. *requirĕre, egēre.*
needful, *necessarius.*
needle, *acus* (*-ūs*).
needless; see unnecessary.
needlework, *opus acu factum.*
needy, *egens, indigens, inops.*
nefarious, *nefarius.*
negation, *negatio, infitiatio.*
neglect, negligence, *neglegentia, incuria.*
negotiate, *agĕre, conloqui*; to — a peace, *pacem componĕre.*
negotiation, *conloquium*; —s are in progress, *agitur (de re).*
negotiator, *legatus, orator, internuntius.*
Negro, *Aethiops.*
neigh, *hinnire.*
neighbour, *vicinus* (f. *vicina*); —s, *vicini, finitimi vicinia*; = fellow man, *alter, ceteri* (plur., = others).
neighbourhood, *vicinia, vicinitas.*
neighbouring, *vicinus, propinquus, finitimus.*
neighbourly, *ut decet vicinum.*
neighing, *hinnitus* (*-ūs*).
neither, pron. *neuter*; in — direction, *neutro.*
neither, conj. *nec* (or *neque*); — . . . nor, *nec . . . nec*; in commands, wishes, etc., *neve* (or *neu*).
nephew, *filius fratris* or *sororis.*
nereid, *Nereis.*
nerve, = vigour, etc., *nervi* (*-orum*).
nervous, = vigorous, *nervosus*; see also timid.
nervousness, *timiditas, trepidatio.*
nest, *nidus.*
nestling, *pullus.*
net, subst. *rete, plaga* (usually plur.).
nettle, *urtica.*
nettled, adj. *offensus, subiratus.*
network, *reticulum.*
neuter, gram., *neuter, neutralis.*
neutral, *medius, neutrius partis.*
never, *nunquam.*
nevertheless, *nihilominus, (at)tamen.*
new, *novus, recens, insolitus* (= unaccustomed). Adv. *nuper, modo, recens.*
new-comer, *advena.*
new-fangled, *mirus, novus.*
newness, *novitas, insolentia.*
news, *res, nuntius*; what —? *quid novi?*
newspaper, *acta* (*-orum*) *diurna* or *publica.*
newt, *lacertus, lacerta* (= lizard).
next, adj. *proximus*; the — year, *proximus* or *insequens annus*; the — day, *posterus dies*; on the — day *postero die, postridie.*
next, adv. *deinceps, deinde, postea.*
nibble, *(ad)rodĕre, gustare* (= to taste).
nice: = pleasant, *suavis, dulcis*; = fastidious, *delicatus*; = discerning, *diligens, subtilis.* Adv. *bene, probe; diligenter, subtiliter.*
nicety: = fastidiousness, *fastidium*; = precision, *subtilitas.*
niche, *aedicula* (for statues).
nick; in the — of time, *in ipso articulo (temporis).*
nickname, *nomen per ludibrium datum*
niece, *fratris* or *sororis filia.*
niggardly; see miserly.
night, *nox*; by —, *nocte, noctu*; in the dead of —, *intempesta nocte.*
nightfall; at —, *sub noctem.*
nightingale, *luscinia.*
nightly, adj. *nocturnus.*
nightmare, *insomnium.*
Nile, *Nilus.*
nimble, *agilis.*
nine, *novem*; — times, *novie(n)s*; — each, *noveni*
nineteen, *undeviginti*; — each, *undeviceni.*
nineteenth, *undevicesimus, nonus decimus.*
ninety, *nonaginta*; — each, *nonageni.*
ninth, *nonus.*
no, adj. *nullus*; often *nihil*, with partitive genit.; by — means, *minime, haudquaquam.*

no, adv.: in answers, *non, minime* (*vero*); — but, *immo* (*vero*); to answer yes or —, *aut etiam aut non respondēre*; to say —, *negare*; with comparatives *non, nihilo.*
nobility: of birth, *nobilitas, genus nobile*; of character, *ingenuus.*
noble, subst. *homo nobilis*; —s, plur., *nobiles, proceres.*
noble, adj.: by birth, *nobilis, generosus*; morally, *ingenuus, honestus, liberalis*; adv. *ingenue, honeste.*
nobody, *nemo*; and —, *nec quisquam.*
nocturnal, *nocturnus.*
nod, subst. *nutus* (*-ūs*).
nod, v. *nutare*; to — assent, *adnuĕre*; = doze, *dormitare.*
noise, subst. *sonitus* (*-ūs*); *strepitus* (*-ūs*; loud); *crepitus* (*-ūs*; = clattering, creaking); *fragor* (= — of breaking); to make a —, *strepĕre,* (*con*)*crepare.*
noise, v.: see publish.
noiseless, *tacitus*; adv. *tacite,* (*cum*) *silentio.*
noisily, noisy; *tumultuosus*; adv. *cum strepitu.*
nomadic, *vagus.*
nominally, *nomine, verbo.*
nominate, *nominare, dicĕre, creare.*
nomination, *nominatio.*
nominative, *casus* (*-ūs*) *nominativus.*
none, *nemo, nullus.*
nonentity, *nihil*; = obscure person, *terrae filius.*
nonsense, *ineptiae* (*-arum*), *nugae* (*-arum*); as interj., nonsense! *gerrae!, fabulae!*; to talk —, *garrire.*
nonsensical, *absurdus, ineptus.*
nook, *angulus.*
noon, *meridies*; of —, adj. *meridianus.*
noose, *laqueus.*
nor, *nec* or *neque*; in commands, *neve* or *neu.*
normal; see regular.
north, subst. *septentrio* (or pl. *septentriones*).
northern, northerly, *septentrionalis, aquilonaris*; — wind, *aquilo.*
north pole, *polus glacialis, arctos.*
North Sea, *Oceanus Germanicus.*
northwards, (*ad*) *septentrionem versus.*
nose, *nasus, nares* (*-ium* = nostrils).
nostrils, *naris* (usually plur.).
not, *non, haud*; — at all, *minime, nullo modo, haudquaquam*; — enough, *parum, minus*; not even . . ., *ne . . . quidem*; and —, = nor, *nec* or *neque*; to say that . . . —, *negare.*
notable; see remarkable.
notary, scriba.
notch, v. *incīdĕre.*
note, subst. *adnotatio*; in music, *sonus, vox*; = letter, *epistula.*
note, v. *adnotare*; see also write, notice.
note-book, *adversaria* (*-orum*), *commentarius.*
noted; see famous.
nothing, *nihil* (*nil*), *nulla res*; — of the kind, *nihil tale*; — new, *nihil novi*; good for —, *nequam*; — but, *nihil aliud nisi.*
notice, subst.: = act of noticing, *animadversio, notatio*; = announcement, warning, *promulgatio, denuntiatio*; as a visible object, *proscriptio, titulus.*
notice, v. *animadvertĕre.*
noticeable; see remarkable.
notification, *promulgatio, denuntiatio.*
notify; see inform.
notion, *notio, suspicio.*
notoriety, *infamia.*
notorious, *notus, infamis.*
notwithstanding, as adv. *nihilominus, tamen*; as prep. see spite.
nought; see nothing.
noun, *nomen.*
nourish, *alĕre, nutrire.*
nourishment, *alimentum, cibus.*
novel, subst. *fabula.*
novel, adj. *novus.*
novelty: = newness, *novitas, insolentia*; = new thing, *res nova.*
November, (*mensis*) *Novembris* or *November.*
novice, *tiro.*
now: as adv. of time, *nunc, iam, hoc tempore, in praesentia*; now . . . now . . ., *modo . . . modo . . .*; — and then, *interdum, nonnunquam*; as a particle of transition, *autem, vero, quidem.*
nowadays, *nunc, hodie.*
nowhere, *nusquam.*
nude, *nudus.*
nudge, *fodicare.*
nuisance, render by adj. *molestus* or *gravis.*
null, *vanus, inritus, inanis.*
nullify, *ad inritum redigĕre.*
numb, adj. *torpens*; to be —, *torpēre*; to grow —, *torpescĕre.*
number, subst. *numerus*; a large —, *multitudo, copia.*
number, v. (*di*)*numerare.*
numbering: a — of the people, *census* (*-ūs*).
numberless, *innumerus, innumerabilis.*
numbness, *torpor.*
numerical, render by subst. *numerus.*
numerous, plur. *multi, plurimi, frequentes, crebri.*
nuptial, *nuptialis*; a — song, *epithalamium, hymenaeus.*
nuptials, subst. *nuptiae* (*-arum*).
nurse, subst. *nutrix* (= children's —).
nurse, v. *nutrire, fovēre*; to — the sick, *curare* (*hominem*), *adsidēre* (*homini*).
nursery, for plants, *seminarium.*
nursling, *alumnus.*
nurture, *educatio.*
nut, *nux.*
nutriment, nutrition; see food.
nutshell, *putamen.*
nymph, *nympha*; water- —, *Naias*; wood- —, *Dryas, Hamadryas*; sea- —, *Nereis.*

O

O! Oh! interj. *o! pro! heu!* — that (in wishes), *utinam, o si.*
oak, *quercus* (*-ūs*), *aesculus* (= winter- —), *ilex* (= holm- —); adj., of —,

quernus; the wood of the —, *robur*; an — -wood, *quercetum*.
oakum, *stuppa*.
oar, *remus*.
oath, *iusiurandum*, *sacramentum* (military).
oats, *avena*.
obdurate; see obstinate.
obedience, *oboedientia*, *obtemperatio*.
obedient, *obediens*, *dicto audiens*, *obtemperans*; adv. *oboedienter*.
obeisance; see bow.
obelisk, *obeliscus*.
obey, *parēre*, *oboedire*, *obtemperare*, *obsequi*.
object, subst. *res*; to be an — of hatred, *odio esse*; = purpose, aim, *consilium*, *propositum*, *finis*; my —, *quod volo* or *sequor*.
object, v.: = feel annoyance, *gravari*, *moleste ferre*; = make objections, *contra dicĕre*, *recusare*, *repugnare*.
objection, *quod contra dicitur*, *contradictio*.
objective, adj. *externus*, *verus* (= true).
oblation; see offering.
obligation, *officium* (= duty), *religio* (= sense of —); under —, adj., *obnoxius*.
oblige: = compel, *cogĕre*; = to put under obligation, *obligare*, *obstringĕre*; = do a favour to, *gratum facĕre*, *commodare*.
obliging, *comis*, *officiosus*; adv. *comiter*, *officiose*.
oblique, *obliquus*. Adv., *oblique*, *in obliquum*; fig., *per ambages*.
obliquity, *obliquitas*; moral —, *pravitas*, *iniquitas*.
obliterate, *delēre*, *abolēre*.
oblivion, *oblivio*, *oblivium*.
oblivious, *immemor*, *obliviosus*.
oblong, *oblongus*.
obloquy, *odium; opprobrium*, (= abuse).
obnoxious: = subject, liable, *obnoxius*; = objectionable, *noxius*, *invisus*.
obscene, *obscenus*, *turpis*; adv. *obscene*, *turpiter*.
obscenity, *obscenitas*, *turpitudo*.
obscure, *obscurus; reconditus* (= abstruse), *ambiguus* (= uncertain); *humilis* (= undistinguished). Adv. *obscure; ambigue*, *per ambages*.
obscure, v. *obscurare*, *tenebras offundĕre*.
obscurity, *obscuritas*; *tenebrae* (= *arum*; = dark).
obsequies; see funeral.
obsequious, (*nimis*) *obsequens*.
obsequiousness, *obsequentia*.
observance, *mos*, *ritus* (-*ūs*); religious —, *cultus* (-*ūs*) *deorum*.
observant, *attentus*; — of, *diligens*, with genit.
observation, *observatio*, *animadversio*, *notatio*; = remark, *dictum*.
observe: = watch, notice, *observare*, *animadvertĕre*, *contemplari*; = keep up, maintain, (*ob*)*servare*, *conservare*.
observer, *spectator* (f. *spectatrix*); *speculator* (f. *speculatrix*).
obsolete, *obsoletus*; to become —, *obsolescĕre*.
obstacle, *impedimentum*, *obex* (= barrier).
obstinacy, *pertinacia*, *pervicacia*, *obstinatio*.
obstinate, *pertinax*, *pervicax*, *obstinatus*; adv. *pertinaciter*, *pervicaciter*, *obstinate*.
obstreperous, *tumultuosus*.
obstruct, *obstruĕre*, *obstare* (with dat.)
obtruction, *impedimentum*, *obstructio*.
obtain, v.: transit., *adipisci*, *consequi*; to — by asking, *impetrare*, *exorare* intransit., see prevail.
obtrude, *ingerĕre*, *inculcare*.
obtuse, *hebes*, *obtusus*.
obviate, *occurrĕre*, *obviam ire*.
obvious, *apertus*, *manifestus*; adv. *aperte*, *manifesto*.
occasion, subst.: = time, *tempus*; = suitable time, opportunity, *occasio*.
occasion, v. *auctorem esse* (with genit.) *creare*, *movēre*.
occasionally, *raro*, *interdum*.
occult, *occultus*.
occupation: = taking, *occupatio*; = business, *occupatio*, *negotium*.
occupy: = take, *capĕre*, *occupare*; = hold, *habēre*, *tenēre*, *obtinēre*, *possidēre*; = engage, keep busy, *occupare*, *tenēre*, *detinēre*.
occur: = come to mind, *in mentem* (*homini*) *venire*, *subire*; = be found in books, *reperiri*, *legi*; = happen, *fieri*, *accidĕre*.
occurrence, *casus* (-*ūs*), *res* (*gesta*).
ocean, *oceanus*.
October, (*mensis*) *October*.
octogenarian, *homo octoginta annos natus*.
odd: = not even, *impar*; see also strange, extraordinary.
ode, *carmen*.
odious, *invisus*, *invidiosus*.
odium, *invidia*; causing —, *invidiosus*.
odour, *odor*.
of, render by genitive; of, = composed of, *ex*, or use special adj. (e.g. of marble, *marmoreus*); of = concerning, *de*.
off, adv. render by compound verbs in *ab-* (*au-*), *de-*, *ex-*; far —, *longe* or *procul*.
off, prep., *contra* (= opposite).
offence: = displeasure, *offensio*, *offensa*; = fault, *peccatum*, *delictum*.
offend: = hurt, displease, *offendĕre*, *laedĕre*: to be —ed, *aegre ferre*; = commit an offence, *peccare*.
offensive: = giving offence, *odiosus molestus*, *gravis*; opp. to defensive, render by *bellum inferre*.
offer, subst. *condicio*; or use verb.
offer, v.: transit., *offerre*, *praebēre*, *porrigĕre* (= hold out); to — violence, *vim adferre*; intransit., = present itself, *offerri*, *dari*, *incĭdĕre*.
office: = duty, function, *munus* (-*eris*, n.), *officium*; = official position, *magistratus* (-*ūs*), *honor*, *provincia*; a good —, = a kindness, *beneficium*, *officium*.

officer, official, *praefectus.*
official, adj. *publicus*; adv. *publice.*
officiate, *munere* (or *officio*) *fungi.*
officious, *molestus*; adv. *moleste.*
officiousness, *nimium studium.*
offspring, *progenies, stirps, liberi* (*-orum*; = children).
oft, often, *saepe, saepenumero*; how —? *quotie(n)s?*; so —, *totie(n)s.*
ogle, *oculis limis intuēri.*
ogre, *larva.*
oil, subst. *oleum*; of —, adj., *olearius.*
oil, v. *oleo ungĕre or perfundĕre.*
ointment, *unguentum.*
old. (1), in gen., = not new, *vetus, vetustus*; an — soldier, *veteranus.* (2), = having lived long, *grandis* (*natu*); an — man, *senex, vetulus*; an — woman, *anus, anicula, vetula*; to grow —, *senescĕre.* (3), = no longer existing, *antiquus, priscus, pristinus*; in the — days, *olim, quondam.*
old age, *senectūs* (*-ūtis*).
older, *grandior, maior* (*natu*).
oldest, *natu maximus.*
old-fashioned, *obsoletus, antiquus, priscus.*
oligarchy, *paucorum dominatio.*
olive, (tree or fruit), *oliva, olea*; an — grove, *olivetum.*
omen, *omen, auspicium.*
ominous, render by phrase, such as *omen infaustum.*
omission, *praetermissio.*
omit, *omittĕre, praetermittĕre, praeterire.*
omnipotent, *omnipotens.*
on, adv. *porro*; or render by compound verb in *pro-*: to go —, *pergĕre, procedĕre*; — to, *in* with acc.
on, prep.: of place, *in* with abl.; sometimes *a, ab* (of sides, etc.), or abl. alone; of time when, abl. alone; = immediately after, *e* (*ex*) or abl. absol.; on, = about, concerning, *de.*
once: as numeral, *semel*; = at one time, *aliquando, olim, quondam*; at —, *simul* (= at the same time), *statim, continuo* (= immediately).
one, *unus, unicus*; — of two, *alter*; — at a time, — by —, *singuli* (*-orum*) or adv. *singillatim*; — or two, *unus vel alter*; it is all — to me, *nihil mea interest*; indef., = a person, *homo*, or render by verb in second pers. sing. (esp. subj.); — another, render by *inter*, with acc. of plur. pron.; — day, *aliquando.*
one-eyed, *luscus, altero oculo captus.*
onerous, *gravis.*
oneself, *ipse.*
one-sided, *iniquus, impar.*
onion, *caepa* or *caepe.*
only, adj. *unus, unicus, solus.*
only, adv. *solum, tantum, modo* (esp. after *si* and *dum*); not — . . . but also, *non solum . . . sed etiam.*
onset, onslaught, *impetus* (*-ūs*), *incursio.*
onward; see on, adv
ooze, subst. *uligo.*
ooze, v. *manare, sudare.*
open, adj. (*ad*)*apertus; patens* or *hians* (= wide —); to stand —, *patēre*; an — space, *propatulum*; in the — air, *sub divo, sub Iove.* Transf., = candid, *apertus, simplex, candidus*; of questions, = undecided, *integer.* Adv. *aperte, palam, manifesto.*
open, v.: transit., *aperire, patefacĕre*; to — a book, *librum* (*e*)*volvĕre*; to — one's mouth, *hiscĕre*; intransit., *aperiri, se aperire, patefieri, dehiscĕre* (= to gape —).
opening: = aperture, *foramen, fenestra*; = opportunity, *occasio, opportunitas, ansa*; = beginning, *initium, exordium.*
operate, *vim* or *effectum habēre*; in war, *rem agĕre* or *gerĕre*; in surgery, *secare.*
operation, *effectio; res* (*gesta* or *gerenda*); a business —, *negotium.*
operative, adj. *efficax.*
opinion, *opinio, iudicium, sententia.*
opponent, *adversarius*; in a lawcourt, my —, *iste.*
opportune, *opportunus*; adv. *opportune, commode.*
opportuneness, *opportunitas, commoditas.*
opportunity, *occasio, facultas, copia.*
oppose: = to set against, *opponĕre, obicĕre*; = to resist, *adversari, resistĕre, obsistĕre, obstare.*
opposed, *adversus, adversarius, contrarius.*
opposite, adj. *adversus, oppositus, contrarius*; — to (or —), as prep., *contra, e regione* (with genit. or dat.).
opposition: = difference, *repugnantia, discrepantia*; = body of opponents, *factio adversa.*
oppress, *premĕre, opprimĕre, vexare.*
oppression, *vexatio, iniuria.*
oppressive, *gravis, iniquus* (= unjust); adv. *graviter, inique.*
oppressor, *tyrannus*; or render by verb.
opprobrious, *probrosus, turpis.*
opprobrium, *dedecus, opprobrium.*
optical, render by *oculorum* (= of eyes).
option, *optio*; see also choice.
opulence, *opulentia*; see wealth.
opulent, *opulentus*; see rich.
or, *aut*; — perhaps, — if you like, *vel, -ve*; — else, *aut, vel*; — rather, *vel* (*potius*); either . . . or, *aut . . . aut, vel . . . vel*; in conditions, whether . . . or . . ., *sive* (or *seu*); in alternative questions, *an*; — not, direct, *an non*, indirect, *necne.*
oracle, *oraculum, sors, responsum* (*oraculi*); to give an —, or oracular response, *oraculum dare.*
oral, render by verb *dicĕre* or *loqui.*
oration, *oratio, contio*; to deliver an —, *orationem* (or *contionem*) *habēre.*
orator, *orator.*
oratorical, *oratorius.*
oratory, *doctrina dicendi, ars oratoria.*
orb, *globus, sphaera, orbis.*
orbit, *orbis, circulus, ambitus* (*-ūs*).
orchard, *pomarium.*
orchid, *orchis.*
ordain; see decree, appoint.
ordeal; see danger, trial.
order: = methodical arrangement, *ordo*; to arrange in —, *ordinare, disponĕre, digerĕre*; in —, *ordine*;

out of —, *extra ordinem*; = class, group, *ordo*; = fraternity, *conlegium*; = a command, *iussum*; by — of the consul, *consulis iussu*; in — that, render by ut with subj. (neg. *ne*), or by *ad* with gerund or gerundive, etc.
order, v.: = arrange, *ordinare, digerĕre, disponĕre*; = command, *iubēre, imperare*; = demand, *imperare* (with acc.).
orderly, adj. *compositus, dispositus*; = well-behaved, *modestus*.
ordinal, adj.: an — number, *numerus ordinalis*.
ordinance, *edictum*.
ordinary, adj. = usual, *usitatus, quotidianus, communis*; = mediocre, *mediocris, vulgaris*. Adv. *ferme, fere, plerumque*.
ore, *aes*.
organ; see instrument, means; musical, *organum*.
organic; render by *animal* or *corpus*.
organization, *descriptio, temperatio*; political —, *reipublicae forma*.
organize, *ordinare, constituĕre, describĕre, temperare*.
orgies; see revelry.
Orient, Oriental; see east, eastern.
origin, *origo, fons*.
original, subst. = pattern, *exemplum, exemplar*.
original, adj.: = primary, *primus, principalis; antiquus, pristinus*; = one's own, *proprius*, (*sui*) *ipsius, novus* (= new). Adv., = at first, *primum, primo, initio*.
originate, v., intransit., (*ex*)*oriri*.
originator, *auctor*.
ornament, subst. *ornamentum, decus* (*-oris*, n.).
ornament, v. (*ex*)*ornare, decorare*.
ornate, (*per*)*ornatus*; adv. *ornate*.
orphan, *orbus* (subst. and adj.).
oscillate, *agitari*; mentally, *dubitare*.
oscillation, *agitatio*; mental, *dubitatio*.
osier; subst. *vimen*; adj. *vimineus*.
ostensible, *simulatus, fictus*; adv. *specie, per speciem*.
ostentation, *iactatio, ostentatio*.
ostentatious, *gloriosus, iactans*; adv. *gloriose*.
ostler, *agaso*.
ostracism, at Athens, *testarum suffragia* (*-orum*); or render by *expellĕre*.
ostrich, *struthiocamelus*.
other: as adj. = different, *alius, diversus*; as pron., *alius*; the — (of two), *alter*; all the —s, *ceteri, reliqui*; belonging to —s, adj., *alienus*; on the — hand, *contra, autem*.
otherwise, *aliter, alioqui*(*n*).
ought, v.: I — to go, *eundum est mihi, ire debeo, ire me oportet*.
ounce, *uncia*: half- —, *semuncia*.
our, ours, *noster*; — people, *nostri* (*-orum*); of — country, *nostras*.
out, adv. *foras* (of going out), *foris* (of being out), *extra*.
out of, prep.: = away from, outside, *e* (*ex*), *extra*; — one's mind, *sui* or *mentis non compos*; = arising from, because of, *propter, per*, or rendered by participle with abl., e.g. — fear, *metu coactus*.
outbid, *licitatione vincĕre*.
outbreak, *eruptio*; = beginning, *initium, principium*; = disturbance, *seditio*.
outcast, *exsul, extorris, profugus*.
outcry, *clamor, vociferatio, convicium*.
outdo, *superare, vincĕre*.
outer, *exterior*.
outflank, *circumire, circumvenire*.
outlandish, *peregrinus, barbarus*.
outlast, *diutius durare* (with *quam* or abl.).
outlaw, subst. *proscriptus*.
outlaw, v. *proscribĕre*, (*homini*) *aqua et igni interdicĕre*.
outlawry, *proscriptio*.
outlay, *sumptus* (*-ūs*), *impensa*.
outlet, *exitus* (*-ūs*); see also mouth.
outline, subst. (*extrema*) *lineamenta* (*-orum*); in a sketch, *adumbratio*.
outline, v. *describĕre, adumbrare*.
outlive, (*homini*) *superesse*.
outlook: physical, render by *spectare*; = prospects, *spes*; = attitude, *animus*.
outlying, *longinquus*.
outnumber, *numero* (or *multitudine*) *superare*.
outpost, *statio*.
outrage, subst. *iniuria, indignitas*.
outrage, v. *violare, iniuriā adficĕre*.
outrageous, *immanis, indignus*; adv. *indigne*.
outright: = at once, *statim, ilico*; = completely, *plane, prorsus, omnino*.
outrun, *cursu superare*.
outset, *initium*.
outside, *superficies* (= surface), *species*; on the —, *extrinsecus*.
outside, adj. *exter* (*exterus*), *externus*.
outside, adv. *extra, extrinsecus, foris* (of rest), *foras* (of motion).
outskirts; see suburb.
outspoken; see frank.
outspread, *patulus, passus*.
outstanding, *reliquus*; see also debt.
outstrip, (*cursu*) *superare*.
outvote, *suffragiis vincĕre*.
outward, adj. *exter* (*exterus*), *externus*; — show, *species*; adv. *extra, extrinsecus*.
outweigh, *praeponderare, vincĕre superare*.
outwit, *circumvenire*.
outworks, *munimenta* (*exteriora*).
oval, adj. *ovatus*.
ovation, *ovatio*; fig., to receive an —, *magnis clamoribus excipi*.
oven, *furnus*.
over, adv. *super, insuper, supra*; to be — (= remain), *superesse, superare*; — and done with, *confectus, peractus*; it is all — with us, *actum est de nobis*.
over, prep.: = across, *super, trans*; = above, *super, supra*; = more than, *super, amplius* (with numerals), *plus quam*.
overawe, (*de*)*terrēre*.
overbalance, *praeponderare*.
overbearing, *adrogans, superbus*.

overboard: to throw —, *iacturam facĕre*; with genit., to fall —, *in mare excīdĕre.*
overcast, of sky, *nubilus.*
overcharge, *nimium exigĕre, nimio vendĕre.*
overcome, (*de*)*vincĕre, superare.*
overdone, (*nimis*) *elaboratus.*
overdraw; to — an account, *aes alienum contrahĕre* (= incur debt).
overdressed, *nimis splendide ornatus.*
overdue, *debitus*; see owing.
overeat, *nimis ĕdĕre, helluari.*
overfill, *supra modum implēre.*
overflow, subst.; see flood.
overflow, v. *redundare, effundi*: to — on to, *inundare.*
overgrown, = covered with foliage, etc., *obsitus*; see also huge, enormous.
overhang, *imminēre, impendēre.*
overhasty, *praeproperus, praeceps;* adv. *praepropere.*
overhaul; see examine; also overtake.
overhead, adv. *supra, insuper*: from —, *desuper.*
overhear, *subauscultare, exaudire.*
overjoyed, *laetitiā exsultans.*
overland, adv. *terrā* (opp. *mari*).
overlap, *imminēre, impendēre.*
overlay, *inducĕre, inlinĕre*; with gold, *inaurare.*
overload, *nimis onerare.*
overlook: = watch, examine, *observare, inspicĕre, intuēri*; = pardon, *ignoscĕre, condonare*; = miss, fail to notice, *praeterire, omittĕre.*
overmuch, adv. *nimis, nimium.*
overpower, *superare, vincĕre, debellare.*
overpowering; see overwhelming.
overrate, *nimis magni facĕre.*
overreach, *circumvenire, circumscribĕre.*
overrule, *vincĕre*; of providence, *gubernare.*
overrun, (*per*)*vagari.*
overscrupulous, *diligentior, religiosior.*
oversee, (*pro*)*curare.*
overseer, *custos,* (*pro*)*curator.*
oversight: = failure to notice, *error, incuria*; = superintendence, *curatio, procuratio, cura.*
oversleep, *diutius dormire.*
overspread, *obducĕre, inducĕre.*
overstate; see exaggerate.
overt, *apertus, manifestus.*
overtake: = catch up with, *consequi*; = surprise, *opprimĕre, deprehendĕre.*
overtax, *iniquis oneribus premĕre.*
overthrow, subst. *clades, ruina, excidium.*
overthrow, v. *deicĕre, adfligĕre, evertĕre.*
overture: diplomatic, *condicio*; musical, *exordium.*
overturn, *evertĕre, subvertĕre.*
overweening, *superbus, insolens.*
overwhelm, *obruĕre, opprimĕre.*
overwork, subst. *labor nimius.*
overwrought, *nimis intentus.*
overzealous, *nimis studiosus.*
owe, v. *debēre.*
owing to, prep. *propter, ob, per*; it was — you that . . . not, *per te stetit quominus.*
owl, *ulula, noctua, strix.*
own: one's —, *proprius*; my —, *meus*; your —, *tuus, vester*; his —, their —, *suus, ipsius* (genit.), *ipsorum.*
own, v.: = confess, *fatēri, confitēri*; = possess, *habēre, possidēre.*
owner, *possessor, dominus.*
ownership, *dominium.*
ox, *bos*; of oxen, adj. *bubulus*; a driver of oxen, *bubulcus.*
oxherd, *armentarius.*
oyster, *ostrea*; — shell, *ostreae testa.*

P

pace, subst.: = a step, *gradus* (*-ūs*), *passus* (*-ūs*); as a measure = *passus* (*-ūs*); = speed, *velocitas, gradus* (*-ūs*); at a quick —, *pleno* or *citato gradu.*
pace, v. *gradi, incedĕre, ambulare, spatiari*; = measure by pacing, *passibus metiri.*
pacific, *pacificus* or *pacis* (genit.).
pacify, *placare, pacare, sedare.*
pack, subst.: = bundle, *sarcina*; = crowd, *turba, grex.*
pack, v. *stipare, co*(*artare*); of luggage, etc., *conligĕre, componĕre.*
packet, *fasciculus.*
pack-horse, *equus clitellarius.*
pack-saddle, *clitellae* (*-arum*).
pact, *pactio, pactum.*
paddle; see oar, row.
Padua, *Patavium.*
page, of a book, *pagina.*
pageant, *spectaculum, pompa.*
pail, *hama, situla.*
pain, subst. *dolor*; violent — *cruciatus* (*-ūs*).
pain, v. transit. *dolore adficĕre, cruciare, angĕre.*
painful, *gravis, acerbus, molestus*; adv. *graviter, acerbe, dolenter.*
painless, *sine dolore, doloris expers.*
pains, = exertion, *opera, labor, studium*; to take —, *operam dare.*
painstaking, *operosus, laboriosus.*
paint, subst. *pigmentum, fucus.*
paint, v.: as an artist, *pingĕre*; = to colour, *inficĕre, fucare.*
paint-brush, *penicillus.*
painter, *pictor.*
painting, *pictura; ars pingendi.*
pair, subst. *par*; of horses or oxen, *iugum*; often *bini* (= two at a time).
pair, v.: transit., (*con*)*iungĕre*; intransit., (*con*)*iungi, coire.*
palace, (*domus*) *regia.*
palatable, *iucundus, suavis, dulcis.*
palate, *palatum.*
palatial, *regius.*
palaver, *nugae* (*-arum*).
pale, subst.: = stake *palus, sudis*; = fence, *saepes.*
pale, adj. *pallidus, luridus*; to be —, *pallēre.*
Palermo, *Panormus.*
palfrey, *equus* or *caballus.*
palimpsest, *palimpsestus.*
palisade, *vallum, vallus.*
pall, v. or render by *taedet.*
pallet, *lectulus, grabatus.*
palliate, *excusare, extenuare.*

pallid; see pale.
pallor, *pallor.*
palm, subst. *palma*; adorned with —, *palmatus.*
palm, v.: to — off, *imponĕre, supponĕre.*
palmer; see pilgrim.
palmy, *florens, optimus.*
palpable, *tractabilis, quod tangi potest*; = obvious, *manifestus, apertus*; adv. *manifesto, aperte.*
palpitate, *palpitare, micare.*
paltry, *vilis, minutus, pusillus.*
pamper, *nimis indulgēre.*
pamphlet, *libellus.*
pan, *patina*; frying- —, *sartago.*
panacea, *panchrestum medicamentum.*
pander, subst. *leno.*
pander, v. *lenocinari*; see flatter, indulge.
panegyric, *laudatio, laudes.*
panegyrist, *laudator, praedicator.*
panel, *tympanum*; a panelled ceiling, *lacunar.*
pang, *dolor.*
panic, subst. *pavor, terror.*
panic, v. *pavēre.*
panic-stricken, *pavidus.*
pannier, *clitellae (-arum).*
panoply; see armour.
panorama; see prospect, view.
pant, v. *anhelare.*
pantheism, *deum in universa rerum natura situm esse credĕre.*
panther, *panthera.*
panting, subst. *anhelitus* (*-ūs*).
pantomime, *mimus.*
pantry, *cella penaria.*
paper, subst. *charta, papyrus*; a written (printed) —, *charta, scriptum, libellus*; public —s, *tabulae publicae*; a news —, *acta* (*diurna*).
papyrus, *papyrus* or *papyrum.*
par: on a — with, *aequus, par.*
parable, *parabola, similitudo.*
parade, subst.: = show, *ostentatio*; milit., *decursus* (*-ūs*).
parade, v.: = display, *ostentare*; milit., intransit., *decurrĕre.*
paradise, *sedes beatorum* or *piorum.*
paradox; render by *admirabilis* or *contra opinionem.*
paragon, *specimen.*
paragraph, *caput* (= section).
parallel, adj.: — to, *e regione*, with genit. or dat.; = similar, *par, (con)similis, congruens.*
paralyse, *debilitare, enervare, adfligĕre.*
paralysed, *pede, manu,* etc., *captus.* Transf., *debilis, torpens, torpidus*; to be —, *torpēre.*
paralysis, *nervorum remissio.* Transf., *debilitas, torpedo.*
paramount, *summus.*
paramour; see lover.
parapet, *pluteus, lorica.*
paraphernalia, *apparatus* (*-ūs*).
paraphrase, subst., *interpretatio, paraphrasis.*
paraphrase, v. *interpretari.*
parasite, *parasitus; adsecula* (=hanger-on).
parasitic, *parasiticus.*
parasol, *umbella, umbraculum.*
parcel, *fascis, fasciculus*; see part, portion.
parcel out, v. *partiri, dividĕre, distribuĕre.*
parch, *torrēre, (ex)urĕre.*
parched, *aridus, torridus.*
parchment, *membrana.*
pardon, subst. *venia.*
pardon, v., (*homini rem*) *ignoscĕre* or *condonare.*
pardonable, *excusabilis.*
pare, (*re*)*secare, subsecare.*
parent, *parens.*
parentage, *stirps, genus* (*-eris,* n.).
parental, *parentum* (genit.).
parenthesis, *interpositio, interclusio.*
Paris, *Lutetia.*
parity; see equality.
park, subst. *vivarium* (= preserve), *horti* (*-orum,* = pleasure-gardens).
parley, subst. *conloquium, sermo.*
parley, v. *conloqui, sermones conferre.*
parliament, *senatus* (*-ūs*); act of — *senatūs consultum*; house of — *curia*; member of —, *senator.*
parliamentary, *senatorius.*
parody, subst. *ridicula imitatio.*
parole, *fides* (*data*).
paroxysm, *febris accessio.* Transf. *vis, impetus* (*-ūs*).
parricide: as person, *parricida*; as act, *parricidium.*
parrot, *psittacus.*
parry, v. = check, ward off, *propulsare, defendĕre, arcēre.*
parsimonious, *parcus, sordidus, tenax*; adv. *parce, sordide.*
parsimony, *parsimonia, tenacitas.*
parsley, *apium.*
part, subst., *pars, membrum*; in two, three —s, *bifariam, trifariam* or *bipartito, tripartito*; for the most —, *maximam partem, fere, plerumque*; to do one's — *officio* or *munere fungi*; to take — in, *partem capĕre* or *participem esse*; —, = side, cause, *partes* (*-ium*); to take a person's —, *homini adesse, favēre*; — in a play, role, *partes* (*-ium*), *persona*; to play the chief —, *primas* (*partes*) *agĕre.*
part, v. transit., *separare, dividĕre, dissociare*; intransit., *digredi, discedĕre.*
partake, *participem esse*; of food, *gustare.*
partaker, *particeps, socius, adfinis.*
partial, = favouring, *studiosus, cupidus.*
partiality, *studium, cupiditas.*
partially, *per studium*; see also partly.
participate, (*rei,* genit.) *esse participem*; (*rei,* dat.) *interesse.*
participation, *societas.*
participator, *particeps, socius, adfinis.*
participle, *participium.*
particle, *particula, frustum* (esp. of food); gram., *particula.*
particoloured, *versicolor, varius.*
particular, adj.: = individual, *proprius, separatus*; = special, outstanding, *singularis, praecipuus*; = exacting, fussy, *elegans, delicatus.* Adv., *magnopere, praesertim, praecipue.*

particularize, *nominare* (= name), *enumerare* (= enumerate).
particulars, subst. *singula* (*-orum*).
parting, subst. *digressus* (*-ūs*), *discessus* (*-ūs*).
partisan, *fautor, homo studiosus.*
partisanship, *studium, favor.*
partition, *partitio*; = wall, barrier, *paries.*
partly, *partim, parte,* (*aliqua*) *ex parte.*
partner, *socius, consors*; in marriage *coniunx.*
partnership, *consortio, societas.*
partridge, *perdix.*
party, *partes* (*-ium*), *factio* (esp. polit.) *secta* (of philosophers, etc.); to belong to a —, *partes sequi*; —, = social gathering, *convivium.*
party-wall, *paries.*
parvenu, *novus homo.*
pass, subst. *angustiae* (*-arum*), *saltus* (*-ūs*), *fauces* (*-ium*); things have come to such a — that . . ., *eo ventum est ut . . .*
pass, v. (1) = go along, go past, *transgredi, transire, praeterire*; to — over, let —, *praeterire, transire, omittěre*; to — off, *abire, deceděre.* (2) of time: to — time, *agěre, degěre,* (*tra*)*ducěre, consuměre*; of time itself, to —, *transire, abire, praeterire.* (3) to — a law, get a law —ed, *legem perferre.* (4) to — down, — along, *traděre, porrigěre, traicěre.* (5) to — a test, be approved, (*ap*)*probari, satisfacěre.*
passable = tolerable, *tolerabilis, mediocris*; adv. *tolerabiliter, mediocriter.*
passage, *transitus* (*-ūs*), *transitio, transgressio*; = way, road, *iter, via*; in a book, *locus.*
passenger, *viator; vector* (on horseback, etc.).
passing; in —, *praeteriens* (partic.), *obiter.*
passion: = suffering, *perpessio, toleratio*; = emotion, *animi motus* (*-ūs*) *commotio*; = uncontrolled emotion, *libido, cupiditas*; = anger, *ira, iracundia*: to fly into a —, *exardescěre*; = extreme fondness, *studium.*
passionate, adj. *cupidus, concitatus, vehemens, ardens*; = hot-tempered, *iracundus, cerebrosus.* Adv. *cupide, vehementer, effuse; iracunde.*
passionless, *cupiditatis expers.*
passive: to remain —, *quiescěre*; gram. *passivus.* Adv. *aequo animo, patienter.*
passiveness, *patientia.*
password, *tessera.*
past, subst. *praeteritum tempus.*
past, adj. *praeteritus, ante actus*; = immediately preceding, *prior, superior, proximus.*
past, adv., render by compound verbs in *praeter-* or *trans-*
past, prep., *praeter, trans.*
pastime, *ludus,oblectamentum.*
pastoral, *pastoralis, pastoricius; agrestis, rusticus*: — poetry, *bucolica* (*-orum*).
pastry, *crustum, crustulum.*
pasture, subst. *pascuum, ager pascuus.*
pasture, v.: transit., *pascěre*; intransit., *pabulari, pasci.*
patch, subst. *pannus.*
patch, v. (*re*)*sarcire.*
patchwork, *cento.*
patent, = open, plain, *manifestus, apertus.*
paternal, *paternus, patrius.*
path, *via, iter, semita, trames.*
pathetic, *flebilis, maestus*; adv. *flebiliter, maeste.*
pathless, *invius.*
pathos, *maestitia, tristitia.*
patience, *patientia, tolerantia, perseverantia* (at work), *aequus animus* (= calmness).
patient, subst. *aeger, aegrotus.*
patient, adj. *patiens, tolerans*; adv. *patienter, toleranter, aequo animo.*
patrician, *patricius.*
patrimony, *patrimonium.*
patriot, *civis bonus.*
patriotic, *patriae* (or *reipublicae*) *amans*; adv. *pro patria.*
patriotism, *patriae amor.*
patrol, v. *circumire, lustrare.*
patron, *patronus, praeses.*
patronage, *patrocinium* (from the patron's side), *clientela* (from the client's); in gen., *praesidium.*
patroness, *patrona.*
patronize, *favēre* (with dat.).
patter, subst. *crepitus* (*-ūs*).
patter, v. *crepare, crepitare.*
pattern, *exemplum, exemplar, specimen, documentum.*
paucity, *paucitas,* or render by adj.
paunch, *abdomen, venter.*
pause, subst. *mora, intervallum, intermissio.*
pause, v. *intermittěre, subsistěre, morari.*
pave, (*viam*) *sterněre* or *munire.*
pavement, *pavimentum, via strata.*
paving, *stratura.*
paving-stone, *saxum quadratum.*
paw, subst. *pes* (= foot), *ungula* (= claw).
paw, v. (*solum*) *pedibus ferire.*
pawn, subst. *pignus* (*-oris,* n.); at chess, *latrunculus, latro.*
pawn, v. (*op*)*pignerare, pignori dare.*
pay, subst. *stipendium, merces.*
pay, v.: transit., (*per*)*solvěre, penděre, numerare*; to — a penalty *poenam dare* or *luěre*; intransit., = be profitable, *prodesse, lucro esse.*
paymaster, *dispensator*; milit., *tribunus aerarius.*
payment, *solutio, repraesentatio* (in cash).
pea, *pisum, cicer.*
peace, subst. *pax, otium, concordia.*
peaceful, *pacatus, placidus, quietus, tranquillus*; adv. *placide, quiete, tranquille.*
peace-offering, *piaculum, placamen.*
peach, (*malum*) *persicum.*
peacock, *pavo.*
peak, *cacumen, apex*; or rendered by adj. *summus.*
peal, subst.: — of laughter, *cachinnus*; — of thunder, *tonitrus* (*-ūs*).
peal, v. *sonare.*

pear, *pirum*; — tree, *pĭrus.*
pearl, *margarita.*
peasant, *rusticus, agrestis.*
pebble, *calculus, lapillus.*
peccadillo, (*leve*) *delictum.*
peck, as measure, *modius.*
peck, v. *vellicare.*
peculation, *peculatus* (-*ūs*).
peculiar: = of one only, *proprius, peculiaris*; = remarkable, *singularis, praecipuus, mirus.* Adv., = especially, *praecipue, praesertim.*
peculiarity, *proprietas.*
pecuniary, *pecuniarius.*
pedagogue, *paedagogus*; = schoolmaster, *magister.*
pedant, pedantic; render by (*nimis*) *diligens.*
pedestal, *basis.*
pedestrian, subst. *pedes.*
pedestrian, adj. *pedester.*
pedigree, *stemma* (-*atis* n.)
pedlar, *institor.*
peel, subst. *cutis, corium.*
peel, v.: transit., *cutem detrahĕre*; intransit., *cutem* (*de*)*ponĕre.*
peep, subst. *aspectus* (-*ūs*), *conspectus* (-*ūs*).
peep, v. (*strictim*) *prospicĕre, inspicĕre.*
peer, subst.: = equal, *par*; = noble, *unus e patriciis* or *nobilibus.*
peer, v.: to — into, *rimari, scrutari.*
peerless, *unicus, singularis.*
peevish, *stomachosus, morosus, difficilis*; adv. *stomachose, morose.*
peevishness, *stomachus, morositas.*
peg, *clavus* (= nail).
pell-mell, *effuse, confuse, passim.*
pellucid; see transparent.
pelt, v.: transit., see throw; of rain, *ferri, descendere*; —ing rain, *maximus imber.*
pen, subst.: for writing, *calamus, stilus*; = fold, *saeptum.*
pen, v.: = write, *scribĕre, litteris mandare*; = fold, *saeptis includĕre.*
penalty, *poena, multa, supplicium.*
penance, *piaculum, poena, satisfactio.*
pence; see penny.
pencil: for drawing *penicillus*; for writing, *stilus.*
pending; adj., the matter is still —, *adhuc sub iudice lis est.*
pending, prep.: = during, *per*; = until, *dum* with subj.
pendulous, *pendulus.*
penetrable, *penetrabilis.*
penetrate, *penetrare, pervadĕre*; by stealth, (*se*) *insinuare*; into a mind, *descendĕre.*
penetrating, adj., of cold, etc., *acutus, acer*; mentally, *sagax, perspicax, subtilis.*
penetration, *acies, acumen.*
peninsula, *paeninsula.*
penitence, *paenitentia.*
penny, *as, nummus* (*sestertius*).
pension, *annua* (-*orum*).
pensive, *in cogitatione defixus.*
penthouse, milit., *vinea.*
penurious, *parcus, sordidus, avarus*; adv. *sordide.*
penury, *inopia, egestas.*
people, subst. (1), = persons, *homines, mortales*; our —, *nostri*; young —, *pueri, adulescentes.* (2), = a community, *populus*; adj., of the —, *publicus*; (3), = race, tribe, *gens, natio.* (4) common —, *plebs, vulgus, multitudo.*
people, v. *frequentare, complēre.*
pepper, *piper.*
perambulate, *perambulare, peragrare, pervagari.*
perceive, *sentire, percipĕre; vidēre* (= see), *audire* (= hear), *intellegĕre* (= understand).
percentage, *pars, portio.*
perceptible, *manifestus; quod percipĕre possis.*
perception; render by verb; = discernment, *iudicium, sagacitas.*
perch, subst., as fish, *perca.*
perch, v. *insidēre.*
percolate, *permanare.*
percussion, *ictus* (-*ūs*; = blow).
perdition, *exitium, pernicies.*
peremptory, *adrogans.* Adv. *adroganter*; in refusals, *praecise.*
perennial, *perennis, iugis.*
perfect, adj. *plenus, absolutus, perfectus, integer* (= sound intact), *merus* (= sheer). Adv. *plene, absolute, perfecte; plane* (= wholly).
perfect, v. *perficĕre, absolvĕre.*
perfection, *absolutio, perfectio.*
perfidious, *perfidus, perfidiosus*; adv. *perfidiose.*
perfidy, *perfidia.*
perforate, *perforare,* (*per*)*terebrare.*
perforce, *vi, per vim, necessario*; or adj. *invitus* (= unwilling).
perform, (*per*)*fungi, exsequi, perficĕre, conficĕre, peragĕre*; on the stage, *partes agĕre.*
performance, (*per*)*functio, confectio*; on the stage, *fabula.*
performer, *actor, auctor, confector*; on the stage, *actor, histrio* (= actor), *acroama* (-*atis*, n.; musical).
perfume, subst. *odor, unguentum.*
perfume, v. *odorare, odore adficĕre.*
perfunctory, *neglegens.*
perhaps, *fortasse, forsitan*; unless —, *nisi forte*, lest —, *ne forte.*
peril; see danger, risk.
period: of time, *tempus, spatium temporis*; = end, *finis, terminus*; rhet. or gram., *periodus,* (*verborum* or *orationis*) *circuitus* (-*ūs*).
periodical, adj. *sollemnis*; adv. *certis* (or *statis*) *temporibus.*
perish, *perire, interire, occĭdĕre.*
perishable, *fragilis, caducus, fluxus.*
perjure, *periurare* (or *peierare*); *periurium facĕre.*
perjured, *periurus.*
perjury, *periurium.*
permanence, *perennitas, stabilitas.*
permanent, *perennis, stabilis*; adv. *perpetuo.*
permissible, *licitus*; it is —, *licet.*
permission, *facultas, potestas, copia, venia*; with your —, *pace tua.*
permit, v. (*hominem*) *sinĕre;* (*homini*) *permittĕre, concedĕre, copiam facĕre.*

permutation, (*per*)*mutatio.*
pernicious, *perniciosus, exitiosus*; adv. *perniciose, exitiose, funeste.*
peroration, *peroratio, conclusio.*
perpendicular, *directus*; adv. *ad lineam, rectā lineā.*
perpetrate, *committĕre, in se admittĕre.*
perpetrator, *auctor; qui facinus in se admisit.*
perpetual, *sempiternus, perennis, adsiduus*; adv. *adsidue, perpetuo.*
perpetuity, *perpetuitas.*
perplex, *distrahĕre, sollicitare.*
perplexed, *dubius, inops consilii.*
perplexing, *difficilis, perplexus, impeditus.*
perplexity, *dubitatio.*
persecute, *insectari, vexare.*
persecution, *insectatio, vexatio.*
persecutor, *vexator, insectator.*
perseverance, *perseverantia, constantia, pertinacia.*
persevere, *perseverare, perstare, persistĕre.*
persevering, *perseverans, constans, pertinax*; adv. *perseveranter, constanter.*
persist; see persevere.
person: = human being, *homo, caput*; in person, *ipse, praesens, coram*; = body, form, *corpus, species, forma*; gram. *persona.*
personal, *privatus, proprius*; to make a — appearance, *ipse adesse.*
personality, *persona, hominis natura, ingenium* (= disposition).
personate, (*hominis*) *partes agĕre.*
personification, *prosopopoeia, personarum fictio.*
personify, *humana specie induĕre.*
perspicacious, *perspicax, sagax, acutus*; adv. *perspicaciter.*
perspicacity, *perspicacitas, acies ingenii.*
perspicuity, *perspicuitas.*
perspicuous, (*di*)*lucidus, perspicuus, apertus*; adv. (*di*)*lucide, perspicue, aperte.*
perspiration, *sudor.*
perspire, *sudare.*
persuade, *persuadēre, adducĕre*; to try to —, *suadēre.*
persuasion, *persuasio.*
persuasive; render by verb.
pert, *protervus, procax*; adv. *proterve.*
pertain, *pertinēre, attinēre.*
pertinacious, *pertinax, obstinatus*; adv. *pertinaciter, obstinate.*
pertinacity, *pertinacia, obstinatio.*
pertness, *protervitas, procacitas.*
perturbation, *perturbatio.*
Perugia, *Perusia.*
perusal, *lectio, perlectio.*
peruse, (*per*)*legĕre, evolvĕre.*
pervade, *permanare.*
perverse, *perversus, pravus*; adv. *perverse, perperam, prave.*
perversion, *corruptio, depravatio.*
perversity, *perversitas, pravitas.*
pervert, v. *depravare, corrumpĕre, detorquēre.*
pest, *pestis, pernicies, lues.*
pester, *sollicitare, vexare.*
pestilence, *pestilentia, pestis, lues, morbus.*
pestilential, *pestilens, foedus.*
pestle, *pilum, pistillum.*
pet, subst. *deliciae* (*-arum*), *amores* (*-um*).
pet, v. *fovēre, in deliciis habēre.*
Peter, *Petrus* (late Latin).
petition; see prayer, request; a formal —, *libellus*; to grant a —, *petenti satisfacĕre.*
petition, v. *petĕre, rogare, implorare.*
petrify, *in lapidem* (*con*)*vertĕre.* Transf., *obstupefacĕre*: to be petrified, *obstupescĕre, stupēre.*
pettifogger, *leguleius, rabula.*
petty, *minutus, tenuis.*
petulance, *petulantia, protervitas.*
petulant, *petulans, protervus.*
phantom, *simulacrum, imago.*
phase, *status* (*-ūs*), *ratio*; different —s, *vices* (plur.).
pheasant, (*avis*) *Phasiana, Phasianus.*
phenomenon; = remarkable event, *prodigium, portentum, miraculum.*
phial; see bottle.
philanthropic, *hominibus amicus, humanus.*
philanthropy, *benevolentia, humanitas.*
Philip, *Philippus.*
philological, *grammaticus.*
philologist, *grammaticus, philologus.*
philology, *grammatica* (*-ae* or *-orum*), *philologia.*
philosopher, *philosophus, sapiens.*
philosophical, *philosophus*; = wise, *sapiens.* Adv. *philosophorum more, sapienter*; = calmly, *aequo animo.*
philosophize, *philosophari; ratiocinari, disputare.*
philosophy, *philosophia.*
philtre, *philtrum.*
phlegm, *pituita*; = coolness, *patientia, lentitudo.*
phlegmatic, *tardus, patiens, lentus*; adv. *patienter, lente, aequo animo.*
phrase, *locutio; verbum.*
phrase, v.; see express, say.
phraseology, *locutio, dicendi genus* (*-eris,* n.).
physic, subst.; see medicine.
physical: = natural, render by genit. *naturae* or *corporis*; = of physics, *physicus.* Adv. *naturā*; = in the manner of physics, *physice.*
physician; see doctor.
physics, *physica* (*-orum*).
physiognomy, *oris habitus* (*-ūs*) or *lineamenta* (*-orum*).
physiology, *physiologia.*
Piacenza, *Placentia.*
pick: = pluck, gather, *legĕre, carpĕre, conligĕre*; to — up, *tollĕre*; to — out, *eligĕre.*
pick-axe, *dolabra.*
picked, *delectus, electus.*
picket, *statio, custodia.*
pickle, subst. *salsura, muria.*
pickle, v. *muriā condire.*
picture, subst. *tabula* (*picta*), *pictura.*
picture, v., = imagine, *cogitatione fingĕre, depingĕre, ante oculos proponĕre.*
picturesque, *amoenus, venustus.*

pie, *crustum.*
piebald, *bicolor.*
piece, *pars, fragmentum* (broken off), *frustum* (esp. of food), *mica* (= crumb); — of cloth, *pannus*; a piece of money, *nummus*; to break into —s, *confringĕre, comminuĕre*; to tear to —s, *discerpĕre, dilacerare, dilaniare*; to fall to —s, *dilabi, (dis)solvi.*
piecemeal, *membratim, minutatim.*
piece together, v. *consuĕre, fabricari.*
pied, *maculosus, versicolor.*
pier, *pila, moles, agger.*
pierce, *pungĕre*; to — through, *perforare, perfodere, transfigĕre.*
piercing, adj. *acer, acutus.*
piety, *pietas* (*erga deos*), *religio* (= religious feeling), *sanctitas* (= holiness).
pig, *porcus, sus.*
pigeon, *columba, columbus, palumbes* (= wood- —).
piggish, *suillus, porcinus.*
pigment; see paint.
pigmy; see Pygmy.
pigsty, *hara.*
pike: the weapon, *hasta, sarissa*; the fish, *lupus.*
pile, subst., *strues, cumulus, acervus*; a — driven into the ground, *sublica, sudis*; a bridge built on —s, *pons sublicius.*
pile, v. *(co)acervare, cumulare, congerĕre, exstruĕre.*
pilfer, *surripĕre, furari.*
pilgrim, *viator, peregrinator.*
pilgrimage, *iter, peregrinatio* (*sacra*).
pill, *pilula.*
pillage, subst. *rapina, direptio, compilatio, expilatio.*
pillage, v. *diripĕre, compilare, expilare, praedari.*
pillager, *praedator, direptor, expilator.*
pillar, *columna, pila*; fig., = support, stay, *columen.*
pillow, *pulvinus, cervical.*
pilot, subst. *gubernator.*
pilot, v. *gubernare.*
pimple, *pustula.*
pin, subst. *acus* (*-ūs*; = needle).
pin, v. *(ad)figĕre.*
pincers, *forceps.*
pinch, subst. *aculeus* (= sting), *morsus* (*-ūs*; = bite).
pinch; v.: = nip, *urĕre*; = stint, confine, *coartare, urgēre.*
pinching, of poverty, *angustus.*
pine, subst. *pinus*; of —, adj. *pineus.*
pine, v. *tabescĕre, confici*; to — for, *desiderare.*
pining, subst. *tabes.*
pinion, subst. of a bird, *penna.*
pinion, v. *(re)vincire.*
pink, *puniceus.*
pinnace, (*navis*) *actuaria, lembus.*
pinnacle, *fastigium.*
pint, perhaps *sextarius*; half a —, *hemina.*
pioneer, *praecursor, explorator*; or render by *primus.*
pious, *pius, religiosus* (= scrupulous), *sanctus* (= saintly). Adv. *pie, religiose, sancte.*
pip, in fruit, *acinus, granum.*
pipe, subst.: = tube, *tubus, canalis, fistula*; = musical instrument, *fistula, tibia, calamus* (= reed- —).
pipe, v. *fistulā* (or *tibiā*) *canĕre.*
piper, *fistulator, tibicen.*
pipkin, *olla.*
piquancy, *sal, vis.*
piquant, *acer*; = stimulating, humorous, *salsus, facetus.*
pique, subst. *offensio, ira.*
pique, v. *vexare, sollicitare.*
piracy, *latrocinium* (*maritimum*).
pirate, *praedo* (*maritimus*).
piratical, *piraticus, praedatorius.*
pit, subst. *fovea, puteus, fossa* (= ditch); in the theatre, *cavea* (*media* or *summa*).
pit against, v. *opponĕre.*
pitch, subst.: the substance, *pix*; of —, adj. *piceus*; = degree, *fastigium, gradus* (*-ūs*); to such a — of madness, *eo amentiae*; in music, *sonus, vox*; = slope, *fastigium.*
pitch, v.: of tents, etc., *ponĕre, constituĕre*; = throw, *iacĕre, conicĕre.*
pitcher, *urceus.*
pitchfork, *furca.*
piteous, pitiable, *miser, miserabilis*; adv. *misere, miserabiliter.*
pitfall, *fovea.*
pith, *medulla.*
pithy, *medullosus.* Transf., *sententiosus, nervosus.*
pitiful: = full of pity, *clemens, misericors*; = mean, *abiectus, humilis, vilis*; see also piteous. Adv. *clementer; abiecte, humiliter.*
pitifulness, *clementia, misericordia*; = meanness, *humilitas.*
pitiless, *immisericors, inexorabilis, inhumanus, crudelis*; adv. *immisericorditer, inhumane, crudeliter.*
pitilessness, *crudelitas, inhumanitas, saevitia.*
pittance, *mercedula, stips, pecunia exigua.*
pity, subst. *misericordia, miseratio.*
pity, v. *misereri, miserari,* or impers. *miseret.*
pivot, *cardo* (= hinge).
placability, *placabilitas.*
placable, *exorabilis, placabilis.*
placard, *libellus, titulus.*
place, subst. (1), = position, spot, *locus, regio*; at, to, from this —, *hic, huc, hinc*; at, to, from that —, *ibi, eo, inde.* (2), = proper position, *locus, sedes, statio*; in — of, (*in*) *loco* with genit., or *pro* with abl. (3), = situation, office, *munus* (*-eris,* n.), *officium.* (4) in the first —, *primo, primum*; in the next —, *deinceps.*
place, v. *ponĕre, (con)locare*; to — oneself, *consistĕre*; to — here and there, *disponĕre.*
placid, *placidus, quietus, tranquillus.*
plagiarism, *furtum.*
plagiarize, *furari.*
plague, subst. *pestis, pestilentia.* Transf., *pernicies, lues, malum.*
plague, v. *vexare, sollicitare, exagitare.*

plain, subst. *campus, planities*; of the —, adj. *campestris.*
plain, adj.: = clear, *clarus, perspicuus, manifestus*; = candid, *simplex, apertus, liber*; = unadorned, *simplex, inornatus*; = not beautiful, *invenustus.* Adv.: = clearly, *clare, perspicue, manifesto*; = candidly, simply, *simpliciter, aperte, libere.*
plainness: = clearness, *perspicuitas*; = candour, simplicity, *simplicitas.*
plaint; see complaint.
plaintiff, *petitor.*
plaintive, *miserabilis, flebilis, queribundus*; adv. *miserabiliter, flebiliter.*
plait, subst.: = fold, *sinus* (*-ūs*), *ruga*; = braid of hair, *gradus* (*-ūs*).
plait, v. *plicare, intexĕre.*
plan, subst.: as drawn, *descriptio*; = layout, scheme, *forma, figura, conformatio*; a — of action, *consilium, propositum, institutum.*
plan, v.: = design, mark out, *designare, describĕre*; = form a — of action, *intendĕre, consilium capĕre* or *inire.*
plane, subst.: = flat surface, *planum, libramentum*; the tool, *runcina*; the tree, *platanus.*
planet, *stella errans* or *vaga.*
plank, *tabula, axis*; to cover with —s, *contabulare.*
plant, subst. *herba, planta.*
plant, v. *serĕre, conserĕre, obserĕre*; in gen., = put in position, *ponĕre, statuĕre, constituĕre.*
plantation, *plantarium* or *seminarium* (= nursery garden), *arbustum, locus arboribus consitus.*
planter, *sator, qui serit.*
planting, subst., as act, *satio, satus* (*-ūs*).
plash, subst. *murmur, sonus.*
plash, v. *murmurare.*
plaster, subst. *gypsum, tectorium*; in medicine, *emplastrum.*
plaster, v. *gypsare, gypso inlinĕre.*
plasterer, *tector.*
plate, subst.: = thin layer of metal, *lam(i)na, bractea*; = wrought metal, at table, *vasa argentea* or *aurea*; = platter, *catillus, patella.*
plate, v.: to — with silver, *argento inducĕre.*
platform, *suggestus* (*-ūs*), *tribunal.*
Platonic, *Platonicus*; the — philosophy, *Academia.*
platter, *catillus, patella.*
plaudit, *plausus* (*-ūs*).
plausibility, *verisimilitudo; simulatio, species.*
plausible: = probable, *veri similis, probabilis*; in bad sense, *speciosus.* Adv. *probabiliter*; in bad sense, *in speciem, simulate.*
play, subst.: = amusement, *ludus, lusus* (*-ūs*), *lusio*; at the theatre, *fabula, ludus scaenicus*; = scope, free action, *campus, area*; = movement, *motus* (*-ūs*), *gestus* (*-ūs*); fair —, *aequum* (*et*) *bonum.*
play, v.: on an instrument, *modulari*; on a stringed instrument, *psallĕre*; = amuse oneself, *ludĕre*; to — a part, *partes agĕre, personam gerĕre*; to — the fool, *ineptire, desipĕre*; to — into the hands of an opponent, *praevaricari.*
player: on strings, *fidicen* (f. *fidicina*), *psaltes, citharista*; on a wind instrument, *tibicen* (f. *tibicina*); see also gambler and actor.
playfellow, playmate, *conlusor.*
playful, *lascivus, iocosus*; adv. *iocose.*
playfulness, *lascivia.*
plaything, *ludibrium.*
playwriter, playwright, *fabularum scriptor.*
plea: at law, *petitio, exceptio, defensio*; in gen., = excuse, *excusatio.*
plead: at law, *causam agĕre, dicĕre, orare*; to — as an excuse, *causari, obtendĕre*; = to beg, entreat, *orare, obsecrare, implorare.*
pleader, *orator, causidicus.*
pleasant, pleasing, *gratus, iucundus, suavis, dulcis*; of places, *amoenus*; of manner, *comis, urbanus.* **Adv.,** pleasantly, *iucunde, suaviter*; = affably, *comiter, urbane.*
pleasantness, *iucunditas, dulcedo, suavitas*; of places, *amoenitas*; of manner, *comitas, urbanitas.*
pleasantry, *facetiae* (*-arum*), *iocus.*
please, v.: = to give pleasure to, *placĕre, delectare,* or impers. *libet*; = to see fit, be disposed, *velle*; if you please, *si placet*; colloq., please! *sis, amabo.*
pleasing; see pleasant.
pleasure: = enjoyment, delight, *voluptas, delectatio, oblectamentum*; fond of —, *voluptarius*; = liking, inclination, *arbitrium, libido.*
plebeian, adj. *plebeius* (opp. *patricius*).
pledge, subst. *pignus* (*-eris* or *-oris*), *cautio, arrabo.*
pledge, v. (*op*)*pignerare, obligare*; to — one's word, *fidem interponĕre, promittĕre, recipĕre.*
plenary; see full, complete.
plenipotentiary, *legatus.*
plenteous, plentiful, *uber, abundans, copiosus*; adv. *abunde, abundanter, copiose.*
plenty, *ubertas, copia, abundantia*; sometimes *satis* with genit.
pliable, pliant, *lentus, flexibilis, mollis.*
pliancy, pliability, *mollitia.*
plight; see condition, and pledge.
plod, *repĕre, tarde progredi.*
plot, subst.: of ground, *agellus, area*; = scheme, conspiracy, *coniuratio*; of a play, etc., *argumentum* (*fabulae*).
plot, v.: intransit., *coniurare*; transit. *machinari.*
plotter; see conspirator.
plough, subst. *aratrum*; **— -man, — -boy,** *arator, bubulcus*; **— -share,** *vomer*; **— -handle,** *stiva.*
plough, v. *arare*; to — up, *exarare*; to — round, *circumarare.*
ploughing, subst. *aratio.*
pluck, subst. *animus, virtūs* (*-ūtis*).
pluck, v. (*e*)*vellĕre*; to — flowers, *flores carpĕre, decerpĕre*; to — up courage, *animum recipĕre.*
plum, *prunum.*

plumage, *plumae, pennae (pinnae).*
plumb-line, plummet, *linea, perpendiculum.*
plume, subst. *pluma, penna (pinna).*
plump, *pinguis.*
plum-tree, *prunus.*
plunder, subst. *praeda, rapina.*
plunder, v. *praedari, diripĕre, expilare, (de)spoliare.*
plunderer, *direptor, praedator.*
plunge, v.: transit., *(sub)mergĕre, immergĕre*; intransit., *se mergĕre*, etc.
plural, *pluralis*; in the —, *pluraliter.*
ply, v. *exercēre.*
Po, the river, *Padus.*
poacher, *fur.*
pocket, subst. *sinus (-ūs*; = fold in the toga); *sacculus* (= a small bag), *crumena* (= purse).
pocket, v. *intercipĕre, avertĕre.*
pocket-book, *pugillares (-ium).*
pod, *siliqua.*
poem, *carmen, poema (-atis,* n.).
poet, *poeta, carminum auctor, vates* (= bard).
poetess, *poetria.*
poetical, *poeticus*; adv. *poetice, poetarum more.*
poetry, *poetice* or *poetica, poesis.*
poignant, *acer.*
point, subst.: = sharp end, *acumen, cuspis, spiculum, mucro*; geograph., *promontorium*; = spot, *locus*; on the — of doing, render by *in eo est ut*, or fut. partic.; the — at issue, *res, caput*; to the —, *ad rem.*
point, v.: = make sharp, *(prae)acuĕre*; to — out, indicate, *(digito) monstrare, indicare.*
point-blank, *directus*: to refuse —, *praecise negare.*
pointed, adj. *(prae)acutus*; = significant, *salsus, aculeatus*; adv. *salse.*
pointless, *insulsus, frigidus, ineptus.*
poise, v. *librare.*
poison, subst. *venenum, virus, toxicum.*
poison, v.: = render poisonous, *venenare, veneno imbuĕre*; = attack with —, *veneno necare, venenum dare.*
poisoner, *veneficus* (f. *venefica*).
poisoning, subst. *veneficium.*
poisonous, *venenatus, veneno imbutus.*
poke, v. *(hominem) fodĕre*; to — the fire, *ignem excitare*; to — about, *rimari, perscrutari.*
polar, *septentrionalis* (= northern).
pole, *contus, pertica, longurius*; of the earth, *axis, cardo, polus*; south —, *axis meridianus*; north —, *axis septentrionalis.*
polecat, *feles.*
polemics, *disputationes (-um), controversiae (-arum).*
police; render by *aediles (-ium)*; —men, *vigiles (-um).*
policy, *ratio rei publicae gerendae, consilia (-orum)*; = prudence, *prudentia, consilium.*
polish, subst., = polished state, *nitor.*
polish, v. *(per)polire, expolire.*
polished, *nitidus, mundus, (per)politus.*
polite, *urbanus, comis, humanus*; adv. *urbane, comiter, humane, humaniter*
politeness, *urbanitas, comitas, humanitas.*
politic, *prudens, circumspectus, providus.*
political, *publicus, civilis*; a — discussion, *sermo de republica habitus*; — science, *ratio civilis, reipublicae gerendae ratio.*
politician, *vir rerum civilium* (or *reipublicae*) *peritus.*
politics, *civilis ratio, respublica*; to take up —, *ad rempublicam accedĕre.*
polity, *reipublicae forma.*
poll, subst. = voting, *suffragium, comitia (-orum).*
pollard, *amputatus.*
polling-booth, *saeptum, ovile.*
poll-tax, *exactio capitum.*
pollute, *polluere, inquinare, contaminare.*
pollution, = filth, *conluvio, impuritas.*
polygamy, *plures uxores habēre.*
polytheism, *multorum deorum cultus (-ūs).*
pomade, *capillare, unguentum.*
pomegranate, *malum granatum* or *Punicum.*
pomp, *apparatus (-ūs).*
pompous, *magnificus, gloriosus*; of style, *tumidus.* Adv. *magnifice, gloriose.*
pomposity, *magnificentia.*
pond, *stagnum, piscina, lacus (-ūs).*
ponder, *considerare, ponderare, secum reputare.*
ponderous, *ponderosus, gravis.*
pontiff, *pontifex.*
pony, *mannus, mannulus.*
pool; see pond.
poop, *puppis.*
poor: = not rich, *pauper*; *inops, egens, mendicus* (= destitute); = inferior, *mediocris, tenuis*; of language, or of soil, *exilis, ieiunus*; = pitiable, *miser, infelix*; = little, *misellus.* Adv. *tenuiter, mediocriter, misere.*
pop, v. *crepare*; to — out, *evadĕre, exsilire.*
poplar, *populus*; of the —, adj. *populeus.*
poppy, n. *papaver (-eris,* n.).
populace, *multitudo, plebs.*
popular: = belonging to the people, *popularis*; the — party, *populares (-ium)*; = liked, *gratiosus, (in vulgus) gratus* or *acceptus.*
popularity, *gratia, populi favor.*
populate; see people, v.
population, *civium* or *incolarum numerus, cives (-ium), incolae (-arum).*
populous, *frequens, celeber.*
porch, *vestibulum.*
pore, subst. *foramen.*
pore, v. *(totum) se abdĕre (re* or *in re).*
pork, *porcina.*
porker, *porcus.*
porous, *rarus.*
porridge, *puls.*
port, = harbour, *portus (ūs).*
portcullis, *cataracta.*
portend, *portendĕre, denuntiare.*
portent, *portentum, prodigium, monstrum, omen.*
portentous, *portentosus, monstr(u)osus*; adv. *monstr(u)ose.*

porter: at a gate, *ianitor*; for luggage, *baiulus*.
portfolio, *scrinium*.
portico, *porticus* (*-ūs*).
portion, *pars, portio*; a marriage —, *dos*.
portmanteau, *vidulus, mantica*.
portrait, *imago* (*picta*).
portray, *depingĕre*.
position: = place, *locus, situs* (*-ūs*), *sedes*; = state, *locus, status* (*-ūs*), *condicio*.
positive; = certain, *certus*; a — statement, *adfirmatio*; adv. *adfirmate* (of assertion), *certe, certo* (of knowing).
possess: = to have, *possidēre, habēre, tenēre*; or render by *esse*, with dat. of possessor; of feelings, etc., = to overwhelm, *invadĕre, occupare*.
possession, *possessio*; to take —, *occupare, capĕre, potiri*.
possessive, *tenax* (*suorum*); gram., *possessivus*.
possessor, *possessor, dominus*.
possibility: render by *posse*; see also opportunity.
possible; render *posse*; it is — for me to live, *vivĕre possum*; it is — that, *fieri potest ut*; as quickly as —, *quam celerrime*. Adv.; see perhaps.
post, subst.; = stake, *palus*; door —, *postis*; milit., *statio, praesidium*; = office, *locus, munus* (*-eris*, n.); for letters, *tabellarii* (*-orum*; = letter-carriers).
post, v.: milit., (*dis*)*ponĕre*; to — a letter, *litteras tabellario dare*.
postage, *vecturae pretium*.
posterior, adj. *posterior*.
posterity, *posteritas, posteri* (*-orum*).
postern, *posticum*.
posthaste, *quam celerrime*.
posthumous; *post patrem mortuum natus*.
postman, *tabellarius*.
postpone, *differre, proferre, prorogare*.
postulate, subst. *sumptio*.
posture: of body, *status* (*-ūs*), *habitus* (*-ūs*); of affairs, *status* (*-ūs*), *condicio, ratio*.
pot; *olla*.
potent; see powerful, efficacious.
potentate, *res, tyrannus, princeps*.
potential; see possible.
pothouse, *caupona*.
potion, *potio*; see also philtre.
potsherd, *testa*.
potter, *figulus*; —'s workshop, *figlina*.
pottery, = pots, etc., *fictilia* (*-ium*).
pouch, *sacculus, saccus*.
poultice, *emplastrum*.
pounce: to — upon, *involare*.
pound, subst.: as measure of weight, *libra*; = enclosure, *saeptum* (*publicum*).
pound, v. (*con*)*tundĕre*, (*con*)*terĕre*.
pour, v.: transit., *fundĕre*; to — in, *infundĕre*; to — out, *effundĕre*; intransit. *fundi, fluĕre, ferri*.
pouring, adj. (of rain), *effusus*.
poverty, *paupertas*; extreme —, *egestas, inopia, mendicitas*.
powder, subst. *pulvis*.
power. (1), = force, vigour, *vis* (plur. *vires*), *robur, lacerti* (*-orum*, physical); military —, *opes* (*-um*). (2), = authority, *imperium, potestas, ius* (*iuris*, n.); unofficial —, *potentia*; in the — of, *penes* (*hominem*), *in manu* (*hominis*); to have great —, *multum posse* or *valēre*.
powerful, *validus, valens, potens, robustus* (physically); of speech, *gravis, nervosus*. Adv. *graviter, vehementer, valde*.
powerless, *invalidus, impotens*; to be —, *nihil posse*.
practicable; see possible.
practical, of a person, (*rerum*) *usu peritus*; — knowledge, *usus* (*-ūs*).
practice: = experience, *usus* (*-ūs*), *tractatio*; = custom, *mos, consuetudo*; = deed, *factum*.
practise: = do, engage in, *facĕre, exercĕre, tractare*; = rehearse, *meditari*.
praetor, *praetor*.
praetorship, *praetura*.
prairie, *campus*.
praise, subst. *laus, laudatio* (= laudatory oration).
praise, v. (*con*)*laudare, laude adficĕre, praedicare*.
praiseworthy, *laudabilis, laude dignus*.
prance, *exsilire, exsultare*.
prank, *iocus*.
prate, prattle, *garrire*.
pray, *precari, rogare, orare, supplicare*.
prayer, *preces* (*-um*), *precatio, votum*.
prayerful, *supplex*.
preach, *docēre, orationem habēre*.
preamble, *exordium*.
precarious, *incertus, dubius*.
precaution; to take —s, *providēre, praecavēre*.
precede, *anteire, antegredi, antecedĕre*.
precedence, *prior locus*; to take —, (*homini*) *antecedĕre*.
precedent, *exemplum*.
preceding, *prior, superior*; = immediately before, *proximus*.
precept, *praeceptum, mandatum*.
preceptor, *magister, praeceptor*.
preceptor, *magister, praeceptor*.
precincts, *termini* (*-orum*), *fines* (*-ium*).
precious, *magni pretii, splendidus, egregius*; a — stone, *gemma*.
precipice, *locus praeceps*.
precipitate, adj. *temerarius, praeceps, inconsultus*. Adv. *temere*.
precipitate, v. *praecipitare, deicĕre, deturbare*.
precipitous, *praeceps, praeruptus*.
precise: of things, *definitus, accuratus*; of persons, *diligens*. Adv. *subtiliter*; see also just.
precision, *subtilitas*; of persons, *diligentia*.
preclude, *prohibēre*.
precocious, *praecox*.
preconceived, *praeiudicatus*.
preconception, *praeiudicata opinio*.
preconcerted, *ex composito factus*.
precursor, *praecursor, praenuntius*.
predatory, *praedatorius, praedabundus*.
predecessor, in an office, *decessor*.

predetermine, *praefinire, praestituĕre.*
predicament, *difficultas, angustiae (-arum).*
predicate, subst. *attributio, attributum.*
predicate, v. *praedicare, dicĕre.*
predict, *praedicĕre.*
prediction, *praedictio, praedictum.*
predilection, *studium.*
predispose, *(animum) inclinare.*
predisposed, *propensus, proclivis.*
predisposition, *(animi) proclivitas, studium.*
predominance, *potentia, principatus (-ūs).*
predominant, *potens, praepollens*; = more numerous, *plures.*
predominate, *(prae)pollēre*; = be more numerous, *plures esse.*
preeminence, *praestantia, eminentia.*
preeminent, *praestans, praecipuus, egregius*; adv. *praecipue.*
preexist, *antea exstare* or *esse.*
preface, *prooemium, praefatio.*
prefatory; to make a few — remarks, *pauca praefari.*
prefect, *praefectus.*
prefecture, *praefectura.*
prefer, *anteponĕre, anteferre, praeferre*; with infin., *malle.*
preferable, *potior, melior*; adv. *potius.*
preferment, *honor* (= office).
prefix, v. *praeponĕre.*
pregnant, *praegnans, gravida*; of language, *pressus*; of events, *magni momenti.*
prejudge, *praeiudicare.*
prejudice, subst.: = premature judgment, *opinio praeiudicata*; = damage, *detrimentum.*
prejudice, v.: to be —d about a matter, *rem praeiudicatam habēre*; see also harm.
preliminary, adj.: a — inquiry, *praeiudicium*; — remarks, *praefatio.*
prelude, *prooemium.* Transf., *prolusio.*
premature, *immaturus, praeproperus*; adv. *ante tempus.*
premeditate, *praemeditari, cogitare.*
premeditation, *praemeditatio.*
premise, premises: in logic, —s, *principia (-orum)*; minor —, *adsumptio*; major —, *propositio*; —s, = building, *aedificium, domus.*
premise, v. *praefari, ponĕre.*
premium, *praemium.*
premonition, *monitio, monitum.*
preoccupation, *animus rei* (dat.) *deditus.*
preoccupy, = seize beforehand, *(prae)-occupare*; to be preoccupied about a thing, *totum in re versari.*
preparation, *praeparatio, apparatus (-ūs), meditatio* (of a lesson, etc.); to make —s, *parare.*
prepare, *(ap)parare, praeparare, instruĕre*; to — for war, *bellum (ap)parare*; to — a speech, lesson, etc., *meditari, commentari.*
preponderate; see predominance.
prepossess, = win over, *delenire, permulcēre.*
prepossession; see prejudice.
preposterous, *praeposterus.*
prerogative; see right.
presage, subst. *praesagium, augurium.*
presage, v.: = foreshow, *portendĕre, significare*; = forebode, *praesagire, augurari.*
prescient, *praesciens, sagax.*
prescribe, *praescribĕre.*
presence, *praesentia*; in my —, *coram me* (abl.); — of mind, *praesens animus.*
present, subst. *donum, munus.*
present, adj.: physically, *praesens*; to be —, *adesse*; of time, *praesens, hic*; at —, *nunc, hoc tempore*; for the —, *in praesentia, in praesens (tempus)*; gram. *praesens.* Adv., soon, *mox, brevi.*
present, v.: = bring forward, *offerre, obicĕre, praebēre*; to — oneself, *occurrĕre, obvenire*; = give, *donare, munerari, dare*; = introduce, *introducĕre, inducĕre.*
presentiment, *praesagitio, augurium*; to have a —, *praesagire.*
preservation, *conservatio*; = safety, *salūs (-ūtis).*
preserve, v. *(con)servare, tuēri* (=watch over), *sustinēre* (= uphold).
preserver, *(con)servator* (f. *servatrix*).
preside, *praesidēre, praeesse.*
presidency, *praefectura.*
president, *praefectus*; or use verb.
press, subst. *prelum, torcular* (for wine, etc.).
press, v.: transit., *premĕre, comprimĕre*; to — out, *exprimĕre*; = urge, harry, *premĕre, urgēre, instare*; intransit., to — on, *pergĕre, contendĕre.*
pressing: see urgent.
pressure, *pressus (-ūs) vis, pondus (-eris, n.).*
prestige, *nomen, gloria, fama.*
presume: = take liberties, *sibi adrogare* or *sumĕre, audēre*; = to suppose, *sumĕre, credĕre.*
presumption: = presumptuousness, *adrogantia*; = supposition, *coniectura, opinio.*
presumptuous, *adrogans*; adv. *adroganter.*
pretence, *simulatio, species*; without —, *sine fuco ac fallaciis.*
pretend, *simulare, fingĕre.*
pretender, *simulator*; to the throne, *qui regnum sibi adrogat.*
pretention: = claim, *postulatio*; = display, *ostentatio.*
preterite, gram., *praeteritum (tempus).*
preternaturally, *praeter naturam, mirabili quodam modo.*
pretext, *causa, simulatio, species*; to use as a —, *praetendĕre.*
prettiness, *concinnitas, venustas.*
pretty, adj. *bellus, pulcher, concinnus, lepidus*; adv. *belle, concinne, lepide.*
pretty, adv. *satis, admodum.*
prevail: = be prevalent, *esse, obtinēre*; = win, *vincĕre, superare*; to — upon, = persuade, *persuadēre, adducĕre.*
prevalent, *(per)vulgatus*; to become —, *increbrescĕre.*
prevaricate, *tergiversari.*
prevarication, *tergiversatio.*

prevent, *prohibēre, impedire.*
previous; see preceding.
prey, subst. *praeda*: a beast of —, *fera.*
prey, v. *praedari*; fig., to — upon, (*animum*) (*ex*)*edĕre, consumĕre.*
price, subst. *pretium*; — of corn, *annona*; at a high —, *magni* (*pretii*); to set a — on, (*rei,* dat.) *pretium constituĕre.*
priceless, *inaestimabilis.*
prick, v. *pungĕre, stimulare*; to — up one's ears, *aures erigĕre.*
prickle, *aculeus, spina.*
prickly, *aculeatus, spinosus.*
pride, *superbia, insolentia, adrogantia*; source of —, *decus* (*-oris*).
priest, *sacerdos, flamen*; high —, *pontifex maximus.*
priestess, *sacerdos.*
priesthood, *sacerdotium.*
prim, (*nimis*) *diligens.*
primal, primeval; see ancient, first.
primary, *primus, principalis*; = chief, *praecipuus.* Adv. *initio, primo; praecipue.*
prime, subst.: of life, *integra aetas*; to be in one's —, *vigēre, florēre*; — of anything, *flos, robur.*
prime, adj.: = first, *primus*; = excellent, *eximius, optimus.*
primitive, *priscus, antiquus.*
prince: = king's son, *filius regis, regulus*; = king, *rex.*
princess, *mulier regii generis, filia regis.*
principal, subst.: of a school, *magister*; = capital, *caput, sors.*
principal, adj., *primus, princeps, praecipuus* (= chief). Adv. *maxime, praecipue.*
principle, *principium, elementum, ratio*; of conduct, *institutum, praeceptum*; a man of —, *homo constans* or *gravis*; want of —, *levitas.*
print, v. *imprimĕre.*
prior, adj. *prior*; see also preceding.
prison, *carcer, vincula* (*-orum,* =chains), *custodia* (=confinement).
prisoner: a — of war, *captivus* (f. *captiva*); in gen. (*homo*) *captus, comprehensus*; = a person on trial, render by *reus.*
pristine, *pristinus, priscus, antiquus.*
prithee! *quaeso, cedo.*
privacy, *solitudo.*
private, *privatus, proprius, domesticus*; = secret, *arcanus, secretus*; a — soldier, *miles gregarius, manipularis.* Adv. *clam, secreto, occulte, privatim* (= in a private capacity).
privateer, *navis praedatoria.*
privation, *inopia, egestas.*
privet, *ligustrum.*
privilege, *ius* (*iuris,* n.), *praecipuum, beneficium.*
privy, adj.: see private; — to, *conscius rei* (genit.); — council, *consilium regis*; — purse, *fiscus.*
prize, subst.: = reward, *praemium, palma*; = prey, *praeda.*
prize, v. *magni aestimare.*
pro and con, *in utramque partem.*
probability, *veri similitudo, probabilitas.*
probable, *veri similis; probabilis* (of guesses, etc.); adv. *probabiliter.*
probe, v. *scrutari, rimari.*
probity, *probitas.*
problem, *quaestio.*
problematical, *dubius, incertus.*
proceed, *pergere, procedĕre, progredi*; = to act, *agĕre, facĕre*; to — from, *emanare, oriri*; to — against, in the courts, *litem intendĕre.*
proceeding, proceedings, in gen., *acta* (*-orum*); legal, *lis, actio.*
proceeds, *reditus* (*-ūs*), *fructus* (*-ūs*).
process, *ratio*; legal, *lis, actio.*
procession, *pompa.*
proclaim, *declarare, pronuntiare, edicĕre* (by decree).
proclamation, *pronuntiatio, declaratio, praedicatio*; = thing proclaimed, *edictum.*
proconsul, *pro consule.*
proconsular, *proconsularis.*
procrastinate, *differre, procrastinare.*
procrastination, *procrastinatio.*
procreate, *procreare.*
procreation, *procreatio.*
procure, (*com*)*parare*; to — in addition, *adquirĕre.*
prodigal, subst. *nepos.*
prodigal, adj. *prodigus, profusus, effusus.*
prodigality, *effusio, prodigentia.*
prodigious, *ingens, immanis.*
prodigy, *prodigium, portentum, miraculum.*
produce, subst. *fructus* (*-ūs*).
produce, v.: = bring forward, *proferre, exhibēre, producĕre*; = bring into existence, (*pro*)*creare, gignĕre, parĕre*; = cause, bring about, *facĕre, efficĕre.*
product, production, *opus* (*-eris* = work); an artistic —, *artificium.*
productive, *ferax, uber.*
productiveness, *ubertas.*
proem, *prooemium.*
profanation, *violatio, nefas.*
profane, adj.: = not sacred, *profanus*; = impious, *impius*; adv. *impie.*
profane, v. *violare, polluĕre.*
profanity, *impietas.*
profess, *profiteri.*
professed, *manifestus, apertus.*
profession: = declaration, *professio*; = employment, *munus* (*-eris,* n.), *ars.*
proffer, v. *promittĕre*; see offer.
proficiency, *scientia, peritia.*
proficient, *peritus, sciens.*
profit, subst. *lucrum, quaestus* (*-ūs*), *fructus* (*-ūs*).
profit, v.: = be of service, *prodesse*; = gain advantage, *proficĕre, lucrum facĕre.*
profitable, *utilis, fructuosus*; adv. *utiliter.*
profitless, *inutilis, vanus.*
profligacy, subst. *homo perditus* or *profligatus.*
profligate, adj. *perditus, flagitiosus, profligatus*; adv. *perdite.*
profound, *altus.* Adv. *penitus* (= completely).
profundity, *altitudo.*
profuse, *effusus, profusus.*

profusion, *largitas, effusio.*
progenitor, *parens.*
progeny, *progenies.*
prognostic, *signum.*
prognosticate; see forebode.
programme, *libellus.*
progress, subst.: = journey, *iter*; = advance, *progressus* (*-ūs*); to make much —, *multum proficĕre.*
progress, v. *progredi, proficĕre.*
progression, *progressus* (*-ūs*).
prohibit, *vetare, interdicĕre.*
prohibition, *interdictum.*
project, subst. *consilium, propositum.*
project, v. *prominēre, eminēre, exstare.*
projectile, (*telum*) *missile.*
proletariat, *proletarii* (*-orum*).
prolific; see fruitful.
prolix, *longus, verbosus.*
prologue, (*pro*)*ducĕre, prorogare, extendĕre.*
prolongation, *productio, prorogatio.*
prolonged, *longus, diuturnus.*
promenade, *ambulatio.*
prominence, *eminentia*; = importance *dignitas, auctoritas.*
prominent: = projecting, *prominens,* or render by verb; = distinguished, *praestans, egregius, inlustris.*
promiscuous, *promiscuus*; adv. *promiscue, temere.*
promise, subst., *promissum, fides.*
promise, v.: = to make a —, *promittĕre, pollicēri, fidem dare*; = to show —, *bonam spem ostendĕre.*
promising, adj. *bonae spei* (genit.).
promissory; a — note, *chirographum.*
promontory, *promontorium*; small —, *lingua, li*(*n*)*gula.*
promote: of person, *provehĕre, producĕre*; of causes, etc., (*ad*)*iuvare, amplificare; consulĕre, prodesse,* with dat.
promoter, *auctor, adiutor, fautor.*
promotion: = rise to higher position, *dignitatis accessio*; = furthering, *amplificatio.*
prompt, *promptus*; adv. *cito.*
prompt, v., = suggest, *subicĕre.*
prompter, *qui rem homini subicit.*
promptitude, *celeritas.*
promulgate, *promulgare.*
promulgation, *promulgatio.*
prone: = face-down, *pronus*; =liable, inclined, *pronus, proclivis, propensus.*
proneness, *proclivitas.*
prong, *dens.*
pronoun, *pronomen.*
pronounce, *enuntiare, exprimĕre, dicĕre*; formally, *pronuntiare, declarare.*
pronunciation, *appellatio, locutio.*
proof, subst.: = act of proving, *probatio, demonstratio*; = means of proving, *argumentum, signum, indicium*; = trial, *experimentum*; to put to the —, *experiri, temptare.*
prop, subst. *adminiculum.*
prop, v. *fulcire*; see support.
propagate: of plants, *propagare, inserĕre*; of living creatures, *gignĕre, procreare*; abstr., *vulgare, serĕre.*
propagation: *propagatio*; abstr., use verb.
propel, *propellĕre, impellĕre.*
propensity, *proclivitas, animus proclivis.*
proper: = peculiar, characteristic, *proprius*; = genuine, *verus, germanus*; = becoming, *decorus, honestus*; it is —, *decet*; = suitable, *aptus, idoneus.* Adv. *proprie, vere; apte.*
property: = characteristic, *proprietas*; = what one owns, *bona* (*-orum*), *res*; private —, *res familiaris*; inherited —, *patrimonium.*
prophecy: the act, *praedictio, vaticinatio*; = what is prophesied, *praedictum.*
prophesy, *praedicĕre, praenuntiare, vaticinari.*
prophet, *vates.*
prophetic, *divinus, fatidicus, vaticinus*; adv. *divinitus.*
propinquity; see nearness.
propitiate, *placare, propitiare.*
propitiation, *placatio*; means of —, *piaculum.*
propitious, *propitius, faustus*; adv. *fauste.*
proportion: = portion, *pars, portio*; = relationship, *ratio*; in —, *pro portione, pro rata parte*; in — to, *pro,* with abl.
proposal, *condicio, sententia, consilium.*
propose: = bring forward for consideration, *ponĕre*; to — a law, *legem ferre* or *rogare*; = intend, *cogitare, in animo habēre.*
proposer: of a law, *legis lator*; in gen., *auctor.*
proposition, in logic, *pronuntiatum, propositio.*
proprietor, *possessor, dominus.*
propriety, *convenientia, decorum, honestas.*
prorogation, *prorogatio.*
prorogue, *prorogare.*
prosaic, *ieiunus, frigidus.*
proscribe, *proscribĕre.*
proscription, *proscriptio.*
prose, (*soluta*) *oratio.*
prosecute: = carry out, *exsequi, perficĕre*; = bring action against, *iudicio persequi, accusare.*
prosecution: = carrying out, *exsecutio*; at law, *accusatio, actio, lis.*
prosecutor, *accusator.*
proselyte, *discipulus.*
prospect: = view, *prospectus* (*-ūs*); = hope, *spes.*
prospective, *futurus*; adv. *in futurum.*
prosper: transit., *fortunare, secundare*; intransit., *florēre, vigēre.*
prosperity, *res* (plur) *secundae* or *prosperae; prosperitas.*
prosperous, *secundus, prosper*(*us*); adv. *bene, prospere.*
prostitute, subst. *meretrix, scortum.*
prostrate, v. (*pro*)*sternĕre*; to — oneself before a person, *ad pedes hominis procumbĕre*; to be —d by grief, *in maerore iacēre.*
protect, *tuēri, defendĕre,* (*pro*)*tegĕre, custodire.*
protection, *tutela, praesidium, custodia;* to take under one's —, *in fidem recipĕre.*

protector, *defensor, propugnator, custos.*
protest, subst. *recusatio.*
protest, v.: = state positively, *adseverare, adfirmare*; to — against, *recusare, intercedĕre.*
prototype, *exemplum, exemplar.*
protract, (*pro*)*ducĕre, prorogare, trahĕre.*
protrude: transit., *protrudĕre*; intransit., *protrudi, prominēre.*
protuberance, *tuber, gibber.*
proud, *superbus, adrogans, fastidiosus*; adv. *superbe, adroganter.*
prove: = show clearly, *probare ostendĕre, docēre*; to — oneself, *se praestare* or *praebēre*; intransit., = to turn out, *fieri, evadĕre, exire.*
provender, *pabulum.*
proverb, *proverbium*; according to the —, *ut aiunt.*
proverbial, proverbially, *proverbii loco* (= as a proverb).
provide: = supply, furnish, (*com*)*parare, praebēre, suppeditare*; to — for, *consulĕre* or *providēre*, with dat.; of laws, = require, order, *iubēre.*
provided that, *dum, dummodo* (with subj.).
provided with, adj. *instructus, ornatus, praeditus.*
providence, *providentia.*
provident, *providus, diligens.* Adv. *diligenter.*
providentially, *divinitus.*
province: = duty, *provincia, officium*; = district, *regio, provincia.*
provincial, *provincialis*; = countrified, *rusticus, agrestis, inurbanus.*
provision, = stipulation, *condicio, cautio.*
provision, v. (*oppidum*) *cibo instruĕre.*
provisional, render by phrase, *ad* or *in tempus.*
provisions, *cibus, cibaria* (*-orum*), *alimentum*; for an army, *commeatus* (*-ūs*).
provoke: = call forth, (*com*)*movēre, ciēre*; = make angry, *inritare, lacessĕre*; to — to action, *incitare, concitare, impellĕre.*
provoking, *molestus.*
prow, *prora.*
prowess, *virtūs* (*-ūtis*).
prowl, *vagari, peragrare.*
proximity; see nearness.
proxy, *procurator, vicarius.*
prudence, *prudentia, cautio, circumspectio.*
prudent, *prudens, cautus, circumspectus*; adv. *caute, considerate.*
prudish, *rusticus, severus, tetricus.*
prune, (*am*)*putare, recidĕre.*
pruner, of trees, *putator.*
pruning, subst. *putatio.*
pruning-hook, *falx.*
pry, *rimari, investigare, scrutari.*
pshaw! *phy!*
public, subst. *homines* (*-um*, plur.), *populus, vulgus.*
public, *publicus, communis* (= not private); to show oneself in —, *in publicum prodire*; — life, *respublica, forum*; the — interest, *respublica*; at the — expense, *sumptu publico, publice*; in a — capacity, *publice*; — opinion, *vulgi opinio.* Adv. publicly, in —, *aperte, palam, coram omnibus.*
publican, *publicanus*; = inn-keeper, *caupo.*
publication, *praedicatio*; of a book, *editio libri*; = book, *liber.*
publicity, *celebritas, lux.*
publish, *proferre, ēdĕre.*
pudding, *placenta.*
puddle, *stagnum.*
puerile, *puerilis, ineptus.*
puff, v. *anhelare*; to — out, = inflate, *inflare.*
pugilism, *pugilatus* (*-ūs*), *pugilatio.*
pugilist, *pugil.*
pull, v.: = twitch, tweak, *vellĕre, vellicare*; = drag, *trahĕre*; to — out, (*e*)*vellĕre, eripĕre.*
pullet, *pullus* (*gallinaceus*).
pulley, *trochlea.*
pulsate, *palpitare, agitari, moveri.*
pulse: of the blood, *venarum pulsus* (*-ūs*); the vegetable, *legumen.*
pulverize, *in pulverem redigĕre.*
pumice, *pumex*; of —, adj., *pumiceus.*
pump, subst. *antlia.*
pump, v. *exhaurire.*
pun, subst. *facetiae* (*-arum*), *logos* (or *-us*).
punch, subst., the drink, *calidum*; — bowl, *cratera*; see also blow.
punch, v. *tundĕre.*
punctilious, *diligens*; in religious matters, *religiosus*; adv. *diligenter, accurate.*
punctual, *diligens*; adv. *diligenter, ad tempus.*
punctuality, *diligentia* (= care).
punctuate, *distinguĕre, interpungĕre.*
punctuation, *distinctio, interpunctio*; — mark, *interpunctum.*
puncture, subst. *punctum.*
puncture, v. (*com*)*pungĕre.*
pungent, *acer, acutus*; adv. *acriter, acute.*
punish, *punire, poenā adficĕre, ulcisci*; to be —ed, *puniri, poenas dare.*
punisher, *vindex, ultor.*
punishment, *castigatio, animadversio*; = what is inflicted, *poena, supplicium, multa.*
puny, *pusillus, exiguus.*
pupil: of the eye, *pupula*; at school, *alumnus* (f. *alumna*), *discipulus* (f. *discipula*).
puppy, *catulus, catellus.*
purchasable, *venalis.*
purchase, subst.: as act, *emptio*; = thing bought, *merx, quod emptum est.*
purchase, v. (*co*)*emĕre, mercari.*
purchaser, *emptor.*
pure: physically, *purus*; pure and simple, *merus, sincerus*; morally, *purus, integer, sanctus, castus.* Adv.: = wholly, *prorsus, plane*; morally, *pure, integre, caste.*
purgation, *purgatio, lustratio.*
purge, *purgare.*
purification, *purgatio*; ceremonial —, *lustratio.*

purify, *(ex)purgare, purum facĕre; lustrare* (with ceremonial).
purity: moral, *integritas, sanctimonia, sanctitas*; of language, *integritas, sinceritas.*
purloin, *avertĕre, surripĕre, furari.*
purple, subst. *purpura, ostrum, conchylium, color purpureus.*
purport; see meaning, mean.
purpose, subst. *propositum, consilium, animus, voluntas*; for the — of, *(eo consilio) ut*; on —, *consulto, de industria*; to no —, *frustra, nequiquam*; to the —, *ad rem.*
purpose, v. *statuĕre, cogitare, in animo habēre.*
purposeless, *vanus, inanis, inritus.*
purposely; see purpose.
purse, *marsupium, zona, crumena.*
pursuant to, *ex* (with abl.), *secundum* (with acc.).
pursue, *(per)sequi, insequi, insectari.*
pursuit: = search, *consectatio*; = occupation, *negotium, occupatio, artificium.*
push, subst. *(im)pulsus (-ūs), impetus (-ūs).*
push, v. *(im)pellĕre, (pro)trudĕre, urgēre*; intransit., to — on, *contendĕre, instare, pergĕre.*
pushing, adj. *protervus, confidens.*
pusillanimity, *timiditas; animus timidus.*
pusillanimous, *timidus, abiectus*; adv. *timide, abiecte.*
put, *ponĕre, (con)locare*; — away, *abdĕre*; — back, *reponĕre*; — down, *deponĕre, demittĕre; comprimĕre* (= suppress); — on, of clothes, *induĕre, sumĕre*; — off, of clothes, *exuĕre, (de)ponĕre*; — off, = postpone, *differre*; — out, *eicĕre, extrudĕre, expellĕre; exstinguĕre* (= quench); — together, *conferre, componĕre*; — up, *erigĕre, statuĕre*; — up with (= tolerate), *ferre, tolerare.*
putative, *falsus; qui dicitur esse.*
putrefy, *putescĕre*; to cause to —, *putrefacĕre.*
putrid, *putridus, putidus.*
puzzle, *quaestio, aenigma, nodus.*
puzzle, v. *dubium facĕre, impedire*; to be —d, *dubitare, haerēre.*
puzzling, *difficilis, ambiguus.*
Pygmy, *pygmaeus*; = any dwarf, *nanus, pumilio, pumilus.*
pyramid, *pyramis.*
pyre, *rogus, pyra.*
Pyrenees, *Pyrenaei montes, Pyrenaeum.*

Q

quadripartite, *quadripartitus.*
quadruped, *quadrupes.*
quadruple, *quadruplex.*
quaff, v. *ducĕre, haurire.*
quag(mire), *palūs (-ūdis).*
quail, subst. *coturnix.*
quail, v. *animo deficĕre, pavēre.*
quaint, *lepidus, facetus, concinnus* = odd, *insolitus, novus.*
quake, *tremĕre, contremiscĕre.*
qualification: = right, *ius (iuris,* n.); = limitation, *exceptio, condicio.*
qualified, *idoneus, aptus, dignus.*
qualify, v.: transit., = make fit, *idoneum reddĕre, instituĕre*; =modify, restrict, *circumscribĕre, deminuĕre*; intransit., *idoneum esse* (or *habēri*).
quality: = nature, character, *natura, ingenium, indoles*; of what —? *qualis?*; of such a —, *talis*; good —, *virtūs (-ūtis)*; bad —, *vitium*; =kind, sort, *genus (-eris,* n.), *nota* (of wine); a lady of —, *generosa femina.*
qualm, *fastidium* (= disgust), *nausea, nauseola* (= squeamishness); — of conscience, *conscientia (mala).*
quantity, = number, *numerus*; a certain —, *aliquot, aliquantum*; a large —, *multitudo, copia, vis*; — in scansion, *mensura, quantitas.*
quarrel, subst. *iurgium, altercatio, rixa.*
quarrel, v. *iurgare, altercari, rixari.*
quarrelsome, *litigiosus, pugnax.*
quarry, subst.: a stone —, *lapicidinae (-arum), lautumiae (-arum)*; = prey, *praeda.*
quart, (as measure) *duo sextarii.*
quartan, adj. *quartanus.*
quarter: = fourth part, *quarta pars, quadrans*; = district, *vicus, regio*; = mercy, *venia.*
quarter, v. *quadrifariam dividĕre*; to — troops, *milites per hospitia disponĕre.*
quarterly, *trimestris*; adv. *tertio quoque mense.*
quarters, *hospitium, habitatio, tectum*; milit., winter — (for troops), *hiberna (-orum)*, summer —, *aestiva (-orum)*; at close —, *comminus*; to come to close —, *manum conserĕre.*
quash, *rescindĕre, infirmare.*
quaver; see tremble.
quay, *margo, crepido.*
queen, *regina.*
queer, *novus, insolitus, mirus.*
quell, *opprimĕre, comprimĕre.*
quench, *exstinguĕre, restinguĕre.*
querulous, *queribundus, querulus.*
query; see question.
quest; see seek, search.
question, subst.: = inquiry, *quaestio, interrogatum*; to ask —s, *(inter)rogare*; = doubt, dispute, *controversia, dubium*; there is no — that, *haud dubium est quin.*
question, v.: = to ask questions, *(inter)rogare, percontari, quaerĕre*; = to doubt, *dubitare.*
questionable, *incertus, ambiguus, dubius.*
questioning, subst. *(inter)rogatio, percontatio.*
quibble, subst. *captio, cavillatio.*
quibble, v. *cavillari.*
quibbling, adj. *captiosus.*
quick, = prompt, active, *promptus, alacer, expeditus*; — witted, *astutus, sagax, catus.* Adv., = fast, *cito, celeriter.*
quicken: = accelerate, *accelerare, maturare*; in gen., = stimulate, *incitare, stimulare, incendĕre.*

quicklime, *calx viva.*
quickness, *velocitas*; of intellect, *ingenii acumen, sagacitas.*
quicksand, *syrtis.*
quicksilver, *argentum vivum.*
quiet, subst. *tranquillitas, pax, otium, silentium.*
quiet, adj. *quietus, tranquillus, taciturnus* (= not talking); to be —, *quiescĕre, silēre, tacēre.* Adv. *quiete, tranquille, silentio* (= in silence).
quiet, quieten, v. *tranquillare, pacare.*
quill, *penna; spina*; for striking strings, *plectrum.*
quinquennial, *quinquennalis.*
quintessence, *flos.*
quip, *dictum.*
quit, *decedĕre* (*de loco*).
quite, adv.: = completely, *admodum, prorsus, omnino, funditus*; = fairly, moderately, *satis.*
quiver, subst. *pharetra.*
quiver, v. *tremĕre, micare.*
quivering, adj. *tremulus.*
quoit, *discus.*
quotation, *prolatio, commemoratio*; = passage quoted, *locus adlatus.*
quote, *adferre, proferre,* (*com*)*memorare.*
quoth he, or she, *inquit, ait.*

R

rabbit, *cuniculus.*
rabble, *multitudo, turba, plebecula.*
rabid, *rabidus*; adv. *rabide.*
race, subst.: = family, people, *genus* (*-eris*, n.), *gens*; = contest of speed, *cursus* (*-ūs*), *certamen, curriculum.*
race, v. (*cursus*) *certare.*
race-course, *curriculum, stadium, circus.*
race-horse, *equus, celes.*
raciness, *sucus, sapor.*
rack, subst., for torture, *eculeus, tormentum.*
rack, v. *torquēre,* (*ex*)*cruciare, vexare.*
racket, = noise, *strepitus* (*-ūs*).
racy, *salsus.*
radiance, *fulgor, candor, splendor.*
radiant, *clarus, candidus, splendidus.*
radiate, *fulgēre, radiare.*
radical, adj.: = innate, *insitus, innatus*; = complete, *totus*; in politics, *novarum rerum cupidus* or *studiosus.* Adv. *radicitus, funditus, prorsus, omnino.*
radish, *raphanus, radix.*
raft, *ratis.*
rafter, *tignum, trabs.*
rag, *pannus.*
rage, subst. *rabies, furor, ira* (= anger).
rage, v. *furĕre, saevire.*
raging, *furens, furibundus, saevus.*
ragged: of people, *pannosus*; of clothes, *lacer.*
rail, subst. *tignum transversum.*
rail, v.: to — off, (*con*)*saepire*; to — at, *maledicĕre, conviciari.*
railing, subst. *saepimentum, saepes.*
raillery, *iocus, cavillatio.*
raiment, *vestis, vestitus* (*-ūs*).
rain, subst. *pluvia, imber.*
rain, v.: it —s, *pluit.*
rainbow, *arcus* (*-ūs*) *pluvius.*
rain-cloud, *nimbus.*
rainy, *pluvius, pluvialis.*
raise: = lift, (*ex*)*tollĕre,* (*e*)*levare, erigĕre*; = increase, *augēre*; = promote, elevate, *producĕre, provehĕre*; = arouse, *excitare, erigĕre, tollĕre.*
rake, subst. *rastellus, pecten*; = prodigal roué, *ganeo, nepos, vappa.*
rake, v. *radĕre, pectine verrĕre.*
rakish, *profligatus, dissolutus.*
rally, v.: transit.; to — troops, *ordines restituĕre*; = banter, *ludĕre, irridēre*; intransit., = recover, *se conligĕre, convalescĕre* (from illness).
ram, subst. *aries.*
ramble, subst. *ambulatio.*
ramble, v. *errare, vagari, ambulare* (= walk about).
rambling, *vagus.*
rampant, *ferox, superbus*; to be — *superbire.*
rampart, *vallum, agger; praesidium.*
rancid, *rancidus.*
rancorous, *malevolus, malignus, invidus*; adv. *maligne, infeste.*
rancour, *odium, invidia, malevolentia.*
random; at —, *temere.*
range, subst.: = row, *ordo, series*; a — of mountains, *montes perpetui*; of a missile, (*teli*) *coniectus* (*-ūs*).
rank, subst.: of soldiers, *ordo*; = degree, station, *ordo, gradus* (*-ūs*), *locus.*
rank, adj.: of plants, *luxuriosus*; of smell, *foetidus, graveolens*; = great, extreme, *maximus, summus.*
rank, v. *numerare, habēre.*
rankle, v. *mordēre, pungĕre.*
ransack: = plunder, *diripĕre, spoliare*; = search thoroughly, *rimari,* (*per*)*scrutari.*
ransom, subst.: = money paid, *pretium, pecunia*; = the arrangement, *redemptio.*
ransom, v. *redimĕre.*
rant, v. *declamare, ampullari.*
rap, subst. *pulsatio.*
rap, v. *pulsare.*
rapacious, *rapax, avidus.*
rapacity, *rapacitas, aviditas.*
rapid, subst. *vertex, gurges.*
rapid, *rapidus, citus, celer*; adv. *rapide, cito, celeriter.*
rapidity, *rapiditas, celeritas.*
rapine, *rapina.*
rapture, (*summa*) *voluptas, exsultatio.*
rare: = uncommon, *rarus, inusitatus*; = thin, *rarus, tenuis*; = exceptional, *singularis, eximius.* Adv. *raro.*
rarefy, *extenuare.*
rarity, = fewness, *raritas, paucitas.*
rascal, *homo scelestus, furcifer, verbero.*
rascality, *scelus* (*-eris*, n.).
rascally, *scelestus, nequam.*
rash, *praeceps, inconsultus, temerarius*; adv. *inconsulte, temere.*
rashness, *temeritas.*
rat, *mus.*
rate, subst.: = price, *pretium*; — of interest, *usura*; — of exchange, *collybus*; = tax, *vectigal, tributum*; at any —, *certe, utique.*

rate, v., = value, *aestimare.*
rather: = in preference, *potius, libentius, prius*; I would —, *malo*; = somewhat, *aliquantum.*
ratification, *sanctio*; or use verb.
ratify, *sancire, ratum facĕre, confirmare.*
ration, *demensum, cibaria* (*-orum*).
rational, *ratione praeditus;* (*rationi*) *consentaneus*; to act —ly, *prudenter agĕre.*
rationality; see *ratio.*
rattle, subst.: = noise, *crepitus* (*-ūs*), *strepitus* (*-ūs*); a child's —, *crepitaculum, crepitacillum.*
rattle, v. *crepare, strepĕre.*
ravage, (*per*)*vastare,* (*de*)*populari.*
ravaging, *vastatio, populatio.*
rave, *furĕre, insanire.*
raven, *corvus.*
ravening, ravenous, *rapax, vorax.*
ravine, *fauces* (*-ium*).
raving, *furens, furibundus, insanus.*
ravish: = carry off, *rapĕre, abducĕre*; = debauch, (*con*)*stuprare.*
ravishing; see delightful.
raw, *crudus*; = inexperienced, *rudis, imperitus*; of weather, *frigidus, humidus.*
ray, *radius, iubar.*
raze, *solo* (*ad*)*aequare.*
razor, *novacula.*
reach, subst.: = grasp, capacity, *captus* (*-ūs*).
reach, v. = touch, get to, *tangĕre, contingĕre, attingĕre*; (*ad locum*) (*per*)*venire, accedĕre.*
react: to — upon, = affect, *adficĕre*; to — to, (*rem*) *ferre* or *accipere,* with adv.
reactionary, *qui* (*rempublicam*) *ad pristinum statum revocare vult.*
read, *legĕre, evolvĕre*; to — through, *perlegĕre*; to — aloud, *recitare*; well —, of a person, *litteratus.*
reader, *legens, qui legit.*
readiness, *animus promptus* or *paratus*; — of speech, *volubilitas linguae, lingua prompta.*
reading, subst. *lectio*; a — aloud, *recitatio.*
ready, *paratus, promptus*; — money, *pecunia praesens* or *numerata*; to make —, (*com*)*parare, instruĕre*; to be —, *praesto esse.* Adv., = willingly, *prompto* or *parato animo, libenter.*
real, *verus, sincerus*; — estate, *fundus, praedium.* Adv. *revera, vere.*
realistic, to be, *veritatem imitari.*
reality, *res* (*vera*), *veritas.*
realization, = completion, *effectus* (*-ūs*).
realize: = effect, *efficĕre, perficĕre*; = understand, *intellegĕre, comprehendĕre*; of money, *pecuniam redigĕre.*
realm, *civitas, respublica, regnum.*
reap, (*de*)*metĕre, messem facĕre*; fig., *fructum capĕre, percipĕre.*
reaper, *messor.*
reaping-hook, *falx.*
reappear, *redire, rursus apparēre.*
rear, subst.; use adj. *extremus* or *novissimus,* with *agmen* or *acies*; to form the — guard, *agmen claudĕre* or *cogĕre.*
rear, v. = bring up, *alĕre, educare.*
reason, subst.: = cause, *causa, ratio*; for this (or that) —, *ideo, idcirco*; by — of, *propter, ob*; there is no — why, *non est cur,* with subj.; for no —, *temere*; as a faculty, *ratio, mens, consilium.*
reason, v. *ratiocinari, reputare*; to — with another person, *disceptare, disputare.*
reasonable: of persons, *rationis particeps, prudens*; = fair, (*rationi*) *consentaneus, aequus, iustus.* Adv. *ratione*; = adequately, *satis.*
reasonableness: = rationality, *ratio*; = fairness, *aequitas, moderatio.*
reasoner, *disputator.*
reasoning, *ratio, ratiocinatio.*
reassert, *iterare* (= repeat).
reassure, (*animum*) *confirmare, erigĕre.*
rebel, subst. *homo seditiosus, hostis patriae.*
rebel, v. *seditionem* (*com*)*movĕre, deficĕre, desciscĕre.*
rebellion, *seditio, defectio, motus* (*-ūs*).
rebellious, *seditiosus, turbulentus, novarum rerum cupidus*; adv. *seditiose, turbulente*(*r*).
rebound, v. *repelli, resilire.*
rebuff, subst. *repulsa.*
rebuff, v. *repellĕre, reicĕre.*
rebuild, *restituĕre, reficĕre.*
rebuke, subst. *reprehensio, vituperatio, obiurgatio.*
rebuke, v. *reprehendĕre, vituperare, obiurgare.*
rebuker, *obiurgator.*
rebut, *redarguĕre, repellĕre, refellĕre.*
recall, subst. *revocatio.*
recall, v. *revocare*; to — to mind, *recordari, in memoriam revocare.*
recant, *recantare.*
recantation, *receptus* (*-ūs*).
recapitulate, *enumerare, commemorare.*
recapitulation, *enumeratio.*
recapture, v. *recipĕre.*
recast, *reficĕre.*
recede, *recedĕre, retro cedĕre.*
receipt, = act of receiving, *acceptio,* or use verb; in a ledger, a —, *acceptum*; to enter as a —, *acceptum referre.*
receive, *accipĕre, excipĕre, recipĕre.*
receiver, *receptor* (f. *receptrix*).
recent, *recens, novus*; adv. *nuper, recens.*
receptacle, *recaptaculum, cella, horreum.*
reception, *acceptio, hospitium* (in a house).
receptive, *docilis.*
receptiveness, *docilitas.*
recess, *recessus* (*-ūs*), *latibulum.*
reciprocal, *mutuus*; adv. *mutuo, invicem.*
reciprocate, *inter se dare.*
recital, *narratio, commemoratio.*
recitation, *recitatio.*
recite, *recitare*; = narrate, (*com*)*memorare, dicĕre,* (*e*)*narrare.*

reckless, *neglegens, temerarius, imprudens*; adv. *neglegenter, temere, imprudenter.*
recklessness, *imprudentia, neglegentia, temeritas.*
reckon, = count, calculate, *computare*; see also consider.
reckoning, subst. *ratio, computatio.*
reclaim, v.: = ask back, *repetĕre; reposcĕre*; = reform, *corrigĕre, emendare.*
recline, v. *se reclinare, recumbĕre.*
recluse, *homo solitarius.*
recognizance, *sponsio, vadimonium.*
recognize: = know again, *agnoscĕre, cognoscĕre, noscitare*; = acknowledge, *noscĕre*; = approve, *(com)probare.*
recoil, *resilire, recellĕre*; to — in horror, *refugĕre.*
recollect, *(com)meminisse, reminisci, recordari.*
recollection, *memoria, recordatio.*
recommence, v.: transit., *redintegrare, renovare*; intransit., *renasci, renovari.*
recommend, *commendare, probare.*
recommendation, *commendatio, laus, laudatio.*
recommendatory, *commendaticius.*
recompense, subst. *remuneratio, praemium.*
recompense, v. *remunerari.*
reconcile, *placare, reconciliare, in gratiam reducĕre*; = make congruous, *accommodare.*
reconciliation, *reconciliatio gratiae.*
recondite, *reconditus, exquisitus.*
reconnoitre, *explorare, (pro)speculari.*
reconsider, *denuo considerare.*
record, v. *perscribĕre, in tabulas referre.*
record-office, *tabularium.*
records, *tabulae (-arum), historia; annales (-ium,* = chronicles).
recount, *referre, (e)narrare, (com)memorare.*
recourse: to have — to, *confugĕre, se conferre (ad)*; = stoop to, *descendĕre (ad).*
recover, v.: transit., *recuperare, recipĕre, reparare*; intransit., *refici, convalescĕre, se conligĕre.*
recovery, *recuperatio*; in health, *salus* or *sanitas restituta.*
recreant; see coward.
recreate, *renovare, recreare.*
recreation, *requies, (animi) remissio.*
recrimination, *(mutua) accusatio.*
recruit, subst. *tiro.*
recruit, v. *recreare, reficĕre*; milit., = enrol, *conscribĕre, delectum habēre.*
recruiting, subst. *delectus (-ūs), conquisitio.*
rectification, *correctio, emendatio.*
rectify, *corrigĕre, emendare.*
rectilinear, *(di)rectus.*
rectitude, *probitas, integritas, honestas.*
recumbent, *(re)supinus, recubans.*
red, *ruber*; of the hair, *rufus, rutilus*; to be —, *rubēre*; the — Sea, *Sinus Arabicus.*
redden, v.: transit., *rubefacĕre*; intransit., *rubescĕre.*
redeem, *redimĕre, liberare* (= set free).
redeemer, *liberator, vindex.*
redemption, *redemptio, liberatio.*
red-hot, *candens, fervens.*
redness, *rubor.*
redolent, *redolens* (with acc.).
redouble, *ingeminare.*
redound, *redundare*; it —s to my credit, *est mihi honori.*
redress, subst. *satisfactio.*
redress, v. *restituĕre, compensare, sarcire.*
reduce: = to bring, *redigĕre, revocare* — to order, *in integrum reducĕre;* to be —ed to, *redire*; = diminish, *(im)minuĕre, deminuĕre*; = conquer, *vincĕre, expugnare.*
reduction, = diminution, *deminutio.*
redundancy, of style, *redundantio.*
redundant, *supervacaneus.*
re-echo, v.: transit., *referre*; intransit. *resonare.*
reed, *harundo, calamus.*
reedy, *harundineus.*
reef, = rocks, *scopuli, saxa.*
reef, v.: to — sails, *contrahĕre vela.*
reek, *fumare.*
reel, subst., = dance, *saltatio.*
reel, v. *titubare, vacillare.*
reestablish, *restituĕre.*
reestablishment, *restitutio.*
refer: to — a matter, *referre, deferre;* — to, = mention, *mentionem facĕre;* — to, = mean, be speaking of, *dicĕre, spectare.*
referee, *arbiter.*
reference, render by verbs; with — to, *quod attinet ad.*
refill, *replēre.*
refine: of liquids, *liquare*; of metals, *purgare.*
refined, *(ex)politus, urbanus, humanus.*
refinement, *urbanitas, humanitas*; of language, etc., *subtilitas.*
reflect, v.: transit., of light, *repercutĕre*; in gen., = show, *ostendĕre;* this —s credit on you, *hoc tibi est honori*; intransit., = think, *considerare, reputare, cogitare.*
reflection: of light, *repercussus (-ūs);* =image reflected, *imago*; =thought, *cogitatio, consideratio*; = blame, *reprehensio, vituperatio.*
reform, v.: of troops, *restituĕre, reficĕre*; = amend, *corrigĕre, emendare*; intransit., = get better, *se corrigĕre.*
reformation, *correctio, emendatio.*
reformer, *corrector, emendator.*
refract, *infringĕre.*
refractory, *contumax.*
refrain, subst. *carmen.*
refrain, v. *(se) abstinēre, temperare.*
refresh, *recreare, reficĕre.*
refreshment: abstr., *refectio*; = food, *cibus.*
refrigerate, *refrigerare.*
refuge, *perfugium, refugium, asylum;* to seek — at, *confugĕre ad.*
refugee, *fugitivus* (= runaway), *exsul* (= exile).
refund, *reddĕre, dissolvĕre.*
refusal, *recusatio, repudiatio.*
refuse, subst. *purgamentum faex, quisquiliae (-arum).*

refuse, v.: to — to give, *(de)negare*; to — to accept, *recusare, respuĕre, repudiare*; to — battle, *pugnam detrectare*; to — to do, *nolle, recusare.*
refutation, *refutatio, dissolutio.*
refute, *refellĕre, redarguĕre, refutare, convincĕre.*
regain, *recipĕre, reciperare.*
regal; see royal.
regale; see entertain, feast.
regalia, *insignia (-ium) regia.*
regard, subst.: = consideration, *respectus (-ūs), cura*; = esteem, *studium, amor*; Cicero sends his —s, *Cicero tibi salutem plurimam dicit*; see also reference.
regard, v.: = look at, *observare, intuēri*; = bear in mind, *respicĕre, spectare*; = consider, *ducĕre, habēre*; = concern, relate to, *attinēre* or *pertinēre ad.*
regardless, *neglegens, incuriosus.*
regency, *regni administratio, interregnum.*
regent, *interrex.*
regicide, *regis caedes* (= deed); *regis interfector* (= person).
regiment, *legio*; of cavalry, *turma (equitum).*
region, *regio, tractus (-ūs), locus.*
register, *liber, tabulae (-arum), album.*
register, v. *perscribĕre, in album referre.*
regret, subst. *dolor, desiderium* (= longing), *paenitentia* (= repentance).
regret, v.: = grieve, *dolēre*; = feel loss of, *desiderare, requirĕre*; = repent of an action, impers. *paenitet*; I — having done it, *paenitet me fecisse.*
regular: = correct, *iustus, legitimus, rectus*; — troops, *milites legionarii*; = constant, even, *certus, constans, aequabilis.* Adv., = correctly, *ordine, iuste, legitime, recte*; = constantly, evenly, *constanter, aequabiliter.*
regularity, *ordo, constantia, aequabilitas.*
regulate, *ordinare, dirigĕre, moderari.*
regulation, *administratio*; = an order, *iussum, praeceptum, lex.*
rehabilitate, *restituĕre.*
reign, subst., *regnum*; in your —, *te regnante* or *rege.*
reign, v. *regnare* (as king), *imperare* (as emperor).
reimburse, *(rem homini) reddĕre.*
rein, subst. *habena, frenum*; to pull in the —s, *habenas adducĕre*; to loosen the —s, *frenos dare.*
rein, v. *frenare.*
reinforce, *(con)firmare, augēre.*
reinforcement, *supplementum, novae copiae (-arum), subsidium.*
reinstate, *restituĕre.*
reiterate, *iterare.*
reject, *reicĕre, repudiare, respuĕre*; to — a bill, *legem antiquare.*
rejection, *reiectio, repudiatio, repulsa* (of a candidate).
rejoice, *gaudēre, laetari*; transit., *laetificare, exhilarare.*
rejoicing, *gaudium, laetitia.*
rejoin; see return or answer.
relapse, v. *recidĕre, relabi.*
relate, v. *(e)narrare, (com)memorare, referre*; — to, = concern, *spectare, pertinere, attinere ad.*
related, *propinquus, cognatus, consanguineus, adfinis* (by marriage).
relation, *ratio*; in — to, *ad, pro, erga*; —s, *familiaritas, necessitudo, amicitia*; see also relative and narrative.
relationship, *propinquitas, cognatio, adfinitas* (by marriage).
relative, subst.; see related.
relative, adj.; render by *spectare ad* (= relate to) or *comparare* (= compare).
relax, v.: transit. *(re)laxare, remittĕre*; intransit., *(re)languescĕre, relaxari.*
relaxation, *(animi) relaxatio, remissio.*
relay, subst. *equi per viam dispositi.*
release, subst. *liberatio, missio.*
release, v. *liberare, (ex)solvĕre, missum facĕre*; to — a slave, *manu mittĕre.*
relent, *molliri, iram remittĕre.*
relentless, *immisericors, inexorabilis, crudelis*; adv. *crudeliter.*
relevant, to be, *ad rem attinēre.*
reliance, *fides, fiducia.*
relic, relics, *reliquiae (-arum).*
relict, *vidua.*
relief: = alleviation, *(ad)levatio, sublevatio, levamen(tum)*; = aid, *auxilium, subsidium*; in art, *asperitas*; to engrave in —, *caelare.*
relieve: = lighten, ease, *(ad)levare, sublevare*; = take another's place, *excipĕre, succedĕre* (with dat.).
religion, *religio, cultus (-ūs) deorum.*
religious: of persons, *erga deos pius, sanctus, religiosus*; — observances, *ritūs (-uum), religiones (-um).* Adv. *pie, sancte, religiose.*
relinquish, *relinquĕre.*
relish, subst., = liking, fondness, *studium.*
relish, v.; see enjoy.
reluctant, *invitus, coactus*; to be —, *nolle.*
rely, *(con)fidĕre, fidem habēre, niti*; —ing upon, *fretus.*
remain: = stay, endure, *(per)manēre, remanēre, durare, morari* (= linger); = be left over, *restare, superesse.*
remainder, *residuum, quod restat.*
remaining, *reliquus, superstes.*
remains, *reliquiae (-arum).*
remand, subst. *comperendinatio.*
remand, v., *remittĕre*; legal, *(reum) ampliare, comperendinare.*
remark, subst. *dictum.*
remark, v.; see observe, say.
remarkable, *singularis, insignis, mirus*; adv. *singulariter, insigniter, mire.*
remedial, *salutaris.*
remedy, *remedium, medicina, medicamen(tum).*
remember, *meminisse, reminisci, recordari, memoriā tenēre.*
remembrance, *memoria, recordatio.*
remind, *(ad)monēre, commonēre, commonefacĕre.*
reminiscence, *recordatio*; —s, written up, *commentarii (-orum).*
remiss, *neglegens.*

remit: = send back, *remittĕre*; = let off (debts, etc.), *remittĕre, condonare.*
remittance, *pecunia.*
remnant; see remainder.
remonstrance, *reclamatio, (ad)monitio.*
remonstrate, *reclamare, reclamitare.*
remorse, *conscientia mala, paenitentia.*
remorseless; see pitiless.
remote, *remotus, disiunctus, longinquus.*
remoteness, *longinquitas.*
removal, *amotio*; to a new home, *(de)migratio.*
remove, v.: transit., *amovēre, submovēre, tollĕre, auferre*; = lead away, *abducĕre*; intransit., *se movēre, discedĕre, abire, migrare.*
remunerate, *remunerari.*
remuneration, *remuneratio, praemium.*
rend, *(di)scindĕre, divellere.*
render: = give (back), *reddĕre, referre, tribuĕre*; to — thanks, *gratias agĕre*; = make, cause to be, *facĕre, reddĕre.*
rendezvous, perhaps *locus ad conveniendum constitutus.*
renegade, *transfuga.*
renew: = make new, *(re)novare, reficĕre*; = begin again, repeat, *renovare, redintegrare, iterare.*
renewal, *renovatio, instauratio.*
renounce, *renuntiare, repudiare, se (re) abdicare.*
renovate: see renew.
renown, *fama, gloria, laus.*
renowned, *clarus, inlustris.*
rent, subst., *reditus (-ūs), vectigal, merces (-edis).*
renunciation, *abdicatio, repudiatio.*
reopen, *iterum aperire.*
repair, v., *reficĕre, reparare, restituĕre*; see also go.
reparation, *satisfactio.*
repast; see meal.
repay, *reddĕre, reponĕre, solvĕre.*
repayment, *solutio*; or use verb.
repeal, subst. *abrogatio.*
repeal, v. *rescindĕre, tollĕre, abrogare.*
repeat, *iterare, redintegrare.*
repeatedly, *identidem, saepenumero, etiam atque etiam.*
repel, *repellĕre, propulsare, reicĕre.*
repent, impers. *paenitet*; I — of having done that, *paenitet me id fecisse*; I — of the crime, *paenitet me sceleris.*
repentance, *paenitentia.*
repentant, *paenitens.*
repetition, *iteratio, repetitio.*
repine, *(con)queri.*
repining, *querela* (= complaint).
replace: = put back, *reponĕre, restituĕre*; to — by another, *substituĕre.*
replenish, *replēre, supplēre.*
replete; see full.
repletion, *satietas.*
reply, subst. *responsum, responsio.*
reply, v. *respondēre*; — by letter, *rescribĕre.*
report, subst.: official, *relatio, renuntiatio*; = rumour, *fama, rumor*; = loud noise, *fragor, crepitus (-ūs).*
report, v. *(re)nuntiare, referre*; it is —ed, *ferunt, traditur, dicitur.*
repose, subst. *(re)quies, otium.*
repose, v.: transit., *(re)ponĕre*; intransit., *quiescĕre.*
repository, *thesaurus, receptaculum.*
reprehend, *reprehendĕre.*
reprehensible, *culpā dignus.*
represent: = portray, *exprimĕre, (ef)fingĕre, (de)pingĕre, adumbrare* (= sketch); = state, *dicĕre, monēre*; = play a part, *personam gerĕre, partes agĕre.*
representation, = image, likeness, *imago, effigies.*
representative, subst. *vicarius, procurator.*
repress, *comprimĕre, cohibēre.*
reprieve, *supplicium differre.*
reprimand, subst. *reprehensio.*
reprimand, v. *reprehendĕre.*
reprisals, *talio*; to make —s, *par pari respondēre.*
reproach, subst. *exprobratio, obiectatio*; in words, *probrum, convicium.*
reproach, v. *increpitare, obiurgare.*
reproachful, *obiurgatorius.*
reprobate, adj. *perditus, profligatus.*
reproduce, *regignĕre, denuo generare.*
reproof, *vituperatio, reprehensio, obiurgatio.*
reprove, *vituperare, reprehendĕre.*
reprover, *reprehensor, obiurgator.*
reptile, *bestia serpens.*
republic, *respublica (libera); civitas.*
republican, *vir liberae reipublicae studiosus.*
republican, adj. *popularis*; or genit. *reipublicae liberae.*
repudiate; see reject.
repudiation, *repudiatio.*
repugnance, *repugnantia, odium* (= hatred).
repugnant, *repugnans, diversus, alienus.*
repulse, subst., of a candidate, *repulsa.*
repulse, v. *repellĕre, propulsare, reicĕre.*
repulsive, *odiosus, foedus.*
reputable, *honestus.*
reputation, *fama, opinio*; good —, *existimatio, gloria*; bad —, *infamia.*
repute; to be in good —, *bene audire.*
request, subst. *preces (-um), rogatio*; at my —, *rogatu meo, me rogante.*
request, v. *precari, orare, rogare.*
require: = demand, *poscĕre, postulare, imperare*; = need, *egēre, requirĕre, desiderare.*
requirement, *postulatio*; or use verb.
requisite, adj. *necessarius.*
requisition, *postulatio*; or render by *imperare.*
requite, *compensare, rependĕre.*
rescind, *rescindĕre, abrogare, tollĕre.*
rescript, *responsum, rescriptum.*
rescue, subst. *liberatio*; or use verb.
rescue, v. *liberare, servare, eripĕre.*
research, *eruditio, investigatio.*
resemblance, *similitudo*; bearing a —, *similis.*
resemble, *similem esse* (with genit. or dat.).
resent, *aegre* or *moleste ferre.*
resentful, *iracundus.*
resentment, *ira, stomachus.*
reservation, *exceptio, condicio.*

reserve, subst.: = store, *copia*; milit., —s, *subsidia* (*-orum*); in —, adj. *subsidiarius*; — of manner, *taciturnitas*; without —, *aperte*.
reserve, *retinēre, reponĕre*.
reserved, *taciturnus, occultus, tectus*.
reservoir, *lacus* (*-ūs*), *cisterna* (underground).
reside, v. *habitare*. Transf., *residēre, inesse*.
residence: act, *habitatio, mansio, commoratio*; place of —, *domus, domicilium, sedes*.
resident, subst. *habitator, incola*.
residue, *quod reliquum est*.
resign, (*magistratu*) *abire* or *se abdicare*; in gen., = give up, (*con*)*cedĕre, deponĕre*; to — oneself, *animum submittĕre*.
resignation, *abdicatio*; = resigned attitude, *animus submissus* or *aequus*.
resin, *resina*.
resist, *resistĕre, repugnare, adversari*.
resolute, *fortis, firmus, constans*; adv. *fortiter, firme, firmiter, constanter*.
resolution: = determination, *constantia, firmitudo*; = a purpose, *sententia, consilium, propositum*.
resolve, v.: = break down, *dissolvĕre, dissipare*; = determine, *statuĕre, constituĕre, decernĕre*; of a deliberative body, *sciscĕre, iubēre*.
resolved, *certus*.
resonant, *resonans*.
resort, subst. = place, *locus*.
resort, v.: to a place, *celebrare, frequentare*; — to, = have recourse to, *confugĕre, decurrĕre, descendĕre*.
resound, *resonare, personare*.
resource, resources, *facultates* (*-um*), *opes* (*-um*; = wealth or power).
respect, subst.: = esteem, *observantia, reverentia*; to pay one's —s to, *salutare*; in all —s, *omnino*; in — of, *ad, de, ab*.
respect, v. *observare,* (*re*)*vereri, colĕre*; see also concern, relate.
respectability, *honestas*.
respectable, *honestus*; adv. *honeste, bene*.
respectful, *observans, verecundus*; adv. *verecunde*.
respecting, *de* with abl.
respective, *proprius, suus* (often with *quisque*).
respiration, *respiratio, spiritus* (*-ūs*).
respite; see reprieve.
resplendent, *splendidus*.
respond, response; see answer.
respondent, legal, *reus*.
responsibility, responsible; render by *rationem reddĕre* (= give an account); to make oneself —, (*rem*) *praestare, in se recipĕre, promittĕre*.
responsive, *apertus* (= open), *facilis* (=tractable).
rest, subst.: = repose, (*re*)*quies, otium, tranquillitas*; = remainder, *reliquum, quod restat*.
rest, v., intransit., (*re*)*quiscĕre, conquiescĕre*; — upon, (*re*) (*in*)*niti*.
restless, *inquietus, turbidus, sollicitus* (=anxious).
restoration, *refectio*; or use verb.
restorative, subst. *medicina*.
restore: = give back, *reddĕre*; = reinstate, replace, *restituĕre, redintegrare, reficĕre*; to — to health, *sanare*.
restrain, *coercēre, continēre, cohibēre, inhibēre*.
restraint, *moderatio, modus*; = hindrance, *impedimentum*.
restrict, *coercēre, circumscribĕre,* (*de*)*finire*.
restriction, *modus, finis*; see restraint.
result, subst. *exitus* (*-ūs*), *eventus* (*-ūs*); the — is that, *evenit ut*; without —, *nequiquam*.
result, v. *fieri, evenire, evadĕre, oriri*.
resume, *repetĕre, recolĕre*.
resuscitate, *ab inferis excitare*; see also revive.
retail, *divendĕre*.
retailer, *caupo*.
retain, *tenēre, retinēre,* (*con*)*servare*.
retainer: = attendant, *cliens, adsectator, satelles*; = retaining fee, *arrhabo*.
retaliate, *par pari respondēre, ulcisci*.
retaliation, *ultio* (=revenge).
retard, (*re*)*morari,* (*re*)*tardare*.
retire, v. *abire,* (*re*)*cedĕre, se removēre*; milit., *pedem referre, se recipĕre*.
retired, adj. *secretus, remotus, solitarius*.
retirement, *solitudo, otium*.
retiring; see modest.
retort; see reply.
retrace, *repetĕre*; — one's steps, *pedem referre*.
retract, *renuntiare*.
retreat, subst. *reditus* (*-ūs*), *recessus* (*-ūs*), *receptus* (*-ūs*), *fuga*; see also refuge.
retreat, v. *se recipĕre, pedem referre, fugĕre* (=flee).
retrench, *sumptūs minuĕre*.
retribution, *poena*.
retrieve; see recover.
retrograde; render by *retro* (= backwards), or *in deteriorem partem* (= for the worse).
retrogression, *recessus* (*-ūs*), *regressus* (*-ūs*).
retrospect, (*praeteritorum*) *memoria*.
retrospective, render by *retro* (= backwards) or by *praeterita* (*-orum*; = the past).
return, subst.: = journey back, *reditus* (*-ūs*), *regressus* (*-ūs*); = giving back, *remuneratio*; = official declaration, *renuntiatio, professio*.
return, v.: transit., *reddĕre, referre*; intransit., *redire, reverti* (= turn back).
returned, adj. *redux*.
reunion, *reconciliatio*; see also assembly.
reunite, *iterum coniungĕre; reconciliare*.
reveal, *patefacĕre, aperire, evulgare*.
revel, revelry, *comissatio, bachatio*.
revel, v. *comissari,* (*per*)*bacchari; luxuriare, exsultare*.
reveller, *comissator*.
revenge, subst. *ultio, vindicta, vindicatio*.
revenge, v. *ulcisci, vindicare*.
revengeful, *ulciscendi cupidus*.

revenue, *vectigal, reditus* (*-ūs*).
reverberate, = resound, *resonare.*
reverberation, *repercussus* (*-ūs*).
revere, (*re*)*verēri, venerari.*
reverence, subst. *reverentia, veneratio, verecundia;* religious —, *religio, pietas erga deos.*
reverend, *venerabilis, reverendus.*
reverent, *verecundus*; in religious sense, *religiosus, pius.* Adv. *verecunde; religiose.*
reverie, *cogitatio.*
reverse, subst.: = change, *conversio,* (*com*)*mutatio, vicissitudo*; = the opposite, *contrarium*; = defeat, *clades*; = hind part, *pars aversa.*
reverse, v. *invertĕre,* (*com*)*mutare, convertĕre.*
reversion, legal, *hereditas.*
revert, *redire, revolvi.*
review, subst. *recognitio*; milit., *recensio, lustratio.*
review, v. *inspicĕre, contemplari*; milit., *recensēre, lustrare.*
revile, *conviciari, insectari, maledicĕre.*
reviler, *conviciator.*
reviling, subst. *maledictio, probrum, convicium.*
revise, *retractare*; see also correct.
revision, *emendatio.*
revisit, *revisĕre.*
revive, v.: transit., *recreare, excitare*; fig. *redintegrare*; intransit., *revirescĕre, recreari*; fig. *renasci.*
revocation, *revocatio, abrogatio.*
revoke, *abrogare, rescindĕre.*
revolt, subst. *defectio, seditio*; of a conquered people, *rebellio.*
revolt, v. *deficĕre, desciscĕre*; of a conquered people, *rebellare.*
revolting, adj. *taeter, foedus, turpis.*
revolution, *conversio, orbis, ambitus* (*-ūs*); political —, *res* (*rerum,* plur.) *novae.*
revolutionary, adj. *seditiosus, turbulentus, novarum rerum cupidus.*
revolutionize, *novare, commutare.*
revolve, *se* (*re*)*volvĕre* or (*re*)*volvi, circumverti.*
revulsion; see disgust.
reward, subst. *praemium, merces.*
reward, v. *remunerari, compensare, praemium dare.*
rewrite, *iterum scribĕre.*
rhetoric, *rhetorica, ars dicendi.*
rhetorical, *rhetoricus, oratorius*; adv. *rhetorice.*
rheumatism, *dolor artuum.*
Rhine, river, *Rhenus.*
Rhone, river, *Rhodanus.*
rhythm, *numerus, modus.*
rhythmical, *numerosus*; adv. *numerose, modulate.*
rib, *costa*; of a ship, *statumen.*
ribald, *obscenus.*
ribbon, *redimiculum, taenia, vitta.*
rich: = possessing wealth, *dives, locuples, opulentus*; to grow —, *ditescĕre*; = costly, sumptuous, *opimus, pretiosus, lautus*; = copious, fertile, *copiosus, abundans, uber, ferax.* Adv. *copiose, abundanter, pretiose.*
riches, *divitiae* (*-arum,* plur.), *opes* (*-um,* plur.); *pecunia* (= money).
richness, *abundantia, ubertas.*
rid, *liberare*; to get — of, — oneself of, *deponĕre, dimittĕre.*
riddance, *liberatio.*
riddle, subst. *aenigma* (*-atis,* n.), *ambages* (*-um,* plur.).
riddled, e.g. with wounds, *confossus.*
ride, v.: on a horse, *equitare,* (*equo*) *vehi*; in a chariot, *ire curru*; at anchor, *in ancoris consistĕre.*
rider, *eques.*
ridge, *iugum, montis dorsum.*
ridicule, subst. *ridiculum.*
ridicule, v. *inridēre, deridēre,* (*in*)*ludĕre.*
ridiculous, *ridiculus*; adv. *ridicule.*
riding, *equitatio*; or use verb.
rife; to become —, *percrebescĕre.*
rifle; see plunder.
rift, *rima.*
rig, subst. *habitus* (*-ūs*).
rig, v. *armare, ornare.*
rigging, *armamenta* (*-orum*), *rudentes* (*-um*).
right, subst. *fas, ius* (*iuris,* n.).
right, adj.: opp. to left, *dexter*; — hand, (*manus*) *dextra*; at — angles *ad pares angulos*; morally —, *rectus iustus, aequus*; = suitable, proper, *rectus, verus*; at the — time, *ad tempus*; you are —, *ita est ut dicis*; it is all —, *bene habet.* Adv. *recte iuste, iure, merito* (= deservedly) *bene* (=well).
righteous, *probus, aequus, iustus*; adv. *probe, iuste.*
righteousness, *probitas.*
rightful, *legitimus, iustus*; adv. *legitime, iuste, iure.*
rigid, *rigidus, durus*; adv. *rigide, dure.*
rigidity, *rigor.*
rigour, *severitas, duritia.*
rill, *rivus, rivulus.*
rim, *ora.*
rime, *pruina.*
Rimini, *Ariminum.*
rind, *cortex, liber* (= inner bark).
ring, subst. *orbis, anulus*; a — of people, *corona.*
ring, v. *tinnire*; = resound, *resonare.*
ringing, subst. *tinnitus* (*-ūs*).
ringing, adj. *tinnulus, canorus.*
ringleader, *auctor, princeps, dux.*
ringlet, *cincinnus, cirrus.*
rinse, *eluĕre.*
riot, subst. *seditio, motus* (*-ūs*), *tumultus* (*-ūs*).
riot, v. *seditionem movēre*; = revel, *comissari, luxuriare.*
rioter, *homo turbulentus.*
riotous, adj. *turbulentus*; = wild, in gen., *luxuriosus*; — living, *luxuria.* Adv. *turbulente.*
rip, *scindĕre, divellĕre.*
ripe, *maturus, tempestivus.*
ripen: transit., *maturare*; intransit., *maturari, maturescĕre.*
ripeness, *maturitas.*
ripple, subst., *unda.*
rise, subst.: = origin, *ortus* (*-ūs*); to give — to, *parĕre, efficĕre*; = increase,

incrementum; = rising ground, *clivus, collis.*
rise, v.: = get up, *(ex)surgĕre, se erigĕre, se levare*; of sun, stars, etc., *oriri*; = originate, start, *(co)oriri, surgĕre, nasci*; = increase, *increbescĕre, crescĕre*; to — in dignity, etc., *crescĕre, emergĕre, ascendĕre*; = rebel, *consurgĕre, cooriri.*
rising, subst. *ortus* (*-ūs*); see also rebellion.
rising, adj.: — ground, *clivus, collis.*
risk, subst. *periculum, discrimen.*
risk, v. *in periculum adducĕre* or *vocare.*
rite, ritual, subst. *ritus* (*-ūs*).
rival, subst. *aemulus* (f. *aemula*), *competitor* (f. *competitrix*); in love, *rivalis.*
rival, adj. *aemulus.*
rival, v. *aemulari, certare* (*cum*).
rivalry, *aemulatio, certamen*; in love, *rivalitas.*
river, subst. *flumen, fluvius, amnis*; adj. *fluviatilis, fluvialis.*
river-bed, *alveus.*
road, *via, iter*; on the — *in itinere, obiter.*
roadstead, *statio.*
roam, *palari, vagari, errare.*
roaming, *vagus, errabundus.*
roar, subst. *fremitus* (*-ūs*), *mugitus* (*-ūs*).
roar, v. *mugire, fremĕre, vociferari* (of persons).
roast, v. *torrēre, frigĕre.*
roasted, *assus*; — meat, *assum.*
rob, *(ex)spoliare, compilare, latrocinari.*
robber, *praedo, latro, fur.*
robbery, *latrocinium, spoliatio, rapina.*
robe, subst.: *vestis, vestimentum*; woman's —, *palla, stola*; — of state, *trabea.*
robe, v. *vestire.*
robust, *robustus, validus.*
rock, subst. *saxum, rupes, scopulus.*
rock, v.: transit., *agitare, quatĕre*; intransit., *agitari, nutare, vacillare.*
rocky, *scopulosus, saxeus.*
rod, *virga, ferula, decempeda* (for measuring).
roe: of fish, *ova* (*-orum*); = female deer, *caprea.*
roebuck, *capreolus.*
rogue, (*homo*) *nequam* or *scelestus*; *veterator.*
roguery, *fraus, dolus, nequitia.*
role, *partes* (*-ium*), *persona.*
roll, subst. *volumen*; = list of names, *album.*
roll, v.: transit., *volvĕre, volutare, versare*; intransit., *volvi, volutari.*
roll-call; to answer a —, *ad nomina respondēre.*
roller, *cylindrus, phalangae* (*-arum*).
rolling, adj. *volubilis.*
Roman, *Romanus.*
romance, subst. *fabula.*
romance, v. *fabulari.*
romantic, *fictus, commenticius* (= imaginary); *mirus, novus* (= strange).
Rome, *Roma.*
roof, subst. *tectum, culmen.*
roof, v. (*tecto*) *tegĕre.*
room: = space, *locus, spatium*; to make —, *locum dare*; = apartment, *conclave, cubiculum.*
roomy, *laxus, spatiosus.*
root, subst. *radix, stirps*: by the —s, *radicitus.*
root, v. to —, or become —ed, *radices agĕre, inveterascĕre*; to be —ed, *inhaerēre*; —ed, *inveteratus*; for — up, see uproot.
rope, *funis, restis.*
rose, *rosa.*
rosemary, *ros marinus*
rosy, *roseus.*
rot, subst. *tabes.*
rot, v. *putescĕre, tabescĕre.*
rotate, *volvi, circumagi.*
rotation, *ambitus* (*-ūs*); in —, *ordine.*
rotatory, *versatilis.*
rotten, *putrefactus, putridus*
rotundity, *figura rotunda.*
rouge, subst. *fucus.*
rouge, v. *fucare.*
rough, *asper, horridus, atrox, hirsutus* (= shaggy). Adv. *aspere.*
roughen, *(ex)asperare.*
roughness, *asperitas*; of style, *salebra.*
round, subst. *orbis*; in fighting, *congressus* (*-ūs*).
round, adj. *rotundus, globosus.*
round, adv. and prep., *circum, circa.*
round, v.: = make round, *rotundare, tornare*; = sail round, *flectĕre*; — off, = complete, *concludĕre, absolvĕre.*
roundabout, *devius*; a — way, *ambages* (*-um*), *circuitus* (*-ūs*).
rounded, *teres.*
roundly, *plane, praecise.*
rouse, *excitare.*
rout, subst. *fuga*; see also mob.
rout, v. *fugare, dissipare, fundĕre.*
route; see way, road, journey.
routine, *usus* (*-ūs*), *ordo.*
rove; see wander.
row, subst.: = line, *ordo, versus* (*-ūs*); in a row, (*ex*) *ordine*; see also quarrel and noise.
row, v. *remigare*; to — a boat, *lintrem remis propellĕre*; to — hard, *remis contendĕre.*
royal: = of a king, *regius*, or *regis* (genit); = like a king, *regalis.* Adv. *regie, regaliter.*
royalty, *regnum, regia potestas.*
rub, *terĕre, conterĕre*; to — down, *(de)fricare*; to — out, *delēre.*
rubbish, *rudus* (*-eris*, n.), *quisquiliae* (*-arum*).
rubble, *rudus* (*-eris*, n.).
rudder, *gubernaculum, clavus.*
ruddy, *rubicundus.*
rude: = unfinished, *rudis, inconditus*; = ill-mannered, *importunus, inhumanus, insolens.* Adv. *incondite; insolenter.*
rudeness, *inhumanitas, importunitas, insolentia.*
rudimentary, *inchoatus.*
rudiments, *elementa* (*-orum*).
ruffian, *latro, sicarius.*
ruffianly, *nefarius, nequam, sceleratus.*
ruffle, v. *agitare*: to be —d, *inhorrescĕre.* Transf., see irritate.

rug, *stragulum.*
rugged, *asper, horridus, praeruptus.*
ruin, subst.: = collapse, *ruina, exitium, pernicies*; concr., —s, *parietinae* (*-arum*), *ruinae* (*-arum*).
ruin, v. *perdĕre, pessum dare, conficĕre.*
ruinous, *exitiosus*; = in ruins, *ruinosus.*
rule, subst: = ruler, *regula, decempeda*; = regulation, *lex, praeceptum*; = government, *imperium, regnum.*
rule, v. *dominari, regĕre, praeesse, imperare*; to — as a king, *regnare*; to — passions, etc., *temperare*, with dat.
ruler, *rector, dominus, rex* (= king); see also rule.
rumble, subst. *murmur.*
rumble, v. (*in*)*sonare, murmurare.*
ruminate, *ruminare.*
rumination, *ruminatio.*
rumour, subst. *rumor, fama, sermo.*
rumour, v.: it is —ed, *fertur, fama est.*
run, subst. *cursus* (*-ūs*) *citatus.*
run, v. *currĕre, cursu ferri*; of fluids, = flow, *fluĕre*; — about, *cursare*; — into, *incurrĕre*; — through, *percurrĕre.*
runaway, *fugitivus.*
runner, *cursor.*
running, of water, *vivus.*
rupture, v. *frangĕre, confringĕre, rumpĕre.*
rural, *rusticus, rusticanus, agrestis.*
ruse, *dolus.*
rush, subst.: the plant, *iuncus, scirpus*: of —es, adj., *iunceus, scirpeus*; = dash, *impetus* (*-ūs*).
rush, v. *ruĕre, ferri, currĕre.*
russet, *fulvus* (poet).
rust, subst. *robigo, ferrugo* (of iron only).
rust, v. *robiginem trahĕre*; fig. *torpescĕre.*
rustic, *rusticus, agrestis.*
rustle, subst. *crepitus* (*-ūs*), *sonus.*
rustle, v. *crepare, crepitare.*
rusty, *robiginosus.*
rut, *orbita.*

S

sable, adj. *niger, ater.*
sabre, *gladius, ensis, acinaces.*
sack, subst.: = bag, *saccus, culeus;* — of a city, *direptio.*
sack, v. *diripĕre, spoliare.*
sacker, *direptor.*
sacred, *sacer, sanctus*; to declare —, *sancire.* Adv. *sancte.*
sacredness, *sanctitas, religio.*
sacrifice, subst. *sacrificium, sacra* (*-orum*); = victim, *victima, hostia.* Transf., = loss, *iactura.*
sacrifice, v. *sacrificare, immolare.* Transf., = give up, *iacturam facĕre*, with genit.; *dedĕre.*
sacrilege, *sacrilegium.*
sacrilegious, *sacrilegus.*
sad, *maestus, tristis*; = causing sadness, *gravis, acerbus, luctuosus.*
sadden, *dolore adficĕre.*
saddle, subst. *ephippium.*
saddle, (*equum*) *sternĕre.*
sadness, *maestitia, tristitia, dolor.*
safe, subst. *armarium, arca.*
safe, adj.: = protected, *tutus*; feeling —, *securus*; — and sound, *incolumis, salvus;* —, = reliable, *fidus.* Adv. *tuto.*
safe-conduct, *fides* (*publica*).
safeguard, *propugnaculum, munimentum.*
safety, *salūs* (*-ūtis*), *incolumitas.*
saffron, *crocus*; adj., *croceus.*
sagacious, *sagax, prudens* ; adv. *sagaciter, prudenter.*
sagacity, *sagacitas, prudentia.*
sage, subst. and adj. *sapiens.*
sail, subst. *velum*; to set —, *vela dare*; to furl one's —s, *vela contrahĕre.*
sail, v. *navigare*; to — past, *praetervehi*: — out, *enavigare.*
sailing, subst. *navigatio.*
sailor, *nauta.*
saintly, *sanctus.*
sake: for the — of, *causā, gratiā* (with genit.); *pro* (with abl.); *ob* or *propter* (with acc.).
salaam, v. *corpus humi prosternĕre.*
salad, *acetaria* (*-orum*).
salary, *merces, salarium.*
sale, *venditio, hasta* (= auction); to offer for —, *venum dare* for —, adj., *venalis.*
salesman, *venditor.*
salient, *praecipuus.*
saline, *salsus.*
sallow, *pallidus, luridus.*
sally, *eruptio.*
sally, v. *erumpĕre, eruptionem facĕre.*
salt, subst. *sal.*
salt, adj. *salsus.*
salt, v. *sale condire.*
salt-cellar, *salinum.*
salt-mine, salt-works, *salinae* (*-arum*).
salubrious, *saluber* or *salubris*; adv. *salubriter.*
salutary, *salutaris, utilis.*
salutation, *salutatio.*
salute, *salutare.*
salvation, *salūs* (*-ūtis*).
salve, *unguentum*; for eyes, *collyrium.*
same, *idem, eadem, idem*; the — as, *idem qui, idem ac* (*atque*); in the — place, *ibidem*; at the — time, *simul, eodem tempore*; it is all the — to me, *meā nihil interest.*
sample, *exemplum, specimen.*
sanctify, (*con*)*secrare, dedicare.*
sanction, subst. *confirmatio, auctoritas*; with the — of a person, *hominis iussu.*
sanctity, *sanctitas, sanctimonia.*
sanctuary: = holy place, *templum, delubrum, fanum*; = refuge, *asylum, receptaculum.*
sand, *harena, saburra.*
sandal, *crepida, solea*; wearing —s, *crepidatus, soleatus.*
sandy, *harenosus.*
sane, *sanus, mentis compos.*
sanguinary, *cruentus, sanguineus, sanguinarius.*
sanguine; see hopeful.
sanity, *mens sana.*
sap, subst. *sucus.*
sap, v. *cuniculos agĕre.* Transf. *corrumpĕre, haurire.*

sapling, *arbor novella.*
sarcastic, *acerbus*; adv. *acerbe.*
sash, *zona.*
satchel, *loculus, pera, sacculus.*
satellite, *satelles.*
satiate, (*ex*)*satiare, explēre, saturare.*
satiety, *satietas, satias.*
satire, *satura* or *satira*; see also satirical.
satirical, *famosus, probrosus, acerbus.*
satirist, *satirarum scriptor; derisor.*
satisfaction, *satisfactio, expletio, voluptas* (= pleasure).
satisfactory, *idoneus*; adv. *bene, ex sententia.*
satisfy, *satisfacěre, placēre*; satisfied, *contentus.*
saturate; see soak.
satyr, *satyrus.*
sauce, *iūs* (*iūris,* n.), *condimentum.*
saucer, *patella.*
sauciness, *protervitas, procacitas.*
saucy, *protervus, procax*; adv. *proterve, procaciter.*
saunter, *ambulare, vagari, repěre.*
sausage, *tomaculum.*
savage, adj. *ferus, saevus, trux, atrox;* adv. *saeve, atrociter.*
savageness, *feritas, saevitia, atrocitas.*
save, prep. and conj.; see except.
save, v.: = preserve, (*con*)*servare, tuēri*; = rescue, *liberare, eripěre, servare*; to — up, *reservare, parcěre.*
saving, subst. *conservatio, compendium.*
saving, adj. *parcus.*
savings, *peculium.*
saviour, (*con*)*servator* (with f. *servatrix*); *liberator.*
savour, subst. *sapor.*
savour, v. *sapěre.*
savoury, adj. *conditus.*
saw: = saying, *dictum, proverbium*; the tool, *serra.*
saw, v. *serrā secare.*
sawdust, *scobis.*
say, *dicěre, loqui, narrare;* to — that not, *negare.*
saying, subst. *dictio*; = thing said, *dictum, verbum.*
scabbard, *vagina.*
scaffold; see execution.
scaffolding, *machina, pegma.*
scale, subst.: of a fish, *squama*; of a balance, *lanx*; a pair of —s, *libra, trutina*; = gradation, *gradus* (*-ūs*).
scale, v. = climb, *ascenděre, conscenděre.*
scaling-ladder, *scalae* (*-arum*).
scalp, *cutis capitis.*
scaly, *squameus, squamosus.*
scamp; see knave.
scamper: see hurry.
scan, = examine, *inspicěre,* (*per*)*scrutari, contemplari*; metrically, *metiri.*
scandal; see disgrace, slander.
scandalize, *offenděre.*
scandalous, *pessimi exempli, probrosus, turpis.*
scantiness, *exiguitas.*
scanty, *exiguus, parvus, tenuis*; adv. *exigue.*
scar, *cicatrix.*
scarce, *rarus*; adv. *vix, aegre.*
scarcity, *paucitas, raritas, inopia.*
scare, *terrēre.*
scarecrow, *formido.*
scarf, *fascia.*
scarlet: subst. *coccum*; adj. *coccineus* or *coccinus.*
scathe; see harm.
scatheless, *salvus, incolumis.*
scathing (of words), *aculeatus, acerbus.*
scatter, v.: transit., *spargěre, dispergěre*; of troops, *dissipare, funděre*; intransit., *dilabi, diffugěre.*
scene: = stage, *scaena*; = place, *locus*; = spectacle, *prospectus* (*-ūs*), *spectaculum.*
scenery: in a theatre, *apparatus* (*-ūs*) *scaenae*; natural —, *loca* (*-orum*).
scent, subst.: = sense of smell, *odoratus* (*-ūs*); = odour, *odor* ; = perfume, *unguentum.*
scent, v.: = detect by —, *odorari*; = perfume, *odorare, odoribus perfunděre.*
scented, adj. *odoratus.*
sceptic, sceptical; render by verb *dubitare.*
sceptre, *sceptrum.*
scheme, subst. *consilium, ratio.*
scholar: = pupil, *discipulus*; = man of learning, *vir doctus* or *litteratus.*
scholarly, *doctus, litteratus, eruditus.*
scholarship, *litterae* (*-arum*), *doctrina, eruditio.*
school, subst. *ludus* (*litterarum*), *schola.*
school, v. *docēre.*
school-fellow, *condiscipulus.*
school-master, school-mistress, *magister, magistra.*
science, *scientia, ars, doctrina, disciplina*; natural —, *physica, rerum naturae scientia.*
scientific, *physicus;* — principles, *artis praecepta*; adv. *physice, ratione.*
scientist, *physicus.*
scimitar, *acinaces.*
scintillate, *scintillare.*
scintillation, *scintilla* (= spark).
scion, *progenies.*
scissors, *forfices* (*-um*).
scoff, v.: to — at, *inridēre, ludibrio habēre*; to be —ed at, *ludibrio esse.*
scoffer, *inrisor.*
scoffing, subst. *inrisio, inrisus* (*-ūs*).
scold, v. *obiurgare, increpare, conviciari.*
scolding, subst. *obiurgatio, convicium.*
scoop, v.: to — out, (*ex*)*cavare.*
scope, = free play, *campus, area.*
scorch, *amburěre, adurěre, torrēre.*
scorched, *torridus.*
score, subst.: = account, *ratio, nomen*; = total, *summa*; = 20, *viginti.*
score, v.: = mark, *notare, signare;* = obtain, q.v.
scorn, subst. *contemptus* (*-ūs*), *fastidium.*
scorn, v. *contemněre, fastidire, sperněre.*
scorner, *contemptor.*
scornful, *fastidiosus*; adv. *fastidiose contemptim.*
scorpion, *scorpio, nepa.*
scot; — -free, *immunis.*
Scotland, *Caledonia.*
Scottish, *Caledonius.*
scoundrel, *homo nefarius* or *nequam.*

scour, (*de*)*tergĕre*, (*ex*)*purgare*; to — the land, *agrum pervagari, percurrĕre.*
scourge, subst. *flagrum, flagellum.* Transf., *pestis.*
scourge, v. *virgis caedĕre, verberare.*
scourging, subst. *verbera* (-*um*).
scout, subst. *explorator, speculator.*
scout, v. *explorare, speculari.*
scowl, v. *frontem contrahĕre.*
scramble, v.; to — up, *scandĕre, escendĕre.*
scrap, *frustum, fragmentum.*
scrape, subst. *angustiae* (-*arum*), *difficultas.*
scrape, v. *radĕre*: to — off, *abradĕre*; to — together, *corradĕre.*
scraper, (for flesh) *strigil, strigilis.*
scratch, v. *scabĕre, radĕre*; to — out, *delēre.*
scream, subst. *vociferatio, ululatus* (-*ūs*).
scream, v. *clamitare, vociferari, ululare.*
screech, v. *ululare.*
screeching, subst. *ululatus* (-*ūs*)
screen, *umbraculum.*
screen, v. (*pro*)*tegĕre, tueri, defendĕre.*
screw, subst. *clavus* (= nail).
scribe, *scriba, librarius.*
scroll, *volumen.*
scrub, (*de*)*tergēre.*
scruple, *religio, scrupulus.*
scruple, v. *dubitare.*
scrupulous, *religiosus*; adv. *religiose.*
scrutinize, (*per*)*scrutari.*
scrutiny, (*per*)*scrutatio.*
scuffle, *rixa, turba.*
scull, subst., = oar, *remus.*
scull, v. *remigare.*
sculptor, *sculptor.*
sculpture, subst.: the art, *ars fingendi, sculptura*; a work of —, *opus* (-*eris*, n.) or *signum* (= statue).
sculpture, v. *sculpĕre.*
scum, *spuma.* Transf., *faex, sentina.*
scurrilous, *contumeliosus, probrosus, scurrilis*; adv. *contumeliose.*
scutcheon, *insigne* (or in plur.).
scythe, *falx.*
sea, subst. *mare, pelagus* (-*i*, n.), *aequor* (poet.), *pontus* (poet.), *altum* (= 'the deep'); on the —, of the —, adj. *maritimus, marinus.*
sea-gull, *gavia.*
seal, subst.: on a letter, *signum*; the animal, *phoca.*
seal, v. (*con*)*signare, obsignare.*
sealing-wax, *cera.*
seam, *sutura.*
seaman, *nauta.*
seamanship, *ars navigandi.*
sear, v. (*ad*)*urĕre.*
search, subst. *investigatio, inquisitio.*
search, v.: to — a place, *investigare, explorare*; a person, *excutĕre*; to — for, *quaerĕre, exquirĕre, petĕre.*
seasickness, *nausea.*
season, subst., *tempus, tempestas, hora*; in due —, *tempore, ad tempus*; for a —, *in tempus.*
season, v.: = flavour, *condire*; = harden, *durare.*
seasonable, *tempestivus, opportunus*; adv. *tempore, tempestive, opportune.*
seasoning, *condimentum.*
seat, subst. *sedes, sella*; a row of —s, *subsellium*; = abode, dwelling, *domicilium, sedes.*
seat, v. *ponĕre, conlocare.*
seaweed, *alga.*
secede, *abire, decedĕre, secedĕre.*
secession, *secessio.*
seclude, *secludĕre, segregare, removēre.*
secluded, *secretus, seclusus.*
seclusion, *solitudo.*
second, subst., of time, *momentum* (*temporis*).
second, adj. *secundus, alter*; for the — time, *iterum.* Adv. *secundo, deinde.*
second, v., = support, *adesse, auxilio esse, suffragari* (all with dat.).
secondary, *secundarius, inferior.*
seconder, *suasor, auctor.*
second-rate, *inferior.*
secrecy, *secretum.*
secret, subst. *res occulta* or *arcana*; in —, *clam.*
secret, adj. *occultus, arcanus, secretus*; = underhand, *clandestinus, furtivus.* Adv. *clam, in occulto, occulte, furtim.*
secretary, *scriba, servus a manu.*
secrete, *celare, occultare, abdĕre.*
sect, *secta, schola.*
section, *pars, portio.*
secure: = carefree, *securus*; = safe, *tutus*; adv. *tuto.*
secure, v.: = make safe, *munire, confirmare*; = arrest, *comprehendĕre.*
security: = safety, *salūs* (-*ūtis*, f.); = pledge, *pignus* (-*eris*, n.), *cautio, vadimonium* (= bail).
sedan, *lectica.*
sedate, *sedatus, gravis*; adv. *sedate, graviter.*
sedentary, render by *sedēre.*
sedge, *ulva.*
sediment, *faex, sedimentum.*
sedition, *seditio, motus* (-*ūs*).
seditious, *seditiosus, turbulentus*; adv. *seditiose.*
seduce, *corrumpĕre.*
seducer, *corruptor, corruptela.*
seduction, *corruptela, stuprum.*
sedulity, *sedulitas, adsiduitas, diligentia.*
sedulous, *sedulus, adsiduus, diligens*; adv. *sedulo, adsidue, diligenter.*
see, *vidēre, cernĕre conspicĕre* (= catch sight of), *aspicĕre* (= look at), *spectare* (= watch); to go to —, *visĕre, visitare*; = to understand, *vidēre, intellegĕre*; to — to, *curare, providēre.*
seed, *semen.*
seed-time, *sementis.*
seedling, *arbor novella.*
seek, *quaerĕre, exquirĕre,* (*ex*)*petĕre*; — to do, = endeavour, *conari, tendĕre.*
seem, *vidēri*; to — good, *vidēri.*
seeming, adj. *fictus, falsus*; adv. *in speciem, ut videtur.*
seemliness, *decorum.*
seemly, *decorus, honestus*; it is —, *decet, convenit.*
seer, *vates.*
seethe, v.: transit., *fervefacĕre, coquĕre*; intransit., *fervēre, aestuare.*

segregate, *segregare, seponĕre, seiungĕre.*
Seine, river, *Sequana.*
seize, *(ap)prehendĕre, rapĕre, corripĕre, occupare.*
seldom, *raro.*
select, adj. *(e)lectus, delectus, exquisitus.*
select, v. *legĕre, eligĕre, deligĕre.*
selection, *electio, delectus* (-*ūs*); = things chosen, *res selectae.*
self: emphatic, *ipse*; reflexive, render by personal pronoun with *ipse* (third person *se* or *sese*); by one—, *solus*; beside one—, *mente captus*; in it—, *per se.*
self-confidence, *fiducia sui.*
self-confident, *confidens.*
self-control, *imperium sui, continentia, temperantia.*
self-evident, *manifestus, apertus.*
self-indulgence, *intemperantia.*
self-indulgent, *impotens sui, intemperans.*
self-love, *amor sui.*
self-satisfied, to be, *sibi placēre.*
self-seeking, *cupiditas.*
self-willed, *pertinax, pervicax.*
selfish, to be, *sibi* (*soli*) *consulĕre.*
sell, *vendĕre, venum dare*; to try to —, *venditare*; to be sold, *venire.*
seller, *venditor, institor, propola.*
semblance, *species, imago.*
senate, *senatus* (-*ūs*); = house, *curia.*
senator, *senator.*
senatorial, *senatorius.*
send, *mittĕre*; — away, *relegare, dimittĕre*; — for, *arcessĕre, accire*; — forward, *praemittĕre.*
senior, = older, (*natu*) *grandior* or *maior.*
sensation, *sensus* (-*ūs*); a — of pain, *dolor*; = excitement, (*animi*) *commotio*; to create a —, *admirationem movēre.*
sensational, *mirificus, mirus*; adv. *mirifice, mire.*
sense: = sensation, feeling, *sensus* (-*ūs*); = understanding, intelligence, *iudicium, prudentia*; out of one's —s, *mentis compos*; = meaning (of a word), *vis, significatio, sententia.*
senseless; = unconscious, (*omni*) *sensu carens*; = foolish, *rationis expers.*
sensible, = intelligent, *prudens*; adv. *prudenter.*
sensitive, *patibilis, sensilis*; emotionally, *mollis.*
sensual, *libidinosus.*
sensuality, *libido.*
sentence, subst. *sententia, enuntiatio*; in court, *iudicium, decretum, sententia.*
sentence, v. *damnare, condemnare.*
sentiment : = opinion, *sententia, opinio*; = feeling, *sensus* (-*ūs*), *animus.*
sentimental, *mollis, effeminatus.*
sentimentality, *mollitia* (*animi*).
sentinel, sentry, *excubitor, vigil*; —s, plur., *stationes, vigiliae, excubiae.*
separable, *separabilis, dividuus.*
separate, adj. *separatus, secretus, disiunctus.* Adv. *separatim, singuli* (adj., = one by one).
separate, v. *separare, seiungĕre, dividĕre.*
separation, *separatio, disiunctio.*
September, (*mensis*) *September.*
sepulchral, *sepulcralis, feralis.*
sepulchre, *sepulcrum.*
sequel, *eventus* (-*ūs*), *exitus* (-*ūs*).
sequence, *ordo, series.*
serene, *serenus, tranquillus.*
serf, *servus.*
serious: of persons, *gravis, severus*; of things, *serius, gravis, magni momenti.* Adv. *serio, graviter.*
seriousness, *gravitas severitas, tristitia.*
serpent, *serpens, anguis.*
serried, *densus, confertus.*
servant, *servus, famulus, puer* (= boy), *ancilla* (= maid).
serve, *servire, praesto esse*; at table, *famulari, ministrare*; to — up food, *apponĕre*; as a soldier, (*stipendia*) *merēre, militare.*
service, *opera, ministerium*; = a helpful action, *officium*; — in the army, *militia, stipendia* (-*orum*).
serviceable, *utilis, opportunus, aptus.*
servile, *servilis.* Transf., *humilis, abiectus.*
servility, *adulatio.*
servitude, *servitus* (-*ūtis*), *servitium.*
session, *conventus* (-*ūs*).
set, subst.; see company, collection.
set, adj. *status, constitutus.*
set, v.: transit. *ponĕre, statuĕre,* (*con*)*locare*; — apart, *secernĕre, seponĕre*; — forth, *exponĕre*; — over, *praeficĕre*; — up, *statuĕre, constituĕre*; intransit., of sun, etc., *occidĕre*; to — out, *proficisci.*
setting, subst., of sun, etc., *occasus* (-*ūs*).
settle, v.: transit., *conlocare, constituĕre, statuĕre, componĕre*; — accounts, *rationes putare* or *conficĕre*; — a debt, *solvĕre, expedire*; intransit., (*con*)*sīdĕre, se conlocare.*
settlement, *constitutio, compositio, pactum*; of a colony, *deductio.*
settler, *advena, colonus.*
seven, *septem*: — at a time, — each, *septeni*; — times, *septie*(*n*)*s.*
seven hundred, *septingenti.*
seventeen, *septemdecim* (*septen-*); — at a time, — each, *septeni deni*; — times, *septie*(*n*)*s decie*(*n*)*s.*
seventeenth, *septimus decimus.*
seventh, *septimus.*
seventieth, *septuagesimus.*
seventy, *septuaginta*: — at a time, — each, *septuageni*; — times, *septuagie*(*n*)*s.*
sever, *dividĕre, dirimĕre, disiungĕre.*
several: = some, *nonnulli,* (*com*)*plures, aliquot*; = respective, *suus, proprius*; adv. *singillatim.*
severe, *severus, austerus, gravis*; adv. *severe, austere*; —ly wounded, *graviter ictus.*
severity, *severitas, gravitas.*
Seville, *Hispalis.*
sew, *suĕre.*
sewer, *cloaca.*
sex, *sexus* (-*ūs*).
shabbiness, *sordes* (-*ium*).
shabby, *obsoletus.* Transf., *sordidus turpis.* Adv. *obsolete*; *sordide.*

shackle, v. *constringĕre, vincire.*
shackles, *vincula, catenae, compedes* (*-um*).
shade, subst. *umbra*; living in —, *umbratilis*; = disembodied spirit, *umbra, simulacrum*; in plur., *manes.*
shade, v. *opacare,* (*in*)*umbrare.*
shadow, *umbra.*
shadowy, *vanus, inanis.*
shady, *umbrosus, opacus.*
shaft: = arrow, *sagitta*; = handle, *hastile*; of a carriage, *temo*; — of a mine, *puteus.*
shake, v.: transit., *quatĕre, concutĕre, agitare, vibrare*; to — hands, *iungĕre dextras*; to — off, *excutĕre*; intransit., *agitari, tremĕre.*
shaking, subst., *quassatio* (act.), *tremor* (pass.).
shallow, subst. *vadum.*
shallow, adj. *humilis, vadosus.* Transf., *levis.*
sham, subst. *fallacia, dolus, fraus.*
sham, adj. *fictus, falsus, simulatus.*
sham, v. *simulare.*
shambles, *laniena, strages* (=massacre).
shame, subst.: = modesty, *pudor, verecundia*; = disgrace, *dedecus* (*-oris,* n.), *ignominia, infamia*; shame! *pro pudor!*
shame, v. *pudorem adferre.*
shameful, *turpis, foedus, inhonestus*; adv. *turpiter, foede, inhoneste.*
shameless, *impudens, inverecundus*; adv. *impudenter.*
shamelessness, *impudentia.*
shank, *crūs* (*crūris,* n.).
shape, subst. *forma, figura, species.*
shape, v. (*con*)*formare, figurare, fingĕre.*
shapeless, *informis.*
shapely, *formosus.*
share, subst. pars, *portio, sors*; of a plough, *vomer.*
share, v. *partiri, communicare.*
sharer, *particeps, socius, consors.*
shark, *pistrix.*
sharp, *acutus*; = bitter, *acer, acerbus*; = acute, keen, *acer, acutus, sagax.* Adv. *acriter, acute, acerbe* (=bitterly).
sharpness, *acerbitas* (= bitterness); of intellect, (*ingenii*) *acumen.*
shatter, *frangĕre, confringĕre.*
shave, (*caput,* etc.) (*ab*)*radĕre, tondēre.*
shavings, *scobis.*
shawl; see mantle.
she, when emphatic, *illa, ea, ista, haec.*
sheaf, *merges.*
shear, *tondēre.*
shearing, subst. *tonsura.*
shears, *forfex.*
sheath, *vagina.*
sheathe, *in vaginam recondĕre.*
shed, subst. *tugurium*; milit., *pluteus, vinea.*
shedding, subst. *effusio*; of tears, *fletus* (*-ūs*).
sheep, *ovis, bidens.*
sheep-fold, *ovile.*
sheepish, *insulsus.*
sheer: = steep, *abruptus, praeruptus*; = pure, *merus.*
sheet, *lodix* (= blanket); of paper, *scheda*; of metal, *lamina*; of a sail, *pes.*
shelf, *pluteus, pegma* (*-atis,* n.).
shell, subst.: of fish, *testa, concha*; of nuts, *putamen, cortex.*
shell-fish, *concha, conchylium.*
shelter, subst. *perfugium, asylum, receptaculum.*
shelter, v.: transit., (*pro*)*tegĕre, defendĕre, tutari*; intransit., *latēre.*
shelving, *declivis, proclivis.*
shepherd, *pastor, upilio*; of a —, adj., *pastoralis, pastoricius.*
shield, subst. *scutum, clipeus, parma.*
shield, v. (*scuto*) *defendĕre,* (*pro*)*tegĕre.*
shift, subst. = expedient, *ratio, consilium, dolus* (= trick).
shift, v., = change, (*per*)*mutare.*
shifty, *versutus, varius.*
shin, *crūs* (*crūris,* n.), *tibia.*
shine, *lucēre, fulgēre, splendēre, nitēre.*
ship, subst. *navis, navigium* (smaller); war- —, *navis longa*; flag- —, *navis praetoria*; merchant- —, *navis oneraria*; of a —, adj., *navalis, nauticus.*
ship, v. *in navem imponĕre.*
shipwreck, *naufragium*; —ed, adj., *naufragus.*
shirk, *dētrectare, subterfŭgĕre.*
shirt, *subucula, tunica.*
shiver, v. *horrēre, tremĕre* (= tremble), *algēre* (= be cold).
shoal = shallow, *vadum.*
shock, subst.: physical, *impetus* (*-ūs*); mental, *stupor, offensio.*
shock, v. *perturbare, offendĕre.*
shocking, *indignus, turpis.*
shoe, *calceus, solea* (= slipper).
shoe-maker, *sutor.*
shoot, subst. *surculus, planta, virga.*
shoot, v.; transit., *iaculari,* (*e*)*mittĕre, iacĕre*; to — at, *telo petĕre*; intransit., *volare.*
shooting-star; see meteor.
shop, *taberna*; work- —, *officina.*
shopkeeper, *tabernarii* (*-orum,* plur. only).
shore, *litus* (*-oris,* n.), *ora.*
short, *brevis*; — of stature, *humilis*; — cut, *via compendiaria*; in —, *denique, ad summam, ne multa*; to fall — of, *non attingĕre.* Adv.: = briefly, *breviter*; = in a short time, *brevi, mox.*
shortness, *brevitas, exiguitas.*
short-sighted, *lusciosus.* Transf., *improvidus.*
shot, (*telum*) *missile, glans* (= bullet).
shoulder, subst. *humerus*; — -blades, *scapulae.*
shoulder, v. *in humeros tollĕre.*
shout, shouting, subst. *clamor, vociferatio.*
shout, v. (*con*)*clamare, vociferari.*
shove, v. *trudĕre, impellĕre.*
shovel, subst. *pala, batillum.*
show, subst.: = exhibition, *spectaculum, ludi* (*-orum*); = display, *ostentatio*; = (mere) appearance, *species.*
show, v.: = point out, (*de*)*monstrare*; = display, *exhibit, ostendĕre, ostentare.*
shower, subst. *imber, pluvia.*
shower, v. *effundĕre.*

showy, *speciosus, magnificus.*
shred, *frustum.*
shrew, *oblatratrix, mulier importuna.*
shrewd, *acutus, perspicax, sagax*; adv. *acute, sagaciter.*
shrewdness, (*ingenii*) *acumen* or *acies*; *sagacitas.*
shriek, subst. *ululatus* (*-ūs*), *clamor.*
shriek, v. *ululare, clamare.*
shrill, *acutus, argutus*; adv. *acute.*
shrine, *aedicula, delubrum, sacellum.*
shrink; transit., *contrahĕre*; intransit., *se contrahĕre*; to — from, *refugĕre, abhorrēre.*
shrivelled, *rugosus, vietus* (=shrivelled).
shroud, v. *involvĕre, velare, tegĕre.*
shrub, *frutex.*
shrubbery, *arbustum.*
shudder, subst. *horror, tremor.*
shudder, v. *horrēre, tremĕre.*
shuffle, *claudicare* (= limp), *tergiversari* (= be evasive).
shuffling, subst. *tergiversatio.*
shun, (*de*)*fugĕre, vitare, declinare.*
shutter, *foricula, valvae* (*-arum*, plur.).
shuttle, *radius.*
shy, adj. *timidus, verecundus*; adv. *timide, verecunde.*
shy, v., of a horse, *consternari.*
shyness, *timor, verecundia, pudor.*
Sicily, *Sicilia.*
sick, *aeger, aegrotus*; to be —, *aegrotare* (= to vomit, *vomĕre*); to feel —, *nauseare.* Transf., of boredom, render by *taedet.*
sickle, *falx.*
sickly, *infirmus.*
sickness: = nausea, *vomitus* (*-ūs*), *nausea*; = illness, *morbus aegrotatio.*
side, subst. *latus* (*-eris*, n.), *pars* (= part or faction); on this —, *hinc*; on this — of, *citra, cis*; on (or from) all —s, *undique*; on both —s, *utrinque.*
side, adj. *obliquus, transversus.*
side, v.: to — with, (*ab homine*) *stare;* (*homini*) *favēre* or *studēre.*
sideboard, *abacus.*
sidelong, *obliquus, transversus, limus.*
sideways, *oblique*; or use *obliquus* as adj.
siege, *oppugnatio* (= attack), *obsidio* (= blockade).
sieve, *cribrum.*
sift, *cribrare.* Transf., *investigare.*
sigh, subst. *suspirium.*
sigh, v. *suspirare, suspiria ducĕre.*
sight, subst. *visus* (*-ūs*), *aspectus* (*-ūs*); to catch — of, *conspicĕre, conspicari*; = view, range of —, *conspectus* (*-ūs*); = thing seen, *species, facies, spectaculum.*
sign, subst. *signum, indicium, vestigium* (= foot-mark), *insigne* (= badge); a good —, *omen faustum*; a bad —, *omen sinistrum.*
sign, v.; to — a document, (*con*)*signare, subscribĕre*; see also signal.
signal, subst. *signum*; to give a —, *signum dare.*
signal, adj. *insignis, maximus, egregius*; adv. *insigniter, egregie.*
signal, v. *significare, signum dare.*
signalize, v. *insignire.*
signature, *nomen* (*subscriptum*).
signet, *signum* (= seal).
significance, *significatio, vis.*
significant: see expressive.
signify, *significare*; of words, *valēre.*
silence, subst. *silentium*; to keep —, *tacēre, silēre.*
silence, v. *in silentium redigĕre, comprimĕre, confutare.*
silent, *silens, tacitus, mutus*; to be —, *silēre* (= make no noise), *tacēre* (=not speak). Adv. *tacite, silentio.*
silk, *bombyx, vestis serica.*
silken, *sericus, bombycinus.*
silk-worm, *bombyx.*
sill, *limen inferum.*
silliness, *stultitia, fatuitas, infacetiae* (*-arum*).
silly, *stultus, fatuus, infacetus.*
silt, subst. *limus.*
silver, subst. *argentum*; adorned with —, *argentatus.*
silver, silvery, adj. *argenteus*; — mine, *argenti metalla* (*-orum*).
silver, silvery, adj. *argenteus.*
silver, v. *argento inducĕre.*
similar, *similis, par*; adv. *similiter, pariter.*
similarity, *similitudo.*
simile, *similitudo, translatio.*
similitude, *similitudo.*
simmer, *fervescĕre, lente fervēre.*
simper, v. *subridēre, inepte ridēre.*
simple, *simplex; sincerus* (= guileless), *inconditus* (= artless), *ineptus* (= silly); adv. *simpliciter.*
simplicity *simplicitas, natura simplex; stultitia* (= folly).
simplify, *simplicem reddĕre.*
simulate, *simulare.*
simulation, *simulatio.*
simultaneously, *eodem tempore, simul, una.*
sin, subst. *peccatum, delictum, nefas.*
sin, v. *peccare, delinquĕre.*
since, adv. *postea, abhinc*; long —, *iamdudum, iampridem.*
since, prep. *ex, ab, post*; — the foundation of the city, *post urbem conditam.*
since, conj.: of time, *cum, postquam, ex quo* (*tempore*); causal, *cum, quandoquidem, quia, quoniam.*
sincere, *sincerus, simplex, candidus, verus*; adv. *sincere, ex animo, simpliciter.*
sincerity, *animus sincerus, veritas, simplicitas.*
sinew, *nervus.*
sinewy, *nervosus.*
sinful, *impius, improbus, pravus, malus.*
sing, *canere, cantare, modulari.*
singe, *amburĕre, adurĕre.*
singer, *cantor, cantator.*
singing, subst. *cantus* (*-ūs*), *concentus* (*-ūs*).
single, adj. *unus, solus, unicus, singularis*; = unmarried, *caelebs*; not a — one, *ne unus quidem.* Adv. *singillatim, viritim*; or adj. *singuli* (= one by one).
singular: opp. to plural, *singularis*; = outstanding, *singularis, unicus,*

egregius, maximus; = strange, *mirus, mirabilis*. Adv. *singulariter, unice, egregie, maxime, mire, mirabiliter*.
sinister, *sinister; infaustus* (= unlucky), *pravus* (= wrong).
sink, v.: transit., (*sub*)*mergĕre, demergĕre, deprimĕre*; intransit. (*con*)-*sīdĕre, desidĕre, submergi, demergi*; of prices, courage, etc., *cadĕre*.
sinuous, *sinuosus*.
sip, v. (*primis labris*) *degustare*.
sir, in addresses, *bone vir, vir optime*.
sire, *pater, genitor*.
sister, *soror, germana*.
sit, v.: transit., to — a horse, *in equo haerēre*; intransit., *sedēre*; to — down, *consīdĕre, adsīdĕre*; of a court, *habēri*.
site, *situs* (*-ūs*).
sitting, subst. *sessio, consessus* (*-ūs*).
situated, *situs, positus, conlocatus*.
situation: *situs* (*-ūs*), *locus*; = state of affairs, (*rerum*) *status* (*-ūs*); = office, *munus* (*-eris*, n.).
six, *sex*; — at a time, — each, *seni*; — times, *sexie*(*n*)*s*.
sixteen, *sedecim*; — at a time, — each, *seni deni*; — times, *sedecie*(*n*)*s*.
sixteenth, *sextus decimus*.
sixth, *sextus*; for the — time, *sextum*.
sixtieth, *sexagesimus*.
sixty, *sexaginta*; — at a time, — each, *sexageni*; — times *sexagie*(*n*)*s*.
size: *magnitudo, amplitudo*; = glue, *gluten*.
skeleton, *ossa* (*-ium*, n.), *ossium compages*.
sketch, subst. *adumbratio, descriptio*.
sketch, v. *describĕre, designare, adumbrare*.
skiff, *scapha, cymba, navicula*.
skilful, *sollers, peritus, callidus*; adv. *sollerter, perite, callide*.
skill, *sollertia, peritia, ars, calliditas*.
skim, *despumare, spumam eximĕre*; to — over a thing, *perstringĕre, percurrĕre, transcurrĕre*.
skin, subst. *cutis, pellis, membrana* (thin).
skin, v. *pellem* or *corium detrahĕre*.
skip, *salire* (= leap); to — for joy, *exsultare*; = pass over, *transilire, praeterire*.
skipper, *navis magister*.
skirmish, subst. *proelium*.
skirmisher, *veles*.
skirt, v. *tangĕre*; — the coast, *oram legĕre*.
skittish, *protervus*; to be —, *lascivire*; adv. *proterve*.
skittishness, *protervitas, lascivia*.
skulk, *latēre, delitescĕre*.
skull, *caput*.
sky, *caelum*; under the open —, *sub divo*.
slack: = loose, *laxus, remissus*; = careless, *remissus, segnis, neglegens*; adv. *laxe, neglegenter*.
slacken, v.: transit., (*re*)*laxare, remittĕre*; intransit., *laxari, remitti*.
slackness, *remissio, neglegentia*.
slake, v., of thirst, *restinguĕre, exstinguĕre, explēre*.
slander, subst. *calumnia*, (*falsa*) *criminatio*.
slander, v. *calumniari, criminari, obtrectare*.
slanderer, *obtrectator*.
slanderous, *maledicus, famosus*; adv. *falso, per calumniam*.
slanting, *obliquus, transversus*.
slash, v. *caedĕre, incidĕre*; see cut.
slate: for writing, *tabula*; = tile, *tegula*.
slaughter, subst. *caedes, occidio, strages*.
slaughterer, *lanius*.
slaughterhouse, *laniena*.
slave, subst. *servus, ancilla* (female), *verna* (home-born), *famulus*; fellow-—, *conservus*; of a —, adj., *servilis*; to be a —, *servire*.
slave-dealer, *venalicius, mango*.
slavery, *servitūs* (*-ūtis*), *servitium*.
slavish, *servilis*; adv. *serviliter*.
slay, *interficĕre, occīdĕre, necare*.
slayer, *interfector*; of a man, *homicida*; of a close relative, *parricida*.
sledge, *trahea*.
sleek, *lēvis, nitidus* (= shining); to be —, *nitēre*.
sleep, subst. *somnus, sopor*; want of —, *vigilia*.
sleep, v. *dormire*.
sleepiness, *veternus, somni cupido*.
sleepless, *insomnis, vigilans*.
sleeplessness, *insomia, vigilia*.
sleepy, *semisomnus, somniculosus, somno gravis*.
sleet, *nix grandine mixta*.
sleeves, *manicae* (*-arum*).
slender, *tenuis, gracilis, exilis*.
slenderness, *tenuitas, gracilitas*.
slice, v. *concīdĕre, secare*.
slide, v. *labi*.
slight, adj. *levis, tenuis, exiguus*.
slight, v. *neglegĕre, contemnĕre*.
slim, *exilis*.
slime, *limus*.
slimy, *limosus*.
sling, subst.: the weapon, *funda*; for the arm, *fascia*.
sling, v. (*fundā*) *mittĕre, torquēre*.
slink, v.: to — away, *sese subducĕre*.
slip, subst. *lapsus* (*-ūs*), *culpa* (= fault), *error* (= mistake); of a plant, *surculus*.
slip, v. *labi*; — away, *se subducĕre, elabi*; to let —, *amittĕre, omittĕre*.
slipper, *crepida, solea*.
slippery, *lubricus*.
slit, subst. *rima*.
slit, v. *incīdĕre, findĕre, scindĕre*.
slope, subst. *clivus, fastigium*; upward, *acclivitas*; downward, *declivitas*.
slope, v. *vergĕre*.
sloping, *acclivis, declivis, pronus*.
sloth, *inertia, segnitia, desidia, ignavia*.
slothful, *iners, segnis, ignavus*; adv. *segniter, ignave*.
slough, *palūs* (*-ūdis*); of a snake, *vernatio, exuviae* (*-arum*).
slovenliness, *sordes* (*-ium*), *neglegentia*.
slovenly, *sordidus, discinctus, neglegens*.
slow, *tardus, lentus*; adv. *tarde, lente, sensim* (= gradually).
slowness, *tarditas, segnitas, pigritia*.

slug, *limax.*
sluggish, *segnis, piger, ignavus*; adv. *segniter, ignave.*
sluggishness, *pigritia, ignavia, inertia.*
sluice, *emissarium.*
slumber; see sleep.
slur; see disgrace.
slur over, v. *extenuare.*
sly, *vafer, subdolus*; adv. *vafre, subdole.*
slyness, *dolus, astutia.*
smack, subst.: = flavour, *sapor, gustus* (-*ūs*); = blow, *alapa*; = small ship, *lenunculus*; fishing- —, *horia.*
smack, v.; to — of, *sapĕre,* (*red*)*olēre.*
small, *parvus, parvulus, exiguus, minutus*; a — mind, *animus pusillus*; so —, *tantulus*; how —? *quantulus?*
smallness, *parvitas, exiguitas.*
smart, subst. *dolor, cruciatus* (-*ūs*).
smart, v. = to feel pain, *dolere, plecti.*
smart, adj.: = active, *acer, alacer*; = witty, *salsus*; = elegant, *lautus, mundus, nitidus.*
smear, v. (*in*)*linĕre, oblinĕre.*
smell, subst. *odor, odoratus* (-*ūs*; = the sense), to have a bad —, *male olēre.*
smell, v.: = perceive a —, *olfacĕre*; = give off a smell, *olēre*; to — of, *redolēre.*
smelt, *fundĕre, coquĕre.*
smile, subst. *risus* (-*ūs*); with a —, *subridens.*
smile, v. (*sub*)*ridēre, renidēre.*
smite, v. *ferire, percutĕre.*
smith, *faber*; black—, *faber ferrarius.*
smithy, *officina, fabrica.*
smoke, subst. *fumus.*
smoke, v. *fumare.*
smoky, *fumosus.*
smooth, adj. *levis, teres*; of style, *lenis*; of manner, *blandus*; of temper, *aequus.* Adv. *leniter.*
smoothness, *levitas, aequabilitas.*
smother, *suffocare, animam intercludĕre.* Transf., *opprimĕre, comprimĕre.*
smuts, *fuligo.*
snail, *cochlea.*
snake, *anguis, serpens, vipera.*
snaky, *vipereus, anguineus.*
snap, v.: transit., = break, *frangĕre*; — the fingers, *digitis concrepare*; — up, *adripĕre, corripĕre*; intransit., *dissilire, frangi.*
snappish, *morosus, difficilis, mordax.*
snare, subst. *laqueus, plaga, insidiae* (-*arum*).
snare, v. *inlaqueare.*
snarl, subst. *gannitus* (-*ūs*).
snarl, v. (*og*)*gannire,* (*sub*)*ringi.*
snatch, *rapĕre, corripĕre*; — at, *captare*; — away, *eripĕre, avellĕre.*
sneak, = go stealthily, (*cor*)*repĕre*; — in, *inrepĕre*; — away, (*furtim*) *se subducĕre.*
sneer, subst., *rhonchus.*
sneer, v. *deridēre, inridēre*
sneeze, *sternuĕre.*
sneezing, *sternumentum.*
snore, *stertĕre.*
snort, v. *fremĕre.*
snout, *rostrum.*
snow, subst. *nix.*
snow, v.: it —s, *ningit.*
snowy, *nivosus, niveus.*
snub; see rebuke.
snub-nosed, *silus, simus.*
snuff, of a candle, *fungus.*
so: adv., = thus, *sic, ita*; = to such an extent, *sic, ita, adeo, tam*; so . . . as, *tam . . . quam*; so that (final), *ut*; so great, *tantus*; so many, *tot*; so many times, *totie*(*n*)*s*; so far as, *quantum*; so long as, *dum* (*modo*), with subjunc.; as conj., so, and so, *itaque, ergo, igitur.*
soak, *madefacĕre*; — up, *bibĕre*; — through, *permanare.*
soap, *sapo.*
soar, *sublime ferri, subvolare.*
sob, subst. *singultus* (-*ūs*).
sob, v. *singultare.*
sober, *sobrius, temperans, temperatus*; adv. *sobrie, temperate.*
sobriety, *sobrietas, temperantia.*
sociable, *comis, facilis, socialis*; adv. *socialiter.*
social, *communis, civilis*; — life, *vitae societas, vita communis.*
socialism, *bona communia habēre.*
society, *homines* (-*um*), *hominum conventus* (-*ūs*); more limited, *societas, sodalitas, conlegium, factio* (political); the — of an individual, *convictus* (-*ūs*), *consuetudo.*
sock; see stocking.
socket, *cavum.*
sod, *caespes.*
soda, *nitrum.*
sodden, *madidus.*
sofa, *lectulus, grabatus.*
soft, *mollis, tener, lenis, effeminatus*; adv. *molliter, leniter.*
soften, v.: transit., (*e*)*mollire, mitigare, lenire*; intransit., *molliri, mitescĕre.*
softness, *mollitia, mollities.*
soil, subst. *solum, terra, humus.*
soil, v. *inquinare, polluĕre, maculare.*
sojourn, subst. *commoratio, mansio.*
sojourn, v. (*com*)*morari, manēre.*
sojourner, *hospes, peregrinus, advena.*
solace, subst. *solatium, consolatio.*
solace, v. (*con*)*solari.*
solar, render by genit. *solis.*
soldier, *miles*; fellow —, *commilito*; foot —, *pedes*; horse —, *eques.*
soldierly, *militaris.*
soldiery, *milites* (-*um*), or coll. sing. *miles.*
sole, subst.: of the foot, *solum, planta*; the fish, *solea.*
sole, adj. *solus, unus, unicus*; adv. *solum, tantum.*
solemn, *sanctus, religiosus*; see also serious. Adv. *sancte, graviter.*
solemnization, *celebratio.*
solemnize, *celebrare.*
solicit: = ask for, *petĕre, poscĕre, captare*; = incite, *sollicitare.*
solicitation, *preces* (-*um*).
solicitous, *sollicitus, anxius*; adv. *sollicite, anxie.*
solicitude, *sollicitudo, cura, anxietas.*
solid, *solidus, stabilis, firmus*; adv. *firme, firmiter.*
solidity, *soliditas.*

solitary, *solus, solitarius*; of places, *desertus.*
solitude, *solitudo.*
solstice: the summer —, *solstitium*; winter —, *bruma.*
solution, (*dis*)*solutio*; of problems, *explicatio.*
solve, (*dis*)*solvĕre, expedire, explicare.*
solvent; to be —, *solvendo esse.*
some, somebody, someone, *aliquis -quid,* pron., and *aliqui -qua -quod,* adj.; *quis, quid,* pron., and *qui, qua, quod,* adj. (indef., usually after *si, nisi, ne* or *num*); *nescioquis,* pron., and *nescioqui,* adj.; *nonnullus* (esp. plur., = — few); *aliquot* (plur., indecl.); distributively, — . . . others, *alii . . . alii*; to — degree, *aliquantum*; at — time, *aliquando.*
somehow, *nescio quomodo, nescio quo pacto.*
something, *aliquid, nonnihil.*
sometimes, *aliquando, nonnunquam, interdum.*
somewhat, *aliquantum, aliquantulum.*
somewhere, *alicubi.*
son, *filius, natus*; — -in-law, *gener*; step- —, *privignus.*
song, *carmen, cantus* (*-ūs*), *canticum.*
sonorous, *canorus, clarus*; adv. *canore, clare.*
soon, *mox, brevi* (*tempore*), *cito*; too —, *ante tempus*; as — as possible, *quam primum*; as — as, *simul ac.*
sooner, *maturius*; = for preference, *potius, libentius.*
soot, *fuligo.*
soothe, *mulcēre, lenire, placare, sedare.*
soothing, *blandus.*
soothsayer, *haruspex, hariolus, auspex.*
soothsaying, subst. *haruspicina, auspicium.*
sop, *frustum, offa* (*panis*).
sophism, sophistry, *captio, sophisma.*
sophistical, *captiosus.*
soporific, adj. *soporifer, soporus.*
sorcerer, *veneficus.*
sorceress, *venefica, maga, saga.*
sorcery, *ars magica.*
sordid, *sordidus, abiectus*; adv. *sordide.*
sordidness, *sordes* (*-ium*).
sore, subst. *ulcus* (*-eris,* n.).
sore, *adj.,* = painful, *gravis, acerbus*; adv. *graviter.*
sorrow, subst. *dolor, maestitia, tristitia, luctus* (*-ūs*).
sorrow, v. *dolēre, maerēre, lugēre.*
sorrowful, *tristis, maestus, lugubris*; adv. *maeste.*
sorry; see sorrowful; I am —, = I regret, *me paenitet*; = I pity, *me miseret.*
sort, subst., = kind, *genus*; of what —? *qualis? cuiusmodi?* of that —, *talis, eiusmodi*; he is not the — of man to, *non is est qui,* with subjunc.
sort, v. *digerĕre.*
sortie, *excursio, eruptio*; to make a —, *erumpĕre.*
sot, *potator, homo ebriosus.*
soul, *anima, animus* (rational or emotional); not a —, *nemo, ne unus quidem.*
sound, subst. *sonus, sonitus* (*-ūs*), *strepitus* (*-ūs*).
sound, adj. *sanus, integer*; safe and —, *incolumis, salvus*; of sleep, *altus, artus*; of arguments, *gravis.* Adv., of sleep, *arte*; of beating, etc., *graviter.*
soundness, *sanitas, integritas*; of arguments, *gravitas.*
sour, adj. *acerbus, amarus.*
sour, v. *exacerbare.*
source, *fons, caput, origo, principium.*
sourness, *acerbitas, amaritudo.*
south, subst. *meridies, regio meridiana.*
south, southern, adj. *meridianus, australis*; — wind, *auster*; — -west wind, *Africus.*
southwards, *in* or *ad meridiem.*
sovereign, subst. *rex, dominus, princeps.*
sovereign, adj. *sui iuris*; — remedy, *remedium efficacissium.*
sovereignty, *summa imperii,* (*summum*) *imperium, dominatio, regnum.*
sow, subst. *sus.*
sow, v. *serĕre, semen spargĕre.*
sower, *sator.*
sowing, subst. *satio, satus* (*-ūs*).
space, *spatium, locus.*
spacious, *amplus.*
spaciousness, *amplitudo, laxitas.*
spade, *pala.*
Spain, *Hispania.*
span, subst., as measure, *palmus*; the — of life, *vitae summa.*
span, v.; see measure; of bridges, *iungĕre.*
spangled, *distinctus.*
Spanish, *Hispanus, Hispanicus, Hispaniensis.*
spar, subst. *asser, longurius.*
spare, v. *parcĕre* (with dat.).
sparing, *parcus;* adv. *parce.*
spark, *scintilla, igniculus.*
sparkle, v. *scintillare, fulgēre, nitēre.*
sparrow, *passer.*
spatter, *spargĕre, aspergĕre.*
speak, *dicĕre, loqui, fari*; — out, — up, *eloqui*; — to, *adfari, appellare, adloqui*; — together, *conloqui.*
speaker, *orator, is qui dicit.*
spear, subst. *hasta.*
spear, v. *hastā transfigĕre.*
special, *praecipuus, proprius, peculiaris;* adv. *praecipue, imprimis, praesertim.*
species, *genus* (*-eris,* n.), *species.*
specific, adj.: = peculiar, *proprius, peculiaris*; = explicit, *disertus*; adv. *diserte.*
specify, *denotare, enumerare.*
specimen, *specimen, documentum, exemplum.*
specious, *speciosus.*
speck, *macula.*
speckled, *maculis distinctus, maculatus.*
spectacle, *spectaculum.*
spectator, *spectator, is qui spectat.*
spectre; see ghost.
speculate, = consider, *cogitare, quaerĕre.*
speculation: = thought, *cogitatio*; scientific —, *rerum contemplatio*; = guess, *coniectura.*
speculative, = conjectural, *coniecturalis.*

speech, *oratio*; a — before the people, *contio*; to deliver a —, *orationem* (or *contionem*) *habēre*.
speechless; see dumb.
speed, subst. *celeritas, velocitas*.
speed, v.: transit., *maturare*; = make prosperous, *fortunare*; intransit., = hasten, *properare, festinare*.
speedy, *citus, celer, velox;* adv. *cito, celeriter, velociter*.
spell, subst. *carmen*.
spellbound, *defixus, stupens, stupefactus*.
spend: of money, *insumēre*; of time, *agēre, degēre, consumēre*.
spendthrift, *nepos, homo prodigus*.
sphere, *sphaera, globus*; = field of activity, *provincia*.
spherical, *globosus*.
spice, *condimentum*.
spicy, *conditus;* fig. *salsus*.
spider, *aranea;* —'s web, *aranea*.
spike, *clavus, cuspis*.
spikenard, *nardus*.
spill, *effundēre*.
spin, *nēre*; — round, transit., *versare, circumagēre*; intransit., use pass.; to — out, = prolong, *ducēre*.
spindle, *fusus*.
spine, *spina*.
spinster, *virgo, innupta*.
spiral, adj. *tortuosus*.
spire, *turris*.
spirit: = character, *animus, ingenium, indoles, natura*; = animation, courage, *animus, spiritus* (*-ūs*), *ferocia*; a disembodied —, *anima*, plur. *manes* (*-ium*); = intention, meaning, *consilium, sententia*.
spirited, *animosus, ferox, acer*.
spiritless, *ignavus*.
spiritual, render by genit., *animi* or *ingenii*.
spit, subst. *veru*.
spit, v. *spuēre*; — out, *respuēre*.
spite, subst. *malignitas, malevolentia, invidia, odium*.
spite, v.; see vex, annoy.
spiteful, *malignus, malevolus*; adv. *maligne*.
splash, v. transit., *aspergēre*.
splendid, *splendidus, egregius,* (*prae*)*clarus*; adv. *splendide,* (*prae*)*clare*.
splendour, *splendor; apparatus* (*-ūs*, = pomp).
splinter, *fragmentum*.
split, subst. *fissura, scissura, rima*.
split, v.: transit., (*dif*)*findēre, scindēre*; intransit., (*dif*)*findi, dissilire*.
spoil, subst. *praeda*; —s of war, *spolia* (*-orum*, plur.).
spoil, v.: — plunder, (*ex*)*spoliare*; = to injure, mar, *corrumpēre, perdēre, vitiare*.
spoiler, *spoliator*.
spoiling, spoliation, *spoliatio*.
spoke, *radius*.
spondee, *spondeus*.
sponge, subst. *spongia*.
sponsor, of measures, etc., *auctor*.
spontaneous, *voluntarius*; adv. (*sua*) *sponte, ultro*.
spoon, *cocleare*.
sport, subst. *ludus, lusus* (*-ūs*); = hunting, *venatio*; = mockery, *ludibrium, inrisio*.
sport, v. *ludēre, lascivire*.
sportive, adj. *lascivus, iocosus, festivus*; adv. *per iocum, iocose*.
sportiveness, *lascivia, iocus*.
sportsman, *venator*.
spot, subst.: = mark, stain, *macula, nota*; = place, *locus*.
spot, v. *notare, maculare*.
spotless, *sine maculis, purus*.
spotted, *maculosus, maculis distinctus*.
spouse, *coniunx*.
spray, subst.: liquid, *aspergo*; on a tree, *virgula*.
spread, v.: transit. (*ex*)*pandēre, explicare, extendēre, spargēre* (= scatter), (*di*)*vulgare* (= publish); intransit., render by pass.
sprig, *surculus, virgula*.
sprightliness, *alacritas, facetiae* (*-arum*, = pleasantries).
sprightly, *alacer*; *facetus* (= humorous).
spring, subst. *fons*; fig., *origo, principium*; the season, *ver, tempus vernum*.
spring, v. = leap, *salire*; to — from, (*ex re*) *nasci*, (*ex*)*oriri*; to — up, of plants, *crescēre*; of winds, *surgēre*.
spring-tide, *aestus* (*-ūs*) *maximus*.
sprinkle, *spargēre, aspergēre, conspergēre*.
sprite, *faunus, nympha*.
sprout, v. *pullulare, germinare*.
spruce, adj. *comptus, bellus, nitidus, elegans*; adv. *belle, nitide, eleganter*.
spur, subst. *calcar*.
spur, v.: to — a horse, *equo calcaria subdēre*.
spurious, *adulterinus, falsus*.
spurn, *fastidire, aspernari, repudiare*.
spy, subst. *explorator, speculator*.
spy, v. *explorare, speculari*.
squabble, subst. *rixa, altercatio, iurgium*.
squabble, v. *rixari*.
squadron, of cavalry, (*equitum*) *turma* or *ala*; of ships, *classis*.
squalid, *sordidus, spurcus*; adv. *sordide*
squall, subst. *procella*; an infant's, *vagitus* (*-ūs*).
squall, v. *vagire*.
squalor, *sordes* (*-ium*).
squander, *profundēre, perdēre, dissipare*.
squanderer, *nepos*.
square, subst. *quadratum, quadra*.
square, adj. *quadratus*.
square, v. *quadrare*.
squash, v. *conterēre, contundēre*.
squat, v. *subsidēre, considēre*.
squeak, subst. *stridor*.
squeak, v. *stridēre*.
squeamish, *fastidiosus, delicatus*.
squeamishness, *fastidium*.
squeeze, subst. *compressio*.
squeeze, v. *premēre, comprimēre*; — out, *exprimēre*.
squint, v. *limis* or *perversis oculis esse*; one who —s, *strabo*.
squirrel, *sciurus*.
stab, v. *confodēre*.
stability, *stabilitas, firmitas, constantia*.
stable, subst. *stabulum*.
stable, adj. *stabilis, firmus, constans*.
stable, v. *stabulare*.

stack, subst. *cumulus, acervus, strues.*
stack, v. *cumulare.*
staff: = stick, *baculum, scipio*; a herald's —, *caduceus*; = assistants, military, *legati* (*-orum*), civil, *adiutores.*
stag, *cervus.*
stage, *proscaenium, scaena*; of the —, *scaenicus*; = degree, *gradus* (*-ūs*).
stagger, v. *titubare, vacillare.*
stagnant, *stagnans, piger, lentus.*
stagnate, *stagnare.* Transf., *hebescĕre, languēre.*
staid; see sober.
stain, subst. *macula, labes, nota.*
stain, v. *maculare, foedare, polluĕre.*
stainless, *purus, integer.*
stair, *gradus* (*-ūs*); —case, *scalae* (*-arum*).
stake, subst.: = post, *palus, stipes, sudes*; = pledge, *pignus* (*-oris*, n.); to be at —, *agi, in discrimine esse.*
stake, v. (*de*)*ponĕre.*
stale, subst. *culmus, caulis, calamus.*
stalk, v.; = strut, *incedĕre.*
stall, subst. *stabulum*; = shop, *taberna.*
stall, v. *stabulare.*
stammer, v. *balbutire, lingua haesitare.*
stammering, adj. *balbus.*
stamp, subst. *nota, signum, imago* (*impressa*); of the foot, *pedis supplosio.*
stamp, v. *signare, notare*; with the foot, *pedem supplodĕre*: to — underfoot, *conculcare.*
stand, subst.: to come to a —, *consistĕre, subsistĕre*; to make a — against, *resistĕre* (with dat).
stand, v. (1) = be upright, *stare, consistĕre*; to — by, *adesse*; — fast, *consistĕre, subsistĕre, restare*; — for office, *petĕre*; stand in the way, *obstare*; — out, *eminēre, exstare*; — up, *surgĕre.* (2) = set upright, place, *statuĕre, constituĕre.* (3) = tolerate, *tolerare, perferre, sustinēre.*
standard: = flag, *vexillum, signum*; = measure, *regula, norma.*
standard-bearer, *vexillarius, signifer.*
standing, subst. *condicio, gradus* (*-ūs*), *locus*; of long —, *vetus.*
standstill: to be at a —, *haerēre.*
star, *stella, astrum.* Transf., *lumen.*
stare, subst. *obtutus* (*-ūs*).
stare, v. *spectare, intuēri*; in astonishment, *stupēre.*
stark, *rigidus.*
starling, *sturnus.*
start, subst.: = sudden movement, *saltus* (*-ūs*); = beginning, *initium, principium*; = setting out, *profectio.*
start, v.: transit., *instituĕre, aggredi, incipĕre*; intransit., = move suddenly, *expavescĕre*; to — up, *exsilire*; = begin, *incipĕre,* (*ex*)*ordiri*; = set out, *proficisci.*
startle; see frighten.
startling, *terribilis*; = strange, *mirus.*
starve, v.: transit., *fame necare*; intransit., *fame confici* or *perire.*
state, subst.: = condition, *status* (*-ūs*), *condicio, locus*; polit., *respublica, civitas*; = grandeur, *apparatus* (*-ūs*), *magnificentia.*
state, adj. *publicus.*
state, v. *adfirmare, adseverare, dicĕre.*
stately, *lautus, magnificus.*
statesman, *vir reipublicae peritus.*
statesmanship, *ars reipublicae regendae.*
station, subst. see position; v. see place, set.
stationary, *immobilis, immotus*; — camp, (*castra*) *stativa* (*-orum*).
statue, *signum, statua, effigies.*
stature, *statura.*
statute, *lex.*
staunch, adj. *firmus, certus, fidus.*
staunch, v. (*sanguinem*) *sistĕre* or *cohibēre.*
stay, subst.: = prop, *adminiculum*; = sojourn, *mansio, commoratio.*
stay, v.: transit., = prop, *fulcire*; = stop, (*de*)*morari, detinēre, cohibēre*; intransit., (*com*)*morari, manēre.*
stead: in— of, *pro,* with abl.: *loco* or *in vicem,* with genit.
steadiness, *stabilitas, firmitas, constantia.*
steady, *stabilis, firmus, constans*; adv. *firme, firmiter, constanter.*
steal, v.: transit., *furari, surripĕre*; intransit., = go stealthily, *subrepĕre*; — in, *inrepĕre*; — away, *se subducĕre.*
stealthy, *furtivus, clandestinus*; adv. *furtim, clam.*
steam, subst. (*aquae*) *vapor, nidor, fumus.*
steam, v. *vaporare.*
steed, *equus.*
steel, subst. *chalybs*; = sword, *ferrum.*
steel, v.: to — oneself, *obdurescĕre.*
steep, adj. *praeruptus, praeceps, arduus.*
steep, v. *madefacĕre, imbuĕre.*
steer, subst. *iuvencus.*
steer, v. *gubernare, regĕre.*
steering, subst. *gubernatio.*
steersman, *gubernator, rector.*
stem, subst.: of a tree, *stirps, truncus*; of a plant, *caulis, calamus*; = race, *stirps, genus* (*-eris*, n.).
stem, v. = check, *cohibēre, coercēre.*
step, subst.: = stair, *gradus* (*-ūs*); = pace, *gradus, passus, gressus* (all *-ūs*); — by —, *gradatim, pedetentim*; = plan, measure, *ratio, consilium.*
step, v. *gradi*; — in, *ingredi*; — forwards, *progredi.*
step-brother, *filius vitrici,* or *novercae.*
step-daughter, *privigna.*
step-father, *vitricus.*
step-mother, *noverca.*
step-sister, *filia vitrici* or *novercae.*
step-son, *privignus.*
sterile, *sterilis.*
sterility, *sterilitas.*
sterling, *verus, bonus.*
stern, subst., *puppis.*
stern, adj. *durus, severus*; adv. *severe, dure.*
sternness, *severitas.*
steward, *procurator*; of an estate, *vilicus.*
stewardship, *cura, procuratio.*
stick, subst. *baculum, virga* (= rod), *fustis* (= cudgel).

stick, v.: transit., *(ad)figĕre*; intransit., *(ad)haerēre, adhaerescĕre*; = get stuck, *haerēre, haesitare, dubitare.*
sticky, *tenax, lentus.*
stiff, *rigidus, durus*; to be —, *rigēre.* Adv., *rigide, dure, duriter.*
stiffen, v.: transit., *rigidum facĕre*; intransit., *rigescĕre.*
stiffness, *rigor.*
stifle, *suffocare.*
stigma, *nota.*
stigmatize, *notare, notam inurĕre.*
still, adj. *tranquillus, quietus, placidus.*
still, adv. *adhuc, etiam*; see also nevertheless.
still, v. *sedare, placare.*
stilling, subst. *sedatio.*
stillness, *silentium, tranquillitas, quies.*
stimulate, *stimulare, excitare, incitare.*
stimulus, *stimulus, incitamentum.*
sting, subst. *aculeus.*
sting, v. *pungĕre, aculeos infigĕre.*
stinginess, *parsimonia, tenacitas.*
stinging, *mordax, acerbus, aculeatus.*
stingy, *parcus, sodidus, tenax*; adv. *parce, sordide.*
stink; see smell.
stint, v. *parce dare, parcĕre.*
stipend; see salary.
stipendiary, *mercenarius, stipendiarius.*
stipulate, *stipulari, (de)pacisci.*
stipulation, *pactum, condicio.*
stir, subst. *motus (-ūs), tumultus (-ūs).*
stir, v.: transit., *(com)movēre, exagitare*; intransit., *se movēre, progredi.*
stitch, v. *(con)suĕre.*
stock, subst.: of a tree, *truncus, stirps*; = family, *genus, stirps*; = store, *copia.*
stock, adj.; see common, trite.
stock, v. *instruĕre, ornare.*
stockade, *vallum.*
stocking, *tibiale.*
stoic, subst. and adj. *stoicus.*
stoical, *ferreus, rigidus, austerus*; adv. *austere, stoice.*
stoicism, *stoicorum ratio* or *doctrina.*
stomach, subst. *stomachus.*
stone, subst. *lapis, saxum*; of —, adj. *lapideus*; in fruit, *nucleus*; precious —, *gemma.*
stone, v. *lapides in hominem conicĕre.*
stony: = of stone, *lapideus, saxeus*; = full of stones, *lapidosus, saxosus.*
stony-hearted, *durus, ferreus.*
stoop, v. *se inclinare* or *demittĕre.*
stooping, adj. *pronus, inclinatus.*
stop, subst.: = stay, *mansio*; = pause, *intermissio, pausa*; as punctuation, *interpunctum.*
stop, v.: transit., *sistĕre, prohibēre, comprimĕre*; — up, *obturare, occludĕre*; intransit., = halt, *(con)sistĕre*; = stay, *manēre, (com)morari*; = cease, refrain, *desinĕre.*
stoppage, *obstructio, impedimentum.*
store, subst. *copia, vis.*
store, v. *coacervare, reponĕre, condĕre.*
store-house, *horreum, thesaurus, apotheca.*
store-room, *cella.*
storey, *tabulatio, tabulatum.*
stork, *ciconia.*
storm, subst. *tempestas, procella.*
storm, v.: transit., *expugnare, vi capĕre*; intransit., *furĕre, saevire.*
storm-cloud, *nimbus.*
storming, subst. *expugnatio.*
stormy, *turbulentus, turbidus*; adv. *turbulente, turbide.*
story: = tale, *fabula, res, narratio*; to tell a —, *narrare*; = falsehood, *mendacium*; see also storey.
stout: = fat, *obesus, pinguis*; = thick, *crassus, densus*; = strong, *validus, robustus*; = brave, *fortis.* Adv. *fortiter, valide, robuste.*
stove, *focus, caminus.*
stow; see store.
straggle, *vagari, deerare, palari.*
straight: adj. *(di)rectus, erectus*; adv. *recta, recto itinere.*
straighten, *corrigĕre.*
straightforward, *simplex, apertus.*
strain, subst.: = exertion, *intentio, contentio*; of music, etc., *modus*; = manner, *modus*; in this —, *ita, sic.*
strain, v. *contendĕre*; see also filter.
strained; see far-fetched.
strait, subst.: = narrow sea, *fretum*; = any narrow passage, or difficulty, *angustiae (-arum,* plur.).
strait, *artus, angustus.*
straiten, *in angustias adducĕre.*
strand, subst. *litus (-oris,* n.), *ripa.*
strand, v. *navem vadis inlidĕre.*
strange, adj.: = foreign, *peregrinus, externus*; = alien, not one's own, *alienus*; = unusual, *insolitus, novus, mirus, mirabilis.* Adv. *mirum in modum, mirabiliter.*
strangeness, *novitas, insolentia.*
stranger, *hospes, advena, peregrinus.*
strangle, *strangulare, gulam laqueo frangĕre.*
strap, subst. *lorum.*
strap, v. *loris (con)stringĕre.*
stratagem, *ars, dolus.*
strategy, *ars belli gerendi.*
straw, *stramentum.*
strawberry, *fragum.*
stray, adj. *errabundus.*
stray, v. *(ab)errare, vagari, palari.*
streak, subst. *linea, nota.*
streak, v. *lineis distinguĕre.*
stream, subst. *flumen, rivus*; up —, *adverso flumine*; down —, *secundo flumine.*
stream, v. *fluĕre, effundi.*
streamer, *vexillum.*
street, *via, vicus.*
strength, *vires (-ium,* plur.), *robur, nervi (-orum).*
strengthen, transit., *(con) firmare, (con)roborare.*
strengthening, subst. *confirmatio.*
strenuous, *strenuus, impiger, (g)navus*; adv. *strenue, impigre.*
strenuousness, *(g)navitas, studium.*
stress, *momentum, vis.*
stretch, subst.: = effort, *contentio, nisus (-ūs)*; at a —, *uno tenore*; = expanse, *tractus (-ūs), spatium.*
stretch, v.: transit., *(ex)tendĕre, contendĕre*; to — out, *porrigĕre*; intransit., render by pass.
strew, *sternĕre, spargĕre.*

strict: = exact, *diligens, religiosus*; = severe, *severus, rigidus*. Adv. *accurate; severe, rigide.*
strictness: = carefulness, *accuratio, diligentia*; = severity, *severitas, rigor.*
stricture, *animadversio, reprehensio.*
stride, subst. *ingens gradus* (*-ūs*).
strife, *certamen, contentio, controversia.*
strike, v.: transit., *ferire, percutĕre, pulsare, caedĕre*; mentally, *percutĕre, percellĕre*; to be struck by lightning, *de caelo tangi*; to — down, *adfligĕre*; — out, *elidĕre, delēre*; intransit., to — against, *offendĕre, incurrĕre.*
striking; see remarkable.
string, subst. *linum, linea, filum*; bow-—, *nervus*; of a musical instrument *nervus, fides* (usually plur.).
string, v. *nervos aptare* (of an instrument); see also bind.
stringent; see severe.
strip, subst.; of paper, *scidula chartae*; of cloth, *lacinia.*
strip, v.: transit., *spoliare, (de)nudare, exuĕre*; intransit., *vestem exuĕre* or *deponĕre.*
stripe; see streak and stroke.
stripling, *adulescens, adulescentulus.*
strive, *(e)niti, contendĕre.*
striving, *nisus* (*-ūs*), *certatio, contentio.*
stroke, subst. *ictus* (*-ūs*), *verber, plaga*; of lightning, *fulmen*; — of fortune, *eventus* (*-ūs*).
stroke, v. *(per)mulcēre, demulcēre.*
stroll, subst. *ambulatio.*
stroll, v. *ambulare, spatiari, reptare.*
strong, adj. *validus, firmus, robustus, fortis*; of flavours, *acer*; of winds, *vehemens*; of arguments, *gravis, firmus*; to be —, *valēre, pollēre.* Adv. *valide, firmiter, fortiter, vehementer.*
stronghold, *arx.*
structure: abstract, *ratio, forma, conformatio*; material, *aedificium, moles, compages.*
struggle, subst. *certamen, luctatio.*
struggle, v. *luctari, niti, contendĕre.*
strut, *(superbe) incedĕre.*
stubble, *stipulae* (*-arum*, plur.).
stubborn, *pertinax, pervicax, obstinatus*; adv. *pertinaciter, pervicaciter, obstinate.*
stubbornness, *pertinacia, pervicacia, obstinatio.*
stud, *bulla.*
studded, *distinctus.*
student; see scholar.
studied, *meditatus, commentatus.*
studious, *litterarum studiosus*; adv. *summo studio, studiose.*
study, subst., *studium, meditatio, commentatio, cognitio* (with genit.).
study, v. *rei* (dat.) *studēre; in rem inquirĕre.*
stuff, subst. *materia, materies*; = gear, *impedimenta* (*-orum*), *supellex*; = fabric, *textile, tela*; — and nonsense! *nugae! gerrae!*
stuff, v. *farcire, refercire, replēre.*
stuffing, *fartum* (in food), *tomentum* (for cushions).
stultify, *ad inritum redigĕre.*
stumble, *offendĕre*; — upon, *incidĕre.*
stumbling, subst. *offensio.*
stump, *stipes* (*-itis*), *truncus.*
stun, *sensu privare.* Transf., *(ob)stupefacĕre.*
stupefaction, *stupor, torpor.*
stupefy; see stun.
stupendous, *ingens, immanis*; *mirus.*
stupid, *stupidus, stolidus, stultus*; adv. *stolide, stulte.*
stupidity, *stupiditas, stupor, stultitia.*
stupor, *stupor, torpor.*
sturdy; see strong, firm.
sturgeon, *acipenser.*
stutter, v. *balbutire.*
sty, *hara, suile.*
style, subst., *genus* (*-eris*, n.), *ratio, modus*; — of dress, *habitus* (*-ūs*); of language, *dicendi* or *scribendi genus, oratio, sermo.*
style, v. *appellare.*
stylish, *speciosus, elegans*; adv. *speciose, eleganter.*
suave, *suavis, urbanus, blandus.*
suavity, *suavitas, urbanitas.*
subdivide, *iterum dividĕre.*
subdivision, *pars.*
subdue, *in imperium redigĕre, domare.*
subject, subst.: of a person, *civis*; = a matter, *res, quaestio*; gram., *subiectum.*
subject, adj. *subiectus, obnoxius.*
subject, v. *subicere, obnoxium reddĕre.*
subject-matter, *materia, res.*
subjection, *servitus* (*-ūtis*), *officium.*
subjective, render by personal pronouns or by *opinio.*
subjoin, *subiungĕre, subicĕre.*
subjugate, *(per)domare, subigĕre.*
subjunctive, *(modus) subjunctivus.*
sublime, *elatus, excelsus*; adv. *elate, excelse.*
sublimity, *elatio, excelsitas.*
submerge, *submergĕre.*
submission, *obsequium, officium.*
submissive, *oboediens, submissus.*
submit, v.: transit., *referre* (*ad senatum*, etc.); — to, = endure, *perferre.*
subordinate, subst. *minister.*
subordinate, adj. *inferior, subiectus* (with dat.).
subordinate, v. *subicĕre, posthabēre.*
subordination, *obsequium, disciplina.*
suborn, *subornare, subicĕre.*
subscribe: = write underneath, *subscribĕre*; = contribute, *conferre.*
subscription, = contribution, *conlatio, conlecta.*
subsequent, *(in)sequens, posterior*; adv. *postea.*
subserve, *(in)servire, obtemperare, obsequi.*
subservience, *obtemperatio.*
subside, *resīdĕre, consīdĕre.*
subsidiary, *subsidiarius.*
subsidy, *subsidium, vectigal, tributum.*
subsist, *esse*; — on a thing, *re vesci.*
subsistence, *victus* (*-ūs*).
substance, *natura, corpus* (*-oris*, n.), *res*; = property, *res, bona* (*-orum*, plur.).
substantial, *verus* (= real), *solidus* (= firm), *gravis* (= important),

amplus (= large). Adv. *firmiter* (=solidly), *magna ex parte* (=largely).
substantiate; see prove, establish.
substantive, gram., *nomen.*
substitute, subst. *vicarius.*
substitute, v. transit., *substituĕre, sufficĕre* (esp. of the replacing of magistrates).
subterfuge, *tergiversatio.*
subterranean, *subterraneus.*
subtle, *subtilis; argutus, acutus.* Adv. *subtiliter, argute, acute.*
subtlety, *ingenii acumen, subtilitas, argutiae* (*-arum*, plur.).
subtract, *deducĕre.*
suburban, *suburbanus.*
subvert, *subvertĕre, evertĕre.*
succeed, v.: transit., = come after, (*sub*)*sequi, excipĕre, succedĕre* (with dat); intransit., = do well, of persons, *rem bene gerĕre, florēre*; of things, *succedĕre, bene evenire.*
success, *res secundae, successus* (*-ūs*).
successful, *felix*; of things, *secundus, prosper.* Adv. *feliciter, prospere, bene.*
succession, *successio*; = series, *continuatio, series*; in —, *ex ordine.*
successive, *continuus*; adv. (*ex*) *ordine, deinceps.*
successor, *successor.*
succinct, *brevis*; adv. *breviter.*
succour, subst. *auxilium, subsidium.*
succour, v. *subvenire, succurrĕre,* with dat.
succumb, *succumbĕre.*
such, adj. *talis; huius modi, eius modi*; such . . . as, *talis . . . qualis*; such that, *talis ut,* with subj.; in — a way, *tali modo, ita, sic.*
suck, v. *sugĕre*; — out, *exsorbēre.*
sucker, *surculus, planta.*
suckle, v. *mammam praebēre.*
suckling, (*infans*) *lactens.*
sudden, *subitus, repentinus, inopinatus*; adv. *subito, repente.*
sue: = entreat, *rogare, orare*; at law, (*hominem*) *in ius vocare.*
suet, *sebum.*
suffer: = endure, *pati,* (*per*)*ferre, tolerare, subire*; = be in pain, *dolorem ferre, dolore adfici*; = be ill, *aegrotare*; = be punished, *plecti, poenas dare*; = allow, *pati, sinere.*
sufferance, *patientia*; on —, *precarius,* adj.
suffering, *dolor, miseria*; see pain.
suffice, *sufficĕre, satis esse.*
sufficient; render by adv. *satis.*
suffocate, *suffocare*; see strangle.
suffrage, *suffragium.*
suffuse, *suffundĕre.*
suggest, (*rem homini*) *subicĕre.*
suggestion, *admonitio, consilium.*
suicide: to commit —, *sibi mortem consciscĕre.*
suit, subst.: at law, *actio, lis, causa*; of clothes, *vestis, vestitus* (*-ūs*).
suit, v.: = adapt, *accommodare*; = fit, be suitable, *convenire, congruĕre.*
suitable, *idoneus, aptus, accommodatus, opportunus*; adv. *idonee, apte, accommodate, opportune.*
suitableness, *opportunitas.*
suite: = retinue, *comitatus* (*-ūs*), *comites* (*-um*); of rooms, *conclavia* (*-ium*).
suitor, = wooer, *procus.*
sulkiness, sullenness, *morositas.*
sulky, sullen, *morosus*; adv. *morose.*
sully, *maculare, inquinare.*
sulphur, *sulfur*; dipped in —, *sulfuratus.*
sulphurous, *sulpureus.*
sultry, *aestuosus.*
sum, subst. *summa*; of money, *pecunia.*
sum up, v. *breviter repetĕre.*
summary, subst. *epitoma* or *epitome.*
summary, adj.: = brief, *brevis*; = quick, *subitus, repentinus.* Adv. *breviter, summatim; statim.*
summer, *aestas*; of —, adj., *aestivus.*
summit, *cacumen, culmen*; or render by adj. *summus.*
summon, (*ad*)*vocare, arcessĕre, accire*; before a court, *appellare, in ius vocare*; to — up courage, *animum conligĕre.*
summons: at a person's —, *hominis accitu.*
sumptuous, *sumptuosus, lautus*; adv. *sumptuose.*
sumptuousness, *apparatus* (*-ūs*), *lautitia.*
sun, subst. *sol*; rising —, *sol oriens*; setting —, *sol occidens.*
sunburnt, *adustus.*
sunder, *separare, disiungĕre.*
sundial, *solarium.*
sundry, *diversus, varius.*
sunny, *apricus.*
sunrise, *solis ortus* (*-ūs*).
sunset, *solis occasus* (*-ūs*).
sunshine, *sol.*
sup, *cenare.*
superannuated, *emeritus, rude donatus.*
superb, *magnificus, lautus*; adv. *magnifice, laute.*
supercilious, *superbus, fastidiosus, insolens.*
superciliousness, *superbia, insolentia.*
superficial, = exterior, *externus*; = shallow, *levis*; adv. *strictim, leviter.*
superfluous, adj. *supervacaneus, supervacuus*; to be —, *superesse.* Adv. *ex supervacuo.*
superhuman, *divinus, maior quam pro homine.*
superintend, *administrare, praeesse.*
superintendent, *praefectus.*
superior, *superior, melior* (= better).
superlative, *optimus, egregius, singularis*; gram., *superlativus.*
supernatural, *divinus, caelestis*; by — agency, *divinitus.*
supernumerary, *praeter* (*iustum*) *numerum*; of soldiers, *ascriptivus*; in plur., *accensi.*
superscription, *inscriptio.*
supersede, *succedĕre* (with dat.).
superstition, *superstitio.*
superstitious, *superstitiosus*; adv. *superstitiose.*
supervene, *supervenire*; see also follow.
supervise, (*pro*)*curare.*
supervision, (*pro*)*curatio.*

supine, subst. *supinum* (gram.).
supine, adj. *supinus.* Transf., *iners, neglegens*; adv. *neglegenter.*
supineness, *neglegentia, inertia.*
supper, *cena.*
supplant, *in alterius locum inrepĕre.*
supple, *mollis, lentus.*
supplement, *supplementum, incrementum.*
suppliant, *supplex.*
supplicate, *supplicare, obsecrare, obtestari.*
supplication, *obsecratio, obtestatio.*
supply, supplies, *copia, facultas*; milit. *commeatus* (-*ūs*).
supply, v. = provide, *suppeditare, ministrare.*
support, subst. *firmamentum*; = maintenance, *alimentum, victus* (-*ūs*); = help, *subsidium, auxilium.*
support, v.: = hold up, *sustinēre, fulcire*; = endure, (*per*)*ferre, tolerare*; = maintain, *alĕre*; = help, *adesse, suffragari,* with dat.
supporter, *adiutor, suffragator, fautor.*
suppose: = assume, *ponĕre, sumĕre*; = believe, *credĕre, putare, opinari.*
supposition, *opinio, coniectura.*
supposititious, *subditus, subditivus.*
suppress, *supprimĕre, comprimĕre.*
supremacy, *principatus* (-*ūs*), *dominatio, imperium.*
supreme, *supremus, summus*; adv. *unice, maxime.*
sure, *certus, tutus* (= safe), *firmus* (= trustworthy); I am —, *pro certo habeo.*
surely, *certe, profecto, scilicet*; in questions, *nonne?* — not? *num?*
surety, *vas, sponsor* (of a person).
surface, *superficies,* or render by adj. *summus.*
surfeit, subst. *satietas.*
surfeit, v.: to — oneself, *se ingurgitare.*
surge, subst. *fluctus* (-*ūs*).
surge, *fluctuare*; — forward, *proruĕre.*
surgeon, *medicus, chirurgus.*
surliness, *morositas, difficultas.*
surly, *morosus, difficilis.*
surmise, subst. *coniectura.*
surmise, v. *suspicari, coniecturam facĕre.*
surmount, *transcendĕre,* (*ex*)*superare.*
surmountable, (*ex*)*superabilis.*
surname, *cognomen, cognomentum.*
surpass, *vincĕre,* (*ex*)*superare, praestare* (with dat.).
surplus, subst. *residuum, quod superest.*
surprise, subst., (*ad*)*miratio*; or render by v. or adj.
surprise, v. *admirationem* (*homini*) *movēre*; to be —d, (*ad*)*mirari*; = take by —, *opprimĕre, necopinantem adoriri.*
surprising, *mirus, mirabilis.*
surrender, subst. *deditio, traditio.*
surrender, v. *dedere, tradere,* (*con*)*cedĕre*; intransit., *se dedĕre.*
surreptitious, *furtivus, clandestinus*; adv. *furtim, clam.*
surround, *cingĕre, circumdare, circumvenire.*
survey, subst. *contemplatio, conspectus* (-*ūs*); of land, *mensura.*
survey, v. *spectare, contemplari*; = measure land, *agrum metiri, mensuram agĕre.*
surveyor, (of land), *decempedator, metator.*
survive, *superesse, superstitem esse.*
surviving, survivor, *superstes.*
susceptible, *mollis.*
suspect, adj. *suspectus.*
suspect, v. *suspicari*; = think, fancy, *putare.*
suspend, *suspendĕre*; = break off, defer, *intermittĕre, differre*; from office, *loco movēre, magistratum abrogare.*
suspense, *dubitatio*: in —, adj., *suspensus.*
suspension, *dilatio* (= delay); — of hostilities, *indutiae* (-*arum*).
suspicion, *suspicio.*
suspicious, *suspiciosus, suspicax*; adv. *suspiciose.*
sustain, *sustinere, sustentare.*
sustenance, *alimentum, victus* (-*ūs*).
sutler, *lixa.*
swaddling-clothes, *fasciae* (-*arum*), *incunabula* (-*orum*).
swagger, *gloriari, se iactare.*
swallow, subst. *hirundo.*
swallow, v. (*ab*)*sorbēre,* (*de*)*vorare.*
swamp, subst. *palus* (-*udis*).
swamp, v. (*de*)*mergĕre, immergĕre.*
swampy, *paluster, paludosus.*
swan, *cygnus, olor*; of a —, *cygneus.*
swarm, subst. of bees, *examen.*
swarm, v. *congregari, confluĕre.*
swarthy, *fuscus, adustus.*
sway, subst. *imperium, dominatio, dicio.*
sway, v., = move to and fro, *agitare, motare*; see also govern.
swear, *iurare*; — falsely, *peierare* or *periurare.*
sweat, subst. *sudor.*
sweat, v. *sudare.*
sweep, subst., = expanse, *ambitus* (-*ūs*), *spatium.*
sweep, v. *verrĕre.*
sweepings, *quisquiliae* (-*arum*).
sweet, *dulcis, suavis*; adv. *dulciter, suaviter.*
sweeten, *dulcem reddĕre* or *facĕre.*
sweetheart, *deliciae* (-*arum*), *amores* (-*um*).
sweetness, *dulcedo, suavitas.*
swell, v.: transit., *tumefacĕre, augēre*; intransit., *tumēre, tumescĕre, crescĕre* (= grow).
swelling, subst. *tumor, tuber.*
swerve, subst. *declinatio.*
swerve, v. *declinare.*
swift, *citus, velox, celer, pernix*; adv. *cito, celeriter, perniciter.*
swiftness, *celeritas, velocitas, pernicitas.*
swim, v. *nare, natare*; — across, *tranare.*
swimmer, *natator.*
swimming, subst. *natatio.*
swindle, subst. *fraus.*
swindle, v. *fraudare, circumvenire.*
swindler, *fraudator.*
swine, *sus, porcus*; adj., of —, *suillus.*
swineheard, *subulcus, suarius.*

swing, v.: transit., *agitare, vibrare, iactare.*
switch, subst. *virga, virgula.*
Switzerland, *Helvetia.*
swoon, v. *animo linqui, conlabi.*
swoop, subst. *impetus* (*-ūs*).
swoop, v. *impetum facĕre, incurrĕre.*
sword, *gladius, ensis, ferrum.*
sycophancy, *sycophantia, adsentatio, adulatio.*
sycophant, *sycophanta, adsentator, adulator.*
syllable, *syllaba.*
sylvan, *silvestris.*
symbol, *symbolum, signum.*
symmetrical, *aequalis, congruens*; adv. *pariter, aequaliter.*
symmetry, *convenientia, congruentia, aequalitas.*
sympathetic, *concors, humanus, misericors.*
sympathize, *congruĕre, consentire, miserēri* (= pity).
sympathy, *consensus* (*-ūs*), *concordia; humanitas.*
symphony, *symphonia, concentus* (*-ūs*).
symptom, (*morbi*) *indicium* or *signum.*
syndicate, *societas.*
synonymous, *idem significans.*
synopsis, *epitome* or *epitoma; breviarium.*
syntax, *syntaxis* (gram.); *verborum constructio.*
Syracuse, *Syracusae* (*-arum*, plur.).
system, *ratio, disciplina.*
systematic, *accuratus, compositus*; adv. *ordine, accurate, composite.*

T

tabernacle, *tabernaculum.*
table, *mensa*; = fare, *cena, victus* (*-ūs*); = list, *index.*
table-napkin, *mappa.*
tablet, *tabula, tabella, album.*
tacit, *tacitus*; adv. *tacite.*
taciturn, *taciturnus.*
taciturnity, *taciturnitas.*
tack, subst., = small nail, *clavulus.*
tack, v., in sailing, *reciprocare*; see also nail and sew.
tackle, subst. *instrumenta* (*-orum*), *armamenta* (*-orum*).
tackle, v. *tractare, obviam ire.*
tact, *dexteritas.*
tactful, *dexter*; adv. *dextere, dextre.*
tactics, *res militaris, belli ratio.*
tactless, *ineptus, insulsus, infacetus.*
tactlessness, *ineptiae* (*-arum*).
tail, *cauda.*
tailor, *textor.*
taint, subst. *contagio, vitium.*
taint, v. *inficĕre, contaminare, corrumpĕre.*
take, *capĕre, sumĕre, accipĕre* (= receive); — away, *auferre, demĕre, adimĕre*; — down, in writing, *litteris mandare*; — in, mentally, *percipĕre, comprehendĕre*; — on, *suscipĕre*; to —, = to move, by carrying, *ferre*; by leading, *ducĕre*; to — in good part, *in bonam partem accipĕre*; intransit., to — to, *se conferre ad*, with acc.
taking, subst. *acceptio, expugnatio* (of a city).
tale, *narratio, fabula, historia.*
tale-bearer, *delator, sycophanta.*
talent: = weight or coin, *talentum;* = faculty, *ingenium,* (*ingenii*) *facultas.*
talented, *ingeniosus, eximii ingenii.*
talk, subst. *sermo, conloquium.*
talk, (*con*)*loqui, sermocinari*; to — to, *adloqui, adfari.*
talkative, *loquax, garrulus*; adv. *loquaciter.*
talkativeness, *loquacitas.*
tall, *longus, procerus,* (*ex*)*celsus.*
tallness, *proceritas, statura procera.*
tally, v. *convenire.*
talon, *unguis, ungula.*
tame, adj. *cicur, mitis, mansuetus*; to grow —, *mitescĕre.* Transf., *demissus*; of language, *frigidus.* Adv. *demisse; frigide.*
tame, v. *mansuefacĕre, domare.*
tamer, *domitor*; f. *domitrix.*
taming, *domitus* (*-ūs*).
tamper; see meddle.
tan, v.: to — skins, *conficĕre*; of the sun, *colorare.*
tangible, *tractabilis; quod tangi potest.*
tangle, subst. *implicatio, nodus.*
tank, *lacus* (*-ūs*).
tantalize; see tease.
tap, v. *leviter ferire*; to — a cask, *relinĕre.*
tape; see ribbon.
taper, subst. *cereus, funalis.*
tapestry, *pictura acu facta, stragulum pictum.*
tar, *pix* (*liquida*).
Taranto, *Tarentum.*
tardiness, *tarditas.*
tardy, *tardus, lentus*; adv. *tarde, lente.*
target, *scopos.*
tarnish, v. transit., *inquinare.*
Tarragona, *Tarraco.*
tarry, (*com*)*morari, cunctari, cessare.*
tart, adj. *acerbus, amarus*; adv. *acerbe.*
tartness, *acerbitas.*
task, subst. *pensum, opus* (*-eris*, n.).
task-master, *operis exactor.*
taste, subst.: = sense of —, *gustatus* (*-ūs*), *palatum*: = flavour, *sapor, gustatus* (*-ūs*). Transf., critical —, *iudicium, intellegentia*; = liking, *gustatus* (*-ūs*), *studium.*
taste, v.: transit., (*de*)*gustare,* (*de*)*libare*; intransit., *sapĕre.*
tasteful, *elegans, scitus, concinnus*; adv. *eleganter, scite.*
tasteless, *sine sapore, insulsus; inelegans*; adv. *insulse, ineleganter.*
tastelessness, *insulsitas.*
tatter, *pannus.*
tattered, *pannosus.*
taunt, subst. *probrum, convicium.*
taunt, v. (*rem homini*) *obicĕre.*
taunting, *contumeliosus*; adv. *contumeliose.*
tavern, *caupona, taberna.*
tavern-keeper, *caupo.*
tawdry, *fucosus.*
tawny, *fulvus.*
tax, taxation, *vectigal, tributum.*

tax, v., *vectigal* or *tributum* (*homini*) *imponěre.*
taxable, *vectigalis, stipendiarius.*
tax-collector, (*vectigalium*) *exactor.*
teach, (*e*)*docēre, instituěre, erudire.*
teachable, *docilis.*
teachableness, *docilitas.*
teacher, *doctor, magister* (with f. *magistra*).
teaching, subst. *doctrina, disciplina, eruditio.*
team, (of horses or oxen), *iugum.*
tear, subst. *lacrima, fletus* (*-ūs,* = weeping).
tear, v. transit. (*di*)*scinděre,* (*di*)*lacerare,* (*di*)*vellěre*; — away, *avellěre*; — down, *rescinděre, revellěre*; — out, *evellěre.*
tearful, *lacrimans, lacrimabundus*; adv. *multis cum lacrimis.*
tearing, tear, subst. *scissura.*
tease, *fatigare, vexare, obtunděre.*
tedious, *lentus, longus, molestus*; adv. *lente, moleste.*
tediousness, *molestia.*
teem, *scatēre.*
tell: = relate, say, *dicěre, narrare, referre,* (*com*)*memorare, docēre* (= inform); = command, *iubēre, imperare*; = count, *numerare*; intransit., = have effect, *valēre.*
temerity, *temeritas.*
temper, subst. *ingenium, animus*; bad —, *iracundia, stomachus.*
temper, v. *temperare, miscēre, lenire.*
temperance, *temperantia, continentia, moderatio.*
temperate, *temperans, continens, moderatus*; adv. *continenter, moderate.*
temperateness, *temperantia.*
tempest, *tempestas, procella.*
tempestuous, *turbidus, violentus, vehemens*; adv. *turbide, violenter, vehementer.*
tempestuousness, *violentia.*
temple, *aedes, templum, fanum, delubrum*; of the head, *tempus* (*-oris,* n.).
temporal, *humanus.*
temporarily, *ad* or *in tempus.*
tempt, (*at*)*temptare, sollicitare, inlicere.*
temptation, *sollicitatio, inlecebra.*
ten, *decem*; — each, — at a time, *deni*; — times, *decie*(*n*)*s.*
tenacious, *tenax, pertinax*; adv. *tenaciter.*
tenacity, *tenacitas, pertinacia.*
tenant, *conductor, inquilinus, incola.*
tend: transit., *colěre, curare*; intransit., *spectare, tenděre.*
tendency, *inclinatio, proclivitas.*
tender, adj. *tener, mollis, indulgens* (= kind, fond); adv. *molliter, indulgenter.*
tender, v. *deferre.*
tenderness, *mollitia*; = affection, *indulgentia, amor.*
tendon, *nervus.*
tendril, *clavicula, pampinus.*
tenour, *tenor*; = drift, purport, *sententia.*
tense, subst. *tempus* (*-oris,* n.).
tense, adj. *intentus, attentus.*
tension, *intentio.*
tent, *tabernaculum*; general's —, *praetorium.*
tenth, *decimus.*
tenure, *possessio.*
tepid, *tepidus*; to become —, *tepescěre*; to be —, *tepēre.*
term, subst.: = limited time, *spatium, dies*; = word, *verbum, vocabulum*; = condition, *condicio, lex*; to be on good —s with, *familiariter uti.*
term, v.: see call, name.
terminate; see end.
termination, *finis, exitus* (*-ūs*), *clausula.*
terrace, *solarium, ambulatio.*
terrestrial, *terrestris, terrenus, humanus.*
terrible, *terribilis, horribilis, atrox;* adv. *terribilem in modum, atrociter.*
terrific; see dreadful, terrible.
terrify, (*per*)*terrēre.*
territory, *fines, ager, regio, terra.*
terror, *terror, formido, metus* (*-ūs*).
terse, *pressus, brevis, angustus*; adv. *presse, breviter, anguste.*
terseness, *brevitas, oratio pressa.*
test, subst.; see trial, examination.
test, v. *temptare, experiri, explorare.*
testament, = will, *testamentum.*
testator, *testator.*
testify, *testari, testificari.*
testimonial, *litterae commendaticiae.*
testimony, *testimonium.*
testy, *morosus.*
text, *oratio, verba* (*-orum*).
textile, adj. *textilis.*
texture, *textura, textus* (*-ūs*).
Thames, *Tamesis* or *Tamesa.*
than, after comparative, *quam,* or abl. case.
thank, v. *gratias agěre*: = feel gratitude, *gratiam habēre*; — you! or No — you! *benigne* (*dicis*).
thankful, *gratus;* adv. *grate, grato animo.*
thankfulness, *animus gratus.*
thankless, adj. *ingratus*; adv. *ingrate.*
thanks, subst. *gratia* or plur. *gratiae, grates.*
thanksgiving, *supplicatio.*
that, demonstr. pron. *ille, illa, illud,* or *is, ea, id,* or *iste, ista, istud.*
that, relat. pron. *qui, quae, quod.*
that, conj.: in indirect statement, render by acc. and infin; after verbs of fearing, *ne* followed by subj.; in final clauses, = in order —, *ut* followed by subj.; in consecutive clauses, *ut* followed by subj.
thatch, *stramentum.*
thaw, v.: transit., (*dis*)*solvěre, liquefacěre*; intransit., (*dis*)*solvi, liquescěre.*
the, no regular equivalent in Latin; — famous, *ille, illa, illud*; — more people have, — more they want, *homines quo plura habent eo ampliora cupiunt.*
theatre, *theatrum, scaena* (= stage).
theatrical, *scaenicus, theatralis*; adv. *more histrionum.*
theft, *furtum.*
their, theirs, *suus* (= — own); *eorum, illorum.*
theme, *res, propositum, quaestio.*

then, *tum, tunc*; = therefore, *ergo, igitur.*
thence, *inde, illinc, istinc.*
thenceforth, *inde, ex eo tempore.*
theory, *ratio, doctrina, ars, scientia.*
there, *ibi, illic, istic*; to be —, *adesse*; — is, *est*; — are, *sunt*; = to that place, *eo, illuc.*
thereabouts, *prope* (= near), *fere* (= nearly).
thereafter, thereupon, *inde, deinde, postea.*
therefore, *igitur, ergo, itaque, ideo.*
therein, *in eo, in ea re.*
they, when emphatic, is rendered by nom. plur. of *is, ea, id* or of *ille, illa, illud.*
thick: = stout, *crassus, pinguis*; = closely packed, *densus, artus, confertus.* Adv. *confertim, crebro.*
thicken, v.: transit., *densare*; intransit., *densari, concrescěre* (= curdle).
thicket, *dumetum, fruticetum.*
thickness, *crassitudo, crebritas.*
thief, *fur.*
thigh, *femur.*
thin, adj.: = slim, *gracilis, exilis, macer*; = rare, *tenuis, rarus.*
thin, v. *attenuare, extenuare.*
thine, *tuus.*
thing, *res, negotium*; often rendered by neuter of adj. or pron.
think, *cogitare*; = believe, suppose, *opinari, creděre, putare*; to — about, (*rem*) *reputare*, (*de re*) *cogitare.*
thinness, *tenuitas, gracilitas, raritas, macies.*
third, *tertius.*
thirst, subst. *sitis.*
thirst, v. *sitire.*
thirsty, *sitiens, siccus.*
thirteen, *tredecim*; — each, — at a time, *terni deni*; — times, *terdecie(n)s.*
thirteenth, *tertius decimus.*
thirtieth, *trice(n)simus.*
thirty, *triginta*: — each, — at a time, *triceni*; — times, *tricie(n)s.*
this, *hic, haec, hoc*; on — side (of), *citra*; of — kind, *huiusmodi.*
thistle, *carduus.*
thither, *eo, illuc, istuc*; hither and —, *huc (et) illuc.*
thong, *lorum.*
thorn, *sentis, spina.*
thorn-bush, *vepres, dumus, sentis.*
thorny, *spinosus.* Transf., *arduus, impeditus.*
thorough; see complete. Adv. *penitus, prorsus, omnino.*
thoroughbred, *generosus.*
thoroughfare, *transitus* (*-ūs*); = road through, *via* (*pervia*).
thou, *tu, tute, tutemet.*
though; see although.
thought, *cogitatio, animus* (= mind), *sententia* (= opinion), *opinio* (= supposition), *consilium* (= view, plan).
thoughtful, *in cogitatione defixus*; *prudens* (= sensible), *providus* (= far-sighted). Adv. *prudenter.*
thoughtless, *neglegens, imprudens, temerarius* (= rash); adv. *neglegenter, imprudenter, temere.*
thoughtlessness, *neglegentia, temeritas* (= rashness).
thousand, *mille*; plur. *milia* (or *millia*); a — times, *millie(n)s.*
thousandth, *mille(n)simus.*
Thrace, *Thracia.*
thraldom, *servitūs* (*-ūtis*).
thrash: to — (or thresh) corn, *terěre*; see also beat.
thrashing, threshing, *tritura.*
thrashing-floor, threshing-floor, *area.*
thrashing-machine, *tribulum.*
thread, subst. *filum, linea, linum.*
thread, v. *inserěre.*
threadbare, *obsoletus, tritus.*
threat, *minae* (*-arum*), (*com*)*minatio.*
threaten, (*com*)*minari, minitari, denuntiare, intentare*; = impend, (*im*)*minēre, instare*; = seem likely to do, render by *vidēri* with fut. infin.
threatening, *minax, minitabundus*; = impending, *instans, imminens.* Adv. *minaciter.*
three, *tres*; — times, *ter*; — each, — at a time, *trini* or *terni*; in — parts, adj. *tripertitus* or *tripartitus.*
threefold, *triplus, triplex.*
three hundred, *trecenti*; — each, — at a time, *treceni*; — times, *trecentie(n)s.*
three hundredth, *trecente(n)simus.*
threshold, *limen.*
thrice, *ter.*
thrift, *frugalitas, parsimonia.*
thrifty, *frugi, parcus*; adv. *frugaliter, parce.*
thrill, subst.: of pleasure, *voluptas, gaudium*; of fear, *horror.*
thrill, v. *commovēre*; intransit., of sounds, *resonare.*
thrilling, *mirificus, mirus.*
thrive, *vigēre, virēre, florēre.*
throat, *fauces* (*-ium*), *iugulum, guttur.*
throb, v. *salire, palpitare, micare.*
throne, (*regale*) *solium, sedes regia*; = royal power, *regnum, imperium.*
throng, subst. *multitudo, frequentia.*
throng, v. *celebrare, stipare, frequentare.*
throttle, *suffocare, spiritum intercluděre.*
through, prep. *per*, with acc.; = on account of, *propter*, or *ob*, with acc.
through, adv., render by compound verb with *trans-* or *per-*; — and —, *penitus, prorsus, omnino.*
throw, throwing, subst. *iactus* (*-ūs*), *coniectus* (*-ūs*).
throw, v. *iacěre, conicěre, mittěre* (esp. of weapons); — away, *abicěre*; — back, *reicěre*; — down, *deicěre, deturbare, proruěre.*
thrower, *iaculator.*
thrust, v. *truděre*; see push, drive.
thumb, (*digitus*) *pollex.*
thunder, subst. *tonitrus* (*-ūs*).
thunder, v. (*in*)*tonare.*
thunder-bolt, *fulmen.*
thunder-struck, *attonitus, obstupefactus.*
thus, *ita, sic.*
thwart, subst. *transtrum.*
thwart, v.: see hinder, prevent.
thy, *tuus.*
thyme, *thymum.*
Tiber, river, *Tiberis.*
ticket, *tessera.*

tickle, *titillare.*
tide, (*maritimus*) *aestus* (*-ūs*); the turn of the —, *commutatio aestūs.*
tidiness, *munditia.*
tidings, *nuntius.*
tidy, *mundus*; adv. *munde.*
tie, subst. *vinculum, nodus.*
tie, v.; see bind; — a knot, *nodum facĕre.*
tier, *ordo*; see row.
tiger, *tigris.*
tight, *strictus, a(d)strictus, artus*; — rope, *funis contentus.*
tighten, v. *stringĕre, contendĕre, adducĕre.*
tile, *tegula, testa;* pan- —, *imbrex.*
till, prep. (*usque*) *ad*; — now, *hactenus.*
till, conj. *dum, donec, quoad.*
till, v. *colere, arare.*
tillage, *cultus* (*-ūs*), *cultura.*
tiller, (*gubernaculi*) *clavus.*
tilt, v. transit. (*in*)*vertĕre.*
timber, *materia* or *materies.*
time, subst. *tempus* (*-oris*, n.), *dies, spatium* (= space of —), *saeculum* (= age), *otium* (= leisure), *occasio* (= opportunity); — of life, *aetas*; for a —, *ad* or *in tempus*; on —, (*in*) *tempore, temperi, tempestive*; from the — when, *ex quo* (*tempore*); at —s, *interdum*; at the same —, *simul, eodem tempore*; — of day, *hora*; — in music, *tempus, numerus.*
timely: adj. *tempestivus, opportunus*; adv. *ad tempus, tempestive, opportune.*
timid, *timidus, verecundus* (= bashful), *ignavus* (= cowardly). Adv. *timide.*
timidity, *timiditas, verecundia* (= shyness).
tin, *plumbum album, stannum.*
tinder, *fomes.*
tinge, v. *imbuĕre, colorare, inficĕre, tingĕre.*
tinkle, v. *tinnire.*
tinkling, subst. *tinnitus* (*-ūs*).
tinkling, adj. *tinnulus.*
tinsel, = metal leaf, *bractea.*
tip, subst. *cacumen, apex*; or render by adj. *extremus.*
tip, v., = head, point, *praefigĕre*; — up, — over, (*in*)*vertĕre, inclinare.*
tipple, (*per*)*potare.*
tipsy, *temulentus, ebrius.*
tiptoe, on, *suspenso gradu.*
tire, v. transit., (*de*)*fatigare.*
tired, (*de*)*fessus, fatigatus*; I am — of saying, *taedet me dicĕre.*
tiresome, *importunus, molestus.*
tit-bits, *cuppedia* (*-orum*), *scitamenta* (*-orum*).
title, *titulus, index* (of a book), *nomen* (= name), *praescriptio* (= heading).
titled, *nobilis.*
titter, v.; see laugh.
Tivoli, *Tibur.*
to, commonly rendered by the Latin dative; for motion to, use *ad* with acc. (except with *domus* and *rus* and names of towns or small islands); —, or up —, a certain time, *ad* or *in* with acc.; to and fro, *huc* (*et*) *illuc.*
toad, *bufo.*
toadstool, *fungus.*
toast, v. *torrēre, frigĕre*; = drink a health, (*homini*) *propinare.*
today: subst. *hodiernus dies*: of —, adj. *hodiernus*; adv. *hodie.*
toe, (*pedis*) *digitus.*
together, *una, simul*; all —, *cuncti, universi.*
toil, subst. *labor, opera.*
toil, v. (*e*)*laborare, sudare.*
toilsome, *laboriosus, operosus.*
token, *signum.*
Toledo, *Toletum.*
tolerable, *tolerabilis, patibilis*; = middling, *tolerabilis, mediocris, modicus*; adv. *mediocriter, modice, satis* (= sufficiently).
tolerance, toleration, *tolerantia; indulgentia, lenitas, facilitas.*
tolerate, *tolerare,* (*aequo animo*) *ferre.*
toll, subst. *vectigal, portorium.*
toll, v. *sonare.*
tomb, *sepulcrum.*
tomb-stone, *lapis, cippus, monumentum.*
tomorrow: subst. *crastinus dies*: of —, adj. *crastinus*; adv. *cras.*
tone, *sonus, sonitus* (*-ūs*), *vox.*
tongs, *forceps.*
tongue, *lingua.*
tonnage, expressed by numbers of *amphorae.*
too: = also, *etiam, quoque, praeterea*; = excessively, render by *nimis* or *nimium* or by comparative; — stupid to know, *stultior quam qui sciat*; — little, *parum.*
tool: an iron-, *ferramentum*; —s, plur., *instrumentum.*
tooth, *dens.*
top, subst.: = summit, *cacumen, culmen*; or render by adj. *summus*; a child's —, *turbo.*
top, adj. *summus.*
topic, *res.*
topical, *hodiernus, hic.*
topography, *locorum descriptio.*
torch, *fax, taeda.*
torment, subst. *cruciatus* (*-ūs*), *tormentum.*
torment, v. (*ex*)*cruciare, torquēre, vexare.*
tormenter, *vexator*; or render by verb.
tornado, *turbo, tempestas.*
torpid, *torpens, lentus, iners.*
torpor, *torpor.*
torrent, *torrens.*
torrid, *torridus.*
tortoise, *testudo.*
torture, *tormentum, cruciatus* (*-ūs*), *dolor, angor.*
torture, v. (*ex*)*cruciare,* (*ex*)*torquēre.*
torturer, *tortor, carnifex.*
toss, tossing, subst. *iactus* (*-ūs*), *iactatio.*
toss, v. *iactare.*
total, subst. *summa, universitas.*
total, adj. *totus, omnis*; adv. *omnino, funditus, penitus.*
totter, v. *labare, vacillare, titubare.*
touch, subst. (*con*)*tactus* (*-ūs*), *tactio.*
touch, v. *tangĕre, attingĕre, contingĕre*; = influence, affect, *tangĕre,* (*com*)*movēre.*
touching, prep. *de*, with abl.

touchy, *inritabilis, iracundus,*
tough, *lentus, durus.*
toughness, *duritia.*
tour, *iter, peregrinatio, lustratio.*
tow, subst. *stuppa*: of —, adj. *stuppeus.*
tow, v. *trahĕre.*
toward, towards, prep.: of motion, *ad* or *adversus* with acc.; of time, = near to, *ad* or *sub,* with acc.; of personal relations, *adversus, erga, in,* with acc.
towel, *mantele.*
tower, subst. *turris*; fig., *arx, praesidium.*
tower, v. *eminēre, exstare*; — over, *imminēre,* with dat.
towering, *arduus.*
town, *urbs, oppidum*; of a —, adj., *urbanus.*
town-hall, *curia.*
townsman, *civis, oppidanus.*
trace, subst. *vestigium, indicium.*
trace, v.: = draw, mark out, *designare, describĕre, adumbrare*; = follow up, track, (*in*)*vestigare.*
track, subst.; see path.
tract: = region, *tractus* (*-ūs*), *regio*; = treatise, *libellus.*
tractable, *tractabilis, docilis, facilis.*
tractableness, *docilitas, facilitas.*
trade, subst., = commerce, *mercatura, commercium*; = any occupation, *ars, artificium.*
trade, v. *mercaturam facĕre,* (*com*)*mercari, negotiari.*
trader, *mercator*; see also merchant.
tradition, *memoria, litterae* (*-arum,* documentary).
traditicnal, (*a maioribus*) *posteris traditus.*
tragedian: = writer, *tragicus*; = actor, *tragoedus, tragicus actor.*
tragedy, *tragoedia*; fig. *casus* (*-ūs*).
tragic, *tragicus*; = sad, *tristis, miserabilis.* Adv. *tragice*; *miserabiliter.*
train, subst.: a robe with a —, *syrma*; = procession, *pompa*; = any series, *ordo, series.*
train, v. (*e*)*docēre, instituĕre*; = drill, *exercēre.*
trainer, *magister*; of horses, *equorum domitor.*
training, *disciplina, exercitatio.*
traitor, *proditor.*
tramp; see walk, march.
trample, *calcare, conculcare.*
trance, render by *animus a corpore abstractus.*
tranquil, *tranquillus, placidus, quietus.*
tranquillity, *tranquillitas, quies.*
tranquillize, *tranquillare, pacare, sedare.*
transact, *gerĕre, agĕre, conficĕre.*
transaction, *res, negotium.*
transcend, (*ex*)*superare, excellĕre.*
transcendent, *praestans, singularis, eximius.*
transcribe, *transcribĕre.*
transcript, *exemplum, exemplar.*
transfer, subst. *translatio, mancipium* (of property).
transfer, v. *transferre, traducĕre.*
transference, *translatio.*
transfix, *transfigĕre, traicĕre, confodĕre.*
transform, (*con*)*vertĕre,* (*com*)*mutare.*
transgress, *transcendĕre, violare*; intransit., *delinquĕre, peccare.*
transgression, *delictum, peccatum.*
transient, adj. *brevis, fugax, caducus, fluxus.*
transit, *transitus* (*-ūs*).
transition, *transitio, transgressio.*
transitive, *transitivus* (gram.).
translate, (*con*)*vertĕre, reddĕre.*
translator, *interpres.*
transmit, *transmittĕre, tradĕre.*
transparent, *perlucidus* (*pell-*), *perspicuus*; to be —, *perlucēre, lucem transmittĕre.* Trans., *evidens, manifestus*; adv. *manifesto.*
transpire, of secrets, etc., (*di*)*vulgari, pervulgari, percrebrescĕre.*
transplant, *transferre, traducĕre.*
transport, subst. as a ship, *navigium vectorium, navis oneraria.*
transport, v. *transportare, transferre*; for banishment, *relegare*; to be —ed with rage, *iracundia exardescĕre,* with delight, *gaudio efferri* or *exsultare.*
transpose, *traicĕre.*
transverse, *transversus, transversarius.*
trap, subst. *laqueus*; see also snare, net.
trap, v. *inretire*; see ensnare.
trappings, *ornamentum, insignia* (*-ium*); of horses, *phalerae* (*-arum*).
trash, *quisquiliae* (*-arum*), *scruta* (*-orum*).
trashy, *vilis.*
travail, v. *parturire.*
travel, subst. *iter, peregrinatio* (abroad); — through, see traverse.
traveller, *viator, vector, peregrinator.*
traverse, *obire, peragrare,* (*per*)*lustrare.*
tray, *ferculum.*
treacherous, *perfidus, perfidiosus*; adv. *perfidiose.*
treachery, *perfidia, fraus.*
tread, subst. (*in*)*gressus* (*-ūs*), *gradus* (*-ūs*).
tread, v. *ingredi, incedĕre, insistĕre.*
treason: in gen., *perfidia, proditio*; high —, *maiestas, perduellio*; to commit —, *maiestatem minuĕre* or *laedĕre.*
treasure, subst. *thesaurus, gaza, opes* (*-um*).
treasure, v.; see value: — up, (*re*)*condĕre.*
treasure-house, *thesaurus.*
treasurer, *praefectus aerarii.*
treasury, *aerarium, fiscus.*
treat, v.: = discuss, (*rem*) *tractare,* (*de re*) *disputare*; medically, *curare*; = entertain, *invitare*; = behave towards (with adv.), *habēre, tractare*; — with, = negotiate, *agĕre* (*cum*).
treatise, *liber, libellus.*
treatment, *tractatio, curatio*; kind —, *comitas*; cruel —, *saevitia.*
treaty, *pactum, foedus* (*-eris,* n.).
Trebizond, *Trapezus* (*-untis*).
treble, adj., see triple; of voices, *acutus.*
treble, v. (*rem*) *triplicem facĕre.*
tree, *arbor*; genealogical —, *stemma* (*-atis,* n.).
tremble, *tremĕre, contremiscĕre, micare* (= flicker); to cause to —, *tremefacĕre.*
trembling, subst. *tremor.*
trembling, adj. *tremebundus, tremulus.*

tremendous, *terribilis*; = huge, *ingens, immanis.* Adv. *valde, magnopere, maxime.*
trench, subst. *fossa*; see also ditch.
trench, v. *fossam foděre* or *facěre.*
Trent, *Tridentum.*
trepidation, *trepidatio.*
trial, *temptatio, experimentum, experientia*; = attempt, *conatus* (*-ūs*); in court, *iudicium, quaestio.*
triangle, *triangulum.*
triangular, *triangulus, triquetrus.*
tribe, at *Rome, tribus* (*-ūs*); by —s, *tributim*; in gen., *natio, gens.*
tribulation, *miseria, incommodum, aerumna.*
tribunal, *tribunal*; = law court, *iudicium.*
tribune, *tribunus.*
tributary, subst., render by verb *influěre.*
tributary, adj. *vectigalis, stipendiarius.*
tribute, *tributum, vectigal, stipendium.*
trick, subst. *dolus, fraus, machina.*
trick, v.: see deceive.
trickery, *fallacia, astutia.*
trickle, v. *manare, rorare, stillare*
trident, *tridens.*
tried, *spectatus, cognitus, probatus.*
Trieste, *Tergeste.*
trifle, subst. *res parvi momenti; nugae* (*-arum*).
trifle, v. *nugari, luděre, ineptire.*
trifler, *nugator.*
trifling, subst. *iocus, ineptiae* (*-arum*).
trifling, adj. *levis, minutus, nugatorius.*
trim, v. *concinnare*; of hair, *coměre*; = prune, (*am*)*putare.*
trimming, subst. *fimbriae* (*-arum*).
trio, = three together, *tres, tria.*
trip, v. transit., — up, *supplantare*; intransit., = stumble, *offenděre.*
tripartite, *tripertitus* or *tripartitus.*
triple, *triplex.*
tripod, *tripūs* (*-podis*).
trite, *tritus, pervulgatus.*
triumph, subst. *triumphus*; = success, *victoria,* = rejoicing, *exsultatio.*
triumph, v. *triumphare, triumphum agěre*; = exult, *exultare*; — over, = conquer, *superare, vincěre.*
triumphal, *triumphalis.*
triumphant, *victor; elatus, exsultans.*
trivial, *levis.*
trochee, *trochaeus.*
Trojan, subst. *Tros*; adj. *Troianus.*
troop, subst. *caterva, grex, manus* (*ūs*); of horsemen, *turma*; —s, *copiae.*
trooper, *eques.*
trophy, *tropaeum.*
tropics, *regiones torridae.*
trot, subst. *gradus* (*-ūs*) *citatus* or *tolutilis.*
troth, *fides*; to plight —, *fidem dare.*
trouble, subst.: = adversity, *molestia, incommodum, calamitas*; of mind, *sollicitudo, anxietas*; — taken, = effort, *opera, negotium, labor.*
trouble, v. *vexare, agitare, sollicitare*; to — oneself, *laborare*; — about, *curare.*
troublesome, *molestus, gravis, incommodus.*
trough, *alveus.*
trousers, *brac*(*c*)*ae* (*-arum*).
truce, *indutiae* (*-arum*).
truckle, *morem gerěre, obtemperare.*
trudge; see walk.
true, *verus, sincerus, germanus*; = loyal, *fidus, fidelis.* Adv. *vere, profecto, certe.*
trumpet, *tuba* (straight); *bucina, lituus, cornu* (curved); a — call, *classicum.*
trumpeter, *tubicen, bucinator.*
trump up, *fingěre.*
truncheon, *scipio, fustis.*
trunk: of a tree, *truncus, stirps*; of the body, *truncus, corpus*; = chest, box, *arca*; of an elephant, *manus* (*-ūs*), *proboscis.*
trust, subst., = confidence, *fiducia, fides.*
trust, v.: = feel confidence, (*con*)*fiděre, creděre*; = entrust, (*con*)*creděre, committěre, mandare.*
trustee, *custos, procurator.*
trustworthiness, *constantia, fides.*
trustworthy, *certus, constans, fidus.*
truth, *veritas*; the —, = the fact(s), *verum, vera.*
truthful, *verus, verax, veridicus.*
truthfulness, *veritas.*
try, subst. *conatus* (*-ūs*).
try, v.: = make trial of, *temptare, experiri*; = attempt, *conari*; in court, to — a case, *iudicare, cognoscěre, quaerěre.*
trying, adj. *molestus, gravis, incommodus.*
tub, *dolium, labrum.*
tube, *tubus.*
tuck, v.: to — up, *succingěre.*
tuft: of hair, *crinis*; of wool, *floccus*; of feathers, *crista.*
tufted, *cristatus.*
tug, v. *trahěre.*
tumble, subst. *casus* (*-ūs*), *ruina.*
tumble, v. = disarrange, (*per*)*turbare, miscěre*; intransit., see fall.
tumid, *tumidus, inflatus, turgidus.*
tumour, *tumor, tuber.*
tumult, *tumultus* (*-ūs*), *motus* (*-ūs*), *turba.*
tumultuous, *tumultuosus, turbulentus, turbidus*; adv. *tumultuose, turbulente.*
tune, *cantus* (*-ūs*), *carmen, modi* (*-orum*); to keep in —, *concentum servare*; out of —, *absonus.*
tuneful, *canorus.*
tunic, *tunica.*
tunnel, *cuniculus.*
turban, *mitra.*
turbid, *turbidus.*
turbot, *rhombus.*
turbulent, *turbulentus, seditiosus, turbidus.*
turf, *caespes, herba.*
turgid, *tumidus.*
Turin, *Augusta Taurinorum.*
turmoil, *turba.*
turn, turning, *conversio, flexus* (*-ūs*); of events, *vicissitudo, commutatio*; to take a — for the better, *in melius mutari*; of alternation, *sors* (= lot): by —s, *alternis, invicem*; a good —, *officium*; a — of speech, *genus dicendi.*

turn, v.: transit., *(con)vertĕre, advertĕre* (= turn towards), *versare, torquēre* (= twist), *flectĕre* (= bend); — aside, *deflectĕre*; — away, *avertĕre*; — round, *circumagĕre, rotare, volvĕre*;— one's attention to, *animum advertĕre, animadvertĕre*; intransit., *(con)verti, se (con)vertĕre*; — out, = issue, end, *evenire, evadĕre, cadĕre*; — up, *incĭdĕre.*
turnip, *rapum.*
turpitude, *turpitudo, dedecus* (*-oris,* n.).
turret, *turris, turricula.*
turtle, turtle-dove, *turtur.*
Tuscany, *Etruria.*
tusk, *dens.*
tutelage, *tutela*; see also protection.
tutor, *magister, praeceptor.*
tweak, *vellĕre, vellicare.*
twelfth, *duodecimus.*
twelve, *duodecim*; — each, — at a time, *duodeni*; — times, *duodecie(n)s.*
twelvemonth, *annus.*
twentieth, *vicesimus.*
twenty, *viginti*; — each, — at a time, *viceni*; — times, *vicie(n)s.*
twice, *bis.*
twig, *surculus, ramulus, virgula.*
twilight; evening, *crepusculum*; morning, *diluculum.*
twin, subst. and adj., *geminus.*
twinge, *dolor.*
twinkle, *micare, fulgĕre, coruscare.*
twinkling, subst. *fulgor*; in the — of an eye, *temporis puncto.*
twist, v. : transit, *(in)torquēre, (in)flectĕre.*
twitch, v. *vellĕre, vellicare.*
two, *duo*; — each, — at a time, *bini*; in — parts, adj. *bipartitus,* adv. *bipartito.*
twofold, *duplex.*
two-footed, *bipes.*
two hundred., *ducenti*; — each, — at a time, *duceni*; — times, *ducentie(n)s.*
type: = model, *exemplar, exemplum*; = character, class, *forma, figura, genus* (*-eris,* n.).
tyrannical, adj. *tyrannicus, superbus*; adv. *tyrannice, superbe, regie.*
tyrannize, *dominari.*
tyranny, *dominatio, tyrannis.*
tyrant, *tyrannus* (= usurper or despot); *dominus superbus.*

U

udder, *uber.*
ugliness, *deformitas, foeditas.*
ugly, *deformis, turpis, foedus.*
ulcer, *vomica, ulcus* (*-eris,* n.).
ulterior, *ulterior*; see also further.
ultimate, *extremus, ultimus*; adv. *ad extremum, ad ultimum, postremo.*
umbrage: see shade, or offence.
umpire, *arbiter, disceptator.*
un-, as a negative prefix, is rendered by the Latin prefix *in-,* or else by *non* or *haud* or *sine.*
unabashed, = shameless, *impudens.*
unabated, *integer* (= whole).
unable, render by *non posse.*
unacceptable, *ingratus, iniucundus.*
unaccompanied, *solus, sine comitatu.*
unaccomplished, *imperfectus, infectus.*
unaccountable, *inexplicabilis, inenodabilis.*
unaccustomed, *insuetus, insolitus.*
unacquainted, *ignarus, imperitus, inscius.*
unadorned, *inornatus, incomptus, simplex.*
unadulterated, *sincerus, merus, integer.*
unadvised, *imprudens, inconsultus*; adv. *imprudenter, inconsulte.*
unaffected: = simple, *simplex, candidus*; = unmoved, *immotus*; to remain —, *non adfici.*
unafraid, *impavidus, intrepidus, interritus.*
unaided, *sine ope, sine auxilio.*
unalloyed, *purus, sincerus, merus.*
unalterable, *immutatus.*
unamiable, *morosus, difficilis.*
unanimity, *unanimitas, consensio, concordia.*
unanimous, *unanimus, concors*; adv. *uno consensu, una voce.*
unappeased, *non satiatus, implacatus.*
unapproachable; of place, *invius*; of persons, *rari aditūs.*
unarmed, *inermis, nudus.*
unasked, *(sua) sponte, ultro.*
unassuming, *modestus, modicus.*
unattempted; to leave nothing —, *nihil inexpertum omittĕre, omnia experiri.*
unattended, *incomitatus, sine comitibus.*
unauthorized, *inlicitus, inconcessus.*
unavailing, *inritus, futilis, vanus.*
unavenged, *inevitabilis; quod evitari non potest.*
unaware, adj. *inscius, nescius, ignarus.*
unaware, unawares, adv. *(de) improviso, (ex) inopinato*; often by adj. agreeing with the person surprised, e.g. *imprudens, necopinans.*
unbar, *reserare.*
unbearable; see intolerable.
unbeaten, *invictus.*
unbecoming, *indecorus, indignus, turpis*; adv. *indecore, turpiter.*
unbeliever, *qui non credit.*
unbelieving, *incredulus.*
unbend, *remittĕre, (re)laxare.*
unbending, *rigidus, durus.*
unbewailed, *in(de)fletus, indeploratus.*
unbiassed, *integer; neutro inclinatus.*
unbidden, *invocatus, iniussus.*
unbind, *(dis)solvere, laxare.*
unblemished, adj. *purus, integer, in(con)taminatus.*
unblushing, *impudens*; — effrontery, *os durissimum.*
unborn, *nondum natus.*
unbosom: to — oneself, *se patefacĕre, (rem) confiteri.*
unbought, *non emptus, inemptus.*
unbound, of hair, *passus, solutus.*
unbounded, *infinitus, immensus.*
unbribed, *incorruptus, integer.*
unbridled, *effrenatus.*
unbroken, *integer, sincerus*; in time *perpetuus*; of horses, *indomitus.*
unbuckle; see unfasten, untie.

unburden, *exonerare, liberare.*
unburied, *inhumatus, insepultus.*
uncalled, *invocatus*; — for, see unnecessary.
uncared for, *neglectus.*
unceasing, *perpetuus, continuus, adsiduus.*
unceremonious, *simplex* (= natural), *inurbanus* (= rude); adv. *simpliciter, inurbane.*
uncertain, *incertus, ambiguus, dubius, anceps*; to be —, *dubitare, haesitare.*
uncertainty, *dubitatio, dubium*; or render by adj.
unchain, *e vinculis eximĕre*; see loose.
unchangeable, *immutabilis, certus, constans*; adv. *constanter.*
unchangeableness, *immutabilitas, constantia.*
unchanged, *immutatus, integer; idem* (= same).
uncharitable, *durus, inhumanus, iniquus*; adv. *inhumaniter.*
uncharitableness, *inhumanitas.*
unchaste, *incestus, impudicus.*
unchastity, *incestum, impudicitia.*
unchecked, *liber.*
uncivil; see rude.
uncivilized, *ferus, barbarus, incultus.*
unclasp, *refibulare*; see also loose.
uncle, *patruus* (= father's brother), *avunculus* (= mother's brother).
unclean, *impurus, inquinatus.*
unclouded, *serenus, tranquillus.*
uncoil, *evolvĕre, explicare.*
uncombed, *impexus, horridus, incomptus.*
uncomfortable, *molestus, incommodus, gravis*; adv. *incommode.*
uncommanded; see unbidden.
uncommon, *rarus, insolitus, inusitatus*; adv. *plus solito, praeter solitum.*
uncommunicative; see silent.
uncomplaining, *patiens.*
uncompleted, *imperfectus.*
unconcerned, *securus, neglegens, incuriosus.*
unconditional, *simplex, purus*; adv. *simpliciter, sine ulla pactione.*
unconfined, *liber.*
uncongenial; see unpleasant.
unconquerable; see invincible.
unconquered, *invictus.*
unconscious: = insensible, (*omni*) *sensu carens*; = ignorant, *inscius, ignarus.*
unconsecrated, *profanus.*
unconsidered, *neglectus.*
unconstitutional, *non legitimus*; adv. *contra legem, contra rempublicam.*
unconstrained, *liber.*
unconsumed, *inconsumptus.*
uncontaminated, *in(con)taminatus.*
uncontrollable, *impotens.*
uncontrolled, *liber, effrenatus.*
uncooked, *crudus, incoctus.*
uncorrupt, *incorruptus, purus.*
uncouth, *rudis, incultus, rusticus.*
uncouthness, *inhumanitas.*
uncover, *detegĕre, recludere, aperire.*
uncultivated; of soil, *incultus, vastus*; of manners, etc., *inhumanus, rudis, agrestis.*
uncurbed; see unbridled.
uncut, *intonsus* (of hair); *integer* (= whole).
undamaged, *inviolatus, integer.*
undaunted, *impavidus, intrepidus.*
undeceive, *errorem* (*homini*) *eripĕre.*
undecided, *incertus, dubius, ambiguus, anceps.*
undefended, *indefensus, nudus.*
undefiled, *incorruptus, purus.*
undefined, *infinitus.*
undeniable, *evidens, haud dubius*; adv. *certe, sine dubio.*
under, prep. *sub* (to be —, *sub* with abl.; to go —, or go along —, *sub* with acc.); *subter; infra* (with acc.); — Teucer's leadership, *Teucro duce*; in size or number, *infra* or *intra* (with acc.) or render as 'less than'; — these circumstances, *quae cum ita sint.*
underestimate, *minoris facĕre* or *aetsimare.*
under-garment, *subucula.*
undergo, *subire, sustinēre, pati*; to — punishment, *poenas dare.*
underground, adj. *subterraneus.*
undergrowth, *virgulta* (*-orum*, plur.).
underhand, *clandestinus, insidiosus.*
undermine, (*cuniculis*) *subruĕre, labefactare.*
undermost, *infimus, imus.*
underneath, adv. *infra, subter.*
underrate, *minoris facĕre* or *aestimare.*
undersell, *minoris* (*quam ceteri*) *vendĕre.*
understand, *intellegĕre;* (*animo* or *mente*) *comprehendĕre.*
understanding, *mens, ingenium*; see also agreement.
undertake, *suscipĕre,* (*in se*) *recipĕre, incipĕre* (= begin).
undertaker, (of funerals), *libitinarius, vespillo.*
undertaking, subst. *inceptum, coeptum, res suscepta.*
undervalue, *minoris facĕre* or *aestimare.*
underwood; see undergrowth.
undeserved, *immeritus, iniustus* (= unjust); adv. *immerito.*
undeserving, *indignus, immerens.*
undesigned, *fortuitus.*
undesigning, *simplex, candidus.*
undesirable; see bad, worthless.
undeveloped, *immaturus, nondum adultus.*
undigested, *crudus, imperfectus.*
undiminished, *inlibatus, integer.*
undisciplined, *inexercitatus, inconditus.*
undisguised, *apertus*; adv. *palam.*
undistinguished, *mediocris, inglorius, ignobilis.*
undisturbed, *otiosus, tutus* (= safe).
undivided, *indivisus, totus, integer.*
undo: of knots, etc., (*dis*)*solvĕre, expedire*; see also ruin.
undone, *infectus*; to leave —, *omittĕre*; = ruined, *perditus.*
undoubted, *certus, haud dubius*; adv. *sine dubio.*
undress, v.: transit., *veste exuĕre* or *nudare*; intransit., *vestem exuĕre* or (*de*)*ponĕre.*

undressed, *nudus*; = unprocessed, *crudus, rudis.*
undue, *nimius, immodicus*; adv. *nimis, nimium.*
undulate, *fluctuare, vacillare.*
undutiful, *impius, officii immemor.*
unearth, *detegĕre, effodĕre.*
unearthly, *plus quam humanus.*
uneasiness, *sollicitudo,* (*animi*) *perturbatio.*
uneasy, in mind, *anxius, sollicitus, trepidus.*
uneducated, *indoctus, ineruditus, rudis.*
unemployed, *otiosus, vacuus.*
unencumbered, *liber, expeditus.*
unendowed, *indotatus.*
unenlightened, *indoctus, humanitatis expers.*
unenterprising, *iners, socors, piger.*
unenviable, *miser, tristis.*
unequal, *impar, dispar, dissimilis*; adv. *inaequaliter, impariter.*
unequalled, *summus, singularis.*
unerring, *certus.*
uneven, *iniquus, impar, inaequalis, asper* (= rough); adv. *inaequaliter.*
unevenness, *iniquitas, asperitas* (= roughness).
unexamined, *inexploratus.*
unexampled, *unicus, singularis, novus, inauditus.*
unexercised, *inexercitatus.*
unexhausted, *indefessus, integer* (= whole), *recens* (= fresh).
unexpected, *inexspectatus, insperatus, improvisus*; adv. (*ex*) *improviso, praeter spem, praeter opinionem.*
unexplored, *inexploratus.*
unfading, *immortalis, semper florens.*
unfailing, *perennis, perpetuus, certus.*
unfair, *iniquus, iniustus, immeritus*; adv. *inique, iniuste, iniuriā.*
unfairness, *iniquitas, iniuria.*
unfaithful, *infidelis, infidus, perfidus;* adv. *infideliter.*
unfaithfulness, *infidelitas, perfidia.*
unfamiliar; see unaccustomed.
unfasten, (*re*)*solvĕre,* (*re*)*laxare, refigĕre.*
unfathomable, *immensus, infinitus.*
unfavourable, *iniquus, adversus*; of omens, *tristis, infaustus.* Adv. *male.*
unfavourableness, *iniquitas*; or render by adj.
unfed, *impastus.*
unfeeling, *durus, ferreus, inhumanus*; adv. *inhumane.*
unfeigned, *verus, sincerus*; adv. *vere, sincere, ex animo.*
unfilial, *impius* (*erga parentes*).
unfinished, *imperfectus*; = crude, *rudis, impolitus.*
unfit, *inutilis, incommodus, indignus.*
unfitness, *inutilitas.*
unfix, *refigĕre.*
unfledged, *implumis.*
unfold, v. transit. *explicare, aperire.*
unforeseen, *improvisus.*
unforgiving, *implacabilis, inexorabilis.*
unforgotten, render by phrase with *oblivio* (= oblivion) or *memoria* (= memory).
unformed, *informis, imperfectus.*
unfortified, *immunitus.*
unfortunate; see unlucky.
unfounded, *vanus, fictus, falsus.*
unfrequented, *avius, devius, desertus.*
unfriendliness, *inimicitia, simultas.*
unfriendly, *inimicus, iniquus, alienus.*
unfruitful, *sterilis, infecundus.*
unfruitfulness, *sterilitas, infecunditas.*
unfulfilled, *inritus, vanus.*
unfurl, of sails, *pandĕre, explicare.*
unfurnished, *imparatus.*
ungainly, *inhabilis.*
ungenerous, *inliberalis, sordidus*; adv. *inliberaliter.*
ungentlemanly, *inliberalis, indecorus.*
ungodly; see impious.
ungovernable, *indomitus, effrenatus, impotens.*
ungraceful, *invenustus, inelegans.*
ungracious, *iniquus, morosus, asper*; adv. *morose, aspere.*
ungrateful, *ingratus, beneficii immemor.*
ungrudging; see liberal.
unguarded, *incustoditus, indefensus*; = imprudent, *incautus, imprudens*; adv. *incaute, temere.*
unguent, *unguentum.*
unhallowed, *profanus.*
unhappiness, *miseria, aegrimonia.*
unhappy, *infelix, infortunatus, miser;* adv. *misere, infeliciter.*
unharmed, *salvus, incolumis.*
unharness, *disiungĕre, solvĕre.*
unhealthy, *infirmae valetudinis, infirmus*; = unwholesome, *pestilens, gravis.*
unheard, *inauditus.*
unheeded, *neglectus.*
unhesitating, *strenuus, confidens*; adv. *strenue, confidenter.*
unhewn, *rudis.*
unhindered, *liber, expeditus.*
unhinged, in mind, *mente, captus.*
unhistorical, *commenticius, fictus.*
unholy, *profanus*; see also impious.
unhonoured, *inhonoratus.*
unhoped for, *insperatus.*
unhurt, *integer, incolumis, salvus.*
uniform, adj. *constans, aequabilis; unius generis.* Adv. *constanter, aequabiliter.*
uniformity, *aequabilitas, constantia.*
unimpaired, *integer, intactus, inviolatus.*
unimpeachable, *sanctus, integer, locuples.*
unimportant, *lĕvis; nullius momenti.*
uninformed, *indoctus.*
uninhabitable, *inhabitabilis.*
uninhabited, *desertus.*
uninitiated, *profanus.* Transf., *ignarus, imperitus.*
uninjured, *incolumis, integer, salvus.*
uninstructed, *indoctus, rudis.*
unintelligible, *obscurus*; adv. *obscure.*
unintentionally, *forte, non sponte*; or render by adj. agreeing with agent, such as *imprudens, insciens.*
uninteresting, *ieiunus, frigidus.*
uninterrupted, *continuus, perpetuus*; adv. *continenter, uno tenore.*
uninvited, *invocatus.*
union, (*con*)*iunctio, consociatio*; = united body, *societas, sodalitas.*
unique, *unicus, singularis.*

unison, *concordia vocum.*
unite, v.: transit., *(con)iungĕre, (con)sociare* (as partners), *miscēre* (= mix); intransit., *coniungi, coire, consentire* (= agree).
united, *coniunctus, consociatus, socius.*
unity, = agreement, *consensio, concordia.*
universal, *universus, communis, omnium* (= of all); adv. *universe, in universum.*
universe, *mundus, rerum natura.*
unjust, *iniustus, iniquus*; adv. *iniuste, inique, iniuria.*
unkempt, *neglectus, incomptus.*
unkind, *inhumanus, severus*; adv. *inhumane, severe.*
unkindness, *inhumanitas, severitas.*
unknowing, *inscius, insciens, ignarus.*
unknown, *ignotus, incognitus, inexploratus*; a person — to me, *nescio quis.*
unlamented, *infletus, indefletus.*
unlawful, *non legitimus, inlicitus*; adv. *contra legem* or *leges.*
unlearn, *dediscĕre.*
unlearned, *indoctus, inlitteratus.*
unless, *nisi* (contracted *ni*).
unlike, *dissimilis, dispar, diversus.*
unlikely; see improbable.
unlimited, *infinitus, immensus.*
unload, *exonerare, onere liberare.*
unlock, *recludĕre, reserare.*
unlooked-for, *inexspectatus, insperatus.*
unloose, *solvĕre.*
unlucky, *infelix*; adv. *infeliciter, secus.*
unmanageable; see ungovernable.
unmanly, *viro indignus, effeminatus, mollis.*
unmannerly, *male moratus, inurbanus.*
unmarried, *caelebs.*
unmask, *detegĕre, patefacĕre.*
unmatched, *unicus, singularis.*
unmentioned; to leave —, *omittĕre, praetermittĕre.*
unmerciful, *immisericors, inclemens, immitis*; adv. *immisericorditer, inclementer.*
unmindful, *immemor.*
unmistakable; see clear, certain.
unmitigated, often to be rendered by the superl. of an adj., e.g. a war of — cruelty, *bellum atrocissimum*; see also complete, absolute.
unmixed, *merus, simplex.*
unmolested, *incolumis, inviolatus.*
unmoved, *immotus.*
unnatural, *monstruosus, portentosus*; of character, *immanis, impius.* Adv. *contra naturam, praeter naturam.*
unnavigable, *innavigabilis.*
unnecessary, *non necessarius, supervacuus, vanus.* Adv. *cum non opus, ex supervacuo, praeter necessitatem*; sometimes *nimis* or *nimium.*
unnerve, *enervare, debilitare.*
unobserved; see unnoticed.
unorganized, *inconditus.*
unostentatious; see modest.
unpaid, *non solutus, residuus.*
unpalatable, *amarus.*
unparalleled, *unicus, singularis.*
unpardonable, *quod excusari non potest.*
unpatriotic, *patriae immemor.*
unpitied, *immiserabilis.*
unpitying, *immisericors, immitis.*
unpleasant, *molestus, ingratus, odiosus*; adv. *moleste, ingrate, odiose.*
unpleasantness, *incommodum, molestia.*
unploughed, *inaratus.*
unpolished, *impolitus, rudis.*
unpolluted, *impollutus, intemeratus, integer.*
unpopular, *invidiosus, ingratus, offensus.*
unpopularity, *invidia, offensio.*
unpractised, *inexercitatus, rudis.*
unprecedented, *novus, inauditus.*
unprejudiced, *integer*; see unbiassed.
unpremeditated, *subitus*; or use phrase *ex tempore.*
unprepared, *imparatus.*
unprepossessing; see unpleasant, ugly
unprincipled, *improbus, nequam.*
unproductive, *infecundus, sterilis.*
unprofitably, *inutiliter, frustra, incassum.*
unprovoked, *non laccessitus*; or render by *ultro.*
unpublished, *nondum editus.*
unpunished, *impunitus, inultus*; or render by adv. *impune.*
unqualified; see unsuitable or unconditional.
unquenchable, *inexstinctus.*
unquestionable, *certus, haud dubius*; adv. *sine dubio.*
unravel, *retexĕre.* Transf., *explicare, enodare.*
unreasonable, *absurdus* (= irrational), *iniquus* (= unfair); adv. *absurde, inique.*
unremitting, *continuus, adsiduus.*
unreserved, = frank, *liber, apertus, simplex*; see also unconditional. Adv. *absolute, sine ulla exceptione.*
unrest; see restlessness.
unrestrained, *effrenatus, effusus, impotens.*
unrevenged, *inultus.*
unrewarded, *sine praemio, inhonoratus.*
unrighteous, *improbus, iniustus, iniquus*; adv. *improbe, inuste, inique.*
unrighteousness, *improbitas.*
unripe, *immaturus, crudus.*
unrivalled, *eximius, unicus, singularis.*
unroll, *evolvĕre, explicare.*
unruffled, *tranquillus, immotus.*
unruly, *effrenatus, ferox, turbidus.*
unsafe, *infestus, intutus, periculosus.*
unsaid, *indictus.*
unsatisfactory, *non idoneus, malus*; adv. *male, minus bene, secus.*
unseal, *resignare.*
unseasonable, *intempestivus, importunus, immaturus*; adv. *intempestive.*
unseasoned, of food, *non conditus*; of wood, *viridis, humidus.*
unseemly; see indecorous.
unseen, *invisus.*
unselfish, *suae utilitatis immemor, liberalis* (= generous).
unserviceable, *inutilis.*
unsettle, *labefacĕre, (per)turbare.*
unsettled, *inconstans, varius, incertus.*
unshaken, *immotus, inlabefactus.*
unshaved, *intonsus.*
unsheathe, *(de)stringĕre, e vagina educĕre.*
unshod, *pedibus nudis.*

unsightly; see ugly.
unskilful, unskilled, *inscitus, imperitus*; adv. *inscite, imperite.*
unskilfulness, *imperitia.*
unsociable, *insociabilis, difficilis.*
unsophisticated, *simplex.*
unsound, *vitiosus, infirmus*; of unsound mind, *insanus.*
unspeakable, *infandus, inenarrabilis.*
unspoiled, *incorruptus, integer.*
unstable, *inconstans, instabilis, incertus.*
unstained, *purus, in(con)taminatus, integer.*
unsteadiness, *inconstantia.*
unstring; to — a bow, *arcum retendĕre.*
unstrung, of nerves, etc., *fractus, debilitatus.*
unstudied, (of style) *simplex.*
unsubdued, *indomitus.*
unsuccessful, *infelix, infaustus*; adv. *infeliciter.*
unsuitable, unsuited, *incommodus, alienus*; adv. *incommode.*
untainted, *incorruptus, non infectus.*
untamed, *indomitus, ferus.*
untasted, *ingustatus.*
untaught, *indoctus.*
unteachable, *indocilis.*
unthankful; see ungrateful.
unthinking; see thoughtless.
untie, *(dis)solvĕre, laxare.*
until, prep. *ad* or *in*, with acc.
until, conj. *dum, donec, quoad.*
untilled, *incultus, inaratus.*
untimely, *immaturus, intempestivus.*
untiring, *adsiduus, indefessus.*
unto; see to.
untouched, *intactus, integer.*
untoward, *adversus.*
untried, *inexpertus, intemptatus.*
untroubled, *tranquillus, placidus, quietus.*
untrue, *falsus*; adv. *falso.*
untruth, *falsum, mendacium.*
unused, see unaccustomed; = not yet used, *recens, integer.*
unusual, *inusitatus, insuetus, insolitus*; in an — manner, *inusitate.*
unutterable, *infandus, inenarrabilis.*
unvarnished, *simplex.*
unveil, *detegĕre, aperire, patefacĕre.*
unversed, *rudis, imperitus.*
unviolated, *inviolatus.*
unwariness, *imprudentia.*
unwarlike, *imbellis.*
unwarrantable, *iniquus, iniustus.*
unwary, *incautus, imprudens;* adv. *incaute, imprudenter.*
unwashed, *inlotus.*
unwatched, *incustoditus.*
unwavering; see firm.
unwearied, *indefessus, integer.*
unweave, *retexĕre.*
unwelcome, *ingratus.*
unwell, *aeger, invalidus, infirmus.*
unwholesome, *pestilens, gravis.*
unwieldy, *inhabilis.*
unwilling, *invitus*; to be —, *nolle.*
unwind, *retexĕre, explicare.*
unwise, *insipiens, stultus*; adv. *insipienter, stulte.*
unwitting, *inscius, insciens.*
unwonted; see unusual.
unworthiness, *indignitas.*
unworthy, *indignus*; adv. *indigne.*
unwounded, *invulneratus, integer.*
unwrap, *evolvĕre, explicare.*
unwrought, *rudis, infectus.*
unyielding; see inflexible.
unyoke, *disiungĕre.*
up, prep.: — the river, *adverso flumine*; — the mountain, *in adversum montem.*
up, adv. *sursum*; — to, *usque ad* (with acc.), *tenus* (after an abl. or genit.); to go —, *ascendĕre.*
upbraid, *reprehendĕre, obiurgare, exprobrare.*
upbraiding, *obiurgatio, exprobratio.*
uphill; adj. *adclivis, arduus*; adv. *adverso colle, adversus collem.*
uphold, *sustinēre, sustentare.*
upland, adj. *editus.*
upon, prep.: in space, *super, in*; in time, = directly after, *e* or *ex* (with abl.); — this subject, *de hac re.*
upper, *superus, superior*; to get the — hand, *superare, vincĕre.*
uppermost, *summus, supremus.*
upright, *(e)rectus*; morally, *probus, honestus*; adv. *recte, probe, honeste.*
uprightness, *probitas, honestas.*
uproar, *tumultus* (-*ūs*); see noise.
uproarious, *tumultuosus.*
uproot, *radicitus tollĕre, evellĕre.*
upset, adj. *adflictus, perculsus.*
upset, v. *evertĕre, subvertĕre.*
upshot, *exitus* (-*ūs*), *eventus* (-*ūs*).
upstart, *novus homo.*
upwards, *sursum.*
urbane, *urbanus.*
urbanity, *urbanitas.*
urge, v. *impellĕre, incitare, urgēre.*
urgency, *gravitas, necessitas.*
urgent; of matters, *gravis, magni momenti*; of persons, *vehemens*; adv. *vehementer, magnopere.*
urn, *urna.*
usage, *mos, consuetudo.*
use, subst. *usus* (-*ūs*), *usurpatio, usura*; to make — of, *(re) uti.*
use, v.: = to make use of, *uti, usurpare, adhibēre*; = to treat, *tractare*; to — up, *consumĕre*; to — wrongly, *abuti.*
useful, *utilis, aptus, commodus*: to be —, *usui esse, prodesse.* Adv. *utiliter, apte, commode.*
usefulness, *utilitas, usus* (-*ūs*), *commoditas.*
useless, *inutilis, vanus, inritus;* adv. *frustra.*
usher, v.: to — in, *introducĕre.*
usual, *usitatus, solitus, consuetus*; more than —, *plus solito.* Adv. *ferme, fere, plerumque.*
usurer, *faenerator, toculio.*
usurp, *adsumĕre, occupare.*
usury, *faeneratio, usura*; to practise — *faenerari.*
utensils, *vasa* (-*orum*), *utensilia* (-*ium*) *supellex.*
utility; see usefulness.
utmost, *extremus, ultimus, summus*; to do one's —, *summis viribus contendĕre.*
utter, adj. *totus* (= whole). Adv. *omnino, penitus, funditus.*
utter, v. *dicĕre, pronuntiare, effari.*

utterance, *dictum* (= saying), *pronuntiatio* (= delivery).

V

vacancy: = empty space, *vacuum, inane, inanitas*; = unoccupied post, render by *vacuus*; — of mind, *stupiditas.*
vacant, *vacuus.*
vacate, *vacuefacĕre*; to — an office, *se magistratu abdicare.*
vacation, *feriae* (*-arum*).
vacillate, *vacillare.*
vacillating, *dubius, incertus.*
vacillation, *dubitatio.*
vagabond, vagrant: subst. *grassator*; adj. *vagus.*
vagary, *ineptiae* (*-arum*).
vague, *incertus, dubius, ambiguus*; adv. *incerte, dubie, ambigue.*
vain: = worthless, *inanis, levis*; = fruitless, *vanus, inritus*; = self-satisfied, *gloriosus*; to be —, *sibi placēre.* Adv. —ly, or in —, *frustra, nequiquam.*
vainglorious, *vaniloquus, gloriosus.*
vale; see valley.
valiant, *fortis, animosus, acer*; adv. *fortiter, animose, acriter.*
valid, *gravis, certus*; of laws, *ratus.*
validity, *gravitas, pondus* (*-eris*, n.).
valley, (*con*)*vallis.*
valour, *virtus* (*-utis*), *fortitudo.*
valuable, *pretiosus, magni pretii.*
valuation, *aestimatio.*
value, subst. *aestimatio, pretium.*
value, v. *aestimare, ducĕre, pendĕre*; to — highly, *magni facĕre.*
valueless; see worthless.
van: of an army, *primum agmen*; as vehicle, see cart.
vanish, (*e*)*vanescĕre.*
vanity: = emptiness, *inanitas*; = self-satisfaction, *gloria, ostentatio.*
vanquish, (*de*)*vincĕre, superare.*
vanquisher, *victor* (f. *victrix*).
vapid, *vapidus, ieiunus, insulsus.*
vapour, *vapor, nebula, exhalatio.*
variable, *varius, mutabilis, inconstans.*
variableness, *mutabilitas*; see change.
variance, *discordia, dissensio, discrepantia*; to be at —, *dissidēre, discordare, discrepare.*
variation, *varietas, vicissitudo.*
variegated, *varius, versicolor.*
variety, *varietas, diversitas.*
various, *varius, diversus*; adv. *varie, diverse.*
vary, v.: transit., *variare, mutare*; intransit., *variari, mutari.*
vase, *vas.*
vassal, *cliens.*
vassalage, *clientela.*
vast, *vastus, ingens, immanis*; adv. *magnopere, valde.*
vastness, *amplitudo, magnitudo.*
vat, *cupa, dolium.*
vault, subst., *fornix, camera*; a — underground, *hypogeum.*
vault, v., in building, *confornicare*; = leap, *salire.*
vaunt; see boast.
veal, (*caro*) *vitulina.*
veer, *se vertĕre, verti.*
vegetable, subst., *planta*; an edible —, *holus* (*-eris*, n.); — market, *forum holitorium.*
vegetate, v., fig., *hebescĕre.*
vegetation, *herbae, plantae* (*-arum*).
vehemence, *vis, contentio, impetus* (*-ūs*), *ardor.*
vehement, *vehemens, acer*; adv. *vehementer, acriter.*
vehicle: see carriage, waggon.
veil, subst. *rica*; bridal —, *flammeum, flammeolum.*
veil, v. *velare, tegĕre.*
vein, *vena.*
vellum, *membrana.*
velocity, *velocitas.*
venal, *venalis, nummarius.*
venality, *animus venalis.*
vend, *vendĕre.*
vendor, *venditor.*
venerable, *venerabilis.*
venerate, *colĕre, observare, venerari.*
veneration, *cultus* (*-ūs*), *veneratio.*
vengeance, *ultio, vindicta*; to take —, *ulcisci, vindicare.*
venial, *veniā dignus.*
venison, (*caro*) *ferina.*
venom, *venenum, virus.*
venomous, *venenatus.*
vent, subst. *foramen, spiramentum, emissarium*; to find —, *erumpĕre.*
vent, v.: to — anger, *stomachum effundĕre, evomĕre.*
ventilate, *ventilare* (= to fan); fig., *in medium proferre.*
venture, *periculum* (= risk); *alea* (= hazard); *facinus* (*-oris*, = bold act).
venture, v.: = dare, *audēre, periclitari*; = endanger, *periclitari.*
venturesome, venturous, *audax, temerarius*; adv., *audacter.*
venturousness, *audacia, temeritas.*
veracious, *verus, verax, veridicus.*
veracity, *veritas.*
veranda, *subdialia* (*-ium*), *porticus* (*-ūs*, f.).
verb, *verbum.*
verbal, render by *verbum* or *vox.*
verbatim, *ad verbum, totidem verbis.*
verbiage, *verba* (*-orum*).
verbose, *verbosus*; adv. *verbose.*
verbosity, *copia* or *ubertas verborum.*
verdant, *viridis, viridans.*
verdict, *sententia, iudicium*; to pronounce a —, *iudicare, sententiam dicĕre.*
verdure, *viriditas.*
verge, subst. *margo, ora*; fig., on the — of, render by fut. partic., or *instare*, or *prope.*
verge, v. *vergĕre, inclinare, appropinquare.*
verification, *confirmatio.*
verify, *confirmare, probare.*
verily, *profecto, sane, certe.*
verisimilitude, *verisimilitudo.*
veritable, *verus.*
vermilion: subst., *minium*; adj. *miniatus.*

vernacular; — tongue, *sermo patrius*.
versatile, *versatilis, varius et multiplex*.
versatility, *facilitas, ingenium facile*.
verse, *versus* (-*ūs*; in sing. = line of poetry).
versed, *versatus, exercitatus, peritus*.
versification, *versuum ratio*.
versify, *versūs* (or *carmina*) *facĕre*.
vertex, *vertex*, or render by *summus*.
vertical, (*di*)*rectus*; a — line, *linea, perpendiculum*; adv. *recte, ad lineam, ad perpendiculum*.
vertigo, *vertigo*.
very, adj. *ipse*; see true, real.
very, adv.; render by superlative, or a special form with the prefix *per*-, or *maxime, summe, admodum*; not (so) —, *non ita, haud ita*; — much, with verbs, *magnopere, maxime, valde*.
vessel, *vas*; a blood —, *arteria, vena*; = ship, *navis*.
vest, v.: see clothe or invest.
vestal; a — virgin, *virgo vestalis*.
vestibule, *vestibulum*.
vestige, *vestigium, indicium*.
vetch, *vicia*.
veteran, subst. and adj. *veteranus*.
veto, subst. *intercessio* (of the tribunes).
veto, v. *intercedĕre, vetare*.
vex, *vexare, sollicitare*; to be —ed at, *aegre ferre*, or render by *piget*.
vexation, *indignatio, stomachus, molestia*.
vexatious, *molestus, gravis*; adv. *graviter*.
viands, *cibus*.
vibrate, *vibrare*; see also shake.
vibration, *motus* (-*ūs*); or render by verb.
vicarious, *vicarius*; adv. render by *loco* with genit., or *pro* with abl.
vice, *vitiositas, vitium, turpitudo*.
vicious, *vitiosus, turpis, flagitiosus*; adv. *turpiter, flagitiose*.
viciousness, *vitiositas*; see vice.
vicissitude, *vicissitudo, varietas, vices* (plur.).
victim, *victima, hostia*.
victor, *victor* (f. *victrix*).
victorious, *victor*, with f. *victrix*; adv., render by adj.
victory, *victoria*; to gain a —, *vincĕre, superare*.
victual, *rem frumentariam providēre* (with dat.).
vie, *certare, contendĕre, aemulari*.
Vienna, *Vindobona*.
view, subst.: = vision, *conspectus* (-*ūs*), *prospectus* (-*ūs*); mental —, = judgment, *sententia, iudicium*; in my —, *meo iudicio, me iudice*.
view, v. *adspicĕre, intuēri, contemplari*.
vigil, *vigilia, pervigilatio, pervigilium*.
vigilance, *vigilantia, diligentia*.
vigilant, *vigilans, intentus, diligens*; adv. *vigilanter, intente, diligenter*.
vigorous, *strenuus, impiger, acer*; adv. *strenue, impigre, acriter*.
vigour, *vis, nervi* (-*orum*).
vile, *abiectus, nequam, turpis*; adv. *abiecte, nequiter, turpiter*.
vileness, *turpitudo*.
vilify; see slander.
villa, *villa* (= country-house).
village, *pagus, vicus*.
villager, *paganus, vicanus*.
villain, *homo scelestus*; colloq., *verbero, scelus* (-*eris*, n.).
villainous, *scelestus, sceleratus, flagitiosus*.
villainy: as disposition, *improbitas, pravitas, nequitia*; as act, *scelus* (-*eris*, n.), *flagitium*.
vindicate: = maintain, *tenēre, obtinēre, defendĕre*; = justify, *probare, purgare*.
vindication, *vindicta, defensio*.
vindicator, *vindex, defensor*.
vindictive, *ulciscendi cupidus*.
vine, *vitis*.
vine-dresser, *vinitor*.
vinegar, *acetum*.
vineyard, *vinea, vinetum*.
vintage, *vindemia*.
vintner, *vinarius*.
violate, *violare, rumpĕre*.
violation, *violatio*.
violator, *violator, ruptor*.
violence, *violentia, vis; ardor* (of passion, etc.); *gravitas* (of weather, etc.).
violent, *violentus, vehemens, gravis* (of illness, weather, etc.): adv. *vi, per vim, violenter, vehementer, graviter*.
violet, subst. *viola*; a bed of —s, *violarium*.
viper, *vipera, aspis*; of a —, adj., *vipereus*.
virgin, subst. *virgo*.
virginity, *virginitas*.
virile, *virilis*; see manly.
virility, *virilitas*; see manhood.
virtual, virtually, *re non verbo*.
virtue: moral —, *virtus* (-*utis*, f.), *probitas*; = chastity, *pudicitia, sanctimonia*; = efficacy, *virtus, vis*, or use verb, e.g. *posse, prodesse*; by — of, *per, ex, pro*.
virtuous, *virtute praeditus, honestus, probus*; = chaste, *pudicus, castus*; adv. *honeste*.
virulence, *vis*; of diseases, *gravitas*; of hostility, *acerbitas*.
virulent, *gravis, acerbus*; adv. *graviter, acerbe*.
viscera, *viscera* (-*um*), *exta* (-*orum*).
viscous, *lentus, tenax*.
visible, *manifestus*; to be —, *apparēre, in conspectu esse*: adv., *manifesto, quod cernĕre possis*.
vision: = faculty of sight, *visus* (-*ūs*); *aspectus* (-*ūs*); = thing seen, *visus* (-*ūs*), *species*; = apparition, *simulacrum, imago*.
visionary: of things, *inanis, fictus, vanus*; of character, *fanaticus*.
visit, subst. *salutatio*.
visit, v.: = go to see, (*in*)*visĕre, visitare, salutare*; = punish, *animadvertĕre, punire*.
visitation; see punishment.
visitor, *salutator, hospes, advena*.
visor, *buccula* (= cheek-piece).
vista, *prospectus* (-*ūs*); see view.
vital, *vitalis;* adv. *vitaliter*; see also essential.
vitality, *vis, animus*.

vitiate, *depravare, corrumpĕre, inritum facĕre* (= invalidate).
vitiation, *corruptio, depravatio.*
vituperate, *vituperare, reprehendĕre.*
vituperation, *vituperatio, reprehensio.*
vivacious, *vividus, alacer, acer*; adv. *acriter.*
vivacity, *alacritas, vigor.*
vivid; see lively.
vixen, *vulpes*; of women, *canis.*
vocabulary, *index verborum* (= list of words), *copia verborum* (= stock or flow of words).
vocation, *officium, munus* (*-eris*, n.).
vociferate, *vociferari, clamare.*
vociferation, *vociferatio, clamor.*
vociferous, vociferously, *magno clamore.*
vogue, *mos.*
voice, subst. *vox.*
voice, v.; see utter, express.
void, subst. *inanitas, inane, vacuum.*
void, adj.: = empty, *inanis, vacuus*; = invalid, *inritus, vanus.*
volatile, *volaticus, levis, mobilis.*
volatility, *levitas, mobilitas.*
volcano, *mons flammas eructans*; or refer to some specific volcano.
volition, *voluntas.*
volley, *tela* (*-orum*) *coniecta.*
voluble, *volubilis*; see also fluent.
volume: = book, *liber, volumen*; = size, *magnitudo, amplitudo*; = quantity, *copia.*
voluminous, *copiosus, magnus, amplus.*
voluntary, *voluntarius*; adv., *ultro,* (*mea*, etc.) *sponte.*
volunteer, subst. *voluntarius* (*miles*).
volunteer, v. *operam suam profitēri.*
voluptuous, *voluptarius, luxuriosus, libidinosus.*
voluptuousness, *voluptas, luxuria.*
vomit, v. (*e*)*vomĕre.*
voracious, *edax,* (*cibi*) *avidus*; adv. *avide.*
voracity, *edacitas,* (*cibi*) *aviditas.*
vortex, *vertex, turbo.*
votary, *cultor.*
vote, subst. *suffragium, punctum, sententia.*
vote, v. *suffragium* or *sententiam ferre; censēre.*
voter, *suffragator, qui suffragium fert.*
voting-tablet, *tabella, suffragium.*
votive, *votivus.*
vouch, v.: to — for a thing, *rem in se recipĕre*; = assert, warrant, *adseverare, testari.*
vouchsafe, *concedĕre.*
vow, subst. *votum, devotio, sponsio.*
vow, v. (*de*)*vovēre*; = to undertake, promise, (*de*)*spondēre, promittĕre.*
vowel, *littera vocalis.*
voyage, subst. *navigatio, cursus* (*-ūs*).
voyage, v. *navigare.*
vulgar, *vulgaris, usitatus, plebeius.*
vulture, *vultur, vulturius.*

W

wade, *vado flumen transire.*
wag, subst. *ioculator, homo iocosus.*
wag, v. *movēre, quassare.*
wage; to — war, *bellum gerĕre.*
wager, subst. *sponsio, pignus* (*-oris*).
wager, v. *sponsionem facĕre, pignore certare.*
wages, *merces, stipendium.*
waggon, *plaustrum, vehiculum, carrus.*
wail, *plorare, plangĕre.*
wailing, subst. *ploratus* (*-ūs*).
wain, *plaustrum.*
wainscot, *paries* (= party-wall).
waist, *corpus* (*-oris*, n.) *medium.*
wait, subst. *mora* (= delay); to lie in — for, *aucupari, insidiari.*
wait, v. *manēre*; to — for, *opperiri, exspectare, praestolari*; to — at table, *ministrare.*
waiter, *famulus, minister, puer.*
waiting, subst.: = delay, *mora, commoratio*; at table, *ministerium.*
waive, (*rem*) *concedĕre,* (*de re*) *decedĕre.*
wake, subst. see watch; in the — of, *post.*
wake, v.: transit., *expergefacĕre, excitare*; intransit., *expergisci, excitari.*
wakefulness, *insomnia, vigilia.*
walk, subst.: a — as taken, *ambulatio*; to go for a —, *ire ambulatum*; = gait, *incessus* (*-ūs*), *ingressus* (*-ūs*).
walk, v. *pedibus ire, ambulare, ingredi, incedĕre.*
wall, subst. *murus, moenia* (*-ium*; of a town), *paries* (= partition).
wall, v. *muro cingĕre, munire.*
wallet, *saccus, crumena.*
wallow, *volutari.*
walnut, (fruit or tree), *iuglans.*
wan, *pallidus, exsanguis.*
wand, *virga, virgula.*
wander, *vagari, palari, errare*: to — through, *pervagari*; to — in mind, *delirare.*
wanderer, *erro, peregrinator.*
wandering, subst. *error, erratio.*
wandering, adj. *errabundus, vagus.*
wane, *decrescĕre, minui.*
want, subst. *penuria, inopia, egestas, desiderium* (— as felt), *defectio*; in —, adj. *inops, egenus, egens.*
want, v.: = lack, need, *egēre, indigēre, requirĕre, desiderare*; = wish, *velle, avēre, cupĕre.*
wanting, = defective, *vitiosus*; to be found —, *deesse, deficĕre.*
wanton, adj. *lascivus, petulans, protervus*; adv. *petulanter, proterve, ultro* (= without provocation).
wanton, v. *lascivire.*
wantonness, *lascivia, petulantia, protervitas.*
war, subst. *bellum*; civil —, *bellum intestinum, domesticum, civile*; a — of extermination, *bellum internecinum*; to declare —, *bellum indicĕre*; to make —, *bellum inferre*; to carry on a —, *bellum gerĕre.*
warble, *canĕre.*
war-cry, *clamor* (*bellicus*), *ululatus* (*-ūs*).
ward, subst.: = a quarter of a town, *regio, vicus*; = custody, *custodia*; = a minor, *pupillus.*
ward, v.; to — off, *arcēre, propulsare, avertere*; by prayers, *deprecari.*

warden, warder, *custos.*
wardrobe, *vestiarium.*
ware, wares, *merx.*
warehouse, *horreum, apotheca.*
warfare, *militia.*
wariness, *prudentia, cautio, circumspectio.*
warlike, *militaris, bellicus, ferox.*
warm, *calidus*; luke- —, *tepidus*; to be warm, *calēre.*
warm, v. *calefacĕre.*
warmth, *calor, fervor.*
warn, (*ad*)*monēre*; in advance, *praemonēre.*
warning, subst. (*ad*)*monitio, monitus* (*-ūs*), *exemplum* (= object-lesson).
warp, subst., in weaving, *stamen.*
warp, v.: of timber, intransit., *pandari.* Transf., *depravare, torquēre*; see also distort.
warrant, subst.: = authority, *auctoritas, potestas*; = written authorization, *mandatum, diploma* (*-atis*, n.).
warrant, v. (*con*)*firmare, promittĕre* (= promise).
warranty, *satisdatio*; see guarantee.
warrior, *miles, homo* (or *vir*) *militaris.*
wary, *providus, circumspectus, cautus.*
wash, subst. *lavatio*; a colour- —, *fucus* (esp. red).
wash, v.: transit., *lavare*; to — out, — away, *abluĕre*; intransit., *lavari.*
wasp, *vespa.*
waste, subst.: = unprofitable expenditure, *effusio, sumptus* (*-ūs*) *effusus, iactura*; = waste land, *vastitas, solitudo*; = discarded material, *ramenta* (*-orum*).
waste, adj. *vastus, incultus, desertus*; to lay —, *vastare,* (*de*)*populari.*
waste, v.: transit., = to spend unprofitably, *consumĕre, perdĕre*; intransit., to — away, (*con*)*tabescĕre, consumi, confici.*
wasteful, *profusus, effusus*; adv. *profuse, effuse.*
wastefulness, *profusio, effusio.*
watch, subst.: = watching, *excubiae* (*-arum*), *vigilantia, vigilia*: to keep —, *vigilare*; concrete, the —, *vigilia, statio*; = quarter of a night, *vigilia*; = timepiece, *horologium.*
watch, v.: = observe or guard, (*ob*)*servare, tuēri*; = stay awake, *vigilare, excubare.*
watchful, *vigilans*; adv. *vigilanter.*
watchfulness, *vigilantia, vigilia.*
watchman, *vigil, excubitor, custos.*
watchtower, *specula.*
watchword, *tessera, signum.*
water, subst. *aqua*; fresh —, *aqua dulcis*; rain —, (*aqua*) *pluvia, aqua caelestis*; to go for —, *aquari*; of the —, adj., *aquatilis, aquarius.*
water, v. (*in*)*rigare, conspergĕre* (= to sprinkle).
water-carrier, *aquator, aquarius.*
water-clock, *clepsydra.*
watering-place, *aquatio*; for bathing, etc., *aquae* (*-arum*).
water-jug, *hydria, urceus.*
water-snake, *hydrus.*
waterspout, *prester, typhon.*
waterworks, *aquae* or *aquarum ductu* (*-ūs*).
watery, *aquatilis, aquosus.*
wattle, subst.; = hurdle, *cratis*; of a cock, *palea.*
wave, subst. *fluctus* (*-ūs*), *unda.*
wave, v.: transit., *agitare, iactare, vibrare*; intransit., *fluctuare, undare.*
waver, *fluctuare, dubitare.*
wavering, subst. *dubitatio, fluctuatio.*
wavering, adj. *incertus, dubius.*
wax, subst. *cera.*
wax, v. = to cover with wax, (*in*)*cerare* intransit., = grow, *crescĕre.*
waxen, *cereus.*
way. (1), abstract: = journey, *via, cursus* (*-ūs*), *iter*: — up to, *aditus* (*-ūs*); = manner, *modus, ratio, via*; in this —, *sic, ita*; = custom, *mos, institutum*; —s and means, *opes* (*-um*; plur.). (2), concrete, = road, *via*; a bye- —, *trames, semita, callis*; in the —, adj. *obvius*; out of the —, *devius, avius, remotus*; the milky —, *orbis lacteus.*
wayfarer, *viator.*
waylay, (*homini*) *insidiari.*
wayward; see wilful.
we, *nos*; but often not expressed.
weak, *infirmus, debilis, imbecillus, invalidus*; *hebes* (= dull, faint, etc.); *levis* (of character, etc.); adv. *infirme.*
weaken, v. transit. *debilitare, enervare, infirmare.*
weakness, *imbecillitas, infirmitas, debilitas*; *levitas* (of arguments, etc.); *vitium* (= fault).
weal: the public —, *respublica.*
wealth, *divitiae* (*-arum*), *opes* (*-um*), *copia.*
wealthy, *dives, locuples, opulentus.*
weapon, *arma* (*-orum*; defensive) *telum* (offensive).
wear, subst. *usus* (*-ūs*).
wear, v.: to — away, (*con*)*terĕre*; = to have on the body, *gerĕre, gestare*; = to last, *durare*; to — off, *evanescĕre.*
weariness, *lassitudo, taedium.*
wearisome, *laboriosus, molestus.*
weary, adj. (*de*)*fatigatus,* (*de*)*fessus.*
weary, v.: transit., (*de*)*fatigare, obtundĕre* (= to bore); intransit., use impersonal *taedet.*
weasel, *mustela.*
weather, subst. *caelum, tempestas.*
weather, v.: to — a cape, *promontorium circumvehi*; to — a storm *vim tempestatis perferre.*
weave, (*con*)*texĕre*
weaver, *textor.*
web, *tela, textum.*
wed; see marry.
wedding, *nuptiae* (*-arum*).
wedge, subst. *cuneus*; — **-shaped,** *cuneatus.*
week, *septem dies.*
week-days, *dies profesti.*
weep, *lacrimare, lacrimas fundĕre, flēre*; to — for, (*de*)*plorare,* (*de*)*flēre, lamentari.*
weeping, subst. *fletus* (*-ūs*), *lamentatio.*
weigh, v.: transit. (lit. and fig.), (*ex*)*pendĕre, pensare, examinare*; to

— down, *opprimĕre*, *gravare*; intransit., to — much, *magni ponderis esse*.

weight, *pondus* (*-eris*, n.), *gravitas*, *momentum*; to have great —, *multum valēre*.

weighty, *gravis* (lit. and fig.).

weir, *moles*, *agger*.

welcome, subst. *salutatio*.

welcome, adj. *acceptus*, *gratus*.

welcome! interj. *salve*.

welcome, v. *salutare*, *salvēre iubēre*.

welfare, *salūs* (*-ūtis*, f.), *commodum*, *utilitas*.

well, subst. *puteus*.

well, adj. *salvus*, *sanus*: to be —, (*bene*) *valēre*; to get —, *convalescĕre*.

well, adv. *bene*, *recte*; very —, *optime*, *praeclare*; it is —, *bene est*, *bene habet*.

well, v.: to — up, *scatēre*.

well-being, *salūs* (*-ūtis*, f.).

well-born, *nobilis*.

well-bred, *comis*, *urbanus*.

well-earned, *meritus*.

well-informed, *doctus*, *eruditus*.

well-known, (*omnibus*) *notus*, *celebratus*.

well-meaning, *benevolus*, *amicus*.

welter, subst. *congeries*.

west, subst, *occidens*, *solis occasus* (*-ūs*).

west, adj. *occidentalis*; — wind, *Zephyrus*, *Favonius*.

westwards, *ad occasum*, *ad occidentem*.

wet, adj. *umidus*, *madidus*; to be —, *madēre*.

wet, v. *madefacĕre*, (*in*)*rigare*.

wether, *vervex*.

whale, *balaena*, *cetus* or *cetos*.

wharf, *navale*, *crepido*.

what: interrog., as pronoun, *quid?*, as adj. *qui*, *quae*, *quod?*; of — sort? *qualis?*; of — size? *quantus?*; relative, = that which, (*id*) *quod*.

whatever, whatsoever: relat. pronoun or adj., *quisquis*, *quicunque*; indef., any —, *quivis*.

wheat, *triticum*; of —, adj., *triticeus*.

wheedle, (*e*)*blandiri*.

wheel, subst. *rota*.

wheel, v.: = turn round, transit., *convertĕre*, intransit., of troops, *signa convertĕre*; = push forward on wheels, *propulsare*.

wheeze, *anhelare*; see also pant.

whelp, *catulus*.

when: interrog., *quando?*; relat., *cum*, *ubi*, *quando*, *ut*, *postquam* (= after).

whence, *unde*.

whenever, *quandocumque*, *quoties*, *cum* (with indic).

where: interrog., *ubi?*; — from, *unde?*; — to, *quo?*; relat., *ubi*, *qua*.

whereas, *quoniam*, *quod*, *cum*.

whereby; render by relative.

wherefore: interrog., *cur?*; relat., *quare*, *quamobrem*, *quapropter*.

wherein, *in quo*, *in quibus*, *ubi*.

whereof, render by genit. of relat.

whereupon, *quo facto*.

wherever, *ubicumque*, *quacumque*.

whet, (*ex*)*acuĕre*.

whether, conj. In single indirect questions, *num*, *-ne* or *an*, followed by subj.; in disjunctive indirect questions, *utrum . . . an*, *-ne . . .an*, followed by subj.; — . . . or not, *utrum . . . necne*. In disjunctive conditional sentences, when a thing is so in either of two conditions, — . . . or, is *sive* (or *seu*) . . . *sive* (or *seu*).

whetstone, *cos*.

whey, *serum*.

which: interrog., *quis?*; — of the two *uter?*; relat., *qui*, *quae*, *quod*.

whiff, *halitus* (*-ūs*; = breath).

while, subst.: for a —, *aliquamdiu*; in a little —, *brevi*, *mox*; for a little —, *parumper*, *paulisper*.

while, whilst, *dum*, *donec*, *quoad* (rare).

while, v.: to — away time, *tempus fallĕre*.

whim, *libido*.

whimsical, *levis* (= fickle).

whine, v. *vagire* (esp. of children).

whining, subst. *vagitus* (*-ūs*).

whinny, *hinnire*.

whip, *flagrum*, *flagellum*, *scutica*.

whip, v. *verberare*.

whirl, v. transit., (*con*)*torquēre*, *rotare*.

whirlpool, *vertex*, *vorago*, *gurges*.

whirlwind, *turbo*, *vertex*.

whirr, subst. *stridor*.

whirr, v. *stridĕre* or *stridēre*.

whisht, interj. *st! tace*, *tacete*.

whisper, subst. *susurrus*.

whisper, v. *susurrare*, *insusurrare*.

whistle, v. *sibilare*.

whit; not a —, *ne minimum quidem*, *minime*.

white, adj. *albus* (= dead —), *candidus* (= shining —), *canus* (= hoary); to be —, *albēre*.

whiten, whitewash, v. transit. *dealbare*.

whiteness, *candor*.

whither: interrog., *quo?*; relat., *quo*.

whithersoever, *quoquo*, *quocunque*.

who: interrog., *quis*, *quid*; relat., *qui*, *quae*, *quod*.

whoever, *quicunque*, *quisquis*.

whole, subst.: the — of a thing, *tota res*; on the —, *plerumque*, *ferme*, *fere*.

whole, adj. *totus*, *omnis*, *universus*, *integer* (= unhurt).

wholesome, *salutaris*, *utilis*.

wholesomeness, *salubritas*, *utilitas*.

wholly, *omnino*, *prorsus*.

whose, *cuius*; plur. *quorum*, *quarum*, *quorum*.

why, *cur*, *quare*, *quamobrem*.

wicked, *improbus*, *malus*, *nefarius*; adv. *improbe*, *male*, *nefarie*.

wickedness, *improbitas*, *scelus* (*-eris*, n.).

wicker, *vimineus*; — work, *crates*.

wide, *latus*, *laxus*, *amplus*; adv. *late*.

widen, v.: transit., *amplificare*, *dilatare*; intransit., *patescĕre*.

widow, *vidua*.

widowed, *viduus*, *orbus*.

width, *latitudo*, *amplitudo*.

wield, *tractare*, *uti* (with abl.).

wife, *uxor*, *coniunx*.

Wight, Isle of, *Vectis*.

wild, adj. *ferus, incultus, ferox*; a — beast, *fera*; adv. *normally* *ferociter, saeve.*
wilderness, wilds, *loca* (*-orum*) *deserta, solitudo, vastitas.*
wildness, *feritas, ferocia.*
wile, *ars, dolus.*
wilful, *contumax, pervicax*; adv. *contumaciter, pervicaciter*; see also deliberately.
wilfulness, *contumacia, pervicacia.*
will, subst.: = volition, *voluntas, animus, arbitrium*; against one's —, *invitus*, adj.; = testament, *testamentum.*
will, v.: = wish, *velle*; = leave property by will, *legare, relinquěre.*
willing, *libens, volens, paratus*; adv. *libenter*, or use adj. *libens.*
willingness, *voluntas.*
willow, *salix.*
wily, *vafer, astutus, versutus.*
win, v.: transit., see get, gain; intransit., *vincěre, superare.*
wind, subst. *ventus.*
wind, v. = turn, twist, *volvěre, torquēre.*
winding, subst. *sinus* (*-ūs*), *flexus* (*-ūs*).
winding, adj. *flexuosus, tortuosus.*
windlass, *sucula, tormentum.*
window, *fenestra.*
windy, *ventosus.*
wine, *vinum*: sour —, *vappa*; undiluted, *merum*; the — god, *Bacchus.*
wine-cellar, *apotheca.*
wine-merchant, *vinarius.*
wing, subst. *ala*; of an army, *cornu, ala.*
wing, v.; to — one's way, *volare.*
winged, *alatus, aliger, pennatus.*
wink, v. *conivēre, nictare.*
winner, *victor.*
winning, *venustus, suavis.*
winnow, *ventilare, evanněre.*
winnowing-fan, *ventilabrum, vannus.*
winter, subst. *hiems, bruma* (lit. = shortest day).
winter, adj. *hiemalis, hibernus.*
winter, v. *hiemare, hibernare.*
winter-quarters, *castra* (*-orum*) *hiberna.*
wipe, (*abs*)*tergēre, detergēre*; to — out, *abolēre, delēre.*
wire, *filum* (*ferreum*).
wisdom, *sapientia, prudentia, consilium.*
wise, *sapiens, prudens* (= sensible); to be —, *sapěre.* Adv. *sapienter, prudenter.*
wish, subst. *optatio, desiderium* (= longing), *votum* (= prayer).
wish, v. *velle, cupěre,* (*ex*)*optare*; not to —, *nolle.*
wistful, render by *desiderium* (= longing).
wit: as a quality, *ingenium,* (*ingenii*) *acumen, facetiae* (*-arum*), *sal*; with one's —s about one, *sanus*; = witty person, (*homo*) *facetus.*
wit, v.: to —, *videlicet, scilicet, dico.*
witch, *venefica, saga.*
witchcraft, *veneficium, ars magica.*
with, prep., *cum* (with abl.); sometimes plain abl.
withal, *simul.*
withdraw, v.: transit., *avertěre, revocare, removēre*; intransit., (*re*)*ceděre, disceděre, se recipěre*; to — from office, *magistratu se abdicare.*
wither, v.: transit., *urěre, corrumpěre*; transit., *marcescěre, marcēre.*
withered, *marcidus.*
withhold, *retinēre, recusare* (= to refuse).
within, prep. *intra* (with acc.), *in* (with abl.); — a period of time, render by plain abl.
within, adv. *intus, intro* (= to the inside).
without, prep. *sine* (with abl.), *extra* (with acc.); to be (or go) — a thing, *re carēre*; — going, — doing, etc., render by clause.
without, adv. *extra, foris* (= out of doors).
withstand, *resistěre, obsistěre* (with dat.).
witness, subst.: = one who gives evidence, *testis*; to call as a —, *testari, antestari*; = evidence, q.v.; = a party present, *arbiter, spectator*; before many —es, *coram multis.*
witness, v.: = give evidence, *testari*; = see, q.v.
witticism, *dictum, facetiae* (*-arum*).
witty, *dicax, facetus, salsus*; adv. *facete.*
wizard, *veneficus, magus.*
woad, *vitrum.*
woe, *dolor, luctus* (*-ūs*); interj., *vae!*
wolf, *lupus, lupa*; of a —, adj. *lupinus.*
woman, *femina* (opp. *vir*), *mulier* (esp. a grown —); an old —, *anus* (*-ūs*); a little —, *muliercula.*
womanish, *muliebris, mollis, effeminatus.*
womanly, *muliebris.*
womb, *alvus, uterus.*
wonder, subst.: as a feeling, (*ad*)*miratio*; = wonderful thing, *miraculum, res mira*; and no —, *nec mirum.*
wonder, v. (*ad*)*mirari*; I — whether, why, etc., *scire velim.*
wonderful, *mirus, mirificus,* (*ad*)*mirabilis*; adv. *mire, mirifice,* (*ad*)*mirabiliter.*
wont, subst. *mos, consuetudo.*
wont: to be —, *solēre, consuevisse.*
woo, *ambire,* (*in matrimonium*) *petěre.*
wood: as substance, *lignum, materia* (*materies*); to get —, *lignari*; = collection of trees, *silva, nemus* (*-oris*, n.).
wooden, *ligneus.*
woodland, *silvae* (*-arum*), *nemora* (*-um*).
woodman, *lignator.*
wood-nymph, (*hama*)*dryas.*
wood-pecker, *picus.*
wood-pigeon, *palumbes.*
woody, wooded, *silvestris, silvosus.*
wooer, *procus.*
woof, *subtemen, trama.*
wool, *lana.*
woollen, woolly, *laneus.*
word, subst. *verbum*; *vocabulum* or *nomen* (= name); *dictum* (= saying) = word of honour, *fides*: to keep one's —, *fidem servare*; to break one's —, *fidem fallěre.*
word, v.; see express.
wordy, *verbosus.*
work, subst. *opus* (*-eris*, n.; = piece of —); *pensum* (= task); *opera,*

labor (= effort); *liber* (= literary —); a small —, *opusculum.*
work, v.: intransit. (*e*)*laborare, operari*; to — at night, *lucubrare*; a —ing day, *dies profestus*; transit., = exercise, ply, *exercēre, exercitare*; = till, *colĕre*; = effect, do, *facĕre, efficĕre.*
workman, *opifex, operarius, artifex, faber.*
workmanship, *ars, opus* (*-eris*, n.).
workshop, *officina.*
world, *rerum natura, mundus; orbis terrarum* or *terrae* (= the globe); *terrae* (*-arum*; = all countries); *gentes, homines, omnes* (all plur., = mankind); the ancient —, *antiquitas, veteres* (*-um*, plur.); a man of the —, *homo rerum peritus*; the lower —, *inferi* (*-orum*).
worm, subst. *vermis, vermiculus, tinea* (in wood, books, etc.).
worm, v.: to — one's way in, (*se*) *insinuare.*
worry, subst.; see anxiety.
worry, v.: = tear, maul, (*di*)*lacerarc,* (*di*)*laniare*; = harass, *vexare, sollicitare.*
worse, adj. *peior*; to grow —, *degenerare, ingravescĕre* (of troubles); adv. *peius, deterius.*
worship, subst. *veneratio, cultus* (*-ūs*): divine —, *cultus deorum*; to attend —, *sacris adesse.*
worship, v. *venerari, colĕre.*
worshipper, *cultor.*
worst: adj. *pessimus*; adv. *pessime.*
worst, v. *vincĕre.*
worth, subst., = merit, *virtūs* (*-ūtis*, f.), *dignitas.*
worth, adj.: render by genit. of value or by *valēre*; it is — while, *operae pretium est.*
worthless, *vilis, inutilis, nequam.*
worthy, *dignus* (with abl., or *qui* and subj.); adv. *digne.*
would; see will, wish; — that, in wishes, *utinam* and subj.
wound, subst. *vulnus* (*-eris*, n.), *cicatrix* (= scar).
wound, v. *vulnerare, sauciare.*
wounded, *vulneratus, saucius.*
wrangle; see quarrel.
wrap, *involvĕre, velare, amicire.*
wrapper, = cover, *involucrum, tegumentum.*
wrath, *ira, iracundia, indignatio.*
wrathful, *iratus, iracundus*, adv. *iracunde, per iram.*
wreath, *corona, serta* (*-orum*).
wreathe, *nectĕre, contorquēre* (= twist).
wreck, wreckage, *naufragium.*
wrecked, *naufragus.*
wrench, wrest, (*rem homini*) *extorquēre* or *eripĕre.*
wrestle, *luctari.*
wrestler, *luctator, athleta.*
wrestling, subst. *luctatio.*
wretch, *homo miser.*
wretched: = unfortunate, *miser, miserabilis*; = bad, *malus, nequam*; adv. *misere, miserabiliter; male* (= badly).
wretchedness, *miseria, aerumna.*
wriggle, *se torquēre, torquēri.*
wring; to — the neck, *gulam, frangĕre,*
wrinkle, subst. *ruga.*
wrinkle, v.; to — the forehead, *frontem contrahĕre.*
wrinkled, *rugosus.*
wrist; render by *manus* (= hand).
writ: Holy —, *Litterae* (*-arum*) *Sanctae*; a legal —, *mandatum, praescriptum.*
write, *scribĕre*; — out, *describĕre*; — back, *rescribĕre*; — often, *scriptitare.*
writer, *scriptor, scriba* (professional); *qui scribit.*
writhe, *torquēri.*
writing, subst.: as act, *scriptio, scriptura*; the art of —, *ars scribendi*; = thing written, *scriptum, litterae* (*-arum*).
writing-case, *scrinium.*
writing-tablet, *tabula, cera.*
wrong, subst.: = injury, *iniuria*; = wickedness, *nefas*; to do wrong, *peccare, delinquĕre.*
wrong, adj. *falsus* (= false), *pravus* (= perverse), *iniquus* (= unfair); to be — (i.e. mistaken), *falli, errare.* Adv. *male, perperam, prave, falso, inique, iniuriā.*
wrong, v. *iniuriā adficĕre.*
wroth, *iratus.*
wrought, *factus, confectus.*
wry, *distortus, perversus, pravus.*

Y

yacht, *celox.*
yard: the measure, *tres pedes* (*-um*); a — long, or wide, *tripedalis*: court —, *area*; sail—, *antenna.*
yawn, v. *oscitare*; = open wide, *scindi, hiare.*
ye; see you.
yea; see yes.
year, *annus, anni spatium*; lasting a —, adj. *annuus*; last —, *superiore* or *priore anno*; next —, *proximo anno*; every —, *singulis annis; quotannis*; every other —, *alternis annis*; a period of two —s, *biennium.*
yearly: adj., *annuus, anniversarius*; adv. *quotannis, singulis annis.*
yearn; to — for, *desiderare.*
yearning, *desiderium.*
yell, subst. *ululatus* (*-ūs*), *eiulatio.*
yell, v. *ululare, eiulare.*
yellow, *flavus, fulvus, aureus* (= golden), *croceus* (= saffron coloured).
yelp, yelping, subst. *gannitus* (*-ūs*).
yelp, v. *gannire.*
yes, *ita* (*est*), *certe, etiam, sane*; I say —, *aio.*
yesterday, adv. *heri*; of —, adj., *hesternus.*
yet: = nevertheless, (*at*)*tamen, at*; = even now, *etiamnunc, adhuc*; not —, *nondum*: with comparatives, = even, *etiam.*
yew, *taxus.*
yield, v.: transit., = produce, (*ef*)*ferre*; = give, *dare, praebēre*; = surrender, *dedĕre,* (*con*)*cedĕre*; intransit., (*con*)-*cedĕre, obsequi.*

yielding, adj., *facilis, indulgens.*
yoke, subst. *iugum.*
yoke, v. *(con)iungĕre.*
yolk, (of an egg) *vitellus.*
yon, yonder, adj. *ille, iste.*
yonder, adv. *illic, istic* (= there, where you are).
yore: of —, *olim, quondam.*
York, *Eboracum.*
you, *tu, te,* etc. (sing.); *vos,* etc. (plur.); but often not expressed.
young, subst. *partus* (*-ūs*; = offspring), *fetus* (*-ūs*) or *proles* (= brood), *pullus* (= a single — animal).
young, adj. *parvus* or *parvulus* (= little), *adulescens* (= growing up), *novus* (= fresh, new); — child, *infans*; — lad, *puer*; — man, *adulescens adulescentulus, iuvenis.*
younger, *iunior,* (*natu*) *minor.*
youngest, (*natu*) *minimus.*
your, yours, *tuus* (of a sing. owner; = thy), *vester* (of plur. owner); that of —s, *iste.*
yourself, *tu ipse, tute, tutemet.*
yourselves, *vos ipsi, vosmet* (*ipsi*).
youth, *pueritia, adulescentia, iuventūs* (*-ūtis,* f.); from one's — up, *ab ineunte aetate, a puero*; collective, = young people, *iuventus* (*-utis,* f.), *iuvenes* (*-um*); = a young man, *puer, adulescens, iuvenis.*
youthful, *iuvenilis iuvenalis, puerilis*; adv. *iuveniliter, iuvenum more.*

Z

zeal, *studium, ardor, fervor, industria.*
zealous, *studiosus, acer*; adv. *studiose, acriter.*
zenith, *vertex.*
Zephyr, *Zephyrus, Favonius.*
zero, render by *nihil.*
zest, *studium.*
zodiac: girdle, *cingulum*; = region *orbis, regio, plaga.*
zoology, *animantium descriptio.*

FINIS